T5-AFQ-133

M., A., M. & S.—Tax. Business Org. UCB—1

University Casebook Series

December, 1990

ACCOUNTING AND THE LAW, Fourth Edition (1978), with Problems Pamphlet (Successor to Dohr, Phillips, Thompson & Warren)

George C. Thompson, Professor, Columbia University Graduate School of Business.
Robert Whitman, Professor of Law, University of Connecticut.
Ellis L. Phillips, Jr., Member of the New York Bar.
William C. Warren, Professor of Law Emeritus, Columbia University.

ACCOUNTING FOR LAWYERS, MATERIALS ON (1980)

David R. Herwitz, Professor of Law, Harvard University.

ADMINISTRATIVE LAW, Eighth Edition (1987), with 1989 Case Supplement and 1983 Problems Supplement (Supplement edited in association with Paul R. Verkuil, Dean and Professor of Law, Tulane University)

Walter Gellhorn, University Professor Emeritus, Columbia University.
Clark Byse, Professor of Law, Harvard University.
Peter L. Strauss, Professor of Law, Columbia University.
Todd D. Rakoff, Professor of Law, Harvard University.
Roy A. Schotland, Professor of Law, Georgetown University.

ADMIRALTY, Third Edition (1987), with Statute and Rule Supplement

Jo Desha Lucas, Professor of Law, University of Chicago.

ADVOCACY, see also Lawyering Process

AGENCY, see also Enterprise Organization

AGENCY—PARTNERSHIPS, Fourth Edition (1987)

Abridgement from Conard, Knauss & Siegel's Enterprise Organization, Fourth Edition.

AGENCY AND PARTNERSHIPS (1987)

Melvin A. Eisenberg, Professor of Law, University of California, Berkeley.

ANTITRUST: FREE ENTERPRISE AND ECONOMIC ORGANIZATION, Sixth Edition (1983), with 1983 Problems in Antitrust Supplement and 1990 Case Supplement

Louis B. Schwartz, Professor of Law, University of Pennsylvania.
John J. Flynn, Professor of Law, University of Utah.
Harry First, Professor of Law, New York University.

BANKRUPTCY, Second Edition (1989), with 1990 Case Supplement

Robert L. Jordan, Professor of Law, University of California, Los Angeles.
William D. Warren, Professor of Law, University of California, Los Angeles.

BANKRUPTCY AND DEBTOR-CREDITOR LAW, Second Edition (1988)

Theodore Eisenberg, Professor of Law, Cornell University.

UNIVERSITY CASEBOOK SERIES—Continued

BUSINESS CRIME (1990)

Harry First, Professor of Law, New York University.

BUSINESS ORGANIZATION, see also Enterprise Organization

BUSINESS PLANNING, Temporary Second Edition (1984)

David R. Herwitz, Professor of Law, Harvard University.

BUSINESS TORTS (1972)

Milton Handler, Professor of Law Emeritus, Columbia University.

CHILDREN IN THE LEGAL SYSTEM (1983) with 1990 Supplement (Supplement edited in association with Elizabeth S. Scott, Professor of Law, University of Virginia)

Walter Wadlington, Professor of Law, University of Virginia.
Charles H. Whitebread, Professor of Law, University of Southern California.
Samuel Davis, Professor of Law, University of Georgia.

CIVIL PROCEDURE, see Procedure

CIVIL RIGHTS ACTIONS (1988), with 1990 Supplement

Peter W. Low, Professor of Law, University of Virginia.
John C. Jeffries, Jr., Professor of Law, University of Virginia.

CLINIC, see also Lawyering Process

COMMERCIAL AND DEBTOR-CREDITOR LAW: SELECTED STATUTES, 1990 EDITION

COMMERCIAL LAW, Second Edition (1987)

Robert L. Jordan, Professor of Law, University of California, Los Angeles.
William D. Warren, Professor of Law, University of California, Los Angeles.

COMMERCIAL LAW, Fourth Edition (1985), with 1990 Case Supplement

E. Allan Farnsworth, Professor of Law, Columbia University.
John Honnold, Professor of Law, University of Pennsylvania.

COMMERCIAL PAPER, Third Edition (1984), with 1990 Case Supplement

E. Allan Farnsworth, Professor of Law, Columbia University.

COMMERCIAL PAPER, Second Edition (1987) (Reprinted from COMMERCIAL LAW, Second Edition (1987))

Robert L. Jordan, Professor of Law, University of California, Los Angeles.
William D. Warren, Professor of Law, University of California, Los Angeles.

COMMERCIAL PAPER AND BANK DEPOSITS AND COLLECTIONS (1967), with Statutory Supplement

William D. Hawkland, Professor of Law, University of Illinois.

COMMERCIAL TRANSACTIONS—Principles and Policies, Second Edition (1991)

Alan Schwartz, Professor of Law, Yale University.
Robert E. Scott, Professor of Law, University of Virginia.

COMPARATIVE LAW, Fifth Edition (1988)

Rudolf B. Schlesinger, Professor of Law, Hastings College of the Law.
Hans W. Baade, Professor of Law, University of Texas.
Mirjan P. Damaska, Professor of Law, Yale Law School.
Peter E. Herzog, Professor of Law, Syracuse University.

COMPETITIVE PROCESS, LEGAL REGULATION OF THE, Fourth Edition (1990), with 1989 Selected Statutes Supplement

Edmund W. Kitch, Professor of Law, University of Virginia.
Harvey S. Perlman, Dean of the Law School, University of Nebraska.

CONFLICT OF LAWS, Ninth Edition (1990)

Willis L. M. Reese, Professor of Law, Columbia University.
Maurice Rosenberg, Professor of Law, Columbia University.
Peter Hay, Professor of Law, University of Illinois.

CONSTITUTIONAL LAW, Eighth Edition (1989), with 1990 Case Supplement

Edward L. Barrett, Jr., Professor of Law, University of California, Davis.
William Cohen, Professor of Law, Stanford University.
Jonathan D. Varat, Professor of Law, University of California, Los Angeles.

CONSTITUTIONAL LAW, CIVIL LIBERTY AND INDIVIDUAL RIGHTS, Second Edition (1982), with 1989 Supplement

William Cohen, Professor of Law, Stanford University.
John Kaplan, Professor of Law, Stanford University.

CONSTITUTIONAL LAW, Eleventh Edition (1985), with 1990 Supplement (Supplement edited in association with Frederick F. Schauer, Professor, Harvard University)

Gerald Gunther, Professor of Law, Stanford University.

CONSTITUTIONAL LAW, INDIVIDUAL RIGHTS IN, Fourth Edition (1986), (Reprinted from CONSTITUTIONAL LAW, Eleventh Edition), with 1990 Supplement (Supplement edited in association with Frederick F. Schauer, Professor, Harvard University)

Gerald Gunther, Professor of Law, Stanford University.

CONSUMER TRANSACTIONS, Second Edition (1991), with Selected Statutes and Regulations Supplement

Michael M. Greenfield, Professor of Law, Washington University.

CONTRACT LAW AND ITS APPLICATION, Fourth Edition (1988)

Arthur Rosett, Professor of Law, University of California, Los Angeles.

CONTRACT LAW, STUDIES IN, Third Edition (1984)

Edward J. Murphy, Professor of Law, University of Notre Dame.
Richard E. Speidel, Professor of Law, Northwestern University.

CONTRACTS, Fifth Edition (1987)

John P. Dawson, late Professor of Law, Harvard University.
William Burnett Harvey, Professor of Law and Political Science, Boston University.
Stanley D. Henderson, Professor of Law, University of Virginia.

CONTRACTS, Fourth Edition (1988)

E. Allan Farnsworth, Professor of Law, Columbia University.
William F. Young, Professor of Law, Columbia University.

CONTRACTS, Selections on (statutory materials) (1988)

CONTRACTS, Second Edition (1978), with Statutory and Administrative Law Supplement (1978)

Ian R. Macneil, Professor of Law, Cornell University.

UNIVERSITY CASEBOOK SERIES—Continued

COPYRIGHT, PATENTS AND TRADEMARKS, see also Competitive Process; see also Selected Statutes and International Agreements

COPYRIGHT, PATENT, TRADEMARK AND RELATED STATE DOCTRINES, Third Edition (1990), with 1989 Selected Statutes Supplement and 1981 Problem Supplement

Paul Goldstein, Professor of Law, Stanford University.

COPYRIGHT, Unfair Competition, and Other Topics Bearing on the Protection of Literary, Musical, and Artistic Works, Fifth Edition (1990), with 1990 Statutory Supplement

Ralph S. Brown, Jr., Professor of Law, Yale University.
Robert C. Denicola, Professor of Law, University of Nebraska.

CORPORATE ACQUISITIONS, The Law and Finance of (1986), with 1990 Supplement

Ronald J. Gilson, Professor of Law, Stanford University.

CORPORATE FINANCE, Third Edition (1987)

Victor Brudney, Professor of Law, Harvard University.
Marvin A. Chirelstein, Professor of Law, Columbia University.

CORPORATION LAW, BASIC, Third Edition (1989), with Documentary Supplement

Detlev F. Vagts, Professor of Law, Harvard University.

CORPORATIONS, see also Enterprise Organization

CORPORATIONS, Sixth Edition—Concise (1988), with 1990 Case Supplement and 1990 Statutory Supplement

William L. Cary, late Professor of Law, Columbia University.
Melvin Aron Eisenberg, Professor of Law, University of California, Berkeley.

CORPORATIONS, Sixth Edition—Unabridged (1988), with 1990 Case Supplement and 1990 Statutory Supplement

William L. Cary, late Professor of Law, Columbia University.
Melvin Aron Eisenberg, Professor of Law, University of California, Berkeley.

CORPORATIONS AND BUSINESS ASSOCIATIONS—STATUTES, RULES, AND FORMS (1990)

CORRECTIONS, SEE SENTENCING

CREDITORS' RIGHTS, see also Debtor-Creditor Law

CRIMINAL JUSTICE ADMINISTRATION, Third Edition (1986), with 1990 Case Supplement

Frank W. Miller, Professor of Law, Washington University.
Robert O. Dawson, Professor of Law, University of Texas.
George E. Dix, Professor of Law, University of Texas.
Raymond I. Parnas, Professor of Law, University of California, Davis.

CRIMINAL LAW, Fourth Edition (1987)

Fred E. Inbau, Professor of Law Emeritus, Northwestern University.
Andre A. Moenssens, Professor of Law, University of Richmond.
James R. Thompson, Professor of Law Emeritus, Northwestern University.

CRIMINAL LAW AND APPROACHES TO THE STUDY OF LAW (1986)

John M. Brumbaugh, Professor of Law, University of Maryland.

CRIMINAL LAW, Second Edition (1986)

Peter W. Low, Professor of Law, University of Virginia.
John C. Jeffries, Jr., Professor of Law, University of Virginia.
Richard C. Bonnie, Professor of Law, University of Virginia.

CRIMINAL LAW, Fourth Edition (1986)

Lloyd L. Weinreb, Professor of Law, Harvard University.

CRIMINAL LAW AND PROCEDURE, Seventh Edition (1989)

Ronald N. Boyce, Professor of Law, University of Utah.
Rollin M. Perkins, Professor of Law Emeritus, University of California, Hastings College of the Law.

CRIMINAL PROCEDURE, Third Edition (1987), with 1990 Supplement

James B. Haddad, Professor of Law, Northwestern University.
James B. Zagel, Chief, Criminal Justice Division, Office of Attorney General of Illinois.
Gary L. Starkman, Assistant U. S. Attorney, Northern District of Illinois.
William J. Bauer, Chief Judge of the U.S. Court of Appeals, Seventh Circuit.

CRIMINAL PROCESS, Fourth Edition (1987), with 1990 Supplement

Lloyd L. Weinreb, Professor of Law, Harvard University.

DAMAGES, Second Edition (1952)

Charles T. McCormick, late Professor of Law, University of Texas.
William F. Fritz, late Professor of Law, University of Texas.

DECEDENTS' ESTATES AND TRUSTS, Seventh Edition (1988)

John Ritchie, late Professor of Law, University of Virginia.
Neill H. Alford, Jr., Professor of Law, University of Virginia.
Richard W. Effland, late Professor of Law, Arizona State University.

DISPUTE RESOLUTION, Processes of (1989)

John S. Murray, President and Executive Director of The Conflict Clinic, Inc., George Mason University.
Alan Scott Rau, Professor of Law, University of Texas.
Edward F. Sherman, Professor of Law, University of Texas.

DOMESTIC RELATIONS, see also Family Law

DOMESTIC RELATIONS, Second Edition (1990)

Walter Wadlington, Professor of Law, University of Virginia.

EMPLOYMENT DISCRIMINATION, Second Edition (1987), with 1990 Supplement

Joel W. Friedman, Professor of Law, Tulane University.
George M. Strickler, Professor of Law, Tulane University.

EMPLOYMENT LAW, Second Edition (1991), with Statutory Supplement

Mark A. Rothstein, Professor of Law, University of Houston.
Andria S. Knapp, Visiting Professor of Law, Golden Gate University.
Lance Liebman, Professor of Law, Harvard University.

ENERGY LAW (1983) with 1986 Case Supplement

Donald N. Zillman, Professor of Law, University of Utah.
Laurence Lattman, Dean of Mines and Engineering, University of Utah.

UNIVERSITY CASEBOOK SERIES—Continued

ENTERPRISE ORGANIZATION, Fourth Edition (1987), with 1987 Corporation and Partnership Statutes, Rules and Forms Supplement

Alfred F. Conard, Professor of Law, University of Michigan.
Robert L. Knauss, Dean of the Law School, University of Houston.
Stanley Siegel, Professor of Law, University of California, Los Angeles.

ENVIRONMENTAL POLICY LAW 1985 Edition, with 1985 Problems Supplement (Supplement in association with Ronald H. Rosenberg, Professor of Law, College of William and Mary)

Thomas J. Schoenbaum, Professor of Law, University of Georgia.

EQUITY, see also Remedies

EQUITY, RESTITUTION AND DAMAGES, Second Edition (1974)

Robert Childres, late Professor of Law, Northwestern University.
William F. Johnson, Jr., Professor of Law, New York University.

ESTATE PLANNING, Second Edition (1982), with 1985 Case, Text and Documentary Supplement

David Westfall, Professor of Law, Harvard University.

ETHICS, see Legal Profession, Professional Responsibility, and Social Responsibilities

ETHICS OF LAWYERING, THE LAW AND (1990)

Geoffrey C. Hazard, Jr., Professor of Law, Yale University.
Susan P. Koniak, Professor of Law, University of Pittsburgh.

ETHICS AND PROFESSIONAL RESPONSIBILITY (1981) (Reprinted from THE LAWYERING PROCESS)

Gary Bellow, Professor of Law, Harvard University.
Bea Moulton, Legal Services Corporation.

EVIDENCE, Sixth Edition (1988 Reprint), with 1990 Case Supplement (Supplement edited in association with Roger C. Park, Professor of Law, University of Minnesota)

John Kaplan, Professor of Law, Stanford University.
Jon R. Waltz, Professor of Law, Northwestern University.

EVIDENCE, Eighth Edition (1988), with Rules, Statute and Case Supplement (1990)

Jack B. Weinstein, Chief Judge, United States District Court.
John H. Mansfield, Professor of Law, Harvard University.
Norman Abrams, Professor of Law, University of California, Los Angeles.
Margaret Berger, Professor of Law, Brooklyn Law School.

FAMILY LAW, see also Domestic Relations

FAMILY LAW Second Edition (1985), with 1991 Supplement

Judith C. Areen, Professor of Law, Georgetown University.

FAMILY LAW AND CHILDREN IN THE LEGAL SYSTEM, STATUTORY MATERIALS (1981)

Walter Wadlington, Professor of Law, University of Virginia.

FEDERAL COURTS, Eighth Edition (1988), with 1990 Supplement

Charles T. McCormick, late Professor of Law, University of Texas.
James H. Chadbourn, late Professor of Law, Harvard University.
Charles Alan Wright, Professor of Law, University of Texas, Austin.

UNIVERSITY CASEBOOK SERIES—Continued

FEDERAL COURTS AND THE FEDERAL SYSTEM, Hart and Wechsler's Third Edition (1988), with 1989 Case Supplement, and the Judicial Code and Rules of Procedure in the Federal Courts (1989)

Paul M. Bator, Professor of Law, University of Chicago.
Daniel J. Meltzer, Professor of Law, Harvard University.
Paul J. Mishkin, Professor of Law, University of California, Berkeley.
David L. Shapiro, Professor of Law, Harvard University.

FEDERAL COURTS AND THE LAW OF FEDERAL-STATE RELATIONS, Second Edition (1989), with 1990 Supplement

Peter W. Low, Professor of Law, University of Virginia.
John C. Jeffries, Jr., Professor of Law, University of Virginia.

FEDERAL PUBLIC LAND AND RESOURCES LAW, Second Edition (1987), with 1990 Case Supplement and 1990 Statutory Supplement

George C. Coggins, Professor of Law, University of Kansas.
Charles F. Wilkinson, Professor of Law, University of Oregon.

FEDERAL RULES OF CIVIL PROCEDURE and Selected Other Procedural Provisions, 1990 Edition

FEDERAL TAXATION, see Taxation

FOOD AND DRUG LAW (1980), with Statutory Supplement

Richard A. Merrill, Dean of the School of Law, University of Virginia.
Peter Barton Hutt, Esq.

FUTURE INTERESTS (1970)

Howard R. Williams, Professor of Law, Stanford University.

FUTURE INTERESTS AND ESTATE PLANNING (1961), with 1962 Supplement

W. Barton Leach, late Professor of Law, Harvard University.
James K. Logan, formerly Dean of the Law School, University of Kansas.

GOVERNMENT CONTRACTS, FEDERAL, Successor Edition (1985), with 1989 Supplement

John W. Whelan, Professor of Law, Hastings College of the Law.

GOVERNMENT REGULATION: FREE ENTERPRISE AND ECONOMIC ORGANIZATION, Sixth Edition (1985)

Louis B. Schwartz, Professor of Law, Hastings College of the Law.
John J. Flynn, Professor of Law, University of Utah.
Harry First, Professor of Law, New York University.

HEALTH CARE LAW AND POLICY (1988)

Clark C. Havighurst, Professor of Law, Duke University.

HINCKLEY, JOHN W., JR., TRIAL OF: A Case Study of the Insanity Defense (1986)

Peter W. Low, Professor of Law, University of Virginia.
John C. Jeffries, Jr., Professor of Law, University of Virginia.
Richard C. Bonnie, Professor of Law, University of Virginia.

INJUNCTIONS, Second Edition (1984)

Owen M. Fiss, Professor of Law, Yale University.
Doug Rendleman, Professor of Law, College of William and Mary.

INSTITUTIONAL INVESTORS, (1978)

David L. Ratner, Professor of Law, Cornell University.

INSURANCE, Second Edition (1985)

William F. Young, Professor of Law, Columbia University.
Eric M. Holmes, Professor of Law, University of Georgia.

INSURANCE LAW AND REGULATION (1990)

Kenneth S. Abraham, University of Virginia.

INTERNATIONAL LAW, see also Transnational Legal Problems, Transnational Business Problems, and United Nations Law

INTERNATIONAL LAW IN CONTEMPORARY PERSPECTIVE (1981), with Essay Supplement

Myres S. McDougal, Professor of Law, Yale University.
W. Michael Reisman, Professor of Law, Yale University.

INTERNATIONAL LEGAL SYSTEM, Third Edition (1988), with Documentary Supplement

Joseph Modeste Sweeney, Professor of Law, University of California, Hastings.
Covey T. Oliver, Professor of Law, University of Pennsylvania.
Noyes E. Leech, Professor of Law Emeritus, University of Pennsylvania.

INTRODUCTION TO LAW, see also Legal Method, On Law in Courts, and Dynamics of American Law

INTRODUCTION TO THE STUDY OF LAW (1970)

E. Wayne Thode, late Professor of Law, University of Utah.
Leon Lebowitz, Professor of Law, University of Texas.
Lester J. Mazor, Professor of Law, University of Utah.

JUDICIAL CODE and Rules of Procedure in the Federal Courts, Students' Edition, 1989 Revision

Daniel J. Meltzer, Professor of Law, Harvard University.
David L. Shapiro, Professor of Law, Harvard University.

JURISPRUDENCE (Temporary Edition Hardbound) (1949)

Lon L. Fuller, late Professor of Law, Harvard University.

JUVENILE, see also Children

JUVENILE JUSTICE PROCESS, Third Edition (1985)

Frank W. Miller, Professor of Law, Washington University.
Robert O. Dawson, Professor of Law, University of Texas.
George E. Dix, Professor of Law, University of Texas.
Raymond I. Parnas, Professor of Law, University of California, Davis.

LABOR LAW, Eleventh Edition (1991), with 1991 Statutory Supplement

Archibald Cox, Professor of Law, Harvard University.
Derek C. Bok, President, Harvard University.
Robert A. Gorman, Professor of Law, University of Pennsylvania.
Matthew W. Finkin, Professor of Law, University of Illinois.

LABOR LAW, Second Edition (1982), with Statutory Supplement

Clyde W. Summers, Professor of Law, University of Pennsylvania.
Harry H. Wellington, Dean of the Law School, Yale University.
Alan Hyde, Professor of Law, Rutgers University.

LAND FINANCING, Third Edition (1985)

The late Norman Penney, Professor of Law, Cornell University.
Richard F. Broude, Member of the California Bar.
Roger Cunningham, Professor of Law, University of Michigan.

LAW AND MEDICINE (1980)

Walter Wadlington, Professor of Law and Professor of Legal Medicine, University of Virginia.
Jon R. Waltz, Professor of Law, Northwestern University.
Roger B. Dworkin, Professor of Law, Indiana University, and Professor of Biomedical History, University of Washington.

LAW, LANGUAGE AND ETHICS (1972)

William R. Bishin, Professor of Law, University of Southern California.
Christopher D. Stone, Professor of Law, University of Southern California.

LAW, SCIENCE AND MEDICINE (1984), with 1989 Supplement

Judith C. Areen, Professor of Law, Georgetown University.
Patricia A. King, Professor of Law, Georgetown University.
Steven P. Goldberg, Professor of Law, Georgetown University.
Alexander M. Capron, Professor of Law, University of Southern California.

LAWYERING PROCESS (1978), with Civil Problem Supplement and Criminal Problem Supplement

Gary Bellow, Professor of Law, Harvard University.
Bea Moulton, Professor of Law, Arizona State University.

LEGAL METHOD (1980)

Harry W. Jones, Professor of Law Emeritus, Columbia University.
John M. Kernochan, Professor of Law, Columbia University.
Arthur W. Murphy, Professor of Law, Columbia University.

LEGAL METHODS (1969)

Robert N. Covington, Professor of Law, Vanderbilt University.
E. Blythe Stason, late Professor of Law, Vanderbilt University.
John W. Wade, Professor of Law, Vanderbilt University.
Elliott E. Cheatham, late Professor of Law, Vanderbilt University.
Theodore A. Smedley, Professor of Law, Vanderbilt University.

LEGAL PROFESSION, THE, Responsibility and Regulation, Second Edition (1988)

Geoffrey C. Hazard, Jr., Professor of Law, Yale University.
Deborah L. Rhode, Professor of Law, Stanford University.

LEGISLATION, Fourth Edition (1982) (by Fordham)

Horace E. Read, late Vice President, Dalhousie University.
John W. MacDonald, Professor of Law Emeritus, Cornell Law School.
Jefferson B. Fordham, Professor of Law, University of Utah.
William J. Pierce, Professor of Law, University of Michigan.

LEGISLATIVE AND ADMINISTRATIVE PROCESSES, Second Edition (1981)

Hans A. Linde, Judge, Supreme Court of Oregon.
George Bunn, Professor of Law, University of Wisconsin.
Fredericka Paff, Professor of Law, University of Wisconsin.
W. Lawrence Church, Professor of Law, University of Wisconsin.

LOCAL GOVERNMENT LAW, Second Revised Edition (1986)

Jefferson B. Fordham, Professor of Law, University of Utah.

MASS MEDIA LAW, Fourth Edition (1990)

Marc A. Franklin, Professor of Law, Stanford University.
David A. Anderson, Professor of Law, University of Texas.

MUNICIPAL CORPORATIONS, see Local Government Law

NEGOTIABLE INSTRUMENTS, see Commercial Paper

NEGOTIATION (1981) (Reprinted from THE LAWYERING PROCESS)

Gary Bellow, Professor of Law, Harvard Law School.
Bea Moulton, Legal Services Corporation.

NEW YORK PRACTICE, Fourth Edition (1978)

Herbert Peterfreund, Professor of Law, New York University.
Joseph M. McLaughlin, Dean of the Law School, Fordham University.

OIL AND GAS, Fifth Edition (1987)

Howard R. Williams, Professor of Law, Stanford University.
Richard C. Maxwell, Professor of Law, University of California, Los Angeles.
Charles J. Meyers, late Dean of the Law School, Stanford University.
Stephen F. Williams, Judge of the United States Court of Appeals.

ON LAW IN COURTS (1965)

Paul J. Mishkin, Professor of Law, University of California, Berkeley.
Clarence Morris, Professor of Law Emeritus, University of Pennsylvania.

PENSION AND EMPLOYEE BENEFIT LAW (1990)

John H. Langbein, Professor of Law, University of Chicago.
Bruce A. Wolk, Professor of Law, University of California, Davis.

PLEADING AND PROCEDURE, see Procedure, Civil

POLICE FUNCTION, Fourth Edition (1986), with 1990 Case Supplement

Reprint of Chapters 1–10 of Miller, Dawson, Dix and Parnas's CRIMINAL JUSTICE ADMINISTRATION, Third Edition.

PREPARING AND PRESENTING THE CASE (1981) (Reprinted from THE LAWYERING PROCESS)

Gary Bellow, Professor of Law, Harvard Law School.
Bea Moulton, Legal Services Corporation.

PROCEDURE (1988), with Procedure Supplement (1989)

Robert M. Cover, late Professor of Law, Yale Law School.
Owen M. Fiss, Professor of Law, Yale Law School.
Judith Resnik, Professor of Law, University of Southern California Law Center.

PROCEDURE—CIVIL PROCEDURE, Second Edition (1974), with 1979 Supplement

The late James H. Chadbourn, Professor of Law, Harvard University.
A. Leo Levin, Professor of Law, University of Pennsylvania.
Philip Shuchman, Professor of Law, Cornell University.

PROCEDURE—CIVIL PROCEDURE, Sixth Edition (1990)

Richard H. Field, late Professor of Law, Harvard University.
Benjamin Kaplan, Professor of Law Emeritus, Harvard University.
Kevin M. Clermont, Professor of Law, Cornell University.

PROCEDURE—CIVIL PROCEDURE, Fifth Edition (1990)

Maurice Rosenberg, Professor of Law, Columbia University.
Hans Smit, Professor of Law, Columbia University.
Rochelle C. Dreyfuss, Professor of Law, New York University.

PROCEDURE—PLEADING AND PROCEDURE: State and Federal, Sixth Edition (1989), with 1990 Case Supplement

David W. Louisell, late Professor of Law, University of California, Berkeley.
Geoffrey C. Hazard, Jr., Professor of Law, Yale University.
Colin C. Tait, Professor of Law, University of Connecticut.

PROCEDURE—FEDERAL RULES OF CIVIL PROCEDURE, 1990 Edition

PRODUCTS LIABILITY AND SAFETY, Second Edition, (1989), with 1989 Statutory Supplement

W. Page Keeton, Professor of Law, University of Texas.
David G. Owen, Professor of Law, University of South Carolina.
John E. Montgomery, Professor of Law, University of South Carolina.
Michael D. Green, Professor of Law, University of Iowa

PROFESSIONAL RESPONSIBILITY, Fifth Edition (1991), with 1991 Selected Standards on Professional Responsibility Supplement

Thomas D. Morgan, Professor of Law, George Washington University.
Ronald D. Rotunda, Professor of Law, University of Illinois.

PROPERTY, Sixth Edition (1990)

John E. Cribbet, Professor of Law, University of Illinois.
Corwin W. Johnson, Professor of Law, University of Texas.
Roger W. Findley, Professor of Law, University of Illinois.
Ernest E. Smith, Professor of Law, University of Texas.

PROPERTY—PERSONAL (1953)

S. Kenneth Skolfield, late Professor of Law Emeritus, Boston University.

PROPERTY—PERSONAL, Third Edition (1954)

Everett Fraser, late Dean of the Law School Emeritus, University of Minnesota.
Third Edition by Charles W. Taintor, late Professor of Law, University of Pittsburgh.

PROPERTY—INTRODUCTION, TO REAL PROPERTY, Third Edition (1954)

Everett Fraser, late Dean of the Law School Emeritus, University of Minnesota.

PROPERTY—FUNDAMENTALS OF MODERN REAL PROPERTY, Second Edition (1982), with 1985 Supplement

Edward H. Rabin, Professor of Law, University of California, Davis.

PROPERTY, REAL (1984), with 1988 Supplement

Paul Goldstein, Professor of Law, Stanford University.

PROSECUTION AND ADJUDICATION, Third Edition (1986), with 1990 Case Supplement

Reprint of Chapters 11–26 of Miller, Dawson, Dix and Parnas's CRIMINAL JUSTICE ADMINISTRATION, Third Edition.

PSYCHIATRY AND LAW, see Mental Health, see also Hinckley, Trial of

PUBLIC UTILITY LAW, see Free Enterprise, also Regulated Industries

REAL ESTATE PLANNING, Third Edition (1989), with Revised Problem and Statutory Supplement (1991)

Norton L. Steuben, Professor of Law, University of Colorado.

REAL ESTATE TRANSACTIONS, Revised Second Edition (1988), with Statute, Form and Problem Supplement (1988)

Paul Goldstein, Professor of Law, Stanford University.

RECEIVERSHIP AND CORPORATE REORGANIZATION, see Creditors' Rights

REGULATED INDUSTRIES, Second Edition, (1976)

William K. Jones, Professor of Law, Columbia University.

REMEDIES, Second Edition (1987)

Edward D. Re, Chief Judge, U. S. Court of International Trade.

REMEDIES, (1989)

Elaine W. Shoben, Professor of Law, University of Illinois.
Wm. Murray Tabb, Professor of Law, Baylor University.

SALES, Second Edition (1986)

Marion W. Benfield, Jr., Professor of Law, University of Illinois.
William D. Hawkland, Chancellor, Louisiana State Law Center.

SALES AND SALES FINANCING, Fifth Edition (1984)

John Honnold, Professor of Law, University of Pennsylvania.

SALES LAW AND THE CONTRACTING PROCESS, Second Edition (1991)

(Reprinted from Commercial Transactions, Second Edition (1991)
Alan Schwartz, Professor of Law, Yale University.
Robert E. Scott, Professor of Law, University of Virginia.

SECURED TRANSACTIONS IN PERSONAL PROPERTY, Second Edition (1987) (Reprinted from COMMERCIAL LAW, Second Edition (1987))

Robert L. Jordan, Professor of Law, University of California, Los Angeles.
William D. Warren, Professor of Law, University of California, Los Angeles.

SECURITIES REGULATION, Sixth Edition (1987), with 1990 Selected Statutes, Rules and Forms Supplement and 1990 Cases and Releases Supplement

Richard W. Jennings, Professor of Law, University of California, Berkeley.
Harold Marsh, Jr., Member of California Bar.

SECURITIES REGULATION, Second Edition (1988), with Statute, Rule and Form Supplement (1988)

Larry D. Soderquist, Professor of Law, Vanderbilt University.

SECURITY INTERESTS IN PERSONAL PROPERTY, Second Edition (1987)

Douglas G. Baird, Professor of Law, University of Chicago.
Thomas H. Jackson, Dean of the Law School, University of Virginia.

SECURITY INTERESTS IN PERSONAL PROPERTY (1985) (Reprinted from Sales and Sales Financing, Fifth Edition)

John Honnold, Professor of Law, University of Pennsylvania.

SELECTED STANDARDS ON PROFESSIONAL RESPONSIBILITY, 1991 Edition

UNIVERSITY CASEBOOK SERIES—Continued

SELECTED STATUTES AND INTERNATIONAL AGREEMENTS ON UNFAIR COMPETITION, TRADEMARK, COPYRIGHT AND PATENT, 1989 Edition

SELECTED STATUTES ON TRUSTS AND ESTATES, 1991 Edition

SOCIAL RESPONSIBILITIES OF LAWYERS, Case Studies (1988)

Philip B. Heymann, Professor of Law, Harvard University.
Lance Liebman, Professor of Law, Harvard University.

SOCIAL SCIENCE IN LAW, Second Edition (1990)

John Monahan, Professor of Law, University of Virginia.
Laurens Walker, Professor of Law, University of Virginia.

TAXATION, FEDERAL INCOME (1989)

Stephen B. Cohen, Professor of Law, Georgetown University

TAXATION, FEDERAL INCOME, Second Edition (1988), with 1990 Supplement (Supplement edited in association with Deborah H. Schenk, Professor of Law, New York University)

Michael J. Graetz, Professor of Law, Yale University.

TAXATION, FEDERAL INCOME, Sixth Edition (1987)

James J. Freeland, Professor of Law, University of Florida.
Stephen A. Lind, Professor of Law, University of Florida and University of California, Hastings.
Richard B. Stephens, late Professor of Law Emeritus, University of Florida.

TAXATION, FEDERAL INCOME, Successor Edition (1986), with 1990 Legislative Supplement

Stanley S. Surrey, late Professor of Law, Harvard University.
Paul R. McDaniel, Professor of Law, Boston College.
Hugh J. Ault, Professor of Law, Boston College.
Stanley A. Koppelman, Professor of Law, Boston University.

TAXATION, FEDERAL INCOME, OF BUSINESS ORGANIZATIONS (1991)

Paul R. McDaniel, Professor of Law, Boston College.
Hugh J. Ault, Professor of Law, Boston College.
Martin J. McMahon, Jr., Professor of Law, University of Kentucky.
Daniel L. Simmons, Professor of Law, University of California, Davis.

TAXATION, FEDERAL INCOME, OF PARTNERSHIPS AND S CORPORATIONS (1991)

Paul R. McDaniel, Professor of Law, Boston College.
Hugh J. Ault, Professor of Law, Boston College.
Martin J. McMahon, Jr., Professor of Law, University of Kentucky.
Daniel L. Simmons, Professor of Law, University of California, Davis.

TAXATION, FEDERAL INCOME, OIL AND GAS, NATURAL RESOURCES TRANSACTIONS (1990)

Peter C. Maxfield, Professor of Law, University of Wyoming.
James L. Houghton, CPA, Partner, Ernst and Young.
James R. Gaar, CPA, Partner, Ernst and Young.

TAXATION, FEDERAL WEALTH TRANSFER, Successor Edition (1987)

Stanley S. Surrey, late Professor of Law, Harvard University.
Paul R. McDaniel, Professor of Law, Boston College.
Harry L. Gutman, Professor of Law, University of Pennsylvania.

TAXATION, FUNDAMENTALS OF CORPORATE, Second Edition (1987), with 1989 Supplement

Stephen A. Lind, Professor of Law, University of Florida and University of California, Hastings.
Stephen Schwarz, Professor of Law, University of California, Hastings.
Daniel J. Lathrope, Professor of Law, University of California, Hastings.
Joshua Rosenberg, Professor of Law, University of San Francisco.

TAXATION, FUNDAMENTALS OF PARTNERSHIP, Second Edition (1988)

Stephen A. Lind, Professor of Law, University of Florida and University of California, Hastings.
Stephen Schwarz, Professor of Law, University of California, Hastings.
Daniel J. Lathrope, Professor of Law, University of California, Hastings.
Joshua Rosenberg, Professor of Law, University of San Francisco.

TAXATION, PROBLEMS IN THE FEDERAL INCOME TAXATION OF PARTNERSHIPS AND CORPORATIONS, Second Edition (1986)

Norton L. Steuben, Professor of Law, University of Colorado.
William J. Turnier, Professor of Law, University of North Carolina.

TAXATION, PROBLEMS IN THE FUNDAMENTALS OF FEDERAL INCOME, Second Edition (1985)

Norton L. Steuben, Professor of Law, University of Colorado.
William J. Turnier, Professor of Law, University of North Carolina.

TORT LAW AND ALTERNATIVES, Fourth Edition (1987)

Marc A. Franklin, Professor of Law, Stanford University.
Robert L. Rabin, Professor of Law, Stanford University.

TORTS, Eighth Edition (1988)

William L. Prosser, late Professor of Law, University of California, Hastings.
John W. Wade, Professor of Law, Vanderbilt University.
Victor E. Schwartz, Adjunct Professor of Law, Georgetown University.

TORTS, Third Edition (1976)

Harry Shulman, late Dean of the Law School, Yale University.
Fleming James, Jr., Professor of Law Emeritus, Yale University.
Oscar S. Gray, Professor of Law, University of Maryland.

TRADE REGULATION, Third Edition (1990)

Milton Handler, Professor of Law Emeritus, Columbia University.
Harlan M. Blake, Professor of Law, Columbia University.
Robert Pitofsky, Professor of Law, Georgetown University.
Harvey J. Goldschmid, Professor of Law, Columbia University.

TRADE REGULATION, see Antitrust

TRANSNATIONAL BUSINESS PROBLEMS (1986)

Detlev F. Vagts, Professor of Law, Harvard University.

TRANSNATIONAL LEGAL PROBLEMS, Third Edition (1986) with 1991 Revised Edition of Documentary Supplement

Henry J. Steiner, Professor of Law, Harvard University.
Detlev F. Vagts, Professor of Law, Harvard University.

TRIAL, see also Evidence, Making the Record, Lawyering Process and Preparing and Presenting the Case

TRUSTS, Fifth Edition (1978)

George G. Bogert, late Professor of Law Emeritus, University of Chicago.
Dallin H. Oaks, President, Brigham Young University.

TRUSTS AND ESTATES, SELECTED STATUTES ON, 1991 Edition

TRUSTS AND SUCCESSION (Palmer's), Fourth Edition (1983)

Richard V. Wellman, Professor of Law, University of Georgia.
Lawrence W. Waggoner, Professor of Law, University of Michigan.
Olin L. Browder, Jr., Professor of Law, University of Michigan.

UNFAIR COMPETITION, see Competitive Process and Business Torts

WATER RESOURCE MANAGEMENT, Third Edition (1988)

The late Charles J. Meyers, formerly Dean, Stanford University Law School.
A. Dan Tarlock, Professor of Law, IIT Chicago-Kent College of Law.
James N. Corbridge, Jr., Chancellor, University of Colorado at Boulder, and Professor of Law, University of Colorado.
David H. Getches, Professor of Law, University of Colorado.

WILLS AND ADMINISTRATION, Fifth Edition (1961)

Philip Mechem, late Professor of Law, University of Pennsylvania.
Thomas E. Atkinson, late Professor of Law, New York University.

WRITING AND ANALYSIS IN THE LAW (1989)

Helene S. Shapo, Professor of Law, Northwestern University
Marilyn R. Walter, Professor of Law, Brooklyn Law School
Elizabeth Fajans, Writing Specialist, Brooklyn Law School

University Casebook Series

FEDERAL INCOME TAXATION OF BUSINESS ORGANIZATIONS

By

PAUL R. McDANIEL
Partner, Hill & Barlow
Boston, Massachusetts

HUGH J. AULT
Professor of Law
Boston College Law School

MARTIN J. McMAHON, Jr.
Leatherman Professor of Law
University of Kentucky

DANIEL L. SIMMONS
Professor of Law
University of California at Davis

Westbury, New York
THE FOUNDATION PRESS, INC.
1991

Library of Congress Cataloging-in-Publication Data

Federal income taxation of business organizations / by Paul R. McDaniel . . . [et al.].
p. cm. — (University casebook series)
Includes index.
ISBN 0-88277-843-9
1. Business enterprises—Taxation—United States—Cases.
2. Corporations—Taxation—Law and legislation—United States—Cases. I. McDaniel, Paul R. II. Series.
KF6450.A7F43 1991
343.7305'268—dc20
[347.3035268] 90-20774

M., A., M. & S.—Tax. Business Org. UCB

PREFACE

This book covers the federal income taxation of partnerships and corporations. It is a successor to Surrey, Warren, McDaniel and Ault, Federal Income Taxation, Volume 2 (2d Ed., 1980), and, in general, covers the same material as that earlier work. Because of significant structural changes in the income tax in the intervening years, however, the relative importance of certain issues has changed and new issues have arisen. The organization and depth of coverage of various topics in this volume reflect those changes. Unlike the predecessor work, this volume is not encyclopedic. The extent of the statutory changes, the corresponding increase in the scope and complexity of detail in Regulations, and the number of cases and rulings issued in the last ten years preclude inclusion of every relevant authority on every topic. Accordingly, these materials are selective. Both students and instructors must bear in mind that the authorities discussed in connection with any particular issue in many instances are only examples of a much larger body of law.

This book is intended for use in a variety of courses, depending upon the portions selected for coverage by the individual instructor. We are well aware that it is no longer possible to cover the entire volume in any single course (at least one of the normal 3–4 hours per semester type). But, depending on the level of detail covered, this volume can be used for as many as four or five separate courses at either the J.D. or L.L.M. level. The arrangement in outline format of both the subdivisions within the chapters and the detailed Illustrative Material following the principal cases is intended to facilitate the assignment by the instructor of selected portions of the material on any particular topic when the book is used in a course which is a broad survey of taxation of business enterprises. At the same time, detailed discussion of complex issues is presented for consideration in advanced courses.

We recognize that teachers of courses dealing with federal income taxation of business organizations approach their courses with different objectives in mind and use different techniques for handling the materials. In selecting and organizing the materials, we have attempted to maximize the usefulness of these materials for whatever approach the teacher wishes to adopt—an intensive technical analysis, a problem oriented method, a consideration of the policies that underlie the technical tax structure, or a survey of the principal elements of the federal income taxation of business organizations. Accordingly, we have not provided any sets of questions or problems within the materials themselves because the nature of the questions which will be appropriate will vary greatly with the type of course for which the materials are being utilized. Most instructors, we believe, prefer to use questions and problems which have been tailored to their own technique and scope of coverage. In addition, we believe that the selection of principal cases and the numerous examples discussed in the Illustrative Materials can, in effect, serve as problems for students and class discussion.

Like its predecessor, this book charts a course between those books that employ primarily textual explanation and those that rely for the most part on cases. Many chapters and sections of chapters are introduced by a textual discussion or outline for the student of the basic issues and structure of the statute for the major area of partnership or corporate taxation covered in the chapter or section. Principal cases have been included to illustrate for the student how the courts have utilized the technical tax tools at their disposal. We have recognized, however, that the dramatic changes in the statutory structure in the last few years, particularly those in the Tax Reform Act of 1986—for example, the elimination of the capital gains preference, repeal of nonrecognition of gain upon the distribution of property by a corporation, the flattening of the personal income tax rates, inversion of the long-standing relative tax rates on individual and corporate income, and the introduction of passive activity loss rules—have changed dramatically the important issues. As a result, many cases long used in teaching materials are no longer helpful to students, even though they remain valid precedents. Thus, the statutory changes in many instances precluded the use of a judicial decision as a principal case to illustrate the application of a significant number of Code provisions. Accordingly, in a number of chapters, the "principal case" is an excerpt from a congressional committee report, which helps the student understand the reasons underlying changes in the statute.

In the Illustrative Material which follows the principal cases, we have attempted to provide sufficient discussion of rulings and cases to give an insight into the endless variety of factual situations to which the highly technical provisions of the Internal Revenue Code governing corporate and partnership taxation must be applied. The Illustrative Material also provides historical background and discussion of sequential amendments to particular provisions of the Code and Regulations where necessary to understand the significance of current provisions. The breadth and detail of the Illustrative Material is such that many instructors may wish to assign only portions of it depending on the scope of the particular course. To assist in selective use of Illustrative Materials, as a rule, we have arranged the Illustrative Material from the general to the more specific as the outline progresses.

Of course, the Internal Revenue Code and Treasury Regulations are the centerpiece of any course in federal taxation. This volume is intended to be used in conjunction with either a complete set of the Code and Regulations or one of the several available edited versions of the Code and Regulations. The statutory and regulatory references at the head of each topic are not intended to be exhaustive. Rather, they represent only the essential sections of the Code and Regulations which the student must understand to obtain the framework for the cases and materials under the particular topic. We have not undertaken completely to explain the operation of the Code and Regulations in the textual notes and Illustrative Material. The student must work with the statute and regulatory materials before undertaking the examination of its application in the materials in this volume.

This book is divided into nine Parts which are further subdivided into Chapters. Each part, in general, represents a block of material in which we think most instructors in a particular course will choose to cover all of the chapters, although the depth of the coverage within each chapter may differ with the overall scope of the course. Many instructors will cover more than one part in a particular course. Alternatively, the entire volume could be used as a source book, without particular assignments, in an advanced problem oriented course such as Business Planning.

Part I (Chapters 1–6) provides complete coverage of partnership taxation, including the impact of rules extrinsic to subchapter K such as the at-risk and passive activity loss rules. This Part may be utilized in either a two or three credit hour course covering that topic. We expect, however, that some material would have to be omitted in a two-hour course.

Part II (Chapters 7–14) covers basic Corporate Taxation—the corporate income tax, classification, formation, capital structure, dividends, redemptions, and liquidations (except in connection with acquisitions). This Part generally will be combined with other parts as one element in a broader course, although it may be used for a separate two-hour course in basic Corporate Taxation.

Part III (Chapter 15) covers Subchapter S. This Part may be combined with Part I in a course on taxation of pass-thru entities or with Part II in a course in basic corporate taxation. Parts I, II, and III, with some selective editing, may be combined in a four-hour course in Basic Taxation of Business Organizations.

Part IV (Chapters 16 and 17) covers taxable and tax free mergers and acquisitions. This Part (particularly Chapter 16 dealing with taxable acquisitions) includes sections on matters such as bootstrap acquisitions and leveraged buyouts, which relate back to, and build upon concepts explored in Part II. Part V (Chapters 18 and 19) deals with single corporation reorganizations and corporate divisions. Part VI (Chapters 20 and 21) discusses carryover of corporate attributes in acquisitions and reorganizations. Part VII (Chapter 22) covers bankruptcy reorganizations. These four Parts may be combined into a two or three credit hour course in Advanced Corporate Taxation or, portions of these parts may be combined with Part II (and possibly Part III) in a four-hour course covering Corporate Taxation generally. Our own experience has demonstrated, however, that it is difficult to cover all of the topics discussed in Parts II through VI even in a four credit hour course. To facilitate selective use of the materials on tax-free acquisitive reorganizations, the first three sections of Chapter 17 provide an overview of corporate reorganizations and the important judicial and administrative limitations superimposed on the statute, while the remaining sections individually examine in detail each different form of acquisition technique. Some instructors may choose to cover only the first three sections in a basic Corporation Taxation course.

Part VIII (Chapter 23 and 24) discusses affiliated corporations and consolidated returns. Part IX (Chapter 25) covers penalty taxes and collapsible corporations. We expect that only a few courses, primarily Advanced Corporate Taxation courses in L.L.M. programs, will cover these Parts in conjunction with a more discrete division of the earlier Parts into a greater number of courses each having a more narrowly focused scope. Some limited reference to these materials may be in order in J.D. level courses in corporate taxation.

In organizing the materials within the Chapters and Parts, we have kept in mind that instructors may wish to vary the order in which topics are covered. Thus, each Chapter does not necessarily assume that the students have read all of the preceding Chapters. For example, stock dividends (Chapter 12) can as easily be covered after redemptions (Chapter 13) as before. Similar principles were followed with respect to the various Parts. Thus, the materials are usable in a course in Basic Taxation of Business Organizations that covers corporate taxation (Part II) before partnership taxation (Part I), although our own bias is clear from the sequential numbering of the Parts. It is expected, however, that Part II will have been covered before any of Parts IV through IX.

As to editorial matters, the statutory references throughout are to the 1986 Code, except where the text expressly indicates otherwise. References in the cases and other primary sources to the 1954 and 1939 Codes and prior statutes have been edited to conform them to the 1986 Code. Generally, the practice is to omit the earlier citation and instead refer to the matter as "the former version," or "the predecessors," or to give the current relevant 1986 Code section if there has been significant change in the statutory language. In general, references to the Code and Regulations are current as of December 31, 1989. Citations to cases and rulings also are current as of December 31, 1989. In some instances, however, later references have been utilized where the materials were particularly important to the topic. Footnotes in cases and quoted materials very frequently have been omitted. Where retained, the original numbering of the footnotes has been kept so that, in many instances, the footnote numbers are not consecutive. Editorial footnotes for cases and materials are so designated and are indicated by an asterisk. References to Tax Court Memorandum (T.C.M.) decisions are to publications by Commerce Clearing House.

We are indebted to Monica Townsend, John Winans, Les Moore, Hunter Whitesell, Calvin Elam, Gary Alberts and Jessica Steele for research and editorial assistance and to Mary Ruth Becker, Joyce Saylor, and Rita Simonelli for aid in preparing the manuscript. We also appreciate the patience and help of the numerous students in classes at the University of Kentucky and the University of California at Davis who have used these materials in manuscript format over the last several years and have contributed many valuable suggestions.

PAUL R. MCDANIEL
HUGH J. AULT
MARTIN J. MCMAHON, JR.
DANIEL L. SIMMONS

July, 1990

SUPPLEMENT TO PREFACE: 1990 LEGISLATION

The Omnibus Budget Reconciliation Act of 1990 was enacted as the pages of this volume were being set. Throughout the text we refer to the impact on specific areas of the preferential treatment for capital gains provided by the Code prior to 1987. The 1990 Act reintroduces a differential between the top ordinary income rate for individuals (31%) and the top rate on long-term capital gains (28%). It seems unlikely, at the time of this writing, that a three percentage point differential will, in the vast majority of transactions, be sufficient to produce the complexity and tax planning engendered by, for example, a twenty percentage point differential. Nonetheless, instructors using this volume may wish to note the reintroduction of a capital gains/ordinary income differential at several points throughout the text. With respect to redemption premium on preferred stock which is redeemable at a fixed time or putable to the issuer by the holder (see pages 535–536), section 305(c) is amended to require amortization of the premium as income to the holder under economic accrual principals of section 1272 (pages 436–437). Redemption premium is subject to amortization if it represents the equivalent of OID of 1/4 of one percent per year or more. The 1990 Act amends sections 108(e)(10) and (11) to change the treatment of debt for debt exchanges and debt for stock exchanges in taxable and nontaxable corporate reorganizations. These changes will have to be taken into account when considering the discharge of indebtedness materials at pages 996 through 1010. As a related matter, section 1275(a)(4), discussed at page 880, is repealed, potentially creating discharge of indebtedness income and original issue discount on a debt for debt exchange in a nontaxable reorganization. With respect to divisive corporate reorganizations, Chapter 19, section 355(c), discussed at page 904, is revised to specify rules regarding the distribution of boot other than qualified stock of the controlled corporation. Section 355(c) now contains its own set of rules rather than merely referring to the rules of sections 311 and 356. There is also a new section 355(d) which requires recognition of corporate level gain in a divisive reorganization with respect to the distribution of stock to a person who acquired a 50 percent or greater interest in either the distributing or controlled corporation within the five year period preceding the transaction. Section 355(d) can be discussed at page 923 preceding the material in Section C.

November 1, 1990

ACKNOWLEDGEMENTS

We gratefully acknowledge the permission extended by the following authors and publishers to reprint excerpts from the materials listed below which appear in this edition:

The American Law Institute, Federal Income Tax Project: Subchapter C Proposals on Corporate Acquisitions and Dispositions (W. Andrews Reporter). Copyright © 1982 by The American Law Institute. Reprinted with the permission of The American Law Institute. A. Bradford, Untangling the Income Tax, Harvard University Press, 1986. Reprinted by permission of the publishers from UNTANGLING THE INCOME TAX, by David F. Bradford, Cambridge, Mass.: Harvard University Press, Copyright © 1986 by the President and Fellows of Harvard College. Caps, What Every Business Lawyer and Accountant Must Know About the Law Regarding Consolidated Returns, 21 So. Calif. Tax Inst. 191 (1969). Copyright © 1969 by Matthew Bender & Co., Inc., and reprinted with permission From University of Southern California *21st Annual Institute on Federal Taxation.* Colby Blackburn and Trier, Elimination of Earnings and Profits From the Internal Revenue Code, 39 Tax Lawyer 285 (1986). Reprinted with the permission of the authors. Graetz, The Tax Aspects of Leveraged Buyouts and Other Corporate Financial Restructurings, 42 Tax Notes 721 (1989). Copyright 1989, Tax Notes. Reprinted with the permission of Tax Notes. Mentz, Carlise, and Nevas, Leveraged Buyouts: A Washington Perspective of the 1989 Legislation and Prospects for 1989, 46 Tax Notes 1047 (1990). Copyright © 1990, Tax Notes. Reprinted with the permission of Tax Notes. McClure, Must Corporate Income Be Taxed Twice. Copyright © 1979, The Brookings Institution. Reprinted with permission of The Brookings Institution. J. Musgrave and P. Musgrave, Public Finance in Theory and Practice, Fifth Edition. Copyright © 1989, McGraw–Hill Publishing Company. Reprinted with the permission of McGraw–Hill Publishing Company. J. Pechman, Federal Tax Policy, Fifth Ed. Copyright © 1987, The Brookings Institution. Reprinted with permission of The Brookings Institution. Podolin, New Problems in Tax Accounting for Mergers and Acquisitions: Pooling of Interests and Generally Accepted Accounting Principals, 29 N.Y.U. Tax Inst. 499 (1971). Reprinted with permission of New York University, School of Continuing Education, Institute on Federal Taxation. Simon and Simmons, The Future of Section 355, 40 Tax Notes 291 (1988). Copyright © 1988, Tax Notes. Reprinted with the permission of Tax Notes.

*

SUMMARY OF CONTENTS

PART VI. CARRYOVER OF CORPORATE ATTRIBUTES IN REORGANIZATIONS AND OTHER TRANSACTIONS

PART VII. BANKRUPTCY TAX ISSUES

PART VIII. AFFILIATED CORPORATIONS

PART IX. SPECIAL RULES TO PREVENT AVOIDANCE OF SHAREHOLDER LEVEL TAX

TABLE OF CONTENTS

PART V. NONACQUISITIVE REORGANIZATIONS

PART VI. CARRYOVER OF CORPORATE ATTRIBUTES IN REORGANIZATIONS AND OTHER TRANSACTIONS

PART VII. BANKRUPTCY TAX ISSUES

PART VIII. AFFILIATED CORPORATIONS

PART IX. SPECIAL RULES TO PREVENT AVOIDANCE OF SHAREHOLDER LEVEL TAX

TABLE OF INTERNAL REVENUE CODE SECTIONS

TABLE OF INTERNAL REVENUE CODE SECTIONS

TABLE OF TREASURY REGULATIONS

TEMPORARY TREASURY REGULATIONS

TEMPORARY TREASURY REGULATIONS

PROPOSED TREASURY REGULATIONS

TREASURY REGULATIONS

TREASURY REGULATIONS

TREASURY REGULATIONS

TREASURY REGULATIONS

TREASURY REGULATIONS

TREASURY REGULATIONS

TREASURY REGULATIONS

*

TABLE OF CASES AND RULINGS

Principal cases are in italic type. Non-principal cases are in roman type. References are to Pages.

FEDERAL INCOME TAXATION
OF
BUSINESS ORGANIZATIONS

*

PART I

TAXATION OF PARTNERS AND PARTNERSHIPS

CHAPTER 1

INTRODUCTION TO PARTNERSHIP TAXATION

SECTION 1. NONTAX ASPECTS OF PARTNERSHIPS

A. GENERAL PARTNERSHIPS

A partnership is a form of business organization in which two or more persons agree to conduct a business jointly in unincorporated form. Partners may contribute money, property, or services to the partnership, all as agreed among the partners. Except as otherwise agreed among the partners, each partner has a right to share in the profits and management of the partnership and has an undivided interest in the partnership property. Partnerships are basically contracts of mutual agency between co-proprietors. Thus, each partner is fully liable to creditors for all debts of the partnership, including those for which another partner has contracted. Among themselves, however, partners who pay more than their share of partnership obligations are entitled to contribution from partners who pay less than their share; and in some instances a partner may be entitled to indemnification from another partner.

Although originally governed almost exclusively by common law, partnerships are now generally established under the Uniform Partnership Act ("UPA") as adopted in the various states. Nevertheless, case law continues to control many aspects of the relationship of partners among themselves and to creditors or other third parties who have dealings with a partnership. Unlike corporations, no formal contract or articles of partnership are required and, unless the partnership conducts business under a fictitious name, the business generally is not required to file documentation of its existence with any state agency. Another significant difference between partnerships and corporations is that general partnership interests, unlike corporate stock, generally are not subject to federal securities laws and state "blue sky" laws.

Section 7(3) of the UPA provides that not all co-ownership of property constitutes a partnership. Sharing of both profits and control of the property, however, generally will establish a partnership for state law purposes, even in the absence of a formal agreement. The essence of a partnership is *co-proprietorship.* While a partnership may be based on an understanding or an oral agreement, the better practice is to reduce a partnership agreement to writing, spelling out the rights and responsibilities of the respective partners. A written agreement is important if the partners have made unequal contributions of capital or services and profits are being divided other than equally, and is even more important when the profits are divided according to a formula rather than on a fractional basis.

B. LIMITED PARTNERSHIPS

Some partnerships must be formed pursuant to a written agreement or certificate filed with appropriate state authorities. The Uniform Limited Partnership Act ("ULPA"), adopted in one form or another in every state, permits the formation of partnerships in which specified partners are not liable for partnership debts beyond their specified contribution to the capital of the partnership. A limited partnership must have at least one general partner whose liability is unlimited, but it may have more. The partnership's business is controlled entirely by the general partners. Unlike general partners, who have a right to participate in management, limited partners generally are prohibited from participating in the management of the partnership's business. If a limited partner does participate in managing the partnership's business, his shield of limited liability is lost under section 2 of the ULPA. Limited partners do have a right, however, to inspect the partnership's books, receive accountings, and to vote on certain organic changes in the partnership, such as the admission of new partners or changes in the partnership agreement. The ULPA allows the partnership some flexibility in the scope of these voting rights.

A limited partner in many respects more nearly resembles a corporate shareholder than a co-proprietor. This resemblance is based on the nature of the voting rights and the limited liability aspects of limited partnership interests. Accordingly, limited partnership interests are generally subject to the federal securities laws and state blue sky laws. Among the partners, the limited partnership format offers all of the flexibility of the general partnership in providing for diverse formulae for sharing the partnership's profits. The general partner's share may be determined in a different manner than the limited partners' shares. Indeed, the shares most frequently are determined differently, because in an arms' length bargain the profit sharing ratios generally should reflect a disproportionate contribution of services by general partners, who manage the business, and a disproportionate contribution of capital by limited partners.

Despite the unlimited liability of general partners, the extraordinary flexibility of the partnership form of doing business makes it a very popular form for conducting small business. Most individuals who join together in a professional practice form a partnership rather than a corporation, as do many other service oriented businesses. The partnership format is not limited to service businesses, however, and many other businesses are conducted in partnership form. As will be seen in examining the following materials, in many instances the pattern of taxation of partnerships also has encouraged their use. Since the partnership is treated as a conduit for tax purposes, profits are taxed only once, in contrast to the taxation of corporate profits, first, when earned by the corporation, and again, when distributed to shareholders. In addition, when the enterprise realizes losses, the partners may deduct the losses currently on their own returns, while losses at the corporate level may not be deducted by shareholders.

SECTION 2. INTRODUCTION TO SUBCHAPTER K

A. GENERAL

The importance of the partnership form of conducting business and the complex tax problems which that form of business operation engenders were statutorily recognized by the income tax law for the first time in the 1954 revision of the Internal Revenue Code. Subchapter K of the 1954 Code, which has been carried forward into the 1986 Code with relatively few statutory changes since its original enactment, presents a coordinated and detailed treatment of partnership transactions. Its provisions are an attempt to solve in the statute the tax problems of partnership operations which had emerged in prior years when there were only a few sketchy statutory provisions specifically dealing with partnership taxation. In enacting Subchapter K, Congress sought "simplicity, flexibility, and equity as between the partners." [1]

Subchapter K is to a considerable extent based on recommendations prepared by the American Law Institute in 1954.[2] In 1984, the American Law Institute proposed a number of changes to Subchapter K,[3] some of which were subsequently adopted, but Congress has not shown any inclination to revise extensively the partnership tax provisions. Only isolated changes have been made to solve particular narrow problems that have emerged. Although Subchapter K is indeed a vast improvement over the vague rules that preceded it, the statutory interrelationships, contradictions, and gaps in coverage are more complex and extensive than is readily apparent on first reading the relatively brief statutory provisions. As noted by one Tax Court Judge:

1. H.Rep. No. 1337, 83d Cong., 2d Sess. 65 (1954); S.Rep. No. 1622, 83d Cong., 2d Sess. 89 (1954).

2. For these recommendations see American Law Institute, Federal Income Tax Project, February 1954 Draft, Vol. II: Jackson, Johnson, Surrey and Warren, A Proposed Revision of the Federal Income Tax Treatment of Partnerships and Partners—American Law Institute Draft, 9 Tax L.Rev. 109 (1954).

3. American Law Institute, Federal Income Tax Project, Subchapter K (1984).

"The distressingly complex and confusing nature of the provisions of subchapter K present a formidable obstacle to the comprehension of these provisions without the expenditure of a disproportionate amount of time and effort even by one who is sophisticated in tax matters with many years of experience in the tax field. * * * If there should be any lingering doubt on this matter one has only to reread section 736 in its entirety * * * and give an honest answer to the question whether it is reasonably comprehensible to the average lawyer or even to the average tax expert who has not given special attention and extended study to the tax problems of partners. Surely, a statute has not achieved 'simplicity' when its complex provisions may confidently be dealt with by at most only a comparatively small number of specialists who have been instituted into its mysteries." [4]

The present statutory treatment of partnerships has been in effect for some time, and there is an ever increasing number of reported court decisions and revenue rulings interpreting the nuances of the sparse statutory structure. The flood of tax shelter cases since the late 1970's is in large part responsible for this judicial and administrative attention. In addition, the Regulations under many of the provisions of Subchapter K are relatively detailed and of broad scope. Many questions that might arise upon examining only the statute, and to which several reasonable answers may be possible, are answered in increasingly detailed Regulations, which are critically important in partnership taxation.

The central theoretical issue in partnership taxation, which leads to most of the difficulties in actual practice, is when and for what purposes a partnership should be treated as an entity separate from the partners or merely as the aggregate of the partners, a conduit. Subchapter K resolves this dilemma by adopting entity treatment for some purposes and aggregate treatment for other purposes. Generally, this approach has been successful, although problems sometimes arise when the two approaches apply to different aspects of the same transaction, and incongruities occur.

The provisions of Subchapter K are highly interrelated. Few, if any of its provisions can be studied or wholly understood in isolation. For example, when the statute allows the partners to affect the current tax liability of one partner through the shaping of the partnership agreement—which Subchapter K does with surprising frequency—there generally will be an offsetting effect on other partners or the affected partner in a later year. Often the offsetting effect is found in the operation of a different provision than that governing the first transaction, one that may be invoked by a seemingly unrelated future transaction. With this in mind, a brief overview of the basic statutory pattern

4. Foxman v. Commissioner, 41 T.C. 535, 551, note 9 (1964) (A), aff'd, 352 F.2d 466 (3d Cir.1965).

of Subchapter K may be helpful before studying any particular provisions in depth.

B. OUTLINE OF THE TAXING PATTERN

A partnership does not pay income tax as such, although it must file a partnership return. Sections 701, 6031. Instead, the separate partners are liable in their individual capacities to pay tax on their share of the partnership's income. But the partnership is an accounting entity for purposes of computing the partnership's taxable income, which is then taxed to the partners as individuals according to the manner in which it is divided among them. Hence the need for a partnership return, which also acts as an information return.[5] A partnership return is more than just an information return, however, because audits and adjustments with respect to partnership items must be conducted at the partnership level, not the individual partner level, except in the case of certain small partnerships. Sections 6221–6233.

Partnership taxable income is computed following the same rules that govern the computation of the taxable income of any individual engaged in business, with a few specific modifications. See section 703(a)(2); Regulations, section 1.703–1(a)(2). Sections 702(a) and 703(a)(1) and Regulations, sections 1.703–1(a), 1.702–1(a)(1)–(8), require certain items entering into the computation of an individual's income tax liability to be segregated and separately stated on the partnership's return. This rule applies to items whose taxable status is affected by the tax situation of the individual partner. Aggregate partnership taxable income or loss, exclusive of the separately stated items and nonallowable deductions, is computed under the general rules regarding gross income and deductions. In this regard, the partnership has its own accounting period and accounting methods, although section 706(b) restricts the partnership's ability to choose a taxable year that does not coincide with the taxable year of a majority of its partners. Although in general partnership business income is computed on an entity basis, because of the passive loss limitations of section 469, it may be necessary for a partnership to state separately the net income or loss from each separate business "activity" that it conducts; and this segregation is always required for limited partnerships. Nevertheless, it is fair to describe the approach so far as more of an entity approach than an aggregate approach. Computation of partnership taxable income is discussed in detail, infra page 72.

Once the taxable income of the partnership is computed, aside from the special modifications treating the partnership itself as an account-

5. For 1985 slightly over 1.7 million partnership returns, with more than 13,000,000 partners, were filed. These returns reflected gross receipts of about $367 billion, and an aggregate taxable loss of about $8.9 billion. Out of the total number of partnerships, somewhat more than one half had net income totaling about $77 billion. Broken down between general and limited partnerships, general partnerships in the aggregate realized about $18 billion of net income and limited partnerships realized net losses of $26.9 billion. 7 S.O.I. Bulletin, No. 1, 33–38 (1987).

ing entity, the approach shifts. Each partner is liable for the tax attributable to his distributive share of the separately stated items and the remaining partnership taxable income, whether or not it is distributed. This result is accomplished by requiring the partner to include his share of income, deductions, or losses on his own return along with the rest of his taxable income. This is so even in the extreme case where the partner reports on the cash method and the partnership uses the accrual method but has not actually received payment of the income item. Likewise, because each partner is entitled to his distributive share of separately stated deduction items and credits, as well as a residual loss, if any, deduction items accrued by the partnership, even if not paid, affect the taxation of a cash method partner. Finally, section 702(c) includes a partner's distributive share of partnership gross income in the partner's gross income whenever it is necessary to determine gross income to apply any Code provision.[6]

Thus, for the purpose of tax liability the entity approach yields to treatment of the partnership as a conduit through which the individual partners are regarded as receiving the income so computed as if they had earned it individually. This quantitative "fragmentation" of the partnership income among the several partners is accompanied by a further "qualitative" division under which all specially treated items retain their qualitative identity when allocated to the several partners. Section 702(b). This qualitative division permits the different items of income and deduction derived from the partnership to be joined with their counterparts derived from the nonpartnership activities of the respective individual partners. But the partnership as an accounting entity still affects aspects of this allocation of distributive shares, such as the time of inclusion of those shares. Since the partnership income is computed on the basis of the partnership accounting period, the attribution to the partners is normally made only at the end of that period. Accordingly, the individual partners must include their share of partnership income for the taxable year of the partnership ending with or within the individual partner's taxable year. Section 706(a). However, as a result of special rules governing the use of fiscal taxable years, a partner and the partnership will usually have the same taxable year. Section 706(b). Moreover, in general, elections affecting the computation of taxable income derived by a partnership must be made by the partnership.

This divergent treatment of a partnership—an accounting entity on the one part, an aggregation of separate individuals on the other—is a practicable and sensible treatment. It avoids on the one hand the confusion that would result from a computation of income based on the different accounting methods of the partners and, on the other, the tax avoidance and tax liability problems that would result from taxing the partnership on its income and postponing taxation of the partners until

6. However, when the partner receives a guaranteed payment under section 707, see discussion, infra, page 167, a double inclusion of that payment in income is prevented.

actual distribution of the income. But this conduit approach does introduce some accounting complexities in requiring the separate computation of the various special items of partnership income, gain, loss or credit, and more importantly, creates the difficult problem of determining the amount and character of the partner's distributive shares of each of the various items.

Significant tax difficulties arise in those aspects of partnership operation in which the choice of the entity as against the aggregate approach would produce material differences. These situations involve the formation of the partnership, the disposition of partnership assets, the distribution of partnership assets to partners, the dissolution of a partnership, sales by a partner of his partnership interest to other partners or outsiders, and so on. Increasingly, the use of detailed statutory and regulatory rules governing most partnership transactions largely resolve the issues as to the aggregate and entity view of the partnership, but these rules in turn introduce an intricate framework engendering its own complexity and difficulties.

Until 1988, all forms of partnership activity were treated under the same set of rules. The partnership provisions covered a wide variety of situations, ranging from small service or business partnerships involving two or three members, to large accounting and law partnerships with hundreds of members, to tax shelter and investment partnerships, which may involve as many owners as publicly held corporations. For taxable years after 1987, however, section 7704 generally treats limited partnerships with publicly traded interests as corporations. Section 7704 is discussed in detail, infra, page 45.

Since subchapter K does not apply at all unless a partnership exists, the logical starting point is an examination of the definition of a partnership for tax purposes. The remainder of this chapter will deal with that issue. Succeeding chapters deal with the formation, operation and liquidation of partnerships, and the transfer of partnership interests by sale or death.

SECTION 3. DEFINITION OF A PARTNERSHIP

A. PARTNERSHIP VERSUS OTHER BUSINESS ARRANGEMENT

INTERNAL REVENUE CODE: Sections 761(a); 7701(a)(2).

REGULATIONS: Sections 1.761–1(a), (b), 2(a); 301.7701–1, –3(a).

MADISON GAS AND ELECTRIC CO. v. COMMISSIONER

United States Court of Appeals, Seventh Circuit, 1980.
633 F.2d 512.

CUMMINGS, CIRCUIT JUDGE.

This is an action under 26 U.S.C. § 7422 for the refund of federal income taxes. The question is whether certain training and related expenses incurred by a public utility in the expansion of its generating capacity through the joint construction and operation of a nuclear plant with two other utilities are deductible as ordinary and necessary expenses in the years of payment or are non-deductible pre-operating capital expenditures of a new partnership venture. The Tax Court in an opinion reported at 72 T.C. 521 held that they are non-deductible capital expenditures. We affirm.

I

All relevant facts have been stipulated by the parties (App. 8–41) and found and set forth at length by the Tax Court. We find it necessary to summarize them only briefly. Taxpayer Madison Gas and Electric Co. (MGE), a Wisconsin corporation, is an operating public utility which has been engaged since 1896 in the production, purchase, transmission and distribution of electricity and the purchase and distribution of natural gas. MGE is subject to the jurisdiction and regulation of the Public Service Commission of Wisconsin (PSC) and the Nuclear Regulatory Commission. The Federal Energy Regulatory Commission (FERC) also has or may have jurisdiction over MGE.

MGE is required to furnish reasonably adequate service and facilities within its service area at rates found reasonable and just by the PSC. During 1969 and 1970, the tax years here in issue, MGE rendered service to some 73,000 residential and commercial customers in a service area of approximately 200 square miles in Dane County, Wisconsin. MGE also sells a small percentage of its electrical power to other utilities in Wisconsin. Its primary responsibility, however, is to its customers in the service area. The number of customers within that area has grown rapidly and continuously during the past 25 years, and the customer demand for electricity has increased with the expansion of commercial and industrial accounts, the substitution of electricity for other forms of energy, and the increasing prevalence of high-energy devices such as air-conditioning units. Thus at the time of trial MGE was servicing almost 90,000 residential, commercial and industrial customers.

MGE has over the years kept pace with the increasing demand for electrical power and provided it at reasonable rates by expanding the generating capacity of its facilities, contracting for the purchase and sale of excess electrical power, interconnecting transmission facilities with those of other Wisconsin utilities, and finally by building and operating additional facilities in conjunction with other utilities. Expenses incurred in connection with one of these joint ventures is the subject of the present suit.

On February 2, 1967, MGE entered into an agreement, entitled "Joint Power Supply Agreement" (Agreement) (App. 42–59), with Wisconsin Public Service Corporation (WPS) and Wisconsin Power and Light Co. (WPL) under which the three utilities agreed, *inter alia,* to construct and own together a nuclear generating plant now known as the Kewaunee Nuclear Power Plant (Plant). Under the Agreement, the Plant is owned by MGE, WPS and WPL as tenants-in-common with undivided ownership interests of 17.8%, 41.2% and 41.0% respectively. Electricity produced by the Plant is distributed to each of the utilities in proportion to their ownership interests. Each utility sells or uses its share of the power as it does power produced by its own individually owned facilities, and the profits thereby earned by MGE contribute only to MGE's individual profits. No portion of the power generated at the Plant is offered for sale by the utilities collectively, and the Plant is not recognized by the relevant regulatory bodies as a separate utility licensed to sell electricity. Each utility also pays a portion of all expenditures for operation, maintenance and repair of the Plant corresponding exactly to its respective share of ownership. Under utility accounting procedures mandated by the PSC and the FERC, these expenses are combined with and treated in the same manner by MGE as expenses from its individually owned facilities. The ownership and operation of the Plant by MGE, WPS and WPL is regarded by the PSC and the FERC as a tenancy-in-common. It was the intention of the utilities to create only a co-tenancy and not a partnership and to be taxed as co-tenants and not as partners.

In its 1969 and 1970 taxable years, MGE incurred certain expenses relating to the nuclear training of WPS employees, the establishment of internal procedures and guidelines for plant operation and maintenance, employee hiring activities, nuclear field management, environmental activities and the purchase of certain spare parts (App. 116–126). MGE had to incur these expenses in order to carry out its Plant activities. Pursuant to order of the PSC, MGE was required to amortize training expenses, net of income taxes, over a 60–month period from the date of commercial operation of the Plant, a date occurring after those in issue here, and the other non-construction expenses associated with the Plant, net of income taxes, over a three-year period beginning January 1, 1978. MGE did not deduct the expenses described above on its tax returns for 1969 and 1970, but in the Tax Court claimed a deduction for them by amendment to its refund petition in the total amounts of $33,418.45 and $114,434.27 for 1969 and 1970 respectively.

MGE's position was, and is, that the claimed expenses were currently deductible under Section 162(a) of the Internal Revenue Code of 1954 (Code) as ordinary and necessary business expenses. The Commissioner's position was, and is, that the claimed expenses were non-deductible capital expenditures. The Tax Court agreed with the Commissioner, holding that the operation of the Plant by MGE, WPS and WPL is a partnership within the meaning of Section 7701(a)(2) of the Code, that the expenses in question were incurred not in the carrying out of an existing business but as part of the start-up costs of the new partnership venture, and that the expenses were therefore not currently deductible but must be capitalized under Section 263(a) of the Code. MGE appeals from this judgment, arguing that its arrangement with WPS and WPL is not a partnership within the meaning of the Code and, alternatively, that even if it is a partnership the expenses are currently deductible.

II

The threshold issue is whether MGE's joint venture with WPS and WPL is a tax partnership. The Commissioner concedes that if it is not, the expenses are currently deductible under Section 162(a). A partnership for federal tax purposes is defined by the Code in Section 7701(a)(2), which provides in pertinent part:

> "The term 'partnership' includes a syndicate, group, pool, joint venture, or other unincorporated organization, through or by means of which any business, financial operation, or venture is carried on, and which is not, within the meaning of this title, a trust estate or a corporation."

MGE's arrangement with WPS and WPL in connection with the Plant clearly establishes an unincorporated organization carrying on a "business, financial operation, or venture" and therefore falls within the literal statutory definition of a partnership. The arrangement is, of course, not taken out of this classification simply because the three utilities intended to be taxed only as a co-tenancy and not as a partnership. While it is well-settled that mere co-ownership of property does not create a tax partnership, see, e.g., Estate of Appleby v. Commissioner, 41 B.T.A. 18 (1940), co-owners may also be partners if they or their agents carry on the requisite "degree of business activities." Powell v. Commissioner, 26 T.C.M. 161 (1967); Hahn v. Commissioner, 22 T.C. 212 (1954).

MGE's argument is that a co-tenancy does not meet the business activities test of partnership status unless the co-tenants anticipate the earning and sharing of a single joint cash profit from their joint activity. Because its common venture with WPS and WPL does not result in the division of cash profits from joint marketing, MGE contends that the venture constitutes only a co-tenancy coupled with an expense-sharing arrangement and not a tax partnership. The Tax Court held that the Code definition of partnership does not require joint venturers to share in a single joint cash profit and that to the extent that a profit motive is required by the Code it is met here by the distribution of profits in kind. We agree.

The definition of partnership in Section 7701(a)(2) was added to the Code by Section 1111(a) of the Revenue Act of 1932 and first appeared in Section 3797(a)(2) of the 1939 Code. The Congressional Reports accompanying the 1932 Act make clear, in largely identical language, that Congress intended to broaden the definition of partnership for federal tax purposes to include a number of arrangements, such as joint ventures, which were not partnerships under state law. H.P.Rep. No. 708, 72d Cong., 1st Sess., 53 (1932); S.Rep. No. 665, 72d Cong., 1st Sess., 59 (1932). In so doing, they briefly discuss the advantages of requiring a partnership return for joint venturers rather than leaving the sole responsibility for reporting annual gains and losses on the individual members. MGE invites us to infer from these discussions that Congress contemplated inclusion only of those joint ventures that are capable of producing joint cash gains and losses. But even if we were inclined to narrow the statutory language on the basis of such slender evidence, the subsequent legislative history would dissuade us from reaching MGE's suggested construction.

In Bentex Oil Corp. v. Commissioner, 20 T.C. 565 (1953), the Tax Court held that an unincorporated organization formed to extract oil under an operating agreement which called for distribution of oil in kind was a partnership within the meaning of Section 3797(a)(2) of the 1939 Code. The Bentex joint venture is not distinguishable from that presented here in any meaningful way. The co-owners there, as here, shared the expenses of production but sold their shares of the production individually. Following *Bentex,* Congress reenacted the definition of partnership in Section 3797(a)(2) of the 1939 Code without change as Section 7701(a)(2) of the 1954 Code. In addition, it repeated the definition verbatim in Section 761(a), which permits certain qualifying organizations to elect to be excluded from application of some or all of the special Subchapter K partnership provisions. A qualifying corporation is one which is used

> "(1) for investment purposes only and not for the active conduct of a business, or
>
> "(2) for the joint production, extraction, or use of property, but not for the purpose of selling services or property produced or extracted, if the income of the members of the organization may be adequately determined without the computation of partnership taxable income."

In short, Section 761(a) allows unincorporated associations such as the Bentex venture and the one in issue here, which fall within the statutory definition of partnership, to elect out of Subchapter K.[2] The Section has generally been interpreted, in the absence of any legislative history, as approving the *Bentex* decision while providing relief from certain resulting hardships. See, e.g., Williams, Joint Operation of Jointly Owned Natural Resources, 10 Oil and Gas Quarterly 149 (1961); Taubman, Oil and Gas Partnerships and Section 761(a), 12 Tax L.Rev. 49 (1956). This interpretation is surely correct for, as the Tax Court observed:

> "[i]f distribution in kind of jointly produced property was enough to avoid partnership status, we do not see how such distribution could be used as a test for election to be excluded from the partnership provisions of subchapter K" (72 T.C. at 563).

MGE also relies on Treasury Regulation Sections 301.7701–3 and 1.761–1(a) (26 C.F.R.) to support its argument that joint marketing is a *sine qua non* of partnership status. These Sections state in identical language that tenants in common

> "may be partners if they actively carry on a trade, business, financial operations, or venture and divided the profits thereof."

In addition, MGE cites to us case law referring to a joint profit motive as a characteristic of partnerships.[3] See, e.g., Commissioner v. Tower, 327 U.S. 280, 286, 66 S.Ct. 532, 535, 90 L.Ed. 670 ("community of interest in the profits and losses"); Ian Allison v. Commissioner, 35 T.C.M. 1069 (1976) ("an agreement to share profits"). Neither the above-quoted Treasury Regulations Sections nor the case law distin-

2. MGE argues that in enacting Section 761(a) Congress had in mind only oil, gas and mineral ventures acting under operating agreements and that therefore the Section should not be automatically construed to include an operating agreement for the production of electricity. In support of this position, MGE inexplicably cites Taubman, Oil and Gas Partnerships and Section 761(a), 12 Tax L.Rev. 49 (1956), in which the author expressly states:

> "Congress thus attempted to establish a workable formula which would be valid not only for oil and gas, but all types of operating agreements, as well as the related and equally difficult field of investment." 12 Tax L.Rev. 49, 67.

The three utilities here in fact did file a partnership return and election-out of Subchapter K (App. 19, 41). The Tax Court held that the filing of a partnership return and election-out under Section 761(a) are not admissions of partnership status (72 T.C. at 558). MGE did not argue below that election-out caused the organization not to be a partnership for non-Subchapter K tax purposes, and the Tax Court declined to decide this possible issue (72 T.C. at 559 n. 9). In its alternative position here, however, MGE contends that the holding below is "inconsistent with the purpose" of Section 761(a) (Br. 41). This argument is indistinguishable from an argument that election-out under Section 761(a) negates partnership status except where the Code explicitly provides to the contrary. Since the issue was not raised and decided below, we do not address it here. We note, however, that Section 7701(a)(2) explicitly states that an organization which is a partnership as defined in that Section is a partnership for the purposes of the entire Code, whereas Section 761(a) provides only for election-out of Subchapter K.

3. The Commissioner takes the position that the presence of a joint profit motive is merely one factor to be considered in determining partnership status, while MGE argues that it is a necessary element. Because we find a joint profit motive here, albeit for in-kind profits, we need not resolve this dispute.

guish between the division of cash profits and the division of in-kind profits, and none of the cited cases involved in-kind profits. Moreover, while distribution of profits in-kind may be an uncommon business arrangement, recognition of such arrangements as tax partnerships is not novel. See, e.g., *Bentex,* supra; Luckey v. Commissioner, 334 F.2d 719 (9th Cir.1965); Bryant v. Commissioner, 46 T.C. 848, affirmed, 399 F.2d 800 (5th Cir.1968).[4]

The practical reality of the venture in issue here is that jointly produced electricity is distributed to MGE and the other two utilities in direct proportion to their ownership interest for resale to consumers in their service areas or to other utilities. The difference between the market value of MGE's share of that electricity and MGE's share of the cost of production obviously represents a profit. Just as obviously, the three utilities joined together in the construction and operation of the Plant with the anticipation of realizing these profits. The fact that the profits are not realized in cash until after the electricity has been channeled through the individual facilities of each participant does not negate their joint profit motive nor make the venture a mere expense-sharing arrangement.[5] We hold therefore that MGE's joint venture with WPS and WPL constitutes a partnership within the meaning of Sections 7701(a)(2) and 761(a) of the Code.

III

On the ultimate issue in this case, the Tax Court held that the claimed expenses were incurred as pre-operational costs of the partnership venture and therefore under settled law were non-deductible capital expenditures. See Richmond Television Corp. v. United States, 845 F.2d 901 (4th Cir.1965), vacated on other grounds, 382 U.S. 68, 86 S.Ct. 233, 15 L.Ed.2d 143.

MGE argues that this holding elevates form over substance in that even if the operating arrangement is technically a tax partnership, the claimed expenses were in actuality simply ordinary and necessary expenses of expanding its existing business. MGE asks us therefore to ignore the partnership entity as lacking economic substance.

In support of its position, MGE relies heavily on First National Bank of South Carolina v. United States, 558 F.2d 721 (4th Cir.1977);

4. See generally, McKee, Nelson & Whitmire, Federal Taxation of Partnerships and Partners, par. 3.02, pp. 3–8, in which the authors conclude: "A partnership may result from a joint extraction or production agreement among co-owners of mineral property or production facilities, even though the co-owners separately take and sell (or reserve the right to take and sell) their shares of production. * * * Despite the absence of an objective to earn a joint cash profit, these ventures are generally considered partnerships" (footnotes omitted).

5. Treasury Regulation Sections 301.7701–3 and 1.761–1(a) (26 C.F.R.) state that a "joint undertaking merely to share expenses is not a partnership," and go on to give the example of neighboring landowners who jointly construct a ditch "merely to drain surface water from their properties." We agree with the Tax Court that the venture here is "in no way comparable to the joint construction of a drainage ditch" (72 T.C. at 560).

First Security Bank of Idaho N.A. v. Commissioner, 63 T.C. 644 (1975); and Colorado Springs National Bank v. United States, 505 F.2d 1185 (10th Cir.1974). In those cases, the respective courts held that the initial costs incurred by banks participating in non-profit associations set up as clearinghouses for a credit card system were deductible as ordinary and necessary business expenses because participation in a credit card system was not a new business venture but merely a new way of conducting an old business. These cases are not on point. Participation in the credit card associations had no extrinsic or marketable value, created no property right and did not entitle the participants to any distribution of profits, either cash or in-kind. There was no suggestion in those cases whatsoever that the banks had by participating in the association created a new partnership venture with other banks, and the courts were not asked to ignore partnership status. The question was whether the costs were necessary and ordinary current expenses or capital investments in future economic benefits.

Here MGE, WPS and WPL are engaged in the joint production of electricity for resale, a joint venture for profit. Because they were each already in the business of selling electricity, it can, of course, be argued that the partnership venture itself is an extension or expansion of their existing businesses. It does not follow from this though that we should ignore the partnership as lacking economic substance. Such reasoning would lead to the absurd conclusion that any partnership established to do collectively what its participants formerly did individually or continue to do individually outside the partnership lacks economic substance and should not be treated as a partnership for tax purposes.

At bottom, MGE's position is that it is not sound policy to treat the entity here as a partnership. But we are not free to rewrite the tax laws, whatever the merits of MGE's position. Under the Internal Revenue Code the joint venture here is a partnership and the expenses were non-deductible, pre-operational start-up costs of the partnership venture. Accordingly, the judgment of the Tax Court is affirmed.

ILLUSTRATIVE MATERIAL

A. PARTNERSHIP VERSUS CO-OWNERSHIP OF PROPERTY

1. *General*

Determining whether co-owners of property are engaged in business as partners is important for a variety of reasons beyond the requirement in section 6031 that a partnership file a return.[7] For example, if the arrangement is a partnership, all tax accounting elections, including cost recovery methods under section 168, must be made by the partnership, not by the individual co-owners. Other provisions whose proper application cannot be determined without first determining if a partnership exists include section 453, governing installment sales, section 1031, governing like kind exchanges (undivided interests in property are subject to section 1031; partner-

7. For the importance of filing partnership returns, see Simons v. United States, 89–1 U.S.T.C. ¶ 9238 (S.D.Fla.1989) (upholding $1,000 per year failure to file penalty under section 6698).

ship interests are not), section 1033, dealing with involuntary conversions, and section 1221 defining capital assets. Also, if ownership is a cotenancy rather than a partnership, deductions, other than depreciation, attributable to the enterprise do not reduce the individual owners' bases in the property, whereas deductions that flow through to partners reduce their bases in their partnership interests. See section 705(a)(2)(A).

A partnership is broadly defined in section 761(a) as any "syndicate, group, pool, joint venture or other unincorporated organization through or by means of which any business, financial operation, or venture is carried on, and which is not * * * a corporation, or a trust or estate." In an important case decided before the enactment of Subchapter K, but which related to a year in which the statutory predecessor of section 761(a) appeared in the Code, the Supreme Court held that the test for determining the existence of a partnership is whether the parties by their actions intended to join together to conduct a business and sharing in the profits and losses, regardless of how they characterized the relationship. Commissioner v. Culbertson, 337 U.S. 733 (1949). Despite the broad definition in the statute, the Regulations provide that a joint undertaking to share expenses or the mere co-ownership of property which is maintained, kept in repair, and leased does not constitute a partnership. However, co-ownership will be treated as a partnership if active business operations are carried on, such as providing services for a tenant either directly or through an agent. Regulations, section 1.761–1(a)(1).

Although the reported cases cite numerous factors which are considered in determining whether persons have entered into a partnership, the single most important factor in all cases is whether the parties are acting as coproprietors. In Levine v. Commissioner, 72 T.C. 780 (1979) (unpublished case), aff'd on other issues, 634 F.2d 12 (2d Cir.1980), the taxpayers owned various commercial real estate properties which they leased to tenants. No partnership returns were filed, and the taxpayers reported the income or loss from the properties pro rata on their individual returns. Even though the parties did not characterize their relationship as a partnership, the Tax Court found that they were partners because they engaged in an active business by leasing the properties to tenants, providing property management services to the tenants, and sharing the gains and losses. These factors were found more indicative of a partnership business than "a mere passive investment." See also Rothenberg v. Commissioner, 48 T.C. 369 (1967) (owners of apartment buildings found to be partners rather than tenants in common where the operation of the buildings constituted the active conduct of a rental business; hence the partnership and not the individuals was the proper taxpayer to make the election under section 453 regarding installment method reporting of gains); Underwriters Insurance Agency of America v. Commissioner, 40 T.C.M. 5 (1980) (co-owners of tuna fishing boats were partners even though boats were registered and transferred in individual names as co-owners rather than in partnership name; boats were operated through employees or agents, not leased, and partnership returns were filed for some vessels for some years); Antonides v. Commissioner, 91 T.C. 686 (1988) (taxpayers were partners in boat chartering business in 1981 even though no written partnership agreement was signed until 1982).

2. *Cases Finding Co-ownership*

In McShain v. Commissioner, 68 T.C. 154 (1977), no partnership existed where co-owners leased unimproved land to a single tenant, who was required to pay rent, all taxes, assessments, utility bills and other assessments relating to the land. The only activities of the lessors were collecting rent and signing applications for permits and licenses. Accordingly, when the land was condemned, section 1033 applied to the co-owners individually.

Revenue Ruling 75–374, 1975–2 Cum.Bull. 261, provides some examples of maintenance and repair activity that allow co-owners to avoid partnership classification under Regulations, section 1.761–1(a)(1). Co-owners of an apartment building hired an unrelated management corporation to manage, operate and maintain the property. The management company negotiated and executed leases, collected rents and other payments from tenants, paid taxes, assessments and insurance premiums with respect to the property, and performed all other customary services to maintain and repair the property on behalf of and at the expense of the co-owners. Services provided to the tenants by the co-owners through the management company included heat, air conditioning, hot and cold water, unattended parking, trash removal, and cleaning of public areas. The management company also provided to tenants *on its own behalf* additional services such as attendant parking, cabanas, gas, and other utilities. The Ruling held that the co-owners were not partners between themselves, and implies that they were not partners with the management company. Since the Regulations apply the same standard whether services are provided directly or through an agent, the result in the Ruling should not have differed if the co-owners had provided maintenance and repairs directly. Those services provided by the management company on its own behalf, however, appear to have gone beyond maintenance and repair and, if the management company had provided those services on behalf of the co-owners or if the co-owners had provided those services directly, they probably would have been found to be partners.

Madison Gas and Electric, supra page 8, turned on whether the joint profit motive requisite for finding a partnership could be satisfied if the venture was organized to produce a product of value which would be divided among the parties to the venture with each party, in turn, independently selling or using his share of the product. This issue was also raised in an earlier case, Allison v. Commissioner, 35 T.C.M. 1069 (1976). In that case X Corporation, which was in the business of arranging financing for commercial property development, entered into an agreement with Y Corporation under which X Corporation would arrange to secure the financing necessary for Y Corporation to purchase and subdivide a tract of land; upon completion of the subdivision, Y Corporation was to deed X Corporation 75 of the subdivided lots. X Corporation claimed that the lots were received in a tax free liquidation of a joint venture; the Commissioner asserted that they were received as compensation for services. Emphasizing that there was no agreement to resell the subdivided lots jointly, the court found that there was no joint profit motive and thus no partnership. In addition, the court noted that no partnership books were kept and no partnership tax returns filed. The different result in this case may be reconciled with *Madison Gas and Electric* because the *Allison* case involved a venture of limited scope and duration rather than the ongoing conduct of a business.

See also Bussing v. Commissioner, 88 T.C. 449 (1987), supplemental opinion, 89 T.C. 1050 (1987), finding a purported "sale-leaseback" transaction to be a partnership between the "lessor" and the "lessee."

3. *Election Out of Partnership Status*

Section 761(a) authorizes regulations under which members of "an unincorporated organization" may elect to be excluded from the operation of subchapter K if the organization is availed of (1) for investment purposes rather than the active conduct of a business; (2) for the joint production, extraction or use of property, but not for the purpose of selling services or property produced or extracted; or (3) by securities dealers engaged in a short term venture to underwrite, sell or distribute a particular issue of securities, provided in all cases that the members' incomes can adequately be determined without the computation of partnership taxable income. See Regulations, section 1.761–2, for further details and the manner for making the election. When a valid section 761 election is made no partnership return must be filed. In addition, the election overrides section 703(b), which requires that all elections (with specified exceptions) be made by the partnership, and thereby permits co-owners to make inconsistent elections with respect to the accounting treatment of items relating to the property. See Rev.Rul. 83–129, 1983–2 Cum.Bull. 105 (election to capitalize and amortize mine development expenses under section 616). But where a provision of the Code outside of Subchapter K specifically refers to the treatment of partnerships wholly apart from subchapter K, a section 761 election has no effect. See Bryant v. Commissioner, 399 F.2d 800 (5th Cir. 1968) (investment credit limitation under section 48(c)(2)(D) of 1954 Code applies to partnership that made 761 election); Rev.Rul. 65–118, 1965–1 Cum.Bull. 30 (same).

B. PARTNERSHIP VERSUS EMPLOYMENT OR AGENCY AGREEMENT

A partnership does not exist if the relationship between the parties is an employment, agency or independent contractor arrangement. See Rev.Rul. 75–43, 1975–1 Cum.Bull. 383 (no partnership where a corporate feedlot owner entered into a service agreement with individual cattle owners to raise cattle for the owners). This issue has arisen most frequently with respect to classifying receipts as ordinary income from compensation or gain from the sale of a capital asset. See Luna v. Commissioner, 42 T.C. 1067 (1964) (taxpayer was found to be an employee of an insurance company rather than a party to a joint venture; hence a lump sum payment to him was taxable as compensation and not as capital gain on the sale of a partnership interest).

In determining whether an arrangement is a partnership or an employment, agency or contractor arrangement, the same standards used to determine if co-owners are partners apply. But because employees, agents, and independent contractors frequently are compensated on the basis of a percentage of the employer's profits, the sharing of profits aspect of the test may be more difficult to apply; sharing of losses, which is not common in employment or similar relationships may be more significant, but is not always necessary. The essential factual inquiry is whether the persons are "coproprietors" of the business. In Wheeler v. Commissioner, 37 T.C.M. 883 (1978), the taxpayer entered into an agreement with Perault to develop specific tracts of land. The taxpayer contributed "know-how" and Perault provided the financing, with the profits to be split 25 percent to the taxpayer and 75 percent to Perault. Although title to all properties was held in Perault's name, the parties did business under the name "Perault and Wheeler." The taxpayer had total authority to manage the day-to-day affairs of the business, but he could not borrow on behalf of the venture. Perault, however, was entitled to receive all of the operating income until he received back his entire investment plus six percent interest and was to bear all losses; consistently, he reported all of the operating income and expenses. Upon the sale of properties, however, Perault reported only his share of gains; he did not report the full gain and claim a deduction for compensation paid to the taxpayer. The Tax Court held that Wheeler and Perault were partners. Accordingly, Wheeler's share of the gains was taxable to him as capital gains, rather than being treated as compensation for services taxable as ordinary income. See also Rev.Rul. 54–84, 1954–1 Cum.Bull. 284 (holding properties in one partner's name and absence of loss sharing did not prevent partnership status).

In Tharp v. Commissioner, 57 T.C.M. 1190 (1989) (unpublished case), no partnership was found to exist despite testimony of both purported partners that they intended to form an equal partnership. The objective evidence indicated that Tharp made all important management decisions without consulting his purported partner, Tharp in fact treated the "partnership" liabilities as his own by making all payments on his own account, and Tharp actually received substantially more than one-half of the profits. Accordingly, all of the unreported income of the business was taxable to Tharp.

Dorman v. United States, 296 F.2d 27 (9th Cir.1961), involved an agreement for a ranching venture under which the taxpayer, who contributed no capital, was to be an equal partner, but his interest was not "vested" until he fully paid promissory notes representing his capital contribution to the partnership. The notes, which were for an amount equal to one half of the other venturer's capital contribution, were payable only out of the taxpayer's share of profits from the venture. In the interim, the taxpayer received a salary. The taxpayer was found to be merely an employee with an executory right to become a partner. Therefore, he was not permitted to deduct any portion of the net operating loss incurred by the venture. See also Smith's Estate v. Commissioner, 313 F.2d 724 (8th Cir.1963) (purported partnership between investment advisors and investors in commodities in which investors contributed all of the capital and bore all of the losses, but shared trading profits with investment advisors were not recognized; investment advisors realized income from compensation).

C. PARTNERSHIP VERSUS LOAN

Occasionally, a transaction otherwise denominated as a loan may be recharacterized as a partnership. This may occur in the case of an unsecured nonrecourse debt which is to be repaid only out of profits from a venture. See Hartman v. Commissioner, 17 T.C.M. 1020 (1958). Even if there is security for the loan, if it is inadequate, the loan may be recharacterized as an equity investment when the debt is convertible into an equity investment. See Rev.Rul. 72–350, 1972–2 Cum.Bull. 394.

Characterization of a transaction as a loan on the one hand or as a partnership on the other hand is significant not only for the purpose of characterizing payments from the "borrower" to the "lender" as interest or as a payment by a partnership to a partner, but also for purposes of determining who is entitled to claim losses incurred by the venture, the treatment of the parties if the "loan" is not repaid, and the "lender's" treatment if he sells his interest.

Even though it is well accepted that interest need not be a fixed rate, but may be a specified portion of the borrower's profits, see Dorzback v. Collison, 195 F.2d 69 (3d Cir.1952), participating loans and shared appreciation mortgages still raise the question of whether the purported lender and borrower are instead partners. Under certain circumstances, the Internal Revenue Service will treat a shared appreciation mortgage entirely as a loan. Rev.Rul. 83–51, 1983–1 Cum.Bull. 48, treats as interest contingent interest equal to a fixed percentage of the appreciation in value of the borrower's personal residence over the term of the loan. In the commercial context, the Service will not rule in advance on whether a shared appreciation mortgage creates a true loan. Rev.Proc. 85–22, 1985–1 Cum.Bull. 550. Cf. Rev.Rul. 76–413, 1976–2 Cum.Bull. 213 (certain contingent interest on a mortgage loan made to a real estate developer by a trust was "interest on obligations secured by real property" under section 856(c), relating to real estate investment trusts, rather than profits from active participation in the operation of the property; the result of the Ruling was changed by amendment of Section 856, but the analysis appears to continue to be relevant).

Shared appreciation mortgages and participation loans also may be held to constitute "equity" or part debt/part equity investments. See infra, page 409.

D. RELEVANCE OF STATE LAW

As the prior material indicates, characterization of an arrangement as a partnership under state law is not controlling for federal income tax purposes; Internal Revenue Code standards control. Regulations, section 301.7701–1(c); Commissioner v. Culbertson, 337 U.S. 733 (1949); Kahn's Estate v. Commissioner, 499 F.2d 1186 (2d Cir.1974). Thus, Rev.Rul. 77–137, 1977–1 Cum.Bull. 178, held that an assignee of a limited partnership interest, who under state law was not admitted to the partnership by virtue of the assignment but who was entitled to distributions of partnership profits, nevertheless would be taxed as the owner of the partnership interest. While local law may distinguish a partnership from a joint venture for some purposes, the latter generally being formed for a single business purpose in contrast to the formation of a partnership to conduct an ongoing business, the distinction is not relevant for tax law; a joint venture is treated the same as a partnership. See Podell v. Commissioner, 55 T.C. 429 (1970). Local law is controlling, however, in determining the rights and responsibilities of the participants which are taken into account in determining the existence of a partnership applying tax law standards.

A partnership may exist for tax purposes even though it could not legally exist under local law. See Nichols v. Commissioner, 32 T.C. 1322 (1959) (finding that a partnership for the practice of medicine existed between a physician and nonphysician, an arrangement that would be proscribed under state law); Rev.Rul. 77–332, 1977–2 Cum.Bull. 484 (partnership between CPAs and non-CPA "principals" in accounting firm; state law prohibits non-CPA partners).

Generally the organization of a business venture as a corporation under state law results in the venture being taxed as a corporation. But see S & M Plumbing Co. Inc. v. Commissioner, 55 T.C. 702 (1971) (A) (joint venture found even though a corporation issued preferred stock to its "partner"); see also, Olmstead Hotel v. Commissioner, 11 T.C.M. 694 (1952) (entity which was a trust under relevant state law was held to be a partnership for tax purposes).

E. REFERENCES

McMahon, The Availability and Effect of Election Out of Partnership Status Under Section 761(a), 9 Va. Tax Rev. 1 (1989); Burnes, The Shared Appreciation Mortgage—A Joint Venture, a Relationship Between Debtor and Creditor, or Both?, 12 J. Real Est. Tax. 195 (1985); Burke & Meyer, Federal Income Tax Classification of Natural Resource Ventures: Co–Ownership, Partnership, or Association?, 37 Sw.L.J. 859 (1984); Nelson, The Tax Classification of Partnerships: Distinguishing From Arm's–Length Economic Arrangements, 40 N.Y.U.Inst. on Fed.Tax. 15–1 (1982); Feder, Either a Partner or a Lender Be: Emerging Tax Issues in Real Estate Finance, 36 Tax Lawyer 191 (1983); Weidner, The Existence of State and Tax Partnerships: A Primer, 11 Fla.St.U.L.Rev. 1 (1983); Baker, Informal Partnerships: Their Status Under Federal and State Tax Law, 59 Neb.L.Rev. 464 (1980).

B. PARTNERSHIP VERSUS ASSOCIATION

INTERNAL REVENUE CODE: Section 7701(a)(3).

REGULATIONS: Sections 301.7701–1, –2(a)–(e), –3(b).

INTRODUCTION

Limited partnerships under the Uniform Limited Partnership Act have many characteristics in common with corporations. A limited partner is liable for partnership debts only to the extent of his capital contribution plus any additional amounts that he has agreed to contribute. Thus there is a strong resemblance to the limited liability of corporate shareholders. On the other hand, all limited partnerships must have at least one general partner who is fully liable for debts of the partnership.

Limited partners have no right to participate in the day-to-day management of the partnership's business; that is the responsibility of the general partner. The limited partners are entitled to examine the partnership's books, receive accountings, and vote on changes in the partnership agreement, rights similar to the rights of corporate shareholders. While general partnership interests, because they represent an agency relationship, are not freely transferable—they cannot be sold and bought like corporate stock—limited partnership interests may or may not be transferable, subject to some statutory limitations, depending on the terms of the partnership agreement.

Finally, the death or withdrawal of a limited partner does not terminate the partnership; both the entity and its business continue.

The death, bankruptcy, or withdrawal of a general partner, however, generally terminates the formal existence of the legal entity under state law, even if the partnership agreement provides that the business will be continued in a newly constituted successor partnership without interruption.

All of these attributes of limited partnerships make this form of business organization a popular vehicle for assembling groups of investors who desire limited liability, transferable interests, and professional management of the business, while avoiding treatment as a corporation for tax purposes.

In addition, limited partnerships enjoyed great popularity as the organization of choice for tax shelters because of the flow through of tax losses. Tax shelter investments came in many forms, including farming and cattle feeding operations, oil and gas exploration and development, equipment leasing, movie production, research and development projects, and, most frequently, commercial and residential rental real estate projects. All of these enterprises shared the feature that for the early years of the business' existence (many years in the case of real estate projects), tax deductions from the business exceeded gross income from the business, even if cash expenditures were not less than cash receipts. Thus, if partnership treatment was available, the investors were able to deduct the losses from the business against unrelated income.

After the Tax Reform Act of 1986, the limited partnership found a new role, providing a substitute for the corporate form of conducting profitable businesses. The changes in the rate structure introduced by the Tax Reform Act of 1986 increased the relative tax burden on retained corporate profits by establishing a corporate tax rate higher than the individual rate. In addition, the Act eliminated the preferential rate for capital gains, thus preventing a reduced rate of shareholder level tax on retained corporate earnings through the sale of corporate shares. Finally, certain technical changes were made in the taxation of gain at the corporate level which increased the tax burden on corporate distributions. This increased taxation of profits realized through the corporate form of business organization made the limited partnership form of investment attractive for potentially profitable operations. In turn, it highlighted the fundamental question of what types of business organizations should be subject to the traditional pattern of "double level" corporate taxation. The following materials trace the developments involving this issue.

Although the Internal Revenue Code provides that the corporate tax applies not only to organizations that are "corporations" under state law, but to any organization that is an "association" as defined in section 7701(a)(3), the statutory definition of "association" is not particularly helpful. Thus, the courts and the Internal Revenue Service have been forced to grapple with the definition of an "association" through years of litigation and administrative action.

MORRISSEY v. COMMISSIONER

Supreme Court of the United States, 1935.
296 U.S. 344.

MR. CHIEF JUSTICE HUGHES delivered the opinion of the Court.

Petitioners, the trustees of an express trust, contest income taxes for the years 1924 to 1926, inclusive, upon the ground that the trust has been illegally treated as an "association." The Circuit Court of Appeals affirmed the decision of the Board of Tax Appeals, which sustained the ruling of the Commissioner of Internal Revenue. 74 F.(2d) 803. We granted certiorari because of a conflict of decisions as to the distinction between an "association" and a "pure trust," the decisions being described in one of the cases as "seemingly in a hopeless state of confusion." Coleman–Gilbert Associates v. Commissioner, 76 F.(2d) 191, 193.

The facts were stipulated. In the year 1921 petitioners made a declaration of trust of real estate in Los Angeles. They were to be designated in "their collective capacity" as "Western Avenue Golf Club." The trustees were authorized to add to their number and to choose their successors; to purchase, encumber, sell, lease and operate the "described or other lands"; to construct and operate golf courses, club houses, etc.; to receive the rents, profits and income; to make loans and investments; to make regulations; and generally to manage the trust estate as if the trustees were its absolute owners. The trustees were declared to be without power to bind the beneficiaries personally by "any act, neglect or default," and the beneficiaries and all persons dealing with the trustees were required to look for payment or indemnity to the trust property. The beneficial interests were to be evidenced solely by transferable certificates for shares which were divided into 2,000 preferred shares of the par value of $100 each, and 2,000 common shares of no par value, and the rights of the respective shareholders in the surplus, profits, and capital assets were defined. "Share ledgers" showing the names and addresses of shareholders were to be kept.

The trustees might convene the shareholders in meeting for the purpose of making reports or considering recommendations, but the votes of the shareholders were to be advisory only. The death of a trustee or of a beneficiary was not to end the trust, which was to continue for twenty-five years unless sooner terminated by the trustees.

During the years 1921 and 1922, the trustees sold beneficial interests and paid commissions on the sales. About 42 acres (of the 155 acres described by the declaration of trust) were plotted into lots which were sold during the years 1921 to 1923, most of the sales being on the installment basis. On the remaining property a golf course and club house were constructed, and in 1923 this property with the improvements was conveyed to Western Avenue Golf Club, Inc., a California corporation, in exchange for its stock. Under a lease from the corporation petitioners continued the operation of the golf course until January 12, 1924. After that date petitioners' activities were confined to collections of installments of principal and interest on contracts of purchase, the receipt of interest on bank balances and of fees on assignments by holders of purchase contracts, the execution of conveyances to purchasers, the receipt of dividends from the incorporated club, and the distribution of moneys to the holders of beneficial interests. On December 31, 1923, the total number of outstanding beneficial interests was 3016, held by 920 persons; by December 31, 1926, the number of interests had been gradually decreased to 2172, held by 275 persons. The holdings by the trustees ranged approximately from 16 to 29 per cent.

Petitioners contend that they are trustees "of property held in trust," within [the predecessor of section 641] and are taxable accordingly and not as an "association." They urge that, to constitute an association, the applicable test requires "a quasi-corporate organization in which the beneficiaries, whether or not certificate holders, have some voice in the management and some control over the trustees and have an opportunity to exercise such control through the right to vote at meetings"; and that, in any event, the activities in which petitioners were engaged, during the tax years under consideration, did not constitute "a carrying on of business" within the rule applied by this Court.

The Government insists that the distinction between associations and the trusts taxed under [section 641] is between "business trusts on the one side" and other trusts "which are engaged merely in collecting the income and conserving the property against the day when it is to be distributed to the beneficiaries"; that Congress intended that all "business trusts" should be taxed as associations.

1. The Revenue Acts of 1924 and 1926 provided:

"The term 'corporation' includes associations, joint-stock companies, and insurance companies." * * *

A similar definition is found in earlier Revenue Acts of 1917 * * * and 1921 * * * and also in the later Acts of 1928 * * * and 1934. * * *

[In Hecht v. Malley, 265 U.S. 144, 44 S.Ct. 462 (1924), we] concluded that, when the nature of the trusts was considered, as the petitioners were "not merely trustees for collecting funds and paying them over," but were "associated together in much the same manner as the directors in a corporation for the purpose of carrying on business enterprises," the trusts were to be deemed associations within the meaning of the Act of 1918. * * *

2. As the statute merely provided that the term "corporation" should include "associations," without further definition, the Treasury Department was authorized to supply rules for the enforcement of the Act within the permissible bounds of administrative construction. * * *

3. "Association" implies associates. It implies the entering into a joint enterprise, and, as the applicable regulation imports, an enterprise for the transaction of business. This is not the characteristic of an ordinary trust—whether created by will, deed, or declaration—by which particular property is conveyed to a trustee or is to be held by the settlor, on specified trusts, for the benefit of named or described persons. Such beneficiaries do not ordinarily, and as mere *cestuis que trustent,* plan a common effort or enter into a combination for the conduct of a business enterprise. Undoubtedly the terms of an association may make the taking or acquiring of shares or interests sufficient to constitute participation, and may leave the management, or even control of the enterprise, to designated persons. But the nature and purpose of the cooperative undertaking will differentiate it from an ordinary trust. In what are called "business trusts" the object is not to hold and conserve particular property, with incidental powers, as in the traditional type of trusts, but to provide a medium, for the conduct of a business and sharing its gains. Thus a trust may be created as a convenient method by which persons become associated for dealings in real estate, the development of tracts of land, the construction of improvements, and the purchase, management and sale of properties; or for dealings in securities or other personal property; or for the production, or manufacture, and sale of commodities; or for commerce, or other sorts of business; where those who become beneficially interested, either by joining in the plan at the outset, or by later participation according to the terms of the arrangement, seek to share the advantages of a union of their interests in the common enterprise.

The Government contends that such an organized community of effort for the doing of business presents the essential features of an association. Petitioners stress the significance of, and the limitations said to be implied in, the provision classifying associations with corporations.

4. The inclusion of associations with corporations implies resemblance; but it is resemblance and not identity. The resemblance points to features distinguishing associations from partnerships as well as from ordinary trusts. As we have seen, the classification cannot be said to require organization under a statute, or with statutory privileges. The term embraces associations as they may exist at common law. We have already referred to the definitions, quoted in that case, showing the ordinary meaning of the term as applicable to a body of persons united without a charter "but upon the methods and forms used by incorporated bodies for the prosecution of some common enterprise." These definitions, while helpful, are not to be pressed so far as to make mere formal procedure a controlling test. The provision itself negatives such a construction. Thus unincorporated joint-stock companies have generally been regarded as bearing the closest resemblance to corporations. But, in the revenue acts, associations are mentioned separately and are not to be treated as limited to "joint-stock companies," although belonging to the same group. While the use of corpo-

rate forms may furnish persuasive evidence of the existence of an association, the absence of particular forms, or of the usual terminology of corporations, cannot be regarded as decisive. Thus an association may not have "directors" or "officers," but the "trustees" may function "in much the same manner as the directors in a corporation" for the purpose of carrying on the enterprise. The regulatory provisions of the trust instrument may take the place of "by-laws." And as there may be, under the reasoning in the *Hecht* case, an absence of control by beneficiaries such as is commonly exercised by stockholders in a business corporation, it cannot be considered to be essential to the existence of an association that those beneficially interested should hold meetings or elect their representatives. Again, while the faculty of transferring the interests of members without affecting the continuity of the enterprise may be deemed to be characteristic, the test of an association is not to be found in the mere formal evidence of interests or in a particular method of transfer.

What, then, are the salient features of a trust—when created and maintained as a medium for the carrying on of a business enterprise and sharing its gains—which may be regarded as making it analogous to a corporate organization? A corporation, as an entity, holds the title to the property embarked in the corporate undertaking. Trustees, as a continuing body with provision for succession, may afford a corresponding advantage during the existence of the trust. Corporate organization furnishes the opportunity for a centralized management through representatives of the members of the corporation. The designation of trustees, who are charged with the conduct of an enterprise,—who act "in much the same manner as directors"—may provide a similar scheme, with corresponding effectiveness. Whether the trustees are named in the trust instrument with power to select successors, so as to constitute a self-perpetuating body, or are selected by, or with the advice of, those beneficially interested in the undertaking, centralization of management analogous to that of corporate activities may be achieved. An enterprise carried on by means of a trust may be secure from termination or interruption by the death of owners of beneficial interest and in this respect their interests are distinguished from those of partners and are akin to the interests of members of a corporation. And the trust type of organization facilitates, as does corporate organization, the transfer of beneficial interests without affecting the continuity of the enterprise, and also the introduction of large numbers of participants. The trust methods also permits the limitation of the personal liability of participants to the property embarked in the undertaking.

It is no answer to say that these advantages flow from the very nature of trusts. For the question has arisen because of the use and adaptation of the trust mechanism. The suggestion ignores the postulate that we are considering those trusts which have the distinctive feature of being created to enable the participants to carry on a business and divide the gains which accrue from their common undertaking,—trusts that thus satisfy the primary conception of association and have the attributes to which we have referred, distinguishing them from partnerships. In such a case, we think that these attributes make the trust sufficiently analogous to corporate organization to justify the conclusion that Congress intended that the income of the enterprise should be taxed in the same manner as that of corporations.

5. Applying these principles to the instant case, we are of the opinion that the trust constituted an association. The trust was created for the development of a tract of land through the construction and operation of golf courses, club houses, etc. and the conduct of incidental businesses, with broad powers for the purchase, operation and sale of properties. Provision was made for the issue of shares of beneficial interests, with described rights and priorities. There were to be preferred shares of the value of $100 each and common shares of no par value. Thus those who took beneficial interests became shareholders in the common undertaking to be conducted for their profit according to the terms of the arrangement. They were not the less associated in that undertaking because the arrangement vested the management and control in the trustees. And the contemplated development of the tract of land held at the outset, even if other properties were not acquired, involved what was essentially a business enterprise. The arrangement provided for centralized control, continuity, and limited liability, and the analogy to corporate organization was carried still further by the provision for the issue of transferable certificates.

Under the trust, a considerable portion of the property was surveyed and subdivided into lots, which were sold and, to facilitate the sales, the subdivided property was improved by the construction of streets, sidewalks and curbs. The fact that these sales were made before the beginning of the tax years here in question, and that the remaining property was conveyed to a corporation in exchange for its stock, did not alter the character of the organization. Its character was determined by the terms of the trust instrument. It was not a liquidating trust; it was still an organization for profit, and the profits were still coming in. The powers conferred on the trustees continued and could be exercised for such activities as the instrument authorized. * * *

The judgment is
Affirmed.

ILLUSTRATIVE MATERIAL

A. GENERAL

Although *Morrissey* involved the question of whether the organization was a "trust" or an "association" for Federal income tax purposes, the factors considered in that case have been applied to distinguish partnerships from associations. In the materials in this section, the distinction between partnerships and associations is considered in the context of limited partnerships, where it is critical that the income and losses for tax purposes be passed through to the investor limited partners and that no entity level tax be imposed on distributions of appreciated property. The partnership-association distinction is also important in the treatment of "professional corporations," considered infra, page 308.

B. INTERNAL REVENUE SERVICE REGULATIONS

In some regards *Morrissey* was a Pyrrhic victory for the Commissioner, because in the 1950's and 1960's unincorporated professionals (e.g., doctors, lawyers, etc.) used that case and Regulations based on *Morrissey* to classify their partnership-like organizations as corporations in order to take advantage of more advantageous pension plan rules. After a number of judicial defeats, see, e.g., United States v. Kintner, 216 F.2d 418 (9th Cir.1954), the Commissioner and Treasury amended the Regulations in 1960 to make it more difficult to classify an unincorporated organization as an association. In turn, these Regulations made it much easier for those engaged in other activities, such as real estate ventures, to avoid association classification.

Under Regulations, section 301.7701–2(a), six characteristics are taken as the criteria for distinguishing corporations from other organizations. These are: (1) the presence of associates; (2) an objective to carry on business and divide the gains therefrom; (3) continuity of life, i.e., the death, resignation, etc. of a member does not cause the dissolution of the organization; (4) centralization of management, i.e., fewer than all the members have exclusive authority to make management decisions; (5) limited liability; and (6) free transferability of interests. To be classified as an association taxable as a corporation, the organization must have more corporate than noncorporate characteristics. Under the Regulations, the corporate characteristics common to the types of organization being compared are ignored in the ultimate decision. Thus, for example, since the presence of associates and an objective to carry on a business for profit are common to both corporations and partnerships, the determination whether an organization is an association taxable as a corporation or is a partnership will be made with reference only to the other four characteristics. While the tax status of an organization as an association or partnership is thus to be determined under Federal tax law, state law is controlling as to the presence or absence of the particular corporate characteristics identified by the Regulations; for example, whether or not an organization has limited liability is determined under the applicable state law.

Although most of the controversy in the partnership versus association area has risen in the context of limited partnerships, the test of the Regulations do apply to determine the status of general partnerships. See, e.g., Rev.Rul. 75–19, 1975–1 Cum.Bull. 382 (a general partnership formed under the Uniform Partnership Act, in which the partners were four corporations that were all subsidiaries of a single parent, was held to be a valid partnership under the tests of the Regulations).

LARSON v. COMMISSIONER

Tax Court of the United States, 1976.
66 T.C. 159.

TANNENWALD, JUDGE: [The taxpayer was a limited partner in two California limited partnerships. One of the partnerships (Mai–Kai), owned and operated an apartment complex. The other (Somis) owned and operated citrus groves. The sole general partner of both partnerships was a corporation (GHL). GHL organized, managed and administered both partnership properties and its net worth varied between $18,000 and $50,000 during the years in question.

Ten limited partners in Mai–Kai purchased their "units" for $9,500 each. The partnership acquired the apartment complex for $450,000, the entire purchase price being represented by a promissory note secured by a nonrecourse mortgage on the apartment complex. The pertinent elements of the limited partnership agreement provided: (1) The partnership would continue for a stated period of 33 years unless extended by a vote of the limited partners entitled to 60% or more of the profits of the partnership. (2) The general partner was entitled to a 20% interest in partnership profits and the partnership cash flow, except that such 20% interest was subordinated to the rights of the limited partners to have returned first their initial investment through a combination of cash flow and tax losses (assuming a 50% tax bracket for the limited partner). (3) The general partner also was entitled to a monthly management fee, a refinancing fee, and reimbursement for its expenses incurred in the operation of the partnership business. (4) No limited partner could withdraw his capital contribution without the consent of the general partner. (5) No limited partner could participate in the management of the partnership business. (6) The general partner could not assign its interest in the partnership. (7) The limited partners could not transfer their right to receive partnership income without the prior written consent of the general partner, which consent could not unreasonably be withheld. (8) The capital interest of a limited partner could be transferred only after prior notification to the general partner. If the proposed sale price were less than the fair market value of the limited partnership interest to be transferred, the interest first had to be offered to the remaining limited partners. (9) The partnership would terminate upon the disposition by the partnership of its entire interest in the apartment complex, upon the bankruptcy of the general partner unless the business was continued by a newly-elected general partner, upon a determination by limited partners entitled to 60% or more of the partnership profits that the partnership should terminate, or upon removal of the general partner by a vote of limited partners entitled to 60% or more of the partnership profits (in which event partnership assets would be distributed unless 100% of the limited partners elected to form a new partnership to continue the partnership business).

There were 44 limited partners in Somis, each having purchased a unit for $10,000. Somis acquired citrus groves for a purchase price of $3,620,000, of which $102,750 was paid in cash and the balance was represented by nonrecourse notes. The partnership agreement for Somis generally followed the provisions described above in the Mai–Kai partnership with the following differences: (1) The initial 15 year term of the partnership could be extended by a vote of 51% of the limited partners. (2) The general partner could not transfer more than 45% of the partnership's assets or refinance the partnership property without the approval of 51% of the limited partners. (3) The general partner was allowed additional compensation for organizational services and an "incentive" fee equal to a specific percentage of partnership cash flow above a stated amount. (4) Profits, sales proceeds, and liquidation proceeds were allocated 15% to the general partner and 85% to the limited partners, with the general partner having no interest in the cash flow. (5) The partnership could be terminated by a vote of 51% of the limited partnership interests and the same percentage could remove the general partner, in which event the partnership would terminate unless 51% of the limited partnership interests elected to continue the business in a new partnership.

No limited partner in either partnership was a stockholder of GHL, except for one limited partner who owned less than a 2% interest in Somis and somewhat over 23% of the stock of GHL. No certificates evidencing ownership interests in the partnerships were issued nor were any meetings of the limited partners held. GHL secured the required permission from the California Corporations Commissioner to permit it to offer for sale the units of partnership interest and offering circulars describing the units as "tax sheltered real estate investments" were prepared for both partnerships.

The partnerships generated extensive tax losses and the taxpayer deducted his distributive share on his individual income tax returns for the years in question. The Commissioner disallowed the deductions on the ground that the "partnerships" were associations taxable as corporations.

In its initial opinion, 65 T.C. No. 10 (1975), a majority of the Tax Court sustained the Commissioner. The majority, in so holding, applied its own view of the *Morrissey* tests and virtually disregarded the Regulations, section 7701–2. Within three weeks after the filing of the original opinion, that opinion was withdrawn and subsequently the Tax Court rendered the following decision.]

OPINION

* * * Petitioners allege that the partnerships fail all of the tests of corporate resemblance established by respondent's regulations (sec. 301.7701–2, Proced. & Admin.Regs.); respondent contends that all those tests are satisfied. Both sides agree that the regulations apply and are controlling, and our opinion and decision are consequently framed in

that context; the validity of respondent's regulations is not before us.[8] In our previous (now withdrawn) opinion dated October 21, 1975, we concluded that respondent should prevail. Upon reconsideration, we have come to the opposite conclusion and hold for petitioners.

The starting point of the regulations' definition of an "association" is the principle applied in Morrissey v. Commissioner, 296 U.S. 344 (1935), that the term includes entities which resemble corporations although they are not formally organized as such. *Morrissey* identified several characteristics of the corporate form which the regulations adopt as a test of corporate resemblance. For the purpose of comparing corporations with partnerships, the significant characteristics are: continuity of life; centralization of management; limited liability; and free transferability of interests. Other corporate or noncorporate characteristics may also be considered if appropriate in a particular case. An organization will be taxed as a corporation if, taking all relevant characteristics into account, it more nearly resembles a corporation than some other entity. Sec. 301.7701–2(a)(1), Proced. & Admin.Regs.; see and compare Bush # 1, 48 T.C. 218, 227–228 (1967), and Giant Auto Parts, Ltd., 13 T.C. 307 (1949). This will be true only if it possesses more corporate than noncorporate characteristics.

The regulations discuss each major corporate characteristic separately, and each apparently bears equal weight in the final balancing. * * * This apparently mechanical approach may perhaps be explained as an attempt to impart a degree of certainty to a subject otherwise fraught with imponderables. In most instances, the regulations also make separate provision for the classification of limited partnerships. Petitioners rely heavily on those provisions, while respondent seeks to distinguish them or to minimize their importance.

1. *Continuity of Life*

Pertinent provisions of the regulation concerning this characteristic are set forth [in Regulations, section 7701–2(b)]. A corporation possesses a greater degree of continuity of life than a partnership, since its existence is not dependent upon events personally affecting its separate members. Because of their more intimate legal and financial ties, partners are given a continuing right to choose their associates which is denied to corporate shareholders. A material alteration in the makeup of the partnership, as through the death or incapacity of a partner, either dissolves the partnership relation by operation of law or permits dissolution by order of court. Uniform Partnership Act, secs.

8. In this connection, we note the following passage from the Supreme Court opinion in Morrissey v. Commissioner, 296 U.S. 344, 354–355 (1935):

"As the statute merely provided that the term 'corporation' should include 'associations,' without further definition, the Treasury Department was authorized to supply rules for the enforcement of the Act within the permissible bounds of administrative construction. Nor can this authority be deemed to be so restricted that the regulations, once issued, could not later be clarified or enlarged so as to meet administrative exigencies or conform to judicial decision."

31 and 32 (hereinafter referred to as UPA). Partners are then free to withdraw their shares from the business, though they may agree to form a new partnership to continue it. A partner is also given the right to dissolve the partnership and withdraw his capital (either specific property or the value of his interest) at will at any time (UPA sec. 31(2)), although he may be unable to cause the winding up of the business and may be answerable in damages to other partners if his act breaches an agreement among them (UPA secs. 37 and 38(2)). The significant difference between a corporation and a partnership as regards continuity of life, then, is that a partner can always opt out of continued participation in and exposure to the risks of the enterprise. A corporate shareholder's investment is locked in unless liquidation is voted or he can find a purchaser to buy him out.

In a partnership subject to the Uniform Limited Partnership Act (hereinafter referred to as ULPA), this right of withdrawal is modified. A limited partner can withdraw his interest on dissolution (ULPA sec. 16), but he can neither dissolve the partnership at will (ULPA sec. 10) nor force dissolution at the retirement, death, or insanity of a general partner if the remaining general partners agree to continue the business in accordance with a right granted in the partnership certificate (ULPA sec. 20). CULPA section 15520 [10] further provides that a new general partner can be elected to continue the business without causing dissolution, if the certificate permits.

The sole general partner in the limited partnerships involved herein was a corporation, whose business was the promotion and management of real estate ventures. As a practical matter, it is unlikely that either Mai–Kai or Somis would have been dissolved midstream and the partners afforded an opportunity to withdraw their investments. Petitioners argue that the partnerships nevertheless lacked continuity of life because they could be dissolved either at will by, or on the bankruptcy of, the general partner. We turn first to the effect of bankruptcy of GHL.

California Uniform Partnership Act section 15031(5) (West Supp. 1976) (hereinafter referred to as CUPA) provides that a partnership is dissolved on the bankruptcy of a partner. CUPA section 15006(2) makes that act applicable to limited partnerships unless inconsistent with statutes relating to them. CULPA nowhere provides for dissolution or nondissolution in the event of bankruptcy. Section 15520, which merely covers dissolution and countervailing action by the remaining partners under certain circumstances, does not provide for such event. See n. 10 supra. CUPA section 15031(5) therefore applies.

10. That section provided during the years in issue:

The retirement, death, insanity, removal or failure of reelection of a general partner dissolves the partnership, unless the business is continued by the remaining general partners and/or the general partner or general partners elected in place thereof

(a) Under a right so to do stated in the certificate, or

(b) With the consent of all members * * * [Cal.Stats.1963, c. 870, sec. 5 at 2112.]

Since the bankruptcy of GHL would bring about dissolution by operation of law, each limited partner would be entitled to demand the return of his contribution (CULPA sec. 15516). Somis and Mai–Kai simply do not satisfy the regulations' test of continuity, which requires that the "bankruptcy * * * of *any member* will *not* cause a dissolution of the organization." (Emphasis supplied.) [11]

The fact that under the agreements involved herein a new general partner might be chosen to continue the business does not affect this conclusion. Respondent seizes upon this aspect of the agreements to argue that the limited partners could anticipate the bankruptcy of GHL [12] and elect a new general partner. But this element does not detract from the hard fact that if GHL became bankrupt while it was the general partner of Somis and Mai–Kai, there would at best be a hiatus between the event of bankruptcy and the entry of a new general partner so that, from a legal point of view, the old partnerships would have been dissolved. Moreover, at least in the case of Mai–Kai, a vote of 100 percent of the limited partners was required to elect a new general partner. Glensder Textile Co., 46 B.T.A. 176 (1942), held that such contingent continuity of life did not resemble that of a corporation. Respondent's regulations * * * incorporate this conclusion.

We hold that the partnerships involved herein do not satisfy the "continuity of life" test as set forth in respondent's regulations. We recognize that our application of respondent's existing regulations to the event of bankruptcy results in a situation where it is unlikely that a limited partnership will ever satisfy the "continuity of life" requirement of those regulations. But the fact that the regulations are so clearly keyed to "dissolution" (a term encompassing the legal relationships between the partners) rather than "termination of the business" (a phrase capable of more pragmatic interpretation encompassing the life of the business enterprise) leaves us with no viable alternative. In this connection, we note that respondent is not without power to alter the impact of our application of his existing regulations. See Morrissey v. Commissioner, n. 8 supra.

In view of our conclusion as to the effect of GHL's bankruptcy, we find it unnecessary to deal with the contentions of the parties as to whether, under California law, GHL had the legal power to dissolve both Mai–Kai and Somis so as to counteract the "continuity of life" elements contained in the rights of the limited partners under the partnership agreements and certificates, or whether, in respect of this

11. In light of our conclusion, infra * * * that GHL has not been shown to have had a substantial interest in the partnerships, it may be argued that it was not a "member" for the purpose of the regulations. Such an argument, however, we find to be structurally incompatible with the regulations, which consider the substantiality of a partner's interest in the partnership only in connection with centralization of management and transferability of interests. Cf. sec. 301.7701–2(d)(2), Proced. & Admin.Regs. * * * (fourth sentence).

12. An assumption which, given the startling instances of unexpected bankruptcies in the current business world and the absence of involvement of the limited partners in the operations of GHL, is questionable.

characteristic, CULPA corresponded to the Uniform Limited Partnership Act. See sec. 301.7701–2(b)(2) and (3), * * *. Indeed, since the California law, as we interpret it, does not permit the partners in Mai–Kai and Somis to contract against dissolution in the event of bankruptcy of GHL, the rights and duties created by the agreements and certificates cannot alter our conclusion on the "continuity of life" issue; this is a quite different situation from that which exists when other corporate characteristics such as centralized management (see * * * infra) and free transferability of interest (see * * * infra) are considered.

2. *Centralized Management*

In the corporate form, management is centralized in the officers and directors; the involvement of shareholders as such in ordinary operations is limited to choosing these representatives. In a general partnership, authority is decentralized and any partner has the power to make binding decisions in the ordinary course (UPA sec. 9). In a limited partnership, however, this authority exists only in the general partners (ULPA secs. 9 and 10), and a limited partner who takes part in the control of the business loses his limited liability status (ULPA sec. 7). From a practical standpoint, it is clear that the management of both Mai–Kai and Somis was centralized in GHL. The sole general partner was empowered by law as well as by the partnership agreements to administer the partnership affairs. However, respondent's regulations specify that—

> In addition, limited partnerships subject to a statute corresponding to the Uniform Limited Partnership Act, generally do not have centralized management, but centralized management ordinarily does exist in such a limited partnership if substantially all the interests in the partnership are owned by the limited partners. [Sec. 301.7701–2(c)(4), Proced. & Admin.Regs.]

In other words, even though there may be centralized administration by a general partner, the "centralization of management" test will not be met if the general partner has a meaningful proprietary interest. See Zuckman v. United States, 524 F.2d 729 (Ct.Cl.1975). In specifying this additional condition, respondent has adopted the theory of Glensder Textile Co., supra, that managing partners with such interests in the business are not "analogous to directors of a corporation" because they act in their own interests "and not *merely* in a representative capacity for a body of persons having a limited investment and a limited liability." (46 B.T.A. at 185; emphasis added.) It is thus necessary to look to the proprietary interest of GHL in order to determine whether the additional condition imposed by respondent's regulations has been met.[14]

14. We need not determine what the consequences would be if the respondent's regulations did not contain this additional condition. Cf. John Provence # 1 Well, 37 T.C. 376 (1961), affd. 321 F.2d 840 (3d Cir. 1963).

Unlike the taxpayers in Zuckman v. United States, supra, petitioners herein have failed to show that the limited partners did not own all or substantially all the interests in the partnerships involved herein within the meaning of the regulations. GHL's interests in Mai–Kai and Somis were subordinated to those of the limited partners. Petitioners have not attempted to demonstrate that GHL's capital interests had any present value during the years in issue, and it is clear that, because of the subordination provisions, it had no present right to income during those years. Petitioners would have us look to the anticipated return on the partnership properties in future years to determine that GHL had a substantial proprietary stake in the business independent of its management role. They have not, however, proved by competent evidence that such a return could in fact be expected, relying instead on unsupported projections; [15] nor have they shown that any such future profit would be reflected in the present value of GHL's interest. Although there was testimony that GHL expected profits from the subordinated interests when the limited partnerships were liquidated, we are not convinced that the possibility of such income at an indefinite future date had value during the years at issue. GHL reported gross income of $906,930.89 from fiscal 1969 to fiscal 1974, out of which only $118 represented a partnership distribution (from a partnership not involved herein).

Furthermore, the limited partners in Somis and Mai–Kai possessed the right to remove GHL as the general partner. Thus, GHL's right to participate in future growth and profits was wholly contingent on satisfactory performance of its management role,[17] and not at all analogous to the independent proprietary interest of a typical general partner. In *Glensder Textile Co.,* supra, our conclusion that centralization of management was lacking rested not only on the fact that management retained a proprietary interest but also on the fact that the limited partners could not "remove the general partners and control them as agents, as stockholders may control directors." 46 B.T.A. at 185.

Petitioners argue that such power of removal and control could be given to limited partners under ULPA,[18] that CULPA (which makes specific reference to such power) is a statute corresponding to ULPA,

15. For example, petitioners blithely assume a 3–percent annual increase in the value of the real estate, which they characterize as "conservative," and, in effect, ask us to take judicial notice that their assumption is valid.

17. On removal, GHL would have been entitled to receive the cash value of its interest, both by statute (CUPA sec. 15038(1)) and, in the case of Somis, by agreement. To the extent of that value, GHL would have a vested present proprietary interest to protect. The petitioners had the burden of showing that such value existed and that it was substantial; they have done neither. GHL did not list any partnership interests as assets on its tax returns and apparently did not report any income either on the receipt of a partnership interest or on the lapse of a subordination clause. See secs. 1.61–2(d)(5) and 1.421–6(d)(2), Income Tax Regs.; Sol Diamond, 56 T.C. 530 (1971), affd. 492 F.2d 286 (7th Cir.1974). Cf. sec. 83. It did, however, report as ordinary income $118 of cash flow received from another partnership.

* * *

18. Cf. UPA sec. 31.

and that accordingly respondent's regulation requires a decision in their favor on this issue. In our opinion, the regulation was not intended to provide a blanket exemption from association status for ULPA limited partnerships, regardless of the extent to which the partners by agreement deviate from the statutory scheme. It states only that a limited partnership in an ULPA jurisdiction *generally* will lack centralized management. See p. 176 supra. We have repeatedly held that an organization is to be classified by reference to the rights and duties created by agreement as well as those existing under State law. Bush # 1, 48 T.C. at 228; Western Construction Co., 14 T.C. 453, 467 (1950), affd. per curiam 191 F.2d 401 (9th Cir.1951); Glensder Textile Co., 46 B.T.A. at 183. The effect of such organic laws as ULPA (and CULPA) is to provide a rule which governs in the absence of contrary agreement. Where the theme is obscured by the variations, it is the latter which set the tone of the composition. Neither ULPA nor CULPA requires that the limited partners be given the right to remove the general partner; in fact, ULPA does not even mention such a possibility. By reserving that right, the limited partners in Mai–Kai and Somis took themselves out of the basic framework of ULPA and hence out of the shelter of the regulation, which is based on *Glensder.*

We conclude that Somis and Mai–Kai had centralized management within the meaning of respondent's regulations.

3. *Limited Liability*

Unless some member is personally liable for debts of, and claims against, an entity, section 301.7701–2(d)(1), Proced. & Admin.Regs., states that the entity possesses the corporate characteristic of limited liability. The regulation provides that "in the case of a limited partnership subject to a statute corresponding to the Uniform Limited Partnership Act, personal liability exists with respect to each general partner, except as provided in subparagraph (2) of this paragraph." The first sentence of subparagraph (2) establishes a conjunctive test, under which a general partner is considered not to have personal liability only "when he has no substantial assets (other than his interest in the partnership) which could be reached by a creditor of the organization *and* when he is merely a 'dummy' acting as the agent of the limited partners." (Emphasis added.) In other words, personal liability exists if the general partner *either* has substantial assets *or* is not a dummy for the limited partners. We do not agree with respondent's assertion, made for the first time in connection with the motion for reconsideration, that the regulation should be read disjunctively. Although the purpose of subparagraph (2) was ostensibly to delineate the conditions under which personal liability of a general partner *does not exist,* practically all the remaining material in the subparagraph outlines the conditions under which such personal liability does exist. In several examples, personal liability is said to exist, either because the general partner has substantial assets or because he is not a dummy for the limited partners. See Zuckman v. United States, supra.

In no instance is there a suggestion that both conditions established by the first sentence of subparagraph (2) need not be satisfied.

In so concluding, we are mindful that in Glensder Textile Co., supra, the apparent source of the language in the regulations, the term "dummy" was arguably considered applicable to any general partner without substantial assets risked in the business. The opinion in *Glensder* states (46 B.T.A. at 183):

> If, for instance, the general partners were not men with substantial assets risked in the business *but* were mere dummies without real means acting as the agents of the limited partners, whose investments made possible the business, there would be something approaching the corporate form of stockholders and directors. * * * [Emphasis added.]

Thus, lack of substantial assets seems to be considered the equivalent of being a dummy—an equivalence which respondent apparently sought to avoid by using the word "and" in his existing regulations.[20]

While it may be doubtful that GHL could be considered to have had substantial assets during the years in issue, we find it unnecessary to resolve this question since it is clear that GHL was not a dummy for the limited partners of Somis and Mai–Kai. Respondent contends that GHL fell within the "dummy" concept because it was subject to removal by the limited partners, and thus was subject to their ultimate control. While it is true that a mere "dummy" would be totally under the control of the limited partners, it does not follow that the presence of some control by virtue of the power to remove necessarily makes the general partner a "dummy." It seems clear that the limited partners' rights to remove the general partner were designed to give the limited partners a measure of control over their investment without involving them in the "control of the business"; the rights were not designed to render GHL a mere dummy or to empower the limited partners "to direct the business actively through the general partners." Glensder Textile Co., 46 B.T.A. at 183. Moreover, the record indicates that the limited partners did not use GHL as a screen to conceal their own active involvement in the conduct of the business; far from being a rubber stamp, GHL was the moving force in these enterprises. With a minor exception, the persons controlling GHL were independent of and unrelated to the limited partners.

In view of the foregoing, we conclude that personal liability existed with respect to GHL, and the partnerships lack the corporate characteristic of limited liability.

20. In this connection, it is of interest to note that the proposed regulations were cast solely in economic terms, i.e., relied entirely on substantiality of assets, without any reference whatsoever to a "dummy" situation. See 24 Fed.Reg. 10,450, 10,452 (1959), * * *.

4. *Transferability of Interests*

A stockholder's rights and interest in a corporate venture are, absent consensual restrictions, freely transferable by the owner without reference to the wishes of other members. A partner, on the other hand, can unilaterally transfer only his interest in partnership "profits and surplus," and cannot confer on the assignee the other attributes of membership without the consent of all partners (UPA secs. 18(g), 26, and 27). Respondent's regulations recognize and rely upon this distinction.[21]

The regulations state that if substantially all interests are freely transferable, the corporate characteristic of free transferability of interests is present. Since we have concluded, for the purposes of this case, that the limited partners should be considered as owning substantially all the interests in Mai–Kai and Somis * * * we turn our attention to the question whether their interests were so transferable.

A transferee of a limited partnership interest may become a substituted limited partner with the consent of all members or under a right given in the certificate. CULPA sec. 15519. The partnership certificates of Mai–Kai and Somis are silent in this regard. However, when the provisions of the agreements relating to transferability and the power of an assignee to obtain a judicial amendment of the partnership certificate (see CULPA secs. 15502(1)(a)X and 15525) are taken into account, it would appear that the agreements rather than the certificates should be considered the controlling documents herein. Indeed, petitioners do not seek to draw any solace from the certificates, positing their arguments as to lack of transferability on the agreements themselves.

Both partnership agreements permit the assignment of a limited partner's income interest with the consent of the general partner, which may not unreasonably be withheld. Petitioners have not suggested any ground on which consent could be withheld. The requirement of consent, circumscribed by a standard of reasonableness, is not such a restriction on transfer as is typical of partnership agreements; nor is it the sort referred to by the regulations. In our opinion, the limited partners' income rights were freely transferable. See Outlaw v. United States, 494 F.2d 1376, 1384 (Ct.Cl.1974).

Petitioners also argue that transferability is limited by the requirement that, in the event of a proposed assignment, a limited partner's capital interest first be offered to other members under certain circumstances. While an assignment for less than fair market value could be prevented in this manner, there was no requirement that such an offer be made if an interest was to be sold to a third party at fair market value. Thus, there was no "effort on the part of the parties to select their business associates," as is characteristic of the usual partnership arrangement. J.A. Riggs Tractor Co., 6 T.C. 889, 898 (1946). We think

21. Sec. 301.7701–2(e) * * *

that these interests possessed considerably more than the "modified" form of free transferability referred to in subparagraph (2) of the regulation.

In sum, an assignee for fair consideration of a limited partner's interest in Somis or Mai–Kai could acquire all of the rights of a substituted limited partner within the framework of the agreement and governing State law, without discretionary consent of any other member. Any restrictions or conditions on such a transfer were procedural rather than substantive. The right of assignment more closely resembles that attending corporate shares than that typically associated with partnership interests. Mai–Kai and Somis therefore possessed the corporate characteristic of free transferability of interests. See also n. 23 infra.

5. *Other Characteristics*

Both parties have identified other characteristics of Mai–Kai and Somis which they allege are relevant to the determination whether those entities more closely resemble partnerships or corporations. Some of these are within the ambit of the major characteristics already discussed. Petitioners point to the fact that, unlike a corporate board of directors, GHL as manager lacked the discretionary right to retain or distribute profits according to the needs of the business. This argument is in reality directed to the issue of centralized management. The same is true of respondent's analogy between the limited partners' voting rights and those of corporate shareholders. To be sure the partnership interests were not represented by certificates but this factor conceivably is more properly subsumed in the transferability issue. See Morrissey v. Commissioner, 296 U.S. at 360. Moreover, those interests were divided into units or shares and were promoted and marketed in a manner similar to corporate securities—an additional "characteristic" which we have not ignored, (see Outlaw v. United States, supra), but which we do not deem of critical significance under the circumstances herein. Similarly, we do not assign any particular additional importance to the facts that the partnerships have not observed corporate formalities and procedures (Morrissey v. Commissioner, supra; Giant Auto Parts, Ltd., 18 T.C. 307 (1949)) or that, unlike general partners, limited partners were not required personally to sign the partnership certificates. Finally, respondent argues that the limited partnerships resemble corporations because they provide a means of pooling investments while limiting the liability of the participants. Cf. Helvering v. Combs, 296 U.S. 365 (1935). As it relates to the facts of this case, this point is subsumed in our earlier discussion. To the extent that it presages an attempt to classify *all* limited partnerships as corporations, it is in irreconcilable conflict with respondent's own regulations.

6. *Conclusion*

The regulations provide that an entity will be taxed as a corporation if it more closely resembles a corporation than any other form of organization. They further state that such a resemblance does not exist unless the entity possesses *more* corporate than noncorporate characteristics. If every characteristic bears equal weight, then Mai–Kai and Somis are partnerships for tax purposes. We have found that they possess only two of the four major corporate characteristics and that none of the other characteristics cited by the parties upsets the balance.[22] On the other hand, if the overall corporate resemblance test, espoused by *Morrissey* and adhered to by the regulations, permits us to weigh each factor according to the degree of corporate similarity it provides, we would be inclined to find that these entities were taxable as corporations. Each possessed a degree of centralized management indistinguishable from that of a pure corporation; the other major factors lie somewhere on the continuum between corporate and partnership resemblance. Were not the regulations' thumb upon the scales, it appears to us that the practical continuity and limited liability of both entities would decisively tip the balance in respondent's favor. However, we can find no warrant for such refined balancing in the regulations or in cases which have considered them. See Zuckman v. United States, 524 F.2d 729 (Ct.Cl.1975); Outlaw v. United States, supra; Kurzner v. United States, 413 F.2d 97, 105 (5th Cir.1969) ("four equally weighted procrustean criteria"); secs. 301.7701–2(a)(3) and 301.7701–3(b)(2), Proced. & Admin.Regs., example (2). Cf. Estate of Smith v. Commissioner, 313 F.2d 724, 736 (8th Cir.1963) ("substantially greater noncorporate characteristics both in number *and in importance* ") (emphasis added). Only in connection with free transferability of interests do the regulations recognize a modified and less significant form of a particular characteristic.[23]

Our task herein is to apply the provisions of respondent's regulations as we find them and not as we think they might or ought to have been written.[24] See and compare David F. Bolger, 59 T.C. 760, 771 (1973). On this basis, petitioners must prevail.

Decisions will be entered under Rule 155.

Reviewed by the Court.

FAY and HALL, JJ., did not participate in the consideration and disposition of this case.

22. Indeed, considering the importance of predictability in applying respondent's regulations, we would not be inclined to give such lesser characteristics controlling weight unless their materiality was unmistakable, a situation which does not obtain in this case.

23. Even if we had found that the interests of the limited partners in Somis and Mai–Kai possessed only such modified form of free transferability, petitioners would still prevail, since the balance would be two characteristics favoring partnership status and something less than two characteristics favoring corporate status.

24. As to respondent's future possibilities, see Morrissey v. Commissioner, n. 8 supra.

[The concurring opinions of five judges and the dissenting opinions of six judges have been omitted.]

ILLUSTRATIVE MATERIAL

A. LIMITED PARTNERSHIPS AND TAX SHELTERS

As noted previously, during the 1960's through the mid–1980's, the limited partnership form was utilized as the primary marketing vehicle for tax shelters. The limited partnership form was used to enable partnership interests to be sold in the same manner as stock, but still obtain for the individual partners the benefits of tax losses through a combination of the application of the *Crane* doctrine in the limited partnership context, see infra page 128, and the allocation of income and deductions to provide maximum tax benefit to the limited partners, see infra page 105. It was essential that the limited partnership be classified as a "partnership" rather than as an "association" taxable as a corporation, since only in the former case are the income and losses which the activity generates passed through to the individual owners.

Amendments to the Internal Revenue Code enacted in the Tax Reform Act of 1986, most particularly the restrictions on deductions from passive activities under section 469, discussed infra page 155, reduced the availability of tax shelters generally. However, these changes did not totally eliminate the desirability of organizing ventures that will produce tax losses in the limited partnership form, and other changes in the Internal Revenue Code enacted in 1986 encourage the organization of profitable ventures in the limited partnership form rather than the corporate form, for the purpose of avoiding the corporate income tax. Therefore, issues involving the classification of limited partnerships as partnerships or associations which arose in the context of tax shelter cases are of continuing importance.

B. SUBSEQUENT DEVELOPMENTS

1. *Judicial Interpretation*

Zuckman v. United States, 524 F.2d 729 (Ct.Cl.1975), was decided just one day after the Tax Court's initial opinion was filed in *Larson.* The Court of Claims had no difficulty finding that a real estate limited partnership had none of the four corporate characteristics of the Regulations. In *Zuckman,* a Missouri limited partnership was formed to construct and operate an apartment building. The general partner was a corporation, which was a wholly owned subsidiary of another corporation. In turn, the parent corporation was wholly owned by one of the three limited partners (Kanter), who held a 29 percent interest in the partnership. The other two limited partners (of which the taxpayer was one) each held less than a one percent interest in the partnership. The corporate general partner held almost a 70 percent interest in the partnership. The parent of the general partner had net assets of over $3.5 million dollars, but the corporate general partner itself was capitalized at $500 and had no other substantial assets. The board of directors of the parent corporation gave to Kanter a proxy to vote all of the stock in his own individual capacity. The Court of Claims held: (1) There was no continuity of life because the partnership was organized under the Missouri Uniform Limited Partnership Act and, under the Regulations, continuity of life can never exist under such circumstances. Moreover, continuity of life did not exist because the bankruptcy of the corporate general partner would have automatically dissolved the partnership. Finally, the partnership agreement itself precluded the continuation of the partnership in the event of the retirement, disability or forfeiture of the charter of the general partner. (2) Centralized management did not exist because the corporate general partner had a substantial interest in the partnership itself, the court rejecting the Government's argument that the corporate general partner's interest in the partnership should be attributable to Kanter. (3) Limited liability did not exist because, in the court's view, limited liability can never exist under the Regulations (i.e., if the general partner has assets, it is personally liable; if a general partner has no assets, but is a dummy, then the limited partners have personal liability; if the general partner has no assets, but is not a dummy, then the general partner is again personally liable). (4) There was no free transferability of interests because, although the 29 percent limited partner's interest was transferable, then the general partner's interest was not because such a transfer would have dissolved the organization unless all the limited partners agreed to substitute a new general partner to continue the enterprise; under the Regulations an interest is not freely transferable if a transfer dissolves the organization.

In Foster v. Commissioner, 80 T.C. 34 (1983), aff'd on other grounds, 756 F.2d 1430 (9th Cir.1985), the taxpayer claimed that a general partnership organized under the Uniform Partnership Act was properly taxable as an association. The court examined each of the four characteristics tested under the regulations, and concluded that the provisions of the Uniform Partnership Act itself, notwithstanding limitations in the partnership agreement on the rights of the partners to dissolve the partnership and on the rights of certain partners to manage the partnership, precluded the presence of any corporate characteristics. Although a general partner may contract away his *right* to dissolve the partnership, he cannot contract away his *power* to dissolve the partnership; and designation of a managing partner does not negate the mutual agency of general partners vis-a-vis third parties.

2. *Internal Revenue Service Rulings*

The Internal Revenue Service has acquiesced in *Larson,* and several aspects of the decision are reflected in subsequent Revenue Rulings. For example, limited partnership agreements frequently contain a provision in which a limited partner's interest purportedly can be assigned only with the consent of the general partner, even though such an assignment without consent can carry with it the right to partnership income and capital distributions. Following the approach in *Larson,* Rev.Rul. 77–137, 1977–1 Cum. Bull. 178, held that even where the general partner did not give his consent under such a provision, the assignee of the partnership interest would be considered a substituted limited partner for Federal income tax purposes, at least where the assignor agreed to exercise any residual powers remaining in him solely in favor of and in the interest of the assignee. Rev.Rul. 79–106, 1979–1 Cum.Bull. 448, following the analysis of the majority in *Larson,* held that the additional factors which the majority in the opinion in *Larson* treated as irrelevant or as subsumed under the other four major characteristics would not be considered "other factors" under Regulations, section 301.7701–2(a)(1). If these factors are not relevant, what are the "other factors" to which the Regulations refer?

An advance ruling from the Internal Revenue Service that an organization will be treated as a partnership and not as an association will render interests in a large limited partnership or a tax shelter offering more readily salable, because investors will be depending on the partnership treatment. The Service has imposed certain limitations on the availability of such rulings.

Rev.Proc. 89–12, 1989–1 Cum.Bull. 798, is the most recent statement of the Service's advance ruling guidelines. It applies not only to entities organized as partnerships, but also to other entities seeking classification as a partnership. See infra, page 44. In addition to providing a check-list of information which must be supplied in order to obtain a ruling, the Revenue Procedure states that the Service will consider ruling that an entity is a partnership only if two specific conditions are satisfied. First, the general partners in the aggregate generally must have at least a one percent interest in each material item of partnership income, gain, loss, and credit at all times during the life of the partnership. Only certain specific deviations are allowed, and temporary noncompliance will preclude a ruling unless the general partner's interest substantially exceeds one percent for a substantial period of time during which the partnership is expected to generate profits. If the partnership has total contributions exceeding $50 million, however, the general partner's interest is adequate if it is at least one percent divided by the ratio of total contributions to $50 million. For example, if total contributions to the partnership were $125,000,000, the general partner's interest must be at least .4 percent (1 percent divided by 125/50). In no event, however, will a ruling be issued if the partner's interest is less than .2 percent at any time.

Second, the general partners, in the aggregate, must maintain a minimum capital account balance equal to the lesser of $500,000 or one percent of total positive capital account balances. The agreement must require the general partners to make additional contributions to meet this minimum required balance whenever a limited partner makes an additional contribution. The minimum capital account balance requirement is waived if at least one general partner has provided substantial services to the partnership in its capacity as a partner (other than services for which it has received a guaranteed payment subject to section 707(c)) *and* the agreement requires the general partners under certain circumstances to make a capital contribution to the partnership in connection with its dissolution.

The requirement that the general partner have a material interest in the partnership profits and capital obviously is important to the classification issue. If a general partner does not have a material interest, he may not be a partner for federal tax purposes. As a result, the limited partnership probably would have the corporate characteristics of continuity of life (because death of a limited partner does not terminate the partnership), centralized management (because management authority is vested in a non-partner who can only be acting in a representative capacity), and limited liability (because no member of the organization would have any potential liability for partnership obligations). The requirement that the general partner have a material interest "at all times" was directed to the type of provision involved in *Larson* where the corporate general partner was not entitled to a share of partnership profits or cash distributions until after specified amounts had been returned to the limited partners.

Rev.Proc. 89–12 also provides standards with respect to certain specific corporate characteristics. A limited partnership formed under the ULPA will not be treated as lacking continuity of life if less than a majority of the limited partnership interests may elect a new general partner or continue the partnership upon removal of a general partner. This requirement has nothing to do with the continuity of life test of Regulations, section 301.7701–2(b), as interpreted by the Tax Court in *Larson,* but appears to be an attempt by the Service in effect to inject a "likelihood of continuity of business enterprise" test in lieu of the continuity of life test for advance ruling purposes.

Whenever limited partnership interests (excluding those held by a general partner) exceed 80 percent of the total partnership interests, the Service will not rule that the partnership lacks centralized management. This appears merely to be an interpretation of when "substantially" all the interests are held by limited partners under Regulations, section 301.7701–2(c)(4).

Finally, if a limited partnership has a corporate general partner, as long as the net worth of the general partner is at least 10 percent of the amount of total contributions to the partnership, the partnership will be deemed to lack limited liability. If the only general partners are corporations and the safe harbor is not met, limited liability will be found to exist unless the corporate general partner has substantial assets other than the partnership interest which could be reached by creditors of the partnership or it is demonstrated that the general partners will act independently of the limited partners.

Rev.Proc. 89–12 sets forth standards for advance rulings only; as *Larson* demonstrates, an organization, even one with a sole corporate general partner, nonetheless may be classified as a partnership even though it fails to meet the requirements of Rev.Proc. 89–12.

See also Rev.Proc. 86–12, 1986–1 Cum.Bull. 534 (IRS will rule on Subchapter K issues without ruling on entity classification issues).

3. *Regulations*

As a result of the decisions in *Larson* and *Zuckman* it is unlikely that a properly drafted partnership agreement under the Uniform Limited Partnership Act ever could result in association status for the organization. Following the not very subtle invitation by the Tax Court in *Larson* to revise the Regulations, the Internal Revenue Service issued Proposed Regulations, section 301.7701–1, 2, 3, 42 Fed.Reg. 1038 (Jan. 5, 1977) which would have resulted in many limited partnerships being classified as associations. These Proposed Regulations were controversial and were quickly withdrawn. There is currently little likelihood that the regulations will be revised to change significantly any of the criteria, although minor changes may be made.

In 1983, Regulations, section 301.7701–2(c)(4), were amended to make it easier to find centralized management. The amended regulations provide that where limited partners own substantially all of the partnership interests and have a substantially unrestricted right to remove the general partner, the power will be a factor to be considered positively in determining whether there is centralized management. Regulations, section 301.7701–2(d)(2), were amended at the same time to provide that if the partnership agreement purports to confer limited liability on a general partner, the provision will be presumed to be effective unless the taxpayer can demonstrate that it is ineffective under local law. In light of *Zuckman,* however, these amendments appear to be of no importance. Under the *Zuckman* analysis, a limited partnership formed under the Uniform Limited Partnership Act never can have limited liability. Both *Zuckman* and *Larson* conclude that under Regulations, section 301.7701–2(b), such a limited partnership never can have continuity of life. Thus, in all cases a limited partnership organized under the Uniform Limited Partnership Act can have no more than two of the four characteristics of an association and lacking a majority never can be classified as an association.

4. *Other Entities Classified as Partnerships*

A business may be conducted by an entity which under state law is neither a corporation nor a partnership. Such a business entity, however, will be classified for federal income tax purposes as either a corporation or a partnership. Rev.Rul. 88–76, 1988–2 Cum.Bull. 360, dealt with the proper classification of a Wyoming "limited liability company." Under state law the limited liability company could be managed either by the members, in proportion to their capital contributions, or by a designated manager. The limited liability company in the Ruling was managed by three designated managers. Under the governing statute, members of the limited liability company could transfer their interests only with the unanimous consent of all other members. If consent was not granted, the assignee could not participate in management, but was entitled to share in profits and a return of contributions. State law provided for the dissolution of the limited liability company upon (1) the expiration of its charter, (2) unanimous consent of the members, or (3) the death, retirement, resignation, expulsion, bankruptcy, or other termination of the membership of a member, unless under a provision in the articles of organization all remaining members consented to continue the business. The Service ruled that the limited liability company lacked continuity of life because consent to continue the business upon withdrawal of a member was not assured. Free transferability of interests did not exist because the members did not have the right to transfer all of the attributes of their membership interest without the consent of the other members. Accordingly, even though the entity had limited liability and centralized management, it was classified as a partnership. The Service declined to weigh the importance of the factors, citing *Larson* for the proposition that each factor bears equal weight.

In Rev.Rul. 88–79, 1988–2 Cum.Bull. 361, the Service ruled that a Missouri business trust was a partnership. The organization in question was formed by six "managers" as a trust under state law, but its object was to carry on the business of buying and selling oil and gas royalty interests, and it offered participation units to the public. The entity was to continue for 20 years unless terminated earlier. The entity would terminate operations upon the death, insanity, bankruptcy, retirement, or resignation of any manager, unless all remaining managers and a majority of the participants agreed to continue the business. The death, insanity, bankruptcy, retirement, or resignation of any participant did not affect the entity. Under the terms of the trust, the affairs of the entity were to be managed solely by the designated managers, except for limited voting rights in the participants with respect to amendments to the agreement or continuation of the business upon withdrawal of the managers. The designated managers were personally liable for the debts of the organization to the extent that they exceeded its assets, and the participants were not liable for the organization's debts. The managers were not entitled to transfer their interests, and the participants' interests were assignable only with the consent of a majority of the managers. If a majority of the managers did not consent to the assignment, the assignee would not acquire any voting rights, but would be entitled to share in the profits and losses and distributions in liquidation. Again, the entity was classified as a partnership. Although it had centralized management, it lacked continuity of life, limited liability, and free transferability of interests. See also Rev.Rul. 88–8, 1988–1 Cum.Bull. 403 (British "limited company" classified as partnership under Regulations).

A business trust sometimes may be classified as a corporation. See *Morrissey,* supra, page 22. It also would appear that a business trust classified as a partnership under the principles applied in Rev.Rul. 88–79 could be subject to classification as a corporation under section 7704, if participation units are publicly traded. Rev.Rul. 88–79 failed to address this issue. (But section 7704(c) and (d)(1)(E) would preclude the particular entity in the Ruling from classification as a partnership under section 7704.)

C. PUBLICLY TRADED PARTNERSHIPS

1. *General*

Section 7704 generally treats as a corporation any partnership the interests in which are traded on an established securities market or are readily tradable on a secondary market or a substantial equivalent of a secondary market. Because under state law general partnership interests cannot be traded, the provision in fact only applies to limited partnerships. The legislative history explains that a secondary market exists if prices are regularly quoted by brokers or dealers who are making a market for such interest. Occasional accommodation trades of partnership interests, a buy-sell agreement between the partners (without more), or the occasional repurchase or redemption by the partnership or acquisition by a general partner of partnership interests will not be treated as a secondary market or the equivalent thereof. However, if the partners have regular and ongoing opportunities to dispose of their interests, the interests are tradable on the equivalent of a secondary market. Meaningful restrictions imposed on the right to transfer partnership interests may preclude classification as a corporation, even if some interests are actually traded. See H.Rep. 100–495, 100th Cong., 1st Sess. 943–950 (1987).

As a corollary to section 7704, Congress amended section 469, dealing with limitations on deductions from passive activities to provide that net income from any publicly traded limited partnerships is treated as portfolio income (like dividends and interest) rather than passive activity income solely for purposes of applying section 469. Net losses from any publicly traded limited partnership may not offset either portfolio income (including net income from another publicly traded limited partnership) or net income from other passive activities, but instead must be separately carried-over and may be deducted only against net income from the same publicly traded limited partnership in future years. Section 469(g). See H.Rep. 100–3545, 100th Cong., 1st Sess. 951–52 (1987). This provision extends to publicly traded limited partnerships even if they are specially excepted from the rules of section 7704. Generally under section 469, all items with respect to limited partnership interests are considered to be passive activity income or loss.

2. *Meaning of "Publicly Traded"*

In Notice 88–75, 1988–2 Cum.Bull. 386, the Internal Revenue Service announced that a partnership interest is treated as readily tradable "if the interest is regularly quoted by persons such as brokers or dealers who are making a market in the partnership interest." In the absence of an identifiable market maker, the substantial equivalent of a secondary market exists if either (1) "the holder of an interest has a readily available, regular and ongoing opportunity to sell or exchange such interest through a public means of obtaining or providing information of offers to buy, sell, or exchange interests;" or (2) "buyers and sellers have the opportunity to buy, sell, or exchange interests in a time frame and with the regularity and continuity that the existence of a market maker would provide." Rather than elaborate on when these conditions are met, the Notice provides several "safe harbor" examples of sales and exchanges that are considered not to result in public trading.

The most broadly applicable safe harbor excludes from the definition of publicly traded partnership so-called "private placements"—that is, any partnership whose interests were not registered under the Securities Act of 1933 if either (1) the partnership does not have more than 500 members, or (2) the initial offering price of each partnership unit was at least $20,000 and the partnership agreement prohibits subdivision of units for resale into units the initial offering price of which would not have been at least $20,000.

In addition, a partnership will not be considered to be publicly traded for any year in which there is a "lack of actual trading." This test can be met under two alternatives. The first alternative is met if, with limited exceptions, no more than five percent of the total interests in partnership capital or profits is sold or disposed of during the year (including repurchases of partnership interests by the partnership). Alternatively, this safe harbor applies if no more than two percent of total interests in partnership profits and capital are sold or otherwise disposed of during the year, even though additional interests, raising the total to over five percent, are disposed of in transactions meeting certain other safe harbors. It is clear from section 7704(f), dealing with the effect of a partnership becoming a corporation, that section 7704 contemplates the possibility that a partnership which is initially recognized as such might in a subsequent year become a corporation under section 7704. The "lack of actual trading" safe harbor, which applies on a year-by-year basis, suggests further that a partnership might be considered to be a corporation in one year and a partnership in the next, when it meets the safe harbor. This result could give rise to a constructive liquidation of the "corporation" with tax consequences to the entity and the investors or conversely, the constructive formation of a new corporation.

3. *Exceptions*

A broad exception to section 7704 allows publicly traded limited partnerships more than ninety percent of whose gross income is from certain "passive sources" to continue to be treated as partnerships. Qualified income for this purpose, with some narrow exceptions, includes, interest, dividends, real property rents, gain from the sale of real property, and income and gains from the exploration, development, extraction, processing, refining, etc. of oil and gas or any other natural resource. While the legislative history is silent as to the reason for this exception, it presumably is based on the historic use of limited partnerships in organizing such ventures and the availability of conduit taxation for other entity forms (e.g., real estate investment trusts) making investments of this type.

Section 7704 applies for all taxable years beginning after 1987. Publicly traded partnerships in existence on December 17, 1987, however, are excepted until 1998, unless there is an addition of a new line of business during that period.

4. *References*

Haney and Holmes, Publicly Traded Partnerships After the Revenue Act of 1987, 66 Taxes 331 (1988).

D. POLICY ASPECTS OF ENTITY CLASSIFICATION ISSUES

The entity classification issues discussed in the previous materials have by and large been resolved through a technical analysis of the various "corporate" factors involved. However, behind these technical issues is the broader policy question of the circumstances in which business profits shall be subject to a "double" level of tax, once at the entity level and again when made available to the participants. When Congress focused on the question in 1987, it found publicly traded interests to be one specific situation in which the corporate taxing pattern should be applicable regardless of the form of business organization. But this obviously is not the only approach which could be taken. The Treasury Department has recommended to Congress on a number of occasions that limited partnerships with more than 35 partners be taxed as corporations. In connection with the 1987 legislation, Congress instructed the Treasury to prepare a report and recommendations on the appropriate tax treatment of all partnerships which "significantly resemble" corporations. In addition, as discussed infra, page 271, not all corporations are subject to a pattern of double taxation. Thus entity classification is only one aspect the broader question of the method by which business profits should be taxed. These issues are considered in more detail in Chapter 7.

CHAPTER 2

FORMATION OF THE PARTNERSHIP

SECTION 1. INTRODUCTION: CONTRIBUTION OF MONEY OR PROPERTY

INTERNAL REVENUE CODE: Sections 721; 722; 723; 704(c); 1223(1) and (2); 1245(b)(3).

REGULATIONS: Sections 1.721–1; 1.722–1; 1.723–1.

Sections 721–723 provide that no gain or loss shall be recognized to the partnership or partners on a contribution of property to a partnership in exchange for a partnership interest, that a partner's basis for his partnership interest shall be equal to his adjusted basis for the contributed property, plus any cash contributed, and that the partnership's basis for the contributed property is equal its adjusted basis in the hands of the contributing partner. The nonrecognition rule of section 721 overrides the rule of section 1001(c), which generally requires that realized gains and losses be recognized. Section 722 prescribes the partner's basis in his partnership interest, which is a separate and distinct asset from the underlying property owned by the partnership. The contributing partner's basis in his partnership interest as determined under section 722 is commonly referred to in tax jargon as "outside basis." Section 723 prescribes the partnership's basis in the assets contributed by the partners. The partnership's basis in the contributed property as determined under section 723 (as well as the partnership's basis in property acquired by purchase) is commonly called "inside basis."

These provisions apply both to contributions to an existing partnership as well as to contributions to a newly formed partnership. Application of these rules is fairly straightforward where only money and unencumbered property are contributed to the partnership, whether the partnership is already in existence or just being formed. If contributed property is encumbered by liens, the partnership otherwise assumes debts of a contributing partner, or cash or other property is distributed to a contributing partner in connection with the contribution, however, the tax treatment of the transaction is more complicated. In these cases some of the rules governing taxation of the operation of partnerships also come into play. These issues are discussed infra, page 68.

As a result of the basis provisions in sections 722 and 723, the gain that goes unrecognized under section 721 does not permanently escape taxation; it is deferred until a later recognition event occurs. Unrecognized losses are similarly deferred. The deferral mechanisms do not work perfectly, however, and in some instances, subsequent events may cause nonrecognition of gain or loss to become permanent. Conversely, because these provisions give rise to two distinct bases in two distinct assets, there may be no double recognition of gain or loss in the future. The provisions of Subchapter K generally prevent these occurrences as long as partnership interests are not bought and sold or otherwise transferred after the initial formation, but these problems frequently arise when partnership interests have been transferred.

Nonrecognition under section 721 is accorded only to contributions of *property* in exchange for a partnership interest. If a partnership interest is received in exchange for services rendered to the partnership or to a partner, section 721 does not apply. Such a transaction generally will be taxable under either section 83 or the general principles of section 61. Receipt of a partnership interest in consideration of services is discussed infra, page 52.

ILLUSTRATIVE MATERIAL

A. CHARACTER AND HOLDING PERIOD

1. *Treatment of Partner*

A partnership interest is a capital asset in the hands of a partner, even though it may have been acquired in exchange for assets that would produce ordinary income upon sale, such as inventory. Section 741. But if a partnership's property consists of inventory or unrealized accounts receivable, section 751 may require the recognition of ordinary income on a sale of the partnership interest notwithstanding its classification as a capital asset.

As a consequence of the exchanged basis rule of section 722, pursuant to section 1223(1) a partner's holding period for his partnership interest includes the period for which he held the contributed property, if the property was a section 1231 or a capital asset. If the property was an ordinary income asset, however, the holding period commences when the partnership interest is received. But if a mix of assets is contributed each with a different holding period, the computation of the holding period of the partnership interest is unclear; fragmentation of the partnership interest, which appears to be the most logical answer, is inconsistent with Subchapter K's general treatment of a partnership interest as a single unitary asset.[1]

2. *Treatment of Partnership*

Property contributed to a partnership in a transaction subject to sections 721–723 is characterized as a capital asset, section 1231 asset, or ordinary income asset (e.g., inventory) according to the purpose for which the partnership holds the property, except as provided in section 724. That section provides three special rules. Unrealized receivables contributed by a partner, such as a cash basis service provider's accounts receivable, retain their ordinary income character permanently. Inventory items contributed by a partner retain their ordinary character for five years, even though not held as inventory by the partnership. Finally, property with a built-in capital loss at the time of the contribution retains its character as a capital asset, to

1. The same question arises where property is contributed in exchange for corporate stock in a transaction governed by section 351. In that case the fragmentation theory has been applied. See Runkle v. Commissioner, 39 B.T.A. 458 (1939).

the extent of the built-in loss, even though the partnership holds the asset as an ordinary income asset.

Because section 723 gives the partnership a transferred basis in property contributed to it, section 1223(2) provides that the partnership's holding period for the property includes the period for which the contributing partner held the property. Thus, section 1231 property contributed to a partnership for use in its trade or business retains its character as section 1231 property even though the partnership has not independently met the holding period requirement.

B. BUILT–IN GAINS AND LOSSES

Under the general rules of section 704, governing the allocation of items of income and deduction among partners, the gain or loss inherent in an asset at the time it is contributed to a partnership would be allocated among the partners according to their general profit sharing ratios. Thus, if A and B formed an equal partnership to which A contributed $10,000 cash and B contributed land with a fair market value of $10,000 and a basis of $3,000, and the land were sold for $10,000, the $7,000 gain would be recognized equally by A and B, $3,500 each. Section 704(c) precludes this result by requiring built-in gains and losses to be allocated for tax purposes to the partner who contributed the property, even though the gains and losses may be allocated otherwise for partnership accounting purposes. See Regulations, section 1.704–1(b)(5), Ex. (13)(i). Section 704(c) is discussed in greater detail, infra, page 113.

C. THE SWAP FUND PROBLEM

Suppose three investors each own a single block of stock in three different corporations and wish to diversify their investments on a tax free basis. Under section 721 as originally enacted, they could each contribute their stock to a newly formed partnership and would then have an undivided one-third interest in the stock of the three corporations. They would have thus obtained a diversification of investment with no current tax. This basic technique was used on a larger scale for the establishment of so-called "swap funds" under which a number of investors wishing to diversify their investment portfolios entered into a partnership formed by an investment manager. Typically, the manager and the potential investor both had the right to withdraw from the transaction before it was consummated if the resulting "mix" of investments was not satisfactory to the manager or the investors. The Internal Revenue Service originally issued private rulings that such funds could in fact achieve diversification on a tax free basis but Congress in 1976 put an end to the practice by enacting section 721(b). That section withdraws the nonrecognition of gain treatment under section 721(a) for transfers of property to a partnership which involve a diversification of investment. Because the contribution of property to a swap fund partnership is a recognition event if gain is realized, section 722 permits the contributing partner to increase his basis in his partnership interest by the recognized gain.

Section 721(b) is intended to apply the same constraints on diversification transfers to partnerships as apply to transfers to corporations or trusts. However, section 721(b) on its face withdraws nonrecognition only if a gain is realized and section 722 adjusts a partner's basis only with respect to recognized gains. Thus, if a loss is realized on a contribution to a swap fund the nonrecognition rules apply and no deduction is allowed currently.

D. PARTNERSHIP ORGANIZATION AND SYNDICATION EXPENSES

Section 709(a) disallows any deduction for partnership organization and syndication expenses. Instead these expenses must be capitalized. Section 709(b) allows the partnership to elect to amortize organization, but not syndication, expenses over a sixty month period beginning with the month in which the partnership commences business. For application of this rule see Aboussie v. United States, 779 F.2d 424 (8th Cir.1985); Diamond v. Commissioner, 92 T.C. 423 (1989). If the partnership is liquidated before the end of the sixty month period, the partnership is allowed a loss deduction under section 165 for the unamortized deferred deduction. But if a section 709(b) election has not been made, the partnership is never allowed a loss deduction for organization expenses regardless of when the partnership is liquidated. Rev.Rul. 87–111, 1987–2 Cum.Bull. 160. Because the unamortized organization expenses are reflected in the partners' bases for their partnership interests, however, an amount equal to those expenses will be taken into account to reduce gain or increase loss on the liquidation of the partnership or to increase the basis of property distributed to the partners in the liquidation. See infra, page 223.

Organizational expenses are defined in section 709(b)(2) and Regulations, section 1.709–2(a), to include items such as legal and accounting fees incident to the negotiation and drafting of the partnership agreement and establishing an accounting system, and filing fees. Expenses to acquire partnership assets are not organization fees.

Syndication fees, as defined in Regulations, section 1.709–1(b), are never amortizable or deductible upon liquidation of the partnership. Such fees encompass brokerage fees incurred to sell partnership interests, legal fees in connection with an underwriting, securities laws registration fees, accounting fees connected with offering materials, printing costs of a prospectus, placement memorandum, or promotional material, etc. Rev.Rul. 85–32, 1985–1 Cum.Bull. 186. See also Rev.Rul. 88–4, 1988–1 Cum.Bull. 264 (attorneys' fees for tax opinion letter included in prospectus of syndicated partnership are syndication fees); Rev.Rul. 89–11, 1989–1 Cum.Bull. 179 (no section 165 loss deduction allowed for syndication expenses incurred in an unsuccessful effort to establish a partnership). For the application of section 709 to a so-called "sponsor's fee" paid by a limited partnership to its promoter, see Driggs v. Commissioner, 87 T.C. 759 (1986).

E. REFERENCES

Keyser, A Theory of Nonrecognition Under an Income Tax: The Case of Partnership Formation, 5 Am.J. of Tax Policy 269 (1986); Boyd and O'Dell, How Do Syndication Costs Affect the Partners' Bases in the Partnership, 3 J. of Partnership Tax. 138 (1986).

SECTION 2. CONTRIBUTION OF PROPERTY VERSUS CONTRIBUTION OF SERVICES

INTERNAL REVENUE CODE: Sections 83(a)–(d), (g), (h); 721.

REGULATIONS: Sections 1.83–1(a), –3(e), –4(b)(2), –6(a)(4), (b); 1.721–1(b); 1.722–1.

If a partner receives a partnership interest in exchange for services, section 721 does not apply to provide nonrecognition. Where the partnership interest received includes an interest in partnership capital, i.e., property contributed by other partners, Regulations, section 1.721–1(b)(1), provide that the fair market value of the partnership interest is includable under section 61 as compensation for services. Correspondingly, the partnership either deducts or capitalizes the same amount, depending on the nature of the services. The same results are obtained by applying section 83. In addition, section 83 provides comprehensive rules regarding the year in which the value of the partnership interest must be included in income if the interest is subject to a risk of forfeiture or other restrictions that prevent it from being fully vested. This aspect of section 83 would apply, for example, if a partner were required to render services to the partnership for a certain period of time before the interest vested. In such a case taxation is deferred, but the amount includable is determined at the time the restrictions lapse rather than on the earlier date that the partnership interest was first received.

Although the basic rules which apply when a service partner receives an interest in partnership capital are clear, receipt of an interest in exchange for services that entitles the service partner only to a share of future profits is more problematic.

Since nonrecognition under section 721 extends only to the receipt of a partnership interest in exchange for "property," a crucial issue in the formation of a partnership is whether a partner's contribution is "property" or services. Neither the Code nor the Regulations define the word "property," and this issue must be resolved on a case by case basis.

A. EXCHANGE OF SERVICES FOR INTEREST IN PARTNERSHIP CAPITAL

UNITED STATES v. FRAZELL

United States Court of Appeals, Fifth Circuit, 1964.
335 F.2d 487.

TUTTLE, CHIEF JUDGE. This is an appeal by the Government from a judgment in favor of the taxpayer. Frazell v. United States, W.D.La. 1963, 213 F.Supp. 457. As the largely undisputed facts are set out at length in the opinion of the district court, only a summary will be presented here. On February 9, 1951, William Frazell, a geologist, entered into a contract with the N.H. Wheless Oil Company, a partnership, and W.C. Woolf, under which Frazell was to check certain areas to determine whether potentially productive oil and gas properties might be procured there. He was to recommend those properties he found suitable to Wheless and Woolf, and upon their joint approval, he was to attempt to acquire such properties, taking title thereto in the names of Wheless and Woolf in equal shares. In return for these services, Frazell was to receive "a monthly salary or drawing account," plus expenses, and specified interests in the property acquired. It was agreed, however, "that Frazell shall not be entitled to, nor shall he be considered as owning, any interest in said properties until such time as Wheless and Woolf shall have recovered their full costs and expenses of said properties" including the amounts paid out to Frazell. 213 F.Supp. at 470.

The arrangement proved successful, and it was evident in the early part of 1955 that Wheless and Woolf would fully recover their costs and expenses by the end of November of that year. In April 1955, the 1951 contract was terminated, and by contract dated April 20, 1955, all the properties acquired under the earlier arrangement were transferred to the W.W.F. Corporation, a Delaware corporation formed specifically to acquire these properties in return for the issuance of debentures to Wheless and Woolf and of stock to Wheless, Woolf, and Frazell. Frazell received 6,500 shares of W.W.F. stock (13% of the total issued), having a fair market value of $91,000.00, but he included no part of this amount in his 1955 income tax return. The Commissioner ruled that the $91,000.00 should have been included in income and assessed a deficiency, which Frazell paid under protest and seeks to recover here.

* * * [The trial court found] that the 1951 contract created a "joint venture" among the three participants. 213 F.Supp. at 468. We take no issue with the trial court's finding of fact in this matter, but it does not follow from the categorization of the 1951 arrangement as a "joint venture" that the April 1955 transactions resulted in no taxable income to Frazell.

It is fundamental that "compensation for services" is taxable as ordinary income under the Internal Revenue Code of 1954. I.R.C.1954 § 61(a)(1). This principle applies whether the one compensated for his services is an employee receiving a salary, fees, or commission (ibid.), one receiving corporate securities (I.R.C.1954 § 351(a)), or a "service partner" receiving an interest in the partnership. (I.R.C.1954 § 721; Treas.Reg. § 1.721–1(b)(1)).

The regulation pertaining to partnerships provides that

"the value of an interest in such partnership capital so transferred to a partner as compensation for services constitutes income to the partner under section 61. The amount of such income is the fair market value of the interest in capital so transferred * * * at the time the transfer is made for past services. * * * The time when such income is realized depends on all the facts and circumstances, including any substantial restrictions or conditions on the compensated partner's right to withdraw or otherwise dispose of such interest."

This rule would have been directly applicable had the 1951 contract continued in effect through November 1955, the date on which Wheless and Woolf would have fully recovered their costs in the venture. The contract made it clear that Frazell would "not have the right to dispose of any rights which may accrue to him" before those costs were recovered. 213 F.Supp. at 472. But after November, he would have received a largely unrestricted [1] interest in about 13% of the partnership properties. That this interest was primarily, if not entirely, in return for Frazell's services to the enterprise is undisputed. Thus, so much of the interest Frazell was to receive in November 1955 as could be attributed to his services for the oil venture would have been ordinary income to him in the year of receipt.

The applicable rule is in no way changed by Frazell's contention that his interest in the enterprise was a "carried interest." There are three recognized varieties of "carried interest," and each "may be created under varied circumstances, e.g., * * * as compensation for services rendered, e.g., by a geologist. * * *" Williams & Meyers, Oil and Gas Law, vol. 2, § 424 (1959). The interest created by the 1951 contract most nearly fits into the "Menahan" category of "carried interests;" that is, "a springing executory interest * * * conveyed by the carrying party [Wheless and Woolf] to the carried party [Frazell], such interest to become possessory upon the satisfaction of * * * [the carrying party's] costs." Williams & Meyers, op. cit. supra § 424.1, p. 423. Even if Frazell is taken to have had some sort of interest in the properties in question from their first acquisition, his interest would not have become possessory until November 1955. Under Treasury Regulation § 1.721–1(b)(1), the value of that interest would have been taxable to him at that time. See also Anderson & Coffee, "Proposed Revision of Partner and Partnership Taxation: Analysis of the Report of the Advisory Group on Subchapter K," 15 Tax L.Rev. 285, 318 (1960).

The fact that the contract was terminated prior to November 1955 should have no effect on the tax consequences of Frazell's arrangements. * * * If Frazell's partnership interest became possessory immediately upon the termination of the 1951 contract, so much of that interest received as compensation for services was taxable to him under the rule of Treasury Regulation § 1.721(b)(1). Thereafter, the transfer of his interest for W.W.F. stock was taxfree under section 351(a). * * *

This is not to say that the full $91,000.00 is ordinary income. The trial court found that, just as Wheless and Woolf contributed large amounts of capital, "Frazell supplied to the venture a very valuable oil map which was his private property." 213 F.Supp. at 461. Indeed the

1. Even after Wheless and Woolf recovered their costs, the contract gave them a right of first refusal should Frazell desire to dispose of any of his interests in the properties in question.

record shows that prior to entering into the 1951 contract Frazell had acquired several maps which apparently proved very helpful to the work of the venture. Among the reasons given by Mr. Wheless for desiring to employ Frazell was that "he had accumulated maps, geological data and various information that was valuable to the arrangement that it would have taken a long time for someone else just moving into the territory to accumulate." And Frazell himself testified that he "had contributed considerable information and maps which resulted in the discovery and production of oil. * * *" Although it is clear that the greater part of the 13% interest received by Frazell was received as compensation for services, the court's finding and the cited testimony suggest that some part of that interest might have been received in return for "property;" namely, the maps. That part of the property Frazell received in 1955 attributable to his contribution of maps is not taxable in 1955 [under the view that] the interest received [was] a partnership interest vesting on the termination of the 1951 contract (I.R.C.1954 § 721) * * *.

Before the nonrecognition rule can be applied to the maps in this case, however, two factual determinations must be made: (1) Did Frazell contribute the maps in question to the oil venture or did he keep them as his own personal property? (2) If he contributed them to the venture, what was their value at the time they were contributed? As the burden of proof on both of these issues lies with the taxpayer, it might be argued that he is foreclosed in these issues because of the silence of the record on these points. However, we prefer to remand the case to the district court to permit it to make findings on these two issues. This disposition is in accord with the action of this court in a number of recent cases. E.g., Bisbee–Baldwin Corp. v. Tomlinson, 5 Cir.1963, 320 F.2d 929.

The judgment is therefore reversed and the case remanded to the district court to determine whether the maps introduced at the original trial were contributed by Frazell to the oil venture created by the 1951 contract. If the court finds that the maps were so contributed, it shall determine their value as of the time of their contribution. Such part of $91,000.00 as exceeds the value of the maps as determined by the trial court is properly taxable to Frazell as ordinary income.

Reversed and remanded.*

* [Ed.: The court held alternatively that if the stock was viewed as received in substitution for the originally contemplated partnership interest, it was still received as compensation for services and would be taxable to Frazell under section 351(a). Judge Hutcheson dissented on the ground that the District Court finding that a tax-free exchange under section 351(a) was present should be sustained.

ILLUSTRATIVE MATERIAL

A. THE MEANING OF PROPERTY

1. *General*

The problem of identifying "property" which qualifies an exchange for nonrecognition under section 721 is not unique; the same issue arises in determining whether stock received in exchange for a contribution to a corporation is eligible for nonrecognition under section 351, although section 351 has some additional requirements not imposed by section 721. Accordingly, the precedents may be applied interchangeably, at least insofar as the issue is determining the meaning of "property."

2. *Property Created by Personal Efforts*

The meaning of the term "property" is quite broad. Not only tangible property and cash, but a variety of intangible property rights, such as patents, may qualify, even if those rights were created by the personal efforts of the person who contributed them. Thus, the term property encompasses business goodwill, Rev.Rul. 70–45, 1970–1 Cum.Bull. 17, secret processes and formulae, even if not patented, Rev.Rul. 64–56, 1964–1 (Part 1) Cum.Bull. 133, and contracts to acquire property, Ambrose v. Commissioner, 15 T.C.M. 643 (1956).

The difference between services and self-created intangible property is not always easy to ascertain, and in some cases both may be present. In United States v. Stafford, 727 F.2d 1043 (11th Cir.1984), the taxpayer obtained from an insurance company a "letter of intent" proposing to lend to the taxpayer or his designee a substantial sum of money on very favorable terms. Although the parties expected that a loan would be made pursuant to the letter of intent, it was not legally enforceable by the taxpayer. After obtaining the letter of intent in his own name, the taxpayer formed a limited partnership of which he was the sole general partner. He contributed $200,000 cash in exchange for two limited partnership shares, and, as required by the partnership agreement, he contributed the letter of intent in exchange for a third limited partnership share.

The government asserted that section 721 did not apply to the limited partnership share received in exchange for the letter of intent because the interest was in fact received in consideration of services rendered to the partnership by the taxpayer in negotiating the loan to the partnership. First, the court concluded that the taxpayer owned the letter of intent, since he was working on his own behalf at the time he acquired it. Turning to the question of whether the letter was "property" within the meaning of section 721, the court concluded that the unenforceability of the letter was no bar to property status, citing Rev.Rul. 64–56, supra. Because the taxpayer transferred all of his rights in the letter the contribution was a transfer of property. However, because the record on appeal contained insufficient evidence to determine whether the third limited partnership interest was in fact received in exchange for the letter, or for services to be rendered to the partnership, or for both, the court remanded the case, with directions that if the value of the letter was less than $100,000, the difference between that amount and the value of the letter represented taxable compensation.

3. *Accounts Receivable and Installment Obligations*

Accounts receivable from performing services for persons other than the partnership also constitute property for purposes of sections 721–723. Hempt Bros., Inc. v. United States, 490 F.2d 1172 (3d Cir.1974) (receivables are property for purposes of section 351); Roberts Co. v. Commissioner, 5 T.C. 1 (1945). Even though accounts receivable are property which generally may be transferred to a partnership without recognition under section 721, the assignment of income doctrine may be applied when a cash basis taxpayer contributes accrued but unpaid items to a partnership and the facts and circumstances suggest tax avoidance. H.Rep. 98–861, 98th Cong., 2d Sess. 857. See Rev.Rul. 80–198, 1980–2 Cum.Bull. 113; Rev.Rul. 80–199, 1980–2 Cum.Bull. 122.

Installment obligations are specifically designated as eligible property in Regulations, section 1.721–1(a). Moreover, section 453B does not require recognition of gain upon a transfer of an installment obligation to a partnership. See Regulations, section 1.453–9(c)(2). Presumably, under section 704(c) the remaining deferred gain must be allocated to the contributing partner when it is recognized.

4. *Partners' Promissory Notes*

Since a partner's personal promissory note contributed to the partnership in exchange for a partnership interest meets the definition of property, the rules of sections 721–723 govern. In this situation, however, Bussing v. Commissioner, 88 T.C. 449 (1987), held that the contributing partner has no basis in the promissory note, and therefore his basis in his partnership interest under section 722 initially is zero (plus the amount of any money and the basis of other property contributed). As payments are made on the note his basis will be increased pro tanto. Regulations, section 1.704–1(b)(2)(iv)*(d)(2)*, provide that in such a case the partner's capital account is to be increased only as payments are made on the note. What is the partnership's basis in the note if it sells the note before any payments have been made?

B. EFFECT OF RECEIPT OF A CAPITAL INTEREST FOR SERVICES

When a person exchanges services for a partnership capital interest section 721 does not apply, and the fair market value of the interest is includable as compensation under section 61 and section 83. See Regulations, section 1.721–1(b)(1). The service partner's basis for his partnership interest is the amount included in income plus any money and the basis of other property contributed to the partnership. Regulations, section 1.722–1. However, if the partnership interest is subject to a substantial risk of forfeiture, the value is not included until the restrictions lapse, unless the taxpayer elects under section 83(b) to include the value in income in the year of receipt. For the meaning of "substantial risk of forfeiture," see Regulations, section 1.83–3(c).

Section 83(h) allows the partnership a deduction or capitalized cost of acquiring an asset (tangible or intangible) equal to the amount includable by the partner under section 83(a). Logically, the service partner should not be entitled to any part of this deduction and a provision in the partnership agreement pursuant to section 704(b) allocating it to the other partners should be respected. See also section 706(c)(2)(B). Any deduction allowed would then reduce the outside bases of the other partners under section 705.

Finally, the partnership may recognize gain (or loss) on the admission of the service partner. In effect, the partnership has transferred an undivided portion of each of its assets to the service partner as payment for services. If its assets are appreciated, gain is recognized on the constructive transfer. This gain should be allocated to the non-service partners. As a corollary, the partnership constructively receives the property back from the service partner and under section 723 takes a basis equal to his "tax cost" basis in the property.

Assume, for example, that C is admitted as a one-third partner to the equal partnership, AB, which has assets with a basis and value of $180,000, in exchange for services; the transaction generates a deductible expense for the partnership. C would have $60,000 of ordinary income, and the partnership a $60,000 deduction which the agreement may allocate to A and B. C's basis for his interest would be $60,000, and A's and B's former bases of $90,000 would each be reduced by virtue of the deduction by $30,000 to $60,000. But assume the assets had a basis of only $96,000 and A's and B's bases for their partnership interests each was only $48,000. The Regulations indicate that C would still have ordinary income of $60,000 and the partnership a deduction of $60,000. This would reduce A's and B's bases for their interests each to $18,000. But the partnership will recognize a gain of $28,000 which should be allocated to A and B, since in effect they have purchased $60,000 worth of services by each transferring to C one-third of each partnership asset with a total cost of $32,000 (⅓ of $96,000). See Regulations, section 1.83–6(b). Hence A's and B's bases for their respective interests would each be then increased by $14,000 to $32,000. The ABC partnership would then hold the assets with a $124,000 basis (⅔ of original $96,000 basis, plus $60,000 basis for the recontributed ⅓).

A similar result was reached in McDougal v. Commissioner, 62 T.C. 720 (1974). McDougal purchased a race horse for $10,000 and at the time of the purchase promised one McClanahan that if the latter would care for and train the horse he would be entitled to a one-half interest in the horse once McDougal had recovered the cost and expenses of the acquisition. In addition, McClanahan would be entitled to the standard trainer's fees for the services performed. The horse raced with success and after McDougal had recovered out of the winnings the cost of acquisition, a partnership was formed which owned the horse and in which McClanahan had a one-half interest. The value of the horse at this time was $60,000. McDougal treated the transaction as generating a capital gain on the difference between the $30,000 value of the one-half interest in the horse and one-half of the basis ($5,000) and at the same time claimed a $30,000 business deduction for the services performed by McClanahan. The Commissioner argued that the transfer to the partnership was governed by sections 721 and 723 and that the partnership's basis in the horse was limited to McDougal's adjusted basis at the time of transfer. The court held for the taxpayer, analyzing the transaction as if McDougal had first transferred an interest in the horse to McClanahan for his services, recognizing capital gain on the transfer ($25,000) and generating a business deduction ($30,000), and then transferred the remaining one-half interest in the horse to the partnership. He thus took a $5,000 basis for his partnership interest and the partnership had a corresponding $5,000 basis for his one-half interest in the horse. McClanahan under this analysis presumably recognized $30,000 of ordinary income and took a $30,000 basis in his one-half interest in the horse. This basis became his basis in his partnership interest under section 722 and the partnership's basis for the other one-half interest in the horse under section 723. Would the result differ if McDougal and McClanahan had agreed to be partners from the outset, but that McDougal would receive all of the partnership's profits until he had recovered the acquisition cost and expenses? See infra, page 98.

B. EXCHANGE OF SERVICES FOR INTEREST IN PARTNERSHIP PROFITS

DIAMOND v. COMMISSIONER

United States Court of Appeals, Seventh Circuit, 1974.
492 F.2d 286.

FAIRCHILD, CIRCUIT JUDGE.

This is an appeal from a decision of the Tax Court upholding the commissioner's assessment of deficiencies against Sol and Muriel Diamond * * *. The Tax Court concluded that Diamond realized ordinary income on the receipt of a right to a share of profit or loss to be derived from a real estate venture * * * in Diamond v. Commissioner, 56 T.C. 530 (1971). * * *

The 1962 Partnership Case.

During 1961, Diamond was a mortgage broker. Philip Kargman had acquired for $25,000 the buyer's rights in a contract for the sale of an office building. Kargman asked Diamond to obtain a mortgage loan for the full $1,100,000 purchase price of the building. Diamond and Kargman agreed that Diamond would receive a 60% share of profit or loss of the venture if he arranged the financing.

Diamond succeeded in obtaining a $1,100,000 mortgage loan from Marshall Savings and Loan. On December 15, 1961 Diamond and Kargman entered into an agreement which provided:

(1) The two were associated as joint venturers for 24 years (the life of the mortgage) unless earlier terminated by agreement or by sale;

(2) Kargman was to advance all cash needed for the purchase beyond the loan proceeds;

(3) Profits and losses would be divided, 40% to Kargman, 60% to Diamond;

(4) In event of sale, proceeds would be devoted first to repayment to Kargman of money supplied by him, and net profits thereafter would be divided 40% to Kargman, 60% to Diamond.

Early in 1962, Kargman and Diamond created an Illinois land trust to hold title to the property. The chief motivation for the land trust arrangement was apparently to insulate Diamond and Kargman from personal liability on the mortgage note.

The purchase proceeded as planned and closing took place on February 18, 1962. Kargman made cash outlays totalling $78,195.83 in connection with the purchase. Thus, under the terms of the agreement, the property would have to appreciate at least $78,195.83 before Diamond would have any equity in it.

Shortly after closing, it was proposed that Diamond would sell his interest and one Liederman would be substituted, except on a 50–50 basis. Liederman persuaded Diamond to sell his interest for $40,000. This sale was effectuated on March 8, 1962 by Diamond assigning his interest to Kargman for $40,000. Kargman in turn then conveyed a similar interest, except for 50–50 sharing, to Liederman for the same amount.

On their 1962 joint return, the Diamonds reported the March 8, 1962 $40,000 sale proceeds as a short term capital gain. This gain was offset by an unrelated short term capital loss. They reported no tax consequences from the February 18 receipt of the interest in the venture. Diamond's position is that his receipt of this type of interest in partnership is not taxable income although received in return for services. He relies on § 721 and Reg. § 1.721–1(b)(1). He further argues that the subsequent sale of this interest produced a capital gain under § 741. The Tax Court held that the receipt of this type of interest in partnership in return for services is not within § 721 and is taxable under § 61 when received. The Tax Court valued the interest at $40,000 as of February 18, as evidenced by the sale for that amount three weeks later, on March 8.

Both the taxpayer and the Tax Court treated the venture as a partnership and purported to apply partnership income tax principles. It has been suggested that the record might have supported findings that there was in truth an employment or other relationship, other than partnership, and produced a similar result, but these findings were not made. See Cowan, The Diamond Case, 27 Tax Law Review 161 (1972). It has also been suggested (and argued, alternatively, by the government) that although on the face of the agreement Diamond appeared to receive only a right to share in profit (loss) to be derived, the value of the real estate may well have been substantially greater than the purchase price, so that Diamond may really have had an interest in capital, if the assets were properly valued. This finding was not made. The Tax Court, 56 T.C. at 547, n. 16, suggested the possibility that Diamond would not in any event be entitled to capital gains treatment of his sale of a right to receive income in the future, but did not decide the question.[3]

Taking matters at face value, taxpayer received, on February 18, an interest in partnership, limited to a right to a share of profit (loss) to be derived. In discussion we shall refer to this interest either as his interest in partnership or a profit-share.

3. Because of the decision we reach, it is also unnecessary for us to consider this possibility and we express no conclusions concerning it.

The Tax Court, with clearly adequate support, found that Diamond's interest in partnership had a market value of $40,000 on February 18. Taxpayer's analysis is that under the regulations the receipt of a profit-share February 18, albeit having a market value and being conferred in return for services, was not a taxable event, and that the entire proceeds of the March 8 sale were a capital gain. The Tax Court analysis was that the interest in partnership, albeit limited to a profit-share, was property worth $40,000, and taxpayer's acquisition, thereof on February 18 was compensation for services and ordinary income. Assuming that capital gain treatment at sale would have been appropriate, there was no gain because the sale was for the same amount.

There is no statute or regulation which expressly and particularly prescribes the income tax effect, or absence of one, at the moment a partner receives a profit-share in return for services. The Tax Court's holding rests upon the general principle that a valuable property interest received in return for services is compensation, and income. Taxpayer's argument is predicated upon an implication which his counsel, and others, have found in Reg. § 1.721–1(1)(b), but which need not, and the government argues should not, be found there.

26 U.S.C.A. § 721 is entitled "Nonrecognition of gain or loss on contribution," and provides: "No gain or loss shall be recognized to a partnership or to any of its partners in the case of a contribution of property to the partnership in exchange for an interest in the partnership." Only if, by a strained construction, "property" were said to include services, would § 721 say anything about the effect of furnishing services. It clearly deals with a contribution like Kargman's of property, and prescribes that when he contributed his property, no gain or loss was recognized. It does not, of course, explicitly say that no income accrues to one who renders services and, in return, becomes a partner with a profit-share.

Reg. § 1.721–1 presumably explains and interprets § 721, perhaps to the extent of qualifying or limiting its meaning. Subsec. (b)(1), particularly relied on here, reads in part as follows:

"Normally, under local law, each partner is entitled to be repaid his contributions of money or other property to the partnership (at the value placed upon such property by the partnership at the time of the contribution) whether made at the formation of the partnership or subsequent thereto. To the extent that any of the partners gives up any part of his right to be repaid his contributions (as distinguished from a share in partnership profits) in favor of another partner as compensation for services (or in satisfaction of an obligation), section 721 does not apply. The value of an interest in such partnership capital so transferred to a partner as compensation for services constitutes income to the partner under section 61. * * *"

The quoted portion of the regulation may well be read, like § 721, as being directly addressed only to the consequences of a contribution of money or other property. It asserts that when a partner making such contributions transfers to another some part of the contributing partner's right to be repaid, in order to compensate the other for services or to satisfy an obligation to the other, § 721 does not apply, there is recognition of gain or loss to the contributing partner, and there is income to the partner who receives, as compensation for services, part of the right to be repaid.

The regulation does not specify that if a partner contributing property agrees that, in return for services, another shall be a partner with a profit-share only, the value of the profit-share is not income to the recipient. An implication to that effect, such as is relied on by taxpayer, would have to rest on the proposition that the regulation was meant to be all inclusive as to when gain or loss would be recognized or income would exist as a consequence of the contribution of property to a partnership and disposition of the partnership interest. It would have to appear, in order to sustain such implication, that the existence of income by reason of a creation of a profit-share, immediately having a determinable market value, in favor of a partner would be inconsistent with the result specified in the regulation.

We do not find this implication in our own reading of the regulation. It becomes necessary to consider the substantial consensus of commentators in favor of the principle claimed to be implied and to look to judicial interpretation, legislative history, administrative interpretation, and policy considerations to determine whether the implication is justified.

The Commentators: There is a startling degree of unanimity that the conferral of a profit-share as compensation for services is not income at the time of the conferral, although little by way of explanation of why this should be so, or analysis of statute or regulation to show that it is prescribed. See publications cited pp. 181–2 of Cowan, The Diamond Case.

One of the most unequivocal statements, with an explanation in terms of practicality or policy, was made by Arthur Willis in a text:

"However obliquely the proposition is stated in the regulations, it is clear that a partner who receives only an interest in future profits of the partnership as compensation for services is not required to report the receipt of his partnership interest as taxable income. The rationale is twofold. In the first place, the present value of a right to participate in future profits is usually too conjectural to be subject to valuation. In the second place, the service partner is taxable on his distributive share of partnership income as it is realized by the partnership. If he were taxed on the present value of the right to receive his share of future partnership income, either he would be taxed twice, or the value of his right to participate in partnership income must be amortized over some period of time." [5]

5. Willis on Partnership Taxation 84–85 (1971). See Cowan, The Diamond Case, 27 Tax Law Review 181 n. 56 (1972).

Judicial Interpretation: Except for one statement by the Tax Court no decision cited by the parties or found by us appears squarely to reach the question, either on principle in the absence of the regulations, or by application of the regulations. In a footnote in Herman M. Hale, 24 T.C.M. 1497, 1502 (1965) the Tax Court said: "Under the regulations, the mere receipt of a partnership interest in future profits does not create any tax liability. Sec. 1.721–1(b), Income Tax Reg." There was no explanation of how this conclusion was derived from the regulations.

Legislative History: The legislative history is equivocal.

An advisory group appointed in 1956 to review the regulations evidently felt concern about whether the provision of Reg. § 1.721–1 that the value of an interest in capital transferred to a partner in compensation for services constitutes income had a statutory basis in the light of § 721 providing that there shall be no recognition of gain or loss in the case of a contribution of property. The group proposed enactment of a new section to provide such basis, and legislation introduced into the 86th Congress in 1959 incorporated this recommendation. The bill, H.R. 9662, would have created a new § 770 providing specifically for the taxation of a person receiving an interest in partnership capital in exchange for the performance of services for the partnership. However, neither proposed § 770 nor anything else in H.R. 9662 dealt with the receipt merely of a profit-share. The lack of concern over an income tax impact when only a profit-share was conferred might imply an opinion that such conferring of a profit-share would not be taxable under any circumstances, or might imply an opinion that it would be income or not under § 61 depending upon whether it had a determinable market value or not.

Several statements in the course of the hearings and committee reports paralleled the first parenthetical phrase in Reg. § 1.721–1(b) and were to the effect that the provision did not apply where a person received only a profit-share.[6] There was, however, at least one specific statement by the chairman of the advisory group (Mr. Willis) that if the service partner "were to receive merely an interest in future profits in exchange for his services, he would have no immediate taxable gain because he would be taxed on his share of income as it was earned." [7] H.R. 9662 passed the House of Representatives, and was favorably reported to the Senate by its finance committee, but never came to a vote in the Senate. Even had the bill become law, it would not have dealt expressly with the problem at hand.

Administrative Interpretation: We are unaware of instances in which the Commissioner has asserted delinquencies where a taxpayer who received a profit-share with determinable market value in return for services failed to report the value as income, or has otherwise acted

6. See, e.g., Senate Rep. No. 1616, 86th Cong., 2d Sess. 117 (1960).

7. See Hearings on Advisory Group Recommendations on Subchapters C, J, and K of the Internal Revenue Code before the House Comm. on Ways and Means, 86th Cong., 1st Sess. 53 (1959).

consistently with the Tax Court decision in *Diamond.* Although the consensus referred to earlier appears to exist, the Commissioner has not by regulation or otherwise acted affirmatively to reject it, and in a sense might be said to have agreed by silence.

Consideration of partnership principles or practices: There must be wide variation in the degree to which a profit-share created in favor of a partner who has or will render service has determinable market value at the moment of creation. Surely in many if not the typical situations it will have only speculative value, if any.

In the present case, taxpayer's services had all been rendered, and the prospect of earnings from the real estate under Kargman's management was evidently very good. The profit-share had determinable market value.

If the present decision be sound, then the question will always arise, whenever a profit-share is created or augmented, whether it has a market value capable of determination. Will the existence of this question be unduly burdensome on those who choose to do business under the partnership form?

Each partner determines his income tax by taking into account his distributive share of the taxable income of the partnership. 26 U.S.C.A. § 702. Taxpayer's position here is that he was entitled to defer income taxation on the compensation for his services except as partnership earnings were realized. If a partner is taxed on the determinable market value of a profit-share at the time it is created in his favor, and is also taxed on his full share of earnings as realized, there will arguably be double taxation, avoidable by permitting him to amortize the value which was originally treated as income. Does the absence of a recognized procedure for amortization militate against the treatment of the creation of the profit-share as income?

Do the disadvantages of treating the creation of the profit-share as income in those instances where it has a determninable market value at that time outweigh the desirability of imposing a tax at the time the taxpayer has received an interest with determinable market value as compensation for services?

We think, of course, that the resolution of these practical questions makes clearly desirable the promulgation of appropriate regulations, to achieve a degree of certainty. But in the absence of regulation, we think it sound policy to defer to the expertise of the Commissioner and the Judges of the Tax Court, and to sustain their decision that the receipt of a profit-share with determinable market value is income.
* * *

ILLUSTRATIVE MATERIAL

A. IMPLICATIONS OF *DIAMOND*

As the Court of Appeals opinion in the *Diamond* case indicates, prior to the Tax Court opinion in that case it had been generally accepted that the receipt of a partnership *profits* interest for services was not currently taxable. See Rev.Rul. 70–435, 1970–2 Cum.Bull. 100, modifying Rev.Rul. 60–31, 1960–1 Cum.Bull. 174 (holding that receipt of future income interest in a joint venture is not taxable). The *Diamond* case presented the court with an appealing situation in which to tax the receipt of a profits interest received for services. The profits interest in that case was easily valued, was paid for past services and was sold shortly after receipt.

Consider, however, some of the implications of the *Diamond* holding. If an associate in a law firm is admitted to partnership and thus becomes entitled to a certain percentage of future profits, should she realize income at that time? While both the associate and Diamond have received a "profits" interest in the sense that they have an interest in a partnership which does not involve a right to be paid out of the capital contributions of the other partners, the two situations intuitively seem quite different. Are the differences substantive or matters of valuation? If the former, are the differences sufficient to support tax distinctions between types of "profits" interests? Some factors which might be considered would include whether the profits interest is for past services, the relation of the service partner's capital contribution to the capital contributions of the other partners and in general whether the service partner seems more like an employee or independent contractor than a joint venturer.

Perhaps the crucial difference is that in *Diamond* the court found that the partnership interest had a "determinable market value," while the value of an interest as a newly admitted law partner (or a partnership interest in any other partnership in which a partner's income is determined largely with reference to income from personal services to be rendered in the future) cannot be readily ascertained. In Vestal v. United States, 498 F.2d 487 (8th Cir.1974), the taxpayer contracted with certain limited partners of a partnership, the sole asset of which was oil and gas rights in a then unproductive but proven field, for the transfer of a portion of their partnership interests after they had recovered their original capital investment in exchange for his services in organizing the partnership. The court held that no income was realized in the year the contract rights were received because the value was speculative. On rehearing, this decision was held to be consistent with *Diamond.*

A different approach was taken in St. John v. United States, 84–1 U.S.T.C. ¶ 9158 (C.D.Ill.1983), where in exchange for services the taxpayer received a current partnership interest entitling him only to future profits. The court concluded that the value of the profits interest was zero because if the partnership were liquidated immediately after receipt, the taxpayer would have received nothing. Applying this analysis to the *Diamond* case suggests that perhaps Diamond in fact received an interest in partnership capital to the extent that the value of the building exceeded the value assigned to it by the partners upon formation of the partnership. Compare Hensel Phelps Construction Co. v. Commissioner, 74 T.C. 939 (1980), aff'd, 703 F.2d 485 (10th Cir.1983), in which the Tax Court valued an interest in partnership capital received in exchange for past services with reference to the fair market value of the services provided.

Should it matter whether the partnership interest is received in exchange for past or future services? If this distinction is to be determinative, are there objective tests which can be used to determine on which side of the line a particular transaction falls? If the value of a partnership interest in future profits received in exchange for future services is taxable in the year of receipt, is the partner also taxable on the income as received in future years? How can double taxation be avoided?

If the court in the *Diamond* case had accepted the taxpayer's argument that the receipt of the interest in future partnership profits was not a taxable event, the subsequent disposition of the partnership interest could nonetheless generate ordinary income. See Hale v. Commissioner, 24 T.C.M. 1497 (1965), so holding, relying on Hort v. Commissioner, 313 U.S. 28 (1941).

B. APPLICATION OF SECTION 83 TO PARTNERSHIP PROFITS INTERESTS RECEIVED FOR SERVICES

Diamond involved tax years before the enactment of section 83. The rules concerning the treatment of a partner who receives a partnership interest as compensation for services must be coordinated with the rules under section 83 which in general are controlling as to the taxability of property transferred in connection with the performance of services. Section 83 requires that the fair market value of the "property" transferred be included in income. However, under section 83 there is a statutory issue whether an interest in partnership profits constitutes "property". Regulations, section 1.83–3(e), define "property" comprehensively and exclude only "an unfunded and unsecured promise to pay money in the future." The Regulations appear to cover any kind of an interest in a partnership, including a profits interest of the type involved in *Diamond.* Proposed Regulations, section 1.721–1(b)(1)(i) (1971), however, seemed to take the position that the transfer of an interest in profits, as opposed to an interest in capital, would not be covered by section 83. The Proposed section 721 Regulations were not made final when the section 83 Regulations were adopted, thus perhaps indicating continuing uncertainty in the Internal Revenue Service as to how the issue should be resolved. The Internal Revenue Service does not appear to have pursued application of section 83 to partnership interests in future profits. General Counsel Memorandum 36,346 (July 25, 1977), suggested that section 83 not be applied to such interests received by service partners and that *Diamond* not be followed. No Revenue Ruling has ever been issued to this effect, however. What is the difference, if any, between an unsecured and unfunded promise to pay money in the future, which is not covered by section 83, and a partnership interest in future profits?

Applying section 83 to a profits only partnership interest in exchange for services raises the same valuation problems as in the *Diamond* case. See St. John v. United States, supra, page 65, which held that section 83 applied to the receipt of an interest in partnership profits, but that the value of the interest was zero. But in Campbell v. Commissioner, 59 T.C.M. 236 (1990), the court rejected the *St. John* valuation method and valued an interest in future partnership profits by computing the discounted value of the stream of income and tax benefits expected to be received by the services partner.

In applying section 83, should it matter whether the services must be performed continuously or only for a specified period of time? If property is received for services and the taxpayer's rights to the property are forfeitable or subject to substantial restrictions on transfer, the value of the property is not includable under section 83 until the property vests or the restrictions lapse. The value of the property is includable at its fair market value at that time. In such a case the service partner might consider an election under section 83(b) to include the value of the property at the time it is received, particularly if the value at the time of receipt is zero. (The Service might then, contrary to *Diamond,* seek to take the position that there was no "transfer" of "property" for section 83 purposes.)

Apart from the problem of the treatment of a profits interest under section 83, there are other questions as to the application of section 83 to the receipt of a partnership interest for services. Suppose that the partnership interest is subject to a substantial risk of forfeiture. Under Regulations, section 1.83–1(a), the transferee is not treated as the owner of the property until the risk of forfeiture lapses. Is the recipient of the partnership interest a partner during this period? If not, how is his share of partnership profits to be treated? Is he taxable on the increase in value of the partnership interest attributable to his services at the time the substantial risk of forfeiture lapses? If section 83 is applied to the receipt of an interest in partnership profits for services, should the partnership be allowed a deduction or capitalized expense under section 83(h) and Regulations, section 1.83–6, in amount equal to the value of the transferred profits interest? Must it also recognize gain in an equal amount? Should the deduction (capitalized expense) and income be allocated only to the preexisting partners? Does the service partner make a constructive contribution to the partnership of the future profits, thereby giving the partnership a basis in that income under section 723 equal to the amount included by the service partner, whose basis in those rights would be the amount included? If so, can (must?) this basis be amortized and the resulting deduction allocated to the service partner under section 704(b) or 704(c) as the future profits are earned? See Regulations, section 1.704–1(b)(5), Ex. (14).

The complexity and seeming artificiality of the computations necessary to deal with these questions if section 83 is applied to a future profits interest indicate that such interests should be treated as unfunded promises to pay money in the future, thereby negating the applicability of section 83. This is consistent with the recommendation of the 1984 American Law Institute, Federal Income Tax Project—Subchapter K, which recommended that a partner who received a profits only interest in exchange for services to the partnership generally should not be taxed upon receipt of the interest and that the partnership not be entitled to any deduction. Under the proposal a profits interest would be any interest other than a capital interest. A capital interest would exist only to the extent that the partner would receive proceeds in a hypothetical liquidation of the partnership. In essence, this recommendation follows the principle of the *St. John* case, supra, page 65.

C. REFERENCES

Cuff, New Partner in Professional Service Partnership Faces Unforeseen Tax Problems, 64 J. of Tax. 302 (1986); Lane, *Sol Diamond:* The Tax Court Upsets the Service Partner, 46 So.Cal.L.Rev. 239 (1973); Cowan, Receipt of an Interest in Partnership Profits in Consideration for Services: The Diamond Case, 27 Tax L.Rev. 161 (1972).

SECTION 3. CONTRIBUTIONS OF ENCUMBERED PROPERTY

INTERNAL REVENUE CODE: Sections 705(a); 722; 723; 731(a) and (b); 733; 752(a)–(c).

REGULATIONS: Sections 1.722–1, Ex. (2); 1.1245–4(c)(4), Ex. (3).

TEMPORARY REGULATIONS: Sections 1.752–1T(a)–(c), (f), (g), –2T.

When property subject to liabilities is contributed to a partnership or the partnership assumes a partner's liabilities in connection with the contribution of property, analysis of the tax consequences of formation of a partnership becomes more complex. Subchapter K has no special provisions dealing with this event. Instead, the results must be determined by piecing together the rules governing contributions to partnerships in sections 721–722, treatment of debt in section 752, partnership distributions in sections 731 and 733, and partners' basis in their partnership interests in section 705. Gain, but not loss, may be recognized upon the contribution of property to the partnership.

The starting point is sections 721–723. Upon contribution of the property the contributing partner takes a basis in his partnership interest equal to his basis in the property, without regard to the amount of the debt. By virtue of the transfer, however, the contributing partner has been relieved from the debt in his individual capacity and all of the partners have indirectly assumed the debt in their capacity as partners. Section 752(a) provides that an increase in a partner's share of liabilities by reason of a partnership transaction is to be treated as contribution of cash to the partnership by the partners. This deemed cash contribution increases the partner's basis in the partner's partnership interest under section 722. Section 752(b) provides that any decrease in a partner's share of liabilities is to be treated as a distribution of money to the partner.[2] Under sections 731 and 733, distributions of money reduce the partner's basis in the partner's partnership interest and are treated as gain to the extent that the distribution exceeds basis. As a consequence of these provisions, the contribution of encumbered property to a partnership by a partner will

2. Under sections 752(a) and (b), a partner contributing encumbered property is simultaneously relieved of the debt encumbering the property and deemed to contribute cash to the partnership in an amount equal to the contributing partner's share of the new partnership debt, determined under Temporary Regulations, section 1.752–1T. See Temporary Regulations, section 1.752–2T. Temporary Regulations, section 1.752–1T(j)(3), provide that where a partner's share of the liabilities is both increased and decreased in the same transaction, only the net increase or decrease is taken into account. Thus, the amount of the deemed distribution to the contributing partner is equal to the portion of the debt for which the other partners bear the economic risk of loss.

reduce the contributing partner's basis in the partnership interest to the extent of the share of the liability assumed by the other partners (or the other partners' share of liability to which the property is subject), and will result in recognized gain to the contributing partner to the extent that amount exceeds the contributing partner's basis in the partner's partnership interest. Each noncontributing partner's basis in the partner's partnership interest will be increased to the extent of the noncontributing partner's share of the liability. Under section 752(c), the same result is achieved even if the partnership merely takes the property subject to the debt and does not assume it. Assuming that either the partnership agreement or controlling state law treats the noncontributing partners as assuming ultimate liability for a share of the debt, the net effect for the contributing partner is the receipt of a deemed cash distribution. The manner in which partners share the economic risk of loss for partnership debts is determined under Temporary Regulations, section 1.752–1T(d), for debts which are with recourse to either the partnership or any partner, and under Temporary Regulations, section 1.752–1T(e), for debts which are without recourse to the partnership or any partner. Determination of partners' shares of partnership debt is discussed in detail infra, page 122. See also Temporary Regulations, section 1.752–2T(b), Ex. (1) (no deemed distribution if contributing partner retains ultimate liability to repay indebtedness encumbering contributed property).

Pursuant to sections 731 and 733 (and section 705) the deemed distribution created by Section 752 reduces the contributing partner's basis in his partnership interest and, to the extent that the deemed distribution exceeds the basis in his partnership interest, the excess is treated as gain from the sale or exchange of his partnership interest. Section 741 directs that this gain be treated as capital gain, subject to certain exceptions provided in section 751. The other partners also are treated by section 752(a) as having contributed cash to the partnership in an amount equal to their respective shares of the debt assumed by the partnership, and they increase their bases in their partnership interests accordingly.

The following examples illustrate the above rules:

(1) Partner A contributes to new partnership ABC property with a basis of $1,000, subject to a mortgage of $900, which is assumed by the partnership. (It is not relevant whether the lien is a purchase money mortgage or one that was placed on the property to secure a loan unrelated to its acquisition.) A's basis for his partnership interest would be $400, i.e., the original $1,000 basis minus the $600 of the indebtedness that was, in effect, assumed by the other partners. B and C each would increase his basis by $300.

(2) If the mortgage amount were $1,800 (regardless of the fair market value of the property), A would recognize a gain of $200, i.e., the excess of the $1,200 of indebtedness that was in effect assumed by

the other partners over the original $1,000 basis.[3] A's basis in his partnership interest is reduced to zero as a result of these computations. B and C each increases his basis again, this time by $600. Note that if ABC were a pre-existing partnership and A's outside basis were at least $200, he would not have recognized any gain on the contribution of the encumbered property.

(3) If A were personally liable for the $900 debt in (1) and the partnership merely took the property subject to the indebtedness without the partnership or B or C agreeing to indemnify A for any repayment of the debt, the debt would be a nonrecourse debt of the partnership which was recourse with respect to A. In this case A bears the entire economic risk of loss. Therefore A would be treated as receiving a distribution of $900 under section 752(b) and making a contribution of $900 under section 752(a). Since only the net contribution or distribution is taken into account, A's basis for his partnership interest remains $1,000. Applying this rule, A would recognize no gain even if the mortgage were $1,800 as in (2).

(4) On the other hand, if the $900 mortgage debt in (1) were a nonrecourse debt as to A, upon the contribution of the property to the partnership, the partnership would be treated as assuming the debt. Because the debt is a nonrecourse debt, under Temporary Regulations, section 1.752–1T(e)(1)(ii), an amount of debt equal to the gain which would be allocated to A under section 704(c)—i.e., the built-in appreciation at the time of the contribution—is allocated to A. In order to determine this amount, it is necessary to ascertain the fair market value of the property at the time it was contributed. Assume that its value was $1,600. In this case $600 of the nonrecourse indebtedness would be allocated to A. The remaining $300 of nonrecourse indebtedness would be allocated among the partners according to their profit sharing ratios; since they are equal partners, $100 would be allocated to each partner. Thus $700 of the indebtedness is allocated to A and $100 to each of B and C. As a result, A's basis in his partnership interest is $800 (the original $1,000 basis in the property minus the $200 of debt in effect assumed by B and C), and B and C each increase their basis by $100. See Temporary Regulations, section 1.752–2T(b), Ex. (2).

The assumption by a partnership of the accounts payable of a cash method sole proprietor who is contributing her business to the partnership presents a special problem. If accounts payable of a cash method partnership were taken into account as liabilities under section 752, a cash method partner who contributed equal amounts of receivables and payables of a previously conducted sole proprietorship, and no other property, would be required to recognize gain. This generally would

3. Pursuant to section 741, this gain would be capital gain. Regulations, section 1.1245–4(c)(4), Ex. (3), however, provide that such gain will be ordinary income to the extent that there is any depreciation recapture inherent in the asset. This result clearly conflicts with the statutory mechanics of Subchapter K, which treat the gain as realized on the sale or exchange of the contributed property.

affect adversely the formation of personal service partnerships. Section 357(c) specifically addresses this problem in the formation of corporations by providing that cash basis payables will not be considered liabilities assumed by the corporation. Subchapter K contains an analogous provision, albeit somewhat vague, in the last sentence of section 704(c). The Conference Report accompanying the enactment of this provision indicated that cash basis accounts payable are not to be treated as liabilities for purposes of section 752. H.Rep. No. 98–861, 98th Cong., 2d Sess. 856–857 (1984). See also Rev.Rul. 88–77, 1988–2 Cum.Bull. 128 (same). Temporary Regulations, section 1.752–1T(g), define liabilities in such a manner as to exclude cash method accounts payable for all purposes under section 752. Thus the assumption of a cash method partner's accounts payable cannot give rise to a constructive distribution to the contributing partner under section 752(b) nor to a constructive contribution by the other partners under section 752(a).

CHAPTER 3

OPERATION OF THE PARTNERSHIP

SECTION 1. PARTNERSHIP TAXABLE INCOME

INTERNAL REVENUE CODE: Sections 61(a)(13); 701; 702; 703; 704(a)–(d); 705; 706(a), (b).

See also sections 6031; 6221–6233; 6698.

REGULATIONS: Sections 1.702–1; 1.703–1.

Subchapter K basically follows a conduit or pass-through approach to taxing partnership operations. Section 701 provides that a partnership is not taxable as an entity, but that the partners are individually liable for income taxes in their separate capacities. The starting point for determining the individual partner's tax liability, however, treats the partnership as a separate entity. Section 703(a) provides for the computation of partnership taxable income in the same manner as individuals, subject to certain exceptions.

After partnership taxable income is determined under section 703, each partner takes into account in computing his individual taxable income his "distributive share" of each of the separately stated items in section 702(a) and the residual taxable income or loss of the partnership. Pursuant to section 704(a), a partner's distributive share is determined with reference to the partnership agreement, except as otherwise required by section 704(b), (c), or (e). Hence, the partners may provide in the agreement for a 50–50 sharing of profits, a 75–25 sharing, etc. Determination of a partner's distributive share is discussed in section 2 of this chapter.

UNITED STATES v. BASYE

Supreme Court of the United States, 1973.
410 U.S. 441.

MR. JUSTICE POWELL delivered the opinion of the Court.

* * *

I

Respondents, each of whom is a physician, are partners in a limited partnership known as Permanente Medical Group, which was organized in California in 1949. Associated with the partnership are over 200 partner physicians, as well as numerous nonpartner physicians and other employees. In 1959, Permanente entered into an agreement with Kaiser Foundation Health Plan, Inc., a nonprofit corporation providing prepaid medical care and hospital services to its dues-paying members.

Pursuant to the terms of the agreement, Permanente agreed to supply medical services for the 390,000 member-families, or about 900,000 individuals, in Kaiser's Northern California Region which covers primarily the San Francisco Bay area. In exchange for those services, Kaiser agreed to pay the partnership a "base compensation" composed of two elements. First, Kaiser undertook to pay directly to the partnership a sum each month computed on the basis of the total number of members enrolled in the health program. That number was multiplied by a stated fee, which originally was set at a little over $2.60. The second item of compensation—and the one that has occasioned the present dispute—called for the creation of a program, funded entirely by Kaiser, to pay retirement benefits to Permanente's partner and non-partner physicians.

The pertinent compensation provision of the agreement did not itself establish the details of the retirement program; it simply obligated Kaiser to make contributions to such a program in the event that the parties might thereafter agree to adopt one. As might be expected, a separate trust agreement establishing the contemplated plan soon was executed by Permanente, Kaiser, and the Bank of America Trust and Savings Association, acting as trustee. Under this agreement Kaiser agreed to make payments to the trust at a predetermined rate, initially pegged at 12 cents per health plan member per month. Additionally, Kaiser made a flat payment of $200,000 to start the fund and agreed that its pro rata payment obligation would be retroactive to the date of the signing of the medical service agreement.

The beneficiaries of the trust were all partner and nonpartner physicians who had completed at least two years of continuous service with the partnership and who elected to participate. The trust maintained a separate tentative account for each beneficiary. As periodic payments were received from Kaiser, the funds were allocated among these accounts pursuant to a complicated formula designed to take into consideration on a relative basis each participant's compensation level, length of service, and age. No physician was eligible to receive the amounts in his tentative account prior to retirement, and retirement established entitlement only if the participant had rendered at least 15 years of continuous service or 10 years of continuous service and had attained age 65. Prior to such time, however, the trust agreement explicitly provided that no interest in any tentative account was to be regarded as having vested in any particular beneficiary. The agreement also provided for the forfeiture of any physician's interest and its redistribution among the remaining participants if he were to terminate his relationship with Permanente prior to retirement.[4] A similar forfeiture and redistribution also would occur if, after retirement, a

4. If, however, termination were occasioned by death or permanent disability, the trust agreement provided for receipt of such amounts as had accumulated in that physician's tentative account. Additionally, if, after his termination for reasons of disability prior to retirement, a physician should reassociate with some affiliated medical group his rights as a participant would not be forfeited.

physician were to render professional services for any hospital or health plan other than one operated by Kaiser. The trust agreement further stipulated that a retired physician's right to receive benefits would cease if he were to refuse any reasonable request to render consultative services to any Kaiser-operated health plan.

The agreement provided that the plan would continue irrespective either of changes in the partnership's personnel or of alterations in its organizational structure. The plan would survive any reorganization of the partnership so long as at least 50% of the plan's participants remained associated with the reorganized entity. In the event of dissolution or of a nonqualifying reorganization, all of the amounts in the trust were to be divided among the participants entitled thereto in amounts governed by each participant's tentative account. Under no circumstances, however, could payments from Kaiser to the trust be recouped by Kaiser: once compensation was paid into the trust it was thereafter committed exclusively to the benefit of Permanente's participating physicians.

Upon the retirement of any partner or eligible non-partner physician, if he had satisfied each of the requirements for participation, the amount that had accumulated in his tentative account over the years would be applied to the purchase of a retirement income contract. While the program thus provided obvious benefits to Permanente's physicians, it also served Kaiser's interests. By providing attractive deferred benefits for Permanente's staff of professionals, the retirement plan was designed to "create an incentive" for physicians to remain with Permanente and thus "insure" that Kaiser would have a "stable and reliable group of physicians."

During the years from the plan's inception until its discontinuance in 1963, Kaiser paid a total of more than $2,000,000 into the trust. Permanente, however, did not report these payments as income in its partnership returns. Nor did the individual partners include these payments in the computations of their distributive shares of the partnership's taxable income. The Commissioner assessed deficiencies against each partner-respondent for his distributive share of the amount paid by Kaiser. Respondents, after paying the assessments under protest, filed these consolidated suits for refund.

The Commissioner premised his assessment on the conclusion that Kaiser's payments to the trust constituted a form of compensation to the partnership for the services it rendered and therefore was income to the partnership. And, notwithstanding the deflection of those payments to the retirement trust and their current unavailability to the partners, the partners were still taxable on their distributive shares of that compensation. Both the District Court and the Court of Appeals disagreed. They held that the payments to the fund were not income to the partnership because it did not receive them and never had a "right to receive" them. * * *. They reasoned that the partnership, as an entity, should be disregarded and that each partner should be treated simply as a potential beneficiary of his tentative share of the retirement fund.[6] Viewed in this light, no presently taxable income could be attributed to these cash basis [7] taxpayers because of the contingent and forfeitable nature of the fund allocations. * * *

We hold that the courts below erred and that respondents were properly taxable on the partnership's retirement fund income. This conclusion rests on two familiar principles of income taxation, first, that income is taxed to the party who earns it and that liability may not be avoided through an anticipatory assignment of that income, and, second, that partners are taxable on their distributive or proportionate shares of current partnership income irrespective of whether that income is actually distributed to them. The ensuing discussion is simply an application of those principles to the facts of the present case.

II

Section 703 of the Internal Revenue Code of 1954, insofar as pertinent here, prescribes that "[t]he taxable income of a partnership shall be computed in the same manner as in the case of an individual." 26 U.S.C. § 703(a). Thus, while the partnership itself pays no taxes, 26 U.S.C. § 701, it must report the income it generates and such income must be calculated in largely the same manner as an individual computes his personal income. For this purpose, then, the partnership is regarded as an independently recognizable entity apart from the aggregate of its partners. Once its income is ascertained and reported, its existence may be disregarded since each partner must pay a tax on a portion of the total income as if the partnership were merely an agent or conduit through which the income passed.[8]

In determining any partner's income, it is first necessary to compute the gross income of the partnership. One of the major sources of gross income, as defined in § 61(a)(1) of the Code, is "[c]ompensation for services, including fees, commissions, and similar items." 26 U.S.C.

6. The Court of Appeals purported not to decide, as the District Court had, whether the partnership should be viewed as an "entity" or as a "conduit." 450 F.2d 109, 113 n. 5, and 115. Yet, its analysis indicates that it found it proper to disregard the partnership as a separate entity. After explaining its view that Permanente never had a right to receive the payments, the Court of Appeals stated: "When the transaction is viewed in this light, the partnership becomes a mere *agent* contracting on behalf of its members for payments to the trust for their ultimate benefit, rather than a *principal* which itself realizes taxable income." Id., at 115 (emphasis supplied).

7. Each respondent reported his income for the years in question on the cash basis. The partnership reported its taxable receipts under the accrual method.

8. There has been a great deal of discussion in the briefs and in the lower court opinions with respect to whether a partnership is to be viewed as an "entity" or as a "conduit." We find ourselves in agreement with the Solicitor General's remark during oral argument when he suggested that "[i]t seems odd that we should still be discussing such things in 1972." Tr. of Oral Arg. 14. The legislative history indicates, and the commentators agree, that partnerships are entities for purposes of calculating and filing informational returns but that they are conduits through which the tax-paying obligation passes to the individual partners in accord with their distributive shares. See, e.g., H.R. Rep. No. 1337, 83d Cong., 2d Sess., 65–66 (1954); S.Rep. No. 1622, 83d Cong., 2d Sess., 89–90 (1954); * * *.

§ 61(a)(1). There can be no question that Kaiser's payments to the retirement trust were compensation for services rendered by the partnership under the medical service agreement. These payments constituted an integral part of the employment arrangement. The agreement itself called for two forms of "base compensation" to be paid in exchange for services rendered—direct per-member, per-month payments to the partnership and other, similarly computed, payments to the trust. * * * Payments to the trust, much like the direct payments to the partnership, were not forfeitable by the partnership or recoverable by Kaiser upon the happening of any contingency.

Yet the courts below, focusing on the fact that the retirement fund payments were never actually received by the partnership but were contributed directly to the trust, found that the payments were not includable as income in the partnership's returns. The view of tax accountability upon which this conclusion rests is incompatible with a foundational rule, which this Court has described as "the first principle of income taxation: that income must be taxed to him who earns it." Commissioner v. Culbertson, 337 U.S. 733, 739–740 (1949). The entity earning the income—whether a partnership or an individual taxpayer—cannot avoid taxation by entering into a contractual arrangement whereby that income is diverted to some other person or entity. Such arrangements, known to the tax law as "anticipatory assignments of income," have frequently been held ineffective as means of avoiding tax liability. The seminal precedent, written over 40 years ago, is Mr. Justice Holmes' opinion for a unanimous Court in Lucas v. Earl, 281 U.S. 111 (1930). There the taxpayer entered into a contract with his wife whereby she became entitled to one-half of any income he might earn in the future. On the belief that a taxpayer was accountable only for income actually received by him, the husband thereafter reported only half of his income. The Court, unwilling to accept that a reasonable construction of the tax laws permitted such easy deflection of income tax liability, held that the taxpayer was responsible for the entire amount of his income.

* * *

The principle of *Lucas v. Earl,* that he who earns income may not avoid taxation through anticipatory arrangements no matter how clever or subtle, has been repeatedly invoked by this Court and stands today as a cornerstone of our graduated income tax system. * * * And, of course, that principle applies with equal force in assessing partnership income.

Permanente's agreement with Kaiser, whereby a portion of the partnership compensation was deflected to the retirement fund, is certainly within the ambit of *Lucas v. Earl.* The partnership earned the income and, as a result of arm's-length bargaining with Kaiser, was responsible for its diversion into the trust fund. The Court of Appeals found the *Lucas* principle inapplicable because Permanente "never had the right itself to receive the payments made into the trust as current income." 450 F.2d, at 114. In support of this assertion, the court relied on language in the agreed statement of facts stipulating that "[t]he payments * * * were paid solely to fund the retirement plan, and were not otherwise available to [Permanente] * * *." Ibid. Emphasizing that the fund was created to serve Kaiser's interest in a stable source of qualified, experienced physicians, the court found that Permanente could not have received that income except in the form in which it was received. * * * We think it clear, however, that the tax laws permit no such easy road to tax avoidance or deferment. Despite the novelty and ingenuity of this arrangement, Permanente's "base compensation" in the form of payments to a retirement fund was income to the partnership and should have been reported as such.

III

Since the retirement fund payments should have been reported as income to the partnership, along with other income received from Kaiser, the individual partners should have included their shares of that income in their individual returns. 26 U.S.C. §§ 61(a)(13), 702, 704. For it is axiomatic that each partner must pay taxes on his distributive share of the partnership's income without regard to whether that amount is actually distributed to him. *Heiner v. Mellon,* 304 U.S. 271 (1938), decided under a predecessor to the current partnership provisions of the Code, articulates the salient proposition. After concluding that "distributive" share means the "proportionate" share as determined by the partnership agreement, id., at 280, the Court stated:

> "The tax is thus imposed upon the partner's proportionate share of the net income of the partnership, and the fact that it may not be currently distributable, whether by agreement of the parties or by operation of law, is not material." Id., at 281.

Few principles of partnership taxation are more firmly established than that no matter the reason for nondistribution each partner must pay taxes on his distributive share. Treas.Reg. § 1.702–1, 26 CFR § 1.702–1 (1972). See, e.g., Hulbert v. Commissioner, 227 F.2d 399 (CA7 1955); Bell v. Commissioner, 219 F.2d 442 (CA5 1955); Stewart v. United States, 263 F.Supp. 451 (SDNY 1967); Freudmann v. Commissioner, 10 T.C. 775 (1948); S. Surrey & W. Warren, Federal Income Taxation 1115 (1960); 6 J. Mertens, Law of Federal Income Taxation §§ 35.01, 35.22 (1968); A. Willis, On Partnership Taxation § 5.01 (1971).

The courts below reasoned to the contrary, holding that the partners here were not properly taxable on the amounts contributed to the retirement fund. This view, apparently, was based on the assumption that each partner's distributive share prior to retirement was too contingent and unascertainable to constitute presently recognizable income. It is true that no partner knew with certainty exactly how much he would ultimately receive or whether he would in fact be entitled to receive anything. But the existence of conditions upon the actual receipt by a partner of income fully earned by the partnership is irrelevant in determining the amount of tax due from him. The fact that the courts below placed such emphasis on this factor suggests the basic misapprehension under which they labored in this case. Rather than being viewed as responsible contributors to the partnership's total income, respondent-partners were seen only as contingent beneficiaries of the trust. In some measure, this misplaced focus on the considerations of uncertainty and forfeitability may be a consequence of the erroneous manner in which the Commissioner originally assessed the partners' deficiencies. The Commissioner divided Kaiser's trust fund payments into two categories: (1) payments earmarked for the tentative accounts of *nonpartner* physicians; and (2) those allotted to *partner* physicians. The payments to the trust for the former category of nonpartner physicians were correctly counted as income to the partners in accord with the distributive-share formula as established in the partnership agreement.[16] The latter payments to the tentative accounts of the individual partners, however, were improperly allocated to each partner pursuant to the complex formula in the retirement plan itself, just as if that agreement operated as an amendment to the partnership agreement.

The Solicitor General, alluding to this miscomputation during oral argument, suggested that this error "may be what threw the court below off the track." It should be clear that the contingent and unascertainable nature of each partner's share under the retirement trust is irrelevant to the computation of his distributive share. The partnership had received as income a definite sum which was not subject to diminution or forfeiture. Only its ultimate disposition among the employees and partners remained uncertain. For purposes of income tax computation it made no difference that some partners might have elected not to participate in the retirement program or that, for any number of reasons, they might not ultimately receive any of the trust's benefits. Indeed, as the Government suggests, the result would be quite the same if the "potential beneficiaries included no partners at all, but were children, relatives, or other objects of the partnership's largesse." [18] The sole operative consideration is that the income had been received by the partnership, not what disposition might have been effected once the funds were received.

16. These amounts would be divided equally among the partners pursuant to the partnership agreement's stipulation that all income above each partner's drawing account "shall be distributed equally."

18. Brief for United States 21. For this reason, the cases relied on by the Court of Appeals, 450 F.2d, at 113, which have held that payments made into deferred compensation programs having contingent and forfeitable features are not taxable until received, are inapposite. Schaefer v. Bowers, 50 F.2d 689 (CA2 1931); Perkins v. Commissioner, 8 T.C. 1051 (1947); Robertson v. Commissioner, 6 T.C. 1060 (1946). Indeed, the Government notes, possibly as a consequence of these cases, that the Commissioner has not sought to tax the nonpartner physicians on their contingent accounts under the retirement plan. Brief for United States 21.

IV

In summary, we find this case controlled by familiar and long-settled principles of income and partnership taxation. There being no doubt about the character of the payments as compensation, or about their actual receipt, the partnership was obligated to report them as income presently received. Likewise, each partner was responsible for his distributive share of that income. We, therefore, reverse the judgments and remand the case with directions that judgments be entered for the United States.

It is so ordered.

MR. JUSTICE DOUGLAS dissents.

ILLUSTRATIVE MATERIAL

A. PARTNERSHIP TAXABLE INCOME AND SEPARATELY STATED ITEMS

Basye demonstrates the relationship between the determination of partnership taxable income and the treatment of the partnership itself as a mere conduit for purposes of imposing tax liability. While partnership taxable income is computed at the entity level, each partner is then currently taxed on his distributive share of that taxable income, even if it has not been distributed to him. This rule is so important to the operation of Subchapter K that it applies, as in *Basye,* even where the partnership agreement or a contractual agreement prevents the current distribution of income.

Partnership taxable income is computed following the same rules that govern the computation of the taxable income of any individual engaged in business, with a few specific statutory modifications. Section 703(a)(2) disallows deductions for personal exemptions, charitable contributions, net operating losses, foreign taxes, depletion on oil and gas wells, and the special deductions allowed to individuals under sections 211–219. In addition, the standard deduction provided for individuals by section 63(b) is disallowed for partnerships. Because capital gains and losses are separately stated and flow through to the individual partners, who may carry over unused capital losses, Regulations, section 1.703–1(a)(2), adds to the list of disallowed deductions the capital loss carryover deduction under section 1212. In addition, sections 702(a) and 703(a)(1) require certain items entering into the computation of an individual's income tax liability to be segregated and separately stated on the partnership's return. These items require separate consideration to determine their character as capital gain or loss or ordinary income or loss at the partner's level or the extent to which they are includable in or excludable or deductible from the partner's gross income. See also Regulations, sections 1.703–1(a), 1.702–1(a)(1)–(8). The separately stated items include capital gains and losses, section 1231 gains and losses, charitable contributions, dividends received (if there is a corporate partner), and foreign taxes. Section 702(a)(1)–(6). Regulations, section 1.702–1(a)(8)(i) and (ii), add to the statutory list bad debt recoveries, wagering gains and losses, expenses for the production of nonbusiness income, medical expenses, dependents' care, alimony, taxes and interest paid to housing cooperatives, oil and gas intangible drilling and development costs, solid mineral exploration expenditures, section 751(b) gains and losses,[1] and any items of income, gain, loss deduction or credit subject to a specific allocation under the partnership agreement which differs from the general profit and loss ratio. Because under Regulations, section 1.702–2, each partner separately computes his individual net operating loss deductions, by taking into account his distributive share of partnership items, any income or deduction item that requires special treatment in computing such deductions must be separately stated. The limitations on the deduction of passive losses under section 469, the disallowance of deductions for personal interest under section 163(h), both added in 1986, and the limitation on the deduction of investment interest under section 163(d), require that interest paid or received be separately stated in many cases. See Rev.Rul. 84–131, 1984–2 Cum.Bull. 37 (requiring that interest paid be separately stated by a partnership which has any partner subject to the investment interest deduction limitations of section 63(d)); Rev.Rul. 86–138, 1986–2 Cum.Bull. 84 (extending the same rule to lower tier partnerships if any partner in an upper tier partnership is subject to section 163(d)).

In general, partnership business income (excluding separately stated items), which, generally speaking is the amount described in section 702(a)(8), is computed by including all of the income and deductions attribute to each separate business of the partnership. Because of the passive loss limitations of section 469, however, it may be necessary for a partnership to state separately the net income or loss from each separate business "activity" that it conducts; and this segregation will always be required of limited partnerships. Furthermore, when this segregation is required, it also is necessary to separately attribute to each such "activity" any partnership items which are separately stated as required by section 702(a)(1)–(7).

B. CHARACTER OF ITEMS AND ACTIVITIES

1. *Determination Based on Partnership Activities*

As previously indicated, section 702(a)(1)–(7) and the Regulations thereunder adopt a conduit approach which requires the partners to report separately their distributive shares of any partnership item of income, credit or deduction receiving specialized treatment under the Code, which items must in turn under section 703 be separately stated on the partnership return. Section 702(b) further amplifies this conduit concept with respect to the segregated items by treating the partners as if "such item were realized directly from the source from which realized by the partnership, or incurred in the same manner as incurred by the partnership". Section 702(b) has been interpreted to require that the determination of the character of an income or deduction item be made by reference to its characterization at the partnership level. Podell v. Commissioner, 55 T.C. 429 (1970) (real property was not a capital asset in the hands of the partnership and hence the partner's share of income on the disposition of the asset was ordinary); Barham v. United States, 301 F.Supp 43 (M.D.Ga.1969), aff'd per curiam, 429 F.2d 40 (5th Cir.1970) (same); Rev.Rul. 68–79, 1968–1 Cum.Bull. 310 (where an asset had a holding period of over six months in the hands of the partnership, the individual partner could treat the gain on disposition of the asset as long-term gain even though he had been a member of the partnership

1. Such gains or losses are those recognized by a partnership possessing substantially appreciated inventory or unrealized receivables upon a disproportionate distribution. See the discussion, infra, page 220.

for less than six months); Regulations, section 1.702–1(b). Consistent application of this approach would ignore the activities of the individual partner, as where, for example, the partnership sells investment real estate and one of the partners in his individual capacity is a dealer in that type of property. Rev.Rul. 67–188, 1967–1 Cum.Bull. 216, held that a loss on real property determined to be section 1231 property at the partnership level retained that character in the hands of the individual partner, who was a real estate dealer; the Ruling, however, did not deal expressly with the effect of the taxpayer's individual activity on the nature of the loss. See also Regulations, section 1.702–1(a)(8)(ii).

As illustrated by *Madison Gas & Electric,* supra, page 8, whether a business has commenced or is in the start-up period also is determined at the partnership level. The resolution of this issue affects whether expenses may be deducted currently or must be capitalized and amortized over sixty months under section 195.

Whether the partnership business is engaged in for profit is likewise determined at the partnership level. Brannen v. Commissioner, 722 F.2d 695 (11th Cir.1984). Where a limited partnership is involved, the relevant intent is that of the general partner. Deegan v. Commissioner, 787 F.2d 825 (2d Cir.1986). This inquiry is important in applying section 183, dealing with so-called "hobby losses" and in determining whether losses incurred by tax shelter partnerships will be disallowed. Unless there is a profit motive, the losses are allowed only to the extent of income from the activity. Note that the absence of a joint profit motive, without which a partnership generally will not be found to exist, does not otherwise affect partnership treatment in these cases, a result which is somewhat difficult to square with the definitional test.

2. *Determination Based on Contributing Partner's Activities*

Section 724 provides special rules under which certain property contributed to a partnership by a partner retains the character that it had in the partner's hands. Unrealized receivables, such as cash basis accounts receivable, retain their ordinary income character. Section 724(a). Inventory, however, retains an ordinary income taint for only five years if the partnership holds the property as a capital asset or as section 1231 property (depreciable or real property held for use in the taxpayer's trade or business). Section 724(b). Similarly, capital assets which have depreciated in value at the time of their contribution retain their capital character for five years after the date of the contribution, but only to the extent of the built-in loss at the time of the contribution. Section 724(c). If the loss is greater because the property further depreciates while held by the partnership, the character of the excess loss is determined with reference to the purpose for which the partnership held the property. These rules were enacted at a time when recognized long-term capital gains were taxed at a preferential rate and long-term capital losses were deductible against ordinary income at a ratio of two to one, subject to an annual maximum offset against ordinary income of $3,000. The purpose of these rules was to prevent the conversion of ordinary income into capital gain or capital loss into ordinary loss through the contribution of the property to a partnership.

C. BASIS OF A PARTNER'S INTEREST

1. *General*

In *Bayse* the partnership income taxed to the physician partners is reflected as an upward adjustment to each partner's basis in his partnership interest under section 705(a). This adjustment to basis, coupled with the rule of section 731 that a partner does not recognize any gain on a partnership distribution unless the amount of money distributed exceeds the basis of the partnership interest, is the heart of the mechanism that assures that partners pay one level of tax on partnership profits. As income is earned by the partnership, the partner pays taxes on it and adjusts his basis upward. When the previously taxed income is distributed, the partner owes no taxes and reduces his basis. Assuming that there have been no other events affecting the partner's basis, the basis after the distribution is identical to what it was before the income was earned. In the absence of a distribution, the partner will recover basis on sale or liquidation of the partner's interest in the partnership.

Section 705(a) prescribes a number of adjustments which must be taken into account in determining the basis of a partner's interest in a partnership. The partner starts with his basis determined under section 722 for contributions to the partnership; the basis is then increased by the partner's distributive share of the partnership profits, tax exempt receipts, and the excess of depletion deductions over the adjusted basis of depletable property; and it is decreased by the partner's distributive share of losses, nondeductible expenditures not properly chargeable to a capital account, and distributions to the partner. See Regulations, section 1.705–1(a)(2)(ii). However, a partner's basis is never reduced below zero. If the adjustment which would otherwise reduce basis below zero is a distribution, section 731 directs that the partner recognize gain.

While section 705(a)(1)(b) refers to "income * * * exempt from tax," Regulations, section 1.705–1(a)(2)(ii), properly refer more broadly to "tax-exempt receipts." Suppose the partnership realizes gain on a transaction which it is not required to recognize because of the operation of a section like 1033, 1031, etc. Is this a "tax-exempt receipt" which results in an upward adjustment of partnership basis? Under section 265, which disallows deductions for expenses allocable to tax-exempt income, it has been held that nonrecognized gain is not income "wholly exempt" from tax and hence no disallowance of deduction was required. See, e.g., Hawaiian Trust Co. Ltd. v. United States, 291 F.2d 761 (9th Cir.1961); Commissioner v. McDonald, 320 F.2d 109 (5th Cir.1963). Presumably the same result would be reached under section 705 since otherwise, for basis purposes, a "double crediting" of the accrued gain would be produced, i.e., once on the exchange and again on disposition of the property.

As for the effect on basis of disallowed deductions, it does not matter whether deductibility is determined at the partnership or individual partner level. See Rev.Rul. 89–7, 1989–1 Cum.Bull. 178 (partner must reduce partnership basis by full amount of section 179 expenditures deducted by partnership even though the partner could not fully deduct his distributive share of such expenditures because of application of section 179(b)(1) limitation at individual partner level).

Why is it necessary to this scheme to increase basis by tax-free receipts and decrease it by nondeductible expenditures not properly chargeable to a capital account (e.g., a fine that is nondeductible under section 162(f))?

2. *Alternative Basis Rules*

When a partnership is liquidated or a partnership interest sold, section 705(a) read literally would require a partner to go back to the beginning and laboriously determine her basis by adjusting each year for the distributive share of each item of the partnership and for each distribution to her. The same computation would be necessary to determine whether a distributive share of loss exceeds basis. The partnership records may or may not make this possible. Moreover, in a simple partnership, these computations are not really necessary. If the partners' profit and loss ratios are the same as their capital ratios, if their contributions were in cash or in properties whose basis and value were the same, if any current distributions were likewise in cash or in such property and were pro rata, and if there have been no retirements or sales of a partner's interest—and many partnerships meet these conditions—then a partner's basis may be obtained by a simple formula. Her basis will be her pro rata share of the total adjusted basis of the partnership's assets. In effect, all the adjustments of section 705(a) would in the end yield this result. Hence, section 705(b) authorizes Regulations permitting the use of this simple formula. It also authorizes variations of this formula taking account of adjustments necessary to reflect any significant discrepancies arising as a result of contributed property, transfers or distributions. See Regulations, section 1.705–1(b).

D. ELECTIONS AND LIMITATIONS

Section 703(b) provides that, in general, elections under the Code are to be made by the partnership, except that the partners individually make separate elections in three cases; (1) elections under section 108(b)(5) to reduce the basis of depreciable property instead of other tax attributes when discharge of indebtedness income is not recognized; (2) elections under section 617 with respect to mine exploration costs, and (3) elections with respect to the foreign tax credit under section 901. Thus, the partnership elects its taxable year and accounting method (including its inventory method), Regulations, section 1.703–1(b)(1), as well as subsidiary elections with respect to ACRS deductions under section 168, the deduction of intangible drilling and development costs under section 263(c), see Rev.Rul. 68–139, 1968–1 Cum.Bull. 311, and election out of installment reporting under section 453.

In Demirjian v. Commissioner, 457 F.2d 1 (3d Cir.1972), a partnership realized a gain on the involuntary conversion of real property. The partners individually replaced the converted partnership property with property similar or related in service or use and attempted to elect nonrecognition of gain under section 1033. The court held that the gain was required to be recognized. Section 703(b) requires that the election under section 1033 be made by the partnership, and to be effective, the partnership, not the partners, must acquire the replacement property. See also McManus v. Commissioner, 583 F.2d 443 (9th Cir.1978) (same).

While Subchapter K is silent as to whether the limitations imposed by the Code on the amount of an item to be taken into account are to be imposed at the partner or partnership level, Regulations, section 1.702–1(a)

(8)(iii), apply the limitations in general at the partner level. Thus, the $3,000 limit on deducting capital losses against ordinary income, the percentage limitations on charitable contributions under section 170, the limitation on the deduction of investment interest under section 163(d), the $25,000 ceiling on the deduction against nonpassive income of losses from active participation real estate activities under section 469(i), and the limitation on percentage depletion of oil and gas under section 613A are applied at the partner level. Section 613A(c)(7)(D) provides detailed rules for computing percentage depletion of oil and gas at the partner level. Section 469, restricting the ability to deduct passive activity losses also is applied at the individual partner level. Section 179(d)(8) applies the $10,000 limit on expensing of depreciable property at *both* the partnership and individual partner level.

In a related area, Resnik v. Commissioner, 66 T.C. 74 (1976), aff'd per curiam, 555 F.2d 634 (7th Cir.1977), disallowed a deduction for prepaid interest expense at the partnership level under section 446(b) on the ground that allowance of the deduction did not clearly reflect the partnership's income. As a result, the interest expense did not pass through to the individual partners. The court intimated that in cases where there was no distortion at the partnership level, section 446(b) might nonetheless apply at the partner level.

E. PARTNERSHIP TAXABLE YEAR

A partnership has its own taxable year under section 706(b)(1), and section 706(a) provides that a partner includes her distributive share of partnership items in her taxable year in which or with which the partnership year ends. If the partnership's freedom to choose its taxable year were unfettered, this rule would permit significant tax deferral. Individual partners, who almost invariably use a calendar year, could cause the partnership to elect a fiscal year ending on January 31. Thus, all of the income of the partnership from February through December would not be reportable by the partners until the next calendar year. To prevent this type of avoidance, section 706(b) restricts the partnership's choice of its taxable year.

In general, a partnership must adopt the same taxable year as any one or more of its partners that have an aggregate interest in partnership profits and capital of more than fifty percent, or, if there is no such partner or majority group with the same year, the same taxable year as *all* of the "principal partners," who are the partners with a five percent or more interest in profits or capital. If neither the majority interest rule nor the principal partner rule can be used to determine a taxable year, the partnership must adopt the calendar year. Because most individuals use the calendar year, any partnership of which a majority of the partners are individuals usually will use a calendar year.

As a result of these rules, the partnership may be compelled to change its taxable year if new partners are admitted or, in some cases, if existing partners' percentage interests change. For example, if the ABC partnership has three equal partners A, with a January 31st fiscal year, B, with a July 31st fiscal year, and C, with calendar year, the partnership must adopt a calendar year under section 706(b)(1)(B)(iii). Now suppose that on February 1, C sells his interest to A, who becomes a two-thirds partner. Under section 706(b)(1)(B)(i) the partnership must adopt a January 31st fiscal year. Section 706(b)(4) provides, however, that if the partnership taxable year must be changed due to the "majority interest" rule, the change need not be made until A has held the majority interest for three consecutive taxable years of the partnership, using the original calendar year.

These strictures on the adoption of fiscal years by partnerships are relaxed by section 706(b)(1)(C), which allows a partnership to adopt a different taxable year with the permission of the Internal Revenue Service if the partnership can establish a business purpose for the fiscal year. The statute specifically provides that "deferral of income to partners shall not be treated as a business purpose." Rev.Proc. 87–32, 1987–2 Cum.Bull. 396, sets forth procedures for approval under section 704(b)(1)(C) of a different taxable year which coincides with the partnership's "natural business year." A partnership's natural business year is any twelve month period in the last two months of which the partnership realizes twenty-five percent of its gross receipts (under the method of accounting used to prepare its tax returns) for three consecutive years. If the partnership has more than one natural business year, it may only adopt the one in which the highest percentage of gross receipts are received in the last two months. Under a grandfather rule, any partnership that between July 1, 1974 and December 31, 1986 received permission to use a fiscal year ending in January through August may retain its year even if it does not meet this test.

Prior to the amendment of section 706(b) by the Tax Reform Act of 1986, the IRS routinely approved requests for partnership fiscal years ending in September, October or November, which resulted in three months or less deferral for calendar year partners. See Rev.Proc. 72–51, 1972–2 Cum.Bull. 832. These taxable years are not grandfathered, and unless the partnership can establish a business purpose for the taxable year, it must change its taxable year to conform to the rules of section 706(b). Rev.Rul. 87–57, 1987–2 Cum.Bull. 117, explains the factors to be considered and deals with eight fact patterns in which the partnership does not have a natural business year under Rev.Proc. 87–32, supra, or desires a taxable year different from its natural business year. Under the facts and circumstances test of Rev.Rul. 87–57, a business purpose for a particular year is not established merely by the use of a particular year for regulatory, financial accounting, or administrative purposes. If the desired taxable year creates deferral or distortion, which according to the ruling always occurs if the requested year differs from the taxable year of the partners, the partnership "must demonstrate compelling reasons for the requested tax year."

To prevent back-door avoidance of the rules restricting the choice of the partnership's taxable year, section 706(b)(2) prohibits a principal partner from changing to a taxable year different from the partnership unless the partner can establish a business purpose for the change.

The rigid rules of section 706, limiting flexibility in choosing the partnership's taxable year, are ameliorated by section 444. This provision, added in 1987, allows a partnership to elect a taxable year other than that required by section 706, provided that the selected year does not end more than three months before the end of the required year, even if there is no business purpose for the selected year. Thus, for example, if a partnership is required to use the calendar year because its partners use the calendar year and it either has no natural business year or no business purpose for a different year, it nevertheless may elect to adopt a fiscal year ending in September, October, or November. However, a partnership which qualifies for a fiscal year under the business purpose rule may not make a section 444 election treating the business purpose based fiscal year as its required year. Section 444 also permits existing partnerships otherwise required to switch from a fiscal year to a calendar year (or from one fiscal year to a different fiscal year) to retain the same fiscal year that they they used for 1986, even though it ends more than three months before the required year.

If an election is made under section 444, the partnership must make a payment computed under section 7519 to compensate the Treasury for the deferral of taxes. This is a nondeductible entity level payment which is not credited against the partners' individual tax liabilities. (This payment in effect converts the interest free loan generated by any tax deferral resulting from the use of a fiscal year into an interest bearing loan.) The payment may, however, be refunded in a future year in which the use of a fiscal year does not effect deferral of taxes. Sections 444 and 7519 do not apply to a partnership which qualifies for a fiscal year under Rev.Proc. 87–32 or Rev. Rul. 87–57.

The effect of termination of a partnership, the sale of a partnership interest, and the death or retirement of a partner on the partnership's and the partner's taxable years are considered later under those topics.

F. PARTNERSHIP TAX RETURNS AND AUDIT PROCEDURES

As previously noted, section 6031 requires that a partnership return be filed. Section 6698 imposes additional penalties, over and above the general failure to file penalty of section 7203, on any partnership that fails to file a *complete* partnership tax return. Individual partners are liable for the penalty to the extent of their liability for partnership debts generally.

Sections 6221 through 6231 establish a procedure under which audits of partnerships, other than certain small partnerships, are conducted at the partnership level instead of by auditing the partners individually. Section 6222 requires a partner to report partnership items on her own return consistently with the treatment on the partnership return, unless the partner has received incorrect information from the partnership or the partner identifies the inconsistent treatment on her return. Any partnership item reported by a partner consistently with the partnership return can be adjusted only in a partnership audit proceeding. Section 6225.

Unless the partnership has more than 100 partners, all partners must be notified by the Internal Revenue Service of the commencement of a partnership audit, are entitled to participate in the proceedings, and must be given notice of the final partnership administrative adjustment resulting from the proceeding. If the partnership has more than 100 partners, generally only partners with a profits interest of at least one percent are entitled to notice from the IRS and to participate in the audit. Partnerships must designate a "tax matters partner," who is responsible for notifying other partners of the audit and the final partnership administrative adjustment and keeping all of the partners informed of the administrative and judicial proceedings with respect to the audit. Sections 6223; 6224(a).

The Internal Revenue Service must offer to settle with all partners on consistent terms, and the tax matters partner generally may settle on behalf of non-notice partners. Section 6224(b), (c). The final partnership administrative adjustment is binding on all partners, subject to judicial review. The tax matters partner has ninety days after the notice of the final partnership administrative adjustment to seek judicial review. If he does not act within sixty days, any partner individually may seek judicial review within 150 days of the date of the final partnership administrative adjustment. Special rules are provided in section 6226 to govern jurisdiction.

Similarly, section 6227 provides special rules governing requests for refunds, termed "administrative adjustment requests," with respect to partnership items. Section 6228 controls judicial review of the denial of such requests. As with audits, the tax matters partner generally may act on behalf of the partnership.

These rules do not apply to partnerships with ten or fewer partners, all of whom are natural persons, as long as each partner's share of all items is identical. Thus, for example, if the AB partnership shares profits equally, but losses are allocated seventy-five percent to A and twenty-five percent to B, the AB partnership is subject to the partnership audit procedures. A partnership not subject to these procedures may elect to be governed by the partnership audit rules, and the election can be revoked only with the consent of the Commissioner. Section 6231(a)(1)(B).

If the Internal Revenue Service issues a statutory notice of deficiency to a partner without complying with the partnership audit procedures in a case to which they apply, the notice of deficiency is not valid with respect to the partnership items. See Maxwell v. Commissioner, 87 T.C. 783 (1986) (portion of Tax Court petition relating to partnership items dismissed for lack of jurisdiction, and IRS barred from assessing a deficiency based on the partnership items prior to the termination of the partnership audit proceedings): Stieha v. Commissioner, 89 T.C. 784 (1987) (Tax Court petition dismissed for lack of jurisdiction). Clovis v. Commissioner, 88 T.C. 980 (1987) held that mere notice of a *proposed* final partnership administrative adjustment, analagous to the "30 day letter" that normally precedes a statutory notice of deficiency, is not a final partnership administrative adjustment; a Tax Court petition based on the proposed final partnership administrative adjustment is premature and will be dismissed for lack of jurisdiction.

G. AGGREGATE OR ENTITY APPROACH

Despite the detailed rules discussed above, a number of situations involving partnerships are not specifically covered by Subchapter K, and in these situations the aggregate-entity dichotomy still prevails in the cases and Rulings.

In Randolph Products Co. v. Manning, 176 F.2d 190 (3d Cir.1949), the income of a corporation was derived exclusively from the rental of property to a partnership consisting of a husband and wife who also owned all of the corporation's stock. The corporation would have been a personal holding company if it could be said that, under the rule of section 543(a)(6), its income was received from "an individual entitled to the use of the property" which "individual" also owns 25% or more of the corporation's stock. The court, in holding that the corporation was a personal holding company, rejected the taxpayer's contention that a partnership is a "separate and distinct business unit or entity".

In Rev.Rul. 60–352, 1960–2 Cum.Bull. 208, the taxpayer, who was a limited partner in a partnership which held installment obligations, donated his partnership interest to a charity. The Service, basing its Ruling in part on the aggregate theory of partnership, held that the transfer of the partnership interest constituted a disposition of the installment obligation and hence required an immediate recognition of gain.

In Foster v. United States, 329 F.2d 717 (2d Cir.1964), an aggregate rather than an entity approach was followed in allocating to a partner working abroad only his proportionate share of the part of the total partnership income earned abroad for purposes of the former section 911 exclusion. The taxpayer had urged that the partnership be treated as an entity paying him for his individual services, which would have resulted in the entire distribution to him qualifying under former section 911. Compare the treatment of guaranteed payments, discussed infra, page 174.

The entity approach, however, was followed in Haughey v. Commissioner, 47 B.T.A. 1 (1942). The court held that the recovery of a deducted item was income to a partnership if it had taxable income in the year of deduction, even though the partners because of other deductions of their own would not have paid any tax on their increased share of distributive income if the partnership deduction had not been taken. M.H.S. Co., Inc. v. Commissioner, 35 T.C.M. 733 (1976), aff'd per curiam, 575 F.2d 1177 (6th Cir.1978), held that a purchase by a taxpayer of an interest in a partnership owning property similar to property of the taxpayer which had been involuntarily converted was not a qualified replacement under section 1033. See also Rev.Rul. 57–154, 1957–1 Cum.Bull. 262 (same); Rev.Rul. 70–144, 1970–1 Cum.Bull. 170 (purchase by 50% partner of the remaining 50% partnership interest, where the partnership held property similar to property of the purchasing partner which had been condemned, qualified under section 1033; the acquisition by the partner of the remaining partnership interest resulted in a termination of the partnership and the direct acquisition by him of partnership property). Compare Estate of Meyer v. Commissioner, 58 T.C. 311 (1972) aff'd per curiam, 503 F.2d 556 (9th Cir.1974), where an exchange of partnership interests qualified under section 1031, the court stressing the fact that the underlying assets of the two partnerships were similar. Rev.Rul. 78–135, 1978–1 Cum.Bull. 256, is to the contrary.

In Rev.Rul. 75–113, 1975–1 Cum.Bull. 19, an accrual basis partnership assigned contract rights to its cash basis partners. The Ruling applied assignment of income principles, treating the partnership as an entity, to require the income to be accrued by the partnership and taxed currently to the partners as part of their distributive share of partnership income, rather than as payments were received by the cash basis partners.

In Holiday Village Shopping Center v. United States, 773 F.2d 276 (Fed.Cir.1985), a corporation liquidated and distributed its interest in a limited partnership which held improved real property subject to section 1250 depreciation recapture. If the corporation had owned the property, recapture income would have been recognized as a result of the liquidating distribution. The taxpayer corporation argued that no recapture income was recognized because it distributed the partnership interest, not the property, and section 751, discussed infra, page 199, did not apply. The court disregarded the partnership and treated the distribution as a distribution of section 1250 property by the corporation, reflecting an aggregate approach which on the facts cannot be reconciled with the entity approach of Subchapter K governing dispositions of partnership interests. Sections 311 and 336, as amended in 1986, discussed infra, pages 477 and 616, now treat most corporate distributions as a sale or exchange, thereby providing a statutory basis for the result in *Holiday Village Shopping Center.* Section 311 and 336 relate to corporate taxation generally, rather than partnership taxation, and do not adopt the aggregate theory of *Holiday Village Shopping Center.* In cases where an exception to those sections applies, the doctrine of *Holiday Village Shopping Center* might nonetheless be applied.

H. REFERENCES

Lewis and Brown, Partnership Audits and Litigation Under TEFRA, 42 N.Y.U.Tax.Inst. 3 (1984); Fellows, Partnership Taxation: Confusion in Section 702(b), 32 Tax L.Rev. 67 (1976); Pusey, The Partnership as an "Entity": Implications of *Basye,* 54 Taxes 143 (1976); Wolfman, Level for Determining Character of Partnership Income—"Entity" v. "Conduit" Principle in Partnership Taxation, 19 N.Y.U.Tax Inst. 287 (1961).

SECTION 2. TAXATION OF PARTNERS

A. DETERMINING PARTNERS' DISTRIBUTIVE SHARES: GENERAL INTRODUCTION

INTERNAL REVENUE CODE: Sections 702; 704(a)–(e); 761(c).

REGULATIONS: Sections 1.702–1; 1.704–1(a); 1.761–1(c).

Section 702(a) requires each partner to take into account his distributive share of each separately stated item and the residual taxable income or loss entering into the partnership's taxable income. Section 704(a) provides that a partner's distributive share is determined by the partnership agreement, except as otherwise provided in Subchapter K. If the partnership agreement does not provide for partners' distributive shares or if the allocation to a partner under the agreement of income, gain, loss, deduction, or credit does not have "substantial economic effect," section 704(b) requires that the partner's distributive share be determined "in accordance with the partner's interest in the partnership (determined by taking into account all facts and circumstances)." A special rule is provided in section 704(c) which allocates items of income, gain, loss and deduction attributable to property contributed to the partnership to take into account differences between fair market value and basis at the time of the contribution. Section 704(d) limits a partner's share of currently deductible losses to that partner's basis in his partnership interest; losses in excess of basis are in effect carried over to be deducted in a subsequent year in which basis has been increased. The Regulations under section 752 provide detailed rules to determine a partner's basis in his partnership interest where debt is involved. Section 704(e) provides special rules governing allocation of items with respect to certain family partnerships.

The partnership agreement is broadly defined as the original agreement plus any modifications agreed to by all the partners or adopted in any other manner provided by the partnership agreement. The modifications may be oral or written and may be made with respect to a particular taxable year subsequent to the close of that year but before the due date for filing the partnership return. Local law governs any matter on which the agreement is silent. Section 761(c); Regulations, section 1.761–1(c).

Section 706(d) provides that if there is a change in a partner's interest in the partnership during the year, each partner's distributive share of income, gain, loss and deduction shall be determined by a method prescribed by regulations which takes into account the varying interests of the partners during the taxable year. See Regulations, section 1.706–1(c)(4). In addition, section 706(d)(2) requires that certain deductions be allocated over the year to which they are attributable, thus preventing a newly admitted partner from sharing in any deduction which had economically accrued prior to admission. This rule applies to interest, taxes, and payments for services or for the use of property, and the Internal Revenue Service has the authority to issue Regulations expanding the items covered. Section 706(d) is discussed in further detail infra, page 134.

Subject to these various restrictions governing the recognition for tax purposes of allocations made by the partnership agreement, partners are free to allocate income, gain, loss and deductions as they choose, and the agreement will be respected for tax purposes. Thus, if two partners agree to split partnership net profits or losses in a 75–25 ratio, their distributive shares of each item in section 702(a) will be in that ratio. If they agree that profits are to be split 50–50, but net operating losses are to be split 75–25, the profit sharing ratio would determine distributive shares in a profitable year, and the loss sharing ratio would control in an unprofitable year. Any agreement must, however, pass muster under the "substantial economic effect test" of section 704(b). But as long as the partnership agreement does not attempt to allocate items differently for tax purposes than for partnership accounting purposes, section 704(b) will not prevent recognition of the distributive shares provided in the partnership agreement.

B. ALLOCATIONS OF PARTNERSHIP ITEMS

INTERNAL REVENUE CODE: Section 704(b); 704(e).

REGULATIONS: Section 1.704–1(b).

ORRISCH v. COMMISSIONER *

Tax Court of the United States, 1970.
55 T.C. 395.

FEATHERSTON, JUDGE. Respondent determined deficiencies in petitioners' income tax for 1966 and 1967 in the respective amounts of $2,814.19 and $3,018.11. The only issue for decision is whether an amendment to a partnership agreement allocating to petitioners the entire amount of the depreciation deduction allowable on two buildings owned by the partnership was made for the principal purpose of avoidance of tax within the meaning of section 704(b).

* The Tax Court decision was affirmed per curiam, 31 A.F.T.R.2d 1069 (9th Cir. 1973).

FINDINGS OF FACT

* * *

In May of 1963, Domonick J. and Elaine J. Crisafi (hereinafter the Crisafis) and petitioners [Stanley C. and Gerta E. Orrisch] formed a partnership to purchase and operate two apartment houses, one located at 1255 Taylor Street, San Francisco, and the other at 600 Ansel Road, Burlingame, Calif. The cost of the Taylor Street property was $229,011.08, and of the Ansel Road property was $155,974.90. The purchase of each property was financed principally by a secured loan. Petitioners and the Crisafis initially contributed to the partnership cash in the amounts of $26,500 and $12,500, respectively. During 1964 and 1965 petitioners and the Crisafis each contributed additional cash in the amounts of $8,800. Under the partnership agreement, which was not in writing, they agreed to share equally the profits and losses from the venture.

During each of the years 1963, 1964, and 1965, the partnership suffered losses, attributable in part to the acceleration of depreciation—the deduction was computed on the basis of 150 percent of straight-line depreciation. The amounts of the depreciation deductions, the reported loss for each of the 3 years as reflected in the partnership returns, and the amounts of each partner's share of the losses are as follows:

Year	Depreciation deducted	Total loss	Each partner's share of the losses—50 percent of the total loss
1963	$ 9,886.20	$ 9,716.14	$4,858.07
1964	21,051.95	17,812.33	[1] 8,906.17
1965	19,894.24	18,952.59	[1] 9,476.30

[1] The amounts of the losses allocated to the Crisafis for 1964 and 1965 were actually $8,906.16 and $9,476.29.

Petitioners and the Crisafis respectively reported in their individual income tax returns for these years the partnership losses allocated to them.

Petitioners enjoyed substantial amounts of income from several sources, the principal one being a nautical equipment sales and repair business. In their joint income tax returns for 1963, 1964, and 1965, petitioners reported taxable income in the respective amounts of $10,462.70, $5,898.85, and $50,832, together with taxes thereon in the amounts of $2,320.30, $1,059.80, and $12,834.

The Crisafis were also engaged in other business endeavors, principally an insurance brokerage business. They owned other real property, however, from which they realized losses, attributable largely to substantial depreciation deductions. In their joint income tax returns for 1963, 1964, and 1965, they reported no net taxable income.

Early in 1966, petitioners and the Crisafis orally agreed that, for 1966 and subsequent years, the entire amount of the partnership's depreciation deductions would be specially allocated to petitioners, and that the gain or loss from the partnership's business, computed without regard to any deduction for depreciation, would be divided equally. They further agreed that, in the event the partnership property was sold at a gain, the specially allocated depreciation would be "charged back" to petitioner's capital account and petitioners would pay the tax on the gain attributable thereto.

The operating results of the partnership for 1966 and 1967 as reflected in the partnership returns were as follows:

Year	Depreciation deducted	Loss (including depreciation)	Gain (or loss) without regard to depreciation
1966	$18,412.00	$19,396.00	($984.00)
1967	17,180.75	16,560.78	619.97

The partnership returns for these years show that, taking into account the special arrangement as to depreciation losses in the amounts of $18,904 and $16,870.76 were allocated to petitioners for 1966 and 1967, respectively, and petitioners claimed these amounts as deductions in their joint income tax returns for those years. The partnership returns reported distributions to the Crisafis in the form of a $492 loss for 1966 and a $309.98 gain for 1967. The Crisafis' joint income tax returns reflected that they had no net taxable income for either 1966 or 1967.

The net capital contributions, allocations of profits, losses and depreciation, and ending balances of the capital accounts, of the Orrisch–Crisafi partnership from May 1963 through December 31, 1967, were as follows:

	Petitioners'	*Crisafis'*
Excess of capital contributions over withdrawals during 1963	$26,655.55	$12,655.54
Allocation of 1963 loss	(4,858.07)	(4,858.07)
Balance 12/31/63	21,797.48	7,797.47
Excess of capital contributions over withdrawals during 1964	4,537.50	3,537.50
Allocation of 1964 loss	(8,906.17)	(8,906.16)
Balance 12/31/64	17,428.81	2,428.81

	Petitioners'	*Crisafis'*
Excess of capital contributions over withdrawals during 1965	4,337.50	5,337.50
Allocation of 1965 loss	(9,476.30)	(9,476.29)
Balance 12/31/65	12,290.01	(1,709.98)
Excess of capital contributions over withdrawals during 1966	2,610.00	6,018.00
Allocation of 1966 loss before depreciation	(492.00)	(492.00)
Allocation of depreciation	(18,412.00)	0
Balance 12/31/66	(4,003.99)	3,816.02
Excess of withdrawals over capital contributions during 1967	(4,312.36)	(3,720.35)
Allocation of 1967 profit before depreciation	309.99	309.98
Allocation of depreciation	(17,180.75)	0
Balance 12/31/67	(25,187.11)	405.65

* * *

In the notice of deficiency, respondent determined that the special allocation of the depreciation deduction provided by the amendment to the partnership agreement "was made with the principal purpose of avoidance of income taxes" and should, therefore, be disregarded. Partnership losses for 1966 and 1967, adjusted to reflect a correction of the amount of depreciation allowable, were allocated equally between the partners.

ULTIMATE FINDING OF FACT

The principal purpose of the special allocation to petitioners of all of the deductions for depreciation taken by the Orrisch–Crisafi partnership for 1966 and 1967 was the avoidance of income tax.

OPINION

The only issue presented for decision is whether tax effect can be given the agreement between petitioners and the Crisafis that, beginning with 1966, all the partnership's depreciation deductions were to be allocated to petitioners for their use in computing their individual income tax liabilities. In our view, the answer must be in the negative, and the amounts of each of the partners' deductions for the depreciation of partnership property must be determined in accordance with the ratio used generally in computing their distributive shares of the partnership's profits and losses.

Among the important innovations of the 1954 Code are limited provisions for flexibility in arrangements for the sharing of income, losses, and deductions arising from business activities conducted through partnerships. The authority for special allocations of such items appears in section 704(a), which provides that a partner's share of any item of income, gain, loss, deduction, or credit shall be determined by the partnership agreement. That rule is coupled with a limitation in section 704(b), however, which states that a special allocation of an item will be disregarded if its "principal purpose" is the avoidance or evasion of Federal income tax. See Smith v. Commissioner, 331 F.2d 298 (C.A.7, 1964), affirming a Memorandum Opinion of this Court; Jean V. Kresser, 54 T.C. 1621 (1970). In case a special allocation is disregarded, the partner's share of the item is to be determined in accordance with the ratio by which the partners divide the general profits or losses of the partnership. Sec. 1.704–1(b)(2), Income Tax Regs.

The report of the Senate Committee on Finance accompanying the bill finally enacted as the 1954 Code (S.Rept. No. 1622, to accompany H.R. 8300 (Pub.L. No. 591), 83d Cong., 2d Sess., p. 379 (1954)) explained the tax-avoidance restriction prescribed by section 704(b) as follows:

> Subsection (b) * * * provides that if the principal purpose of any provision in the partnership agreement dealing with a partner's distributive share of a particular item is to avoid or evade the Federal income tax, the partner's distributive share of that item shall be redetermined in accordance with his distributive share of partnership income or loss described in section 702(a)(9) [i.e., the ratio used by the partners for dividing general profits or losses]. * * *
>
> Where, however, a provision in a partnership agreement for a special allocation of certain items has substantial economic effect and is not merely a device for reducing the taxes of certain partners without actually affecting their shares of partnership income, then such a provision will be recognized for tax purposes. * * *

This reference to "substantial economic effect" did not appear in the House Ways and Means Committee report (H.Rept. No. 1337, to accompany H.R. 8300 (Pub.L. No. 591), 83d Cong., 2d Sess., p. A223 (1954)) discussing section 704(b), and was apparently added in the Senate Finance Committee to allay fears that special allocations of income or deductions would be denied effect in every case where the allocation resulted in a reduction in the income tax liabilities of one or more of the partners. The statement is an affirmation that special allocations are ordinarily to be recognized if they have business validity apart from their tax consequences. Driscoll, "Tax Problems of Partnerships—Special Allocation of Specific Items," 1958 So.Cal.Tax Inst. 421, 426.

In resolving the question whether the principal purpose of a provision in a partnership agreement is the avoidance or evasion of Federal income tax, all the facts and circumstances in relation to the provision must be taken into account. Section 1.704–1(b)(2), Income Tax Regs., lists the following as relevant circumstances to be considered:

> Whether the partnership or a partner individually has a business purpose for the allocation; whether the allocation has "substantial economic effect", that is, whether the allocation may actually affect the dollar amount of the partners' shares of the total partnership

> income or loss independently of tax consequences; whether related items of income, gain, loss, deduction, or credit from the same source are subject to the same allocation; whether the allocation was made without recognition of normal business factors and only after the amount of the specially allocated item could reasonably be estimated; the duration of the allocation; and the overall tax consequences of the allocation. * * *

Applying these standards, we do not think the special allocation of depreciation in the present case can be given effect.

The evidence is persuasive that the special allocation of depreciation was adopted for a tax-avoidance rather than a business purpose. Depreciation was the only item which was adjusted by the parties; both the income from the buildings and the expenses incurred in their operation, maintenance, and repair were allocated to the partners equally. Since the deduction for depreciation does not vary from year to year with the fortunes of the business, the parties obviously knew what the tax effect of the special allocation would be at the time they adopted it. Furthermore, as shown by our Findings, petitioners had large amounts of income which would be offset by the additional deduction for depreciation; the Crisafis, in contrast, had no taxable income from which to subtract the partnership depreciation deductions, and due to depreciation deductions which they were obtaining with respect to other housing projects, could expect to have no taxable income in the near future. On the other hand, the insulation of the Crisafis from at least part of a potential capital gains tax was an obvious tax advantage. The inference is unmistakably clear that the agreement did not reflect normal business considerations but was designed primarily to minimize the overall tax liabilities of the partners.

Petitioners urge that the special allocation of the depreciation deduction was adopted in order to equalize the capital accounts of the partners, correcting a disparity ($14,000) in the amounts initially contributed to the partnership by them ($26,500) and the Crisafis ($12,500). But the evidence does not support this contention. Under the special allocation agreement, petitioners were to be entitled, in computing their individual income tax liabilities, to deduct the full amount of the depreciation realized on the partnership property. For 1966, as an example, petitioners were allocated a sum ($18,904) equal to the depreciation on the partnership property ($18,412) plus one-half of the net loss computed without regard to depreciation ($492). The other one-half of the net loss was, of course, allocated to the Crisafis. Petitioners' allocation ($18,904) was then applied to reduce their capital account. The depreciation specially allocated to petitioners ($18,412) in 1966 alone exceeded the amount of the disparity in the contributions. Indeed, at the end of 1967, petitioners' capital account showed a deficit of $25,187.11 compared with a positive balance of $405.65 in the Crisafis' account. By the time the partnership's properties are fully depreciated, the amount of the reduction in petitioners' capital account will approximate the remaining basis for the buildings as of the end of 1967. The Crisafis' capital account will be adjusted only for contributions, withdrawals, gain or loss, without regard to depreciation, and similar adjustments for these factors will also be made in petitioners' capital account. Thus, rather than correcting an imbalance in the capital accounts of the partners, the special allocation of depreciation will create a vastly greater imbalance than existed at the end of 1966. In the light of these facts, we find it incredible that equalization of the capital accounts was the objective of the special allocation.[5]

Petitioners rely primarily on the argument that the allocation has "substantial economic effect" in that it is reflected in the capital accounts of the partners. Referring to the material quoted above from the report of the Senate Committee on Finance, they contend that this alone is sufficient to show that the special allocation served a business rather than a tax-avoidance purpose.

According to the regulations, an allocation has economic effect if it "may actually affect the dollar amount of the partners' shares of the total partnership income or loss independently of tax consequences." [6] The agreement in this case provided not only for the allocation of depreciation to petitioners but also for gain on the sale of the partnership property to be "charged back" to them. The charge back would cause the gain, for tax purposes, to be allocated on the books entirely to petitioners to the extent of the special allocation of depreciation, and their capital account would be correspondingly increased. The remainder of the gain, if any, would be shared equally by the partners. If the gain on the sale were to equal or exceed the depreciation specially allocated to petitioners, the increase in their capital account caused by the charge back would exactly equal the depreciation deductions previously allowed to them and the proceeds of the sale of the property would be divided equally. In such circumstances, the only effect of the

5. We recognize that petitioners had more money invested in the partnership than the Crisafis and that it is reasonable for the partners to endeavor to equalize their investments, since each one was to share equally in the profits and losses of the enterprise. However, we do not think that sec. 704(a) permits the partners' prospective tax benefits to be used as the medium for equalizing their investments, and it is apparent that the economic burden of the depreciation (which is reflected by the allowance for depreciation) was not intended to be the medium used.

This case is to be distinguished from situations where one partner contributed property and the other cash; in such cases sec. 704(c) may allow a special allocation of income and expenses in order to reflect the tax consequences inherent in the original contributions.

6. This language of sec. 1.704–1(b)(2), Income Tax Regs., listing "substantial economic effect" as one of the factors to be considered in determining the principal purpose of a special allocation, is somewhat similar to the material quoted in the text from S.Rept. No. 1622, to accompany H.R. 8300 (Pub.L. No. 591), 83d Cong., 2d Sess., p. 379 (1954). But the latter is broader. It is an explanation of the "principal purpose" test of sec. 704(b), and contemplates that a special allocation will be given effect only if it has business validity apart from its tax consequences. Driscoll, "Tax Problems of Partnerships—Special Allocation of Specific Items," 1958 So.Cal. U.Tax Inst. 421, 429 fn. 17; Willis, Handbook of Partnership Taxation 141 (1957).

allocation would be a trade of tax consequences, i.e., the Crisafis would relinquish a current depreciation deduction in exchange for exoneration from all or part of the capital gains tax when the property is sold, and petitioners would enjoy a larger current depreciation deduction but would assume a larger ultimate capital gains tax liability. Quite clearly, if the property is sold at a gain, the special allocation will affect only the tax liabilities of the partners and will have no other economic effect.

To find any economic effect of the special allocation agreement aside from its tax consequences, we must, therefore, look to see who is to bear the economic burden of the depreciation if the buildings should be sold for a sum less than their original cost. There is not one syllable of evidence bearing directly on this crucial point. We have noted, however, that when the buildings are fully depreciated, petitioners' capital account will have a deficit, or there will be a disparity in the capital accounts, approximately equal to the undepreciated basis of the buildings as of the beginning of 1966.[7] Under normal accounting procedures, if the building were sold at a gain less than the amount of such disparity petitioners would either be required to contribute to the partnership a sum equal to the remaining deficit in their capital account after the gain on the sale had been added back or would be entitled to receive a proportionately smaller share of the partnership assets on liquidation. Based on the record as a whole, we do not think the partners ever agreed to such an arrangement. On dissolution, we think the partners contemplated an equal division of the partnership assets which would be adjusted only for disparities in cash contributions or withdrawals.[8] Certainly there is no evidence to show otherwise. That being true, the special allocation does not "actually affect the dollar amount of the partners' share of the total partnership income or loss independently of tax consequences" within the meaning of the regulation referred to above. * * *

In the light of all the evidence we have found as an ultimate fact that the "principal purpose" of the special allocation agreement was tax avoidance within the meaning of section 701(b). Accordingly, the deduction for depreciation for 1966 and 1967 must be allocated between the parties in the same manner as other deductions.

Decision will be entered for the respondent.

ILLUSTRATIVE MATERIAL

A. STATUTORY RULES GOVERNING ALLOCATIONS

The provisions of the partnership agreement dealing with allocations of items of income, gain, loss and credits may range from a simple percentage division of all items on the same basis to complex arrangements with separate

7. This assumes, of course, that all partnership withdrawals and capital contributions will be equal.

8. We note that, in the course of Orrisch's testimony, petitioners' counsel made a distinction between entries in the taxpayers' capital accounts which reflect actual cash transactions and those relating to the special allocation which are "paper entries relating to depreciation."

allocations of profit and loss, cash flow, distributions from refinancing, liquidation distributions, etc., in different periods and at different levels of income. Section 704(b) requires that allocations of the items in the partnership agreement have "substantial economic effect." If the attempted tax allocations in the partnership agreement do not meet the substantial economic effect test, the partner's share of the item in question will be determined in accordance with the partner's overall interest in the partnership, including a consideration of items which are not specially allocated. Prior to its amendment by the Tax Reform Act of 1976, section 704(b) provided that special allocations would not be recognized if the "principal purpose" of the allocation was tax avoidance. The Regulations under section 704(b), discussed in the *Orrisch* case, which were issued prior to the 1976 statutory changes, focused on whether or not the attempted special allocation had substantial economic effect. The Tax Reform Act of 1976 specifically incorporated the substantial economic effect test in the statute, dropping the reference to tax avoidance purpose. The legislative history indicates that there was no intention to change the previously existing law as to what constitutes the requisite economic effect. S.Rep. No. 94–938, 94th Cong., 2d Sess. 100 (1976). Thus the prior case law may have some continuing relevance. The greatest emphasis, however, is on the detailed tests in the regulations promulgated under the 1976 version of Section 704(b).

The Committee Report also left some room for the argument that a (presumably nontax) business purpose for a special allocation has some significance. The statutory stress, however, is clearly on the substantial economic effect of the allocation and the presence of a "business purpose" should not protect an allocation which does not have the necessary economic effect. Indeed, it is difficult to imagine what the nontax business purpose could be and there is no provision in the regulations sustaining an allocation based upon its alleged business purpose.

Prior to 1976 there was some question whether the limitations of section 704(b) applied to so-called "bottom line" allocations of the *entire* profit or loss of the partnership. See Kresser v. Commissioner, 54 T.C. 1621 (1970). The 1976 amendments to section 704(b) made it clear that the substantial economic effect limitation applies both to the allocation of a particular item of income or deduction as well as to shifts in the general ratio on which profits and losses are allocated.

In addition to section 704(b), the Commissioner has also successfully used section 482 to upset partnership allocations where the partners were related parties. Rodebaugh v. Commissioner, 33 T.C.M. 169 (1974), aff'd per curiam, 518 F.2d 73 (6th Cir.1975).

B. THE SECTION 704(b) REGULATIONS

1. *General*

Regulations to reflect the 1976 Act amendments were proposed in 1983 and were promulgated in final form in 1986 and 1987; the Regulations were amended in 1989. Regulations, section 1.704–1(b); Temporary Regulations, section 1.704–1T(b) (applying to nonrecourse debt). The organizing theme of the Regulations is that an allocation "must be consistent with the underlying economic arrangement of the partners" in order to have "substantial economic effect." "This means that in the event there is an economic benefit or economic burden that corresponds to an allocation, the partner to whom the allocation is made must receive such economic benefit or bear such economic burden." Regulations, section 1.704–1(b)(2)(ii). In general, the Regulations adhere to the capital account analysis in *Orrisch,* but prescribe detailed rules which must be followed in making the capital account analysis required if a partnership allocation is to be recognized, particularly where nonrecourse debt is involved. By requiring that tax allocations be reflected in the changes in value of each partner's capital account, the Regulations assure that the tax consequences to each partner accurately reflect the economic gain or loss realized by the partners.

Given the detailed nature of the section 704(b) regulations, it is important to keep in mind that the tax rules do not determine the economic deal between the partners. Rather, the rules are intended to insure that the tax results follow the economics, i.e., the partners cannot set up one reality for economic purposes and then try to construct another and different reality solely for tax purposes.

Under the Regulations, there are three alternative methods by which an allocation can satisfy section 704(b): (1) the allocation has "substantial economic effect" under Regulations, section 1.704–1(b)(2); (2) taking into account all of the facts and circumstances, the allocation is in accordance with the partners' interests in the partnership under Regulations, section 1.704–1(b)(3); or (3) the allocation is deemed under Regulations, section 1.704–1(b)(4), or Temporary Regulations, section 1.704–1T(b)(4)(iv), to be in accordance with the partners' interests in the partnership under a special rule. The application of the facts and circumstances test of Regulations, section 1.704–1(b)(3), is not clearly delineated and, in order to be respected, partnership allocation provisions are generally written to meet one of the mechanical tests.

Temporary Regulations, section 1.704–1T(b)(4)(iv)(*a*)(1), provide that allocations attributable to nonrecourse debt never can have economic effect and always must be allocated among the partners in accordance with their interests in the partnership. However, the Regulations provide a "safe harbor" under which allocations attributable to nonrecourse debt will be deemed to be made in accordance with the partners' interests in the partnership. Temporary Regulations, section 1.704–1T(b)(4)(iv)(*d*).

Although section 704(b) frequently is said to deal with *special* allocations, it is important to note that the Regulations test *all* allocations for substantial economic effect, including straightforward identical fractional allocations of every item. As long as each partner is entitled to a fractional share of each and every item that does not vary from item to item for the partner, however, the allocation always will have substantial economic effect under the tests of the Regulations, even though the partners' fractional shares may differ. But if any partner is entitled to a share of any item that differs from his share of any other item, including his liability for partnership debts, then a detailed analysis under the Regulations is required. This analysis is required regardless of whether the specially allocated item is identified by its tax characteristics or its financial characteristics.

2. *Partners' Capital Accounts*

Regulations, section 1.704–1(b)(2)(iv), provide detailed rules regarding the maintenance of partners' capital accounts which must be followed throughout the life of the partnership for an allocation to have economic effect. In applying these rules, a partner who has more than one interest in the partnership is treated as having a single capital account that reflects all of the partner's interests, even if one interest is as a general partner and the other is as a limited partner, and without regard to the time or manner of acquisition of the interests.

A partner's capital account must be increased by the amount of any money contributed by the partner and by income (including tax exempt income) allocated to the partner; and it must be decreased by the amount of any money distributed to the partner and by the partner's share of loss, deduction, and section 705(a)(2)(B) expenditures (nondeductible expenditures not chargeable to a capital account). In addition, a partner's capital account must be increased by the fair market value (not the basis) of any property contributed by the partner to the partnership. A partner's own promissory note contributed to the partnership is not taken into account, however, until the disposition of the note by the partnership or the partner pays the principal. Regulations, section 1.704–1(b)(2)(iv)(*d*)(*2*). If property is distributed to a partner, the partner's capital account must be reduced by the fair market value of the property. Regulations, section 1.704–1(b)(2)(iv)(*e*). If property that is contributed to the partnership or distributed by the partnership is subject to a debt, the effect of the debt must be taken into account. Regulations, section 1.704–1(b)(2)(iv)(*c*).

Upon liquidation of the partnership, all capital accounts must be adjusted to reflect appreciation and depreciation of partnership property. In addition, partners' capital accounts may (but are not required to) be increased or decreased to reflect a revaluation of the partnership's property on the happening of certain events, such as the admission of a new partner, the distribution of property, or the liquidation of a partner's interest. Regulations, section 1.704–1(b)(2)(iv)(*f*). If the partnership elects to reflect current values in the capital accounts, the partnership must thereafter adjust capital accounts to reflect certain items (such as depreciation) as computed for book purposes rather than for tax purposes. Regulations, section 1.704–1(b)(2)(iv)(*g*). In general, the partners' determination of the fair market value of property will be accepted if it is determined in arm's length negotiations in which the partners' have sufficiently adverse interests. Regulations, section 1.704–1(b)(2)(iv)(*h*).

Because capital accounts are maintained with reference to the fair market value of property contributed to the partnership and property distributed by the partnership, and in some cases are increased or reduced by income or gain and deductions or losses as measured for book accounting rather than tax accounting, see Regulations, section 1.704–1(b)(2)(iv)(*g*), a partner's capital account is not the same as his basis in his partnership interest.

3. "*Substantial Economic Effect*"

(a) *Economic effect*

Whether an allocation has "substantial economic effect" is determined under a two part test. First, Regulations, section 1.704–1(b)(2)(ii), require that the allocation have "economic effect." As noted above, this means that the partner receiving the allocation of the tax item must also bear the economic benefit or burden that corresponds to the allocation. Under the Regulations, an allocation has economic effect only if three conditions are satisfied: (1) the allocation is reflected by an appropriate increase or decrease in the partner's capital account; (2) liquidation proceeds are, throughout the term of the partnership, to be distributed in accordance with the partners' positive capital account balances; and (3) any partner with a deficit capital account following the distribution of liquidation proceeds is required to restore the amount of that deficit to the partnership for distribution to partners with positive account balances or payment to partnership creditors. A partner's obligation to restore a negative capital account need not be unlimited; an allocation that creates or increases a negative capital account balance will be respected to the extent that the deficit does not exceed the amount that the partner is obligated to restore.

The determination whether an allocation has economic effect is made annually. Regulations, section 1.704–1(b)(2)(i). Thus, an allocation may be respected one year, but not the next, or may be respected only in part under Regulations, section 1.704–1(b)(2)(ii)(*e*).

The requirement of restoration of negative capital accounts presents a serious problem for recognition of allocations in limited partnerships, particularly where deduction items are disproportionately allocated to limited partners. The essence of a limited partnership interest is that there is no obligation to restore a negative capital account balance. A number of special rules are provided, however, which allow recognition of allocations that do not create a negative capital account for a limited partner, Regulations, sections 1.704–1(b)(2)(ii)(*e*) and (*i*), or which create a temporary negative capital account for a limited partner, Regulations, section 1.704–1(b)(2)(ii)(*c*). In addition, in some instances an obligation to make future contributions will be treated as an obligation to restore a negative capital account balance to the extent of the required contribution. Regulations, section 1.704–1(b)(2)(ii)(*c*).

Regulations, section 1.704–1(b)(2)(ii)(*d*), provide a special rule for recognizing allocations which do not create or increase a capital account deficit when the partner does not have an unlimited obligation to restore the negative capital account upon liquidation. To qualify under this provision, the partnership must maintain the required capital accounts and liquidate according to capital account balances. When determining whether an allocation creates a deficit capital account balance under this test, reasonably anticipated distributions to be made in future years which will not be offset by future income allocations must be taken into account. More specifically, a partnership agreement must provide that a limited partner with a negative capital account balance (or who would have a negative capital account balance as a result of the allocation) cannot be allocated items of deduction while other partners have positive capital account balances. Finally, the partnership agreement must provide for a "qualified income offset." This required provision must allocate to any partner who has a negative capital account as a result of an *unexpected* distribution sufficient income or gain to eliminate the deficit as soon as possible.

The operation of the basic rules can be illustrated by the following example. Suppose A and B each contribute $15,000 to the AB Partnership, which then borrows $170,000 on a recourse basis and buys depreciable property for $200,000. A and B each have a capital account of $15,000 since partnership liabilities have no effect on partners' capital accounts. In the first year the partnership has no taxable income or loss except for a $20,000 depreciation deduction. If the full $20,000 depreciation deduction is specially allocated to B, the allocation will be recognized if two conditions are met: first, B's capital account must be reduced to negative $5,000; and second, assuming that the building were sold for $180,000 at the beginning of the second year and the partnership liquidated, B must be required to contribute $5,000 to the partnership so that A will receive $15,000 on the liquidation. If, however, the agreement of the partners was that B would not be required to restore any negative capital account, the special allocation will be partly recognized; only $15,000 of depreciation could be specially allocated to B, because A would bear the economic risk of the remaining $5,000 of depreciation. In this case, however, since the first year's special allocation reduced B's capital account to zero and A's capital account to $10,000, in year two the first $10,000 of depreciation must be allocated to A and the remaining depreciation must be allocated equally between A and B. Finally, if the agreement of the parties was that notwithstanding the capital account balances (or if the partnership did not maintain capital accounts) the net proceeds from the sale of the building would be divided equally, then the special allocation fails entirely and the depreciation must be allocated equally, because A and B share the economic risk equally.

Regulations, section 1.704–1(b)(2)(ii)(*i*), provide that an allocation that does not have economic effect under the stringent rules prescribed in Regulations, section 1.704–1(b)(2)(ii), will be deemed to have economic effect if as of the end of each partnership year a liquidation of the partnership at the end of that year or at the end of any future year would produce the same economic results to the partners as would occur if the detailed requirements had been satisfied, regardless of economic performance of the partnership. This provision will assure the recognition of any allocation that allocates a consistent fraction of all items to each partner, as long as the partners are fully liable for partnership debts.

(b) *Substantiality*

Assuming an allocation has economic effect under the above described test, that effect must also be "substantial." To be considered "substantial" the economic effect of the allocation must have a reasonable possibility of affecting the dollar amounts to be received by the partners independent of the tax consequences of the allocation. Regulations, section 1.704–1(b)(2)(iii)(*a*). An allocation is not substantial if, as a result of the allocation, the after-tax economic consequences to at least one partner may, in present value terms, be enhanced, and there is a strong likelihood that the after-tax consequences of no partner will, in present value terms, be diminished.

Regulations, section 1.704–1(b)(2)(iii)(*b*), elaborate this general rule by providing that an allocation that merely shifts tax consequences within a given year and does not affect the economic consequences to the partners will not be substantial. This special rule addresses allocations which when viewed together with other allocations result in a net increase or decrease in the partners' capital accounts which does not differ substantially from what would have resulted without the special allocations, but which have the effect of reducing the partners' total tax liability. This test requires an examination of factors extrinsic to the partnership, such as the individual partners' income tax brackets. Assume, for example that C and D are equal partners. In the year in question, the CD partnership realizes a $10,000 capital loss and an operating loss of $10,000. In that same taxable year C individually realizes capital gains of $10,000 and D individually realizes no capital gains. If both items were allocated equally between the partners, C and D each would decrease her capital account by $10,000. C would be able to personally deduct $5,000 of the operating loss and $5,000 of the capital loss. D would be able to deduct $5,000 of the operating loss, but due to section 1211(b) only $3,000 of the capital loss. If the partners amended the partnership agreement to allocate the entire capital loss to C and the entire operating loss to D, C and D each would still decrease her capital account by $10,000. Thus such an allocation has economic effect. However, since the net decreases in the partners' capital accounts do not differ substantially from the net decreases that would have occurred without the allocation, and due to the ability of C to deduct currently all of the capital losses, the total tax liability of the partners' will be less than it would be without the allocation, the allocation does not have "substantial" effect. The allocation will not be respected, and each item will be allocated in proportion to the net decreases in the partners' capital accounts—in this case, equally. If, on the other hand, at the time the partnership agreement was amended to provide for the above described allocation there was not a strong likelihood that the partnership would have substantially equal amounts of capital losses and operating losses, then the allocation would have substantial economic effect. See Regulations, section 1.704–1(b)(5), Ex. (6), (7), and (10).

Regulations, section 1.704–1(b)(2)(iii)(*c*), provide another special application of the substantiality rule by treating transitory allocations as insubstantial. An allocation is transitory if: (1) the allocation may be offset by another allocation; (2) at the time the allocations are included in the partnership agreement there is strong likelihood that the net increases and decreases in the partners' respective capital accounts will not differ substantially from what they would have been absent the allocation and the offsetting allocation; and (3) the total tax liability of the partners will be less than it would have been if the allocations were not in the partnership agreement. If, however, there is a strong likelihood that the offsetting allocations will not be made within five years of the original allocation, the allocations will not be insubstantial.

The transitory allocation rule applies, for example, in the following circumstances. Assume that the EFGH partnership owns and operates a rental property which can be predicted to produce net income of $12,000 per year for each of the next four years. Each partner has a one-quarter capital interest. E has a net operating loss carryover under section 172 from an unrelated business that is about to expire. The partnership agreement is amended to allocate to E all of the partnership net income for the last year in which E can use his net operating loss carryover, and to allocate the net income of the partnership equally among F, G, and H for each of the next three years. As a result, E is allocated an additional $9,000 of net income in the first year, while each of the other partners is allocated $3,000 less net income than they otherwise would have been allocated. Over the next three years, E is allocated a total of $9,000 less than he would otherwise have been allocated, and each of the other partners is allocated a total of $3,000 more. On these facts, there was at the time the allocations were made a strong likelihood that over the four year span each partner would be allocated $12,000 of net income. The allocation to E of all of the income in the first year was cancelled out by the allocation to him of none of the income in any of the next three years. Thus the allocation is transitory and, since it reduced the partners' taxes over the four year span by allowing E to use his net operating loss carryover, it will not be respected. The net income of the partnership will be allocated equally in each of the four years. See Regulations, section 1.704–1(b)(5), Ex. (8).

An important element in applying the transitory allocation rule is the presumption in Regulations, section 1.704–1(b)(2)(iii)(*c*), that the actual fair market value of property decreases by tax depreciation. In some cases this rule is necessary to prevent a special allocation of depreciation coupled with a "gain chargeback" on the disposition of property from giving rise to a transitory allocation. As a result of this assumption, any gain which may be realized on the sale of depreciable property is not taken into account in determining whether there was a strong likelihood that an allocation of gain offsetting the depreciation deductions within five years.

A "gain chargeback" is a provision in a partnership agreement providing that if depreciable property is sold at a gain, the partner who received a special allocation of depreciation with respect to the property will be specially allocated the gain, up to the amount of depreciation deductions previously allocated to him. The operation of a gain chargeback provision can be illustrated by continuing the AB Partnership example discussed supra, page 101. Suppose that at the beginning of the second year, when the property had a basis of $180,000, the property were sold for $200,000. If the special allocation of the $20,000 depreciation deduction to B had been fully recognized (because B was obligated to restore a negative capital account), all of the $20,000 gain would be allocated to B. On the other hand, if only $15,000 of the special allocation of depreciation had been recognized, then only $15,000 of the gain would be allocated to B under the gain chargeback; the remaining $5,000 would be allocated to A. The allocations of gain would be reflected in the partners' capital accounts so that in either case each partner's capital account immediately prior to liquidation would be $15,000. Accordingly, the net proceeds of the sale would be divided equally since the liquidating distributions would be in accordance with positive capital account balances. Thus, while B initially bore the economic loss of the depreciation (which is assumed to have occurred in fact), that loss was made up by the subsequent allocation of a corresponding amount of income to B.

Gain chargeback provisions are not created by the Regulations, but by the partnership agreement; and whether or not an allocation of depreciation will be respected is determined without regard to the existence of a gain chargeback provision, except in the case of deductions based on nonrecourse debt, as discussed infra, page 105. However, because liquidating distributions must be made in accordance with positive capital account balances, economic considerations of the partners dictate that gain chargebacks be part and parcel of provisions in partnership agreements specially allocating depreciation deductions. As the *Orrisch* opinion points out, if the property is sold for at least its original cost, the special allocation of deductions and the corresponding "chargeback" of gain only affect tax liabilities and do not affect the proceeds received by each partner. The cash proceeds are distributed as if no special allocation had been made. The Regulations, however, take the position that this does not mean that there is no substantial economic effect to the allocations if there is a strong likelihood that the offsetting allocations will not be made within five years. The theory underlying this rule appears to be that an allocation which has effect for such a time interval interposes sufficient risk that the partnership will suffer an actual loss that cannot be eliminated by offsetting a future special allocation, such as a gain chargeback. Furthermore, due to the conclusive presumption in Regulations, section 1.704–1(b)(2)(iii)(*c*), that the fair market value of the property decreased by tax depreciation, even if a sale of the property within five years at a price equal to its original cost is a virtual certainty, the allocation of depreciation coupled with the gain chargeback is not transitory, since there conclusively is no strong likelihood of the gain occurring.

An allocation which has economic effect and is neither a transitory allocation under Regulations, section 1.704–1(b)(2)(iii)(*c*), nor one that shifts tax consequences under Regulations, section 1.704–1(b)(2)(iii)(*b*), may nonetheless fail the substantiality test under the general principles of Regulations, section 1.704–1(b)(2)(iii)(*a*). This result would occur, for example, on the following facts. I and J contribute equal amounts to become partners in an investment partnership. The partnership distributes currently all income credited to the partners' capital accounts. I expects consistently to be subject to tax at the 15 percent bracket, and J expects consistently to be subject to tax at the 28 percent bracket. There is a strong likelihood that over the next several years the IJ partnership will realize $500 of tax-exempt interest and $500 of taxable interest and dividends on its investments. If all items were allocated equally between I and J, which would be consistent with their capital interests, each would have $250 of tax-exempt income and $250 of taxable income. As a result, I would realize $462.50 of after-tax income, and J would realize $430 of after-tax income. If, however, the tax-exempt interest was allocated 42 percent to I and 58 percent to J, and the taxable income was allocated 60 percent to I and 40 percent to J, and each partner's capital account was increased according to those percentages, I would realize $210 of tax-exempt income and $300 of taxable income, and J would realize $290 of tax exempt income and $200 of taxable income. On an after-tax basis, however, I would realize a total of $465 and J would realize a total of $444. Each of them would have more after-tax income as a result of the allocation than they would have had if the allocation had been consistent with their capital interests. Therefore, even though it has economic effect, the allocation is not "substantial," and it will not be respected for tax purposes. Because under the allocation, I's capital account is credited with $510 and J's capital account is credited with $490, all items will be allocated 51 percent to I and 49 percent to J. See Regulations, section 1.704–1(b)(5), Ex. (5).

4. *Allocations Attributable to Nonrecourse Debt*

Temporary Regulations, section 1.704–1T(b)(4)(iv), take the position that an allocation of deductions attributable to nonrecourse debt never can have economic effect because only the creditor bears the burden of economic loss. Accordingly, losses and deductions attributable to nonrecourse debt, which are termed "nonrecourse deductions," must be allocated in accordance with the partners' interests in the partnership. However, allocations will be deemed to be made in accordance with the partners' interest in the partnership, and thus given effect, if four requirements are met. These requirements are based on the fact that under Commissioner v. Tufts, 461 U.S. 300 (1983), the partnership always will recognize gain on the disposition of the property equal to the depreciation deductions attributable to nonrecourse debt. The object of these rules is to allocate the gain on the disposition to the partners who enjoyed the benefit of the earlier depreciation deductions.

First, capital accounts must be maintained as required under the rules of Regulations, section 1.704–1(b)(2)(ii)(*b*)(*1*), and liquidating distributions must be made in accordance with positive capital account balances under the rules of Regulations, section 1.704–1(b)(2)(ii)(*b*)(*2*), as described above. Second, beginning in the first year of the partnership in which the partnership has deductions attributable to nonrecourse indebtedness, and for all partnership years thereafter, the partnership agreement must provide for allocations of nonrecourse deductions among the partners in a manner that is reasonably consistent with allocations which have substantial economic effect of some other significant partnership item attributable to the property securing the nonrecourse liability (other than minimum gain realized by the partnership). The Regulations do not provide any guidance to assist in identifying a "significant partnership item," but partnership gross income clearly should qualify. It is reasonable to assume that allocations of deductions attributable to nonrecourse debt in the same proportion as deductions attributable to the partners' capital accounts are allocated also would qualify. Third, beginning with the year in which nonrecourse deductions are first claimed or the proceeds of a nonrecourse borrowing are first distributed, the partnership agreement must provide for a "minimum gain chargeback," described below. Fourth, all other material partnership allocations and capital account adjustments must be recognized under Regulations, section 1.704–1(b). This final requirement means that allocations of net income or of losses attributable to partners' capital accounts must have substantial economic effect.

The amount of nonrecourse deductions of a partnership equals the increase, if any, in the amount of partnership "minimum gain" during the year. Nonrecourse deductions are treated as consisting first of cost recovery or depreciation deductions attributable to properties giving rise to the increase in "minimum gain," and then of a pro rata share of other partnership deductions. Temporary Regulations, section 1.704–1T(b)(4)(iv)(*b*). "Minimum gain" is the sum of the amounts, computed separately with respect to each item of partnership property, that would be realized if in a taxable transaction the partnership disposed of the property in full satisfaction of the nonrecourse liability secured by it. Temporary Regulations, section 1.704–1T(b)(4)(iv)(*c*). For example, if the AB partnership purchased an apartment building for $100, paying $20 of the purchase price with partnership capital and $80 with the proceeds of a nonrecourse mortgage and, when the adjusted basis of the property was $60 and the balance due on the mortgage was $75, the partnership deeded the property to the mortgagee in satisfaction of the debt, the minimum gain is $15. If a property is properly carried on the books of the partnership at a book value that differs from its tax basis, the book value basis is used to compute minimum gain. See Regulations, section 1.704–1(b)(5), Ex. (22). The result of these rules is that deductions are attributed first to the partners' equity contributions, second to partnership debt on which there is personal liability, and finally to nonrecourse debt.

A partnership agreement contains a "minimum gain chargeback" only if it provides that if there is a net decrease in partnership minimum gain during a partnership year, each partner must be allocated income or gain in proportion to the greater of the deficit in the partner's capital account (excluding a deficit the partner must restore) or the partner's share of the decrease in minimum gain allocable to the disposition of a property subject to a nonrecourse mortgage. Temporary Regulations, section 1.704–1T(b)(4)(iv)(*e*). This rule requires a gain chargeback as the mortgage loan is amortized or upon disposition of the property (but the chargeback also can be triggered by other events, e.g., by a capital contribution by one partner which is invested to increase the basis of partnership assets or by one partner guaranteeing all or part of a previously nonrecourse debt). The gain chargeback must be allocated before any other allocation of any partnership items for the year is made under section 704(b). The Regulations provide rules for determining a partner's share of minimum gain, as well as certain exceptions to the general rules and specific rules to cover a variety of particular transactions. Temporary Regulations, section 1.704–1T(b)(4)(iv)(*f*). The purpose of the minimum gain chargeback rule is to assure that an offsetting amount of gain is allocated to the partners who received the economic benefit which gave rise to partnership minimum gain. That benefit could have been in the form of either nonrecourse deductions or distributions of proceeds from nonrecourse refinancings of partnership property. Temporary Regulations, section 1.704–1T(b)(4)(iv)(*a*)(*2*).

Operation of the basic rules governing special allocations of nonrecourse deductions is illustrated in the following example. Suppose that C and D respectively contribute $20,000 and $80,000 to the CD Partnership, which then borrows $900,000 from an unrelated lender on a nonrecourse promissory note secured by depreciable property for which the partnership pays $1,000,000. Also suppose that no principal payments are due on the note for the first five years and that $50,000 of depreciation is allowable on the property each year. The partnership agreement requires that capital accounts be maintained in accordance with the Regulations and that liquidation be in accordance with capital accounts, and that C, but not D (who is a limited partner), is required to restore a negative capital account. Because the partnership has $100,000 of equity, the first two years' depreciation deductions (assuming that the partnership does not have any income or loss from other items) are not nonrecourse deductions. At the end of two years the basis of the property will be $900,000 and the mortgage lien will be the same amount; there is no "minimum gain." Accordingly, D may be allocated up to $80,000 of the first two year's depreciation, and C must be allocated at least $20,000 of depreciation. (C may be allocated more than $20,000 of depreciation, and D may be allocated correspondingly less depreciation.)

In the third year, the depreciation deduction reduces the property's basis to $850,000, and $50,000 of minimum gain arises, since if the partnership transferred the property subject to the mortgage (and for no additional consideration), it would recognize this amount of gain. See Regulations, section 1.704–1(b)(4)(iv)(*c*). Neither partner bears the economic risk of loss with respect to this deduction, and no allocation of the deduction can have substantial economic effect. Nevertheless, an allocation will be deemed to have substantial economic effect if the partnership agreement contains a minimum gain chargeback provision. The deduction could be allocated between C and D in any proportion, as long the resulting minimum gain were allocated between them correspondingly. For example, if the entire $50,000 of minimum gain were allocated to D, an allocation of all of the depreciation to D will be respected. Any special allocation formula, however, must be reasonably consistent with some other significant allocation that has substantial economic effect. Thus a special allocation of depreciation alone, with all other items being allocated according to a different consistent fraction, will not be recognized. However, partnership agreements often provide for different allocations of items at different times. For example, the agreement may provide that all items of income and deduction and all distributions will be allocated 80 percent to D and 20 percent to C until D has received distributions of $100,000, and thereafter all items and distributions will be allocated fifty-fifty (a so-called "flip-flop"). In this case depreciation may be allocated either equally or 80 percent to D and 20 percent to C, or anywhere in the range between those two allocations. In any case, C and D must be allocated the proper amount of minimum gain chargeback. Note that an allocation of minimum gain chargeback alone is not another significant item with substantial economic effect.

Assume, then that the agreement allocates the depreciation 80 percent to D and 20 percent to C. At the end of the third year, D has a deficit in his capital account of $40,000, and C has a deficit of $10,000. If the property were deeded to the lender in lieu of foreclosure of the mortgage on the first day of year four, the partnership would recognize a gain of $50,000—the "minimum gain," which would be allocated $40,000 to D and $10,000 to C, thereby restoring their respective capital accounts to a zero balance.

A minimum gain chargeback must occur not only when the property is sold, but anytime that there is a decrease in partnership minimum gain. Thus, loan principal amortization requires that income be allocated to the partners in the same ratio as the special allocation of depreciation. For example, suppose that CD did not sell the property at the beginning of year four, but continued to hold the property and paid $100,000 of principal on the first day of year six. At that time the basis of the property would be $750,000. Reduction of the loan principal from $900,000 to $800,000 reduces partnership minimum gain from 150,000 to $50,000, and assuming that the partnership has at least $100,000 of taxable income, that amount must be allocated among C and D in the same ratio that nonrecourse depreciation deductions previously had been specially allocated. Thus if in years three through five, D had been allocated $120,000 of depreciation and C had been allocated $30,000 of depreciation, D must be allocated $80,000 of the income, and C must be allocated $20,000. Note that the depreciation allocated in the first two years which had actual substantial economic effect is not considered in allocating the minimum gain chargeback.

Despite the fact that nonrecourse depreciation deductions never can have any substantial economic effect because they cannot affect the actual dollar amounts received by any partner, the Regulations allow them to be allocated among the partners as long as the corresponding income items are allocated in the same manner. Through the minimum gain chargeback provision, the regulations assure that allocations of nonrecourse depreciation ultimately will be entirely offset by future income allocations. This system is justifiable because otherwise there would be no way to allocate such deductions to *any* partner, even though the deductions must be taken into account in computing partnership taxable income. The requirement that allocations of nonrecourse deductions be reasonably consistent with allocations having substantial economic effect of some other significant partnership item attributable to the secured property is designed to prevent abusive special allocations designed to specially allocate deductions (but not income) to one or more partners when the minimum gain which will eventually offset those deductions is not expected to be realized until many years in the future.

For special rules governing the allocation of deductions attributable to debt which is nonrecourse as to the partnership but for which a partner bears the economic risk of loss, see Temporary Regulations, section 1.704–1T(b)(4)(iv)(*h*).

C. JUDICIAL INTERPRETATION OF SECTION 704(b)

Ogden v. Commissioner, 84 T.C. 871 (1985), aff'd per curiam, 788 F.2d 252 (5th Cir.1986), applied current section 704(b) before the Regulations were promulgated. Using the capital account analysis approved in *Orrisch,* the court invalidated the special allocations. The taxpayer had argued that capital account analysis should not apply in two situations: where allocations are proportionate to the partners' capital interests at the end of the partnership year (but before the allocation is made); and where the partnership contains a gain chargeback provision. The Tax Court rejected the taxpayer's first argument because allocations proportionate to year-end capital accounts fail to take into account partners' varying interests during the year, as is required by section 706(c)(2)(B), discussed infra, page 134. Turning to the second argument, the court found, as in *Orrisch,* that the gain chargeback was not sufficient to save the allocation because there was no evidence that partners would be required to restore capital account deficits, and thus, upon liquidation the partnership's assets would not be distributed according to the capital accounts.

In Elrod v. Commissioner, 87 T.C. 1046 (1986), a special bottom line allocation of 25 percent of partnership gains to a partner with a 5 percent share of partnership losses was partially recognized. Losses were charged to capital accounts and distributions in liquidation of the partnership would be in accordance with capital accounts, but the partner was not required to restore any deficit in his capital account. Accordingly, the loss allocation was recognized only to the extent that it did not create a capital account deficit; for years in which the taxpayer maintained a positive capital account, the allocation was recognized in full. Because *Elrod* involved years before the publication of the section 704 Regulations, the court did not apply the Regulations. Rather, it applied the judicially developed capital account analysis, which the Regulations expressly permit to be applied to validate allocations for partnership years beginning before May 1, 1986 or before January 1, 1987 in the case of allocations of nonrecourse deductions. See Regulations, section 1.704–1(b)(1)(ii). The court noted that it was "unclear" whether the same result would be reached under the Regulations. Nothing in stated facts of the published opinion, however, indicates that the same result would not be reached under the Regulations.

In Gershkowitz v. Commissioner, 88 T.C. 984 (1987), the Tax Court again applied the judicial capital account analysis for substantial economic effect, but its reasoning illustrated the close relationship of that analysis to the tests of the Regulations. In that case the partnership agreement was amended in December, 1977 to provide that for all transactions on or after January 1, 1977, net profits and losses from capital transactions would first be allocated among the partners to eliminate any deficits in their capital accounts, and after such deficits were eliminated, 95 percent of profits would be allocated to the limited partners relative to their contributions and 5 percent would be allocated to the general partner. Prior to the amendment the partnership agreement provided that all gains and losses were to be allocated 95 percent to the limited partners in proportion to their capital contributions and 5 percent to the general partner, until all limited partners had received distributions equal to his capital contribution, and thereafter among all partners relative to their capital contributions. At the time the partnership agreement was amended, the partnership was insolvent, had ceased to conduct business, was in the process of liquidation, and during 1977 had realized discharge of indebtedness income under section 61(a)(12) and gain from the transfer of property subject to nonrecourse mortgages in excess of adjusted basis. All of the partners had negative capital account balances, and the purpose of the special allocation was to bring all partners' capital accounts to a zero balance. The Commissioner asserted that the allocations lacked substantial economic effect because their sole purpose was to limit the tax liability of the partners. The taxpayer asserted that the allocations should be recognized because they were designed to leave each partner with a capital account of zero, which accurately reflected the economic status of the partnership at the time of liquidation. After first noting that "the purpose underlying the 1976 amendments to section 704(b) was to permit partnerships to use special allocations for bona fide business purposes, but not for tax avoidance purposes," the Tax Court concluded that the effect of the special allocation was to defeat the requirement in Regulations, section 1.704–1(b)(2)(ii)(*b*)(*2*), that liquidating distributions be made in accordance with capital accounts. Accordingly, without any more detailed explanation of its reasoning, it invalidated the allocations.

The Commissioner's argument in *Gershkowitz* that the allocation should be disregarded because it had a tax avoidance purpose and the court's recitation that the purpose of the 1976 amendment to section 704(b) was to permit partnerships to use special allocations for bona fide business purposes, but not for tax avoidance purposes, raises the question of whether an allocation which meets the mechanical tests of the Regulations may be invalidated if it has a tax avoidance purpose. Judicial interpretation of the pre–1976 version of section 704(b), which disallowed allocations if the principal purpose was tax avoidance or evasion focused primarily on the substantial economic effect test, but sometimes the partners' tax avoidance motives were considered as well. See Goldfine v. Commissioner, 80 T.C. 843 (1983). The statutory stress of section 704(b) after the 1976 amendment, however, is on an objective economic test for determining the validity of partnership allocations. But the Senate Finance Committee Report states that the intent of the 1976 version of section 704(b) is "to prevent the use of special allocations for tax avoidance purposes while allowing their use for bona fide business purposes." Arguably, this leaves room to consider the partners' purpose for the allocation. Nevertheless neither the Committee Report nor the *Gershkowitz* opinion should be read to stand for the proposition that an allocation which has substantial economic effect under the regulations will be invalidated if it has a tax avoidance purpose. Any allocation that meets the mechanical tests of the Regulations must accurately reflect the economic gain or loss realized by the partners. No more accurate alternative allocation which will more accurately reflect the economic results is available.

Close examination of the facts in *Gershkowitz* reveals that on its particular facts, involving an amended allocation, the result was correct, even without resort to the purpose for the allocation. Superficially, it appears that since all of the partnership's income from the year in question was from discharge of indebtedness and gain from the transfer of mortgaged property, the partnership was, in effect, applying the "gain chargeback" concept of Regulations, section 1.704–1(b)(4)(iv)(*e*), to bring all partners' capital accounts to zero.

But because gain was allocated under the amended agreement using a formula which did not correlate the gain allocated to a particular partner with the deductions previously allocated to that partner, this was not a true gain chargeback. Since *Gershkowitz* involved nonrecourse debt, which could not have had any *real* economic effect, the allocation could be treated as having economic effect only if it matched the gain realized by each partner with prior deductions allocated to that partner. The effect of the amended allocation, however, was to defeat that matching.

D. FAMILY PARTNERSHIPS

1. *General*

Allocations of partnership items in partnerships in which the partners are family members present additional problems that are not present when the partnership allocations are bargained at arms' length. In so-called family partnerships, allocations may reflect an attempt to shift income for tax purposes in a manner inconsistent with the principles of Lucas v. Earl, 281 U.S. 111 (1930), and Helvering v. Horst, 311 U.S. 112 (1940). The principal problems involved partnerships where one (or more) partner's capital interest was derived by gift from a family member partner and partnerships in which personal services were important but one or more partners did not provide any significant services.

The landmark case dealing with family partnerships is Commissioner v. Culbertson, 337 U.S. 733 (1949). That case involved a ranching partnership composed of a father and four sons, two of whom were minors. The sons had received their interests partly by gift from the father and partly by contribution of funds loaned to them by the father, which were repaid from the proceeds of partnership operations. The Court articulated the relevant test as follows:

"The Tax Court read our decisions in Commissioner v. Tower, (327 U.S. 280), and Lusthaus v. Commissioner, (327 U.S. 29), as setting out two essential tests of partnership for income-tax purposes: that each partner contribute to the partnership either vital services or capital originating with him. Its decision was based upon a finding that none of respondent's sons had satisfied those requirements during the tax years in question. * * *

"The question is not whether the services or capital contributed by a partner are of sufficient importance to meet some objective standard supposedly established by the *Tower* case, but whether, considering all the facts the agreement, the conduct of the parties in execution of its provisions, their statements, the testimony of disinterested persons, the relationship of the parties, their respective abilities and capital contribution, the actual control of income and the purposes for which it is used, and any other facts throwing light on their true intent–the parties in good faith and acting with a business purpose intended to join together in the present conduct of the enterprise. There is nothing new or particularly difficult about such a test. Triers of fact are constantly called upon to determine the intent with which a person acted. * * *

"Unquestionably a court's determination that the services contributed by a partner are not 'vital' and that he has not participated in 'management and control of the business' or contributed 'original capital' has the effect of placing a heavy burden on the taxpayer to show the bona fide intent of the parties to join together as partners. But such a determination is not conclusive, * * * ". (737, 742–44).

Two years after the *Culbertson* decision, Congress enacted the predecessor of section 704(e).

This section provides that a donee of a partnership interest is to be treated as the owner of the interest unless the facts and circumstances attending the gift, including the conduct of partnership affairs before and after the transfer, indicate that the purported gift was a sham or that the donor retained so many incidents of control that he would be treated as the owner of the interest under Helvering v. Clifford, 309 U.S. 331 (1940). Powers retained by the donor in his capacity as managing partner, however, do not generally indicate lack of true ownership in the transferee. Retained powers are closely scrutinized, and a power exercisable for the benefit of the donee partner (such as a power exercisable as a custodian under the Uniform Gifts to Minors Act) is distinguishable from a power vested in the transferor for his own benefit.

Because section 704(e) recognizes the donee of a partnership interest as the true owner of the interest, it incorporates express rules to prevent the deflection to the donee of partnership income in excess of the share properly attributable to his capital interest. Partnership allocations under section 704(a) which do not take into account a proper allowance for services rendered to the partnership are not respected. Similarly, if the partnership agreement provides for partnership allocations disproportionate to the partners' capital interests, section 704(e) reallocates partnership income in proportion to partnership capital. See S.Rep. No. 82–81, 82d Cong., 1st Sess. (1951).

The incentive to engage in the income-shifting activities to which section 704(e) was directed was greatly reduced by the adoption in 1986 of generally flat rates of tax and the enactment of the so-called "kiddie tax" in section 1(i) where minor children are involved.

2. *Relationship of Section 704(e) and Culbertson*

Section 704(e) applies only when a partnership interest is acquired by gift or in a transfer between family members, see section 704(e)(2), (3), *and* capital is a material income producing factor in the partnership. See Regulations, section 1.704–1(e)(4), for the application of section 704(e) to purchased partnership interests. Carriage Square, Inc. v. Commissioner, 69 T.C. 119 (1977), held that capital was not a material income producing factor and section 704(e) did not apply where the partners contributed only de minimis capital and the balance of the partnership's income producing capital was borrowed on the strength of corporate general partner's credit.

If the partnership is a service partnership, the *Culbertson* test is still determinative as to whether the partnership will be recognized. See Poggetto v. United States, 306 F.2d 76 (9th Cir.1962); Payton v. United States, 425 F.2d 1324 (5th Cir.1970). In such cases a putative partnership in which one family member fails to perform services generally will fail the *Culbertson* test. Id.

3. *Application of Section 704(e) Where Partners Perform Services*

Even where capital is a material income producing factor and section 704(e) applies, due regard must be given to the performance of services by the partners in allocating partnership income. Section 704(e)(2) provides that distributive shares that do not make an "allowance of reasonable compensation for services rendered to the partnership by the donor" will not be respected. Regulations, section 1.704–1(e)(3), extend the reasonable allowance for services concept to take services performed by the donee into account in determining the donor's distributive share. See Woodbury v. Commissioner, 49 T.C. 180 (1967), in which an allowance was made for the services of both the donor and donee partners.

4. *Restrictions on Donees's Control*

Regulations, section 1.704–1(e)(2), set forth a number of factors to be taken into account in determining whether the donee actually has acquired ownership of a partnership interest. More stringent standards are applied when a partnership interest is held by a trustee or a minor child, and when the donated interest is a limited partnership interest. See Virgil v. Commissioner, 47 T.C.M. 692 (1983) (failure to appoint trustees or guardians for minor children who were donee partners resulted in taxation of their distributive share to donor parent).

Cirelli v. Commissioner, 82 T.C. 335 (1984), involved a partnership in which five children (four of whom were minors) were equal partners in an equipment leasing partnership. The children contributed no capital and performed no services. The partnership leased property only to a corporation controlled by the children's father, and financed its purchases through loans from the father or rental receipts. The father in fact had total control over the partnership's affairs. Even though section 704(e) was not directly applicable, the Tax Court applied the factors enumerated in Regulations, section 1.704–1(e)(2), to determine that purported partnership was a sham.

5. *Reference*

Banoff, Long, Steele and Smith, Family Partnerships: Capital As a Material Income–Producing Factor, 37 Tax Lawyer 275 (1984).

E. REFERENCES

Marich, Substantial Economic Effect and the Value Equals Basis Conundrum, 42 Tax L.Rev. 509 (1987); Close & Kusnetz, The Final Section 704(b) Regulations: Special Allocations Reach New Heights of Complexity, 40 Tax Lawyer 307 (1987); Gunn, The Character of a Partner's Distributive Share Under the "Substantial Economic Effect" Regulations, 40 Tax Lawyer 121 (1986); Lokken, Partnership Allocations, 41 Tax L.Rev. 545 (1986); Weidner, Partnership Allocations and Capital Accounts Analysis, 42 Ohio St. L.J. 467 (1981); McKee, Partnership Allocations: The Need for an Entity Approach, 66 Va.L.Rev. 1039 (1980).

C. ALLOCATIONS WITH RESPECT TO CONTRIBUTED PROPERTY

INTERNAL REVENUE CODE: Section 704(c)(1).

REGULATIONS: Section 1.704–1(c).

Assume that A and B form a partnership in which they will share profits and losses equally. A contributes property with a basis of $400

and a value of $1,000, and B contributes $1,000 cash. As between the partners each has contributed property of equal value and each has a capital account of $1,000. But from a tax standpoint, the low basis of A's property presents problems. This basis carries over to the partnership since gain or loss is not recognized on the formation of the partnership. Hence, if the property is later sold the partnership will have a tax gain of $600, though on the partnership's non-tax accounts no gain has resulted. How should the tax gain be allocated between the partners? If the property is not sold but is held by the partnership as depreciable property, the depreciation on the partnership books will differ from that allowable for tax purposes because, among other things, the depreciable cost will be $1,000 for book purposes, but the depreciable basis for tax purposes will be only $400. How should this disparity be handled?

These problems are addressed by section 704(c), which, as amended in 1984, is explained below.

GENERAL EXPLANATION OF THE TAX REFORM ACT OF 1984

Staff of the Joint Committee on Taxation, 211–215 (1984).

[Pre–1984] Law

Partnership allocations generally

Under [pre–1984] law, a partner's distributive share of partnership income, gain, loss, deduction, or credit (or items thereof) generally is governed by the partnership agreement. However, if the allocation provided for by the partnership agreement does not have substantial economic effect, these items are reallocated for tax purposes in accordance with the partner's interest in the partnership, determined by taking into account all facts and circumstances. Proposed Treasury regulations provide that, in general, an allocation has economic effect (whether or not substantial) if (1) the allocation is reflected by an appropriate increase or decrease in the partner's capital account, (2) liquidation proceeds (if any) are to be distributed in accordance with the partners' capital account balances, and (3) any partner with a deficit in his capital account following the distribution of liquidation proceeds is required to restore the amount of such deficit to the partnership. The economic effect of the allocation must be substantial in relation to the tax effect for the allocation provided for in the agreement to have substantial economic effect.

Property contributed to a partnership

Under [pre–1984] law (sec. 704(c)(2)), when property was contributed to a partnership, the partnership could (but was not required to) allocate depreciation, depletion, or gain or loss with respect to the contributed property so as to take account of the variation between the basis of the property to the partnership and its fair market value at the time of contribution. If the partnership did not make allocations on this basis, the allocations were made as if the property had been purchased by the partnership.

Under [pre–1984] law, a shifting of income or losses among partners that did not reflect the economic burdens borne by the parties could occur if a partnership did not elect to allocate depreciation, depletion, and gain or loss with respect to contributed property so as to take account of the variation between the basis and the fair market value of the contributed property. For example, assume that partner A contributed property with a basis of $200 and a value of $100 while partner B contributed $100 in cash to a partnership, and the initial capital accounts of the partners were each set at $100 (the fair market value of their contributions). Under the general rule, it was thought that a subsequent sale of the property for $100 would result in an allocation of $50 of loss to each partner, thereby shifting $50 of loss from A to B. This shifting of the loss could remain effective so long as the partnership remained in existence, although the pre-contribution loss would be effectively reallocated to the contributing partner if his interest in the partnership were liquidated or sold. Generally, it was thought that a similar shifting of gain could be accomplished in the case of a contribution of appreciated property to a partnership.

Reasons for Change

Although Congress believed that the underlying theory of the present law partnership provisions, that taxpayers should be able to pool their resources for productive uses without triggering taxable gain or loss, is appropriate, it also believed that special rules were needed to prevent an artificial shifting of tax consequences between partners with respect to pre-contribution gain or loss. This is particularly important since the various partners may have different tax positions. For example, a partner to whom gain could have been shifted in the absence of the Act's provisions could be tax-exempt, could have a lower marginal rate than the contributing partner, or could have an expiring net operating loss carryover.

Congress was also concerned that the transfer to a partnership of accounts receivable, accounts payable, or other accrued but unpaid items of a partner who uses the cash method of accounting should not result in effectively transferring some or all of the transferor partner's tax benefits or burdens (attributable to the future deduction or income) to other partners.

In addition to the cases described above, Congress was aware of the similar situation which exists when cash is contributed to an ongoing partnership which has property with a value greater than, or less than, its adjusted basis in the hands of the partnership. However, Congress did not provide a new rule in this case because it believed that this issue may have been adequately dealt with in proposed Treas.Reg. section 1.704–1(b)(4)(i) (concerning allocations when there are disparities between tax and book capital accounts).

Explanation of Provision

* * *

Contributed property

The Act replaces the [pre–1984] law elective treatment of allocations with respect to contributed property with a new rule under which items of income, gain, loss, and deduction with respect to contributed property are to be shared among the partners, under Treasury regulations, so as to take account of the difference between the partnership's basis for the property and the fair market value of the property at the time of the contribution. Although Congress intended that partnerships could continue to rely on the regulations issued under former section 704(c)(2) until new regulations are provided, Congress provided authority to modify significantly those rules.[3]

Under the provision, a partnership is generally required, rather than being permitted (as under prior law), to allocate "built-in" gain or loss on contributed property to the contributing partner. In determining the amount of built-in gain or loss, the fair market value of contributed property generally is to be determined by reference to the arm's-length dealings of the various partners as reflected in their capital accounts (if the parties have sufficiently adverse interests). This determination normally will not be upset by the Treasury except in cases of manipulation or abuse. It is anticipated that the regulations may require a partnership to file a statement of the agreed fair market value of contributed property with the partnership return for the year in which the contribution is made.

It was anticipated that Treasury regulations may permit partners to agree to a more rapid elimination of disparities between the value and adjusted basis of contributed property (determined at the time of contribution) among partners than is required by the new rules, by substituting items not described in section 704(c) for items described in section 704(c) and vice versa, provided that there is no tax avoidance potential.[4] Similarly, to limit the burden of recordkeeping requirements for small operating partnerships, if no tax avoidance potential exists, the regulations may permit (1) aggregation of properties with fair market values greater than their respective adjusted basis that are contributed by a single partner; (2) aggregation of properties with fair market values less than their respective adjusted basis that are contributed by a single partner; (3) differences of less than 15 percent (but not

3. With respect to contributions made before the regulations are proposed, Congress expected that the regulations will provide specifically that the partnership has complied with the requirements of this mandatory allocation if allocations with respect to contributed property were made in accordance with the regulations under section 704(c)(2) of prior law.

4. In addition, it may be appropriate to amend example (2) of Treas.Reg. section 1.704–1(c)(2) to provide that if the property there is sold for a price exceeding $9,000, the taxable gain represented by the first $200 of such excess would be allocated to partner C. This would allow the effect of the ceiling rule limitations to be offset by subsequent gain allocations.

exceeding $10,000) between the adjusted basis and the fair market value of any aggregated properties to be accounted for in a manner consistent with section 704(c)(1) as it existed under prior law; and (4) differences between the adjusted basis and the fair market value of contributed properties to be eliminated more slowly than required by the new rules through allocations solely of gain or loss on the disposition of such properties (i.e., permitting allocations of depreciation, depletion, or similar items with respect to such property, to be governed solely by section 704(b)), provided that this flexibility is not likely to result in the contributing partner avoiding the effect of the allocation of built-in gain or loss (such as when the property is expected to be held by the partnership until it has little, if any, fair market value).

The examples above were intended by Congress to be illustrative of, rather than a limitation on, the Treasury's authority to provide reasonable rules as long as no abuse potential is present. Thus, although partnerships may continue to rely on the regulations issued under [pre–1984] law section 704(c)(2) until new regulations are proposed, the Treasury Department has the authority to modify or expand those rules significantly. These modified regulations may take into account situations not addressed by the [pre–1984] law rules, including those involving contributions of (1) more than one item of property with built-in gain or loss by a single partner (as described above), (2) properties with built-in gain or loss by more than one partner, (3) property with built-in gain that would constitute ordinary income under the various recapture provisions, (4) property which is disposed of by the partnership in exchange for "substituted basis" property as defined in new section 7701(a)(42), (5) property when there are disproportionate profit and loss sharing arrangements contained in the partnership agreement, and (6) property which is not disposed of prior to the contributing partner's disposition of his partnership interest.

Under [pre–1984] law, an election could be made to allocate depreciation or depletion with respect to contributed property so as to reflect any amount of built-in gain or loss on the contributed property. For example, if in a 50–50 partnership, A contributed property with a fair market value of $100 and a basis of $50 to a partnership and B contributed $100 cash which was used to purchase a depreciable asset, the regulations under prior law permitted AB to elect to allocate depreciation of the $50 basis to B. Such an allocation would be sensible from the viewpoint of A and B. First, if the contributed property will, in fact be exhausted, the allocation is the only mechanism available to compensate B for the fact that he had to contribute value by reference to the property's fair market value rather than its basis. Secondly, the aggregate amount of basis invested in the partnership is $150 ($100 cash plus $50 basis). If depreciation with respect to the purchased property is shared equally ($50 and $50), then A will recover his original contributed basis even with the allocation of depreciation on the contributed property to B. Thus, the allocation of depreciation or depletion was, under prior law, simply one way of eliminating the difference between the value and basis of contributed property. Congress intended that the regulatory authority granted to the Treasury would be construed broadly enough to give the Treasury discretion to permit mandatory allocations of depreciation and depletion when necessary to eliminate a built-in gain or loss, and to permit allocation solely of gain or loss when foregoing an allocation of depletion or depreciation does not create significant avoidance potential.

* * *

Accrued but unpaid cash items

The Act authorizes the Treasury to provide for mandatory allocations of items of income and deduction, as well as gain or loss, with respect to contributed property and authorizes the Treasury to prescribe similar rules when a partner using the cash receipts and disbursements method of accounting transfers accounts payable or other accrued but unpaid liabilities to a partnership. By referring to items of income and deduction, it was not intended that Treasury regulations require variations between the basis and fair market value of contributed property to be eliminated by allocations of operating income and loss attributable to the property (other than depreciation, depletion, and similar items). Rather, this expansion of the scope of section 704(c) was intended primarily to address situations in which a cash method partner contributes accounts receivable, accounts payable, or other accrued but unpaid items to a partnership. Thus, for example, if a cash-method taxpayer contributes accounts payable to a partnership, the deductions attributable to those items generally are allocated, if possible, to the contributing partner and, if not, are capitalized (see the discussion of retroactive allocations below). Congress intended that, parallel to the amendments recently made to section 357(c) (and contrary to Rev.Rul. 60–345, 1960–2 C.B. 211), these accrued but unpaid items will not be treated as partnership liabilities for purposes of section 752. Congress expected that the Treasury Department will provide regulations which reach a consistent result in situations in which the partnership is on the accrual method of accounting. These changes, and the changes contained in new section 724 (regarding character of gain or loss on disposition of certain contributed property), were not intended to override the anticipatory assignment of income doctrine in those situations in which such doctrine would apply to a cash-method partner's contribution of accrued but unpaid items to a partnership (see, e.g., Rev.Rul. 80–198, 1980–2 C.B. 113 and Rev.Rul. 80–199, 1980–2 C.B. 122, and the cases cited therein). These changes complement, and are consistent with, the modifications to the retroactive allocation provisions adopted by Congress which prevent a cash-method partnership from shifting its accrued deductions to partners who are admitted to the partnership after such deductions are accrued.

ILLUSTRATIVE MATERIAL

A. ALLOCATION OF GAIN AND LOSS

Reconsider the example, supra, page 113. If the AB partnership sells the contributed property for $1,000, under section 704(c) the $600 gain recognized by the partnership must be allocated entirely to A, even though that gain is not added to A's capital account. This rule does not conflict with the requirement of section 704(b) that an allocation have substantial economic effect to be recognized because the pre-contribution appreciation is already reflected in capital accounts under Regulations, section 1.704–1(b)(2)(iv)(*d*). See also Regulations, section 1.704–1(b)(2)(iv)(*g*). Suppose the partnership sold the property for $1,200, realizing an $800 gain. Section 704(c) requires that $600 of gain be allocated to A, while the balance of the $200 gain is allocated under section 704(a), subject to the substantial economic effect rules of section 704(b). Since A and B are equal partners, $100 of the remaining gain is allocated to each of A and B. Thus A is allocated $700 of gain and B $100. For book purposes, however, the partnership realized a gain of only $200, which is allocated equally between A and B.

B. DEPRECIABLE PROPERTY

Allocations of depreciation and of gain or loss on depreciable property under the principles of section 704(c) are more complex. Perhaps that is why Congress authorized the Treasury to promulgate Regulations liberalizing the application of section 704(c) to depreciation. In the absence of regulations specifying when section 704(c) does not apply to depreciation deductions, however, there is no basis for computing depreciation deductions without regard to section 704(c), even though the computations may be burdensome.

Suppose that C and D form a partnership to which C contributes $1,000 cash and D contributes depreciable property with a basis of $600 and a fair market value of $1,000. Each partner has a fifty percent interest in partnership capital and profits. Assume, for simplicity, that the property has a five-year cost recovery period for tax purposes and an identical useful life for book depreciation, and in both cases the cost is recoverable using the straight line method. (Tax depreciation and book depreciation generally must be computed using the same methods in order to maintain capital accounts in the required manner. See Regulations, section 1.704–1(b)(2)(iv)(*g*)(*3*).) Tax depreciation would be $120 per year and book depreciation would be $200 per year. Applying Regulations, section 1.704–1(c)(2) Ex. (1), $100 of the tax depreciation should be allocated to C, who contributed the cash. In effect, C purchased a one-half interest in the asset for $500; since the property has a five year life, using the straight line method, C should be entitled to $100 of depreciation per year. The additional $20 of tax depreciation is allocated to D. C and D each have $100 of book depreciation. This approach to allocating depreciation deductions between the partners gives C, the partner contributing cash to the partnership, the tax benefits of acquiring by purchase an interest in the property contributed by D, while preserving for D the nonrecognition treatment accorded by section 721. As discussed below, however, there are limitations on the extent to which section 704(c) accords to a partner contributing cash to the partnership the tax benefits usually obtained by purchasing assets directly. This occurs when the partnership's basis in the property under section 722 is less than the hypothetical purchase price paid by the cash partner for his interest in the partnership property.

Section 704(c) applies to the allocation of depreciation deductions not only when one partner contributes cash and the other property, but also when both contribute property. Assume that E and F form a partnership in which each partner has a fifty percent interest in partnership profits and capital. E contributes depreciable property # 1 with a basis of $750 and a fair market value of $1,000. The property has a remaining cost recovery period of five years and is depreciated under the straight line method. F contributes depreciable property # 2 with a basis of $1,500 and a fair market value of $1,000. The property has a remaining cost recovery period of ten years and is depreciated using the straight line method. The tax depreciation of $150 on property # 1 is allocated $50 to E and $100 to F. The tax depreciation of $150 on property # 2 is allocated $50 to E and $100 to F. The total book depreciation of $250 is allocated equally between E and F.

Suppose that after the CD Partnership in the earlier example held the property for two years and claimed $240 of tax depreciation deductions, which reduced the tax basis of the property to $360 and $400 of book depreciation, which reduced the book basis to $600, the partnership sold the property for $900, recognizing a $540 gain for tax purposes and a $300 gain for book purposes. How should this gain be allocated between C and D? Regulations, section 1.704–1(c)(2)(i), Ex. (2), promulgated under the prior version of section 704(c), indicate that to the extent of taxable gain in excess of book gain, the gain is allocated to the contributing partner. The tax gain equal to the book gain is allocated according to the partnership agreement, subject to section 704(b). Thus, the $240 of tax gain ($540) in excess of book gain ($300) would be allocated to D; the remaining tax gain would be allocated equally, $150 to each partner. D recognizes total gain of $390 and C recognizes total gain of $150. Each partner's capital account should be increased by $150. The capital accounts of C and D thus are $950 each and their respective bases in their partnership interests are also $950. Note that if there is a loss for book purposes but a gain for tax purposes, the entire gain is allocated to the contributing partner.

C. THE CEILING LIMITATION

Suppose that the property in the AB partnership example above were sold by the partnership for $800. For tax purposes, the gain recognized is $400, but for partnership book purposes, there is a $200 loss. Theoretically, A should be allocated $600 of gain and A and B should each be allocated $100 of loss. But Regulations, section 1.704–1(c)(2)(i), prohibit any partner from being allocated gain greater than the gain actually recognized by the partnership, the so-called "ceiling" on gain which may be allocated. See Regulations, sections 1.704–1(c)(2)(i); 1.704–1(b)(5), Ex. (18)(v). Therefore, A may not be allocated $500 of net gain, offset by a $100 loss allocated to B. Instead A may be allocated only $400 of gain. This result is not consistent with economic reality. It has been suggested that Regulations should be promulgated under section 704(c) to allow the partnership in such a case to allocate specially to A $100 of gain from sales of other property, without following the capital account maintenance rules of Section 704(b), so as to eliminate the disparity between the partnership tax and book capital accounts. See Marich and McKee, Sections 704(c) and 743(b): The Shortcomings of Existing Regulations and the Problems of Publicly Traded Partnerships, 41 Tax Law Rev. 627 (1986).

The ceiling rule also presents problems with respect to the allocation of depreciation under section 704(c). Suppose that the property contributed by D in the CD Partnership example above had a basis of only $400. In that case tax depreciation would be only $80 per year, but C's share of book depreciation would be $100 per year. It is impossible, however, to allocate to C under section 704(c) more than the partnership's $80 of tax depreciation. Regulations, section 1.704–1(c)(2)(i), Ex. (1). A theoretically proper result would be to allocate $100 of depreciation to C and require D to recognize $20 of income per year, in addition to his distributive share of partnership income with respect to all other items.

This latter approach, which eliminates the problems inherent in the ceiling rule, is called the "deferred sale" approach. It is applicable, as well, upon the sale by the partnership of contributed property. Recall the example in which the AB partnership sold contributed property with a basis of $400 and a book value of $1,000 for $800. Section 704(c) allocates the entire $400 taxable gain to A, when in economic reality he should have a $500 gain. The deferred sale approach achieves this result by allocating a $600 gain to A and a $100 loss each to A and B.

While the current effects of the ceiling rule approach and the deferred sale approach differ, when the current effects are balanced with the results upon liquidation, the overall amount of gain or loss recognized by each partner will be identical. Under the deferred sale approach, the partner who contributed the low basis-high value asset would include year by year a part of the pre-contribution appreciation in his income as the asset depreciated, or would include the amount of pre-contribution appreciation when the asset was sold. Consequently, on liquidation he would not have any remaining pre-contribution gain to account for with respect to the asset. The other partner, as under current law, would not be taxed on this pre-contribution appreciation when the asset was sold, but unlike current law always would have the benefit of its full value at contribution to compute his annual depreciation. Under the current section 704(c) rules, when the ceiling rule applies, the partner contributing low basis property recognizes less current gain, while the other partner is entitled to less depreciation (or no loss on a sale). However, because of the effect of basis adjustments under section 705, the contributing partner recognizes a pro tanto greater gain (or smaller loss) on final liquidation, while the other partner has a smaller gain (or greater loss). There are two additional differences. First, the character of the gain or loss may be transmuted from ordinary to capital under the current approach, while the deferred sale approach does not permit this result. Second, if the partners receive property other than cash in liquidation, recognition of gain or loss may be further postponed. See section 731(a), discussed infra, page 223. These problems could be cured by requiring in such a case that the partnership allocate specially to the partner who contributed the low basis-high value asset gain from sales of other ordinary income property, without following the capital account maintenance rules of section 704(b), so as to eliminate the disparity between the partnership tax and book capital accounts. See Marich and McKee, Sections 704(c) and 743(b): The Shortcomings of Existing Regulations and the Problems of Publicly Traded Partnerships, 41 Tax Law Rev. 627 (1986).

D. CONTRIBUTIONS TO PARTNERSHIP POSSESSING APPRECIATED OR DEPRECIATED PROPERTY

The same problem as is dealt with by section 704(c) arises when a new partner contributes cash to enter an existing partnership that holds appreciated or depreciated property. Suppose that E contributes $150 cash to partnership FG, which owns property having a basis of $180 and a fair market value of $300, to become a one-third partner. E has in effect paid $100 for a one-third interest in the property and should not recognize any gain if it were sold for $300; all of the gain should be recognizable by E and F. Section 704(c) does not expressly apply to this situation, but Regulations, sections 1.704–1(b)(2)(iv)(f) and 1.704–1(b)(4)(i), require the application of section 704(c) principles in allocating tax items whenever the partnership property is revalued and existing partnership capital accounts adjusted in connection with the admission of a new partner. See Regulations, section 1.704–1(b)(5), Ex. (14)(i)–(ii). (See also Regulations, section 1.704–1(b)(5), Ex. (18), applying these principles to depreciation.) The same result may be achieved by a special allocation of gain to F and G without increasing their capital accounts at the time of E's admission. Regulations, section 1.704–1(b)(5), Ex. (14)(iv). If neither of these alternatives is utilized by the partnership, the result will be that E will be allocated gain of $40 when the property is sold for $300 and his capital account will be increased by the same amount, even though based on the economics of the transaction his share of both should have been zero. In this circumstance, Regulations, section 1.704–1(b)(1)(iii), authorize the recharacterization of the transaction under other provisions of the Code. For example, the amount allocated to E may constitute compensation.

E. DISTRIBUTIONS OF SECTION 704(c) PROPERTY

Section 704(c)(1)(B), added by the 1989 Act, requires the contributing partner to recognize gain or loss upon the distribution of property by the partnership to another partner within five years of the date the property was contributed to the partnership. This provision is discussed infra, page 219.

F. REFERENCES

Turlington, Section 704(c) and Partnership Book-Tax Disparities—The Ceiling Rule and the Art of Tax Avoidance, 46 N.Y.U. Tax Inst. 26–1 (1988); Jones and Jackson, How to Handle Property Contributions to a Partnership Under Mandatory Allocation, 64 J.Tax. 205 (1986).

D. EFFECT OF PARTNERSHIP INDEBTEDNESS ON PARTNERS' BASES IN PARTNERSHIP INTERESTS

INTERNAL REVENUE CODE: Sections 704(d); 705; 733; 752.

REGULATIONS: Sections 1.705–1.

TEMPORARY REGULATIONS: Section 1.752–1T.

Section 752(a) provides that any increase in a partner's share of partnership liabilities is treated as a cash contribution. Thus, an increase in a partner's share of partnership liabilities requires that his outside basis be increased pursuant to sections 705 and 722. A partner's outside basis is crucial to the conduit theory of partnership taxation because his outside basis is the ceiling on the amount of partnership losses that can be passed through to the partner's individual return. See section 704(d), discussed infra, page 140. If a partner's share of partnership liabilities decreases or his individual liabilities decrease as a result of assumption of those liabilities by the partnership, the amount by which such liabilities is decreased is treated by section 752(b) as a partnership distribution of cash. This deemed cash distribution reduces the partner's basis in his partnership interest pursuant to sections 705(a) and 733. To the extent that the deemed distribution exceeds outside basis gain is recognized. Section 731.

The Code provides no rules for determining a partner's share of partnership liabilities. Temporary Regulations, section 1.752–1T, provide the guiding principles. These rules are intended to treat as a partner's share of the partnership liabilities only that portion of those liabilities for which he bears the ultimate economic risk of loss. Thus, recourse and nonrecourse debts are treated differently.

Section 752 and the Regulations thereunder apply whenever the partnership borrows money or repays a loan. For example, if A and B form a general partnership to which each contributes $20,000 and the AB general partnership then borrows $100,000, A and B each increases her basis in the partnership by $50,000. If $20,000 of the loan subsequently is repaid, A and B each reduces her basis in the partnership by $10,000; and if either or both had a basis of less than $10,000 at that time, she recognizes gain. Because section 752 is Subchapter K's way of incorporating the principles of Crane v. Commissioner, 331 U.S. 1 (1947), and its progeny, section 752(c) applies the above rules to liabilities attached to property which are not assumed when the property is transferred subject to the liabilities. When the transfer is between the partnership and partners, liabilities to which the property is taken subject, but which are not assumed, are taken into account under sections 752(a) and (b) only to the extent of the fair market value of the property; but if the property is sold by the partnership, pursuant to section 752(d) liabilities in excess of the fair market value are taken into account as well. See Commissioner v. Tufts, 461 U.S. 300 (1983).

ILLUSTRATIVE MATERIAL

A. ALLOCATION OF RECOURSE LIABILITIES

1. *General*

A partner's share of any recourse liability is the portion of the economic risk of loss for the liability borne by the partner. Temporary Regulations, section 1.752–1T(a)(1)(i). Temporary Regulations, section 1.752–1T(d)(2), define a "recourse liability" as any liability "to the extent * * * that one or more partners bear the economic risk of loss * * * for such liability." See also Temporary Regulations, section 1.752–1T(a)(1). The term "liability" is defined for purposes of section 752 in Temporary Regulations, section 1.752–1T(g), as limited to debts that: (1) create or increase basis (including cash balances); (2) give rise to a deduction (e.g., accrual method accounts payable); or (3) give rise to a nondeductible expenditure not chargeable to a capital account (under section 263 or 263A). Thus cash method accounts payable are not liabilities for purposes of section 752 and do not increase the partners' bases in their partnership interests.

The economic risk of loss concept is capsulized in Temporary Regulations, section 1.752–1T(a)(1)(ii), and is defined in Temporary Regulations, section 1.752–1T(d)(3). Generally speaking, a partner's share of partnership recourse liabilities is the amount of the partnership's liabilities for which the partner bears the ultimate burden of payment if the partnership is unable to make the payment. This ultimate burden is determined by taking into account the net effect of: (1) partners' obligations to restore negative capital accounts; (2) partners' obligations to pay notes to the partnership executed by them; (3) partners' obligations to creditors under guarantee agreements; (4) partners' obligations to other partners under any agreement; (5) partners' rights to contribution or indemnification under the partnership agreement or any other agreement; and (6) rights of contribution or indemnification arising by operation of law (e.g., subrogation rights of a guarantor). See Temporary Regulations, section 1.752–1T(a)(1)(iii). In addition, Temporary Regulations, section 1.752–1T, treat an economic risk of loss borne by a person related to a partner as borne by the partner for purposes of allocating partnership debt among the partners. Related persons for this purpose are identified in Temporary Regulations, section 1.752–1T(h), through cross references to sections 267(b) and 707(b), with certain modifications.

2. *Economic Risk of Loss*

(a) *General*

Economic risk of loss, which is the linchpin for determining whether a debt is recourse or nonrecourse and for allocating recourse debt among partners, is defined in Temporary Regulations, section 1.752–1T(d)(3). The definition corresponds to the economic risk of loss rules under the section 704(b) regulations, supra, page 98. A partner bears the economic risk of loss with respect to a debt that is recourse to the partnership if upon a hypothetical liquidation of the partnership in which all of its assets are treated as worthless (as described in Temporary Regulations, section 1.752–1T(d)(3)(iii)), the partner would be required either: (1) to make a "net payment to a creditor or other person" with respect to the liability, or (2) to make a "net contribution to the partnership" with respect to the liability. A partner also bears the economic risk of loss with respect to a debt that is nonrecourse to the partnership if the partner or a related party (as defined in Temporary Regulations, section 1.752–1T(h)) is the creditor with respect to the nonrecourse liability. Temporary Regulations, section 1.752–1T(d)(3)(i). If the sum of the economic risk of loss of the partners exceeds the partnership's liabilities, then each partner's economic risk of loss is a pro rata share of the partnership liabilities (determined with reference to his proportionate share of the aggregate economic risk of loss). Temporary Regulations, section 1.752–1T(d)(3)(i), (k), Ex. (9)(iv).

Because the partners' risk of loss is determined largely by analyzing the amounts which the partners would be required to contribute to the partnership upon a hypothetical liquidation in which the partnership's assets are deemed to be worthless, and that required contribution is determined with reference to negative balances in partners' capital accounts, it cannot always be said that general partners share partnership recourse liabilities in the same proportion as they share partnership losses. For examples of situations in which recourse indebtedness of a general partnership is allocated unequally among equal general partners, see Temporary Regulations, section 1.752–1T(k), Ex. (12) and (13).

(b) *Constructive Liquidation of Partnership*

Temporary Regulations, section 1.752–1T(d)(3)(iii), prescribe the rules governing constructive liquidation analysis for determining partners' economic risk of loss. The following events are considered to happen in the constructive liquidation: (1) all of the partnership's assets (other than property contributed to the partnership solely for the purpose of securing a partnership obligation) become worthless; (2) all of the partnership's liabilities become due and payable in full; (3) the partnership transfers any property contributed to the partnership solely for the purpose of securing a partnership obligation to the creditor in partial or full satisfaction of the debt; (4) the partnership transfers its remaining assets for no consideration, except that property subject to nonrecourse mortgage liens is treated as transferred to the creditor in satisfaction of the debt; and (5) the partnership allocates all items of income, gain, deduction, loss, and credit among the partners as provided in the partnership agreement. For this purpose partnership assets do not include any obligations of partners (or related persons) to make contributions or payments to the partnership. (Thus, such obligations are not considered valueless). The constructive liquidation analysis will provide the final capital account balances, both positive and negative, of all partners, prior to any contributions required to wind up the partnership. Partners with a capital account of zero or more generally are not obligated to make any contribution to the partnership. Thus, they will not be allocated any share of partnership recourse liabilities unless they have an independent obligation to make a payment to a creditor or another party, including a partner. Partners having negative capital accounts will have an economic risk of loss and generally will be allocated an amount of partnership recourse liabilities equal to the negative capital account, unless they are entitled to reimbursement from a partner or other person. In addition, the constructive liquidation triggers deemed satisfaction of all obligations to make payments to creditors and reimbursements to other partners and persons related to other partners. The net effect of the constructive settlement of capital accounts and these other payments equals each partner's economic risk of loss.

(c) *Obligation to Make Net Contribution to Partnership*

Temporary Regulations, section 1.752–1T(d)(3)(ii)(B)(*3*), provide that a partner's required net contribution to the partnership in a constructive liquidation equals the aggregate amount that he would be required to contribute to the partnership, minus reimbursements that the partner is entitled to receive from other partners or persons as a result of making such contributions. As is the case with rights to reimbursement for payments to creditors, Temporary Regulations, section 1.752–1T(d)(3)(ii)(D)(*2*), deem all persons to be capable of making a reimbursement. Thus, the *right* to reimbursement controls, without regard to the actual financial condition of the obligor.

A partner's net contribution with respect to any particular liability is the total required net contribution multiplied by a fraction: the numerator is the outstanding liability of the partnership on the debt, and the denominator is the sum of all of the partners' obligations to the partnership. The Regulations provide rules for determining which partnership liabilities are taken into account in this above proration. Nonrecourse debts are not counted. Nor are any amounts treated as obligations of a partner to make payments to a creditor. Temporary Regulations, section 1.752–1T(d)(3)(ii)(B)(*1*).

A partner is treated as being required to contribute only those amounts: (1) represented by the partner's (or a related party's) promissory note to the partnership (other than a note readily tradable on an established market, which is treated as a property contribution); (2) due to the partnership under the partnership agreement or by operation of law (such as an obligation to restore a negative capital account balance); or (3) due to another partner to reimburse the other partner for making a contribution to the partnership under either of the first two categories. Temporary Regulations, section 1.752–1T(d)(3)(ii)(B)(*2*). An obligation to make a payment will be recognized only to the extent that the amount is determinable with reasonable certainty and is not subject to contingencies that would make it unlikely that it ever would be discharged. Temporary Regulations, section 1.752–1T(d)(3)(ii)(D).

If an obligation to make an additional contribution is not required to be satisfied by the end of the taxable year in which the partner's interest is liquidated (if there were to be such a liquidation) or, if later, 90 days after such liquidation, then the obligation will be taken into account only at its discounted value. Temporary Regulations, section 1.752–1T(d)(3)(ii)(E). If the obligation bears interest at the applicable Federal rate, its value is its face value. Otherwise, the imputed principal amount is determined under section 1274(b).

See also Temporary Regulations, section 1.752–1T(d)(3)(ii)(E)(*4*), governing satisfaction of an obligation with a promissory note, discussed infra, page 127.

(d) *Obligation to Make Net Payment to Creditor or Other Person*

A partner's obligation to pay a creditor or other person equals: (1) the payments that the partner or a related person would be obligated to make to creditors or other persons on a constructive liquidation minus (2) the reimbursement that the partner and any related persons are entitled to receive. Temporary Regulations, section 1.752–1T(d)(3)(ii)(A). Temporary Regulations, section 1.752–1T(d)(3)(ii)(D)(*2*), provide that all persons are deemed financially able to satisfy their obligations to pay or to reimburse any other person for a payment to any person. (As discussed above, for purposes of determining the economic risk of loss in a constructive liquidation, the partnership is deemed to be unable to make any payments to its creditors. Temporary Regulations, section 1.752–1T(d)(3)(iii).)

Payments which a partner would be obligated to make to creditors include payments to other partners or persons related to other partners, or to the partnership, pursuant to an obligation of the partner, related person, or partnership, under an agreement or under state law (other than an obligation to make additional contributions to the partnership) to reimburse such person or the partnership for payments to creditors, other persons, or contributions to the partnership. This category includes, for example, payments to reimburse another partner for paying more than his share of partnership debts, or payments pursuant to an agreement by one partner to indemnify another partner against loss. (However, payments to another partner to reimburse the other partner for making a contribution to the partnership, as distinguished from a payment directly to a creditor or other person, are treated under the rules governing additional contributions to the partnership, discussed above.) If a partner guarantees a partnership obligation, but is subrogated to the creditor's rights against the partnership if he pays the obligation, the right of reimbursement under the subrogation rights partially or entirely offsets the obligation on the guarantee depending on the nature of the partnership. For example, if a limited partner guarantees a partnership recourse debt and is required to pay the debt, she acquires a right under state law to be reimbursed by the partnership, i.e., by the general partner. Thus, the guarantor limited partner does not bear the economic risk of loss. See Temporary Regulations, section 1.752–1T(k), Ex. (4). Accordingly, the guarantor partner does not increase her outside basis as a result of the guarantee and the other partners' bases remain unaffected. For results of guarantees and indemnification agreements under prior law, see, e.g., Proesel v. Commissioner, 77 T.C. 992 (1981) (general partner allocated debt guaranteed by limited partners because limited partners would be subrogated to creditor's claims against general partner if they paid the debt); Smith v. Commissioner, 84 T.C. 889 (1985), aff'd, 805 F.2d 1073 (D.C.Cir.1986) (general partner who agreed to indemnify partnership for amounts paid on nonrecourse debt was allocated entire debt). But see Rev.Rul. 69–223, 1969–1 C.B. 184 (limited partner agreed to indemnify general partner for part of recourse loan; no amount of debt allocated to limited partner because indemnification agreement was not agreement to make additional contribution to partnership). Under the Temporary Regulations, Rev.Rul. 69–223 clearly no longer is correct. See also Temporary Regulations, section 1.752–1T(d)(3)(iv), regarding arrangements tantamount to a guarantee.

An obligation to make a payment to a creditor or other person is recognized only to the extent that the creditor or other person has a legally enforceable right to such payment. In addition, the obligation will be recognized only to the extent that the amount is determinable with reasonable certainty and is not subject to contingencies that would make it unlikely that it ever would be discharged. Temporary Regulations, section 1.752–1T(d)(3)(ii)(D).

If an obligation to make a payment to a creditor is not required to be satisfied within a reasonable time after the partnership liability becomes due and payable, only the discounted value of the obligation will be taken into account. Temporary Regulations, section 1.752–1T(d)(3)(ii)(E). If the obligation bears interest at the applicable Federal rate, its value is its face value. Otherwise, the imputed principal amount is determined under section 1274(b).

Temporary Regulations, section 1.752–1T(d)(3)(ii)(E)(*4*), provide that satisfaction of an obligation to make a payment to a creditor with a promissory note is not satisfaction for purposes of the Regulations. However, because this rule is contained in the provisions governing "time of satisfaction," its effect appears merely to be to require that promissory notes used to satisfy such obligations bear interest at the applicable Federal rate where it has been agreed upon in advance that an obligation may be satisfied with a note.

If a partner's obligation is limited to the value of property, as where the partner makes an accommodation pledge of his individual property to secure a partnership debt without guaranteeing the debt itself, the amount of the obligation is the fair market value of the property (but not more than the partnership debt) determined (1) at the time the amount of the obligation is determined if the property has a readily ascertainable value (e.g., marketable securities) or by its terms decreases in value (e.g., self-amortizing debt instrument), or (2) at the time the liability was incurred or assumed, or the last time the property was revalued for purposes of the liability. Temporary Regulations, section 1.752–1T(d)(3)(ii)(F).

Temporary Regulations, section 1.752–1T(d)(3)(ii)(A)(*2*)(*ii*), provide a special rule that treats the contribution of property to a partnership for the purpose of using the property to secure a debt of the partnership as an obligation to make a payment to the creditor.

B. NONRECOURSE DEBT

1. *General*

The rules governing allocations of nonrecourse debt for basis purposes are considerably more complex. First, partnership indebtedness is not considered to be nonrecourse debt except to the extent that neither the partnership nor any partner bears the economic risk of loss for the liability. Temporary Regulations, section 1.752–1T(e)(2). See also Temporary Regulations, section 1.752–1T(a)(2)(i). Thus a debt which is nonrecourse to the partnership but which is guaranteed by a partner is subject to the rules governing partners' shares of recourse debt rather than nonrecourse debt. Partners generally share nonrecourse liabilities in the proportion which they share partnership profits. Temporary Regulations, section 1.752–1T(a)(2). Thus limited partners are allocated a share of partnership nonrecourse liabilities. However, Temporary Regulations, section 1.752–1T(e)(1), provide that before allocating nonrecourse liabilities among partners according to their profit sharing ratios, each partner first must be allocated an amount of partnership nonrecourse debt to reflect his share of "minimum gain" under Temporary Regulations, section 1.704–1T(b)(2)(iv)(*f*)(4). Minimum gain is the amount of gain which would be recognized if the partnership's property subject to nonrecourse mortgages were disposed of in satisfaction of the mortgages and for no additional consideration. Although in many cases these required preliminary allocations may be complex, in any case in which each partner's share of each item of income, gain, deduction, loss, and credit is a uniform fraction (or percentage), each partner's share of partnership nonrecourse debt will be equal to the total partnership nonrecourse debt multiplied by his fractional profits interest.

The purpose of providing in Temporary Regulations, section 1.752–1T(e)(3)(i), that nonrecourse indebtedness is first allocated among the partners relative to minimum gain under the section 704(b) Regulations is to assure that each partner has sufficient basis to be able to claim his share of deductions based on nonrecourse debt without running afoul of the section 704(d) limitation, discussed infra, page 140. This debt allocation rule also assures that partners will not recognize gain where the proceeds of a nonrecourse mortgage loan are distributed, because Temporary Regulations, section 1.704–1T(b)(4)(iv)(*f*) provide that a partner's share of minimum gain is increased by any such distribution. The cat chasing its tail aspect of the relationship of basis being determined by minimum gain, minimum gain being generated by deductions, and deductions being allowable only to the extent of basis is solved by Temporary Regulations, section 1.752–1T(e)(3) (i), which provide that for purposes of determining basis, any increase of any partner's share of minimum gain is deemed to occur before the event that causes the increase.

Allocation under Temporary Regulations, section 1.752–1T(e)(1)(iii), of the residual nonrecourse debt is dependent upon determining the partners' respective profit shares, which may present problems if their interests in various types of profits differ. This problem may be avoided by specifying in the partnership agreement the partners' respective shares in partnership profits for purposes of allocating residual partnership nonrecourse debt. The specified shares will be respected as long as they are reasonably consistent with some other significant item of partnership income or gain which has substantial economic effect under the section 704(b) Regulations. See Temporary Regulations, section 1.752–1T(e)(3)(ii)(C). It is important to note that unless the partnership agreement takes advantage of this provision to specify that the residual profit sharing ratio for purposes of allocating nonrecourse debt is the same as any *disproportionate* allocation of depreciation deductions based on nonrecourse debt, as the partnership claims depreciation deductions which increase minimum gain, the share of partnership debt allocated to the partners receiving the special allocation will increase. The other partners will have a corresponding decrease in partnership debt which will give rise to a deemed distribution under section 752(b) and may cause gain recognition.

Temporary Regulations, section 1.704–1T(e)(1)(ii), provide for the allocation of partnership nonrecourse debt among partners relative to their respective shares of section 704(c) gain prior to the allocation of any nonrecourse debt in proportion to the partners' shares of partnership profits (except minimum gain). This allocation prevents immediate recognition of gain to a partner upon contribution to the partnership of property encumbered by a nonrecourse mortgage because any deemed distribution under section 752(b) will not exceed the contributing partner's basis for her partnership interest. This is illustrated supra, page 70.

Temporary Regulations, section 1.704–1T(e)(1)(ii), also govern allocations of partnership nonrecourse debt when Regulations, section 1.704–1(b)(2)(ii)(*f*) or (b)(4)(i), require the application of section 704(c) principles to determine allocations after partnership property has been revalued in connection with the admission of a new partner. In this context, Temporary Regulations, section 1.704–1T(e)(1)(ii), allocate nonrecourse debt to the preexisting partners. This allocation avoids a deemed distribution to the original partners under section 752(b) arising from shifting a portion of the nonrecourse debt to the new partner, and the consequent possibility that gain would result to the original partners under section 731.

The rules governing allocation of nonrecourse debt are based on the premise that none of the partners suffers an actual risk of individual loss from nonrecourse debt. The debt will be repaid, if at all, only out of partnership profits. For example, assume a limited partnership composed of a general partner and two limited partners who share profits equally acquires property subject to a nonrecourse mortgage of $15,000. Each partner increases his basis in his partnership interest by $5,000. As the loan is repaid out of partnership profits, each partner increases his basis by the amount of profits, see section 705(a), and decreases his basis by the reduction in partnership liabilities. Thus, when the loan is fully repaid, each partner's basis is unchanged. However, if the mortgage were recourse to the partnership, thus making the general partner but not the limited partners liable on the mortgage, he would be treated as solely responsible for the mortgage and would be entitled to the full basis adjustment. This result is justified by the fact that the debt, if not satisfied out of partnership profits, ultimately is the responsibility of the general partner.

Occasionally, limited partners seek to disavow the form of partnership borrowing structured as recourse financing in an attempt to come within the special rules governing allocation of nonrecourse debt. In Kingbay v. Commissioner, 46 T.C. 147 (1966), limited partners were not allowed to include liabilities in the basis for their partnership interest where the general partner was liable on the mortgage obligation. The taxpayers argued that the corporate general partner should be disregarded since it was a corporation with capital of only $1,000 and was wholly owned by one of the partners. But the court held the taxpayers were bound by their own form of the transaction; they could not argue that in substance no partner was personally liable on the mortgage obligation, thereby increasing their bases.

2. *Liabilities That Are Part Recourse and Part Nonrecourse*

Temporary Regulations, section 1.752–1T(j)(3), provide that if one or more partners bear an economic risk of loss for only part of a partnership liability, the liability will be treated as a recourse liability to the extent that any partner bears an economic risk of loss and the excess will be treated as a nonrecourse liability. This rule applies, for example, when one or more partners personally guarantee part, but less than all, of a partnership nonrecourse debt. Thus, assume the ABC limited partnership borrows $1,000 on a nonrecourse basis and A, the sole general partner guarantees $800 of the debt. The Temporary Regulations treat $800 of the indebtedness as a recourse loan the economic risk of loss of which is borne by A. This result follows because if A pays the debt pursuant to the guarantee, A's subrogation rights are limited to the rights of a nonrecourse lender and, under the Regulations, the property secured by the loan is deemed to be worthless for purposes of determining which partners bear the economic risk of loss. Under this test, only A would bear the risk of loss of the $800. Thus, only $200 of the debt would be allocated among the partners according to their profit sharing ratios. The results would be similar if B, a limited partner guaranteed the debt: $800 of the debt would be treated as a recourse debt allocated to B. Rev.Rul. 84–118, 1984–2 Cum.Bull. 120, reached this result under predecessor Regulations. See Abramson v. Commissioner, 86 T.C. 360 (1986) (for a year prior to the effective date of Regulations, section 1.752–1T, limited partners who pro rata personally guaranteed a partnership nonrecourse debt were allowed to increase their basis in their partnership interests under section 752(a) by the amount of debt which they had guaranteed). Temporary Regulations, section 1.752–1T(j)(3), also apply, for example, if a partner sells property to the partnership for a nonrecourse obligation that wraps around a primary nonrecourse mortgage. The excess of the debt from the partnership to the partner is a recourse debt, the economic risk of loss of which is borne by the selling partner. The underlying debt is a nonrecourse debt. See Temporary Regulations, section 1.752–1T(k), Ex. (19).

C. OTHER PROBLEMS CONCERNING PARTNERSHIP INDEBTEDNESS

1. *Transfer of Encumbered Property*

Suppose that a partnership owns property with a basis of $1,000 and a fair market value of $2,000, which is subject to a nonrecourse mortgage debt of $2,500. If the partnership transfers the property to an unrelated person for no cash payment, is the amount realized on the disposition $1,000 or $1,500 under the doctrine of Crane v. Commissioner, 331 U.S. 1 (1947)? Section 752(c) provides that for purposes of applying section 752, a liability to which property is subject is considered as a liability of the owner only to the extent of the fair market value of the property. Does this limit the amount realized to $2,000? In Commissioner v. Tufts, 461 U.S. 300 (1983), the Supreme Court made the following observations on the role of section 752(c):

"Relying on the Code's § 752(c), 26 U.S.C. § 752(c), however, respondents argue that Congress has provided for precisely this type of asymmetrical treatment [i.e., including the mortgage in basis but not accounting for the proceeds on the transfer of the encumbered property] in the sale or disposition of partnership property. Section 752 prescribes the tax treatment of certain partnership transactions, and § 752(c) provides that '[f]or purposes of this section, a liability to which property is subject shall, to the extent of the fair market value of such property, be considered as a liability of the owner of the property.' Section 752(c) could be read to apply to a sale or disposition of partnership property, and thus to limit the amount realized to the fair market value of the property transferred. Inconsistent with this interpretation, however, is the language of § 752(d), which specifically mandates that partnership liabilities be treated 'in the same manner as liabilities in connection with the sale or exchange of property not associated with partnerships.' The apparent conflict of these subsections renders the facial meaning of the statute ambiguous, and therefore we must look to the statute's structure and legislative history.

"Subsections (a) and (b) of § 752 prescribe rules for the treatment of liabilities in transactions between a partner and his partnership, and thus for determining the partner's adjusted basis in his partnership interest. Under § 704(d), a partner's distributive share of partnership losses is limited to the adjusted basis of his partnership interest. 26 U.S.C. § 704(d) (1976 ed., Supp. V); see Perry, Limited Partnerships and Tax Shelters: The *Crane* Rule Goes Public, 27 Tax L.Rev. 525, 543 (1972). When partnership liabilities are increased or when a partner takes on the liabilities of the partnership, § 752(a) treats the amount of the increase or the amount assumed as a contribution by the partner to the partnership. This treatment results in an increase in the adjusted basis of the partner's interest and a concomitant increase in the § 704(d) limit on his distributive share of any partnership loss. Conversely, under § 752(b), a decrease in partnership liabilities or the assumption of a partner's liabilities by the partnership has the effect of a distribution, thereby reducing the limit on the partner's distributive share of the partnership losses. When property encumbered by liabilities is contributed to or distributed from the partnership, § 752(c) prescribes that the liability shall be considered to be assumed by the transferee only to the extent of the property's fair market value. Treas.Reg. § 1.752–1(c), 26 CFR § 1.752–1(c) (1982).

"The legislative history indicates that Congress contemplated this application of § 752(c). Mention of the fair market value limitation occurs only in the context of transactions under subsections (a) and (b).[15] The sole reference to subsection (d) does not discuss the limitation.[16] While the legislative history is certainly not conclusive, it indicates that the fair market value limitation of § 752(c) was directed to transactions between a partner and his partnership.[17] 1 A. Willis, J. Pennell, & P. Postlewaite, Partnership Taxation § 44.03, p. 44–3 (3d ed. 1981); Simmons, Tufts v. Commissioner: Amount Realized Limited to Fair Market Value, 15 U.C.D.L.Rev. 577, 611–613 (1982).

"By placing a fair market value limitation on liabilities connected with property contributions to and distributions from partnerships under subsections (a) and (b), Congress apparently intended § 752(c) to prevent a partner from inflating the basis of his partnership interest. Otherwise, a partner with no additional capital at risk in the partnership could raise the § 704(d) limit on his distributive share of partnership losses or could reduce his taxable gain upon disposition of his partnership interest. See Newman, The Resurgence of Footnote 37: Tufts v. Commissioner, 18 Wake Forest L.Rev. 1, 16, n. 116 (1982). There is no potential for similar abuse in the context of § 752(d) sales of partnership interests to unrelated third parties. In light of the above, we interpret subsection (c) to apply only to § 752(a) and (b) transactions, and not to limit the amount realized in a sale or exchange of a partnership interest under § 752(d).

* * *

"When a taxpayer sells or disposes of property encumbered by a nonrecourse obligation, the Commissioner properly requires him to include among the assets realized the outstanding amount of the obligation. The fair market value of the property is irrelevant to this calculation. We find this interpretation to be consistent with Crane v. Commissioner, 331 U.S. 1 (1947), and to implement the statutory mandate in a reasonable manner. National Muffler Dealers Assn. v. United States, 440 U.S. 472, 476 (1979)."

15. "The transfer of property subject to a liability by a partner to a partnership, or by the partnership to a partner, shall, to the extent of the fair market value of such property, be considered a transfer of the amount of the liability along with the property." H.R.Rep. No. 1337, 83d Cong., 2d Sess., A236 (1954); S.Rep. No. 1622, 83d Cong., 2d Sess., 405 (1954).

16. "When a partnership interest is sold or exchanged, the general rule for the treatment of the sale or exchange of property subject to liabilities will be applied." H.R.Rep. No. 1337, at A236–A237; S.Rep. No. 1622, at 405. These Reports then set out an example of subsection (d)'s application, which does not indicate whether the debt is recourse or nonrecourse.

17. The Treasury Regulations support this view. The regulations interpreting § 752(c) state:

"Where property subject to a liability is contributed by a partner to a partnership, or distributed by a partnership to a partner, the amount of the liability, to an extent not exceeding the fair market value of the property at the time of the contribution or distribution, shall be considered as a liability assumed by the transferee." § 1.752–1(c), 26 CFR § 1.752–1(c) (1982).

The regulations also contain an example applying the fair market limitation to a contribution of encumbered property by a partner to a partnership. Ibid. The regulations interpreting § 752(d) make no mention of the fair market limitation. § 1752.1(d). Both regulations were issued contemporaneously with the passage of the statute, T.D. 6175, 1956–1 Cum.Bull. 211, and are entitled to deference as an administrative interpretation of the statute. See Commissioner v. South Texas Lumber Co., 333 U.S. 496, 501 (1948).

2. *Discharge of Indebtedness Income*

Income from discharge of indebtedness under section 61(a)(12) which is realized by the partnership is passed through to each partner under section 702. Suppose the partnership is insolvent at time such discharge of indebtedness income is realized? Does the insolvency exception in section 108 apply or must the status of each partner be examined? Stackhouse v. United States, 441 F.2d 465 (5th Cir.1971), implied that the insolvency exception should be applied at the partnership level. Gershkowitz v. Commissioner, 88 T.C. 984 (1987), however, held that the insolvency exception is applied at the individual partner level and for years after 1980, section 108(d)(6) permits the application of the insolvency exception only at the individual partner level.

D. BASIS IN TIERED PARTNERSHIP

Suppose that A contributes $25 to the AB limited partnership in exchange for an interest as a 20 percent limited partner. The AB limited partnership in turn contributes $100 to become a one third limited partner in the ABC limited partnership, which acquires a building subject to a nonrecourse liability of $1,200. In the year in question, the ABC limited partnership incurs a loss of $600, of which $200 is allocable to the AB limited partnership. In addition, the AB limited partnership loses an additional $50. A's distributive share of the $250 loss of the AB limited partnership is $50. Does he have sufficient basis in the AB limited partnership to deduct currently the entire loss? Rev.Rul. 77–309, 1977–2 Cum. Bull. 216, held that the AB limited partnership is entitled to include one-third ($400) of the nonrecourse liability of the ABC partnership in its basis for its interest in that partnership, and that A is, in turn, entitled to include 20 percent of that amount ($80) in his basis for his interest in the AB limited partnership. Thus, A's basis for his interest is $105 and he can deduct the entire amount of the loss. This approach now is incorporated in Temporary Regulations, section 1.752–1T(j).

E. REFERENCES

Levine, Loffman and Presant, A Practical Guide to the Section 752 Temp.Regs.—Part I, 70 J.Tax'n. 196 (1989), Part II, 70 J.Tax'n. 260 (1989); Carman and Niemann, *Abramson* and Regulation section 1.752–1(e)—The Best of Both Worlds, 3 J.Partnership Tax. 379 (1987); Coven, Limiting Losses Attributable to Nonrecourse Debt: A Defense of the Traditional System Against the At–Risk Concept, 74 Cal.L.Rev. 41 (1986); Burke and Friel, Allocating Partnership Liabilities, 41 Tax L.Rev. 173 (1986); Katz, Inclusion of Liabilities in the Basis of a Partnership Interest and Related Issues, 41 N.Y.U.Inst.Fed.Tax. 13–1 (1983); Epstein, The Application of the *Crane* Doctrine to Limited Partnerships, 45 So.Cal.L.Rev. 100 (1972).

E. ALLOCATIONS WHERE INTERESTS VARY DURING THE YEAR

INTERNAL REVENUE CODE: Section 706(c)(2)(B), (d).

REGULATIONS: Section 1.706–1(c)(2), (4).

ILLUSTRATIVE MATERIAL

A. GENERAL

Section 706(c)(1) provides that a partnership's taxable year does not close on admission of a new partner, the liquidation of a partner's interest, or the sale of a partnership interest.[2] This rule, coupled with the ability of partnerships to provide for special allocations of tax items, raises the question whether an allocation to a partner of items attributable to a portion of a taxable year during which he was not a partner will be respected. This problem most frequently arises on the admission of a new partner, either by contribution or by purchase of a partnership interest from a partner, but it may also arise when an existing partner increases his interest through contribution or purchase.

Suppose, for example, that a calendar year cash method partnership has incurred a loss of $100,000 prior to December 1, and on that date admits a new partner to whom all of the loss is specially allocated. Prior to the Tax Reform Act of 1976, there was some judicial support for giving effect to such retroactive allocations, see Smith v. Commissioner, 331 F.2d 298 (7th Cir. 1964), although the Tax Court disapproved such allocations. Moore v. Commissioner, 70 T.C. 1024 (1978). The 1976 Act expressly prohibited such retroactive allocations. In 1984, section 706 was amended again to tighten further the restrictions on retroactive allocations and give the Commissioner broad authority to promulgate regulations governing the allocation of items to take into account the varying interests of the partners in the partnership during the taxable year.

Section 706(d)(1) requires that if there is any change in a partner's interest in the partnership during the year, each partner's distributive share of any partnership item of income, gain, loss, deduction or credit must be determined using a method prescribed by the Regulations which takes into account the varying interests of the partners in the partnership during the year. Although this section does not on its face require that in the absence of Regulations partners' distributive shares be determined so as to take into account the partner's varying interests during the year, and Regulations have not yet been promulgated, Congress intended that section 706(d)(1) be treated as directly imposing this requirement. The language of section 706(d)(1) is substantially similar to that of the 1976 version of section 706(c)(2)(B), which directly imposed a similar requirement. The 1984 changes were intended to extend the application of the pre–1984 rules to situations in which they arguably did not apply, not to narrow the application of the rule. The old rules were expressly triggered by sales and exchanges of partnership interests and admission of a new partner, but the statutory language applied only to the old partners; extension of the rules to new partners was by necessary implication. Under current section 706(d)(1), however, the dis-

2. Section 706(c)(2)(A) provides that the taxable year of the partnership closes with respect to a partner who retires or sells or exchanges his *entire* partnership interest.

tributive share of "each partner" must be determined taking into account the varying interests of the partners if there is a change in "any partner's interest." See H.Rep. No. 98–432, 98th Cong., 2d Sess. 1213 (1984).

B. INTERIM CLOSING OF THE BOOKS VERSUS PRORATION

1. *General*

Regulations, section 1.706–1(c)(2), prescribe two methods for taking into account the partners' varying interests during the year when a partner sells his entire interest or retires. These regulations were issued under the pre–1976 version of section 706 and do not specifically address the method to be used on admission of a new partner by contribution or on a disposition of less than all of a partner's interest, but the legislative history of pre–1984 section 706(c)(2)(B), the 1976 statutory predecessor to section 706(d)(1), indicates that the same methods are to be used, S.Rep. No. 94–938, 94th Cong., 2d Sess. 97–98 (1976), and judicial application of pre–1984 section 706(c)(2)(B) employed these methods. See Richardson v. Commissioner, 76 T.C. 512 (1981), aff'd, 693 F.2d 1189 (5th Cir.1982).

Under these Regulations, the interim closing of the books method is mandatory, unless the partners agree to use the proration method when a partner retires or sells his entire interest in the partnership. Presumably, the election is now available whenever section 706(d)(1) applies. Under the proration method, the partnership's items for the entire year are prorated over the days in the taxable year and are allocated among the partners based on their respective percentage interests on each day. To avoid undue complexity, in 1976 Congress authorized the Internal Revenue Service to promulgate regulations under which changes in partnership interests would be accounted for using a semi-monthly convention, but no regulations to this effect have been published yet.

Rev.Rul. 77–310, 1977–2 Cum.Bull. 217, illustrates the computation of allocations under the proration method as follows. Assume that A, B, and C each have both a profits and a capital interest in the ABC partnership of 90 percent, 5 percent, and 5 percent, respectively. The ABC partnership uses the calendar year. On December 1, B and C contribute additional cash and the partnership agreement is amended to reduce A's profits and capital interest to 30 percent and increase the interest of each of B and C to 35 percent. During the year the partnership sustained a loss from business operations of $1,200. The partners must compute their distributive shares as follows:

Partner	Profit/Loss Percent-ages	Months Held	Computations	Distributive Shares of Loss
A	90	11	.90 × 11/12 × 1200 =	$ 990
	30	1	.30 × 1/12 × 1200 =	30
B	5	11	.05 × 11/12 × 1200 =	55
	35	1	.35 × 1/12 × 1200 =	35
C	5	11	.05 × 11/12 × 1200 =	55
	35	1	.35 × 1/12 × 1200 =	35
				$1,200

Under the interim closing of the books method, the partnership would determine the exact amount of the operating loss incurred from January 1 through November 30, using its normal method of accounting, except as described below, and that loss would be allocated 90 percent to A and 5 percent to each of B and C. The actual loss incurred in December would be allocated 30 percent to A and 35 percent to each of B and C. Thus, if $1,000 of the loss was incurred before December 1 and $200 was incurred during December, the loss would be allocated among the partners as follows:

Partner	Profit/Loss Percent-ages	Loss Incurred During Months Held	Distributive Shares of Loss
A	90	$1,000	$ 900
	30	200	60
B	5	1,000	50
	35	200	70
C	5	1,000	50
	35	200	70
			$1,200

The interim closing of the books is the more accurate method for apportioning income between the period before a change in the partners' interests and the period after the change. The proration method, however, is more convenient. In deciding whether to agree to use the proration method, each partner must consider the effect of its inaccuracies on his tax liability for the year. When a partnership interest is disposed of in its entirety, the selling partner must bear in mind that if the proration method is used, events occurring after the sale can significantly and unexpectedly affect his tax liability for the year of the sale.

Where the Commissioner asserts a deficiency under section 706(d) he may apply either the proration or closing of the books method. Johnsen v. Commissioner, 84 T.C. 344 (1985), rev'd on other grounds, 794 F.2d 1157 (6th Cir.1986). If the Commissioner applies the proration method, the taxpayer may prove at trial that the interim closing of the books method is more reasonable. See Sartin v. United States, 5 Cl.Ct. 172 (1984); Richardson v. Commissioner, 76 T.C. 512 (1981) aff'd, 693 F.2d 1189 (5th Cir. 1982). However, if the taxpayer elects to use the interim closing of the books method, he has the burden of establishing the date on which each item was earned, received, accrued, or paid. Sartin v. United States, supra; Moore v. Commissioner, 70 T.C. 1024 (1978).

2. *Allocable Cash Basis Items*

(a) *General*

When the interim closing of the books method is applied by a cash method partnership, certain items are not taken into account on the date of payment. Section 706(d)(2), added by the 1984 Act to reverse the result in Richardson v. Commissioner, 76 T.C. 512 (1981), requires the proration over the taxable year by cash method partnerships of deductions for interest, taxes, rents, and other items which may be specified in the Regulations. This provision reflects the fact that these items may accrue over extended periods either before or after payment, and taking them into account on the date of payment may result in a significant misstatement of the partners' taxable incomes. Thus, for example, if the ABC partnership in the preceding example had operated without any gain or loss except for a $1,200 rent payment attributable to the entire year made in arrears on December 31, the interim closing of the books method would result in the same allocation as results under the proration method since $100 of the rent must be attributed to each month. If the rental payment were attributable to only the last six months of the year, however, then $200 of rent would be allocated to each of the last six months of the year. As a result, A's distributive share of the loss would be $960 ((.9 × 5/6 × $1,200) + (.3 × 1/6 × $1,200)), and B's and C's shares would be $120 ((.05 × 5/6 × $1,200) + (.35 × 1/6 × $1,200)).

In addition to the items specified in section 706(d)(2), cash method partnerships are required to apportion depreciation ratably over the year, rather than attributing it entirely to the last day of the year. See Hawkins v. Commissioner, 713 F.2d 347 (8th Cir.1983).

Accrual method partnerships are required to prorate deductions for interest, rent, taxes, depreciation, and similar items over the year without any specific statutory directive. See Williams v. United States, 680 F.2d 382 (5th Cir.1982).

(b) *Items Attributable to Prior or Future Years*

Suppose that the $1,200 rent paid in December by the ABC partnership in the preceding example was attributable to the year preceding the year in which it was paid and in which there was a change in partnership interests. Since the ABC partnership uses the cash method, the payment must be taken into account in the year in which it was paid, but for purposes of determining the partners' distributive shares, section 706(d)(2)(C) requires that the payment be treated as paid on the first day of the taxable year. Section 706(d)(2)(D) then provides that it is allocated among the partners according to their interests in the prior year to which the payment was attributable. Thus, A's distributive share of the loss would be $1,080 (.9 × $1,200) and B's and C's shares would be $60 (.05 × $1,200). If any person who was a partner in the prior year is no longer a partner in the year in which the item is paid, the distributive share of the item attributable to that partner is not deductible by the partnership. It must be capitalized and allocated to the basis of partnership assets under the rules of section 755. (Section 755 is discussed infra, page 208.)

Similarly, if in a year in which there is a change in partnership interests, a cash method partnership makes a deductible payment of an item attributable to a future year, the item is attributed to the last day of the year. Assume that the ABC partnership in the preceding examples had neither a profit nor a loss for the taxable year of the change except for a $1,200 payment on July 1 of local real property taxes for the year beginning July 1. The $600 attributable to the current year is allocated ratably over the last six months of the year, and the remaining $600 is attributed to the last day of the year. Accordingly, A's distributive share of the loss is $660 (($600 × 5/6 × .9) + ($600 × 1/6 × .3) + ($600 × .30)), and B's and C's shares each are $270 (($600 × 5/6 × .05) + ($600 × 1/6 × .35) + ($600 × .35)).

C. RELATIONSHIP OF SECTION 706(d) TO SECTION 704(b)

Suppose that C is admitted to the AB partnership on December 30 as a one-third partner with A and B, and the partnership agreement specially allocates all of the depreciation on the partnership's property for the year to C. The ABC partnership maintains capital accounts as required by the section 704(b) regulations, charges the depreciation to C's capital account, will liquidate according to the partners' capital accounts, and C is required to restore any deficit in his capital account upon liquidation. The allocation has substantial economic effect. Will it be recognized? Ogden v. Commissioner, 84 T.C. 871 (1985), aff'd per curiam, 788 F.2d 252 (5th Cir.1986), held that section 704(b)(2) does not override the requirements of section 706(d). A retroactive allocation is ineffective even if it has substantial economic effect. See also Regulations, section 1.704–1(b)(1)(iii), providing that section 704(b)(2) does not override section 706(d).

Snell v. United States, 680 F.2d 545 (8th Cir.1982), rejected the taxpayer's argument that section 706(d) applies only when the partnership agreement does not expressly provide for allocation of an item for the year. However, section 706(d) does not apply to retroactive reallocations of items among existing partners where the reallocation is not attributable to a capital contribution that results in the reduction of the interest of one or more partners. Lipke v. Commissioner, 81 T.C. 689 (1983). Regulations, section 1.761–1(c), permit amendments to a partnership agreement made after the close of the taxable year, but on or before the due date for the partnership's return, to be given retroactive effect. In such a case, however, the reallocation must have substantial economic effect under section 704(b)(2). Thus, for example, if the DEF law partnership, in which each partner had a one-third interest in profits and capital, amended its partnership agreement on April 14, 1990, effective January 1, 1989, to give D a one half interest in partnership profits and E and F each a one-quarter interest, for the purpose of more accurately reflecting the relationship of their services to firm profits for the year, the amended allocation would be effective.

D. RELATIONSHIP OF SECTION 706(d) TO GENERAL ASSIGNMENT OF INCOME DOCTRINE

In Cottle v. Commissioner, 89 T.C. 467 (1987), the taxpayer held a 1 percent limited partnership interest and a 25 percent general partnership interest in a partnership organized to acquire an apartment building and convert it to condominiums. Almost all of the effort required to effect the conversion and sale of the units occurred prior to October 21, 1977, but none of the sales of units had been closed. On that day, the taxpayer transferred his 25 percent general partnership interest to his wholly owned corporation in a transaction subject to section 351. On November 15, 1977 the partnership closed the sale of most of the condominium units. Applying the interim closing of the books method, the taxpayer reported no income for the year attributable to the general partnership interest which he held until October 21. The Commissioner asserted that the taxpayer and not the corporation was taxable on all of the partnership income attributable to the units sold on November 15 because "due to the assignment of income doctrine, the interim closing of the books was not a reasonable method of determining who should report the income in question." Neither the taxpayer nor the Commissioner urged use of the proration method. Because the taxpayer retained his 1 percent limited partnership interest, the statutory predecessor of section 706(d) rather than section 706(c)(2)(A) applied. Nevertheless, relying on the legislative history of the statutory predecessor of section 706(d), the court allowed the taxpayer to apply Regulations, section 1.706–1(c)(2), mandating the closing of the books method. The court reasoned that Subchapter K dictates that the timing of the includability of income (and of deductions) is determined at the partnership level under the method of accounting used by the partnership. Because there were contingencies attached to the closing of the sales by the partnership, the court concluded that the income was not earned by the partnership until November 15. Thus, as of October 21, when the partnership closed its books, it had no income and, accordingly, there was no partnership income to be allocated to the taxpayer at that time. The court then turned to the applicability of more general assignment of income principles, which it described as follows:

"Respondent argues that the principles of Commissioner v. Court Holding Co., 324 U.S. 331 (1945), as applied in Murry v. Commissioner, T.C. Memo. 1984–670, should govern the instant case to cause petitioners rather than DRC to be taxable on the profits from the condominium sales.

"In *Murry,* the taxpayer owned an apartment complex that was to be converted to a condominium, and the units therein would subsequently be sold. The taxpayer's wholly-owned corporation was to undertake the development of the property as a condominium. Because of certain financial difficulties, the taxpayer had to sell the apartment complex to the lender. However, in order to accommodate the taxpayer's tax considerations, the lender agreed to buy the property from the taxpayer's corporation. The taxpayer thus agreed to make a capital contribution of the property to the corporation, if the corporation agreed to sell the property immediately thereafter to the lenders.

"We held in *Murry* that the taxpayer and not the corporation was taxable on the sale of the property to the lender. In so holding, we applied the *Court Holding* doctrine which provides that 'a sale by one person cannot be transformed for tax purposes into a sale by another by using the latter as a conduit through which to pass title.' Commissioner v. Court Holding Co., 324 U.S. at 334.

"We agree with petitioners that *Murry* is not relevant to this case. Associates in the instant case was the owner and developer of the property. It converted the property to condominium units, sold the units therein, and reported the profits from these sales on its partnership return. There is no question in this case, as was present in *Murry,* as to who earned the income. No conduit was used by Associates to sell the condominium units. The parties agree that Associates earned the income; the only question in the instant case is how that income is to be allocated among the partners. And that question is resolved solely by application of section 706(c)(2)(B), which governs the allocation of partnership items when there are transfers of partial partnership interests during the tax year. The rules thereunder are specifically designed to avoid assignments of income and retroactive allocation of losses between transferor and transferee partners. Moore v. Commissioner, 70 T.C. at 1032–1033. We think they adequately resolve the question in the instant case, and that their use is specifically mandated by Richardson v. Commissioner, 76 T.C. at 526–527.

"We hold for petitioners on this issue." (499–500).

What would have been the result in the *Cottle* case if the partners had agreed to use the proration method?

E. TIERED PARTNERSHIPS

Prior to the enactment of section 706(d)(3) in 1984 it arguably was possible to sidestep the prohibition on retroactive allocations through the use of tiered partnerships. Assume for example that the UT partnership held a 90 percent interest in the LT partnership, and both partnerships used the calendar year. LT had a $10,000 loss for the year. UT's share of that loss was $9,000. On December 30, A contributed cash to UT in exchange for an eighty percent interest, and UT used the interim closing of the books method to apply section 706(d). Arguably, UT's $9,000 loss from LT was incurred on December 31, the last day of LT's taxable year, and A's distributive share of the loss would be $7,200. Section 704(d)(3) prevents this avoidance technique by, in effect, ignoring UT, the upper tier partnership, for allocation purposes and flowing through to the partners of UT in accordance with their effective interests in LT on the close of each day UT's distributive share of each LT item. Thus, in the example, if UT's entire $9,000 loss from LT was attributable to depreciation, since A was a partner for two days of LT's taxable year within UT's taxable year, A's share would be $49, which is 2/365 of the loss. These principles apply whether the upper tier partnership uses the cash or the accrual method. In addition, the rules governing allocable cash basis items must be applied in allocating lower tier partnership items to the partners of the upper tier partnership by the flow through method. Section 706(d)(3) generally adopts the position of the Internal Revenue Service set forth in Rev.Rul. 77–311, 1977–2 Cum.Bull. 218.

F. LIMITATIONS ON ALLOWANCE OF PARTNERSHIP LOSSES

Even if all allocations of tax items have complied with the rules discussed in the preceding materials, special rules are provided which may limit the ability of a partner to deduct her distributive share of partnership *losses* in a given year. The following materials consider those limitations.

(1) BASIS LIMITATION

INTERNAL REVENUE CODE: Sections 704(d); 752.

REGULATIONS: Section 1.704–1(d).

TEMPORARY REGULATIONS: Section 1.752–1T.

REVENUE RULING 66–94

1966–1 Cumulative Bulletin 166.

Advice has been requested as to the manner in which a partner should compute the basis of his partnership interest under section 705(a) of the Internal Revenue Code of 1954 for purposes of determining the extent to which his distributive share of partnership losses will be allowed as a deduction, and the extent to which gain will be realized by a partner upon the distribution of cash to him by the partnership.

During the taxable year, *A*, a member of the partnership, contributed 50*x* dollars to the partnership as his initial capital contribution, and received 30*x* dollars as a cash distribution from the partnership. *A* 's distributive share of partnership losses at the end of its taxable year was 60*x* dollars.

Section 705(a) of the Code provides, in part, that the adjusted basis of a partner's interest in a partnership shall be the basis of such interest determined under section 722 of the Code (relating to contributions to a partnership)—(1) increased by the sum of his distributive share for the taxable year and prior taxable years of taxable income of the partnership, tax exempt income of the partnership, and the excess of depletion deductions over the basis of depletable property, and (2) decreased, but not below zero, by distributions by the partnership as provided in section 733 and by the sum of his distributive share of partnership losses and nondeductible partnership expenditures not chargeable to capital account.

Section 1.704–1(d)(1) of the Income Tax Regulations provides, in part, that a partner's distributive share of partnership loss will be allowed only to the extent of the adjusted basis (before reduction by current year's losses) of such partner's interest in the partnership at the end of the partnership taxable year in which such loss occurred.

Section 1.704–1(d)(2) of the regulations provides, in part, that in computing the adjusted basis of a partner's interest for the purpose of ascertaining the extent to which a partner's distributive share of partnership loss shall be allowed as a deduction for the taxable year, the basis shall first be increased under section 705(a)(1) of the Code and decreased under section 705(a)(2) of the Code, except for losses of the taxable year and losses previously disallowed.

Section 1.731–1(a) of the regulations provides, in part, that where money is distributed by a partnership to a partner, no gain or loss shall be recognized to the partner except to the extent that the amount of money distributed exceeds the adjusted basis of the partner's interest in the partnership immediately before the distribution. For purposes of sections 731 and 705 of the Code, advances or drawings of money or property against a partner's distributive share of income shall be treated as current distributions made on the last day of the partnership taxable year with respect to such partner.

Based on the foregoing, it is concluded that:

(1) In computing *A* 's adjusted basis for his interest in the partnership under section 705(a) of the Code, *A* 's original basis, which is determined under section 722 relating to contributions to the partnership, should be decreased by first deducting distributions made to *A* by the partnership and thereafter, by deducting his distributive share of partnership losses. However, *A* 's basis for his interest in the partnership may not be reduced below zero. Thus:

A 's contribution to the partnership	50 x dollars
Deduct cash distributions made to A by the partnership	– 30 x dollars
	20 x dollars
Deduct A 's distributive share of losses (60 x dollars) but only to the extent that A 's basis is not reduced below zero	– 20 x dollars
A 's basis for his interest in the partnership under section 705 of the Code	– 0

(2) In order to determine the extent to which A 's distributive share of partnership losses will be allowed as a deduction, A 's basis for his interest in the partnership computed in accordance with section 705(a) of the Code, should be determined without taking into account his distributive share of partnership losses for the taxable year. Thus:

A's contribution to the partnership	50 x dollars
Deduct cash distribution made to A by the partnership	– 30 x dollars
	20 x dollars
A 's distributive share of partnership losses for the taxable year are not taken into account	– 0
A 's basis for determining the amount of his allowable partnership losses	20 x dollars

(3) In order to determine the extent to which gain will be realized by A upon the distribution of cash to him by the partnership, A 's basis for his interest in the partnership computed in accordance with section 705(a) of the Code, should be determined without taking into account cash distributions made to him by the partnership during its current taxable year. Thus:

A 's contribution to the partnership	50 x dollars
Cash distributions made by the partnership to A during the taxable year are not taken into account	– 0
	50 x dollars
Deduct A 's distributive share of partnership losses to the extent allowed by section 704(d) of the Code. (See examples (1) and (2).)	– 20 x dollars
A 's basis for determining the amount of gain he realized upon the distribution of cash to him by the partnership	30 x dollars

A may deduct his distributive share of the partnership loss to the extent of 20 x dollars (see example 2) and he realizes no gain from the cash distribution of 30 x dollars because his basis for determining the amount of gain upon such distribution is 30 x dollars (example 3).

SENNETT v. COMMISSIONER

United States Court of Appeals, Ninth Circuit, 1985.
752 F.2d 428.

PER CURIAM.

Taxpayers William and Sandra Sennett claimed an ordinary loss deduction of $109,061 on their 1969 tax return. This loss represented William Sennett's share of the ordinary losses incurred in 1968 by Professional Properties Partnership ("PPP") when it repurchased his interest in the partnership. The Commissioner of Internal Revenue disallowed the deduction asserting *inter alia* that in 1969 Sennett had no basis in an interest in PPP since he had left the partnership in 1968 and is precluded by 26 U.S.C. § 704(d) and Treas.Reg. § 1.704–1(d) from claiming any loss. The Tax Court, 80 T.C. 825, ruled against petitioners. It held that a former partner may not invoke the loss carryover provisions of section 704(d) in the tax year after the withdrawal from the partnership of that partner. We agree and affirm.

FACTS

Sennett entered PPP as a limited partner in December 1967. PPP's total capital at that time was approximately $402,000. Sennett contributed $135,000 and received a 33.5% interest in the partnership. In 1967 PPP reported an ordinary loss of $405,329, and Sennett reported his allowable distributive share of $135,000.

Sennett sold his interest in PPP on November 26, 1968, with an effective date of December 1, 1968. The contract provided that PPP would pay Sennett $250,000, in annual installments with interest. Sennett agreed to pay PPP within one year the total loss allocated to Sennett's surrendered interest. PPP then sold twenty percent of Sennett's interest to a third party. PPP's return in 1968 reported a negative capital account of $109,061, corresponding to the eighty percent portion of the partnership interest PPP bought from Sennett and retained.

On May 15, 1969, Sennett and PPP executed an amended agreement which reduced PPP's obligation to $240,000, without interest if paid in full by December 31, 1969, or if paid one-half in 1969 and the rest in 1970, at seven percent interest. PPP executed a promissory note to Sennett for $240,000, which Sennett signed as paid in full. Sennett meanwhile paid PPP $109,061, which was eighty percent of his share of PPP's 1967 and 1968 losses. On his 1969 return Sennett reported $240,000 long-term capital gain and $109,061 as his distributive share of PPP's ordinary loss. The Commissioner disallowed the ordinary loss and maintained that, instead, there should be a long-term capital gain reported of $130,939 ($240,000 – $109,061). The Tax Court agreed and the Sennetts took this appeal.

ANALYSIS

* * *

In deciding whether Sennett can deduct a $109,061 loss, we must look to 26 U.S.C. § 704(d). The statute provides:

> LIMITATION ON ALLOWANCE OF LOSSES.—A partner's distributive share of partnership loss (including capital loss) shall be allowed only to the extent of the adjusted basis of such partner's interest in the partnership at the end of the partnership year in which such loss occurred. *Any excess of such loss over such basis shall be allowed as a deduction at the end of the partnership year in which such excess is repaid to the partnership.* (Emphasis added.)

Treas.Reg. § 1.704–1(d)—in force in 1969 and having substantively the same effect now—interprets the statute as allowing only a partner to benefit from the carry-over allowed by subsection 704(d). The Commissioner relies upon this regulation in disallowing the deduction, since Sennett was not a partner in the year he repaid the excess. Sennett does not deny this. Nor does he deny that his basis was zero when PPP purchased his interest and incurred the loss in 1968. Sennett argues instead that the regulation is merely an "interpretive regulation," and entitled to little or no weight. Sennett points to statutory language which allows the taxpayer to claim a deduction in the amount of the excess of basis in the partnership. He claims he repaid the loss in 1969 and is entitled to the deduction regardless of his lack of partner status.

This circuit has held that an interpretive regulation will be given effect if "it is a reasonable interpretation of the statute's plain language, its origin, and its purpose." First Charter Financial Corp. v. United States, 669 F.2d 1342, 1348 (9th Cir.1982). "A Treasury regulation 'is not invalid simply because the statutory language will support a contrary interpretation.' " *Id.* (quoting United States v. Vogel Fertilizer Co., 455 U.S. 16, 26, 102 S.Ct. 821, 828, 70 L.Ed.2d 792 (1982)). As will be explained below, restricting carryover to partners is a reasonable interpretation in light of the wording of the statute and the legislative history.

Statutory language supports the Treasury Regulation. For example, the presence of the word "partner" at the beginning of subsection 704(d) strongly implies that a taxpayer must be a partner to take advantage of the carryover.

The Treasury Regulation's interpretation is also supported by a review of the legislative history of the statute. Section 704(d), as initially adopted by the House, allowed for deduction of the distributive share to the extent of adjusted basis. There was no provision for a carryover of the excess loss until the excess was repaid. H.R.Rep. No. 1337, 83d Cong., 2d Sess. 1, reprinted in 1954 U.S.Code Cong. & Ad. News 4017, 4364. The bill the Senate passed, which was the version Congress enacted, provided for carryover. The accompanying Senate

Report sums up both sentences of subsection 704(d) in a fashion that demonstrates the committee felt the subsection limited carryover to partners. It states:

> Your committee has revised subsection (d) of the House bill to provide that any loss in excess of the basis of a *partner's* partnership interest may be allowed as a deduction only at the end of the partnership year in which the loss is repaid, either directly, or out of future profits.
>
> Subsection (d), as amended, may be illustrated as follows. Assume that a partner has a basis of $50 for his interest, and his distributive share of partnership loss is $100. Under the subsection, the partner's distributive share of the loss would be limited to $50, thereby decreasing the basis of his interest to zero. The remaining $50 loss would not be recognized, unless the partner makes a further contribution of $50. If, however, the *partner* repays the $50 loss to the partnership *out of his share of partnership income for the following year,* then the additional $50 loss will be recognized at the end of the year in which such repayment is made.

S.Rep. No. 1622, 83d Cong., 2d Sess. 1, reprinted in 1954 U.S.Code Cong. & Ad.News 4621, 5025 (emphasis added).

Limiting carryover to those who are partners at the time of repayment, as Treas.Reg. § 1.704–1(d) does, effectuates congressional intent to allow deductions only to the extent of adjusted basis. When a partner repays the excess loss, it is, as the Senate Report notes, "a further contribution" to the partnership. The partner thereby increases his basis by an amount equal to the loss and reduces it to zero by taking the loss. Nor is the partnership element merely a formal distinction, since the partner repaying the excess loss increases his interest in the partnership and his exposure to loss. Sennett's position, in contrast, was that of a debtor with rights superior to those of partners.

CONCLUSION

Since Sennett was not a member of the partnership at the time he attempted to invoke the loss carryover provisions of section 704(d) by repaying his claimed share of the loss, he was not entitled to deduct a portion of PPP's 1967 and 1968 losses. The decision of the Tax Court rejecting the $109,061 deduction and setting taxpayer's long-term capital gain for the 1969 taxable year at $130,939 is affirmed.

ILLUSTRATIVE MATERIAL

A. LIMITATION ON ALLOWANCE OF LOSSES IN GENERAL

Section 704(d) limits the deductibility of a partner's distributive share of a partnership loss to the partner's basis for his partnership interest. Any excess is held in suspense, to be allowed when a basis exists, as by additional contributions, a future share of partnership earnings left in the partnership, or the incurring of a partnership liability. See Regulations, section 1.704–1(d). Thus, suppose A contributes $100,000 cash and B contributes $50,000 cash, but they agree to share profits and losses equally since B will also contribute services. The partnership spends $125,000 on deductible research costs. A can deduct $62,500, but B can deduct only $50,000 currently. He may deduct an additional $12,500 when he obtains sufficient basis. Suppose the partnership realizes a loss in 1989 but an individual partner wishes to postpone the recognition of the loss until 1990. Can he withdraw his partnership capital at year end, hold the loss in the suspense account, and then recognize it in 1990 upon a recontribution of the capital to the partnership, an action which would thereby reestablish his basis? See Rev. Rul. 66–94, supra (reduction in basis for distributions under sections 733 and 705(a)(2) is made before applying section 704(d)).

Suppose that the CD partnership realizes a $10,000 loss in 1989, and D, whose distributive share of that loss is $2,500 (25%), has a zero basis. If the partnership were to borrow $10,000, under section 752(a), D would be treated as contributing $2,500 in cash and his basis would be increased by that amount. Will year end borrowing for the purpose of increasing basis to permit the deduction of losses be recognized? See Corum v. United States, 268 F.Supp. 109 (W.D.Ky.1967), in which a road building partnership borrowed funds on December 28th and repaid the loan on the following January 15th. The business purpose for the loan was to improve the liquidity on the partnership's year end balance sheet, which was used by governmental authorities to determine the financial capability of the contractors bidding on jobs. The taxpayer was permitted to include his share of the indebtedness in basis for purposes of applying section 704(d) and thereby could deduct his entire distributive share of the partnership's loss for the year.

If a new partner is admitted during a year in which the partnership incurs a loss and, as a result, existing partners are treated under section 752(b) as receiving a cash distribution that reduces basis, when should the partners' basis be determined for purposes of applying section 704(d)? Suppose that G is admitted to the EF partnership on December 31. Before G's admission E and F each had a basis in his partnership interest of $160 and the partnership had debts of $300. During the current year prior to December 31, the AB partnership incurred a loss of $300, all of which will be allocated to E and F under section 706(d). As a result of G's admission, on December 31, before taking into account the loss, E and F each have a basis of $110 ($160 minus the $50 of debt of which each was relieved on C's admission) and a distributive share of the loss of $150. If they can use their December 30 basis the entire loss is deductible by them. Richardson v. Commissioner, 693 F.2d 1189 (5th Cir.1982), held that the end of year basis was controlling for applying section 704(d). Hence, E and F may each deduct only $110 of the loss. C cannot deduct any of the loss by virtue of section 706(d), discussed supra page 134.

Even if a loss is not limited by section 704(d), deductions may be restricted by section 465, the at-risk rules, or section 469 dealing with passive losses. Both of these provisions are particularly applicable to limited partners, but may also affect general partners. Sections 465 and 469 are discussed infra, pages 147 and 155.

B. REFERENCES

Burke and Friel, Allocating Partnership Liabilities, 41 Tax L.Rev. 173 (1986); Cohen and Millman, Partnership Debt: Liability and Basis, 43 N.Y.U.Tax.Inst. 27 (1985).

(2) THE AT–RISK RULES OF SECTION 465

INTERNAL REVENUE CODE: Sections 465(a)(1) and (2), (b), (1) and (3), (d).

PROPOSED REGULATIONS: Sections 1.465–6(b), –24(a)(2).

PRITCHETT v. COMMISSIONER

United States Court of Appeals, Ninth Circuit, 1987.
827 F.2d 644.

SKOPIL, CIRCUIT JUDGE:

We must decide in this case whether taxpayers, limited partners in five similar partnerships engaged in oil and gas drilling operations, were "at risk" pursuant to 26 U.S.C. § 465 on certain recourse notes and thus entitled to deduct distributive shares of non-cash partnership losses. The Tax Court in a reviewed, split decision held that each taxpayer was at risk only to the extent of actual cash contribution. Pritchett v. Commissioner, 85 T.C. 580 (1985). We reject the Tax Court's rationale in holding that taxpayers were not at risk on the recourse debt. We remand to allow the Tax Court to consider the Commissioner's alternative theory that taxpayers were not at risk because the creditor had an impermissible role in the activity at issue. See 26 U.S.C. § 465(b)(3).

FACTS AND PROCEEDINGS BELOW

Taxpayers are each members in similar limited partnerships formed to conduct oil and gas operations. All five partnerships entered into agreements with Fairfield Drilling Corporation ("Fairfield") whereby Fairfield agreed to drill, develop, and exploit any productive wells. Fairfield provided all necessary equipment and expertise. Pursuant to a "turnkey" agreement, each partnership paid cash and executed a recourse note to Fairfield. Each note was non-interest-bearing and matured in fifteen years. Each was secured by virtually all of the maker-partnership's assets. The principal for each note was to be paid from net income available to each partnership if the drilling operations proved successful. Only the general partners were personally liable under the notes. Nevertheless, each partnership agreement provided that if the notes were not paid off at maturity, the limited partners would be personally obligated to make additional capital contributions to cover the deficiency when called upon to do so by the general partners.

Each partnership elected to use accrual accounting and to deduct intangible drilling costs as an expense. The partnership agreements provided that all losses were to be allocated among limited partners in proportion to their respective capital contributions. Because there was no income in the tax year in question, each limited partner deducted from taxable income a distributive share of partnership loss. The Commissioner disallowed that portion of the deduction based on the note.

The Tax Court affirmed by a 9–7 vote the Commissioner's action. The majority held that under the partnership agreements the limited partners had no personal liability on the notes for the tax year in question and therefore they were at risk under section 465 only for the actual cash contribution made to the partnerships. Pritchett, 85 T.C. at 590. Any potential liability was "merely a contingency" since in the first year of the partnership it was not known whether income would be sufficient to pay off the note or even whether the general partners would in fact exercise their discretion to make a cash call on an unpaid balance fifteen years later. Id. at 588.

Seven judges dissented in three separate opinions. One judge reasoned that for federal tax purposes, "both general and limited partners are personally liable for a pro rata portion of the partnership's recourse obligation to Fairfield." Id. at 594 (Whitaker, J., dissenting). Another found nothing in the agreements to indicate the general partners had unilateral discretion to waive the cash call. Id. at 599 (Cohen, J., dissenting). A majority of the dissenting judges apparently believed, however, that the Commissioner's actions might be affirmed on the alternative ground that section 465(b)(3)(A) provides that amounts borrowed are not at risk if the money is borrowed from someone with an interest in the activity at issue. E.g., id. at 593 (Whitaker, J., dissenting) ("majority may have inadvertently reached the right result, although for the wrong reasons"). The majority notes this alternative ground but expressly does not adopt it. Id. at 590.

These timely appeals followed.

DISCUSSION

In 1976 Congress added section 465 to the Internal Revenue Code to combat abuse of tax shelters caused by nonrecourse financing. See Commissioner v. Tufts, 461 U.S. 300, 309 n. 7, 103 S.Ct. 1826, 1832 n. 7, 75 L.Ed.2d 863 (1983). Section 465 forbids a taxpayer from taking a loss in excess of amounts at risk in the investment.

The limited partners argue that the notes create at risk debt because each limited partner is personally liable. The contract provisions provide that if the notes are not paid off by the successful drilling operations, "the General Partners will by written notice call for additional capital contributions in an amount sufficient to pay the outstanding balance" and that "[e]ach Limited Partner shall be obligated to pay in cash to the Partnership" the amount called. (Emphasis added). It is clear, however, as the majority opinion notes, that the limited partners are not directly and personally liable to Fairfield. Pritchett, 85 T.C. at

587–88. Even assuming a third party beneficiary right, Fairfield had no recourse against the limited partners until the end of the note's fifteen year term.

Whether the Tax Court's decision is correct hinges on its characterization of taxpayers' obligation as indirect and secondary. In a decision rendered shortly after *Pritchett,* the Tax Court sought to distinguish between direct and indirect liability. Abramson v. Commissioner, 86 T.C. 360, 375–76 (1986). In that reviewed decision, the Tax Court, by a 15–1 vote, held that limited partners' pro rata shares of partnership debt that was to be repaid in whole or in part out of partnership revenues was at risk. Id. The limited partners had a direct contractual liability to a third party seller of goods. *Abramson* distinguished *Pritchett* by noting:

> In *Pritchett* the limited partners were not directly liable to the lender on the partnership obligation. Rather, the general partner was personally liable to the lender on the recourse obligation, and the limited partners were, if anything, potential indemnitors of the general partner. The limited partners were not obligated on any debt for purposes of section 456 until the general partner called for contributions to the partnership. Consequently, in *Pritchett,* the limited partners had not borrowed any amount within the meaning of section 465(b)(2). In this case, to the contrary, each partner is personally and directly liable for a pro rata part of the amount owed to the seller * * *. Because each partner's liability for the partnership debt (in the words of the statute, for the "amounts borrowed") ran directly to the seller and each partner's liability was personal, each partner is at risk for his proportionate share of amount owed to the seller.

Id. at 376.

We agree that Congress intended to condition section 465's exclusion of deductions in part on whether the liability for borrowing is primary or secondary. The statute expressly requires that the taxpayer be "personally liable for the repayment." 26 U.S.C. § 465(b)(2)(A). In debate on the Deficit Reduction Act of 1984, a House Report explained that section 465 limits an at-risk loss to, *inter alia,* "amounts borrowed for use in the activity with respect to which the taxpayer has *personal* liability." H.R.Rep. No. 98–432, Part II, 98th Cong., 2d Sess. 1506, reprinted in 1984 U.S.Code Cong. & Admin.News 697, 1146 (emphasis added). If the limited partnership agreements here create only contingent liability, we will affirm the Tax Court's decision to disallow taxpayers' deductions.

We conclude, however, that the liability of the limited partners was unavoidable and hence not contingent. In Melvin v. Commissioner, 88 T.C. 63 (1987), the Tax Court appeared to answer the question posed here by concluding that

> the fact that the partnership or other partners remain in the "chain of liability" should not detract from the at-risk amount of

> the parties who do have the ultimate liability. The critical inquiry should be who is the obligor of last resort, and in determining who has the ultimate economic responsibility for the loan, the substance of the transaction controls.

Melvin, 88 T.C. at 75 (citing United States v. Raphan, 759 F.2d 879, 885 (Fed.Cir.1985)). Applying that standard we have no reservation in concluding that taxpayers, by virtue of their contractual obligations, have ultimate responsibility for the debt. See Bennion v. Commissioner, 88 T.C. 684, 695 (1987) (applying the *Melvin* standard to taxpayer's "Guarantee Agreement" to determine that taxpayer was ultimately liable on a debt obligation even though the obligation flowed through others). Furthermore, we are not dissuaded by the Tax Court's reasoning that the debt is contingent because the general partners may elect to not make the cash calls. The contracts made the call mandatory and "economic reality" dictates that the partners would do so. See Durkin v. Commissioner, 87 T.C. 1329, 1879 (1986) (concluding that economic reality assured that promissory notes of limited partners to the partnership would be enforced).

The Tax Court also reasoned that the debt was contingent since it was not known in the tax year in question whether sufficient partnership revenues would satisfy the notes prior to or on maturity. We find the Tax Court's reasoning on this point faulty. If the notes required balloon payments upon maturity, the limited partners' obligation to contribute additional funds would be "certain." The acceleration of payments should not be a factor in the taxation analysis. In *Abramson*, like this case, early payment was tied to the success of the operation. No mention was made in *Abramson* that the debt was contingent. Furthermore, the fact that the obligation may not become due for several years in the future is of no significance to the allocation of a pro rata share of the taxpayers' debt in the tax year in question. See Taube v. Commissioner, 88 T.C. 464, 487 (1987) (debt due years in future is nevertheless genuine indebtedness fully includable in basis); Melvin, 88 T.C. at 73 ("debt obligations of a partnership that are payable in later years generally are to be included in the at-risk amounts").

The Commissioner argued below and on appeal that taxpayers' deductions are alternatively barred by section 465(b)(3). That subsection provides that "amounts borrowed shall not be considered to be at risk with respect to an activity if such amounts are borrowed from any person who * * * has an interest (other than an interest as a creditor) in such activity." 26 U.S.C. § 465(b)(3)(A). The legislative history suggests that "*any type of financial interest* in the activity (other than as a creditor) would constitute a prohibited 'other interest' under section 465." Bennion, 88 T.C. at 696 (citing to Staff of Joint Committee on Taxation, General Explanation of Tax Reform Act of 1976 at 39, 1976–3 C.B. (Vol. 2) 51) (emphasis in original). Furthermore, proposed Treasury regulations provide that a lender will be deemed to have a prohibited interest if it has either a capital interest or an interest in the net profits of the activity. See id. (citing Sec. 1.465–8(b), Proposed Income Tax Regs., 44 Fed.Reg. 32239 (June 5, 1979)).

The agreements here provided that Fairfield would receive twenty percent of the gross sales of oil and gas, payable if the partnerships achieved certain profit levels. Judge Simpson concluded that these arrangements gave Fairfield a "substantial interest" in the partnership. Pritchett, 85 T.C. at 592 (Simpson, J., concurring). Judge Cohen stated that she shared Judge Simpson's impression that Fairfield appears to be a person having an interest in the activity, but that "[t]his should be explored further by the finder of facts." Id. at 599 (Cohen J., dissenting). We agree with Judge Cohen's suggestion that this possibility should be explored further. Although we may affirm a correct decision on any basis supported by the record, remand is appropriate when a lower court's "application of an incorrect legal standard leaves * * * an inadequate factual record on which to affirm." United States v. Washington, 641 F.2d 1368, 1371 (9th Cir.1981), cert. denied, 454 U.S. 1143, 102 S.Ct. 1001, 71 L.Ed.2d 294 (1982).

Finally, the Commissioner argues that even if the debts are at risk and thus deductible, the amounts should nevertheless be limited to the present value of the notes. Section 465(b)(4) provides that "a taxpayer shall not be considered at risk with respect to amounts protected against loss through nonrecourse financing, guarantees, stop loss agreements, *or other similar arrangements*.["] 26 U.S.C. § 465(b)(4) (emphasis added). The Commissioner argues that interest-free notes should be regarded as a "similar arrangement."

Our review of the record indicates that this issue was not raised below. "As a general rule, we will not consider an issue raised for the first time on appeal." Bolker v. Commissioner, 760 F.2d 1039, 1042 (9th Cir.1985). Although there are exceptions to the rule, the better practice is to remand to allow the Tax Court to address such an issue first. See id. (trial tactics and legal arguments may have been different if the Commissioner had argued the issue below). Accordingly, we also remand this issue for the Tax Court's consideration.

Reversed and remanded.

ILLUSTRATIVE MATERIAL

A. COVERED ACTIVITIES

Section 465 applies to any activity conducted as a business or for profit by individuals (including trusts and estates), whether as a proprietor, a partner, or as a shareholder in an S corporation. Section 465(c). See Peters v. Commissioner, 77 T.C. 1158 (1981). Prior to 1987, section 465 did not apply to the activity of holding real estate, but this exemption was repealed in the Tax Reform Act of 1986. However, because many real estate activities are financed through nonrecourse borrowing which meets the definition of "qualified nonrecourse financing" in section 465(b)(6), discussed below, most real estate investments continue to be effectively exempted.

Identifying the scope of each activity conducted by the taxpayer is an important issue in applying the at-risk rules. Section 465(c)(2) specifically provides that certain activities will be treated as separate, but most business activities are subject to the vague aggregation rules of section 465(c)(3)(B). Suppose that a limited partnership operates a hotel and a shopping center located on the same tract of land. Is it engaged in one activity or two activities? No regulations governing this issue have been promulgated. Compare Temporary Regulations, section 1.465–1T (permitting partnerships and S corporations to aggregate, by type, activities described in section 465(c)(2)(A)(i), and (iii)–(v) during 1984); Ann. 87–26, 1987 I.R.B. 15, 39 (extending application of Temporary Regulations, section 1.465–1T, to certain later taxable years).

B. AT RISK AMOUNT

1. *General*

Section 465(b) prescribes the rules for determining the amount that a taxpayer has at risk. Any money contributed to the activity (e.g., the partnership) is at risk, as is the *basis* of any contributed property. Generally, amounts borrowed with respect to the property are at risk to the extent that the taxpayer is personally liable for payment of the debt or has pledged property, other than property used in the activity, to secure the debt. Amounts borrowed from any person with an interest in the activity are not at risk. Section 465(b)(3). For application of this rule, see Waddell v. Commissioner, 86 T.C. 848 (1986). Thus, if Partner A borrows $50,000 from Partner B, with full recourse, to invest in the ABC Partnership, A is not at risk for the $50,000. Presumably, this result rests on the view that B is the one at risk. But if A has adequate resources to stand behind the liability, as long as the debtor-creditor relationship is not a sham, it is difficult to see how the situation presents the problem to which section 465 is addressed.

Suppose that A, B, and C each contribute $10,000 to the ABC Partnership. Thereafter, A loans the partnership $170,000, with full recourse, and the partnership purchases depreciable property for $200,000. Under section 707(a), discussed infra page 167, A's loan generally is treated as if it were made by a person other than a partner. In addition, Temporary Regulations, section 1.752–1T, supra, page 123, treat the liability as a recourse liability of the partnership allocable among the partners according to their economic risk of loss. Under those Regulations, each of A, B and C would be entitled to increase their bases in their partnership interests on account of the borrowing. Proposed Regulations, section 1.465–7(a) (1979), however, take the position that with respect to any loan by a partner to the partnership, only the lender partner is at risk. Thus, B and C are at risk only with respect to their $10,000 contributions. A presumably is at risk with respect to his contribution of $10,000 plus the portion of the debt not allocable to B and C under Regulations, section 1.752–1T, although those regulations make no attempt to explain the relationship of economic risk of loss under Temporary Regulations, section 1.752–1T and Proposed Regulations, section 1.465–7(a).

A partner is not at risk with respect to nonrecourse partnership indebtedness, unless the debt is "qualified nonrecourse financing" as defined in section 465(b)(6). This term generally includes only nonrecourse borrowing related to the holding of real property, which is borrowed from an unrelated party, other than the seller of the mortgaged property or the promoter of the partnership, who is regularly engaged in the lending business. Borrowing from related parties regularly engaged in the lending business qualifies only if the terms are commercially reasonable and on substantially the same terms as loans from unrelated persons. In addition, borrowing guaranteed by the federal, state or local government qualifies.

A partner's at risk amount is increased by his distributive share of partnership income items and is decreased by distributions to him and his distributive share of partnership deductions. See Proposed Regulations, section 1.465–22 (1979); Lansburgh v. Commissioner, 92 T.C. 448 (1989). When a partnership makes principal payments in a nonrecourse loan out of net partnership income, a partner's at risk amount increases. To the extent that loan principal payments are out of partnership capital, however, a partner's at risk amount is unaffected. See generally Proposed Regulations, section 1.465–25 (1979); Cooper v. Commissioner, 88 T.C. 84 (1987).

2. *Partner's Guarantee of Partnership Debt*

Generally, a partner's guarantee of a nonrecourse loan made to the partnership avoids the application of section 465, and the entire loan is allocated to the guarantor partner's basis in his partnership interest under Temporary Regulations, section 1.752–1T. See supra page 130. As illustrated in *Pritchett,* guarantees by limited partners of a portion of a loan to a partnership is a method of limiting each limited partner's liability to the partnership's creditors to the partner's pro rata share of the specific debt and rendering the partner at risk as to that amount.

Partners' guarantees do not always work to avoid section 465, however. In Peters v. Commissioner, 89 T.C. 423 (1987), the taxpayer, along with other limited partners, guaranteed a portion of the partnership's nonrecourse indebtedness. Each partner's guarantee extended only to an amount equal to the aggregate deductions that the partner expected to claim. Relying on Brand v. Commissioner, 81 T.C. 821 (1983), the court concluded that Congress did not intend that a guarantor entitled to reimbursement from the primary obligor would be personally liable under section 465(b)(2)(A). Accordingly, because under the applicable state law the guarantor partners were entitled to reimbursement from the partnership if they made good the partnership debt, they were not at risk under section 465(b)(4). The court distinguished its earlier opinion in *Abramson,* discussed in *Pritchett,* supra, on the ground that under the agreements in that case "the limited partners were primarily and ultimately liable because neither the partnership nor its general assets (other than the motion picture film in question) was subject to the nonrecourse obligation. Thus, there was no primary obligor against whom the taxpayers would have had a right of subrogation." In contrast, in *Peters* the court concluded that the partnership was the only primary obligor, as evidenced by the manner in which the amounts of the guarantees were computed; the guarantees "having in effect been voluntarily given, were at most lagniappe as far as [the lender] was concerned."

Is the difference between *Peters* and *Pritchett* merely form? Suppose that the partners were called upon to make good on their guarantees. The *Peters* court acknowledged that in such event it would be unlikely that the partnership would have any assets with which to reimburse the guarantor-partners. Nevertheless, it concluded that since the taxpayers chose the use of guarantees "as their means of making an end run around the rules of section 465," they could not selectively ignore their legal rights as guarantors. The opinion in *Peters* indicates that the court was influenced by the blatancy of the method of computing the guaranteed amounts.

In Melvin v. Commissioner, 88 T.C. 63 (1987), a limited partner contributed his own $70,000 recourse promissory note to a limited partnership to reflect his obligation to make future capital contributions. The partnership then borrowed over $3,000,000 from an unrelated lender on a nonrecourse basis, pledging most of its property, including the taxpayer's promissory note, to secure the loan. The taxpayer stipulated that the mere contribution of the note did not increase his at risk amount under section 465, and court approved the stipulation, noting that the contributed promissory note reflected neither a cash contribution nor a borrowing under section 465(b)(1). Nevertheless, the taxpayer argued that because his note had been pledged to secure the nonrecourse loan from the third party lender, he was personally liable on that debt to the extent of his note to the partnership and therefor was at risk for that amount. Since he bore the ultimate liability for repayment of the debt if the partnership's funds were insufficient, the court agreed with the taxpayer. It noted that a critical factor in its holding was that the partner had no right of reimbursement from the partnership if the lender proceeded directly against the partner on his note after the partnership defaulted.

Despite the taxpayer's stipulation in *Melvin,* given the holding in *Pritchett,* it is not clear why the contribution of a partner's promissory note should not increase the partner's at risk amount. Even if the contributed promissory note is not pledged, the contributing partner does not appear be in a significantly different economic position from the taxpayer in *Pritchett,* who was obligated under the partnership agreement to make additional contributions to pay partnership debts. Perhaps the crucial distinction is one of form in that the contributed promissory note is "property," but its basis to the contributing partner is zero. Hence, the limitation of a partner's at risk amount to the basis of contributed property in section 456(b)(1)(A) applies.

C. EFFECT OF AT RISK LIMITATION

In general, the effect of section 465 is to defer deductions attributable to nonrecourse debt until the debt is repaid. In computing allowable deductions for the year, however, the taxpayer is permitted to treat deductions as being wholly attributable to his at risk amount—his equity investment or share of recourse debt—until that at risk amount has been exhausted. Thereafter, deductions in excess of current increases in the taxpayer's at risk amount are suspended until the taxpayer increases his at risk amount.

Section 465 operates independently of the rules governing a partner's basis in his partnership interest. Even though a partner has sufficient basis to avoid the application of section 704(d), discussed supra, page 134, deduction of his distributive share of partnership losses will be postponed if his at risk amount is insufficient. Nevertheless, his basis in his partnership interest is reduced by the full amount of his distributive share of partnership losses. Assume, for example, that A contributes $5,000 cash to acquire a one third interest in profits and capital of the ABC general partnership. The partnership then borrows $285,000 on a nonrecourse basis to drill an oil well. A's basis in his partnership interest, applying the rules of section 752, discussed supra, page 122, is $100,000 ($5,000 + (⅓ × $285,000)). His at risk amount, however, is only $5,000. Thus, if for the current year A's distributive share of partnership items is a $100,000 loss from drilling a dry hole, he may deduct currently only $5,000 of the loss; section 465 defers the remaining $95,000 deduction. But under section 705, A must reduce the basis of his partnership interest by the full $100,000 loss. Thus, his basis for his partnership interest is zero. If the oil property is abandoned to the mortgagee the following year, A's distributive share of partnership income will be $95,000, but he will be entitled to claim the $95,000 deduction previously suspended by section 465. The basis of A's partnership interest is unaffected by the allowance of the deduction in the later year under section 465. Basis is increased by his $100,000 share of partnership income, and is reduced by a like amount due to the cancellation of the partnership debt, leaving A with a basis of zero.

D. REFERENCES

Wolf, At–Risk as Applied to Partnerships: Recent Developments, 43 N.Y.U. Tax Inst. 26–1 (1985); Comment: Elliston v. Commissioner, Tiered Partnerships and the Aggregation Rules of Section 465, 38 Tax Lawyer 779 (1985).

(3) THE PASSIVE ACTIVITY LOSS RULES OF SECTION 469

INTERNAL REVENUE CODE: Sections 469(a), (b), (c)(1)–(4), (d)(1), (e)(1), (g), (h)(1) and (2), (i), (*l*)(3).

TEMPORARY REGULATIONS: Section 1.469–2T(d)(6)(ii)(A), –5T(e).

SENATE FINANCE COMMITTEE REPORT, TAX REFORM ACT OF 1986

S.Rep. No. 99–313, 99th Cong., 2d Sess. 713–718 (1986).

[Pre–1987] Law

In general, no limitations are placed on the ability of a taxpayer to use deductions from a particular activity to offset income from other activities. Similarly, most tax credits may be used to offset tax attributable to income from any of the taxpayer's activities.

* * *

In the absence of more broadly applicable limitations on the use of deductions and credits from one activity to reduce tax liability attributable to other activities, taxpayers with substantial sources of positive income are able to eliminate or sharply reduce tax liability by using deductions and credits from other activities, frequently by investing in tax shelters. Tax shelters commonly offer the opportunity to reduce or avoid tax liability with respect to salary or other positive income, by making available deductions and credits, possibly exceeding real economic costs or losses currently borne by the taxpayer, in excess or in advance of income from the shelters.

Reasons for Change

In recent years, it has become increasingly clear that taxpayers are losing faith in the Federal income tax system. This loss of confidence has resulted in large part from the interaction of two of the system's principal features: its high marginal rates (in 1986, 50 percent for a single individual with taxable income in excess of $88,270), and the opportunities it provides for taxpayers to offset income from one source with tax shelter deductions and credits from another.

The prevalence of tax shelters in recent years—even after the highest marginal rate for individuals was reduced in 1981 from 70 percent to 50 percent—has been well documented. For example, a recent Treasury study [1] revealed that in 1983, out of 260,000 tax returns reporting "total positive income" [2] in excess of $250,000, 11 percent paid taxes equaling 5 percent or less of total positive income, and 21 percent paid taxes equaling 10 percent or less of total positive income. Similarly, in the case of tax returns reporting total positive income in excess of $1 million, 11 percent paid tax equaling less than 5 percent of total positive income, and 19 percent paid tax equaling less than 10 percent of total positive income.[3]

Such patterns give rise to a number of undesirable consequences, even aside from their effect in reducing Federal tax revenues. Extensive shelter activity contributes to public concerns that the tax system is unfair, and to the belief that tax is paid only by the naive and the unsophisticated. This, in turn, not only undermines compliance, but encourages further expansion of the tax shelter market, in many cases diverting investment capital from productive activities to those principally or exclusively serving tax avoidance goals.

The committee believes that the most important sources of support for the Federal income tax system are the average citizens who simply report their income (typically consisting predominantly of items such as salaries, wages, pensions, interest, and dividends) and pay tax under the general rules. To the extent that these citizens feel that they are bearing a disproportionate burden with regard to the costs of government because of their unwillingness or inability to engage in tax-oriented investment activity, the tax system itself is threatened.

Under these circumstances, the committee believes that decisive action is needed to curb the expansion of tax sheltering and to restore to the tax system the degree of equity that is a necessary precondition

1. Treasury Department, "Taxes Paid by High-Income Taxpayers and the Growth of Partnerships," reprinted in IRS Statistics of Income Bulletin (Fall 1985), beginning at page 55.

2. Total positive income was defined as the sum of salary, interest, dividends, and income from profitable businesses and investments, as reported on tax returns.

3. Other studies have similarly reached the conclusion that tax shelters, by flowing through tax benefits to individuals with positive sources of income, have permitted some taxpayers with sizeable economic incomes substantially to reduce their tax liabilities. See Joint Committee on Taxation, Tax Reform Proposals: Tax Shelters and Minimum Tax (JCS-34-85), August 7, 1985.

to a beneficial and widely desired reduction in rates. So long as tax shelters are permitted to erode the Federal tax base, a low-rate system can provide neither sufficient revenues, nor sufficient progressivity, to satisfy the general public that tax liability bears a fair relationship to the ability to pay. In particular, a provision significantly limiting the use of tax shelter losses is unavoidable if substantial rate reductions are to be provided to high-income taxpayers without disproportionately reducing the share of total liability under the individual income tax that is borne by high-income taxpayers as a group.

The question of how to prevent harmful and excessive tax sheltering is not a simple one. One way to address the problem would be to eliminate substantially all tax preferences in the Internal Revenue Code. For two reasons, however, the committee believes that this course is inappropriate.

First, while the bill reduces or eliminates some tax preference items that the committee believes do not provide social or economic benefits commensurate with their cost, there are many preferences that the committee believes are socially or economically beneficial. This is especially true when such preferences are used primarily to advance the purposes upon which Congress relied in enacting them, rather than to avoid taxation of income from sources unrelated to the preferred activity.

Second, it would be extremely difficult, perhaps impossible, to design a tax system that measures income perfectly. For example, the statutory allowance for depreciation, even under the normative system used under the bill for alternative minimum tax purposes, reflects broad industry averages, as opposed to providing precise item-by-item measurements. Accordingly, taxpayers with assets that depreciate less rapidly than the average, or that appreciate over time (as may be the case with certain real estate), may engage in tax sheltering even under the minimum tax, unless Congress directly addresses the tax shelter problem.

* * *

The question of what constitutes a tax shelter that should be subject to limitations is closely related to the question of who Congress intends to benefit when it enacts tax preferences. For example, in providing preferential depreciation for real estate or favorable accounting rules for farming, it was not Congress's primary intent to permit outside investors to avoid tax liability with respect to their salaries by investing in limited partnership syndications. Rather, Congress intends to benefit and provide incentives to taxpayers active in the businesses to which the preferences were directed.

* * *

The availability of tax benefits to shelter positive sources of income also has harmed the economy generally, by providing a non-economic return on capital for certain investments. This has encouraged a flow of capital away from activities that may provide a higher pre-tax economic return, thus retarding the growth of the sectors of the economy with the greatest potential for expansion.

The committee believes that, in order for tax preferences to function as intended, their benefit must be directed primarily to taxpayers with a substantial and *bona fide* involvement in the activities to which the preferences relate. The committee also believes that it is appropriate to encourage nonparticipating investors to invest in particular activities, by permitting the use of preferences to reduce the rate of tax on income from those activities; however, such investors should not be permitted to use tax benefits to shelter unrelated income.

There are several reasons why it is appropriate to examine the materiality of a taxpayer's participation in an activity in determining the extent to which such taxpayer should be permitted to use tax benefits from the activity. A taxpayer who materially participates in an activity is more likely than a passive investor to approach the activity with a significant nontax economic profit motive, and to form a sound judgment as to whether the activity has genuine economic significance and value.

A material participation standard identifies an important distinction between different types of taxpayer activities. In general, the more passive investor is seeking a return on capital invested, including returns in the form of reductions in the taxes owed on unrelated income, rather than an ongoing source of livelihood. A material participation standard reduces the importance, for such investors, of the tax-reduction features of an investment, and thus increases the importance of the economic features in an investor's decision about where to invest his funds.

Moreover, the committee believes that restricting the use of losses from business activities in which the taxpayer does not materially participate against other sources of positive income (such as salary and portfolio income) addresses a fundamental aspect of the tax shelter problem. As discussed above, instances in which the tax system applies simple rules at the expense of economic accuracy encourage the structuring of transactions to take advantage of the situations in which such rules give rise to undermeasurement or deferral of income. Such transactions commonly are marketed to investors who do not intend to participate in the transactions, as devices for sheltering unrelated sources of positive income (e.g., salary and portfolio income). Accordingly, by creating a bar against the use of losses from business activities in which the taxpayer does not materially participate to offset positive income sources such as salary and portfolio income, the committee believes that it is possible significantly to reduce the tax shelter problem.

Further, in the case of a nonparticipating investor in a business activity, the committee believes that it is appropriate to treat losses of the activity as not realized by the investor prior to disposition of his interest in the activity. The effort to measure, on an annual basis, real economic losses from passive activities gives rise to distortions, particularly due to the nontaxation of unrealized appreciation and the mismatching of tax deductions and related economic income that may occur, especially where debt financing is used heavily. Only when a taxpayer disposes of his interest in an activity is it possible to determine whether a loss was sustained over the entire time that he held the interest.

The distinction that the committee believes should be drawn between activities on the basis of material participation bears no relationship to the question of whether, and to what extent, the taxpayer is at risk with respect to the activities.[4] In general, the fact that a taxpayer has placed a particular amount at risk in an activity does not establish, prior to a disposition of the taxpayer's interest, that the amount invested, or any amount, has as yet been lost. The fact that a taxpayer is potentially liable with respect to future expenses or losses of the activity likewise has no bearing on the question whether any amount has as yet been lost, or otherwise is an appropriate current deduction or credit.

At-risk standards, although important in determining the maximum amount that is subject to being lost, are not a sufficient basis for determining whether or when net losses from an activity should be deductible against other sources of income, or for determining whether an ultimate economic loss has been realized. Congress' goal of making tax preferences available principally to active participants in substantial businesses, rather than to investors seeking to shelter unrelated income, can best be accomplished by examining material participation, as opposed to the financial stake provided by an investor to purchase tax shelter benefits.

In certain situations, however, the committee believes that financial risk or other factors, rather than material participation, should be the relevant standard. A situation in which financial risk is relevant relates to the oil and gas industry, which at present is suffering severe hardship due to the worldwide collapse of oil prices. The committee believes that relief for this industry requires that tax benefits be provided to attract outside investors. Moreover, the committee believes that such relief should be provided only with respect to investors who are willing to accept an unlimited and unprotected financial risk proportionate to their ownership interests in the oil and gas activities. Granting tax shelter benefits to investors in oil and gas activities who did not accept unlimited risk, proportionate to their ownership investments in the activities, would permit the benefit of this special exception to be diverted unduly to the investors, while providing less benefit to oil and gas activities and threatening the integrity of the entire rule limiting the use of nonparticipatory business losses.

4. The at-risk rules of present law, while important and useful in preventing overvaluation of assets, and in preventing the transfer of tax benefits to taxpayers with no real equity in an activity, do not address the adverse consequences arising specifically from such transfers to nonparticipating investors.

A further area in which the material participation standard is not wholly adequate is that of rental activities. Such activities predominantly involve the production of income from capital. * * *

Rental activities generally require less ongoing management activity, in proportion to capital invested, than business activities involving the production or sale of goods and services. Thus, for example, an individual who is employed full-time as a professional could more easily provide all necessary management in his spare time with respect to a rental activity than he could with respect to another type of business activity involving the same capital investment. The extensive use of rental activities for tax shelter purposes under present law, combined with the reduced level of personal involvement necessary to conduct such activities, make clear that the effectiveness of the basic passive loss provision could be seriously compromised if material participation were sufficient to avoid the limitations in the case of rental activities.

A limited measure of relief, however, is believed appropriate in the case of certain moderate-income investors in rental real estate, who otherwise might experience cash flow difficulties with respect to investments that in many cases are designed to provide financial security, rather than to shelter a substantial amount of other income.

Further, additional considerations apply in the case of limited partnerships. In order to maintain limited liability status, a limited partner generally is precluded from materially participating in the business activity of the partnership; in virtually all respects, a limited partner more closely resembles a shareholder in a C corporation than an active business entrepreneur. Moreover, limited partnerships commonly are used as vehicles for marketing tax benefits to investors seeking to shelter unrelated income. In light of the widespread use of limited partnership interests in syndicating tax shelters, the committee believes that losses from limited partnership interests should not be permitted, prior to a taxable disposition, to offset positive income sources such as salary.

* * *

ILLUSTRATIVE MATERIAL

A. GENERAL

Section 469 applies to individual partners, not directly to the partnership. Section 469 does not apply to a partner which is a C corporation, unless the corporation is "closely held." Section 469(a)(2)(B). The rules of section 469 may disallow a partner's deduction of his distributive share of a partnership loss, even though the loss is allowable under both section 704(d) and section 465. For rules governing the coordination of section 469 with section 704(d) and section 465, see Temporary Regulations, section 1.469–2T(d)(6). When section 469 disallows a partner's distributive share of a partnership loss the partner's basis in his partnership interest should be reduced by the full distributive share of partnership losses notwithstanding that section 469 defers the deduction. See S.Rep. No. 99–313, 99th Cong., 2d Sess. 723, n. 9 (1986).

B. PASSIVE ACTIVITY LOSSES

1. *Treatment of Passive Activity Losses*

Mechanically, section 469(a) disallows any "passive activity loss." A passive activity loss is defined in section 469(d)(1) as the aggregate losses from all passive activities for the year in excess of the aggregate income from such activities for the year. In this context, the term losses means the amount by which all otherwise allowable deductions exceed gross income; and income means the amount by which gross income exceeds deductions. Thus, if Passive Activity A generates $1,000 of income and $1,200 of deductions, and Passive Activity B generates $500 of deductions and $600 of gross income, the taxpayer has a $100 passive activity loss for the year which will be disallowed. Temporary Regulations, section 1.469–1T(f), provide rules for allocating the disallowed loss among the various passive activities that contributed to it, and then allocating the loss attributable to each activity among the component deductions. The disallowed loss carries over to the next year, where it enters the computation again; and this carry-over continues until the loss is allowed or permanently disallowed. Section 469(b). Thus, section 469, like section 465, generally operates only to defer, not totally disallow, deductions attributable to passive activities. Furthermore, it allows a full current deduction for passive activity losses to the extent the taxpayer has current passive activity income from other sources.

2. *Definition of "Passive Activity" and "Material Participation"*

A "passive activity" generally is any trade or business activity in which the taxpayer does not "materially participate." Section 469(c)(1). However, all rental activities are deemed to be passive activities regardless of the level of the taxpayer's participation. Section 469(c)(2). For the definition of rental activity, see Temporary Regulations, section 1.469–1T(e)(3). Section 469(h) defines material participation as regular, continuous, and substantial involvement in the operations of the activity. In addition, section 469(h)(2) specifically provides that except as provided in Regulations, "no interest in a limited partnership as a limited partner shall be treated as an interest with respect to which a taxpayer materially participates." The Temporary Regulations generally test for material participation by counting the number of hours devoted to the activity each year by the taxpayer and permit limited partners to be treated as materially participating under certain circumstances. Temporary Regulations, section 1.469–5T(a). In applying these rules it is important to remember that each partner's individual participation must be tested separately.

Under Temporary Regulations, section 1.469–5T(a), a taxpayer materially participates in an activity if any of the following tests are met: (1) the taxpayer devotes more than 500 hours to the activity in the year; (2) the taxpayer's participation constitutes all of the participation in the activity of any individual; (3) the taxpayer participates in the activity for more than 100 hours during the year and his participation is not less than that of any other individual; (4) the activity is a trade or business, the taxpayer participates in the activity for more than 100 hours (but not more than 500 hours) during the year, and the taxpayer's total participation in all such trade or business activities during the year exceeds 500 hours; (5) the taxpayer materially participated in the activity for five of the preceding ten taxable years; (6) the activity is a personal service activity in which the taxpayer materially participated for any three preceding years; or (7) based on all the facts and circumstances, the individual participates in the activity on a regular, continuous, and substantial basis. Work not customarily performed by the owner of a business is not taken into account if one of the principal purposes of performing such work is to meet the material participation requirement. Unless an individual also participates in the day-to-day management or operations of the business, work performed in the capacity of an investor is not counted. Temporary Regulations, section 1.469–5T(f)(2). A taxpayer who participates in an activity for 100 hours or less during the year cannot qualify as materially participating under the facts and circumstances test. Temporary Regulations, section 1.469–5T(b)(2)(iii). Management services are taken into account in determining material participation only to a limited extent in applying the facts and circumstances test. Temporary Regulations, section 1.469–5T(b)(2)(ii).

3. *"Significant Participation Activities"*

Temporary Regulations, section 1.469–2T(f)(2), define as a "significant participation activity" any activity in which the taxpayer participates for more than 100 hours during the year, but in which he does not materially participate. If gross income for the year from all significant participation activities exceeds passive activity deductions from such activities, all of the activities are aggregated into a single passive activity that did not produce a loss for the year. Temporary Regulations, section 1.469–1T(f)(2)(i)(C). In addition, Temporary Regulations, section 1.469–2T(f)(2), recharacterize as active income a portion of the income from any significant participation activity, if all such activities in the aggregate produce net income.

4. *Application to Partners*

It is clear from these rules that a general partner does not qualify as materially participating merely because of his status as a general partner. The level of participation in each activity in which the partnership is engaged must be tested separately. A partner may be active as to some partnership activities and passive as to others.

Temporary Regulations, section 1.469–5T(e), provide two exceptions to section 469(h)(2), which generally require that a limited partner be treated as not materially participating in any partnership activity. First, a limited partner materially participates in a partnership activity if any one of tests (1), (5), or (6) for material participation described above are met. Second, a limited partnership interest held by a general partner is not treated as a limited partnership interest in applying section 469; whether the partner materially participates is determined for both interests together under the above described tests. This final rule appears to contradict the statutory language of section 469(h)(2), but the Treasury has authority under that section virtually to rewrite the statute.

5. *Special Rule for Oil and Gas Working Interests*

Section 469(c)(3) provides that any working interest in an oil or gas property is treated as not being a passive activity if the taxpayer holds the interest in a form that does not limit liability, even though the taxpayer does not materially participate. Thus, a general partnership interest qualifies as active, but a limited partnership interest does not. If any losses from a property are treated as active under this rule, all income from the property in future years must be treated as active income. Section 469(c)(3)(B); see Temporary Regulations, section 1.469–2T(c)(6).

C. APPLICATION ON ACTIVITY–BY–ACTIVITY BASIS

1. *General*

Whether a partner's distributive share of any partnership item is treated as active or passive is determined by whether the taxpayer materially participated in the particular activity that gave rise to the item during the *partnership's* taxable year. Temporary Regulations, section 1.469–2T(e)(1). The Code does not provide any guidance for determining the scope of an activity, but such a determination is crucial in applying section 469. The Committee Reports indicate that a single activity consists of those "undertakings [that] consist of an integrated and interrelated economic unit, conducted in coordination with or reliance upon each other, and constituting an appropriate unit for the measurement of gain or loss." S.Rep. No. 99–313, 99th Cong., 2d Sess. 739 (1986). Thus, it is clear that a single partnership may be engaged in more than one activity. It is also clear that two related partnerships may be engaged together in a single activity. Under this standard, a partner may materially participate with respect to one partnership activity, but not with respect to a different partnership activity during the same year. In such a case, the partner's distributive share of partnership items attributable to the activity in which he did not materially participate would be passive income or loss. Regulations, section 1.469–4T, provide detailed rules regarding the scope of activities for purposes of section 469.

2. *Scope of "Activity"*

Temporary Regulations, section 1.469–4T(a)(3), classify all business endeavors conducted by the same person at the same location (or in close proximity) as an "undertaking," which is the smallest unit which may be classified as an "activity." For example, if at a single location the taxpayer conducts a hardware store and a construction business, both together constitute an undertaking. However, rental endeavors generally will not be grouped with nonrental endeavors; they constitute separate undertakings. Temporary Regulations, section 1.469–4T(a)(3)(iv). For example, if at the same location the taxpayer operates a retail automobile business and an automobile leasing business which leases vehicles on a long-term basis, the two endeavors are separate undertakings. But Temporary Regulations, section 1.469–4T(d)(2), provide aggregation if either operation generates more than 80 percent of the combined gross income. Business endeavors conducted at different locations generally are separate undertakings, even though conducted by the same person. See Temporary Regulations, section 1.469–4T(c)(2)(iii)(C), (c)(3). Endeavors in which the ownership is not congruent, even though there may be some overlapping ownership, constitute separate undertakings. Each undertaking is initially treated as a separate activity. Temporary Regulations, section 1.469–4T(a)(4).

Trade or business and professional service undertakings are subject to mandatory aggregation rules. Trade or business undertakings (generally defined as all undertakings other than professional service, oil and gas, or rental undertakings, Temporary Regulations, section 1.469–4T(a)(4)(ii)(A)) will be aggregated if (1) more than one-half of their operations are in the same line of business or they are vertically integrated, *and* (2) they are controlled by the same persons. Temporary Regulations, section 1.469–

4T(a)(4)(ii)(B), (f). In addition, a group of undertakings will be aggregated into a larger activity if they are part of a group of undertakings constituting an "integrated business" and are controlled by the same interests. Temporary Regulations, section 1.469–4T(a)(4)(ii)(C), (g). This rule would apply, for example, to a chain of virtually identical stores. Common control is determined under a facts and circumstances test, but if five or fewer persons own more than a 50 interest in each of two or more undertakings, taking into account only the common ownership of each individual, they are reputably presumed to be commonly controlled. Temporary Regulations, section 1.469–4T(j)(1) and (2). A partner's interest in an undertaking conducted by the partnership is measured by the greater of the partner's interest in partnership capital (as a percentage of value) or the partner's largest distributive share of any item of partnership income or gain (disregarding section 707(c) payments). Temporary Regulations, section 1.469–4T(j)(3). A special rule permits disaggregation of multiple undertaking activities into two or more separate activities, as long as the person conducting the undertakings so elects for the first taxable year of the activity. Where the undertakings are conducted by a partnership the election is made by the partnership. Temporary Regulations, section 1.469–4T(*o*).

Professional service undertakings are aggregated if they are controlled by the same interests and either (1) more than 20 percent of their operations are in the same field or one of the undertakings earns more than 20 percent of its gross income from persons who are customers of the other. Temporary Regulations, section 1.469–4T(a)(4)(iii), (h). Rental real estate undertakings generally are not aggregated unless the taxpayer elects to aggregate them. This election is made by the partnership. Temporary Regulations, section 1.469–4T(a)(4)(iv), (k). Rental undertakings may be fragmented and reaggregated, subject to year-to-year consistency rules. Temporary Regulations, section 1.469–4T(k)(2)(i).

D. ACTIVE PARTICIPATION RENTAL REAL ESTATE ACTIVITIES

Section 469(i) relaxes the restrictions on deducting losses from passive activities with respect to losses from rental real estate activities in which the taxpayer "actively participates." If this participation standard is met, a taxpayer may deduct against income that is not passive income up to $25,000 of rental real estate losses. These losses must first be offset against any passive income, however; and the $25,000 ceiling is reduced by one half of the amount by which the taxpayer's adjusted gross income (without taking such losses into account) exceeds $100,000. Thus a partner who fails the material participation standard, but who meets the active participation standard may be able to deduct currently all or a part of his distributive share of partnership losses attributable to rental real estate activities. Section 469(i)(6) defines "active participation." Under this provision no partner with less than a 10 percent interest (by value) in the activity (as distinguished from the partnership) may be considered as actively participating. In addition, no limited partner, regardless of the extent of his interest can be treated as actively participating.

E. PORTFOLIO INCOME

Even if a partner does not materially participate in the activities of a partnership, her distributive share of portfolio income items (defined generally as all income other than income derived in the ordinary course of a trade or business) received by the partnership is not passive income. Temporary Regulations, section 1.469–2T(c)(3). Thus, for example, interest on a reserve maintained in connection with a partnership activity with respect to which a partner is passive is not passive activity income for the partner. See Temporary Regulations, section 1.469–2T(c)(3), Ex. (2).

F. PAYMENTS TO PARTNERS

Payments received by a partner in a transaction subject to section 707(a) are never treated as passive activity income with respect to the partnership activity. Temporary Regulations, section 1.469–2T(e)(2)(i). Payments to a partner subject to section 707(c) are treated as compensation or interest in applying the passive loss rules. Temporary Regulations, section 1.469–2T(e)(2)(ii)(A). For sections 707(a) and (c), see infra, pages 167 and 174.

Payments to a retired partner or a deceased partner's successor in interest which are subject to section 736(b) are treated as passive income only if they would have been characterized as passive income if received at the time the liquidation of the partner's interest commenced. Temporary Regulations, section 1.469–2T(e)(2)(iii). Payments subject to section 736(a) which are attributable to unrealized receivables (as defined in section 751(c)) and goodwill are treated as passive activity income only if the activity to which they are attributable was a passive activity of the partner for the partnership taxable year in which payments commenced. Temporary Regulations, section 1.469–2T(e)(2)(ii)(B). Section 736 payments are discussed infra, page 231.

G. EFFECT OF DISPOSITION OF ACTIVITY

Section 469(g) allows the taxpayer to deduct previously disallowed losses attributable to any activity in the year in which she makes a fully taxable disposition of his entire interest in the activity. Generally a sale of all of the assets used in the activity is required. The sale by a partner of all of her interest in a partnership will permit the partner to deduct suspended losses attributable to all partnership activities in which she did not materially participate. If the partnership was engaged in two or more activities in which the partner did not materially participate and the partnership sells all of the assets used in one activity, the suspended losses attributable to that activity may be claimed by the partner, but suspended losses attributable to other activities of the partnership remain in suspense. It is important to bear in mind that if the partner sells her entire interest in the partnership, she should be allowed to deduct all suspended losses notwithstanding that she has no remaining basis. This result is required because a partner's outside basis should be reduced by her full distributive share of partnership losses notwithstanding that section 469 may operate to defer the deduction. See supra, page 140. Thus, allowing the loss despite the lack of any basis for the partnership interest is not inconsistent with Sennett v. Commissioner, supra, page 143.

Gain or loss on the sale or other taxable disposition of a partnership interest is characterized as passive or active by looking through the partnership entity to its activities. Temporary Regulations, section 1.469–2T(e)(3). However, the gain or loss realized on the sale of the entire interest is a ceiling on the look-through computation. A sale at a gain may be treated as composed of both passive gain and active gain; a sale at a loss include both passive loss and active loss; but a sale at no gain, for example, will not be treated as composed of equal amounts of active gain and passive loss (or passive gain and active loss). See Temporary Regulations, section 1.469–2T(e)(3)(vii) Ex. (1). For the sale of a partnership interest, see infra, chapter 5.

H. REFERENCES

Banoff, Sales and Redemptions of Partnership Interests Under the Passive Loss Regulations, 68 J.Tax. 332 (1988); Brode, Structuring Real Estate Entities in View of the New Limitation on Loss Rules, 65 J.Tax. 290 (1986).

SECTION 3. TRANSACTIONS BETWEEN PARTNERS AND THE PARTNERSHIP

A. INTRODUCTION

The question of whether a partner could deal with the partnership in a capacity other than as a partner, e.g., as a provider of or payor for services and as a buyer from or seller of property to the partnership arose in the early days of the income tax. Resolution of the issue turned on whether the entity or aggregate approach were adopted with respect to such transactions.

Suppose A, an equal partner in the AB partnership, pays the partnership a $200 commission for stock purchased for his individual account, $20 of which is attributable to transfer taxes. Under the aggregate approach A will not be taxed on any part of the $180 partnership profit; $90 of the profit is properly allocated to B and the other $90 is attributable to services A has performed for himself. Instead, he will be regarded as having contributed $90 to the partnership, and he will add $110 to the cost of his stock. ($20 taxes plus $90 paid to B). B will be taxed on $90. Benjamin v. Hoey, 139 F.2d 945 (2d Cir.1944), adopted this approach. Under the entity theory, A and B would each be taxed on his $90 share of the $180 partnership profit and A would add $200 to the basis of his stock. Wegener v. Commissioner, 119 F.2d 49 (5th Cir.1941) (partner received income from drilling wells for partnership); Shirley v. O'Malley, 91 F.Supp. 98 (D.Neb.1950) (partnership deducted rent on assets leased from partner); Rev.Rul. 72–504, 1972–2 Cum.Bull. 90 (individual may deduct rent paid to the partnership for the use of a building in his individual business provided he includes the rental income in his distributive share of partnership profits).

Similar problems arise where B sells an asset to the partnership: B, having a basis for her partnership interest of $75, sells the partnership property worth $200 but with a $100 basis. Under the aggregate theory, she has sold a one-half interest, so she has a $50 gain, and contributed a one-half interest, increasing her basis to $125. She is regarded as receiving a distribution of $100, reducing her basis to $25. If the partnership sells the property it has a gain of $50, which is allocable to B under section 704(c), increasing her basis to $75. If the partnership then liquidates with B receiving $100, she will be taxed on $25 so that she is finally taxed on a total of $125. Under the entity approach, she would have been taxed on an immediate $125 gain.

The difference in the two approaches is essentially a matter of timing, although the character of items may be affected as well. The entity approach is not only simpler, but better preserves the proper character of items and is, therefor, adopted in section 707(a)(1) as the general method for dealing with transactions in which a partner deals with the partnership "other than in his capacity as a member of such partnership." In Heggestad v. Commissioner, 91 T.C. 778 (1988), the Tax Court held that section 707(a) expressly overrules any precedential value of Benjamin v. Hoey, supra.

The basic rule of section 707(a)(1) is supplemented by two special provisions. Section 707(a)(2) recharacterizes certain allocations and distributions related to the performance of services by a partner or the transfer of property to the partnership as transactions subject to section 707(a)(1). Section 707(b) disallows loss deductions on sales between a partner and a 50 percent or more controlled partnership (or between two partnerships each of which is 50 percent or more controlled by the same persons). In addition, gain on a sale of property other than a capital asset (i.e., section 1231 property) between a partner and a related partnership is recharacterized as ordinary income.

Some of the same problems that arise in transactions governed by section 707(a) also arise when a partner is entitled to a "salary" or guaranteed payment from the partnership that is unrelated to partnership net income. Accordingly, section 707(c) applies the entity theory to determine the includability of such payments by the partner and the deductibility of such payments by the partnership.

B. TRANSACTIONS IN WHICH A PARTNER DOES NOT ACT AS A PARTNER

INTERNAL REVENUE CODE: Sections 707(a), (b); 1239(a)–(c); 267(a)(2), (e)(1)–(4)

REGULATIONS: Sections 1.267(a)–2T(c); 1.707–1(a), (b)

REVENUE RULING 81–301

1981–2 Cumulative Bulletin 144.

Is an allocation based on a percentage of gross income paid to an advisor general partner subject to section 707(a) of the Internal Revenue Code, under the circumstances described below?

FACTS

ABC is a partnership formed in accordance with the Uniform Limited Partnership Act of a state and is registered with the Securities and Exchange Commission as an open-end diversified management company pursuant to the Investment Company Act of 1940, as amended. Under the partnership agreement, *ABC*'s assets must consist only of municipal bonds, certain readily-marketable temporary investments, and cash. The agreement provides for two classes of general partners: (1) "director general partners" (directors) who are individuals and (2) one "adviser general partner" (adviser) that is a corporate investment adviser registered as such in accordance with the Investment Advisers Act of 1940, 15 U.S.C.A., section 80b–5 (1971).

Under the partnership agreement, the directors are compensated and have complete and exclusive control over the management, conduct, and operation of *ABC*'s activities. The directors are authorized to appoint agents and employees to perform duties on behalf of *ABC* and these agents may be, but need not be, general partners. Under the partnership agreement, the adviser has no rights, powers, or authority as a general partner, except that, subject to the supervision of the directors, the adviser is authorized to manage the investment and reinvestment of *ABC*'s assets. The adviser is responsible for payment of any expenses incurred in the performance of its investment advisory duties, including those for office space and facilities, equipment, and any of its personnel used to service and administer *ABC*'s investments. The adviser is not personally liable to the other partners for any losses incurred in the investment and reinvestment of *ABC*'s assets.

The nature of the adviser's services are substantially the same as those it renders as an independent contractor or agent for persons other than *ABC* and, under the agreement, the adviser is not precluded from engaging in such transactions with others.

Each general partner, including the adviser general partner, is required to contribute sufficient cash to *ABC* to acquire at least a one percent interest in the partnership. The agreement requires an allocation of 10 percent of *ABC*'s daily gross income to the adviser. After reduction by the compensation allocable to the directors and the adviser, *ABC*'s items of income, gain, loss, deduction, and credit are divided according to the percentage interests held by each partner.

The adviser's right to 10 percent of *ABC*'s daily gross income for managing *ABC*'s investment must be approved at least annually by a majority vote of the directors or a majority vote of all the partnership interests. Furthermore, the directors may remove the adviser as investment manager at any time on 60 days written notice to the adviser. The adviser can terminate its investment manager status by giving 60 days written notice to the directors. The agreement provides that the adviser will no longer be a general partner after removal or withdrawal as investment manager, but will continue to participate as a limited partner in the income, gains, losses, deductions, and credits attributable to the percentage interest that it holds.

LAW AND ANALYSIS

Section 61(a)(1) of the Code provides that, except as otherwise provided by law, gross income means all income from whatever source derived, including compensation for services, including fees, commissions, and similar items.

Section 702(a) of the Code provides that in determining the income tax of a partner each partner must take into account separately such partner's distributive share of the partnership's items of income, gain, loss, deduction, or credit.

Section 707(a) of the Code provides that if a partner engages in a transaction with a partnership other than as a member of such partnership, the transaction shall, except as otherwise provided in section 707, be considered as occurring between the partnership and one who is not a partner.

Section 1.707–1(a) of the Income Tax Regulations provides that a partner who engages in a transaction with a partnership other than in the capacity as a partner shall be treated as if not a member of the partnership with respect to such transaction. Such transactions include the rendering of services by the partner to the partnership. In all cases, the substance of the transaction will govern rather than its form.

Section 707(c) of the Code provides that to the extent determined without regard to the income of the partnership, payments to a partner for services shall be considered as made to one who is not a member of the partnership, but only for purposes of section 61(a) and, subject to section 263, for purposes of section 162(a).

Although the adviser is identified in the agreement as an "adviser general partner," the adviser provides similar services to others as part of its regular trade or business, and its management of the investment and reinvestment of *ABC*'s assets is supervised by the directors. Also it can be relieved of its duties and right to compensation at any time (with 60 days notice) by a majority vote of the directors. Further, the adviser pays its own expenses and is not personally liable to the other partners for any losses incurred in the investment and reinvestment of *ABC*'s assets. The services performed by the adviser are, in substance, not performed in the capacity of a general partner, but are performed in the capacity of a person who is not a partner.

The 10 percent daily gross income allocation paid to the adviser is paid to the adviser in its capacity other than as a partner. Therefore, the gross income allocation is not a part of the adviser's distributive share of partnership income under section 702(a) of the Code or a guaranteed payment under section 707(c).

HOLDING

The 10 percent daily gross income allocation paid to the adviser is subject to section 707(a) of the Code and taxable to the adviser under section 61 as compensation for services rendered. The amount paid is deductible by the partnership under section 162, subject to the provisions of section 265.

* * *

ILLUSTRATIVE MATERIAL

A. PERFORMANCE OF SERVICES UNRELATED TO CAPACITY AS PARTNER

1. *General*

In Pratt v. Commissioner, 64 T.C. 203 (1975), aff'd, 550 F.2d 1023 (5th Cir.1977), the taxpayers were general partners in two limited partnerships which were formed to construct and operate shopping centers. Under the terms of the partnership agreements, the general partners were to receive 5 percent of the gross rental receipts of the partnerships in exchange for the performance of management services with respect to the partnership properties. The partnerships used the accrual method of accounting while the individual general partners used the cash basis method. For the three years in question the partnership accrued and deducted the management service fees but did not pay them over to the general partners and the partners did not include the fees in income. The cash method taxpayers argued that the fees were governed by section 707(a) and were, therefor, not includable in income because not paid. The Commissioner argued that the fees were includable in income because they were part of the partners' distributive shares of partnership income. The Tax Court agreed with the Commissioner:

"Since we conclude that the management fees are not guaranteed payments under section 707(c), we must decide whether the provisions for such fees in the partnership agreement might be considered as a 'transaction' engaged in by petitioners with the partnership in a capacity other than as a partner within the meaning of section 707(a). Initially, it might be noted that since section 707(c) deals specifically with continuing payments to a partner for services such as salary payments or the management fees here in issue, it is far from clear that such continuing payments were ever intended to come within the provisions of section 707(a). Section 707(a) refers to 'transactions' between a partner and a partnership and is susceptible of being interpreted as covering only those services rendered by a partner to the partnership in a specific transaction as distinguished from continuing services of the partner which would either fall within section 707(c) or be in effect a partner's withdrawal of partnership profits. * * *

"However, we need not decide whether a continuing payment to a partner for services was ever contemplated as being within the provisions of section 707(a).

"Section 1.707–1(a) of the Income Tax Regulations with respect to a 'partner not acting in capacity as partner' states that 'In all cases, the substance of the transaction will govern rather than its form.' Here, the record indicates that in managing the partnership petitioners were acting in their capacity as partners. They were performing basic duties of the partnership business pursuant to the partnership agreement. Although we have been unable to find cases arising under the 1954 Code concerning when a partner is acting within his capacity as such, a few cases arising under the provisions of the 1939 Code dealt with whether a payment to a partner should be considered as paid to him in a capacity other than as a partner. See Leif J. Sverdrup, 14 T.C. 859, 866 (1950); Wegener v. Commissioner, 119 F.2d 49 (5th Cir.1941), affg. 41 B.T.A. 857 (1940), cert. denied 314 U.S. 643 (1941). * * *

"Petitioners in this case were to receive the management fees for performing services within the normal scope of their duties as general partners and pursuant to the partnership agreement. There is no indication that any one of the petitioners was engaged in a transaction with the partnership other than in his capacity as a partner. We therefore hold that the management fees were not deductible business expenses of the partnership under section 707(a). Instead, in our view the net partnership income is not reduced by these amounts and each petitioner's respective share of partnership profit is increased or loss is reduced by his credited portion of the management fees in each year here in issue." (208–212)

Note the speculation in the excerpt from *Pratt,* quoted above, that section 707(a) might not have been intended to apply to continuing payments to a partner. In affirming the Tax Court the Court of Appeals stressed the fact that "in order for the partnership to deal with one of its partners as an 'outsider' the transaction dealt with must be something outside the scope of the partnership." (550 F.2d at 1026). However, Rev.Rul. 81–301, appears to reject this theory, since the services rendered in *Pratt* do not appear to be substantially different from the services in Rev.Rul. 81–301. Should section 707(a) be confined to isolated transactions as suggested in *Pratt?* If not, it is difficult to find a workable distinction between a section 707(a) payment and a section 707(c) payment. Section 707(a)(2)(A), enacted in 1984, clearly extends section 707(a) to continuing payments under certain circumstances. See infra, page 182. See also Zahler v. Commissioner, 41 T.C.M. 1074 (1981), rev'd on other grounds, 684 F.2d 356 (6th Cir.1982), holding that commissions paid to a partner in a securities brokerage firm, which paid sales commissions to partner and nonpartner sales personnel alike, were not subject to section 707(a)); S.Rep. No. 83–1622, 83d Cong., 2d Sess. 386 (1954). Rev.Rul. 72–504, 1972–2 Cum.Rul. 90, allowed a partner whose individual business paid rent to a partnership of which he was a member to deduct the full amount of the rent paid.

Suppose the ABC Partnership is a calendar year, accrual method partnership engaged in the real estate business. B, a lawyer, performs legal services for the partnership in November of year 1 and sends the partnership a bill for $200. The partnership pays B the $200 in January of year 2. Section 267(a)(2), which controls the timing of deductions for amounts paid to related taxpayers, defers the payor's deduction until the year in which the item is properly includable by the payee. Section 267(e)(1) treats a partnership and each partner as related for purposes of applying section 267(a)(2), regardless of the percentage interest which the partner has in the partnership. Thus the ABC partnership may not deduct the amount until year 2. See Temporary Regulations, section 1.267(a)–2T(c), Q & A.1. In addition, section 267(e)(3) invokes attribution rules. Thus, the partnership's deduction also would be deferred if in the above example the services were performed by B's child or spouse and payment was similarly delayed. The attribution rules also result in deferral of deductions for amounts due to a cash method partnership from a related accrual method partnership. See Temporary Regulations, section 1.267(a)–2T(c), Q & A.3.

In Armstrong v. Phinney, 394 F.2d 661 (5th Cir.1968), the court held that the entity approach adopted in section 707 was also applicable for purposes of the section 119 exclusion for meals and lodging provided to employees. Thus it would be possible as a matter of law for a partner to qualify as an employee entitled to the exclusion; the case was remanded for findings of fact concerning the partner's employee status. Wilson v. United States, 376 F.2d 280 (Ct.Cl.1967), consistent with prior law, reached the opposite conclusion on the ground that "[a] partnership is not a legal entity separate and apart from the partners, and, accordingly, a partnership cannot be regarded as the employer of a partner for the purposes of Section 119", with no discussion of section 707. Does section 707(c) have any bearing on the section 119 issue? See also Rev.Rul. 69–184, 1969–1 Cum.Bull. 256, holding that members of a partnership are not employees of the partnership for employment tax (FICA) purposes.

2. *Payments for Capital Expenditures*

Payments by a partnership to a partner governed by section 707(a) are not automatically deductible. If the payment is a capital expenditure, the partnership must capitalize it. Even though there is no deduction, the payee partner nevertheless realizes gross income by reason of the payment. See Rev.Rul. 75–214, 1975–1 Cum.Bull. 185, holding that payments by a limited partnership to the general partner as compensation for organizing the partnership were subject to section 707 and were required to be capitalized by the partnership pursuant to section 263. (For years after 1975, the same result is reached under section 709, discussed supra, page 51.)

B. SALES AND EXCHANGES OF PROPERTY

1. *Loss Situations*

Section 707(b)(1)(A) disallows any loss on a sale or exchange between a person and a partnership in which the person owns, directly or indirectly, more than 50 percent of either a capital or a profits interest. Section 707(b)(1)(B) applies the same rule to sales or exchanges between two partnerships in which the same persons own more than 50 percent of either a capital or a profits interest.

Davis v. Commissioner, 866 F.2d 852 (6th Cir.1989), illustrates two aspects of the breadth of section 707(b)(1)(B). A bank foreclosed on real property held by a limited partnership and one month later the bank sold the property to another partnership the profits and capital interests in which were 100 percent owned directly or indirectly by the same persons as the first partnership. First, section 707(b)(1)(B) applied to the sale even though it was indirect. Second, and more importantly, in applying section 707(b)(1)(B) to deny the first partnership a loss on the foreclosure, the court did not analyze the percentage ownership of each partner in each partnership, even though it appears from the stated facts that the partner in question did not have more than a 50 percent interest in each partnership. For section 707(b)(1)(B) to apply, however, it is not necessary that the *commonly owned interests* of each partner in each partnership total more than 50 percent. Thus, section 707(b)(1)(B) applies to deny the loss if the AB partnership in which A holds a 99 percent interest and B holds a 1 percent interest sells property at a loss to the BA partnership in which B owns a 99 percent interest and A holds a 1 percent interest.

The American Law Institute has recommended that section 707(b)(1)(B) be applied to disallow losses on sales between related partnerships only if the same persons owned more than 50 percent of either the profits or capital interests in each partnership, taking into account only the common holdings in each partnership. A partner's common holding is his percentage ownership in the partnership in which he has a smaller interest. American Law Institute, Federal Income Tax Project, Subchapter K (1984). Assume, for example, that the profits and capital interests in the ABCDE partnership are held as follows: A, 5 percent, B, 10 percent, C, 15 percent, D, 20 percent, and E, 50 percent; and the profits and capital interests in the EDCBA partnership are held as follows: E, 5 percent, D, 10 percent, C, 15 percent, B, 20 percent, and A, 50 percent. The common holdings in the two partnerships are as follows: A, 5 percent, B, 10 percent, C, 15 percent, D, 10 percent, and E, 5 percent. The aggregate common holdings are 45 percent, and therefore, the partnerships would not be under common control. The ALI proposal appears to implement better the policy of disallowing losses where there has not been a significant change in beneficial interest, while allowing losses where there is some relationship between the buyer and seller but there has been a significant change in beneficial interest.

Section 707(b)(3) applies the constructive ownership rules of section 267(c)(1), (2), (4), and (5) apply to determine who is a partner when applying section 707(b)(1)(A). Thus a loss on a sale between a partnership and a person who does not actually own any interest in the partnership may be disallowed. Thus, if G holds a 51 percent interest in both profits and capital of the GH partnership and the partnership sells property with a basis of $1000 to I, who is G's spouse for $500, the loss will be disallowed under section 707(b)(1) because I constructively owns more than a 50 percent interest in the partnership. However, if G holds only a 50 percent or less interest in the GH partnership, then section 707(b) does not apply; but the general rule of section 267 still applies to disallow a portion of the loss based on the related partner's percentage interest in the partnership. See Regulations, section 1.267(b)–1(b). For example, if G was a 40 percent partner, 40 percent of the loss would be disallowed. When a portion of the loss is disallowed under section 267 on the sale of property by a partnership to a related person, the disallowed loss should be allocated to the partner related to the purchaser. See Casel v. Commissioner, 79 T.C. 424 (1982).

2. *Gain Situations*

If gain is recognized on a sale or exchange between a person and a more than 50 percent controlled partnership, section 707(b)(2) requires that the gain be treated as ordinary gain if the property is not a capital asset in the hands of the *transferee.* Section 707(b)(2) was adopted when capital gains were taxed at a lower rate than ordinary income and was designed to prevent the transferee from claiming deductible depreciation on a stepped-up basis at the reduced price of a capital gains tax. On this rationale, section 707(b)(2) is overinclusive to the extent that it applies to land, apart from improvements, which will be held for use in the transferee's trade or business. The 1984 ALI Subchapter K project recommended excepting land from the rules of section 707(b)(2). The same attribution rules that are used to apply section 707(b)(1) are used to apply section 707(b)(2). See Rev.Rul. 67–105, 1967–1 Cum.Bull. 167, for the application of the attribution rules.

Section 1239 overlaps with section 707(b)(2), in part, and provides for ordinary gain treatment for property sold between a person and a more than fifty percent controlled partnership if the property is depreciable in the hands of the purchaser. Section 1239 also invokes the attribution rules of section 267(c).

In addition, section 453(g) denies installment sale treatment on any sale between a partner and a partnership in which the partner owns, directly or indirectly, more than 50 percent of either a capital or a profits interest, unless the transferor establishes that the transaction did not have tax avoidance as one of its principal purposes. Section 453(g) does not apply, however, to sales between related partnerships. There is no administrative or judicial guidance as to what establishes the absence or presence of a tax avoidance purpose in this context.

C. REFERENCES

Starr and Perine, To What Extent Can Partners and S Corporation Shareholders Receive Nontaxable Fringe Benefits?, 65 J.Tax. 40 (1986); Vogel, Distinguishing a Section 707(a) Payment From a Section 707(c) Payment, 2 Tax L.J. 65 (1984); Cowan, Compensating the General Partner: The *Pratt* Case, 56 Taxes 10 (1978).

C. GUARANTEED PAYMENTS

INTERNAL REVENUE CODE: Section 707(c).

REGULATIONS: Section 1.707–1(c).

GAINES v. COMMISSIONER

Tax Court of the United States, 1982.
45 T.C.M. 363.

PARKER, JUDGE.

* * *

Issue No. 2: Guaranteed Payments

Findings of Fact

On their partnership returns for the year 1973, Lincoln Manor, Brookwood, Gaines Realty, and Riverbend each claimed as deductions certain guaranteed payments to partners. Gaines Properties was a general partner in each of these partnerships. The amounts claimed by the limited partnerships as deductions for guaranteed payments to partners and Gaines Properties' share of those guaranteed payments were as follows:

Partnership	Amount Claimed	Gaines Properties' Share
Lincoln Manor	$ 74,131.26	$ 23,750.00
Brookwood	109,666.00	88,666.00
Gaines Realty	125,881.00	91,006.00
Riverbend	216,087.00	104,168.50

Each of the four limited partnerships accrued and claimed deductions for these guaranteed payments. Lincoln Manor, Brookwood, Gaines Realty, and Riverbend all used the accrual method of accounting on their 1973 partnership returns. Gaines Properties reported its income using the cash receipts and disbursements method of accounting.

Gaines Properties never received any of the guaranteed payments and did not report them in its income.

Respondent determined that Gaines Properties should have reported as income the guaranteed payments accrued and deducted by the four limited partnerships. Respondent, however, disallowed portions of the deductions that the four limited partnerships claimed for these guaranteed payments, on the ground that some portions were capital expenditures and not currently deductible.[14]

Issue No. 2: Guaranteed Payments

Opinion

Lincoln Manor, Brookwood, Riverbend, and Gaines Realty accrued and claimed deductions on their partnership returns for certain "guaranteed payments," including guaranteed payments to Gaines Properties, a general partner of each limited partnership. Gaines Properties never received these guaranteed payments. Respondent disallowed to the limited partnership portions of the claimed deductions for guaranteed payments, including some of the deductions attributable to the guaranteed payments to Gaines Properties. Notwithstanding this partial disallowance of deductions at the partnership level, respondent determined that the entire amount of the guaranteed payments to Gaines Properties, including the portion disallowed as deductions at the partnership level, should be included in Gaines Properties' income. Petitioners argue that the guaranteed payments that Gaines Properties did not receive, or at least such payments to the extent that the deductions therefor were disallowed at the partnership level, were not includable in Gaines Properties' income. Respondent argues that Gaines Properties' share of these guaranteed payments was includable in its income regardless of the fact that the deduction was partially disallowed at the partnership level and regardless of the fact that Gaines Properties, which used the cash method of accounting, never received the payments. We agree with respondent.

Section 707(c), as in effect in 1973, provided:

> To the extent determined without regard to the income of the partnership, payments to a partner for services or the use of capital shall be considered as made to one who is not a member of the partnership, but only for the purposes of section 61(a) (relating to gross income) and section 162(a) (relating to trade or business expenses).

This case does in fact involve "guaranteed payments" to a partner within the meaning of section 707(c) of the Code. The fact that no

14. It appears that respondent disallowed deductions of at least $40,000 of Gaines Properties' share of Brookwood's guaranteed payments, at least $24,000 of its share of Riverbend's guaranteed payments, and at least $22,641.56 of its share of Gaines Realty's guaranteed payments, a total disallowance of at least $66,641.56. In view of our holding on the guaranteed payments issue, we need not determine the exact amounts of Gaines Properties' share of guaranteed payments that respondent disallowed as deductions to the limited partnerships.

actual payments were made does not affect the status of these transactions as section 707(c) guaranteed payments. "[D]espite the use of the word 'payments' in both § 707(c) and the Regulations thereunder, it is clear that no actual payment need be made; if the partnership deducts the amount under its method of accounting, the 'recipient' partner must include the amount in income in the appropriate year." W. McKee, W. Nelson and R. Whitmire, Federal Taxation of Partnerships and Partners (hereinafter McKee, Nelson and Whitmire), par. 13.03[2], pp. 13–16. See also Pratt v. Commissioner, 64 T.C. 203, 213 (1975), affd. on this point and revd. on other grounds 550 F.2d 1023 (5th Cir.1977); sec. 1.707–1(c), Income Tax Regs. The parties stipulated that each of the four limited partnerships deducted "guaranteed payments." The partnership agreements of Brookwood and Gaines Realty expressly stated that certain payments to partners "shall constitute guaranteed payments within the meaning of section 707(c) of the Code." While the descriptions of such payments in the partnership agreements are not binding upon us (Doyle v. Mitchell Bros. Co., 247 U.S. 179, 187 (1918)), the payments referred to in those two partnership agreements are clearly fixed sums determined without regard to partnership income. See Sec. 707(c); Sec. 1.707–1(c), Income Tax Regs. Furthermore, it is equally clear that the payments to the partners were for services in their capacities as partners.[15] Respondent in his notices of deficiency determined that these payments were in fact guaranteed payments under section 707(c), and petitioners did not dispute this determination. Accordingly, we hold that the payments here were guaranteed payments within the meaning of section 707(c).

The statutory language of section 707(c) addresses only the character of the guaranteed payments and not the timing. Respondent's regulation under section 707(c), section 1.707–1(c), Income Tax Regs., addresses the timing question, as follows:

> Payments made by a partnership to a partner for services or for the use of capital are considered as made to a person who is not a partner, to the extent such payments are determined without regard to the income of the partnership. However, a partner must include such payments as ordinary income for his taxable year within or with which ends the partnership taxable year in which the partnership deducted such payments as paid or accrued under its method of accounting. See section 706(a) and paragraph (a) of § 1.706–1.

As the regulation makes clear, the statutory authority for the timing of the inclusion of these guaranteed payments is section 706(a), which provides:

15. Transactions between a partner and his partnership when the partner is not acting in his capacity as a partner are governed by section 707(a), not section 707(c). W. McKee, W. Nelson, and R. Whitmire, Federal Taxation of Partnerships and Partners, par. 13.01[2]. See also Pratt v. Commissioner, 64 T.C. 203, 210–211 (1975), aff'd on this issue 550 F.2d 1023 (5th Cir.1977).

> In computing the taxable income of a partner for a taxable year, the inclusions required by section 702 and section 707(c) with respect to a partnership shall be based on the income, gain, loss, deduction, or credit of the partnership for any taxable year of the partnership ending within or with the taxable year of the partner.

The separate reference of section 707(c) guaranteed payments in the timing provisions of section 706(a) was explained by the Senate Report as simply—

> to make clear that payments made to a partner for services or for the use of capital are includible in his income at the same time as his distributive share of partnership income for the partnership year when the payments are made or accrued * * *. (S.Rept. No. 1622, to accompany H.R. 8300 (Pub.L. No. 591), 83d Cong., 2d Sess. 385 (1954)).

In Cagle v. Commissioner, 63 T.C. 86 (1974), affd. 539 F.2d 409 (5th Cir. 1976), we held that includability and deductibility of guaranteed payments are two separate questions, and specifically that guaranteed payments are not automatically deductible simply by reason of their being included in the recipient's income. In *Cagle,* we stated 63 T.C. at 95:

> We think that all Congress meant was that guaranteed payments should be included in the recipient partner's income in the partnership taxable year ending with or within which the partner's taxable year ends and in which the tax accounting treatment of the transaction is determined at the partnership level. S.Rept. No. 1622, supra at pp. 94, 385, 387.

We believe our statement in *Cagle* is an accurate description of the Congressional intent. We have found nothing in the statutory language, regulations, or legislative history to indicate that includability in the recipient partner's income was intended to be dependent upon deductibility at the partnership level.

Petitioners seem to argue that there is a patent unfairness in taxing them on nonexistent income, namely income that they have neither received nor benefitted from (e.g. through a tax deduction at the partnership level). Their argument has a superficial appeal to it, but on closer analysis must fail. Except for certain very limited purposes, guaranteed payments are treated as part of the partner's distributive share of partnership income and loss. Sec. 1.707–1(c), Income Tax Regs. For timing purposes guaranteed payments are treated the same as distributive income and loss. Sec. 706(a); sec. 1.706–1(a) and sec. 1.707–1(c), Income Tax Regs. A partner's distributive share of partnership income is includable in his taxable income for any partnership year ending within or with the partner's taxable year. Sec. 706(a). As is the case with a partner's ordinary distributive share of partnership income and loss, any unfairness in taxing a partner on guaranteed payments that he neither receives nor benefits from results from the conduit theory of partnerships, and is a consequence of the taxpayer's choice to do the business in the partnership form.[16] We find no justification in the statute, regulations, or legislative history to permit these petitioners to recognize their income pro rata as deductions are allowed to the partnership. See also Pratt v. Commissioner, 64 T.C. 203, 213 (1975), affd. on this ground 550 F.2d 1023 (5th Cir. 1977). We hold for respondent on the guaranteed payments issue.

ILLUSTRATIVE MATERIAL

A. INCLUSION AND DEDUCTION OF GUARANTEED PAYMENTS

1. *General*

Suppose A and B decide to form the AB Partnership but A, as a condition of participating in the venture, insists on being paid a salary of $5,000 a year whether or not the partnership makes a profit. The partnership has no income for the year, and A is paid $5,000. Under the aggregate approach as applied in situations arising prior to 1954, assuming each partner's capital account is reduced $2,500, A will be taxed on $2,500 income and B has a $2,500 loss. G.C.M. 6582, VIII–2 Cum.Bull. 200 (1929): "Partners are working for themselves, and, in contemplation of law, a man may not constitute himself his own employee. (Estate of Tilton v. Commissioner, 8 B.T.A., 914 (C.B. VII–1, 31); Appeal of Harriet Taylor, 2 B.T.A., 1159 (C.B. VII–1, 31).) Therefore, whatever is received by a partner in the form of or under the name of salary constitutes nothing more or less than a withdrawal from the partnership of anticipated profits, and if, at the end of the taxable period of the partnership, it is discovered that the total of the amounts so withdrawn by the partners exceeds the apparent profits, it is evident that the true net profit realized is ascertained only by eliminating from the calculation the total amount withdrawn as salary. * * * (Any) sums in excess thereof withdrawn by them must be considered as withdrawals from capital investment, as there is no other source from which the withdrawals could be derived." See also I.T. 2503, VIII–2 Cum.Bull. 145 (1929); Commissioner v. Banfield, 122 F.2d 1017 (9th Cir.1941), adopting this approach as to interest paid on the capital contribution of a partner.

Section 707(c) here, however, adopts the entity approach, under which A has $5,000 compensation, the partnership has a $5,000 loss, and A and B each have a $2,500 loss, leaving A with a net income of $2,500. While this usually leaves the same dollar result as under the aggregate approach, the tax results may differ where the partnership has special income items. Thus, assume that the partnership had $5,000 of capital gain. Under the aggregate approach, A presumably would merely have a distributive share of $5,000 capital gain. Under the entity approach of section 707(c), A has $5,000 compensation, A and B each have a distributive share of $2,500 of the capital gain and a distributive share of $2,500 of the partnership $5,000 ordinary loss. See Regulations, section 1.707–1(c), Ex. (4).

Section 707(c) applies the entity approach only as respects inclusion in gross income and allowance as a deduction. Thus, the guaranteed payment is not considered an interest in profits under sections 706(b)(3), 707(b), and 708(b). See Regulations, section 1.707–1(c). The statute retains the aggre-

16. As part of a partner's distributive share of profit and loss, the guaranteed payments included in his income increase the partner's basis in his partnership interest. Sec. 705(a)(1) and (2).

gate concept as to other aspects of the situation. Thus, suppose A is on a calendar year and the partnership is on a fiscal year ending July 31. Under section 706(a) a partner reports his distributive share of partnership income as part of his own income for the year with or within which the partnership year ends. As *Gaines* indicates, Regulations, section 1.706–1(a)(1), require guaranteed payments to be similarly reported, i.e., to be included in the year with or within which the partnership year of the payment ends. If the payment is made in August 1988, A would include it in 1989 along with the rest of his distributive share for the year ended July 31, 1989.

A guaranteed payment is not covered by the deferred compensation rules of sections 404(a) and (b) or the withholding rules. Regulations, section 1.707–1(c). However, Miller v. Commissioner, 52 T.C. 752 (1969), held that guaranteed payments received by a partner for services performed abroad were excludable under former section 911 as income earned abroad and not, as urged by the Commissioner, simply as a distributive share of partnership income. Carey v. United States, 427 F.2d 763 (Ct.Cl.1970), reached the same result. Compare also Armstrong v. Phinney, supra, page 171.

2. *Guaranteed Minimum*

Suppose that A and B are partners in the AB Partnership, in which A is a 25 percent partner, but that the partnership agreement provides that A is entitled to receive not less than $100 per year. If the partnership's income for the year is $400 or more, no portion of A's distributive share is a guaranteed payment. Regulations, section 1.707–1(c), Ex. (2). This is true even if the partnership agreement provides that A's minimum is to be treated as an expense item in computing partnership profits. Rev.Rul. 66–95, 1966–1 Cum.Bull. 169. If, however, partnership profits were only $200, then $50 (25% of $200) would be A's distributive share, and $50 would be a guaranteed payment. Suppose further that the partnership's taxable income, apart from A's guaranteed payment, consists of $120 of ordinary income and $80 of capital gains. In this case the $50 guaranteed payment would be deducted from the $120 of ordinary income, leaving $70 of ordinary income and $80 of capital gains to be apportioned between A and B in the ratio that they share partnership profits for the year after deducting the guaranteed payment. A's share is $50/$150 and B's share is $100/$150. Thus, in addition to $50 of ordinary income from the guaranteed payment, A has $23.33 of ordinary income and $26.67 of capital gain; B has $46.67 of ordinary income and $53.33 of capital gain. See Rev.Rul. 69–180, 1969–1 Cum.Bull. 183.

3. *Capitalization*

Guaranteed payments are subject to the usually applicable requirements of section 263 and cannot be deducted simply because the expenditures take the form of guaranteed payments. Section 707(c). Cagle v. Commissioner, 539 F.2d 409 (5th Cir.1976), reached the same result under a prior version of section 707(c) which did not expressly subject guaranteed payments to section 263. For application of the capitalization rule to guaranteed payments in consideration of services in organizing a partnership and syndicating interests, see Tolwinsky v. Commissioner, 86 T.C. 1009 (1986). Rev.Rul. 80–234, 1980–2 Cum.Bull. 203, treated a finder's fee paid to a partner for finding acceptable loan applicants as a guaranteed payment. The partner was required currently to include the payment in income, but the partnership was required to capitalize it as a cost of the loan amortizable over the life of the loan.

B. IDENTIFYING GUARANTEED PAYMENTS

Section 707(c) frequently has been applied to amounts withdrawn by partners as "salary." In Falconer v. Commissioner, 40 T.C. 1011 (1963), payments to a partner referred to in the partnership agreement as "salary" were classified as section 707(c) payments where the partnership had been operating at a loss when the payments were made. The taxpayer unsuccessfully argued that the amounts were advances that he was obligated to repay to the other partners. Clark v. Commissioner, 44 T.C.M. 492 (1982), reached the same result on similar facts. At a time when the taxpayer-partner had a negative capital account, the partnership made payments to him by, first, increasing his capital account by an amount that was unrelated to partnership profits and, second, distributing to him an identical amount, which reduced his capital account and left it at its original negative balance.

In Pratt v. Commissioner, supra, page 170, a general partner of a limited partnership was entitled to a real property management fee equal to 5% of gross rents from the property. The Tax Court held that the payments were not section 707(c) payments:

"Section 707(c) refers to payments 'determined without regard to the income.' The parties make some argument as to whether payments based on 'gross rentals' as provided in the partnership agreements should be considered as payments based on 'income.' In our view there is no merit to such a distinction. The amounts of the management fees are based on a fixed percentage of the partnership's gross rentals which in turn constitute partnership income. To us it follows that the payments are not determined without regard to the income of the partnership as required by section 707(c) for a payment to a partner for services to be a 'guaranteed payment.' " (210).

The Internal Revenue Service rejected this aspect of *Pratt* in Rev.Rul. 81–300, 1981–2 Cum.Bull. 143, which held that "a payment for services determined by reference to an item of gross income will be a guaranteed payment if, on the basis of all of the facts and circumstances, the payment is compensation rather than a share of partnership profits." Whether the same method of payment would have been a reasonable method to compensate an unrelated party is an important factor. Thus, because it is not unusual for the compensation paid to a real estate manager to be computed as a percentage of rents, the Ruling specifically concluded that the fees in *Pratt* were section 707(c) guaranteed payments. The legislative history of section 707(a)(2)(A), discussed infra, page 182, endorses the conclusion in Rev.Rul. 81–300 that compensation measured as by a percentage of gross income may be a section 707 payment, but states that by virtue of section 707(a)(2)(A), the transaction in the Ruling should be governed by section 707(a) rather than section 707(c). S.Rep. No. 98–169, 98th Cong., 2d Sess. 230 (1984). There is no express explanation of the rationale for this conclusion.

This sequence of events has left the scope of section 707(c) unclear. There is no clear demarcation of the line between a partner acting in the capacity of a partner and a partner acting in a capacity other than as a partner. Regulations, section 1.707–1(a), provide that "the substance of the transaction will govern rather than its form," but fails to give any guidance as to what aspects of the "substance" are relevant. Prior to the 1984 Act, the inquiry focused on the nature of the services provided, see *Pratt,* supra, but the direction in the Senate Finance Committee Report accompanying the 1984 Act that the payment in Rev.Rul 81–300 is a section 707(a) payment indicates that this may no longer be the relevant inquiry. The piecemeal modifications of section 707 have left the provision with no clear focus.

C. GUARANTEED PAYMENTS FOR THE USE OF CAPITAL

1. *General*

Section 707(c) expressly contemplates guaranteed payments by the partnership for the use of a partner's capital. Guaranteed payments for the use of capital which are subject to section 707(c) are distinguishable from interest on a loan which is subject to section 707(a) in that section 707(c) governs payments in the nature of interest paid with respect to contributed capital, while section 707(a) governs interest payments on a bona fide loan. See Pratt v. Commissioner, supra, page 170. A bona fide loan from a partner to the partnership exists only if there is an unconditional obligation to pay a sum certain at a determinable date. Rev.Rul. 73–301, 1973–2 Cum.Bull. 215. A contribution credited to a partner's capital account, repayable only as a distribution from partnership capital under the terms of the partnership agreement, is not a loan even though it may bear "interest."

Guaranteed payments for the use of partnership capital are used by partnerships which, for example, desire generally to allocate profits to reflect services provided to the partnership, while providing a proper allowance for disproportionate capital contributions. Assume, for example, that D, E, and F desire to form a partnership in which both capital and profits will be a material income producing factor. D, E, and F intend to be "equal" partners, but the partnership requires $300,000 of capital, and E and F each can contribute only $50,000. The solution is for D to contribute $200,000, while E and F each contribute $50,000, and to provide in the partnership agreement that D will receive an annual guaranteed payment equal to a specified percentage of the amount by which his capital contribution exceeds that of the other partners. Thus, the partnership agreement may provide that D is to receive a guaranteed payment of $15,000 (10% × $150,000) after which the profits of the partnership are to be split equally.

A more flexible formula can be devised to take into account the possibility that the partners desire ultimately to equalize their capital contributions. Thus, the partnership agreement might provide that any partner who has contributed more than any other partner is entitled to an annual guaranteed payment equal to 10 percent of the partner's excess contribution. As the partnership earns profits, D and F may leave a portion of the distributive shares in the partnership, thereby increasing their capital accounts, while E withdraws not only his share of profits, but a portion of his original capital contribution. Thus, if at the end of the end of a future year the respective capital account balances of the partners are D, $120,000, E, $100,000, and F, $80,000, E would be entitled to a guaranteed payment of $4,000 (10% × ($120,000 – $80,000)) and F would be entitled to a guaranteed payment of $2,000 (10% × ($100,000 – $80,000)). When all partners' capital accounts were equalized, any guaranteed payments would cease.

2. *Characterization*

Guaranteed payments for the use of capital raise characterization questions analogous to some of the characterization questions relating to guaranteed payments for services. In general, guaranteed payments for the use of capital easily are classified as ordinary income (see Regulations, section 1.707–1(c)), but whether they are interest is not clear. Characterization of guaranteed payments for the use of capital as interest may be relevant to both the recipient partner and to the partnership. From the partner's perspective, characterization as interest is relevant for purposes of applying rules such as the investment interest limitation of section 163(d). From the partnership's perspective, determining whether the deduction is to be treated as an ordinary and necessary business expense under section 162 or as an interest expense under section 163 may be relevant in applying the uniform capitalization rules of section 263A. There is no authority on the proper characterization of guaranteed payments for capital, although in private letter rulings, as far as the recipient is concerned, the Internal Revenue Service has characterized such payments with reference to the character of the partnership's ordinary income from which they were made. See, e.g., Private Letter Ruling 8728033. In so far as guaranteed payments for services are treated as earned income where that distinction is relevant, see supra, page 165, it would be consistent to treat guaranteed payments for the use of capital as interest. However, as far as characterization from the perspective of the partnership is concerned, section 707(c) expressly refers to section 162. This raises the possibility that such payments may be characterized differently from the perspective of the recipient and the partnership, since characterization of a deduction as a section 162 deduction is not helpful in characterizing the nature of the receipt.

D. REFERENCES

Postlewaite and Cameron, Twisting Slowly in the Wind: Guaranteed Payments After the Tax Reform Act of 1984, 40 Tax Lawyer 649 (1987); Banoff, Determining the Character of Guaranteed Payments for Partners' Capital, 67 J.Tax. 284 (1987); Davis and Vogel, Guaranteed Payments: Strategies for Avoiding Pitfalls in Their Use, 2 J. Partnership Tax. 332 (1986).

D. DISGUISED TRANSACTIONS BETWEEN PARTNERS AND THE PARTNERSHIP

INTERNAL REVENUE CODE: Section 707(a)(2).

ILLUSTRATIVE MATERIAL

A. DISGUISED SALES AND EXCHANGES OF PROPERTY

1. *Background*

In Otey v. Commissioner, 70 T.C. 312 (1978), aff'd per curiam, 634 F.2d 1046 (6th Cir.1980), the taxpayer and another individual formed a partnership to construct housing on property owned by the taxpayer. Under the partnership agreement the taxpayer contributed the property to the partnership with an agreed value of $65,000 and an FHA-insured construction loan was taken out in an amount greater than that needed for the construction. The taxpayer then withdrew $65,000 of the excess mortgage proceeds from the partnership. The Commissioner argued that the taxpayer in effect sold his property to the partnership and recognized gain under section 707(a), supra, page 172. The Tax Court, however, held that sections 721 and 731 controlled with the result that the money distribution merely reduced the taxpayer's basis in his partnership interest: "Were there no partnership at all, a taxpayer could borrow funds on the security of appreciated property and apply them to his personal use without triggering gain. Had the distributed funds come directly from the other partner, [the Commissioner's] case would be stronger. While it may be argued that the funds have come indirectly from [the partner] because his credit facilitated the loan, the fact is that the loan was a partnership loan on which the partnership was primarily liable, and both partners were jointly and separately liable for the full loan if the partnership defaulted. We do not view the factual pattern here as constituting a disguised sale of the land to [the other partner] or the partnership."

Similar results were reached in slightly different contexts in Communications Satellite Corp. v. United States, 625 F.2d 997 (Ct.Cl.1980), and Jupiter Corp. v. United States, 2 Cl.Ct. 58, 83–1 U.S.T.C. ¶ 9168 (Cl.Ct.1983), where the I.R.S. unsuccessfully attempted to recharacterize distributions to old partners in connection with contributions by new partners as sales of partnership interests.

2. *The Legislative Response*

Congress disagreed with the courts' conclusions that the transactions in *Otey, Communications Satellite Corp.,* and *Jupiter Corp.* did not resemble sales, and in 1984 enacted section 707(a)(2)(B), authorizing the Treasury to promulgate regulations treating as a sale subject to section 707(a) any transaction in which there is a direct or indirect distribution of money or property to a partner related to his direct or indirect transfer of money or property to the partnership. The Senate Finance Committee Report indicates that the regulations should apply this rule only to attempts to disguise sales and not to "non-abusive transactions that reflect the various economic contributions of the partners." S.Rep. No. 98–169, 98th Cong., 2d Sess. 230 (1984). It gives the following example of circumstances in which the rule may be applied:

"For example, when a partner contributes appreciated property to a partnership and receives a distribution of money or property within a reasonable period before or after such contribution, that is approximately equal in value to the portion of contributed property that is in effect given up to the other partner(s) the transaction will be subject to this provision. However, the distribution would not be so subject if there is a corresponding partnership allocation of income or gain, but that arrangement may instead be subject to the new provision relating to partnership payments for property or services described above. The disguised sale provision also will apply to the extent (1) the transferor partner receives the proceeds of a loan related to the property to the extent responsibility for the repayment of the loan rests, directly or indirectly, with the partnership (or its assets) or the other partners, or (2) the partner has received a loan related to the property in anticipation of the transaction and responsibility for repayment of the loan is transferred, directly or indirectly, to the partnership (or its assets) or the other partners.

"Although the rule applies to sales of property to the partnership, the committee does not intend to prohibit a partner from receiving a partnership interest in return for contributing property which entitles him to priorities or preferences as to distributions, but is not in substance a disguised sale. Similarly, the committee generally does not intend this provision to adversely affect distributions that create deficit capital accounts (maintained in a manner consistent with Treasury regulations under section 704(b)) for which the distributee is liable, regardless of the timing of the distribution, unless such deficit capital account is improperly understated or not expected to be made up until such a distant point in the future that its present value is small. However, if this deficit creating distribution is coupled with an allocation of income or gain, the distribution/allocation arrangement may be subject to the new provision relating to partnership payments for services or property. Similarly, the contribution of encumbered property to a partnership would not suggest a disguised sale to the extent responsibility for the debt is not shifted, directly or indirectly, to the partnership (or its assets) or to the non-contributing partners. The committee anticipates that the Treasury regulations will treat transactions to which the provision applies as a sale of property or partnership interests among the partners or as a partial sale and partial contribution of the property to the partnership, with attendant tax consequences, depending upon the underlying economic substance of the transaction. These regulations may provide for a period, such as three years, during which contributions by and distributions to the same or another partner normally will be presumed related. Finally, it is anticipated that the regulations will take into account the effect of liabilities which may accompany effective sales of property to a partnership or another partner." (231).

The excerpt from the Committee Report quoted above suggests that the Regulations might provide a presumption that contributions and distributions occurring within a three year period are related. Should this presumption apply to all distributions or only to disproportionate distributions to the contributing partner?

It is not entirely clear from the legislative history exactly how a transaction subject to section 707(a)(2)(B) is to be treated. The statutory language indicates that the normal sale or exchange treatment of section 707(a)(1) should apply. The Senate Finance Committee Report, however, states that it is expected that the regulations should treat transactions to which section 707(a)(2)(B) applies "as a sale of property or partnership interests among the partners or as a partial sale and partial contribution of the property to the partnership, with attendant tax consequences, depending on the underlying economic substance of the transaction." The part sale—part contribution analysis also appears in the Committee Report's discussion of the treatment of liabilities in the above quoted excerpt.

Suppose that A, a one-third partner in the ABC Partnership transfers Blackacre, which has a basis of $180,000 and a fair market value of $300,000, to the partnership; immediately thereafter, the partnership mortgages Blackacre for $300,000 and distributes the loan proceeds to A. Under the normal section 707(a) rules, A would recognize a gain of $120,000. Under the part sale—part contribution approach described in the Senate Finance Committee Report, however, A presumably would recognize a gain of only $80,000, on a sale of an undivided two-thirds of the property. In addition, A would be treated as contributing an undivided one-third of the property to the partnership, thereby increasing her basis in the partnership interest by $60,000 (the basis in an undivided one-third of the property) pursuant to section 722, and receiving a distribution of $100,000. The distribution would reduce her basis, and she would recognize gain to the extent that her basis immediately prior to the distribution (but after taking into account the increase in basis attributable to the contribution of a one-third interest in the property) was less than $100,000.

Section 707(a)(2)(B) also may recharacterize a contribution by one partner coupled by a distribution to another partner as a transaction between the two partners acting in capacities other than as a partner. This may apply where one partner transfers property to the partnership while another transfers cash, followed by the distribution of cash to the partner who contributed property and property to the partner who contributed cash, or in situations such as that presented in *Communications Satellite Corp.* and *Jupiter Corp.*, supra.

To some extent, section 707(a)(2)(B) is redundant. Regulations, section 1.731–1(c)(3), long have provided that a contribution to a partnership followed "within a short period" by a distribution of other property to the contributing partner or a distribution of the contributed property to another partner may be treated as a taxable exchange. The existing Regulations, which the courts failed to apply, would have been adequate to treat as taxable sales or exchanges the contributions and distributions in *Otey, Communications Satellite Corp.*, and *Jupiter Corp.*

B. DISGUISED PAYMENTS FOR SERVICES OR PROPERTY

Suppose A, who is a one third partner in the ABC partnership, performs services for the partnership related to the acquisition of a new building. If A is paid a fixed sum for performing these services under either section 707(a) or section 707(c), the partnership will be required to capitalize the payment and A will be required currently to include the payment in income. On the other hand, if the partnership makes a special income allocation to A, which is subsequently distributed, B's and C's distributive shares will be reduced proportionately, in effect allowing the capital expenditure for A's services to be deducted by B and C. In Ellison v. Commissioner, 80 T.C. 378 (1983), the Tax Court rejected the use of a similar technique. To provide the Treasury with more authority to attack such transactions, in the 1984 Act Congress added section 707(a)(2)(A), which authorizes regulations treating as a section 707(a)(1) transaction the performance of services for or contribution of property to the partnership by a partner coupled with a related allocation *and* distribution to the partner if, when viewed together, the two events are more properly characterized as a transaction occurring between the partnership and a partner acting in his capacity other than as a partner.

The Senate Finance Committee Report indicates that section 707(a)(2)(A) may apply both to one-time transactions and to continuing arrangements which use allocations and distributions in lieu of direct payments. The provision is specifically intended to apply to partnership organization and syndication fees which must be capitalized pursuant to section 709. Furthermore, the Regulations may recharacterize a purported partner as not being a partner. The Committee Report lists the following six factors as relevant in determining whether a partner is receiving a putative allocation and distribution in his capacity as a partner: (1) whether the amount of the payment is subject to appreciable risk; (2) whether the partnership status of the recipient is transitory; (3) whether the allocation and distribution are close in time to the performance of services for, or the transfer of property to, the partnership; (4) whether considering all of the facts and circumstances it appears that the recipient became a partner primarily to obtain for himself or the partnership benefits which would not have been available if he had rendered services to the partnership in a third party capacity; (5) whether the value of the recipient's interest in general and in continuing partnership profits is small relative to the allocation in question; and (6) whether the requirements for maintaining capital accounts under section 704(b) makes it unlikely that income allocations are disguised payments for capital because it is economically unfeasible. Transitory special allocations are particularly suspect when coupled with the existence of another factor. Furthermore, the mere fact that the amount of an allocation is contingent does not insulate it under section 707(a)(2)(A). Contingent allocations generally will be recharacterized as fees, however, only where the partner in question normally performs, has previously performed or is capable of performing similar services for third parties. S.Rep. No. 98–169, 98th Cong., 2d Sess. 226–229 (1984).

The Senate Finance Committee Report gives the following example of the application of section 707(a)(2)(A):

"A commercial office building constructed by a partnership is projected to generate gross income of at least $100,000 per year indefinitely. Its architect, whose normal fee for such services is $40,000, contributes cash for a 25–percent interest in the partnership and receives both a 25–percent distributive share of net income for the life of the partnership, and an allocation of $20,000 of partnership gross income for the first two years of partnership operations after leaseup. The partnership is expected to have sufficient cash available to distribute $20,000 to the architect in each of the first two years, and the agreement requires such a distribution. The purported gross income allocation and partnership distribution should be treated as a fee under sec. 707(a), rather than as a distributive share. Factors which contribute to this conclusion are (1) the special allocation to the architect is fixed in amount and there is a substantial probability that the partnership will have sufficient gross income and cash to satisfy the allocation/distribution; (2) the value of his interest in general and continuing partnership profits is relatively small in relation to the allocation in question; (3) the distribution relating to the allocation is fairly close in time to the rendering of the services; and (4) it is not unreasonable to conclude from all the facts and circumstances that the architect became a partner primarily for tax motivated reasons. If, on the other hand, the agreement allocates to the architect 20 percent of gross income for the first two years following construction of the building a question arises as to how likely it is that the architect will receive substantially more or less than his imputed fee of $40,000. If the building is pre-leased to a high credit tenant under a lease requiring the lessee to pay $100,000 per year of rent, or if there is low vacancy rate in the area for comparable space, it is likely that the architect will receive approximately $20,000 per year for the first two years of operations. Therefore, he assumes limited risk as to the amount or payment of the allocation and, as a consequence, the allocation/distribution should be treated as a disguised fee. If, on the other hand, the project is a 'spec building,' and the architect assumes significant entrepreneurial risk that the partnership will be unable to lease the building, the special allocation might (even though a gross income allocation), depending on all the facts and circumstances, properly be treated as a distributive share and partnership distribution." (228–29).

C. REFERENCE

Turlington, Transfers of Encumbered Property to Partnerships: Disguised Sales Under Section 707(a)(2)(B), 4 J. Partnership Tax. 187 (1987).

CHAPTER 4

SALE OF PARTNERSHIP INTEREST BY PARTNER

SECTION 1. THE SELLER'S SIDE OF THE TRANSACTION

INTERNAL REVENUE CODE: Sections 706(c); 708; 741; 751(a), (c), (d), (f); 752(d); 1031(a)(2)(D).

REGULATIONS: Sections 1.741–1; 1.751–1(a), (c), (d), (g), Ex. (1).

TEMPORARY REGULATIONS: Section 1.752–3T.

When a partner disposes of his partnership interest by sale or exchange, another aspect of the entity versus aggregate treatment of the partnership arises. Should the partnership interest be treated as a unitary asset in its own right, like corporate stock, independent of the assets owned by the partnership, with a resulting capital gain or loss? Or should the partner on selling his partnership interest be viewed as selling his proportionate share of all of the assets held by the partnership, with the nature of the gain or loss to be determined by reference to the particular partnership assets involved? Subchapter K provides a compromise solution. Generally, under the entity approach of section 741, the sale or exchange of a partnership interest results in capital gain or loss. However, in certain circumstances section 751(a) overrides section 741 to impose a modified aggregate approach, under which a partner is treated as having sold his share of certain types of partnership assets which produce ordinary income.

Section 751 is sometimes called the "collapsible partnership" provision, in an analogy to section 341, which treats gain on the sale of corporate stock in so-called "collapsible corporations" as ordinary income in certain cases. Its purpose is to prevent the conversion of ordinary income into capital gain. Accordingly, it was of significant importance prior to the Tax Reform Act of 1986. With the repeal of preferential tax rates for capital gains, the importance of section 751 is greatly reduced. Nevertheless, section 751(a) is not entirely anachronistic. There are continuing differences between capital gains and losses on the one hand and ordinary gains and losses on the other, the most important being that capital losses are deductible only against capital gains, plus, in the case of individuals, against $3,000 of ordinary income. In this regime the primary importance of section 751 is its ability to create ordinary income and a related capital loss when a partnership interest is sold at no gain or an overall net loss.

Several other aspects of the sale of a partnership interest present computational problems. When a partnership interest is sold part-way through the partnership's taxable year, how is the selling partner's taxable income and basis of her partnership interest to be computed? What if the partner sells only a portion of her partnership interest? Finally, how are partnership liabilities taken into account in computing gain or loss on the sale of a partnership interest?

In contrast to the sale of a partnership interest, the mere admission of a new partner to an existing partnership is governed by the rules applicable to the formation of a partnership. See supra, page 48. Thus the threshold issue is distinguishing a sale of a partnership interest from the mere admission of a new partner, since despite the economic similarity of the two transactions, the tax consequences can be very different.

COLONNADE CONDOMINIUM, INC. v. COMMISSIONER

Tax Court of the United States, 1988.
91 T.C. 793.

WRIGHT, JUDGE: [Colonnade Condominium, Inc. was a limited partner in Georgia King Associates, holding a 50.98 percent interest. The shares of Colonnade were held equally by Bernstein, Feldman, and Mason. Prior to April 1978, Colonnade was obligated to make capital contributions to Georgia King in a series of installments in the total amount of $1,330,300. At that time it had actually contributed less than $400,000. Colonnade's basis in its partnership interest was $8,262,710. Its share of partnership liabilities was $10,074,456. Colonnade had a negative capital account balance. In April, 1978 the partnership agreement of Georgia King was amended to admit each of Bernstein, Feldman, and Mason as a 13.66 percent general partner. Colonnade's interest was reduced from 50.98 percent to 10 percent. Bernstein, Feldman, and Mason each assumed responsibility for contributing $272,000 of the future capital contribution previously required from Colonnade. At that time the fair market value of a 40.98 percent interest in Georgia King was $4,999,560. Colonnade did not treat the April 1, 1978 transfer of its 40.98 percent partnership interest to Bernstein, Feldman, and Mason as a taxable event. The Commissioner asserted that the transaction was a sale of a portion of Colonnade's partnership interest.]

OPINION

Respondent contends that Colonnade's transfer of a portion of its partnership interest in Georgia King Associates to its three shareholders pursuant to the April 1, 1978, amendment to the partnership agreement resulted in the sale of a 40.98–percent general partnership interest by Colonnade in return for the discharge of recourse and nonrecourse partnership liabilities. Accordingly, respondent argues that such disposition should be governed by sections 741 and 1001.

* * * Petitioner, on the other hand, asserts that the April 1, 1978, amendment merely provided for the admission of new partners in an existing partnership and is a nontaxable event.

We agree with respondent.

* * *

The statutory scheme under subchapter K gives partners great latitude in selecting the form the partnership takes and in allocating economic benefits and tax burdens of partnership transactions among themselves. See, e.g., Hamilton v. United States, 231 Ct.Cl. 517, 524–525, 687 F.2d 408, 412–413 (1982); Foxman v. Commissioner, 41 T.C. 535, 551 (1964), affd. 352 F.2d 466 (3d Cir.1965); McKee, Nelson & Whitmire, Federal Taxation of Partnerships and Partners, par. 1.03 (1977), citing H.Rept. 1337, 83d Cong., 2d Sess. 65 (1954). Under the partnership provisions of the Code, this flexibility is achieved by, inter alia, allowing a partner to choose either to sell his partnership interest to a third person or to reorganize the partnership to allow the admission of the third person as a new partner.

This flexibility, however, is not unlimited. The form of the transaction must be in keeping with its true substance and the intent of the parties. See Commissioner v. Court Holding Co., 324 U.S. 331 (1945); Gregory v. Helvering, 293 U.S. 465 (1935) (the substance, rather than the form, of the transaction is controlling). In this regard, the provisions of written documents are not necessarily conclusive for tax purposes. Highland Hills Swimming Club, Inc. v. Wiseman, 272 F.2d 176 (10th Cir.1959). Nor will a "label" attached by a tax-conscious litigant control the proper characterization of a transaction involving the disposition of a partnership interest. Crenshaw v. United States, 450 F.2d 472, 476–477 (5th Cir.1971). In short, "the legislative policy of flexibility does not permit a taxpayer to avoid the tax ramifications of a sale of a partnership interest simply by recasting the intended or constructive sale in the form of a reorganization to a partnership. Jupiter Corp. v. United States," 2 Cl.Ct. 58, 79 (1983).

Section 741 provides that in the case of the sale or exchange of a partnership interest, gain or loss shall be recognized to the transferor partner. The gain or loss, except to the extent that section 751 applies, is capital. Section 741 shall apply whether the partnership interest is sold to a member or nonmember of the partnership. Sec. 1.741–1(b), Income Tax Regs.

Section 721(a) states the general rule that gain or loss is not recognized through contributions of property to a partnership in exchange for partnership interests. Correspondingly, in a distribution by a partnership to a partner under section 731(a)(1), gain shall not be recognized except to the extent the distribution exceeds adjusted basis. Decreases in a partner's liabilities or share of the partnership's liabilities are considered distributions under section 752(b). Section 705(a)(2) provides that a partner's adjusted basis is decreased by his distributions from the partnership as well as the partner's distributive share of partnership losses. Petitioner argues that, as of April 1, 1978, three new partners were admitted to the partnership and, as a result, petitioner received a distribution as a result of being relieved of its share of partnership liabilities. Petitioner's basis in the partnership was reduced pursuant to section 705(a)(2).

The Code and regulations do not offer any guidance for distinguishing between an admission of new partners (pursuant to a contribution of property which is nontaxable under section 721), as petitioner contends is the correct characterization of the transaction before us, and a sale of a partnership interest under section 741, taxable as respondent urges. In one of the few cases addressing this issue, this Court in Richardson v. Commissioner, 76 T.C. 512 (1981), affd. 693 F.2d 1189 (5th Cir.1982), connected on the difference between the admission of a new partner into a partnership and the sale or exchange of a partnership interest:

> Admission of new partners is not in all respects identical to a sale or exchange of a partnership interest. In the former situation, the transaction is between the new partners and the partnership. The latter situation involves a transaction between a new partner and an existing partner. * * * [76 T.C. at 528.]

In *Richardson,* the taxpayers unsuccessfully maintained that they had sold their interest in three partnerships on December 30, 1974. 76 T.C. at 527–528. The admission of the new partners in *Richardson* corresponded with the infusion of large amounts of new capital into the partnership, although capital was not reduced with respect to the old partners. The transaction was essentially between the new partners and the partnership. Upon the admission of the new partners, the interests of all the original partners were reduced substantially. This Court viewed the transaction as an admission rather than a sale.

Unlike *Richardson,* the form and substance of the transaction at issue herein reflects transfers between an existing partner, Colonnade, and new partners, Bernstein, Feldman, and Mason and, therefore, was a sale of a partnership interest. The partnership as a whole was essentially unaffected. Prior to the April 1, 1978, amendment, Colonnade held a 50.98–percent partnership interest. As a result of the amendment, Colonnade divested itself of a 40.98–percent interest, which was acquired collectively by Bernstein, Feldman, and Mason at 13.66 percent each. Colonnade was left with a 10–percent interest, but together with its three shareholders, Colonnade still controlled the partnership as the majority general partner. The interests of the other partners in Georgia King were unchanged by the amendment.

Similarly, Colonnade divested itself of its rights under sections 10.03(c) and 10.05(a)(vi) of the partnership agreement (allocations of certain gains and losses) to the extent of 30 percent which were acquired collectively by Bernstein, Feldman, and Mason at 10 percent each. Again, the allocations under these two sections remained unchanged with respect to To–Sault, CRHC, and CHP–XX. Most notably, the aggregate capital contributions of Georgia King, $2,226,800, remained the same before and after the April 1, 1978, amendment. No additional contributions were required under the April 1, 1978, amendment to the partnership agreement. Colonnade, however, was discharged of its recourse obligation to contribute $816,060 in the future, an obligation which was acquired equally between Bernstein, Feldman, and Mason at $272,020 each. The total payment schedule for the contributions (in yearly installments) remained unchanged and continued to mirror the total equity payments required of the partnership. Colonnade was also discharged of 40.98 percent of its partnership nonrecourse liabilities, which were acquired by the three individual shareholders.

The fact that the three shareholders of Colonnade expressly assumed Colonnade's liabilities, in return for partnership interests which are capital assets under section 741, is especially significant. In determining whether an actual or constructive sale or exchange took place, we note that the touchstone for sale or exchange treatment is consideration. In LaRue v. Commissioner, 90 T.C. 465, 483–484 (1988), we noted that where liabilities are assumed as consideration for a partnership interest, a sale or exchange exists:

> If, in return for assets, any consideration is received, even if nominal in amount, the transaction will be classified as a sale or exchange. Blum v. Commissioner, 133 F.2d 447 (2d Cir.1943). * * * When the transferee of property assumes liabilities of the transferor encumbering the property, the liability is an amount realized by the transferor. Crane v. Commissioner, [331 U.S. 1 (1947)]; Commissioner v. Tufts, [461 U.S. 300 (1983)]. Assumption of liabilities by the transferee constitutes consideration making the transaction a sale or exchange. Wilkinson v. United States, 177 F.Supp. 101 (S.D.Ala.1959).
>
> * * * Where assets are transferred to third parties, assumption of liabilities constitutes consideration. * * *
>
> * * * the assumption of liabilities by a third party transferee constitutes an amount realized, and this is consideration to the transferor. *Crane v. Commissioner,* [supra]; *Tufts v. Commissioner,* [supra].

In arguing that the form of the arrangement reflects the substance, petitioner points out that the documents show that Bernstein, Feldman, and Mason were admitted to the partnership upon obtaining the required approval of NJHFA, as well as To–Sault, the managing general partner. Petitioner contends that the documents demonstrate an agreement between the partnership and the partners for the admission of new partners and do not reflect a transaction between petitioner and the new general partners. However, as we noted earlier, labels, semantics, technicalities, and formal documents do not necessarily control the tax consequences of a given transaction. * * * To look solely to the documents in this case and ignore the substance and reality of the transaction would exalt form over substance.

Aside from the transfer of a portion of Colonnade's partnership interest to the three new partners in return for a discharge of liabilities, there were no other changes in the structure or the operation of the Georgia King partnership as a result of the April 1, 1978, amendment. The substance of the transaction did not transpire between the partnership and the new partners, but rather, between Colonnade, an existing partner, and three new partners. Because there was no new or additional capital transferred to the partnership, there were no modifications of the partnership assets and liabilities. The only change was the transfers from the transferor partner's capital account to the transferees' capital accounts. As such, the transaction warrants sale and exchange treatment under section 741.

* * *

REVENUE RULING 84–53

1984–1 Cumulative Bulletin 159.

Issue. What are the tax consequences of the sale of a partnership interest in the situations described below?

Facts. *Situation 1.* In 1978, *Y* was formed as a limited partnership under the Uniform Limited Partnership Act of State *N* for the purpose of investing and trading in stocks and securities. *Y* has a calendar taxable year. *A* contributed $50x to *Y* in exchange for a general partner interest, entitling *A* to a 50 percent interest in all partnership distributions and in partnership income, gain, loss, and deduction. *B* contributed $50x to *Y* in exchange for a limited partner interest, entitling *B* to a 50 percent interest in all partnership distributions and in partnership income, gain, loss, and deduction.

On January 1, 1980, when the stock and securities of *Y* had decreased in value from $100x to $64x, *B* sold to *A* one-half of *B's* limited partner interest for $16x, which interest *A* holds as a limited partner.

On January 1, 1982, when the stock and securities of *Y* has risen in value from $64x (its 1980 value) to $120x, *A* sold to *C* one-half of *A's* general partner interest for $30x. Immediately prior to the sale, *A's* entire partnership interest had a fair market value of $90x and the transferred portion of the interest had a fair market value of $30x. Since formation, the partnership has made cash distributions in an amount equal to its total income (including tax-exempt income). Assume that all partnership allocations (in all situations) are valid, and that *A, B,* and *C* are unrelated parties.

Situation 2. The facts are the same as in *Situation 1* except that, in 1981, *Y* borrowed $80x recourse which was invested in securities that became worthless on December 31, 1981. Furthermore, immediately prior to *A's* sale to *C, A's* entire partnership interest had a fair market value of $30x and the transferred portion of *A's* interest had a fair market value of $10x.

Situation 3. The facts are the same as in *Situation 2* except that, on January 1, 1982, *A* sold *A's* entire limited partner interest to *C* for its fair market value of $10x (rather than one-half of *A's* general partner interest).

Situation 4. The facts are the same as in *Situation 1* except that, in 1981, *Y* borrowed $96x recourse which is invested in securities that become worthless on December 31, 1981. Furthermore, immediately prior to *A's* sale to *C, A's* entire partnership interest had a fair market value of $18x and the transferred portion of *A's* interest had a fair market value of $6x.

Law and analysis. Section 705 of the Internal Revenue Code provides rules for determining the adjusted basis of a partner's interest in a partnership.

Section 722 of the Code provides that the basis of an interest in a partnership acquired by a contribution of property equals the transferor partner's adjusted basis in the contributed property.

Section 752(a) of the Code provides that any increase in a partner's share of the partnership's liabilities is considered to be a contribution of money by the partner to the partnership.

Section 752(b) of the Code provides that any decrease in a partner's share of a partnership's liabilities is considered to be a distribution of money by the partnership to the partner.

Section 1.752–1[T] of the Income Tax Regulations provides rules for determining a partner's share of partnership liabilities with respect to both limited partnerships and general partnerships.

Section 752(d) of the Code provides that in the case of a sale or exchange of an interest in a partnership, liabilities shall be treated in the same manner as liabilities in connection with the sale or exchange of property not associated with partnerships.

Section 1.1001–2 of the regulations provides that the amount realized from a sale or other disposition of property includes the amount of liabilities from which the transferor is discharged as a result of the sale or disposition.

Section 1.61–6(a) of the regulations provides that when a part of a larger property is sold, the basis of the entire property shall be equitably apportioned among the several parts for purposes of determining gain or loss on the part sold.

Consistent with the provisions of Subchapter K of the Code, a partner has a single basis in a partnership interest, even if such partner is both a general partner and a limited partner of the same partnership. See Rev.Rul. 84–52, [1984–1 Cum.Bull. 157]. Thus, for example, in applying the limitations of section 704(d) of the Code, losses allocated with respect to a partner's limited partner interest will be allowed so long as they do not exceed the partner's basis in the entire partnership interest.

Under section 1.61–6(a) of the regulations, when a partner makes a taxable disposition of a portion of an interest in a partnership, the basis of the transferred portion of the interest generally equals an amount which bears the same relation to the partner's basis in the partner's entire interest as the fair market value of the transferred portion of the interest bears to the fair market value of the entire interest. However, if such partnership has liabilities, special adjustments must be made to take into account the effect of those liabilities on the basis of the partner's interest.

In cases where the partner's share of all partnership liabilities does not exceed the adjusted basis of such partner's entire interest (including basis attributable to liabilities), the transferor partner shall first exclude from the adjusted basis of such partner's entire interest an amount equal to such partner's share of all partnership liabilities, as determined under section 1.752–1[T] of the regulations. A part of the remaining adjusted basis (if any) shall be allocated to the transferred portion of the interest according to the ratio of the fair market value of the transferred portion of the interest to the fair market value of the entire interest. The sum of the amount so allocated plus the amount of the partner's share of liabilities that is considered discharged on the disposition of the transferred portion of the interest (under section 752(d) of the Code and section 1.1001–2 of the regulations) equals the adjusted basis of the transferred portion of the interest.

On the other hand, if the partner's share of all partnership liabilities exceeds the adjusted basis of such partner's entire interest (including basis attributable to liabilities), the adjusted basis of the transferred portion of the interest equals an amount that bears the same relation to the partner's adjusted basis in the entire interest as the partner's share of liabilities that is considered discharged on the disposition of the transferred portion of the interest bears to the partner's share of all partnership liabilities, as determined under section 1.752–1[T].

Holdings. *Situation* 1. Prior to the sale of one-half of *B*'s limited partner interest to *A*, the adjusted basis of *B*'s entire partnership interest was $50x. Because the fair market value of the transferred portion of *B*'s interest ($16x) is one-half of the fair market value of *B*'s entire partnership interest ($32x), $25x (1/2 of $50x) of adjusted basis must be allocated to the interest transferred by *B*. *B* sustained a $9 loss ($16x–$25x) on the sale of *A*. The adjusted basis of the remainder of *B*'s partnership interest is $25x.

Prior to the sale of one-half of *A*'s general partner interest to *C*, the adjusted basis of *A*'s entire partnership interest was $66x. Because the fair market value of the transferred portion of *A*'s interest ($30x) is one-third of the fair market value of *A*'s entire partnership interest ($90x), $22x (1/3 of $66x) of the adjusted basis must be allocated to the portion of the interest transferred by *A*. *A* realizes an $8x gain ($30x–$22x) on the sale of *C*. The basis of the remainder of *A*'s partnership interest is $44x. The results would be the same to *A* if *A*, instead, sold to *C* the limited partner interest acquired earlier from *B*.

Situation 2. The tax consequences of *B* 's sale of one-half of *B* 's limited partner interest to *A* are identical to those described in *Situation* 1.

In 1981, *A* 's basis in *A* 's entire partnership interest was increase[d] from $66x to $146x as a result of the $80x recourse borrowing (which increases only the basis of *A*, the sole general partner, under section 1.752–1(e) of the regulations and sections 752(a) and 722 of the Code) and was decreased to $86x as a result of the $60x loss allocated to *A* that year when the securities became worthless. Thus, prior to the sale of one-half of *A* 's general partner interest to *C*, the adjusted basis of *A* 's entire partnership interest was $86x. To take into account the effect of the liability sharing rules of section 1.752–1(e) of the regulations on *A* 's adjusted basis, $80x (*A* 's share of all partnership liabilities) is subtracted from $86x, leaving $6x. Because the fair market value of the transferred portion of *A* 's interest ($10x) is one-third of the fair market value of the entire interest ($30x), $2x (1/3 of $6x) of the remaining adjusted basis must be allocated to the transferred portion of *A* 's general partner interest. The sum of that amount ($2x) plus the amount of partnership liabilities from which *A* is discharged on the disposition of the transferred portion of A's general partner interest ($40), or $42x, equals the adjusted basis of the transferred portion of the interest. *A* realizes an $8x gain ($10x + $40x – $42x) on the sale to *C*. The basis of the remainder of *A* 's partnership interest is $44x ($86x – $42x).

Situation 3. The tax consequences of *B* 's sale of one-half of *B* 's limited partner interest to *A* are identical to those described in *Situation* 1.

As in *Situation* 2, prior to the sale of *A* 's limited partner interest to *C*, the adjusted basis of *A* 's entire partnership interest was $86x. To take into account the effect of the liability sharing rules of section 1.752–1[T] of the regulations on *A* 's adjusted basis, $80x (*A* 's share of all partnership liabilities) is subtracted from $86x, leaving $6x. Because of the fair market value of the transferred portion of *A* 's limited partner interest ($10x) is one-third of the fair market value of *A* 's entire interest ($30x), $2x (1/3 of $6x) of the remaining adjusted basis must be allocated to the transferred limited partner interest. The sum of that amount ($2x) plus the amount of partnership liabilities from which *A* is discharged on the disposition of the transferred limited partner interest ($0x), or $2x, equals the adjusted basis of the transferred portion of the interest. *A* realizes an $8x gain ($10x – $2x) on the sale to *C*. The basis of the remainder of *A* 's partnership interest is $84x ($86x – $2x).

Situation 4. The tax consequences of *B* 's sale of one-half of *B* 's limited partner interest to *A* are identical to those described in *Situation* 1.

In 1981, *A* 's basis in *A* 's entire partnership interest was increased from $66x to $162x as a result of the $96x recourse borrowing and was decreased to $90x as a result of the $72x loss allocated to *A* that year when the securities became worthless. Thus, prior to the sale of one-half of *A* 's general partner interest to *C,* the adjusted basis of *A* 's entire partnership interest was $90x. In this situation, *A* 's share of all partnership liabilities ($96x) exceeds the adjusted basis of *A* 's entire interest ($90x). Thus, the adjusted basis of the transferred portion of *A* 's general partner interest equals $45x, the amount which bears the same relation to A's adjusted basis in the entire interest ($90x) as the amount of partnership liabilities from which *A* is discharged on the disposition of the transferred portion of the general partner interest ($48x) bears to *A* 's share of all partnership liabilities ($96x). *A* realizes a $9x gain ($48x + $6x – $45x) on the sale of *C.* The basis of the remainder of *A* 's partnership interest is $45x ($90x – $45x).

ILLUSTRATIVE MATERIAL

A. TREATMENT OF PARTNERSHIP LIABILITIES

As explained in *Colonnade Condominium, Inc.* and Rev.Rul. 84–53, supra, section 752(d) requires the selling partner to include his share of partnership liabilities, determined under Regulations, section 1.752–1T, in the amount realized on the sale or exchange of a partnership interest. This reflects the inclusion of the partner's share of partnership liabilities in the basis of his partnership interest and incorporates the doctrine of Crane v. Commissioner, 331 U.S. 1 (1947), into Subchapter K. Furthermore, in Commissioner v. Tufts, 461 U.S. 300 (1983), the Supreme Court held that section 752(d) applied to nonrecourse liabilities in excess of the fair market value of the mortgaged property. This rule was applied to compute the amount of gain recognized on the sale in *Colonnade Condominium.* *Tufts* is discussed supra, page 131.

In Slavin v. Commissioner, 57 T.C.M. 343 (1989), the taxpayer assigned his 50 percent partnership interest to the other partner for no cash consideration and was discharged by the partnership's creditors from liability on partnership mortgage indebtedness. The taxpayer argued that the transaction gave rise to discharge of indebtedness income under section 61(a)(12), which was excludable under section 108 because he was insolvent. The court found a sale because the debt was not extinguished, it was assumed by the other partner.

B. TREATMENT OF PARTNERSHIP INCOME PRIOR TO SALE OF INTEREST

Under section 708(b)(1)(B), if 50 percent or more of the partnership interests in capital and profits are sold within a 12–month period, the partnership is considered as terminated. As a result, under section 706(c)(1) the taxable year of the partnership closes and each partner, whether or not she is a partner who has sold her interest, must include her distributive share of the partnership income. If less than 50 percent of the interests are sold, the partnership's taxable year does not close as a general matter. However, under section 706(c)(2)(A)(i) the partnership's taxable year does close as to the partner who sells her interest. As a result she must include in her income her distributive share of the partnership profits of the year up to that point, and is thus prevented from obtaining capital gain treatment respecting that share through a sale of her partnership interest. This income is characterized as ordinary or capital under section 702(b), supra, page 80. Under Regulations, section 1.705–1(a)(1), the selling partner adjusts her basis in her partnership interest to reflect her distributive share of partnership income (or loss) so taken into account.

If the partner does not sell her entire partnership interest, her partnership year does not close under section 706(c)(2)(A)(i). See section 706(c)(2)(B). Instead, section 706(d)(1) applies, requiring that her distributive share for the year be determined by taking into account her varying interests. Section 706(d)(1) is discussed supra, page 134.

In Smith v. Commissioner, 331 F.2d 298 (7th Cir.1964), one partner purchased the partnership interest of the other partner and, as part of the negotiations over the purchase price, the partners modified the partnership agreement to allocate all of the income of the partnership for the fiscal year of the sale to the purchasing partner. At the time of the modification, it was not clear whether the partnership would have a profit or a loss for the period in question. The court held that the modification was valid under section 704(b) and taxed the purchasing partner on the entire partnership income for the year. Such an agreement should be recognized under the current section 704(b) Regulations, discussed supra, page 98, if the selling partner's entire partnership interest is sold. However, Ogden v. Commissioner, 84 T.C. 871 (1985), aff'd per curiam, 788 F.2d 252 (5th Cir.1986), held that section 706(d)(1) disallows retroactive allocations to a new partner, even though the allocation is otherwise valid under section 704. Suppose that the purchaser is already a partner. Lipke v. Commissioner, 81 T.C. 689 (1983), allowed retroactive allocations to continuing partners when other partners interest varied. Should a retroactive allocation to the seller be valid, but one to the buyer be invalid?

C. SALES CAUSING CONSTRUCTIVE TERMINATIONS

1. *General*

As noted above, section 708(b)(1)(B) treats a partnership as terminated if 50 percent or more of the total interest in partnership profits *and* capital is sold or exchanged within a twelve month period. The Internal Revenue Service applies this rule to all exchanges, even though the exchange itself may be subject to a nonrecognition provision. See Rev.Rul. 81–38, 1981–1 Cum.Bull. 386 (transfer of 50 percent partnership interest to wholly owned subsidiary in transaction entitled to nonrecognition under section 351); Rev. Rul. 87–110, 1987–2 Cum.Bull. 159 (acquisition of corporate 50 percent partner in corporate reorganization entitled to nonrecognition under section 368).

Compare Rev.Rul. 84–52, 1984–1 Cum.Bull. 157, which held that the transfer of 50 percent of the general partnership interests in a general partnership to effect the conversion of those interests to limited partnership interests, pursuant to an amendment to the partnership agreement, did not result in termination of the partnership under section 708(d)(1). The Ruling also held that the exchange is accorded nonrecognition by section 721. Does this mean that no transfer of a partnership interest that is governed by section 721 is an exchange for purposes of section 708(d)(1)? Suppose that A is a

50 percent partner in the AB Partnership and he contributes his interest to the DEF Partnership in exchange for a 10 percent partnership interest in DEF. If an entity theory of partnership taxation is applied, the AB partnership is terminated. If the aggregate theory is applied to look through the DEF partnership, A has retained a 5 percent interest in the AB partnership, with the result that there has been an exchange of only 45 percent of the interests of the AB partnership. Accordingly, the AB partnership does not terminate. If, however, A held a 60 percent interest in the AB partnership, which he exchanged for a 10 percent interest in the DEF partnership, A has retained a six percent interest in the AB partnership and a 54 percent interest in the AB partnership has been exchanged. In this case, the AB partnership terminates.

The sale to the other partner of a partnership interest in a two-person partnership terminates the partnership and immediately ends the partnership's taxable year, even if the selling partner owned less than a 50 percent interest. Rev.Rul. 55–68, 1955–1 Cum.Bull. 372. McCauslen v. Commissioner, 45 T.C. 588 (1966), held that when a partnership terminates and is liquidated in this manner, the purchaser is treated as having acquired by direct purchase the portion of partnership assets attributable to the acquired partnership interest. For the seller, however, Regulations, section 1.741–1(b), provide that the transferor partner is treated as selling his partnership interest, not an undivided share of the partnership assets. This same rule would apply whenever all of the interests in a partnership are sold to one or more purchasers in an integrated transaction.

In contrast to the sale of a partnership interest, when a new partner is admitted and acquires a 50 percent interest by virtue of a contribution to the partnership, section 708(d)(1)(B) is inoperative. Rev.Rul. 75–423, 1975–2 Cum.Bull. 260.

2. *Tiered Partnerships*

The sale of an interest in an upper tier partnership (UTP) is treated as a sale of an interest in the lower tier partnership (LTP) only if the sale of the upper tier partnership causes its termination under section 708(b)(1)(B). Compare Rev.Rul. 87–50, 1987–1 Cum.Bull. 157, with Rev.Rul 87–51, 1987–1 Cum.Bull. 158. Thus, if G sells his 40 percent interest in the LTP Partnership to H, and I sells to J his 40 percent percent interest in UTP Partnership, which is a 40 percent partner of LTP, the LTP Partnership does not terminate, even though, in effect, there has been a sale of 56 percent of beneficial interest in the partnership. If, however, I had owned and sold a 50 percent interest in UTP, then UTP would have terminated, and its 40 percent interest in LTP would be treated as sold. As a result, LTP would terminate. This result would be true even if G had owned and sold only 10 percent of UTP, notwithstanding that, in effect, the beneficial interest in only 30 percent of the interests in LTP had been sold.

3. *Effect of Termination*

The effect of a section 708(b) "termination" is stated in the Regulations as follows: "If a partnership is terminated by a sale or exchange of an interest, the following is deemed to occur: The partnership distributes its properties to the purchaser and the other remaining partners in proportion to their respective interests in the partnership properties; and, immediately thereafter, the purchaser and the other remaining partners contribute the properties to a new partnership * * *." Regulations, section 1.708–1(b)(1)(iv).

This constructive "distribution-recontribution" approach of the Regulations has some important implications. As discussed supra, page 84, the "new" partnership may be required to change its taxable year to comport with the taxable years of the "new" partners. Elections made by the "old" partnership are no longer in effect, and new elections must be made. But see Rev.Rul. 86–73, 1986–1 Cum.Bull. 282 (section 754 election of "old" partnership applies to adjust basis of assets under section 743(b) immediately prior to deemed liquidating distribution). As a result of the operation of section 732, governing the basis of distributed property, the basis of the partnership property of the "new" partnership may be reallocated among the assets in a different manner than in the "old" partnership. Depending on various facts, this basis reallocation may either eliminate the application of section 704(c) or give rise to its application. Finally, if the partnership has cash, partners receiving a constructive cash distribution in excess of basis will recognize gain under section 731.

D. CAPITAL GAIN OR ORDINARY INCOME: SECTION 751

1. *Background*

Section 741, premised on the entity treatment of a partnership, as a general rule treats a partnership interest as a capital asset per se, so that its sale results in capital gain or loss. When capital gains were taxed at a preferential rates, this approach gave rise to tax avoidance possibilities. When a sole proprietor sells his business, Williams v. McGowan, 152 F.2d 570 (2d Cir.1945), requires that each asset be classified separately as to capital gain or loss and ordinary gain or loss; the business is not regarded as a unitary capital asset. The treatment of a partnership interest as a unitary capital asset would allow the comminution rule of Williams v. McGowan to be avoided, even though some of the partnership assets are ordinary assets. Accordingly, section 751(a) is designed to limit the tax avoidance possibilities of the general rule of section 741.

With the elimination of preferential rates for capital gains in 1986, the scope of the problem to which section 751(a) is directed was substantially reduced, through residual differences in the treatment of capital gains and ordinary income still exist, which at least arguably justify the continued existence of the provision.

2. *Operation in General*

Where a partnership has unrealized receivables or has inventory which has substantially appreciated in value (as defined in section 751(d)), a sale by a partner of his interest in the partnership is treated, as respects these items, on an aggregate approach. The partner is regarded as having sold pro tanto his interest in each of those ordinary assets. In effect, the result reached is the same as if the partnership had sold those assets and distributed to the partner his distributive share of the ordinary income. The items selected, unrealized receivables and substantially appreciated inventory, represent the significant ordinary income items held by a business or personal service partnership.

Where the inventory has appreciated in value but not to an extent that results in classification as a substantial appreciation under section 751(d), then capital gain results under section 741 if a partnership interest has been sold. Here, as in case law prior to the enactment of section 751, the issue of whether partnership interests or partnership assets are sold is relevant. See e.g., Kinney v. United States, 358 F.2d 738 (5th Cir.1966) (on the facts, there was a sale of a partnership interest and not of the individual assets; therefore the taxpayer was limited to a capital loss under section 741, despite the fact that some of the assets, if sold separately, would have generated an ordinary loss); Barran v. Commissioner, 334 F.2d 58 (5th Cir.1964) (sale treated as sale of partnership interest for holding period purposes).

3. *Unrealized Receivables*

Unrealized receivables are broadly defined in section 751(c) to include any rights to payment for goods delivered or to be delivered or for services rendered or to be rendered, to the extent not previously includible in income. This broad interpretation has been followed by the courts. Logan v. Commissioner, 51 T.C. 482 (1968), held, in connection with the sale of a partnership interest in a law firm, that unbilled fees for work in progress constituted unrealized receivables. The taxpayer argued that the partnership had no express contractual rights against the clients and that claims in quantum meruit were not covered by section 751(c). The court held to the contrary, finding a Congressional intent for a broad interpretation of 751(c), and stressing the fact that the partner, if he had remained in the partnership, would have realized ordinary income on the collection of the fees.

Ledoux v. Commissioner, 77 T.C. 293 (1981), aff'd per curiam, 695 F.2d 1320 (11th Cir.1983), ascribed an even broader meaning to the term "unrealized receivables." In that case the taxpayer sold an interest in a partnership which had a contract entitling it to operate a dog racing track for a 20 year period in consideration of paying the track owner the first $200,000 of net profit. The taxpayer argued that the agreement was more in the nature of a leasehold than a right to receive payments for services, or that the portion of the purchase price attributable to the agreement was in the nature of a payment for going concern value. The Tax Court concluded that to be an unrealized receivable the agreement need not obligate the partnership to perform services; it is sufficient that the partnership have the right to perform future services for compensation. However, the analysis of the court left open the possibility that unrealized receivable classification might have been avoidable, at least in part, if the purchase and sale agreement had indicated that a portion of the price had been attributable to partnership goodwill.

The following cases also found that the items involved were unrealized receivables: Roth v. Commissioner, 321 F.2d 607 (9th Cir.1963) (right to proceeds from distribution of motion picture); Wolcott v. Commissioner, 39 T.C. 538 (1962) (uncompleted architectural contracts); Frankfort v. Commissioner, 52 T.C. 163 (1969) (real estate commissions which were to become due when closings took place); Blacketor v. United States, 497 F.2d 928 (Ct.Cl.1974) (fifteen year agreement entitling taxpayer to commissions on sales of wood products); United States v. Woolsey, 326 F.2d 287 (5th Cir.1963) (twenty-five year management contract); Rev.Rul. 79–51, 1979–1 Cum.Bull. 225 (right to payments for work to be performed under long-term construction contracts which were being reported for tax purposes on the completed contract method). Hale v. Commissioner, 24 T.C.M. 1497 (1965), held that the sale of a profits interest in a partnership resulted in ordinary income, without discussion of section 751, under the authority of Hort v. Commissioner, 313 U.S. 28 (1941), and Commissioner v. P.G. Lake, Inc., 356 U.S. 260 (1958).

Miller v. United States, 181 Ct.Cl. 331, 67–2 U.S.T.C. ¶ 9685 (1967), held that a partnership had no unrealized receivables where it merely had the expectancy of continuing to represent a client which generated most of its income. The contract with the client was on a day-to-day basis and cancellable at any time. See also Phillips v. Commissioner, 40 T.C. 157 (1963), and Baxter v. Commissioner, 433 F.2d 757 (9th Cir.1970), both finding no section 751 property where the contracts were cancellable at will or with a short notice period. Aliber v. Commissioner, 52 T.C.M. 1316 (1987), held that accounts receivable representing rights to reimbursement for real estate taxes paid by the partnership on behalf of owners of condominium properties managed by the partnership were not unrealized receivables.

"Unrealized receivables" include gain which would have been treated as ordinary income under the various recapture rules (e.g., section 1245(a)) on the sale of an asset by the partnership. For purposes of section 751, the amount of potential recapture income is treated as an unrealized receivable with a basis of zero. Regulations, section 1.751–1(c)(4), (5).

4. *Substantially Appreciated Inventory*

Under section 751(d)(2), "inventory" includes, in addition to stock in trade, all non-capital assets except depreciable property and land governed by section 1231. In determining whether property is to be classified as inventory, the activities of the selling partner are taken into account. For a series of cases dealing with different partners in the same partnership and reaching different results on the section 751 question as to the status of real property held by the partnership, see Morse v. United States, 371 F.2d 474 (Ct.Cl. 1967) (capital asset); Estate of Freeland v. Commissioner, 393 F.2d 573 (9th Cir.1968) (inventory); Ginsburg v. United States, 396 F.2d 983 (Ct.Cl. 1968) (capital asset). Regulations, section 1.751–1(d)(2)(ii), include within the definition of inventory all accounts receivable, including those of both cash and accrual method taxpayers. Inventory does not include other "unrealized receivables," as defined in section 751(c), such as depreciation recapture. The gain attributable to accounts receivable included in inventory is not taxed twice. Rather, including these items in inventory affects the calculation to determine whether the inventory is substantially appreciated.

A partnership owns inventory which has "appreciated substantially in value" if the inventory itself has appreciated in value by more than 20 percent and if its value also exceeds 10 percent of the fair market value of the partnership's total assets other than money. Even though inventory had not actually appreciated economically it was held to be appreciated inventory where it had been treated as an expensed item and hence had a zero tax basis. Yourman v. United States, 277 F.Supp. 818 (S.D.Cal.1967). The inclusion in inventory of accounts receivable of an accrual method partnership makes it more difficult to meet the 20 percent test for substantial appreciation, while making it easier to meet the more than 10 percent of fair market value test. Assume, for example, that an accrual method partnership holds actual inventory, having a basis of $79 and a fair market value of $100, accounts receivable having a basis and fair market value of $30, and a capital asset having a fair market value of $900. If the accounts receivable were not treated as inventory, the 20 percent appreciation test is measured by the $79 basis and $100 fair market value benchmarks, and that test would be met. But the 10 percent of fair market value test is not met, since $100 is not more than 10 percent of total assets of $1,030. When the accounts receivable are included in inventory, however, the 10 percent test is met, since $130 is more than 10 percent of $1,030, but the 20 percent test is not met because the $130 fair market value of the inventory does not exceed its $109 basis by more than 20 percent.

The ratio tests in section 751(d) may be easily circumvented. For example, the 10 percent test might be avoided by borrowing money and investing it in a low risk investment such as government bonds; or the ratio between adjusted basis and fair market value of inventory might be reduced by subjecting the property to a mortgage liability.

5. *Tiered Partnerships*

Prior to 1984 tiered partnerships were used to avoid section 751. The lower tier partnership would hold the tangible assets and the upper tier partnership would own an interest in the lower tier partnership. When a partner of the upper tier partnership sold his interest, arguably section 751 did not apply. The 1984 Act added section 751(f), which prevents the use of this technique by looking through the upper tier partnership to the assets of the lower tier partnership to apply section 751 on a sale of an interest in the upper tier partnership. Madorin v. Commissioner, 84 T.C. 667 (1985), reached this result without the benefit of statutory authority.

6. *Computational Aspects*

Regulations, section 1.751–1(a)(2), provide that the section 751(a) gain is the difference between the portion of the amount realized allocable to section 751 assets and the portion of the selling partner's basis for his partnership interest allocable to those assets. The portion of the selling partner's basis for his partnership interest allocable to section 751 assets is equal to the bases such assets would have under section 732, discussed infra, page 217, if the partnership had currently distributed those assets to the partner. Since section 732 calls for a carryover of partnership basis on distribution and since only the selling partner's pro rata share of section 751 assets will be involved, the selling partner's pro rata share of the partnership basis for the section 751 assets generally will determine the basis allocable to the assets.

For example, assume that A, with a basis for her one-third interest in the ABC partnership of $75, sells that interest for $100. ABC owns inventory having a basis of $150 and a value of $210, and a capital asset having a basis of $75 and a value of $90. Of the $100 realized by A, $70 is attributable to the inventory (which is substantially appreciated). If one-third of the inventory, having a fair market value of $70, had been distributed to A, her basis in that inventory under section 732, discussed infra, page 217, would have been $50. Accordingly, under section 751(a), A recognizes $20 of ordinary income. Having accounted for $70 of the total of $100 realized on the sale and $50 of A's total basis of $75, the residual gain taxed as capital gain under section 741 is $5, which is the excess of the remaining amount realized, $30, over A's remaining basis, $25.

This treatment of basis is satisfactory where the seller's basis for his partnership interest is equivalent to his pro rata share of partnership basis. But where the seller's basis may differ, as the result for example of his previous purchase of his partnership interest, the allocated basis of section 751 assets may be lower than the selling partner's actual cost allocable to the assets unless the partnership has elected to adjust basis pursuant to an election under section 754 (infra, page 207), or the sale is made within two years after his original purchase. (A transferee partner selling or receiving a distribution within two years of his purchase may elect to treat the partnership basis of the assets as though an inside basis adjustment had been made, section 732(d)). For example, suppose that the partnership assets consist of inventory with a zero basis but worth $100,000, and that partner A's basis for his one-fourth partnership interest is $25,000 because of his previous purchase of the interest at that price. If A sells his interest for $25,000, he will recognize $25,000 ordinary income and $25,000 capital loss in the absence of an inside basis adjustment. This result can be avoided, however, if a section 743(b) or section 732(d) election to adjust basis is in effect, in which case he would have a $25,000 basis for his interest in the assets and no gain or loss would be recognized as a result of the sale. Basis adjustments are discussed, infra, page 206.

7. *Loss Situations*

Section 751(a) may apply even though the partnership interest is not sold at an overall gain. For example, assume A, with a basis for his interest of $75, sells for $65 his interest in partnership AB, owning inventory having a basis of $50 and a value of $100 and securities with a basis of $100 and a value of $30. Although he has realized an overall loss of $10, he must fragment that overall loss into $25 of ordinary income and $35 of capital loss, since the partnership inventory has met the test of substantial appreciation. Regulations, section 1.751–1(a)(2).

The aggregate approach under section 751 applies only on the gain side; where the inventory has substantially depreciated, a capital loss results. This different treatment apparently is the result of a desire not to further complicate the matter.

8. *Policy Analysis of Section 751*

In 1984 the American Law Institute recommended the replacement of the section 741 and section 751(a) approach to taxation of the sale of partnership interests with the fragmentation approach to the sale of a business adopted in Williams v. McGowan, supra, page 199. The change was principally justified on simplicity grounds. However, the subsequent elimination of the capital gain preference has so reduced the problems at which the section was aimed that its complete elimination may be the most likely result of future developments.

E. DISPOSITIONS OTHER THAN SALES

1. *Exchanges of Partnership Interests*

Section 1031(a)(2)(D) specifically excludes partnership interests from the categories of property which may be exchanged without recognition of gain or loss. This provision, which was enacted in 1984, overruled Long v. Commissioner, 77 T.C. 1045 (1981), and other cases which treated an exchange of a general partnership interest in a partnership holding rental real property for a general partnership interest in a different partnership holding similar properties as a tax-free like kind exchange. See also Estate of Meyer v. Commissioner, 58 T.C. 311 (1972), aff'd per curiam, 503 F.2d 556 (9th

Cir.1974) (denying section 1031 treatment to an exchange of a general partnership interest for a limited partnership interest for a year prior to the enactment of section 1031(a)(2)(D)). Section 751(a) applies to taxable exchanges of partnership interests. For the treatment of an exchange of a partnership interest for real property, see Aliber v. Commissioner, 52 T.C.M. 1316 (1987).

2. *Gifts*

Section 751(a) does not apply where a partnership interest is disposed of by gift. However, Rev.Rul. 60–352, 1960–2 Cum.Bull. 208, held that a where a partner made a charitable contribution of an interest in a partnership holding section 453 installment obligations, the partner was required to recognize the gain attributable to his share of the partnership's installment obligations. This Ruling is consistent with the policy of section 453B, but it is not consistent with the mechanics of sections 741 and 751(a). A section 453 installment obligation is not substantially different than any other unrealized receivable.

In Madorin v. Commissioner, 84 T.C. 667 (1985), the taxpayer established a grantor trust of which he was treated as the owner under section 674 because of certain retained powers. The trust acquired a partnership interest and during the period that the partnership reported losses, the taxpayer properly included the trust's distributive share of those losses in his return. When the partnership began to show income, the taxpayer renounced his retained powers, thereby completing the transfer. At that time the trust's share of partnership liabilities exceeded its basis in the partnership interest and the partnership had unrealized receivables. The termination of the grantor trust status was treated as a part gift-part sale transaction, applying Regulations, section 1.1001–2(a), Ex. (5), and the gain was characterized as ordinary gain under section 751. See also Rev.Rul. 75–194, 1975–1 Cum. Bull. 80 (applying part gift-part sale analysis to charitable contribution of partnership interest where partner's share of debt exceeded basis).

3. *Corporate Distributions*

Suppose that a corporation owns an interest in a partnership holding unrealized receivables or substantially appreciated inventory and it distributes the partnership interest to its shareholders either as a dividend or in liquidation. If the distribution is a dividend and the fair market value of the partnership interest exceeds its basis to the corporation, or if the distribution is in liquidation of the corporation, section 751 applies because sections 311 and 336, respectively treat such corporate distributions of property as a sale or exchange of the property. But if the distribution is not in liquidation of the corporation and the fair market value of the partnership interest is less than its basis, section 311 does not treat the distribution as a sale or exchange, and section 751 presumably does not apply even though the partnership holds unrealized receivables or substantially appreciated inventory. However, section 761(e), enacted in 1984, which treats any distribution of a partnership interest by a corporation or a trust as an exchange for purposes of section 708 (relating to termination of a partnership) and section 743 (relating to optional basis adjustments), also authorizes the Treasury Department to promulgate regulations treating such a distribution as an exchange for purposes of section 751. As of yet no such Regulations have been promulgated.

In Holiday Village Shopping Center v. United States, 773 F.2d 276 (Fed.Cir.1985), a corporation liquidated and distributed its interest in a limited partnership which held property subject to depreciation recapture. On the facts, section 751 did not apply. The court disregarded the partnership and treated the distribution as a distribution of property directly by the corporation, reflecting an aggregate approach which cannot be reconciled with the entity approach governing dispositions of partnership interests where section 751 does not apply.

F. INSTALLMENT SALES OF PARTNERSHIP INTERESTS

Gain realized on the sale of a partnership interest sold for deferred payments may be reported on the installment method under section 453. See Rev.Rul. 76–483, 1976–2 Cum.Bull. 131. Section 453 is not difficult to apply as long as a partnership does not hold any property that could not be sold on the installment method if the property were owned and sold directly by the partner. On the other hand, if the partnership holds property which may not be sold on the installment method under section 453 (such as inventory, see section 453(b)(2)(A)), the analysis is more complex and the existing statutory pattern is unclear.

Denying installment reporting entirely if the partnership holds any assets ineligible for installment treatment is inconsistent with the basic entity theory of section 741 as modified by section 751(a). On the other hand, allowing installment reporting on the full gain in such cases may be seen as circumventing the restrictions of section 453. Section 453 itself provides a partial answer in section 453(i)(2) which treats as recapture income for purposes of disallowing installment sale treatment under section 453(i) any ordinary income realized on the sale of a partnership interest under section 751 which is attributable to depreciation recapture under section 1245 or section 1250. On the one hand, this statutory structure might be read to imply that absent a specific statutory directive, the entity approach is to be applied in the case of installment sales of partnership interest, and only depreciation recapture will be denied installment reporting. On the other hand, section 453(i)(2) was a minor technical correction to the depreciation rules, inserted in Conference Committee. See H.Rep. No. 99–841, 99th Cong., 2d Sess. II–845 (1986). The relative obscurity of this amendment supports an argument that it does not preclude a more comprehensive melding of the policies of sections 453, 741 and 751. Rev.Rul. 89–108, 1989–2 Cum.Bull. 100, held that installment reporting is not available for the gain on the sale of a partnership interest to the extent that the gain is attributed to substantially appreciated inventory and taxed as ordinary income under section 751. The Ruling is silent, however, as to the treatment of section 741 gain which is attributable to partnership inventory which is not substantially appreciated. The facts of the Ruling indicate that the partnership held no unrealized receivables and thus provides no guidance on that issue.

A compromise solution, which would be consistent with the basic structure of the section involved, but which is without any clear statutory basis, would be to require current recognition the entire portion of the gain attributable to partnership property ineligible for installment method reporting. That portion of the gain may or may not correspond to the portion of the gain characterized as ordinary income under section 751(a), given the difference in the definitional provisions.

G. SALE VERSUS LIQUIDATION

While section 741 generally allows capital gain treatment to the selling partner on the sale of a partnership interest, amounts paid in liquidation of a partnership interest may result in ordinary income under section 736. Thus, the characterization of the transaction as a "sale" or as a "liquidation" is of crucial importance. This problem is considered, infra, page 242.

H. REFERENCES

Erickson, An Appeal for Repeal of Section 751, 65 Taxes 365 (1987); Birkeland & Postlewaite, Constructive Termination of a Partnership—A Fresh Look, 39 Tax Lawyer 701 (1986); Nad, Dispositions of Partnership Interests and Partnership Property, 43 N.Y.U.Inst. on Fed.Tax. 29 (1985); Brier, Like-Kind Exchanges of Partnership Interests: A Policy Oriented Approach, 38 Tax.L.Rev. 389 (1983); James, The Installment Sale of Partnership Interest, 43 Tenn.L.Rev. 307 (1976).

SECTION 2. THE PURCHASER'S SIDE OF THE TRANSACTION: BASIS ASPECTS

INTERNAL REVENUE CODE: Sections 732(d); 742; 743; 752(a); 754; 755; 761(e).

REGULATIONS: Sections 1.732–1(d); 1.742–1; 1.743–1; 1.754–1; 1.755–1(a), (b)(2), (c).

TEMPORARY REGULATIONS: Section 1.755–2T.

Where an individual acquires an interest in a partnership by purchase, the aggregate versus entity issue again presents a problem. Here the problem arises in connection with determining the basis of the buying partner, both as to his partnership interest and his share of the bases of the partnership assets. Once again, Subchapter K adopts a dual approach, with the entity approach providing the general rule under sections 742 and 743(a), but aggregate treatment being permitted under section 743(b) at the election of the partnership.

ILLUSTRATIVE MATERIAL

A. BUYING PARTNER'S BASIS

Section 742 provides that a person buying an interest in a partnership has a basis for her partnership interest equal to its cost. The buying partner's concern, however, is not limited to the basis for her partnership interest. It is also important to her that the price she paid for that interest be reflected in the basis of the partnership's assets since that basis will determine the amount of gain or loss recognized on a sale of the assets or the amount of depreciation allowable with respect to the assets.

Suppose the ABC partnership has inventory worth $1,500 but with a basis of $600, and other assets worth $3,000 with a basis of $3,000. A sells his one-third interest to D for $1,500. The partnership now sells the inventory for $1,500. The partnership would have a $900 profit and B, C and D would each be taxed on ordinary income of $300. But economically D has not realized any profit, since she in effect paid $500, the fair market value, for her share of the inventory. To avoid any such result, the partnership basis for her share of the inventory should be $500, leaving only B and C each with a $300 profit on their respective shares. In response to this problem, section 743 keeps the entity approach as the standard rule but, in section 743(b), allows the partnership to elect under section 754 an aggregate approach whereby the basis of the partnerships assets may be affected. As applied to the example above, the section 754 election would allow the partnership to make a special upward adjustment in the basis of the partnership inventory to reflect D's cost. On the other hand, if D's proportionate share of the basis in the partnership assets were greater than the amount paid for the partnership interest, a section 754 election would require a downward adjustment in the basis of partnership property under section 743(b). Although the adjustment applies to "partnership property," the adjustment is applied only with respect to the transferee partner; it does not affect the "inside" basis of the other partner(s).

The desirability of an election from the point of view of the incoming partner is thus a function of whether or not the partnership assets have appreciated or declined in value. Since the election, once made, applies to a number of different situations, it is difficult to generalize as to when it is appropriate for a particular partnership. Some partnerships experiencing frequent changes in partner personnel might find the aggregate approach which the election provides too bothersome a complication. On the other hand, from the point of view of an incoming partner, it may be important that he have a commitment from the partnership to make the requisite election or else the basis adjustment which he may desire will not be available.

The statutory mechanics of the election are somewhat complicated.[1] The election is made by the partnership—not the incoming partner—under section 754 and, when made, applies both to sales of partnership interests under section 743(b), discussed in Part B., infra, and to the basis adjustments under section 734, attributable to distributions of partnership property, discussed, infra, page 237.

B. BASIS OF PARTNERSHIP PROPERTY UNDER SECTION 743(b)

Section 743(b) allows the partnership to elect to adjust the basis of partnership assets upon the transfer of a partnership interest by sale or at death in an amount equal to the difference between the transferee's basis in his partnership interest and his pro rata share of the partnership's aggregate basis for all of its assets. This basis adjustment is solely for the benefit of the transferee. A partner's share of the partnership's adjusted basis is equal to his share of partnership capital plus surplus (i.e., his capital account under the section 704(b) Regulations), plus his share of partnership liabilities. Regulations, section 1.743–1(b)(1). The effect of any required allocations under

1. The Regulations require the election to be made in the partnership return "for the taxable year during which the distribution or transfer occurs." Regulations, section 1.754–1(b)(1). The Regulations originally provided that the election be made "for the first taxable year to which the election applies" and was the subject of some dispute. Neel v. United States, 266 F.Supp. 7 (N.D.Ga.1966), held the original Regulation invalid. See also Estate of Dupree v. United States. 391 F.2d 753 (5th Cir.1968) (election not effective when not made within statutory time for filing the original return). Jones v. United States, 553 F.2d 667 (Ct.Cl.1977), upheld the validity of the present Regulations in a situation in which an election was filed in 1969 with respect to a transfer which had taken place in 1967 on the death of a partner.

section 704(c) reflecting the difference between the basis and book value of contributed property must be given effect. See Regulations, section 1.743–1(b)(2)(i). Because the buyer succeeds to his seller's capital account, Regulations, section 1.704–1(b)(2)(iv)(*l*), prior special allocations under section 704(b) also are taken into account. Thus, a purchasing partner's pro rata share of the partnership's basis does not necessarily equal the sum of the total basis of partnership property multiplied by the partner's percentage interest, see Regulations, section 1.743–1(b)(1), Ex. (1), although absent special allocations or section 704(c) allocations that relationship generally will hold true. Finally, after the purchase, capital account adjustments under the section 704 regulations to reflect gain, loss, income, and deductions are made as if there had been no basis adjustment. Regulations, section 1.704–1(b)(2)(iv)(*m*)(*2*). Thus, the purchasing partner's capital account may be credited with book gain even though his distributive share of the partnership's gain on a subsequent sale of the property is less than that amount. See Regulations, section 1.704–1(b)(5), Ex. (13)(iii).

Section 755 provides for the allocation of the basis adjustment to the various assets of the partnership, including goodwill. First, the adjustment is divided into two portions, that attributable to section 1231(b) assets and capital assets (other than goodwill) and that attributable to other types of property. The adjustment to each class of property is then allocated to the properties of that class so as to reduce proportionately the difference between the fair market value and the adjusted basis of each partnership asset. If the overall adjustment is an upward adjustment and one of the classes of property has appreciated while the other has depreciated, the entire adjustment must be allocated to the appreciated class. This rule presents problems when the class of assets that has depreciated in value overall contains some assets that have appreciated. The basis of these appreciated assets cannot be increased. See Regulations, section 1.755–1(c), Ex. (3). The entire adjustment is allocated to appreciated assets in the class that has net appreciation. If, however, a single class of assets consists of both appreciated and depreciated assets, Regulations, section 1.755–1(a)(2), permits the basis of some assets to be decreased while the basis of other assets is increased, so as to reduce the difference between basis and fair market value. The net amount of the adjustments must equal the Section 743(b) adjustment. See Regulations, section 1.755–1(a)(2).

The operation of the special basis adjustment rules is illustrated in the following example, based on Regulations, section 1.755–1(c), Ex. (3). Suppose that the ABC Partnership has three assets: a capital asset having a basis of $1,000 and a fair market value of $1,500; a depreciable asset having a basis of $1,000 and a value of $700; and inventory having an adjusted basis of $700 and a value of $800. A sells his one third interest to D for $1,000 and the partnership makes a section 754 election. D's share of the partnership's basis in its assets is $900 ($\frac{1}{3}$ × $2,700), and his section 743(b) special basis adjustment is $100. The class of capital and section 1231 assets has $200 of net appreciation; and the class of all other assets (the inventory) has $100 of appreciation. Two thirds of the appreciation is attributable to the class including capital and section 1231 assets. Thus a $67 special basis adjustment is allocated to those assets. Since the depreciable asset has a fair market value of less than basis, no adjustment is made to its basis; the entire $67 is allocated to the capital asset. The inventory represents one-third of the appreciation, so $33 of the basis adjustment is allocated to it.

Suppose now that the partnership sells the capital asset for $1,500. D has a basis for his one-third interest in that asset of $400 (⅓ of the partnership's $1,000 basis plus his $67 basis adjustment). Thus his distributive share of the gain is only $100, while B's and C's shares are each $167. If the inventory is sold for a $100 gain, D's distributive share is zero, because his one-third share of the partnership's basis, which is $233, plus his $33 adjustment offsets his $266 share of the sales price. Note that in this example, the normal allocation rules of section 755 prevented each asset from being assigned a basis equal to its fair market value. The excess gain recognized by D on the sale of the capital asset, however, is offset by the higher depreciation allowed on the section 1231 asset, since he did not adjust its basis down. Under Regulations, section 1.755–1(a)(2), the partnership can request a special basis increase of $100 for the capital asset and a special basis decrease of $67 for the section 1231 asset. If the IRS granted the request, D would not recognize any gain on the sale of the capital asset. Should D have asked the partnership to make the request?

If the assets of the partnership constitute a trade or business, for purposes of applying the apportionment rules of Regulations, section 1.751–1, the fair market value of partnership goodwill must be determined using the residual method required by section 1060 for applicable asset acquisitions." Temporary Regulations, section 1.755–2T. Under this valuation method, the fair market value of partnership goodwill is the amount which if assigned to the goodwill would result in a liquidating distribution to the purchasing partner equal to the basis in his partnership interest, reduced by the portion of that basis attributable to partnership liabilities, if immediately after the purchase all partnership property, including intangible assets other than goodwill (e.g., patents, secret processes, trademarks, etc), were sold at fair market value and, after the payment of partnership debts, the proceeds were distributed to the partners. This method of valuing partnership goodwill overruled United States v. Cornish, 348 F.2d 175 (9th Cir.1965). That case held that where the purchaser paid a premium for the partnership interest, the premium was spread among all of the partnership assets, including goodwill which was independently valued, with the result that the basis of tangible assets was increased above their fair market value.

In Mushro v. Commissioner, 50 T.C. 43 (1968) (NA), the receipt of insurance proceeds by the deceased partner's wife was treated as payment by the remaining partners for the deceased partner's partnership interest and hence a section 743 basis adjustment was allowed.

In Rev.Rul. 79–92, 1979–1 Cum.Bull. 180, a section 754 election was in effect and as a result under section 743(b) one partner had a higher basis in partnership assets than the other partners. The Ruling held that if the partnership sold the assets for deferred payments and the partner with the higher basis realized a loss while the other partners realized a gain, partners could report the gain on the installment method under section 453.

C. APPLICATION TO TIERED PARTNERSHIPS

Suppose that A purchases from B for $50 a one-fourth partnership interest in UTP Partnership which owns inventory having a basis of $40 and a fair market value of $80 and a one-third interest in LTP Partnership, having a basis of $80 and a fair market value of $120. LTP's sole asset is a capital asset having a basis of $330 and a fair market value of $360. UTP's basis in LTP is less than its pro rata basis in LTP's assets because UTP purchased its interest in LTP at a time when LTP did not have a section 754 election in effect. Assuming that B's pro rata share of UTP's basis in its assets is $30, if UTP has a section 754 election in effect, B is entitled to a section 743(b) basis adjustment of $20, of which $10 is attributable to UTP's interest in LTP.

Rev.Rul. 87–115, 1987–2 Cum.Bull. 163, held that a section 743(b) adjustment to the basis of LTP's asset also is available if LTP also has a section 754 election in effect. In that case the sale of A's interest in UTP to B is treated as a deemed sale of an interest in LTP. If LTP does not have a section 754 election in effect, no basis adjustment is allowed. Similarly, if LTP has a section 754 election in effect, but UTP does not, no basis adjustment is allowed.

If a section 743(b) adjustment is available to LTP, it is determined as follows. The deemed price paid by B for an indirect interest in LTP is $30 (1/4 of UTP's $80 basis in LTP plus B's $10 special adjustment). B's share of the adjusted basis of LTP's asset is $27.5 (1/4 of $110). Thus, B's section 743(b) adjustment in the basis of LTP's asset is only $2.5. What happened to the remaining $7.5 of B's section 743(b) adjustment to UTP's basis in LTP? What would be B's basis adjustment in LTP's basis for its asset if UTP's basis in LTP had been $110, an amount equal to one third of its pro rata basis of LTP's assets?

D. EFFECT OF CONSTRUCTIVE TERMINATION

Rev.Rul. 86–73, 1986–1 Cum.Bull. 282, held that a section 754 election applied to the purchase of a partnership interest in a transaction which caused a constructive termination of the partnership under section 708, discussed supra, page 197. Rev.Rul. 88–42, 1988–1 Cum.Bull. 265, extended this principle to permit a partnership to make a section 754 election on its final return when a sale of a partnership interest causes a constructive termination of the partnership. As a result, the basis of the partnership's assets is adjusted under section 743(b) prior to the deemed distribution, and the purchasing partner's basis in the assets, determined under section 732, will take into account the adjustment. Similarly, the reconstituted partnership's basis in the assets under section 723 will reflect the adjustment. The same result would be effected by a valid section 732(d) election by the purchasing partner, but the Service has not ruled on whether section 732(d) elections are available with respect to deemed distributions under section 708.

E. PURCHASE OF PARTNERSHIP INTEREST VERSUS PURCHASE OF PARTNERSHIP ASSETS

Suppose that A and B are equal partners and that A purchases B's entire partnership interest. Since the purchase results in the termination of the partnership, A could either take a cost basis in an undivided one-half of the partnership assets, as if she purchased them directly from B, and a basis in the other-half determined under section 732, or she could take a basis in the assets determined by treating the transaction first as the purchase of a partnership interest to which sections 742 and 743 apply, followed by the liquidation of the partnership, in which A's basis in all of the assets is determined under section 732. McCauslen v. Commissioner, 45 T.C. 588 (1966), held that the purchaser is treated as having acquired by direct purchase the portion of partnership assets attributable to the acquired partnership interest. Rev.Rul. 67–65, 1967–1 Cum.Bull. 168 followed *McCauslen.*

Although Rev.Rul. 67–65 has not been revoked, Rev.Rul. 84–111, 1984–2 Cum.Bull. 88, indicates that the Internal Revenue Service might not follow *McCauslen* if the issue were raised currently. The 1984 Ruling involved the incorporation of a partnership and set forth three alternative transactions. In the first situation, the partnership transferred its assets to the corporation for stock and then contributed the stock to the partners in liquidation. In the second situation, the partnership distributed its assets in liquidation, and the partners then contributed the assets to the corporation for its stock. In the third situation, the partners contributed their partnership interests to the corporation in exchange for stock. The form of each transaction was respected. In the third situation the partners were treated as exchanging their partnership interests for stock in a transaction governed by section 351. Although the partnership was terminated under section 708(b)(1)(A) upon the transfer of the partnership interests, the corporation was held to have acquired the partnership assets by virtue of liquidation of the partnership. If *McCauslen* were followed, the assets would have been acquired in exchange for stock.

F. SPECIAL CASE OF DISTRIBUTION OF ASSETS TO BUYING PARTNER

For the special rule of section 732(d) applicable where a section 743(b) election has not been made, but the partnership assets are distributed in kind to a buying partner within two years from the date but the partnership assets are distributed in kind to a buying partner within two years from the date of purchase, see infra, page 222.

G. REFERENCES

Weidner, Transfers of Partnership Interests and Optional Adjustments to Basis, 10 N.M.L.Rev. 51 (1980); Rudolph, Collapsible Partnerships and Optional Basis Adjustments, 28 Tax L.Rev. 211 (1973); Caso and Epstein, An Analysis of the Optional–Basis–Adjustment Rules for Partners and Partnerships, 42 J.Tax. 234 (1975).

CHAPTER 5

PARTNERSHIP DISTRIBUTIONS

SECTION 1. CURRENT DISTRIBUTIONS

INTERNAL REVENUE CODE: Sections 704(c)(1)(B); 731; 732; 733; 734; 735; 741; 751(b)–(d); 761(d).

REGULATIONS: Sections 1.731–1(a)(1) and (3), (b); 1.732–1, –2; 1.733–1; 1.734–1; 1.735–1; 1.751–1(b); 1.761–1(d).

TEMPORARY REGULATIONS: Section 1.752–1T(f), (j)(3), –2T.

Under the conduit approach to the taxation of partnership income adopted by Subchapter K, a partner is taxed currently on his share of the partnership income whether that income is distributed or not. Thus, unlike the corporate situation, the distribution of cash or property by the partnership to the partner is not the event which causes the partner to take into account the income earned at the partnership level. Rules must be provided, however, to coordinate the conduit approach to the taxation of partnership income with the fact that actual distributions will be made by the partnership to the individual partners. Sections 731–736 set forth the rules applicable to partnership distributions. In general, distributions of cash, unless made to a retiring partner, do not result in gain to the partner on receipt until they exceed her adjusted basis for her partnership interest. Distributions of property likewise, in general, do not result in gain to the partner, even if the fair market value of the distributed property exceeds the partner's basis for her partnership interest. Instead the distributed property takes a carryover basis in the partner's hands. These rules are subject to several limitations and qualifications. Section 751(b), for example, creates a constructive taxable exchange whenever a partner receives a current distribution which alters the partners' respective interests in unrealized receivables or substantially appreciated inventory.

REVENUE RULING 81–242

1981–2 Cumulative Bulletin 147.

ISSUE

May gain be recognized to each partner when mortgaged property owned by a partnership is involuntarily converted even though the partnership elects to defer the recognition of gain under section 1033 of the Internal Revenue Code?

FACTS

P is a general partnership of five individuals. In 1969, *P* purchased a building for commercial use. Through depreciation and other adjustments and distributions, the bases of the partners' interests had been reduced below their share of liabilities.

In 1980, City *Y*, through appropriate proceedings, acquired by condemnation the building owned by *P* for 20x dollars. At the time of the condemnation, the mortgage debt owed by *P* was 15x dollars, and *P*'s basis in the property was 10x dollars. The award made by City *Y* was used to pay off the mortgage debt.

P elected to replace the building within the meaning of section 1033(a)(2) of the Code and within the time prescribed by section 1033(a)(2)(B).

LAW AND ANALYSIS

Section 1033(a)(2) of the Code provides that if property is involuntarily converted into money by condemnation, then any gain shall be recognized. However, section 1033(a)(2)(A) provides that if replacement property is purchased (under circumstances that comply with the pertinent provisions of section 1033), then, at the election of the taxpayer, gain shall be recognized only to the extent that the amount realized on the conversion exceeds the cost of the replacement property.

Section 703(b) of the Code provides that any election affecting the computation of taxable income derived from a partnership must be made by the partnership.

Furthermore, Rev.Rul. 66–191, 1966–2 C.B. 300, holds that the election under section 1033 of the Code not to recognize gain from an involuntary conversion can be made only by the partnership and not by the partners individually.

Section 731(a)(1) of the Code provides that when there is a distribution by a partnership to a partner, gain shall not be recognized to that partner, except to the extent that any money distributed exceeds the adjusted basis of that partner's interest in the partnership immediately before the distribution.

Section 752(b) of the Code provides that any decrease in a partner's share of the liabilities of a partnership, or any decrease in a partner's individual liabilities by reason of the assumption by the partnership of the individual liabilities, shall be considered as a distribution of money to the partner by the partnership.

In this case, *P* realized 10x dollars of gain from the condemnation of its building. Because *P* elected to replace the condemned building within the meaning of section 1033(a)(2) of the Code and within the time prescribed by section 1033(a)(2)(B). *P* is not required to recognize the 10x dollars gain realized from the condemned building.

The award by City *Y* was used to pay off the 15x dollars of liability on the condemned building, resulting in a decrease in each partner's share of the liability of *P*. Under section 752(b) of the Code, the decrease is treated as a distribution of money to each partner. Thus, under section 731(a)(1), gain is recognized to each partner to the extent that the deemed distribution to each partner exceeds the adjusted basis of each partner's interest in *P* immediately before the distribution.

The transaction described above is distinguishable from that considered in Rev.Rul. 79–205, 1979–2 C.B. 255. In that ruling, a partnership made nonliquidating distributions of property to its two equal partners. Because the properties in question were subject to liabilities, the distributions resulted in a decrease in the liabilities of the partnership (a deemed distribution to each partner under section 752(b)), and an increase in each partner's individual liabilities (a deemed contribution by each partner under section 752(a)). The ruling concludes that the distributions were part of a single transaction and that the properties were treated as having been distributed simultaneously to the two partners. Thus, the resulting liability adjustments were treated as having occurred simultaneously.

In this case, the condemnation of the building and the subsequent reinvestment of the proceeds were separate transactions that did not occur simultaneously. When *P* subsequently acquired replacement property that was subject to a liability, each partner's share of the liability of *P* increased. Because this increase resulted from a separate transaction, it may not be netted against the decrease in liability on the prior condemnation of the original property. Therefore, the full amount of the decrease in liability was a deemed distribution of money to the partners.

HOLDING

Under section 1033 of the Code, the 10x dollars of gain from the condemnation of *P*'s building is not recognized in 1980. However, under section 731(a)(1), gain is recognized to each partner to the extent that that partner's proportionate share of the deemed distribution of the 15x dollars of liability exceeds the adjusted basis of that partner's interest in *P* immediately before the distribution.

ILLUSTRATIVE MATERIAL

A. DEFINITION OF CURRENT DISTRIBUTIONS

Subchapter K distinguishes between distributions "in liquidation of the partner's interest" and distributions to a partner "other than in liquidation of the partner's interest." The term "liquidation" has reference to the entire interest of the partner and hence applies to the complete dissolution of a partnership or one of a series of distributions in complete termination of a partner's interest. Regulations, section 1.761–1(d). Any other distribution to a partner falls within the second category, that of distributions other than in liquidation. This latter category—referred to as current distributions—thus includes the distribution of a partner's distributive share of profits, as well as distributions from a partner's capital account which reduce the amount which the partner is entitled to receive upon the dissolution of the partnership but which do not otherwise affect the partner's interest in future partnership profits, and distributions in partial liquidations, i.e., which reduce a partner's interest but which do not end that interest, as where a partner having a 10 percent interest in capital becomes one with a 5 percent interest. Regulations, section 1.761–1(d). See Chase v. Commissioner, 92 T.C. 874 (1989), holding that a loss could not be recognized by a partner who received a cash distribution of $929,582 in liquidation of an 11.72 percent limited partnership interest having an adjusted basis of $1,710,344, because the taxpayer continued to hold a general partnership interest. (The excess of the basis of the limited partnership over the amount of the distribution presumably would be added to the partner's basis in his general partnership interest.)

A receipt of money or property by a partner under an obligation to repay such amount or return the property to a partnership is treated as a loan under section 707 rather than as a current distribution. A withdrawal will not be treated as a loan, however, unless there is a definite obligation to repay a sum certain at a determinable time. The fact that the distribution creates a deficit in the partner's capital account which must be restored on liquidation or will otherwise be taken into account in making liquidating distributions does not alone establish that the transaction is a loan. Rev.Rul. 73–301, 1973–2 Cum.Bull. 215. See also Rev.Rul. 81–241, 1981–2 Cum. Bull. 146. Of course, if the distribution is treated as a loan and the obligation is later canceled, the obligor partner will be considered to have received a distribution of money or property at the time of the cancellation. Regulations, section 1.731–1(c)(2). But where a partner's indebtedness to the partnership is satisfied by the partnership setting off the debt against a distribution otherwise due to the partner, there has been no forgiveness of indebtedness; the transaction is a constructive distribution. See Zager v. Commissioner, 53 T.C.M. 230 (1987).

B. CASH DISTRIBUTIONS

Current distributions generally consist of cash distributions of partnership earnings already taxed to the partners. Such distributions reduce the basis of the partner's interest, under sections 733 and 705(a)(2), but otherwise have no tax effect. Since the partner's basis had been adjusted upwards under section 705(a)(1) by reason of the partner's distributive share in the earnings, the distribution of necessity must give rise to a downward adjustment. The two adjustments cancel out, leaving the partner's basis the same as it was before the partnership earned and distributed the amount. In this simple case, the basis adjustments merely eliminate any possibility of recognition of gain.

Where a current cash distribution is a partial liquidation or reduces the partner's capital account, section 731(a)(1) provides for recognition of gain to the extent that the cash exceeds the partner's basis in her partnership interest, since otherwise the excess cash would go untaxed. The gain recognized under section 731 when distributions of cash exceed a partner's basis is treated as gain on the sale of a partnership interest and hence, under section 741, is capital gain, unless the partnership has unrealized receivables or substantially appreciated inventory so that section 751(b) applies.

Interim distributions of earnings might exceed a partner's basis at the time of the distribution. Because a partner's distributive share of income and hence the basis increase on account of that share is not computed until the end of the year, Regulations, section 1.731–1(a)(1)(ii), treat advances or drawings against a partner's distributive share of income as made on the last day of the partnership year for the purposes of sections 731 and 705. Thus, any basis increase attributable to a partner's distributive share of partnership income for the year is available to offset the distribution.

Section 731(a)(2) denies any loss recognition on a current distribution. Because the partner's interest has not been liquidated, there has been no closed and completed transaction—the prerequisite for a loss deduction—and the partner's remaining basis can attach to his remaining partnership interest.

When a current distribution of cash results in recognition of gain, the bases of the other partners in their partnership interests do not change, even though the distribution has reduced the partnership's aggregate basis for its assets. In effect, some of their partnership interest basis, represented by the amount by which the cash distributed by the partnership exceeded the distributee partner's proportionate share, has been used to acquire an increased interest in the remaining partnership assets. As a general rule, section 734 provides that the basis of the remaining partnership property is not affected by the distribution. However, if the partnership has made an election under section 754, then the bases of the partnership assets will be adjusted upwards under section 734(b) by the amount of the gain recognized. This adjustment, in effect, reflects the transfer of the basis from the distributed cash to the remaining assets. A current distribution can only effect an increase in basis of partnership assets; it cannot cause a decrease. Section 734(b) is discussed in more detail, infra, page 237.

C. CONSTRUCTIVE CASH DISTRIBUTIONS

As discussed supra, page 122, section 752(a) treats any increase in a partner's share of partnership liabilities as a contribution of money by the partner to the partnership thus increasing his basis in the partnership interest. Correspondingly, as indicated in Rev.Rul. 81–242, supra, section 752(b) treats a decrease in the partner's share of partnership liabilities as a distribution of money to the partner by the partnership, thus bringing into play the rules of section 731. The reduction in liabilities will reduce the partner's basis pro tanto and will result in the recognition of gain if the constructive distribution exceeds the partner's basis in his partnership interest.

Partnership liabilities can be reduced not only by repayment, but by the transfer (or distribution) of encumbered property, the abandonment of encumbered property, or by discharge through compromise. A partner's share of partnership liabilities also will be reduced upon the admission of a new partner to the partnership who assumes liability for a proportionate share of partnership liabilities, thereby resulting in a constructive distribution under section 752(b) to the original partners, which may cause gain to be recognized under section 731(a). See Rev.Rul. 84–102, 1984–2 Cum.Bull. 119. As discussed, supra, page 68, when a partner contributes encumbered property to a partnership, he generally is treated as receiving a current distribution to the extent that the liability attached to the property is allocated to other partners. If that portion of the liability exceeds the contributing partner's basis in his partnership interest, he recognizes gain under section 731(a), and his basis in his partnership interest is reduced to zero. See Rev. Rul. 84–15, 1984–1 Cum.Bull. 158.

In Stackhouse v. United States, 441 F.2d 465 (5th Cir.1971), a partnership liability to a third party was compromised for an amount some $97,000 less than its face amount. The court held that the reduction in partnership liabilities constituted a distribution to the partners under section 752(b) and the tax results were controlled solely by section 731(a). The court rejected the Government's argument that $97,000 reduction in liabilities should be treated as forgiveness of indebtedness income under section 61(a)(12), and held that section 731(a) alone controlled the taxation of the partners. The correct analysis of the *Stackhouse* situation would seem to be that there was forgiveness of indebtedness income at the partnership level with a corresponding increase in the taxpayer's partnership interest basis under section 705 followed by the constructive distribution under 752(b) of a like amount, resulting in gain to the extent that it exceeded basis. Rev.Rul. 71–301, 1971–2 Cum.Bull. 256, and Rev.Rul. 72–205, 1972–1 Cum.Bull. 37, are consistent with this analysis although they do not address the point directly. Section 108(d)(6), added in 1980, requires the application at the individual partner level of the exceptions to recognition of discharge of indebtedness income provided in section 108. This provision adopts the Commissioner's position in the *Stackhouse* case.

D. DISTRIBUTIONS CONTROLLED BY SECTION 707

Section 707(a)(2), as discussed, supra, page 185, treats as section 707(a) payments certain distributions related to the performance of services for the partnership or the transfer of property to the partnership. When section 707(a)(2) applies, no part of the distribution is treated as a distribution of partnership earnings or the partner's capital account under section 731. Section 707(a) payments received in exchange for services are ordinary income to the payee partner and are deductible, subject to the general capitalization rules, to the partnership. If, as suggested in footnote 16 of *Gaines,* supra, page 174, the inclusion of a section 707(c) guaranteed payment increases the partner's basis for his partnership interest, then the distribution of a guaranteed payment is governed by section 731.

E. PROPERTY DISTRIBUTIONS WHICH DO NOT ALTER INTERESTS IN SUBSTANTIALLY APPRECIATED INVENTORY OR UNREALIZED RECEIVABLES

1. *General*

Where a property distribution, other than in liquidation of the partner's interest, is pro rata among all the partners, the effect in the normal case is that the basis of the distributed asset carries over to the partners, section 732(a)(1), and each partner reduces the basis of her partnership interest pro tanto. Section 733. If the distribution is not pro rata, in effect there has been an exchange among the partners, just as in the case of a complete liquidation. Unless the distribution alters the partners' interests in substantially appreciated inventory or unrealized receivables, however, Subchapter K does not so regard a non-pro rata distribution. Instead, in the case of any distribution of property which is not in complete termination of a partner's interest, it applies a simpler rule and merely carries over the basis of the partnership asset, as in a pro rata distribution. See Regulations, section 1.732–1(a), Exs. (1) and (2). Basis in the partnership interest is likewise reduced by the amount of the carried-over basis of the distributed asset. Section 733. In contrast, the section 704(b) regulations, discussed supra, page 98, which govern the maintenance of capital accounts, require that the distributee partner's capital account be reduced by the fair market value of the distributed property. To do this requires that the property be revalued and that the capital accounts of *all* partners be adjusted to reflect the gain or loss that would have been allocated to each partner if the property had been sold. See Regulations, section 1.704–1(b)(2)(iv)(*e*).

Section 732(a)(2) provides that if the distributee partner's basis for his partnership interest (less any cash received) is less than the basis of the asset in the partnership's hands, then the basis of the asset in the partner's hands is limited to the partner's basis in his partnership interest (less the cash received). This limitation eliminates the necessity of having to recognize a gain to the distributee partner on a distribution of property other than in liquidation. In the case of a distribution of several properties having an aggregate partnership basis greater than the distributee partner's basis for her partnership interest (less any cash received), the substituted basis is allocated among the properties as follows: first to any inventory and unrealized receivables, in an amount equal to the partnership basis therefor, with any remaining substituted basis then allocated to any other distributed assets in proportion to their respective bases in the hands of the partnership. If the partnership basis of the distributed inventory and unrealized receivables exceeds the substituted basis to be allocated, then that basis is allocated first to the inventory and unrealized receivables in proportion to the partnership's basis therefor and any remaining assets have a zero basis. Section 732(c); Regulations, section 1.732–1(c)(2). This allocation scheme is designed to prevent inventory and unrealized receivables from ever receiving a higher basis in the hands of the distributee than they had at the partnership level. As will be seen, these allocation rules apply equally to liquidating property distributions.

If the distributed asset is an unrealized receivable, section 735 provides a perpetual carryover of its non-capital character. The character of partnership inventory, however, is retained for only five years. See Luckey v. Commissioner, 334 F.2d 719 (9th Cir.1964), and Sanford Homes, Inc. v. Commissioner, 52 T.C.M. 310 (1986), both, applying this rule to inventory sold within the five-year period. Section 735(c)(2) extends these characterization rules to substituted basis property received by the partner in a partially or wholly tax free exchange for the tainted distributed property, other than a transfer to a C corporation in a section 351 transaction. Finally, these carryovers of asset character apparently apply only to the distributee, and not to a donee of the distributee.

Under the allocation rules for current distributions of property, the same overall amount of gain is recognized whether the partners sell after the distribution or the partnership sells before the distribution. But these rules do result in a different allocation of that gain or loss among the partners. If partners A and B each receive property worth $100, but A's property has a carryover basis of $50 while B's has a carryover basis of $150, upon a later sale of the property by the partners A would realize a gain of $50 and B a loss of $50. On the other hand, if the partnership had first sold the property, no gain or loss would have resulted. The partners should be able to resolve any inequities resulting from this possible shifting of gains and losses by arm's-length negotiations, e.g., an arrangement to compensate the partner currently receiving disproportionately low basis property. On the other hand, it should be noted that the partners might find that a disproportionate allocation of the burdens is desirable, in that the low basis property might be currently distributed to a low bracket taxpayer or to one with compensating losses. Under section 751(b) however, the degree of tax avoidance which can be achieved by distributing appreciated inventory or unrealized receivables to low basis partners is considerably diminished. When a current distribution is non-pro rata, if the partnership has unrealized receivables or substantially appreciated inventory, gain may be recognized to both the distributee partner and the partnership. See infra, page 220.

Where the distributee partner's basis in the distributed property is limited by section 732(a)(2), the remaining partners, by utilizing property with a basis higher than the distributee partner's basis, have in effect purchased part of his interest with that excess amount. Under sections 754 and 734(b) this excess may be reflected in the bases of the remaining partnership assets.

2. *Distributions of Encumbered Property*

Because of the rules of section 752(a) and (b), a distribution of encumbered property gives rise to three simultaneous events; a distribution of property; a deemed distribution of cash; and a deemed contribution of cash. The tax results can differ dramatically, depending on the order in which these events are deemed to occur. Normally, when cash and property are distributed simultaneously, the cash is deemed to have been distributed first and the property second. See Regulations, section 1.732–1(a), Ex. (1). This ordering minimizes the potential for recognition of gain. Treatment of the deemed cash contribution and deemed cash distribution is also crucial. Temporary Regulations, section 1.752–1T(j)(3), hold that only the *net* effect of liabilities is taken into account. Rev.Rul. 79–205, 1972–2 Cum.Bull. 255, reached the same result, even in the case of simultaneous distributions of encumbered property to different partners, before the Regulations were promulgated.

Suppose that the AB Partnership distributes to A property having an adjusted basis to the partnership of $2,000, which is subject to liabilities of $1,600. A's basis for his partnership interest prior to the distribution is $1,000. The partnership distributes to B property having an adjusted basis of $3,200, subject to liabilities of $2,800. B's adjusted basis for his partnership interest is $1,500. As a result of these distributions, each partner reduced his share of partnership liabilities by $2,200 (½ of $1,600 plus $2,800); A's individual liabilities treated as a contribution under section 751(a) increased by $1,600; B's individual liabilities increased by $2,800. A is treated as receiving a net cash distribution of $600, which reduces his basis in his partnership interest from $1,000 to $400; the property then takes a basis of $400; and A has a zero basis in his partnership interest. B is treated as having contributed $600 to the partnership. The basis adjustment attributable to this deemed contribution is treated as occurring before the property distribution, with the result that the basis for his partnership interest is increased from $1,500 to $2,100. Then under section 732(a)(2) the distributed property takes a $2,100 basis, and A's basis in his partnership interest is reduced to zero.

3. *Distributions of Section 704(c) Property*

Section 704(c)(1)(A), discussed supra, page 113, requires the partnership to allocatc gain or loss on the sale of contributed property to the contributing partner to the extent of the built-in gain or loss at the time of the contribution of the property. To prevent avoidance of such an allocation through the subsequent distribution to a different partner of contributed property having a built-in gain or loss, section 704(c)(1)(B) treats the distribution of such property within five years of its contribution to the partnership as a recognition event to the contributing partner. The amount of the gain or loss is the same amount as would have been allocated to the contributing partner if the partnership had sold the property to the distributee partner at its fair market value. Even though the gain or loss is recognized directly by the contributing partner, and not as a distributive share of partnership income, section 704(c)(1)(B)(iii) requires that the contributing partner's basis in her partnership interest be increased or decreased appropriately. Similarly, in applying section 732 and section 705 to determine the distributee partner's basis for the property and her partnership interest after the distribution, the partnership's basis in the property immediately before the distribution is increased by the gain (or decreased by the loss) recognized by the contributing partner.

F. UNREALIZED RECEIVABLES AND SUBSTANTIALLY APPRECIATED INVENTORY

Where the partnership has unrealized receivables or substantially appreciated inventory and makes a non-pro rata distribution, whether it be of assets of either type or of any other asset (including cash), then the provisions of section 751(b) apply if the distribution is "in exchange for" the partner's interest in other partnership property. Whether a non-pro rata distribution is to be considered "in exchange for" an interest in other property depends upon the effect of the distribution on the partners' interests in particular partnership assets. Assuming that partnership capital accounts generally are maintained in accordance with the principles of the section 704(b) regulations, any non-pro rata distribution which is charged to a partner's capital account—which is to say all non-pro rata distributions—should have the effect of a distribution in exchange for an interest in other partnership property. Furthermore, if different partners receive distributions of like amounts, but the distributions are disproportionate as to unrealized receivables and inventory, section 751(b) will apply. If section 751(b) is applicable, the distribution is treated as a sale or exchange between the distributee partner and the partnership, as constituted after the distribution.

Section 751(b) generally is intended to prevent partners from allocating among themselves the character of the gain recognized from sales of partnership property. Without this provision a partnership would be free, for example, to distribute capital gain property to a partner who had capital losses to be offset, while the partnership recognized and allocated to the other partners an offsetting amount of ordinary income. Conversely, the partnership might distribute ordinary income property to a low tax bracket partner, while retaining capital gain property. In this role, section 751(b), like section 751(a) discussed in the preceding chapter, was of much greater importance prior to 1986 when capital gains were subject to preferential treatment and there was a relatively large range in individual rate brackets. Today, it remains something of a complex anachronism, given the general decision in section 751 not to treat all non-pro rata distributions as constructive exchanges.

The following example illustrates the operation of section 751(b). Suppose that C and D are equal partners in the CD partnership, which owns two assets: a capital asset having a basis of $60 and a fair market value of $100; and an item of inventory having a basis of $210 and a fair market value of $300. C's basis for her partnership interest is $135. Suppose further that the partnership distributes the capital asset to C to effect the reduction of her interest to that of a one-third partner. Because the inventory is "substantially appreciated" as defined in section 751(d), section 751(b) treats C as having received in a distribution subject to section 731 an undivided one half of the capital asset, for which she takes a basis of $30, and one-sixth of the inventory, having a value of $50, for which she takes a basis of $35. She is then treated as exchanging the distributed inventory for the other one-half interest in the capital asset. As a result, C recognizes ordinary gain of $15 and the partnership recognizes capital gain of $20. C's basis for the capital asset is $85 ($35 for one-half under section 732(a) plus $50 purchase price for one-half), and her basis in her partnership interest is reduced from $135 to $70. The partnership's basis for the inventory is increased from $210 to $225 ($175 for undistributed five-sixths plus $50 purchase price for one-sixth).

Section 751(b) can require recognition of gain in some unexpected situations due to the deemed distribution rule of section 752(b). Suppose that the EFG partnership, of which E, F, and G are equal partners, has assets with a value of $175, of which $40 are unrealized receivables (having a basis of zero), and liabilities of $100. Suppose further, that H contributes $25 to the partnership to become a one quarter partner. Because E, F, and G each have reduced their share of partnership liabilities from $33.33 to $25, each has a deemed distribution of $8.33. Furthermore, because each has reduced his interest in the partnership's unrealized receivables from $13.33 to $10, section 751(b) applies. E, F, and G are each treated as having received $3.33 of receivables in a distribution to which section 731(a) applies. Under section 732 each takes a zero basis in the receivables. Section 751(b) then treats them each as having sold the receivables to the partnership for $3.33, and each must recognize that amount of gain. The remaining $5 deemed distribution to each of E, F and G is treated as a distribution of cash under section 731. H did not receive a constructive distribution, so section 751(b) does not apply to him. See Rev.Rul. 84–102, 1984–2 Cum.Bull. 119. The partnership now has a $10 basis for its unrealized receivables. Although section 743(b) does not apply to give H a $10 basis in his share of the unrealized receivables, Regulations, section 1.704–1(b)(5), Ex. (14)(iv), indicates that a special allocation to E, F and G of all of the income subsequently realized with respect to the receivables will be respected.

Regulations, section 1.751–1(b)(2)(ii), and (b)(3)(iii), allocate partnership gain recognized on a constructive section 751(b) exchange to the nondistributee partners. The distributee partner recognizes gain on his own side of the exchange. Thus, in the CD partnership example, above, all of the partnership gain on the exchange of the capital asset would be allocated to D. The Regulation does not apply in the EFG partnership example, however, because the partnership recognized no gain under section 751(b); all of the gain was recognized by D, E, and F individually on the constructive sale of the unrealized receivables to the partnership.

The mechanics of section 751(b) are discussed in further detail under distributions in liquidation governed by section 736(b), infra, page 229, where section 751(b) applies in a slightly different manner due to its interaction with section 736(a). For a more detailed example of the application of section 751(b) to current distributions, see Regulations, section 1.751–1(g), Ex. (5).

G. CURRENT DISTRIBUTIONS OF PROPERTY WHERE BASIS ADJUSTMENTS ARE IN EFFECT

Where a section 754 basis adjustment election is in effect, any basis adjustments previously made under section 743(b) (upon a transfer of a partnership interest) or under section 734(b) (upon a partnership distribution) are taken into account in determining the partnership's basis for distributed assets. Regulations, section 1.732–2. For example, assume C acquired B's interest in partnership AB for $1,000 at a time when the partnership had a nondepreciable capital asset with a basis and value of $1,000 and depreciable property with a basis of $500 and a value of $1,000. Under section 743(b), the basis of the depreciable property is increased for C's benefit by $250. If the partnership later distributes the depreciable asset to C, the basis carried over to him will be $750. If the depreciable asset is distributed to A, however, his basis in the asset will still be $500, and C's special basis adjustment of $250 will be shifted to the nondepreciable capital asset, so that C's basis for his interest in that asset will become $750. Regulations, section 1.732–2(b) and 1.743–1(b)(2)(ii). This basis shift can only be made to property of the same class as the property having the special basis adjustment. As noted previously, section 755 divides property into two classes: capital assets and depreciable property in one class, and all other property in the other class. Hence, if the partnership had no other capital assets or depreciable property at the time of the distribution to B, C's $250 special basis adjustment would stay in abeyance until the partnership acquired property of the required character. Regulations, section 1.755–1(b)(4).

H. CURRENT DISTRIBUTIONS OF PROPERTY TO TRANSFEREE PARTNER WHERE ELECTION TO ADJUST BASIS NOT IN EFFECT

If a distribution is made to a transferee partner within two years from the time he acquired his partnership interest and the partnership did not elect to adjust basis, section 732(d) allows the transferee to elect to treat the partnership basis for the distributed property as if the basis adjustment had been in effect. See Regulations, section 1.732–1(d)(1)(iii).

The transferee-distributee is required to apply the special basis rule of section 732(d) in situations where not applying it would result in a shift of basis to depreciable property. However, in order for section 732(a) to apply, the fair market value of the partnership property (other than money) at the time of the transfer must exceed 110 percent of its adjusted basis to the partnership. See Regulations, section 1.732–1(d)(4), Ex. (2), and the discussion infra, page 226.

I. REFERENCES

McGuire, Tax Shelters: *Tufts* and Partnership Property Distributions, 14 J. Real Estate Tax. 182 (1987); Seago and Horvitz, Some Subtle Effects of the Partnership Constructive Distribution Rules, 58 Taxes 97 (1980); Parker and Lee, Constructive Cash Distributions In a Partnership: How and When They Occur, 41 J.Tax. 88 (1974).

SECTION 2. DISTRIBUTIONS IN LIQUIDATION OF A PARTNER'S INTEREST

The treatment of distributions in liquidation of a partner's interest is somewhat more complicated than that of current distributions. Liquidating distributions must be divided into two categories: distributions liquidating a partner's interest in a continuing partnership and liquidating distributions in dissolution of the partnership. With one exception, the same rules govern distributions in complete dissolution of the partnership and distributions in complete termination of a particular partner's interest. When the interest of a partner is liquidated other than in liquidation of the partnership, the partner is referred to as a "retiring partner." See Regulations, section 1.736–1(a)(1)(ii). In the case of a retiring partner, section 736 applies to determine the treatment of payments or property distribution received in liquidation of his interest, whether the distribution is a lump sum payment, single property distribution, or a series of payments representing a continuing interest in partnership income. See Smith v. Commissioner, 313 F.2d 16 (10th Cir.1962) (section 736 applied to lump sum payment).

A. RECOGNITION OF GAIN OR LOSS TO DISTRIBUTEE PARTNER—SUBSTITUTION OF BASIS

INTERNAL REVENUE CODE: Sections 731; 732; 734; 735; 736; 741; 751(b), (c), (d).

REGULATIONS: Sections 1.731–1; 1.732–1, –2; 1.734–2; 1.736–1.

ILLUSTRATIVE MATERIAL

A. CLASSIFICATION OF PAYMENTS

To the extent that distributions to a withdrawing partner equal the fair market value of her interest in partnership assets other than goodwill and cash-method accounts receivable, the payments are treated under section 736(b) as a liquidating distribution and are subject to the rules of sections 731, 732 and 751. To the extent that the amount distributed exceeds that value, as long as the partnership has maintained capital accounts as required by section 704(b), it will be attributable to the distributee's interest in unrealized receivables or in goodwill of the partnership. In the absence of provision in the partnership agreement calling for a payment to the retiring partner for her interest in goodwill, such excess payments are taxed under section 736(a) as income to the distributee. However, Regulations, section 1.736–1(b)(1) and (2), provide that payments attributable to unrealized receivables are governed by section 736(b) to the extent of the retiring partner's basis in any unrealized receivables, generally basis resulting from any special basis adjustments under section 743(b). Otherwise, as noted previously, payments for a retired partner's interest in unrealized receivables are governed by section 736(a) and not by section 751, even though, they would fall within the definition of section 751 assets. If a section 736(a) payment is dependent on partnership income, it is taxed as a distributive share of partnership income. If not, it is treated as a guaranteed payment subject to section 707(c), discussed supra, page 174. In either case, the effect is that the continuing partners are not taxed on the amount paid to the distributee which is taxable to him under section 736(a).

B. LIQUIDATING DISTRIBUTIONS IN GENERAL

As a general rule, assuming that section 751(b) is inapplicable, liquidating distributions classified as section 736(b) payments or made in complete dissolution of a partnership do not result in the recognition of gain to the distributee partner unless cash in excess of the partner's basis for the partnership interest is received. Section 731(a)(1). Any property distributed generally will take a substituted basis equal to the distributee's basis for his partnership interest less any cash received. Section 732(b). Of course, if that cash exceeds the distributee's basis, gain will result and any property distributed will take a zero basis. Loss will result only if (1) a distribution consists solely of cash which is less than the distributee's basis for his partnership interest; or (2) the distributee partner receives only cash, unrealized receivables, and inventory, and the sum of the amount of the cash and the distributee partner's basis under section 732(a)(2) for the unrealized receivables and inventory—which cannot exceed the partnership's basis therefor—is less than the partner's basis for the partnership interest. Section 731(a)(2). Any gain or loss recognized under section 731(a) will be capital gain or loss under section 741. (For recognition of gain when section 751(b) applies, see infra, page 229.) The substituted basis, i.e., partnership interest basis less cash received, is then allocated among the distributed assets in proportion to their bases in the hands of the partnership. As previously indicated, any section 734(b) or 743(b) basis adjustments previously made with respect to the distributee partner's basis for those assets are taken into account in determining the partnership basis for its assets for this purpose. Regulations, section 1.732–2.

Thus, in the simple case of a complete dissolution where the distribution is pro rata and the partners' bases do not differ from their pro rata share of the aggregate partnership basis for its assets (e.g., there were no contributions of assets having differing bases and credited value, no transfers of partnership interest or non-pro rata distributions without basis adjustments being made), the dissolution results in no alteration of the bases of the properties involved and no gain or loss consequences.

As with current distributions, the effect of changes in the partners' shares of partnership liabilities must be taken into account. A distributee partner has a deemed cash distribution under section 752(b) equal in amount to his entire share of partnership liabilities prior to the liquidation of his interest. When a partnership is terminated and the partnership distributes encumbered property to the partners, the increases and decreases in each partner's share of partnership liabilities under sections 752(a) and (b) are treated as occurring simultaneously. Thus, only the net decrease in liabilities is treated as a cash distribution; and if a partner assumes a greater amount of partnership liabilities than he is relieved of, he increases his basis in his partnership interest by the net increase prior to determining the basis of distributed property. Temporary Regulations, section 1.752–1T(j)(3); Rev.Rul. 87–120, 1987–2 Cum.Bull. 161.

Under state law a general partner who has withdrawn from a partnership may remain liable to partnership creditors for debts incurred before his withdrawal. Generally, however, the continuing partners agree to indemnify the withdrawing partner if he is required to pay any debts other than those which he has agreed to pay. Barker v. Commissioner, 47 T.C.M. 131 (1983), held that where such an agreement between the partnership and the retiring partner is not entered into until a taxable year following the year in which the retiring partner withdraws from the partnership and receives an actual liquidating distribution, the deemed distribution under section 752(b) attributable to the assumption by the continuing partners of the retiring partner's share of partnership indebtedness does not occur until the subsequent year in which the agreement becomes effective.

The Internal Revenue Service has ruled that where a partnership with no assets terminates without distributing property, section 731 applies as if a distribution had actually taken place. Since "no property" other than money, unrealized receivables or inventory has been received, section 731 gives the taxpayer a current capital loss. Rev.Rul. 76–189, 1976–1 Cum.Bull. 181. See Tapper v. Commissioner, 52 T.C.M. 1230 (1986), holding that a partnership organized to construct and sell a particular building was liquidated upon the sale of the building even though no actual distribution of cash or property was received by the partners; the taxpayer received a distribution equal to his share of the mortgage assumed by the buyer. In O'Brien v. Commissioner, 77 T.C. 113 (1981), the taxpayer "abandoned" an interest in a joint venture that held real estate encumbered by nonrecourse mortgages and claimed an ordinary loss deduction. The court upheld the Commissioner's treatment of the transaction as a liquidating distribution, resulting in capital loss under sections 731 and 741. Relying on section 752(c), the court rejected the taxpayer's argument that there was no constructive distribution under section 752(b).

In Neubecker v. Commissioner, 65 T.C. 577 (1975), the court held that no loss was currently recognized by a partner who received assets other than money, receivables and inventory. The court also rejected the taxpayer's argument that he was entitled to an ordinary loss under section 165 for the forfeiture or abandonment of his partnership interest. The court found that section 731 precluded any recourse to the general loss provisions of section 165 as to a fact situation falling within the ambit of section 731. Compare Johnson v. Commissioner, 66 T.C. 897 (1976), which held that where the taxpayer received the proceeds of a life insurance policy on the life of his partner, he was not entitled to a loss deduction under section 731(a)(2) and section 741 on the liquidation of the partnership following the partner's death. The court rested its decision on the ground that under section 165(a) no deduction is allowed for a loss which is "compensated for by insurance or otherwise." Implicit in this reasoning is the premise that section 731 does not provide a statutory ground for claiming losses independently of section 165, but instead establishes further limitations on the availability of a loss deduction on the liquidation of a partnership interest. These two cases may be reconciled on the theory that a loss is allowable to a retiring partner with respect to his partnership interest only where the conditions of both section 165 and section 731 have been met; these two sections are not to be viewed as alternative grounds for establishing a loss.

C. DISTRIBUTION OF INVENTORY AND ACCOUNTS RECEIVABLE NOT SUBJECT TO SECTION 751(b)—CARRYOVER OF BASIS, ALLOCATION OF BASIS AND RECOGNITION OF LOSS

The general rule, discussed in B., supra, is subject to certain modifications when distributions of inventory or unrealized receivables are made but where sections 736(a) and 751(b) remain inapplicable. This situation will occur, for example, where inventory and unrealized receivables, on an aggregate basis, are distributed pro rata to the partners in a complete liquidation or where distributed inventory is not substantially appreciated. As previously indicated in the discussion of current property distributions, section 732(c) generally requires a carryover of the partnership basis for such assets and section 735 requires the same carryover of asset character as occurs on current distributions. See Wilmot Fleming Engineering Co. v. Commissioner, 65 T.C. 847 (1976), for an application of this rule. Thus, in the allocation of the partner's basis in her partnership interest (less cash received) among the various assets, that basis is first allocated to the inventory or unrealized receivables in an amount equal to the partnership's basis, with any remaining basis of the partner allocated to the remaining assets in proportion to their respective partnership bases. But if no other property is distributed and the partner's basis in her partnership interest exceeds the carried-over basis for the distributed inventory or unrealized receivables, then a capital loss is recognized equal to the excess of the partner's basis over any cash received plus the partnership's basis for the distributed inventory and unrealized receivables. This recognized loss compensates for the loss of basis resulting from the carryover of basis and has no relation to whether any economic loss is sustained. For example, assume that A's basis in her partnership interest is $1,000 and that she received a liquidating distribution of $500 in cash and inventory having a zero basis to the partnership and a value of $1,000. Although A has realized a $500 gain, she will take the inventory at a zero basis and recognize a $500 capital loss.

If other non-inventory assets are distributed, no loss will be recognized and those assets, as noted above, will acquire the entire remaining basis of the partner in her partnership interest. In extreme situations, assets with a very low value may receive a very high basis. For example, if partner A, above, in addition to receiving cash and the inventory item had received an additional non-inventory asset, A's basis for the asset would be $500. While no loss would be recognized on the distribution, if the asset were then sold for $50, she would recognize a $450 loss. The character of that loss would be determined with respect to the character of the distributed property in the partner's hands.

If a partner's basis for his partnership interest (less any cash received) is less than the partnership's basis for distributed inventory or unrealized receivables, section 732(c) does not apply to provide a carryover basis to the distributee partner. Instead, the substituted basis rule again applies, and the partner allocates the basis of his partnership interest among the inventory and unrealized receivables in proportion to their bases in the hands of the partnership. Any other distributed assets take a zero basis. Regulations, section 1.732–1(c)(2), Ex. (1).

D. SPECIAL ALLOCATION OF BASIS UNDER SECTION 732(d)

As previously indicated, section 732(d) applies a special basis allocation rule where the retiring partner obtained his interest by purchase, death or other transfer within the prior two years. If the partnership had elected to adjust the basis of partnership assets at the time of the acquisition, then the purchase price he paid on buying the partnership interest would under section 743(b) be reflected in his share of the basis of those assets, and the allocation rule of section 732(c)(1) would be coordinated with his purchase cost. Regulations, section 1.732–2. But if the partnership did not so elect (the election is that of the partnership and not the partner), then the partnership basis would not reflect his purchase cost and the allocation limitation under section 732(c)(1) to that basis might operate unfairly. Section 732(d) allows the retiring partner to elect a hypothetical adjustment to the basis of the assets to reflect his purchase cost and then applies the allocation rules of section 732(c) discussed above. Regulations, section 1.732–1(d).

Where the absence of an election would result in a shift of basis to depreciable property and at the time of the transfer the value of partnership property (other than money) exceeds 110 percent of its adjusted basis to the partnership, the partnership's basis in its assets must be determined as though the section 732(d) election had been made by the distributee partner. See Regulations, section 1.732–1(d)(4), Ex. (1).

In Rudd v. Commissioner, 79 T.C. 225 (1982) (A), section 732(d) was applied to give a partner a substantial basis in partnership goodwill, which was found to have been distributed to the partners in liquidation of a professional accounting partnership. Upon abandonment of the use of the partnership name following the liquidation of the partnership, the individual partner who had succeeded to the right to use the name was allowed an ordinary loss under section 165 for the portion of the basis of the goodwill allocated to the partnership name. Because the business of the partnership was continued by a new partnership, no loss was allowed with respect to the remaining partnership goodwill. Compare O'Brien v. Commissioner, supra, page 225, denying an ordinary loss on a purported abandonment of a partnership interest.

E. EFFECT OF RETIREMENT ON PARTNERSHIP TAXABLE YEAR

The liquidation of a partner's interest does not usually close the taxable year of partnership with respect to the remaining partners. Section 706(c)(1). However, a liquidation of an interest in a two-person partnership may result in a termination of the partnership under section 708(b)(1) "because no part of any business * * * continues to be carried on * * * in a partnership." A termination would result in a closing of the partnership taxable year for all the partners. The Regulations, however, provide that such a termination will not occur so long as payments are being made under section 736, since the recipient is deemed a continuing partner until those payments cease. Regulations, section 1.736–1(a)(6); 1.708–1(b)(1)(i)(b).

F. LIQUIDATION ASPECTS OF THE INCORPORATION OF A PARTNERSHIP

In Rev.Rul. 84–111, 1984–2 Cum.Bull. 88, the Internal Revenue Service concluded that the form followed in the incorporation of a partnership determines whether the partnership is viewed as liquidated by the partners, who then contribute the assets to the corporation, or by the corporation, following the transfer to it of all of the partnership interests. The Ruling sets forth three alternative transactions.

In the first situation, the partnership transferred its assets to the corporation for stock and then distributed the stock to the partners in liquidation. The transfer was tax free under section 351. Thus, the corporation took a basis in the partnership's assets equal to the partnership's basis in those assets as provided in section 362(a). Under section 358 the partnership took a basis in the corporate stock equal to its basis in the transferred assets, reduced by partnership liabilities assumed by the corporation. In addition, the assumption by the corporation of partnership liabilities reduced the partners' bases in their partnership interests. Sections 752 and 733. Upon distribution of the stock to the partners, the partnership terminated under section 708(b)(1)(A), and each partner took a basis in the stock received in the distribution equal to the partner's basis in his partnership interest.

In the second situation, the partnership distributed its assets in liquidation and the partners each contributed the assets received in the liquidating distribution to the corporation for its stock. Upon distribution of the assets, the partnership terminated under section 708(b)(1)(A), and under section 732(b) each partner took a basis in his share of the assets equal to the basis of his partnership interest, reduced by any cash received. The decrease in each partner's share of partnership liabilities was offset by each partner's assumption of a proportionate share of partnership liabilities, so that each partner's basis for his partnership interest was unaffected. Under section 351 no gain or loss was recognized by the partners on the contribution of the assets to the corporation. The corporation's basis in the assets under section 362 was equal to the former partner's basis in the assets. Under section 358 each former partner's basis in the corporate stock was equal to the basis of the assets contributed by the partner to the corporation, reduced by any liabilities of the former partner assumed by the corporation.

In the third situation, the partners contributed their partnership interests to the corporation in exchange for stock. The partners exchanged their partnership interests for stock in a transaction governed by section 351. Each partner's basis in the stock received was equal to the partner's basis in his partnership interest, reduced by his share of partnership liabilities. On the transfer of all of the partnership interests to the corporation, the partnership terminated under section 708(b)(1)(A). The corporation acquired the partnership assets by virtue of liquidation of the partnership and the corporation's basis in the assets of the partnership was equal to the aggregate basis of the partners in their partnership interests under section 732(b), allocated as provided in section 732(c). See section 362(a).

A partner may recognize gain under section 357(c) if at the time she transfers her partnership interest to a corporation in exchange for stock (as in situation 3 in Rev.Rul. 84–111) her share of partnership liabilities exceeds her basis for her partnership interest. Smith v. Commissioner, 84 T.C. 889 (1985).

B. PARTNERSHIP HAVING SUBSTANTIALLY APPRECIATED INVENTORY OR UNREALIZED RECEIVABLES

INTERNAL REVENUE CODE: Section 751.

REGULATION: Section 1.751–1(b).

ILLUSTRATIVE MATERIAL

A. TREATMENT OF DISTRIBUTEE PARTNER AND REMAINING PARTNERS

The section 732 carryover basis rules prevent the conversion by a distributee partner into capital gain of ordinary income attributable to inventory and unrealized receivables. Section 736(a) assures that a retiring partner is taxed on not less than his share of unrealized receivables if he is paid for them. However, sections 732 and 736 do not assure that the distributee partner and the partnership are each taxed on a proportionate share of the ordinary income attributable to the partnership's inventory at the time of the distribution. In an attempt to remedy this failure, the deemed exchange rules of section 751(b), discussed supra, page 220, apply to non-pro rata liquidating distributions as well as to certain current distributions. As a result, most non-pro rata liquidating distributions are partially taxable at the time of the distribution.

Section 751(b) applies if the distribution is non-pro rata and the distributee partner receives less than his share of unrealized receivables and substantially appreciated inventory, and hence more of his share of other property or cash. Under section 736(a) the distributee is treated as having been paid his share of the receivables. Under section 751(b)(1)(B) the distributee is treated as having sold to the partnership his interest in the substantially appreciated inventory retained by the partnership. The distributee recognizes ordinary income as a result of this deemed sale. The partnership will recognize gain or loss with respect to the deemed sale by it of the other property or money to the distributee partner in exchange for his interest in the inventory and makes an adjustment in the basis of its remaining inventory reflecting its purchase from the distributee partner. The gain or loss recognized by the partnership will be characterized with reference to the character of the property in its hands. These results for the partnership occur even though no election had been made under section 754. The partnership generally may not adjust its basis for the distributee's share of the receivables which it retained, even if a section 754 election is in effect, because section 743 adjustments are not allowable for amounts taxed to a distributee under section 736(a). See infra, page 234.

Section 751(b) also applies if the distributee partner receives more than his share of the receivables and inventory and hence less of his share of other property or money. In this case, under section 751(b)(1)(A) the partnership is regarded as having sold its interest in the distributed receivables or inventory. (Section 736(a) has no application to the receivables in this case.) The partnership will recognize ordinary income on the imputed sale, and the basis of its remaining assets will be adjusted to reflect the purchase of the distributee partner's share. Likewise, the distributee partner will recognize gain or loss on the imputed sale of other property to the partnership. This gain or loss will be characterized as ordinary or capital with respect to the character of the property.

Section 751(b) can apply to one part of a distribution while the general distribution rules of section 731 and 732 apply to the balance of the distribution. This result occurs because the operational premise of section 751(b) is that the distributee partner is treated as receiving a distribution of his pro rata share of every partnership asset prior to the deemed exchange. The general rules for determining gain or loss under sections 731 and 741 and basis under section 732 are applied to this preliminary deemed pro rata distribution. The partner and the partnership are then treated as exchanging the assets which were not actually distributed, but which were included in the deemed distribution, for the assets which were actually distributed, but were not included in the deemed distribution. This hypothetical exchange is taxed under section 1001, using normal characterization rules, as modified by sections 724 and 735. See, Regulations, section 1.751–1(g), Ex. (2), (3), (4) and (5).

The application of section 751(b) generally requires a determination of the assets in which the distributee partner and the other partners have relinquished their respective interests, a valuation of such properties, and a determination of the partners' bases for their respective interests. However, not every non-pro rata distribution will trigger section 751(b). For example, if the ABC partnership held inventory with a basis of $120 and a value of $180 and unrealized receivables of $90, a liquidating distribution of all of the unrealized receivables would not invoke section 751(b) because the distributee partner did not receive a disproportionate share of the partnership's section 751 assets. Similarly, a liquidating distribution of $90 of inventory would not bring section 751 into play, see Regulations, section 1.751–1(b)(1)(ii), although section 736(a) would apply to $30 of the distribution.

Section 751(b) is theoretically flawed because it measures disproportionality by the value of substantially appreciated inventory and accounts receivable rather than by the excess of value over basis. Thus, it fails to fulfill completely its stated purpose. In the above example, each partner's share of unrealized ordinary income is $50. However, if the unrealized receivables are distributed to A, who then collects them, A will recognize $90 of ordinary income, which will be partially offset by a capital loss on the liquidation of A's partnership interest. B and C will then recognize only $30 of ordinary income on the sale of the inventory.

Another problem in the application of section 751(b) is whether effect should be given to agreements between the partners which specify the particular assets which have been exchanged. Regulations, section 1.751–1(g), Ex. (3) and Ex. (5), appear to sanction an agreement between the partners specifying the "other property" in which the distributee partner has relinquished an interest where he receives section 751 assets in the distribution. In the converse situation, where the distributee relinquishes an interest in section 751 assets, the Regulations are silent. Allowing such a designation, either of section 751 assets or of other assets, permits the partners to select assets for the exchange that will minimize the gain realized on the deemed exchange. To permit this with respect to the capital and section 1231 assets retained by the partnership is not inconsistent with the purpose of section 751. But to permit such selection if the withdrawing partner surrenders his share of ordinary income assets is inconsistent with its purpose.

Section 751(b) does not apply to a distribution of property which the distributee partner contributed to the partnership, since the status quo prior to the contribution is being restored. Section 751(b)(2)(A).

B. PARTNERSHIP LIQUIDATION

It is not clear on the face of section 751 and the Regulations thereunder whether section 751 applies to disproportionate distributions on dissolution of the partnership. This ambiguity arises because section 751(b) requires distributions representing an exchange of a distributee's interest in section 751 assets for other partnership property (or vice versa) "to be considered as a sale or exchange of such property between the distributee and the partnership (as constituted after the distribution)." Obviously, in a complete liquidation no partnership would exist after the distribution and the exchange would have to be between the distributee and the other partners. Yourman v. United States, 277 F.Supp. 818 (S.D.Cal.1967), held that section 751(b) was applicable to a non-pro rata distribution of assets on the dissolution of a partnership. Rev.Rul. 77–412, 1977–2 Cum.Bull. 223, is to the same effect, treating the exchange as between the partner and the partnership, "even though after the distribution the partnership consists of a single individual." See also Wolcott v. Commissioner, 39 T.C. 538 (1962).

C. DEFINITION OF UNREALIZED RECEIVABLES AND SUBSTANTIALLY APPRECIATED INVENTORY

Unrealized receivables and substantially appreciated inventory are defined in section 751(c) and (d) respectively. Note that unrealized receivables include recapture income, which significantly expands the sweep of section 751(b). For discussion of the meaning of unrealized receivables and substantially appreciated inventory, see supra, pages 200–202.

C. TREATMENT OF SECTION 736(a) PAYMENTS

INTERNAL REVENUE CODE: Sections 706(c), (d); 708; 734; 736; 751(b); 761(b).

REGULATIONS: Sections 1.706–1(c); 1.736–1; 1.761–1(d).

As noted supra, page 223, distributions from a continuing partnership to a retiring partner which are governed by section 736(a) are ordinary income to the distributee and are deductible or excludable by the partnership. In many cases a partner's separation from the partnership is effected by means of distributions representing a continuing interest in the partnership income for a period of time. When continuing payments are received, the application of section 736 is somewhat more complex than when a partner's interest is liquidated by a lump sum distribution.

ILLUSTRATIVE MATERIAL

A. EFFECT OF RETIREMENT ON TAXABLE YEAR

Where a retiring partner has no continuing interest in partnership profits, section 706(c) provides for the closing of the taxable year of the partnership as respects the distributee partner and the result is similar to the sale of his interest. If, on the other hand, a retiring partner is to receive continuing payments, the distributee is treated as a partner so long as the section 736(a) payments continue. Regulations, section 1.736–1(a)(1)(ii) and (6).

The liquidation of a partner's interest does not usually close the taxable year of partnership with respect to the remaining partners. Section 706(c)(1). However, a liquidation of an interest in a two-person partnership may result in a termination of the partnership under section 708(b)(1) "because no part of any business * * * continues to be carried on * * * in a partnership." A termination would result in a closing of the partnership taxable year for all the partners. The Regulations, however, provide that such a termination will not occur so long as payments are being made under section 736, since the recipient is deemed a continuing partner until those payments cease. Regulations, sections 1.736–1(a)(6); 1.708–1(b)(1)(i)(b).

B. CLASSIFICATION OF PAYMENTS BETWEEN INCOME PAYMENTS AND DISTRIBUTIONS IN LIQUIDATION

1. *General*

Suppose the partnership agreement provides that a retiring partner will receive one-third of the partnership profits for the next three years in payment for his interest in the partnership. How should the annual payments be treated by the retiring partner and the remaining partners? The first problem is one of classification. As to the retiring partner, the payments could be regarded as a distributive share of partnership profits for the next three years and hence as ordinary income. Or they could be treated as a distribution in liquidation of his partnership interest, so that the rules applicable to distributions, discussed supra, page 224, would control and capital gain or loss treatment could result. As to the remaining partners, under the first view, the payments would reduce the distributive shares on which they were taxable. Under the second view, the remaining partners would be taxable on the entire partnership profits without any subtraction of a distributive share for the retiring partner. Then, the partnership as constituted after the distribution would be regarded as making a distribution to the retiring partner in exchange for his interest, so that the basis adjustment under section 734(b) could be made.

Section 736 meets this problem by classifying payments as distributions to the extent that the payments equal the fair market value of the retiring partner's interest in partnership assets other than unrealized receivables and goodwill. These payments are treated under section 736(b) as a liquidating distribution and are subject to the rules of sections 731, 732 and 751. See Part A., supra. Payments in excess of that value either may be attributable to the distributee's interest in unrealized receivables or in goodwill of the partnership or they may be in the nature of mutual insurance. In the absence of a provision in the partnership agreement calling for a payment to the retiring partner for his interest in goodwill, the excess payments (except to the extent attributable to basis in unrealized receivables) are taxed under section 736(a) as income to the distributee. If the payments are dependent on partnership income, they are taxed as a distributive share of partnership income. If not, they are treated as a guaranteed payment subject to section 707(c), discussed supra, page 174.

The factors that determine whether payments attributable to goodwill are treated as section 736(a) payments or as section 736(b) payments are discussed, infra, page 235.

2. *Allocation of Payments Between Sections 736(a) and 736(b)*

When distributions consist of both section 736(a) payments and section 736(b) payments, the portion of each payment subject to the respective rules must be determined. Specific rules for the allocation of payments between sections 736(a) and 736(b) are provided by Regulations, section 1.736–1(b)(5)(iii), which, however, allow the parties to provide for any other reasonable method of allocation.

Where the total payments to be made are fixed in amount, that portion of each annual payment which the total agreed section 736(b) payments bear to the total payments to be received is taxed as a section 736(b) distribution. Any balance is treated as a section 736(a) income payment. Regulations, section 1.736–1(b)(5)(i). Any gain realized with respect to the section 736(b) payments can be reported ratably as the section 736(b) payments are received if the recipient so elects. Regulations, section 1.736–1(b)(6). Otherwise, the normal recovery of basis rule applies.

If the total amount to be received is not fixed, e.g., the retiring partner is merely to receive a certain percentage of the partnership income for a period of time, then the Regulations prescribe a return of capital treatment. The first payments received are treated as distributions until they equal the fair market market value of the retiring partner's interest in tangible personal property plus any amount called for in the partnership agreement for goodwill. Thereafter section 736(a) applies. Regulations, section 1.736–1(b)(5)(ii). In such a case, gain under section 731 is not realized until the retiring partner's basis has been recouped. Regulations, section 1.736–1(b)(6).

C. DISTRIBUTEE'S TREATMENT OF PAYMENTS AFTER CLASSIFICATION

1. *Income Payments*

Once the classification is made, the next step is the tax treatment of the payments as classified. Section 736(a) payments which are dependent on partnership income are taxed to the retiring partner as a distributive share of partnership income and, of course, are excludable by the remaining partners when they compute their distributive shares. In this case the character of income, determined at the partnership level, flows through to the distributee partner. If the payments are fixed, they are ordinary income taxed to the retiring partner as guaranteed payments taxable to the retiring partner under section 707(c) and are deductible by the partnership. Regulations, section 1.736–1(a)(4).

If the retiring partner receives only section 736(a) payments and he has a basis for his partnership interest, presumably under section 731(a)(2) he would have a loss equal to that basis. The loss would be considered as loss from the sale of the partnership interest and, accordingly, is a capital loss under section 741. The exception in section 741 regarding substantially appreciated inventory (governed by section 751) could not apply to payments that had been classified under section 736(a). Since the payments made for unrealized receivables are treated as distributive shares, section 751(b) is not needed and hence is not applicable. See section 751(b)(2)(B).

2. *Payments for Interest in Partnership Property*

If the payments are classified under section 736(b) as made in exchange for the retiring partner's interest in partnership property, then the payments are considered a "distribution." Under section 731(a), if the amount of the cash payments so classified exceeds the partner's basis for his interest, the excess is recognized as a gain. If it is less, the excess of basis over cash is recognized as a loss. The gain or loss is treated as arising from the sale or exchange of the partnership interest. Under section 741, the gain or loss accordingly would be capital gain or loss. But where the partnership holds substantially appreciated inventory, ordinary income might result under section 751(b), discussed supra, page 229. If property is received, the substituted basis rules of section 732 apply, subject, of course, to the rules of section 751(b) respecting substantially appreciated inventory.

Holman v. Commissioner, 564 F.2d 283 (9th Cir.1977), held that the rules of section 736 apply even where the partner has been expelled from the partnership. He is still treated as a "retiring partner" for tax purposes despite the involuntary nature of his "retirement". See also Milliken v. Commissioner, 72 T.C. 256 (1979), aff'd by order, 612 F.2d 570 (1st Cir. 1979).

D. TREATMENT OF REMAINING PARTNERS

1. *Payments Treated as Distributive Share or Guaranteed Payments*

Where the payments to the retiring partner are classified under section 736(a) as a distributive share or guaranteed payment, the payments reduce the income of the remaining partners. The retiring partner's distributive share is taxed directly to him; the guaranteed payment is a deductible partnership expense. Regulations, section 1.736–1(a)(4). If the partnership is terminated and the withdrawing partners assume the liability to continue the guaranteed payments owing to a former retired partner, those payments are deductible by them under section 162. Rev.Rul. 75–154, 1975–1 Cum. Bull. 186. Similarly, if the business of the partnership is incorporated and the corporation succeeds to the obligation to make section 736(a) payments to a retired partner, the payments are deductible by the corporation. Rev. Rul. 83–155, 1983–2 Cum.Bull. 38.

Section 736(a) payments treated as section 707(c) guaranteed payments in effect represent the purchase price to the partnership of the retiring partner's share of unrealized receivables and partnership goodwill, and thus seemingly should be capitalized as are other section 707(c) payments to acquire an asset. However, the legislative history of the 1976 amendments to section 707(c), expressly imposing the capitalization requirement, indicate that section 736(a) payments treated as section 707(c) payments are to be deductible in all events. See S.Rep. No. 94–938, 94th Cong., 1st Sess. 94, n. 7 (1976). The continued deductibility of these payments thus obviates the need for any optional basis increase under section 734(b). See infra, page 237.

2. *Payments Treated for Interest in Partnership Property*

Where the payments to the retiring partner are classified under section 736(b) as in exchange for the retiring partner's interest in partnership property, then the remaining partners are taxable on the partnership income unreduced by the payments. To the extent that the payments are made out of partnership capital, these payments appropriately do not increase the partners' bases in their partnership interests. But if the payments are made from partnership income, the partners' bases in their partnership interests are increased by their distributive shares of partnership income so paid to the retiring partner. This too is appropriate. The remaining partners, however, may desire that the cost of the additional interests purchased from the retiring partner to be reflected directly in the bases of the partnership assets as well. While the standard rule in section 734(a) does not permit that reflection, section 734(b) does provide on an elective basis for adjusting the basis of partnership assets, as discussed infra, page 237.

E. STANDARDS FOR CLASSIFICATION BETWEEN SECTION 736(a) AND SECTION 736(b)

1. *Payments Attributable to Goodwill*

Payments for goodwill are classified as section 736(a) payments "except to the extent that the partnership agreement provides for a payment with respect to good will." If the partnership agreement specifically provides for payments to a retiring partner with respect to partnership goodwill, such payments are classified as section 736(b) payments. Section 736(b)(2)(B). In Smith v. Commissioner, 313 F.2d 16 (10th Cir.1962), the court required the retiring taxpayer to treat as an ordinary income payment a "premium" paid in excess of the book value of his interest in the partnership property on the date of withdrawal. The taxpayer argued that the premium was a payment for goodwill entitled to capital gain treatment, but the court held that the failure of the partnership agreement to refer expressly to payments for goodwill required the distribution to be treated under section 736(a): "Paragraph (2)(B) of subsection (b) exempts from ordinary income treatment payments made for goodwill only when the partnership agreement so provides specifically and does not permit an intent to compensate for goodwill to be drawn from the surrounding circumstances as the taxpayer here urges us to do." (19)

In Commissioner v. Jackson Investment Co., 346 F.2d 187 (9th Cir. 1965), the original partnership agreement did not make any provision for payment for goodwill on liquidation of a partner's interest. Subsequently, one of the partners withdrew and the partners entered into an agreement referring to a $40,350 payment to the withdrawing partner as "a guaranteed payment or a payment for good will." The Tax Court held, 41 T.C. 675 (1964) (NA), that the subsequent agreement did not constitute a modification of the original partnership agreement; hence the payment was controlled by section 736(a)(2) and was deductible by the partnership. The Court of Appeals reversed, finding that the partners' subsequent agreement was a modification of the original partnership agreement. The language of the agreement was internally inconsistent since "payment for goodwill" and "guaranteed payment" in this context were mutually exclusive, but the court concluded that the parties intended the payments to be governed by section 736(b)(2)(B) and as such were not deductible by the partnership.

In Elser v. Commissioner, 56 T.C.M. 41 (1988) (unpublished case), the court cited the absence of interest on deferred payments to a withdrawing partner as evidence that the payments were for goodwill rather than for partnership property. The partnership agreement was oral and the court found more creditable the testimony of the remaining partners that the payments were not attributable to partnership property other than goodwill.

2. *Valuation of Partnership Assets*

Determining the amount taxable as income under section 736(a) or treated as a distribution under section 736(b) requires a valuation of the distributee's interest in all the partnership's assets, including the work in progress (unrealized receivables) held by the partnership at the time of the distribution and, if the partnership agreement provides for payments with respect to goodwill, the partnership's goodwill. Regulations, section 1.736–1(b)(1), state: "Generally, the valuation placed by the partners upon a partner's interest in partnership property in an arm's length agreement will be regarded as correct." Regulations, section 1.736–1(b)(3), similarly allow the valuation placed on goodwill, whether the valuation is specific in amount or based on a formula, to be fixed for purposes of section 736(b) by an arm's length agreement among the partners. However, Temporary Regulations, section 1.755–2T (discussed supra, page 209), provide that for purposes of determining the fair market value of all partnership property when allocating any section 734(b) basis adjustment available to the partnership as a result of a section 736(b) distribution (discussed infra, page 237), the fair market value of all partnership property other than goodwill is to be determined taking into account all the facts and circumstances, and the fair market value of goodwill must be determined using the residual method. Whether the broad discretion under that Temporary Regulation to ignore arms' length agreements to as value will be extended to the operation of section 736 is unclear as a matter of statutory interpretation. It would be incongruous, however, to respect a bargained for allocation for purposes of section 736, but not for purposes of sections 743 and 755.

F. POLICY BASIS FOR FLEXIBLE RULES

The approach of section 736 should be completely reassessed. The relative flexibility given the parties with respect to the allocation between section 736(a) and section 736(b) payments historically was bottomed on the parties conflicting tax interests when capital gains were taxed at a preferential rate. Prior to the Tax Reform Act of 1986, the then existing capital gain preference lead the retiring partner to prefer that such payments be treated as section 736(b) payments. The continuing partners, on the other hand, sought to classify payments for partnership goodwill as section 736(a) payments, so as to be able to deduct or exclude them from income. With the flattening of the rate structure and the repeal of the capital gains preference in the Tax Reform Act of 1986, the prior conflict of interests generally has disappeared. While the continuing partners still prefer treating payments as section 736(a) payments, the retiring partner is relatively indifferent, as long as he receives section 736(b) payments at least equal to his basis for his partnership interest. As a result it generally can be expected that most partnership agreements will not specifically provide for payments to a retiring partner for partnership goodwill, even though the partners may take the value of partnership goodwill into account in determining the amount to be paid to a retiring partner. Thus, payments for the retiring partner's interest in partnership goodwill generally will be treated as section 736(a) payments deductible or excludable by the remaining partners. In this light the flexibility of section 736 may no longer be appropriate.

As previously noted, the rules of section 736 are not limited to cash distributions or to payments made over a period of time. They apply as well to lump sum distributions and to property distributions. To avoid the classification complexities in these types of cases, as well as the possibilities for manipulation, due in large part to the immediate deduction or exclusion available to the continuing partners for section 736(a) payments, the 1984 ALI Subchapter K Study proposed the repeal of section 736 for all payments to a partner other than payments to a general partner in a partnership in which capital is not a material income producing factor. Under the ALI proposal, payments to a retired partner would be treated as received in exchange for his interest in the partnership assets under a fragmentation theory. American Law Inst., Federal Income Tax Project—Subchapter K, Proposals on the Taxation of Partners (1984).

SECTION 3. BASIS ADJUSTMENTS TO REMAINING PARTNERS

INTERNAL REVENUE CODE: Sections 731(b); 754; 734; 755.

REGULATIONS: Sections 1.734–1, –2; 1.754–1; 1.755–1.

ILLUSTRATIVE MATERIAL

A. PURPOSE OF BASIS ADJUSTMENTS

1. *General*

If an election is in effect under section 754, then the partnership is entitled to adjust the basis of its remaining assets in the case of a distribution as well as when a partnership interest is transferred. The formula by which the aggregate adjustment is computed is provided by section 734(b), which governs both current and liquidating distributions, although in the latter case it is applicable to more situations. Under this section, remaining partnership basis is increased by any gain recognized to the distributee partner under section 731 and by any excess of partnership basis for distributed assets over their basis to the distributee. Conversely, remaining partnership basis is decreased by any loss recognized to the distributee and by any excess of the basis of distributed assets to the distributee over their basis to the partnership. While section 734(b) applies to all distributions, only the increases can apply in the case of a current distribution since loss cannot be recognized, and the distributee's basis with respect to the assets cannot exceed that of the partnership. After the aggregate adjustment is computed, it must be spread among the partnership assets under the allocation rules of section 755.

The purpose of the section 734(b) adjustment is to reflect the fact that where the distribution is not pro rata, there has in effect been an exchange of properties between the distributee partner and the remaining partners. If a distributee partner receives a pro rata share of each asset, then no problem exists as respects the remaining partners since they simply own the remaining assets to the same extent as they did before. But where the distribution is non-pro rata, and if the assets which are distributed to the distributee partner have appreciated or depreciated in value then, as respects the remaining partners' prior share of those assets, there is in effect a realization of gain or loss to them because by distributing the assets to the distributee partner they acquire his prior share of the remaining partnership assets. Section 731(b) prevents recognition of this gain or loss, but the adjustments required by section 734(b) to the bases of the remaining assets are designed to reflect that unrecognized gain or loss in a case in which the partnership under section 754 has elected to reflect immediately the effect of the liquidating distribution at the partnership asset level.

Moreover, in a non-pro rata distribution, if the remaining assets have appreciated or depreciated in value, the remaining partners, by distributing assets presumably reflecting the current fair market value of the distributee's interest in those remaining assets, have in effect purchased the distributee's interest with their interests in the distributed assets. (See Regulations, section 1.704–1(b)(2)(iv)(*e*), discussed, supra, page 100, requiring that distributed property be revalued, all partners' capital accounts be adjusted to reflect the gain or loss which would have been allocated to each partner if the property had been sold by the partnership, and the distributee partner's capital account be reduced by the fair market value of the distributed property.) The section 734(b) adjustments are also designed to reflect the cost to the remaining partners of purchasing the distributee's interest. The use of a basis adjustment thus is a device for incorporating the aggregate view of a non-pro rata distribution or a retirement as an exchange of interests between the distributee partner and the remaining partners without, however, requiring the immediate recognition of gain or loss that a fully taxable exchange would entail.

2. *Example*

Assume that partnership ABC holds asset X with a basis of $0 and value of $90; asset Y with a basis and value of $90; and $90 cash. Each partner has a $60 basis for his partnership interest. Asset X is distributed to partner A on his retirement. When the remaining partners transferred their interest in asset X to A, in effect they paid $60, the value of their interest in asset X. They received one-third of the $90 cash, or $30, and also A's interest in asset Y, worth $30. Hence, $30 of the $60 value paid to A is allocable to the cash and $30 to the interest in asset Y. Thus, the basis of asset Y is the remaining partners' original basis of $60 in asset Y, plus the $30 paid for A's interest. But the remaining partners have also realized $60 gain when they transferred their interest in asset X, which had a basis of zero, and received $60 value. To reflect the postponed recognition of this gain, their $90 cost basis of asset Y must be reduced by $60, leaving a $30 basis. In effect the net adjustment in the partnership basis for asset Y is thus negative $60 and the partnership's basis is $30. The section 734(b) formula will produce this result, since A's pro rata share of the aggregate partnership basis was $60, while X's basis to the partnership was zero. Since A's reduction in his interest in the basis of the partnership assets exceeds the partnership's basis by $60, section 734(b) calls for a $60 decrease.

Suppose, instead, that asset Y had been distributed to partner A. Here the remaining partners transferred $60 worth of property (their two-thirds interest in asset Y having a basis to them of $60) in exchange for $30 cash (the distributee partner's interest in the $90 partnership cash) and his interest in asset X, worth $30. Hence, they paid $30 value for the distributee partner's interest in asset X. The zero basis of asset X should, therefore, be increased by the $30 cost of that interest. It need not then be reduced since the remaining partners' original bases for their interest in asset Y, $60, were exactly equal to the amount they realized on the exchange and they therefore had no gain on the exchange. Here again, section 734(b) will produce this result since the $90 partnership basis for Y exceeds the $60 interest in partnership basis for its assets relinquished by A by $30.

Finally, suppose the $90 cash had been distributed to partner A. Here the remaining partners have transferred $60 (their two-thirds interest in the cash) in exchange for the distributee partner's interest in assets X and Y. They paid $30 for A's one-third interest in asset Y and $30 for his one-third interest in asset X. Expressing the adjustment in terms of cost, it is $30 as to asset X and as to asset Y it is $60, the remaining partners' original basis in asset Y, plus the $30 paid for A's interest, or $90. Only a $30 basis adjustment is necessary, since Y already has a $90 basis. Thus the basis of asset X should be increased by $30. Again, this is the result under section 734(b).

It should be noted that after A's retirement, B's and C's aggregate bases for their partnership interests will be $120 and that by virtue of the foregoing basis adjustments, the aggregate bases for all of the partnership's assets will also be $120. Thus, the partners could still apply the alternative rule of section 705(b) and compute the basis for their partnership interest with reference to their pro rata share of the partnership's basis for its assets. Where the partner's aggregate outside basis equals the aggregate basis for partnership assets prior to the distribution, the section 734(b) adjustment works to maintain that equality after the distribution. But where outside basis and inside basis are not equal prior to the distribution (due to a transfer of distributions at a time when there was not a section 754 election in effect) the section 743(b) adjustment cannot restore that equality.

B. ALLOCATION OF BASIS ADJUSTMENT UNDER SECTION 755: SOME PROBLEMS UNDER SECTION 734 RULES

Section 734(b)(1) only roughly approximates the foregoing results. As previously indicated in the discussion of section 743 adjustments, supra, page 207, under section 755(b) any overall adjustment first is divided into an adjustment attributable to section 1231 assets and capital assets and an adjustment attributable to all other assets. The overall adjustment then is allocated to property of each class so as to reduce differences between basis and value. The Regulations interpret this provision to require adjustments to remaining property having the same character as that of distributed assets which have a basis in the hands of the distributee different from that of the partnership's. Regulations, section 1.755–1(b)(1)(i). If the adjustment is attributable to the distributee partner recognizing either a gain or a loss, then the adjustment is allocated solely to capital and section 1231 assets. Regulations, section 1.755–1(b)(1)(ii). These rules present a problem because, in fact, the adjustment may have been attributable to an increase or decrease in the value of a remaining asset having a character different from that of the distributed assets, or to a cash distribution which resulted in gain or loss to the distributee partner which was attributable to ordinary income assets of the partnership (although in most cases a cash distribution attributable to ordinary inventory will trigger the application of section 751(b), thereby obviating the need for a section 734(b) adjustment).

Where a cash distribution to a retiring partner is attributable to unrealized receivables and is taxed under section 736(a), section 743(b) does not appear to apply to permit any increase in the basis of the retained unrealized receivables. In this case, however, a basis adjustment is unnecessary because the remaining partners have, in effect, received a deduction for the amount paid for the unrealized receivables. See Regulations, section 1.736–1(a)(4). Therefore, it is appropriate that the partnership's basis in the receivables not be increased. See supra, page 234. If the partnership owns "no property of the character required to be adjusted" or a downward adjustment has been limited by the fair market value floor of Regulations, section 1.755–1(b)(3), the remaining adjustment is held in suspense and applied when the partnership acquires property to which the adjustment can be applied. Regulations, section 1.755–1(b)(4). If an upward adjustment to the basis of capital and section 1231 assets is required, and the partnership owns such assets, but they are not appreciated sufficiently to utilize the entire adjustment, the Regulations do not provide for any carryover.

Thus, in the second example in A.2., above, the basis of asset X should be increased to reflect its acquisition cost and the character of the distributed asset should be immaterial. Under the Regulations, however, if asset Y was inventory and asset X was a section 1231 asset, no adjustment would be made at the time of the distribution, but one could be made when the partnership later acquired an asset other than a capital or section 1231 asset. If, on the other hand, asset Y was a capital asset and asset X was neither a capital asset nor a section 1231 asset (and assuming, somewhat unrealistically that section 751(b) did not apply), then the $30 basis adjustment would be totally lost to the partnership. This defect could be cured by providing that the adjustment be made to property of the same character as that to which the adjustment is attributable and not as that of the distributed property. See H.Rep. No. 86–1231, 86th Cong., 2d Sess. 98 (1960).

The formula in section 734(b) will provide the correct overall adjustment in most cases. But it appears inadequate in some instances since it is essentially based on the distributee's basis for his partnership interest—which governs gain or loss or basis to the distributee. The formula will not produce the correct result if the basis for the distributee partner's interest differs from his share of the partnership's basis for its assets. Thus, if in the above example A had purchased his interest from a previous partner, paying $90, or if A was an estate succeeding to a decedent partner's interest and having a $90 basis, there would be no adjustment under the formula.

This defect is most glaring where an estate's interest in the partnership is terminated by a distribution of cash and no gain is recognized to the estate to the extent section 1014 applies to give it a stepped-up basis for its partnership interest. No adjustment is allowed even though the partnership is paying for the estate's interest in assets which have increased in value. Had the formula in section 734(b) been related to the distributee's pro rata share of the partnership's aggregate basis for its assets (as is done in section 743(b)), the formula would work correctly.

C. SPECIAL PROBLEM OF TIERED PARTNERSHIPS

Suppose that the AB Partnership holds two assets: asset X with a basis of zero and a fair market value of $100 and asset Y with a basis of $100 and a fair market value of $100. If asset Y was distributed to A, who has a zero basis for her interest, she would take a zero basis for asset Y, and, if a section

754 election was in effect, the partnership would increase its basis for asset X to $100. As a result, the $100 basis of asset Y has been transferred to asset X, and $100 of total gain will be recognized if they are both sold. Now suppose that instead the AB Partnership contributes asset Y to another partnership (LT) in which it has a 99 percent interest, following which it distributes its interest in the LT Partnership to A. She will take a zero basis for her interest in LT, but the basis of asset Y remains $100. If the AB Partnership can make a section 743(b) adjustment to the basis of asset X, then both assets can be sold without the recognition of any gain, although A would recognize gain if the proceeds were distributed to her by LT. Congress perceived this result as abusive, and in 1984 added the last sentence of section 743(b), disallowing an upward section 743 adjustment for the upper tier partnership, in this case AB, if the distributed property is an interest in another partnership, in this case LT, unless the other partnership also has a section 754 election in effect. Because section 761(e), also added in 1984, treats the distribution of a partnership interest as an exchange, Congress intended that section 743(b) require that the distributed partnership reduce the basis of its assets. See Staff of the Joint Committee on Taxation, 98th Cong., 2d Sess., General Explanation of the Tax Reform Act of 1984, at p. 249 (1984).

As is apparent from the example in B., supra, however, the adjustment allocation rules of Regulations, section 1.755–1(a)(1)(iii), may not produce the results intended by the 1984 legislation. Although A's basis for her interest in LT is zero, thereby requiring a section 743(b) adjustment reducing LT's basis for its assets by $100, the section 755 Regulations require that this basis reduction be applied only to assets with a fair market value less than their basis. LT holds no such assets, so the basis of asset Y remains $100. Furthermore, the unused basis reduction is not held in suspense; it must be made at the time of the transfer or not at all. Thus, unless the distributed partnership holds depreciated property, the Congressional "solution" to this problem is not effective. The Treasury Department could remedy this problem by amending the section 755 Regulations under the authority in section 755(a)(2) to require under these circumstances that LT make a downward adjustment in the basis of its assets regardless of the value of those assets.

D. REFERENCES

Barber, Optional Basis Adjustments to Partnership Property: An Analysis of the Special Elections, 3 J. Partnership Tax. 242 (1986); Pennell, Problems Involving the Optional Adjustment to Basis of Partnership Assets, 34 So.Calif.Tax Inst. 8 (1982).

SECTION 4. SALE OF INTEREST TO OTHER PARTNERS VERSUS LIQUIDATION

INTERNAL REVENUE CODE: Sections 736; 741.

FOXMAN v. COMMISSIONER

Tax Court of the United States, 1964.
41 T.C. 535.

The principal issue common to all three cases is whether an agreement dated May 21, 1957, between petitioner Jacobowitz and petitioners Foxman and Grenell resulted in a "sale" of Jacobowitz's interest in a partnership to the two remaining partners under section 741, I.R.C.1954, or whether the transaction must be considered a "liquidation" of Jacobowitz's partnership interest under sections 736 and 761(d).*

FINDINGS OF FACT

* * * Prior to 1954, Abbey Record Manufacturing Co. was a partnership composed of petitioner Jacobowitz and two associates named Zayde and Brody, engaged in the business of custom manufacturing of phonograph records. The enterprise had been founded about 1948, with Jacobowitz as the active principal. Prior to 1954 the partnership, hereinafter referred to as Abbey, manufactured primarily 10-inch 78 r.p.m. records on contract for various companies. Petitioner Grenell purchased the interests of Zayde and Brody on December 31, 1953, and became an equal partner with Jacobowitz on January 2, 1954. Early in 1954 the partners agreed to enter the business of manufacturing 12-inch long playing records, known as LPs. Petitioner Foxman, who had been a consultant to the business when it was originally formed in 1948, was hired as a salaried employee in June 1954 to provide the necessary technical assistance for the changeover in machinery and production methods. Thereafter, as a result of certain agreements dated February 1, 1955, and January 26, 1956, Foxman, Grenell, and Jacobowitz became equal partners in Abbey, each with a one-third interest.

Abbey kept its accounts and filed its Federal income tax returns on an accrual basis of accounting and on the basis of a fiscal year ending February 28.

A related venture commenced by Jacobowitz, Foxman, and Grenell, individually, was represented by Sound Plastics, Inc., a corporation in which each owned one-third of the stock; it was engaged in the business of manufacturing "biscuits" or vinyl forms used in the making of records.

* [Ed.: Two other issues are omitted. The decision of the Tax Court on the issue set forth in the text was affirmed in 352 F.2d 466 (3d Cir.1965), on the ground that the issue before the Tax Court was one of fact and its decision was not shown to be clearly erroneous.]

During the early period of the changeover to LPs, Abbey faced many problems in production and quality control. However, with Foxman and Jacobowitz in charge of production and with Grenell responsible for much of the selling, Abbey's fortunes were on the upswing. Its net income for the fiscal year ending February 29, 1956, was approximately $108,000, and for the fiscal year ending February 28, 1957, was approximately $218,000. Grenell, who acted as consultant and repertory director for two mail-order record companies, Music Treasures of the World and Children's Record Guild, was able to get these companies as customers of Abbey and they accounted for approximately 50–75 percent of Abbey's business.

The Agreement of May 21, 1957

Notwithstanding Abbey's success there was considerable disharmony among and between the partners. As a result there were discussions during the spring of 1956 relating to the withdrawal of Jacobowitz from Abbey. These negotiations did not lead to any agreement and the partners continued to work and to quarrel. Early in 1957, Foxman and Grenell decided to resolve the conflict by continuing the partnership without Jacobowitz and discussions were resumed again in March 1957. It was at about this time that Foxman offered Jacobowitz $225,000 in cash, an automobile which was in Abbey's name, and Foxman's and Grenell's interest in Sound Plastics, Inc., for Jacobowitz's interest in Abbey. Jacobowitz prepared a draft of an option agreement providing for Foxman's purchase of his one-third interest in the partnership and sent it to Foxman. Foxman never signed the option agreement. During the latter part of March or early April 1957, the negotiations of the three partners led to a tentative agreement whereby Jacobowitz's partnership interest would be purchased for $225,000 plus the aforementioned auto and stock in Sound Plastics, Inc. Jacobowitz, who did not trust either Foxman or Grenell, initially desired cash. Foxman and Grenell explored the possibilities of a $200,000 bank loan from the First National Bank of Jersey City, hereinafter referred to as First National, and informed First National of their tentative agreement to buy Jacobowitz's interest for $225,000; they had further discussions with First National concerning a possible loan on May 1, 1957, and on May 3, 1957. First National indicated, on the basis of an examination of the financial assets of Abbey, that it would consider a loan of approximately only $50,000.

The negotiations of the three partners culminated in an agreement dated May 21, 1957, for the "sale" of Jacobowitz's partnership interest; the terms of this agreement were essentially the same terms as the terms of the option agreement which Foxman did not execute.

Relevant portions of the May 21, 1957, agreement are as follows:

> Agreement, made this 21st day of May 1957, between NORMAN B. JACOBOWITZ, hereinafter referred to as the "First Party", and HORACE W. GRENELL, and DAVID A. FOXMAN indi-

vidually, jointly and severally, hereinafter referred to as the "Second Parties" and ABBEY RECORD MFG. CO., hereinafter referred to as the "Third Party", Witnesseth: * * *

Whereas, the first party is desirous of selling, conveying, transferring and assigning all of his right, title and interest in and to his one-third share and interest in the said ABBEY to the second parties; and

Whereas, the second parties are desirous of conveying, transferring and assigning all of their right, title and interest in and to their combined two-thirds shares and interest in SOUND PLASTICS, INC. to the first party;

Now, Therefore, it is Mutually Agreed as Follows:

FIRST: The second parties hereby purchase all the right, title, share and interest of the first party in ABBEY and the first party does hereby sell, transfer, convey and assign all of his right, title, interest and share in ABBEY and in the moneys in banks, trade names, accounts due, or to become due, and in all other assets of any kind whatsoever, belonging to said ABBEY, for and in consideration of the following:

A) The payment of the sum of TWO HUNDRED FORTY TWO THOUSAND FIVE HUNDRED & FIFTY ($242,550.00) DOLLARS, payable as follows:

$67,500.00, on the signing of this agreement, the receipt of which is hereby acknowledged;

$67,500.00 on January 2nd, 1958;

$90,000.00 in eighteen (18) equal monthly installments of $5,000.00 each, commencing on February 1st, 1958 and continuing on the first day of each and every consecutive month thereafter for seventeen (17) months;

$17,550.00, for services as a consultant, payable in seventy-eight (78) equal weekly installments of $225.00 each, commencing on February 1st, 1958 and continuing weekly on the same day of each and every consecutive week thereafter for seventy-seven (77) weeks.

The balance set forth hereinabove is represented by a series of non-interest bearing promissory notes, bearing even date herewith, and contain an acceleration clause and a grace period of ten (10) days.

Said balance is further secured by a chattel mortgage, bearing even date herewith and contains a provision that same shall be cancelled and discharged upon the payment of the sum of $67,500.00 on or before January 2nd, 1958.

The right is hereby granted to the second parties to prepay all or part of the balance due to the first party. If prepayment is made of both of the sums of $67,500.00 and $90,000.00 set forth above, prior to February 1st, 1958, there shall be no further liability for the balance of $17,550.00 or any of the payments of $225.00 weekly required thereunder. If such prepayment is made after February 1st, 1958, the first party shall be entitled to retain payments made to date of payment of the full sums of $67,500.00 and $90,000.00 (plus any weekly payments as aforesaid to date of payment) and there shall be no further liability for any remaining weekly payments.

B) In addition to the payments required under paragraph "A" hereof, the second parties hereby transfer, convey and assign all of their right, title and interest in SOUND PLASTICS, INC. to the first party. Simultaneously herewith, the second parties have delivered duly executed transfers of certificates of stock, together with their resignations as officers and directors of said SOUND PLASTICS, INC. Receipt thereof by the first party is hereby acknowledged.

C) In addition to the payments required under paragraph "A" hereof and the transfer of stock referred to in paragraph "B" hereof, the second parties hereby transfer, convey and assign all of their right, title and interest in and to one, 1956 Chrysler New Yorker Sedan, as evidenced by the transfer of registration thereof, duly executed herewith, the receipt of which by the first party is hereby acknowledged.

SECOND: So long as a balance remains due to the first party, the second parties agree to continue the partnership of ABBEY and each of the second parties agree to devote the same time, energy, effort, ability, endeavors and attention to furthering the business of said ABBEY and to promote its success as heretofore and will not engage in any other business or effort, except that HORACE W. GRENELL shall be permitted to continue to create master records for other persons or companies.

The second parties further agree not to substantially change the form of business, engage in a new business, assign or transfer any of the assets or the lease of ABBEY, without the written consent of the first party, unless such new business and/or assignee and/or transferee, by an agreement in writing, assumes all the obligations, terms, covenants and conditions of this agreement and delivers such assumption agreement to the first party in person or by registered mail, within five (5) days from the date of the commencement of such new business and/or assignment and/or transfer. It is expressly understood and agreed that such assumption agreement shall in no wise release the second parties from any of their obligations hereunder.

* * *

FOURTH: All parties do hereby agree that the true and accurate status of ABBEY and SOUND PLASTICS, INC. as to liabilities and assets are reflected in the balance sheets attached

> hereto and made a part hereof and represent the true condition of the companies as of March 1, 1957. *First party shall not be entitled to any further share of profits that may accrue since March 1, 1957 and may retain any sums received therefrom to date hereof.* [Italicized words inserted by hand.]
>
> FIFTH: Except as herein otherwise expressly provided, the second parties do hereby forever release and discharge the first party from any and all liability of whatsoever nature, description, character or kind arising out of any transaction or matter connected directly or indirectly between themselves or in connection with ABBEY and/or SOUND PLASTICS, INC.
>
> * * *
>
> ELEVENTH: The second parties agree that they will forever indemnify and save the first party, free, clear and harmless of and from all debts, taxes (other than personal income taxes) claims, damages or expenses, upon, or in consequence of any debt, claim or liability, of whatsoever kind or nature due or claimed by any creditor to be due from ABBEY and/or the first party, by reason of the first party having been a member of the partnership of ABBEY, except as set forth in paragraphs "EIGHTH" and "FOURTH" hereof. The first party likewise agrees that he will forever indemnify and save the second parties, free, clear and harmless of and from all debts, taxes (other than personal income taxes) claims, damages or expenses, upon or in consequence of any debt, claim or liability of whatsoever kind or nature due or claimed by any creditor to be due from SOUND PLASTICS, INC., and/or the second parties, by reason of the second parties having been stockholders, officers and directors of said corporation, except as provided in paragraph "FOURTH" hereof.

Paragraph Twelfth of the agreement provides that "The first party [Jacobowitz] hereby retires from the partnership." The part of the agreement designating payment of $17,550 in weekly installments of $225 per week found in paragraph "First: A)" was embodied in a separate document also dated May 21, 1957; it was signed by Abbey, Foxman, and Grenell, respectively.

The chattel mortgage mentioned in "First A)" of the agreement, in describing the [transaction] provided for in the agreement of May 21, 1957, stated in part:

> the party of the second part [Jacobowitz] has sold, transferred, assigned and conveyed all his right, title and interest as a partner * * * to the parties of the first part [Foxman and Grenell, individually and trading as Abbey].

Samuel Feldman, a New York City attorney who represented Foxman and Grenell, drafted the agreement of May 21, 1957; at Feldman's suggestion, Abbey was added as a party to the agreement. An earlier draft of the proposed agreement did not include Abbey as a party. During the negotiations leading to the May 21, 1957, agreement, the words "retirement" or "liquidation of a partner's interest" were not mentioned. There was no specific undertaking by the third party (Abbey) any place in the instrument. A sale of a partnership interest was the only transaction ever discussed.

Jacobowitz unsuccessfully tried to obtain guarantees of payment of the notes he held from the wives of Foxman and Grenell; he was also unsuccessful in trying to obtain the homes of Foxman and Grenell as security on the notes.

The first $67,500 payment due on the signing of the agreement was made by cashier's check. On the promissory note due January 2, 1958, the name of Abbey appears as maker; the signatures of Foxman and Grenell appear on the face of the note as signatories in behalf of Abbey and on the back of it as indorsers. The 18 promissory notes, each in the amount of $5,000, also bear the signatures of Foxman and Grenell on the face of the instrument as signatories in behalf of Abbey, the maker, and on the back of the instrument as indorsers.

Payments to Jacobowitz pursuant to the May 21, 1957, agreement were timely made. Foxman and Grenell made an election to prepay pursuant to "First A)" of the May 21, 1957, agreement, and Jacobowitz returned the series of 18 promissory notes of Abbey, in the amount of $5,000 each, and the promissory note of Abbey in the amount of $17,550 payable in 78 weekly installments of $225. Jacobowitz was paid this $90,000 amount by check with Abbey's name appearing as drawer and the names of Foxman and Grenell appearing as signatories in behalf of Abbey; they did not indorse this check. Payments made to Jacobowitz for his interest were charged to Abbey's account. The parties did not contemplate any performance of services by Jacobowitz in order for him to receive the $17,550 under the May 21, 1957, agreement; this amount was considered by the parties either as a penalty or in lieu of interest if Foxman and Grenell failed to pay the $90,000 amount prior to February 1, 1958.

Just prior to May 21, 1957, Abbey borrowed $9,000 from each of four savings banks and also borrowed $9,000 from Foxman and Grenell. On December 27, 1957, Abbey borrowed $75,000 from First National. * * *

On May 21, 1957, Foxman and Grenell entered into an agreement providing for a continuation of the Abbey partnership which recited that Abbey had purchased the interest of Jacobowitz in Abbey. * * *

The reported earnings of Abbey for the fiscal year ending February 28, 1958, without reduction for alleged payments to partners, were $303,221.52.

In its tax return for the fiscal year ending February 28, 1958, Abbey treated the sum of $159,656.09 as a distribution of partnership earnings to Jacobowitz in the nature of a guaranteed payment under Section 736. * * * Jacobowitz, on the other hand, treated the transaction as a sale in his return for 1957, reporting a long-term capital gain * * *.

OPINION

RAUM, JUDGE: 1. *Tax consequences of termination of Jacobowitz's interest in Abbey; the agreement of May 21, 1957.*—On May 21, 1957, Jacobowitz's status as a partner in Abbey came to an end pursuant to an agreement executed on that day. The first issue before us is whether Jacobowitz thus made a "sale" of his partnership interest to Foxman and Grenell within section 741 of the 1954 Code, as contended by him, or whether the payments to him required by the agreement are to be regarded as "made in liquidation" of his interest within section 736, as contended by Foxman and Grenell. Jacobowitz treated the transaction as constituting a "sale," and reported a capital gain thereon in his return for 1957. Foxman and Grenell, on the other hand, treated the payments as having been "made in liquidation" of Jacobowitz's interest under section 736, with the result that a substantial portion thereof reduced their distributive shares of partnership income for the fiscal year ending February 28, 1958.

The Commissioner, in order to protect the revenues, took inconsistent positions. In Jacobowitz's case, his determination proceeded upon the assumption that there was a section 736 "liquidation," with the result that payments thereunder were charged to Jacobowitz for the partnership fiscal year ending February 28, 1958, thus not only attributing to Jacobowitz additional income for his calendar year 1958 but also treating it as ordinary income rather than capital gain. In the cases of Foxman and Grenell, the Commissioner adopted Jacobowitz's position that there was a section 741 "sale" on May 21, 1957, to Foxman and Grenell, thus disallowing the deductions in respect thereof from the partnership's income for its fiscal year ending February 28, 1958; as a consequence, there was a corresponding increase in the distributive partnership income of Foxman and Grenell for that fiscal year which was reflected in the deficiencies determined for the calendar year 1958 in respect of each of them.

As is obvious, the real controversy herein is not between the various petitioners and the Government, but rather between Jacobowitz and his two former partners. We hold, in favor of Jacobowitz, that the May 21, 1957, transaction was a "sale" under section 741.

The provisions of sections 736 and 741 of the 1954 Code have no counterpart in prior law. They are contained in "Subchapter K" which for the first time, in 1954, undertook to deal comprehensively with the income tax problems of partners and partnerships.

That a partnership interest may be "sold" to one or more members of the partnership within section 741 is not disputed by any of the parties. * * * See Regulations, section 1.741–1(b). * * * And it is clear that in such circumstances, sections 736 and 761(d), do not apply. See regulations, sec. 1.736–1(a)(1)(i).

* * * Did Jacobowitz *sell* his interest to Foxman and Grenell, or did he merely enter into an arrangement to receive "payments * * *

in liquidation of [his] * * * interest" from the partnership? We think the record establishes that he sold his interest.

At first blush, one may indeed wonder why Congress provided for such drastically different tax consequences, depending upon whether the amounts received by the withdrawing partner are to be classified as the proceeds of a "sale" or as "payments * * * in liquidation" of his interest.[7] For, there may be very little, if any, difference in ultimate economic effect between a "sale" of a partnership interest to the remaining partners and a "liquidation" of that interest. In the case of a sale the remaining partners may well obtain part or all of the needed cash to pay the purchase price from the partnership assets, funds borrowed by the partnership or future earnings of the partnership. See A.L.I., Federal Income Taxation of Partners and Partnerships 176 (1957). Yet the practical difference between such transaction and one in which the withdrawing partner agrees merely to receive payments in liquidation directly from the partnership itself would hardly be a meaningful one in most circumstances. Why then the enormous disparity in tax burden, turning upon what for practical purposes is merely the difference between Tweedledum and Tweedledee, and what criteria are we to apply in our effort to discover that difference in a particular case? The answer to the first part of this question is to be found in the legislative history of subchapter K, and it goes far towards supplying the answer to the second part.

In its report on the bill which became the 1954 Code the House Ways and Means Committee stated that the then "existing tax treatment of partners and partnerships is among the most confused in the entire tax field"; that "partners * * * cannot form, operate, or dissolve a partnership with any assurance as to tax consequences"; that the proposed statutory provisions [subchapter K] represented the "first comprehensive statutory treatment of partners and partnerships in the history of the income tax laws"; and that the "principal objectives have been simplicity, flexibility, and equity as between the partners." H.Rept. No. 1337, 83d Cong., 2d Sess., p. 65. Like thoughts were expressed in virtually identical language by the Senate Finance Committee. S.Rept. No. 1622, 83d Cong., 2d Sess., p. 89. * * *

* * * [O]ne of the underlying philosophic objectives of the 1954 Code was to permit the partners themselves to determine their tax burdens *inter sese* to a certain extent, and this is what the committee reports meant when they referred to "flexibility." The theory was that

7. If the transaction were a "sale" under section 741, Jacobowitz's gain would be taxed as capital gain (there being no section 751 problem in respect of unrealized receivables or inventory items which have appreciated substantially in value), and would be reportable in 1957 rather than in 1958. On the other hand, if the transaction were a section 736 "liquidation," the amounts received by him (to the extent that they were not for his "interest * * * in partnership property" pursuant to section 736(b)(1) would be taxable as ordinary income and would be reportable by him in 1958, rather than in 1957. The tax liabilities of the remaining partners, Foxman and Grenell, would be affected accordingly, depending upon whether section 736 or 741 governed the transaction.

the partners would take their prospective tax liabilities into account in bargaining with one another. * * *

Recurring to the problem immediately before us, this policy of "flexibility" is particularly pertinent in determining the tax consequences of the withdrawal of a partner. Where the practical differences between a "sale" and a "liquidation" are, at most, slight, if they exist at all, and where the tax consequences to the partners can vary greatly, it is in accord with the purpose of the statutory provisions to allow the partners themselves, through arm's-length negotiations, to determine whether to take the "sale" route or the "liquidation" route, thereby allocating the tax burden among themselves.[11] And in this case the record leaves no doubt that they intended to and in fact did adopt the "sale" route.

The agreement of May 21, 1957, indicates a clear intention on the part of Jacobowitz to sell, and Foxman and Grenell to purchase, Jacobowitz's partnership interest. The * * * "whereas" clause refers to Jacobowitz as "selling" his interest and part "First" of the agreement explicitly states not only that the "second parties [Foxman and Grenell] hereby purchase * * * the * * * interest of * * * [Jacobowitz] * * * in Abbey," but also that "the first party [Jacobowitz] does hereby sell" his interest in Abbey. Thus, Foxman and Grenell obligated themselves *individually* to purchase Jacobowitz's interest. Nowhere in the agreement was there any obligation on the part of Abbey to compensate Jacobowitz for withdrawing from the partnership. Indeed, a portion of the consideration received by him was the Sound Plastics stock, not a partnership asset at all. That stock was owned by Foxman and Grenell as individuals and their undertaking to turn it over to Jacobowitz as part of the consideration for Jacobowitz's partnership interest reinforces the conclusion that *they as individuals* were buying his interest, and that the transaction represented a "sale" of his interest to them rather than a "liquidation" of that interest by the partnership. Moreover, the chattel mortgage referred to in part "First" of the agreement of May 21, 1957, states that Jacobowitz "has sold * * * his * * * interest as a partner."

In addition to the foregoing, we are satisfied from the evidence before us that Foxman and Grenell knew that Jacobowitz was interested only in a sale of his partnership interest. The record convincingly establishes that the bargaining between them was consistently upon

11. See S.Rept. No. 1616, 86th Cong., 2d Sess., in respect of the proposed "Trust and Partnership Income Tax Revision Act of 1960" (H.R.9662):

"under present law even though there is no economic difference it is possible for partners to arrange different tax effects for the disposition of the interest of a retiring or deceased partner, merely by casting the transaction as a sale rather than a liquidating distribution (p. 76).

"* * * Under present law, if the transaction is in the form of a sale of an interest, then section 741 (rather than section 736) would govern, even though the interest of the selling partner is transferred to the other member of a two-man partnership (p. 103)."

the basis of a proposed sale.[13] And the agreement of May 21, 1957, which represents the culmination of that bargaining, reflects that understanding with unambiguous precision. The subsequent position of Foxman and Grenell, disavowing a "sale," indicates nothing more than an attempt at hindsight tax planning to the disadvantage of Jacobowitz.

Foxman and Grenell argue that Jacobowitz looked only to Abbey for payment, that he was in fact paid by Abbey, that there was "in substance" a liquidation of his interest, and that these considerations should be controlling in determining whether section 736 or section 741 applies. But their contention is not well taken.

Jacobowitz distrusted Foxman and Grenell and wanted all the security he could get; he asked for, but did not receive, guarantees from their wives and mortgages on their homes. Obviously, the assets of Abbey and its future earnings were of the highest importance to Jacobowitz as security that Foxman and Grenell would carry out their part of the bargain. But the fact remains that the payments received by Jacobowitz were in discharge of their obligation under the agreement, and not that of Abbey. It was they who procured those payments in their own behalf from the assets of the partnership which they controlled. The use of Abbey to make payment was wholly within their discretion and of no concern to Jacobowitz; his only interest was payment. The terms of the May 21, 1957, agreement did not obligate Abbey to pay Jacobowitz.

Nor is their position measurably stronger by reason of the fact that Jacobowitz was given promissory notes signed in behalf of Abbey. These notes were endorsed by Foxman and Grenell individually, and the liability of Abbey thereon was merely in the nature of security for their primary obligation under the agreement of May 21, 1957. The fact that they utilized partnership resources to discharge their own individual liability in such manner can hardly convert into a section 736 "liquidation" what would otherwise qualify as a section 741 "sale." It is important to bear in mind the object of "flexibility" which Congress attempted to attain, and we should be slow to give a different meaning to the arrangement which the partners entered into among themselves than that which the words of their agreement fairly spell out. Otherwise, the reasonable expectations of the partners in arranging their tax burdens *inter sese* would come to naught, and the purpose of the statute would be defeated. While we do not suggest that it is never possible to look behind the words of an agreement in dealing with problems like the one before us, the considerations which Foxman and

13. Various items of evidence support this conclusion. Of particular interest is the fact that the first payment to Jacobowitz, $67,500, was computed so as to enable him to report his gain as having been derived from an installment sale. However, a miscalculation (by failing to take into account the Sound Plastics stock and the Chrysler automobile) resulted in Jacobowitz's receiving more than the permissible 30 percent in 1957 (section 453(b)(2)(A)(ii), 1954 Code), and he therefore reported his entire gain in his 1957 return. The point remains, nevertheless, that a "sale" was planned and executed.

Grenell urge us to take into account here are at best of an ambiguous character and are in any event consistent with the words used. We hold that the Commissioner's determination in respect of this issue was in error in Jacobowitz's case but was correct in the cases involving Foxman and Grenell. Cf. Charles F. Phillips, 40 T.C. 157; Karan v. Commissioner, 319 F.2d 303 (C.A. 7). * * *

Decision will be entered under Rule [155].

ILLUSTRATIVE MATERIAL

A. SALE VERSUS LIQUIDATION

As the court in *Foxman* indicated, historically the real controversy in this area has been between the withdrawing partner, who preferred a sale classification with the resulting capital gain treatment, and the remaining partners, who prefer a "liquidation" classification since the payments would then reduce their distributive share of partnership income. With the repeal of preferential rates for long-term capital gains, this tension between the withdrawing partner and the continuing partnership is greatly diminished. As far as the partnership is concerned, the stakes are unchanged. But after the 1986 Act the withdrawing partner is now much less concerned with the characterization issue. Unless there would be a capital loss on sale of the partnership interest, in which case liquidation treatment might nevertheless generate ordinary income under section 736(a) or section 751(b), the retiring partner's concerns generally are now limited to the timing of basis recovery.

The Internal Revenue Service is of course concerned that, however characterized, the transaction be treated the same by both parties. It was able to obtain this result in *Foxman* by joining all of the parties in the same suit. The I.R.S. was not so fortunate, however, in another situation where the same transaction was treated by the Tax Court as a capital gain-generating sale under section 741 for the withdrawing partner, Phillips v. Commissioner, 40 T.C. 157 (1963) (NA), while the remaining partners were allowed deductions under a section 736 liquidation theory by the Court of Claims, Miller v. United States, 181 Ct.Cl. 331 (1967). The *Phillips–Miller* situation involved a two-person partnership and the Court of Claims, following Regulations, section 1.736–1(b)(6), had no difficulty in treating the payments by the remaining partner as liquidation distributions by the partnership despite the fact that no partnership was actually in existence after the withdrawal. To the same effect is Stilwell v. Commissioner, 46 T.C. 247 (1966).

The taxpayer in Spector v. Commissioner, 71 T.C. 1017 (1979), rev'd and remanded, 641 F.2d 376 (5th Cir.1981), was a partner in an accounting partnership with Wilson. To effect Spector's withdrawal from the partnership, the Spector–Wilson partnership was merged with another accounting partnership, following which Spector withdrew from the merged partnership in consideration of four equal annual payments. The withdrawal agreement specifically stated that one half of each payment was a payment subject to section 736, none of which was for partnership property, and the other one half of the payment was for a covenant not to compete. Finding that the taxpayer had adduced "strong proof" that the form of the transaction did not reflect its substance, the Tax Court held that the payments were not controlled by section 736. Instead, the court concluded that in essence the partnership into which the Spector–Wilson partnership had merged had purchased the taxpayer's share of the goodwill of the Spector–Wilson partnership, and it allowed the taxpayer capitai gains treatment. The Court of Appeals reversed the Tax Court, on the grounds that it had applied an erroneous standard. Economic reality does not provide a ground to set aside the structure chosen to effect a partner's withdrawal. The court explained that the fundamental theory underlying Subchapter K is that given the substantial, if not total, identity in terms of economic net result between a sale and a liquidation, the withdrawing and continuing partners should be allowed to allocate the tax benefits and burdens as they see fit. It then remanded the case for a determination of whether the taxpayer had adduced proof of mistake, fraud, undue influence, or any other ground, that in an action between the parties to the agreement, would be sufficient to set it aside or alter its construction. On remand, the Tax Court concluded that this burden had not been met. Accordingly, section 736 controlled treatment of the payments. 44 T.C.M. 631 (1982).

The following are some other cases on the sale versus liquidation issue, arising where the parties have taken differing positions with respect to the nature of their agreement: Coven v. Commissioner, 66 T.C. 295 (1976) (payments were found to be for the partnership interest and not in liquidation or as compensation despite the fact that they were paid under an agreement entitled "Consulting Contract" which nominally obligated the withdrawing partner to perform consulting services); Cooney v. Commissioner, 65 T.C. 101 (1975) (liquidation found where the agreement was in terms of liquidation of the partnership interest and amounts paid were paid by the partnership and not by the other partners).

In Sloan v. Commissioner, 42 T.C.M. 1606 (1981), the Commissioner challenged the treatment by the partnership of payments to a withdrawn partner as section 736(a) payments deductible by the partnership. The agreement called for the specifically named remaining partners to make "retirement" payments to the withdrawing partner. Examining the agreement, the court concluded that its language indicated that the agreement was a liquidation, not a sale; its form on the other hand, indicated that the transaction was a sale. The court looked to the treatment of the payments by the withdrawing partner in his tax return as evidence of the parties' intent. Because the withdrawing partner had treated all of the retirement payments as ordinary income, the court concluded that the parties intended that the transaction be a liquidation. Accordingly, the remaining partners were allowed a deduction for the payments.

In Crenshaw v. United States, 450 F.2d 472 (5th Cir.1971), the taxpayer desired to sell her interest in a partnership. A transaction was arranged whereby she received a distribution of real property from the partnership, which she then transferred to the estate of her deceased husband in exchange for another parcel of real estate. The estate subsequently sold the property back to the original partners for cash, after which it was recontributed to the old partnership. The taxpayer argued that the transaction should be treated as a liquidating distribution under section 736 followed by a tax-free like-kind exchange under section 1031. The Court of Appeals, reversing the District Court, applied the step transaction doctrine and held that the net result of the various exchanges was in effect a sale of her partnership interest for cash which was taxable under section 741.

In contrast, Harris v. Commissioner, 61 T.C. 770 (1974), declined to recharacterize as a sale a transaction carefully structured to avoid a capital loss on the sale of a partnership interest. To effect the taxpayer's withdrawal from a partnership in which he held a forty percent interest, the partnership first sold to a trust for the benefit of children of another partner an undivided ten percent interest in the real estate which was its principal asset. The trust immediately leased its undivided interest back to the partnership. The loss on the sale was specially allocated to the taxpayer, and the sales proceeds were distributed to him; his capital account was reduced by the loss and the distribution, and his partnership interest was reduced to thirty-three percent. The following year, the partnership distributed to the taxpayer in full liquidation of his partnership interest an undivided thirty percent interest in the real estate, which the taxpayer immediately leased back to the partnership. About two months later the taxpayer sold the undivided thirty percent interest to the trust which had purchased the ten percent interest the prior year. Because the trust did not become a partner and the taxpayer's partnership interest did not survive the transaction, the court distinguished *Crenshaw* and allowed the taxpayer a section 1231 loss on the sale of the real estate.

The problem of the retiring partner and the partnership taking inconsistent positions regarding characterization of a transaction as a sale versus the liquidation of a partnership interest in many cases may be solved by application of the partnership level audit rules. See supra, page 86.

B. REFERENCES

Swihart, Tax Problems Raised by Liquidations Of Partnership Interests, 44 Texas L.Rev. 1209 (1966); Skeehan, Transfer of a Partnership Interest; Problems on Admission of a New Partner and Withdrawal of Old Partner, 28 N.Y.U.Inst. on Fed.Tax. 541 (1970); Martin, Liquidation and Sale of a Partnership Interest, 25 So.Calif.Tax Inst. 433 (1973).

CHAPTER 6

DEATH OF A PARTNER

SECTION 1. INTRODUCTION

Upon the death of a general partner, under state law the partnership technically is dissolved, but under section 708, the partnership continues for federal tax purposes as long as the business of the partnership is continued, unless the partnership had only two partners. The deceased partner's interest in the partnership typically is disposed of in one of three ways: his estate (or other designated successor in interest) may receive a liquidating distribution; his interest may be purchased by the surviving partners, frequently pursuant to a prearranged agreement; or his designated successor may be substituted as a partner. Limited partnership interests are generally subject to the same treatment, but a limited partnership generally is not automatically dissolved by the death of a limited partner.

When a deceased partner's interest is liquidated, the rules regarding distributions in liquidation, discussed supra, chapter 5 generally govern the taxation of the liquidating distributions and their effect on the partnership. Similarly, if the interest is sold to the remaining partners, the rules governing sales of partnership interests, discussed, supra, chapter 4, generally govern. In both cases, however, either section 1014, providing that the basis of property acquired by bequest or inheritance is the fair market value at the decedent's date of death, or section 691, which denies a date of death basis to "income in respect of a decedent," must be taken into account. Where the deceased partner's successor in interest is substituted as a partner, there is no distribution or taxable transfer, but the transfer nevertheless has important effects. For example, if a section 754 election is in effect, a section 743(b) adjustment to the basis of partnership property is required.

In all three cases consideration must be given to the effect of the partner's death on the taxable year of the partner and of the partnership. As far as the individual partner in her own right is concerned, section 443(a)(2) closes her taxable year on the date of death. Section 706, however, not only provides the rules governing the partnership's taxable year, but modifies the application of section 443(a)(2) with respect to the deceased partner's distributive share of partnership items. Most controversy in this area involves the allocation of partnership income or loss between the decedent's final return and the income tax return of her estate.

SECTION 2. ALLOCATION OF PARTNERSHIP INCOME BETWEEN THE DECEASED PARTNER AND THE ESTATE

INTERNAL REVENUE CODE: Sections 706(c); 736(a); 753.

REGULATIONS: Sections 1.706–1(c)(3); 1.708–1(b)(1)(I); 1.736–1; 1.742–1; 1.753–1.

ESTATE OF APPLEBAUM v. COMMISSIONER

United States Court of Appeals, Third Circuit, 1983.
724 F.2d 375.

JAMES HUNTER, III, CIRCUIT JUDGE:

This appeal arises from a dispute over the short taxable year of Joseph R. Applebaum ("Applebaum"). Applebaum was a general partner in Phoenix Plaza Associates, a limited partnership ("the partnership"). Midway through 1975, Applebaum died. That year the partnership suffered a substantial loss. The question presented here is how Applebaum's share of that loss should be allocated between his final income tax return, filed by his widow, Florence K. Applebaum, and the income tax return filed by his estate.

The applicable statutory provision, I.R.C. § 706 (1976), plainly requires that all of Applebaum's share of the partnership loss be allocated to his estate. Appellants in this case, Florence K. Applebaum and Estate of Joseph R. Applebaum ("appellants"), urge us to disregard the statutory requirement so that they may allocate the partnership loss between them on a pro rata basis. They advance a number of policy reasons in support of their position. Appellants presented similar arguments to the United States Tax Court, sitting below, which rejected their position in a thorough and well-reasoned opinion. Applebaum v. Commissioner, 43 T.C.M. (CCH) ¶ 39,034(M) (1982). We will affirm the judgment of the Tax Court substantially for the reasons expressed in that opinion.

I.

Phoenix Plaza Associates was organized in 1968 to develop and operate a shopping center in Phoenixville, Pennsylvania. Applebaum, one of several general partners, owned 59.52 percent of the partnership at the time of his death on August 22, 1975.

Section X of the partnership agreement provided in part that upon the death of a general partner, that partner's general interest "shall be converted into that of a Limited Partner and be subject to the provisions of the agreement relating to a Limited Partner's interest * * *." Following Applebaum's death, however, a substantial disagreement arose between the remaining general partners and Applebaum's estate regarding the estate's continuing liability for certain partnership obligations incurred prior to Applebaum's death. As a result of this dispute, the remaining general partners refused to amend the Certificate of Limited Partnership to reflect the change in status of Applebaum's interest from general to limited. This dispute dragged on for nearly three years, spawning litigation in the federal and the state courts. The estate and the remaining partners eventually settled their dispute, but continued to disagree whether Applebaum's interest had converted from general to limited on his death.

In 1975, the year of Applebaum's death, the partnership suffered a loss of $313,684.79. Applebaum's 59.52 percent share amounted to $186,705.19. Because Applebaum's estate succeeded to his interest in the partnership midway through the year, the issue arose how that loss should be allocated between Applebaum's short taxable year and the estate's. Appellants' solution was to divide the loss pro rata between them, based on the portion of the year (234 days) that Applebaum was alive. The tax return filed by Florence K. Applebaum claimed $119,696 of the loss, and the estate's return claimed the remaining $67,009.19.[1]

Appellee, the Commissioner of Internal Revenue ("Commissioner"), disallowed the portion of the partnership loss claimed on Applebaum's final return by his widow. The Commissioner contends that the entire $186,705.19 loss must be allocated to the estate. Appellants contested the Commissioner's determination in the United States Tax Court and following that court's adverse determination, appealed to this court. They raise the same contentions here as below, and we affirm the Tax Court in rejecting them.

II.

Appellants contend first that we must overlook the plain statutory language of I.R.C. § 706(c)(2)(A)(ii), which states in relevant part that "the taxable year of a partnership with respect to a partner who dies *shall not close* prior to the end of the partnership's taxable year." (emphasis added) If the partnership's taxable year is not deemed closed prior to the end of its usual taxable year, all of the income or loss attributable to the deceased partner's share for that year must be allocated to his estate. Treas.Reg. § 1.706–1(c)(3)(ii). If the partnership year is deemed to close on a partner's death, then the pro rata allocation urged by appellants would be proper.

Section 706(c)(2)(A)(ii) unequivocally states that the death of a partner will not close the partnership year. Appellants nevertheless advance two policy arguments for disregarding this plain language. The first is that subsection 706(c)(2)(A) runs counter to the broad tax policy of allowing partnerships great freedom in allocating profits and losses among partners. See I.R.C. §§ 704(a), 761(c) (1976). According to appellants, no other section of the Internal Revenue Code denies

1. The estate declared no income in 1975, so the partnership loss was of no benefit to the estate.

partnerships this "flexibility." They contend also that section 706(c)(2)(A)(ii) violates assignment-of-income principles by retroactively allocating all of a deceased partner's loss or income to his estate, even though the estate was only a partner for part of the taxable year.[4] In making both arguments, appellants seek to override plain, particular statutory language by citing to overarching policy concerns.

The courts have repeatedly rejected such efforts with respect to closely related provisions of the Code. See, e.g., Rodman v. Commissioner, 542 F.2d 845, 858 (2d Cir.1976); Marriott v. Commissioner, 73 T.C. 1129, 1139 (1980); Moore v. Commissioner, 70 T.C. 1024, 1030–32 (1978). In Hesse v. Commissioner, 74 T.C. 1307 (1980), the Tax Court squarely rejected a taxpayer's attempt to circumvent the clear command of the provision at issue in this case, section 706(c)(2)(A)(ii). The Tax Court in the present case followed *Hesse* in rejecting appellants' claim. In each of these cases the courts have stressed the unambiguous import of the enacted language. While on occasion reproving the sometimes harsh result, they have declined to create an exception where Congress had not.

Appellants urge us to examine the legislative history of section 706(c)(2)(A)(ii), which they contend demonstrates that Congress did not intend to deny the widows of deceased partners the tax benefits of their husband's partnership losses. The Senate and House reports accompanying this provision do indicate that Congress was mainly concerned with the bunching of income that occurred when mid-year decedent partners realized income from their partnership interests,[5] and was not concerned with the provision's effect where, as here, the partnership showed a loss. S.Rep. No. 1622, 83d Cong., 2d Sess. 91 (1954); H.R.Rep. No. 1337, 83d Cong., 2d Sess. A225–26 (1954), U.S.Code Cong. & Admin. News 1954, p. 4017.

However enlightening this legislative history, we simply cannot ignore the unequivocal language of the provision. Section 706(c)(2)(A)(ii) could have excluded partnerships that declared losses rather than income, but it does not. Moreover, we cannot ignore the fact that Congress has not in the ensuing thirty years amended the provision to correct its "error." [6]

4. It is well-established that one taxpayer may not assign income to another taxpayer. Helvering v. Horst, 311 U.S. 112, 61 S.Ct. 144, 85 L.Ed. 75 (1940). This principle has been applied to prevent partnerships from retroactively assigning income or losses from a full taxable year to a partner who entered the partnership after the start of the year. Rodman v. Comm'r, 542 F.2d 845, 857–58 (2d Cir.1976); Moore v. Comm'r, 70 T.C. 1024 (1978).

5. It was once common for partnerships to have taxable years different from their partners. Before the passage of § 706(c)(2)(A)(ii), consequently, the final tax returns for decedent partners could contain up to 23 months of partnership income. By providing that a partner's death would not close his taxable year, Congress ensured that a decedent partner's final return would reflect no more than one year's partnership income; income from a taxable year closing after the partner's death would be reflected on the tax return of his estate. See Hesse v. Comm'r, 74 T.C. 1307 (1980).

6. The Advisory Group on Subchapter K recommended, shortly after the passage of § 706(c)(2)(A)(ii), that the provision be repealed and replaced with a provision that would have permitted a *pro rata* allocation like that sought by appellants. An-

Congress has been aware for many years of the problem faced by taxpayers in appellants' situation, but has neither amended nor repealed section 706(c)(2)(A)(ii). The plain language of that section prevents appellants from making the *pro rata* allocation they seek. We reject appellants' efforts to circumvent the plain language of section 706(c)(2)(A)(ii).

III.

Appellants present a second argument to support their attempted allocation. I.R.C. § 706(c)(2)(A)(i) states that a partnership's taxable year shall close "with respect to a partner who sells or exchanges his entire interest in a partnership." Appellants argue first that Applebaum's partnership interest converted on his death from a general to a limited interest, and second that this conversion constituted a "sale or exchange" sufficient to close Applebaum's taxable year.

The court below rejected appellants' argument at the first stage, finding that because of the intrapartnership dispute following Applebaum's death, his general interest never in fact converted to a limited one. Given the intensity of that dispute, the multiple lawsuits it engendered, and the continued refusal of the surviving general partners to amend the Certificate of Limited Partnership to reflect any change in the status of Applebaum's interest in the partnership, we cannot say that the Tax Court erred. Consequently, we need not reach appellants' further and highly controversial argument that such a conversion would constitute a sale or exchange for purposes of section 706(c)(2)(A)(i).

The opinion and decision of the Tax Court will be affirmed.

ADAMS, CIRCUIT JUDGE, concurring.

Although I join in the result reached by the majority, I write separately because I am persuaded that this case requires more than simply applying the plain language of I.R.C. § 706(c) (1976).[1]

As I read the statute, § 706(c) prohibits only the early closing of a partnership's tax year as the result of a partner's death. Granted that the partnership tax year must continue after a partner's death, § 706(c) nonetheless leaves open the possibility of allocating gain or loss between a deceased partner and his successor-in-interest during the

derson & Coffee, Proposed Revision of Partner and Partnership Taxation: Analysis of the Report of the Advisory Group on Subchapter K, 15 Tax.L.Rev. 285, 309–10 (1960). A bill embodying this recommendation passed the House of Representatives in 1960, and was favorably reported out of the Senate Finance Committee. However, the bill was never passed by the full Senate. 1 A. Willis, Partnership Taxation § 3.05, at 28 (2d ed. 1976).

1. Section 706(c) includes two subsections, §§ 706(c)(1) and 706(c)(2)(A)(ii), both of which contain the language applicable to the present dispute: "the taxable year of a partnership shall not close as the result of the death of a partner." For simplicity in this opinion, "§ 706(c)" is used to refer specifically to this prohibition, even though the full text of § 706(c) includes many provisions unrelated to nonclosure of the tax year at a partner's death. See § 706(c) reprinted in full, Maj.Op. at 376–377 n. 2.

course of an ongoing partnership tax year. Yet in its regulation, the IRS has precluded the option of making such an allocation. Instead, the IRS has by regulation chosen a construction of § 706(c) which frustrates the Congressional intent underlying the statute and prevents a fair reflection of a deceased partner's economic activities. Thus to my mind, this case involves not the application of the plain meaning of a statute, but rather the validity of a regulation. While I am troubled by the harsh result compelled by the IRS regulation, I cannot say—in view of the deference owed agency interpretations—that the regulation is sufficiently contrary to the 1954 Code to require its invalidation.[2]

No one contests the fact that Congress enacted § 706(c) with one evident purpose—to provide relief from the unfair tax burden imposed when a partner dies during the partnership tax year. Prior to 1954, the tax year of a partnership generally had to close with respect to a deceased partner at the time of death. See Guaranty Trust Co. v. Comm'r, 303 U.S. 493, 58 S.Ct. 673, 82 L.Ed. 975 (1938); Hesse v. Comm'r, 74 T.C. 1307, 1311 (1980). Accordingly, if the partnership had a tax year which ran from January 31 to January 31, and the decedent reported income on a calendar-year basis, then a partner who died on December 31 would have to report not only the twelve months of partnership income that had accrued by the preceding January 31, but also the eleven additional months of partnership income which accrued at the time of the partner's death. Consequently, under the pre–1954 rule, a partner could be taxed for up to 23 months of "bunched" income [3] on his final pre-death return.

In 1954, Congress enacted § 706(c) to provide relief from this "bunching" of income. See H.R.Rep. No. 1337, 83d Cong., 2d Sess. at A225–A226, reprinted in 1954 U.S.Code Cong. & Ad.News 4017, 4092–4093; S.Rep. No. 1622, 83d Cong., 2d Sess. 91, reprinted in 1954 U.S. Code Cong. & Ad.News 4621, 4723–4724; see also Hesse, supra, 74 T.C. at 1311–12. As the Tax Court in this case recognized, the legislative history reveals no evidence suggesting that Congress intended § 706(c) to do anything other than provide relief from the inequitable effects of bunching. Applebaum v. Comm'r, 43 T.C.Memo ¶ 39,034 (1982) at 1425–26.[4] In construing § 706(c) to prohibit the allocation attempted

2. I do not take issue with the majority's treatment of the other argument raised by Applebaum on appeal: that the partnership tax year ended at Applebaum's death pursuant to I.R.C. § 706(c)(2)(A)(i) (1976). Like the majority, I cannot say that the Tax Court erred in finding that Applebaum's partnership interest did not convert from a general to a limited interest at his death.

3. Because almost two years' income was reported on a single year's tax return, the earnings of such deceased partners would be taxed at a higher rate than would apply if they had lived for the rest of the partnership taxable year. It was this phenomenon that rendered "bunching" of income a problem. See Hesse, supra, 74 T.C. at 1311.

4. Although the Tax Court sought to supplement this evidence with post-enactment history, that approach proves very little. In 1960, Congress considered a bill, H.R. 9662, which included a provision expressly giving partners the option of electing to allocate partnership income between the pre-death period and the estate's return. H.R.Rep. No. 1231, to accompany H.R. 9662, 86th Cong., 2d Sess. 3, 30, 91 (1960); S.Rep. No. 1616, to accompany H.R. 9662, 86th Cong., 2d Sess. 80–81, 114 (1960). Unlike the Tax Court, I am not

by the Applebaums, the IRS has taken a relief measure and turned it into an additional tax burden on its intended beneficiaries—deceased partners.

The IRS interpretation of § 706(c) also contradicts economic common sense, preventing in this case a fair portrayal of Mr. Applebaum's pre-death income. Through August 22, 1975, the date of Mr. Applebaum's death, his share of the partnership loss was $110,000. Appellant's Br. at 16. Had Mr. Applebaum lived until January 1, 1976, no one would have questioned the right of his widow to deduct both the $110,000 lost through August and the remaining $76,000 lost by the end of 1975. But because Mr. Applebaum did not live an extra four months, his widow was denied all tax deductions stemming from the partnership for the entire year, even for that 8–month period when her husband was alive and was sustaining a partnership loss. The tax consequences of this distorted picture of Mr. Applebaum's pre-death income have been correctly described by the Tax Court as "both illogical and unfair." Hesse, supra, 74 T.C. at 1316.

This type of misallocation of losses has been prohibited by the courts under another subsection of § 706(c). See, e.g., Richardson v. Comm'r, 693 F.2d 1189 (5th Cir.1982), Williams v. U.S., 680 F.2d 382 (5th Cir.1982); Snell v. U.S., 680 F.2d 545 (8th Cir.1982); Marriott v. Comm'r, 73 T.C. 1129 (1980); Moore v. Comm'r, 70 T.C. 1024 (1978); and Rodman v. Comm'r, 542 F.2d 845 (2d Cir.1974). Specifically, the line of case law beginning with *Rodman* bars tax-shelter arrangements whereby a successor partner obtains an interest late in the partnership taxable year and is then allowed to assume a full year's worth of losses. Relying in part on the assignment-of-income principle, *Rodman* and its progeny hold that a partnership may not allocate gains or losses to a successor partner for a period during which the successor held no interest in fact. Similarly, the assignment-of-income principle—which in essence mandates that partnership distributions realistically reflect a partner's participation in the firm—suggests that the Applebaums' allocation of losses should be permitted. If Applebaum's estate is conceived to be a successor partner, assignment-of-income principles should prohibit the allocation of the entire 1975 loss to Applebaum's estate, which held an interest in fact only after August 22, 1975. Thus, if Mr. Applebaum had sought to sell his partnership interest on the day before his death, in order to give the purchaser a tax loss, the IRS would not permit it.

As I view it, therefore, the IRS construction of § 706(c) is at odds both with economic reality and the congressional policy underlying the provision. The majority upholds this construction solely on the ground

persuaded that Congress's failure to pass H.R. 9662 indicates Congressional approval of the result in this case. See Applebaum, supra, ¶ 39,034 at 1426. First, it is generally agreed that H.R. 9662 failed to pass the Senate because of controversy over a provision completely unrelated to § 706(c). Willis, Partnership Taxation § 305 (2d ed. 1976). Second, Congress's failure to approve an amendment six years after passage of § 706(c) proves nothing about congressional intent in 1954.

that it is mandated by the plain and unequivocal language of § 706(c). I cannot agree.

Although § 706(c) clearly prohibits the closing of a partnership tax year at a partner's death, it simply does not address whether partnership income may be allocated between a deceased partner and his successor-in-interest during a continuing tax year. To be sure, § 706(c)'s language is mandatory: the provision states unequivocally that "the taxable year of a partnership shall not close as a result of the death of a partner." But in view of the legislative history of § 706(c), it would appear that Congress chose this preemptory language because it was statutorily overturning the old rule that had created the bunching problem, not because it sought to produce the result reached today. The only language which plainly prevents the allocation attempted by the Applebaums is in Treasury Regulation § 1.706–1(c)(3)(ii):

> The last return of a decedent partner shall include *only* his share of partnership taxable income for any partnership taxable year or years ending within or with the last taxable year for such decedent partner * * *. (emphasis added)

The key issue, then, is whether this regulation can be upheld as a permissible interpretation of the tax code. Admittedly the burden of showing a tax regulation's invalidity is heavy: ordinarily courts owe deference to a regulation that "implement[s] the congressional mandate in some reasonable manner." U.S. v. Vogel Fertilizer Co., 455 U.S. 16, 24, 102 S.Ct. 821, 827, 70 L.Ed.2d 792 (1982), quoting U.S. v. Correll, 389 U.S. 299, 307, 88 S.Ct. 445, 450, 19 L.Ed.2d 537 (1967). Even so, "this general principle of deference, while fundamental, only 'sets the framework for judicial analysis; it does not displace it.'" Id., quoting U.S. v. Cartwright, 411 U.S. 546, 550, 93 S.Ct. 1713, 1716, 36 L.Ed.2d 528 (1973). As the Supreme Court recently cautioned,

> the "deference owed to an expert tribunal cannot be allowed to slip into a judicial inertia which results in the unauthorized assumption by an agency of major policy decisions properly made by Congress." Accordingly, while reviewing courts should uphold reasonable and defensible constructions of an agency's enabling Act, they must not "rubber-stamp * * * administrative decisions that they deem inconsistent with a statutory mandate or that frustrate the congressional policy underlying a statute."

Bureau of Alcohol, Tobacco & Firearms v. Federal Labor Relations Authority, [464] U.S. [89], [97], 104 S.Ct. 439, 444, 78 L.Ed.2d 195 (1983) (citations omitted).

Thus a prime purpose of judicial review of administrative agencies must be to insure compliance with congressional policy as expressed in both the language of the enabling act and its legislative history. Despite the deference owed administrative agencies, a regulation is not a statute, and the IRS is not the Congress. Where, as here, the IRS appears to have subtly subverted the policy underlying a particular provision of the tax code, a court must carefully scrutinize the regulation's fidelity to the overall statutory framework. See note 5 supra.

Section 704(a) provides the strongest argument that the 1954 Code requires the IRS to permit allocations such as that attempted by the Applebaums. That provision, which commands that "A partner's distributive share * * * shall * * * be determined by the partnership agreement," embodies a fundamental policy decision to permit partners flexibility in allocating the tax burden among themselves. H.R.Rep. No. 1337, 83d Cong., 2d Sess. 65 (1954); 1 McKee, Nelson & Whitmire, Federal Taxation of Partnerships and Partners § 1.03 (1977). Indeed, the McKee treatise calls allocative flexibility "[o]ne of the principal legislative objectives of Subchapter K." Id. See also I.R.C. § 761(c) (1976). To the extent that Treas.Reg. § 1.706(c)(3)(ii) prevents a partnership from agreeing to a reasonable allocation of its tax loss, the regulation would appear to conflict with the statutory mandate of § 704(a).[6]

Several other code provisions not mentioned by the majority or the Tax Court do, however, indicate that the IRS may preclude the allocation sought to be made by the Applebaums. Section 691(a)(1) requires that "all income not properly includible" in a decedent's pre-death income must be reported by some other entity, generally the estate. Whether Mr. Applebaum's allocation of partnership losses is "properly includible" on his pre-death tax return is addressed by §§ 702(a), 706(a) and 443(a). Section 702(a)(9) provides that "[i]n determining his income tax, each partner shall take into account separately his distributive share of a partnership's * * * taxable income or loss." Section 706(a) states in turn that "the inclusions required by" Subchapter K shall be based on partnership income "for any taxable year of the partnership ending within or with the taxable year of the partner."[7] Finally, § 443(a)(2) mandates that a "taxpayer in existence during only part of what would otherwise be his taxable year" shall make a tax return for that "short period." Since Applebaum's tax year therefore closed on August 22, 1975, and since the partnership's tax year did not terminate until December 31, 1975, these provisions make it clear that no partnership gain or loss for 1975 is an "inclusion required" on Applebaum's 1975 pre-death return. While I am not persuaded that the 1954 Code compels the additional step taken by the IRS—i.e., absolutely prohibiting other reasonable inclusions such as Mr. Applebaum's loss allocation—I must conclude, albeit reluctantly, that Treas.Reg. § 1.706–1(c)(3)

6. The Tax Court rejected the significance of § 704(a)'s flexibility principle, reasoning that a series of decisions suggest that § 706(c) supersedes § 704(a). Applebaum, supra, ¶ 39,034 at 1425. See cases cited supra at 12. This analysis is, however, inapposite. In the present case, the question is not whether § 704(a) allocations should override § 706(c), but instead whether § 704(a) allocations may override a regulation, § 1.706–1(c)(3)(ii).

7. Section 706(a) provides in full:

In computing the taxable income of a partner for a taxable year, the inclusions required by section 702 and section 707(c) with respect to a partnership shall be based on the income, gain, loss, deduction, or credit of the partnership for any taxable year of the partnership ending within or with the taxable year of the partner.

(ii) is not so inconsistent with these latter tax statutes as to require its invalidation.

Even though I believe that the Applebaums' allocation faithfully implements the congressional policy behind § 706(c) and accurately depicts his economic participation in the partnership, there is nonetheless sufficient support for today's conclusion in other sections of the tax code to sustain it. Accordingly, I concur in the result reached by the majority.

ILLUSTRATIVE MATERIAL

A. TREATMENT IN GENERAL

Suppose that a partnership is on a February 1–January 31 fiscal year and a partner is on a calendar year. A partner dies on November 30, 1991. Under section 443(a)(2) the deceased partner's executor must file an income tax return for the decedent partner for the period January 1–November 30, 1991, including therein income of the decedent allocable to that period under the decedent's method of accounting. The executor must therefore include the decedent's distributive share of the partnership income for the previous February 1, 1990–January 31, 1991 fiscal year. The partnership income for the period February 1, 1991–November 30, 1991 must also be accounted for. If this share must also be included, then twenty-two months income will be bunched in the decedent's final return. This result is avoided by section 706(c), which provides that the partnership year does not close for the decedent partner, or for the partnership, unless the partnership actually ceases on the decedent's death so that a termination occurs under section 708(b)(1)(A). The decedent partner's year does not close even though the partnership agreement does not provide for continuance of the partnership and even if the estate does not continue as a partner or have an interest in its profits, if the partnership activities continue. The partnership income thus falls in the estate's return and, under section 753, is treated as income in respect of a decedent. Regulations, section 1.706–1(c)(3)(ii); Rev.Rul. 68–215, 1968–1 Cum.Bull. 312.

Section 706 prevents the bunching in the tax year of death of more than one year of partnership income, where the tax years of the partnership and the decedent differ. It is intended to be a relief provision. Currently, however, the rules of section 706(c)(2)(A)(ii) are at least as likely to produce a hardship for the taxpayer as they are to provide relief, as is illustrated in *Estate of Applebaum.* Because allowing the partnership to use a fiscal year while the partners are on a calendar year permits postponement of tax, section 706(b), considered supra, page 84, severely limits the situations in which a partnership may have a taxable year which differs from those of the partners. Thus the bunching problem which section 706(c)(2)(A)(ii) has largely been eliminated by changes to other provisions of Subchapter K since its enactment.

Consider the case of a calendar year decedent in a calendar year partnership which, after the amendments to section 706(b) discussed supra, page 84, is the most frequently occurring situation. When the partner and partnership are on the same taxable year, there is no bunching problem. Since the partnership year does not automatically close on the day of the partner's death, the estate in its return will report the decedent's final distributive share. The primary effect of section 706(c)(2)(A)(ii) in this case is to isolate partnership income or loss on the estate's income tax return. As a result, the decedent's personal deductions and exemptions will not be offset against that distributive share of partnership income. Where the deceased partner was married, this treatment also denies the benefit of the lower joint return rates for his distributive share of partnership income. Where the partnership has a loss, as was the case in *Estate of Applebaum,* section 706(c)(2)(A)(ii) may defer the effective deduction of partnership losses at the individual partner level. If the partnership loss is allowable on the decedent's final return (or joint return with his spouse), and the loss exceeds the income on that return, the excess may be carried back three years under section 172. If the loss must be reported on the estate's return and it exceeds the estate's income, however, it can only be carried forward. See Hesse v. Commissioner, 74 T.C. 1307 (1980), which on similar facts reached the same result as *Estate of Applebaum.* Note that the beneficiaries of the deceased partner's estate might not be his surviving spouse. As a result, not only is the deduction deferred but the incidence of the tax benefit of the deduction is shifted from the surviving spouse to the beneficiaries of the estate.[1]

The Regulations take cognizance of these problems by applying section 706(c)(2)(A)(i) to allow a closing of the partnership year with respect to the decedent partner on the date of death if there is an agreement in effect calling for a sale of the decedent's interest to the remaining partners as of that day. Regulations, section 1.706–1(c)(3)(iv). In addition, the partnership agreement may provide for a named individual to succeed to the decedent's interest in the partnership, and the entire distributive share for the year will be taxed to the named successor. Regulations, section 1.706–1(c)(3)(iii). Where the spouse of the deceased partner is the successor, the spouse's share of the distributive income for the taxable year may be included in a joint return in accordance with section 6013(a)(3). But even where the designated successor in interest is other than the deceased partner's spouse, the distributive share for the entire year is reported on the successor's return. Rev.Rul. 71–271, 1971–1 Cum.Bull. 206.

Rev.Rul. 86–101, 1986–2 Cum.Bull. 94, held that the conversion of a deceased general partner's interest into a limited partnership interest did not close the partnership taxable year with respect to the deceased partner under section 706(a)(2)(A) since the conversion was not an exchange of the partner's entire interest.

Section 706(c)(2)(A)(ii) is inconsistent with the rules of section 706(d), discussed supra, page 134, which require that a partner's distributive share take into account his varying interests during the year. Consider the situation if A holds a limited partnership interest in a partnership in which her interest is 25 percent of capital, profits, and losses. Both A and the partnership report on the calendar year. Suppose that B purchases A's interest on July 1 of a year in which the partnership has income of $400, which accrued ratably during the year. Under section 706(d), A and B must each include $50. They are powerless to vary this by special allocations. But if A died on July 1 and bequeathed her interest to B, assuming that A's estate had distributed the interest to B before December 31, A would include

1. Under section 642(h), the beneficiaries of the estate are entitled to deduct in their returns the estate's unused net operating losses when the estate terminates.

zero and B would include $100. Under *Estate of Applebaum,* A and B may not change this result by special allocations.

B. TWO PERSON–PARTNERSHIPS

A special problem exists in the case of a two-person partnership. If a partner of a two-person partnership dies, and his interest is purchased by the surviving partner who continues the business as a sole proprietor, the partnership is terminated because no part of its operations continues to be carried on "in a partnership." However, the partnership continues for tax purposes so long as the estate or other successor in interest continues to share in the profits or losses of the partnership business or receives payments under section 736. Regulations, sections 1.708–1(b)(1)(i)(a), 1.736–1(a)(6); see also Rev.Rul. 66–325, 1966–2 Cum.Bull. 249; Estate of Skaggs v. Commissioner, 672 F.2d 756 (9th Cir.1982).

C. REFERENCES

Gunn, Federal Tax Problems of Income In Respect of a Deceased Partner, 3 J. Partnership Tax. 23 (1986); Nave, The Inherent Inequities in Section 706(c) Relating to the Tax Treatment of A Deceased Partner's Final Year, 61 Taxes 756 (1983); Wallace, Selected Post–Death Problems of Partnerships and Partners, 33 So.Calif.Tax.Inst. 18 (1981).

SECTION 3. EFFECT ON BASIS OF PARTNERSHIP ASSETS AS RESPECTS DECEDENT PARTNER'S SUCCESSOR IN INTEREST

INTERNAL REVENUE CODE: Sections 732; 742; 743; 753; 754; 755.

REGULATIONS: Sections 1.742–1; 1.743–1(b); 1.734–2; 1.754–1; 1.755–1.

ILLUSTRATIVE MATERIAL

A. TREATMENT IN GENERAL

The basis problems and the Subchapter K solutions to those problems on the death of a partner are essentially the same as in the case of the sale of a partnership interest, supra, page 206. In the death situation, section 742 refers to the general basis rules of section 1011 and following for determining the basis of a partnership interest acquired at death. Thus, under section 1014 the successor's basis for the partnership interest is the fair market value of the partnership interest at the deceased partner's date of death. Under section 743(a), the basis of partnership assets is not affected. However, if the estate or successor continues as a partner and a section 754 election has been made, then the basis of the partnership assets will be adjusted under section 743(b) to eliminate any difference between the basis in the partnership interest and the new partner's share of the basis in the partnership assets.

Rev.Rul. 79–124, 1979–1 Cum.Bull. 224, held that an adjustment to the basis of partnership assets under section 743(b) is to be made with respect to the partnership property attributable to the entire interest of a deceased partner which was held as community property where pursuant to section

1014(b)(6) the entire interest is treated as received by the surviving spouse from the decedent.

Under section 761(e) the distribution of a partnership interest from an estate to the beneficiary may be an exchange for purposes of section 743(b), and, if a section 754 election is in effect, a basis adjustment may be required. However, since the distribution is a nonrecognition event to the estate and under section 643(e)(1) the distributee takes a transferred basis, unless the estate elects under section 643(e)(3) to treat the distribution as a recognition event, generally no adjustment will be made.

B. PARTNERSHIP ASSETS INCLUDE UNREALIZED RECEIVABLES

The basis rules of section 1014 and section 743(b) present problems where the assets of the partnership include accounts receivable with a zero basis. If the basis for such a partnership interest were the estate tax value determined under section 1014(a), it would be attributable in part to a value represented by the accounts receivable. Ordinarily, however, accounts receivable of a decedent are carryover basis items under section 691, thereby preserving their inherent ordinary income. In the case of a partnership holding accounts receivable, if a basis adjustment under section 743(b) were allowed to the decedent's successor, then realization of the potential ordinary income in the accounts receivable could be permanently avoided. The Regulations attempt to close this obvious loophole by providing that the basis of the partnership interest acquired from a decedent is the fair market value of the interest reduced to the extent that such value is attributable to items constituting income in respect of a decedent under Section 691. Regulations, section 1.742–1. Assuming that this is a fair interpretation of the reference in section 742 to the general basis provisions, the question remains whether accounts receivable in this situation would constitute income in respect of a decedent. Clearly, if the accounts receivable had been held by the partner individually, they would have represented income in respect of a decedent in the hands of his estate or heirs. Here, however, the receivables are technically property of the partnership, and not of the individual partner. Section 691(e) refers to section 753 for the application of section 691 to income in respect of a deceased partner and that section merely provides that section 736(a) payments in liquidation of the deceased partner's interest are to be treated as income in respect of a decedent.

The obvious inadequacy of the statutory treatment of the problem has not prevented the courts from achieving the correct result. In Quick's Trust v. Commissioner, 54 T.C. 1336 (1970), aff'd per curiam, 444 F.2d 90 (8th Cir.1971), the court held that the right of a successor partner to share in the collection of accounts receivable could be separated from the general "bundle of rights" represented by the partnership interest and such right was covered by section 691. The reference in section 753 to section 736(a) payments was not to be treated as exclusive. As a result, the new basis of the partnership interest was reduced by the fair market value of the accounts receivable and the increase in the basis of the accounts receivable under section 743(b) was eliminated. A similar analysis was applied in Woodhall v. Commissioner, 454 F.2d 226 (9th Cir.1972), involving the sale of a partnership interest received from a decedent partner where the partnership held unrealized receivables at the time of the partner's death.

C. REFERENCES

Chillag, Section 743(b): A Second Basis Adjustment Following the Death of A Partner, 62 Taxes 156 (1984); Kalish and Schneider, Is There Partnership Basis After Death?, 35 Tax Lawyer 143 (1981).

SECTION 4. PAYMENTS OR DISTRIBUTIONS TO DECEDENT PARTNER'S SUCCESSOR IN INTEREST

A. TREATMENT OF DECEDENT PARTNER'S SUCCESSOR IN INTEREST

INTERNAL REVENUE CODE: Sections 736; 731(a), (c); 741; 732(b), (c), (d), (e); 735; 751(c); (d)(2); 753; 761(d).

REGULATIONS: Sections 1.732–1(d); 1.736–1; 1.753–1.

ILLUSTRATIVE MATERIAL

A. CASH PAYMENTS

1. *Initial Classification of Payments*

When a partner dies, under state law the partnership is dissolved, and his estate is entitled to distribution of his capital account, unless the partnership agreement provides otherwise. If such a liquidating distribution is made, the general rules governing liquidating distributions under sections 731–736 and section 751 control. Of course, due to the determination of basis under section 1014, gain or loss generally will not be recognized, even where the entire distribution is in cash. In addition, partnership agreements often provide that the estate of a deceased partner will receive a percentage of the profits for several years or a fixed annual amount, or some combination of the various alternatives. These payments are in liquidation of the decedent's interest in the partnership assets and goodwill, or in the nature of mutual insurance. These classification problems are identical with those considered earlier on the retirement of a partner, and the Subchapter K solution is the same. Section 736(a), considered supra, page 223, classifies these payments between those considered to be the estate's distributive share of partnership income or a guaranteed payment to the estate, and those considered as in exchange for the estate's interest in partnership property. See Regulations, section 1.736–1(a)(2) and 1.736–1(b). While payment made for a decedent's share of substantially appreciated inventory is treated as a section 736(b) distribution, section 751(b) will apply and result in ordinary income unless basis adjustments under sections 754 and 743(b) have been made.

2. *Aspect of Income in Respect of a Decedent*

Section 753 provides that the amounts classified under section 736(a) shall be considered income in respect of a decedent under section 691. The Regulations also include as section 691 income any amounts paid by a third party in exchange for rights to future partnership section 736(a) payments. Regulations, section 1.753–1(a). *Quick Trust* and *Woodhall,* supra, indicate that the statutory reference to section 736(a) in section 753 is not exclusive.

Where the estate receives section 736(a) payments which are treated as income in respect of a decedent, Regulations, section 1.742–1, discussed supra, page 267 require any section 1014 basis of the partnership interest to be reduced by the amount of the payments, thus preventing the estate from realizing a loss equal to the amount of the section 736(a) payments, i.e., the difference between any section 1014 basis and the section 736(b) payments.

The income in respect of a decedent treatment provided by section 753 implies that the value of the section 736(a) payments, e.g., for unrealized receivables, in the nature of mutual insurance and for goodwill in the absence of an agreement, will be subject to estate tax and, consequently, will qualify for the deduction under section 691 for estate tax paid. See Rev.Rul. 71–507, 1971–2 Cum.Bull. 331.

As discussed above, the partnership year does not close as to the decedent partner, so that the estate will include in its income the distributive share for the entire year. Only the value of the decedent's distributive share as of the date of death, however, is an asset of the estate for estate tax purposes. The Regulations provide that the amount of distributive share included in the estate's income will be treated as income in respect of a decedent. Regulations, section 1.753–1(b).

3. *Treatment of Payments After Classification*

The rules applicable to the treatment of the payments in the hands of the estate are the same as those applied in the case of a retiring partner and are discussed, supra, page 223.

B. PROPERTY DISTRIBUTIONS

Property distributions to an estate in liquidation of the interest of a deceased partner are subject to the general rules governing recognition of gain or loss by the distributee, the basis of property distributed, and the disposition of the property by the distributee discussed supra, page 223. The section 1014 date of death value basis of the partnership interest is used in assigning basis to the distributed property under section 732.

B. TREATMENT OF REMAINING PARTNERS

INTERNAL REVENUE CODE: Sections 731(b); 734; 736; 754; 755.

ILLUSTRATIVE MATERIAL

A. IN GENERAL

The rules applicable to the treatment of the remaining partners on the retirement of a partner are equally applicable to the liquidation of a deceased partner's interest. These rules are discussed supra, page 237.

If as a result of an election under section 754, the partnership must adjust the bases of the partnership assets, the formula of section 734(b) does not provide the correct result. The gain or loss to the estate is affected by the application of section 1014(a). To the extent that section 1014 produces a step-up in basis for the estate, gain that would otherwise be recognized on a liquidating distribution of cash is reduced pro tanto and hence the premise of the formula of section 743(b) is not satisfied. Conversely, if basis is stepped down, loss that otherwise would be recognized is eliminated. This problem is corrected to some extent by the Regulations in allowing any special basis adjustment the estate may have by virtue of section 743(b) or 732(d) to shift to the remaining assets for the benefit of the remaining partners. Regulations, section 1.734–2(b)(1). But this is not a principled compensation and the results are not theoretically correct.

In Estate of Skaggs v. Commissioner, 672 F.2d 756 (9th Cir.1982), the surviving partner of a husband-wife partnership, who inherited the deceased partner's interest, unsuccessfully asserted that the partnership automatically terminated upon the death of the deceased partner and that under section 1014 the basis of an undivided one half of the partnership's assets should be increased to the fair market value on the date of death. The court found that the partnership continued for purposes of paying its debts and winding up its affairs, and that absent a valid section 754 election, no basis adjustment was allowable with respect to the partnership assets.

For the possibility of filing a section 754 election on an amended partnership return for the year of the partner's death on facts similar to *Estate of Skaggs,* see Rev.Rul. 86–139, 1986–2 Cum.Bull. 95.

PART II

TAXATION OF CORPORATIONS AND SHAREHOLDERS

CHAPTER 7

TAXATION OF CORPORATE INCOME

SECTION 1. THE REGULAR CORPORATE INCOME TAX

When we turn from partnerships to corporations, we encounter a complete change in tax treatment. Under the Internal Revenue Code, a corporation is a taxpaying entity, separate and distinct from its shareholders. Except in certain limited situations, a corporation must pay an income tax on its profits even if the corporation currently or subsequently distributes those profits to its shareholders as dividends taxable to them individually as a part of their taxable income.[1]

The corporate income tax predates the current individual income tax. The modern corporate income tax originated in 1909, four years before the adoption of the Sixteenth amendment and the broad based individual income tax which it made possible. In Flint v. Stone Tracy Company, 220 U.S. 107 (1911), the Supreme Court upheld the 1909 corporate income against a constitutional challenge alleging that it was direct tax that was not apportioned among the states according to population as required by Article I, Section 9, Clause 4 of the Constitution. Rather, the Court held that the corporate income tax was an excise tax on the privilege of doing business in the corporate form. Ever since the enactment of the individual income tax in 1913, corporate income generally has been taxed twice, first when earned by the corporation and again when distributed to the shareholders as dividends or in liquidation, although prior to 1936 there was partial exclusion of dividends under the individual income tax and during 1936 and 1937 corporations were allowed a deduction for the amount of dividends paid out to shareholders. From 1954 through 1986 individuals were permitted by former section 116 to exclude from income a relatively small portion of dividends received (the original exclusion was $50; this amount had increased to $100 per taxpayer immediately

1. For 1985 nearly 3.3 million corporate income tax returns were filed. Approximately 1.8 million returns reported aggregate taxable income of almost $364 billion. The remaining returns reported operating losses of nearly $124 billion. Before allowing credits, corporations owing tax paid income taxes of about $111 billion; the allowance of nearly $48 billion of credits, however, reduced net income tax receipts to $63 billion. 1985 Statistics of Income, Corporation Income Tax Returns (Pub. 16) 18, 30 (1989).

prior to repeal of the exclusion). In addition, from 1954 until 1963 shareholders were allowed a credit equal to 4 percent of dividends received (in excess of the exclusion).[2]

Under current law the most significant exception to taxation of the corporation as a separate entity is the election under Subchapter S (sections 1371–1379) to treat the corporation as a pass-through entity with gains and losses being reported on the shareholders' individual returns.[3] A number of restrictive conditions limit the availability of this election. Corporations which do not make an election under subchapter S, which are the majority of corporations, are called "C corporations;" corporations which make the election are called "S corporations."

The policy decision to treat a corporation as a taxpaying entity separate and distinct from its shareholders entails certain structural requirements. A separate rate structure, currently specified in section 11, is applicable to corporations. The rate of tax on corporate income has varied over the years. Under the 1986 Act, the rates are: 15 percent on the first $50,000 of taxable income, 25 percent on the next $25,000, and 34 percent on taxable income in excess of $75,000. If taxable income exceeds $100,000, a 5 percent surtax is imposed on the excess over $100,000, up to a maximum additional tax of $11,750, which occurs when taxable income reaches $335,000. Thus, in effect the tax rate on taxable income in excess of $100,000, but not exceeding $335,000, is 39 percent, and when taxable income exceeds $335,000 the rate drops to 34 percent again. The purpose of this surtax, or "rate hump," is to phase out the benefit of the graduated rates for corporations having taxable income in excess of $100,000, so that corporations with taxable income exceeding $335,000 pay a 34 percent flat rate.[4]

Taxable income of a corporation basically is determined by applying the same rules that govern taxation of individuals, so that the gross

2. See Shoup, The Dividend Exclusion and Credit in the Revenue Code of 1954, 8 Nat'l Tax J. 136 (1955).

3. Subchapter S applies only to "small business corporations" having a limited number of shareholders. While Subchapter S is loosely referred to as permitting a corporation to elect to be taxed as a partnership, the operational effects under the Subchapter are somewhat different from partnership treatment. Subchapter S is discussed infra, page 636.

4. In 1909, when the corporate income tax was introduced, the rate was 1%. During World War I, it reached 12%; a 40% top rate was applicable during World War II; and a 52% rate was imposed during the Korean War. In 1964, the rate was reduced to 50% for that year and to 48% beginning in 1965. The rates and brackets were modified several times during the 1970's and 1980's. See J. Pechman, Federal Tax Policy, 135–137, 302–305, 321–322 (5th ed. 1987).

For many years the corporate income tax provided a relatively large portion of federal tax receipts, being as much as 42.2 percent in 1929, 36.8 percent in 1944, and 32.4 percent in 1954. In more recent years, however, due to structural provisions of the general tax laws, such as accelerated capital cost recovery provisions, which have a disproportionate effect on corporations as compared with individuals, the percentage of federal tax receipts attributable to the corporate income tax has fallen. By 1960 corporate taxes were only 24.8 percent of total receipts; by 1980 only 13.9 percent; and from 1982 through 1986 ranged from 8 to 10 percent. Some of the revisions in the Tax Reform Act of 1986 were intended to shift the tax burden relatively more to corporations.

income rules, the deduction rules, the accounting provisions, and the capital gain and loss provisions are all pertinent.[5] But there are a number of important variations from these basic income tax provisions that are applicable only to corporations. Thus, for example, application of the deduction sections, such as sections 162(a) and 165(a), to corporations generally is guided by the premise that all corporations are engaged in trade or business.[6] In addition, there are a number of special provisions which apply only to corporations, such as the dividends received deduction in section 243 for intercorporate dividends, which effectively excludes all or part of such dividends from a corporation's taxable income. The treatment of capital gains and losses recognized by corporations also differs. Under section 1212(a), capital losses are allowed only to the extent of capital gains, with a five-year carryover and a three-year carryback of any excess losses. Section 1201 provides that for any year in which the maximum tax rate under section 11 exceeds 34 percent (excluding the 5 percent surtax), the maximum rate of tax on long term capital gains is limited to 34 percent.[7]

The nonapplicability to most corporations of the passive activity loss rules of section 469, supra, page 155, is a very significant difference between individual and corporate taxation. Section 469 applies to a closely held C corporation, defined in section 469(j)(1)(B) as a C corporation more than 50 percent of the stock of which is held at some time during the last half of the taxable year by five or fewer persons, taking into account certain attribution rules. It also applies to "personal service corporations" defined in section 469(j)(2). Section 469 does not apply to S corporations, but it does apply to the shareholders in taking into account their shares of S corporation income or loss. Special rules govern the determination of whether a closely held C corporation or personal service corporation "materially participates" in an activity. See section 469(h)(4), (j)(2).

The rules governing choice of accounting methods and taxable years also differ for corporations. Most C corporations are required to

5. As with individuals, corporations are subject to the alternative minimum tax provided by sections 55 through 59 in any year in which the alternative minimum tax exceeds the regular tax. The alternative minimum tax rate for corporations is 20 percent, and the tax is imposed on "alternative minimum taxable income," a tax base that differs substantially from "taxable income". The alternative minimum tax is discussed infra, page 276.

6. But see, e.g., International Artists, Ltd. v. Commissioner, 55 T.C. 94 (1970) (A), where a corporation was denied deductions for expenses relating to a personal residence which it purchased for its principal officer and shareholder; Riss v. Commissioner, 57 T.C. 469 (1971), denying a loss deduction to a corporation with respect to a loss sustained by the corporation on the sale of property used solely as a personal residence by a shareholder. Generally, corporate expenditures for the personal benefit of shareholders are treated as nondeductible dividends, see infra, page 482.

7. Of course, there is nothing to prevent Congress from amending section 1201 to provide a higher maximum rate of tax on capital gains at the same time it amends section 11 to increase the general rate. Conversely, section 1201 might be amended to provide, as it did prior to the 1986 Act, for a maximum tax rate on capital gains lower than the then current maximum rate under section 11.

use the accrual method of accounting. Exceptions are provided for corporations with average annual gross receipts of less than $5 million and personal service corporations. See section 448. Although most C corporations are free to choose any taxable year, personal service corporations and S corporations generally are required to adopt a calendar year. See sections 441(i), 1378(b). These corporations may adopt a fiscal year, however, if the corporation can establish a business purpose for the fiscal year or if it makes an election under section 444, which requires that the corporation make an advance deposit of taxes.[8]

Special problems also result from transactions unique to the corporate form, such as the tax consequences to a corporation of the issuance of its stock or of dealings by it in its stock. Section 1032 solves this problem by providing that a corporation does not realize income upon the sale or issuance of its own shares for money or property. Further, there is the necessity of classifying as either stock or debt the securities issued by a corporation, since payment of interest generates a deduction to the corporation under section 163 while the distribution of a dividend does not. This classification issue is a matter of considerable controversy.

Because the corporation is a separate tax entity, rules must be provided to specify the tax treatment for various events in the life of the corporation, e.g., upon the formation of the corporation. Speaking generally, if an individual, group of individuals or partnership desires to incorporate a business and accordingly transfers the assets to a corporation formed for that purpose, no gain or loss will result from the change in the form of his ownership of the assets. The transferor now owns stock of a corporation holding the assets instead of holding the assets themselves; but the Code expressly provides that any gain or loss inherent in those assets is not to be recognized when they are so exchanged for stock. The transferor's basis for the assets now becomes the basis for the stock, and this asset basis likewise carries over to the corporation and becomes its basis for the assets. The rules governing formation of a corporation are discussed in Chapters 9 and 10.

Problems also arise as to the proper tax relationship between the ongoing corporation and its shareholders. The corporation may distribute cash, property, or its own stock. It is necessary to establish a standard for ascertaining the extent to which distributions represent corporate earnings, and thus are appropriately taxed to the shareholders as dividends, or a return of capital which should be applied against the basis of the shareholder's stock and taxable as gain if the distribution exceeds that basis. It also is necessary to decide whether the distribution of property by the corporation is an event which should result in the recognition of gain or loss to the corporation when the property is either appreciated or depreciated. The rules governing the tax treatment of dividends are considered in Chapter 11. Special

8. The rules governing adoption of a fiscal year by a taxpayer generally required to adopt a calendar year are discussed in connection with partnerships, supra, page 84 and S corporations, infra, page 668.

problems presented by dividends paid in the distributing corporation's own stock are discussed in Chapter 12.

Some of the shares of a shareholder, or all of the shares of some shareholders, may be redeemed by the corporation for cash or other property. In this case it is necessary to determine whether the transaction more nearly resembles a sale of the stock, thereby giving rise to recovery of basis and capital gain treatment, or a dividend with the attendant ordinary income consequences. It also is necessary to determine whether it is appropriate for the corporation to recognize gain or loss if property, rather than cash, is distributed to the shareholder in such a transaction. The rules required to determine the proper tax treatment of these transactions at the corporate and the shareholder level are considered in Chapter 13.

The shareholders later may decide to sell or liquidate the corporation. Again, it is necessary to provide rules for determining the gain or loss realized in such cases, and whether that gain or loss will be recognized at the corporate level, the shareholder level, or both. Special rules may be appropriate where the liquidated corporation is a subsidiary corporation, most of the stock of which is owned by another corporation. In this case nonrecognition of gain and loss to both corporations may be appropriate. Furthermore, consideration must be given to treatment of sales and purchases of corporate assets in connection with a liquidation. The purchase of all of the stock of a corporation and the purchase of all of its assets as a going business may be alternatives from a non-tax perspective. To what extent should the tax system treat these transactions identically and to what extent should the form chosen by the parties govern the transaction? Chapters 14 and 16 consider these matters.

It would be possible to "integrate" the tax treatment of the corporation with the tax treatment of its shareholders. Thus, it is not essential to an income tax system that corporations be subject to a separate tax structure, in the sense that both the corporation and its shareholders bear tax on the same income. The tax systems of some countries have varying degrees of integration of the corporate and individual income taxes. The policy arguments for a separate corporate income tax versus integration of the taxation of corporations and their shareholders are discussed infra, page 286. The limited integration offered by Subchapter S is considered infra in Chapter 15.

Undoubtedly new rules would be required if the corporate and individual income taxes were integrated, but one method of understanding the United States corporate tax structure is to consider which of the present rules are required because of the policy decision to treat the corporation as a taxpaying entity independent of its shareholders. Also, note should be taken of the situations in which there has been a decision to depart from the separate tax treatment of corporations and shareholders, as in Subchapter S or mutual funds, and a different set of rules has been shaped for this purpose. Are these situations an appropriate part of an otherwise separate structure, or are they aberrations inconsistent with that separate structure? In addition, which rules in the corporate tax area result from the decision not to tax the appreciation in the value of assets on an accrual basis? It is also interesting to identify the rules that result from the decision prior to the 1986 Act to give special treatment to "capital gains and losses." Which of the corporate-shareholder tax rules can be modified or repealed as a result of the repeal of the capital gains preference in the 1986 Act? Which rules stem from a decision to aid "small business"? What other policy decisions may have influenced the rules?

Still another way of viewing the materials is from the standpoint of business planning requirements. What are the various routes to implement a given business decision when tax consequences are taken into consideration? Which are more or less expensive from a tax standpoint? Which are the situations in which business needs appear to have shaped the tax rules, and conversely, where the development of the tax law has determined the manner in which certain business transactions must be carried out? The materials on the sale and purchase of the corporate business in Chapter 16, acquisitive tax free reorganizations in Chapters 17 and 21, single corporation reorganizations in Chapter 18, and corporate divisions in Chapter 19 raise planning as well as structural questions.

SECTION 2. THE ALTERNATIVE MINIMUM TAX

INTERNAL REVENUE CODE: Sections 53(a)–(c); 55(a)–(c), (d)(2); 56(a), (c)(1), (g); 57(a).

ILLUSTRATIVE MATERIAL

A. GENERAL

The alternative minimum tax (AMT) applies both to individuals and to corporations (other than S Corporations), but certain structural features of the AMT make it a much more important consideration for corporate taxpayers than for individual taxpayers. Most individuals do not have to make AMT computations each year. On the other hand, many corporations can be expected to incur AMT liability and the possibility that a corporation may be liable for the AMT is so significant that most corporations must make AMT computations on an annual basis even though no AMT liability may arise for the year. The purpose of the AMT is to assure that a taxpayer with substantial economic income cannot escape significant tax liability through exclusions, deductions, and credits under the regular tax that are provided as incentives for economic behavior which Congress intends to encourage rather than which serve accurately to measure economic income. See S.Rep. No. 99–313, 99th Cong, 2d Sess. 518–20 (1986).

Mechanically, under section 55(a) the AMT is an "add on" tax, but structurally the AMT is a "shadow" tax system which applies a lower uniform rate to a more broadly defined tax base than is used in computing the regular income tax. The corporation generally is required to pay the greater of the regular income tax or the AMT.

B. COMPUTATION

1. *AMT Rate and Exclusion*

Generally speaking, the tax base for the AMT is the corporation's regular taxable income increased by the "tax preferences" specified in section 57 and adjusted as required under section 56 by recomputing certain deductions, such as ACRS depreciation under section 168, to negate to some extent the acceleration of these deductions which is provided under the regular income tax. The resulting tax base is termed "alternative minimum taxable income" (AMTI) and, after an allowance of an exemption, AMTI is taxed at a flat 20 percent rate. Section 55(b). The exemption allowed to a corporation is $40,000, but it is reduced by 25 percent of the amount by which the corporation's AMTI exceeds $150,000. Section 55(d)(2), (3). Thus, for a corporation with AMTI of $310,000 or more, no exemption is available. The amount resulting from this computation is termed "tentative AMT" by section 55(b). Technically, the AMT liability is the amount by which this tentative AMT exceeds regular tax liability for the year. Thus in a year in which the corporation is liable for AMT it also is liable for regular tax.

2. *Alternative Minimum Taxable Income*

In computing AMTI, section 57 adds back to taxable income the following items: (1) natural resource depletion deductions under section 611 to the extent that the deductions exceed the taxpayer's basis for the property at the end of the year (this applies only to percentage depletion, but not to all percentage depletion over cost depletion); (2) between 90 and 99.17 percent of the amount by which intangible drilling and development costs deducted under section 263(c) for drilling oil and gas or geothermal steam wells exceeds income from such wells for the year; (3) certain bad debt reserve deductions by banks; (4) interest on private activity bonds exempt from tax under section 103; (5) the excess of the fair market value over the basis of any capital gain property donated to a charity; and (5) certain accelerated depreciation taken on property placed in service before 1987.

The adjustments in section 56 are far more complex. They may either increase or decrease AMTI relative to taxable income, and may produce different results in different years. For example, section 56(a)(1) prescribes that in computing AMTI, taxable income be "adjusted" by recomputing depreciation using the extended cost recovery periods of section 168(g) and applying, except in the case of real property, the 150 percent declining balance method, switching to straight line. (Most tangible personal property is depreciated for regular tax purposes under the 200 percent declining balance method, switching to straight line; real estate is depreciated using the straight line method for both regular tax and AMT purposes.) As a result, AMTI is increased relative to regular taxable income in the early years of an asset's cost recovery period, but is decreased relative to regular taxable income in later years. Section 56(a) prescribes a variety of other timing adjustments relating to mine exploration and development expenses, long term construction contracts, and disallowance of installment reporting under section 453 for dealers.[9] In addition, for AMT purposes, a special net operating loss carryover rule, prescribed in section 56(d), must be used instead of the normal net operative loss carryover rule of section 172. Under section 56(d), a net operating loss carryover is not permitted to reduce AMTI to zero; the maximum AMT net operating loss carryover deduction equals 90 percent of AMTI without regard to the deduction.

The complexities caused by the AMT extend beyond the face of its own provisions. For example, section 56(a)(7) recognizes that property may have a different basis for AMT purposes than for regular tax purposes because of the slower cost recovery permitted under the AMT. Thus, the gain or loss on the sale of property often is different for AMT purposes than for regular tax purposes. This result always will be true if depreciable property is sold prior to full cost recovery under the AMT.

The most complex, and most significant, adjustment, however, is the "adjusted current earnings" (ACE) adjustment in section 56(g). This provision adds to AMTI an amount equal to 75 percent of the excess of the corporation's "adjusted current earnings" over its AMTI (computed without reference to the ACE adjustment or the AMT net operating loss deduction). If AMTI exceeds adjusted current earnings, then the ACE adjustment is negative. "Adjusted current earnings" is defined in section 56(g)(4) as AMTI with numerous complex adjustments. These adjustments, which include further adjustments to depreciation deductions and the recomputation of income and deduction items to reflect the extent to which items are includable or deductible in determining the corporation's "earnings and profits" under section 312,[10] are intended to cause AMTI more accurately to reflect the corporation's economic income. In particular, Congress was concerned with taxing corporations which report earnings to shareholders and pay dividends but have no taxable income under the regular tax. See S.Rep. No. 99–313, 99th Cong. 2d Sess. 519 (1986). Unfortunately, however, the rules for computing earnings and profits are not certain in every instance. Section 312, governing earnings and profits does not proscribe a comprehensive set of rules; rather it merely specifies some adjustments to taxable income which must be made to compute earnings and profits. Numerous possible adjustments, not specified in the statute, are required and appropriate. See infra, page 462.

2. *Credit Against Regular Tax*

Because many of the adjustments in section 56 and tax preferences in section 57 taken into account in computing AMTI reflect timing differences with respect to regular taxable income, rather than permanent exclusions from taxable income, in the interest of fairness the AMT is treated to some extent as a prepayment of regular taxes. Section 53 allows a credit against regular tax liability, to the extent it exceeds tentative AMT, as defined in section 55(b), of a portion of AMT liability for prior years. For most corporations the creditable portion of the prior minimum tax paid is limited to portion of prior AMT liability attributable to adjustments and preferences

9. Section 56(c)(2) and (3) also provides two very narrowly focused adjustments of importance to only a small percentage of corporations.

10. Earnings and profits computed under section 312 are used to measure a corporation's dividend paying capacity for tax purposes. The rules governing the computation of earnings and profits are discussed infra, page 462.

includable in AMTI *other than* the excess depletion deduction, private purpose tax-exempt bond interest, and appreciated charitable contributions. Section 53(d). Here it is important that mechanically AMT is not the entire amount resulting from multiplying AMTI by the AMT tax rate but only the amount by which tentative AMT exceeds regular tax liability for the year. AMT from any number of prior years may be credited against regular tax in a particular year, but the carryover credit available for future years is, of course, reduced by the amount of the credit claimed. Section 53(a). The carryover credit is available in the first year the corporation incurs regular income tax liability regardless of whether or not the items that gave rise to prior AMT liability are brought back into the regular income tax base in that year. The operation of the credit can be illustrated by the following example. Suppose that in year one an accelerated deduction of $100 reduces regular taxable income and is treated as a tax preference item subject to the AMT. In a later year, regular taxable income will be $100 higher than it would have been if the deduction had not been accelerated. The additional $34 of regular tax on the $100 can be partially off set by a credit of $20 of minimum tax paid in year one.

C. REFERENCES

Shapiro, Perception, Reality and Strategy: The New Alternative Minimum Tax, 66 Taxes 91 (1988); Gould, The New Corporate AMT: Where We Are Today; Where We May Be Tomorrow, 46th Annual N.Y.U. Inst. on Tax'n 36–1 (1988); Zimbler, The Corporate Alternative Minimum Tax: Another Look, 65 Taxes 846 (1987).

SECTION 3. SELECTED TAX POLICY ISSUES

A. THE INCIDENCE OF THE CORPORATION INCOME TAX

J. PECHMAN, FEDERAL TAX POLICY

The Brookings Institution (Fifth ed. 1987).

There is no more controversial issue in taxation than the question, "Who bears the corporation income tax?" On this question, both economists and businessmen differ among themselves. The following quotations are representative of these divergent views:

> Corporate taxes are simply costs, and the method of their assessment does not change this fact. Costs must be paid by the public in prices, and corporate taxes are thus, in effect, concealed sales taxes. (Enders M. Voorhees, chairman of the Finance Committee, U.S. Steel Corporation, address before the Controllers' Institute of America, New York, September 21, 1943.)
>
> The initial or short-run incidence of the corporate income tax seems to be largely on corporations and their stockholders. * * * There seems to be little foundation for the belief that a large part of the corporate tax comes out of wages or is passed on to consumers in the same way that a selective excise [tax]

tends to be shifted to buyers. (Richard Goode, The Corporation Income Tax, Wiley, 1951, pp. 71–72.)

* * * The corporation profits tax is almost entirely shifted: the government simply uses the corporation as a tax collector. (Kenneth E. Boulding, The Organizational Revolution, Harper, 1953, p. 277.)

It is hard to avoid the conclusion that plausible alternative sets of assumptions about the relevant elasticities all yield results in which capital bears very close to 100 percent of the [corporate] tax burden. (Arnold C. Harberger, "The Incidence of the Corporation Income Tax," Journal of Political Economy, vol. 70, June 1962, p. 234.)

* * * An increase in the [corporate] tax is shifted fully through short-run adjustments to prevent a decline in the net rate of return [on corporate investment], and * * * these adjustments are maintained subsequently. (Marian Krzyzaniak and Richard A. Musgrave, The Shifting of the Corporation Income Tax, Johns Hopkins Press, 1963, p. 65.)

* * * There is no inter-sector inefficiency resulting from the imposition of the corporate profits tax with the interest deductibility provision. Nor is there any misallocation between safe and risky industries. From an efficiency point of view, the whole corporate profits tax structure is just like a lump sum tax on corporations. (Joseph E. Stiglitz, "Taxation, Corporate Financial Policy, and the Cost of Capital," Journal of Public Economics, vol. 2, February 1973, p. 33.)

* * * If the net rate of return is given in the international market place, the burden of a tax on the income from capital in one country will not (in the middle or long run) end up being borne by capital (which can flee) but by other factors of production (land, labor, and to a degree, perhaps, old fixed capital). (Arnold C. Harberger, "The State of the Corporate Tax: Who Pays It? Should It Be Replaced?" in Charls E. Walker and Mark A. Bloomfield, eds., New Directions in Federal Tax Policy for the 1980s, Ballinger, 1983.)

Unfortunately, economics has not yet provided a scientific basis for accepting or rejecting one side or the other. This section presents the logic of each view and summarizes the evidence.

The Shifting Mechanism

One reason for the sharply divergent views is that the opponents frequently do not refer to the same type of shifting. It is important to distinguish between short- and long-run shifting and the mechanisms through which they operate. The "short run" is defined by economists as a period too short for firms to adjust their capital to changing demand and supply conditions. The "long run" is a period in which capital can be adjusted.

The Short Run. The classical view in economics is that the corporation income tax cannot be shifted in the short run. The argument is as follows: all business firms, whether they are competitive or monopolistic, seek to maximize net profits. This maximum occurs when output and prices are set at the point where the cost of producing an additional unit is exactly equal to the additional revenue obtained from the sale of that unit. In the short run, a tax on economic profit should make no difference in this decision. The output and price that maximized the firm's profits before the tax will continue to maximize profits after the tax is imposed. (This follows from simple arithmetic. If a series of figures is reduced by the same percentage, the figure that was highest before will be the highest after.)

The opposite view is that today's markets are characterized neither by perfect competition nor by monopoly; instead, they show considerable imperfection and mutual interdependence or oligopoly. In such markets, business firms may set their prices at the level that covers their full costs *plus* a margin for profits. Alternatively, the firms are described as aiming at an after-tax target rate of return on their invested capital. Under the cost-plus behavior, the firm treats the tax as an element of cost and raises its price to recover the tax. (Public utilities are usually able to shift the tax in this way, because state rate-making agencies treat the corporation tax as a cost.) Similarly, if the firm's objective is the after-tax target rate of return, imposition of a tax or an increase in the tax rate—by reducing the rate of return on invested capital—will have to be accounted for in making output and price decisions. To preserve the target rate of return, the tax must be shifted forward to consumers or backward to the workers or partly forward and partly backward.

It is also argued that the competitive models are irrelevant in most markets where one or a few large firms exercise a substantial degree of leadership. In such markets, efficient producers raise their prices to recover the tax, and the tax merely forms an "umbrella" that permits less efficient or marginal producers to survive.

When business managers are asked about their pricing policies, they often say that they shift the corporation income tax. However, even if business firms intend to shift the tax, there is some doubt about their ability to shift it fully in the short run. In the first place, the tax depends on the outcome of business operations during an entire year. Businessmen can only guess the ratio of the tax to their gross receipts, and it is hard to conceive of their setting a price that would recover the precise amount of tax they will eventually pay. (If shifting were possible, there would be some instances of firms shifting more than 100 percent of the tax, but few economists believe that overshifting actually occurs.)

Second, businessmen know that should they attempt to recover the corporation income tax through higher prices (or lower wages), other firms would not necessarily do the same. Some firms make no profit or have large loss carry-overs and thus pay no tax; among other firms, the ratio of tax to gross receipts differs. In multiproduct firms, the producer has even less basis for judging the ratio of tax to gross receipts for each product. All these possibilities increase the uncertainty of response by other firms and make the attempt to shift part or all of the corporation income tax hazardous.

The Long Run. In the long run, the corporation income tax influences investment by reducing the rate of return on corporate equity. If the corporation income tax is not shifted in the short run, net after-tax rates of return are depressed, and the incentive to undertake corporate investment is thereby reduced. After-tax rates of return tend to be equalized with those in the noncorporate sector, but in the process corporate capital and output will have been permanently reduced. Thus, if there is no short-run shifting and if the supply of capital is fixed, the burden of the tax falls on the owners of capital in general. If the depressed rate of return on capital reduces investment, productivity of labor decreases and at least part of the tax may be borne by workers.

Where investment is financed by borrowing, the corporation tax cannot affect investment decisions because interest on debt is a deductible expense. If the marginal investment of a firm is fully financed by debt, the corporation tax becomes a lump-sum tax on profits generated by previous investments and is borne entirely by the owners of the corporation, the stockholders. In view of the recent large increase in debt financing (see the section on equity and debt finance below), a substantial proportion of the corporation income tax may now rest on stockholders and not be diffused to owners of capital in general through the shifting process just described.

The Corporation Tax in an Open Economy. The foregoing analysis assumed that the corporation tax was imposed in a closed economy. In an open economy, the rate of return on capital is set in the international marketplace. If the tax in one country is higher than it is elsewhere, capital will move to other countries until the rate of return is raised to the international level. Thus the burden of the tax would not be borne by capital but by other factors of production (land, labor, and old fixed capital) that cannot move. Since labor is the largest input into corporate products, wage earners would bear most of the burden of the corporation tax through lower real wages.

In the years immediately after World War II, most countries imposed tight capital controls and currencies were not convertible. As capital controls were dismantled and many foreign currencies other than the U.S. dollar became acceptable in international transactions, the open economy model became more realistic. During this later period, the effective corporation tax rates have been declining in the United States. It follows that recent U.S. tax policy has probably reduced any adverse effect of the corporation income tax on real wages, not increased it as some allege.

The Evidence

The evidence on the incidence of the corporation income tax is inconclusive. The data do not permit a clear determination of the factors affecting price and wage decisions. Different authors examining the same set of facts have come to diametrically opposite conclusions.

Over the long run, unincorporated business has not grown at the expense of incorporated business in the United States. Corporations accounted for 58.7 percent of the national income originating in the business sector in 1929; their share reached 75.6 percent in 1986 * * *. Much of the increase came from the relative decline in industries, particularly farming, in which corporations are not important; but even in the rest of the economy, there is no indication of a shift away from the corporate form of organization. The advantages of doing business in the corporate form far outweigh whatever deterrent effects the corporation tax might have on corporate investment.

Beyond this, the data are conflicting. On the one hand, before- and after-tax rates of return reported by corporations have been higher since the end of World War II than in the late 1920s, when the corporation income tax was much lower * * *. On the other hand, except for recession years, the share of pre-tax property income (profits, interest, and capital consumption allowances) in the corporate gross product changed little * * *. Corporations have been able to increase their before-tax profits enough to avoid a reduction in the after-tax return without increasing their share of income in the corporate sector. This suggests that corporations have increased pre-tax rates of return not by marking up prices or lowering wages, but by making more efficient use of their capital. But what might have occurred without the tax is unknown, and its long-run effect remains unclear.

The burden of corporate taxation borne by individuals is strikingly different under the different incidence assumptions. The tax is regressive in the lower income classes and mildly progressive in the higher ones if as much as one-half is shifted forward to consumers in the form of higher prices and the remainder is borne by owners of capital in general. If the entire tax is borne by capital, progressivity increases in the higher income classes * * *.

ILLUSTRATIVE MATERIAL

A. BRADFORD, UNTANGLING THE INCOME TAX (Harvard University Press 1987):

"Confusion between nominal and real incidence is particularly common in the case of the corporation income tax. There is no doubt that this tax is borne by persons, not by the institutions that file the tax returns and send in the checks. But there is doubt and controversy about how the corporation income tax affects the burdens on individuals in their roles as workers, consumers, savers, and so on. The problem of determining the true incidence of the corporation income tax is a classic in public finance. In a famous treatment of the problem, Arnold Harberger (1962) [11] conceived of the tax as an extra levy on the use of capital (machines, buildings, inventories, and so on) in the corporate sector. His analysis of the tax has been so widely accepted that it can now be considered the traditional view.

"As with an excise tax on telephone calls, a levy on an input to a single sector—in this case, capital services in the corporate sector—discourages the use of that input and leads to shifts in prices for inputs and outputs throughout the economy. (The price of capital services can be thought of as the interest rate a borrower must pay a lender for the use of the funds required to purchase and maintain a building, a machine, a bit of inventory, and the like.) Just as the process of adjustment of wages, prices, output, and employment generates the ultimate distribution of the burden of a tax on telephone calls, a similar process spreads the burden of a tax on corporate capital. The distribution after full adjustment of the economy has taken place will depend on the details of how demand for the outputs of the corporate sector varies with the prices of goods produced there and how the corporate and noncorporate sectors make use of the services of capital and labor.

"Two things are clear in Harberger's characterization of the situation. First, no special burden can result for owners of capital employed in the corporate sector (corporate shareholders). Because resources are free to move between sectors, they must receive the same return in both. Economists use the term "shifting" to describe the difference between the nominal and the real incidence of a tax. In this instance, the tax on uses of capital in the corporate sector will certainly be shifted. The question is: onto whom? Second, the tax must be shifted to individuals in some combination of their roles as capitalists (owners of wealth) and workers. (Consumers as such can bear no special burden in the Harberger model, because he does not distinguish purchasers of corporate goods from purchasers of noncorporate goods.) That is, the tax will change both the after-tax return to savers and the wages received by workers. It is even possible that a tax on the use of capital in the corporate sector could raise the wages of workers (if lots of capital and not many workers are released by the tax-induced contraction of the corporate sector), in which case we would say capitalists (who might, of course, also be workers) bear more than 100 percent of the tax. Similarly, it is theoretically possible that capitalists could *gain* from the tax.

"Harberger's famous conclusion, based on educated guesses about critical features of the production technology and demand behavior, was that the tax probably did not affect the wages of workers. The tax was thus probably borne entirely by individuals as owners of wealth and not as workers. The technique employed by Harberger involved describing mathematically the interrelationships of demand and supply throughout the economy, along with the ways in which inputs are combined by firms to produce goods and services.[12] Since the time of Harberger's first contributions, advances in computer technology have allowed other researchers to produce greatly refined versions of his analysis (see Ballard et al., 1985).[13]

11. [Ed.: Harberger, The Incidence of the Corporate Income Tax, 70 J.Pol.Econ. 215 (1962).]

12. The technique is referred to as "general equilibrium analysis," because of its attempt to encompass all the balancing relationships in the economy and thereby account for the full range of ripple effects of a policy change.

13. [Ed.: Ballard, Shoven & Whalley, *General Equilibrium Computations of the Marginal Welfare Cost of Taxes in the United States,* 75 Am.Econ.Rev. 128 (March 1985).]

"More recent treatments have been able to distinguish many different industries, to allow for interindustry transactions, to recognize the existence of many other taxes, and to include individual workers/consumers of varying types. The primary inputs, however, have in most cases been held to two: capital and labor. These detailed models, increasingly comprehensive in coverage, have typically supported Harberger's original conclusion about the incidence of a tax on the use of capital by corporations.

"I have been careful in this discussion to refer to a tax 'on the use of capital by corporations,' rather than to the corporation income tax. In recent years the view of the corporation income tax has been changing (see Bradford, 1980b).[14] Although researchers are not challenging the correctness of the earlier work as to the effect of a tax on corporate capital, they have begun to question the adequacy of conceiving of the corporation income tax as a tax on corporate capital. They emphasize the importance of looking at the details of the tax as it affects various transactions, such as payment of dividends or undertaking an investment project. These details can be analyzed correctly only if the corporation income tax is seen as an element in the income tax system as a whole, that is, jointly with the personal income tax. Together, the two sets of rules determine how the corporation tax influences investment and financial decisions, employment practices, and so on.

"This rethinking can be related to the view I have often encountered among businesspeople, that the corporation income tax amounts to a sales tax applied to corporations. To some extent this view is simply an expression of the point already emphasized here: taxes paid by corporations are borne not by institutions as such, nor by their stockholders as such, but by a wide class of individuals. The proceeds from a company's sales must cover taxes paid by the company, the cost of hired inputs (including labor and capital), and a residual profit or loss accruing to the owners of the company. In a competitive economy, owners will insist on receiving a competitive return, including compensation for bearing risk. (If they do not get it, they will change the firm's decisions.) Conversely, owners who regularly earn supernormal profits find them eroded by the entry of competitor firms. The tendency of the system is toward a situation in which owners who contribute capital to firms obtain a return equivalent to that of owners who hire out their capital—not more, not less. (*Equivalent* return is not necessarily the identical return. There are typically differences in risk.)

"Thus taxes paid by corporations must ultimately be reflected in changes in prices paid by customers and received by suppliers (including suppliers of finance and of labor services). This is true whether the tax is a sales tax, a corporation income tax, or a payroll tax. Whether the tax that is labeled a corporation income tax is equivalent to a sales tax on corporations depends on the details. A cash-flow tax of the sort proposed by Henry Aaron and Harvey Galper[15] would be based effectively on the difference between the sales and purchases of the corporate sector to and from the noncorporate economy. It would thus, indeed, have the character of a corporate sales tax. Yet a tax levied on the income of corporations, calculated according to accrual-income principles except with no deduction for interest paid (or

14. [Ed.: Bradford, "The Economics of Tax Policy Towards Saving," in *The Government and Capital Formation* (G. von Furstenberg ed. 1980).]

15. [Ed.: Aaron & Galper, Reforming the Federal Tax System, 24 Tax Notes 285 (1984).]

taxation of interest received), would clearly be a double tax on corporate income and not equivalent to a sales tax. The effect of the existing system * * * with its deduction for corporate interest paid, its accelerated depreciation of investment, investment tax credit, inadequate inflation indexing, and so on, is unfortunately, difficult to determine." (136–139)

B. REFERENCES

Shoven, The Incidence and Efficiency Effects of Taxes on Income from Capital, 84 J. of Pol.Econ. 1261 (1976); McLure & Thirsk, A Simplified Exposition of the Harberger Model I: Tax Incidence, 28 Nat'l Tax J. 1 (1975); Stiglitz, Taxation, Corporate Financial Policy and the Cost of Capital, 2 J. of Pub.Econ. 1 (1973); Musgrave & Krzyzaniak, Incidence of the Corporate Income Tax in U.S. Manufacturing, 58 Amer.Econ.Rev. 1358 (1968); Klein, The Incidence of the Corporation Income Tax: A Lawyer's View of a Problem in Economics, 1965 Wisc.L.Rev. 576; Harberger, The Incidence of the Corporate Income Tax, 70 J.Pol.Econ. 215 (1962).

B. INTEGRATION OF THE CORPORATION AND PERSONAL INCOME TAXES

INTRODUCTION

Every industrialized country has been required to deal with the policy questions of whether a corporation should pay an income tax separate from, and in addition to, that on its shareholders; whether the corporate and individual income taxes should be fully "integrated," so that only a single tax at the shareholder level ultimately is borne by income earned in corporate form; or whether some in-between position should be adopted. The United States has chosen a system of completely separate taxation of corporations and shareholders, except in those limited circumstances in which a corporation can, and does, make a Subchapter S election. Furthermore, certain provisions of the 1986 Act, particularly those dealing with distributions of property by the corporation to its shareholders, whether as dividends or in liquidation, see infra pages 477 and 616, were designed to strengthen the system of double taxation of corporate profits. Other industrialized countries have reached policy decisions falling somewhere between the poles of completely separate taxation and full integration. The following materials present background on this subject, review the recent history of treatment of this issue in the United States, and give a brief survey of some positions which have been taken in other countries.[16]

16. See also J. Pechman, ed., Comparative Tax Systems: Europe, Canada and Japan 49–53, 100, 161–167, 221–222, 270–271, 309–310, 357–362, 412–414 (Tax Analysts 1987).

(1) Role of the Corporate Income Tax

J. MUSGRAVE AND P. MUSGRAVE, PUBLIC FINANCE IN THEORY AND PRACTICE

The role of the corporation tax in a good tax system is by no means obvious. If the appropriate tax base is viewed in terms of consumption, there is clearly no case for a corporation tax. Corporate source income should then become taxable only if and when it is distributed and spent by the recipient. But the case for a corporation tax may be questioned even in the context of an income-based approach. Here taxation at the corporate level may be viewed as a mere device for integrating corporate source income into the individual income tax, or it may be viewed as an additional "absolute" tax on corporate source income, to be imposed before net income is allocated to the shareholder. Under U.S. law, the latter view continues to apply. The federal corporation tax of 34 percent is taken out first and cannot be credited against the shareholder's personal income tax on dividend income. Proposals to integrate corporate income into the individual income tax were rejected in the tax reform of 1986.

The Integrationist View

Those who take the integrationist position view the problem of taxation at the corporate level merely as a way of including all corporate-source income in the individual income tax base. Their basic proposition is that in the end, all taxes must be borne by people and that the concept of equitable taxation can be applied to people only. Moreover, they hold that income should be taxed as a whole under a global income concept, independently of its source. Proceeding on the assumption that the corporation income tax falls on profits, they criticize such a tax because profits when distributed are taxed twice—first at the corporation level under the corporation tax and then at the personal level as dividends under the individual income tax.

Consider taxpayer A who pays personal income tax at the 28 percent rate. Her share in the profits of corporation X is $100 on which the corporation pays a tax of $34. The remainder, or $66, is distributed in dividends to A, who then pays an income tax of $18.48. The combined tax equals $52.48. In the absence of a corporation tax, the income tax paid on $100 of dividends would have been $28, thus leaving an "excess tax" of $24.48. Next consider shareholder B, who pays personal income tax at a rate of 15 percent. For him, the combined tax equals $34 plus $9.90, or $43.90. The income tax under an integrated system would have been $15, thus leaving an excess tax of $28.90, somewhat above that of A. Failure to integrate imposes an additional burden and that burden per dollar of corporate source income is larger for the smaller shareholder whose individual income tax is lower. At the same time, note that dividends are likely to comprise a larger share of A's than of B's income. This being the case, the extra tax as a percent of total income may be larger for A than for B. However this may be, the extra tax is unjustified from the integrationist's point of view, because all income (including that derived from corporate source) should be taxed at the same rate. In place of the corporation tax, there should be source withholding of individual income tax on corporate source income.

The preceding illustration has assumed that profits after tax are in fact distributed as dividends. In reality such is not the case, because at least half of profits after corporation tax tend to be retained. In the absence of imputing retained earnings to the shareholder (as would be the case under the integrated system) the corporation tax thus serves the purpose of reaching retained earnings. With the new sets of rates introduced in 1986, the corporate rate of 34 percent now exceeds the individual income tax rate applicable on distribution, but (except for the low-income shareholder) the margin has become slight.

The Absolutist View

Those who take an opposing position believe that the integrationist approach rests on an unrealistic view of the corporation. The large widely held corporation—which accounts for the great bulk of corporation tax revenue—is not a mere conduit for personal income. It is a legal entity with an existence of its own, a powerful factor in economic and social decision making, operated by a professional management subject to little control by the individual shareholder. From this it is concluded that being a separate entity, the corporation also has a separate taxable capacity which is properly subject to a separate and absolute tax. Whether profits after tax are distributed or retained is irrelevant in this context.

This "absolute" or "classical" view of the tax is hardly tenable. Corporations do indeed act as distinct decision-making units, only more or less vaguely related to the wishes of the shareholders, thus calling for a regulatory policy at the corporate rather than the shareholder level. Moreover, tax devices may be useful under certain circumstances for such regulatory purposes. However, this is quite a different matter from proposing that a corporation has an ability to pay of its own and should be subject to a distinct tax.[2] Obviously, all taxes must in the end fall on somebody, i.e., on natural persons. Corporate profits are part of the income of the shareholders and, in the spirit of the accretion approach to the income tax, should be taxed as part of their income. There is no reason why they should either bear an extra tax or be given preferred treatment.

2. One may, of course, speak of the ability of a corporation to pay a certain tax without going bankrupt or without curtailing its operations. The concept of capacity to pay as used in this sense, however, relates to the economic effects of the tax rather than to ability to pay as used in the context of equity considerations.

Once more, note that this view of the corporation tax rests on the assumption that the tax falls on profits and is not passed on to consumers or wage earners. To the extent that such shifting occurs, the intent of the absolutists to impose an extra tax on corporate source income is thwarted. The tax, in this case, becomes an inferior and arbitrary sales or wages tax, without a rational place in an equitable tax structure.[3]

Other Reasons for Corporation Tax

Even though there is no valid argument for an absolute corporation tax on individual ability-to-pay grounds, a number of other considerations might justify such a tax. However, it would hardly be of the same order of magnitude or structure as the federal profits tax.

Benefit Consideration Corporations may be called upon to pay a benefit tax. Government renders many services which benefit business operations by reducing costs, broadening markets, facilitating financial transactions, and so forth. Most of these services, however, do not accrue solely to corporations but to other forms of business organization as well. The rationale would therefore be for a general tax on business operations rather than for a tax on corporations only. Although there are certain governmental costs incurred in connection with corporations in particular, these costs are a minor factor and hardly justify a tax. The privilege of operation under limited liability is, of course, of tremendous value to corporations, but the institution of limited liability as such is practically costless to society and hence does not justify imposition of a benefit tax. The purpose of benefit taxes is to allocate the cost of public services rendered, not to charge for costless benefits.

To the extent that a benefit tax is appropriate, two further questions arise. One relates to the level at which such a tax should be imposed. Since most public services which accrue as benefits to business are rendered at the state and local levels, it is evident that such a tax would not be primarily a federal matter. The other relates to the appropriate tax base. This will differ with the service rendered, but in most cases it will not be profits. Thus, real property would best reflect the value of fire protection; employment would reflect the input of school expenditures; transportation would reflect road services; and so forth. If a general proxy is to be used, total costs incurred in the state or locality might be the best overall measure, with value added (which includes profits as well as other factor costs) being a second possibility.

Regulatory Objectives A different case for an absolute corporation tax may be made if the tax is viewed as an instrument of control over corporate behavior. The appropriate form of corporation tax then depends on the particular policy objective that is to be accomplished.

3. It is inferior because the implicit rates of sales or payroll taxation will vary arbitrarily with the profit-sales ratio (margin) or the profits-wage bill ratio of particular corporations.

1. The control of monopoly has been traditionally undertaken through regulatory devices, but a tax approach might be used. This, however, would not call for a general tax on profits, which would not be effective in correcting monopolistic behavior. Rather, it would call for a more complex tax, related to the degree of monopolistic restriction.

2. If it were desired to restrict the absolute size of firms or bigness (which is not the same as restricting monopoly or market shares), a tax might again be used for this purpose. Here, a progressive business tax would be called for. The reason for progression, however, would not be ability to pay, as in the individual income tax. Large firms might be owned by small investors and small firms might be owned by wealthy investors. Rather, progression would be used to discriminate against the large firm and curtail what are considered to be undesirable social effects of bigness. The question then arises about whether such a tax should not be on asset size or sales rather than on profits. Even if bigness is held undesirable, it is not a reason for penalizing the profitable big firm in particular.

Although we have no full-fledged experience with such an approach (a progressive corporation tax was recommended by the Roosevelt administration in 1936 but rejected), a limited application is found in the three-rate schedule which applies various lower rates to small firms. This is a subject to which we will return later on.

3. An excess profits tax may be imposed in periods of emergency (such as wars) when direct controls over wages and prices are needed. Wage constraints under such conditions cannot be applied effectively without corresponding profit constraints, and a tax on excess profits is a helpful tool in this connection. The United States imposed such a tax in both world wars as well as during the Korean war. Although sound in principle, the excess profits tax is difficult to administer since excess profits are not readily defined. Such profits may be measured by comparison with a base period, but inequities may result from differences in initial position; or, a standard rate of return may be used, in which case risk differentials can hardly be overlooked, thus posing the difficult problem of what rates are appropriate for what industries.

A different type of situation in which a selective excess profits tax may be called for was created by the recent oil crisis and the removal of price controls on oil, leading to the imposition of a windfall profits tax.

4. As a stimulus to capital formation and growth, it may be desirable to encourage corporate saving and to discourage dividend distribution. This objective may be accomplished by imposing a tax on dividends paid out while exempting earnings retained. Alternatively, it may be held desirable to encourage corporate

distributions and to discourage retentions in order to improve the functioning of the capital market or to increase consumption expenditures. This goal may be achieved by imposing a tax on undistributed profits while exempting profits which are paid out as dividends. Such a tax was imposed in the late thirties with the intention of stimulating consumer spending.

5. Finally, the corporation tax may be used to provide incentives or disincentives to investment, as distinct from corporate savings. Devices like accelerated depreciation and, prior to 1986, the investment tax credit may be used for this purpose, and they may be applied on a cyclical or a secular basis. The effectiveness of such measures will be considered in more detail later on, but it should be noted here that such incentives may also be given directly—i.e., in the form of investment subsidies or grants—rather than as relief under the profits tax.

In all, these considerations suggest that tax instruments may be helpful devices in controlling corporate behavior but in most cases, a form of taxation would be required which differs from the profits tax. (371–375)

(2) ISSUES IN CORPORATE TAX INTEGRATION

The following reading, excerpts from books by Charles McLure and Joseph Pechman, respectively, explores first the policy issues involved in the integration of the corporate and individual income taxes, and second, devices to accomplish that integration.

McLURE, MUST CORPORATE INCOME BE TAXED TWICE?

The Brookings Institution, 1979.

Integration of the corporate and individual income taxes—a policy long favored by some public finance economists, but few others in the United States—has suddenly moved to the forefront in discussions of tax policy. It was raised on two different occasions by the Ford administration, it was expected to be the key proposal in the Carter administration's 1978 tax reform package, and Chairman Al Ullman of the House Committee on Ways and Means proposed it in early 1978.[1]

1. William E. Simon, Testimony in Tax Reform (Administration and Public Witnesses), Hearings before the House Committee on Ways and Means, 94 Cong. 1 sess. (Government Printing Office, 1975), pt. 5, pp. 3846–61, and U.S. Department of the Treasury, Blueprints for Basic Tax Reform (GPO, 1977), especially pp. 68–75 and 194–200; "Tax Reform Option Papers Prepared by Treasury Department, September 2, 1977, for the White House," Bureau of National Affairs, Daily Report for Executives (Special Supplement), DER 196 (October 7, 1977), especially pp. 48–53; and Congressional Record, daily ed., February 2, 1978, pp. H 640–42, and ibid., March 22, 1978, pp. H 2337–38. The Simon proposal, the anticipated Carter proposal, and the Ullman proposal were for relief from double taxation of dividends, while the "proposal" in Blueprints (which strictly speaking was not an official proposal, though it is generally considered one) was for full integration (this distinction is explained below). It should be noted that the present study was basically completed before the expected Carter proposals were leaked to the press in early September 1977.

Yet to most Americans, and perhaps even to most economists, lawyers, accountants, politicians, and public officials, integration is so novel that they would have considerable difficulty in answering such questions as: What is integration? What are its advantages? Why the sudden interest in integration? Not to mention: How is integration achieved? What are the issues of tax policy it involves? Are there any unusual practical problems? This book is primarily devoted to the second group of questions. But for background it will be useful to answer the first three questions briefly and give some indication of the importance of the others, as well as to consider some terminology.[2]

* * *

Pros and Cons of Integration

Those who object to the pattern of taxation resulting from the separate, unintegrated income taxes on income originating in investments in corporate shares argue that the separate taxation of corporate-source income is logically indefensible, that it creates both horizontal and vertical inequities, that it distorts the allocation of investment between the corporate sector and the noncorporate sector, that it encourages corporations to rely too heavily on debt financing and retain too great a share of net corporate income, and that it depresses the nation's rates of capital accumulation and economic growth. Against this rather impressive list of indictments, it is countered that the separate taxation of corporate income *can* be defended on basic tax principles, especially because it adds significantly to the progressivity of the income tax; that the distortions of resource allocation and corporate financial policy have not been firmly documented and would not be very important, in any event; and that integration of the income taxes, because it would encourage distribution of corporate profits, is likely to increase the rates of private capital accumulation and economic growth only if the substantial loss of revenue it would entail were made up in a distinctly regressive way—or not made up at all. Furthermore, say the skeptics, full integration, having never been tried in any country and having been rejected explicitly in at least two, involves considerable practical problems, and even dividend relief, which they view as inequitable, raises many problems, as European experience shows.

Interest in Integration

Interest in integration, which had largely been dormant in the United States since the penalty tax on undistributed profits was repealed in 1939, can be traced to the confluence of several forces.

2. For more extensive discussion of the arguments for and against integration, see chapter 2; Charles E. McLure, Jr., "Integration of the Personal and Corporate Income Taxes: The Missing Element in Recent Tax Reform Proposals," Harvard Law Review, vol. 88 (January 1975), pp. 532–82; and George F. Break and Joseph A. Pechman, Federal Tax Reform: The Impossible Dream? (Brookings Institution, 1975), chapter 4, which was reprinted, with a few changes, in George F. Break and Joseph A. Pechman, "Relationship between the Corporation and Individual Income Taxes," National Tax Journal, vol. 28 (September 1975), pp. 341–50. For further explanation of terms relating to integration, see the glossary of this book.

Perhaps the most visible of these has been the much-discussed capital shortage.[12] Businessmen (and some economists) have argued that the tax system in general, and the double taxation of corporate dividends in particular, is responsible for what they take to be an undesirable shortfall in capital formation. Relief from double taxation of dividends, they argue, would go far in relieving the capital shortage.

A second important reason for the recent American interest in integration is the increased tendency for other developed countries to provide at least partial dividend relief.[14] In 1965 France began to allow shareholders credit for half the corporate tax attributable to dividends, and in 1973 the United Kingdom returned to a system of partial relief from double taxation of dividends after using a classical system from 1965 to 1973. Finally, on January 1, 1977, West Germany, which since 1953 had applied a lower rate of tax to dividends than to retentions, became the first member of the European Community to provide complete relief from the double taxation of dividends.* And of perhaps

12. This is not the place to attempt to judge whether the "capital shortage" is real or imaginary (or indeed what the term is intended to mean). Among attempts to do so are: Leonall C. Andersen, "Is There a Capital Shortage: Theory and Recent Empirical Evidence," Journal of Finance, vol. 31 (May 1976), pp. 257–68; Barry Bosworth, James S. Duesenberry, and Andrew S. Carron, Capital Needs in the Seventies (Brookings Institution, 1975); Allen Sinai and Roger E. Brinner, The Capital Shortage: Near–Term Outlook and Long–Term Prospects (Lexington, Mass.: Data Resources, Inc., 1975); Paul Wachtel, Arnold Sametz, and Harry Shuford, "Capital Shortages: Myth or Reality?" Journal of Finance, vol. 31 (May 1976), pp. 269–85; and New York Stock Exchange, The Capital Needs and Savings Potential of the U.S. Economy: Projections Through 1985 (New York Stock Exchange, 1974). See also Joint Committee on Taxation, Tax Policy and Capital Formation, prepared for the Task Force on Capital Formation of the House Committee on Ways and Means by the Staff of the Joint Committee on Taxation (GPO, 1977); and Eli Shapiro and William L. White, eds., Capital for Productivity and Jobs (Prentice–Hall, 1977).

14. Much of the descriptive information on foreign systems has appeared in International Bureau of Fiscal Documentation, European Taxation (Amsterdam), various issues, and in International Fiscal Association, Cahiers de Droit Fiscal International (Rotterdam), various issues. In addition, for details of integration schemes used in other countries, see Organization for Economic Co-operation and Development, Company Tax Systems in OECD Member Countries (Paris: OECD, 1973); Richard M. Hammer, "The Taxation of Income from Corporate Shareholders: Review of Present Systems in Canada, France, Germany, Japan and the U.K.," National Tax Journal, vol. 28 (September 1975), pp. 315–34; and Hugh J. Ault, "Germany: The New Corporation Tax System," Intertax: European Tax Review (August 1976), pp. 262–75. These are reviewed in chapter 3.

* [Ed.: The two-rate or "split-rate" system is not currently employed as the sole method of integration in any major industrialized country. As discussed below, however, Germany has employed a split-rate system in conjunction with its imputation system.

The imputation system is utilized, for example, in France, The United Kingdom, Belgium, Ireland and Canada, with each system producing variations on the method. Thus, France gives the shareholder a credit for 50% of the dividend, which credit is grossed-up. The United Kingdom similarly gives a credit of approximately 50%. Canada provides a $33\frac{1}{3}\%$ credit, again with the credit being grossed-up. Germany is the only industrialized country which completely integrates the corporate and individual taxes with respect to distributed dividends. Germany also employs a split-rate system in connection with its imputation system. Thus, a rate of 56% is imposed on undistributed corporate profits, which is reduced to 36% for dividend distributions. The 36% rate tax is then credited by the shareholder, with the amount of the credit being included in income (grossed-up). See Ault and Rädler, The German Corporation Tax Reform Law 1977 (1976).]

even greater ultimate importance, in its 1975 proposal for a directive on the harmonization of company income taxes, the Commission of the European Communities suggested that all nine member countries should eventually provide relief for from 45 to 55 percent of the double taxation of dividends.[15] This suggestion was not approved by the European Parliament.[16]

* * *

Policy Issues in Integration

The three most obvious issues in the debate over integration are whether or not to have some kind of integration; if so, whether it should involve all corporate income or only distributed income; and whether integration or dividend relief should be complete or only partial. But positions on these basic issues depend crucially on how less obvious questions are resolved.

First, corporations, like other business taxpayers, benefit from an array of tax preferences that reduces the effective rate of taxation of corporate economic income—to an average rate of only about 36 to 38 percent. The proper treatment of tax preferences, usually overlooked in elementary discussions of integration and dividend relief, permeates any detailed discussion of dividend relief, and it can do so for integration, too, if a decision is not made at an early stage to eliminate all preferences from the tax code. Among the policy questions that must be settled are whether tax preferences should be eliminated so far as corporate-source income is concerned, passed through to shareholders on all corporate-source income, or passed through only on income that is not distributed; and, beyond that, whether exclusion preferences (such as interest on municipal bonds) and deductible preferences (such as the excess of accelerated depreciation over economic depreciation) should be treated differently from creditable preferences (such as the investment tax credit). Additional questions that must be addressed, especially in the case of dividend relief, include whether preference income is to be assumed to be paid out, or "stacked," first (so that dividends are attributed initially to tax-preferred income) or last (so that dividends are attributed initially to fully taxed income) or to be split proportionately between dividends and retentions. Whereas economic reasoning may point to certain answers to some of these questions, administrative realities may point elsewhere.

* * * [D]ecisions on the treatment of preferences (especially rules for stacking and washout) involve serious questions of economic policy and not mere technical details. Commercial banks and regulated public utilities, for example, would be hit hard by a system that washed

The classical one-rate system is in effect, for example, in the Netherlands, Switzerland and the United States.]

15. Commission of the European Communities, "Proposal for a Council Directive Concerning the Harmonization of Systems of Company Taxation and of Withholding Taxes on Dividends," Bulletin of the European Communities, Supplement 10/75: Harmonization of Systems of Company Taxation (Luxembourg: Office for Official Publications of the European Communities, 1975), article 3.

16. Intertax (January 1978), p. 1.

out tax preferences (especially if the foreign tax credit were treated as a preference), even if preference income were stacked last. Considerations such as this may help to explain the adoption of liberal stacking and transition rules in Europe.

Second, some 20 to 25 percent of all corporate stock is held by tax-exempt organizations, including pension funds, foundations, and educational and religious organizations.[18] Should the burden of the corporate income tax be removed from these otherwise tax-exempt organizations if the income taxes are integrated? The revenue consequences of doing so is enormous (for example, some $12 billion [1976 dollars] under total integration).[19]

Third, any scheme involving integration of the corporation and personal income taxes will have important implications for other components of the income tax system. In some cases the relation will be direct * * *. In other instances the tie will be less direct, but still very strong; full integration, for example, may be unacceptable without a withholding tax levied at the corporate level at a rate that is coordinated with the top marginal rate under the personal income tax. Furthermore, whether any form of integration is politically acceptable will depend on the tax reforms that accompany it. Dividend relief, for example, would substantially reduce the distributional progressivity of the tax system and would be acceptable among liberals only if packaged with a large reduction of the tax preferences currently enjoyed by high-income households; total integration, by comparison, because it would reach retained earnings on a current basis, might be acceptable to this group even if accompanied by less extensive tax reform.

Fourth, any form of integration involves incredibly complicated questions about the proper taxation of international flows of corporate earnings. How, for example, should dividends flowing between two countries that provide dividend relief be taxed? Should the relief be granted by the source country or the residence country? Does it matter whether direct or portfolio investment is involved? What if the two countries employ different means of providing dividend relief? What if only one country allows dividend relief and the other has a classical system? A fully integrated system? These basic questions must be settled—and the answers agreed upon by the countries—before it is possible to proceed to technical problems of implementation.

* * *

International Considerations

One of the few subjects commonly encountered by tax economists that is more complicated than integration is the tax treatment of income flowing across international boundaries; unfortunately the

18. This estimate is based on figures for the receipt of dividends contained in Marshall E. Blume, Jean Crockett, and Irwin Friend, "Stockownership in the United States: Characteristics and Trends," Survey of Current Business, vol. 54 (November 1974), pp. 16–40.

19. See Simon, Tax Reform, pp. 3856–57, and Break and Pechman, Federal Tax Reform: The Impossible Dream? p. 103.

proper tax treatment of such income poses major problems for either integration or dividend relief. Clearly, international tax relations are simplest if all countries employ classical systems. But the United States' most important trading partners use tax systems that provide at least partial relief from the double taxation of dividends; therefore, it may become increasingly difficult to negotiate tax treaties if the United States retains an unintegrated classical system. Yet international considerations, as well as administrative difficulties, tend to militate against the adoption of full integration. Given the present interpretation of "reciprocity" in double taxation conventions, the difficulty of not allowing the benefits of integration to foreign shareholders in U.S. firms might dictate against the use of the dividend-paid deduction method of dividend relief, which many observers find to be the most natural and most easily administered approach if appraised only in terms of its domestic attributes. Thus the very choice between the shareholder credit approach and the dividend-paid deduction might be in large part predetermined by U.S. treaty obligations and foreign practices. Unless the United States could persuade other major countries to change from the shareholder credit approach to the dividend-paid deduction (or the equivalent split-rate system), use of the second approach might be effectively foreclosed.

J. PECHMAN, FEDERAL TAX POLICY

The Brookings Institution (Fifth ed. 1987).

Taxation of corporate earnings continues to be controversial. Some people regard taxation of total profits under the corporation tax and of distributed profits under the individual income tax as inequitable. Others believe that taxation of the corporation as a separate entity is justified. Whether something needs to be done depends on an evaluation of the economic issues discussed earlier and on the effect of the proposed changes on the distribution of tax burdens. The problem is tricky and there is no easy solution.

The Additional Burden on Dividends

On the assumption that all, or a significant portion, of the corporation tax rests on the stockholder, the effect of the tax is to impose the heaviest burden on dividends received by persons in the lowest income classes. This can be seen by examining the illustrative calculations in table 5–9, which show the total and additional tax burden on stockholders who receive $66 of dividends under present tax rates. Given the present rate of 34 percent, the corporation income before tax from which the $66 of dividends were paid must have amounted to $100. If this $100 had been subject to individual income tax rates only, the tax on these dividends would go from zero at the bottom of the income scale to 33 percent in the zone where the benefit of the first bracket rate and the exemption are phased out (see chapter 4) and 28 percent at the top. With the corporation tax, the combined individual and corporation income tax increases from $34 for those subject to a zero rate to $55.78

Table 5–9. Additional Burden of the Corporation Income Tax on $100 of Corporation Income [a]

Dollars

Marginal individual income tax rate (percent) (1)	*Corporate income before tax* (2)	*Corporation tax at 34 percent* (3)	*Dividends received by stockholders* (4)	*Stockholder's individual income tax* (5)	*Total tax burden* (6)	*Additional burden of the corporation tax* (7)
0	100	34	66	0	34.00	34.00
10	100	34	66	6.60	40.60	30.60
20	100	34	66	13.20	47.20	27.20
28	100	34	66	18.48	52.48	24.48
33	100	34	66	21.78	55.78	22.78
40	100	34	66	26.40	60.40	20.40
50	100	34	66	33.00	67.00	17.00

Column 3 = 0.34 × column 2.
Column 4 = column 2 − column 3.
Column 5 = column 4 × column 1.
Column 6 = column 3 + column 5.
Column 7 = column 6 − column 1 × column 2.
a. Assumes that corporation income after tax is devoted entirely to the payment of dividend.

for those subject to the 33 percent rate and $52.48 for those subject to the 28 percent rate (table 5–9, column 6).

However, the *additional* burden resulting from the corporation tax falls as income rises. For example, the taxpayer subject to a zero individual rate would have paid no tax on the $66 of dividends; the additional corporation income tax burden in this case is the full $34 tax. By contrast, a taxpayer subject to the 28 percent rate pays an individual income tax of $18.48 on the dividend, and the total tax burden on the original $100 of corporate earnings is $52.48. But since the taxpayer would have to pay $28.00 under the individual income tax in any case, the additional burden is only $24.48. For the taxpayer subject to the 33 percent rate, the additional burden is $22.78 (table 5–9, column 7).

One test of an equitable method of moderating or eliminating the additional tax burden on dividends is to ask whether the method removes a uniform percentage of the additional burden shown in table 5–9. If the percentage removed is the same for dividend recipients in every individual income tax bracket, the method deals evenly at all levels. Deviations from a constant percentage indicate the dividend recipients who are favored or penalized by the method.

A second test is whether the method increases or reduces the progressivity of the tax system as a whole. Since corporate ownership is heavily concentrated in the high income classes * * *, moderation or reduction of the additional tax burden on dividends alone would reduce progressivity, unless the change were accompanied by rate increases or revisions in the individual income tax base to prevent large tax cuts for the minority of taxpayers who have large stockholdings.

Methods of Integration

Five methods of integrating the corporation and individual income taxes have been used at various times in different countries: (1) a dividend-received credit for individuals; (2) a deduction for dividends paid by the corporation in computing the corporation income tax; (3) a "split-rate" corporation income tax, which applies a higher tax rate to undistributed than to distributed corporate earnings; (4) a method that considers all or a portion of the corporation income tax to be withholding on dividends at the source; and (5) an exclusion of all or a portion of the dividends received from the individual income tax base. These methods would only partially integrate the corporation and individual income taxes because the relief would be given only to distributed earnings. A sixth method would be to treat all corporations like partnerships and tax their income to the stockholders whether distributed or not. This is the only method that would fully integrate the corporation and individual income taxes on both distributed and undistributed corporate earnings and would rely entirely on the individual income tax for the taxation of corporate profits. Of the various methods, the second, third, fourth, and sixth would remove the same proportion of the additional burden of the corporation tax at all individual income levels. All the methods would make the federal tax system less progressive without offsetting changes. It is assumed that there is no shifting of the corporation income tax.

THE DIVIDEND–RECEIVED CREDIT. Under this method, dividend recipients are allowed to deduct a percentage of their dividends as a credit against their individual income tax. Between 1954 and 1963, U.S. taxpayers were allowed a credit of 4 percent for dividends after a $50 exclusion ($100 for joint returns).

Although the credit grants the same relief on a dollar of dividends at all income levels, it removes an increasing proportion of the additional burden of the corporation tax as incomes rise. For those subject to a zero rate, the credit is worthless. For a taxpayer subject to a 10 percent rate, the 4 percent credit would remove 8.6 percent of the additional burden, and for a taxpayer subject to the maximum 33 percent rate, the credit would remove 11.6 percent (table 5–10). This regressive pattern of relief led to its repeal.

THE DIVIDEND–PAID DEDUCTION. This is the simplest method of dealing with the problem; it was used in the United States in 1936 and 1937 as a basis for a surtax on corporate earnings. Corporations deduct from their taxable income all or a portion of the dividends they pay out, and the corporation tax applies to the remainder. Table 5–11 shows the relief that would be granted under this method if the corporation were allowed a deduction of 25 percent of dividends paid. As shown in column 6, the relief would be 17.9 percent of the additional tax imposed by the corporation income tax at all income levels.

Table 5–10. Portion of the Additional Burden of the Corporation Income Tax Removed by the 4 Percent Dividend–Received Credit

Marginal individual income tax rate (percent) (1)	*Additional burden resulting from corporation tax (dollars)* (2)	*Dividend-received credit (dollars)* (3)	*Percentage of additional burden removed by the dividend credit* (4)
0	34.00	a	a
10	30.60	2.64	8.6
20	27.20	2.64	9.7
28	24.48	2.64	10.8
33	22.78	2.64	11.6
40	20.40	2.64	12.9
50	17.00	2.64	15.5

Column 2 = column 7 of table 5–9.

Column 3 = 4 percent of $66.

Column 4 = column 3 – column 2.

a. The credit has no value for those subject to a zero tax rate.

Table 5–11. Portion of the Additional Burden of the Corporation Income Tax Removed by the Dividend–Paid Deduction

Assuming the corporation deducts 25 percent of dividends paid

		Tax benefit of dividend-paid deduction (dollars)			
Marginal individual income tax rate (percent) (1)	*Additional burden resulting from corporation tax (dollars)* (2)	*Reduced corporation tax (paid to stockholders as additional dividends)* (3)	*Tax on additional dividends* (4)	*Net benefit* (5)	*Percentage of additional burden removed by the dividend-paid deduction* (6)
0	34.00	6.09	0	6.09	17.9
10	30.60	6.09	0.61	5.48	17.9
20	27.20	6.09	1.22	4.87	17.9
28	24.48	6.09	1.71	4.38	17.9
33	22.78	6.09	2.01	4.08	17.9
40	20.40	6.09	2.44	3.65	17.9
50	17.00	6.09	3.05	3.04	17.9

Column 2 = column 7 of table 5–9.

Column 3 = amount of additional dividends corporations could pay out with a 25 percent dividend-paid deduction.

Column 4 = column 1 × column 3.

Column 5 = column 3 – column 4.

Column 6 = column 5 – column 2.

Aside from granting the same proportionate relief at all income levels, the dividend-paid credit has the merit of treating dividends like interest. (If a full deduction were allowed, the treatment would be identical.) This would increase the attractiveness of equity financing by corporations.

The surtax on undistributed profits raised a storm of protest when it was used briefly in the United States during the 1930s. Corporations complained that by encouraging payouts of earnings it reduced their ability to save and invest at a time when the market for corporate equities was almost dried up. The method is also criticized on the ground that it discourages internal financing by corporations and might reduce total saving and investment. On the other hand, some believe it unwise to permit corporations to avoid the capital markets for financing their investment programs. Forcing them "to stand the test of the marketplace" might exercise a desirable restraint on bigness and also give investors more control over the disposition of their funds.

An alternative method of equalizing the treatment of dividends and interest would be to eliminate the deduction for interest in computing the taxable income of corporations. Since the base of the tax would be raised, the tax rate could be reduced substantially. (At 1988 income and borrowing levels, the 34 percent rate could be reduced by over half.) Such a plan has merit if a separate tax on corporate capital—whether financed by debt or equity capital—is justified. Such a tax has not been seriously considered in the United States because it would drastically alter the distribution of the corporation tax burden among firms and industries. In general, manufacturing corporations, which rely mainly on equity capital, would benefit; utilities and transportation and financial companies, which rely heavily on borrowed capital, would pay much higher taxes.

THE SPLIT-RATE CORPORATION INCOME TAX. A number of countries tax undistributed earnings at a higher rate than distributed earnings. This split-rate plan is similar in effect to a deduction for dividends paid. For example, a 50–25 percent split rate would be equivalent to a 50 percent tax on total corporate earnings with a deduction of 50 percent for dividends paid. The percentages actually used by various countries differ greatly, reflecting the absence of accepted criteria for establishing the split rates. The split-rate system is used in Austria, Japan, Norway, and other countries.

THE IMPUTATION METHOD. Under this method, all or a portion of the individual income tax is regarded as having been paid at the source (through the corporation tax). For example, if 10 percent of the dividend were regarded as having been withheld, a shareholder receiving a $66 dividend would "gross up" the dividend by adding $6.60 (0.10 × 66) to taxable income and then take the $6.60 as a credit against tax. In this illustration, the portion of the additional burden of the corporation income tax removed is 19.4 percent at all income levels (table 5–12). Thus, with a corporate rate of 34 percent, a dividend

Table 5–12. Portion of the Additional Burden of the Corporation Income Tax Removed by the Imputation Method

Assuming 10 percent of dividends received regarded as withheld

		Withholding credit (dollars)			
Marginal individual income tax rate (percent) (1)	*Additional burden resulting from corporation tax (dollars) (2)*	*Amount withheld at source (3)*	*Tax on amount withheld (4)*	*Net credit (5)*	*Percentage of additional burden removed by the dividend credit (6)*
0	34.00	6.60	0	6.60	19.4
10	30.60	6.60	0.66	5.94	19.4
20	27.20	6.60	1.32	5.28	19.4
28	24.48	6.60	1.85	4.75	19.4
33	22.78	6.60	2.18	4.42	19.4
40	20.40	6.60	2.64	3.96	19.4
50	17.00	6.60	3.30	3.30	19.4

Column 2 = column 7 of table 5–9.
Column 3 = 10 percent of $66.
Column 4 = column 1 × column 3.
Column 5 = column 3 − column 4.
Column 6 = column 5 − column 2.

gross-up of 10 percent at the individual level is somewhat more generous than a 25 percent dividend deduction at the corporate level (compare column 6 of tables 5–11 and 5–12).

The imputation method achieves the same result as the dividend-paid deduction for corporations but is likely to discourage corporate saving somewhat less. This advantage frequently makes the imputation method more attractive, even though it is more difficult to understand and would also complicate the individual income tax return. Variants of the imputation method are used in a number of countries, including the United Kingdom, France, Italy, and West Germany.

THE DIVIDEND EXCLUSION. This method permits individual income taxpayers to exclude all or a portion of their dividends from taxable income. In the United States, between 1964 and 1986 there was an individual exclusion of $100 ($200 on joint returns), which was a vestige of the compromise adopted when the 4 percent dividend credit was repealed. The deduction was eliminated beginning in 1987, when the tax base was broadened to provide revenue for rate reductions. Like the dividend-received credit, the exclusion grants an increasing amount of relief on a dollar of dividends as incomes rise. Accordingly, it cannot remove the same proportion of the additional tax burden at all levels of income.

THE PARTNERSHIP METHOD, OR FULL INTEGRATION. The most far-reaching solution is to regard the income of corporations as belonging to their stockholders in the year in which it is earned, regardless of whether the earnings are distributed. The corporation income tax as such would be abolished, but a tax would be retained at the corporate level as a withholding device for the individual income tax. Stockholders would pay individual income tax on their prorated share of the earnings of corporations in which they held stock and would receive credit for the amount of tax withheld at the source, just as in the case of wages and salaries.

This method would automatically apply the correct individual income tax rates to all corporate earnings and thus equalize the tax rates on corporate and noncorporate earnings. It would also be less regressive and less costly than partial integration for dividends alone, because retained as well as distributed corporate earnings would be subject to the individual income tax.

A major drawback of the plan is that, unless the withholding rate was set at a high level, some stockholders would not have funds to pay tax on earnings they did not receive. This would force them to liquidate security holdings or apply pressure on corporations to distribute a much larger portion of their retained earnings. In the former case, stock ownership among people with modest means would be discouraged; in the latter, corporate saving would be reduced.

Treatment approximating this method is available under present law for closely held corporations with no more than thirty-five shareholders. These corporations operate much like partnerships and can arrange to distribute enough earnings to the partners to avoid forced liquidations. The decision to be treated like a partnership for tax purposes is made only if it is advantageous to the shareholders. Experts agree that it would not be practical to extend the partnership method to large, publicly held corporations with complex capital structures, frequent changes in ownership, and thousands or millions of stockholders.

A procedure that would approximate the effect of the partnership method and avoid its liquidity problems would be to permit corporations to allocate all or a portion of their undistributed earnings to their shareholders. The corporation income tax would be converted to a withholding tax for the individual income tax, and the corporate rate would be set at the top-bracket individual income tax rate. Shareholders would include the allocated dividends as well as cash dividends in their taxable income and would deduct the amount of tax withheld as a credit against their income tax. The only difference between this procedure and the original partnership method is that the allocation of earnings by corporations to shareholders would not be mandatory. But since shareholders would be denied immediate credit for the withheld tax, the pressure on corporate management to allocate all undistributed earnings would probably be irresistible. The procedure, which was originally proposed by a Canadian Royal Commission in 1966, has merit (if a separate corporation tax is considered inappropriate), but it has not been seriously considered anywhere.

Practical Problems. Integration of the corporation and individual income taxes raises a number of difficult issues. First, it would be inappropriate to assume that all corporate earnings were subject to a 34 percent rate in crediting individuals with the amount of tax paid on their corporate earnings. For one thing, all corporations are taxed at reduced rates on the first $75,000 of earnings. For another, special provisions (such as accelerated depreciation, the deduction for intangible drilling and development costs, deferral of tax on foreign income, and so on) reduce the effective rate of the corporation tax. If an attempt were made to distinguish such sources of earnings from taxable sources in designing the integration scheme, the mechanics would be extremely complicated. Moreover, the objectives of the special provisions would be thwarted by making such distinctions and the groups affected would object strongly. On the other hand, if distinctions are not made, relief from the corporate tax would be provided when in fact the tax was not paid.

Second, it would be difficult to decide how to treat foreign shareholders and tax-exempt organizations under an integration plan. The corporation income tax now applies to the earnings of the entire corporation, including those that would be allocated to foreign shareholders and tax-exempt organizations under an integration plan. If foreign shareholders and tax-exempt organizations were not eligible for refunds, the cost of the plan would be greatly reduced.

Third, the partial integration schemes—imputation or the split-rate integration schemes, particularly the latter—would have the effect of encouraging larger dividend payouts by corporations. The retained earnings of corporations are a large source of saving in the United States; many would regard it unwise to encourage a reduction in this source of saving. A reduction in the corporation income tax rate would be simpler than partial integration and might do less damage to saving and investment.

Fourth, full integration through the partnership method is impractical for a number of reasons. An adjustment of the basis of all shareholdings for the amount of corporate tax withheld would be required so that individuals would be able to calculate capital gains and losses. It would be virtually impossible to allocate losses satisfactorily among part-year and full-year shareholders and to attribute adjustment of tax through audits or amended returns to the right shareholders. Furthermore, many, if not most, taxpayers would resent paying full tax on income they did not receive.

ILLUSTRATIVE MATERIAL

A. STATUS OF INTEGRATION IN THE UNITED STATES

After receiving some governmental attention during the mid–1970's, see supra, page 291, note 1, interest in integration of the corporate and personal income taxes and/or dividend relief diminished after 1978 as tax policy attention turned to matters of rate reductions, dealing with the effect of inflation in constructing capital cost recovery provisions, and finally, in the mid–1980's, to broadening the tax base. In the Tax Reform Act of 1986 Congress adopted several provisions, e.g., repealing the so-called *General Utilities* rule which previously had permitted corporations to distribute appreciated property to their shareholders without recognition of corporate level gain, which strengthened the double taxation system. When the double taxation system was threatened by a rapid proliferation of publicly traded limited partnerships, portending a move by business to "self-help" integration, Congress intervened in 1987 by enacting section 7704, discussed supra, page 45, which taxes many publicly traded limited partnerships as corporations.

This declining interest in integration also coincided with a growing appreciation of the extraordinarily complex and difficult technical issues which would be entailed in implementing any form of integration system. See McLure, A Status Report on Tax Integration in the United States, 31 Nat'l Tax J. 313 (1978). Moreover, it became apparent that various components of the political process had strongly differing interests in the extent and characteristics of any form of integration that might be adopted. See McClure and Surrey, Integration of Income Taxes: Issues For Debate, 55 Harv.Bus.Rev. 169 (Sept.–Oct. 1977). Academic interest in the issue, has continued and the Treasury Department is actively studying the matter.

How does the issue of who economically bears the burden of the corporate tax relate to the desirability of integration? Would integration be less appropriate if the burden is shifted primarily to workers or consumers than it would be if the burden is borne primarily by shareholders?

Among the arguments made in favor of integration is that the current double taxation system distorts the corporation's choice as to whether to fund new investment by issuing shares to raise equity capital or by borrowing. This problem was addressed by Professor William Andrews, the Reporter for the American Law Institute, Federal Income Tax Project, Subchapter C: Proposals on Corporate Acquisitions and Dispositions (1980), in his Study on Distributions (1980), published with the adopted ALI proposals. Professor Andrews adopted a different approach to the proper relationship between the corporate and individual tax systems as reflected in the following excerpt:

"Most of the troubles with existing law arise from two main uncompensated biases: 1) the bias against new equity investment, and 2) the bias in favor of nondividend distributions. The main proposals in this Study are to alleviate those biases by providing relief for the former and imposing a compensatory excise on the latter. If these proposals were adopted, all distributions would be subjected to more nearly comparable tax burdens, and contributions to corporate equity (negative distributions) would attract a comparable benefit (negative burden). In such a system, the difficult definitional problems with which present law struggles would be eliminated or reduced substantially in significance.

"While the proposals complement one another in important ways, an effort has been made to analyze and present them separately, as follows:

"1) *Relief for new equity.* Reporter's Proposal R1 is to relieve the bias against new equity by provision of a deduction based on newly contributed equity capital. The main proposal is for a corporate dividends-paid deduction, limited to a specified rate on the amount of net newly contributed equity capital, akin to the interest deduction that would have resulted from a debt investment. Adoption of this proposal would move a long way toward eliminating problems of differentiation between debt and equity, since it would attach comparable tax consequences to any investment of outside funds.

"The main problem in implementing this proposal is defining net newly contributed investment in a manner that will exclude mere refinancing of accumulated earnings or previously contributed capital. This problem would be minimized if an appropriate tax burden were imposed generally on nondividend distributions.

"2) *Nondividend distributions.* Reporter's Proposal R2 would deal with the present bias in favor of nondividend distributions by imposing some increased tax on them. One possibility would be to impute redemption distributions pro rata to continuing shareholders, as if they had received a dividend and used it to buy out redeeming shareholders. The proposal offered is simply to impose a flat-rate, compensatory excise on nondividend distributions, to be withheld and paid over to the government by the distributing corporation.

"Adoption of this proposal would take much of the pressure off questions of dividend equivalence, with which present law struggles, and make it possible to be much more lenient about stock dividends and spin-offs, and the bailout opportunities they generate under existing law.

"3) *Intercorporate investments and distributions.* A corporation can now purchase dividend-paying stock of another corporation and enjoy 85 or 100 percent exemption from corporate income tax on the dividends received from this investment. A purchase of shares from noncorporate shareholders represents an indirect way of distributing funds out of corporate solution, and the intercorporate dividend deduction operates to contract the corporate income tax base accordingly, but all without any distribution, as such, by either corporation. Reporter's Proposal R3 would distinguish between direct and mere portfolio investment. In the case of portfolio investment, the dividend-received deduction and cognate provisions would be made inapplicable; with respect to direct investment those provisions would continue in effect, but purchases of shares would be treated as nondividend distributions subject to the compensatory excise in Reporter's Proposal R2." (353–355)

Note how the ALI Subchapter C Study Reporter's proposals deal with the transition problem that would arise if an integration proposal were adopted. Assuming that the shareholders bear some substantial portion of the corporate tax and that such tax burden is capitalized into, i.e., depresses, the value of corporate stock and hence the price at which the current owners purchased the stock, adoption of full integration or dividend relief would give rise to a windfall economic gain for those shareholders. By limiting relief to the portion of the yield on new equity which approximates interest, the Reporter's approach eliminates this problem. How does the proposal for a corporate level excise tax on nondividend distributions increase the fairness or the efficiency of taxation of corporate income? It appears that the perceived problem is that a greater price can be obtained for shares sold back to the corporation than for shares sold to another investor because the other investor could be expected to discount the value of the shares to an amount below the value of a proportionate amount of the corporation's assets to reflect the double taxation of a flow of dividends from those assets. Are the

ALI Reporter's proposals intended to solve the same problems as are perceived by those who favor integration?

B. REFERENCES

Andrews, Tax Neutrality Between Equity Capital and Debt, 30 Wayne L.Rev. 1057 (1984); McClure, Comments on "Tax Neutrality Between Equity Capital and Debt," 30 Wayne L.Rev. 1073 (1984); Warren, The Relation and Integration of Individual and Corporate Income Taxes, 94 Harv.L.Rev. 719 (1981); Auerbach, Tax Integration and the "New View" of the Corporate Tax, a 1980's Perspective, Proceedings of the 74th Annual Conf. on Taxation 21 (1981); Beghe, The American Law Institute Subchapter C Study: Acquisitions and Distributions, 33 Tax Lawyer 743 (1980); Ault, International Issues in Corporate Tax Integration, 10 Law and Policy in Internat'l Bus. 461 (1977); Comm. on Corporations of the Tax Section of the New York Bar Association, Report on the Integration of Corporate and Individual Income Taxes, 31 Tax Law. 37 (1977); Gabinet & Coffey, The Implications of the Economic Income Concept of Income for Corporation–Shareholder Income Tax Systems, 27 Case W.Res.L.Rev. 895 (1977); Gourevitch, Corporate Tax Integration: The European Experience, 31 Tax. Law. 65 (1977); NTA–TIA Symposium, The Taxation of Income From Corporate Shareholdings, 28 Nat'l Tax J. 255–381 (1975).

CHAPTER 8

IDENTIFYING TAXABLE CORPORATE ENTITIES

SECTION 1. INTRODUCTION

Under current law, corporate income is taxed at a maximum rate of 34 percent. On the other hand, the maximum individual tax rate is 28 percent. A maximum corporate tax rate higher than the maximum individual tax rate, coupled with the double taxation of corporate earnings, serves as a disincentive to organizing businesses in the corporate form unless nontax factors strongly indicate that the corporate form is necessary or desirable.

Prior to the 1986 Act, the maximum individual rate exceeded the maximum corporate rate. In addition, although corporate earnings were taxed twice, if the distribution of earnings was delayed until liquidation of the corporation or of the shareholder's entire interest in the corporation, the shareholder level tax was incurred at the preferential rates which applied to long term capital gains. These factors, coupled with the pre–1987 statutory provisions which permitted corporations to distribute appreciated property to shareholders without recognizing a corporate level taxable gain on the appreciation, served as a strong tax inducement to incorporate a profitable business venture that was going to accumulate and reinvest earnings, even if no nontax factors indicated that incorporation was preferable to the partnership or sole proprietorship form. Conversely, if the venture was expected to produce a tax loss, for example a business experiencing tax losses in its early years in part because of tax preferences, it was advantageous to be taxed as a partnership or sole proprietorship, even though the use of the corporate form would have been desirable to accomplish some nontax objective.

Prior to 1987, in the case of a profitable business there was a tax incentive for individuals to shift income to a corporation (or obtain other tax benefits available only in corporate form). On the other hand, there was an incentive to keep a loss business in non-corporate form until it began showing a profit. These objectives gave rise to controversies regarding whether income should be taxed to the corporation or directly to its owners. The materials in this chapter examine the resolution of this issue in several contexts. Note, however, that under the current rate structure in many instances the positions of the government and the taxpayer have been reversed, i.e., the government will seek to tax income at the corporate rather than the individual rate; individual taxpayers may have the opposite objective.

SECTION 2. WHAT IS A "CORPORATION" UNDER THE INCOME TAX?

INTERNAL REVENUE CODE: Section 7701(a)(3); 7704.

REGULATIONS: Sections 301.7701–1, –2(a) – (e), –4(b).

In general, any business organized under the incorporation statute of a state will be treated as a corporation for federal income tax purposes. But some classification problems can arise. For example, can a group of professionals—lawyers, doctors, architects, etc.—"incorporate" and obtain the benefits of corporate status for federal income tax purposes? If so, should they so incorporate—are there burdens as well as benefits?

The question whether a business organization constitutes a partnership or a corporation has been considered, supra, page 20. The status of an organization as a "trust" or a "corporation" was involved in *Morrissey,* supra, page 22, and the following materials discuss subsequent developments in the classification issues where a trust entity is involved.

ILLUSTRATIVE MATERIAL

A. PROFESSIONAL CORPORATIONS AND ASSOCIATIONS

After the Commissioner's successful assertion of corporate status in *Morrissey,* and some subsequent cases, some taxpayers began to seek corporate treatment for their organizations. Doctors and other professionals, who were prevented by state law from incorporating and thus could not obtain the benefits of qualified pension and profit-sharing plans, formed associations intended to qualify as "corporations" under the tests in the *Morrissey* case. These entities were sustained as corporations for tax purposes. See, e.g., United States v. Kintner, 216 F.2d 418 (9th Cir.1954). In *Kintner,* the taxpayer, along with other doctors with whom he was associated in a medical partnership, formed an unincorporated association for the practice of medicine and established a pension plan. The articles of association attempted to give the organization the "attributes of a corporation" as defined in *Morrissey.* Applying the *Morrissey* tests, the District Court found the association taxable as a corporation. The Court of Appeals affirmed, rejecting the Government's contention that because of a state law prohibition against the practice of medicine by a corporation, the organization could not be classified as an association taxable as a corporation for federal tax purposes. The Internal Revenue Service refused to follow *Kintner* and in November, 1960 issued Regulations effective in 1961 stating a series of more refined tests of "corporateness" based on the *Morrissey* decision, see supra, page 27. Regulations, section 301.7701–2, often are referred to as the *Kintner* regulations.

Since the difficulties in qualifying as a corporation under the *Kintner* Regulations resulted from the application of certain provisions of state law, professionals desiring to obtain corporate status to qualify for federal income tax benefits were soon able to convince state legislatures to change the state law consequences applicable to their organizations. See, e.g., Mass.Gen.Laws ch. 156A (1970); Ohio Rev.Code ch. 1785 (1964).

In 1965, the Internal Revenue Service promulgated new Regulations which made it impossible for professional corporations to be taxed as corporations. These regulations, however, uniformly were held invalid. See, e.g., Empey v. United States, 406 F.2d 157 (10th Cir.1969); O'Neill v. United States, 410 F.2d 888 (6th Cir.1969); Kurzner v. United States, 413 F.2d 97 (5th Cir.1969). The Service then issued Rev.Rul. 70–101, 1970–1 Cum.Bull. 278, stating that it "generally will treat organizations of doctors, lawyers, and other professional people organized under state professional association arts as corporations for tax purposes."

While the battle over corporate status for professional corporations was thus over, some problems remained in adapting the day-to-day operations of a professional practice to the corporate form. See Roubik v. Commissioner, 53 T.C. 365 (1969) (though professional service organization qualified as a "corporation", the individual doctors were taxed on the income since, as a factual matter, the business was not "actually *carried on* by the incorporated organization"). See also the discussion of the applicability of section 482 to single shareholder corporations, infra, page 333.

Ironically, the issue which generated the controversy over professional service corporations in the first place—the efforts of professionals to obtain the benefits of corporate pension plans—has become moot. Over the years the disparity between the treatment of qualified pension plans for corporations, on the one hand, and for partnerships and other self employed individuals, on the other hand, was gradually narrowed; and since 1982 qualified pension plans for corporations, partnerships, and sole proprietors all have been subject to substantially similar rules.

See generally, Kalish and Lewis, Professional Corporations Revisited (After The Employee Retirement Income Security Act of 1974), 28 Tax Lawyer 471 (1975); Siegel, The Utility of the Professional Corporation: A Rejoinder, 29 Tax Lawyer 265 (1976); Panel Discussion on Professional Corporations, 24 Tax Lawyer 223 (1971); Eaton, Operation of a Professional Service Corporation, 28 N.Y.U.Tax Inst. 1243 (1970); Worthy, What Lies Ahead for Professional Corporations, 32 J.Tax. 88 (1970).

B. TRUST VERSUS ASSOCIATION TAXABLE AS A CORPORATION

Regulations, sections 301.7701–4(a) and (b), distinguish between "ordinary" trusts whose purposes are the protection or conservation of trust property and trusts which are in effect a joint enterprise of the beneficiaries for the conduct of business for profit. To determine if a trust falls in the latter category, and hence is taxable as an association, the six tests specified in Regulations, section 301.7701–2(a)(1), must be applied. The Regulations are not entirely clear how the tests should be applied in trust versus association cases. Regulations, section 301.7701–(a)(2), note that centralization of management, continuity of life, free transferability of interests, and limited liability are generally common both to trusts and to corporations; hence, "the determination of whether a trust *which has such characteristics* is to be treated for tax purposes as a trust or as an association depends on whether there are associates and an objective to carry on business and divide the gains therefrom." (Emphasis added). Thus it is clear that the essential prerequisites for classification of a trust as an association are associates and a business objective. See Estate of Bedell v. Commissioner, 86 T.C. 1207 (1986) (testamentary trust which conducted a manufacturing business lacked "associates" because the beneficiaries had "not planned a common effort or entered into a combination for the conduct of a business enterprise," only a few of the beneficiaries participated in trust affairs, and their interests were not transferrable); Elm Street Realty Trust v. Commissioner, 76 T.C. 803 (1981) (A) (inter vivos estate planning trust which received rent from net lease of real estate had business objective because trustee had *unexercised* power to sell real estate and purchase and improve other real estate; but lacked associates because donee beneficiaries had no role in creation of trust, only limited powers to participate in the trust's activities, and beneficial interests were transferable only under restrictive conditions). But see Hynes v. Commissioner, 74 T.C. 1266 (1980), holding that a trust created to develop and sell real estate was to be taxed as an association even though the grantor held 100 percent of the beneficial interest; the term "associates" in the regulations encompasses "one-man corporations."

In Outlaw v. United States, 494 F.2d 1376 (Ct.Cl.1974), after first finding the presence of associates and a business purpose, the court went on to examine the other four characteristics and concluded that all six corporate characteristics were present. A trust was formed to own and manage some 10,000 acres of farm land and employed 18 to 20 full time plus 60 to 70 temporary workers to engage in a full scale agricultural operation. The court tested the status of the "trust" under the Regulations and found (1) associates (27 original investors increasing to 41); (2) an objective to carry on business (owning, developing and exploiting agricultural lands for income); (3) continuity of life (no provision for terminating the organization at will or upon the death, bankruptcy, etc. of an investor); (4) centralization of management (all decisions were made by an operating committee); (5) limited liability (beneficiaries were liable only to the extent of their proportionate interests in the trust assets); and (6) free transferability of interests (investors could transfer interests after giving notice to the trustee). See also Rev.Rul. 80–75, 1980–1 Cum.Bull. 314 (trust established by promoter to conduct business activity and to which beneficiaries contributed cash in exchange for income interests and remainder to person designated by holder of income interest was classified as an association; the holding was based on the presence of associates and an object to carry on a business and divide the profits; the other four factors were deemed to be present). Compare Rev. Rul. 78–371, 1978–2 Cum.Bull. 344 (trust was treated as an association upon a determination that there were associates and an objective to carry on business and divide the gains therefrom; the Ruling did not consider the other four characteristics); Rev.Rul. 79–77, 1979–1 Cum.Bull. 448 (likewise applying only the two tests, but concluding that a trust formed to hold land was a trust and not an association); Rev.Rul. 88–79, 1988–2 Cum.Bull. 361 (trust formed by investors to conduct business classified as partnership because, on facts, the particular trust did not enjoy limited liability, free transferability of interests, or continuity of life).

Regulations, section 301.7701–4(d), make an exception for "liquidating" trusts which will not be held to be associations taxable as corporations as long as the primary purpose of the trust is the liquidation and distribution of the assets transferred to it. See Abraham v. United States, 406 F.2d 1259 (6th Cir.1969), where the court found the trust to be an association taxable as a corporation and not a liquidating trust; the trustees were given broad powers to conduct the prior business, although the powers were not actually exercised. In Walker v. United States, 194 F.Supp. 522 (D.Mass.1961), an irrevocable trust was set up to hold property, an office building, as part of a family settlement of a dispute over the property. The court found the arrangement was a trust; it had centralized management but no transferability of interests or continuity of life because of the power of the beneficiaries to revoke the arrangement. The purpose of the trust was the liquidation of the property and not the carrying on of business for profit. See also Rev.Rul. 75–379, 1975–2 Cum.Bull. 505, and Rev.Rul. 63–228, 1963–2 Cum.Bull. 229, finding certain trusts which engaged in business activities to fall within the "liquidation" exception; Rev.Proc. 82–58, 1982–2 Cum.Bull. 247 (guidelines for advance rulings on classification of liquidation trusts).

See Rands, Organizations Classified as Corporations for Federal Tax Purposes, 59 St. John's L.Rev. 657 (1985); Note, Determining the Taxable Status of Trusts That Run Businesses, 70 Cornell L.Rev. 1143 (1985); Westin, Shareholders' Liquidating Trusts After Revenue Procedure 80–54, 9 J.Corp.Tax. 63 (1982); Fox, The Maximum Scope of the Association Concept, 25 Tax.L.Rev. 311 (1970); Stephens and Freeland, The Federal Tax Meaning of Estates and Trusts, 18 Tax L.Rev. 251 (1963); Lyons, Comments on the New Regulations on Associations, 16 Tax L.Rev. 441 (1961).

C. SPECIAL CLASSES OF CORPORATIONS

1. *Conduit Corporations Relieved of Federal Tax*

Regulated investment companies investing in securities—mutual funds-are in effect relieved of corporate tax liability as respects the dividends and capital gains from their stock investments if they currently distribute this income to their shareholders. A mutual fund to this extent is thus treated as a conduit rather than a taxable entity. See sections 851–855. In 1958 Congress refused to permit regulated investment companies to "pass through" to their shareholders the exemption for interest from tax-exempt securities; however, in 1976, section 852(b)(5) was added to permit conduit treatment for tax-exempt interest received by mutual funds in certain situations.

In 1960 Congress extended conduit treatment to real estate investment trusts (REITs) otherwise taxable as corporations (see sections 856–860); and in 1986 conduit treatment was extended to real estate mortgage investment conduits (REMICs) (sections 860A–860G).

2. *Other Special Corporate Treatment*

Certain classes of corporations are given special treatment as respects the computation or treatment of taxable income, e.g., banks, insurance companies, and foreign corporations; or exemption from tax, e.g., the various tax-exempt organizations (as to which, however, the corporate income tax is applicable to the extent of "unrelated business taxable income," sections 511–514).

SECTION 3. REGARD AND DISREGARD OF THE CORPORATE ENTITY

STRONG v. COMMISSIONER

United States Tax Court, 1976.
66 T.C. 12.

TANNENWALD, JUDGE: * * *

Petitioners formed a partnership for the purpose of constructing and operating an apartment complex on real estate contributed by several partners. In order to obtain financing for the project, it was necessary to transfer the property to a corporation wholly owned by the partnership so that mortgage loans could be made at an interest rate in excess of the limit imposed by State usury laws on loans to individuals. Construction and operation of the apartments generated net operating losses during the years in issue which were reported on the partnership's returns and as distributive shares on the individual returns of the petitioners. The respondent determined that the corporation, as owner of the property, was the proper party to report those losses. Petitioners allege that the corporation was a nominee whose ownership should be disregarded for tax purposes. The crux of petitioners' case is that the corporation was merely a sham or device used for the purpose of avoiding the New York usury statute, that it performed no acts other than those essential to that function, and that to treat it as the actual owner of the property would be to exalt form over substance.

The use of sham or dummy corporations to avoid application of the usury laws is a recognized practice in New York. Hoffman v. Lee Nashem Motors, Inc., 20 N.Y.2d 513, 231 N.E.2d 765, 285 N.Y.S.2d 68 (1967); Leader v. Dinkler Management Corp., 20 N.Y.2d 393, 230 N.E. 2d 120, 283 N.Y.S.2d 281 (1967). There is no doubt that petitioners sought to do business in partnership form and that the corporation was, at least in their eyes, a mere tool or conduit. Their argument is not without some appeal, but we conclude that it should not be accepted.

The principal guidepost on the road to recognition of the corporate entity is Moline Properties v. Commissioner, 319 U.S. 436 (1943). In that case, a corporation was organized as part of a transaction which included the transfer of mortgaged property to it by the shareholder, the assumption by it of the outstanding mortgages, and the transfer of its stock to a voting trustee named by the mortgagee as security for additional advances. Later the indebtedness was repaid and the shareholder reacquired control of the corporation. Thereafter it mortgaged and sold some of the property it held, and leased another portion. The Court held that the corporation was a separate entity from its inception, and stated its rule of decision as follows:

> The doctrine of corporate entity fills a useful purpose in business life. Whether the purpose be to gain an advantage under the law of the state of incorporation or to avoid or to comply with the demands of creditors or to serve the creator's personal or undisclosed convenience, *so long as that purpose is the equivalent of business activity or is followed by the carrying on of business by the corporation,* the corporation remains a separate taxable entity. * * * In Burnet v. Commonwealth Improvement Co., 287 U.S. 415, this Court appraised the relation between a corporation and its sole stockholder and held taxable to the corporation a profit on a sale to its stockholder. This was because the taxpayer had adopted the corporate form for purposes of his own. The choice of the advantages of incorporation to do business, it was held, required

the acceptance of the tax disadvantages. [319 U.S. at 438–439. Fn. refs. omitted; emphasis supplied.]

Cases following *Moline Properties* have generally held that the income from property must be taxed to the corporate owner and will not be attributed to the shareholders, unless the corporation is a *purely passive dummy* or is used for a tax-avoidance purpose. Harrison Property Management Co. v. United States, 475 F.2d 623 (Ct.Cl.1973); Taylor v. Commissioner, 445 F.2d 455 (1st Cir.1971); National Investors Corp. v. Hoey, 144 F.2d 466 (2d Cir.1944); Collins v. United States, 386 F.Supp. 17 (S.D.Ga.1974), affd. per curiam 514 F.2d 1282 (5th Cir.1975). This is particularly true where the demand that the corporate entity be ignored emanates from the shareholders of a closely held corporation. See Harrison Property Management Co. v. United States, supra at 626; David F. Bolger, 59 T.C. 760, 767 n. 4 (1973).[8] It has been suggested that the prevailing approach misses the point by focusing (as do the parties herein) on the viability of the corporate entity rather than the situs of real beneficial or economic ownership. Kurtz & Kopp, "Taxability of Straw Corporations in Real Estate Transactions," 22 Tax Lawyer 647 (1969). However, the thrust of the case law, as we read it, is to leave the door open to the argument that a corporation played a purely nominal or "straw" role in a transaction, while closing it firmly against any contention that a corporation may be disregarded simply because it is the creature of its shareholders. See cases collected and analyzed in Kronovet, "Straw corporations: When will they be recognized; what can and should be done," 39 J.Tax. 54 (1973).

The Supreme Court has held that shareholder domination, even to the extent that a corporation could be said to lack beneficial ownership of its assets and income, is insufficient to permit taxpayers to ignore the corporation's existence. National Carbide Corp. v. Commissioner, 336 U.S. 422, 433–434 (1949); Moline Properties v. Commissioner, supra. The Court of Appeals for the Second Circuit, to which appeal will lie herein, has similarly refused to disregard the interposition of a corporate entity between shareholders and their property, except where the corporation has not purported to deal with the property in its own right. The focus is on business purpose or activity with respect to the particular property whose ownership is in question.

In Paymer v. Commissioner, 150 F.2d 334 (2d Cir.1945), two brothers formed a pair of corporations (Raymep and Westrich) to which they transferred legal title to certain real estate. Their purpose was to deter execution against the property by their individual creditors. Neither corporation engaged in any business activity except that Raymep obtained a loan and as part security "assigned to the lender all the

8. See also Higgins v. Smith, 308 U.S. 473 (1940). Cf. Colin v. Altman, 39 App. Div.2d 200, 333 N.Y.S.2d 432, 433–434 (1st Dept.1972): "the corporate veil is never pierced for the benefit of the corporation or its stockholders. * * * [The sole stockholder] is not the corporation either in law or fact and, having elected to take the advantages [of incorporation], it is not inequitable to subject him to the disabilities consequent upon his election."

lessor's rights, profits and interest in two leases on the property and covenanted that they were in full force and effect and that it was the sole lessor." 150 F.2d at 336. Westrich was disregarded on the ground that it "was at all times but a passive dummy which did nothing but take and hold title to the real estate conveyed to it. It served no business purpose *in connection with the property.*" 150 F.2d at 337. (Emphasis added.) Raymep, however, was not disregarded, because it did perform a business function as the owner of the property.

In Jackson v. Commissioner, 233 F.2d 289 (2d Cir.1956), affg. 24 T.C. 1 (1955), the Court of Appeals disregarded holding companies which lacked separate business purpose or activity, stating that the situation was encompassed within the foregoing language in its opinion in *Paymer* and further observing:

> A natural person may be used to receive income which in fact is another's. So, too, a corporation, although for other purposes a jural entity distinct from its stockholders, may be used as a mere dummy to receive income which in fact is the income of the stockholders or of someone else; in such circumstances, the company will be disregarded. [233 F.2d at 290 n. 2.]

Finally, in Commissioner v. State–Adams Corp., 283 F.2d 395 (2d Cir. 1960), revg. 32 T.C. 365 (1959) (which involved a different factual situation), the court characterized its holding in *Paymer* as "nothing more than a restatement of the fundamental rule that income from real estate held in the name of a nominee will be taxed to the beneficial owner, not to the nominee." 283 F.2d at 398 (fn. ref. omitted). The mere fact that some of the documents herein speak in terms of a corporate nominee is not sufficient to bring petitioners within the exception to the general rule. Harrison Property Management Co. v. United States, supra; Collins v. United States, supra; cf. Tomlinson v. Miles, 316 F.2d 710 (5th Cir.1963).

In short, a corporate "straw" may be used to separate apparent from actual ownership of property, without incurring the tax consequences of an actual transfer; but to prevent evasion or abuse of the two-tiered tax structure, a taxpayer's claim that his controlled corporation should be disregarded will be closely scrutinized. If the corporation was intended to, or did in fact, act in its own name with respect to property, its ownership thereof will not be disregarded.

The degree of corporate purpose and activity requiring recognition of the corporation as a separate entity is extremely low. Thus, it has been stated that "a determination whether a corporation is to be considered as doing business is not necessarily dependent upon the quantum of business" and that the business activity may be "minimal." See Britt v. United States, 431 F.2d 227, 235, 237 (5th Cir.1970).

In this case, the corporation's purpose and activities were sufficient to require recognition of its separate ownership of the property in question and, a fortiori, of its existence as a taxable entity. The purpose to avoid State usury laws is a "business purpose" within the meaning of *Moline Properties.* Collins v. United States, supra; David F. Bolger, supra.[9] The corporation had broad, unrestricted powers under its charter. Compare Collins v. United States, supra. Its activities were more extensive than those which required recognition of Raymep in Paymer v. Commissioner, supra. Like Raymep, it borrowed money on the security of rents; in addition, it mortgaged the property itself and it received and applied the loan proceeds. It engaged in the foregoing activities on more than one occasion and is more vulnerable than was the corporation in Collins v. United States, supra, which was also formed to avoid usury law restrictions and placed only a single mortgage. These activities, carried out in its own name, go beyond "transactions essential to the holding and transferring of title." See Taylor v. Commissioner, 445 F.2d at 457. The fact that the corporation in this case, unlike those in other cases, did not enter into any leases does not, in our opinion, constitute a sufficient basis for distinguishing their thrust.[10]

Furthermore, the corporation was otherwise treated by the partnership in a manner inconsistent with petitioners' contention that the two were the same entity. The partnership agreement required that deeds, loan agreements, and mortgages "executed by or on behalf of the partnership" be signed by both Jones and Strong; property standing in the corporate name was so dealt with on Jones' signature alone. Separation of title to the various parcels permitted the creation of mutual easements, an act which would have been prevented by the doctrine of merger had the properties been under common ownership. See Parsons v. Johnson, 68 N.Y. 62 (1877); Snyder v. County of Monroe, 2 Misc.2d 946, 153 N.Y.S.2d 479, 486 (Monroe County Sup.Ct.1956), affd. mem. 6 App.Div.2d 854, 175 N.Y.S.2d 1008 (4th Dept.1958). The corporation applied for and received insurance on the property in its own name.

Finally, although not determinative, an element to be considered is the fact that the corporate vehicle in this case, whatever the parties' intentions, carried with it the usual baggage attending incorporation, including limitation of the shareholders' personal liability during construction. Jones alone was potentially responsible (as guarantor) for repayment of the construction loans.

In the final analysis, the corporation herein fits the mold articulated in Collins v. United States, supra:

> The fact remains, however, that the corporation did exist and did perform the function intended of it until the permanent loan was consummated. It was more than a business convenience, it was a business necessity to plaintiffs' enterprise. As such, it came

9. See also Daniel E. Rogers, T.C. Memo, 1975–289.

10. In Raymep Realty Corp., 7 T.C.M. 262 (1948), relied upon by petitioners we held the execution of a lease in the name of a corporate nominee titleholder did not require the corporation to be recognized as a taxable entity. We characterized that single act as "a purely nominal adjunct to the holding of title." Here, by contrast, the business activity was the raison d'etre of the corporation.

into being. As such, it served the purpose of its creation. [386 F.Supp. at 21.]

The fact that the purpose and use of the corporation was limited in scope is beside the point. See Sam Siegel, 45 T.C. 566, 577 (1966).

The tide of judicial history is too strong to enable petitioners to prevail, albeit that the activities of the corporation were substantially less than those involved in most of the decided cases with the exception of Collins v. United States, supra.

Having set up a separate entity through which to conduct their affairs, petitioners must live with the tax consequences of that choice. Indeed, the very exigency which led to the use of the corporation serves to emphasize its separate existence. See Moline Properties v. Commissioner, 319 U.S. at 440; David F. Bolger, 59 T.C. at 766. Our conclusion is not based upon any failure of the petitioners to turn square corners with respondent; they consistently made clear their intention to prevent separate taxation of the corporation if legally possible. They took most precautions consistent with business exigency to achieve that end. We simply hold that their goal was not attainable in this case.

Reviewed by the Court.

Decisions will be entered for the respondent.*

COMMISSIONER v. BOLLINGER

Supreme Court of the United States, 1988.
485 U.S. 340.

JUSTICE SCALIA delivered the opinion of the Court.

Petitioner the Commissioner of Internal Revenue challenges a decision by the United States Court of Appeals for the Sixth Circuit holding that a corporation which held record title to real property as agent for the corporation's shareholders was not the owner of the property for purposes of federal income taxation. 807 F.2d 65 (1986). We granted certiorari, 482 U.S. 913, 107 S.Ct. 3183, 96 L.Ed.2d 672 (1987), to resolve a conflict in the courts of appeals over the tax treatment of corporations purporting to be agents for their shareholders. Compare George v. Commissioner, 803 F.2d 144, 148–149 (CA5 1986), cert. pending, No. 86–1152; Frink v. Commissioner, 798 F.2d 106, 109–110 (CA4 1986), cert. pending, No. 86–1151.

I

Respondent Jesse C. Bollinger, Jr., developed, either individually or in partnership with some or all of the other respondents, eight apartment complexes in Lexington, Kentucky. (For convenience we will refer to all the ventures as "partnerships.") Bollinger initiated development of the first apartment complex, Creekside North Apartments, in 1968. The Massachusetts Mutual Life Insurance Company agreed to

* [Ed.: The decision was affirmed by memorandum, 553 F.2d 94 (2d Cir.1977.]

provide permanent financing by lending $1,075,000 to "the corporate nominee of Jesse C. Bollinger, Jr." at an annual interest rate of eight percent, secured by a mortgage on the property and a personal guaranty from Bollinger. The loan commitment was structured in this fashion because Kentucky's usury law at the time limited the annual interest rate for noncorporate borrowers to seven percent. Ky.Rev. Stat. §§ 360.010, 360.025 (1972). Lenders willing to provide money only at higher rates required the nominal debtor and record title holder of mortgaged property to be a corporate nominee of the true owner and borrower. On October 14, 1968, Bollinger incorporated Creekside, Inc., under the laws of Kentucky; he was the only stockholder. The next day, Bollinger and Creekside, Inc., entered into a written agreement which provided that the corporation would hold title to the apartment complex as Bollinger's agent for the sole purpose of securing financing, and would convey, assign, or encumber the property and disburse the proceeds thereof only as directed by Bollinger; that Creekside, Inc., had no obligation to maintain the property or assume any liability by reason of the execution of promissory notes or otherwise; and that Bollinger would indemnify and hold the corporation harmless from any liability it might sustain as his agent and nominee.

Having secured the commitment for permanent financing, Bollinger, acting through Creekside, Inc., borrowed the construction funds for the apartment complex from Citizens Fidelity Bank and Trust Company. Creekside, Inc., executed all necessary loan documents including the promissory note and mortgage, and transferred all loan proceeds to Bollinger's individual construction account. Bollinger acted as general contractor for the construction, hired the necessary employees, and paid the expenses out of the construction account. When construction was completed, Bollinger obtained, again through Creekside, Inc., permanent financing from Massachusetts Mutual Life in accordance with the earlier loan commitment. These loan proceeds were used to pay off the Citizens Fidelity construction loan. Bollinger hired a resident manager to rent the apartments, execute leases with tenants, collect and deposit the rents, and maintain operating records. The manager deposited all rental receipts into, and paid all operating expenses from, an operating account, which was first opened in the name of Creekside, Inc., but was later changed to "Creekside Apartments, a partnership." The operation of Creekside North Apartments generated losses for the taxable years 1969, 1971, 1972, 1973, and 1974, and ordinary income for the years 1970, 1975, 1976, and 1977. Throughout, the income and losses were reported by Bollinger on his individual income tax returns.

Following a substantially identical pattern, seven other apartment complexes were developed by respondents through seven separate partnerships. For each venture, a partnership executed a nominee agreement with Creekside, Inc., to obtain financing. (For one of the ventures, a different Kentucky corporation, Cloisters, Inc., in which Bollinger had a 50 percent interest, acted as the borrower and titleholder. For convenience, we will refer to both Creekside and Cloisters as "the corporation.") The corporation transferred the construction loan proceeds to the partnership's construction account, and the partnership hired a construction supervisor who oversaw construction. Upon completion of construction, each partnership actively managed its apartment complex, depositing all rental receipts into, and paying all expenses from, a separate partnership account for each apartment complex. The corporation had no assets, liabilities, employees, or bank accounts. In every case, the lenders regarded the partnership as the owner of the apartments and were aware that the corporation was acting as agent of the partnership in holding record title. The partnerships reported the income and losses generated by the apartment complexes on their partnership tax returns, and respondents reported their distributive share of the partnership income and losses on their individual tax returns.

The Commissioner of Internal Revenue disallowed the losses reported by respondents, on the ground that the standards set out in National Carbide Corp. v. Commissioner, 336 U.S. 422, 69 S.Ct. 726, 93 L.Ed. 779 (1949), were not met. The Commissioner contended that *National Carbide* required a corporation to have an arm's length relationship with its shareholders before it could be recognized as their agent. Although not all respondents were shareholders of the corporation, the Commissioner took the position that the funds the partnerships disbursed to pay expenses should be deemed contributions to the corporation's capital, thereby making all respondents constructive stockholders. Since, in the Commissioner's view, the corporation rather than its shareholders owned the real estate, any losses sustained by the ventures were attributable to the corporation and not respondents. Respondents sought a redetermination in the United States Tax Court. The Tax Court held that the corporations were the agents of the partnerships and should be disregarded for tax purposes. Bollinger v. Commissioner, 48 TCM 1443 (1984), ¶ 84, 560 P–H Memo TC. On appeal, the United States Court of Appeals for the Sixth Circuit affirmed. 807 F.2d 65 (1986). We granted the Commissioner's petition for certiorari.

II

For federal income tax purposes, gain or loss from the sale or use of property is attributable to the owner of the property. See Helvering v. Horst, 311 U.S. 112, 116–117, 61 S.Ct. 144, 147, 85 L.Ed. 75 (1940); Blair v. Commissioner, 300 U.S. 5, 12, 57 S.Ct. 330, 333, 81 L.Ed. 465 (1937); see also Commissioner v. Sunnen, 333 U.S. 591, 604, 68 S.Ct. 715, 722, 92 L.Ed. 898 (1948). The problem we face here is that two different taxpayers can plausibly be regarded as the owner. Neither the Internal Revenue Code nor the regulations promulgated by the Secretary of the Treasury provide significant guidance as to which should be selected. It is common ground between the parties, however, that if a corporation holds title to property as agent for a partnership, then for tax purposes the partnership and not the corporation is the owner.

Given agreement on that premise, one would suppose that there would be agreement upon the conclusion as well. For each of respondents' apartment complexes, an agency agreement expressly provided that the corporation would "hold such property as nominee and agent for" the partnership, App. to Pet. for Cert. 21a, n. 4, and that the partnership would have sole control of and responsibility for the apartment complex. The partnership in each instance was identified as the principal and owner of the property during financing, construction, and operation. The lenders, contractors, managers, employees, and tenants—all who had contact with the development—knew that the corporation was merely the agent of the partnership, if they knew of the existence of the corporation at all. In each instance the relationship between the corporation and the partnership was, in both form and substance, an agency with the partnership as principal.

The Commissioner contends, however, that the normal indicia of agency cannot suffice for tax purposes when, as here, the alleged principals are the controlling shareholders of the alleged agent corporation. That, it asserts, would undermine the principle of Moline Properties v. Commissioner, 319 U.S. 436, 63 S.Ct. 1132, 87 L.Ed. 1499 (1943), which held that a corporation is a separate taxable entity even if it has only one shareholder who exercises total control over its affairs. Obviously, *Moline* 's separate-entity principle would be significantly compromised if shareholders of closely held corporations could, by clothing the corporation with some attributes of agency with respect to particular assets, leave themselves free at the end of the tax year to make a claim—perhaps even a good-faith claim—of either agent or owner status, depending upon which choice turns out to minimize their tax liability. The Commissioner does not have the resources to audit and litigate the many cases in which agency status could be thought debatable. Hence, the Commissioner argues, in this shareholder context he can reasonably demand that the taxpayer meet a prophylactically clear test of agency.

We agree with that principle, but the question remains whether the test the Commissioner proposes is appropriate. The parties have debated at length the significance of our opinion in *National Carbide Corp. v. Commissioner,* supra. In that case, three corporations that were wholly owned subsidiaries of another corporation agreed to operate their production plants as "agents" for the parent, transferring to it all profits except for a nominal sum. The subsidiaries reported as gross income only this sum, but the Commissioner concluded that they should be taxed on the entirety of the profits because they were not really agents. We agreed, reasoning first, that the mere fact of the parent's control over the subsidiaries did not establish the existence of an agency, since such control is typical of all shareholder-corporation relationships, id., 336 U.S. at 429–434, 69 S.Ct., at 730–732; and second, that the agreements to pay the parent all profits above a nominal amount were not determinative since income must be taxed to those who actually earn it without regard to anticipatory assignment, id., at

435–436, 69 S.Ct., at 733–734. We acknowledged, however, that there was such a thing as "a true corporate agent . . . of [an] owner-principal," id. at 437, 69 S.Ct., at 734, and proceeded to set forth four indicia and two requirements of such status, the sum of which has become known in the lore of federal income tax law as the "six *National Carbide* factors":

> "[1] Whether the corporation operates in the name and for the account of the principal, [2] binds the principal by its actions, [3] transmits money received to the principal, and [4] whether receipt of income is attributable to the services of employees of the principal and to assets belonging to the principal are some of the relevant considerations in determining whether a true agency exists. [5] If the corporation is a true agent, its relations with its principal must not be dependent upon the fact that it is owned by the principal, if such is the case. [6] Its business purpose must be the carrying on of the normal duties of an agent." Id., at 437, 69 S.Ct., at 734 (footnotes omitted).

We readily discerned that these factors led to a conclusion of nonagency in *National Carbide* itself. There each subsidiary had represented to its customers that it (not the parent) was the company manufacturing and selling its products; each had sought to shield the parent from service of legal process; and the operations had used thousands of the subsidiaries' employees and nearly $20 million worth of property and equipment listed as assets on the subsidiaries' books. *Id.,* at 425, 434, 438, and n. 21, 69 S.Ct., at 728, 732–733, 734, and n. 21.

The Commissioner contends that the last two *National Carbide* factors are not satisfied in the present case. To take the last first: The Commissioner argues that here the corporation's business purpose with respect to the property at issue was not "the carrying on of the normal duties of an agent," since it was acting not as the agent but rather as the owner of the property for purposes of Kentucky's usury laws. We do not agree. It assuredly was not acting as the owner in fact, since respondents represented themselves as the principals to all parties concerned with the loans. Indeed, it was the lenders themselves who required the use of a corporate nominee. Nor does it make any sense to adopt a contrary-to-fact legal presumption that the corporation was the principal, imposing a federal tax sanction for the apparent evasion of Kentucky's usury law. To begin with, the Commissioner has not established that these transactions were an evasion. Respondents assert without contradiction that use of agency arrangements in order to permit higher interest was common practice, and it is by no means clear that the practice violated the spirit of the Kentucky law, much less its letter. It might well be thought that the borrower does not generally require usury protection in a transaction sophisticated enough to employ a corporate agent—assuredly not the normal *modus operandi* of the loan shark. That the statute positively envisioned corporate nominees is suggested by a provision which forbids charging the higher corporate interest rates "to a corporation, the principal asset of which shall be the ownership of a one (1) or two (2) family dwelling," Ky.Rev.Stat. § 360.025(2) (1987)—which would seem to prevent use of the nominee device for ordinary home-mortgage loans. In any event, even if the transaction did run afoul of the usury law, Kentucky, like most States, regards only the lender as the usurer, and the borrower as the victim. See Ky.Rev.Stat. § 360.020 (1987) (lender liable to borrower for civil penalty), § 360.990 (lender guilty of misdemeanor). Since the Kentucky statute imposed no penalties upon the borrower for allowing himself to be victimized, nor treated him as *in pari delictu,* but to the contrary enabled him to pay back the principal without any interest, and to sue for double the amount of interest already paid (plus attorney's fees), see Ky.Rev.Stat. § 360.020 (1972), the United States would hardly be vindicating Kentucky law by depriving the usury victim of tax advantages he would otherwise enjoy. In sum, we see no basis in either fact or policy for holding that the corporation was the principal because of the nature of its participation in the loans.

Of more general importance is the Commissioner's contention that the arrangements here violate the fifth *National Carbide* factor—that the corporate agent's "relations with its principal must not be dependent upon the fact that it is owned by the principal." The Commissioner asserts that this cannot be satisfied unless the corporate agent and its shareholder principal have an "arm's-length relationship" that includes the payment of a fee for agency services. The meaning of *National Carbide's* fifth factor is, at the risk of understatement, not entirely clear. Ultimately, the relations between a corporate agent and its owner-principal are *always* dependent upon the fact of ownership, in that the owner can cause the relations to be altered or terminated at any time. Plainly that is not what was meant, since on that interpretation all subsidiary-parent agencies would be invalid for tax purposes, a position which the *National Carbide* opinion specifically disavowed. We think the fifth *National Carbide* factor—so much more abstract than the others—was no more and no less than a generalized statement of the concern, expressed earlier in our own discussion, that the separate-entity doctrine of *Moline* not be subverted.

In any case, we decline to parse the text of *National Carbide* as though that were itself the governing statute. As noted earlier, it is uncontested that the law attributes tax consequences of property held by a genuine agent to the principal; and we agree that it is reasonable for the Commissioner to demand unequivocal evidence of genuineness in the corporation-shareholder context, in order to prevent evasion of *Moline.* We see no basis, however, for holding that unequivocal evidence can only consist of the rigid requirements (arm's-length dealing plus agency fee) that the Commissioner suggests. Neither of those is demanded by the law of agency, which permits agents to be unpaid family members, friends, or associates. See Restatement (Second) of Agency §§ 16, 21, 22 (1958). It seems to us that the genuineness of the agency relationship is adequately assured, and tax-avoiding manipulation adequately avoided, when the fact that the corporation is acting as agent for its shareholders with respect to a particular asset is set forth in a written agreement at the time the asset is acquired, the corporation functions as agent and not principal with respect to the asset for all purposes, and the corporation is held out as the agent and not principal in all dealings with third parties relating to the asset. Since these requirements were met here, the judgment of the Court of Appeals is

Affirmed.

JUSTICE KENNEDY took no part in the consideration or decision of this case.

ILLUSTRATIVE MATERIAL

A. APPLICATION OF THE BUSINESS ACTIVITY TEST

1. *General*

In cases involving the issue whether a corporation should be taxed as a separate entity, the taxpayer and the Commissioner may be on different sides, depending on the tax stakes involved. Thus, for example, a taxpayer whose personal tax bracket exceeds the corporate rate (an unlikely occurrence after 1986) will urge that the corporation be recognized for tax purposes so as to postpone imposition of his higher individual rate on the income; the Commissioner may seek to disregard the corporate entity. Conversely, as in *Strong* and *Bollinger,* the taxpayer who seeks to deduct directly losses that result from activities of the "corporation" or who utilizes the corporate form only for nominal purposes, will urge that the formal existence of the corporation be ignored; the Commissioner will assert that the activities of the corporation warrant its recognition as a separate taxable entity. Historically, taxpayers generally had little success in attempts to assert that the corporation which they created should be disregarded for tax purposes; the courts generally upheld the Commissioner's position that the activities of the corporation were sufficient to warrant its being regarded as a separate entity for tax purposes. (Note that even in *Bollinger,* in which the taxpayer prevailed, the corporation was not ignored for tax purposes; it was treated as the shareholders' agent.) On the other hand, the corporate entity should be disregarded to prevent tax avoidance. The following cases illustrate the results reached by the courts in this area.

2. *Insufficient Business Activity—Corporate Entity Disregarded*

In National Investors Corp. v. Hoey, 144 F.2d 466 (2d Cir.1944), the taxpayer, an investment trust, owned four subsidiaries, one of which (Investors Fund) though organized in 1931 had issued no shares and conducted no business. The taxpayer decided to unite itself and its subsidiaries into one corporation, and in furtherance of this plan transferred its assets on December 17, 1934 to the Investors Fund for 10 shares of the latter's stock (increased to 20 by a stock dividend on December 7, 1935). The plan was not accepted by the taxpayer's stockholders in 1935 and on December 21, 1935 it started to liquidate Investors Fund by surrendering two shares for 1/10th of the assets. The assets had fallen in value and the taxpayer desired to realize in 1935 only as much loss as it could utilize against its gains of that year. The balance of the shares was surrendered in January 1936. The

Commissioner contended that the 1935 loss was not allowable. In an opinion by Judge Learned Hand, the court stated:

"This result depends upon whether, in the situation just disclosed, we should recognize a transaction of sale or exchange between a corporation and its sole shareholder; and our decision turns upon three decisions of the Supreme Court: Burnet v. Commonwealth Improvement Co., 287 U.S. 415, 53 S.Ct. 198; Higgins v. Smith, 308 U.S. 473, 60 S.Ct. 355, and Moline Properties, Inc. v. Commissioner, 319 U.S. 436, 63 S.Ct. 1132. In the first of these the question was whether it was proper to tax a corporation for profits upon transactions between itself and a decedent's estate which owned all its shares. The court merely declared that, since a corporation was for most purposes recognized as a separate jural person, and since the situation was not one of the exceptions where the 'corporate form' should be 'disregarded,' it should be taxed upon its gains, regardless of the fact that no living person had gained or lost a cent. When Higgins v. Smith, supra, was before us (Smith v. Higgins, 2 Cir., 102 F.2d 456) we assumed that this rule held good in a case where the Commissioner had refused to allow a deduction to the sole shareholder of losses sustained in transactions between him and his corporation. In this we were in error, however, for the Supreme Court held that, although the Treasury might insist upon the separate personality of the corporation when it chose, it might also disregard it, when it chose. It explained Burnet v. Commonwealth Improvement Co., supra, 287 U.S. 415, 53 S.Ct. 198, by saying that 'a taxpayer is free to adopt such organization of his affairs as he may choose and having elected to do some business as a corporation, he must accept the tax disadvantages. On the other hand, the Government may not be required to acquiesce in the taxpayer's election of that form for doing business which is most advantageous to him. The Government may look at actualities and upon determination that the form employed of doing business or carrying out the tax event is unreal or a sham may sustain or disregard the effect of the fiction as best serves the purposes of the tax statute. * * * It is command of income and its benefits which marks the real owner of property.' [Higgins v. Smith, 308 U.S. 473, 60 S.Ct. 358.] This language we later interpreted as meaning that 'the Treasury may take a taxpayer at his word, so to say; when that serves its purpose, it may treat the corporation as a separate person from himself; but that is a rule which works only in the Treasury's own favor; it cannot be used to deplete the revenue.' United States v. Morris & Essex R. Co., 2 Cir., 135 F.2d 711, 713. Again we were wrong; we neglected to observe that the corporate 'form' must be 'unreal or a sham,' before the Treasury may disregard it; we had taken too literally the concluding language that it was the 'command of income and its benefits which marks the real owner of property.'

"This error was made plain in the third decision of the Supreme Court—Moline Properties, Inc. v. Commissioner, supra, 319 U.S. 436, 63 S.Ct. 1132. In that case the question was whether the corporation might insist upon the Treasury's including capital gains within the gross income of its sole shareholder, and the court decided that it might not. That was the same situation as existed in Burnet v. Commonwealth Improvement Co., supra, 287 U.S. 415, 53 S.Ct. 198. The gloss then put upon Higgins v. Smith, supra, was deliberate and is authoritative: it was that, whatever the purpose of organizing the corporation, 'so long as that purpose is the equivalent of business activity or is followed by the carrying on of business by the corporation, the corporation remains a separate taxable entity.' 319 U.S. 439, 63 S.Ct. 1134. That, as we understand it, is the same interpretation which was placed upon corporate reorganizations in Gregory v. Helvering, 293 U.S. 465, 55 S.Ct. 266, which has sometimes been understood to contradict the doctrine that the motive to avoid taxation is never, as such, relevant. In fact it does not trench upon that doctrine; it merely declares that to be a separate jural person for purposes of taxation, a corporation must engage in some industrial, commercial, or other activity besides avoiding taxation: in other words, that the term 'corporation' will be interpreted to mean a corporation which does some 'business' in the ordinary meaning; and that escaping taxation is not 'business' in the ordinary meaning.

"If the law be so understood, it seems to us that the plaintiff at bar has not proved that it was entitled to the deduction. [While being used as a means of putting through the consolidation plan was a 'business' activity, as soon as that plan was rejected] any continued retention of the securities longer than was necessary for liquidation was not a 'business' activity as, indeed, the plaintiff itself recognized by proceeding to liquidate. Any decrease in the value of the securities until the shareholders rejected the 'Plan,' and for a reasonable time thereafter, the plaintiff might count as part of its loss—it was not bound to begin liquidation on the very day of the rejection. But any decrease thereafter it was not entitled to include, for the whole purpose of acquiring the shares was to put through the 'Plan,' and when that was known to be impossible, there was no longer any 'business' for the Investors Fund to do. That any later decreases should not be 'recognized' is the inevitable corollary of the doctrine that the Treasury may disregard transactions with a wholly owned corporation, not engaged in any 'business' activity." (467–68)

In Greenberg v. Commissioner, 62 T.C. 331 (1974), aff'd per curiam, 526 F.2d 588 (4th Cir.1975), two individuals formed five corporations to develop large residential subdivisions. All the corporations performed identical functions. Following a disagreement between the two shareholders, four corporations were liquidated, and one of the shareholders was redeemed out of the remaining corporation. The taxpayer was left as the sole shareholder of the remaining corporation. The taxpayer reported capital gains on the amounts received in liquidation of the four corporations. The court held that the four liquidated corporations were merely shams; all the income earned by those corporations was the income of the continuing corporation; and the amounts distributed to the taxpayer were simply a dividend: "These [liquidated] corporations served no purpose except to obtain a tax benefit which is not 'business' sufficient to grant them recognition as separate 'taxworthy' entities for Federal tax purposes." (345) See also Kimbrell v. Commissioner, 371 F.2d 897 (5th Cir.1967) (Commissioner's contention upheld that corporations involved were "mere depositories" for the individual shareholder's income where the corporation engaged in no business activities but merely received the income for the services performed by the individual taxpayer); Patterson v. Commissioner, 25 T.C.M. 1230 (1966), aff'd per curiam, 68–2 USTC ¶ 9471 (2d Cir.1968) (the corporation performed no useful function and the taxpayer, a professional boxer, "simply did not put flesh on the bones of the corporate skeleton").

In Noonan v. Commissioner, 52 T.C. 907 (1969), aff'd per curiam, 451 F.2d 992 (9th Cir.1971), a corporation received income as a limited partner from a business enterprise in which the sole shareholder was a general partner. The Tax Court acknowledged that the corporation had been properly organized, but it refused to recognize the separate corporate entity where the record was devoid of evidence showing any active business purpose. Compare the cases in *3.(b),* infra.

3. *Sufficient Business Activity—Corporate Entity Respected*

(a) *General*

In situations similar to that in Strong v. Commissioner, supra, the courts have rejected taxpayers' attempts to have a corporation holding title to real estate disregarded and treated as a "mere dummy" for tax purposes. In Bolger v. Commissioner, 59 T.C. 760 (1973), the taxpayer was engaged in real estate investment and finance. The taxpayer would locate a building which a business desired to lease. The following transactions would take place, often all on the same day: Taxpayer would organize a nominally capitalized corporation with the shareholders being himself and other individuals; the corporation would purchase the building and enter into a lease with the user; the corporation would then issue its notes, secured by a mortgage on the property and an assignment of the lease, to an institutional lender to obtain funds for the purchase. The term of the mortgage notes and the primary term of the lease were usually coextensive. The mortgage provided that the property could be transferred, with the transferees being obligated to fulfill the terms of the mortgage and the lease except that the transferees would assume no personal financial obligation for the payment of principal and interest on the note. Such transferees were also obligated to keep the corporation in existence. Immediately after these transactions, the corporation would then convey the property to its shareholders subject to the lease and mortgage and without any cash payment to the corporation. The transferee shareholders would assume the corporation's obligation under the lease and mortgage, but they had no personal liability thereon except to the extent of the property they received. The taxpayers claimed that they were entitled to the depreciation deductions generated by the properties. The Commissioner asserted that only the corporation had a depreciable interest in the property. The court first held that both at the time the corporation was created and after the transfer of the property to the shareholders, the corporation was a viable business entity. Although at the latter point the corporation was stripped of its assets and, by virtue of its various agreements could not engage in any business activity, the court held it was sufficient that the corporation continued to be liable on its obligations to the lender and remained in existence with full powers to own property and transact business. The court went on to hold, however, that because of the transfer of the property to the shareholders the individual taxpayers were entitled to the depreciation deductions. The case presaged the Tax Court's position in *Strong* that there is very little room for a taxpayer successfully to assert disregard of the corporate form which the taxpayer has adopted.

See also Tomlinson v. Miles, 316 F.2d 710 (5th Cir.1963) (corporation formed to hold title to real estate to facilitate its ultimate sale held taxable on the gain from such sales although the corporation held title "for the use and benefit" of the shareholders); Taylor v. Commissioner, 445 F.2d 455 (1st Cir.1971) (opening of a checking account and the execution of deeds and a mortgage constituted "business activity": "If [the corporation] were to serve only as a straw, it should have only performed those transactions essential to the holding and transferring of title." (457); Commissioner v. State–Adams

Corp., 283 F.2d 395 (2d Cir.1960) (court rejected the taxpayer's argument that the holding of title did not warrant recognition of the corporate entity since the corporate functions of collecting money with respect to the land constituted "business activity"); Britt v. United States, 431 F.2d 227 (5th Cir.1970) (where the court held, for the taxpayer, that the corporation was a separate entity since the corporate activity in signing notes and collecting dividends constituted "business activity").

Recognition of the corporate entity because the corporation conducts sufficient business activity does not preclude a *Bollinger* type argument that the corporation nevertheless was acting merely as the agent of its shareholders. See infra, page 327.

(b) *Investment Activity*

Taxpayers have sometimes been successful in having their corporations recognized as separate entities under the *Moline Properties* concept of "business activity" even though the corporate function consisted only of a single investment asset rather than active business operations. In Siegel v. Commissioner, 45 T.C. 566 (1966) (A), the taxpayer, wishing to limit his potential liability, established a Panamanian corporation to invest in a farm joint venture in Cuba. The taxpayer had no immediate need for the profits and his plan at the time of the incorporation was ultimately "to obtain the fruits of the venture through liquidation of the corporation". Although the other members of the joint venture actively participated in the farming operation, the corporation's only activity was to receive money from the venture, deposit it in its account, and periodically invest and reinvest the funds in the Cuban farming venture. The Tax Court concluded that there was a sufficient amount of business activity: "Nor may it be said that [the corporation's] minimal activity did not constitute the conduct of business. The point is that [the corporation] was formed for only a limited purpose, namely, to invest in the joint venture * * *." (577)[1] See also Bateman v. United States, 490 F.2d 549 (9th Cir.1973) (one dissent) (corporation which owned a limited partnership interest in a partnership in which its sole shareholder was active and conducted no business other than this passive investment was treated as a separate taxable entity; a trial court finding that the business purpose for the corporation was to build a cash reserve fund to buy out retiring or deceased partners' interests was upheld as not clearly erroneous).

B. THE ASPECT OF ACTUAL DIRECTION OF CORPORATE ACTIVITIES

In attempting to have the corporation disregarded for tax purposes, the Commissioner has argued unsuccessfully that the corporation is not engaged in "business activity" where the shareholder-owner has completely dominated the corporate activities. For example, in Bass v. Commissioner, 50 T.C. 595 (1968), the taxpayer organized a Swiss corporation to which he transferred working interests in oil and gas leases. The Commissioner attempted to discount the business actions of the corporation on the theory that the taxpayer "actually made the business decisions for the corporation." The Tax Court concluded that the corporation was a viable business entity since it had "acted" like a genuine corporation in paying the expenses of the business

1. Section 951, added in 1962, would now deal with the situation in *Siegel* to the extent that the utilization of a foreign rather than a domestic corporation was involved.

and filing returns. The *Bass* opinion emphasized the Supreme Court's language in National Carbide Corp. v. Commissioner, 336 U.S. 422 (1949), that "the fact that the owner retains direction of its affairs down to the minutest detail * * * [makes] no difference tax-wise." A like result was reached in Ross Glove Co. v. Commissioner, 60 T.C. 569 (1973) (A).

After failing in his attempt to prevent the classification of professional service corporations as corporations for tax purposes, see supra, page 308, the Commissioner began to attack professional service corporations generally on the basis that such corporations were shams that did not actually earn their incomes. However, as long as corporate formalities were followed and the shareholder-employees respected the corporate form in conducting business, the Commissioner met with little success. Compare Achiro v. Commissioner, 77 T.C. 881 (1981) (corporate form of management services company respected at taxpayer's behest even though shareholders were sole employees and primary purpose of forming corporation was to reduce income taxes) with Jones v. Commissioner, 64 T.C. 1066 (1975) (court reporter who formed personal service corporation taxed individually because court rules required reporter to be an individual rather than a corporation).

C. APPLICATION OF THE AGENCY RATIONALE

The *Moline Properties* doctrine makes it difficult to disregard the corporate entity if the corporation conducts any business and, as discussed supra, the requisite activity threshold is low. Taxpayers often have sought to achieve the same result as is produced by the disregard of corporate entity theory on the ground that a principal-agent relationship exists between the shareholder and the corporation. Therefore the income involved is the shareholder's rather than the corporation's. As explained in the *Bollinger* opinion, this argument was based on language in National Carbide Corp. v. Commissioner, 336 U.S. 422, 437–39 (1949).

Prior to the *Bollinger* decision, most cases turned on application of the fifth *National Carbide* factor, whether the relations between the principal and the agent depended on the principal's ownership of the agent. For example, in Harrison Property Management Co., Inc. v. United States, 475 F.2d 623 (Ct.Cl.1973), three partners transferred title to oil-bearing property to the corporation, retaining all beneficial rights and interests in the property in themselves. The primary reason for the formation of the corporation was the orderly management of the property in the event of the death of one of the individuals. The corporation received the income from oil leases, paid expenses incident thereto, and filed a fiduciary income tax return showing all net income distributed to the three individuals. The individuals reported the amounts in their individual returns. The Commissioner contended that the corporation should be treated as a separate entity and was taxable on the income. The court first held that the corporation was a taxable entity under the *Moline Properties* test and then rejected the taxpayer's alternative contention that an agency relationship existed between the corporation and the three individuals:

"*National Carbide* makes it clear that the formal designation of 'agency agreement' is not conclusive; the significant criteria, as we understand them, are whether the so-called 'agent' would have made the agreement if the so-called 'principals' were not its owners, and conversely whether the 'principals' would have undertaken the arrangement if the 'agent' were not their corporate creature. * * *

"[W]e do not doubt that the present plaintiffs fail the test. It is inconceivable that Harrison Property Management Co., Inc. would have made its alleged 'agency' contract with property owners other than its own shareholders, the Harrisons, or that the latter would have agreed to such an arrangement with the corporation if they did not own and control it. Obviously the agreement was deliberately drawn, in conjunction with the special provisions of the corporate charter, so that the company would service its owners alone, and was made solely because they were its owners. The entire operating arrangement was custom-made for that very purpose. * * * In other words, all of the corporation's relations with the beneficial owners of the managed property were wholly dependent on the fact that they were the sole shareholders. * * *" (625–628)

The courts of appeals decisions preceeding *Bollinger* viewed the six *National Carbide* factors as being of greater importance than did the Supreme Court in *Bollinger,* and also emphasized the fifth factor. Roccaforte v. Commissioner, 708 F.2d 986 (5th Cir.1983), rev'g, 77 T.C. 263 (1981), held that while the first four factors were relevant, in order to establish an agency relationship it was mandatory that the final two factors—relations between the principal and agent must be arms' length and the business purpose of the corporation must be to carry on the normal duties of an agent—be met. Because the Tax Court had found that the relations between the shareholders and the corporation were dependent on the fact that the "agent" was owned by the principals, the court held that a true agency had not been established. The facts upon which the nonarms' length relationship conclusion was based were that the corporation was owned by its shareholders in the same percentages which the shareholders held their interests in the partnership which they claimed owned the property for tax purposes, the sole function of the "agent" was to borrow money in avoidance of state usury laws, and it was not compensated for its services. Similar results were reached in Ourisman v. Commissioner, 760 F.2d 541 (4th Cir.1985); Vaughn v. United States, 740 F.2d 941 (Fed.Cir.1984); Jones v. Commissioner, 640 F.2d 745 (5th Cir.1981); Frink v. Commissioner, 798 F.2d 106 (4th Cir.1986), vacated 485 U.S. 977 (1988); George v. Commissioner, 803 F.2d 144 (5th Cir.1986), vacated 485 U.S. 973 (1988). In all of these cases the court concluded that a corporation which is not compensated and which is owned by one or more of its principals could not be a true agent under the fifth *National Carbide* factor.

Several Courts of Appeals decisions, however, applied an agency rationale to avoid corporate taxation. In general, these decisions focused on the fact that the corporation was not owned proportionately by the principals. The Sixth Circuit in its opinion in *Bollinger* distinguished *Roccaforte* because in *Bollinger* the corporation's stock was not owned by the same individuals who claimed to be the principals. 807 F.2d 65 (6th Cir.1986). See also Moncrief v. United States, 730 F.2d 276 (5th Cir.1984) (corporation wholly owned by 25 percent partner was true agent of partnership; *Roccaforte* distinguished); Raphan v. United States, 759 F.2d 879 (Fed.Cir.1985) (principals owned no stock of agent corporation).

Are the above Courts of Appeals decisions of any relevance after *Bollinger* or does the *Bollinger* opinion signal that form may control? The opinion stresses that a written agency agreement, the terms of which are respected, should be sufficient to establish the agency. Apparently these facts should suffice even in the case of an individual claiming that her wholly owned corporation is her agent. If so, the analysis in *Harrison Property Management Co.*, supra, page 327 is no longer valid. From the perspective of preventing tax avoidance through self-serving labelling of transactions, which is the preferable rule, that in *Bollinger* or that in *Harrison Property Management Co.?* Is one test more administratable than the other? If no written agreement exists should the agency argument be rejected on the grounds that form has not been followed, or should the courts engage in a facts and circumstances search for a "real" agency relationship? Heaton v. Commissioner, 57 T.C.M. 1412 (1989), held that under *Bollinger* the absence of a written agency agreement was fatal to the taxpayer's agency claim, but the court also examined other factors to find that the taxpayer failed to satisfy every one of the *Bollinger* standards. The importance of form under the *Bollinger* standards also was emphasized in Greenberg v. Commissioner, 56 T.C.M. 1030 (1989).

In light of the *Bollinger* opinion's casual treatment of the *National Carbide* factors, what standards, other than form, ought the courts to use for guidance? For some pre-*Bollinger* approaches, see Stillman v. Commissioner, 60 T.C. 897 (1973), rejecting a taxpayer's argument that a corporation was simply the agent of its individual shareholders where the corporation held legal title to a leasehold interest, assertedly on behalf of a partnership which was comprised of four individuals, three of whom were the shareholders of the corporation, but there was no agency contract, and no compensation was paid to the corporation for the services it performed. See also Red Carpet Car Wash, Inc. v. Commissioner, 73 T.C. 676 (1980) (corporation was mere nominee where its name was used in a partnership agreement solely for purpose of hiding from associates in other businesses the participation of the individual partner and the partnership otherwise treated individual owner as the partner).

Apart from the broader issue of what factors generally establish a true agency relationship or, conversely, preclude a true agency relationship, is the *Bollinger* opinion flawed on its particular facts in finding an agency relationship? The sole purpose and activity of the corporation was to obtain a loan at a rate that would have been usurious under state law if the loan had been made to an individual. According to the opinion in *Bollinger,* the individual rather than the corporation was taxed because the corporation was a genuine agent. If that is true, then the principal—an individual—was the true borrower, and the loan was usurious under state law. Thus the lender would have violated state law. In Commissioner v. First Security Bank of Utah, N.A., 405 U.S. 394 (1972), the Supreme Court refused to apply section 482, discussed below, to tax a bank on income received by a commonly controlled insurance company. A key element in the Court's reasoning was that it would have been illegal for the bank to have received the income. Is *Bollinger* inconsistent with *First Security Bank of Utah?*

D. RELATED ASPECTS

Section 269, infra, page 993, section 482, and section 1561, infra, page 1016, involve situations in which a corporation, though treated as a separate entity for tax purposes, may nonetheless lose some tax attributes otherwise available to corporations.

E. REFERENCES

Note: The Continued Validity of the Separate Entity Doctrine: The Remaining Issues After Commissioner v. Bollinger, 42 Tax Law. 773 (1989); Note: Recent Developments in the Federal Tax Law Treatment of Nominee Corporations, 13 Fla.St.U.L.Rev. 361 (1985); Kurtz and Kopp, Taxability of Straw Corporations in Real Estate Transactions, 22 Tax Lawyer 647 (1969); Fuller, Business Purpose, Sham Transactions and the Relation of Private Law to the Law of Taxation, 37 Tul.L.Rev. 355 (1963); Miller, The Nominee Conundrum: The Live Dummy is Dead, But The Dead Dummy Should Live!, 34 Tax.L.Rev. 213 (1979).

SECTION 4. REALLOCATION OF INCOME

INTERNAL REVENUE CODE: Section 482.

ILLUSTRATIVE MATERIAL

A. SECTION 482 IN GENERAL

Section 482 authorizes the Commissioner to reallocate items of income, deduction, or credit among two or more organizations, trades or businesses under common control when necessary to prevent evasion of taxes or clearly to reflect income. This provision may apply in a variety of contexts, but the common theme is that when related entities deal with one another at less than arm's length the Commissioner can adjust their taxable incomes to reflect the income that each would have earned had they dealt at arm's length. Thus an increase in the income of one of the related parties, reflecting a payment which would have been made in an arm's length relationship but which was not made, must be accompanied by a correlative deduction or capitalized item for the other related party. Regulations, section 1.482–1(d)(2).[2]

B. APPLICATION TO TRANSACTIONS INVOLVING INDIVIDUAL SHAREHOLDERS AND THEIR CONTROLLED CORPORATIONS

In the context of transactions involving individual shareholders and their controlled corporations the provision most frequently has been applied to dealings such as leases at inadequate or excessive rent and to dealings between commonly controlled corporations at an inadequate or at an excessive price, such as the sale of goods or services from X Corporation to Y Corporation, both of which are owned by the same shareholders. See Regulations, section 1.482–2(b)–(e); Peck v. Commissioner, 752 F.2d 469 (9th Cir.1985) (reallocation between corporation at less than arm's length rental); Fegan v. Commissioner, 71 T.C. 791 (1979) (79 percent shareholder of a corporation leased a motel to the corporation for less than its fair rental value). Section 482 also has been applied where a shareholder served as an employee of a controlled corporation for an inadequate salary, thereby artificially inflating the corporation's income. See Rubin v. Commissioner, 429 F.2d 650 (2d Cir.1970), on remand, 56 T.C. 1155 (1971), aff'd per curiam, 460 F.2d 1216 (2d Cir.1972).

2. Regulations, section 1.482–1(d)(3), permit taxpayers whose incomes have been adjusted under section 482 to make payments or setoffs reflecting the adjustments without further tax consequences. See Rev.Proc. 65–17, 1965–1 Cum.Bull. 833; Rev.Rul. 82–80, 1982–1 Cum.Bull. 89.

The 1986 Act inverted the corporate and individual top marginal rates. Accordingly, those cases discussed below which involved an allocation of income from a corporation to individual shareholders seem unlikely to arise with much frequency. The Commissioner after 1986 has the incentive to allocate income from the individual shareholders to the corporation. The cases (involving both income allocations to and from corporations) do indicate how the Commissioner and the courts have applied section 482 in the individual shareholder-corporation context.

In Cooper v. Commissioner, 64 T.C. 576 (1975), the taxpayer transferred a construction business to a corporation and retained the depreciable assets. The taxpayer did not charge the corporation with any rent. The court upheld the Commissioner's allocation of the fair rental value of the depreciable assets to the individual taxpayer under section 482; the taxpayer was still engaged in a trade or business by virtue of retention of assets essential to the conduct of the construction business. See also Powers v. Commissioner, 724 F.2d 64 (7th Cir.1983) (shareholder leased property from one corporation at greater than arm's length rental and subleased to another corporation at less than arm's length rental; reallocations from both corporations to shareholders upheld); Dolese v. Commissioner, 811 F.2d 543 (10th Cir.1987) (partnership items reallocated between 100 percent shareholder-employee of 51 percent partner and the shareholder-employee, who was a 49 percent partner); Foster v. Commissioner, infra, page 371.

In Miles–Conley Co. v. Commissioner, 10 T.C. 754(148)(A), aff'd, 173 F.2d 958 (4th Cir.1949), the sole stockholder of a corporation engaged in business as a commission merchant in fruit and vegetables decided to conduct the vegetable business as an individual. The principal element of both businesses was the individual's services. The expenses of facilities used in common were pro rated. The Tax Court disallowed the Commissioner's allocation to the corporation of the income from the vegetable business:

"Here we have a 'one man' corporation engaged in the business of buying and selling, or selling on commission, fruits and vegetables. The corporation could have continued its business in fruits and vegetables. However its controlling stockholder decided that petitioner should relinquish its active conduct of the business relating to vegetables and that he, as an individual, should organize and carry on the vegetable business as a sole proprietor, and this was done. He carried on the vegetable business as a sole proprietor, but shared offices and expenses with the corporation. The result of this transaction was to reduce the income of the corporation, and also to reduce the amount of taxes collected by the Commissioner of Internal Revenue. However, we know of nothing in the Internal Revenue Code, and no cases have been called to our attention, which would justify a disregard of the existence of a sole proprietorship because of any lack of business purpose *quoad* the corporation. In this instant case we assume, *arguendo,* that the purpose of A. Carlisle Miles in causing the petitioner to relinquish its dealing in vegetables and in organizing and conducting the business in vegetables as a sole proprietorship was not to further the best interests of the corporation, but was to further his own best interests (including the minimizing of total taxes payable by him and his controlled corporation). We are, nevertheless, unable to conclude that these assumed facts compel us to merge the actuality of the sole proprietorship into the fiction of the corporation for tax purposes, or to disregard A. Carlisle Miles as a separate taxable entity. This is not the case of an individual organizing a solely owned corporation which, as a fiction and a sham, may be disregarded for tax purposes; Cf. Higgins v. Smith, 308 U.S. 473. The respondent, in this case, recognizes the corporation, but disregards the individual. Even his disregard of the individual is provisional and paradoxical. His position appears to be that the sole proprietorship is recognized for the purpose of invoking [section 482] and that the reason [section 482] is applicable is that, in reality, the sole proprietorship does not exist because it is not useful to the legal fiction of the corporation.

"In the instant case it may be that the sole stockholder of the corporation received from the corporation something of value at the time of and by reason of the relinquishment of part of its business by the corporation. This something of value, in the nature of good will, might have been taxable to the sole stockholder in the year in which its was received as a distribution of a dividend or a distribution in partial liquidation. Such an issue is not before us. The fact, if it be a fact, that the sole stockholder received something of value from the petitioner in 1943 which he used in the operation of a sole proprietorship in 1944 would not require or justify the taxing of the income of the proprietorship to the corporation." (762–3)

In some situations in which section 482 might be invoked, other principles are applied. These other rules do not necessarily require correlative adjustments such as those required under section 482. Thus, when an employee-shareholder is paid an excessive salary, the Internal Revenue Service often simply disallows a deduction to the corporation under section 162(a)(1) rather than invoking section 482. When a shareholder purchases or leases property from a corporation at a bargain price, the Service asserts that the bargain element is a dividend to the shareholder. See infra, pages 482. Finally, below market rate of interest loans are subject to the rules of section 7872, although 482 also may be relevant. See Regulations, section 1.482–2(a).

C. THE EXISTENCE OF "CONTROL"

Where two unrelated taxpayers each owned 50 percent of the stock in a subsidiary corporation, the Tax Court originally held that the predecessor of section 482 was not applicable since the subsidiary was not "controlled" by the same interests despite the fact that they were acting in furtherance of their common purposes. Lake Erie & Pittsburg Railway Co. v. Commissioner, 5 T.C. 558 (1945). The Service initially acquiesced in this decision (1945 Cum.Bull. 5), but in 1965 reexamined its position and indicated that it would no longer follow the *Lake Erie* holding. Rev.Rul. 65–142, 1965–1 Cum. Bull. 223. *Lake Erie* was likewise rejected by B. Forman Co. v. Commissioner, 453 F.2d 1144 (2d Cir.1972). In that case, two unrelated corporations formed a subsidiary, in which they each owned 50 percent of the stock, to build and operate a shopping center next to their department stores. The court held section 482 was applicable to allow the Commissioner to allocate to the shareholders interest income on non-interest bearing loans made to the subsidiary: "Whether [the two shareholders] are regarded as a partnership or joint venture, *de facto,* in forming [the subsidiary], the conclusion is inescapable that they acted in concert in making loans without interest to a corporation, all of whose stock they owned and all of whose directors and officers were their alter egos. They were not competitors in their dealings with one another or with [the subsidiary]. Their interests in [the subsidiary] were identical. When the Commissioner withdrew his acquiescence in *Lake*

Erie, he gave reality of control as one of the reasons for doing so * * *. We agree." (1155)

In Hall v. Commissioner, 32 T.C. 390 (1959), the taxpayer as a sole proprietorship sold goods manufactured by him to a foreign corporation at a price considerably below his usual list price, the stock of the corporation according to the taxpayer being owned by his son and another. The court said that section 482 was applicable regardless of the legal ownership of the stock, since the taxpayer in fact exercised control over the corporation and dominated it. The court therefore allocated a part of the corporation's income to the taxpayer by treating the sales as if made in accordance with the taxpayer's list prices.

In Ach v. Commissioner, 358 F.2d 342 (6th Cir.1966), the proprietor of a profitable clothing business sold the assets of a dress business to a corporation with loss carryovers controlled by her son. The Government argued that the sale should be ignored completely and the income from the dress business taxed directly to the proprietor. The Tax Court refused to take this approach, ("The corporation was actually in existence, and there was a genuine transfer of assets to it that were actually used in the conduct of the dress business," 42 T.C. 114, 123 (1964), but went on to allocate 70 percent of the profits of the dress business to the proprietor because of her continuing management activities. The Court of Appeals sustained the allocation.

D. APPLICABILITY OF SECTION 482 TO INADEQUATE SALARY SITUATIONS

1. *Background*

Prior to 1987, a sole shareholder, who was also the principal officer of his corporation, might not have taken any salary from the corporation, planning instead to build up the value of the corporation and then sell the stock, paying tax at capital gain rates. The question was whether section 482 was applicable to permit the Commissioner to allocate a fair salary to him—which he then recontributed to the corporation—but on which he must pay tax. Similar issues arose where the corporation was a personal services corporation through which the shareholder-employee rendered services which he previously performed as a sole proprietor. Could the Commissioner apply the principles of section 61 and Lucas v. Earl, 281 U.S. 111 (1930), as well as section 482 to tax the corporation's income to the shareholder-employee? Of course, after the 1986 Act, an individual has little incentive to avoid taking a salary from his wholly-owned corporation except to the extent of the benefit provided by the 15 and 25 percent corporate rate brackets. The following cases illustrate how the courts dealt with the issues prior to the 1986 Act.

2. *Judicial Doctrine*

In Foglesong v. Commissioner, 35 T.C.M. 1309 (1976), the taxpayer was a sales representative for a pipe company. He formed a corporation which issued 98 percent of its common stock to him. The taxpayer's children were issued preferred stock with a stated value of $400. Thereafter the corporation entered into an employment contract with the taxpayer and into contracts with the pipe manufacturers for whom the taxpayer sold pipe products; commissions earned on sales were paid by the manufacturers directly to the corporation, from which the taxpayer received a salary. The taxpayer's compensation over the next several years was less than two-thirds of the commissions paid to the corporation, which had no other employees or sources of income. During that period dividends of $32,000 were paid on the preferred stock; no dividends were paid on the common stock. The Tax Court weighed the legitimate business purposes for the arrangement against its tax avoidance potential and held that the taxpayer so controlled and directed the earning of the income of the corporation that he was personally taxable on 98 percent of such income under the principles of Lucas v. Earl.

On appeal, the Seventh Circuit Court of Appeals vacated and remanded the case. 621 F.2d 865 (7th Cir.1980). The Court of Appeals concluded that applying section 61 was imprecise and directed the Tax Court to reconsider the case based on the Commissioner's power to reallocate income under section 482. On remand, the Tax Court held that section 482 was properly applied to allocate 98 percent of the corporation's income to the taxpayer because his salary was unreasonably low. 77 T.C. 1102 (1981). The Tax Court applied its earlier decision in Keller v. Commissioner, 77 T.C. 1014 (1981), to hold that the requisite "two organizations" existed: Foglesong was in the trade or business of selling pipe as an employee of the corporation, and the corporation was in the trade or business of selling pipe (through the efforts of Foglesong). The taxpayer appealed again, and the Court of Appeals vacated and remanded the decision a second time. A different panel held that section 482 could not be invoked to allocate income from a personal service corporation to its shareholder-employee who performs services solely for the corporation. The Court of Appeals did not consider the "two organizations" requirement to have been met.

The Internal Revenue Service does not follow the most recent Court of Appeals decision in *Foglesong.* Rev.Rul. 88–38, 1988–1 Cum.Bull. 246. Similarly, notwithstanding the reversal by the Seventh Circuit in *Foglesong,* the Tax Court continues to hold that section 482 can be applied to allocate income between a corporation and a shareholder-employee who performs services solely for a controlled corporation, at least where appeal does not lie to the Seventh Circuit. See Haag v. Commissioner, 88 T.C. 604 (1987) (income of professional service corporation reallocated to physician-sole shareholder who drew nominal salary). See also Borge v. Commissioner, 405 F.2d 673 (2d Cir.1968).

In determining whether a reallocation of income is appropriate under section 482, the inquiry is whether the shareholder-employee's total compensation (including salary, bonuses, deferred compensation, and other fringe benefits) approximates the amount he would have received absent incorporation of the business. See Keller v. Commissioner, 77 T.C. 1014 (1981), aff'd, 723 F.2d 58 (10th Cir.1983) (section 482 applicable, but on facts no reallocation was warranted because total compensation approximated preincorporation earnings).

3. *Applicability of Assignment of Income Principles*

Because it relies on section 482 in cases of nominal compensation to controlling-shareholder employees, the Tax Court applies section 61 and Lucas v. Earl only in the cases where the corporation does not control the income. In Johnson v. Commissioner, 78 T.C. 882 (1982), aff'd without published opinion, 734 F.2d 20 (9th Cir.1984), the Tax Court promulgated a two part test for determining when the corporation controls the income: "First, the service-performer employee must be just that—an employee of the corporation whom the corporation has the right to direct or control in some meaningful sense. Second, there must exist between the corporation and the person or entity using the services a contract or other similar indicium recognizing the corporation's controlling position." (891) In that case the individual taxpayer, a professional basketball player, was held to control the income because even though the team for which he played paid the salary directly to the corporation, the only contract was between the player and the team. In contrast, in *Haag,* supra, the corporation was treated as controlling the income, because the individual and corporation entered into an employment contract and the recipients of services treated the services as being rendered by the corporation.

For other cases in which the Tax Court has used assignment of income principles rather than section 482 to tax shareholders see, e.g., Sargent v. Commissioner, 93 T.C. 572 (1989) (holding that a professional hockey player was an employee of the hockey team for which he played, not his wholly owned corporation which had contracted with the hockey team to provide the player's services under an exclusive personal services contract, because the nature of the services was unique to the individual); Jones v. Commissioner, 64 T.C. 1066 (1975); Ronan State Bank v. Commissioner, 62 T.C. 27 (1974) (bank marketed credit life insurance through its employees but, believing that it was prohibited from engaging in the insurance business under state law, it assigned that business to its two principal shareholders who reported the commission income; the Tax Court upheld the Commissioner's allocation of the commission income to the bank solely under section 61 principles, thus avoiding the Supreme Court decision in Commissioner v. First Security Bank of Utah N.A., 405 U.S. 394 (1972), that section 482 could not be employed to allocate income to a corporation where it would have been illegal for the corporation to have received that income directly). But see Salyersville National Bank v. United States, 613 F.2d 650 (6th Cir.1980) (no reallocation under section 482 on facts substantially similar to *Ronan State Bank,* citing *First Security Bank of Utah*).

What difference in result does it make whether the theory of the reallocation is the disregard of the intervening corporate entity, section 61 principles, or the application of section 482?

4. *Section 269A—Reallocation of Personal Service Corporation Income*

In Keller v. Commissioner, supra, page 334, the physician shareholder of the professional service corporation involved in the case had been a partner in a medical partnership prior to formation of the corporation. Thereafter, Dr. Keller's professional service corporation was substituted for him as a partner. Thereafter, the professional service corporation was substituted for the physician as a partner. The purpose of this arrangement was to permit Dr. Keller to custom tailor a deferred compensation and fringe benefit plan for himself, which could permit evasion of the nondiscrimination rules with respect to pension plans and statutory fringe benefits. Congress responded to the *Keller* decision with the enactment of section 269A. See H.R.Rep. No. 97–760, 97th Cong., 2d Sess. 633–34 (1982). This provision authorizes reallocation of income from a personal service corporation to the employee-owner if (1) the principal purpose of forming or using the corporation is the avoidance of federal income tax by reducing the income of any employee-owner; (2) the corporation performs substantially all of its services on behalf of *one* other corporation, person, or partnership; and (3) substantially all of the services provided by the corporation are performed by employees who own more than 10 percent of the stock. Thus, section 269A does not apply to personal services corporations with more than one customer, which is normally the case or, for example, if ten physicians form a corporation to provide emergency room services exclusively to one hospital and each physician owns 10 percent of the stock. For the mechanics of the reallocation under section 269A, see Proposed Regulations, section 1.269A–1 (1983). As noted previously, the 1982 Act made several changes in the treatment of qualified deferred compensation plans that greatly reduced the tax benefits from personal service corporations. In concert with the effect of the rate reductions in the 1986 Act, these changes have reduced the number of incorporations to which section 269A might be applied.

E. COMBINING INCOME OF CONTROLLED ORGANIZATIONS OR BUSINESSES

Prior to the enactment in 1969 of the predecessor of current section 1561, discussed infra, page 1016, taxpayers often formed multiple corporations to conduct different facets of a related business for the purpose of splitting income to take advantage of graduated tax rates for each corporation. The Commissioner frequently attacked such arrangements under section 482 and met with mixed success. Compare Hamburgers York Road, Inc. v. Commissioner, 41 T.C. 821 (1964) (upheld the Commissioner's allocation of *all* of the income and deductions of a subsidiary to its parent) and Wisconsin Big Boy Corp. v. Commissioner, 452 F.2d 137 (7th Cir.1971) (where all the income and deductions of a chain of restaurant subsidiaries were allocated to parent) with Your Host, Inc. v. Commissioner, 58 T.C. 10 (1972), aff'd on other issues, 489 F.2d 957 (2d Cir.1973) (Commissioner was not justified in allocating all of the income from a chain of restaurant subsidiaries to the parent) and Bush Hog Manufacturing Co. v. Commissioner, 42 T.C. 713 (1964) (A) (Commissioner's reallocation of all of the income of eight regional sales corporations to a manufacturing corporation based on the common control of all of the corporations by a four shareholder group was rejected because each corporation had its own employees, books and records, and there was no artificial shifting of income).

Since the enactment of section 1561 in 1969, far fewer cases involving reallocations between domestic corporations under common control have arisen. In the context of controlled groups of corporations, section 482 now most often is applied to reallocate income among domestic and foreign corporations within the group. See, e.g., Eli Lilly & Co. v. Commissioner, 856 F.2d 855 (7th Cir.1988) (Commissioner's application of section 482 rejected); G.D. Searle & Co. v. Commissioner, 88 T.C. 252 (1987) (reallocation upheld).

For other situations in which section 482 is applicable, see infra, page 1026.

F. REFERENCES

Manning, The Service Corporation—Who Is Taxable On Its Income: Reconciling Assignment of Income Principles, Section 482, and Section 351, 37 U.Miami L.Rev. 653 (1983); Wood, The *Keller, Foglesong,* and *Pacella* Cases: Section 482 Allocations, Assignments of Income, and New Section 269A, 10 J.Corp. Tax'n 65 (1983); Lee, Section 482 and the Integrated Business Enterprise, 57 Va.L.Rev. 1376 (1971); Kauder, The Service Corporation as the Taxpayer's Alter Ego: Variations on the *Borge* Theme, 28 N.Y.U. Tax Inst. 1109 (1970); Eustice, Tax Problems Arising From Transactions Between Affiliated or Controlled Corporations, 23 Tax L.Rev. 451 (1968).

CHAPTER 9

FORMATION OF THE CORPORATION

SECTION 1. TAX ASPECTS OF INCORPORATION OF BUSINESS

A. INTRODUCTION

INTERNAL REVENUE CODE: Sections 351; 357; 358(a), (b)(1); 362(a); 1032; 1223(1), (2).

REGULATIONS: Sections 1.358–2(b)(2); 1.1032–1(a), (d).

When its requirements are met, section 351 permits the incorporation of a proprietorship, a partnership, or a new business without the recognition of gain, and prevents the recognition of loss. Under section 351 gain or loss is not recognized on the transfer of property to a corporation solely in exchange for stock [1] of the corporation if the transferor or transferors control at least 80 percent of the stock of the transferee corporation immediately after the transaction. Section 358 provides that the basis of stock received in exchange for property contributed to the corporation in a nonrecognition transaction under section 351 will be the same as the basis of property transferred to the corporation. Section 362(a) generally provides the corporation with a basis in the property equal to the transferor's basis.

In the absence of section 351, incorporation would constitute a taxable exchange since the transferor's change of status from the owner of an asset to the owner of shares of a corporation which owns the asset is a realization event. Burnet v. Commonwealth Improvement Co., 287 U.S. 415 (1932). Section 351 is intended to defer recognition of gain or loss in "transactions where gain or loss may have accrued in a constitutional sense, but where in popular and economic sense there has been a mere change in the form of ownership and the taxpayer has not really 'cashed in' on the theoretical gain, or closed out a losing venture." Portland Oil Co. v. Commissioner, 109 F.2d 479, 488 (1st Cir.1940). This "tax-free" incorporation is important where the assets to be transferred to the corporation have increased in value so that a gain would be present on a taxable exchange. The section also permits the tax-free creation of a subsidiary corporation by another corporation. In addition, it permits the transfer of property to an existing corporation without the recognition of gain, either where the existing corporation is controlled by an individual or by a corporation.

In the situations covered by section 351, if the taxpayer is seeking the advantage of nonrecognition of gain on the transfer, the conditions of the

1. Prior to the amendment of section 351 in 1989, section 351 nonrecognition treatment likewise applied if the corporation issued "securities," generally long-term debt. As a result of the 1989 amendment, the transfer of appreciated property for anything other than stock is a recognition event (cash, of course, can be transferred for securities without gain recognition).

section represent requirements to be satisfied.[2] But the taxpayer may have a different goal. If the assets to be transferred have depreciated in value, so that a loss would be realized on their transfer, the transferor may be seeking recognition. If section 351 applies, however, the loss will not be recognized. Here, the conditions of the section represent factors to be avoided if the loss is to be obtained. Similarly, since the corporation takes over the transferor's basis if section 351 applies, the taxpayer may in some limited cases be willing to recognize gain in order to obtain for the corporation a depreciable basis equal to the fair market value of the transferred assets instead of the lower basis that would obtain if the gain were not recognized. Here also, the conditions of the section must be avoided if such a stepped-up basis is to be obtained. Section 351 is applicable regardless of the intent of the taxpayer if the conditions of the section are in fact satisfied. Gus Russell, Inc. v. Commissioner, 36 T.C. 965 (1961).

Although by its terms section 351(a) applies only if the transferor receives stock as the sole consideration for the transfer of property to a controlled corporation, section 351(b) allows for the receipt of cash or other property, "boot" in tax jargon. The transferor's realized gain is recognized to the extent of money and the fair market value of property received as boot.[3] Loss, however, is never recognized even though boot may be present. Section 351(b)(2). Under section 358(a) the transferor's basis in stock received is adjusted to reflect receipt and taxation of the boot. The corporation's basis in property received is increased by gain recognized to the transferor. Section 362(a).

The main requirement of section 351, apart from the question of boot, is acquisition of control by the transferors. As defined in section 368(c), control requires that the transferors own at least 80 percent of the stock of the transferee corporation immediately after the exchange. This requirement normally will be satisfied on an incorporation, with problems arising only if there is an immediate transfer of stock to a person not transferring property to the corporation. As a result, the control requirement is most significant with respect to transfers to an existing corporation.

Where incorporation of a proprietorship or partnership is contemplated, it is very likely that the properties involved will be subject to liabilities. Since ordinarily the assumption of a liability or the taking of property subject to a liability is regarded as consideration moving from the transferee to the transferor in the amount of the liability, the application of this rule to section 351 transactions in many cases would produce boot in the amount of the liabilities. The presence of that boot, giving rise to the possibility of taxable gain, would impede the free transition from the unincorporated to the corporate form, thereby frustrating the underlying policy of section 351. Consequently, section 357 provides that the assumption of a liability or the acquisition of property subject to a liability does not constitute boot for the purpose of section 351, unless a tax avoidance scheme is involved or unless the liabilities assumed exceed the basis of the property transferred. While the liability is not considered boot, its assumption by the corporation has the

2. Taxpayers seeking an advance ruling from the Internal Revenue Service regarding the applicability of section 351 must supply the information specified in Rev. Proc. 83–59, 1983–2 Cum.Bull. 575. See also Regulations, section 1.351–3, for information to be filed with the tax return of a taxpayer who received stock in a section 351 transaction.

3. In this regard, section 351 operates in much the same manner as section 1031.

effect of the receipt of money by the stockholder. Accordingly, section 358(d) provides that for basis purposes liabilities are treated as money, which has the effect of decreasing the transferor's basis for the stock received in the exchange.

Nonrecognition principles also apply to the corporate transferee. Section 1032 provides nonrecognition treatment to a corporate transferee on the issuance of its stock in exchange for property or services. Under section 362(a)(1) the basis of transferred property in the hands of the transferee corporation is the same as the basis of the transferred property in the hands of the transferor, plus any gain recognized to the transferor on the exchange. Thus, suppose A transfers an apartment building worth $100,000 but with an adjusted basis of $10,000, to a newly created corporation in return for its stock. A's basis for the stock is $10,000 under section 358(a). The corporation's basis for the apartment building under section 362(a)(1) is likewise $10,000. If the corporation had been in existence and had issued both stock and $30,000 cash for the apartment, A would have had a recognized gain of $30,000 (the extent of the boot, assuming that the value of the stock was $70,000 and assuming that no dividend was involved), a basis of $10,000 for the stock, and a basis of $30,000 for the cash; the corporation would have had a basis of $40,000 ($10,000 basis in transferor A's hands plus gain of $30,000 recognized to A). If for some reason, such as lack of control because of a prearranged transfer of some of the stock, the incorporation was not under section 351 at all, the entire gain would be recognized, and the basis of the apartment in the corporation's hands under general cost principles would be the fair market value of the stock issued for the assets. Regulations, section 1.1032–1(d). The fair market value of the assets would be relevant in determining that value, though it would not be controlling.[4]

The corporation's basis under section 362(a) is thus dependent on the basis of the transferring stockholders and the amount of gain, if any, that is recognized to them. It does not depend upon nor is it affected by any actual cost which the corporation may have. Hence, in the immediately preceding example, where the corporation paid out $30,000 cash as well as stock, if the basis of the stockholder for the apartment house had been higher than the value of the stock and the cash received so that the stockholder realized but did not recognize a loss, the corporation's basis for the apartment house would still be the same as that of the stockholder. The corporation's basis for the apartment house would not be increased by the $30,000 cash which it paid. The loss, not being recognized, would not reduce that basis.

Sections 1223(1) and (2), following the basis provisions, give both stockholder and corporation the holding period of the assets transferred to the corporation. The stock obtains such holding period and may on a sale be treated as held for the period of the transferred property only if the property was itself a capital asset or an asset that could obtain capital gain treatment under section 1231.

Where section 351 is applicable the combined effect of the two basis provisions, sections 358(a) and 362(a)(1), is to produce the possibility of two gains or two losses where only one existed before. However, a subsequent recognition of the stockholder's gain may be postponed if the stock is later

4. Rev.Rul. 56–100, 1956–1 Cum.Bull. 624.

transferred in a tax-free transaction, e.g., a reorganization. Furthermore, if the stock is held by the transferor until death, one of the two gains or losses is eliminated by the rule of section 1014 which provides for a basis equal to the value of the stock at the date of death.

ILLUSTRATIVE MATERIAL

A. ALLOCATION OF BASIS TO STOCK

The stockholders' basis in the stock must be allocated among stock of different classes in proportion to the fair market values of the stock in each class. Section 358(b)(1); Regulations section 1.358–2(b)(2). Thus, for example, if A transfers real property with a basis of $20 and fair market value of $100 to X, a controlled corporation, in a nonrecognition transaction under section 351, and A receives in exchange common stock with a value of $80 and preferred stock with a value of $20, A's substituted basis in the common stock is $16 ($20 X $80/$100) and A's substituted basis in the preferred stock is $4 ($20 X $20/100). The stockholder cannot allocate the basis of some transferred assets to one block of stock, for example, preferred stock, and the lower basis of other assets to another block of stock. See Rev.Rul. 85–164, 1985–2 Cum.Bull. 117.

As to the corporation, the transferor's basis in each transferred asset carries over to become the corporation's basis in that asset. P.A. Birren & Son v. Commissioner, 116 F.2d 718 (7th Cir.1940). The problems encountered in allocating basis increases attributable to the transferor's recognized gain when multiple assets are involved are discussed infra, page 378.

B. TAX CONSEQUENCES TO THE CORPORATE TRANSFEREE—TRANSACTIONS OF A CORPORATION INVOLVING ITS OWN STOCK

1. *General*

The Regulations had long provided, e.g., Regulations 118, section 22(a)–15(a), that the original issue of its stock is not a taxable event for the corporation. In Realty Bond & Mortgage Co. v. United States, 16 F.Supp. 771 (Ct.Cl.1936), the court held that part payments on stock subscriptions retained by the corporation when the subscription agreements were forfeited for nonpayment of the full amounts did not constitute income to the corporation, but rather were capital payments. Section 1032, adopted in 1954, codifies this rule.

The Regulations in effect prior to the enactment of section 1032 also provided that if a corporation dealt in its own shares as it might in the shares of another corporation, the corporation could realize taxable gain or loss. Thus where treasury stock, i.e., previously purchased but unretired stock, was sold gain or loss could result. The prior case law had limited the application of the Regulations to situations in which the corporation was in effect investing or speculating in its own stock as opposed to purchasing the stock for a "corporate" purpose. See United States v. Anderson, Clayton & Co., 350 U.S. 55 (1955).

Section 1032, however, applies both to newly-issued stock and treasury stock. Regulations, section 1.1032–1(d), appear not to treat property received for the stock in these situations as paid-in surplus or a contribution to capital, and thus in general fix the basis of the property at its "cost" to the corporation unless the transaction falls under section 351 or the reorganization nonrecognition sections which generally provide for a carryover of basis from the transferor.

2. *Transfer of Stock for Services*

Suppose a corporation pays an employee a bonus in the form of its stock, which it had previously purchased in the market and whose value is in excess of the basis of the stock. While presumably the value of the stock would otherwise be a deductible expense (see section 83(h)), does the nonrecognition treatment of section 1032 relieving the gain from inclusion (Regulations, section 1.1032–1(a) (last sentence)) bring into play section 265, which disallows expenses allocable to income "wholly exempt"? (This question assumes that an "exchange" is present of the stock for the value of services, fixed at the value of the stock; see International Freighting Corp. v. Commissioner, 135 F.2d 310 (2d Cir.1943).) In Hercules Powder Co. v. United States, 180 F.Supp. 363 (Ct.Cl.1960), after holding that stock so distributed did not result in gain to the corporation under the pre-section 1032 Regulations, the court then allowed the deduction as against the Commissioner's assertion of the rule of section 265:

"We think that the words 'gives rise to neither taxable gain nor deductible loss' in the regulation concerning the original issue of shares did not create an exemption of income from taxation. That could not be accomplished by regulation. That language must mean that such an issue does not give rise to income, within the meaning of [section 61]." (367)

Subsequently, the Internal Revenue Service ruled that a transfer of appreciated stock or newly issued stock to employees as compensation for services is fully deductible under section 162. Although not discussing section 265, the Rulings stated that the nonrecognition provisions of section 1032 have no effect on business expense deductions otherwise allowable under section 162. Rev.Rul. 62–217, 1962–2 Cum.Bull. 59; Rev.Rul. 69–75, 1969–1 Cum.Bull. 52.

In Affiliated Government Employees' Distributing Co. v. Commissioner, 322 F.2d 872 (9th Cir.1963), and United States v. Federal Employees' Distributing Co., 322 F.2d 891 (9th Cir.1963), membership fees received by nonstock membership corporations were held to constitute taxable income and not payments for stock under section 1032; the fees were paid for the privilege of shopping at the taxpayers' stores and the memberships did not have the normal indicia of stock. Similarly, in Community T.V. Ass'n of Havre v. United States, 203 F.Supp. 270 (D.Mont.1962), payments to a television service corporation by subscribers for its "Class B stock" were held to be for services to be rendered by the corporation and not for stock.

3. *Transfer of Appreciated Property as Boot*

The 1988 Act added section 351(f) to the Code. This section provides that in the case of a section 351 transaction gain is to be recognized under section 311(b) on a transfer by the corporation of appreciated property as a part of the exchange. Section 311(b) requires recognition of gain as if the property transferred by the corporation had been sold for its fair market value. Thus corporate level gain will be recognized on a transfer of appreciated property to a stockholder as boot in a section 351 exchange.

4. *The Corporation's Basis in its Own Stock*

Before the enactment of section 1032, the Tax Court held in Firestone Tire & Rubber Co. v. Commissioner, 2 T.C. 827 (1943), that a corporation which acquired its own shares in the open market and held them as treasury shares maintained its cost basis for the shares. The corporate transferee of such treasury stock in a transaction providing for carryover basis under the predecessor to section 362 thereby obtained the stock with a carryover basis equal to the transferor's cost basis. In Rev.Rul. 74–503, 1974–2 Cum.Bull. 117, however, the Internal Revenue Service ruled that the rationale of *Firestone* was rendered invalid by the enactment of section 1032 in the 1954 Code. The Service held that a corporation's treasury stock is no different than previously unissued stock. Thus, for tax purposes, the corporation's basis in treasury stock as well as originally issued stock is zero. Nevertheless, when a corporation issues its own stock in exchange for assets in a taxable transaction, the corporation takes a "purchase price" basis in the assets equal to the fair market value of the stock. Regulations, section 1.1032–1(d).

C. REFERENCES

Manning, The Issuer's Paper: Property or What? Zero Basis and Other Income Tax Mysteries, 39 Tax L.Rev. 159 (1984); Kirkpatrick, Tax Consequences of a Corporation Dealing in Its Own Stock, 13 Tul.Tax Inst. 85 (1964).

B. TRANSFER OF "PROPERTY"

INTERNAL REVENUE CODE: Section 83; 351(d)(1).

REGULATIONS: Sections 1.351–1(a)(i), (ii).

In dealing with the provisions of Subchapter C, the tax advisor must pay meticulous attention to the language of the applicable statutory provision. Virtually every word or phrase has been subject to judicial and administrative interpretation with which the tax advisor must be familiar. The materials in this and the following sections are designed to illustrate, in the context of section 351 transactions, the way in which the tax advisor must deal with the provisions covering corporate transactions on a word-by-word and phrase-by-phrase approach. For example, section 351 applies only to the transfer of "property" in exchange for stock. While "property" in section 351 includes cash, Rev.Rul. 69–357, 1969–1 Cum.Bull. 101, "property" for section 351 purposes does not include all interests that may be considered property interests for other purposes. Section 351(d)(1) specifically provides that stock issued for services is not issued for property.

ILLUSTRATIVE MATERIAL

A. EFFECT OF STOCK FOR SERVICES ON OTHER TRANSFERORS

The presence of a transfer of services to the corporation for stock will not defeat the section 351 transaction as to other parties unless the transferor of services receives more than 20 percent of the stock since transferors of "property" would still be in "control" of the corporation. See Mojonnier & Sons, Inc. v. Commissioner, 12 T.C. 837 (1949) (NA) (Section 351 did not apply to any transferor where upon incorporation of a sole proprietorship former employees received more than 20 percent of stock in consideration for past services). A transferor of services who receives more than 20 percent of the stock for his services and who also transfers some property to the corporation for stock will qualify as a "transferor of property," so that both the stock received for services and the stock received for property will be counted in determining whether the control test is met. However, Regulations, section 1.351–1(a)(ii), warn that if the primary purpose of the property transfer is to qualify the stock received for services and the property transferred constitutes only a "relatively small value" in comparison to the value of the services stock, the services stock will not be counted in determining the control group. Rev.Proc. 76–22, 1976–1 Cum.Bull. 562, indicates that for advance ruling purposes the property transferred will not be considered to be of "relatively small value" if it has a value equal to at least 10 percent of the value of the stock received for services by the person providing services (i.e., the value of the property is at least 9.09 percent of the total value of the stock received).

The question of control is discussed infra at page 360. A related problem, which involves attempts by taxpayers to count previously acquired stock in determining the members of the control group in order to qualify a current property contribution, is discussed infra at page 368.

B. "PROPERTY" DISTINGUISHED FROM SERVICES AND SERVICE FLAVORED ASSETS

The question whether assets that have been produced as the result of the taxpayer's personal efforts constitute "property" for purposes of section 351 is identical to that encountered in exchanges of property for a partnership interest accorded nonrecognition treatment under section 721, discussed supra page 52, and is similar to that encountered in connection with whether an asset constitutes "property" for purposes of capital gain treatment under section 1221. Thus, the term "property" includes secret processes and formulae whether patentable or not. Rev.Rul. 64–56, 1964–1 (Part 1) Cum. Bull. 133. Under that Ruling, if the transferred information qualifies as property, then section 351 applies even though services are to be performed in connection with the transfer; the services, however, must be ancillary and subsidiary to the property transfer. Continuing technical assistance, employee training, and construction assistance will ordinarily be considered services for purposes of section 351 transfers. Rev.Rul. 71–564, 1971–2 Cum.Bull. 179, holds that trade secrets are property for purposes of section 351 transfers as long as the transferee corporation receives an exclusive right to the trade secret until it becomes public knowledge and is no longer protectable under applicable law. E.I. Du Pont de Nemours & Co. v. United States, 471 F.2d 1211 (Ct.Cl.1973), held, however, that the transfer of a royalty free, nonexclusive license qualified as a transfer of "property" in a section 351 exchange. The fact that a taxable transfer of the nonexclusive license would not have qualified for capital gain treatment did not prevent section 351 from applying.

Rev.Rul. 70–45, 1970–1 Cum.Bull. 17, provides that business goodwill is property. In Rev.Rul. 79–288, 1979–2 Cum.Bull. 139, the Internal Revenue Service ruled further that a corporate name registered in a foreign country and protected under the laws of the foreign country is property for section 351 purposes, but that an unregistered, unprotected name with no goodwill value is not property.

In United States v. Frazell, 335 F.2d 487 (5th Cir.1964), supra, page 52, the court alternatively held that the taxpayer realized ordinary income under section 351 on the theory that, if the stock were a substitution for the partnership interest originally contemplated, it would be compensation for services (and not received in exchange for "property"), and hence taxable under section 351. To the extent that the geological maps constituted "property," the taxpayer was entitled to section 351 nonrecognition treatment as to these items.

In James v. Commissioner, 53 T.C. 63 (1969), the taxpayer and one Talbot entered into an agreement to develop a real estate project. Talbot was to contribute land and the taxpayer was to promote the project and obtain the necessary FHA commitment and financing for the project. The taxpayer obtained the commitments in the name of the corporation and the taxpayer and Talbot then transferred the land and financing commitments to a corporation. The stock of the corporation was issued 50–50 to taxpayer and Talbot. The taxpayer argued that he had transferred contract rights (analogous to patents or secret processes) to the corporation and therefore section 351 controlled. Following *Frazell,* the court held that the stock was received for services and was therefore ordinary income to the taxpayer. Furthermore, the only transferor of "property" was Talbot, who owned only 50 percent of the stock after the transaction. Thus section 351 did not apply to Talbot's transfer because the 80 percent control test was not met and taxable gain resulted.

James was distinguished in United States v. Stafford, 727 F.2d 1043 (11th Cir.1984), supra page 56, which held that an unenforceable letter of intent to provide financing was property under section 721, which provides for nonrecognition of gain or loss on the contribution of property to a partnership. The court indicated that it would reach the same result under section 351. The court pointed out that Stafford had developed the letter of intent for his own account and owned the letter of intent individually. The financing commitment in *James* was in the name of the corporation.

In Hospital Corp. of America v. Commissioner, 81 T.C. 520, 587–590 (1983), the Tax Court held that the transfer of an opportunity to negotiate a management contract in Saudi Arabia was not the transfer of "property". In Roberts Company, Inc. v. Commissioner, 5 T.C. 1 (1945), however, a contingent fee agreement in favor of attorneys conveying an interest in land in the event of a successful litigation was held to constitute a property interest in the land involved, so that the attorneys could qualify as transferors of property.

Specific provisions of section 351 address the transfer of stock in discharge of certain indebtedness of the corporation. The Bankruptcy Tax Act of 1980 added sections 351(d)(2) and (3) to provide that stock issued to satisfy an indebtedness of the issuing corporation not evidenced by a security, or to pay interest on indebtedness of the issuing corporation, is not considered as issued in return for property. Similarly, section 351(e)(2) provides that section 351 is not applicable where a corporation in a bankruptcy or insolvency proceeding transfers assets to another corporation and then distributes the stock received to its creditors. The transaction is treated as if the assets had first been distributed to the creditors and the creditors had then transferred the property to the new corporation.

C. REFERENCES

Fleming, Domestic Section 351 Transfers of Intellectual Property: The Law as It Is vs. the Law as the Commissioner Would Prefer It to Be, 16 J.Corp.Tax. 99 (1989); Goodman, How to Avoid Tax Problems Under Section 351 When Transferring Services In Exchange For Stock, 55 Taxes 112 (1977); Corneel, Tax Problems of the Business Promoter, 26 N.Y.U. Tax Inst. 1171 (1968); Herwitz, Allocation of Stock between Services and Capital in the Organization of a Close Corporation, 75 Harv.L.Rev. 1098 (1962).

C. EXCHANGE "SOLELY FOR STOCK"—THE RECEIPT OF OTHER PROPERTY

INTERNAL REVENUE CODE: Sections 351(b); 267; 453(c), (f)(6), (g); 1239.

PROPOSED REGULATIONS: Section 1.43–1(f)(1)(iii), (f)(3)(ii).

REGULATIONS: Sections 1.301–1(1); 1.351–2(d).

The nonrecognition rule of section 351 is limited to an exchange of property "solely for stock" of the controlled corporation. Section 351(b) permits the receipt of other property, commonly termed "boot", but requires that the transferee recognize gain to the extent of the fair market value of other property plus the amount of money received. The basis rules of section 358 adjust the transferor's basis in the stock of the controlled corporation to account for boot by decreasing basis in an amount equal to the fair market value of property and the amount of money received, and increasing basis by the amount of any gain recognized. The transferee corporation's basis in transferred assets is also increased under section 362(a) by the amount of gain recognized by the transferor on the section 351 exchange.

In some circumstances, a taxpayer may desire to treat the transfer of property to a controlled corporation as a "sale" rather than as an exchange governed by section 351. If the taxpayer has property which has declined in value, a "sale" may be desirable to enable the transferor to recognize a loss on the depreciated assets. Sale treatment may be achieved only if the property is transferred in exchange for property other than stock. If the transaction qualifies as a section 351 transaction, even where boot is received, no loss can be recognized in the transaction.

Before 1987, when the Code provided a tax preference for long term capital gains, the transferor might have been willing to pay a capital gain tax on the sale of appreciated assets to permit the corporation to obtain a step-up in basis for the assets, thereby reducing in some circumstances potential ordinary income upon subsequent sales of the property by the corporation, or providing higher depreciation or capital recovery deductions against ordinary income (but see section 1239). The receipt of "property" other than stock in a section 351 transaction would provide the same increase in basis to the extent of gain recognized under section 351(b).

Where property is transferred to a controlled corporation for stock and debt obligations, whether or not the debt is a security, no part of the transaction should constitute a sale with a resulting recognition of loss. The debt instrument constitutes "other property" (boot) and the tax consequences thus are governed by section 351(a) and (b). Gain is recognized on the transaction to the extent of the fair market value of other property, but no loss is recognized. The taxpayer cannot alter these tax consequences by attempting to denominate part of the transaction as a "sale" of some assets and the balance as a transfer under section 351. See, e.g., Nye v. Commissioner, 50 T.C. 203 (1968).

Where the transferor receives only cash or property (and no stock), the transaction is a sale or exchange and gain or loss will be recognized accordingly. Thus the taxpayer can achieve sale treatment by transferring property for debt instruments ("securities") rather than stock. However, if the transferor is in control of the corporation sale treatment will not be accorded the transaction if the purported debt instrument is in fact "equity," see infra, page 387, thus bringing section 351 into play.

ILLUSTRATIVE MATERIAL

A. EXCHANGE OF PROPERTY FOR CORPORATE DEBT

1. *Sale Versus Exchange Treatment*

In Burr Oaks Corp. v. Commissioner, 365 F.2d 24 (7th Cir.1966), three individuals transferred land to a controlled corporation and received in exchange therefore three two-year 6 percent notes each in the amount of $110,000 (although the land was found to be worth only one-half of the face value of the notes). The taxpayers asserted that the transaction was a sale, but the Tax Court found the transaction was an equity contribution to the corporation and the notes were treated as preferred stock rather than debt. The paid-in capital of the corporation was only $4,500 at a time that the corporation incurred "liabilities" of eighty times that amount. The Court of Appeals upheld the Tax Court: "When the payment to the transferors is dependent on the success of an untried undercapitalized business with uncertain prospects, a strong inference arises that the transfer is an equity contribution." (27) The requirements of section 351 being otherwise met, the corporation received only a transferred basis in the land transferred to the corporation. The opposite result was reached in Gyro Engineering Corp. v. United States, 417 F.2d 437 (9th Cir.1969). The principal stockholders transferred three apartment buildings to a corporation for $30,000 cash and $2,343,000 in notes. The transaction was treated as a sale and not as a contribution to capital since the property was generating revenue sufficient to pay the notes. See also J.I. Morgan, Inc. v. Commissioner, 30 T.C. 881 (1958) (A), rev'd and remanded on other issues, 272 F.2d 936 (9th Cir. 1959) (sustaining a "sale" of assets by a majority stockholder to his corporation in return for an installment contract payable in seven years); Piedmont Corp. v. Commissioner, 388 F.2d 886 (4th Cir.1968) (corporation with paid-in capital of $60 acquired from its two stockholders options to purchase land, giving unsecured notes therefor with terms ranging from three to seven years; corporation exercised the options and sold the land; Tax Court upheld the Commissioner's contention that the notes were equity, but the Court of Appeals reversed and upheld sale treatment, concluding that the notes represented valid debt).

In Adams v. Commissioner, 58 T.C. 41 (1972), the taxpayer was a minority stockholder in a corporation (Western). He individually owned some uranium property which he desired to sell to Western, but Western could not buy because of credit restrictions. The taxpayer formed a new wholly-owned corporation (Wyoming) and within 3 days sold his uranium property to Wyoming for a $1 million, 2-year note. Wyoming then leased the property to Western and received a $945,000 advance royalty which was used to pay off the taxpayer's note. The taxpayer reported the payment as long-term capital gain and the corporation included the amount of the note in its basis for cost depletion purposes. While the court upheld the Commissioner's treatment of the transaction under section 351, since both the creation of Wyoming and the "sale" of the uranium property to it were "interdependent steps" in the formation of Wyoming, the note was treated as boot under section 351(b) and not as equity as urged by the Commissioner. See also D'Angelo Associates, Inc. v. Commissioner, infra, page 363.

2. *Installment Sale Treatment*

The receipt of corporate debt obligations by the shareholder as boot may not require the immediate recognition of gain. A disposition of property for payments which are received after the close of the taxable year in which disposition occurs is an installment sale subject to deferred recognition of gain under the rules of section 453. Under section 453(c) the gain recognized with respect to any payment in an installment sale is an amount which bears the same ratio to the payment as the gross profit on the installment sale bears to the total contract price. Section 453(f)(6) provides, with respect to a like-kind exchange under section 1031(b), that payments and total contract price do not include property that may be received without recognition of gain. Proposed Regulations, section 1.453–1(f)(3)(ii) (1984), apply the rules of section 453(f)(6) to a section 351 exchange. Proposed Regulations, section 1.453–1(f)(1)(iii) (1984), allocate the transferor's basis in transferred property first to the stock received without recognition under section 351, to the extent of the fair market value of the stock. Any remaining basis is used to offset gain recognized on the installment sale. In effect, this is the same as stating that payments and total contract price do not include stock permitted to be received under section 351 without recognition of gain.

Assume, for example, that A transfers property with an adjusted basis of $40 and a fair market value of $100 to a corporation controlled by A in exchange for stock worth $70 and a note for $30, payable in three annual installments, with adequate interest, beginning in the year following the transfer. Assuming that the fair market value of the note is $30, section 351(b) requires that A recognize $30 of A's $60 realized gain. Under section 453, however, since "payments" do not include the stock received in the year of the exchange, no gain is recognized immediately. Under the Proposed Regulations, A's $40 basis is allocated to the stock, leaving no basis to reduce gain on the installment sale. Recognition is deferred until the receipt of each $10 payment whereupon A recognizes the full $10 ($10 × $30/$30). Alternatively, if A's basis in the property transferred were $85 dollars, $70 of basis would be allocated to the stock, leaving $15 of basis to offset A's installment gain. A would recognize $15 of gain under section 351(b) but the recognition would be deferred under section 453. A would recognize $5 of gain on each $10 payment ($10 × $15/$30).

Proposed Regulations, section 1.453–1(f)(3)(ii) (1984), provide that the transferor's basis in stock as determined under section 358 includes the deferred gain recognized under the installment method. Thus in the first example above, A's basis in the stock is $40 consisting of A's basis in the property transferred increased by the gain recognized and decreased by the fair market value of the note. A's basis in the second example is $70. With respect to the transferee corporation's basis under section 362(b), however, Proposed Regulations, section 1.453–1(f)(3)(ii) (1984), provide that the transferor's recognized gain under the installment method will not be included in the transferee's basis until the deferred gain is actually recognized by the transferor. Section 453(d) allows the transferor to elect out of installment sale treatment in which case the full fair market value of the note is recognized as gain in the year of the exchange. The election would permit the corporation to immediately step-up its basis in transferred property under section 362(a).

Section 453(g) restricts use of the installment method in the case of a transfer of depreciable property to a corporation if the transferor owns more than 50 percent of the stock of the corporation, a transaction to which section 1239 applies. In addition, section 453(i) requires immediate recognition of any gain subject to depreciation recapture under sections 1245 or 1250. Thus installment treatment frequently is not available for transfers of depreciable property. In addition, Section 453 does not apply to transfers of inventory or property held for sale to customers. Installment sale treatment also is not available if the securities received by the transferor are publicly traded.

B. THE RECEIPT OF STOCK RIGHTS AND CONTINGENT INTERESTS

Regulations, section 1.351–1(a)(1)(ii), provide that stock rights or stock warrants are not "stock" for section 351 purposes. In Hamrick v. Commissioner, 43 T.C. 21 (1964) (Acq. in result only, 1966–2 Cum.Bull. 5), the taxpayer transferred property to a controlled corporation in exchange for stock plus a contingent right to additional stock dependent upon the performance of the corporation. The Tax Court held that the taxpayer's subsequent receipt of the contingent stock qualified for nonrecognition treatment under section 351. The Tax Court followed the decision in Carlberg v. United States, 281 F.2d 507 (8th Cir.1960), holding that transferable contingent rights to receive stock were stock for purposes of section 354 (nonrecognition treatment for an exchange of stock for stock in corporate reorganizations). In both cases the opinions conclude that the contingent rights received by the taxpayers could represent either stock or nothing at all. The Internal Revenue Service has indicated that it will follow the result of *Hamrick,* but only because the rights received by the taxpayer were nonassignable and nonmarketable, and could only give rise to the receipt of additional stock by one who was a party to the transfer. Rev.Rul. 66–112, 1966–1 Cum.Bull. 68, 70.

C. TRANSFERS TO CONTROLLED CORPORATIONS

1. *Dividend Distributions*

Since section 351 applies to an existing corporation, a taxpayer might be tempted to combine a transfer of property with a distribution of cash that is equivalent to a dividend. For example, a sole stockholder transfers a capital asset worth $10,000 to a corporation for $10,000 fair market value of stock plus $1,000 cash. The $1,000 cash could be classified as a dividend under section 301 rather than being considered as boot resulting in capital gain. While section 351(g) does not include a cross-reference to the dividend sections, it would seem that dividend treatment is appropriate in such a case. See Regulations, sections 1.351–2(d) and 1.301–1(1).

If property worth $10,000 is sold by a sole stockholder to an existing corporation for $10,000 cash, the transaction presumably is a sale. However, if the stockholder cannot establish a business purpose for the transfer, the stockholder might be regarded as making a contribution to capital of $10,000 and receiving a dividend of $10,000. But see Curry v. Commissioner, 43 T.C. 667 (1965) (NA), where the court summarily disposed of the Commissioner's contention that there was no "business purpose" for a sale of real estate to a controlled corporation: "It would seem that the mere desire to sell, even if the sole purpose was to realize capital gains, should be a sufficient business purpose (assuming always that the substance complies with the form). * * * Indeed, it is difficult to imagine what added business purpose respondent would require for a sale of property." (695)

2. *Contributions to Capital*

Where a stockholder, without receiving shares of stock in return, contributes additional capital to the corporation in the form of assets that have appreciated or depreciated in value, presumably no gain or loss will be regarded as realized since nothing is received in return.

Moreover, even if a constructive "exchange" were regarded as present because of the increase in value resulting to the existing shares, cf. Scanlon v. Commissioner, 42 B.T.A. 997 (1940), section 351 would usually be applicable to provide nonrecognition treatment. The transferor adds the basis of the contributed property to the basis for his stock; the corporation under section 362(a)(2) uses the transferor's basis. Where property is transferred as a contribution to capital by persons other than stockholders, as where a community organization transfers property to a corporation to induce it to locate in the area, under section 362(c) the corporation's basis in the property is zero.

The distinction between an exchange subject to section 351 and a contribution to capital could be significant in the case of a contribution of property encumbered with a liability in excess of basis. See infra, page 356.

D. CONTINUITY OF INTEREST

Unlike the requirement for nonrecognition treatment in corporate reorganizations, see infra, page 764, there is no express requirement that the transferor in a section 351 exchange maintain a continued interest in the transferred property. See Rev.Rul. 83–34, 1983–1 Cum.Bull. 79 (section 351 transfer to a controlled subsidiary followed by a transfer of the property to another subsidiary pursuant to an integrated plan); Rev.Rul. 83–156, 1983–2 Cum.Bull. 66 (section 351 transfer to a controlled subsidiary followed by a transfer of the property to a partnership).

In Rev.Rul. 84–71, 1984–1 Cum.Bull. 106, P, a public corporation, wanted to acquire the stock of T Corporation. A, who held 14 percent of T's stock, was willing to participate only in a nonrecognition transaction. The remainder of T's stockholders would accept cash. P and A formed a new S Corporation. P transferred sufficient cash to purchase 86 percent of the T stock and A transferred his T stock in a transaction qualified under section 351. S transferred the cash to a new subsidiary, again under section 351. The new subsidiary used the cash to acquire T stock from the remaining T stockholders. The transaction could not have qualified for tax-free reorganization treatment to A because of a lack of continuity of interest, see infra, page 764. The Ruling, however, states that application of section 351 to transfers that are part of the larger transaction will not be precluded by the fact that the larger acquisitive reorganization is taxable due to the absence of the continuity of interest in transferred assets that is required in corporation reorganizations. See Freeman, Corporate Organizations and Reorganizations (Part I), 6 J.Corp.Tax 332 (1980).

E. RECEIPT OF STOCK DISPROPORTIONATE TO PROPERTY TRANSFERRED

The 1939 Code predecessor of section 351 required that for the section to be applicable the nonrecognition property received by each transferor had to be substantially in proportion to the transferor's interest in the transferred property prior to the exchange.

The 1954 Code dropped the proportionate interest requirement as a factor in the nonrecognition of gain, but retained it as a factor indicating the possible existence of compensation or a gift. See the cross-references in section 351(g), and Regulations, section 1.351–1(b)(1), stating that "in appropriate cases" the stock will be treated as if first received in proportion to assets transferred, and then transferred to the ultimate recipients by way of gift or compensation if the facts so warrant. In such a situation, this view of the transaction may defeat the application of section 351 under a step transaction approach if the ultimate recipients are not "transferors of property". The example in the Regulations avoids this issue, since both of the stockholders were transferors of property. However, Rev.Rul. 76–454, 1976–2 Cum.Bull. 102, applied Regulations, section 1.351–1(b)(1), to find a dividend where a stockholder and his controlled corporation formed a new corporation with the stockholder receiving a disproportionately large amount of the stock of the newly formed corporation.

In Weisbart v. Commissioner, 79 T.C. 521 (1982), the Commissioner unsuccessfully claimed that the taxpayer recognized gain on the receipt of more than his proportionate share of the stock of a holding company formed by the taxpayer and a group of family members each of whom contributed the stock of various family corporations engaged in the cattle business. The transferors agreed that their percentage interest in the new corporation was to be based upon the relative book values of their interests in the contributed corporations. The taxpayer's interest was increased to reflect the superior earning power of the particular corporation transferred by him to the combined entity. The Commissioner attempted to require the taxpayer to recognize this excess value. The Tax Court found as a matter of fact that the fair market value of the taxpayer's contribution greatly exceeded its book value and concluded that the taxpayer did not receive more than his fair share. The court applied the express language of Regulations section 1.351–1)(b)(1), to hold that "the entire transaction will be given tax effect in accordance with its true nature":

"If a person were to contribute two pieces of property to a corporation in a single transaction, receiving $75 in stock in exchange for one piece of property and $25 in stock for the other, with each property having a fair market value of $50, no reasonable person would suggest that each of the person's contributions should be viewed separately so that he received $25 as a gift or compensation on the favorable disproportionate distribution. Economic reality cannot be perceived by isolating one piece of a transaction and ignoring the whole. The 'true nature' of the Weisbart transaction must be discerned by viewing the transaction as a whole." (539)

F. PRIOR LAW—TRANSFER IN EXCHANGE FOR STOCK AND SECURITIES

With respect to transfers of property to a controlled corporation made before October 2, 1989, section 351 provided for the receipt of both stock and securities without recognition of gain. Allowing securities to be treated as nonrecognition property in effect deferred the recognition of the gain inherent in the transferred property until the time that the principal amount of the securities was paid. However, this deferral of gain recognition until payment was not subject to the interest and pledging rules of section 453A and other limitations with respect to installment obligations. The 1989 Act amended section 351(a) to remove securities as nonrecognition property. The securities are thus treated as boot which brings the principal payments made on the securities under the installment sales rules, discussed supra, page 348. See H.Rep. No. 108–247, 101 Cong. 1st Sess. 1226–1228 (1989).

There are significant differences in the tax treatment of the transferor and the controlled corporation which result from treating securities as installment obligations rather than nonrecognition property. Before the 1989 change, the transferor's exchanged basis under section 358 was allocated between nonrecognition stock and securities in proportion to their relative fair market values. Section 358(b)(1); Regulations, section 1.358–2(b)(2). As a result of the 1989 change treating securities as boot, under Proposed Regulations, section 1.453–1(f)(1)(iii), the transferor's exchanged basis is first allocated to stock to the extent of its fair market value, and only the remainder is allocated to the securities in computing installment gain. Consequently, a lower basis will be allocated to securities than was previously the case, which results in greater recognition of gain on payment of the obligation.

On the other hand, there is a significant benefit to the corporate transferee as a result of the 1989 change. Under section 362(a), the corporation's basis in assets received in a section 351 exchange is the transferor's basis increased by gain recognized by the transferor on the exchange. Under prior law, the transferee's basis did not include gain recognized by the transferor with respect to the principal payments made on the securities. However, after 1989, the corporate transferee is entitled to increase the basis of transferred assets by the gain recognized by the transferor with respect to securities treated as a boot and subject to installment sales treatment. Proposed Regulations, section 1.453–1(f)(3)(ii), require the transferee to defer its basis adjustment until gain is recognized by the transferor on receipt of installment payments. For example, before the 1989 amendment to section 351(a), if A transferred an asset with a fair market value of $100 and an adjusted basis of $10 to a controlled corporation in exchange for $20 of stock and $80 of securities (with adequate stated interest), A took an $8 adjusted basis for the securities and A recognized $72 of gain at the time of payment of the $80 principal of the securities; the corporation had a $10 basis in property transferred by A. Under the 1989 revision, the receipt of the securities is boot and A will recognize $80 of gain on retirement of the securities. However, since the entire basis of $10 in the transferred property would be allocated to the stock received in the section

351 transaction, A's recognized gain will permit the corporation to increase its basis in the transferred assets to $90. The benefit of the basis increase to a controlled corporation may outweigh the detriment to taxpayers from subjecting securities to the installment sales rules.

Before the 1989 Act, the tax treatment of the transfer of property to a controlled corporation in exchange for corporate debt turned on a determination whether the debt obligations qualified as "securities" and were thus covered by section 351 or were simply treated as boot. In broad terms, the question depended upon whether the obligation represented a continuing participation in the affairs of the corporation. D'Angelo Assoc., Inc. v. Commissioner, 70 T.C. 121 (1978). Where payment of the debt obligation was reasonably certain within a moderately short period of time, the obligation would not be treated as a security. See e.g., Bradshaw v. United States, 683 F.2d 365 (Ct.Cl.1982). Long term obligations where payment was dependent upon the success of the corporate business generally were recognized as securities. See Camp Wolters Enterprises, Inc. v. Commissioner, 230 F.2d 555 (5th Cir.1956) (holding for the Commissioner that five and nine year subordinated notes were "securities;" United States v. Hertwig, 398 F.2d 452 (5th Cir.1968) (unsecured twelve-year notes in amount of $3 million where capital was $10,000 constituted securities and corporation denied a step-up in basis); United States v. Mills, 399 F.2d 944 (5th Cir. 1968) (jury verdict that a one-year unsecured note was a "security" affirmed where the note was renewed twice and the taxpayer testified that it was his intention that the note be a long-term obligations; taxpayer obtained tax-free treatment on exchange).

G. REFERENCES

Cain, Taxation of Boot Notes in a 351/453 Transaction, 27 S.Texas L.Rev. 61 (1985); Jacobs, Something Simple: A Tax–Free Incorporation, 37 Tax Lawyer 133 (1983); Freeman, Corporate Organizations and Reorganizations (Part I), 6 J.Corp.Tax 332 (1980); Blanchard, The Service's Recent Attack: Taxation of Section 351 Exchanges Between Stockholders and Newly Organized Holding Companies, 35 Tax Lawyer, 163 (1981); Freeman, Corporate Organizations and Reorganizations: Holding Companies—Part I: Section 351 as a Lever to Avoid Restrictions Inherent in Section 368, Section 306, and Section 304 and 302, 6 J.Corp.Tax 332 (1980); Part II: Restructuring as a Public Holding Company; Statutory Overlaps; Effect of Intercompany Distributions, 7 J.Corp.Tax 283 (1980); Part III, The Empire Strikes Back, 8 J.Corp.Tax 45 (1981).

D. "SOLELY" FOR STOCK: ASSUMPTION OF LIABILITIES

INTERNAL REVENUE CODE: Sections 357; 358(d).

REGULATIONS: Section 1.357–1, –2; 1.358–3.

(1) SECTION 357(a)

In United States v. Hendler, 303 U.S. 564 (1938), the Supreme Court held that an assumption of liabilities in certain reorganizations constituted boot under the then applicable nonrecognition provisions. The assumption of liabilities thus resulted in recognition of gain to the extent of the liability.

Prior to the time *Hendler* was decided, it was generally thought that an assumption of liabilities was within the scope of nonrecognition provisions applicable to corporate organizations and reorganizations. As a consequence, taxpayers did not report gain with respect to transferred liabilities in transactions pre-dating *Hendler.* The Treasury Department recognized that gain which should have been reported by transferors under *Hendler* (in transactions outside of the statute of limitations) would allow a basis increase to the corporate recipients. The result would have been a substantial revenue loss to the government from higher depreciation deductions and lower gains on subsequent sale of the transferred property. Treasury thus convinced Congress in 1939 to enact the predecessor to section 357(a).

Under section 357(a), the assumption of a liability, or receipt of property subject to a liability, is not treated as the receipt of money or other property. Section 357(a) is subject to two exceptions. Section 357(b), enacted in 1939 as part of the original provision, treats liabilities as boot if either (1) a tax avoidance purpose is present or (2) there is no bona fide business purpose for transferring the liabilities. Second, under section 357(c), enacted in 1954, if the amount of liabilities assumed exceeds the basis of the property transferred, gain results to the extent of such excess, regardless of the purpose of the debt or the assumption. For purposes of determining the transferor's basis in nonrecognition property received in the exchange, section 358(d) treats the assumption of a liability of the transferor or a transfer of property subject to a liability as the receipt of cash by the transferor, without regard to how the debt is treated under section 357. The result is a reduction in the transferor's basis to the extent of the liability.

For a history of section 357, see Surrey, Assumption of Indebtedness in Tax–Free Exchanges, 50 Yale L.J. 1 (1940).

(2) Section 357(b) Situations

Under section 357(b), the total amount of liabilities assumed or to which transferred property is subject is treated as money received unless the taxpayer can show that the principal purpose of the assumption or transfer subject to liabilities was not tax avoidance and that the purpose was a bona fide business purpose. Section 357(b)(2) adds that the taxpayer must meet the burden of proof by "the clear preponderance of the evidence." Under the express terms of the statute, if any liability is found to be transferred to the corporation for the forbidden tax avoidance purpose, or without a bona fide business purpose, all liabilities are treated as money. Regulations, section 1.357–1(c).[5]

ILLUSTRATIVE MATERIAL

A. IN GENERAL

The scope of section 357(b) is not entirely clear. An assumption of liabilities incurred initially to acquire business assets transferred to the transferee should satisfy the bona fide business purpose requirement. See Jewell v. United States, 330 F.2d 761 (9th Cir.1964) (not applying the

5. Regulations, section 1.351–3(a)(6) and (b)(7), require both the transferor and the transferee corporation to describe on their income tax returns for the year of the transfer the business reason of each with respect to the corporation's assumption of liabilities.

predecessor of section 357(b) to the transfer of assets to a corporation which assumed notes due from the taxpayer to a trust). Suppose, however, that a liability, such as a loan from a bank, is incurred just before a transfer of property to a controlled corporation so that the stockholder obtains cash, the corporation assumes the debt, and then pays the bank. The whole transaction really is equivalent to a payment of cash for the property by the corporation to the stockholder, and the assumption of the liability in such a case would appear to fall under section 357(b). For example, in Drybrough v. Commissioner, 376 F.2d 350 (6th Cir.1967), the taxpayer in 1957 transferred real estate to four corporations, each assuming a portion of the mortgage debt on the property that had been incurred in 1953. Another property was transferred to a fifth corporation subject to a mortgage which had been placed on the property in 1957, just three months prior to the transfer. The proceeds of the 1957 mortgage had been invested in tax-exempt bonds. About one-half of the 1953 mortgage proceeds had been used to pay off an earlier indebtedness and most of the balance was also invested in tax-exempt bonds. The court held that the assumption of the 1953 indebtedness was not governed by section 357(b); the use to which the proceeds of the mortgage were put was not relevant in determining whether there was a tax avoidance purpose on the exchange. There was a valid business purpose for placing the real estate subject to the mortgage in the corporation. On the other hand, the assumption of the 1957 indebtedness was governed by section 357(b); the creation of the debt was directly in anticipation of having the corporation assume the indebtedness and constituted a plan to avoid recognition of gain. See also Bryan v. Commissioner, 281 F.2d 238 (4th Cir.1960) (finding a tax avoidance purpose and lack of business purpose on transfer of real estate to a controlled corporation subject to liabilities incurred just prior to the transfer; the court, however, treated as boot only the amount of the liabilities in excess of basis, although the case arose prior to the enactment of section 357(c)); Thompson v. Campbell, 64–2 U.S.T.C. ¶ 9659 (N.D.Tex.1964), aff'd per curiam, 353 F.2d 787 (5th Cir. 1965) (transfer to a controlled corporation of assets subject to liabilities incurred the day before incorporation resulted in boot under section 357(b)).

In some cases a borrowing immediately before the transfer has been found not to run afoul of the business purpose requirement. In Easson v. Commissioner, 33 T.C. 963 (1960), rev'd on other grounds, 294 F.2d 653 (9th Cir.1961), the Tax Court construed the predecessor of section 357(b) not to apply on the facts of the case to a mortgage placed on the assets shortly before incorporation because the taxpayer had a valid business purpose for the corporate assumption of the mortgage (i.e., insulation of personal assets from potential liabilities and facilitation of management of the real estate and estate planning), and the corporation was an active business entity. In Rev. Rul. 79–258, 1979–2 Cum.Bull. 143, the Internal Revenue Service concluded that in a type (D) reorganization,[6] a nonrecognition transaction which is also subject to section 357, there was no tax avoidance motive where the transferor refinanced a portion of an existing long-term debt on the eve of assumption of the debt by the transferee corporation. The refinanced indebtedness was attributable to business assets received by the transferee.

Section 357(b) also has been applied to treat assumed debt as money in cases involving the assumption of personal nonbusiness liabilities of the

6. Section 368(a)(1)(D) is discussed infra, page 891.

transferor. In Estate of Stoll v. Commissioner, 38 T.C. 223 (1962), the taxpayer transferred all the assets of a newspaper business to a corporation, which assumed a $1,015,000 liability of the taxpayer. To the extent of $600,000, the liability represented a refinancing that took place just prior to the incorporation and was secured by property transferred to the corporation. The $415,000 balance of the liability was secured by life insurance policies on the taxpayer's life that were not transferred to the corporation. The Tax Court held that the predecessor of section 357(b) applied to treat the $415,000 of indebtedness as boot because there was no business purpose for the assumption of the liability by the corporation and the liability was not related to the business transfer. However, the predecessor of section 357(b) did not apply to treat the $600,000 liability as boot. (Note that section 357(b)(1) now requires that the total liability be treated as boot if there is a tax avoidance purpose or if there is no bona fide business purpose for the assumption of any liability). In Campbell v. Wheeler, 342 F.2d 837 (5th Cir.1965), the taxpayer transferred a partnership interest to a corporation subject to liabilities which had been incurred just prior to the transfer in order to pay the personal income tax liability of the taxpayer. The court held that the transaction was governed by section 357(b) and the amount of the liabilities assumed constituted boot.

In Simpson v. Commissioner, 43 T.C. 900 (1965), the taxpayer transferred the assets of two department stores, cash, and securities to a corporation in a section 351 transaction. The corporation also assumed liabilities in an amount which was slightly less than the aggregate basis of the assets transferred. The Commissioner asserted that section 357(b) applied, but the court held that the arrangement of the assumption of liabilities in an amount slightly less than basis in order to avoid section 357(c) was not a tax avoidance purpose.

B. REFERENCES

Griener, Behling, and Moffett, Assumption of Liabilities and The Improper Purpose—A Re-examination of Section 357(b), 32 Tax Lawyer 111 (1978).

(3) Section 357(c) Situations

Suppose that A owned an asset worth $100,000, which cost $10,000, and which was subject to a mortgage of $50,000 to secure a bank loan of $50,000 obtained by A in a separate transaction. Unless section 357(b) applies, if A is permitted to transfer the asset to a controlled corporation subject to the liability without recognition of gain, A avoids tax on $40,000, the difference between A's original investment of $10,000 and the $50,000 cash received by A from the borrowing. Before 1954 some authorities concluded that the assumption of liabilities in excess of basis was covered by the predecessor to section 357(b). Bryan v. Commissioner, supra, 281 F.2d 238 (4th Cir.1960); Easson v. Commissioner, supra, 33 T.C. 963 (1960), rev'd, 294 F.2d 653 (9th Cir.1961). Under this view, A would be required to treat the $40,000 of liabilities in excess of basis as money resulting in recognition of gain. The Tax Court in *Easson* described recognition as necessary because property cannot have a negative basis, the Code cannot be applied to produce absurd results, and immediate taxation was thus necessary to prevent exemption of part of the gain. The Court of Appeals, however, disagreed and reversed, holding that the literal language of the predecessor of section 351 had been complied with and the existence of a negative basis was no impediment to qualification under the nonrecognition provisions. The problem is resolved by section 357(c)(1), added in 1954, which provides that the excess of liability over basis shall be considered a gain to the transferor arising from the sale of an asset.[7] In turn, the basis of the corporation is increased by the gain recognized.

ILLUSTRATIVE MATERIAL

A. EFFECT OF TRANSFEROR'S CONTINUED LIABILITY

Rosen v. Commissioner, 62 T.C. 11 (1974), held that section 357(c) applies even in situations in which the transferor remains personally liable on the obligation assumed by the transferee corporation. There is no requirement in section 357(c) that the transferor be relieved of liability.[8] In Owen v. Commissioner, 881 F.2d 832 (9th Cir.1989), the taxpayers incorporated a partnership by transferring partnership assets subject to liabilities in excess of basis. The liabilities had been personally guaranteed by the transferors who remained liable for the full amount of the debt. The Court held that the transferor's continuing personal liability for the loans secured by the transferred property is irrelevant. Section 357(c) applies as long as the property received by the corporation is subject to the debt. See also Smith v. Commissioner, 84 T.C. 889 (1985), reaching the same result.

B. DETERMINATION OF TRANSFEROR'S BASIS

In Alderman v. Commissioner, 55 T.C. 662 (1971), the taxpayers transferred assets to their corporation which assumed liabilities in excess of the transferors' basis for the assets. In order to increase the assets of the corporation and avoid gain under section 357(c), the taxpayers executed a note payable to the corporation in an amount slightly in excess of the amount by which the assumed liabilities exceeded the basis of the transferred assets. The court held that the basis of the note was zero, since the taxpayers incurred no cost in making it. Gain therefore resulted under section 357(c). Presumably, payment of the note in *Alderman* would provide additional basis for the stock in the stockholders' hands as additional capital is actually contributed to the corporation. Arguably, the corporation is not required to recognize gain on this capital contribution. See also Rev.Rul. 68–629, 1968–2 Cum.Bull. 154 (same conclusion as *Alderman*).

In Lessinger v. Commissioner, 872 F.2d 519 (2d Cir.1989), the court refused to follow *Alderman.* Lessinger transferred the assets of a sole proprietorship to his wholly owned corporation in a transaction to which section 351 applied. The proprietorship was insolvent in that its liabilities exceeded the value of transferred assets. Liabilities also exceeded Lessinger's basis in the transferred assets. The transferee corporation created a "loan receivable" due from Lessinger on the corporate books in the amount that the liabilities of the proprietorship exceeded the value of the transferred

7. The gain is capital or ordinary according to the ratio of capital assets to ordinary assets transferred. Regulations, section 1.357–2(b).

8. In Rosen the gain realized as a result of the application of section 357(c) was taxed as ordinary income because of the operation of the section 1245 recapture provisions.

assets. Reversing the Tax Court (85 T.C. 824 (1985)), the Court of Appeals held that Lessinger was not required by section 357(c) to recognize gain. The court agreed with the *Alderman* holding that a taxpayer has no basis in the taxpayer's own promise to pay, but also concluded that the basis of Lessinger's obligation in the hands of the corporate transferee was equal to the face amount of the obligation. The court reasoned that the transferee corporation "incurred a cost in the transaction involving the transfer of the obligation by taking on the liabilities of the proprietorship that exceeded its assets." The court also pointed out that unless the corporation had a basis in *Lessinger's* obligation, it would have to recognize gain on payment of the debt. The court then held that "where the transferor undertakes genuine personal liability to the transferee, 'adjusted basis' in section 357(c) refers to the transferee's basis in the obligation which is its face amount." (526) Finally, the court also noted that Lessinger did not avoid recognition of real gain on the transaction because of his liability to the corporation. The court's decision is questionable. First, in total disregard of section 362(b), the court concluded that the corporation took a basis in the transferor's promissory note equal to its face amount. Second, the court's reasoning that gain under section 357(c) is computed with reference to the transferee's basis in the transferred property rather than the transferor's basis is contrary to the otherwise universally accepted rule that gain is computed with reference to the transferor's basis.

C. CONTRIBUTIONS TO CAPITAL AND SECTION 357(c)

By its terms, section 357(c) does not apply to a contribution to capital. This omission raises the possibility that the taxpayer may transfer property subject to liabilities in excess of basis to a corporation, whether or not controlled by the taxpayer, as a capital contribution rather than in an exchange for stock and avoid recognition of gain. In Jackson v. Commissioner, 708 F.2d 1402 (9th Cir.1983), the taxpayer transferred an interest in a joint venture (partnership) to his wholly owned corporation. The court treated the transfer as a section 351 exchange even though there was no exchange of stock because the transfer was to the taxpayer's wholly owned corporation. An actual stock issue would be a mere formality in such a case. The Ninth Circuit refused to apply section 357(c), however, based on the Tax Court's finding that the corporation did not assume or take property subject to partnership loans on which the taxpayer remained personally liable and the partnership interest was subject to no other liabilities. See also Lessinger v. Commissioner, discussed supra (transfer of assets subject to liabilities in excess of basis to wholly owned corporation which did not issue stock treated as a section 351 exchange subject to section 357(c); an actual issuance of stock would be a mere formality when the corporation is wholly owned).

D. ASSUMPTION OF TRANSFEROR'S DEBT TO TRANSFEREE CORPORATION

In Kniffen v. Commissioner, 39 T.C. 553 (1962) (Acq.), the taxpayer transferred assets and liabilities of a sole proprietorship to a pre-existing corporation. Among the liabilities assumed was a debt from the taxpayer to the corporation. The assumption eliminated the taxpayer's debt by operation of law. The Commissioner asserted that the taxpayer realized cancellation of indebtedness income as boot under section 351(b) and that there was no assumption of debt to bring section 357 into play. The court held for the taxpayer; the debt was assumed and then discharged so that section 357(c) applied.

E. REFERENCE

Cooper, Negative Basis, 75 Harv.L.Rev. 1352 (1962).

(4) Accounts Payable

INTERNAL REVENUE CODE: Section 357(c)(3).

Prior to the Revenue Act of 1978, special problems were present when accounts receivable and accounts payable were transferred by a *cash method* taxpayer in a section 351 transaction. Since the accounts receivable would not have been included in income at the time of the transfer, their tax basis in the hands of the transferor is zero. On the other hand, the accounts payable, by definition not yet paid or deducted by a cash method taxpayer, would, under the literal language of section 357(c), constitute "liabilities" assumed by the corporation in the incorporation transaction. As a result, a cash method taxpayer could realize income in a section 351 transaction where the accounts payable were transferred to a corporation in connection with accounts receivable or other assets with a low tax basis. Raich v. Commissioner, 46 T.C. 604 (1966). The courts struggled with different approaches to avoid this result. See Bongiovanni v. Commissioner, 470 F.2d 921, 924 (2d Cir.1972) (although the payables of a cash basis taxpayer are liabilities for accounting purposes, payables should not be considered liabilities for tax purposes under section 357(c) until they are paid); Thatcher v. Commissioner, 533 F.2d 1114 (9th Cir.1976) (if receivables are transferred, the payables are deemed assumed by the transferee in exchange for the receivables in a taxable transaction in which the deductible payables offset the taxable gain on disposition of receivables); and Focht v. Commissioner, 68 T.C. 223 (1977) (the Tax Court abandoned its position in *Raich* and held that payables are not liabilities under section 357(c) to the extent the payables would be deductible when paid).

The Revenue Act of 1978 added section 357(c)(3), which follows the Tax Court's logic in *Focht* by providing that liabilities which would give rise to a deduction on payment are not to be considered in determining the amount of liabilities to which section 357(c)(1) applies. A complementary provision in section 358(d)(2) provides that such payables are not to be treated as cash received for purposes of determining the transferor's basis in stock or securities received.

ILLUSTRATIVE MATERIAL

A. GENERAL

Accounts payable include trade accounts payable and other cash method liabilities, such as interest and taxes, which relate to the transferred trade or business. Whether a transferor is a cash method taxpayer is determined separately for each item. For example, a taxpayer using a hybrid method of accounting, which utilizes inventories and the accrual method in computing income from purchases and sales and which utilizes the cash method in computing all other items of income and expenses, is considered a cash basis taxpayer for purposes of applying section 357(c) to accounts payable for items computed on the cash method of accounting, but not with respect to liabilities relating to inventory. See Staff of the Joint Committee on Taxation, General Explanation of the Revenue Act of 1978, 218–20 (Comm.Print 1978).

Not all of the potential problems with payables are resolved by section 357(c)(3). In Orr v. Commissioner, 78 T.C. 1059 (1982), which arose before the effective date of section 357(c)(3), the taxpayer transferred to a newly formed corporation customers' cash deposits for travel received in the course of taxpayer's business as a travel agent. The deposits were refundable and had not been taken into income by the taxpayer. The taxpayer's liability to refund deposits exceeded the amount of cash, and hence the basis of property, transferred to the new corporation. The Tax Court held that the taxpayer recognized gain under section 357(c)(1) to the extent the liabilities exceeded the taxpayer's basis in transferred property. The Tax Court refused to allow nonrecognition under its decision in *Focht* because refunds of the deposits would not have been deductible by the taxpayer. Presumably the same result would be reached under section 357(c)(3).

In Rev.Rul. 80–199, 1980–2 Cum.Bull. 122, the Internal Revenue Service announced that it would apply the logic of *Focht* to transactions that occurred before the effective date of section 357(c)(3).

E. THE "CONTROL" REQUIREMENT

INTERNAL REVENUE CODE: Sections 351(a); 368(c).

AMERICAN BANTAM CAR CO. v. COMMISSIONER

United States Tax Court, 1948.
11 T.C. 397.*

[A group of individuals, called the "associates," purchased the assets of a bankrupt automobile company in 1935. The "associates" then organized the taxpayer corporation in 1936 to take over the assets. The associates were to transfer the assets (subject to certain liabilities) to the corporation in return for 300,000 shares of no par common stock. Ninety thousand shares of the preferred stock of the corporation (each share having three votes) were to be sold to the public through underwriters at $10 a share. The underwriters were to receive as compensation, in addition to discounts and commissions, certain amounts of the common stock issued to the associates based on a schedule determined by the progress of the sale of the preferred stock. The transfer of the assets to the corporation was made on June 3, 1936, in return for the common stock. On June 8, 1936, the associates and the underwriters agreed on the details of the compensation schedule. On August 16, 1936, the associates placed their 300,000 common stock shares in escrow until the public offering of the preferred stock was completed. In October 1937, the associates, pursuant to the agreement, transferred to the underwriters 87,900 common stock shares and the underwriters sold 1,008 of these shares to the public. As a consequence of the

* Ed.: The decision was affirmed per curiam, 177 F.2d 513 (3d Cir.1949).

underwriters' stock sales, the associates held 212,100 shares of the common stock (less than 80%), the underwriters held 86,892 shares, and the public 1,008 shares. The public also held 83,618 shares of preferred stock. The issue before the court was the corporation's basis for depreciation of the acquired assets in the years 1942 and 1943. The taxpayer claimed depreciation should be based on cost to the taxpayer in 1936, i.e., the market value of the assets in 1936; the Commissioner claimed depreciation should be based on the basis of the assets in the hands of the associates prior to the transfer to the taxpayer, which basis was lower than the 1936 fair market value. The determination of the basis turned on the question whether the original transfer qualified under section 351. If all the elements of the transaction were taken together under a step transaction approach, then the associates were not in control and the corporation received a stepped-up basis for the assets; if the 1936 and 1937 transactions were treated as separate, then the associates were in control "immediately after" the initial stock transaction and section 351 would apply to carry over the old basis of the assets to the corporation.]

During all of 1936 the associates retained ownership over the 300,000 shares of common stock and during that interval the underwriters sold only 14,757 shares of preferred stock which did not entitle them to any common stock under the agreement of June 8, 1936. The corporation's by-laws provided that each share of preferred stock should have three votes while each share of common stock should have one vote. Therefore, at the end of 1936, out of 344,271 possible stock votes, the total combined voting power of all outstanding stock, the associates owned 300,000 or over 80 per cent. It was not until October 1937 when the [underwriters] received 87,900 shares of the associates' common stock in fulfillment of the underwriting agreement that the associates lost "control" of petitioner within the statutory definition of the word. Retention of "control" for such a duration of time satisfies the governing provision of [section 351]. * * *

In determining whether a series of steps are to be treated as a single indivisible transaction or should retain their separate entity, the courts use a variety of tests. Paul, Selected Studies in Federal Taxation, 2d series, pages 200–254. Among the factors considered are the intent of the parties, the time element, and the pragmatic test of the ultimate result. An important test is that of mutual interdependence. Were the steps so interdependent that the legal relations created by one transaction would have been fruitless without a completion of the series?

Using these tests as a basis for their decisions the courts in Hazeltine Corp. v. Commissioner, 89 F.2d 513, and Bassick v. Commissioner, 85 F.2d 8, treated the series of steps involved in each case as parts of a unified transaction and therefore determined that the transferors of assets to the new corporation did not acquire the requisite control. An analysis of the fact situations involved shows salient distinguishing features from the present facts. In each of the above cases there was a written contract prior both to the organization of the new corporation and the exchange of assets for stock which bound the transferors unconditionally to assign part of the stock acquired to third parties after the exchange. Thus at the moment of the exchange the recipient of the stock did not own it, but held it subject to a binding contractual obligation to transfer a portion. The court in each case thought that the incorporation and exchange would never have been agreed upon without the supplemental agreement turning over stock to a third party. In such situations it is logical for the courts to say that the exchange and the subsequent transfer are part of one and the same transaction so that the transferor never actually owned the shares he later assigned.

A close examination of the facts surrounding the exchange in the present case makes it clear that the exchange of assets for stock and the subsequent transfer of a portion of that stock to [the underwriters] therein involved should not be considered part of the same transaction so as to deprive the associates of "control" immediately after the exchange. The facts are distinguishable from those existing in the *Hazeltine* and *Bassick* cases on three grounds. First, there was no written contract prior to the exchange binding the associates to transfer stock to the underwriters. At the most there was an informal oral understanding of a general plan contemplating the organization of a new corporation, the exchange of assets for stock, and marketing of preferred stock of the new corporation to the public. A written contract providing for the transfer of shares from the associates to the underwriters did not come until five days after the exchange. Secondly, when the transfer of shares to the underwriters was embodied specifically in a formal contract, the underwriters received no absolute right to ownership of the common stock, but only when, as and if, certain percentages of preferred stock were sold. How clearly contingent was the nature of their rights is illustrated by the fact only one underwriter, Grant, met the terms of the agreement and became entitled to any shares. Thirdly, the necessity of placing the 300,000 shares in escrow with a bank is indicative of complete ownership of such stock by the associates following the exchange.

The standard required by the courts to enable them to say that a series of steps are interdependent and thus should be viewed as a single transaction do not exist here. It is true all the steps may have been contemplated under the same general plan of May 1936; yet the contemplated arrangement for the sale of preferred stock to the public was entirely secondary and supplemental to the principal goal of the plan—to organize the new corporation and exchange its stock for the Austin assets. * * *

Thus we conclude that in the present case the exchange of assets for stock between the associates and petitioner on June 3, 1936, was a separate completed transaction distinct from the subsequent transfer of common stock to [the underwriters] so that the associates were in control of petitioner immediately after the exchange within the provisions of [section 351]. * * *

D'ANGELO ASSOCIATES, INC. v. COMMISSIONER

United States Tax Court, 1978.
70 T.C. 121.

WILBUR, J. * * *

This controversy has its origin in events occurring during June 1960. Petitioner was organized on June 21, 1960. Shortly thereafter, initial capital in the amount of $15,000 in cash was transferred to petitioner by Dr. D'Angelo, and petitioner issued 60 shares of common stock, 10 shares to Mrs. D'Angelo and 10 shares each in the names of the five D'Angelo children. On June 30, 1960, Dr. and Mrs. D'Angelo, in a transaction formally designated a sale, transferred various property to petitioner, including the building and equipment whose basis is now at issue. In exchange for this property, the D'Angelos received $15,000 in cash; the assumption by petitioner of a liability of the D'Angelos, secured by a mortgage on property transferred to petitioner; and a 6 percent interest bearing demand note payable to Dr. D'Angelo in the amount of $96,727.85. Thereafter, in claiming depreciation, petitioner treated the transfer as a sale.

We must determine the proper basis for depreciation of the rental property (building and equipment) transferred to petitioner. This issue depends on whether or not section 351 applies to the transfer of this property to the petitioner. Section 351 applies when property is conveyed to a corporation solely in exchange for stock or securities,* and immediately after the exchange, the transferors control the corporation. If section 351 is applicable, petitioner must depreciate the transferred assets using the transferors' basis. See section 362(a)(1). If section 351 is inapplicable, and the transfer of assets to petitioner was, as petitioner contends, a sale, depreciation would be based on the purchase price of those assets, a figure concededly greater than the transferors' adjusted basis. Petitioner would accordingly realize larger depreciation deductions. See sections 167(g), 1011, and 1012.

Respondent contends that the transfer of the rental property to petitioner was pursuant to a nontaxable exchange under section 351(a). He argues that the transfer of cash for stock and the exchange of the rental property for cash and notes were contemporaneous events that were in substance integral parts of a single transaction. * * *

Petitioner, on the other hand, contends that section 351 is inapplicable to the transfer for several reasons. Petitioner asserts that the transfer of the rental property was a transaction separate from the contributions of cash and should be characterized as a taxable sale. Petitioner argues that Dr. and Mrs. D'Angelo never owned more than

* [Ed.: Before October 2, 1989, securities could be received without recognition of gain, see supra, page 352.]

10 of the 60 shares outstanding in petitioner (the 50 shares constituting "control" being issued to non-transferors prior to the sale) * * *

For the following reasons, we agree with respondent.

a. *Sale or Exchange:* It is well established that the economic substance of a transaction must govern for tax purposes rather than the time sequence or form in which the transaction is cast. Gregory v. Helvering, 293 U.S. 465 (1935). Where a series of closely related steps are taken pursuant to a plan to achieve an intended result, the transaction must be viewed as an integrated whole for tax purposes. See Redwing Carriers, Inc. v. Tomlinson, 399 F.2d 652, 658 (5th Cir. 1968); Atlee v. Commissioner, 67 T.C. 395 (1976).

Petitioner has failed to convince us that a sale took place. The events significant to the creation of petitioner occurred almost simultaneously. The formation of petitioner, the transfer of $15,000 cash to petitioner for the issuance of 60 shares of stock, and the transfer of the rental property to petitioner for the return of the $15,000 in cash and the notes all occurred within an interval of less than 10 days. See section 1.351–1(a)(1), Income Tax Regs. The evidence demonstrates that these steps were integral parts of a plan designed by Dr. D'Angelo to transfer the assets used primarily in his dental practice from individual to corporate ownership.

Any reason for petitioner's existence would have vanished absent the transfer of the rental property in accordance with the overall plan. * * * We believe this record demonstrates a continuing interest by Dr. D'Angelo in the transferred rental property consistent with the policy underlying the nonrecognition provisions of section 351 and unlike that contemplated by a sale. See Portland Oil Co. v. Commissioner, 109 F.2d 479, 488 (1st Cir.1940), cert. denied 310 U.S. 650 (1940); Bittker & Eustice, Federal Income Taxation of Corporations and Shareholders, par. 3.01, p. 3–4 (3d ed. 1971).

Sequential protocol is of marginal relevance in determining whether contemporaneous events should be viewed as a single integrated transaction or as independent transactions. Rather, the boundaries are defined by including events contemplated for the success of the business plans from which they emanate. Commissioner v. Court Holding Co., 324 U.S. 331 (1945); United States v. Cumberland Public Service Co., 338 U.S. 451 (1950). In this light it is clear that the success of the corporate undertaking motivated both the transfer of cash for stock and the transfer of the rental property for the corporate obligation. As we noted in Nye v. Commissioner, 50 T.C. 203, 212 (1968):

> [T]hey gave no reason why the transaction was divided into two parts, the transfer of cash for stock and the purported sale of the business assets for the note. Such evidence might have confirmed that the form in which the transaction was cast was consistent with its true nature. * * * Lack of such evidence is worthy of note because it fails to negate the inference to be drawn from other facts indicating that the two parts of the transaction were in-

separably related. * * * In the absence of evidence of a business reason for dividing the transaction, we conclude that a separate sale has not been shown. [Citations omitted]

b. *Control:* We view the events before us as equivalent to the formation and capitalization of the corporation, followed by a gift to the D'Angelo children of the controlling interest when Dr. and Mrs. D'Angelo caused petitioner to directly issue the 50 shares to the children. At the end of the series of transactions on June 30, 1960, all of the assets remaining in the corporation were contributed by Dr. and Mrs. D'Angelo, including the $15,000 in cash.[6] This cash was in the possession of Dr. and Mrs. D'Angelo both before and after the transfers with the petitioner merely issuing stock directly to Mrs. D'Angelo and in the names of the children. The D'Angelo children did not purchase the stock issued in their names, but were simply the beneficiaries of a gift from their parents.[7]

The loss of control of petitioner resulting from the gift of stock does not preclude the application of section 351(a), which requires that the transferors be in control of the transferee corporation "immediately after the exchange." This requirement is satisfied where, as here, the transferors transfer by gift the stock they were entitled to receive in exchange for the property they transferred to the corporation, regardless of whether such disposition was planned before or after acquiring control. See Wilgard Realty Co. v. Commissioner, 127 F.2d 514, 516 (2d Cir.1942), affg. 43 B.T.A. 557 (1941), cert. denied 317 U.S. 655 (1942), Stanton v. United States, 512 F.2d 13, 17 (3d Cir.1975); Bittker & Eustice, Federal Income Taxation of Corporations and Shareholders, par. 3.10 pp. 3–37, 3–38 (3d ed. 1971). The issuance of the stock by

6. In all likelihood, the $15,000 in cash remained in the corporation, and was evidenced by the $15,000 demand note payable to Dr. D'Angelo issued by petitioner on June 30, 1960, the same day the $96,727.85 note was issued. Under this assumption the consideration received from petitioner corresponds with the stated "sales" price; if the cash was distributed as well as the $15,000 note, there is an unexplained $15,000 discrepancy. Accordingly, we find that no adjustment in the adjusted basis of the rental property is needed on account of the $15,000 cash. Additionally, since the $15,000 note is a security for the same reasons we find the $96,727.85 note a security (see infra), no adjustment in basis would be required.

If in fact, the $15,000 was returned to the D'Angelos along with the $15,000 demand note, the same result would be required, since the consideration for the transfer of the rental property would be the $15,000 note (along with the stock and other notes), rather than the contemporaneous return of the same $15,000 contributed a few days earlier.

We also note that petitioner does not contend that the assumption of liability for the mortgage by petitioner should be treated as money received by the transferors by reason of sec. 357(b).

7. As noted earlier, the stock was issued to Dr. D'Angelo as trustee for the children pursuant to the New York State Uniform Gift to Minors Act. Respondent does not argue that the transferors retained control because the trust was illusory or because of the powers Dr. D'Angelo exercised as trustee. In view of respondent's position, we assume for purposes of this case that the trustee acted independently and solely on behalf of the best interests of the beneficiaries, although there is considerable evidence to the contrary. We therefore do not base our decision to any extent on the circumstance that Dr. D'Angelo as trustee acted on behalf of the children; the result would be precisely the same if the children had reached majority when the stock was issued and received title to the stock in their own names.

petitioner to the D'Angelo children is the direct consequence of "the absolute right" of Dr. and Mrs. D'Angelo to designate who would receive all of the stock. Stanton v. United States, supra, at 17; Wilgard Realty Co. v. Commissioner, supra, at 516. Since it is possession of this power which is essential under section 351 for control, it follows that the transferors herein, Dr. and Mrs. D'Angelo were in control of petitioner immediately after the exchange. See American Bantam Car Co. v. Commissioner, 11 T.C. 397 (1948), affd. per curiam 177 F.2d 513 (3d Cir.1949), cert. denied 339 U.S. 920 (1950).

Petitioner nevertheless argues that since the stock was issued directly to Mrs. D'Angelo and the children, Dr. D'Angelo never held any stock in the corporation. We recognize that the *Wilgard* decision was predicated on the transferor's freedom of action *after* he acquired the stock, and that Fahs v. Florida Machine & Foundry Co., 168 F.2d 957 (5th Cir.1948) may be read to support petitioner's viewpoint. See also Heberlein Patent Corporation v. United States, 105 F.2d 965 (2d Cir.1939). Additionally, in Mojonnier & Sons, Inc. v. Commissioner, 12 T.C. 837 (1949), in distinguishing *Wilgard*, this Court stated:

> In the instant proceeding, however, the stock, exclusive of the 1,490 shares issued to Mojonnier and his wife, was not issued to the transferors and then conveyed by them to members of their family, but was issued directly to the members of the family in accordance with the plan and offer of F.E. Mojonnier. Thus, the transferors were never the owners or holders of a sufficient amount of stock to place them in "control" of the corporation within the meaning of section 112(j). Cf. Heberlein Patent Corporation v. United States, supra. [Id. at 850]

Nevertheless, the decisions in both *Wilgard* and *Stanton* were clearly predicated on the power of the transferor to designate who will receive the stock rather than the precise moment that the power was exercised. These cases do not turn on whether the tune Dr. D'Angelo called was written in two/four time, but on his power to call the tune. And it is on this score that both Florida Machine & Foundry Co. and Mojonnier & Sons, Inc., are distinguishable from *Wilgard, Stanton,* and the facts before us.[8] Cf. Culligan Water Conditioning of Tri–Cities, Inc.,

8. If immediately prior to forming the corporation, five-sixths of the rental properties was given to the children and transferred to the corporation in return for the controlling interest (along with their parents' remaining one-sixth interest) petitioner's basis would be the basis of Dr. and Mrs. D'Angelo. Similarly, if the transfers were made directly to the corporation by Dr. and Mrs. D'Angelo in return for stock and the stock then given to the children, petitioner does not seriously contend section 351 would be inapplicable. That this transaction has been squeezed into the seemingly non-existent time interval between these two situations surely cannot produce a different result. Cf. sec. 1.351–1(b)(1), Income Tax Regs., and S.Rept. No. 1622, to accompany H.R. 8300 (Pub.L. No. 591), 83d Cong., 2d Sess. 264, 265 (1954), which, although not addressing the control problem directly, at least suggest the result we reach. Additionally, the prior precedents, by making the power to designate the distributee of the stock dispositive, avoid potential abuses inherent in options that would otherwise be available to taxpayers. Bittker & Eustice, Federal Income Taxation of Corporations and Shareholders, par. 3.01, p. 3–4 (3d ed. 1971). Culligan Water Conditioning of Tri–Cities, Inc. v. United States, 567 F.2d 867 (9th Cir.1978).

v. United States, 567 F.2d 867 (9th Cir.1978); Intermountain Lumber Co. v. Commissioner, 65 T.C. 1025 (1976).

* * *

We conclude * * * that section 351(a) therefore applies to the transfers of rental property as contended by the respondent.

ILLUSTRATIVE MATERIAL

A. CONTROL IMMEDIATELY AFTER THE TRANSFER

In Mojonnier & Sons, Inc. v. Commissioner, 12 T.C. 837 (1949) (NA), discussed in *D'Angelo,* a father had agreed that if his sons and a foreman worked in his business they would receive some stock when he incorporated his business a few years later. On that later incorporation, shares of stock were issued directly to the sons and foreman, so that the father received less than 80 percent of the stock. The court held, with the taxpayer, that section 351 did not apply in view of the absence of control. It rejected the Commissioner's argument that the father should be regarded as receiving all of the stock and then making gifts to the others, the court stating that the transfers of stock were not gifts but rewards for past services and, moreover, had been made directly to the others in accordance with the prior agreement. In May Broadcasting Co. v. United States, 200 F.2d 852 (8th Cir.1953), a transfer of a radio station to a newly formed corporation for its stock and then a sale of one-fourth of the stock to a third party, who also contributed cash to the corporation, was held not to be a section 351 exchange since the sale was pursuant to a contract existing at the time of incorporation, although the requirement of Federal Communications Commission approval delayed the sale until nine months after the first transaction.

Commissioner v. National Bellas Hess, Inc., 220 F.2d 415 (8th Cir. 1955), is similar to the *American Bantam* case, in that an unexercised option held by the employees of the transferee corporation to purchase some stock from the transferors did not prevent control from residing in the transferors; nor did a sale of stock to the public within three months. In Federal Grain Corp. v. Commissioner, 18 B.T.A. 242 (1929), an agreement that the transferors would place the stock of the corporation in a voting trust for five years was said not to defeat the "control" of the transferors, since the definition of "control" relates to ownership of stock rather than actual control through the exercise of voting rights.

Intermountain Lumber Co. v. Commissioner, 65 T.C. 1025 (1976), held that the requisite control immediately after the exchange was not present where, as part of the incorporation transaction, the transferor was obligated under an agreement of sale to sell almost half of the shares of the corporation to a third party. The court formulated the control requirement of section 351 as follows: "A determination of 'ownership,' as that term is used in section 368(c) and for purposes of control under section 351, depends upon the obligations and freedom of action of the transferee with respect to the stock when he acquired it from the corporation. * * * If the [stockholder], as part of the transaction by which the shares were acquired, has irrevocably foregone or relinquished at that time the legal right to determine whether to keep the shares, ownership in such shares is lacking for purposes of section 351. By contrast, if there are no restrictions upon freedom of action at the time he acquires the shares, it is immaterial how soon thereafter the [stockholder] elects to dispose of his stock or whether such disposition is in accord with a preconceived plan not amounting to a binding obligation." (1031)

Since the stockholder was under an obligation to sell the shares, section 351 was not applicable and the corporate transferee obtained a stepped-up basis in the property involved in the transaction. The third party in *Intermountain* did not transfer property to the corporation in the transaction.

Under the standard of *Intermountain,* did the taxpayer in *D'Angelo,* supra page 363, retain control immediately after the corporation's issuance of stock to his children?

B. WHO ARE THE TRANSFERORS?

Section 351 applies when one or more persons who transfer property to the corporation are in control immediately after the transfer. The control requirement thus requires identification of the group of transferors who are to be counted. As discussed, supra at page 343, a person receiving stock or securities for services is not counted as a member of the control group.

In some cases taxpayers have attempted to count existing stockholders as members of the control group in order to classify an exchange of appreciated property for stock by non-controlling persons as a nonrecognition transaction under section 351. For example, in Kamborian v. Commissioner, 469 F.2d 219 (1st Cir.1972), the taxpayers holding 76 percent of the stock of a corporation transferred appreciated property to the corporation in exchange for additional stock. A trust which held 13 percent of the stock of the transferee corporation purchased a small number of shares for cash in an attempt to qualify the transfer under section 351. The taxpayers claimed that the trust was a transferor so that together the combined holdings of transferors exceeded 80 percent. The court held that it is "permissible to consider transfers by other owners only if those transfers were, in economic terms, sufficiently related to * * * make all of the transfers parts of a single transaction." (221) The court added that, "The trustees' desire to help the [other] stockholders avoid taxes, warrantably found by the Tax Court to have been the primary motive for the trust's purchase cannot be used to make a single transaction out of otherwise unrelated transfers." (222)

In Rev.Rul. 79–70, 1979–1 Cum.Bull. 144, X Corporation transferred property to newly organized Y Corporation and, pursuant to a prearranged binding contract, sold 40 percent of the Y stock to Z Corporation. Simultaneously, Z purchased securities for cash from Y. The Ruling held that Z Corporation was not a transferor of property because it received only securities from Y. Z's ownership of the Y stock acquired by purchase from X Corporation could not be counted in determining whether the control requirement of section 351 was satisfied. Since Z therefore received only securities for cash and was not a stockholder prior to the exchange, it was not a member of the control group for section 351 purposes. X was the only transferor of property, it received only 60 percent of the stock, and the transaction therefore did not qualify under section 351.

On the other hand, Rev.Rul. 79–194, 1979–1 Cum.Bull. 145, holds that a pre-arranged sale between two transferors of property for stock does not affect the control requirement. Z Corporation transferred property to

Newco for 80 percent of Newco stock. A group of investors transferred property for 20 percent of Newco stock. Following the transfers to Newco, Z sold stock to the investors. At the end of the transaction, Z owned 49 percent of the Newco stock. The Ruling holds that since Z and the investors were transferors, the persons transferring property to Newco in exchange for Newco stock owned 100 percent of Newco stock immediately after the exchange. However, where the investor group transferred property in exchange for only 1 percent of the Newco stock, with Z receiving 99 percent, the investors were disregarded as transferors and the control requirement was not satisfied because of the subsequent sale of stock by Z to the investors.

In the *American Bantam* case, supra page 360, accepting the taxpayer's unitary view of the transaction, the Commissioner might have replied that the public stockholders and the underwriter were "transferors of property" to be counted in the control group so that sections 368(c) and 351 were satisfied, especially since the shares they held were being counted in determining the total against which the requisite 80 percent was to be computed. Rev.Rul. 78–294, 1978–2 Cum.Bull. 141, described the circumstances under which the public stockholders and the underwriter can be considered as members of the control group for purposes of section 351. If the underwriting agreement involves a firm commitment on the part of the underwriter to purchase the stock, then the underwriter will be treated as part of the transferor group even though it is clear that the underwriter intends to sell the stock to the public as part of the overall financing transaction. If the underwriter is not required to purchase the stock but only to use its "best efforts" to sell the stock to the public, the public investors themselves will belong to the transferor group if "the movement of property from the public investors to the corporation is direct and uninterrupted." The Ruling stresses the fact that the sale to the public was within a short period of time and there was no change in the terms of the offering.

Rev.Rul. 84–44, 1984–1 Cum.Bull. 105, provides that section 351 is not applicable to the transferor of property to a corporate subsidiary in exchange for stock of the transferee subsidiary's parent corporation, which is in turn controlled by the transferor. However, the same result can be accomplished by restructuring the transaction as a transfer to the controlled parent corporation first, followed by a transfer by the parent corporation in exchange for stock of its controlled subsidiary. Rev.Rul. 83–34, 1983–1 Cum.Bull. 79, holds that although these transfers may be undertaken pursuant to an integrated plan, each transfer is treated as a separate transaction that satisfies section 351. See also Rev.Rul. 83–156, 1983–2 Cum.Bull. 66, holding that section 351 applies to a transfer of assets to a wholly owned subsidiary which then transfers the assets to a partnership. Compare Rev.Rul. 70–140, 1970–1 Cum.Bull. 73 (no section 351 treatment for the transfer of assets of a sole proprietorship to a controlled corporation followed immediately by an exchange of the stock of the controlled corporation for the stock of another corporation; because of the integrated nature of the two transactions, the original transferor was not in control.)

Although nonrecognition of gain or loss under section 351 is based in principle on the transferors' continued investment in the transferred property, and requires a continued proprietary interest in the transferee corporation through the receipt of stock representing control, there is no express requirement that the transferors maintain a continued interest in the transferred assets.

C. CONTROL WHEN THERE ARE MULTIPLE CLASSES OF STOCK

The existence of multiple classes of voting stock requires a determination regarding the relative voting power of each class in order to determine whether the transferors of property are in control. There is little available guidance regarding the meaning of "total combined voting power of all classes of stock entitled to vote." In Rev.Rul. 63–234, 1963–2 Cum.Bull. 148, the Internal Revenue Service ruled under section 368(c) (in a type (D) reorganization) that preferred stock which entitled its holders to elect two of twelve directors was voting stock in that "it conferred upon the holders of such stock the right to significant participation in the management of the affairs of the corporation." The Service relied on its earlier ruling in I.T. 3896, 1948–1 Cum.Bull. 72 (declared obsolete in Rev.Rul. 68–100, 1968–1 Cum.Bull. 572), which considered voting control for purposes of membership in an affiliated group, holding that the voting power of preferred stock was in proportion to the number of directors elected by the preferred stockholders. Thus preferred stock with the right to elect two of twelve directors possessed 2/12, or 16.7 percent of voting control. See also Rev.Rul. 69–126, 1969–1 Cum.Bull. 218, applying the same analysis for purposes of defining voting control under section 1504. Under this standard, a stockholder who receives common stock for services might receive more than 20 percent of the common stock by value without defeating section 351 nonrecognition treatment for transferors of property if the common stock transferred to the service stockholder represents a separate class of stock with limited voting rights.

The Internal Revenue Service also has ruled in Rev.Rul. 59–259, 1959–2 Cum.Bull. 115, that "control" under section 368(c) requires that in addition to 80 percent of the combined voting power of all classes of voting stock, the transferor stockholders must also own 80 percent of the number of shares of *each* class of nonvoting stock. Ownership of 80 percent of the total number of shares outstanding is not sufficient.

D. REFERENCE

Tillinghast and Paully, The Effect of the Collateral Issuance of Stock or Securities on the Control Requirement of Section 351, 37 Tax L.Rev. 251 (1982).

SECTION 2. SPECIAL PROBLEMS IN THE INCORPORATION OF AN EXISTING BUSINESS

A. "PROPERTY" AND MIDSTREAM TRANSFERS OF INCOME ITEMS

INTERNAL REVENUE CODE: Sections 446(b); 482.

FOSTER v. COMMISSIONER

United States Court of Appeals, Ninth Circuit, 1985.
756 F.2d 1430.

J. BLAINE ANDERSON, CIRCUIT JUDGE:

In 1955, Jack Foster and his three sons formed a partnership, T. Jack Foster and Sons (Partnership), for the general purpose of dealing in property, with Jack as the managing partner. In 1958, the Partnership began to investigate the reclamation potential of Brewer's Island, a 2,600 acre undeveloped and partially submerged tract of land located about 12 miles south of San Francisco. After commissioning engineering studies, the Partnership determined that the tract could be transformed into a self-contained city (Foster City) of 35,000.

In December, 1959, the Partnership acquired an option to purchase the property for $12.8 million; in May, 1960, it secured enabling legislation from the California legislature for a municipal improvement district known as Estero, which was coterminus with Brewer's Island; and, in August, 1960, it exercised its option to purchase the tract. Thereafter, the Partnership and Estero began developing the property by neighborhood.

* * *

C. *Application of § 482 to the Disposition of Property Acquired in a Nonrecognition Transaction*

The first of the nine neighborhoods to be developed was Neighborhood One. In October, 1962, before any sales to builders were consummated, the Partnership transferred an undivided one-quarter interest in 127 acres of Neighborhood One to each of four newly formed corporations as tenants in common. Each of the four corporations, referred to collectively by the Tax Court as the Alphabets, was solely owned by one of the Fosters.

In August, 1966, the Partnership transferred 311 lots in Neighborhood Four, which had been improved to a lesser extent than Neighborhood One, to Foster Enterprises, a corporation owned by the Fosters in equal shares. Foster Enterprises, which was incorporated in 1960 to take title to a hotel in Hawaii, had accumulated a net operating loss of $1.2 million.

The Neighborhood One transaction was an exchange of property for stock under § 351. The Neighborhood Four transaction was a contribution to capital under § 1032. Under both sections, neither the transferor nor the transferee recognize gain or loss on the transfer, and the basis of the property does not change. The transferee therefore inherits the potential gain or loss inherent in the property at the time of its transfer.

The Tax Court was correct in its determination that the Commissioner may employ § 482 to reallocate income derived from the disposition of property previously acquired in a nonrecognition transaction. Rooney v. United States, 305 F.2d 681, 686 (9th Cir.1962) (Section 482 will control when it conflicts with § 351 as long as the discretion of the Commissioner in reallocating is not abused.); Treas.Reg. § 1.482–1(d)(5) (1984); see also Stewart v. Commissioner, 714 F.2d 977, 989 (9th Cir. 1983).

D. *Section 482 Reallocation*

The Tax Court, pursuant to § 482, reallocated all the income from the sale of the lots in Neighborhood One and Neighborhood Four from the Alphabets and Foster Enterprises to the Partnership. The income reallocated was divided into two parts, income due to appreciation in value before the transfers and income due to appreciation after the transfers.

1. *Pre-transfer Appreciation*

The Tax Court reallocated the income attributable to appreciation before the transfers on the ground that the purpose of the transfers was to avoid taxes. It found that A.O. Champlin, the Fosters' long-time tax advisor, decided it was advantageous from a tax standpoint for the Fosters to undertake the development of Foster City in a partnership form. Losses incurred during the early years could then be used by the partners to reduce income on their personal tax returns. Later, as the land was developed, certain lots were transferred from the Partnership to its controlled entities in an effort to shift income. As noted by the Tax Court, "only highly appreciated inventory pregnant with income was conveyed." Foster, 80 T.C. at 179. Moreover, according to the testimony of Champlin, the value of money on hand to the Fosters far exceeded any interest that might eventually have to be paid on a tax deficiency, particularly when the rate of interest charged by the Government was less than that charged by commercial banks.

In the case of the Alphabets, which were formed within a month of the transfer, the Tax Court determined that the object was to shift from the Partnership the income from the sale of the lots and split it among taxpayers subject to a lower rate of tax. The Fosters argue that the transfer could not have been tax motivated because it would have increased taxes; the income reported by the Alphabets was not offset by any losses, whereas if the income had been reported by the Partnership, it would have been offset by the operating losses which the

Partnership claimed on its returns. The Tax Court, however, found that "the tax savings to an individual realized by preserving a partnership loss may very well exceed the tax cost to his corporation incurred by reporting the income." Id., 80 T.C. at 173.

The Fosters contend that although the Neighborhood Four transfer may have resulted in a tax saving, it was made for a business purpose. There was evidence that Rex Johnson, a senior vice president of Republic National Bank who was in charge of monitoring the Fosters' account, insisted that the lots be conveyed to Foster Enterprises as a condition to Republic's renewing the Partnership's loans. The Tax Court discounted this as the motivation behind the transfer, and we find its reasoning persuasive.

Foster Enterprises was not indebted to Republic. It had borrowed money from Likins–Foster Honolulu Corporation and Roy Turner Associates, Ltd., a subsidiary of Likins–Foster. Both Likins–Foster and the Partnership were indebted to Republic.

According to Johnson, the transfer was necessary to improve the liquidity of Foster Enterprises and thereby (1) enhance the collectibility of the indebtedness of Likins–Foster to Republic, (2) improve the bank's security in the Likins–Foster stock, and (3) insulate the bank from the fortunes of the Foster partnership. The Tax Court, however, found that a special audit report prepared by the bank stated that the Likins–Foster loans were being paid according to schedule. Moreover, if Johnson were concerned about the ability of Likins–Foster to repay its loan, it would have made more sense to transfer the lots directly to that corporation because it was the Likins–Foster stock that had been pledged as security. The transfer of the lots obviously weakened the Partnership's ability to repay its loan to Republic, noted the Tax Court, and certainly exacerbated its cash flow problem.

The sales proceeds were not used by Foster Enterprises to liquidate its debts to Likins–Foster and Turner Associates. Rather, they were loaned to the Partnership to further develop Foster City. Although Foster Enterprises still had an asset, it was now, continued the Tax Court, an unsecured receivable from the Partnership. Collectibility was therefore dependent upon the Partnership's overall success with the Foster City undertaking, precisely the risk against which Johnson ostensibly wanted to protect.

The Tax Court found that the purpose of the Neighborhood Four transaction was to shift to Foster Enterprises the income earned from the sale of the lots so that it could be absorbed by that corporation's losses. The record contains ample evidence to support the Tax Court's conclusions concerning both the Neighborhood Four and the Neighborhood One transactions.[2] We therefore find that the Commissioner did not abuse his discretion in reallocating to the Partnership that portion

2. The Fosters move to augment the record with an additional deposition of A.O. Champlin. The deposition is not properly before this court; the motion is therefore denied. Karmun v. Commissioner, 749 F.2d 567, 570 (9th Cir.1984).

of the sales income due to appreciation before the date of transfer. See Rooney v. United States, 305 F.2d 681, 684–85 (9th Cir.1962).

2. *Post-transfer Appreciation*

Because Neighborhoods One and Four were both further developed after the transfers, a part of the income derived from the sale of lots was created after the transfer date. The Tax Court concluded that Estero was controlled by the Partnership, and was used by it as its instrument for the development of Foster City. Thus Estero's efforts were to be viewed as those of the Partnership, and the gain was to be attributed to it.

Estero, a Municipal Improvement District, was created in 1960 by a special act of the California legislature. It was authorized to tax and to issue tax-exempt bonds to finance its activities in reclaiming and improving Brewer's Island. It was also vested with a broad array of general governmental powers. As enumerated by the Tax Court:

> It was empowered to reclaim land, make provision for street lighting, sewage, storm drainage, garbage and water service, and parks and playgrounds. It was also empowered to construct small craft harbors, provide fire and police protection, condemn land, enter into contracts, and make and enforce such regulations as were necessary and proper to the exercise of its enumerated powers. A violation of such regulation constituted a misdemeanor.

Foster, 80 T.C. at 58.

We agree with the Tax Court that during the years in issue, the Fosters, as the principal landowners and developers, controlled Estero. Indeed, the California Supreme Court has recognized that the Estero Act was designed by the California legislature to place control of the district in the landowner/developer. Cooper v. Leslie Salt Co., 70 Cal. 2d 627, 451 P.2d 406, 408–409, 75 Cal.Rptr. 766, 768–769, cert. denied, 396 U.S. 821, 90 S.Ct. 62, 24 L.Ed.2d 64 (1969). The Tax Court stated:

> There is no question that Estero added value to Brewer's Island. However, it never realized that value because it did not own the land or receive the proceeds from its sale. All we are deciding here is whether the value added by Estero is allocable to the Foster partnership because of the legislatively conferred control that the partnership exercised over the district. To answer that question in the affirmative does not require that we ignore Estero's legal identity as a public agency.

Foster, 80 T.C. at 169. Estero was the Partnership's creature, used by it to improve the land and thus increase its value. That is what it was designed to be and do. Because it is a public body, validly created, its own income, if any, belongs to it, and would not be allocable to some other entity.

* * *

The Tax Court stated that its finding that the Partnership controlled Estero did not conflict with the district's status as a "juristic entity," and therefore [Commissioner v. Birch Ranch & Oil Co., 192 F.2d 924 (9th Cir.1951)] was inapposite. 80 T.C. at 169. We agree. The primary question here is not whether Estero is an independent entity. The primary question is whether the Commissioner can allocate to the Partnership the income arising from value created by Estero that would have gone to the Partnership but for the transfers to the Alphabets and Foster Enterprises. The Alphabets' and Foster Enterprises' function was to divert what would normally be the income of the Partnership away from it and to the Alphabets and Foster Enterprises. If the transfers had not been made, the income in question would not have been Estero's; it would have been that of the Partnership. The relationship between the Partnership and its creatures, the Alphabets and Foster Enterprises, was precisely the same, whether the appreciation in value occurred before the transfers or after them. Under section 482, the Commissioner may allocate income earned subsequent to the income evading event or transfer. The fact that some of it is attributable to a time following the transfers makes no difference. Because Estero did not own the land, the gain in value would never accrue to Estero, but would have accrued to the Partnership, the landowner, but for the transfers. By the transfers, the Partnership shifted that income away from itself and to the Alphabets, which had nothing, and to Foster Enterprises, which had large losses from unrelated ventures. By that device, the Partnership sought to get out from under large tax liabilities and yet retain control of Foster City. Under § 482, the Commissioner could reallocate to the Partnership the income that the Partnership had shifted to the Alphabets and Foster Enterprises. The transfers had no business function; their purpose was tax avoidance. The Tax Court properly upheld the Commissioner's reallocation.

* * *

E. *Penalty*

The Tax Court affirmed the Commissioner's assessment of a penalty against Jack and Gladys Foster for negligent or intentional disregard of income tax rules and regulations. 26 U.S.C. § 6653(a) (1976). We vacate the assessment. This is a case of first impression with no clear authority to guide the decision makers as to the major and complex issues. The positions taken by the Fosters were reasonably debatable. Under all of the circumstances, we do not believe it can be fairly said that the Fosters acted negligently or intentionally in disregard of the law.

AFFIRMED in part, VACATED in part.

ILLUSTRATIVE MATERIAL

A. SECTION 482 ALLOCATIONS

As the Ninth Circuit held in *Foster,* section 482 overrides section 351, allowing the Commissioner to allocate subsequent income back to the transferor or previously incurred expenses to the transferee corporation. See also

Regulations section 1.482–1(d)(5); Rooney v. United States, 305 F.2d 681 (9th Cir.1962).

In G.D. Searle & Co. v. Commissioner, 88 T.C. 252 (1987), and Eli Lilly & Co. v. Commissioner, 84 T.C. 996 (1985), the Commissioner attempted to invoke section 482 to reallocate income from subsidiary corporations to their parent corporations following section 351 transfers of intangible property rights. The parent corporations in both cases were pharmaceutical manufacturers who transferred patents and other intangibles to newly formed subsidiaries in Puerto Rico in order to take advantage of tax credits provided to manufacturing income from United States possessions.[9] In *G.D. Searle* the Tax Court held that where there is no tax avoidance motive, section 482 cannot be used by the Commissioner to disregard the subsidiary's ownership interest in intangibles that were transferred in a valid section 351 transaction. However, the court applied section 482 to require the parent corporation to recognize royalty income equal to 25 percent of the subsidiary's net sales as consideration for the transfer of intangibles developed by the parent. The court concluded that receipt of the subsidiary's stock alone was inadequate consideration for the intangibles transferred to the subsidiary. As a result there was a distortion in the parent's income which could be corrected under section 482.

Eli Lilly & Co. was similar. The Tax Court upheld the Commissioner's reallocation of profits between the parent and its Puerto Rican subsidiary under section 482. The Commissioner required an adjustment of intercompany pricing to reflect adequate consideration for the value of the transferred intangibles which had been developed by the parent corporation. The price paid by the subsidiary was increased to reflect the parent corporation's research and development activities. The Court of Appeals for the Seventh Circuit reversed this holding, however. 856 F.2d 855 (7th Cir. 1988). The Seventh Circuit affirmed the Tax Court's conclusion that the Puerto Rican subsidiary's ownership of the intangibles could not be disregarded under section 482, but rejected the Tax Court's holding that the transferred stock was not adequate consideration for the full value of the transferred receivables. The Court of Appeals approach seems the appropriate one; as long as assignment of income principles, discussed in B. below, would not allow attribution of income to the transferor, the section 351 exchange by definition must be at "arm's length" and should prevent income allocation under section 482.

B. ASSIGNMENT OF INCOME

In the case of a transfer to the corporation of contract rights or other property with accrued but uncollected income, the Commissioner has invoked assignment of income principles to force the transferor to recognize earned income on the transfer of the right to collect that income. See Weinberg v. Commissioner, 44 T.C. 233 (1965), aff'd per curiam sub nom. Commissioner v. Sugar Daddy, Inc., 386 F.2d 836 (9th Cir.1967). However, Hempt Bros. Inc. v. United States, 490 F.2d 1172 (3d Cir.1974), held, however, that application of the assignment of income doctrine to tax the transfer of receivables by a cash basis taxpayer would frustrate the policy of

9. Subject to certain qualifications, section 936 provides a tax credit for the tax (even if not paid) of a United States domestic corporation attributable to income derived from the active conduct of a trade or business in a possession of the United States.

section 351 which is to facilitate incorporation of a going business.[10] Rev. Rul. 80–198, 1980–2 Cum.Bull. 113, adopts the holding of *Hempt Brothers,* but adds that assignment of income principles will apply to tax the transfer of receivables if that is the only asset transferred to the corporation. Cf. Brown v. Commissioner, 40 B.T.A. 565 (1939), aff'd, 115 F.2d 337 (2d Cir.1940).

C. TAX BENEFIT RULE

In Nash v. United States, 398 U.S. 1 (1970), the Commissioner relied on the tax benefit rule to assert that in a section 351 transfer of accrued accounts receivable that were subject to a reserve for bad debts,[11] the amount of the reserve should be restored to income in the year of the transfer: the reserve was no longer needed by the transferor and the transferor had received a tax benefit in the year of deduction, which benefit was required to be restored to income in the year of recovery. The Supreme Court, however, held that the transfer of the reserve for bad debts did not trigger recognition of income in the hands of the transferors:

"Deduction of the reserve from the face amount of the receivables transferred conforms to the reality of the transaction, as the risk of noncollection was on the transferee. Since the reserve for purposes of this case was deemed to be reasonable and the value of the stock received upon the transfer was equal to the *net value* of the receivables, there does not seem to us to have been any 'recovery.' A tax benefit was received by the partnership when the bad debt reserve was originally taken as a deduction from income. There would be a double benefit to the partnership if securities were issued covering the face amount of the receivables. We do not, however, understand how there can be a 'recovery' of the benefit of the bad debt reserve when the receivables are transferred less the reserve. That merely perpetuates the status quo and does not tinker with it for any double benefit out of the bad debt reserve." (4–5)

In Hillsboro National Bank v. Commissioner, 460 U.S. 370 (1983), the Supreme Court abandoned its strict adherence to the presence of a "recovery" as a prerequisite to the application of tax benefit rule, holding that "the tax benefit rule will 'cancel out' an earlier deduction only when a careful examination shows that the later event is indeed fundamentally inconsistent with the premise on which the deduction was initially based." (383) In United States v. Bliss Dairy, Inc., which was consolidated with *Hillsboro National Bank,* the Court applied the tax benefit rule to override a specific nonrecognition provision of the Code.[12] The Court in *Bliss Dairy* noted that in *Nash* there was no event inconsistent with the transferor's deductions for contributions to the reserve because the bad debt reserve in *Nash* was an accurate estimate of the debts that would ultimately prove uncollectible by the transferee corporation.

10. The corporation will have a zero basis in the receivables and will thus be required to recognize on collection the full amount as income. See P.A. Birren & Son v. Commissioner, 116 F.2d 718 (7th Cir. 1940), infra at page 380.

11. For years prior to 1987, section 166(c) allowed a deduction for a reserve for bad debts.

12. The provision was former Section 336 which provided before 1987 for nonrecognition of gain to the corporate distributee in a complete liquidation. The taxpayer in *Bliss Dairy* was required to recapture previously expensed supplies under the tax benefit rule. Such a recapture is not appropriate in a section 351 transaction because the transferor's zero basis carries over to the transferee.

D. CHANGE OF ACCOUNTING METHOD

The Commissioner may invoke his powers under section 446(b) to require proper accounting for income as between the transferor and the transferee corporation. In Palmer v. Commissioner, 267 F.2d 434 (9th Cir. 1959), the transferor was forced to switch from the completed contract method to the percentage of completion method of accounting for long term construction contracts when it attempted to transfer the contracts to a controlled corporation before payment for completed work came due. Mathis v. United States, 430 F.2d 158 (7th Cir.1970), however, rejected the Commissioner's assertion of section 446(b) to force the transferor off of the completed contract method since both the transferor and transferee were paying tax at the same corporate rates on the income in question.

E. REFERENCES

Brown, Incorporating Transfers & Anticipatory Assignments, 38 U.Pitt. L.Rev. 589 (1977); O'Connor, Tax Problems on Transfers of Assets to Corporations, 52 Taxes 756 (1974); White, Sleepers That Travel with Section 351 Transfers, 56 Va.L.Rev. 37 (1970); Lyon and Eustice, Assignment of Income: Fruit and Tree as Irrigated by the P.G. Lake Case, 17 Tax L.Rev. 295, 424 (1962).

B. TRANSFERS OF MULTIPLE ASSETS

REV.RUL. 68–55

1968–1 Cum.Bull. 140.

Advice has been requested as to the correct method of determining the amount and character of the gain to be recognized by Corporation *X* under section 351(b) of the Internal Revenue Code of 1954 under the circumstances described below.

Corporation *Y* was organized by *X* and *A*, an individual who owned no stock in *X*. *A* transferred 20*x* dollars to *Y* in exchange for stock of *Y* having a fair market value of 20*x* dollars and *X* transferred to *Y* three separate assets and received in exchange stock of *Y* having a fair market value of 100*x* dollars plus cash of 10*x* dollars.

In accordance with the facts set forth in the table below if *X* had sold at fair market value each of the three assets it transferred to *Y*, the result would have been as follows:

	Asset I	*Asset II*	*Asset III*
Character of asset	Capital asset held more than 6 months.	Capital asset held not more than 6 months.	Section 1245 property.
Fair market value	$22*x*	$33*x*	$55*x*
Adjusted basis	40*x*	20*x*	25*x*
Gain (loss)	($18*x*)	$13*x*	$30*x*
Character of gain or loss	Long-term capital loss.	Short-term capital gain.	Ordinary income.

The facts in the instant case disclose that with respect to the section 1245 property the depreciation subject to recapture exceeds the amount of gain that would be recognized on a sale at fair market value.

Therefore, all of such gain would be treated as ordinary income under section 1245(a)(1) of the Code.

Under section 351(a) of the Code, no gain or loss is recognized if property is transferred to a corporation solely in exchange for its stock and immediately after the exchange the transferor is in control of the corporation. If section 351(a) of the Code would apply to an exchange but for the fact that there is received, in addition to the property permitted to be received without recognition of gain, other property or money, then under section 351(b) of the Code gain (if any) to the recipient will be recognized, but in an amount not in excess of the sum of such money and the fair market value of such other property received, and no loss to the recipient will be recognized.

The first question presented is how to determine the amount of gain to be recognized under section 351(b) of the Code. The general rule is that each asset transferred must be considered to have been separately exchanged. See the authorities cited in Revenue Ruling 67–192, C.B. 1967–2, 140, and in Revenue Ruling 68–23, page 144, this Bulletin, which hold that there is no netting of gains and losses for purposes of applying sections 367 and 356(c) of the Code. Thus, for purposes of making computations under section 351(b) of the Code, it is not proper to total the bases of the various assets transferred and to subtract this total from the fair market value of the total consideration received in the exchange. Moreover, any treatment other than an asset-by-asset approach would have the effect of allowing losses that are specifically disallowed by section 351(b)(2) of the Code.

The second question presented is how, for purposes of making computations under section 351(b) of the Code, to allocate the cash and stock received to the amount realized as to each asset transferred in the exchange. The asset-by-asset approach for computing the amount of gain realized in the exchange requires that for this purpose the fair market value of each category of consideration received must be separately allocated to the transferred assets in proportion to the relative fair market values of the transferred assets. See section 1.1245–4(c)(1) of the Income Tax Regulations which, for the same reasons, requires that for purposes of computing the amount of gain to which section 1245 of the Code applies each category of consideration received must be allocated to the properties transferred in proportion to their relative fair market values.

Accordingly, the amount and character of the gain recognized in the exchange should be computed as follows:

	Total	*Asset I*	*Asset II*	*Asset III*
Fair market value of asset transferred	$110x	$22x	$33x	$55x
Percent of total fair market value	—	20%	30%	50%
Fair market value of *Y* stock received in exchange	$100x	$20x	$30x	$50x
Cash received in exchange	10x	2x	3x	5x
Amount realized	$110x	$22x	$33x	$55x
Adjusted basis	—	40x	20x	25x
Gain (loss) realized	—	($18x)	$13x	$30x

Under section 351(b)(2) of the Code the loss of 18*x* dollars realized on the exchange of Asset Number I is not recognized. Such loss may not be used to offset the gains realized on the exchanges of the other assets. Under section 351(b)(1) of the Code, the gain of 13*x* dollars realized on the exchange of Asset Number II will be recognized as short-term capital gain in the amount of 3*x* dollars, the amount of cash received. Under section 351(b)(1) and 1245(b)(3) of the Code, the gain of 30*x* dollars realized on the exchange of Asset Number III will be recognized as ordinary income in the amount of 5*x* dollars, the amount of cash received.

ILLUSTRATIVE MATERIAL

A. THE CORPORATION'S BASIS

The seller of multiple assets must compute gain or loss on an asset-by-asset basis instead of comparing the total amount realized with the combined bases of the transferred assets. See Williams v. McGowan, 152 F.2d 570 (2d Cir.1945). Similarly, Rev.Rul. 68–55, requires that cash or other property received in addition to stock be allocated to each asset in proportion to fair market value in order to determine the gain or loss realized and gain recognized with respect to each asset. See also Rev.Rul. 67–192, 1967–2 Cum.Bull. 140; Regulations, section 1.1245–4(c). Computing the corporation's basis in multiple assets received in a section 351 exchange in which the transferor recognizes gain is more of a problem.

It is reasonably clear from the language of section 362(b) that the transferor's basis in each transferred asset carries over to the corporation. See P.A. Birren & Son v. Commissioner, 116 F.2d 718 (7th Cir.1940); Gunn v. Commissioner, 25 T.C. 424, 438 (1955), aff'd per curiam, 244 F.2d 408 (10th Cir.1957). The carryover basis is increased by the transferor's recognized gain which requires an allocation of the gain to different assets. There are three methods by which this allocation might be made: (i) in proportion to the relative fair market values of the different assets, (ii) in proportion to adjusted basis, or (iii) in proportion to the excess of fair market value over basis. Each of the first two allocation methods has the effect of increasing the difference between the value and basis of loss assets. The second method has the advantage of not requiring an appraisal of the assets to determine relative values. The third method allocates recognized gain to assets with built-in gain in proportion to the gain realized on each asset. Under this third the basis of each asset is increased in proportion to each asset's contribution to the recognized gain.

A different set of problems arises when the controlled corporation assumes liabilities subject to section 357. If section 357(b) applies to treat liabilities as boot, the recognition of gain is no different than in the case of cash or other property. Thus the basis increase for the corporation could be allocated to assets in proportion to the difference between the value of each asset and its adjusted basis. The allocation of gain recognized by the transferor under section 357(c) is more difficult. For example, assume that A transfers two assets to X, a controlled corporation. One asset is real property with a fair market value of $75 and a basis of $15, and the second asset is equipment with a value of $25 and a basis of $30. X assumes unsecured liabilities of $50, which requires that A recognize $5 of gain under section 357(c). Here the recognized gain occurs because in the aggregate the basis of transferred assets is less than liabilities. Unlike the case where boot is received, the recognized gain is not attributable to specific assets. Nonetheless, an allocation of A's $5 gain to the real property rather than an apportionment between the two assets has some appeal because the allocation will not cause an increase in the difference between the fair market value and adjusted basis of any asset. If a liability is secured by a particular asset, however, gain recognized by the transferor under section 357(c) with respect to the liability should be allocated to the encumbered asset.

For a discussion of the problems of incorporating partnerships under section 351 see supra, page 227.

B. INSTALLMENT OBLIGATIONS

Under Regulations, section 1.453–9(c)(2), in general no gain or loss results from the transfer of installment obligations to a corporation in an exchange to which section 351 applies despite the fact that part of the tax on the installment gain may in effect be shifted to the other shareholders. However, if the obligor on the installment obligation is the corporation *itself*, then the section 351 transaction constitutes a "satisfaction" of the installment obligation and results in a tax to the transferor. Rev.Rul. 73–423, 1973–2 Cum.Bull. 161, following dicta in Jack Ammann Photogrammetric Engineers, Inc. v. Commissioner, 341 F.2d 466 (5th Cir.1965).

C. TRANSFERS OF DEPRECIABLE PROPERTY: SECTION 1239 AND RECAPTURE UNDER SECTIONS 1245 AND 1250

Prior to 1987, when there was a tax preference for capital gains, a taxpayer owning an asset with a low basis but a high value might attempt to step-up the basis for depreciation by selling the asset to another taxpayer under the taxpayer's control, the larger depreciation deductions offsetting the capital gain. Section 1239, applicable to sales between a corporation and a more than 50 percent stockholder (and between a husband and wife), and section 707(b)(2), applicable to sales between a partner and the partnership, meet this problem to the extent they are applicable by providing ordinary income treatment on the sale. Section 1239 applies to the gain recognized under section 351(b) (boot) and thus also to the gain required to be recognized under section 357(c) (liabilities in excess of basis). Rev.Rul. 60–302, 1960–2 Cum.Bull. 223; Alderman v. Commissioner, 55 T.C. 662 (1971).

Sections 1245(b)(3) and 1250(d)(3) provide that there is no recapture of depreciation in section 351 transactions except to the extent of the gain required to be recognized by section 351. Under Regulations section 1.47–3(f), there is no recapture of the investment credit in a section 351 transfer if the tests described in the Regulations are met, notably that the transfer must be of a trade or business in which the assets are used and the transferor must retain a substantial interest in that trade or business through his shareholdings.

D. REFERENCE

Rabinovitz, Allocating Boot in Section 351 Exchanges, 24 Tax L.Rev. 337 (1969).

SECTION 3: THE SWAP FUND PROBLEM

INTERNAL REVENUE CODE: Section 351(e)(1).

REGULATIONS: Section 1.351–1(c).

Should the section 351 tax-free treatment cover all transfers to controlled corporations? Suppose that an individual owns a large amount of a particular stock which has greatly appreciated in value. The taxpayer would like to diversify that investment but feels that the tax on capital gains is too high a price to pay for diversification. There are many other individuals in a similar situation, but with different stocks. An investment house forms a regulated investment company (mutual fund)—which is a corporation for Federal tax purposes—and invites an exchange of the stocks of the individuals in return for stock of the fund. This exchange would provide the individuals with the desired diversification, since they would now have, through their participation in the mutual fund, an interest in many different stocks, including their former shares. In 1960, the Internal Revenue Service issued letter rulings to the effect that such a transaction would qualify under section 351. The investment funds organized to achieve such purposes were known as "swap funds." In Rev.Proc. 62–32, 1962–2 Cum.Bull. 517, the Internal Revenue Service announced that it would no longer issue rulings on such transactions. However, swap funds continued to flourish, relying upon the opinions of counsel that section 351 made the transaction tax-free to the transferors. In 1966 the Treasury issued Proposed Regulations to the effect that future swap fund transactions would constitute taxable exchanges. In the Foreign Investors Tax Act of 1966, Congress ratified the tax-free treatment of transfers to swap funds which were made prior to June 30, 1967, but excluded "investment companies" from the definition of "corporation" under section 351 for transfers after that date. The Tax Reform Act of 1976 changed the statutory structure but not the result, by providing in what is now section 351(e) that section 351 does not apply to transfers to investment companies. As a result gain (but not loss) is recognized by the transferors in such transactions.[13]

Regulations, section 1.351–1(c), provide that a transferee will be considered to be to an "investment company" if the transaction results, directly or indirectly, in a diversification of the transferor's interest and the transferee is a regulated investment company, a real estate investment trust, or a corporation more than 80 percent of the value of the assets of which is held in readily marketable stocks or securities or similar transferable interests. Under Regulations, section 1.351–1(c)(5), a transaction ordinarily results in diversification "if two or more persons transfer nonidentical assets to a corporation in the exchange." The Internal Revenue Service has taken the position that the requirement that two or more persons transfer nonidentical assets to the corporation is satisfied if one group of transferors transfer the stock of a single corporation and another group transfers cash. Rev.Rul. 87–27, 1987–1 Cum.Bull. 134. The statutory changes and the Regulations thus extend to situations beyond the mutual fund problem which caused those changes.

In Rev.Rul. 88–32, 1988–1 Cum.Bull. 113, the Internal Revenue Service ruled that a transfer of stock does not result in diversification unless diversification is the result of a nonrecognition transaction. Thus, there is no

13. In addition, the 1976 Act added section 683 to provide similar rules for transfers to trusts used as swap funds and also dealt with the problem of diversification through partnership formation. See supra, page 50.

proscribed diversification if the transferor transfers stock of a single corporation to a controlled investment company which sells the stock in a taxable transaction and reinvests the sales proceeds in a diverse portfolio of stock.

SECTION 4. PROPOSALS FOR CHANGE

The American Law Institute, the Staff of the Senate Finance Committee and the Treasury Department have published major proposals for the revision of subchapter C of the Code. Some of the specific recommendations concern section 351 transactions.

The American Law Institute, Federal Income Tax Project, Subchapter C (W. Andrews Reporter, 1982), recommended extending the nonrecognition rules of section 351 to any transfer of property to a corporation whose stock is not publicly traded if the transferor is or becomes a 20 percent stockholder. (189) The Project also would revise section 357(c) to exclude the basis of corporate stock transferred in a section 351 exchange for purposes of determining whether liabilities exceed the basis of property transferred to the controlled corporation. (195)

The recommendations of the Subchapter C Revisions Act of 1985, Senate Finance Committee (Staff Report), Final Report on Subchapter C (1985), are somewhat more extensive. The Study proposed to change the definition of control to conform with the definition of section 1504(a), which is used by the Code to define an affiliated group of corporations. (212) Under that provision, control requires ownership of stock representing both 80 percent of voting control and 80 percent of the value of the corporation. In addition, "control immediately after" the transaction will be deemed to exist if, following a transfer to a controlled corporation, the controlled corporation is acquired in a qualified reorganization, but only if the transferor is a corporation and the assets transferred to the controlled corporation are sufficient for the active conduct of a trade or business by the controlled corporation. (212) The step transaction doctrine would not be applied to recharacterize the transaction.

The Study would treat an installment sale to a 20 percent owned corporation as a section 351 exchange to the extent of the installment notes received by the transferor. The proposal is intended to prevent a basis increase for the corporation where the transferor is permitted to defer recognition of gain. However, for a transferor with less than 80 percent control the receipt of stock in addition to notes would continue to result in a taxable exchange to the extent of the stock.

The Senate Finance Committee Study also recommends revising section 358 to limit the transferor's basis in stock and securities received to the lesser of the basis of property given up or the fair market value of the transferred property, decreased, as under present law, by the fair market value of nonrecognition property and increased by gain recognized. (220)

CHAPTER 10

THE CAPITAL STRUCTURE OF THE CORPORATION

SECTION 1. DEBT VERSUS EQUITY: DEDUCTIBLE INTEREST OR NONDEDUCTIBLE DIVIDEND DISTRIBUTION

INTRODUCTORY NOTE

The tax treatment of the various forms which an investment in a corporation can take is a central issue in the pattern of corporate taxation. Unlike the partnership situation discussed in Part I, the return on capital invested in ownership interests in the corporation, i.e., corporate stock, are subject to two levels of tax, once in the hands of the corporation and again when dividends are distributed to individual shareholders. On the other hand, the return on an investment in a corporation as a creditor, i.e., the interest paid by the corporation for the funds advanced, is only subject to a single level of tax since the interest payment, unlike a dividend, is deductible by the corporation and thus avoids the corporate level tax.[1]

This tax "bias" in favor of investment as a creditor has been a source of great strain on the tax system. Taxpayers and their advisors have attempted to structure obligations which qualify as debt for tax purposes, with the attendant single level of tax on the return, while at the same time giving the investor an opportunity to participate in the growth of the business enterprise—a typical aspect of an ownership or equity investment.

As an investment matter, the investor generally is indifferent to the formal classification of the investment instrument. From the investment perspective, the question is the yield on the investment in relation to the level of risk involved and the formal classification of the return as "interest" or "dividend" is not a matter of concern (except, of course, from a tax point of view). As a general matter, the higher the level of legal and economic protection provided in the instrument, the lower the investment return. In addition, given the imagination of the marketers of financial products, the possible combinations of ownership and creditor interests in a particular financial instrument are almost infinite.

The development of tax principles in this area has lagged far behind the development of investment products. This lag may be

1. If the investor is a tax-exempt entity, such as a pension fund, debt classification generally eliminates the yield from the corporate tax base entirely. Some congressional actions in the area have been motivated by that fact. See infra, page 411.

traceable to two causes. In the first place, the legal rules for the classification of investment instruments as debt or equity have developed primarily in the context of small, closely held corporations in cases where the investors were both shareholders and "lenders." The method of analysis developed by the courts in that context has been largely inadequate to deal with situations such as large venture capital firms investing in an emerging business or the issuance of highly complex and sophisticated financial instruments by publicly traded companies. Secondly, and closely related, is the fact that, in developing the debt-equity rules, the courts generally have applied an "all or nothing" approach. That is, a particular instrument is either a debt instrument in its entirety for tax purposes or an equity instrument in its entirety. This, of course, is totally at odds with the various combinations of debt and equity features which can be employed in a particular financial instrument. Nonetheless, except when Congress has been willing to provide a legislative alternative (which it has been increasingly forced to do), the all-or-nothing approach continues to prevail. This approach has made it relatively easy for sophisticated investors and their equally sophisticated tax advisors to craft instruments which combine the desirable legal features of ownership and creditor status with the most advantageous tax treatment.

The material in this chapter first considers the "traditional" debt-equity classification issues primarily as they have developed in the context of closely-held corporations. It then deals with the classification issues which are raised by more complex financial instruments and the more specific Congressional responses to those issues.

As the materials are considered, keep in mind the issues raised by the proposals for the integration of corporation and personal taxes discussed in Chapter 7. Which of the problems encountered in this Chapter would disappear under integration? What new issues would be raised?

The present distinction between debt and equity capital presents the corporation and its investors with different tax issues and planning possibilities. As respects the corporation issuing the obligation,[2] if the obligation is debt, interest is deductible, retirement at a discount may result in cancellation of indebtedness income, or retirement at a premium may provide an additional interest deduction. If the obligation is stock, dividends are not deductible and the corporation does not recognize income or loss on retirement. Retention of earnings to retire debt will generally not run afoul of the section 531 penalty tax on improperly accumulated earnings, infra, page 1064, but such retention might result in that tax in the case of stock. Also the availability of the deduction for original issue discount requires that the obligation be classified as debt; no such deduction is allowed for the issuance of stock.

2. The term "obligation" is used in the following materials to include stock, debt, and instruments with attributes of both stock and debt whose proper classification is in doubt.

Gain or loss recognized by a corporate or individual stockholder on the sale, exchange or retirement of stock will be capital. Loss incurred on worthless stock is also capital. However, section 1244 allows individuals an ordinary loss on stock in certain small business companies, and a corporation is allowed an ordinary loss on the worthless stock of a controlled subsidiary. Gain or loss recognized on the sale, exchange or retirement of a debt obligation is also capital to a corporate or individual holder (unless there is an element of original issue or market discount involved). Loss on a worthless debt obligation which is classified as a "security" is treated as a capital loss to both the corporate and individual holder. For this purpose, a debt obligation is a "security" if it is in registered form or has coupons attached.[3] An individual's loss on a debt obligation which is not a security is a short-term capital loss, unless the debt arose in the individual's trade or business, in which case the loss is ordinary. Loss incurred by a corporate holder on a non-security debt obligation is ordinary. See sections 165(g), 166(a) and (d). Loss incurred by a corporate holder with respect to worthless securities of a controlled subsidiary generally is ordinary. Section 165(g)(3).

Payments on an obligation will also produce different tax results for the holder depending on the character of the obligation. If the payment constitutes interest it will be includible in the recipient's income whether or not the corporation has earnings and profits, whereas inclusion of the payment on stock as a dividend depends on the presence of earnings and profits. If a corporation holds the obligation, the intercorporate dividends received deduction (infra, page 507) depends on the presence of a "dividend" which requires that the obligation be treated as stock. If the advances to the corporation are regarded as contributions to capital, i.e., additional stock investment, repayment usually will be a dividend to the stockholder, but if regarded as loans, the repayment will not be taxable. Where the obligation is retired, if it is stock, the retirement under some circumstances will be a dividend under section 301; if a debt, retirement will produce capital gain or loss (in the absence of original issue discount or premium). Further, the classification of the obligation as stock or debt is important in determining the applicability of the personal holding company tax, infra, page 1074.

The above discussion is not exhaustive, and there are other facets to the problem. For example, the classification of the obligation as stock or debt is important under the reorganization provisions to both the investor and the corporation. Also, if a foreign subsidiary is involved, the classification will be important, for example, with respect to the foreign tax credit.

3. No loss is allowed in the case of a worthless debt which is a "registration required debt" but which has not been registered. Section 165(j).

SLAPPEY DRIVE INDUSTRIAL PARK v. UNITED STATES

United States Court of Appeals, Fifth Circuit, 1977.
561 F.2d 572.

GOLDBERG, CIRCUIT JUDGE.

This tax refund suit involves seven closely held real estate development corporations that Spencer C. Walden, Jr. organized and manages. The first issue * * * is whether certain purported debts that the corporations owed their shareholders should be treated for tax purposes as contributions to capital. * * * The district court, Cairo Developers, Inc. v. United States, D.C., 381 F.Supp. 431, resolved [the] issue in the government's favor. We affirm.

I. Facts

Spencer C. Walden, Jr. is a successful real estate developer in Albany, Georgia, a city of some 100,000 located less than 50 miles southeast of Plains. Acting primarily through the partnership of Walden & Kirkland, Walden has developed numerous residential subdivisions and various commercial properties. This case concerns a subset of his activities.

Among the properties Walden has developed are several tracts originally owned by his father-in-law, J.T. Haley, and Haley's descendants. With Walden directing organizational efforts, members of the Haley family formed six corporations over a fifteen year period. Those corporations were Pecan Haven, Inc. (Pecan Haven), Lake Park, Inc. (Lake Park), Sherwood Acres, Inc. (Sherwood), Lake Park Additions, Inc. (Additions), Forest Estates, Inc. (Forest Estates) and Slappey Drive Industrial Park, Inc. (Slappey). Each of these is a party to this case. The other corporate party is Cairo Developers, Inc. (Cairo Developers), which Walden formed in conjunction with two individuals not members of the J.T. Haley family.

Walden was the moving force behind each of these corporations. He was president of each enterprise, and his partnership, Walden & Kirkland, handled their development work. All but Slappey were to develop residential subdivisions; Slappey's project was an industrial park.

On this appeal the government * * * contends that purported debts that each corporation owed its shareholders should receive equity treatment. The debts arose from eight transfers of land (ostensibly credit sales) and three transfers of money (ostensibly loans) that the shareholders made to the corporations. [Ed.: The gain on transfers of property for notes would be subject to current taxation under post–1989 law, see supra page 347. The court's discussion of the debt-equity issue remains relevant.] We develop the facts relevant to these contentions by discussing the corporations in the order of their incorporation, referring to the contested transfers by alphabetical labels.

Pecan Haven. Pecan Haven was formed in June 1947. The shareholders were Walden (1 share), his wife Cornelia Haley Walden (59 shares) and her twin sister Loretta Haley (60 shares). They paid $12,000 for their shares. Pecan Haven developed several tracts obtained from Loretta and Cornelia and later developed a tract purchased from their father J.T. Haley.

Transfer A occurred July 26, 1960. Spencer Walden transferred 69.435 acres to the corporation in exchange for its $65,000 five-year 3% installment notes. Appellants assert that the corporation's book net worth at that time was $83,000 and that its "true" net worth, taking into account the appreciated value of its real estate holdings, was $476,000. The corporation failed to make timely payments of principal or interest, and $20,000 remains outstanding.

Lake Park. J.T. Haley's three children—Joel T. Haley, Jr., Cornelia and Loretta—organized Lake Park in November 1950 intending to develop lands they held jointly. They took equal shares of the corporation's stock, for which they paid a total of $28,000. The corporate books reflected the contributions as $9,000 paid-in capital and $19,000 paid-in surplus. The corporation immediately acquired land from its shareholders that it developed.

Transfer B occurred September 7, 1954. The shareholders transferred 100 acres to the corporation in exchange for $10,000 cash and a $40,000 demand note bearing 4% interest. Appellants contend that at the time of the transfer the corporation's net worth was $50,000 and that its "true" net worth was $78,000. Lake Park made irregular principal payments and retired the note in 1959. The corporation did not pay interest as provided in the note, making only a single $2,500 interest payment in 1956.

Sherwood. The Lake Park shareholders—Joel, Cornelia and Loretta—formed Sherwood in September 1954. Each took one-third of the new corporation's stock, for which they paid a total of $21,000. The next day they made transfer C, conveying to the corporation 48 acres in which each owned a one-third undivided interest. In exchange the corporation paid $6,000 cash and an $18,000 demand note bearing 4% interest. The corporation made irregular principal payments and a single interest payment, retiring the debt in 1960.

By the time of the second contested Sherwood transaction, Joel had died, leaving to his wife Katherine and his two children equal portions of his stock and the remaining property owned in conjunction with the other shareholders. This new lineup of shareholders made transfer D in January 1960. In exchange for 126.48 acres, the corporation issued five-year 3% notes to each shareholder totalling $189,720.02. Appellants assert that at that time the corporation had a book net worth of $62,000 and a "true" net worth of $206,000. Sherwood made irregular principal and interest payments, and a $32,000 balance remains outstanding.

Transfer E occurred in December 1964 when Sherwood's shareholders conveyed an additional 84.252 acres to the corporation. In exchange they received five-year 5% notes totalling $126,000. Appellants contend that the corporation had a $117,000 book net worth and a $240,000 "true" net worth. In September 1965 the corporation retired the notes held by Katherine and her two children. The corporation has made no payments on the notes held by Loretta and Cornelia. The corporation made an interest payment to Katherine and her children in 1965 and made annual interest payments to Loretta and Cornelia from 1967 through 1971. * * *

Additions. In June 1959 Loretta, Cornelia and Katherine formed Additions, each taking one-third of its shares and contributing a total of $36,900 paid-in capital. Katherine's two children did not participate. The shareholders and Katherine's children immediately made transfer F, conveying 268.8 acres to the corporation in exchange for five-year 3% notes totalling $368,200.[8] The corporation made no principal or interest payments until 1964. From 1964 until 1969 it made annual interest payments. It has made a single principal payment, for $5,000 in 1965.

Transaction G occurred August 2, 1961. Loretta advanced the corporation $61,250, taking in return its one-year 5% note. The corporation made its first payment on the note in 1964 and retired the note in 1965.

After conducting a topographical survey of the land it had received from its shareholders in 1959, Additions discovered that nearly three acres could not be incorporated into the planned residential subdivision because of drainage problems. The corporation abandoned its initial plan regarding this tract and did not subdivide it into lots. The corporation did not break the parcel out separately on its books but carried it in the same account that included all undeveloped land. In 1963 Georgia Power Company approached Additions and bought two acres for a substation, and the City of Albany contacted Additions and purchased the remainder of the tract for a pumping station. Georgia Power paid $7,500 for its parcel and the city $2,500. Additions claims that this land had been held for investment, making capital gains treatment appropriate.

Forest Estates. In September 1959 Loretta Haley and Marjorie Scherberger formed Forest Estates, each taking half its stock, for which they paid a total of $25,000. They immediately effected transfer H, conveying to the corporation 43.93 acres that they owned jointly in exchange for five-year 4% notes totalling $100,000. Forest Estates made no principal payments on the notes until 1971, and $70,000 remains outstanding. The corporation made small and irregular inter-

8. The notes of Cornelia, Loretta and Katherine were subordinated to the children's notes.

est payments from 1961 through 1967. Forest Estates suffered losses in 1965 and 1966 and apparently abandoned development plans.

Cairo Developers. Spencer C. Walden, Jr., George M. Kirkland, Jr., and J. Norwood Clark formed Cairo Developers in April 1961. Kirkland was Walden's partner in Walden & Kirkland. Clark was a real estate broker from Cairo, Georgia, who owned the bulk of the land that Cairo Developers was to develop. Each organizer took one-third of the corporation's stock, paying in a total of $5,100. From May 1961 through January 1964, the corporation received ostensible loans from the three shareholders, the Walden & Kirkland partnership, a corporation that Walden and Kirkland owned, and two of Walden's children. These advances together constitute transfer J. Most of these notes were due in one year; a few were payable on demand. The corporation made no payments of principal or interest until 1971.

Slappey. On July 7, 1962, Cornelia Haley Walden organized Slappey, paying $9,000 for all its issued stock. On July 9 she transferred the stock in equal segments to her three children. The next day Cornelia made transfer K, conveying 80.78 acres to the corporation in exchange for $6,366.50 cash and an eight-year 4% note for $75,000. Slappey planned to develop the land for industrial and commercial establishments. The corporation made irregular principal and interest payments, failing to pay the debt on its due date.

Transfer L occurred May 27, 1963. Each of the three shareholders advanced the corporation $5,000 in exchange for one-year 6% notes. Slappey has made no payments of principal or interest on these notes.

Overview. We may assume, as appellants contend, that in each ostensible sale of property to a corporation the price reflected the fair market value.[11] Nonetheless, the recurring pattern in regard to all the loans has been the corporations' failure to adhere to the announced repayment schedules. Although the corporations did make some principal and interest payments, in not a single case did the payments conform to the terms included in the notes. In addition, Spencer Walden's deposition testimony makes clear that the creditor-shareholders viewed their situation not at all as normal creditors would. The shareholders entered no objections to the passing of payment dates and requested payments only when the corporations had "plenty of cash." In explaining the willingness to tolerate delinquencies even when interest was not being paid, Walden candidly stated that the individuals were more concerned with their status as shareholders than in their status as creditors.

11. Debt–Equity

The tax code provides widely disparate treatment of debt and equity. In regard to a typical transfer at issue here, involving an

11. We note also that the ostensible lenders took no security interests in the transferred property or otherwise and that, with a single exception, see note 8 supra, the debts at issue were not subordinated to other corporate obligations.

individual's transfer of property to his corporation in exchange for the instrument in question, the classification as debt or equity may affect the taxation of the original transaction,[12] the resulting bases and hence the taxation of subsequent transfers,[13] and the taxation of payments the corporation makes to the shareholder with respect to the instrument.[14] In the case at bar debt classification would greatly benefit the taxpayers.

Unfortunately, the great disparity in the tax treatment of debt and equity does not derive from a clear distinction between those concepts. The problem is particularly acute in the case of close corporations, because the participants often have broad latitude to cast their contributions in whatever form they choose. Taxpayers have often sought debt's advantageous tax treatment for transactions that in substance more closely resembled the kind of arrangement Congress envisioned when it enacted the equity provisions. See Nassau Lens Co. v. Commissioner, 308 F.2d 39, 44–46 (2d Cir.1962) (Marshall, J.). Thus, the labels that parties attach to their transactions provide no guarantee of the appropriate tax treatment. See, e.g., Tyler v. Tomlinson, 414 F.2d 844, 850 (5th Cir.1969); Berkowitz v. United States, 411 F.2d 818, 820 (5th Cir.1969).

Articulating the essential difference between the two types of arrangement that Congress treated so differently is no easy task. Generally, shareholders place their money "at the risk of the business" while lenders seek a more reliable return. See Midland Distributors, Inc. v. United States, 481 F.2d 730, 733 (5th Cir.1973); Dillin v. United States, 433 F.2d 1097, 1103 (5th Cir.1970). That statement of course glosses over a good many considerations with which even the most inexperienced investor is abundantly familiar. A purchaser of General Motors stock may bear much less risk than a bona fide lender to a small corporation. See Fin Hay Realty Co. v. United States, 398 F.2d 694, 697 (3d Cir.1968).

Nevertheless, the "risk of the business" formulation has provided a shorthand description that courts have repeatedly invoked. Contribu-

12. See I.R.C. § 351. That section provides that no gain or loss is recognized when persons transfer property to their controlled corporation solely in exchange for "stock or securities." The term "stock" would include the instruments here if they were characterized as equity. The term "securities" might or might not extend to them if characterized as debt; the term encompasses some debt instruments but not others. As an alternative to its argument that the transactions here are equity, the government contends that even if characterized as debt the property transfers come within § 351 as "securities." In light of our acceptance of the government's primary argument, we need not pass on its alternative contention.

13. See, e.g., I.R.C. § 362. In the instant case the transferring shareholders' bases in their land were significantly lower than the sales prices. Thus the difference between new basis and carryover basis is important.

14. The corporation may deduct interest on indebtedness, see I.R.C. § 163, but if the transaction is characterized as equity, ostensible interest payments become nondeductible dividends. In general, the recipient is not taxable on loan principal payments but is taxable if the transaction constitutes equity; in that instance the purported principal payments come in for dividend treatment. See I.R.C. § 316.

tors of capital undertake the risk because of the potential return, in the form of profits and enhanced value, on their underlying investment. Lenders, on the other hand, undertake a degree of risk because of the expectancy of timely repayment with interest. Because a lender unrelated to the corporation stands to earn only a fixed amount of interest, he usually is unwilling to bear a substantial risk of corporate failure or to commit his funds for a prolonged period. A person ordinarily would not advance funds likely to be repaid only if the venture is successful without demanding the potential enhanced return associated with an equity investment. See Curry v. United States, 396 F.2d 630, 634 (5th Cir.), cert. denied, 393 U.S. 967, 89 S.Ct. 401, 21 L.Ed.2d 375 (1968); DuGro Frozen Foods, Inc. v. United States, 481 F.2d 1271, 1272 (5th Cir. 1973).

These considerations provide only imperfect guidance when the issue relates to a shareholder's purported loan to his own corporation, the usual situation encountered in debt-equity cases. It is well established that shareholders may loan money to their corporations and achieve corresponding tax treatment. See United States v. Snyder Bros. Co., 367 F.2d 980, 983 (5th Cir.1966), cert. denied, 386 U.S. 956, 87 S.Ct. 1021, 18 L.Ed.2d 104 (1967); Rowan v. United States, 219 F.2d 51 (5th Cir.1955). When making such loans they could hardly be expected to ignore their shareholder status; their motivations will not match those of potential lenders who have no underlying equity interest. The "risk of the business" standard, though, continues to provide a backdrop for our analysis. While we should not expect a creditor-shareholder to evidence motivations and behavior conforming perfectly to those of a mere creditor, neither should we abandon the effort to determine whether the challenged transaction is in substance a contribution to capital masquerading as debt.[15]

Rather than attempt to measure concrete cases against an abstract formulation of the overriding test, we have identified numerous observable criteria that help place a given transaction on one side of the line or the other. We have always recognized, however, that the various factors are not equally significant. "The object of the inquiry is not to count factors, but to evaluate them." Tyler v. Tomlinson, 414 F.2d 844, 848 (5th Cir.1969). Each case turns on its own facts; differing circumstances may bring different factors to the fore. See In re Indian Lake Estates, Inc., 448 F.2d 574, 579 (5th Cir.1971); Tomlinson v. The 1661 Corp., 377 F.2d 291, 295 (5th Cir.1967).

With that preliminary caveat, we note the factors that prior cases have identified:

15. In emphasizing the usefulness of comparing the challenged transaction to the type arrangement that a disinterested lender would have entered, the Third Circuit has noted that disregarding the shareholder-lender's personal interest in his own corporation is fairer than presumptively construing all such transactions adversely to the shareholder. See Fin Hay Realty Co. v. United States, 398 F.2d 694, 697 (3d Cir.1968).

(1) the names given to the certificates evidencing the indebtedness;

(2) the presence or absence of a fixed maturity date;

(3) the source of payments;

(4) the right to enforce payment of principal and interest;

(5) participation in management flowing as a result;

(6) the status of the contribution in relation to regular corporate creditors;

(7) the intent of the parties;

(8) "thin" or adequate capitalization;

(9) identity of interest between creditor and stockholder;

(10) source of interest payments;

(11) the ability of the corporation to obtain loans from outside lending institutions;

(12) the extent to which the advance was used to acquire capital assets; and

(13) the failure of the debtor to repay on the due date or to seek a postponement.

Estate of Mixon v. United States, 464 F.2d 394, 402 (5th Cir.1972).[16] As indicated above, these factors are but tools for discerning whether a transaction more closely resembles the type arrangement for which Congress provided debt or equity treatment.[17]

In the case at bar the most telling of the *Mixon* factors is the corporate debtors' consistent failure to repay the debts on the due dates or to seek postponements. More generally, that failure and the corresponding absence of timely interest payments combine with Walden's testimony regarding the parties' view of their relationship to make clear that these transactions were in substance not at all the type arrangements for which debt treatment is appropriate.

The individuals' failure to insist upon timely repayment or satisfactory renegotiation indicates that the compensation they sought went beyond the announced interest rate, for an investor would not ordinarily undertake such a risk for so limited a return. See Tyler v. Tomlinson, 414 F.2d 814, 850 (5th Cir.1969). The failure to insist that the corporations pay the interest that the agreements provided underscores the inference; "a true lender is concerned with interest." Curry v. United States, 396 F.2d 630, 634 (5th Cir.), cert. denied, 393 U.S. 967, 89 S.Ct. 401, 21 L.Ed.2d 375 (1968). See also National Carbide Corp. v.

16. The list is not exhaustive; our cases undoubtedly mention considerations that have yet to take a number. Congress has recently authorized the Secretary to promulgate regulations setting forth appropriate factors. See I.R.C. § 385. For the time being, however, we must rely on our own pronouncements.

17. The issue is primarily one of law. We must uphold the district court's findings of basic facts unless clearly erroneous, but the ultimate characterization of the transactions as debt or equity receives no such protection. See Estate of Mixon v. United States, 464 F.2d 394, 402–03 (5th Cir.1972).

Commissioner, 336 U.S. 422, 435 n. 16, 69 S.Ct. 726, 93 L.Ed. 779 (1949). When a corporate contributor seeks no interest, it becomes abundantly clear that the compensation he seeks is that of an equity interest: a share of the profits or an increase in the value of his shareholdings. See Estate of Mixon v. United States, 464 F.2d 394, 409 (5th Cir.1972).

Walden's testimony confirms these conclusions. He acknowledged that the individuals sought payments of principal or interest only when the corporations had "plenty of cash" and that the investors did so because they were more concerned with their status as shareholders than as creditors. That statement of how the individuals viewed their situation corresponds almost perfectly to the classic equity situation. A corporation normally declares dividends only when it has "plenty of cash." Shareholders ordinarily acquiesce in such dividend policies because their primary concern is the health and long-term success of the enterprise. Walden's statement indicates that the individuals here possessed precisely those motivations and that they believed it appropriate for the corporations to decide when to make payments on the same basis that corporations customarily make dividend decisions. See Berkowitz v. United States, 411 F.2d 818, 821 (5th Cir.1969). The taxpayers' pattern of conduct belies any intention to structure their affairs as parties to a debt transaction ordinarily would. In the circumstances here, these factors indicate that all the transactions should be characterized for tax purposes as equity arrangements.

In reaching this conclusion we have not ignored the other factors our cases have identified. Appellants place particular reliance on the intent of the parties. Here, appellants contend, the form in which the parties cast the transactions conclusively demonstrates their intent to create a debt relationship. In relying so heavily on this factor, however, appellants misconceive its import. The question is not whether the parties intended to call their transaction "debt" and thus to achieve advantageous tax treatment; that a person wants to pay less tax rather than more provides little basis for discerning how much tax Congress decided he should pay. Instead, the relevant inquiry is the actual manner, not the form, in which the parties intended to structure their relationship. If the intended structuring accords with the type arrangement that qualifies for taxation as debt, that intent supports a finding of debt. Here, however, the parties intended to structure their relationship in a manner placing funds at the prolonged risk of the businesses; they intended decisions whether to make payments on the advances to be based on the criteria usually associated with dividend decisions. To the extent that intent is relevant, it favors equity classification.[18]

18. Walden testified that the corporations intended to repay the indebtedness. Even accepting that testimony as true, the parties' conduct makes clear that they intended to repay only after a prolonged period, at which time repayment would be likely only if the enterprises have proved successful. Thus they intended to repay in the same sense that corporations might intend their dividends eventually to total up to the original price of the stock. Walden's testimony in this regard provides only the barest support for debt classification.

Another *Mixon* factor to which appellants look for support is the extent to which the advance was used to acquire capital assets. They argue that here the corporations used none of the advances for that purpose. Instead, appellants note, the corporations used the contributions primarily for land, which constitutes the inventory of these real estate development firms. Whatever force this factor might have in other settings, appellants here can garner little support from it. Most of these advances, while perhaps not used for capital assets, nonetheless served "to finance initial operations." Plantation Patterns, Inc. v. Commissioner, 462 F.2d 712, 722 (5th Cir.1972). See Aqualane Shores, Inc. v. Commissioner, 269 F.2d 116 (5th Cir.1959) (shareholder's credit "sale" of land to real estate development corporation held to constitute equity contribution). Providing the bulk of the necessary first assets without which a corporation could not begin functioning is as traditional a usage of capital contributions as is purchasing "capital assets."

Another factor from *Mixon* that sometimes proves most instructive is the identity of interest between creditor and stockholder. Courts and commentators have often discussed this criterion under the rubric "proportionality." When each shareholder owns the same proportion of the company's stock as he does of the ostensible shareholder debt, the parties' framing of the transaction contributes little to the analysis. See Fin Hay Realty Co. v. United States, 398 F.2d 694 (3d Cir.1968). In that situation the owners' decision regarding how much of their contribution to cast as equity and how much as debt does not affect the distribution of control over the company. Non-tax considerations may play little role in the choice, and reviewing courts accordingly must scrutinize carefully the resulting transaction. When, on the other hand, an individual holds different percentages of the corporation's stock and shareholder debt, the casting of debt in that form ordinarily will affect substantial non-tax interests. There is thus reason to believe that the parties' debt characterization has substance as well as form.[19]

Appellants argue in the case at bar that many of the challenged transfers exhibited imperfect proportionality and that some displayed none at all.[20] While that argument would carry weight in the usual

19. Even when a corporation incurs bona fide debt, of course, the opportunity to advance the funds and earn the corresponding return provides both tax and other advantages to the shareholder. Individual shareholders may therefore insist upon receiving their share of such advantages. Thus "proportionality" justifies courts in applying careful examination of the transactions but is not necessarily inconsistent with a finding of bona fide debt.

20. Transfers B, C, H and L exhibited perfect proportionality; each shareholder took the same percentage of shareholder debt as he or she held of the corporation's stock. Transfers D and E originally showed complete proportionality but became somewhat disproportional when the corporations made principal payments in different amounts to the different shareholders. Transfer F was not completely proportional; Katherine's children made loans but held no shares. Treating Katherine and her children as a unit, however, transfer F exhibited perfect proportionality. Similarly, transfer K evidenced no proportionality but was totally proportional treating Cornelia and her children as a unit. Transfer J was only roughly proportional. While different shareholders (or their businesses) made advances at different times, each of the three equal share-

case, it has little force here. The disproportional holdings all occurred among close relatives. Although we do not treat the various shareholding members of the J.T. Haley family as an indivisible unit, neither do we treat them as unrelated individuals. For all that appears in this record, relations among the various family members were completely harmonious. Because shareholding family members were thus less likely to attribute major significance to departures from strict equality in their positions, the instances of disproportionate debt and equity holdings provide a much weaker inference than they ordinarily would that the ostensible debt was in fact what it purported to be.[21]

Finally, appellants strenuously urge that the level of the corporations' capitalization does not undermine their position. We have not, however, based our decision on the inadequacy of the corporate capitalization. While some of the purported loans were made to corporations with woefully inadequate capital, others were not. In some cases, as the taxpayers note, capitalization was adequate.[22] These facts strengthen our conclusion as to some transactions, weaken it for others. They do not, however, suffice to change the conclusion we have derived from the parties' pattern of conduct and from Walden's testimony.[23]

holders put up roughly one-third of the funds when considered in conjunction with their other loans to the corporation. Transfer G was not proportional; a one-third shareholder made the entire advance. Transfer A was completely disproportional; Spencer made the loan but held no stock.

21. In Estate of Mixon v. United States, 464 F.2d 394 (5th Cir.1972), we examined proportionality by looking to the family attribution provisions of I.R.C. § 318. See 464 F.2d at 398 n. 3, 409. Even using those provisions to increase the individual's shareholdings, he held only 15.3% of the corporation's stock while making 80% of the challenged advance. Thus taking the view of attribution most favorable to the government in that case, the low proportionality favored the taxpayer.

In the case at bar, unlike in *Mixon,* the approach taken to attribution affects the direction in which the proportionality factor cuts. We think the proper approach is the practical one outlined in the text. Rather than rigidly apply the § 318 attribution rules—an approach that *Mixon* does not require and that would contravene the limitation of that section to "those provisions * * * to which [it is] expressly made applicable," I.R.C. § 318(a)—we treat the familial relationships as factors affecting the impact to be accorded the results of the proportionality inquiry. We of course accord careful scrutiny to intra-family transactions. See Dillin v. United States, 433 F.2d 1097, 1103 (5th Cir.1970).

22. Taxpayers urge that these businesses involved little risk and therefore needed little capital. The apparent failure of Forest Estates, however, belies their assertion. The ventures incurred development expenses running into six figures and required as much as two or three years to begin receiving any revenues by selling lots. These considerations demonstrate the inadequacy of, for example, the initial capitalizations of $5,100 for Cairo Developers, $9,000 for Slappey, and $21,000 for Sherwood. Thus the capitalization factor favors the government with respect to transfers made to those corporations upon their formation.

In regard to transfers made at later times, however, we agree with appellants that net worth, not initial capitalization, provides the relevant data. See Tomlinson v. The 1661 Corp., 377 F.2d 291, 299 n. 18 (5th Cir.1967). At the time of transfer E. Sherwood's net worth was $117,000. That figure would become much greater if we were to take into account the appreciated value of Sherwood's real estate holdings or if we added the amounts of the earlier purported debts (originating from transfers C and D) that we reclassify as equity. We need not decide the propriety of these steps, for we agree with appellants that in any event Sherwood's capitalization at the time of transfer E was adequate.

23. The *Mixon* factors not discussed in text carry little weight in this case. The source of principal and interest payments

Because the parties to the transactions in question intended to conduct and did conduct their affairs in a manner that the tax code labels equity rather than debt, taxation of the transactions as equity is appropriate. Contrary to appellants' assertions, in reaching that result we do not disapprove their decisions concerning how to organize the corporations, and we do not substitute our business judgment for theirs. We merely announce the tax consequences that attach to their decisions. While appellants are correct that they were free to decide without our supervision how much of the corporate financing to derive from loans and how much from capital contributions, they were not free to decide for themselves what tax consequences would attach to their conduct. * * *

CONCLUSION

The district court properly characterized the eleven purported corporate debts as contributions to capital. * * * The district court's decision is Affirmed.

ILLUSTRATIVE MATERIAL

A. HISTORICAL BACKGROUND

The earlier cases involving debt-stock classification concerned "hybrid securities" having some of the formal characteristics of debt and some of the formal characteristics of stock. The Supreme Court considered the status of "income debenture bonds" in John Kelley Co. v. Commissioner, 326 U.S. 521 (1946). In *Kelley* the obligations in question involved the following features: 8 percent interest, which was non-cumulative and was to be paid if earnings were sufficient; 20 years maturity; subordination to all creditors, but priorities over stockholders; and no right to participate in management. The Supreme Court upheld a Tax Court finding that the hybrid securities constituted debt. The Court emphasized to some extent the fact that a substantial amount of capital had been invested in the stock of the corporation so that the corporation was not "thinly capitalized": "As material amounts were invested in stock, we need not consider the effects of extreme situations such as normal stock investment and obviously excessive debt structure." (326 U.S. at 526). This observation led the lower courts to consider debt-equity ratios as the determinative factor in the debt-equity characterization question. Subsequently the courts ceased relying on the debt-equity ratio as the exclusive test for determining whether an obligation

and the questionable availability of similar loans from outside lenders provide slight support to the government. That most of the obligations possessed fixed maturity dates would favor appellants had they not consistently ignored those dates. Similarly, the individuals' legal right to enforce payment does not aid appellants in light of the apparent understanding, as manifested in observable behavior, that they would not enforce those rights. The lenders already controlled corporate management; that they derived no more control as a result of the ostensible loans does not cut against the equity classification. See Dillin v. United States, 433 F.2d 1097, 1101 (5th Cir.1970). Finally, that appellants did not subordinate their loans to other corporate obligations, see note 11 supra, provides slight support for appellants but does not undermine the conclusion we have drawn from the more significant indicia discussed in text.

constituted debt or equity and began to apply the multi-factor approach used in the principal case.

Gilbert v. Commissioner, 248 F.2d 399 (2d Cir.1957), was the first case to approach the problem using a multi-factor approach. The court in *Gilbert* identified debt as an unqualified obligation to pay a sum certain at a reasonably close fixed maturity date along with a fixed percentage in interest payable regardless of the debtor's income or lack thereof. (402.) The courts, following the *Gilbert* analysis, began to search for factors which would help to distinguish the unqualified obligation to repay from an equity investment. As a result, formidable lists of factors began to be developed against which obligations could be measured to determine if they more resembled debt or equity. At one point, this "factor check-off list" approach threatened to become as mechanical as the earlier obsession with debt-equity ratios. However, it is now settled that the trier of fact must weigh the various factors in the light of the entire evidence presented and not give undue weight to any one factor. The courts' refusal to sanction a relatively mechanical test such as the debt-equity ratio, however, has resulted in a great deal of uncertainty for tax advisors and the government, with the inevitable consequence that a substantial amount of litigation has been generated in the debt-equity area.

B. SOME ILLUSTRATIVE CASES

In analyzing debt-equity cases under the factors listed in *Slappey Drive Industrial Park,* it is tempting simply to categorize the cases which involve a given factor showing, for example, that in some cases the factor of subordination of shareholder loans resulted in a finding of equity, but in other cases it did not prevent a finding of debt. The temptation to create such legal shopping lists must be resisted. It is the factors *in relationship* which appear to determine the results in debt-equity cases, even in those cases where the court may emphasize particular factors. For instance, where a court considers subordination significant, it is generally subordination in relation to the absence of other factors that would demonstrate debt which is determinative, not subordination as such. It is important to recognize that each of the factors considered by the courts contributes in varying degree to the resolution of the classification issue. For example, in Fin Hay Realty Co. v. United States, 398 F.2d 694 (3d Cir.1968), the court listed sixteen factors to be considered in distinguishing debt from equity, but described the factors as "only aids in answering the ultimate question whether the investment, analyzed in terms of its economic reality, constitutes risk capital entirely subject to the fortunes of the corporate venture or represents a strict debtor-creditor relationship. Since there is often an element of risk in a loan, just as there is an element of risk in an equity investment, the conflicting elements do not end at a clear line in all cases. . . ."

In Lane v. United States, 742 F.2d 1311 (11th Cir.1984), the court stated: "In order for an advance of funds to be considered a debt rather than equity, the courts have stressed that a reasonable expectation of repayment must exist which does not depend solely on the success of the borrower's business." The taxpayer advanced funds to three failing corporations for demand notes, many of which contained no provision for the payment of interest. The taxpayer testified in the trial court that he expected repayment when the corporations were in a position to retransfer the funds without damage to their ongoing businesses. The court concluded from the taxpayer's testimony that repayment was dependent upon the success of the business. As a consequence the advances constituted equity rather than debt.

See also Berkowitz v. United States, 411 F.2d 818 (5th Cir.1969) (debt-equity ratio of 21:1, when ignoring loans from third parties; the due dates for interest payments on the notes were disregarded and there was no repayment of principal; the interest rate was "declared" at the end of each year like dividends; debt was held proportionate to shareholdings; there was no likelihood of repayment in the foreseeable future and then only from income of the property acquired through the use of debt).

In Tomlinson v. 1661 Corp., 377 F.2d 291 (5th Cir.1967), the court held that the shareholder advances constituted debt. The shareholders advanced funds to their corporation on a pro-rata basis, with a resulting debt-equity ratio of approximately 4:1. The evidence indicated that the corporation could have borrowed from outside sources but would have had to have paid a higher rate of interest to do so. The shareholder notes were subordinated only to secured mortgage debt. The interest was accrued but unpaid; however, interest was cumulative and all interest had to be paid before dividends could be paid. The proportionality of debt and equity was not conclusive because the debt was freely transferable whereas the stock was not because of shareholder agreements, and thus the proportionality could be destroyed at any time. The notes were not subordinated to general creditors. Even including third party mortgage debt, the debt-equity ratio was only 14.6:1. The court declined to speculate on the business reasons for the nonpayment of interest.

See also Hardman v. United States, 827 F.2d 1409 (9th Cir.1987) (shareholder "sold" property to a controlled corporation in exchange for an assumption of liabilities plus a note for one-third of the corporate profits on its disposition of the property; distribution of sales proceeds to the shareholder were treated as repayment of the note resulting in long-term capital gain attributable to the shareholder's sale of the property to the corporation; payment of the note was not dependent on the fortunes of the business nor lacking a fixed maturity date because repayment was tied to "a fairly certain event—sale of the property").

For a case in which the positions of the Commissioner and taxpayer were reversed, see Segel v. Commissioner, 89 T.C. 816 (1987), in which the Commissioner asserted that advances to a Subchapter S corporation were loans so that repayment could not be treated as tax-free distributions to S corporation shareholders under the predecessor to section 1368. The court rejected the Commissioner's argument based primarily on the analysis adopted by the Third Circuit in *Fin Hay Realty Co.*, supra, page 398, that an outside lender would not have advanced funds to the corporation on the same terms.

The Internal Revenue Service will not "ordinarily" rule on whether advances to a corporation constitute debt or equity. Rev.Proc. 89–3, 1989–1, Cum.Bull. 761.

C. ANALYSIS OF PARTICULAR FACTORS

1. *Proportion of Debt to Stockholdings*

When debt and equity obligations are held in the same proportion individual stockholders are, apart from tax considerations indifferent with respect to whether distributions from the corporation are made in the form of interest or dividends. In the event of cash flow problems which make the payment of the fixed obligations of debt instruments difficult for the corporation, controlling stockholders who hold debt obligations in the same proportion as equity may forego repayment rather than threaten the continued value of their equity investment. In all cases, therefore, it can be said that payment of proportionately held debt is subject to the fortunes of the business. But the pro rata holding of debt and equity is not an absolute barrier to recognition of debt status, even when a sole stockholder is present. Whether proportionately held debt obligations will be paid in a timely fashion depends on other factors such as the existence of adequate equity capital to insure debt repayment or an income stream sufficient to meet payments of interest and principal. Compare Wilshire & Western Sandwiches, Inc. v. Commissioner, 175 F.2d 718 (9th Cir.1949), with Reed v. Commissioner, 242 F.2d 334 (2d Cir.1957). In some cases, the absence of proportional holdings of stock and debt has been considered as a factor favoring debt status. Adelson v. United States, 737 F.2d 1569 (Fed.Cir.1984) (taxpayer advances to clients in which the taxpayer held only a minor equity interest treated as debt; taxpayer was dealing with client companies as an outsider whose dominant motive was not to further an equity interest in the companies).

2. *Thin Capitalization*

A high proportion of debt relative to shareholder equity is an indication that the corporation lacks reserves to pay interest and principal on debt when corporate income is insufficient to meet current payments. In such a case, the debt holders' potential recovery is subject to entrepreneurial risk as repayment is dependent on the success of the venture. Thus a high ratio of debt to equity is a factor favoring equity classification.

While generally the decisions mention the debt-equity ratio, they offer little discussion of the rules governing its determination. Note that in *Slappey Drive Industrial Park,* supra, the court looked at the relation of the debt both to the book value of the corporation's assets and to their actual fair market value. In Bauer v. Commissioner, 748 F.2d 1365 (9th Cir.1984), the court held that the debt to equity ratio compares total liabilities to the stockholders' equity which includes both initial paid-in capital plus accumulated earnings. The court reversed the Tax Court's holding that shareholder loans were contributions to capital. The Tax Court had based its holding, in part, on a stipulation by the parties that the corporate debt/equity ratio was 92 to 1, the ratio of liabilities to the shareholders' initial capital contributions. Comparing liabilities with total shareholder equity, determined by including both paid in capital and accumulated earnings, produced debt to equity ratios ranging from 2 to 1 to 8 to 1. See also Liflans Corp. v. United States, 390 F.2d 965 (Ct.Cl.1968), and Allen H. Dahme Associates, Inc. v. United States, 436 F.2d 486 (Ct.Cl.1971).

As respects debt, the courts may consider all of the outstanding indebtedness of the corporation even though it is typically shareholder debt which is being tested for equity equivalence. Thus an outstanding bank loan can have an influence on the "thinness" of the corporation's capital structure. See, e.g., Berkowitz v. United States, 411 F.2d 818 (5th Cir.1969).

A high ratio of debt to equity is not automatically fatal to debt status. In Bradshaw v. United States, 683 F.2d 365 (Ct.Cl.1982), notwithstanding a very high ratio of debt to equity (the corporation's capital consisted of an automobile valued at $4,500), the court classified as debt five notes, each in the face amount of $50,000, given to a sole shareholder of the debtor corporation in exchange for real property transferred to the corporation by the shareholder. The court emphasized the fact that the corporation's cash flow was sufficient to meet its obligations under the notes to pay interest and principal on fixed dates and that the corporation paid principal and interest on the notes when due.

3. *Subordination to Other Creditors*

In P.M. Finance Corp. v. Commissioner, 302 F.2d 786 (3d Cir.1962), the court held that shareholder "loans" were equity by placing heavy reliance on the fact that the loans were subordinated to all "present and future bank loans." Complete subordination, the court noted, "tends to wipe out a most significant characteristic of the creditor-debtor relationship, the right to share with general creditors in the assets in the event of dissolution or liquidation, * * * but it also destroys another basic attribute of creditor status: i.e., the power to demand payment at a fixed maturity date." (790) See also, Jones v. United States, 659 F.2d 618 (5th Cir.1981) (debt status upheld despite state regulations requiring subordination to insurance corporation's policy holders); Federal Express Corp. v. United States, 645 F.Supp. 1281 (W.D. Tenn.1986) (debt status sustained for obligations subordinate only to senior debt; the challenged obligations were negotiated at arm's length by sophisticated institutional investors and were on a parity with trade debt).

4. *Intent, Business Purpose and Tax Avoidance*

Although courts frequently list the taxpayer's "intent" as a factor in determining whether an obligation constitutes debt or equity, most of the courts in the cases discussed above recognize that "intent" is simply a way of stating the conclusion, and examine more objective factors to determine the debt-equity status of the particular obligation. In general, earlier cases in which taxpayer "intent" or "business purpose" appeared to take on an independent status have not been followed. See, e.g., Gooding Amusement Co. v. Commissioner, 236 F.2d 159 (6th Cir.1956); Tomlinson v. 1661 Corp., 377 F.2d 291 (5th Cir.1967). In Estate of Mixon v. United States, 464 F.2d 394 (5th Cir.1972), however, the court sustained the taxpayer's treatment of an interest-free shareholder advance to a bank, as required by bank examiners, as debt under a 13 factor analysis; the court indicated that where the objective signs point in all directions, the trial court was correct in looking to the subjective intent of the parties to decide which direction to follow. (407)

5. *Absence of New Investment*

Where the corporation has been in existence for some time, and then issues a dividend in the form of a debt obligation, or, by recapitalization, issues a debt obligation in exchange for previously outstanding stock, the Commissioner has attempted to treat the new obligation as stock on the ground that there is no new investment to permit the obligation to be considered as debt. Compare Sayles Finishing Plants, Inc. v. United States, 399 F.2d 214 (Ct.Cl.1968) (notes issued for stock in a reorganization held to constitute equity since no new funds were added to the corporation by issuing the debt and the only benefit to the business was the obtaining of the interest deduction); Monon Railroad v. Commissioner, 55 T.C. 345 (1970) (debentures issued to acquire outstanding shares of stock held to be valid debt; it was not necessary that new funds be received by the corporation in exchange for the debt where other factors pointed to debt classification). Debt incurred by a corporation to purchase its own stock in a leveraged buy-out may be suspect under this factor. The issuing corporation may not be able to satisfy debt obligations except through sale of assets. See Bittker & Eustice, Federal Income Taxation of Corporations and Shareholders, 4–25 (5th Ed.1987).

D. STANDARD OF REVIEW

Since debt-equity cases turn on factual issues, the Courts of Appeal generally treat the trial court's conclusion as a finding of fact which can be set aside only if it is clearly erroneous. Fed.R.Civ.P. 52(a); Commissioner v. Duberstein, 363 U.S. 278 (1960). See, for example, Charter Wire, Inc. v. United States, 309 F.2d 878 (7th Cir.1962); Ragland Investment Co. v. Commissioner, 435 F.2d 118 (6th Cir.1970); Adelson v. United States, 737 F.2d 1569 (Fed.Cir.1984); Roth Steel Tube Co. v. Commissioner, 800 F.2d 625 (6th Cir.1986); Hardman v. U.S. 827 F.2d 1409 (9th Cir.1987).

In the Fifth and Eleventh Circuits, however, the ultimate inference from the facts as to whether an obligation constitutes debt or equity is a matter of law, not of fact. In Texas Farm Bureau v. United States, 725 F.2d 307 (5th Cir.1984), rehearing denied, 732 F.2d 437 (1984), the Fifth Circuit reversed a jury verdict finding that advances from one nonprofit corporation to a related nonprofit corporation constituted debt, holding that questions of fact arise only when an analysis of the objective criteria fails to resolve the issue and the courts must look to the parties' subjective intent. See also Slappey Drive Industrial Park, footnote 17, supra, page 393; Alterman Foods, Inc. v. United States, 505 F.2d 873 (5th Cir.1974); Lane v. United States, 742 F.2d 1311 (11th Cir.1984). In the Eighth Circuit, the issue is considered to be one of mixed law and fact. J.S. Biritz Construction Co. v. Commissioner, 387 F.2d 451 (8th Cir.1967).

E. SHAREHOLDER–GUARANTEED LOANS AND OTHER LOANS BY NONSHAREHOLDERS

Suppose that instead of borrowing from a shareholder, the corporation borrows from a commercial lending institution, which agrees to make the loan only upon the condition that the shareholder personally guarantees the corporate obligation. Does such an arrangement escape the debt-equity imbroglio? In Murphy Logging Co. v. United States, 378 F.2d 222 (9th Cir. 1967), two partners formed a corporation which purchased logging equipment from the partnership. The corporation borrowed money from a bank to make the acquisition and the shareholders guaranteed the bank note. The Commissioner treated the transaction as if the bank loan had gone directly from the bank to the shareholders, who had then made a contribution to the capital of the corporation in a section 351 transaction. Payments by the corporation on the bank loan were thus treated as constructive dividends to the shareholders (who presumably would also be treated as having made the bank payments, with corresponding interest deductions to the shareholders individually). The District Court upheld the Commissioner, 239 F.Supp. 794 (D.Or.1965). The Court of Appeals, however, reversed and held that the debt ran from the bank to the corporation and allowed the corporate interest deduction. Although the shareholders had placed only $1500 in the corporation and had sold the equipment to the corporation for $238,150, the court included the integrity and reputation of the shareholders as intangible assets to be considered in valuing the equity capital of the corporation. With this factor added, the court concluded that there was no thin capitalization. In addition, the transaction by which the corporation acquired the logging equipment was treated as a sale rather than a section 351 transaction, which permitted the corporation to use a cost basis for the equipment. See also Smyers v. Commissioner, 57 T.C. 189 (1971) (in the absence of thin capitalization, the shareholder guarantee did not convert a loan to equity even though it was "reasonable to assume that these unsecured loans would not have been made without petitioners' guarantee").

In Plantation Patterns, Inc. v. Commissioner, 462 F.2d 712 (5th Cir. 1972), the wife of one Jemison owned all the shares of stock of the taxpayer corporation, which had been capitalized at $5,000. The company was completely run by her husband. The taxpayer acquired the business of another corporation and issued notes to the shareholders of the acquired corporation in a transaction that called for a purchase price of almost $650,000 in excess of the book net worth of the acquired corporation. All but $100,000 of the notes were subordinated to the corporate debt of the taxpayer, but the notes were personally guaranteed by Jemison. The debt-equity ratio of the taxpayer corporation was 100.5:1. The court held that the notes were in fact those of the guarantor (Jemison) which he contributed as capital to the corporation; therefore, the interest deduction was disallowed to the taxpayer corporation. The wife-shareholder, correspondingly, received dividends on the note payments. The court based its decision on the facts that the notes were used to purchase capital assets of the taxpayer corporation; the guarantee by Jemison was essential to the transaction; subordination was present; the complete identity of interest between the shareholder and the guarantor, Jemison being regarded as the "constructive owner" of his wife's shares; and no value was given to the intangible financial skills of Jemison in determining the debt-equity ratio. On the last point the court stated: "[W]e conclude that intangible assets such as those claimed for Mr. Jemison have no place in assessing debt-equity ratio unless it can be shown by convincing evidence that the intangible asset has a direct and primary relationship to the well-being of the corporation. Additionally, it is clear to us that the assets sought to be valued must be something more than management skills and normal business contacts. These are expected of management in the direction of any corporation." (723)

On the other hand, the existence of a shareholder guarantee presumably would not be fatal to a bank loan if it could be established that the bank probably would have made the loan in any event and the guarantee was only additional security for the bank or part of the bank's general policy of requiring shareholder guarantees on loans to closely held corporations.

F. PARENT–SUBSIDIARY LOANS

Transactions between parent and subsidiary corporations also give rise to debt-equity problems. In Jack Daniel Distillery v. United States, 379 F.2d 569 (Ct.Cl.1967), the taxpayer, a subsidiary, issued its $3.5 million note to its parent corporation. The parent corporation contributed another $2 million in cash to the capital of the subsidiary. The court held that the subsidiary's note was a valid debt obligation because it was an unconditional obligation to pay regardless of earnings; interest was accrued for both book and tax purposes; the note was subordinated only to specific debts and not to creditors generally; the subsidiary had the ability to, and did in fact, borrow from unrelated banks (the parent having borrowed the $3.5 million contributed to the subsidiary with knowledge on the part of the lenders that the funds were going to be utilized by the subsidiary); further advances to the subsidiary were not necessary and the loan was repaid in full; despite the fact that the note was unsecured, there was a reasonable expectation that the amounts would be repaid; and substantial equity contributions had been made by the parent.

But in National Farmers Union Service Corp. v. United States, 400 F.2d 483 (10th Cir.1968), a parent's advance to a subsidiary was treated as an equity contribution where there was no acceleration clause, the note was unsecured, the funds were used to supply capital, some notes were cancelled prior to maturity, the likelihood of repayment was remote, no sinking fund had been established, and a third party would not have made the loan. Although the parent had borrowed the money which was transferred to the subsidiary, the lenders did not know that the funds were going to be placed in the subsidiary, thus distinguishing the case from *Jack Daniel,* supra. On similar grounds, the court in Roth Steel Tube Co. v. Commissioner, 800 F.2d 625 (6th Cir.1986), upheld the Tax Court's ruling that advances to a 62 percent subsidiary, acquired by the taxpayer following a bankruptcy reorganization, were contributions to capital. The appellate court stated that neither the fact that 38 percent of the subsidiary's stock was owned by shareholders who did not make proportionate advances, nor the fact that the advances were used for operating funds, was sufficient justification for rejecting the Tax Court's determination that the advances were equity.

Related problems arise with respect to advances between brother-sister corporations. In Stinnett's Pontiac Service, Inc. v. Commissioner, 730 F.2d 634 (11th Cir.1984), the court denied the taxpayer corporation's bad debt deduction for advances to another corporation owned in part by the taxpayer's 74 percent shareholder. The purported loans lacked a fixed maturity date, no interest payments were made, there was no written evidence of indebtedness for a majority of the loans, repayment was subordinate to other creditors, and the borrower was thinly capitalized. The court held that the advances represented a contribution to capital. The court also held that the advances were taxable dividends to the taxpayer's major shareholder because the shareholder benefited from the advances in the form of an economic improvement in the shareholder's equity interest in the borrower. The court reached the opposite conclusion on similar facts in Mills v. Internal Revenue Service, 840 F.2d 229 (4th Cir.1988). The court was impressed with the group's regular history of repaying intercorporate advances and the testimony of the controlling shareholders that the advances were intended as loans.

G. TRANSMUTATION OF DEBT TO EQUITY

Even if an obligation represents a valid debt obligation at the time of its issue, its character can change to equity as the result of the passage of time or a change in circumstances. For example, in Cuyuna Realty Co. v. United States, 382 F.2d 298 (Ct.Cl.1967), the taxpayer corporation between 1912 and 1914 incurred debt to its parent corporation of over $1.4 million. Interest was accrued but never paid. In 1956 the parent forgave the unpaid accrued interest and principal because the taxpayer had been insolvent since its organization and future repayment was impossible. The Commissioner disallowed the interest deduction to the taxpayer for the years beginning in 1952. The court upheld the Commissioner, concluding that, while the notes were intended to create a valid debt in the 1912–1914 period, they had changed their character to equity. No debtor-creditor relation existed long before 1956 since there was no maturity date, there was thin capitalization, no attempts were made to enforce the creditor's rights, and no outside lender would have made the loans: "A rule that the original intention of the parties should control the character of an instrument for all time would be completely inconsistent with the purpose of the statute. Interest, like an ordinary business expense, is allowed as a deduction from income because it is a cost of producing income. It ceases to be a real cost, if with the passage of time it becomes apparent that the parties had no intention of continuing the debtor-creditor relationship." (301)

In Edwards v. Commissioner, 415 F.2d 578 (10th Cir.1969), the taxpayer acquired a corporation for $75,000, with $5,000 of the purchase price being allocated to acquisition of the stock of the acquired corporation and $70,000 to the acquisition of the corporation's notes in the face amount of $241,904 that had been issued by the acquired corporation to its previous sole shareholder. The acquired corporation proved successful and the notes were repaid out of earnings. The taxpayer treated the amounts received as long-term capital gains under the predecessor to section 1271(a). The Commissioner asserted that the payments constituted dividends. The Commissioner did not contest that the notes were originally valid corporate debt, but argued that they changed to equity in the hands of the taxpayer. The court held that the notes represented debt in the hands of the taxpayer and that the predecessor to section 1271(a) applied. The court found that there was no sham, no thin capitalization, and the purchase by the taxpayer did not convert the notes to equity.

Similarly, in Imperial Car Distributors, Inc. v. Commissioner, 427 F.2d 1334 (3d Cir.1970), four investors acquired the stock of the taxpayer corporation from the former owner and also notes of the corporation previously issued to him. New notes were then issued by the corporation pro rata to the investors to replace the former notes. Payments to retire the notes were treated as capital gains by the investors under the predecessor to section 1271(a) and the taxpayer corporation deducted the interest on the notes. The Commissioner conceded that the original notes were valid debt, but urged that the notes became part of the capital of the taxpayer upon their transfer to the investors. The court held that the notes constituted valid debt obligations, reversing a Tax Court determination to the contrary, concluding that where a debt was valid when originally issued, the later transfer did not change its character to equity. See also Jennings v. United States, 272 F.2d 842 (7th Cir.1959) (series of shareholder loans made between 1935 and 1940, with no repayment of principal or interest until 1948, held not to have been changed in equity in 1942 when the liabilities were transferred on the books of the corporation to "Contributed or Paid–In Surplus"; thus, repayments in 1948 did not, constitute dividends).

H. TAXPAYER EFFORTS TO RECLASSIFY OBLIGATIONS

1. *"Preferred Stock Reclassified as Debt*

The classification problem can be presented in reverse, with the taxpayer claiming that "preferred stock" is really debt. In Bowersock Mills & Power Co. v. Commissioner, 172 F.2d 904 (10th Cir.1949), a family corporation had defaulted on its interest and principal payments to the bondholders, members of another family, and consequently could not obtain bank credit.

The bondholders and the corporation agreed to a recapitalization under which preferred stock was issued for the bonds, with 3 percent cumulative dividends payable if earnings were sufficient. The shareholders and the bondholders agreed that the former would purchase a certain number of preferred stock shares annually, and in default of such purchase or upon failure of the corporation to pay preferred dividends, the common stock would be turned over to the bondholders. The court, one judge dissenting, construed the two contracts as one transaction, in view of the family character of the corporation, and held that the "preferred stockholders remained creditors of the corporation, and that the payment on the obligation was deductible as interest."

But in Lee Telephone Co. v. Commissioner, 260 F.2d 114 (4th Cir. 1958), the court rejected the taxpayer's attempt to classify as debt shares of preferred stock issued to finance an expanding telephone business after a public utility commission thought that the debt ratio had grown too large; the shares had a sinking fund but otherwise closely resembled stock. Similarly, in Miele v. Commissioner, 56 T.C. 556 (1971), the corporation decided to purchase a new barge but needed a guarantee from the United States Maritime Commission on a first mortgage loan in order to make the acquisition. The Maritime Commission required $150,000 of additional capital from private sources before it would guarantee the loan and the corporation issued preferred stock to shareholders in proportion to their common stock holdings to secure the needed funds. Subsequently, the preferred stock was redeemed pro rata, and the taxpayer shareholder treated the preferred stock as debt in order to avoid dividend treatment under section 302(a). The court held the taxpayers to their classification.

2. *"Debt Instruments" Reclassified as Equity*

The courts sometimes have permitted taxpayers to obtain a classification of debt instruments different from the formal characterization the parties themselves initially gave to the instruments. For example, in Mercantile Bank & Trust Co. v. United States, 147 F.Supp. 956 (Ct.Cl.1957), a bank, prohibited by state law from issuing preferred stock, issued a "capital note" to the Reconstruction Finance Corporation ("RFC") which closely resembled the usual preferred stock instrument taken by the RFC. The court, with one dissent, permitted the bank to claim that the instrument was stock for excess profits tax purposes. But in Zilkha & Sons, Inc. v. Commissioner, 52 T.C. 607 (1969), where shareholders were urging that hybrid securities constituted preferred stock (the corporation having no earnings and profits, so that all payments with respect to the securities would have constituted nontaxable distributions), the court upheld the Commissioner's determination that the securities constituted debt resulting in taxation of payments received by the security holders as interest. See also J.A. Maurer, Inc. v. Commissioner, 30 T.C. 1273 (1958) (corporation successfully asserted that advances by a shareholder in the form of debt constituted equity capital, so that no cancellation of indebtedness income resulted on the settlement of the advances for less than their face amount); Joseph Lupowitz Sons, Inc. v. Commissioner, 497 F.2d 862 (3d Cir.1974) (taxpayer successfully argued that open account advances were contributions to capital and not loans thus avoiding imputation of interest income).

I. DEBT–EQUITY CLASSIFICATION IN THE CODE AND REGULATIONS

Attempts in Congress to define debt and equity when the 1954 Code was enacted were rejected by the Senate. The Senate Finance Committee Report stated that "any attempt to write into the statute precise definitions which will classify for tax purposes the many types of corporate stocks and securities will be frustrated by the numerous characteristics of an interchangeable nature which can be given to these instruments." S.Rep. No. 1622, 83d Cong., 2d Sess. 42 (1954). In the 1969 Act, however, Congress enacted section 385 in an attempt to transfer the problem of definition to the Secretary of the Treasury.

Excerpt from GENERAL EXPLANATION OF THE TAX REFORM ACT OF 1969, Joint Committee on Internal Revenue Taxation (1970):

"*Explanation of* [*section 385*].—The Act deals with the [debt-equity] problems * * * by adding two different provisions to the tax laws, one which is of general application under the tax laws and a second which relates only to corporate acquisitions.

"The first of these [section 385] provides the Secretary of the Treasury or his delegate with specific statutory authority to promulgate regulatory guidelines, to the extent necessary or appropriate, for determining whether a corporate obligation constitutes stock or indebtedness for all purposes of the Internal Revenue Code. These guidelines are to set forth factors to be taken into account in determining in a particular factual situation whether a debtor-creditor relationship exists or whether a corporation-shareholder relationship exists. The provision specifies certain factors which may be taken into account in these guidelines. However, it is not intended that only these factors be included in the guidelines or that, in a particular situation, any of these factors must be included in the guidelines, or that any of the factors which are included by statute must necessarily be given any more weight than other factors added by regulations. The factors specifically listed are as follows:

(1) Whether there is a written unconditional promise to pay on demand or on a specified date a sum certain in money in return for an adequate consideration in money or money's worth, and to pay a fixed rate of interest;

(2) Whether there is subordination to, or preference over, any indebtedness of the corporation;

(3) The ratio of debt to equity of the corporation;

(4) Whether there is convertibility into the stock of the corporation; and

(5) The relationship between holdings of stock in the corporation and holdings of the interest in question."

"In developing these guidelines, the Secretary of the Treasury is not bound or limited by the specific rules which the Act provides for distinguishing debt from equity in the corporate acquisition context [section 279]. Thus, an obligation the interest on which is not disallowed under the corporate acquisition section nevertheless might be found to constitute equity (and hence the interest disallowed) under the general debt-equity regulatory guidelines. Moreover, unlike the rules provided by the Act in a corporate acquisition context, which deal only with the allowability of the interest deduction, the guidelines to be promulgated by the Secretary of the Treasury are applicable for all purposes of the Internal Revenue Code." (123–24.)

Regulations were not issued until 1980 and were eventually withdrawn before becoming effective. The Regulations drafted by Treasury focused primarily on proportionality and valuation as the keys to debt/equity distinctions. An instrument in the form of debt which was not held in proportion to stock was generally treated as debt. Proportionately held obligations were treated as debt if the debt was not excessive (thin capitalization), the interest rate was commercially reasonable, or if interest was not reasonable, the obligation was issued for money repayable at a fixed time.

The Regulations also dealt with hybrid instruments, i.e., obligations convertible into stock. Proportionately held convertible instruments were debt only if independent creditors owned at least 20 percent of the obligations and the debt features of the instrument represented at least 50 percent of the value of the obligation. Hybrid instruments not held in proportion to stock were treated as debt if the debt feature was 50 percent or more of the total value of the instrument. The Regulations also provided for conversion to equity of obligations initially classified as debt if the corporation failed to make timely payments of interest and principal. Publicly traded obligations, obligations held by independent creditors, and obligations issued in a qualified stock redemption were classified as debt under the Regulations. If the purported debt instrument did not meet the "safe harbor" tests, the Regulations provided for an analysis based on present value principles to identify the various components or the obligation.

The final section 385 regulations were issued in December 1980, applicable to instruments issued after April 30, 1981. T.D. 7747, 1981–1 Cum.Bull. 141. The effective date was extended several times and the Regulations were withdrawn on August 5, 1983. T.D. 7920, 1983–2 Cum. Bull. 69. The Regulations, though elegant in structure and theoretical underpinning, were extremely difficult to apply in the myriad of situations which they were required to cover. The section 385 Regulations expired under the weight of their complexity, particularly in the small business context, and from the fact that enterprising taxpayers developed financial instruments which would have successfully taken advantage of the Regulations' bright line classification of hybrid instruments. See Rev.Rul. 83–98, 1983–2 Cum.Bull. 40, infra.

In the 1989 Act, Congress reentered the fray with an amendment to section 385(a) authorizing the Treasury to promulgate regulations classifying an obligation as part debt, part equity. Bifurcation of debt and equity features of a single obligation is discussed infra, page 409.

J. HYBRID SECURITIES AND OTHER FINANCIAL INSTRUMENTS

1. *Convertible Obligations*

With debt instruments that are convertible into corporate stock, an investor may achieve both the certainty of a fixed payment of principal and interest, and the potential to share in economic growth if the corporation is successful. From the point of view of the corporation, hybrid securities are a way to attract investors interested in long term appreciation while providing deductible interest payments to the issuer. Convertibility is listed in section 385 as one of the facts and circumstances to be considered in determining whether a financial instrument is debt or equity.

Rev.Rul. 83–98, 1983–2 Cum.Bull. 40, considers a hybrid instrument referred to as an "adjustable rate convertible note" (ARCN). Under the facts of the ruling, X Corporation, with a single class of common stock outstanding, issued $10 million of ARCN's. An ARCN could be purchased for $1,000 of cash or 50 shares of X stock, which at the time of the offering was worth $1,000. At the option of the holder, each ARCN was convertible into 50 shares of stock. Otherwise, the ARCN would pay $600 at the end of the 20 year term of the note. The ARCN was callable for $600 by X at any time after the first two years. X was required to pay annual interest on each ARCN equal to the dividends paid on 50 shares of X stock, plus 2 percent of the issue price ($20). The interest was not to be less than $60 nor more than $175. In order to qualify the instrument as debt under the section 385 regulations, the ARCN was designed so that the present value of its debt features was worth more than one-half of its $1,000 issue price. Disregarding the Regulations under section 385 (which were withdrawn one month after Rev.Rul. 83–98 was issued), the Internal Revenue Service held that the ARCN's were equity. The Service found that the ARCN's were structured so that under most likely eventualities they would be converted into common stock. Because of the high probability of conversion, the Service concluded that the ARCN's did not in reality represent a promise to pay a sum certain. The Service also noted that the guaranteed annual interest of $60 per $1,000 of capital was unreasonably low in comparison to the return available on nonconvertible, noncontingent instruments, that based on the level of dividends on X common stock more than 65 percent of the potential annual yield on the instruments was discretionary, and that the instruments were subordinate to the claims of general creditors.

In Rev.Rul. 85–119, 1985–2 Cum.Bull. 60, the Internal Revenue Service allowed interest deductions for payments with respect to publicly traded notes with a mandatory conversion feature adopted to comply with banking regulations. At maturity the notes were convertible into stock of the issuing corporation with a value at the time of conversion equal to the principal of the notes. However, if a note holder elected not to accept stock, the issuer was required to undertake a secondary stock offering on the open market and deliver cash to the note holder in an amount equal to the note principal. The notes required quarterly interest payments in an amount that varied with the market rate payable on comparable subordinated instruments. Factors supporting debt treatment included the facts that the notes were publicly held and not in proportion to equity ownership, interest was payable without regard to earnings, the notes had a fixed maturity at the end of a limited period of time, the issuer was not thinly capitalized, note holders had no vote or participation in management, and, as distinguished from Rev.Rul. 83–98 supra, the amount of stock to be issued in exchange for the notes at maturity was based on the face amount of the notes rather than the value of stock. These debt factors outweighed the fact that the notes were subordinated to other creditors, but not equity interests, and were in form payable only in the issuer's stock.

2. *Bifurcation of Debt and Equity Features*

(a) *Court Decisions*

In two cases, the courts bifurcated the debt and equity components of a single financial instrument. In Helvering v. Richmond, F. & P. R.R. Co., 90 F.2d 971 (4th Cir.1937), the corporation was allowed an interest deduction for guaranteed 7 percent dividends paid on preferred stock, but payments in excess of the guarantee were treated as dividends, a return on equity. The preferred stock provided for participation in corporate earnings above the 7 percent guaranteed dividends and possessed full voting rights. The guaranteed dividends were a first lien on corporate assets and took precedence over all creditors, including general creditors.

In Farley Realty Corp. v. Commissioner, 279 F.2d 701 (2d Cir.1960), the corporation borrowed money from a nonshareholder to acquire a building. The obligation required fixed payment of interest and had a fixed maturity date. In addition, the obligation holder was entitled to 50 percent of the appreciation on sale of the building, whether this event occurred before or after the maturity date. The Commissioner allowed the corporation to deduct fixed interest payments on the loan but disallowed any deduction for payment in settlement of the creditor's interest in appreciation.

In Rev.Rul. 83–51, 1983–1 Cum.Bull. 48, the Internal Revenue Service ruled that contingent interest in the form of shared appreciation paid by the borrower to the mortgagee on a home residence loan is deductible interest. The loans provided for a fixed interest rate plus 40 percent of appreciation on sale of the residence or at the end of the 10 year term of the loan. The Ruling described the interest as ascertainable because it was dependent on fixed events. The Ruling expressly provides that it is not applicable in a commercial context.

In the context of computing original issue discount, the courts have uniformly refused to bifurcate convertible debt into separate debt and equity portions. See for example Chock Full O'Nuts Corp. v. United States, 453 F.2d 300 (2d Cir.1971), discussed infra, page 441.

(b) *Bifurcation by Statute*

(i) *Section 385*

The 1989 Act amended section 385(a) to authorize regulations classifying different portions of obligations as debt in part and equity in part. The legislative history indicates that "such treatment may be appropriate in circumstances where a debt instrument provides for payments that are dependent to a significant extent (whether in whole or in part) on corporate performance, whether through equity kickers, contingent interest, significant deferral of payment, subordination, or an interest rate sufficiently high to suggest a significant risk of default." H.Rep. No. 101–247, 101st Cong., 1st Sess. 1235–1236 (1989).

(ii) *High Yield Discount Obligations*

The 1989 Act also required bifurcation of the return on so-called "high yield discount obligations" into an interest portion and, at least for some purposes, a dividend portion. In general, when a bond or other debt instrument is issued for an amount less than its stated redemption price (or face amount), the difference is defined as original issue discount and amortized as interest over the term of the obligation. The original issue discount is included in income by the holder and deducted by the issuer even though the interest element is not actually paid until the obligation is redeemed for its face amount. Original issue discount is discussed in Section 3, infra, page 432. As part of its investigation of leveraged buy-outs, discussed infra, page 734, Congress expressed the view that heavily discounted bonds sufficiently resemble equity to be treated as preferred stock when the bonds provide a high rate of interest which is not actually paid for long periods of time. H.Rep. No. 101–247, 101st Cong., 1st Sess. 1220 (1989). The legislative history points out that the long-term deferral of interest on original issue discount bonds is riskier than other forms of debt investment and that the presence of a high rate of return suggests that payment of interest is dependent on the profitability of the issuer's business. As a result, section 163(e)(5) disallows entirely the interest deduction for a portion of the original issue discount on a "high yield original issue discount obligation," and defers the interest deduction on the remainder until the interest is actually paid. The holder of a high yield original issue discount obligation must continue to report the accrued original issue discount as income over the term of the obligation as required by section 1272, infra, page 436, but a corporate holder is permitted to treat the disqualified portion of the accrued original issue discount as a dividend for purposes of the dividends received deduction of sections 243–246A. Thus, to a limited extent, the disqualified portion of the return on a high yield original issue discount obligation is treated as a dividend while a portion of the return is given interest treatment, though with deduction deferred to actual payment.

A high yield original issue discount obligation is defined in section 163(i) as an obligation with a term in excess of five years, which has a yield to maturity in excess of a fixed rate (referred to as the "applicable federal rate," see infra, page 436) plus five percent, and which has significant original issue discount. In highly simplified terms, an obligation has significant original issue discount if in any period ending more than five years after the obligation is issued, the obligation has accrued but unpaid interest in excess of the amount of the obligation's annual yield to maturity. Section 163(i)(2). This disqualified portion of a high yield original issue discount obligation (the portion for which no current interest deduction is allowed and which is treated as a dividend to a corporate holder) is the lesser of the original issue discount of the obligation or the amount by which original issue discount exceeds the applicable federal rate plus six percent. Section 163(e)(5)(C). Thus actual interest paid, plus original issue discount up to the applicable federal rate plus six percent, remains deductible as interest, but only when actually paid. The excess is given the equivalent of dividend treatment.

Section 279 limits the allowability of the interest deduction in situations where corporate debt is used to acquire the stock or assets of another corporation. These rules are discussed infra, page 993.

(iii) *Excess Interest Paid to Related Tax Exempt Persons*

Another example of a sort of bifurcation related to thin capitalization concepts is found in section 163(j), added in 1989. Under that section, "excess" interest paid to related parties who are tax exempt may not be deducted currently by the paying corporation if the corporation has a debt-equity ratio in excess of 1.5 to 1. The provision is applicable to interest paid to more than 50 percent shareholders who are domestic tax exempt organizations or foreign persons who are not subject to United States tax on interest payments. "Excess" interest is defined as interest in excess of 50 percent of the corporation's adjusted taxable income. Excess interest can be carried forward indefinitely and deducted in subsequent years to the extent the 50 percentage threshold is not met in those years. In addition, the 50 percent limitation itself can be carried forward for three years.

The Congressional concern here was that the corporation's earnings were being "stripped" out in the form of deductible interest payments but not being taxed in the hands of the tax exempt recipients. In effect, the portion of the interest which is disallowed is included in the corporate tax base in the same way as earnings used to pay dividends.

See also infra, page 734.

K. TRACKING STOCK

A different form of equity, referred to as tracking stock, has been used in certain acquisitions. For example, when General Motors acquired Electronic Data Systems (EDS) in 1984, EDS shareholders were given the option to receive in exchange for each share of EDS stock either $44 of cash, or a combination of $35.20 cash plus one-fifth share of General Motors series E stock and a contingent note. General Motors also distributed series E stock to common shareholders pro rata in order to create a liquid market for the series E stock. Dividends payable on the series E stock are dependent on EDS earnings. The contingent notes are designed to guarantee a fixed return to former EDS shareholders if the price of EDS stock falls below a fixed level. The notes are payable only if insufficient dividends are paid on the series E stock to maintain its market price at a certain level. Since the dividends on the series E stock are dependent on EDS earnings, the value of General Motors series E stock is dependent on the stand-alone value of EDS rather than the value of General Motors as a whole. This arrangement is intended to allow the former EDS shareholders to continue to participate in the rapid growth potential of a high technology company and create a public market that reflects the growth potential of EDS. However, the series E stock has several features that are tied to General Motors. After 1994 General Motors may force conversion of the series E stock into General Motors common stock at a rate based on the then relative values of EDS and General Motors common stock. On liquidation or bankruptcy of General Motors the series E stock would share proportionately in General Motors net assets. Thus, the liquidation value of the series E stock is not tied to the stand alone value of EDS. The series E stock is subordinate to all of General Motors' general creditors. General Motors used the same technique to acquire Hughes Aircraft corporation, issuing a new class H stock which tracked the performance of the Hughes Aircraft assets and General Motors Delco Electronics division, both of which were transferred to a new General Motors subsidiary.

There is a question whether the tracking stock is stock of the acquiring corporation, or whether the attributes of the stock are so tied into the tracked corporation that the stock should be treated as the stock of the tracked corporation. Major tax consequences follow from the identity of the issuer including whether the nominal issuer can avoid recognition of gain under section 1032 of the issue of its own stock for property, whether gain is recognized on the distribution of appreciated property (the stock or other property interest in the tracked subsidiary) under section 311, or whether the distribution of tracking stock to common stockholders is a tax-free stock dividend under section 305(a). In Rev.Proc. 87–59, 1987–2 Cum.Bull. 764, the Internal Revenue Service indicated that it is studying the status of tracking stock and that no rulings will be issued. The Service has, however, issued at least one private letter ruling indicating that such stock would be treated as the stock of the issuing corporation in a statutory merger. Pvt.Ltr. Rul. 8817007 (April 29, 1988).

L. PLANNING CONSIDERATIONS

In view of the number of factors considered by the courts in resolving debt-equity cases and the unpredictable weight given to any particular factor, the tax advisor faces a difficult problem in advising clients as to the proper mix of debt and equity in determining the capital structure of a corporation. In some cases, the client simply may wish to avoid any problem and take his entire investment in the corporation in the form of equity interests. Where other corporate planning considerations—or the more adventurous nature of the client—indicate the use of debt, the tax planning problems are more difficult.

Some of the various factors in the debt-equity equation are clearly within the control of the taxpayer. Thus, proper attention to the form of the debt obligation should create no problem. But how, for example, can the tax advisor establish that outside lenders would have made a loan, a factor which many of the cases consider significant? Here it would be important at the outset to determine through an analysis of the corporation's projected cash flow and operating capital requirements that a bank would have considered a loan under these circumstances and perhaps some documentation from a bank that it would have made such a loan. Other factors may be more difficult to control. For example, where shareholder debt is to be combined with some outside financing, a bank may insist on subordination of the shareholder debt and this factor cannot be "planned around".

Once the formalities indicating a debtor-creditor relationship between the corporation and its shareholders are established, it is important that the formalities be followed. For example, interest and principal should in fact be paid according to the terms of the instrument. But here the planning considerations become more complicated. While payment of principal may be helpful in establishing the debt character of the obligation, it also exposes the shareholder to the risk of dividend taxation should the tax advisor have "guessed wrong" on the debt-equity question. Would it be better to provide in the original instrument that no principal payments will be made for a period of time, with larger payments to be made later in the term of the note? If such a course is taken, however, the taxpayer loses the argument that principal payments were in fact made, a factor sometimes stressed by the courts. On the other hand, even if principal payments are postponed, complete assurance is still not possible. Even though the corporation has been audited and the loans accepted as debt for purposes of the interest deduction, the Service could still challenge the status of the obligation in subsequent years when principal payments are made. In the end, there is no sure escape from the difficult decisions which the current status of the tax law on debt and equity require.

Retaining ownership and transferring property subject to a license or by lease is an alternative to debt. Lease or royalty payments will be deductible by the corporation.

M. REFERENCES

For general references, see Warren, The Corporate Interest Deduction: A Policy Evaluation, 83 Yale L.J. 1585 (1974); Plumb, The Federal Income

Tax Significance of Corporate Debt: A Critical Analysis and Proposal, 26 Tax L.Rev. 369 (1971); Canellos, The Overleveraged Acquisition, 39 Tax Lawyer 91 (1985); Comment, The Intractable Debt/Equity Problem: A New Structure for Analyzing Shareholder Advances, 81 Nw.L.Rev. 452 (1987).

With respect to section 385, see Recommendations as to Federal Tax Distinction between Corporate Stock and Indebtedness, N.Y. State Bar Association Tax Section Committee on Reorganization Problems, 25 Tax Lawyer 57 (1971); Note, Towards New Modes of Tax Decisionmaking—The Debt–Equity Imbroglio and Dislocations in Tax Law Making Responsibility, 83 Harv.L.Rev. 1695 (1970); Sax, The Conglomerate and Tax Reform; A Brief Review, 25 Tax L.Rev. 235 (1970); Eustice, Corporations and Corporate Investors, 25 Tax L.Rev. 509 (1970); Lefevre and Lee, Debt or Equity, Stock Dividends, and Other Corporate Problems, 23 Tax Lawyer 511 (1970); Popkin, A Critique of the Rule–Making Process in Federal Income Tax Law with Special Reference to Conglomerate Acquisitions, 45 Ind.L.J. 453 (1970); Panel, Convertible Debentures and Strange Securities, 28 N.Y.U. Tax Inst. 331 (1970); Gabinet, The Interest Deduction: Several New Installments in a Continuing Saga, 21 Case W.Res.L.Rev. 466 (1970). For a description of the withdrawn Regulations see Bloom & Bush, Final Regulations Under Section 385 Contain Complex Rules and Safe Harbors, 54 J.Tax. 274 (1981). See also Stone & McGeehan, Distinguishing Corporate Debt From Stock Under Section 385, 36 Tax L.Rev. 341 (1981); Kaplan & Yoder, New Variations On An Old Enigma: The Treasury Department's Debt–Equity Regulations, 1981 U.Ill.L.Rev. 567; Boyles & Rush, The Regulations Under Section 385: A Review, Evaluation, and Suggested Approach, 27 Vill.L.Rev. 52 (1981–82).

With respect to hybrid securities and other financial instruments, see Comment, Hybrid Instruments and the Debt–Equity Distinction, 52 U.Chi.L. Rev. 118 (1985); Madison, The Deductibility of "Interest" on Hybrid Securities, 39 Tax Lawyer 465 (1986); Robertson and Burckel, When is Debt Synonymous with Equity? Recent Developments in the Classification of Hybrid Securities, 66 Taxes 784–790 (1988); Sheppard, GM's Class E Stock: Tax Planning in Second Gear, 36 Tax Notes 130 (1987); Walter & Strasen, General Motors Class E and Class H Common Stock, 64 Taxes 365 (1986); Sheppard, Status of Alphabet Stock Remains Unclear, 39 Tax Notes 1252 (1988); Sheffield & St. Clair, An Abecedarium on Alphabet Stock, 66 Taxes 954 (1988); New York State Bar Tax Section, Tracking Stock Arrangements, 43 Tax L.Rev. 51 (1988).

For legislative recommendations with respect to the debt-equity problem, see American Law Institute, Income Tax Problems of Corporations and Shareholders: Report of Working Views of a Study by the American Law Institute Staff and American Bar Association, Section of Taxation Liaison Committee 56–63 (1958) (also in 14 Tax L.Rev. 1, 43 (1958)); Advisory Group Recommendations on Subchapters C, J, and K of the Internal Revenue Code, Hearings before the House Ways and Means Committee, 86th Cong., 1st Sess. 933–35 (1959).

SECTION 2. DEBT VERSUS EQUITY: LOSS ON INVESTMENT IN A CORPORATION

INTERNAL REVENUE CODE: Sections 165(g)(1), (2); 166(a); (b), (d), (e); 1244; 1271(a)(1).

REGULATIONS: Section 1.166–5.

UNITED STATES v. GENERES

Supreme Court of the United States, 1972.
405 U.S. 93.

MR. JUSTICE BLACKMUN delivered the opinion of the Court.

A debt a closely held corporation owed to an indemnifying shareholder-employee became worthless in 1962. The issue in this federal income tax refund suit is whether, for the shareholder-employee, that worthless obligation was a business or a nonbusiness bad debt within the meaning and reach of §§ 166(a) and (d) of the Internal Revenue Code of 1954, as amended, 26 U.S.C.A. §§ 166(a) and (d), and of the implementing Regulations § 1.166–5.

The issue's resolution is important for the taxpayer. If the obligation was a business debt, he may use it to offset ordinary income and for carryback purposes under § 172 of the Code, 26 U.S.C.A. § 172. On the other hand, if the obligation is a nonbusiness debt, it is to be treated as a short-term capital loss subject to the restrictions imposed on such losses by § 166(d)(1)(B) and §§ 1211 and 1212, and its use for carryback purposes is restricted by § 172(d)(4). The debt is one or the other in its entirety, for the Code does not provide for its allocation in part to business and in part to nonbusiness.

In determining whether a bad debt is a business or a nonbusiness obligation the Regulations focus on the relation the loss bears to the taxpayer's business. If, at the time of worthlessness, that relation is a "proximate" one, the debt qualifies as a business bad debt and the aforementioned desirable tax consequences then ensue.

The present case turns on the proper measure of the required proximate relation. Does this necessitate a "dominant" business motivation on the part of the taxpayer or is a "significant" motivation sufficient?

Tax in an amount somewhat in excess of $40,000 is involved. The taxpayer, Allen H. Generes, prevailed in a jury trial in the District Court. See Generes v. United States, 67–2 U.S.T.C. ¶ 9754 (E.D.La.). On the Government's appeal, the Fifth Circuit affirmed by a divided vote. 427 F.2d 279 (5th Cir.1970). Certiorari was granted 401 U.S. 972, 91 S.Ct. 1189 (1971), to resolve a conflict among the Circuits.[4]

4. Compare the decision below and Weddle v. Commissioner, 325 F.2d 849 (2d Cir.1963), with Niblock v. Commissioner, 417 F.2d 1185 (CA7 1969). In Smith v. Commissioner, 55 T.C. 260, 268–271 (1970), reviewed without dissent, the Tax Court felt constrained, under the policy expressed in Golsen v. Commissioner, 54 T.C. 742 (1970), aff'd, 445 F.2d 985 (10th Cir. 1971), to apply the Fifth Circuit test but

I

The taxpayer as a young man in 1909 began work in the construction business. His son-in-law, William F. Kelly, later engaged independently in similar work. During World War II the two men formed a partnership in which their participation was equal. The enterprise proved successful. In 1954 Kelly–Generes Construction Co., Inc., was organized as the corporate successor to the partnership. It engaged in the heavy-construction business primarily on public works projects.

The taxpayer and Kelly each owned 44% of the corporation's outstanding capital stock. The taxpayer's original investment in his shares was $38,900. The remaining 12% of the stock was owned by a son of the taxpayer and by another son-in-law. Mr. Generes was president of the corporation and received from it an annual salary of $12,000. Mr. Kelly was executive vice president and received an annual salary of $15,000.

The taxpayer and Mr. Kelly performed different services for the corporation. Kelly worked full time in the field and was in charge of the day-to-day construction operations. Generes, on the other hand, devoted no more than six to eight hours a week to the enterprise. He reviewed bids and jobs, made cost estimates, sought and obtained bank financing, and assisted in securing the bid and performance bonds that are an essential part of the public-project construction business. Mr. Generes, in addition to being president of the corporation, held a full-time position as president of a savings and loan association he had founded in 1937. He received from the association an annual salary of $19,000. The taxpayer also had other sources of income. His gross income averaged about $40,000 a year during 1959–1962.

Taxpayer Generes from time to time advanced personal funds to the corporation to enable it to complete construction jobs. He also guaranteed loans made to the corporation by banks for the purchase of construction machinery and other equipment. In addition, his presence with respect to the bid and performance bonds is of particular significance. Most of these were obtained from Maryland Casualty Co. That underwriter required the taxpayer and Kelly to sign an indemnity agreement for each bond it issued for the corporation. In 1958, however, in order to eliminate the need for individual indemnity contracts, taxpayer and Kelly signed a blanket agreement with Maryland whereby they agreed to indemnify it, up to a designated amount for any loss it suffered as surety for the corporation. Maryland then increased its

stated that it agreed with the Seventh Circuit. Cases where the resolution of the issue was avoided include Stratmore v. United States, 420 F.2d 461 (3d Cir.1970), cert. denied, 398 U.S. 951, 90 S.Ct. 1870; Kelly v. Patterson, 331 F.2d 753, 757 (5th Cir.1964); and Gillespie v. Commissioner, 54 T.C. 1025, 1032 (1970). See, also, Millsap v. Commissioner, 387 F.2d 420 (8th Cir. 1968). For commentary on the present case, see 3 Sw.U.L.Rev. 135 (1971); 2 Tex. Tech.L.Rev. 318 (1971); and 28 Wash. & Lee L.Rev. 161 (1971).

line of surety credit to $2,000,000. The corporation had over $14,000,000 gross business for the period 1954 through 1962.

In 1962 the corporation seriously underbid two projects and defaulted in its performance of the project contracts. It proved necessary for Maryland to complete the work. Maryland then sought indemnity from Generes and Kelly. The taxpayer indemnified Maryland to the extent of $162,104.57. In the same year he also loaned $158,814.49 to the corporation to assist it in its financial difficulties. The corporation subsequently went into receivership and the taxpayer was unable to obtain reimbursement from it.

In his federal income tax return for 1962 the taxpayer took his loss on his direct loans to the corporation as a nonbusiness bad debt. He claimed the indemnification loss as a business bad debt and deducted it against ordinary income.[5] * * *

In due course the claims were made the subject of the jury trial refund suit in the United States District Court for the Eastern District of Louisiana. At the trial Mr. Generes testified that his sole motive in signing the indemnity agreement was to protect his $12,000-a-year employment with the corporation. The jury, by special interrogatory, was asked to determine whether taxpayer's signing of the indemnity agreement with Maryland "was proximately related to his trade or business of being an employee" of the corporation. The District Court charged the jury, over the Government's objection, that *significant* motivation satisfies the Regulations' requirement of proximate relationship.[6] The court refused the Government's request for an instruction that the applicable standard was that of *dominant* rather than significant motivation.

After twice returning to the court for clarification of the instruction given, the jury found that the taxpayer's signing of the indemnity agreement was proximately related to his trade or business of being an employee of the corporation. Judgment on this verdict was then entered for the taxpayer.

The Fifth Circuit majority approved the significant-motivation standard so specified and agreed with a Second Circuit majority in Weddle v. Commissioner, 325 F.2d 849, 851 (1963), in finding comfort for so doing in the tort law's concept of proximate cause. Judge Simpson dissented. 427 F.2d, at 284. * * *

5. This difference in treatment between the loss on the direct loan and that on the indemnity is not explained. See, however, Whipple v. Commissioner, 373 U.S. 193, 82 S.Ct. 1168 (1963).

6. "A debt is proximately related to the taxpayer's trade or business when its creation was significantly motivated by the taxpayer's trade or business, and it is not rendered a non-business debt merely because there was a non-qualifying motivation as well, even though the non-qualifying motivation was the primary one.

II

A. The fact responsible for the litigation is the taxpayer's dual status relative to the corporation. Generes was both a shareholder and an employee. These interests are not the same, and their differences occasion different tax consequences. In tax jargon, Generes' status as a shareholder was a nonbusiness interest. It was capital in nature and it was comprised initially of tax-paid dollars. Its rewards were expectative and would flow not from personal effort, but from investment earnings and appreciation. On the other hand, Generes' status as an employee was a business interest. Its nature centered in personal effort and labor, and salary for that endeavor would be received. The salary would consist of pre-tax dollars.

Thus, for tax purposes it becomes important and, indeed, necessary to determine the character of the debt that went bad and became uncollectible. Did the debt center on the taxpayer's business interest in the corporation or on his nonbusiness interest? If it was the former, the taxpayer deserves to prevail here. Trent v. Commissioner, 291 F.2d 669 (2d Cir.1961); Jaffe v. Commissioner, T.C.Memo ¶ 67,215; Estate of Saperstein v. Commissioner, T.C.Memo ¶ 70,209; Faucher v. Commissioner, T.C.Memo ¶ 70,217; Rosati v. Commissioner, T.C.Memo ¶ 70,343; Rev.Rul. 71–561, 1971–50 Int.Rev.Bull. 13.

B. Although arising in somewhat different contexts, two tax cases decided by the Court in recent years merit initial mention. In each of these cases a major shareholder paid out money to or on behalf of his corporation and then was unable to obtain reimbursement from it. In each he claimed a deduction assertable against ordinary income. In each he was unsuccessful in this quest:

1. In Putnam v. Commissioner, 352 U.S. 82, 77 S.Ct. 175 (1956), the taxpayer was a practicing lawyer who had guaranteed obligations of a labor newspaper corporation in which he owned stock. He claimed his loss as fully deductible in 1948 under § 23(e)(2) of the 1939 Code. The standard prescribed by that statute was incurrence of the loss "in any transaction entered into for profit, though not connected with the trade or business." The Court rejected this approach and held that the loss was a nonbusiness bad debt subject to short-term capital loss treatment under § 23(k)(4). The loss was deductible as a bad debt or not at all. See Rev.Rul. 60–48, 1960–1 Cum.Bull. 112.

2. In Whipple v. Commissioner, 373 U.S. 193, 83 S.Ct. 1168 (1963), the taxpayer had provided organizational, promotional, and managerial services to a corporation in which he owned approximately an 80% stock interest. He claimed that this constituted a trade or business and, hence, that debts owing him by the corporation were business bad debts when they became worthless in 1953. The Court also rejected that contention and held that Whipple's investing was not a trade or business, that is, that "[d]evoting one's time and energies to the affairs of a corporation is not of itself, and without more, a trade or business of

the person so engaged." 373 U.S. at 202, 83 S.Ct., at 1174. The rationale was that a contrary conclusion would be inconsistent with the principle that a corporation has a personality separate from its shareholders and that its business is not necessarily their business. The Court indicated its approval of the Regulations' proximate-relation test:

> "Moreover, there is no proof (which might be difficult to furnish where the taxpayer is the sole or dominant stockholder) that the loan was necessary to keep his job or was otherwise proximately related to maintaining his trade or business as an employee. Compare Trent v. Commissioner, supra [291 F.2d 669 (CA2 1961)]." 373 U.S., at 204, 83 S.Ct., at 1175.

The Court also carefully noted the distinction between the business and the nonbusiness bad debt for one who is both an employee and a shareholder.[8]

These two cases approach, but do not govern, the present one. They indicate, however, a cautious and not a free-wheeling approach to the business bad debt. Obviously, taxpayer Generes endeavored to frame his case to bring it within the area indicated in the above quotation from Whipple v. Commissioner.

III

We conclude that in determining whether a bad debt has a "proximate" relation to the taxpayer's trade or business, as the Regulations specify, and thus qualifies as a business bad debt, the proper measure is that of dominant motivation, and that only significant motivation is not sufficient. We reach this conclusion for a number of reasons:

A. The Code itself carefully distinguishes between business and nonbusiness items. It does so, for example, in § 165 with respect to losses, in § 166 with respect to bad debts, and in § 162 with respect to expenses. It gives particular tax benefits to business losses, business bad debts, and business expenses, and gives lesser benefits, or none at all, to nonbusiness losses, nonbusiness bad debts, and nonbusiness expenses. It does this despite the fact that the latter are just as adverse in financial consequence to the taxpayer as are the former. But this distinction has been a policy of the income tax structure ever since the Revenue Act of 1916, § 5(a), 39 Stat. 759, provided differently for trade or business losses than it did for losses sustained in another transaction entered into for profit. And it has been the specific policy with respect to bad debts since the Revenue Act of 1942 incorporated into § 23(k) of the 1939 Code the distinction between business and nonbusiness bad debts. 56 Stat. 820.

8. "Even if the taxpayer demonstrates an independent trade or business of his own, care must be taken to distinguish bad debt losses arising from his own business and those actually arising from activities peculiar to an investor concerned with, and participating in, the conduct of the corporate business." 373 U.S., at 202, 83 S.Ct., at 1174.

The point, however, is that the tax statutes have made the distinction, that the Congress therefore intended it to be a meaningful one, and that the distinction is not to be obliterated or blunted by an interpretation that tends to equate the business bad debt with the nonbusiness bad debt. We think that emphasis upon the significant rather than upon the dominant would have a tendency to do just that.

B. Application of the significant-motivation standard would also tend to undermine and circumscribe the Court's holding in *Whipple* and the emphasis there that a shareholder's mere activity in a corporation's affairs is not a trade or business. As Chief Judge Lumbard pointed out in his separate and disagreeing concurrence in *Weddle,* supra, 325 F.2d, at 852–853, both motives—that of protecting the investment and that of protecting the salary—are inevitably involved, and an inquiry whether employee status provides a significant motivation will always produce an affirmative answer and result in a judgment for the taxpayer.

C. The dominant-motivation standard has the attribute of workability. It provides a guideline of certainty for the trier of fact. The trier than may compare the risk against the potential reward and give proper emphasis to the objective rather than to the subjective. As has just been noted, an employee-shareholder, in making or guaranteeing a loan to his corporation, usually acts with two motivations, the one to protect his investment and the other to protect his employment. By making the dominant motivation the measure, the logical tax consequence ensues and prevents the mere presence of a business motive, however small and however insignificant, from controlling the tax result at the taxpayer's convenience. This is of particular importance in a tax system that is so largely dependent on voluntary compliance.

D. The dominant-motivation test strengthens and is consistent with the mandate of § 262 of the Code, 26 U.S.C.A. § 262, that "no deduction shall be allowed for personal, living, or family expenses" except as otherwise provided. It prevents personal considerations from circumventing this provision.

E. The dominant-motivation approach to § 166(d) is consistent with that given the loss provisions in § 165(c)(1), see, for example, Imbesi v. Commissioner, 361 F.2d 640, 644 (3d Cir.1966), and in § 165(c)(2), see Austin v. Commissioner, 298 F.2d 583, 584 (2d Cir.1962). In these related areas, consistency is desirable. See also, Commissioner v. Duberstein, 363 U.S. 278, 286, 80 S.Ct. 1190 (1960).

* * *

G. The Regulations' use of the word "proximate" perhaps is not the most fortunate for it naturally tempts one to think in tort terms. The temptation, however, is best rejected, and we reject it here. In tort law factors of duty, of foreseeability, of secondary cause, and of plural liability are under consideration, and the concept of proximate cause has been developed as an appropriate application and measure of these factors. It has little place in tax law where plural aspects are not usual, where an item either is or is not a deduction, or either is or is not a business bad debt, and where certainty is desirable.

IV

The conclusion we have reached means that the District Court's instructions, based on a standard of significant rather than dominant motivation, are erroneous and that, at least, a new trial is required. We have examined the record, however, and find nothing that would support a jury verdict in this taxpayer's favor had the dominant-motivation standard been embodied in the instructions. Judgment n.o.v. for the United States, therefore, must be ordered. See Neely v. Eby Construction Co., 386 U.S. 317, 87 S.Ct. 1072 (1967).

As Judge Simpson pointed out in his dissent, 427 F.2d, at 284–285, the only real evidence offered by the taxpayer bearing upon motivation was his own testimony that he signed the indemnity agreement "to protect my job," that "I figured in three years' time I would get my money out," and that "I never once gave it [his investment in the corporation] a thought."

The statements obviously are self-serving. In addition, standing alone, they do not bear the light of analysis. What the taxpayer was purporting to say was that his $12,000 annual salary was his sole motivation, and that his $38,900 original investment, the actual value of which prior to the misfortunes of 1962 we do not know, plus his loans to the corporation, plus his personal interest in the integrity of the corporation as a source of living for his son-in-law and as an investment for his son and his other son-in-law, were of no consequence whatever in his thinking. The comparison is strained all the more by the fact that the salary is pre-tax and the investment is tax-paid. With his total annual income about $40,000, Mr. Generes may well have reached a federal income tax bracket of 40% or more for a joint return in 1958–1962. §§ 1 and 2 of the 1954 Code, 68A Stat. 5 and 8. The $12,000 salary thus would produce for him only about $7,000 net after federal tax and before any state income tax. This is the figure, and not $12,000, which has any possible significance for motivation purposes, and it is less than 1/5 of the original stock investment.

We conclude on these facts that the taxpayer's explanation falls of its own weight, and that reasonable minds could not ascribe, on this record, a dominant motivation directed to the preservation of the taxpayer's salary as president of Kelly–Generes Construction Co., Inc.

The judgment is reversed and the case is remanded with direction that judgment be entered for the United States.

MR. JUSTICE POWELL and MR. JUSTICE REHNQUIST took no part in the consideration or decision of this case.

[The concurring and dissenting opinions of Justices Marshall, White, Brennan and Douglas are omitted.]

ILLUSTRATIVE MATERIAL

A. TREATMENT OF SHAREHOLDER ADVANCES TO CORPORATION IN GENERAL

1. *Introduction*

Although the 1986 Act eliminated the preference for long-term capital gain, the capital versus ordinary distinction remains important to both individual and corporate taxpayers who suffer losses. Deduction of a corporate capital loss is limited to capital gain. Section 1211(a). Capital loss deductions of noncorporate taxpayers are limited to the taxpayer's capital gain plus $3,000 annually. Section 1211(b). Therefore, classification of a loss as a bad debt for a corporation, or a business bad debt for an individual, remains important to obtain ordinary loss treatment. Deduction of a capital loss on an equity investment, or loss on a nonbusiness bad debt as in *Generes,* is limited by section 1211.

2. *Worthless Securities*

There are two ways in which worthless corporate obligations can give rise to capital loss deductions. Section 165(g) in general treats a loss on worthless *securities* as capital loss. In contrast, section 166(a) provides ordinary loss treatment on debts not represented by securities. However, section 166(d), at issue in *Generes,* requires short-term capital loss treatment for *nonbusiness bad debt* held by a noncorporate taxpayer. Thus, the trade or business question addressed in *Generes* is raised only if the obligation is not classified as a "security."

Section 165(g)(2) defines securities as stock, rights to acquire stock, and any bond, debenture, note, or other evidence of indebtedness issued by a corporation (or a governmental entity) which is in registered form or has interest coupons attached. An obligation is in registered form if the rights to principal and stated interest are transferable through a book entry system maintained by the issuer. See, e.g., Regulations, section 5f.103–1(c). Section 163(f) disallows an interest deduction with respect to obligations issued by a person other than an individual which are offered to the public unless the obligation is in registered form.[4] If a "registration required obligation" is not issued in registered form, section 165(j) further disallows a deduction for any loss sustained by the holder.

Under section 165(g)(3), the corporate holder of a worthless security of an "affiliated corporation" is entitled to ordinary loss treatment. A corporation is an affiliated corporation for this purpose if the corporate security holder directly owns 80 percent of the voting power of all classes of stock entitled to vote and 80 percent of the stock of each class of nonvoting stock. In addition, the affiliated corporation must have derived 90 percent of its aggregate gross receipts for all taxable years from sources other than passive investments such as rents, royalties, dividends and interest. Regulations, section 1.165–5(d)(2)(iii), provide that the term gross receipts includes all corporate receipts without reduction for the cost of goods sold, except that gross receipts from the sale or exchange of stock or securities are taken into account only to the extent of the gains from such sales.

4. There is an exception for obligations which are not held by a United States person on which interest is payable only outside of the United States, so-called "Eurodollar" obligations. Section 163(f)(2)(B).

3. *Debt–Equity Aspects*

The initial question to be answered in considering the loss character of shareholder advances to a corporation not represented by a security is whether the corporate obligation involved is classified as debt or equity. The rules of section 166 are applicable only if a true debt is created. If the advances are found to constitute a contribution to capital, the capital loss limitations of section 165(g) are generally applicable and the issue of business versus nonbusiness bad debt which concerned the Court in *Generes* is not reached. The characterization of an advance as debt or equity for purposes of section 166 requires the same analysis used to determine whether payments with respect to an obligation are dividends or deductible interest, discussed in Section 1, supra. For example, see Thompson v. Commissioner, 73 T.C. 878 (1980) (advances from shareholders evidenced by written demand notes treated as contributions to capital; small amount of initial capital compared to amounts claimed as debt indicated that the corporation was undercapitalized; no evidence that the holders had ever demanded payment); Recklitis v. Commissioner, 91 T.C. 874, 900–905 (1988) (cash advances to controlled corporation held to be contributions to capital; the advances were interest free, contained no specific repayment terms, and were not evidenced by a written agreement); Adelson v. United States, 737 F.2d 1569 (Fed.Cir.1984), supra, page 400 (advances to client companies in which taxpayer held only minor equity interests held to be debt).

4. *Existence of a "Trade or Business"—The Promoter Cases*

If the advance qualifies as a debt and hence is not a contribution to capital, the question then shifts to whether the noncorporate debtor-investor is engaged in a trade or business, so that the loss falls under sections 166(a) and (b) as a business bad debt and avoids the limitation of section 166(d).

In Whipple v. Commissioner, 373 U.S. 193 (1963), discussed in the majority opinion in *Generes,* the Supreme Court considered whether an investor was engaged in a trade or business. The court denied a business bad debt deduction for advances made by the taxpayer to a company which he had formed and to which he had leased property he owned:

"Devoting one's time and energies to the affairs of a corporation is not of itself, and without more, a trade or business of the person so engaged. Though such activities may produce income, profit or gain in the form of dividends or enhancement in the value of an investment, this return is distinctive to the process of investing and is generated by the successful operation of the corporation's business as distinguished from the trade or business of the taxpayer himself. When the only return is that of an investor, the taxpayer has not satisfied his burden of demonstrating that he is engaged in a trade or business since investing is not a trade or business and the return to the taxpayer, though substantially the product of his services, legally arises not from his own trade or business but from that of the corporation. Even if the taxpayer demonstrates an independent trade or business of his own, care must be taken to distinguish bad debt losses arising from his own business and those actually arising from activities peculiar to an investor concerned with, and participating in, the conduct of the corporate business.

"If full-time service to one corporation does not alone amount to a trade or business, which it does not, it is difficult to understand how the same service to many corporations would suffice. To be sure, the presence of more than one corporation might lend support to a finding that the taxpayer was engaged in a regular course of promoting corporations for a fee or commission, see Ballantine, Corporations (rev. ed. 1946), 102, or for a profit on their sale, see Giblin v. Commissioner, 227 F.2d 692 (C.A. 5th Cir.), but in such cases there is compensation other than the normal investor's return, income received directly for his own services rather than indirectly through the corporate enterprise * * *. On the other hand, since the Tax Court found, and the petitioner does not dispute, that there was no intention here of developing the corporations as going businesses for sale to customers in the ordinary course, the case before us inexorably rests upon the claim that one who actively engages in serving his own corporations for the purpose of creating future income though those enterprises is in a trade or business. That argument is untenable * * *." (202–203)

Despite the suggestion in *Whipple* that promotional services provided to a number of corporations might constitute a trade or business, subsequent cases have in general refused to find a trade or business in such situations. See, e.g., Townshend v. United States, 384 F.2d 1008 (Ct.Cl.1967) (over a 20–year period the taxpayer had investigated a number of business opportunities and had organized five corporations; although he was considered a "promoter" for securities law purposes, the court refused to allow a business bad debt deduction for advances made by the taxpayer; there was no showing that fees or commission from promotional activities were received and the taxpayer realized no profits from a quick turnover of the investments); Compare Elliott v. United States, 268 F.Supp. 521 (D.Or.1967) (taxpayer's advances to a wholly-owned corporation were held to qualify for business bad debt treatment on a finding that he was in the business of seeking out business opportunities which he could successfully promote or finance; in a 12–year period the taxpayer made five loans and four investments).

5. *Is the Debt Incident to an Admitted Trade or Business?*

Assuming that the advance qualifies as a debt and is not a contribution to capital, and that the taxpayer is in a trade or business, the issue then is whether the taxpayer has established the necessary degree of connection between the debt and the business to qualify the debt as a business bad debt. Here the Supreme Court's decision in *Generes* makes matters much more difficult for the taxpayer. For examples of cases applying the *Generes* test and refusing to find the necessary connection between the taxpayer's business and the advance, see Miles Production Co. v. Commissioner, 457 F.2d 1150 (5th Cir.1972); Holland v. Commissioner, 728 F.2d 360 (6th Cir.1984).

As one factor in the determination, the *Generes* opinion stressed the relation between the taxpayer's (after-tax) salary and the amount of his investment. In Adelson v. United States, 737 F.2d 1569 (Fed.Cir.1984), the Court of Appeals concluded that the dominant motive test of *Generes* requires the trial court to compare the potential risk and reward of the taxpayer's equity interest in client companies to which the taxpayer advanced funds with the taxpayer's interest in his salary as a financial consultant. On remand the Claims Court found that the taxpayer's dominant motive was business, but the Court of Appeals again remanded the case to the Claims Court for specific findings comparing the potential profits that might have inured to the taxpayer's business interest with the potential profits from the taxpayer's equity interests. The court stressed language in its initial opinion, however, that determination of dominant motive need not depend upon a mathematical analysis of relative benefits. Adelson v. United States, 782 F.2d 1010 (Fed. Cir.1986). After a reevaluation of the record, the Claims Court determined that the taxpayer established that advances to three corporations were business debts, but did not prove that loans to three other corporations had a dominant business motive. Adelson v. United States, 12 Cl.Ct. 231 (1987). The Claims Court based its determinations on a specific comparison of the taxpayer's potential fee income with the potential return on the taxpayer's equity investment in each corporation.

In Bowers v. Commissioner, 716 F.2d 1047 (4th Cir.1983), the taxpayer advanced funds to a major client of the taxpayer's real estate brokerage firm. The taxpayer's corporation derived commission income from transactions undertaken by the debtor corporation and a substantial part of the commission income was paid to the taxpayer as an employee. The court allowed the taxpayer to claim a business bad debt deduction when the taxpayer's claim for repayment of the advances became worthless. Reversing the Tax Court, the appellate court concluded that the taxpayer's dominant motive in making the advances was to protect the income of his controlled corporation and thereby the taxpayer's own enhanced income. The court thus held that the debt was a business bad debt. On somewhat similar facts, however, business bad debt treatment was denied in Tennessee Securities, Inc. v. Commissioner, 674 F.2d 570 (6th Cir.1982). The taxpayers in *Tennessee Securities* were the principal shareholders of a stock brokerage corporation. The taxpayers individually guaranteed loans to an unrelated corporation which they hoped would undertake a public stock offering utilizing the taxpayer's brokerage corporation as the underwriter. When the debtor corporation declared bankruptcy, the taxpayers caused their brokerage corporation to make payments in satisfaction of the taxpayers' guarantees. The court upheld the Commissioner's determination that the taxpayers recognized ordinary income when their corporation satisfied the taxpayers' obligation under their guarantees. In addition, the court held that since the taxpayers' guarantees were given to enhance their investment in their brokerage corporation, the taxpayers' were treated as recognizing a loss on payment of the guarantees which was a nonbusiness bad debt.

The taxpayer successfully established his dominant business motive under the *Generes* standard in Estate of Mann, 731 F.2d 267 (5th Cir.1984). The taxpayer was allowed a business bad debt deduction for advances to his brother's corporation in which the taxpayer had only a negligible stock interest. The taxpayer had earned substantial commissions from his brother's corporation which had utilized the taxpayer as a broker in several corporate acquisitions. The court upheld the Tax Court's findings that the taxpayer's advances were motivated by the taxpayer's interest in protecting his brokerage commissions.

6. *Shareholder Guarantee of Corporate Debts*

In Putnam v. Commissioner, 352 U.S. 82 (1956), the Supreme Court held that payments by a guarantor because of the default of the primary obligor are subject to the limitations of section 166 and are thus deductible only as capital losses unless the obligation can qualify as a business bad debt: "The familiar rule is that, *instanter* upon the payment by the guarantor of the debt, the debtor's obligation to the creditor becomes an obligation to the guarantor, not a new debt, but by subrogation, the result of the shift of the original debt from the creditor to the guarantor who steps into the creditor's shoes. Thus, the loss sustained by the guarantor unable to recover from the debtor is by its very nature a loss from the worthlessness of a debt." (85)

Subsequently, some cases refused to require nonbusiness bad debt treatment if the payment in connection with the guarantee did not result in a right to subrogation under state law. See, e.g., Rietzke v. Commissioner, 40 T.C. 443 (1963). Other cases, however, emphasized the language in the *Putnam* opinion that "[t]here is no real or economic difference between the loss of an investment made in the form of a direct loan to a corporation and one made indirectly in the form of a guaranteed bank loan" (352 U.S. at 92–93), and applied section 166 to payments on guarantees regardless of whether a state law right of subrogation existed. See, e.g., Stratmore v. United States, 420 F.2d 461 (3d Cir.1970); Horne v. Commissioner, 523 F.2d 1363 (9th Cir.1975). In re Vaughan, 719 F.2d 196 (6th Cir.1983), applied the same rule to payments made under an agreement to release the taxpayer from his obligations under a guarantee. The court concluded that the payments to creditors in release of the taxpayer's guarantee were intended as payments of the guaranteed corporate debts.

The *Putnam* decision does not itself insure that payments made by a stockholder in satisfaction of a guarantee of corporate debt will be deductible as a nonbusiness bad debt under section 166. If a stockholder's guarantee of a loan from an outside lender is found to be a substitute for the infusion of additional equity capital, the stockholder's payment under the guarantee will be treated as a capital contribution. See Lane v. United States, 742 F.2d 1311 (11th Cir.1984) (applying the 13 factor test of *Slappey Drive Industrial Park,* supra, page 387, to distinguish debt from equity, the court concluded that the stockholder's intent at the time the guarantees were extended was to use the guarantees as short-term substitutes for more capital stock; the stockholder's payment was treated as a contribution to capital); Casco Bank & Trust Co. v. United States, 544 F.2d 528 (1st Cir.1976) (stockholder advances to corporation in order to avoid default on bonds guaranteed by the stockholder held to be equity contributions; the stockholder's deduction of a nonbusiness bad debt was not allowed; at the time of the stockholder advances, there was little reasonable expectation that the stockholder would be repaid; unsatisfied advances made in discharge of a guaranty are not as a matter of law bad debt losses; the guaranteed debt was a substitute for equity contributions); Thompson v. Commissioner, 73 T.C. 878, 893–895 (1980) (bad debt deduction denied, advances to corporation treated as capital contributions; stockholder advances represented by the corporation's demand note were the principal source of corporate capital; advances were proportionate to stockholdings; no evidence that the stockholders contemplated a demand for repayment); Kavich v. United States, 507 F.Supp. 1339, 1342 n. 2 (D.Neb.1981) ("In the court's opinion, *Putnam* only says that loans and guarantees should be treated alike. Thus, it would be anomalous to then say that payments made pursuant to guarantees are not subject to the bona fide debt requirement.")

Putnam also raises a question with respect to the deductibility of interest paid by a guarantor following default by the principal obligor. In B.B. Rider Corp. v. Commissioner, 725 F.2d 945 (3rd Cir.1984), the taxpayer sought to deduct under section 163 interest payments to creditors on obligations of the taxpayer's bankrupt corporation which the taxpayer had guaranteed. The court suggested that under *Putnam* the interest payments by the guarantor are payments on the corporation's indebtedness and are thus deductible only as bad debts under section 166. The court remanded the case to the Tax Court for a finding with respect to whether the taxpayer's interest payments were made on the obligation of the bankrupt corporation or on a new obligation assumed by the taxpayer following the bankruptcy reorganization. The court also rejected under *Generes* the taxpayer's argument that payment required by the taxpayer's guarantee was a business bad debt because the guarantee was offered to protect the taxpayer's salary as a corporate employee. On remand the Tax Court held that the taxpayer's interest payments were made on the guarantees rather than under a separate obligation, and treated the interest payments as a bad debt under section 166. Stratmore v. Commissioner, 48 T.C.M. 1369 (1984). The Third Circuit reversed on appeal, 785 F.2d 419 (1986), holding that when the original obligor is released by bankruptcy, and therefore is no longer liable for the debt to either the original creditors or to the guarantor, the obligation becomes a debt of the guarantor and interest payments are deductible under section 163. This conclusion seems to revive the distinction, rejected in the cases discussed above, at least with respect to the interest deduction, between the guarantor who is entitled to a right of subrogation against the primary obligor and one who is not.

For cases denying a deduction for interest see Abdalla v. Commissioner, 647 F.2d 487, 503–504 (5th Cir.1981) (interest deductions denied to stockholder who endorsed a corporate note prior to the corporate debtor's discharge in bankruptcy; even though the stockholder was primarily liable to the creditor as a result of his endorsement he was secondarily liable vis-a-vis the corporation); Nelson v. Commissioner, 281 F.2d 1 (5th Cir.1960) (interest deductions denied and loss of controlling stockholder guarantor treated as nonbusiness bad debt; interest and principal treated as a single obligation subject to the rule of *Putnam*); Golder v. Commissioner, 604 F.2d 34 (9th Cir.1979) (in a case not involving bankruptcy, interest deduction not allowed for payments of interest pursuant to taxpayer's guarantee of debt of taxpayer's controlled corporation).

7. *Section 1271—Exchange Treatment on Retirement*

Section 1271(a)(1) provides that amounts received on the retirement of any debt instruments shall be considered as amounts received in an exchange, thus supplying the exchange element necessary for capital gain or loss treatment. The provision does not independently characterize gain or loss. Under section 1271(a), gain or loss on retirement of a debt instrument which is a capital asset in the hands of the debt-holder will be treated as gain or loss on the exchange of the capital asset resulting in capital gain or loss treatment; gain or loss on retirement of a debt obligation which is not a capital asset is ordinary. A debt is "retired" for this purpose even if the debt is settled for less than its full amount. McClain v. Commissioner, 311 U.S. 527 (1941). Section 1271(a)(2) goes on to require ordinary income treatment for any element of original discount involved in the retirement of the bond; see infra, page 432. See also section 1276, discussed infra, page 446.

B. ORDINARY LOSS ON STOCK

1. *Section 1244 Stock*

Section 1244 allows a stockholder to treat a loss on certain small business stock, called section 1244 stock, as an ordinary loss rather than a capital loss. The loss is also available in computing the stockholder's net operating loss deduction. This ordinary loss treatment is limited to $50,000 per year, or $100,000 on a joint return. The ordinary loss treatment is available only to the individual (not including a trust) or partnership to whom the stock was issued, and in the case of a partnership the loss may be passed through to the individual partners with the dollar limitations applying at the partner level.

Section 1244 stock is defined essentially as stock of a "small business corporation". The stock must be issued for money or other property, other than stocks or securities and, under Regulations, section 1.1244(c)–1(f), other than for services. In Adams v. Commissioner, 74 T.C. 4 (1980), section 1244 stock issued to third party was reacquired by the corporation and then reissued to the taxpayer. Ordinary loss treatment was not allowed to the taxpayer when the stock became worthless. The taxpayer failed to demonstrate that the stock purchase price paid by the taxpayer was anything more than a substitution for capital paid out by the corporation on reacquisition of stock from the first holder. There was no flow of funds into the corporation.

A corporation is a "small business corporation" if, at the time of the issuance of the stock for which an ordinary loss is claimed, the aggregate amount of equity capital received by the corporation does not exceed $1 million. If a qualified corporation issues common stock in excess of $1 million, Regulations, section 1.1244(c)–2(b)(2), provide for designation of shares which were issued before the limit was exceeded as "section 1244 stock".

If a corporation is a small business corporation when the stock was issued, it may lose that status thereafter without disqualifying the stock previously issued. The number of shareholders or the existence of several classes of stock is not material. In addition to being a small business corporation, however, the corporation also must have derived more than 50 percent of its gross receipts from operating income for a period up to five years prior to the loss on the stock, unless its deductions exceed its gross income. Section 1244(c)(1)(C) and (2)(C). Regulations, section 1.1244(c)–1(e)(2), provide that, even if deductions exceed gross income, ordinary loss treatment will be denied if the corporation is not "largely an operating company". The validity of the Regulations was upheld and ordinary loss treatment denied in Davenport v. Commissioner, 70 T.C. 922 (1978), where the corporation derived more than 50 percent of its aggregate gross receipts from interest during the five years preceding the loss, but during those years its deductions exceeded gross income; seven dissenters would have held for the taxpayer on the basis that the corporation was a small loan company and hence was an "operating company" even though its income was interest income. Special provisions regarding section 1244 stock cover stock dividends, recapitalizations and reorganizations and disallow any loss attributable to property with a basis in excess of the value of property contributed to the corporation in exchange for section 1244 stock.

Since the benefits of section 1244 do not extend to debt, the provision creates an advantage for equity capital, which must be weighed against the present tax advantages accorded to debt obligations. Under section 1244 "thick capitalization" is more important than "thin capitalization" since the hedge against loss provided by section 1244 within its limits of $50,000 or $100,000 a year, is valuable in that ordinary loss treatment avoids the section 1211 limitations on deducting a capital loss.

Taxpayer attempts to avoid the limitations of section 166 by having their insolvent corporate debtors issue section 1244 stock on which an ordinary loss was when claimed have been unsuccessful. See Morgan v. Commissioner, 46 T.C. 878 (1966); Hollenbeck v. Commissioner, 50 T.C. 740 (1968), aff'd, 422 F.2d 2 (9th Cir.1970) (stock received in exchange for release of purported debt obligation did not qualify where the "debt" was found to be equity). In addition, notes issued in exchange for section 1244 stock do not retain ordinary loss treatment. Benak v. Commissioner, 77 T.C. 1213 (1981) (worthless note issued on redemption of section 1244 resulted in non-business bad debt treatment).

2. *Small Business Investment Company Stock*

The Small Business Investment Act of 1958 provides for the formation of small business investment companies organized to provide equity capital to small businesses through the purchase of their convertible debentures. These small business investment companies are private corporations with a paid-in capital and surplus of at least $300,000. The Small Business Administration is authorized to lend such a company up to $150,000 through the purchase of the latter's subordinated debentures. Under section 1242, if a stockholder investing in the stock of a small business investment company suffers a loss on the stock, the loss is treated as an ordinary loss and may be utilized in a net operating loss deduction. Also, under section 1243, if the small business investment company itself suffers a loss on stock acquired by it pursuant to the conversion privilege on convertible debentures, the loss is treated as ordinary.

C. LOSS ON SURRENDER OF STOCK VERSUS CONTRIBUTION TO CAPITAL

In Commissioner v. Fink, 483 U.S. 89 (1987), the Supreme Court held that controlling stockholders cannot recognize a loss on surrender of a portion of their stock to the corporation. The taxpayers, husband and wife, owned 72.5 percent of the common stock of the corporation. They surrendered some of their shares reducing their ownership interest to 68.5 percent in order to make the corporation's capital structure more attractive to outside investors. The taxpayers claimed an ordinary loss under section 165 to the extent of the basis in their surrendered shares. The Sixth Circuit allowed the taxpayer's loss deduction by treating each share of stock as a separate investment. Under the "fragmented" view of stock ownership accepted by the Sixth Circuit, gain or loss is recognized separately on the sale or other disposition of each share of stock. Fink v. Commissioner, 789 F.2d 427, 431–432 (1986). The Supreme Court, however, treated the controlling stockholder's stock as a unitary investment:

"A shareholder who surrenders a portion of his shares to the corporation has parted with an asset, but that alone does not entitle him to an immediate deduction. Indeed, if the shareholder owns less than 100 percent of the corporation's shares, any non pro rata contribution to the corporation's capital will reduce the net worth of the contributing shareholder. A shareholder who surrenders stock thus is similar to one who forgives or surrenders a debt owed to him by the corporation; the latter gives up interest, principal, and also potential voting power in the event of insolvency or bankruptcy. But, * * * such forgiveness of corporate debt is treated as a contribution to capital rather than a current deduction. * * * The Finks' voluntary surrender of shares, like a shareholder's voluntary forgiveness of debt owed by the corporation, closely resembles an investment or contribution to capital * * *." (96–97)

For cases reaching the same result see Frantz v. Commissioner, 784 F.2d 119 (2d Cir.1986) (controlling stockholder's voluntary surrender of preferred stock for the purpose of enhancing the value of retained common stock treated as a contribution to capital; because the overall change in the taxpayer's retained interest in the company was miniscule compared to the interest surrendered, there was no justification for treating the change in value as a capital loss, much less as an ordinary one); Schleppy v. Commissioner, 601 F.2d 196 (5th Cir.1979) (non pro rata surrender of stock to improve financial condition of the corporation did not result in an immediate ordinary loss); Tilford v. Commissioner, 705 F.2d 828 (6th Cir.1983) (stockholder denied a capital loss deduction on the transfer of stock to corporate employees; the court upheld Regulations, section 1.83–6(d), which provides that a stockholder transfer of stock to an employee for services rendered to the corporation shall be treated as a stockholder contribution to the corporation's capital followed by a transfer of property to the employee).

In his dissent in *Fink,* Justice Stevens argued that the majority erred in reversing a longstanding interpretation of the Code embodied in the Tax Court's decisions. The Tax Court's opinion in Frantz v. Commissioner, 83 T.C. 162 (1984), adopting the unitary view followed by the Supreme Court, reversed 40 years of Tax Court rulings accepting the fragmentary view that surrender of stock permitted a controlling stockholder to deduct an ordinary loss. See Miller v. Commissioner, 45 B.T.A. 292 (1941); Budd International Corp. v. Commissioner, 45 B.T.A. 737 (1941); Estate of Foster v. Commissioner, 9 T.C. 930 (1947); Downer v. Commissioner, 48 T.C. 86 (1967); Smith v. Commissioner, 66 T.C. 622 (1976), rev'd sub nom. Schleppy v. Commissioner, supra. The Internal Revenue Service acquiesced in the Tax Court's holdings in *Miller,* 1941–2 Cum.Bull. 9, and *Budd International,* 1942–2 Cum.Bull. 3, and did not withdraw the acquiescences until 1977, 1977–1 Cum.Bull. 2. Justice Stevens pointed out that the Commissioner's acquiescence to the Tax Court's position was still on the books at the time the Finks surrendered their stock. According to Justice Stevens: "The value of certain and predictable rules of law is often underestimated. Particularly in the field of taxation, there is a strong interest in enabling taxpayers to predict the legal consequences of their proposed actions, and there is an even stronger general interest in ensuring that the responsibility for making changes in settled law rests squarely on the shoulders of Congress. In this case, these interests are of decisive importance for me." 483 U.S. at 101.

D. SUMMARY OF TREATMENT OF INVESTMENT LOSSES OF INDIVIDUALS

The following is the general pattern of loss treatment for individuals on the worthlessness of their investments in corporations:

1. Stocks, bonds, and other securities (except section 1242 and 1244 items) result in capital losses, allowable in full but only against capital gains plus $3,000 of ordinary income, with an unlimited carry-over of excess losses.

2. Nonbusiness bad debts not represented by "securities", i.e., advances and notes not qualifying under section 165(g)(2)(C), result in short-term capital losses, also allowable in full but only against capital gains (and offset first against short-term gains) and $3,000 of ordinary income with an unlimited carry-over of excess losses.

3. Business bad debts not represented by "securities" (section 165(g)(2)(C)), i.e., advances related to a trade or business of the investor, result in ordinary losses under section 166(a), allowable in full against ordinary income or capital gain and included in the net operating loss deduction.

4. Section 1244 small business stock losses and section 1242 small business investment company stock losses result in ordinary losses, allowable in full against ordinary income or capital gain and included in the net operating loss deduction.

E. SUMMARY OF TREATMENT OF INVESTMENT LOSSES OF CORPORATIONS

The following is the general pattern of loss treatment for corporations when their investments in other corporations become worthless:

1. Stocks, bonds, and other securities (except those in certain subsidiaries) result in long-term capital losses, allowable in full but only against capital gains with a three year carryback and a five year carryforward.

2. Bad debts not represented by "securities," i.e., advances and notes not qualifying under section 165(g)(2)(C), result in ordinary losses, allowable in full against ordinary income or capital gain and included in the net operating loss deduction.

3. Stocks or securities in affiliated (80 percent owned) operating subsidiaries result in ordinary losses (under section 165(g)(3)), allowable in full against ordinary income or capital gain and included in the net operating loss deduction. (If the stock is not worthless, then on liquidation of the subsidiary no loss is allowed on the stock under section 332 but the subsidiary's asset bases and its net operating loss carryovers go to the parent.)

4. Certain corporations, such as small business investment companies and banks, have special rules providing ordinary losses in some situations.

F. REFERENCES

Natbony, Worthlessness, Debt–Equity, and Related Problems, 32 Hast. L.J. 1404 (1981); Young, Income Tax Consequences of Investment Losses of Individuals, 27 Tax L.Rev. 1 (1971); Cohen, Tax Treatment of Shareholder Guarantees of Third Party Loans to Corporations, 39 George Washington L.Rev. 321 (1970); Ohl, The Deduction for Bad Debts: A Study in Flexibility and Inflexibility, 22 Tax Lawyer 579 (1969); Note, Guaranteed Loans and Direct Loans: Equal Treatment under the Law, 16 U.C.L.A.L.Rev. 421 (1969); Note, Shareholder–Creditor Bad Debts under Section 166 of the Internal Revenue Code, 75 Harv.L.Rev. 589 (1962).

With respect to section 1244 stock, see Naples, Section 1244, Small Business Stock Losses: A Reacquaintance That Will Survive Tax Reform and a Proposal for Change, 71 Marq.L.Rev. 283 (1988); Johnson & Cochran, Looking a Gift–Horse in the Mouth: Some Observations and Suggestions for Improving Internal Revenue Code Section 1244, 39 Sw.L.J. 975 (1986); Barrack & Dodge, Section 1244: Is the Intent of Congress Finally Achieved?

6 J.Corp.Tax. 283 (1980); Fleming, The Unfinished Business of Section 1244: Removing the Remaining Traps, 58 Taxes 713 (1980).

SECTION 3. BOND DISCOUNT AND PREMIUM

A. ORIGINAL ISSUE DISCOUNT

INTERNAL REVENUE CODE: Sections 163(e); 483; 1272(a); 1273; 1274(a)–(d); 1275(a)(1), (a)(2), (b), (c).

TAX REFORM ACT OF 1984 GENERAL EXPLANATION OF THE REVENUE PROVISIONS

Staff of the Joint Committee on Taxation 108 (1984).

[Pre–1984] Law

Timing of inclusion and deduction of interest: the OID rules

If, in a lending transaction, the borrower receives less than the amount to be repaid at the loan's maturity, the difference represents "discount." Discount performs the same function as stated interest; that is, it compensates the lender for the use of its money. Sections 1232A and 163(e) of prior law (the "OID rules") generally required the holder of a discount debt obligation to include in income annually a portion of the original issue discount on the obligation, and allowed the issuer to deduct a corresponding amount, irrespective of whether the cash method or the accrual method of accounting was used.[7]

Original issue discount was defined as the excess of an obligation's stated redemption price at maturity over its issue price. This amount was allocated over the life of the obligation through a series of adjustments to the issue price for each "bond period" (generally, each one-year period beginning on the issue date of the bond and each anniversary). The adjustment to the issue price for each bond period was determined by multiplying the "adjusted issue price" (the issue price increased by adjustments prior to the beginning of the bond period) by the obligation's yield to maturity, and then subtracting the interest payable during the bond period. The adjustment to the issue price for any bond period was the amount of OID allocated to that bond period.

7. The premise of the OID rules was that an OID obligation should be treated in the same manner as a nondiscount obligation requiring current payments of interest for tax purposes. To accomplish this result, the rules in essence treated the borrower as having paid the lender the annual unpaid interest accruing on the outstanding principal balance of the loan, which amount the borrower was allowed to deduct as interest expense and the lender was required to include in income. The lender was then deemed to have lent this amount back to the borrower, who in subsequent periods was deemed to pay interest on this amount as well as on the principal balance. This concept of accruing interest on unpaid interest is commonly referred to as the "economic accrual" of interest, or interest "compounding."

The OID rules did not apply to obligations issued by individuals,[8] obligations with a maturity of one year or less, or obligations issued in exchange for property where neither the obligation nor the property received for it was traded on an established securities exchange.

Measurement of interest in deferred-payment transactions involving property: the imputed interest rules

A deferred-payment sale of property exempt from the OID rules was generally subject to the unstated interest rules of section 483. If the parties to the transaction failed to state a minimum "safe-harbor" rate of interest to be paid on the loan by the purchaser-borrower, section 483 recharacterized a portion of the principal amount as unstated interest. This "imputation" of interest was performed by assuming that interest accrued at a rate higher than the safe-harbor rate.

The safe-harbor rate was a simple interest rate; the imputation rate was a compound rate. The safe-harbor and imputation rates were 9 percent and 10 percent, respectively, when the Act became law. The safe-harbor interest rate applicable to certain transfers of land between members of the same family was 6 percent.

* * *

If interest was imputed under section 483, a portion of each deferred payment was treated as unstated interest. The allocation between unstated interest and principal was made on the basis of the size of the deferred payment in relation to the total deferred payments. Amounts characterized as unstated interest were included in the income of the lender in the year the deferred payment was received (in the case of a cash method taxpayer) or due (in the case of an accrual method taxpayer). The borrower correspondingly deducted the imputed interest in the year the payment was made or due.

Reasons for Change

Mismatching and noneconomic accrual of interest

Enacted in 1969, the OID rules were designed to eliminate the distortions caused by the mismatching of income and deductions by lenders and borrowers in discount lending transactions. Prior to that time, an accrual method borrower could deduct deferred interest payable to a cash method lender prior to the period in which the lender included the interest in income. Although the OID rules prevented mismatching in many situations, the potential for distortion continued to exist where the obligation was excepted from the OID rules. Some taxpayers attempted to exploit these exceptions, particularly the exception relating to nontraded obligations issued for nontraded property, to achieve deferral of tax on interest income and accelerated deductions of interest expense.

8. Prior to 1982, the OID provisions applied only to corporate and taxable government obligations. The Tax Equity and Fiscal Responsibility Act of 1982 (TEFRA) extended these provisions to noncorporate obligations other than those of individuals.

For example, in a typical transaction, real estate, machinery, or other depreciable property was purchased for a promissory note providing that interest accrued annually but was not payable until the note matured. The issuer, who used the accrual method of accounting, would claim annual interest deductions for accrued but unpaid interest. The holder, a cash method taxpayer, would defer interest income until it was actually received.

Such a mismatching of income and deductions had serious revenue consequences, since the present value of the income included by the lender in the later period was less than the present value of the deductions claimed by the borrower. The greater the length of time between the borrower's deduction and the lender's inclusion, the greater the loss of tax revenues.

This revenue loss was magnified if the accrual-method purchaser computed its interest deduction using a noneconomic formula such as straight-line amortization, simple interest, or the "Rule of 78's". In Rev.Rul. 83–84, 1983–1 C.B. 9, the Internal Revenue Service stated that interest may be deducted only to the extent it has accrued economically, using a constant yield-to-maturity formula. Some taxpayers, however, took the position that the ruling incorrectly interpreted existing law. Other taxpayers construed the ruling narrowly, as applying only to the precise facts set forth in the ruling.

In light of the significant distortions occurring under prior law, both in the form of mismatching of interest income and deductions and in the form of noneconomic accruals of interest, Congress believed it appropriate to extend the periodic inclusion and deduction rules of sections 1232A and 163(e) of prior law to nontraded debt instruments issued for nontraded property. The same policy objectives that led to the application of these rules to interest on traded debt instruments or instruments issued for cash—namely, better compliance by holders and clearer reflection of income—were believed to apply equally in the case of nontraded instruments issued for nontraded property.

The principal obstacle to applying the OID rules to a transaction in which neither side is traded is the difficulty of determining the issue price of the debt instrument directly. Both the issue price and the redemption price of an instrument must be known to compute the amount of OID. In a transaction involving the issuance of an note for cash, the issue price is simply the amount of cash received. Where the issuer receives nontraded property, however, the fair market value of the property determines the obligation's issue price.[14] Using a "facts and circumstances," case-by-case analysis to determine fair market value in these situations was considered impracticable. Congress believed that the valuation problem could best be resolved by incorporating into the OID rules a mechanism for testing the adequacy of interest in a sale of property already present in the Code—the unstated interest

14. The issue price of the obligation in such a transaction is the value of the property received by the issuer, less any cash down payment made to the holder.

rules of section 483—with certain modifications. An approximation of the maximum fair market value of property (and hence the issue price of the obligation issued in exchange for it) could be arrived at by assuming a minimum rate of interest which parties dealing at arm's-length and without tax motivations could be expected to agree upon.

* * *

Finally, Congress believed there was no justification for continuing the exemption from the OID rules for holders of obligations not constituting capital assets in the holder's hands. Sales of ordinary income assets may involve deferred interest to the same degree as sales of capital assets, and the timing of income in such sales is as important as its character.

While acknowledging the complexity of the OID rules, Congress believed that the rules could be extended to a broader range of transactions without disrupting the routine, legitimate transactions of individuals or small businesses, which might have difficulty applying the rules. The Act exempts many such routine transactions.

Mismeasurement of interest in transactions involving nontraded property

Congress recognized that, under prior law, it was possible for taxpayers in a sale of nontraded property for nontraded debt to achieve unwarranted tax benefits not only by mismatching interest income and deductions, but by manipulating the principal amount of the debt. This could be accomplished by artificially fixing interest at a below-market rate. Although economically the parties were in the same position as if interest had been accurately stated, significant tax advantages often resulted from characterizing the transaction as involving a lower rate of interest and a larger loan principal amount. If recognized for tax purposes, this mischaracterization of interest as principal resulted in an overstatement of the sales price and tax basis of the property. In cases where the property was a capital asset in the hands of the seller, the seller was able to convert interest income, which should have been taxable as ordinary income in the year it accrued, into capital gain taxable at lower rates (and, under the installment method provided in sec. 453, generally only as installment payments were made). If the property was depreciable in the hands of the purchaser, the inflated basis enabled the purchaser to claim excessive cost recovery (ACRS) deductions and, if the property constituted section 38 property, investment tax credits.

These same tax advantages accrued to taxpayers who engaged in low-interest transactions entirely for nontax reasons.

Explanation of Provisions

a. Extension of OID rules

Overview

The Act extends the rules for periodic inclusion and deduction of original issue discount by lenders and borrowers to debt instruments that are issued for property that is not publicly traded, and that are themselves not publicly traded. The Act also repeals * * * the exemption from the income accrual requirement for cash-method holders of obligations not constituting capital assets in the holder's hands. Exceptions from the rules are provided to ensure that they will not apply to * * * *de minimis* transactions * * *.

If either the debt instrument or the property for which it is exchanged is publicly traded, the amount of OID is determined as under [pre–1984] law. The market value of the traded side determines the issue price of the obligation, and the excess of the redemption price over the issue price is original issue discount. Where neither side is traded, the transaction is tested for the adequacy of stated interest in a manner similar to that prescribed in section 483 of [pre–1984] law.

If the stated rate of interest is not equal to or greater than a safe-harbor rate, the issue price is determined by imputing interest to the transaction at a higher rate. The safe-harbor rate and the imputation rate are equal to * * * [the "applicable Federal rate,"] a rate based on the yields of marketable securities of the United States government. [Ed.: The original 1984 legislation imputed interest of 120 percent of the applicable federal rate if the parties failed to specify interest of at least 110 percent of the applicable federal rate. The 1988 Act adopted the applicable federal rate as both the safe-harbor and imputed interest rate.]

* * *

Regulatory authority

The Act authorizes the Treasury Department to issue regulations dealing with the treatment of transactions involving varying interest rates, put or call options, indefinite maturities, contingent payments, assumptions of debt instruments, or other circumstances.

* * *

ILLUSTRATIVE MATERIAL

A. ECONOMIC ACCRUAL OF INTEREST

The ratable deduction and inclusion of original issue discount under the 1969 legislation did not accurately reflect the economic accrual of interest over the life of the bond. For example, a three-year bond with a face amount of $1,418.52 issued for $1,000 reflects an interest rate of 12 percent compounded semiannually (or an effective annual rate of 12.36 percent). Accounting for the $418.52 of original issue discount ratably over the three years would result in a deduction of $139.51 each year for three years.

However, in economic terms, the original issue discount transaction is the same as if the borrower had borrowed additional money each year to pay interest. Interest in each period is computed on the original principal plus the borrowed interest. Using a constant interest rate, the amount of the interest should be lower in the early years and then grow as the outstanding "principal" of the loan increases due to the interest which has been "borrowed" back.[5] This calculation allows the interest expense to be "compounded", i.e., interest is charged on the interest which is borrowed back. The following table illustrates the difference between ratable treatment and economic accrual treatment.

	Ratable Interest	Economic Interest	"Principal" Outstanding
Year 1	$139.51	$123.60	$1,123.60
Year 2	139.51	138.88	1,262.48
Year 3	139.51	156.04	1,418.52

In 1984, the treatment of original issue discount was modified to require that original issue discount deductions and inclusions be calculated on a compounding or constant interest basis. Under section 1272(a)(3), original issue discount is calculated by determining the "yield to maturity" based on semiannual compounding (12 percent in the above example). That rate is then applied to the "adjusted issue price" of the bond. The adjusted issue price is the amount originally paid for the bond plus the amount of the accrued but unpaid interest. Thus, at the beginning of year 3, the adjusted issue price is $1,262.48, reflecting the original issue price of $1,000 and the accrued interest for years 1 and 2. The amount of original issue discount deducted by the borrower and included by the lender for year 3 is $156.04.

The holder of an original issue discount bond is required to include the daily portions of original issue discount for each day the bond is held. Section 1272(a)(1). The daily portion is determined by ratably allocating to each day in a semiannual accrual period the interest increment occurring during that period. Section 1272(a)(3). The issuer deducts original issue discount in the same manner. Section 163(e).

The bond holder's basis in the original issue discount obligation is increased to reflect the amount included in income by the holder. Section 1272(d)(2). If the holder of the obligation disposes of it before maturity, the purchaser steps into the original bondholder's shoes with respect to the remaining original issue discount attributable to the bond. The original bondholder treats any amount received in excess of the adjusted basis as gain on disposition; the second owner is entitled to deduct any such excess over the remaining life of the bond from the amount of original issue discount otherwise required to be included in income. Section 1272(a)(7).

B. ORIGINAL ISSUE DISCOUNT OBLIGATIONS ISSUED FOR PROPERTY

1. *Introduction*

When A sells property to B in a transaction in which some of the payments for the property are deferred, two separate economic transactions

5. This would be the result when a three-year note required annual interest payments but provided that in any year in which interest was not paid, the unpaid interest would be added to principal and would bear interest at the rate stated in the note.

are involved. A is both selling the property to B and loaning B the amount of the unpaid purchase price while B is correspondingly purchasing the property and simultaneously borrowing the unpaid purchase price from A. Original issue discount is present if the stated principal amount of B's obligation is greater than the fair market value of the transferred property.

Prior to the Tax Reform Act of 1969, the courts reached conflicting conclusions on the question of whether original issue discount is created upon the issuance of bonds for property (as opposed to cash) where the value of the property received was less than the face amount of the obligation issued. Compare Nassau Lens Co., Inc. v. Commissioner, 308 F.2d 39 (2d Cir.1962) (original issue discount created), with Southern Natural Gas Co. v. United States, 412 F.2d 1222 (Ct.Cl.1969) (original issue discount not created). In other cases arising under pre–1969 law, the courts were also divided on whether original issue discount could arise on the issue of debentures in exchange for stock of the corporation. In Commissioner v. National Alfalfa Dehydrating & Milling Co., 414 U.S. 817 (1973), the Court declined to pass on the broad question of whether original issue discount could, under pre–1969 law, arise on the issuance of debt obligations in exchange for property other than cash. The Court held that original issue discount did not arise in the case before it upon the issuance of the debentures for the corporation's own preferred stock. The transaction merely constituted the exchange of one form of participation in the corporation for another; the corporation did not incur any additional cost for the use of capital which might be denominated "interest". Further, there was no evidence as to the fair market value of the bonds issued or of the price at which the preferred shares could have been bought on the open market, so that there was a failure to prove the existence of a debt discount in fact. However, in Cities Service Co. v. United States, 522 F.2d 1281 (2d Cir.1974), also a pre–1969 Act case, the court distinguished *National Alfalfa* where the face amount of the debentures exceeded both the stated value of the preferred stock and the original consideration paid in at the time of the issuance of the preferred stock. Thus, the corporation incurred an additional cost in order to retain the use of the capital represented by the preferred stock. The Court of Appeals held that the proper measure of the discount must be determined by reference to the fair market value of the debentures issued (not the property received) and remanded the case for a determination of that fact. See 443 F.Supp. 392 (S.D.N.Y.1978), aff'd per curiam, 586 F.2d 967 (2d Cir.1978). In Texstar Corp. v. United States, 688 F.2d 362 (5th Cir.1982), the court interpreted *National Alfalfa* as permitting original issue discount only if a public market in the corporation's stock or bonds exists to establish the existence of issue discount on the exchange of bonds for stock.

2. *Publicly Traded Bonds or Property*

Some of the problems of the pre–1969 Act cases were resolved by the predecessor to section 1273(b)(3), enacted in the 1969 Act, which adopted the position of the Fifth Circuit in *Texstar.* Section 1273(b)(3) provides that original issue discount arises in the case of bonds issued for property when either the bonds or the property (in the form of stock or securities) is traded on an established securities market and the face amount of the bonds issued exceeds the fair market value of the property received. Regulations, section 1.163–4(a)(1), provide that, for purposes of determining the deduction for the issuer, the term "original issue discount" under section 163 has the same meaning as in the predecessor to section 1273.

3. *Discount Obligations Issued for Other Property*

Presumably the restriction of the original issue discount rules in the 1969 Act to situations involving bonds or property traded on an established securities market was for administrative convenience to avoid some of the difficult valuation problems experienced by the courts in the pre–1969 cases. As described in the Joint Committee Staff's General Explanation of the Tax Reform Act of 1984, supra, page 432, before 1984 the approach of the Code to this problem was to impute interest under section 483 to each payment made in the case of a deferred payment sale in which stated interest was inadequate. In section 1274 Congress dealt with the valuation issue by using the present value of obligations determined by a fixed rate of return as the reference point.

In effect, section 1274 requires that if the stated interest in sales of property on a deferred basis is less than a stipulated interest rate, the rate paid on Federal obligations with a similar maturity,[6] the original issue discount rules apply. For purposes of determining the issue price of the original issue discount obligation, the present value of all payments to be made under the instrument is calculated on the basis of the applicable federal rate. The resulting difference between the hypothetical issue price and the actual payments to be made under the instrument is original issue discount which must be currently included by the seller and deducted by the buyer using a constant interest rate as described above, supra, page 437.

Section 1274A(a) and (b) provide that the discount rate for purposes of section 1274 is not to exceed 9 percent, compounded semiannually, if the stated principal of the obligation is not in excess of $2.8 million, and the obligation is not issued as consideration for the sale or exchange of certain tangible personal property used in a trade or business (section 38 property within the meaning of section 48(b) which, in general, includes depreciable machinery and equipment and certain limited classes of improvements to real property).

The following example illustrates the application of section 1274. Suppose that A agrees to sell property to B for $1,000 on the following terms. Payment for the property will be due three years from the date of the sale and will bear simple interest at 8 percent with all interest to be paid at the end of the third year. Assume that the applicable federal rate is 9 percent. The first question is whether the obligation bears "adequate stated interest". It does not since (a) the stated rate is only 8 percent, (b) the interest is not compounded, and (c) the interest is only payable at the maturity of the obligation. By using a below-market interest rate, A and B have attempted to convert a portion of the financing transaction into a sales transaction. Thus, under section 1274(a)(2), the "imputed principal amount" is treated as the issue price for purposes of determining the original issue discount. The imputed principal amount is defined in section 1274(b) as the present value of all payments due on the debt instrument, using as a discount rate the

6. The applicable Federal rate is determined on a monthly basis. The rate used is the lowest Federal rate for similar obligations in effect in the 3 months prior to the date of the contract of sale. Section 1274(d)(2).

applicable Federal rate.[7] On this basis, the present value of the $1,240 payment to be made in year 3 is $952.19. This amount is then treated as the issue price of the obligation for purposes of determining the original issue discount on the financing portion of the transaction and as the sales price for the sales portion of the transaction.

Section 1274 thus isolates the unstated interest element in the transaction, using the applicable federal rate as the applicable norm. It indicates that economically A sold the property to B for $952.19 and loaned B that amount in return for a promise to pay $1,240 in three years reflecting a 9 percent interest rate, compounded semiannually. B has a basis of $952.19 in the property for purposes of depreciation and sale. On the financing side of the transaction, A is required to include currently the appropriate amount of original issue discount income and B is given a deduction for a corresponding amount, thus matching deduction and inclusion.

If the rate of interest charged and payable under the contract had been equal to the applicable federal rate (or 9 percent in the case of a qualified instrument to which section 1274A(a) applies), the original issue discount rules would not have applied.[8] The agreed price for the property would determine A's gain on the sales portion of the transaction and B's basis for the property. The interest deduction and interest income would likewise be matched because the interest payments must be made currently to prevent the application of the original issue discount rules, thus requiring current inclusion by the cash basis seller.

By using the applicable federal rate to identify the interest element of the transaction, section 1274 avoids the necessity of directly valuing non-traded property for purposes of calculating the original issue discount. In effect, it requires the buyer and seller to use at least the appropriate federal rate on the financing portion of the transaction. The remainder of the payments are then considered to be the price paid for the underlying property. The section thus works backward from a given interest rate to calculate the current value of the property.

4. *Exceptions to Section 1274 and the Application of Section 483*

Some deferred payment sales are not subject to section 1274: sales of a farm or small business by an individual for less than $1 million; the sale of a principal residence; any sale or exchange of property if the total amount receivable under the obligation does not exceed $250,000; and certain sales of patents to the extent the sale price is contingent on income from the patent. Transactions not covered by section 1274 are subject to the imputed interest rules of section 483.

With some exceptions, the amount of imputed interest is calculated for purposes of section 483 in the same manner as under section 1274. Imputed

7. As originally enacted, section 1274 used as the testing rate 110 percent of the applicable Federal rate. If the stated interest was inadequate, then the imputed principal amount was determined on the basis of 120 percent of the applicable federal rate. Thus, in effect, a penalty was imposed if the taxpayers had provided for inadequate interest. Changes in 1985 established the applicable Federal rate as both the testing rate and the rate to be used in determining the imputed principal amount.

8. Under section 1274(d)(1)(D), regulations may be promulgated to permit the taxpayer to use a rate lower than the applicable Federal rate if it can be established that it would have been possible for the taxpayer to borrow in an arm's length transaction at such lower rate.

interest under section 483 is the difference between issue price and the present value of the payments required by the obligation using the applicable federal rate, compounded semiannually, as the discount rate. Section 483(b). Unlike original issue discount under section 1274, however, imputed interest under section 483 is taken into account by a cash basis taxpayer only when payment is received or paid, and by an accrual basis taxpayer when payment is due. Regulations, section 1.483–2(a)(1)(ii). Unstated interest must be allocated to each payment using the constant interest method of section 1272(a). Section 483(a).

Under section 1274A(c), interest on an obligation subject to section 1274 may be reported on the cash method if the stated principal does not exceed $2 million. Cash method reporting must be elected by both the lender and borrower. The election is available only if the lender does not use the accrual accounting method and is not a dealer with respect to the property.

Neither section 1274 nor section 483 applies to hidden interest payable by the issuer with respect to property purchased for personal use. Interest is deductible by the issuer only when paid. Section 1275(b). The holder of the obligation, however, remains subject to reporting interest income under section 1274 or 483 as appropriate. Section 483(e) provides an additional exception for sales of a personal residence between related persons. To the extent that the aggregate sales price of all such sales does not exceed $500,000, the discount rate for computing unstated interest is not to exceed six percent, compounded semiannually.

C. ORIGINAL ISSUE DISCOUNT AND HYBRID SECURITIES

The determination of original issue discount with respect to hybrid securities and investment unit packages, which have been increasingly favored by acquisition-oriented corporations, present difficult conceptual and computational problems. Debentures can be issued with warrants attached, or convertible bonds can be issued with the bondholder given the right to acquire common or preferred stock in the corporation. Some portion of the original issue price of convertible securities may be attributable to the value of the warrants or conversion features. Regulations, section 1.163–3(a), and Proposed Regulations, section 1.1272–2(e) (1986) (continuing the rule of Regulations, section 1.1232–3(b)(2), issued in 1968), provide that, in the case of convertible obligations, no original issue discount is created with respect to the conversion feature. All of the consideration is deemed to be paid for the debt portion of the transaction. In Chock Full O'Nuts Corp. v. United States, 453 F.2d 300 (2d Cir.1971), the court reached the same result as the Regulations for convertible obligations issued in years prior to 1968. Hunt Foods and Industries, Inc. v. Commissioner, 57 T.C. 633 (1972), aff'd per curiam, 496 F.2d 532 (9th Cir.1974), sustained the validity of regulations, section 1.1232–3, holding that no original issue discount was created with respect to the conversion feature in the case of convertible debt obligations. AMF Inc. v. United States, 476 F.2d 1351 (Ct.Cl.1973), is to the same effect. In Honeywell Inc. v. Commissioner, 87 T.C. 624 (1986), the Tax Court applied the same theory to the bonds of a foreign finance subsidiary convertible into common stock of its parent corporation. The court refused to reduce the issue price of the bonds by the value of the conversion feature.

The Regulations provide different treatment for obligations issued as part of an investment unit package that includes a separate option, security or other severable property such as stock warrants. The original issue price of the obligation includes only the consideration paid for the debt portion of the package. The 1969 Act ratified the Regulations' treatment of bonds issued with investment unit packages such as warrants with the predecessor to section 1272(c)(2). The Regulations' treatment of convertible debt also appeared to be approved, since Congress did not extend original issue discount treatment to convertible debentures.

D. CONTINGENT INTEREST AND VARIABLE RATE INTEREST

1. *General*

In the case of obligations issued for cash or marketable securities, original issue discount is the difference between the issue price of the obligation and the amount to be paid at maturity. In the case of obligations issued for property subject to section 1274, the computation of original issue discount depends upon the present value of all payments under the note. Both of these computations require knowledge of the time and amount of payments under the obligations. Determination of the amount of original issue discount is more complex when either the time or amount of payment under the obligation is contingent on some future event, such as the performance of property transferred in exchange for the obligation, or when the interest rate stated in the obligation is variable in accordance with some outside measure of interest, such as the prime rate of a specific financial institution. Proposed Regulations, sections 1.1275–4 and –5 (1986), provide complex devices for dealing with these problems. The following material provides an overview of the Proposed Regulations.

2. *Obligations for Cash or Publicly Traded Property*

With respect to a contingent payment obligation issued for cash or publicly traded property, the obligation is separated into its contingent and noncontingent elements. If noncontingent payments under the obligation are equal to or exceed the issue price, the noncontingent obligation is subject to the original issue discount rules of sections 1271 through 1275. Proposed Regulations, section 1.1275–4(e)(2) (1986). The issue price is the price for the entire obligation, including amounts paid for the contingent portion. As long as the stated noncontingent redemption price does not exceed the issue price, there is no original issue discount. Original issue discount will exist if the noncontingent payments exceed the issue price. Fixed interest payments will be taken into account by the holder and the issuer under their methods of accounting. Contingent interest payments are treated as interest in their entirety, and are taken into income by the holder and deducted by the issuer when the payments become fixed. Proposed Regulations, section 1.1275–4(e)(3)(i) (1986). If the payment of contingent interest is deferred for six months or more beyond the date the interest becomes fixed, the obligation to pay interest is treated as a separate obligation issued on the date the obligation to pay interest becomes fixed and maturing on the date the payment is due. Original issue discount is computed on this separate obligation by treating the fixed interest payment as the stated redemption price and the present value of the future payment as the issue price. Proposed Regulations, section 1.1275–4(e)(3)(ii) (1986).

Proposed Regulations, section 1.1275–4(e)(4), Ex. (1) (1986), illustrate the application of this rule as follows: A sells publicly traded property, with a fair market value of $5,000,000, to B for B's debt instrument calling for payment of $5,000,000 in five years with six percent fixed interest and contingent interest of up to eight percent. Interest is payable annually. The issue price of the entire instrument, and thus the issue price of the noncontingent portion of the instrument, is $5,000,000. The stated redemption price at maturity is also $5,000,000. There is no original issue discount under section 1273(a)(1). The contingent interest payments are interest in their entirety, accounted for by A and B in their taxable years in which the interest becomes fixed.

If a contingent payment on the obligation described in the preceding paragraph became fixed at $100,000 as of December 31, 1986, but is not payable until March 31, 1991, and the deferred interest payment does not bear additional interest, B's obligation to pay the deferred interest is an additional debt obligation subject to the original issue discount rules. The stated principal amount and the stated redemption price at maturity of this separate debt are $100,000. The issue price is the present value of the deferred payment as of the date the interest becomes fixed using the applicable federal rate appropriate to that date. Discounting $100,000 from March 31, 1991 to December 31, 1986, using 11 percent compounded annually as the discount rate, yields a present value of $64,176.69. B is thus treated as issuing a separate debt instrument with an issue price of $64,176.69 to A in satisfaction of the contingent interest under B's original note. A has $64,176.69 of interest income as of the date this obligation is issued, December 31, 1986. The interest on this separate debt instrument is original issue discount allocated to A and deductible by B under the constant interest rate method of section 1272(a)(3), discussed supra, page 437. Proposed Regulations, section 1.1275–4(e)(4), Ex. (3) (1986).

If a debt obligation issued for cash or publicly traded property fails to provide noncontingent payments in an amount equal to the issue price of the obligation (the amount of cash or fair market value of the publicly traded property), all noncontingent payments under the obligation will be treated as payments of principal without regard to whether the payments are designated as interest or principal under the terms of the obligation. Proposed Regulations, section 1.1275–4(f)(1) (1986). Contingent payments must be allocated between principal and interest. The interest element is determined by multiplying the issue price, adjusted in later accrual periods for accrued interest and payments, by the applicable federal rate. Proposed Regulations, section 1.1275–4(f)(2)(ii) (1986). The applicable federal rate is the rate in effect for the date on which the obligation is issued based on the due date for the final payment. The interest portion of contingent payments is taken into account by the holder and the issuer on the date the payment becomes fixed. Contingent payments in excess of interest are treated as principal. Deferred payment of contingent interest that has become fixed in amount as of a certain date is treated as a separate obligation which may in turn generate original issue discount. Proposed Regulations, section 1.1275–4(f)(2)(v) (1986).

Proposed Regulations, section 1.1275–4(f)(4), Ex. (3) (1986), illustrate the operation of this rule as follows: On January 1, 1988, C loans D $2,000,000 in exchange for D's 18 month debt obligation maturing on June 30, 1989. D's obligation provides for three semiannual payments of

$600,000 each, plus contingent payments based on the profits from D's business. Since the last payment is due within three years, the federal short term rate is used as the discount rate. Assume that the federal short term rate for January 1, 1988, is 10 percent. The issue price of D's obligation is $2,000,000, the amount of cash received in exchange for the note. The noncontingent payments total $1,800,000, an amount less than the issue price for the obligation. Thus all of the noncontingent payments will be treated as a return of principal. If C receives a payment of $600,000 on June 1, 1988, without any contingent payment, the full $600,000 is treated as payment of principal. In addition, the obligation will be treated as having $100,000 of accrued interest, computed by multiplying the issue price times the applicable federal rate for the six-month accrual period ($2,000,000 × [10%/2]). The adjusted issue price of D's obligation at the beginning of the second six-month accrual period is the original issue price of $2,000,000, increased by the interest accrued during the first six-month accrual period, and decreased by C's payment of $600,000. The adjusted issue price at the beginning of the second accrual period is thus $1,500,000.

On December 31, 1988, D pays $600,000 plus a contingent payment of $350,000. The $600,000 noncontingent payment is treated as a payment of principal. The $350,000 contingent payment is treated as a payment of interest to the extent of interest accrued on the obligation as of the end of the second accrual period which has not been allocated to a previous payment. Interest accrued during the second accrual period is $75,000 computed by multiplying the adjusted issue price at the beginning of the accrual period, $1,500,000, by the applicable federal rate for the six month accrual period, 10%/2. The total accrued and unpaid interest is thus $175,000 ($100,000 from the first period plus $75,000 from the second period). Thus, $175,000 of the contingent payment is interest and the remaining $175,000 is treated as a payment of principal. The adjusted issue price as of the beginning of the third accrual period is $625,000: the initial issue price, $2,000,000, plus accrued interest, $100,000 + $75,000, less payments of $600,000 and $950,000. This figure also may be derived by subtracting the amounts allocated to principal, $1,375,000 from the original issue price.

At the end of the third accrual period D makes a noncontingent payment of $600,000 plus a contingent payment of $75,000. Proposed Regulations, section 1.1275–4(f)(3) (1986), provide that if the final payment at maturity of an obligation exceeds the outstanding principal amount, the obligation shall be treated as retired for the outstanding principal amount, and the remainder of the final payment is treated as interest. Conversely, if the final payment is less than the outstanding principal, the entire amount of the final payment is treated as principal. In the example, the final payment at maturity exceeds the outstanding principal, which is the same as the adjusted issue price at the beginning of the third and final accrual period, $625,000. Thus D's obligation is retired for $625,000. The remaining $50,000 of the final payment is treated as interest by both C and D on the date of the payment.

3. *Obligations Subject to Section 1274*

If an obligation which provides for both contingent and noncontingent payments is subject to section 1274 (issued for property other than cash or publicly traded securities) or section 483, the noncontingent payments are treated as a separate instrument under the rules of section 1274. Proposed Regulations, section 1.1275–4(c)(2) (1986). The present value of noncontingent payments is used to determine the issue price of this separate obligation. For purposes of computing original issue discount under sections 1272 and 1274, the stated redemption price and the yield to maturity of the obligation are also based on the fixed payments. Contingent payments are separately allocated between interest and principal based upon a present value computation discounted from the time the contingent payment becomes fixed back to the issue date. The amount allocated to principal is the present value of the fixed payment determined as of the issue date of the obligation using the appropriate applicable federal rate as the discount rate. Proposed Regulations, section 1.1275–4(c)(3) (1986). The amount allocable to principal is limited to any fixed or maximum principal amount stated in the obligation. The remainder of the payment is interest which is accounted for by the buyer and seller as of the date the obligation becomes fixed. Payments of contingent amounts which are delayed beyond the date on which the contingent obligation becomes fixed are treated as a separate debt instrument which in turn may require an allocation of imputed interest. Proposed Regulations, section 1.1275–4(c)(3)(iii) (1986).

If an obligation subject to section 1274 states fixed or minimum payments to be made within a specified period of time, but the actual date for payment is not fixed, the issue price, the principal amount of the obligation (and thus the buyer's basis in the property purchased) and the allocation of interest, is to be determined as if the fixed payments are made at the latest date permitted by the instrument. Proposed Regulations, section 1.1275–4(d)(2) (1986). This rule will overstate interest if actual payments are made in advance of the last permissible date. Proposed Regulations, section 1.1275–4(d)(2)(ii)(B) (1986), thus contain provisions for the adjustment of the buyer's basis which is recomputed based on the present value of the payments actually made from the date the obligation was issued.

4. *Variable Interest Rates*

Rather than stating a fixed rate of interest, debt obligations commonly will base the interest rate on some external publicly available standard such as the prime rate of a particular financial institution or the London Interbank Offered Rate (LIBOR). Proposed Regulations, section 1.1275–5 (1986), provide rules for obligations with a variable interest rate that is based on a published objective interest rate available to unrelated borrowers from a financial institution. Interest paid under a variable interest rate which does not satisfy the Proposed Regulation's definition of an objective interest rate is treated as contingent interest subject to the rules discussed in subsections 1 and 2 above. Proposed Regulations, section 1.1275–5(a) and (b) (1986).

If the issue price of an obligation with a variable interest rate equals the stated redemption price, and the stated interest is payable periodically, there is no original issue discount and interest is taken into account by the creditor and issuer under their methods of accounting. If part or all of the stated interest is not payable periodically, original issue discount is determined with respect to unpaid interest based on the amount of interest which accrues on the obligation using the variable interest rate, less any periodic interest actually paid. Proposed Regulations, section 1.1275–5(d)(1) (1986).

If the issue price of a variable interest rate obligation is less than the stated redemption price, the original issue discount attributable to the obligation must be recomputed for each accrual period based on the variable interest rate used for that period. The accrued interest for any period is determined from a "hypothetical adjusted issue price," which is the amount that would have been the issue price of the obligation had the obligation been issued for a fixed rate of interest equivalent to the interest rate on the issue date under the objective interest rate for the obligation. "Hypothetical yield" and "hypothetical interest" are calculated on the basis of this amount to determine the original issue discount element. Proposed Regulations, section 1.1275–5(d)(2)(i), (3)(i) and (3)(iii) (1986).

E. MARKET DISCOUNT

There is an interest element similar to original issue discount present on the purchase of a debt obligation in the market for a price below its stated redemption price. Congress enacted section 1276 in the 1984 Act to insure that this "market discount" is treated as ordinary income on disposition of the bond.

Market discount is defined in section 1278(a)(2) as the excess of the stated redemption price at maturity over the taxpayer's basis in the bond upon acquisition. Gain on any disposition of a market discount bond is treated as ordinary income to the extent of the accrued market discount. Section 1276(a)(1). Market discount accrues to the bondholder ratably for each day the holder owns the bond. Section 1276(b)(1). Alternatively, the bondholder may elect under section 1276(b)(2) to accrue market discount using the economic accrual method of section 1272(a), supra, page 437.

F. REFERENCES

Eustice, Corporations and Corporate Investors, 25 Tax L.Rev. 509, 535 (1970); Reiling, Warrants in Bond–Warrant Units: A Survey And Assessment, 70 Mich.L.Rev. 1411 (1972); Madison, The Deductibility of "Interest" on Hybrid Securities, 39 Tax Law 465 (1986); Lokken, The Time Value of Money Rules, 42 Tax L.Rev. 1 (1986); Spooner, Original Issue Discount: Fundamental Principles and Their Impact upon Marketable Securities, 44 N.Y.U.Inst. on Fed. Tax'n, 32 (1986); ABA Section of Taxation, Report on the Proposed Original Issue Discount Regulations, 40 Tax Law. 481 (1987); Moore, Analyzing the Complex New Proposed Regs. on Imputed Interest and Original Issue Discount, 65 J. Tax'n 14 (1986); Strasen, The Taxation of Convertible and Other Equity–Flavored Debt Instruments, 65 Taxes 937 (1987).

B. BOND PREMIUM

INTERNAL REVENUE CODE: Section 171(a), (b).

REGULATIONS: Section 1.163–12(c)(2).

ILLUSTRATIVE MATERIAL

A. PREMIUM AT ORIGINAL ISSUE

The issuer of a bond with a stated interest rate in excess of prevailing market rates may be in a position to demand a premium for the bond, i.e., consideration in excess of the stated principal amount of the bond. This premium is income to the issuer and is taken into account ratably over the life of the bond. Regulations, section 1.61–12(c)(2). As to the creditor, the premium in effect reduces the interest income. Section 171, as amended in 1986, requires the creditor to amortize premium over the term of the obligation using the constant interest method of section 1272(a). Strangely, the 1986 legislation, which imposed the constant interest method on the creditor, does not address the issuer's income allocation. Section 171(b) requires the holder to amortize bond premium over the full term to maturity, even though the bond may be callable at an earlier date.

Bond premium may also arise as the creditor pays an additional consideration for the privilege of converting the obligation into stock. Section 171(b)(1) excludes from bond premium "any amount attributable to the conversion features."

B. PREMIUM PAID BY THE ISSUER ON REDEMPTION

Bond premium paid by the issuer on redemption of an obligation is deductible by the issuer as additional interest on the obligation. In the case of convertible obligations, however, section 249 limits the deduction for redemption premium to an amount representing a "normal call premium" on obligations that are not convertible. The balance is a capital transaction. Thus, in the case of bond premium paid to redeem convertible bonds, the creditor is not allowed to amortize any portion of the premium attributable to the conversion feature, nor is the issuer allowed an interest deduction for that portion of a premium paid upon redemption of its bonds which is attributable to the conversion feature.[9] This result presumably corresponds to the parallel treatment of original issue discount between issuer and holder, discussed, supra, page 437. However, it should be noted that the treatment of the convertibility feature is different as between original issue discount and bond premium in the case of convertible bonds. The Regulations adopt the view that in the case of convertible bonds, the conversion feature is not separable from the debt for purposes of determining original issue discount, hence preventing a larger original issue discount from resulting; on the other hand, in the case of bond premiums the conversion feature is deemed under the Code to be a feature separable from the debt portion of the obligation and hence the amount, if any, attributable to the conversion element is not deductible as interest.

In Tandy Corp. v. United States, 626 F.2d 1186 (5th Cir.1980), the court denied a deduction under section 163 for premium on conversion of debt into stock. The taxpayer claimed that the excess of the fair market value of the stock issued over the face of the bonds was deductible as interest. The court concluded that under the terms of the indenture conversion extinguished the obligation to pay accrued interest or bond premium. Thus no accrued interest or bond premium was involved. The court did not consider the application of section 249.

In National Can Corp. v. United States, 687 F.2d 1107 (7th Cir.1982), an overseas finance subsidiary issued debentures convertible into the stock of its parent corporation. The parent redeemed its subsidiary's debentures with

9. In Head Ski Co., Inc. v. United States, 323 F.Supp. 1383 (D.Md.1971), aff'd per curiam, 454 F.2d 732 (4th Cir.1972), the court held, contrary to the position of the Internal Revenue Service, that the premium paid to repurchase convertible debentures constituted an ordinary and necessary business expense under the law as it existed prior to the enactment of section 249 in the Tax Reform Act of 1969. The Service then revoked its prior position, and stated that it would follow the decisions in Roberts & Porter, Inc. v. Commissioner, 307 F.2d 745 (7th Cir.1962), and *Head Ski Co.* in situations not covered by section 249. On the other hand, the Service apparently will challenge deductibility where the premium paid is unreasonable in amount. Rev.Rul. 74–210, 1974–1 Cum. Bull. 48.

its own stock, the fair market value of which exceeded the issue price of the debentures. The parent claimed a deduction for the difference as premium under sections 171 and 162. The parent corporation argued that the limitation of section 171(b)(1) applied only to obligations convertible into the stock of the issuing corporation, and not to obligations convertible into the stock of another. The court broadly interpreted section 171(b)(1) to limit deduction of premium attributable to any conversion feature. The court concluded that the premium was due to the unexercised conversion feature of the bonds so that amortization of premium is barred by section 171(b)(1) and Regulations, section 1.171–2(c). The court also disallowed the taxpayer's claimed deduction under section 162 holding that under section 1032 the corporation recognizes no gain or loss when it issues stock in satisfaction of a conversion obligation of the bonds of a subsidiary. (1116) In the District Court the taxpayer also asserted that the value of the conversion feature at the time the bonds were issued reduced the issue price of the bonds thereby creating amortizable original issue discount in an amount equal to the value of the conversion rights. The District Court refused to treat the conversion rights as a separate asset capable of valuation apart from the debt component of the bonds. National Can Corp. v. United States, 520 F.Supp. 567 (N.D.Ill.1981). The taxpayer abandoned this claim on appeal.

CHAPTER 11

DIVIDEND DISTRIBUTIONS

SECTION 1. INTRODUCTION

The income tax treatment of corporate distributions to the shareholder is a complex matter and the rules must be traced through many sections. We start with section 301(a), which generally covers all distributions of property by a corporation to its shareholders in their capacity as shareholders. There are two exceptions: (1) as respects the content of the distribution, stock or rights to stock of the corporation are not considered "property" for this purpose, and (2) as respects the purpose of the distribution, distributions in redemption of stock under certain circumstances and complete liquidations are not considered section 301 distributions. See section 301(f). Section 301(a) is applicable to a broader range of distributions than just dividends in the corporate law sense. Section 301(a) refers to section 301(c), which classifies distributions within the ambit of section 301, between dividends in the tax sense, which are included directly in gross income (section 301(c)(1)), and distributions that are not dividends in the tax sense, which are treated as a return of capital applied against the stock basis (section 301(c)(2)), and if in excess of that basis usually are treated as gain from the sale or exchange of property (section 301(c)(3)), thus bringing the capital gain provisions into play. Section 61(a)(7) also requires that dividends in the tax sense be included in gross income.

Section 243(a)(1) provides corporations with a deduction equal to 70 percent of intercorporate dividends, i.e., dividends distributed by one corporation to another corporation; section 243(c) increases the deduction to 80 percent if the shareholder corporation owns at least twenty percent of the stock of the payor corporation; and section 243(a)(3) extends this deduction to 100 percent for affiliated corporations which so elect. There are numerous limitations on the intercorporate dividends deduction, which is discussed infra, page 507.

Section 316(a) provides the tax definition of a dividend. This definition is in terms of the "earnings and profits" of the corporation. The statutory dividend test is two-fold: any distribution to a shareholder is a dividend if it is out of either (1) earnings and profits accumulated after February 28, 1913, or (2) earnings and profits of the current year regardless of a lack of, or deficit in, accumulated earnings and profits. Earnings and profits differ substantially from taxable income, being more akin to net income in a financial accounting sense. But, because some significant adjustments to earned surplus in the corporate sense are not taken into account in computing earnings and profits, it would not be entirely accurate to say that the taxability of the shareholder depends essentially on the earned surplus account of the corporation.

If the distributing corporation has neither current earnings and profits nor earnings and profits accumulated after February 28, 1913, so that there is not a dividend in the tax sense, then the distribution is applied against the basis of the recipient shareholder's stock under section 301(c)(2), and any excess is taxed as a capital gain under section 301(c)(3). This result would follow where the corporate distribution is from capital or from earnings and profits accumulated prior to March 1, 1913, If the distribution, however, represents an increase in value accrued prior to March 1, 1913, then the excess is not taxable by virtue of section 301(c)(3)(B). The retention of February 28, 1913, as a reference point is a legislative policy decision, not a constitutional requirement.

Section 316(a) eliminates most tracing requirements by specifying in the second sentence that if any earnings and profits exist, the distribution is deemed to be out of such earnings and profits rather than from any other source, and first from the most recently accumulated earnings and profits. But while tracing difficulties are largely avoided, the problem of ascertaining the amount of a corporation's earnings and profits remains. If the earnings and profits of the current year exceed the distribution, the amount of the accumulated earnings and profits is irrelevant. If accumulated earnings and profits are present, the precise determination of the earnings and profits of the current year is likewise unnecessary. But in some situations the precise dollar amount of either current or accumulated earnings and profits may be crucial and it is here that the exact scope of the statutory phrase "earnings and profits" must be determined. As will be seen later, the phrase is only partially defined in section 312, so that resort is frequently made to judicial and administrative interpretation.

Section 301(b) determines the amount of the distribution where property or liabilities are involved, and section 301(d) establishes the basis of the distributed property in the shareholder's hands.

The scope of section 301(a) is qualified by various other sections dealing with corporate distributions, as the cross-references in section 301(g) indicate. Section 302 excepts specified distributions *in redemption of stock* including a distribution *not essentially equivalent to a dividend*—which pretty much presents a statutory cat chasing its tail around. Here the distribution, if not of a dividend character, is treated as in exchange for the stock, which makes applicable the capital gain or loss provisions. Section 331 excepts distributions in complete liquidation of the corporation; and section 302(b)(4) exempts distributions to noncorporate shareholders in partial liquidation of the corporation. In these situations, the distribution also is treated as in exchange for the stock. The definitions of complete and partial liquidations, while having nontax antecedents, are tax words of art, that are somewhat confusing. Thus, the definition of partial liquidation in section 302(e) is likewise, at least in part, stated in terms of a distribution not essentially equivalent to a dividend—again the statutory cat. Certain distributions in corporate reorganizations also are specially treated (sections 354 et seq.), as are certain distributions in redemption of stock to pay death taxes (section 303) and involving related corporations (section 304).

Sections 305, 306, and 307 relate to the distribution of a "stock dividend." In general, these sections treat the distribution as a nontaxable event for the shareholder. However, there are many exceptions which can cause the receipt of the stock dividend to be taxable. In addition, some stock dividends, though they possess a nontaxable character on receipt, may on disposition generate ordinary income to the extent of the amount realized rather than capital gain.

This statutory pattern provides many opportunities for controversies to flourish. Dividend distributions produce ordinary income to the recipient. The shareholder's basis in his stock cannot be offset against dividend distributions. Liquidations, whether partial or complete, and certain stock redemptions achieve exchange treatment in which the shareholder may apply the basis of the redeemed stock against the amount realized. Any gain is capital gain, against which capital losses may be deducted. But since a transaction cast in the form of a partial liquidation or other stock redemption may amount realistically to no more than the distribution of a dividend, the line cannot be clearcut. The differing treatment of dividends, on the one hand, and liquidations, partial liquidations, and redemptions, on the other hand, was of great significance prior to 1987 when long-term capital gains were taxed at a preferential rate. But an equal strain remains on those sections, particularly, section 302(b) and its predecessors, which must distinguish situations in which basis recovery is allowed from those in which the full amount of the distributions is taxable. Further, but also now of importance primarily as a timing matter, the statutory exemption from taxation as current ordinary income of the receipt of many stock dividends provided the shareholder with the opportunity to create capital gain situations through the later sale of the dividend stock unless effective safeguards to prevent this tactic were placed in the statute.

Another facet of the taxation of corporate distributions which has shaped the historical development of Subchapter C should be noted at this point. Where the corporate earnings have not been realized but are represented by appreciation in value of corporate assets, realization by the corporation of that appreciation will produce a corporate level tax on the profit. The corporation then will be faced with distributing its earnings to its shareholders subject to the statutory provisions governing the various methods whereby corporate earnings are transformed into cash in the shareholders' hands. But the corporation-shareholder group may desire to avoid the double tax inherent in this system by avoiding the initial corporation tax. If the appreciated asset is distributed in kind to the shareholders, has realization of profit to the corporation and hence the corporate tax been avoided? For many years prior to the enactment of the 1954 Code, this was a troublesome question. In 1954, the predecessors of section 311 and 336 were enacted specifically to provide for nonrecognition treatment to the corporation with respect to gain or loss inherent in distributed assets, whether by dividend, redemption, or liquidation.

Over the years, numerous limitations were imposed on nonrecognition of gain with respect to distributed property. Finally, the Tax Reform Act of 1986 amended sections 311 and 336 to require that *gain* be recognized by the corporation on the distribution of property, other than in liquidation of the corporation, and that both *gain and loss* be recognized on liquidating distributions. Much of the logic behind the shape of the current provisions, and some of the historical cases to be encountered in the following chapters can be understood only if the existence of these former rules is kept in mind. As section 311 was tightened to limit nonrecognition on distributions of appreciated property, corporate taxpayers attempted to devise increasingly complex schemes to come within the remaining nonrecognition rules, and the courts and Congress were forced to respond. Even after the Tax Reform Act of 1986, there is every indication that corporate taxpayers will continue to seek possible holes in the recognition rules of section 311 so as to avoid the tax on appreciation at the corporate level.

The background of controversial areas involves two other statutory provisions, relating to the corporation rather than the shareholder, which appear in the Code outside of Subchapter C. If corporations are taxed at rates lower than individuals, which was the case for years prior to 1987, retention of corporate earnings and consequent postponement of the shareholder tax are the inevitable results of the treatment of the corporation as a taxpaying entity. As a force in the other direction, the Code contains in sections 531–537 a special tax (at 28 percent) on a corporation which accumulates its earnings for the purpose of avoiding the imposition of the individual tax on its shareholders. Such a special tax presents its own problems of application. By its presence it also precipitates some of the controversial transactions mentioned above when the accumulation of earnings approaches the danger zone created by the section 531 tax, since the shareholders will then usually act to draw some of the earnings out of the corporation. Where the accumulation of earnings largely reflects passive investments by the corporation, such as the holding of stocks and other securities, the statute moves on from the special section 531 tax to a special 28 percent tax (70 percent prior to 1982 and 50 percent from 1982 through 1986) on the undistributed income of a closely-held corporation whose passive income receipts meet the objective standards of sections 541–547.

Both of these penalty taxes were enacted at a time when the maximum rate of tax on individual income substantially exceeded the maximum rate of tax on corporate income, thereby giving rise to an incentive to earn income through a corporation which retained that income. However, under the present rate structure, with corporate rates higher than individual rates, there is no longer an incentive to cause earnings that might otherwise be realized directly by an individual to be realized and accumulated by a corporation. In these circumstances,[1] the reason for these penalty taxes has largely disappeared. Nevertheless, they have not been repealed and remain as traps for the unwary.

The material in this chapter deals with cash and property dividend distributions by the ongoing corporation with respect to its continuing shareholders. Subsequent chapters deal with stock dividends, corporate distributions in redemption of stock, distributions in liquidation of the corporation, and the accumulated earnings tax and the personal holding company tax.

SECTION 2. DIVIDEND DISTRIBUTIONS IN GENERAL

INTERNAL REVENUE CODE: Sections 61(a)(7); 301(a), (b), (c); 312(a), (c), (f)(1) (omitting subparagraph (A)), (k)(1)–(3), (*l*), (n)(2), (4), (5); 316(a); 317(a).

REGULATIONS: Sections 1.301–1(a), (b), (c); 1.312–6(a), (b), (d); 1.312–7(b)(1); 1.316–1(a)(1), (e) Ex. (1); 1.316–2(a), (b), (c).

ESTATE OF DeNIRO v. COMMISSIONER

United States Court of Appeals, Sixth Circuit, 1984.
746 F.2d 327.

WELLFORD, CIRCUIT JUDGE.

The estate of Vincent DeNiro appeals from the tax court's determination that the payment of the estate's tax liability in 1969 by two corporations constituted income to the estate in the form of a constructive dividend. * * * We affirm in part and remand for further proceedings.

I.

The parties to this controversy have been litigating tax matters for many years following the death of Vincent DeNiro under mysterious circumstances in the Cleveland area in 1961.[1] This court first considered matters relating to the DeNiro estate in a review of the convictions of Frank, Louis, and Michael DeNiro, brothers of the deceased, for conspiracy and wilfully attempting to evade federal estate taxes due

1. By requiring distributions, the provisions could perhaps be justified as enforcing the basic policy decision to have a "double" tax on corporate profits on a reasonably current basis, but historically their function was more to prevent accumulations at lower corporate rates.

1. DeNiro died as a result of a bomb detonation when he endeavored to start his car. United States v. DeNiro, 392 F.2d 753, 754 (6th Cir.), cert. denied, 393 U.S. 826, 89 S.Ct. 89, 21 L.Ed.2d 97 (1968).

from Vincent DeNiro's estate. The convictions were affirmed. See United States v. DeNiro, 392 F.2d 753 (6th Cir.), cert. denied, 393 U.S. 826, 89 S.Ct. 89, 21 L.Ed.2d 97 (1968). The court observed that the deceased, known as Vince, "had accumulated wealth in the numbers business in Youngstown, Ohio." Id. at 754. While the gross estate was found to exceed $311,000, no estate tax return had ever been filed. The court also found that Vince was "careful to keep record title of his property in the names of others." Id. at 755. Although during the IRS investigation concerning estate taxes the brothers denied that Vince left any estate, the court found that Vince entirely owned the stock in both Valley Land, Inc. (VLC), a duplex-rental operation, and Cicero's, a restaurant and bar, and owned a majority interest in National Cigarette Service, Inc. (NCS), a vending service corporation. Id. at 754–55 n. 1. The trial judge in the criminal case found that the DeNiro brothers agreed "to gather together and secure permanent possession of these and all other properties which had belonged to their deceased brother to the exclusion of his rightful heirs," the brothers' nieces. Id. at 756. In short, the DeNiro brothers appropriated VLC and NCS and all the assets represented by these corporations after Vince DeNiro's death. The district judge also found that, to cover their conspiracy and the appropriation of their nieces' properties, the DeNiro brothers lied to IRS investigators and forged ownership papers. For reasons not discernible, however, the district judge imposed as punishment only a relatively modest fine and probation. Not until September 1977 were decedent's daughters appointed co-administratrices of decedent's estate by the Mahoning County, Ohio, Probate Court. * * *

This appeal involves income taxes allegedly due from the estate, represented by the official representatives and by the DeNiro brothers as transferees. The tax court upheld assessments of income tax against the estate for the year 1969 * * *. See Estate of DeNiro v. Commissioner, 44 T.C.M. (CCH) 981 (1982). It found as follows:

> During 1969, petitioner owned 65 percent of the stock of NCS and 100 percent of the stock of VLC. At all times relevant hereto, however, the DeNiro brothers controlled the operations of both NCS and VLC. * * * Frank DeNiro, Jr., was the president of both NCS and VLC, and Louis DeNiro was secretary-treasurer of NCS. NCS was in the business of operating vending machines, and VLC was in the business of owning and operating rental apartments.
>
> On or about April 9, 1969, respondent made jeopardy assessments for estate tax, addition to tax, and interest of $1,188,000 against petitioner and the DeNiro brothers, as transferees of the estate. * * *
>
> On or about May 9, 1969, * * * the DeNiro brothers signed a Form 890 (Estate Tax Waiver of Restriction on Assessment and Collection of Deficiency and Acceptancy of Overassessment) consenting to the assessment and collection of an estate tax deficiency

of $81,000, plus interest thereon. Subsequently, respondent made a partial abatement of the original jeopardy assessments and the amount of the assessment remaining after abatement, $104,577.04, was paid by NCS and VLC in 1969.

NCS and VLC paid $89,257.04 and $15,320, respectively, of the assessment. The payment made by VLC represented proceeds of an insurance claim filed by VLC with respect to fire damage to one of its apartment units, while NCS borrowed $69,757.04 of the amount it paid. * * *

Id. at 982.

* * *

II.

Petitioners argue that the tax court erred in characterizing the payments at issue here as constructive dividends to the estate. * * * They also argue that NLS had insufficient earnings and profits to pay a dividend of $89,257.

Receipt of a dividend constitutes gross income under I.R.C. § 61(a)(7); and a dividend is defined under *id.* § 316(a) as "any distribution of property made by a corporation to its shareholders" out of certain funds.

* * *

The tax court concluded that,

> We hold that NCS's and VLC's payment of the assessment made against petitioner for its estate tax liability constituted a taxable dividend to the extent of the respective earnings and profits of each corporation.

[44 T.C.M. (CCH)] at 987.

We affirm the tax court's conclusions as being based upon substantial evidence.

* * *

Having decided that the corporate payments were [subject to section 301], we must next determine the extent of the earnings and profits of NLS [7] at the time of the payment as a potential limiting factor in the amount subject to income tax in 1969. A corporation can distribute a dividend only when its earnings and profits are sufficiently large to allow the payment to come from that category. See I.R.C. § 316(a). Otherwise, a distribution to a stockholder is merely a recovery from his basis in his shares to the extent that he has such a basis; to the extent that the payments exceed the basis, the payments amount to a gain. See id. §§ 316(a), 301(c). Petitioners argue that the earnings and profits available for payment of dividends from NCS were less than the $89,257.04 payment. Petitioners point out that NCS borrowed

7. Petitioners concede that if the payment by VLC is considered a constructive dividend, "the entire $15,320 paid by Valley Land to the estate would constitute a taxable dividend under I.R.C. §§ 301 and 316."

$69,757.04 of the $89,257.04 that it paid. They contend that the current earnings and profits of National Cigarette would permit $41,762.99 to be taxable as ordinary income and $6,544.05 as capital gain, because the estate's basis in NCS stock was $40,950, and $41,762.99 was reflected by NCS's accountant to be the adjusted net income after provision for income taxes for the period ending as of the date of the tax payment, September 17, 1969. The tax court held that the evidence was "insufficient to establish the accumulated earnings and profits of either corporation," and "since petitioner has failed to prove the amount of either corporation's earnings and profits, we must sustain respondent's determination that petitioner had taxable income of $104,577.04 as a result of the payments by NCS and VLC." 44 T.C.M. (CCH) at 987. The commissioner's deficiency determination is presumed to be correct, and the taxpayer has the burden of showing error in the determination. Helvering v. Taylor, 293 U.S. 507, 515, 55 S.Ct. 287, 290, 79 L.Ed. 623 (1935).

The problem with petitioners' position concerning NCS is that while there is a purported deficit in accumulated earnings and profits as of January 1, 1969, claimed to be $96,335, substantial taxable income is reflected for the years 1966, 1967, and 1968, as well as in 1969 if the estate tax payment is deemed not deductible. See Jt.App. at 184. It is difficult to reconcile the claim of accumulated deficit with a consistent pattern of earnings from 1966 through 1969.

In reaching its conclusion, however, the tax court was cryptic. It stated, "the evidence contained in the record is insufficient to establish the accumulated earnings and profits of either corporation." 44 T.C.M. (CCH) at 987. The tax court did not say why the exhibits and the accountant's testimony, substantially unrebutted, were "insufficient" as to NCS; it simply reiterated the above statement and added, "petitioner has failed to prove the amount of either corporation's earnings and profits." Id. The tax court therefore did not address the Commissioner's argument that payment of the estate tax liability by NCS constituted ordinary income to the estate "regardless of whether the corporations had sufficient earnings and profits to make the payment taxable as constructive dividends." Id. at 987 n. 6.

We conclude that this matter should be remanded to the tax court for further consideration and a more specific determination about the sufficiency or insufficiency of the earnings and profits of NCS. If, upon reconsideration, the tax court concludes that NCS's contention is correct at least in part and that some portion of the $89,257 considered as a constructive dividend should be treated as a reduction in basis, it should so indicate and set forth how the sum should be allocated. If the tax court considers that the evidence is insufficient to support the petitioners' contention, it should set out in what respect petitioners have failed to meet the necessary criteria to establish the amount of 1969 earnings and profits. It may also consider further the Commissioner's argument that the entire payment by NCS is taxable as income to the estate regardless whether it is considered a constructive dividend under the rationale of Davis v. United States, 226 F.2d 331 (6th Cir. 1955), cert. denied, 350 U.S. 965, 76 S.Ct. 432, 100 L.Ed. 838 (1956), Weir v. Commissioner, 283 F.2d 675 (6th Cir.1960), and United States v. Goldberg, 330 F.2d 30, 38 (3d Cir.), cert. denied, 377 U.S. 953, 84 S.Ct. 1630, 12 L.Ed.2d 497 (1964). Cf. DiZenzo v. Commissioner, 348 F.2d 122, 125–27 (2d Cir.1965).

* * *

ESTATE OF DeNIRO v. COMMISSIONER

Tax Court of the United States, 1985.
49 T.C.M. 1004.

WILES, JUDGE: The Court of Appeals for the Sixth Circuit remanded this case for us to reconsider the sufficiency or insufficiency of the earnings and profits of National Cigarette Service, Inc. (NCS), for purposes of determining the proper tax treatment of a constructive dividend received by petitioner, Estate of Vincent DeNiro, during 1969.

* * *

The dispute herein involves NCS's $89,257.04 payment in 1969 to satisfy the estate's tax liability. Petitioners argue that NCS's earnings and profits were less than the $89,257.04 payment and, therefore, only part of the payment can be considered a constructive dividend. In our original opinion, we found "the evidence contained in the record is insufficient to establish the accumulated earnings and profits of * * * [NCS] * * *." As directed by the Sixth Circuit, we must make "a more specific determination about the sufficiency or insufficiency of the earnings and profits of NCS." Estate of DeNiro v. Commissioner, 746 F.2d 327, 333 (6th Cir.1984). * * *

After careful reconsideration of the entire record, we must conclude, as we did in our original opinion, that petitioners have failed to carry their burden of proof in establishing NCS's accumulated earnings and profits and, accordingly, we must sustain respondent's determination. Rule 142(a), Tax Court Rules of Practice and Procedure; Welch v. Helvering, 290 U.S. 111 (1933).

The term earnings and profits is not defined in the Internal Revenue Code and does not correspond exactly to taxable income or any of the corporate accounting concepts. See Commissioner v. Wheeler, 324 U.S. 542 (1945), rehearing denied 325 U.S. 892 (1945). "[Earnings and profits] is not an account which will appear on a corporation's books or even on its tax return, and the earnings and profits account will probably be different from the retained earnings or earned surplus accounts that appear on financial balance sheets." Jacoby, Earnings and Profits: A Not So Theoretical Concept—Some Winds of Change, 29 NYU Inst.Tax 649, 653 (1971, Part 1). A corporation's earnings and profits may be derived by making adjustments for items and transactions that are treated one way in computing taxable income and another way in computing earnings and profits. * * * For example, to derive a corporation's earnings and profits its taxable income must be adjusted for: (1) certain items excluded from taxable income which must be included in earnings and profits such as interest from state and local obligations [see sec. 1.312–6(b), Income Tax Regs.]; (2) certain items deducted in computing taxable income which are not deducted in computing earnings and profits such as the section 243 dividends received deduction [see section 1.312–11(a), Income Tax Regs.], and the section 172 net operating loss deduction [see section 1.312–5(d), Income Tax Regs.]; and (3) certain items that cannot be deducted in computing taxable income which may be deducted in computing the earnings and profits such as Federal income taxes, excess charitable contributions, and nondeductible losses [see section 1.312–7(b)(1), Income Tax Regs.].

* * *

A distribution of property by a corporation to its shareholders is taxable as a dividend to the extent of its current earnings and profits calculated at the end of its taxable year, and then to the extent of its earnings and profits accumulated since February 28, 1913, or the date of its incorporation, whichever is later. Section 316(a)(1); section 1.316–2(a)(b), Income Tax Regs. The amount of the distribution which exceeds a corporation's earnings and profits is characterized as a return of capital to the extent of a shareholder's basis in his stock [sections 316(a), 301(c)(2)]; to the extent that the payments exceed the shareholder's basis in his stock, the excess is treated as capital gains [sections 316(a), 301(c)(3)].

We begin our analysis with a computation of NCS's current earnings and profits calculated at the end of its 1969 taxable year; it is undisputed that, to the extent thereof, the $89,257.04 payment is taxable as ordinary income. We agree with petitioner's computation that at the end of its 1969 taxable year NCS had current earnings and profits in the amount of $41,762.99. Thus, that amount of the $89,257.04 payment is taxable as ordinary income; the excess is taxable as ordinary income to the extent of NCS's accumulated earnings and profits.

In the instant case, the only evidence petitioners submitted to establish NCS's accumulated earnings and profits consists of the following: (1) NCS's 1969 U.S. corporate income tax return; (2) NCS's 1969 amended corporate income tax return; and (3) the testimony of Mr. Rogan, NCS's accountant, that as of January 1, 1969, NCS had a "deficit balance of $96,335.90." For the reasons set forth below, we believe that this evidence is insufficient to establish NCS's accumulated earnings and profits.

NCS was incorporated in 1955 and to arrive at a correct determination of its accumulated earnings and profits, adjustments need to have been made to the taxable income and retained earnings of the corporation from 1955 through 1969. Petitioner did not produce any evidence that the proper adjustments were made to NCS's taxable income and retained earnings since 1955 to derive NCS's accumulated earnings and profits as of January 1, 1969. What petitioner did present at trial was a schedule, attached to NSC's 1969 amended corporate tax return, titled "Reconciliation of Retained Earnings Account." According to this schedule, the balance of retained earnings as of December 31, 1967, was ($105,484.64). NCS made various adjustments, based upon an IRS audit for the years 1962 through 1967, to the retained earnings account and arrived at a revised balance as of December 31, 1968, of ($96,335.90).

We are not bound to accept testimony at face value even when it is uncontroverted if it is improbable, unreasonable, or questionable. * * * Mr. Rogan's assertion, that as of January 1, 1969, NCS had an accumulated earnings and profits deficit of $96,335.90, although uncontroverted, nonetheless is highly questionable. As we stated earlier, accumulated earnings and profits does not correspond exactly to a retained earnings account, and Mr. Rogan used these terms synonymously. Indeed, the schedule attached to NCS's amended return is titled "Reconciliation of Retained Earnings Account." Petitioners failed to submit any evidence which established that NCS's retained earnings were the same as its accumulated earnings and profits. Moreover, no corroborating evidence was presented to substantiate that the alleged $105,484.64 deficit in retained earnings as of December 31, 1967, was the result of proper adjustments to NCS's taxable income and retained earnings from 1955 through 1967.[5] Nor did petitioners adequately explain the nature of the adjustments made to the deficit for the years 1967 through 1969. Finally, on NCS's 1969 amended return, it reported that it earned taxable income for the years 1966, 1967, and 1968 in the respective amounts $19,309.61, $35,401.60, and $9,719.91. We find it difficult to reconcile petitioners' claim of an accumulated earnings and profits deficit with NCS's consistent pattern of earnings from 1966 through 1969. This was unexplained by Mr. Rogan and makes his testimony concerning NCS's accumulated earnings and profits deficit even less believable. Accordingly, we must hold, as we did in our original opinion, that petitioners have failed to carry their burden of proof on this issue. * * *

To reflect the foregoing,

Our prior decision will be reentered.

ILLUSTRATIVE MATERIAL

A. DISTRIBUTIONS OUT OF EARNINGS AND PROFITS

1. *General*

Regulations, section 1.316–2, provide rules for ascertaining the source of a distribution. Under the Regulations, the accumulated earnings and profits are significant only if the earnings and profits of the current year do

5. Mr. Rogan has been NCS's accountant since 1969 or 1970. He was initially engaged by NCS's officers "to participate in a tax situation involving the years 1962 through 1967." There is no evidence that Mr. Rogan ever examined the corporate books and records for the years 1955 through 1967 in order to make the proper adjustments to the retained earnings account which would be necessary to derive NCS's earnings and profits, as of December 31, 1967.

not cover the total distributions for the year. See Regulations, section 1.316–1(a)(1). In the latter event, the Regulations provide that if there are some current earnings and profits then the current earnings and profits are prorated among all of the year's cash distributions and the remaining amount of the distributions is charged against accumulated earnings and profits as of the beginning of the year in the order in which the distributions were made. Although the Regulations do not expressly apply this rule if one or more of the distributions is of property, no other rule is provided to govern such a case, and logically the same rule should be applied. Suppose that as of January 1, Y Corporation had no accumulated earnings and profits. From January 1 through June 30 it had operating profits (for earnings and profits purposes) of $50,000, and on July 1 it distributed $40,000 in cash to its shareholders. As of December 31, Y Corporation had only $30,000 of current earnings and profits for the year. Only $30,000 of the July 1 distribution is taxable as a dividend because current earnings and profits always are determined at the end of the year, not at the time of the distribution.

If the operating result for the current year is a loss, so no current earnings and profits exist, then a distribution during the year will be charged against accumulated earnings and profits computed to the date of the distribution. If the actual current earnings and profits or loss to the date of the distribution cannot be ascertained, then the current loss of the year is prorated and applied to the accumulated earnings and profits as of the beginning of the year. See Rev.Rul. 74–164, 1974–1 Cum.Bull. 74, for examples applying the foregoing rules. Suppose that on January 1, X Corporation had accumulated earnings and profits of $40,000. For the period January 1 through June 30, it had an operating loss (for earnings and profits purposes) of $50,000, but as of December 31, it had current earnings and profits for the year of $10,000. On July 1, X Corporation distributed $50,000 of cash to its shareholders. Even though as of July 1, the operating loss incurred during the first half of the year would have eliminated the accumulated earnings and profits if the corporate books had been closed at that time, the entire distribution is a dividend. Since the corporation did not in fact incur a loss for the year, but rather earned $10,000, the loss accrued as of July 1 did not reduce accumulated earnings and profits, which as of July 1 remained $40,000.

Allocation of earnings and profits among distributions with respect to different classes of stock presents more difficult problems where one class of stock has dividend priorities established by the corporate charter. Rev.Rul. 69–440, 1969–2 Cum.Bull. 46, involved a corporation which had three classes of stock, the first two of which had priority with respect to dividend payments. The corporation distributed amounts to the first two classes of stock in excess of earnings and profits. The Ruling held that if the preferred stock, the first priority stock, had dividend priority under the corporate charter, then earnings and profits were first to be allocated to all of the dividends paid on the preferred stock. If this treatment exhausted earnings and profits and distributions were made with respect to other classes of stock, then those distributions simply reduced the basis of that stock.

2. *Timing of Dividend Inclusion*

A dividend is included in the shareholder's gross income when "received," regardless of whether the shareholder uses the cash receipts or accrual method. See Commissioner v. American Light & Traction Co., 156 F.2d 398 (7th Cir.1946), relying on the rule in Regulations, section 1.301–1(b), and rejecting the other possible dates such as declaration or record; Rev.Rul. 64–290, 1964–2 Cum.Bull. 465. See also Bush Bros. & Co. v. Commissioner, 73 T.C. 424 (1979), aff'd, 668 F.2d 252 (6th Cir.1982) (on facts, shareholders did not constructively receive dividends prior to distribution where shareholder control over payment date was minimal); Caruth Corp. v. United States, 865 F.2d 644 (5th Cir.1989) (dividend on stock transferred by charitable gift after declaration date but before record date was taxable to charitable donee, not donor). Similarly, the date of payment (and not the date of declaration) is the date of distribution from the standpoint of the corporation and, accordingly, dividends are taken into account to reduce earnings and profits in the year of payment, Rev.Rul. 62–131, 1962–2 Cum. Bull. 94. Contra, Commissioner v. Goldwyn, 175 F.2d 641 (9th Cir.1949). Dividend checks payable and mailed on December 31 affect earnings and profits for the corporation in that year, even though the shareholder does not include the dividend in income until the following year. Rev.Rul. 65–23, 1965–1 Cum.Bull. 520.

B. DISTRIBUTIONS NOT OUT OF EARNINGS AND PROFITS

1. *General*

A distribution not out of earnings and profits, i.e., where there are neither earnings and profits of the current year nor accumulations since February 28, 1913, is regarded as a distribution of capital under section 316(a) and it falls under the phrase "is not a dividend" in section 301(c)(2). The distribution is applied first to reduce the shareholder's basis for the stock to zero, section 301(c)(2), and any excess results in capital gain, section 301(c)(3). Johnson v. United States, 435 F.2d 1257 (4th Cir.1971), held that where the taxpayer had several blocks of stock with different bases, a distribution on the stock not out of earnings and profits was required to be treated as if made pro rata among the blocks of stock in order to determine the gain realized by the taxpayer on the distribution; he was not allowed to aggregate the total basis in the stock and offset that total against the amount of the distribution.

2. *Pre–March 1, 1913 Profits*

Distributions traceable to pre-March 1, 1913 profits are likewise treated as a return of capital. Since section 316(a) provides that for tax purposes all of the earnings and profits accumulated after February 28, 1913 must be distributed before a distribution may be regarded as out of the pre-March 1, 1913 profits, such latter distributions are unlikely to occur in the case of profitable corporations. In addition, as respects other corporations, most pre-March 1, 1913 situations have passed from the tax picture. The favored treatment accorded pre-March 1, 1913 earnings and increases in value is pure Congressional generosity, not constitutional mandate. See Lynch v. Hornby, 247 U.S. 339 (1918).

3. *Parent and Subsidiary Earnings and Profits*

The earnings and profits of parent and subsidiary corporations are generally not consolidated for purposes of determining whether distributions by the parent corporation to its shareholders are out of earnings and profits and hence taxable as dividends. But compare the result where the corporations file a consolidated return, discussed infra, Chapter 24. As a result, it is possible for the parent corporation to make distributions to its shareholders which will not be treated as dividends despite the existence of earnings and profits in the subsidiary corporation. Suppose that X Corporation, which has earnings and profits, wishes to make cash available to a shareholder but the shareholder does not want the distribution treated as a dividend. The shareholder transfers the stock of X Corporation to Y Corporation, a newly formed holding company, in a section 351 exchange. Y Corporation then obtains a loan from a bank, secured by the X Corporation stock, and distributes the loan proceeds to the shareholder. Dividends are then paid by X Corporation to Y Corporation, which it uses to pay off the bank loan. Assuming that the distribution by Y Corporation to the shareholders is made in a taxable year which ends before dividends are paid to it by X Corporation, and if the form of the transaction is respected the taxpayer would have achieved return of basis treatment (section 301(c)(2)) for what is in effect a distribution of the subsidiary's profits. However, Rev.Rul. 80–239, 1980–2 Cum.Bull. 103, held that the distribution from Y Corporation was in fact a disguised dividend paid by X Corporation. Section 304, discussed infra, page 592, was amended in 1982 specifically to govern such transactions, and reaches substantially the same result as the Ruling through different mechanics.

C. DETERMINATION OF EARNINGS AND PROFITS

1. *General*

The earnings and profits of a year are not synonymous with taxable income, but rather are closer to book net income. Recent statutory rules governing the determination of earnings and profits increasingly have moved the concept closer to economic income than to either taxable or book income. Nevertheless, the starting point for computing earnings and profits is taxable income, which must then be adjusted to take into account income items excluded from taxable income, expenses (not chargeable to a capital account) which are disallowed as deductions, and myriad differences regarding the timing of income and deductions. Taxable income is used as a starting point, in part, because it is an amount which must be computed in any event based on an ascertainable standard. However, taxable income must be adjusted to account for items of economic income and expenditure not reflected in the income tax base. Accumulated earnings and profits is not earned surplus, in the corporate sense, but the aggregate of annual earnings and profits, as adjusted for distributions and certain other transactions involving shareholders.

2. *Treatment of Income Items*

Most of the items of wholly or partially exempt income, such as tax-exempt interest, life insurance proceeds, and intercorporate domestic dividends, are included in earnings and profits. Regulations, section 1.312–6(b). But some items excluded from gross income are also excluded in the computation of earnings and profits. Thus, those subsidies or payments to a corporation regarded as nontaxable contributions to capital under section 118 do not constitute earnings and profits, Rev.Rul. 66–353, 1966–2 Cum.Bull. 111. But if payments are includible in income, then earnings and profits are affected. Cf. Hayutin v. Commissioner, 31 T.C.M. 509 (1972). Where receipts are treated as contributions to capital rather than as taxable income for services, and thus have no effect on earnings and profits, no depreciation deduction is allowed with respect to the property under Rev.Rul. 66–353, and hence earnings and profits in subsequent years would be increased correspondingly. Gifts presumably should not be included in earnings and profits. Diebold v. Commissioner, 12 T.C.M. 167 (1953). But see Cummings v. Commissioner, 73 F.2d 477, 480 (1st Cir.1934). Although there is no express authority on point, it appears that section 312(f)(1), discussed infra, applies to exclude permanently from earnings and profits amounts received on the issuance of the corporation's own stock or on the exercise of certain stock options, which are excluded from income by section 1032.

A bad debt previously deducted without an income tax benefit, but which nevertheless reduced earnings and profits, increases earnings and profits on its recovery. Rev.Rul. 58–546, 1958–2 Cum.Bull. 143; but see Lasater's Estate v. Scofield, 74 F.Supp. 458 (W.D.Tex.1947).

A cancellation of indebtedness of the corporation will increase earnings and profits if the cancellation results in taxable income. Schweppe v. Commissioner, 168 F.2d 284 (9th Cir.1948), aff'g 8 T.C. 1224 (1947). The same is true if the cancellation is excluded from income because of the tax benefit rule. Rev.Rul. 58–546, supra. But where the cancellation is excluded from income under section 108 (which for years after 1986 applies only if the corporation is insolvent or the debt is discharged in a Title XI bankruptcy proceeding) and there is a corresponding basis adjustment under section 1017, then no current increase in earnings and profits results from the cancellation. Section 312(1); see also Rev.Rul. 58–546, supra. To the extent that there is no basis reduction, however, earnings and profits must be increased, even though other tax attributes are reduced under section 108(b).

3. *Treatment of Deduction Items*

Most deduction items disallowed in computing taxable income are nonetheless subtracted in determining earnings and profits. Such items include federal income taxes, unreasonable compensation (to the extent not recharacterized as a dividend), excess charitable contributions, disallowed capital losses, and deductions disallowed on grounds of public policy under sections 162(c), (e), (f), and (g). See Rev.Rul. 77–442, 1977–2 Cum.Bull. 264.

A deduction arising from a net operating loss carryover does not reduce current earnings and profits, because the adjustment to earnings and profits was made in the year the loss was incurred. Similar treatment is accorded to capital loss carryovers under section 1212. See also Rev.Rul. 71–165, 1971–1 Cum.Bull. 111 (amortizable bond premium on tax-exempt bonds which is nondeductible under section 171(a)(2) reduces earnings and profits in the year to which the amortizable bond premium is attributable).

Some deductions permitted in computing taxable income are eliminated in computing earnings and profits. Regulations, section 1.312–6(c), provide that a percentage depletion deduction allowed in computing taxable income must be adjusted to the cost depletion method for the computation of earnings and profits. Similarly, the intercorporate dividends received deduction is disallowed. Although a charitable contribution deduction contribution equal to the fair market value of property donated to charity may be allowable under section 170, Rev.Rul. 78–123, 1978–1 Cum.Bull. 87, held that a corporation's earnings and profits are reduced only by the adjusted basis of the property since the appreciation element had never entered into earnings and profits. Kaplan v. Commissioner, 43 T.C. 580 (1965) (NA), is to the contrary.

4. *Treatment of Matters of Timing*

In matters of timing, earnings and profits follow taxable income, unless Congress acts to change this result. Bangor & Aroostook R. Co. v. Commissioner, 193 F.2d 827 (1st Cir.1951). Hence, a reserve for estimated future expenses, while proper under accounting principles, would not reduce earnings and profits if not deductible for tax purposes. See Rev.Rul. 66–35, 1966–1 Cum.Bull. 63 (amortizable bond premium and bond discount on taxable bonds are reflected in earnings and profits in the same year in which includible or deductible in computing taxable income); Rev.Rul. 60–123, 1960–1 Cum.Bull. 145 (corporation deducted interest and taxes for tax purposes, but capitalized such items on its books for regulatory purposes; held, such items are deductible in computing earnings and profits in the same manner and year as allowed for purposes of computing taxable income).

Section 312(f)(1) directs that realized gains and losses be taken into account in computing earnings and profits in the year which they are recognized. Thus, for example, gain deferred on a like-kind exchange under section 1031 does not increase earnings and profits. On the other hand, when gain realized on the sale of property is reported on the installment basis under section 453, the entire gain is added to earnings and profits in the year of the sale, rather than as each installment is received. Section 312(n)(5). For installment sales made prior to September 30, 1984, gain increases earnings and profits only as installments are received. See Regulations, section 1.312–6(a). If it ultimately is determined that the taxpayer has realized an overall loss on the transaction, earnings and profits are decreased in the year the loss is realized. Luckman v. Commissioner, 56 T.C. 1216 (1971).

In computing taxable income, accelerated depreciation deductions are allowed under section 168, and section 179 permits up to $10,000 of certain capital expenses to be deducted currently. For computing earnings and profits, however, section 312(k)(3) provides that: (1) amounts expensed under section 179 must be deducted ratably over a five-year period; and (2) depreciation deductions for tangible property to which section 168 applies (after deducting from basis amounts expensed under section 179) must be computed under the less accelerated alternative depreciation system of section 168(g)(2). For property placed in service before 1987, section 312(k)(1) provides that depreciation generally will be computed for earnings and profits purposes as if straight-line depreciation had been taken, even though the corporation may have utilized accelerated depreciation in computing taxable income. Section 312(k) is designed to prevent the distribution of nontaxable dividends attributable to the excess of accelerated depreciation over the lesser amount of depreciation considered more accurately to reflect economic decline in value. See S.Rep. No. 91–552, 91st Cong., 1st Sess. 176 (1969). Under Regulations, section 1.312–15(a), section 312(k) also applies to amortization under section 169, 184, 187, 188, or "any similar provision."

Because depreciation is allowed at a different rate for earnings and profits purposes, depreciable property has a different basis for this purpose. Accordingly, the gain or loss on the sale of depreciable property for earnings and profits purposes will differ from the taxable gain or loss. Also, because depreciation on manufacturing plant and equipment must be treated as an inventory cost under section 263A, inventories will differ for earnings and profits purposes from those used in computing taxable income.

Section 312(n) requires a number of other adjustments to earnings and profits to reflect more accurately a corporation's economic gain or loss. Among the most significant are that: (1) earnings and profits be increased annually by the "LIFO recapture amount," which generally speaking is tantamount to requiring that earnings and profits be computed using only the first in-first out inventory method; (2) deductible intangible drilling and development costs and solid mineral exploration and development costs be capitalized and amortized in future years; and (3) long term contracts be reported on the percentage of completion method rather than the completed contract method.

5. *Stock Option Situations*

In Luckman v. Commissioner, 418 F.2d 381 (7th Cir.1969), a shareholder in 1961 received a cash distribution from a corporation which he treated as a nontaxable return of capital. Between 1957 and 1962, the corporation had sold to its employees stock under restricted stock options (see section 424(b)), at a purchase price which was about $3.4 million less than the fair market value of the stock at the time of sale. The taxpayer argued that the difference between the option price and the fair market value reduced the earnings and profits of the corporation, creating a deficit in the corporation's earnings and profits account, and thus rendered the distributions received by the taxpayer nontaxable. The Tax Court held that earnings and profits should not be so reduced as the result of the exercise of the stock options (50 T.C. 619 (1968)), but the Court of Appeals reversed:

"As used in federal taxation, [the earnings and profits] concept represents an attempt to separate those corporate distributions with respect to stock which represent returns of capital contributed by the stockholders from those distributions which represent gain derived from the initial investment by virtue of the conduct of business. The crucial issue is whether a given transaction has a real effect upon the portion of corporate net worth which is not representative of distributed capital and which results from its conduct of business. In order to make this determination it is necessary to scrutinize the economic effects of the a particular transaction as well as its character and relation to the corporate business. * * *"

"Had the compensation been paid in cash and then used to purchase stock, there could be no question that the corporation had incurred a true economic expense which reduced earnings and profits. The amount of corporate assets available for distribution to those who owned the stock at the time of the transaction is reduced to the same extent in either case. The economic effect of the two transactions is identical." (383–84)

In Divine v. Commissioner, 59 T.C. 152 (1972), the Tax Court again considered the proper treatment for earnings and profits purposes of the issuance of stock pursuant to the exercise of a restricted stock option. Divine was a shareholder in the same corporation as was involved in *Luckman.* Since the appeal in *Divine* did not go to the Seventh Circuit, the Tax Court reaffirmed its view that earnings and profits were not reduced by the aggregate difference between the option price and the market value of the

stock options were essentially capital transactions and were not viewed by Congress as compensatory in nature. Accordingly, unlike compensatory non-statutory options, no earnings and profits reduction should be allowed. The Tax Court was again reversed. 500 F.2d 1041 (2d Cir.1974) (one dissent). The Court of Appeals concluded that, while Congress changed the income tax treatment of a recipient of a stock option in section 421–424, it did not change the compensatory character of a stock option transaction. See also Anderson v. Commissioner, 67 T.C. 522 (1976), aff'd per curiam, 583 F.2d 953 (7th Cir.1978) (where a subsidiary granted an employee an option to purchase stock of the parent corporation, the subsidiary's earnings and profits were reduced under the *Luckman* rule, not the earnings and profits of the parent corporation; the Tax Court viewed the transaction as if the parent had contributed cash to the subsidiary, the subsidiary purchased the parent's stock, and then issued that stock upon the exercise of the option by the subsidiary's employee).

The results in *Luckman* and *Divine* should be the same for options that are now governed by section 422A or by section 83 and Regulations, section 1.421–6.

6. *Treatment of Capital Surplus Items*

Items which for an accountant would be treated as some form of capital surplus may for tax purposes be included in the computation of earnings and profits. Thus, taxable gains or losses on the sale of donated property (donated surplus) will enter into earnings and profits. Variations will also appear when there is a capitalization of earned surplus through the issuance of an exempt stock dividend, since earnings and profits are not affected by the capitalization, infra, page 531. Query how gains or losses on the sale of treasury stock (treasury stock surplus) should be treated since those gains or losses are not recognized under section 1032 and, where cash is received on the sale, will never enter the tax account. See Deutsch v. Commissioner, 38 T.C. 118 (1962), where the court held that the transfer on the books of the corporation of an amount from the surplus account to the capital account upon the issuance of new stock did not reduce earnings and profits for tax purposes.

7. *Method of Accounting–Federal Income Tax Costs*

Regulations, section 1.312–6(a), first sentence, state that the computation of earnings and profits is determined basically by the method of accounting used by the taxpayer. However, in the case of cash method taxpayers, the treatment of federal income taxes has proved troublesome. Helvering v. Alworth Trust, 136 F.2d 812 (8th Cir.1943); Webb v. Commissioner, 67 T.C. 1008 (1977), aff'd per curiam, 572 F.2d 135 (5th Cir.1978), and Rev.Rul. 70–609, 1970–2 Cum.Bull. 78, held that a cash basis corporation, in computing earnings and profits for the year, could not subtract the federal income tax attributable to that year but not paid until a following year. But Drybrough v. Commissioner, 238 F.2d 735 (6th Cir. 1956), and Demmon v. United States, 321 F.2d 203 (7th Cir.1963), permitted such subtraction. For an accrual basis corporation, federal income taxes are taken into account in determining earnings and profits for the year to which the tax relates, even in the case of a deficiency which is not discovered and paid until a later year. Deutsch v. Commissioner, 38 T.C. 118 (1962). An income tax refund arising from a net operating loss carryback is taken into account for purposes of earnings and profits in the year in which the net operating loss occurred, not in the year to which it is carried back. *Deutsch,* supra; Rev.Rul. 64–146, 1964–1 (Part 1) Cum.Bull. 129.

8. *Effect of Distributions*

Accumulated earnings and profits represents a running account, which is based upon the algebraic sum of the yearly earnings and profits or loss figures from the commencement of the corporate life, reduced by distributions chargeable to earnings and profits. Thus, distributions of taxable dividends reduce the accumulated earnings and profits. Section 312(a). Deficits in the accumulated earnings and profits resulting from operating losses must be made up by subsequent earnings and profits before the account will be on the plus side. But an impairment of capital resulting from capital distributions need not be restored. Hence a distribution treated as a dividend under corporation law but not constituting a dividend for tax purposes because the requisite earnings and profits do not exist, does not produce a deficit in the earnings and profits account and does not prevent subsequent earnings from producing a plus figure for accumulated earnings and profits. Meyer v. Commissioner, 7 T.C. 1381 (1946) (involving stock redemptions); Estate of Uris v. Commissioner, 68 T.C. 448 (1977) (same result; deficit in earnings and profits can be created only by operating losses).

The cancellation by a corporation of a shareholder's debt to the corporation is a distribution of property to the shareholder that reduces earnings and profits, Shephard v. Commissioner, 340 F.2d 27 (6th Cir.1965). In Maher v. Commissioner, 55 T.C. 441 (1970), the Tax Court held that the assumption of a shareholder's liability on a note constituted a distribution which was the equivalent of money and was therefore a taxable dividend in the year of the assumption to the extent of earnings and profits, which were reduced accordingly. The Court of Appeals reversed, holding that a dividend resulted, not in the year the liability was assumed, but in the year payments were actually made by the corporation on the principal obligation; the taxpayer had remained secondarily liable on the note assumed by the corporation and hence the dividend arose only at the time of payment. 469 F.2d 225 (8th Cir.1972). The Internal Revenue Service announced in Rev. Rul. 77–360, 1977–2 Cum.Bull. 86, that it would follow the Court of Appeals decision in cases involving similar facts.

Rev.Proc. 75–17, 1975–1 Cum.Bull. 677, provides guidelines for the treatment of distributions which are claimed to be nontaxable in whole or in part.

D. EARNINGS AND PROFITS CONCEPT IN OTHER SITUATIONS

For taxable years beginning in 1990 and thereafter, earnings and profits principles are used, in part, in determining adjustments includable in alternative minimum taxable income for corporations. See supra, page 276.

The computation of earnings and profits presents special problems in connection with other corporate transactions, such as dividends in kind, infra, page 479, stock redemptions, infra, page 590, S Corporations, infra, page 672, corporate reorganizations, infra, page 800, consolidated returns, infra, page 1042, and the accumulated earnings tax, infra, page 1064.

E. DESIRABILITY OF USE OF EARNINGS AND PROFITS CONCEPT AS A TEST OF A TAXABLE DIVIDEND

A number of commentators,[2] as well as a report prepared by the staff of the Senate Finance Committee,[3] have recommended elimination of the earnings and profits concept. These sources argue that the concept is both unnecessary to prevent avoidance of two-level taxation and undesirable from the standpoint of complexity of tax administration. In general, the proposals recommend that all corporate distributions simply be treated as ordinary income.

The following excerpt from Colby, Blackburn and Trier, Elimination of "Earnings and Profits" from the Internal Revenue Code, 39 Tax Lawyer 285 (1986) analyzes some additional aspects of the earnings and profits issue:

* * *

"IV. THE EARNINGS AND PROFITS LIMITATION ON CORPORATE DISTRIBUTIONS

"The dual corporate-shareholder nature of the E & P regime leads to several intractable problems in determining the taxability of corporate distributions. These problems arise, in part, because the relationship between the amount of E & P at the corporate level and the economics of the shareholder investment can be altered by sales of stock and other transactions. Moreover, because of the dual orientation of the concept, the effects of distortions in the computation of earnings are either permanent, or are reversed much later than would be the case if only the treatment of the corporation were at issue.

* * *

"We conclude that the E & P limitation should be eliminated. The limitation causes a considerable amount of complexity, both in formulating the proper rules for computation of E & P and in applying the rules once formulated. It also appears impossible to formulate a more easily administrable set of rules that does not compromise some policy objective, however the purpose of the statute is interpreted. Finally, because of these problems, the limitation permits a considerable amount of abuse—i.e., the bailout of corporate earnings without policy justification.

"A. The Two–Tiered System

"A central facet of the current taxation of corporate distributions is the two-tiered method of computation. * * *

"There are two common criticisms of the two-tiered test that do not alone warrant the rejection of the E & P concept. The first concerns the computation of current E & P with respect to distributions to a shareholder who is not a shareholder for the entire year. Under section 316(a)(2), such a shareholder will be subject to dividend treatment if E & P arise by the end of the year, even though the corporation had no E & P at the time of a distribution to him. This aspect of the regime should be viewed as a mere

2. Andrews, Out of Its Earnings and Profits: Some Reflections on the Taxation of Dividends, 69 Harv.L.Rev. 1403 (1956); Blum, The Earnings and Profits Limitation on Dividend Income: A Reappraisal, 53 Taxes 2, 68 (1975).

3. Staff of Senate Comm. on Finance, 98th Cong., 1st Sess., Report on the Reform and Simplification of the Income Taxation of Corporations 77–78 (Comm.Print 1983).

administrative accommodation, analogous to the annual accounting concept for determining taxable income.

"The second criticism relates to the shareholder who is taxed at ordinary income rates on distributions from accumulated earnings, although no earnings accrued after he bought the stock. Many commentators justify this result by claiming that if the rule were otherwise, trafficking in the stock of corporations without accumulated E & P would result. Furthermore, the selling price of the stock of a corporation with accumulated E & P will reflect the tax disability purchased by the buyer, so that the purchasing shareholder who receives taxable distributions of accumulated E & P will not truly be disadvantaged. A more important point, however, is that this aspect of the rule is consistent with either of the two purposes noted—i.e., to obviate dividend treatment when the distribution is a return of the capital of the corporation or to tax (subject to special exemptions) all earnings of the corporation twice.

"Because the aspects of the two-part regime relating to these alternative purposes more clearly reflect the problems inherent in the E & P regime, an in-depth analysis of those features is warranted.

"1. *The Two-Part Regime and the Reduction in Capital Concept*

"The two-part regime often results in the treatment of distributions of current earnings as dividends although the corporation has an accumulated E & P deficit. This treatment is usually explained by the 'reduction in capital concept'—i.e., distributions out of current earnings indicate that the corporation previously reduced its capital and is now distributing out of current E & P as opposed to capital. In this respect, the two-part regime supports the goal of taxing distributions that do not constitute a return of corporate capital.

"The reduction in capital concept is criticized as unfair to those shareholders who held their interest at the time of the reduction in capital because they receive insufficient credit for that reduction. At the time of the E & P deficit, the corporation may be forced to borrow money to continue operations. In that case the losses may have been associated with the reduction in net equity. It seems unfair to characterize future earnings of the corporation used to pay off these debts and restore the original net equity of the shareholder as E & P. It is difficult to allow credit for the prior reduction, however, because the corporation is a different entity for shareholders who acquire their interest after the reduction. Extending the effect of the deficit, therefore, would encourage trafficking in deficit corporations.

"A more serious difficulty is that the two-part regime does not always operate consistently with the reduction in capital concept. If any deficit in accumulated E & P remains after one or more profitable years, a distribution greater than E & P in any given year could receive capital gain treatment even though made out of E & P accumulated after the 'reduction in capital.' This result may occur because, once the profitable year ends, the only role of earnings during that year is to reduce a prior deficit in accumulated E & P.

"Alternative approaches appear just as unworkable. A comprehensive factual inquiry as to whether a reduction in capital had occurred would, of course, be virtually impossible to implement. * * * [I]t is insuperably difficult to construct a regime that would perfectly implement the purpose of permitting return-of-capital treatment for distributions solely of capital.

"2. *Rationale for the Two–Part Test: The Double Taxation of Earnings*

"A second justification for the two-part test is that it is an administratively simple means of assuring that all distributed earnings of a corporation are taxed twice. Thus, the E & P requirement could be viewed as administrative—it guarantees dividend treatment, at least to the extent of current earnings, without a wide ranging factual inquiry into the accumulated E & P of the corporation.

"This justification poses at least two problems. First, the test is vastly over-inclusive if the sole purpose is to tax distributed net earnings twice. Distributions from a corporation with a large accumulated deficit will be subject to ordinary income treatment, even though historically the corporation has no net earnings. Second, the administrative burden is often not alleviated, because accumulated E & P must be computed any time a distribution exceeds current E & P.

"B. Tax Accounting Aspects of the Modified Taxable Income Base

"Generally, E & P are computed using taxable income as the base, and adjustments are made to reflect realized not nontaxable receipts and nondeductible but actual disbursements. * * *

"Whether viewed simply as an administratively efficient way of computing economic earnings, or as a hybrid of taxable earnings with adjustments made for tax deductible expenditures intended to reduce taxable earnings only at the corporate level, the modified taxable income base employed by the E & P regime is aimed at serving at least one or the other of the alternative purposes of the regime. The question is whether it is possible, as a matter of policy and administrative practicality, to adequately serve those purposes of the E & P regime with the modified taxable income base.

"Much has been made of the complexity associated with making the necessary adjustments to taxable income. The literature on E & P illustrates the complexity of the adjustments, including those with respect to the proceeds of life insurance, interest on federal, state, and municipal obligations taxable under section 103, compensation for injuries or sickness exempt under section 104(a), the dividends received deduction, and the net operating loss deduction.

"A more serious problem than the complexity associated with these myriad adjustments, however, is the possibility for abuse due to inevitable reliance on general precepts of income tax accounting in computing the base. Analysis of the following four tax accounting aspects of the modified taxable income base for computing E & P is particularly instructive in this regard: (1) the computation of the modified taxable income base according to the taxable year tax accounting convention; (2) incorporation of the realization requirement from general income tax principles into the computation of E & P; (3) utilization of the taxpayer's accounting method for making the computation; and (4) the treatment of cost recovery deductions (depreciation, depletion, etc.) with respect to the taxpayer's assets for E & P purposes.

"The problems inherent in the E & P regime arise from the conjunction of these tax accounting aspects of the system with its dual corporate-shareholder orientation. As a result, the character of distribution may be permanently altered. Moreover, the potential distortion of the timing of recognition, already inherent in the computation of earnings for tax purposes, is magnified significantly.

* * *

"V. THE ELIMINATION OF 'EARNINGS AND PROFITS'

"Given the above analysis of problems with the computation of E & P, which seem incapable of fair and workable solutions, we have concluded that it would be a desirable goal to eliminate the E & P concept from the Code, both to improve the rules governing the taxation of distributions and for purposes of simplification. It now remains to analyze specifically the impact that this would have on the various Code provisions that employ the concept.

"There are a number of basic premises underlying the current system of taxing corporations and shareholders that any proposal for elimination of the E & P concept need not disturb or reexamine. First, elimination of the concept need not affect the general system of double taxation of earnings. Elimination of the concept will, however, accentuate the effect of the double tax, because corporate distributions will be taxable regardless of the corporation's profitability.

* * *

"Finally, the Code differentiates between transactions that involve a return on a shareholder's investment and those that are a disposition of that investment. If a transaction is determined to be an actual disposition, it is entitled to capital gain or loss treatment. However, if the transaction, regardless of its form, involves a mere return on a shareholder's investment, it is taxed as an ordinary income dividend or a return of capital, depending upon whether or not the corporation has current or accumulated E & P. The tests for distinguishing between dispositions of and returns upon investment need not be reexamined. Only the rules for taxing returns on investment would be changed, not those concerning the taxation of dispositions.

* * *

"A. Subchapter C

"1. *Distributions—Section 301,* * * *

"The elimination of the E & P concept will result in the taxation of all corporate distributions as ordinary income dividends, other than distributions made in connection with a disposition of the stock itself. This result is generally equitable. Whether shareholders have economic income when they receive a distribution has little or nothing to do with whether the corporation has E & P, particularly when the stock has changed hands since its original issue. The proposal simply treats an equity investment in a corporation like most other investments—e.g., rents are always ordinary income, regardless of whether the property is declining in value, and interest payments are always ordinary income even though the principal of the loan may never be repaid." (285–292, 297–299)

For the opposite conclusion regarding the desirability of retaining the earnings and profits test, see Cohen, Surrey, Tarleau and Warren, A Technical Revision of the Federal Income Tax Treatment of Corporate Distributions to Shareholders, 52 Col.L.Rev. 1 (1952), discussing American Law Institute, Federal Income Tax Statute, Tentative Drafts Nos. 5 (1951) and 7 (1952).

F. REFERENCES

McDaniel, Earnings and Profits: More Than a Cold Accounting Concept: Additions to and Subtractions From, 32 N.Y.U.Tax Inst. 445 (1974); Note, Employee Stock Options: The Effect Upon A Corporation's Earnings and Profits, 22 Md.L.Rev. 190 (1973); Jacoby, Earnings and Profits: A Not So Theoretical Concept—Some Winds of Change, 29 N.Y.U.Tax Inst. 649 (1971); Zarky and Biblin, The Role of Earnings and Profits in the Tax Law, 1966 So.Calif.Tax Inst. 145; Rudick, "Dividends" and "Earnings or Profits" Under the Income Tax Law: Corporate Non–Liquidating Distributions, 89 U.Pa.L.Rev. 865 (1941).

SECTION 3. DISTRIBUTION OF A DIVIDEND IN KIND

A. TREATMENT OF THE CORPORATION—THE SITUATION PRIOR TO 1986

GENERAL UTILITIES & OPERATING CO. v. HELVERING *

Supreme Court of the United States, 1935.
296 U.S. 200.

MR. JUSTICE MCREYNOLDS delivered the opinion of the Court.

January 1, 1927, petitioner, General Utilities, a Delaware corporation, acquired 20,000 shares (one-half of total outstanding) common stock Islands Edison Company, for which it paid $2,000. Gillet & Company owned the remainder.

During January, 1928, Whetstone, president of Southern Cities Utilities Company, contemplated acquisition by his company of all Islands Edison common stock. He discussed the matter with Lucas, petitioner's president, also with Gillet & Co. The latter concern agreed to sell its holdings upon terms acceptable to all. But Lucas pointed out that the shares which his company held could only be purchased after distribution of them among stockholders, since a sale by it would subject the realized profit to taxation, and when the proceeds passed to the stockholders there would be further exaction. Lucas had no power to sell, but he, Gillet, and Whetstone were in accord concerning the terms and conditions under which purchase of all the stock might become possible—"it being understood and agreed between them that petitioner would make distribution of the stock of the Islands Edison Company to its stockholders and that counsel would prepare a written agreement embodying the terms and conditions of the said sale, agreement to be submitted for approval to the stockholders of the Islands Edison Company after the distribution of said stock by the petitioner."

Petitioner's directors, March 22, 1928, considered the disposition of the Islands Edison shares. Officers reported they were worth $1,122,500, and recommended an appreciation on the books to that

* [Ed.: The case arose under a statute which did not contain section 311.]

figure. Thereupon a resolution directed this change; also "that a dividend in the amount of $1,071,426.25 be and it is hereby declared on the Common Stock of this Company payable in Common Stock of The Islands Edison Company at a valuation of $56.12½ a share, out of the surplus of the Company arising from the appreciation in the value of the Common Stock of The Islands Edison Company held by this Company, viz., $1,120,500.00, the payment of the dividend to be made by the delivery to the stockholders of this Company, pro rata, of certificates for the Common Stock of The Islands Edison Company held by this Company at the rate of two shares of such stock for each share of Company Stock of this Corporation."

Accordingly, 19,090 shares were distributed amongst petitioner's thirty-three stockholders and proper transfers to them were made upon the issuing corporation's books. It retained 910 shares.

After this transfer, all holders of Islands Edison stock sold to Southern Cities Utilities Company at $56.12½ per share. Petitioner realized $46,346.30 net profit on 910 shares and this was duly returned for taxation. There was no report of gain upon the 19,090 shares distributed to stockholders.

The Commissioner of Internal Revenue declared a taxable gain upon distribution of the stock in payment of the dividend declared March 22d, and made the questioned deficiency assessment. * * *

[The opinion of the Board of Tax Appeals] recites: The Commissioner's "theory is that upon the declaration of the dividend on March 22, 1928, petitioner became indebted to its stockholders in the amount of $1,071,426.25, and that the discharge of that liability by the delivery of property costing less than the amount of the debt constituted income, citing United States v. Kirby Lumber Co., 284 U.S. 1, 52 S.Ct. 4." "The intent of the directors of petitioner was to declare a dividend payable in Islands Edison stock; their intent was expressed in that way in the resolution formally adopted; and the dividend was paid in the way intended and declared. We so construe the transaction, and on authority of First Savings Bank v. Burnet, supra [17 B.T.A. 804; aff'd, 60 App. D.C. 307, 53 F.2d 919], we hold that the declaration and payment of the dividend resulted in no taxable income." * * *

[On appeal the] court stated: "There are two grounds upon which the petitioner urges that the action of the Board of Tax Appeals was wrong: First, that the dividend declared was in effect a cash dividend and that the respondent realized a taxable income by the distribution of the Islands Edison Company stock to its stockholders equal to the difference between the amount of the dividend declared and the cost of the stock. Second, that the sale made of the Islands Edison Company stock was in reality a sale by the respondent (with all the terms agreed upon before the declaration of the dividend), through its stockholders who were virtually acting as agents of the respondent, the real vendor." [This latter ground had not been stated in the petition for review by the Circuit Court]

Upon the first ground, it sustained the Board. Concerning the second, it held that, although not raised before the Board, the point should be ruled upon.

"When we come to consider the sale of the stock of the Islands Edison Company we cannot escape the conclusion that the transaction was deliberately planned and carried out for the sole purpose of escaping taxation. The purchaser was found by the officers of the respondent; the exact terms of the sale as finally consummated were agreed to by the same officers; the purchaser of the stock stated that the delivery of all the stock was essential and that the delivery of a part thereof would not suffice; the details were worked out for the express and admitted purpose of avoiding the payment of the tax and for the reason that the attorneys for the respondent had advised that unless some such plan was adopted the tax would have to be paid; and a written agreement was to be prepared by counsel for the respondent which was to be submitted to the stockholders; all this without the stockholders, or any of them, who were ostensibly making the sale, being informed, advised or consulted. Such admitted facts plainly constituted a plan, not to use the harsher terms of scheme, artifice or conspiracy, to evade the payment of the tax. For the purposes of this decision it is not necessary to consider whether such a course as is here shown constituted a fraud, it is sufficient if we conclude that the object was to evade the payment of a tax justly due the government.

"The sale of the stock in question was, in substance, made by the respondent company, through the stockholders as agents or conduits through whom the transfer of the title was effected. The stockholders, even in their character as agents, had little or no option in the matter and in no sense exercised any independent judgment. They automatically ratified the agreement prepared and submitted to them."

A judgment of reversal followed.

Both tribunals below rightly decided that petitioner derived no taxable gain from the distribution among its stockholders of the Islands Edison shares as a dividend. This was no sale; assets were not used to discharge indebtedness.

The second ground of objection, although sustained by the court, was not presented to or ruled upon by the Board. The petition for review relied wholly upon the first point; and, in the circumstances, we think the court should have considered no other. Always a taxpayer is entitled to know with fair certainty the basis of the claim against him.

* * *

Here the court undertook to decide a question not properly raised. Also it made an inference of fact directly in conflict with the stipulation of the parties and the findings, for which we think the record affords no support whatever. To remand the cause for further findings would be futile. The Board could not properly find anything which would assist the Commissioner's cause.

The judgment of the court below must be reversed. The action of the Board of Tax Appeals is approved.

Reversed.

ILLUSTRATIVE MATERIAL

A. "*GENERAL UTILITIES* RULE" JUDICIALLY FOLLOWED PRIOR TO 1954 CODE REVISION

The *General Utilities* case was generally regarded as standing for the proposition that no gain or loss was realized under the predecessor of section 1001 by a corporation which distributed property as a dividend. (In view of the procedural situation, however, the court was not called upon to decide this question but only whether the dividend declared was in effect a cash dividend.) The Commissioner steadily attacked this rule, but his arguments were consistently rejected by the courts. See, e.g., Transport, Trading & Terminal Corp. v. Commissioner, 9 T.C. 247 (1947) (NA). In Natural Gasoline Corp. v. Commissioner, 219 F.2d 682 (10th Cir.1955), a taxpayer unsuccessfully attacked the *General Utilities* rule in a case where the asset distributed had depreciated in value.

B. CODIFICATION OF "*GENERAL UTILITIES* RULE" UNDER 1954 CODE

In the 1954 revision of the Internal Revenue Code Congress codified the *General Utilities* approach in section 311, governing distributions not in liquidation, and section 336, governing distributions in liquidation of the corporation. Both of these sections provided for nonrecognition of both gain and loss at the corporate level on the distribution of property by a corporation. Over the next thirty years, however, Congress slowly but steadily added exceptions to the nonrecognition of gain rule in section 311 (and to a lesser extent section 336), while leaving nonrecognition of losses wholly intact. By 1984, the exceptions had nearly swallowed the general rule as recognition of gain was extended to almost all dividend and redemption distributions. Nonrecognition generally was limited to partial liquidation distributions received by certain individuals and dividend or redemption distributions of capital (or section 1231) assets if specific restrictive conditions had been met. Nonrecognition to the corporation on liquidating distributions as provided under section 336, however, continued unchanged. The reason given for the 1984 amendments to section 311, in Staff of the Joint Committee on Taxation, General Explanation of the Tax Reform Act of 1884, 98th Cong., 2d Sess. (Comm.Print, Dec. 31, 1984), was straightforward.

"Under a double tax system, corporate income generally is taxed twice. Such income is taxed first to the corporation that earns it. It is taxed a second time to the ultimate shareholders of such corporation when it is distributed to them. Any failure to treat distributions of appreciated property as taxable events to the distributing corporation, however, provided opportunities for deferring, or even avoiding, corporate level tax. The Congress believed that such a result was inappropriate under a double-tax system." (148–149).

This explanation left something to be desired. If virtual repeal of the *General Utilities* doctrine was necessary to protect the double tax system, why were any exceptions to recognition retained in section 311, and why should section 336 continue to provide nearly complete nonrecognition of gain and loss at the corporate level on liquidating distributions? Congress responded to this inconsistency in the Tax Reform Act of 1986 by, in effect, replacing the *General Utilities* rule with one of gain recognition on distribution of appreciated property by a corporation.

C. "*GENERAL UTILITIES* RULE" SIDESTEPPED—THE DISTRIBUTION OF INCOME CASES

The Commissioner's tenacity in attacking the *General Utilities* rule prior to its codification in 1954 produced success in situations in which the anti-assignment of income doctrine of Helvering v. Horst, 311 U.S. 112 (1940), proved stronger than the *General Utilities* approach. See, e.g., Commissioner v. First State Bank of Stratford, 168 F.2d 1004 (5th Cir.1948) (a bank that charged off certain notes as worthless in a prior year was required to include amounts collected on the notes by shareholders to whom the notes had been distributed as a dividend in kind when the bank determined that the notes would be repaid); United States v. Lynch, 192 F.2d 718 (9th Cir.1951) (corporation declared dividend in kind of inventory but did not deliver it to the shareholders; instead it sold the inventory for the shareholders' account; the net profit from the sale was taxed to the corporation); Bush Bros. & Co. v. Commissioner, 73 T.C. 424 (1979), aff'd, 668 F.2d 252 (6th Cir.1982) (corporation taxed where it purchased beans stored in a warehouse, declared a dividend payable in the beans and delivered bills of sale to the shareholders, who immediately sold the beans to the warehouse).

The Commissioner was not uniformly successful, however. See Hines v. United States, 477 F.2d 1063 (5th Cir.1973), which refused to tax the corporation on gain from the disposition of property sold by the shareholder shortly after its distribution as a dividend. The court said that taxation of the corporation was appropriate [o]nly if the corporation in fact participated in the sale transaction, by negotiation, prior agreement, post distribution activities or participated in any other significant manner". (1070–1071)

The Commissioner also has had some success arguing that the income of the shareholder should be reallocated to the corporation under section 482, discussed supra, page 330. See Southern Bancorporation, Inc. v. Commissioner, 67 T.C. 1022 (1977) (where bonds and notes were distributed by a bank to its parent to avoid the income tax consequences which would have resulted from a sale by the bank, the income from the subsequent sale of the bonds and notes by the parent corporation could be attributed to the bank under section 482); Rev.Rul. 77–83, 1977–1 Cum.Bull. 139, reaching a similar result; Ruddick Corp. v. United States, 3 Cl.Ct. 61 (1983), aff'd by order 732 F.2d 168 (Fed.Cir.1984) (where subsidiary distributed stock of third corporation to parent immediately prior to sale so as to enable parent to use net operating loss carryovers against gains on sale, income from the sale was attributed to the subsidiary).

The importance of these lines of cases is greatly reduced because of the 1986 revisions to sections 311 and 336. They continue to be relevant, however, in the case of distributions in liquidation of 80 percent controlled corporations, See infra, page 622.

B. THE TAX REFORM ACT OF 1986

INTERNAL REVENUE CODE: SECTIONS 301(a), (b), (c), (d), (e); 311; 312(a)(3), (b), (c); 336(a).

HOUSE WAYS AND MEANS COMMITTEE REPORT, TAX REFORM ACT OF 1986

H.Rep. No. 99–426, 99th Cong., 1st Sess., 281–82 (1985).

The committee believes that the *General Utilities* rule, * * * produces many incongruities and inequities in the tax system. First, the rule may create significant distortions in business behavior. Economically, a liquidating distribution is indistinguishable from a nonliquidating distribution; yet the Code provides a substantial preference for the former. A corporation acquiring the assets of a liquidating corporation is able to obtain a basis in assets equal to their fair market value, although the transferor recognizes no gain (other than possibly recapture amounts) on the sale. The tax benefits may make the assets more valuable in the hands of the transferee than in the hands of the present owner. The effect may be to induce corporations with substantial appreciated assets to liquidate and transfer their assets to other corporations for tax reasons, when economic considerations might indicate a different course of action. Accordingly, the *General Utilities* rule may be responsible, at least in part, for the dramatic increase in corporate mergers and acquisitions in recent years. The committee believes that the Code should not artificially encourage corporate liquidations and acquisitions, and believes that repeal of the *General Utilities* rule is a major step towards that goal.

Second, the *General Utilities* rule tends to undermine the corporate income tax. Under normally applicable tax principles, nonrecognition of gain is available only if the transferee takes a carryover basis in the transferred property, thus assuring that a tax will eventually be collected on the appreciation. Where the *General Utilities* rule applies, assets generally are permitted to leave corporate solution and to take a stepped-up basis in the hands of the transferee without the imposition of a corporate-level tax. Thus, the effect of the rule is to grant a permanent exemption from the corporate income tax.

ILLUSTRATIVE MATERIAL

A. SCOPE OF RECOGNITION AT THE CORPORATE LEVEL

1. *General*

Section 311(a) continues to set forth a general rule of nonrecognition at the corporate level for distributions by a corporation "with respect to its stock" of its stock (or rights to acquire its stock) and "property." Section 311(b) then reverses this rule if the distribution is subject to sections 301 or 302 *and* the fair market value of the property exceeds its basis to the corporation. In such cases, the corporation is required to recognize gain as if it had sold the property to the distributee at fair market value. Section 311(a) continues to prevent the recognition of a loss.

2. *Character of Gain*

Section 311(b) specifies that gain should be recognized as if the corporation had sold the distributed property. This rule should control characterization of the gain as ordinary or capital, as well as its amount. Thus, gain recognized by the corporation on the distribution of appreciated capital assets can be offset by recognized capital losses. See section 1211. Gain on the distribution of section 1231 assets may be capital or ordinary, subject to the section 1231 computation and the applicability of the various recapture rules (primarily section 1245). Section 1239 may recharacterize gain as ordinary when the property is distributed to a more than 50 percent shareholder (taking into account attribution) in whose hands the property is depreciable.

3. *Losses*

Congress in the 1986 Act did not eliminate all of the anomalies in the treatment of property distributions by corporations. Section 336 allows the recognition of loss at the corporate level, subject to certain exceptions, on liquidating distributions. But under section 311, no loss is allowed when depreciated property is distributed. Suppose that X Corporation purchased two parcels of land: Tract 1 for $5,000 in 1987, and Tract 2 for $7,000 in 1988. In 1989, when each parcel had a fair market value of $6,000, X Corporation distributed both parcels as a dividend. X Corporation cannot offset the loss on Tract 2 against the gain on Tract 1.

Since X Corp. cannot offset the loss against the gain, can the nonrecognition of the loss on Tract 2 be sidestepped by selling it to the shareholders? A sale might be accomplished in either of two ways. First, the shareholders could pay the corporation cash for the property. Alternatively, the corporation could declare a $6,000 cash dividend, thereby creating a debt to the shareholders, and then distribute the property in satisfaction of the debt. Should it matter which form is followed? See the Commissioner's first argument described in the *General Utilities* case, supra, page 472.

If a sale is to a more than fifty percent shareholder, section 267(a)(1) disallows any loss at the corporate level. But if the shareholder later sells the property at a gain, the gain will not be recognized to the extent of the previously disallowed loss. Section 311 does not permit the transferee in effect to use the disallowed loss in this fashion. If section 311 were amended to provide for recognition of loss to the distributing corporation, should section 267 apply to disallow the loss in proper circumstances?

Congress did not explain why the 1986 revisions retained the *General Utilities* rule as to current distributions of depreciated property. Is there any sound policy reason for denying the loss deduction? Since under section 301(d) the shareholder's basis for distributed property is its fair market value at the time of distribution, the loss is eliminated forever. The disallowance of the loss may be avoided by selling the property to a third party and distributing the proceeds to the shareholders or, assuming section 267 does not apply, by selling the property to the shareholders. In the first case, however, the shareholders may desire the actual property, not its equivalent value. In the second case, the transaction is economically different. Perhaps the unarticulated reason for disallowing the recognition of losses is Congressional concern with tax avoidance transactions in closely held corporations.

If the tax avoidance potential of allowing corporations a loss on distributions of property to majority shareholders is the concern, it would appear that the problem could have been addressed by subjecting losses at the corporate level resulting from distributions to shareholders to the same rules that govern losses realized on sales to shareholders.

4. *Distributions of Encumbered Property*

Section 311(b)(2), through a cross reference to section 336(b), provides that if the distributed property is subject to a lien or the shareholder assumes a corporate liability in connection with the distribution, then the fair market value of the property will be treated as not less than the amount of the liability. If the corporate debt secured by the property is nonrecourse, this rule is merely duplicative of section 7701(g). See also Commissioner v. Tufts, 461 U.S. 300 (1983). But where a recourse liability greater than the fair market value of the property is assumed by the shareholder, it converts what might otherwise be ordinary income from discharge of indebtedness under Regulations, section 1.1001–2(a)(2), into gain from the sale or exchange of property.

B. THE EFFECT OF DIVIDENDS IN KIND ON EARNINGS AND PROFITS

Accounting for the proper adjustments to earnings and profits as a result of dividends in kind entails several steps. Because a distribution in kind of appreciated property results in the recognition of gain to the corporation under section 311, earnings and profits automatically should be increased by the recognized gain under the normal rules basing earnings and profits on taxable income. Redundantly, section 312(b)(1) provides that earnings and profits be increased in the amount by which the fair market of the distributed property exceeds its basis. (Read literally, section 312(b)(1) results in a double addition to earnings and profits; it is unlikely, however, that it will be so interpreted.) The distribution itself requires a downward adjustment to earnings and profits in an amount equal to the fair market value of the distributed property. See sections 312(a)(3) and 312(b)(2). Why are earnings and profits increased by only the gain but decreased by the fair market value of the distributed property?

Note that section 312(b)(1) excepts from the rule requiring an increase in earnings and profits the distribution of the corporation's own promissory note. Similarly, section 311(b) excepts such a distribution from its gain recognition rule. The distribution, however, does effect a reduction in earnings and profits. The upward adjustment occurs when the corporation earns the income used to pay the indebtedness; there is no downward adjustment when the note is paid.

If depreciated property is distributed, section 312(a)(3) allows earnings and profits to be reduced by the basis of the property, even though section 311(a) disallows recognition of the loss. Note that as far as the net effect on earnings and profits is concerned, this treatment achieves the same result as allowing the loss and reducing earnings and profits by the fair market value of the distributed property.

The increase in current earnings and profits for the year resulting from the gain attributable to the distributed property is taken into account as provided in Regulations, section 1.316–2, in determining the extent to which any distributions (including that of the property itself) made during the year are taxable as dividends. Thus the current earnings and profits resulting from a distribution of appreciated property may be used to support dividend treatment of a portion of an unrelated cash distribution. Suppose that X Corporation has neither accumulated nor current earnings and profits, except as generated by property distributions during the current year. During the year it distributes property having a fair market value of $100 and a basis of $20 to Shareholder 1 and $100 cash to Shareholder 2. Presumably, only $40 of the distribution to each shareholder is a dividend. See Regulations, section 1.316–2.

Where the distributed property is subject to liens or the distributee shareholder assumes a corporate liability in connection with the distribution, section 312(c) requires that a "proper adjustment" be made. Regulations, section 1.312–3, interpret the statutory language to mean that the downward adjustment to earnings and profits under section 312(a) or 312(b) should be reduced by the amount of the liability. Again, because of the manner in which Regulations, section 1.316–2, apportion earnings and profits among distributions during the year to determine the extent to which each distribution is a dividend, the result is not always the same as making the section 312(a) and 312(b) adjustments and then simply increasing earnings and profits by the amount of the liability.

C. TREATMENT OF SHAREHOLDERS

Section 301(b)(1) provides that in the case of both corporate and individual shareholders the amount of any distribution which is a dividend is the fair market value of the distributed property. However, where the property is subject to a lien or the shareholder assumes a corporate indebtedness in connection with the distribution, section 301(b)(2) directs that the amount of the debt reduce the amount of the distribution. In all cases, nevertheless, the shareholder's basis in the distributed property is its fair market value. Section 301(d). Suppose that a corporation with sufficient earnings and profits to support dividend treatment of the entire distribution distributes property having a fair market value of $100, subject to a mortgage of $60. The shareholder has a dividend of $40, but takes a basis in the distributed property for $40 of cash plus an assumption of the mortgage. If the shareholder then sells the property for $100, he realizes no gain. Why is this the correct result?

D. DISTRIBUTION OF RIGHTS TO PURCHASE STOCK OF ANOTHER CORPORATION

Rev.Rul. 70–521, 1970–2 Cum.Bull. 72, treats rights to purchase stock of another corporation as "property" under section 317(a) and as a currently taxable dividend under section 301. Palmer v. Commissioner, 302 U.S. 63 (1937), prior to 1954 Code, had held that the issuance by a corporation of rights to purchase stock in another corporation was not a dividend at the time of issuance, a result which, in the view of the Internal Revenue Service, was changed in 1954 by the comprehensive definition of "property" provided in section 317(a). Although the Supreme Court in Commissioner v. Gordon, 391 U.S. 83 (1968), infra, page 932, described the status of rights to purchase stock in other corporations under the 1954 Code as "not affirmatively settled," the Internal Revenue Service approach in the above Ruling seems to be the correct one and is consistent with the general approach to options in other areas, as for example, in section 83. This approach was followed by the Tax Court in Weigl v. Commissioner, 84 T.C. 1192 (1985). See also Baumer v. United States, 580 F.2d 863, 878–881 (5th Cir.1978), for a discussion of the status of *Palmer* under the 1954 Code.

Rev.Rul. 70–521, supra, also held that where the distributed stock purchase rights had no basis to the distributing corporation (because the distributing corporation created the option), no adjustment to the distributing corporation's earnings and profits was proper. Under current section 312(a)(3) and 312(b)(2), however, the distributing corporation reduces earnings and profits by the fair market value of the rights. Section 311(b) requires the distributing corporation to recognize gain in the amount by which the fair market value of the rights exceeds its basis in the rights; a correlative increase in earnings and profits would be required.

E. DISTRIBUTION OF CORPORATION'S OWN SECURITIES

1. *Debt Instruments*

Suppose that a corporation distributes its own promissory note in the face amount of $10,000. As far as the shareholder is concerned, a distribution of the corporation's own debt instrument generally is treated in the same manner as any other distribution of property. Regulations, section 1.301–1(d), provide that the amount of the distribution is the fair market value of the instrument, and the shareholder takes a fair market value basis in the distributed obligation pursuant to Regulations, section 1.301–1(h)(2)(i).

The distributing corporation receives substantially different treatment when it distributes its own debt instrument than it does when it distributes other property. Because its basis for its own promissory note is zero, if the general rule applied, the distributing corporation would be required to recognize gain. However, the parenthetical in section 311(b)(1)(A) provides nonrecognition treatment to the distributing corporation. Earnings and profits adjustments are governed by section 312(a)(2), which reduces earnings and profits by the face amount of an obligation other than an obligation bearing original issue discount (OID). If the distributed instrument bears OID, then earnings and profits are reduced only by the "issue price." Section 312(o) incorporates the OID rules of sections 1271–1275 for purposes of applying section 312(a)(2). Section 1275(a)(5) treats an OID instrument distributed by a corporation with respect to its stock as an OID instrument issued in exchange for property. Therefor, section 1274 applies, and the issue price is determined with reference to the sum of the present values (discounted at the appropriate AFR) of all payments due under the obligation. See supra, page 439. As a result, earnings and profits are reduced by the lesser of the fair market value of the obligation or its face amount. See S.Rep. No. 98–169, 98th Cong., 2d Sess. 188–89 (1984).

Discount obligations distributed to shareholders in a section 301 distribution are thereafter subject to the OID rules, as if they had been issued for cash consideration equal to their fair market value at the time of distribution. As the corporation deducts interest on the obligation under section 163(e) when it economically accrues, earnings and profits eventually will be charged with the full face amount of the obligation. For the operation of the OID rules, see supra, page 432.

2. *Stock or rights to acquire stock*

Distributions to shareholders of a corporation's own stock or rights to purchase such stock are subject to special rules under section 305. See infra, Chapter 12.

F. REFERENCES

Zolt, The *General Utilities* Doctrine: Examining the Scope of the Repeal, 65 Taxes 819 (1987); Yin, Taxing Corporate Liquidations (and Related Matters) After the Tax Reform Act of 1986, 42 Tax L.Rev. 573 (1987); Lyons, Corporate Liquidations and the "*General Utilities* Rule", 38 Sw.L.J. 1081 (1985); Block, Liquidations Before and After the Repeal of *General Utilities,* 21 Harv.J.Legis. 307 (1984): Steines, Taxation of Corporate Distributions—Before and After TEFRA, 68 Iowa L.Rev. 937 (1983); Carlson, Taxation of "Taxable" Stock Rights: The Strange Persistence of Palmer v. Commissioner, 23 Tax.L.Rev. 129 (1968).

SECTION 4. DISGUISED DIVIDENDS

INTERNAL REVENUE CODE: Sections 61(a)(7); 301(a), (b); 316(a); 317(a).

REGULATIONS: Section 1.301–1(c), (j), (m).

BAUMER v. UNITED STATES

United States Court of Appeals, Fifth Circuit, 1978.
580 F.2d 863.

GOLDBERG, CIRCUIT JUDGE:

This appeal presents a novel variation of the recurrent problem of determining the tax consequences of transactions between closely held corporations and their shareholders. Here a corporation granted an option to purchase a one-half interest in a parcel of real estate to the son of the corporation's sole shareholder for nominal consideration. In the proceedings below, the district court held that the grant of this option resulted in a constructive dividend from the corporation to the father, measured by the ascertainable value of the option.

The government argues on appeal that the option was simply a device for shifting to the son half of the corporation's gain on the subsequent sale of the property to a third party purchaser. Accordingly, for federal tax purposes the option itself should be ignored and the transaction treated as a sale of the entire property by the corporation to the ultimate purchaser accompanied by the distribution of a constructive dividend to the father. The government contends that the value of this dividend should be the difference between the price paid by the son to exercise the option (the "exercise price") and the actual fair market value of the property interest acquired by the son. In the alternative, the government argues that even if the district court correctly held that no tax is owed by the corporation and that the grant of the option, rather than the sale of the property to son, gave rise to the constructive dividend to the father, the court erred in its valuation of the benefit conferred by the option.

The father, son, and corporation ("taxpayers") cross appeal from the judgment of the district court. They maintain that the option was granted to the son in an arm's-length transaction and that the district court erred in treating the option as a constructive dividend by the corporation to the father.

We find that the record supports the district court's conclusion that the grant of the option constituted neither an arm's-length transaction on the one hand, nor an illusory event designed to shift the corporation's gain on the ultimate sale of the property to the son on the other. On these issues we affirm the decision of the district court. However, treating the grant of the option itself as a constructive dividend, we substantially agree with the government that the district court erred in its valuation of the benefit conferred on the son. We therefore remand the actions involving the son and the father for redetermination of the value of the constructive dividend.

I. *The Transaction*

The facts of this case are largely undisputed, although the proper characterization of these facts is far from clear. Taxpayer Erwin G. Baumer ("Father") is the father of taxpayer Erwin H. Baumer ("Son"), and, during the period in question, was the sole shareholder of taxpayer Seven Eighty–Eight Greenwood Avenue Corporation ("Corporation"), a Georgia corporation which owned and leased real estate in the Atlanta, Georgia area. Son is a real estate attorney. In early 1965, Son became interested in purchasing a parcel of residential property on Piedmont Road in Atlanta. In November, 1965, Son was offered the Piedmont property for $175,000. Father, who was knowledgeable about property in the area, advised Son not to accept the offer.[2] Son followed this advice.

Shortly thereafter, in January, 1966, Father was advised that an attractive investment property on Piedmont Road was for sale. This turned out to be the same property that Son had been interested in just a few months earlier. Corporation accepted an offer to purchase the property for $175,000 in late January, 1966. The property was then zoned for residential use.

The district court found that the value of the Piedmont property for residential use was somewhat less than $175,000, but noted that at the time of the purchase, the neighborhood was ripe for transition to commercial use. While the court could not determine whether the actual fair market value of the property was in excess of $175,000, it

2. Father testified that his advice was not based on the investment value of the particular property under consideration; rather, (1) he felt Son had not sufficiently recovered from his wife's death in January, 1965 to make such a significant investment decision; (2) he doubted the financial capacity of Son's partner; and (3) he was hesitant to advise Son to make such a purchase when Son was contemplating a possible change in law firms.

did find that the realization of any potential value in excess of $175,000 depended upon favorable rezoning to commercial uses.

When Father informed Son of this transaction, Son requested that the Corporation sell him an interest in the property. Father agreed, and the Board of Directors authorized Corporation to sell Son a one-half interest in the property. Father testified that he made this offer because he had originally advised Son against purchasing what Father later considered to be an attractive investment property. Subsequently, the proposed transaction was modified and a written option was executed by Corporation and accepted by Son in early May, 1966. The exercise price of the option for purchase of a one-half interest in the property was set at $88,000, approximately one-half of the corporation's cost basis, plus 5½ percent interest calculated from the effective date of the option, February 7, 1966.[3] The stated term of the option was one year from the effective date. The option was exercisable immediately and without conditions, and the option privilege was assignable by Son. The stated consideration for the option privilege was $10.00, which Son did not recall actually paying.

The district court found that Father and Son intended to use the Piedmont property to develop a motel. Son, who had substantial legal experience in zoning matters, began investigating the possibility of rezoning the property for commercial use. Upon discovering that the property could not be rezoned unless sewer services were provided, Son located an adjacent parcel of real estate on Old Ivy Road which had access to sewer facilities. According to the district court's findings, Son's efforts were inspired by the fact that "he considered that he had an interest in the property." In August, 1966, Corporation purchased the Old Ivy property for $25,000.

Because of this purchase, the combined properties became eligible for rezoning to a commercial classification. Consequently, the value of the Piedmont property was substantially increased. On January 12, 1967, approximately one month prior to the termination of the original options, the corporation granted Son an amended option which covered both the Piedmont and Old Ivy properties; set a new exercise price of $100,000, approximately one-half of Corporation's purchase price for the two properties, plus 5½ percent interest; and extended the period during which the option could be exercised until June 30, 1969. The amendment further provided that the option privilege was assignable by Son. The stated consideration for these modifications was $10.00, which Son did not recall having paid.

In January 1967, Pope & Carter Co., Inc. ("Pope & Carter"), an Atlanta real estate brokerage company, informed Father that it was interested in purchasing the Piedmont–Old Ivy property. After negotiations participated in by Father, Son, and Pope & Carter, Corporation

3. The record indicates that the five and one-half percent purchase price escalation factor reflected the interest rate then being paid by Corporation on its borrowed funds.

granted Pope & Carter an option to purchase the combined properties. This option, which took effect on January 25, provided in relevant part that: (1) Pope & Carter was required to expend reasonable time and effort to obtain favorable C–1 zoning, which would permit motel use; (2) the option would remain open for six months without the payment of a cash consideration and could be extended for up to six additional months by paying Corporation $3,000 per month; (3) the option purchase price was $500,000; (4) any option extension payments were to be applied against the purchase price; and (5) the option was assignable. Pope & Carter was aware of Son's interest in the property when it negotiated this option.

Pursuant to its obligations under the option, Pope & Carter expended substantial time and money to obtain the desired zoning. The results were encouraging and beginning in July, 1967, Pope & Carter exercised its right to purchase monthly extensions on its option. At the end of the one year option period, the Pope & Carter option was extended from January 24, 1968 through April 24, 1968 for a consideration of $1,000 per month. From April 24, 1968 through December 27, 1968, additional extensions were granted for the nominal consideration of $1 per month "in view of the impending favorable zoning action."

On December 4, 1968, Pope & Carter's rezoning application was approved, with certain conditions, with respect to the Piedmont property. The Old Ivy property was not rezoned. Two days later, Son exercised his amended option on the Piedmont–Old Ivy properties. On December 18, Son purchased a one-half undivided interest in the properties and tendered to Corporation a note for $114,501.23, bearing interest at 6½ percent. Nine days later, on December 27, Pope & Carter exercised its option to purchase the properties. The district court found that the fair market value of the properties at that time at least equalled Pope & Carter's exercise price of $500,000. The sale was closed on July 1, 1969, with an assignee of Pope & Carter actually making the purchase.

Son received $252,700 for his interest in the properties. Most of this sum was payable in installments by Pope & Carter's assignee, Crow, Pope & Carter Construction Co. Son's note to Corporation was subsequently modified to provide for payment coinciding with these installments. The purpose of this modification was to permit Son to use the payments he would receive from Pope & Carter's assignee to satisfy the obligations arising from his purchase of the property.

On its federal tax return for the fiscal year ending November 30, 1969, Corporation reported a sale to Son of a one-half interest in the combined properties, showing no gain on this transaction. Corporation also reported a sale to Pope & Carter's assignee of its second one-half interest in the combined properties. On this transaction, Corporation reported a gain of one-half of the difference between its purchase price of the properties and the approximately $500,000 option purchase price paid by Pope & Carter's assignee. Son reported on his 1969 income tax return a sale of one-half interest in the Piedmont–Old Ivy properties and a gain thereon valued at the difference between his own option price and one-half the amount paid by Pope & Carter's assignee for the property. Father reported no income on any of these transactions.

The Commissioner concluded that this option transaction constituted a device for transferring half of Corporation's gain on the properties at issue to Son and, accordingly, assessed additional taxes based on the determinations (1) that Corporation should be taxed on the entire gain from the sale to Pope & Carter's assignee and (2) that Father received a constructive dividend on Son's exercise of his option in 1968 and that such dividend was taxable to Father in the amount of the difference between the "bargain price" paid by Son on exercise of his option and the fair market value of the property as reflected by the Pope & Carter sale.[5] Taxpayers paid the resulting deficiencies and instituted these refund proceedings in the district court.

District Court

The district court rejected the government's contention that the option was merely a device for transferring Corporation's gain on the sale of the properties to Son. Accordingly, the court held that Corporation was not liable for the gain on the sale of Son's interest in the properties. The court also rejected, however, the taxpayers' position that the grant of the option to Son was an arm's-length transaction. The court found that the grant of the option, and its amendment, constituted distributions in 1966 and 1967 of corporate property resulting in a dividend to Father and a gift by him to Son. These distributions "were without consideration and by virtue of Father's position as sole shareholder of the corporate plaintiff." Finding the value of the distributions to be indeterminable in 1966 and 1967, the court applied the "open transaction" doctrine of Burnet v. Logan, 283 U.S. 404, 51 S.Ct. 550, 75 L.Ed. 1143 (1931), to defer recognition of the gain and consequent tax liability until 1968. The court then valued the Son's option with reference to the $3,000 per month consideration paid by Pope & Carter for monthly extensions of its option.

The government now appeals from the district court's judgment. It maintains that the district court erred in not treating the option as a sham. Thus according to the government, the entire gain from the sale to Pope & Carter's assignee is taxable to Corporation. Since half of that gain was distributed to Son by means of the option sale of corporate property at a price far below the market value, Father should be liable for a constructive dividend of that amount. Alternatively, the government asserts that the tax consequences to Father are the same even if the district court is correct in holding that no tax is owed by Corporation and that it was the grant of the option, and not the "bargain sale" of the property to Son, that gave rise to a constructive dividend. According to the government, the district court erred in valuing the option with reference to the Pope & Carter option and

5. The Commissioner also determined that Son received a gift from Father in the amount of this dividend. The Commissioner's assessment of gift tax liability against Father is the subject of separate litigation and is not before us on this appeal.

under the open transaction doctrine, the value of the option should be determined by the spread between the option price and the fair market value of the property acquired at the time of exercise.[7]

Taxpayers cross appeal from the district court's conclusion that the grant of the option to Son resulted in a constructive dividend to Father, arguing that the option was granted in an arm's-length transaction. Taxpayers also maintain that even if the grant of the option to Son was a taxable event, the resulting dividend to Father occurred in 1966 or 1967, years which are not in issue in these proceedings.

II. *Imputing Son's Income to Corporation*

We first examine the government's contention that the sale by Corporation to Son of a one-half interest in the property immediately prior to the exercise of the Pope & Carter option was a sham transaction designed to shift half of Corporation's gain on that impending sale to Son. The government maintains that under the doctrine of Commissioner v. Court Holding Co., 324 U.S. 331, 65 S.Ct. 707, 89 L.Ed. 981 (1945), the district court should have taxed the Corporation on the entire gain from the sale to Pope & Carter.

[The court affirmed the District Court holding that the gain on the sale was not taxable to the Corporation under the *Court Holding Co.* doctrine discussed infra, page 690.]

III. *The Arm's-Length Transaction or Constructive Dividend?*

Our conclusion that income from the sale of Son's interest in the Piedmont–Old Ivy property is not imputable to Corporation under *Court Holding* requires us to examine the government's alternative theory that the ascertainable value of property conferred by Corporation on Son without adequate consideration is taxable to Father as a constructive dividend.[17] The district court substantially agreed with this theory and held that Father received a constructive dividend when Corporation granted the option to Son in 1966 and amended it in 1967. However, finding that the value of the option was not ascertainable in 1966 or 1967, the court deferred recognition of the dividend and liability for the tax until Son exercised his option in 1968. The court then valued the option with reference to the consideration paid by Pope & Carter for monthly extensions of its option.

7. The district court found that the fair market value of the property on December 27, 1968, the day Pope & Carter exercised its option, at least equalled the Pope & Carter exercise price of $500,000. Son exercised his option 21 days earlier, on December 6, 1968.

17. Had we imputed the entire gain from the sale of the Piedmont–Old Ivy property to Corporation, the distribution of half of that gain to Son would have constituted a constructive dividend to Father. * * * In this section we reach the government's alternative theory that even if no constructive dividend resulted from Corporation's distribution of the profits of the Pope & Carter sale to Son, a constructive dividend occurred when Corporation distributed the option to Son.

Our review of the court's holding involves several district inquiries. In subsection III(A) we discuss why, as a general matter, the district court was correct in refusing to assume at once that a transaction between a corporation and the sole shareholder's son was an arm's-length transaction. We then consider in subsection III(B) whether constructive dividend treatment was warranted in this case. Finally, in subsection III(C) we examine the district court's valuation of the constructive dividend.

We note at the outset that our journey through the constructive dividend area of tax law is a difficult one, often with no clear precedents to guide our way. In seeking to divine congressional intent, we must view the Code as a coherent whole, gleaning whatever rules and policies it may offer for deciding the issues before us. We attack these issues with a full arsenal of judicial weapons, including our own precedents, the Treasury Regulations, the Code sections which apply directly and those which indicate congressional purpose by analogy.

A. *Judicial Scrutiny of Transactions Between Closely Held Corporations and Their Shareholders: A General Discussion*

We begin by considering taxpayers' contention that the option to Son was granted by Corporation at a fair price in an arm's-length transaction. According to taxpayers no tax consequences should attach either to the grant or to the exercise of the option. In taxpayers' view, Son's option should be treated no differently than the option granted to Pope & Carter. We conclude that this argument is untenable. In order to elucidate our views on the oft-perplexing problem of the conferral of benefits on a controlling shareholder by a closely held corporation, we begin with first principles.

Distributions of "property" made by a corporation to a shareholder with respect to its stock are dividends to the extent of the corporation's current and accumulated earnings and profits, 26 U.S.C.A. §§ 301(a)(c), 316(a),[18] and must be included by the shareholder in gross income. 26 U.S.C.A. §§ 301(a), 301(c)(1).

For purposes of corporate distributions, the Code defines "property" as

> money, securities, and other property; except that such term does not include stock in the corporation making the distribution (or rights to acquire such stock).

26 U.S.C.A. § 317(a). In accordance with this broad definition of property, dividends may be "in cash or in kind, and may also result when the corporation makes a 'bargain sale' of its property to the shareholder at less than fair market value. When there is a 'bargain sale,' the shareholder receives a dividend in the amount of the difference between the fair market value and the price paid for the corporate

18. In the instant case, taxpayers do not contend that Corporation lacked sufficient earnings and profits to support the dividend assessed by the Commissioner. Thus the option granted to Son represents a dividend to the extent that the other requirements of section 301 are met.

property * * *." Green v. United States, 460 F.2d 412, 419 (5th Cir. 1972). As the Supreme Court has recognized, "a sale, if for substantially less than the value of the property sold, may be as effective a means of distributing profits among stockholders as the formal declaration of a dividend." Palmer v. Commissioner, 302 U.S. 63, 58 S.Ct. 67, 82 L.Ed. 50 (1937). No such formal declaration is required for a shareholder to be charged with a constructive dividend. Crosby v. United States, 496 F.2d 1384 (5th Cir.1974).

Two other guiding principles require mention at this stage. It is clear that the intent of the parties does not govern the characterization of a distribution. Instead, courts have looked to the economic *effect* of the transaction at issue in determining the existence of a dividend. See id.; Loftin and Woodard, Inc. v. United States, 577 F.2d 1206, at 1214 (5th Cir.1978). It is also well settled that a dividend does not escape taxation "simply because it fails to pass through the hands of the particular taxpayer when * * * the dividend is diverted at the behest of the shareholder into the hands of others." Green v. United States, supra, 460 F.2d at 419, quoting Sammons v. United States, 433 F.2d 728, 730 (5th Cir.1970), cert. denied, 402 U.S. 945, 91 S.Ct. 1621, 29 L.Ed.2d 113 (1971).

In the *Green* case, supra, this court reviewed a district court's judgment that, as a matter of law, a sale of property by a closely held corporation to the children of the corporation's controlling shareholder did not constitute a constructive dividend. The government had contended that the property was sold to the children at less than fair market value. We reversed the district court, holding that if the corporation did in fact consummate a transaction with favorable consequences for a controlling shareholder's immediate family, "only in the most extraordinary circumstances" would it be possible to conclude that the shareholder had not heavily influenced the corporation's decision. For that reason, we held that the sale was a constructive dividend. 460 F.2d at 420–21.

Likewise, in Crosby v. United States, 496 F.2d 1384 (5th Cir.1974), this court closely examined a transaction to determine whether constructive dividend treatment was warranted. There the corporation made improvements to its stockholder's land after the stockholder had conveyed the land by deed to the corporation. The court determined, however, that the only property right which the corporation had acquired through the transfer of the deed was the right to sell the property. An investigation of the substance of this transaction convinced the court that the underlying purpose of many of the improvements was to benefit the stockholder. We therefore remanded the case for a determination of "which improvements were for a corporate purpose and which were not." Those that were not, we said, were to be treated as constructive dividends. As we recently remarked in *Loftin and Woodard, Inc.*, supra, at 1216.

> "[h]ad the *Crosby* court merely accepted this transaction at face value, it would have overlooked the existence of an economic benefit conferred by the corporation without expectation of repayment and, as a result, overlooked a potential constructive dividend."

This comment is particularly apposite to the instant case. See also Commissioner v. Gordon, 391 U.S. 83, 88 S.Ct. 1517, 1521, 20 L.Ed.2d 448 (1968); Hardin v. United States, 461 F.2d 865 (5th Cir.1972); Honigman v. Commissioner, 466 F.2d 69 (6th Cir.1972). See generally Commissioner v. LoBue, 351 U.S. 243, 76 S.Ct. 800, 803, 100 L.Ed. 1142 (1956) (sale of corporation's own stock to employee at a bargain price pursuant to an employee stock option did not constitute an arm's-length transaction and employee realized taxable gain when he purchased the stock).

These expansive principles governing the treatment of constructive dividends reflect an awareness by Congress and the courts of the ingenious methods which have been devised by owners of closely held corporations trying to escape taxes at the corporate or shareholder level. "Instances of 'constructive' or 'disguised' distributions are commonly encountered in the context of closely held corporations whose dealings with their stockholders are, more often than not, characterized by informality." B. Bittker & J. Eustice, Federal Income Taxation of Corporations and Shareholders 7–24 (3d ed. 1971). As a consequence, courts have generally examined dealings between a closely held corporation and its shareholders or relatives of shareholders with a jaundiced eye and microscopic vision. Such transactions are simply not entitled to the presumption that they are conducted at arm's length. Indeed, they call for special scrutiny. We suggest that the metaphor of a corporation and its sole shareholder walking arm-in-arm is more descriptive of reality than the vision of the corporation and shareholder holding each other apart at arm's length.[20]

The district court, then, was properly skeptical when taxpayers insisted that Corporation and Son dealt at arm's length. Both law and common sense require us not to presume that the option granted to Son was entitled to the same treatment as, for example, the Pope & Carter option, which all concede was negotiated at arm's length. We now proceed to an examination of Son's option to determine whether the district court properly held Father taxable on a constructive dividend in the circumstances of this case.

B. *The Grant of the Option as a Constructive Dividend*

Our inquiry is in two parts. First, we must focus on whether, in fact, the grant of the option conferred a benefit on Son by distributing valuable rights without consideration. If we determine that the option conferred such a benefit, we must then examine whether the resulting

20. The more commonly used image of the "corporate veil" may itself suggest that the nexus between the corporation and its shareholders is often more intimate than taxpayers would have us believe.

corporate distribution constituted a constructive dividend to Father. "[W]hether or not a corporate distribution is a dividend or something else, such as a gift, compensation for services, repayment of a loan * * * or payment for property purchased, presents a question of fact to be determined in each case." Hardin v. United States, 461 F.2d 865, 872 (5th Cir.1972) quoting Lengsfield v. Commissioner, 241 F.2d 508, 510 (5th Cir.1957).

1. *The Option: Valuable Rights or Fair Bargain?*

Our initial task of valuing the option to determine whether the corporation distributed valuable rights to Son is greatly complicated by the unsettled state of the law in this area. Neither the Code nor the applicable case law provides clear guidance. Taxpayers maintain that under the Supreme Court's decision in Palmer v. Commissioner, 302 U.S. 63, 58 S.Ct. 67, 82 L.Ed. 50 (1937), there is no dividend if the exercise price of the option represents the fair market value of the underlying property at the time the option is issued, even if the value of the underlying property has appreciated greatly by the time the option is exercised. Taxpayers argue that the $100,000 exercise price of the option on the combined properties was a reasonable valuation of the fair market value of those properties at the time the option was granted to Son. Thus, according to taxpayers, no valuable rights constituting a dividend were distributed by Corporation.

The government responds first that taxpayers' argument rests on an erroneous reading of *Palmer*, and second, that the 1954 Code has modified this aspect of the *Palmer* decision in any event. We agree with the government that the position contended for by taxpayers is justified neither by good sense [23] nor by the applicable case law.

[The court concluded that the decision in *Palmer* was distinguishable because it involved an option of only 15 days' duration. In addition, the court concluded that the definition of property in section 317(a) includes an option to acquire corporate property and the distribution of the option may constitute a dividend under section 301.]

The 1954 Code also specifies the method for determining the value of a distribution. Under section 301(b)(1)(A), the amount of the distribution is measured by the *fair market value* of the property received. Thus, in the case at bar the amount of the distribution should be measured by the *fair market value* of the option, rather than by the spread between the exercise price and the value of the underlying

23. The government argues that it is unrealistic to believe that the option was of no economic value to Son. Any determination of whether the grant of an option to purchase property constitutes a distribution of valuable rights must consider not only the "spread" between the exercise price of the option and the fair market value of the underlying property, but also the length of time during which the rights can be exercised and the potential for appreciation during that period. The government maintains that where, as here, the option remained open for a period of over two years, during which time favorable zoning action substantially increasing the value of the underlying property was a significant possibility, the option must have been valuable to Son.

property at the time of grant.[25] See Rev.Rul. 70–521. While that spread in some cases may approximate the fair market value of the option,[26] here the duration of the option period and the likelihood of obtaining favorable rezoning must also be considered in determining the option's fair market value. See Treasury Regulation 1.421–6, discussed infra. Thus the determination of whether the grant of the option conferred a benefit on Son is governed by the value of the option, rather than by the spread between the exercise price and the value of the underlying property.

Applying this standard, we are in complete agreement with the district court's finding that the rights granted under the option were of great value to Son. The option entitled Son to reap the benefits of the contemplated rezoning without incurring any of the risks associated with the real estate venture. He paid no consideration for his rights. If, during the two and one half year option period the properties appreciated in value, Son would realize a gain. If the value of the property decreased or remained the same, Son would be no worse off. Son was truly in a "heads I win, tails I don't lose" position. This "option privilege" represented valuable property to Son. As Treasury Regulation 1.421–6, which addresses an analogous question in the employee stock option area, explains:

> [I]rrespective of whether there is a right to make an immediate bargain purchase of the property subject to the option, the fair market value of the option includes the value of the option privilege. The option privilege is the opportunity to benefit at any time during the period the option may be exercised from any appreciation during such period in the value of the property subject to the option without risking any capital.

Any doubts that Corporation distributed valuable rights to Son when it granted the option are dispelled by comparing Son's option with that received by Pope & Carter. Pope & Carter agreed to pay substantial amounts to keep its option open and, in addition, obligated itself to devote reasonable time and effort to obtaining favorable rezoning. In return it received the right to acquire the property for

25. In Commissioner v. Gordon, 391 U.S. 83, 88 S.Ct. 1517, 20 L.Ed.2d 448 (1968) the Supreme Court had occasion to examine the applicability of *Palmer* under the 1954 Code. The question before the Court in *Gordon* was whether a corporate distribution of rights to purchase stock of another corporation constituted a dividend. The Court held that the distribution of valuable rights resulted in a dividend. But because the value of the shares exceeded the exercise price when the rights were distributed, the court did not consider whether the distribution of valuable rights results in a dividend when the exercise price equals the reasonable value of the shares on the date that the rights are distributed. 88 S.Ct. at 1521 and n. 4. The Court also declined to decide whether the dividend occurs at the time of grant or at the time of exercise. See 88 S.Ct. at 1521.

26. *Palmer* itself may be such a case. Indeed, the *Palmer* decision could be explained on the basis that where the option period was limited to a few days and no appreciation in the underlying property during the option period was contemplated, virtually the entire value of the option was reflected in the spread between the exercise price of the option and the market value of the underlying property.

$500,000, a price far in excess of the fair market value of the property at the time the option was granted. Son's option, on the other hand, remained in effect for a longer period, imposed no obligations on Son, and allowed him to purchase a one-half interest in the property for only $100,000 plus 5½ percent interest. Even if we ignore the fact that the amendment to Son's option, which extended the exercise period for an additional two years without increasing the exercise price, was granted a mere thirteen days before the grant of the Pope & Carter option, see footnote 22 supra, it is apparent that in granting the option, Corporation conferred a benefit on Son by distributing valuable rights.

2. *The Corporate Distribution: a Constructive Dividend?*

Having concluded that Corporation distributed valuable rights to Son, we can easily dispose of taxpayers' contention that the grant of the option should not result in a constructive dividend to Father. Whether a corporate distribution is a dividend presents a question of fact to be determined in each case. Hardin v. United States, supra, 461 F.2d at 872. A crucial consideration in characterizing a distribution is whether it primarily served a corporate purpose or a shareholder purpose.[28] The tasks of weighing the evidence, drawing inferences from the facts, *and choosing between* conflicting inferences are, of course, part of the function of the district court. We must not disturb that determination unless we are convinced that there is "clear error" in the district court's findings. Loftin and Woodard, Inc. v. United States, supra, at 1214; Honigman v. Commissioner, 466 F.2d 69, 74 (6th Cir.1972). See Lengsfield v. Commissioner, 241 F.2d 508, 510 (5th Cir.1957).

Here the district court found that the distribution to Son was made "by virtue of Father's position as sole stockholder of the corporate plaintiff" and therefore resulted in a dividend to Father. The record does not require the contrary finding that a corporate purpose was served by giving Son an option to purchase property at Corporation's cost when all parties recognized that the value of the property would

28. In constructive dividend cases involving expenditures which confer a benefit on a shareholder, this court has held that the determination of a constructive dividend *vel non* turns on whether the payments are "primarily for corporate benefit." *Loftin and Woodard Inc.*, supra, at 1215; Sammons v. Commissioner, 472 F.2d 449 (5th Cir.1972). These cases have generally involved corporate payments, ostensibly for corporate purposes, which improve the value of a shareholder's property, see *Loftin and Woodard, Inc.*, supra; Crosby v. United States, supra; or a transfer of funds between related corporations, see Sammons v. Commissioner, 472 F.2d 449 (5th Cir.), cert. denied, 402 U.S. 945, 91 S.Ct. 1621, 29 L.Ed.2d 113 (1971). See also Hardin v. United States, supra (no business purpose for corporate payments to widow of controlling shareholder's brother, a former employee, even though taxpayer alleged that corporation had a duty to widow because of her husband's past services on behalf of the corporation).

In Green v. United States, supra, a case involving a sale of property to a shareholder at less than fair market value, we held that the sale would constitute a constructive dividend if the taxpayer in his personal capacity exercised "substantial influence" over the corporate decision to sell the property at a bargain price. 460 F.2d at 420–21. This standard has the same purpose as the "primary benefit" test; in both instances the issue is whether the distribution was made for a corporate, rather than a shareholder, purpose.

substantially appreciate if favorable rezoning were obtained. Taxpayers maintain that the option was granted because of Corporation's interest in obtaining the benefit of Son's services. The evidence, however, more than adequately supports the conclusion that the grant of the option primarily served the personal interests of Father in his shareholder capacity. Indeed, taxpayers admit that the option was granted to satisfy the moral obligation of Father to compensate Son for taking advantage of a business opportunity Father had personally discouraged Son from pursuing. Taxpayers' Brief at 7. No legitimate business purpose is served by the distribution of funds to satisfy the personal or moral responsibilities of a shareholder. Hardin v. United States, supra, 461 F.2d at 872–73.

Essentially taxpayers urge this court to draw inferences from the evidence different from those drawn by the district court. This we decline to do under the record in this case. As we held in United States v. Green, supra, where a corporation consummates a transaction with favorable consequences for a controlling shareholder's immediate family, "only in the most extraordinary circumstances" would it be possible to conclude that the shareholder had not exercised "substantial influence" in causing a diversion of corporate assets, thereby justifying constructive dividend treatment. No such circumstances are present here. 460 F.2d at 420–21.

Since we hold that there is no clear error in the findings of the district court, we affirm the district court's conclusion that Father received a constructive dividend from the grant by Corporation to Son of the option on the Piedmont–Old Ivy property.

C. *Valuing the Dividend*

The final issue presented by this appeal is whether the district court properly valued Father's constructive dividend. In particular, questions have been raised concerning the district court's use of the consideration paid by Pope & Carter in valuing Son's option. To resolve this issue, we must first examine whether the dividend occurred upon the grant of the option or upon its exercise by Son. If we determine that *grant* of the option constituted a dividend, we must then consider both the district court's finding that the option had no ascertainable value at the time of grant and the Court's subsequent valuation of the option at the time of exercise in 1968. If, on the other hand, the dividend arose only upon Son's *exercise* of the option, we need only consider the proper valuation of the option at that time. * * *

[The court concluded that the dividend occurred at the time of the grant of the option. Because the taxpayers had failed to prove that the option had an ascertainable fair market value at the time of grant, the District Court properly applied the "open transaction" doctrine and deferred the recognition of the dividend income until the option was exercised. Burnet v. Logan, 283 U.S. 404 (1931). However, the court held that the District Court had erred in valuing the dividend by reference to the Pope & Carter option and remanded the case to determine the value of the option by subtracting the $100,000 exercise price from the fair market value of the underlying property on the date the option was exercised. On remand, the District Court concluded that the option could have been valued in the year that it was granted and entered judgment for the taxpayer because the Commissioner had not asserted a deficiency for that year. 518 F.Supp. 813 (N.D.Ga.1981). On appeal, the Court of Appeals again reversed, concluding that under the law of the case its prior decision controlled the determination of the year in which the distribution occurred. 685 F.2d 1318 (11th Cir.1982).]

ILLUSTRATIVE MATERIAL

A. CONSTRUCTIVE DIVIDENDS IN GENERAL

1. *Generally*

As long as sufficient earnings and profits exist for a distribution to be characterized as a dividend under section 316(a), any distribution to shareholders in their capacity as shareholders, see Regulations, section 1.301–1(c), which is not excluded from dividend treatment under section 301(f), will be taxed as a dividend, even if not distributed in proportion to stock ownership. As the court in *Baumer* found, if there is a direct benefit to the individual shareholders as a result of the corporate distribution, the benefit is a dividend for tax purposes—a so-called "constructive" dividend—although it may not be a formal dividend as far as state corporation law is concerned. See Paramount–Richards Theatres, Inc. v. Commissioner, 153 F.2d 602 (5th Cir. 1946), in which the court described this doctrine as follows:

"Corporate earnings may constitute a dividend notwithstanding that the formalities of a dividend declaration are not observed; that the distribution is not recorded on the corporate books as such; that it is not in proportion to stockholdings, or even that some of the stockholders do not participate in its benefits. Nothing in the statute or decisions warrants the view that a dividend distribution loses its character as such and becomes a deductible business expense merely because stockholders do not benefit equally from the distribution." (604)

In some situations, as in the material, supra, page 384, dealing with characterization of shareholder investment in the corporation as debt or equity, there may be an actual payment to the shareholder but which is termed interest, rent, compensation, or something else. See Hutchins Standard Service, Inc. v. Commissioner, 41 T.C.M. 777 (1981), holding that repayment of a purported loan from the shareholder to the corporation, which was recharacterized as an equity contribution, was a dividend. Here, for the most part, the principal stakes in the characterization issue are the deductibility to the corporation of the payment. Interest, compensation and rent are deductible by the corporation; dividends are not deductible. The shareholder would be taxed on the payment as ordinary income regardless of the characterization. But if the shareholder is a corporation, if the payment is a dividend, the section 243 intercorporate dividend deduction may be available. See infra, page 507.

In other situations the corporation may make a clearly nondeductible distribution to the shareholder which the shareholder claims is nevertheless a nontaxable receipt, such as loan proceeds or a return of capital. In Rev.Rul. 83–141, 1983–2 Cum.Bull. 65, a corporation distributed earnings and profits to its shareholders in proportion to the volume of business done by the shareholders with the corporation in their capacity as customers, rather than in proportion to shareholdings. Nevertheless, because the distribution was made to them in their capacity as shareholders, rather than in their capacity as customers, the distribution was characterized as a dividend, rather than as a nontaxable price rebate. In still other situations the disguised dividend is in the form of a benefit obtained by the shareholder as a result of corporate action not involving an actual monetary distribution to the shareholder, such as permitting the shareholder to use an automobile or personal residence owned by the corporation. In many of these cases the corporation nevertheless claims a deduction as an ordinary and necessary business expense for its costs incurred in providing the benefit to the shareholder. At the same time, the shareholder often does not report any income.

While in some cases nonreporting by the shareholder may be based on a good faith belief that the distribution was a loan or that nothing of value was received from the corporation, many cases involve deliberate tax avoidance. There is an increasing tendency for the courts to impose negligence and civil fraud penalties in cases where the corporation distributes cash to the shareholder or corporate expenditures provide a clear economic benefit to the shareholder and the shareholder fails to include the value of the benefit in income. See, e.g., Hagaman v. Commissioner, 54 T.C.M. 992 (1987) (fraud penalty imposed where shareholder diverted cash receipts of corporation for payment of personal expenses and did not report distribution as income); McCabe v. Commissioner, 49 T.C.M. 572 (1985) (penalties for negligence and for instituting primarily for delay Tax Court proceedings contesting deficiency imposed where shareholder did not report as income payment by corporation of shareholder's personal travel expenses).

If the expenditure serves a corporate purpose, even though a shareholder is benefited, the payment of an expense by the corporation may not always be a constructive dividend. In Magnon v. Commissioner, 73 T.C. 980, 993–94 (1980), the Tax Court explained the test as follows: "Where a corporation confers an economic benefit on a shareholder without the expectation of repayment, that benefit becomes a constructive dividend, taxable to the shareholder, even though neither the corporation nor the shareholder intended a dividend. However, 'not every corporate expenditure which incidentally confers economic benefit on a shareholder is a constructive dividend.' The crucial test of the existence of a constructive dividend is whether the 'distribution was primarily for the benefit of the shareholder.'" Applying this standard, the court found that corporate payments for construction work on the shareholder's residence were constructive dividends but that payments to another corporation owned by the shareholder were not. In addition, where the "distribution" is regarded as having no measurable value to the shareholders, a dividend will not result. Thus, in Wilkinson v. Commissioner, 29 T.C. 421 (1957), a bank required to divest itself of stock placed the stock in trust for its stockholders, the beneficial interest in the trust being locked-in with the bank stock so that the two had to be dealt with jointly. The court said that a dividend did not result since the rights of the shareholders had not substantially changed.

2. *Significance of earnings and profits*

As with the case of formally declared dividends, a constructive distribution is a dividend for tax purposes only to the extent that the corporation has either accumulated or current earnings and profits. In Truesdell v. Commissioner, 89 T.C. 1280 (1987), the Tax Court rejected the Commissioner's argument that corporate income diverted to a sole shareholder's personal account was taxable in full without regard to the corporation's earnings and profits, and instead applied constructive dividend analysis. In so doing the Tax Court rejected its prior decision in Benes v. Commissioner, 42 T.C. 358 (1964), aff'd 355 F.2d 929 (6th Cir.1966), and followed the approach adopted by the Ninth Circuit in Simon v. Commissioner, 248 F.2d 869 (8th Cir.1957). In *Simon,* black market profits not reported by the corporation and diverted to the shareholders were taxable to the latter only to the extent of corporate earnings and profits. The Sixth Circuit, however, appears to adhere to a contrary position, taxing such shareholder diversions in full, without regard to the earnings and profits of the corporation, on the theory that the shareholder has asserted dominion and control over the funds. See Weir v. Commissioner, 283 F.2d 675 (6th Cir.1960). But if a shareholder's diversion of corporate income is more in the nature of embezzlement or diversion of funds to defraud other shareholders or corporate creditors, the diverted funds will be fully taxable rather than treated as corporate distributions. See Leaf v. Commissioner, 33 T.C. 1093 (1960), aff'd per curiam, 295 F.2d 503 (6th Cir.1961). Where the Commissioner asserts that a constructive distribution is taxable in full as a dividend, the taxpayer bears the burden of establishing that the corporation had insufficient earnings and profits to support treatment of the entire distribution as a dividend. DiZenzo v. Commissioner, 348 F.2d 122 (2d Cir.1965).

B. COMPENSATION TO SHAREHOLDERS

1. *Salary and Bonuses*

Disguised dividends very frequently take the form of excessive salary and bonus payments made to shareholder-employees. Recharacterization of excessive salaries and compensation to shareholder-employees is facilitated by section 162(a)(1) allowing a deduction of "a reasonable allowance for salaries or other compensation for personal services actually rendered." Regulations, section 1.162–7(b)(1), re-enforce this message by specifically providing that "[a]n ostensible salary paid by a corporation may be a dividend on its stock." Cases involving the recharacterization of purported compensation as dividends of necessity turn on the particular facts of each case. Although there are many formulations of the relevant factors, the following are among those most frequently enumerated: (1) the extent and importance of the shareholder-employee's role in corporate management and activities; (2) the comparability of the purported compensation with that paid to employees performing similar services for other employers; (3) the size, complexity, and economic condition (profitability) of the corporate business; (4) the relationship of the purported compensation to shareholdings (e.g., proportionality); and (5) the corporation's dividend policy. See Elliotts, Inc. v. Commissioner, 716 F.2d 1241 (9th Cir.1983), in which the court also considered whether the corporate profits remaining after paying the purported compensation would provide an acceptable rate of return to a hypothetical investment in the corporation's stock by an outside investor.

In Charles McCandless Tile Service v. United States, 422 F.2d 1336 (Ct. Cl.1970), the Claims Court recharacterized as dividends a portion of the compensation paid to shareholder-employees, even though the amount of the compensation was found to be reasonable, because the corporation had a history of paying little or no dividends. The Tax Court and several Courts of Appeals refused to follow this "automatic dividend" rule, see, e.g., Laure v. Commissioner, 70 T.C. 1087 (1978); Charles Schneider & Co. v. Commissioner, 500 F.2d 148 (8th Cir.1974); and Edwin's, Inc. v. United States, 501 F.2d 675 (7th Cir.1974). In Rev.Rul. 79–8, 1979–1 Cum.Bull. 92, the Internal Revenue Service concluded that although "the failure of a closely held corporation to pay more than an insubstantial portion of its earnings as dividends on its stock is a very important consideration," deductions for compensation to shareholder-employees found to be otherwise reasonable in amount will not be denied solely on that ground.

Contingent compensation to shareholder-employees based on corporate profitability, particularly when combined with infrequent dividend payments or compensation in proportion to shareholdings, frequently results in recharacterization of the contingent compensation as dividends. See, e.g., Charles Schneider & Co., Inc., supra; Paul E. Kummer Realty Co. v. Commissioner, 511 F.2d 313 (8th Cir.1975). Contingent compensation arrangements are accorded some protection by Regulations, section 1.162–7(b)(2), which provide that a deduction will be allowed for otherwise excessive compensation paid under an arm's length contingent compensation agreement the terms of which are reasonable at the time it is entered into. See Kennedy v. Commissioner, 671 F.2d 167 (6th Cir.1982) (contingent compensation reasonable where not in proportion to shareholdings); *Elliots, Inc.*, supra. Even though contingent compensation contracts sometimes are recognized in the case of sole shareholder-employees, the underlying rationale for recognizing such contracts is not as strong in those cases as in cases involving nonshareholder employees. A sole shareholder needs no additional incentive to give his best efforts in managing his business. This was noted in University Chevrolet Co. v. Commissioner, 16 T.C. 1452, 1455 (1951), aff'd 199 F.2d 629 (5th Cir.1952), as follows: "For the sole owner to pay himself a bonus to do his best in managing his own business is nonsense." However, although contingent compensation contracts between a corporation and its sole shareholder may be suspect, under the *Moline Properties* doctrine, discussed supra, page 322, which treats a corporation and its shareholders as separate entities, such contracts cannot be subjected to an automatic dividend rule.

2. *Fees*

Tulia Feedlot, Inc. v. United States, 513 F.2d 800 (5th Cir.1975), held that corporate payments to shareholders for their becoming guarantors of corporate debt were constructive dividends since the "guarantee" fees had no reasonable connection with the amount of loans guaranteed. For a subsequent year, however, the taxpayer was able to prevail in a different forum because it established that the guarantees were necessary to obtain the loans, the guarantees would not have been given without the payment of fees to the guarantor shareholders, and the fees were paid in proportion to the amount of debt guaranteed rather than in proportion to shareholdings. Tulia Feedlot, Inc. v. United States, 3 Cl.Ct. 364 (1983). See also Olton Feed Yard, Inc. v. United States, 592 F.2d 272 (5th Cir.1979) (affirming jury verdict that loan guarantee fees paid to shareholders were constructive dividends where payments were in proportion to stock ownership of a profitable corporation which never paid any dividends).

C. LOANS TO SHAREHOLDERS

1. *Loan versus distribution*

The question whether shareholder withdrawals from a corporation constitute loans or dividends also frequently arises. The ultimate factual inquiries in such cases are whether there is a reasonable expectation of repayment and an intent to enforce the repayment of the disbursed funds. See Pierce v. Commissioner, 61 T.C. 424 (1974) (advances to shareholders held to be loans where an intent to repay was found and substantial repayments were in fact made). To ascertain these subjective facts, the courts examine numerous subsidiary "objective" facts and circumstances. Among the most important "objective" facts are the following: (1) the extent of shareholder control over the corporation; (2) the retained earnings and dividend history of the corporation; (3) the size of the withdrawals; (4) the presence or absence of conventional indicia of debt, such as promissory notes with a determinable maturity date, collateral, and provision for interest; (5) the treatment of the advances in the corporate records; (6) the history of payment of interest and principal; and (7) the shareholder's use of the funds. See, e.g., Busch v. Commissioner, 728 F.2d 945 (7th Cir.1984). These factors are similar to those used to distinguish debt from equity in the case of shareholder contributions, discussed, supra, page 384, and, as is the case there, no one factor is determinative. For example, in Turner v. Commissioner, 49 T.C.M. 1107 (1985), aff'd 812 F.2d 650 (11th Cir.1987), advances to the shareholder were loans where they were evidenced by interest bearing notes, secured by mortgages, treated as loans by independent auditors, and the corporation credited shareholder-employee's salary against the debt. However, other advances initially debited to an "advance" account but subsequently credited and reclassified as business expenses were constructive dividends because there was no evidence of intent to repay the amounts; other advances evidenced only by a book account entry as "due from officers" were dividends.

On the other hand, in Livernois Trust v. Commissioner, 433 F.2d 879 (6th Cir.1970), the existence of demand notes bearing 6 percent interest did not control the characterization of advances to a shareholder as loans rather than dividends. In Berthold v. Commissioner, 404 F.2d 119 (6th Cir.1968), a dividend distribution was found where no security was given, no notes were drawn, no interest was paid, and there were no repayments or efforts to enforce the "indebtedness". Electric & Neon, Inc. v. Commissioner, 56 T.C. 1324 (1971), held that advances were dividends rather than loans where there was no express obligation evidencing the indebtedness and it was unrealistic to expect that the corporation would demand payment from its 97 percent shareholder.

2. *Below market rate of interest loans*

Section 7872 requires the imputation of a dividend where a corporation makes a below-market or interest-free loan to a shareholder. The shareholder may then be entitled to an offsetting interest deduction under section 163. The deductibility of such imputed interest by the shareholder, however, is subject to all of the limitations that generally apply to the deductibility of the interest depending on the use to which the loan proceeds are applied by the shareholder. See, e.g., section 163(d) (limiting deductions for investment interest); section 163(h) (disallowing deductions for personal interest); section 263A(f) (requiring capitalization of certain production period interest); section 265 (disallowing deduction of interest incurred with respect to tax-free bonds); section 469 (restrictions on deductions of passive losses). The corporation recognizes interest income but, of course, obtains no offsetting deductions for the imputed dividend. When the loan is payable on demand, both payments are deemed to have been made on December 31st of each year the loan is outstanding, and the amount of the dividend and the deemed interest payment equals the forgone interest for the year. Section 7872(a). But where the loan is for a specified term, section 7872(b) provides that the dividend distribution is made on the date the loan is made, and its amount is determined by subtracting the net present value, using a specified rate, of the payment due to the corporation from the amount of the loan; the imputed interest payments are treated as occurring over the term of the loan by applying OID principles, discussed supra, page 382.

D. CORPORATE EXPENDITURES RESULTING IN ECONOMIC BENEFIT TO SHAREHOLDERS

1. *General*

There are a variety of situations in which corporate expenses ostensibly incurred in furtherance of the business enterprise have been found to be nondeductible constructive dividends because of the personal benefits derived therefrom by the shareholders. Constructive dividends often take the form of the rent free use of corporate property by shareholders for personal purposes. See, e.g., Dean v. Commissioner, 187 F.2d 1019 (3d Cir.1951) (rent free use of residence owned by corporation); Melvin v. Commissioner, 88 T.C. 63 (1987) (use of corporate automobiles for personal purposes); Finney v. Commissioner, 39 T.C.M. 938 (1980) (use of boats owned by corporation; negligence penalty imposed on corporation for deducting operating costs of boats).

Expenditures for goods and services delivered to shareholders are another frequently encountered example of constructive dividends. Thus, improvements made to a shareholder's land by a corporation were held to constitute a constructive dividend in Gibbs v. Tomlinson, 362 F.2d 394 (5th Cir.1966), where the court found a lack of intent to pay the corporation for the improvements. In Greenspon v. Commissioner, 229 F.2d 947 (8th Cir. 1956), a dividend was found because there was no corporate purpose for a corporation selling industrial pipe to pay for landscaping and maintaining the farm home of the sole stockholder; the Tax Court stated that the "relationship between the aesthetic stimulation of a potential customer from the view of an unusual array of shrubbery and flowers and his order for pipe is much too oblique." The same principle applies to payments of a shareholder's personal living expenses. See Bennett v. Commissioner, 53 T.C.M. 403 (1987) (shareholder's personal telephone and credit card bills; fraud penalty imposed); Meridian Wood Products Co., Inc. v. United States, 725 F.2d 1183 (9th Cir.1984) (shareholder's personal travel and entertainment expenses); Larkin v. Commissioner, 394 F.2d 494 (1st Cir.1968) (payments for health plan covering shareholder-officers, since the benefits were not related to services as employees). See also Sachs v. Commissioner, 277 F.2d 879 (8th Cir.1960) (corporate payment of fine imposed on stockholder-president for filing a false corporate tax return, where he and his brothers owned almost all of stock).

The same disbursement can have both a "business expense" aspect and a dividend aspect because the corporation may deduct the expenditure as a business expense while the shareholder fails to include in income any amount attributable to the expense. Some cases involve only an assertion by the Internal Revenue Service that the shareholder received a dividend; others involve only the issue of whether the expense is properly deductible by the corporation. In most instances, however, the Internal Revenue Service asserts deficiencies against both the corporation and the shareholder. In such cases, disallowance of the corporation's deduction does not always result in a constructive dividend to the shareholder. Often corporate travel and entertainment expenses are disallowed because of a failure to satisfy the substantiation requirements of section 274, but the shareholder is found to have no constructive dividend because the expenditures served a corporate purpose. For example, in Ashby v. Commissioner, 50 T.C. 409 (1968), the shareholder received a constructive dividend on account of the personal use of a boat owned by the corporation. The fact that all deductions with respect to the boat were disallowed to the corporation under section 274(d) for failure to substantiate that the boat was used primarily in business did not prevent the taxpayer from reducing the amount of the dividend in proportion to the actual business use of the boat.

Curiosities, of course, are found in this area. Thus, Peacock v. Commissioner, 256 F.2d 160 (5th Cir.1958), found a gift to its two shareholders rather than income where a corporation permitted the shareholders, a mother and son, to occupy a residence owned by the corporation at a rental considerably below a fair rental.

2. *Valuation of Constructive Distributions Attributable to Corporate Expenditures*

The fair use (rental) value is the generally preferred measure of the amount of a dividend if the shareholder receives the rent free use of corporate property for personal purposes. However, the Internal Revenue Service and the courts frequently use the costs incurred by the corporation to provide such property as a surrogate for the fair use value. In Cirelli v. Commissioner, 82 T.C. 335 (1984), the Tax Court held that a shareholder received a constructive dividend equal to the expenses of maintaining a yacht that were disallowed as corporate deductions, while noting that the proper measure of the amount of the dividend when the distribution is in the form of the use of property is fair rental value of the property. It did not apply that measure, however, because the taxpayer failed to prove that the fair rental value was less than the disallowed expenses. But in Ireland v. United States, 621 F.2d 731 (5th Cir.1980), the court held that the amount of a constructive dividend arising from free use of a corporate airplane was the fair charter value of the flights, where the taxpayer proved that that value was less than the disallowed corporate expenses. See also Melvin v. Commissioner, 88 T.C. 63 (1987), in which shareholders who obtained the use of corporate vehicles for personal purposes by reimbursing the corporation for its costs incurred with respect to the automobiles were found to have a dividend equal to the amount by which the fair rental values of the automobiles exceeded the costs incurred by the corporation; Loftin and Woodard, Inc. v. United States, 577 F.2d 1206, 1222 (5th Cir.1978): "The cases supporting the use of cost stand for the proposition that cost is an *acceptable* measure of value when there is no credible evidence of fair market value or when evidence of fair market value exists but is clearly rebutted."

3. *Payment of Shareholder's Debts*

Payment by a corporation of a shareholder's debt generally constitutes a constructive dividend. In Gaines v. Commissioner, 45 T.C.M. 363 (1982), a corporation paid expenses incurred by a predecessor partnership. Because the court found that the debts of the predecessor partnership had not been assumed by the corporation upon formation, the payment constituted a constructive dividend to the shareholders who were the former partners. If there is a corporate purpose for the payment, it might not be a dividend even though the shareholder is also benefitted. Thus, in Dolese v. United States, 605 F.2d 1146 (10th Cir.1979), the payment by four corporations of legal fees incurred by their shareholder with respect to his divorce were held to be constructive dividends. But the portion of those legal fees that related to clarification of an injunction, issued in the course of the divorce proceedings, restraining the corporations from engaging in any transactions outside the ordinary course of business, even though part of the divorce proceedings, was not a constructive dividend because those costs were incurred to resist actions that were detrimental to the corporation. Mere corporate liability on the obligation, however, does not preclude treatment of payment as a constructive dividend. In Yelencsics v. Commissioner, 74 T.C. 1513 (1980), the corporation cosigned a note with its shareholder without receiving any consideration and without any corporate business purpose. When the corporation paid the note, the shareholder received a constructive dividend.

A constructive dividend has been found where corporate funds were used to discharge an obligation which the shareholder had personally guaranteed. See Wortham Machinery Co. v. United States, 521 F.2d 160 (10th Cir.1975). Miller v. Commissioner, 48 T.C.M. 931 (1984), found a constructive dividend where a medical professional corporation paid a debt of a bankrupt hospital that had been guaranteed by the corporation's sole shareholder, even though the purpose of the loan was to enable the doctor to practice at the hospital through the corporation.

4. *Insurance on Shareholder's Lives*

In Prunier v. Commissioner, 248 F.2d 818 (1st Cir.1957), eight insurance policies were taken out on the lives of two brothers who had each owned one-half the stock of their corporation. Technical ownership of the policies and the right to change the beneficiaries were in the hands of the brothers. However, the minutes of the corporation indicated that upon the death of either brother, the policy proceeds on his life were to go to the corporation, the funds to be used to purchase the stock interest of the decedent brother. The corporation paid the premiums on the policies and the Commissioner asserted that the shareholders were in receipt of constructive dividends as a result. The Court of Appeals, reversing the Tax Court, found that under state law the corporation would have been treated as the equitable owner of the insurance policies. Since it was also the beneficiary of the policies, by virtue of the stockholder agreement, the payment of the premiums did not constitute constructive dividends to the shareholders.

Casale v. Commissioner, 247 F.2d 440 (2d Cir.1957), involving an insurance policy obtained by a corporation on the life of the sole shareholder (in effect), who was also president of the corporation, to provide funds to meet the corporation's liability under a deferred compensation contract made at the same time with the shareholder, and Sanders v. Fox, 253 F.2d 855 (10th Cir.1958), a stock purchase case similar to *Prunier*, also found no dividend to the shareholders involved. Rev.Rul. 59–184, 1959–1 Cum.Bull. 65, follow these decisions. Where the shareholder, or the beneficiaries designated by him have irrevocable rights in the policy, then the corporate payment of the premiums will constitute a dividend. See, e.g., Genshaft v. Commissioner, 64 T.C. 282 (1975).

The receipt of the insurance proceeds by the corporation on the death of the insured is not taxable income to it under section 101. If the insurance proceeds are then distributed by the corporation to the shareholders on the death of the insured, the tax consequences depend on the distribution transaction. In Ducros v. Commissioner, 272 F.2d 49 (6th Cir.1959), the proceeds of a policy as to which the corporation had reserved the right to change the beneficiary were paid directly by the insurance company to two named beneficiary-shareholders on the death of the insured. The court found the proceeds exempt to the recipients under section 101 and not a dividend to them since the distribution was made directly to them by the insurance company. The decision seems erroneous and the Internal Revenue Service will not follow it. Rev.Rul. 61–134, 1961–2 Cum.Bull. 250. Estate of Horne v. Commissioner, 64 T.C. 1020 (1975), reached the same result as *Ducros* on the ground that, for estate tax purposes, the deceased controlling shareholder was treated as owning the policy directly and it would be inconsistent to treat the policy proceeds as a corporate distribution. Instead, either (1) the premium payments on the policy during lifetime should have been constructive dividends to the decedent, or (2) the policy proceeds constituted a dividend to the estate, followed by a transfer to the heir under the shareholder's will. See also Golden v. Commissioner, 113 F.2d 590 (3d Cir.1940), reaching essentially the opposite result from *Ducros.*

5. *Charitable Contributions*

A charitable contribution made by a closely held corporation could be viewed as a constructive dividend to the controlling shareholders of the corporation if the contribution served only the personal charitable interests of the shareholders. But Knott v. Commissioner, 67 T.C. 681 (1977), held that a bargain sale by a corporation to a charitable foundation controlled by the corporation's principal shareholders did not result in constructive dividends to the shareholders because "[t]he [shareholders] did not receive money or other property from the corporation; their personal debts were not assumed by the corporation; the corporation did not purchase and maintain property for the [shareholders'] personal use and enjoyment; and the [shareholders'] family members did not obtain property or other benefits." (694). Thus, in the court's view, the personal interest of the principal shareholders in seeing that the charitable contribution was made was not sufficient to result in a constructive dividend. The Internal Revenue Service follows the *Knott* case, Rev.Rul. 79–9, 1979–1 Cum.Bull. 125.

Payments by subsidiaries to parent corporations which are tax-exempt institutions have been held to be dividends and not deductible charitable contributions. For example, in Crosby Valve & Gage Co. v. Commissioner, 380 F.2d 146 (1st Cir.1967), the taxpayer, a business corporation wholly owned by a charitable foundation, transferred bonds to its parent without receiving consideration in return. The taxpayer asserted that it was entitled to a deduction for a charitable contribution. The court found the distribution to be a nondeductible dividend: "[W]ere petitioner's deduction to be allowed it would be able to make a partially tax-free distribution of its earnings to its sole shareholder-something denied to its competitors * * *." (149).

Baumer

E. INDIRECT BENEFITS TO SHAREHOLDERS: PAYMENTS TO SHAREHOLDER'S RELATIVES

1. *General*

As *Baumer* illustrates, a distribution of money or property to a relative of a shareholder that serves a personal purpose of the shareholder rather than a corporate business purpose can be a constructive dividend to the shareholder, even though the shareholder personally did not receive anything. See, e.g., Snyder v. Commissioner, 47 T.C.M. 355 (1983) (shareholder received constructive dividends as result of use of corporation's automobiles by shareholder's daughters for nonbusiness purpose, payment by corporation to shareholder's son of salary in excess of the amount deductible under section 162(a)(1) as reasonable compensation, payment by corporation of credit card charges incurred by shareholder's son to pay living expenses while at college, and payment of alimony to shareholder's ex-wife). Constructive dividends of this nature arise most commonly when a corporation pays excessive compensation to a relative of a shareholder and the corporation's deduction is disallowed under section 162(a)(1). The distributee relative is then treated as having received a tax free gift, and the shareholder may be liable for a gift tax as well. But see Caledonian Record Publishing Co., Inc. v. United States, 579 F.Supp. 449 (D.Vt.1983) (excessive compensation paid by a corporation to the son of the controlling shareholder was treated as a gift from the corporation to the son; I.R.S. did not assert deficiency against father based on constructive dividend theory); Smith v. Manning, 189 F.2d 345 (3d Cir.1951) (excessive salaries paid by father to daughters taxed to daughters as compensation, notwithstanding disallowance of father's deduction).

2. *Surviving Spouse*

Corporate distributions to shareholder-surviving spouses after the death of their spouse-executives raise a number of issues. If the payment is characterized as additional salary for the past services of the executive, the amount is taxable to the surviving spouse and deductible at the corporate level. On the other hand, if the payment can qualify as a gift, it is tax-free in the hands of the recipient, and the corporation's deduction is limited by section 274(b). Finally, if the payment is viewed as a dividend distribution, it is taxable to the recipient and nondeductible by the corporation. Resolution of these issues tends to be fact specific, and no one factor is determinative. For example, Rubber Associates, Inc. v. Commissioner, 335 F.2d 75 (6th Cir.1964), held that a payment was deductible deferred compensation rather than a dividend distribution because it was made as part of a plan to pay additional compensation for the past services of deceased officer-shareholders. In contrast, Barbourville Brick Co. v. Commissioner, 37 T.C. 7 (1961), held that payments to a widow who was the principal shareholder were dividends, not deductible expenses, despite the fact that they were related in amount to her husband's previous salary.

F. BARGAIN TRANSACTIONS

A sale of property to a shareholder at a price below fair market value will result in the "bargain" element being taxed as a dividend. In Honigman

v. Commissioner, 466 F.2d 69 (6th Cir.1972), the shareholder purchased a hotel from the corporation for $661,000. The Internal Revenue Service on audit took the position that the hotel was worth $1,300,000 and asserted the tax on the excess of that amount over the actual purchase price as a dividend. Appraisal evidence submitted at the trial showed a range of values between $625,000 and $1,300,000. The Tax Court, affirmed by the Court of Appeals, found the fair market value of the property was $830,000 and accordingly taxed $169,000 as a dividend. The Court of Appeals rejected the taxpayer's argument that in a bargain purchase situation there must be an intent to distribute a dividend before dividend characterization of the bargain element is possible. But see Lehman v. Commissioner, 25 T.C. 629 (1955), in which a corporation transferred to its shareholders warrants to buy whiskey at the price at which the whiskey could be sold by the corporation under price regulations. Since this price was less than the price at which the shareholders could sell the whiskey, they made a profit. The court said that the resulting benefit was not a dividend, since the sale by the corporation was at its top price.

Leases of corporate property to shareholders at less than fair rental value similarly are constructive dividends. A lease by a corporation to a stockholder of a theatre at a rental obviously too low in view of the profits from the property was held to result in the profits being taxed to the corporation and then to the shareholder as a dividend. 58th Street Plaza Theatre, Inc. v. Commissioner, 195 F.2d 724 (2d Cir.1952).

A lease of the shareholder's property to the corporation for a rental in excess of fair rental value also gives rise to a constructive dividend. In Lucas v. Commissioner, 71 T.C. 838 (1979), aff'd 657 F.2d 841 (6th Cir.1981), the shareholders leased a coal deposit from a third party for a royalty of 25 cents per ton and subleased the coal to another party who agreed to pay royalties of 50 cents per ton on coal sold to the lessors' wholly owned corporation and 25 cents per ton on coal sold to unrelated parties. The additional 25 cents per ton royalty on coal sold to the corporation was held to be a dividend from the corporation. In Omholt v. Commissioner, 60 T.C. 541 (1973), the taxpayer received an excessive royalty payment in the form of cash and notes from his corporation. Because of the corporation's financial situation it was unable to pay the notes at the time they were issued. The Tax Court found the taxpayer received a constructive dividend when the payments on the notes were made and not on the receipt of the notes themselves.

G. TRANSACTIONS BETWEEN RELATED CORPORATIONS

Transactions between commonly controlled corporations, for example, the lease or sale of property or the provision of services for inadequate consideration, the making of a loan, etc., may involve constructive dividend issues. Most cases involve loans between related corporations in which the Commissioner attempts to treat the entire loan as a constructive distribution by the "lender" to the controlling shareholder coupled with a capital contribution by the shareholder to the "borrower." Not all loans between related corporations are susceptible to such recharacterization. The "loan" first must be found not to constitute bona fide indebtedness. Even then, a constructive dividend to the shareholder will be found only if the shareholder receives a direct benefit, distinct from an indirect benefit as a shareholder, from the making of the loan. Transfers that discharge an obligation of the shareholder generally are found to serve a shareholder purpose. See, e.g., Gilbert v. Commissioner, 74 T.C. 60 (1980) (purported loan the proceeds of which were used to redeem stock of other 50 percent shareholder was constructive dividend to continuing shareholder); Stinnett's Pontiac Service, Inc. v. Commissioner, 730 F.2d 634 (11th Cir.1984) (loan to related corporation satisfying common shareholder's obligation to make additional capital contributions to "borrower" corporation was a constructive dividend). Transfers to a related corporation that serve a corporate business purpose generally escape constructive dividend treatment. See, e.g., Magnon v. Commissioner, 73 T.C. 980 (1980) (no constructive dividend where loan was bona fide and for purpose of improving relations with lender's largest customer, who desired that common shareholder of lender and borrower establish new, separate business); Mills v. Internal Revenue Service, 840 F.2d 229 (4th Cir.1988) (no constructive dividend where purpose of loan was to further financial stability of integrated business conducted through related corporations). See also Schwartz v. Commissioner, 69 T.C. 877 (1978) (no constructive dividend resulted from intercorporate transfers between six commonly controlled corporations where the transfers were pursuant to consolidated bankruptcy proceedings even though the transferred funds were used to discharge debts of the related corporations guaranteed by the shareholder).

A sale of property from one commonly controlled corporation to another at less than an arm's length price may be treated as if the selling corporation had made a distribution in an amount equal to the bargain element to its shareholders who in turn contributed that amount to the capital of the buying corporation. Rev.Rul. 69–630, 1969–2 Cum.Bull. 112, held that this result automatically followed if section 482 was applied to reallocate income between the related corporations to reflect an arms' length price. (Section 482 is discussed infra, page 1026). The case law usually has applied this approach when there has been an intentional diversion of funds from one corporation to the other. In Worcester v. Commissioner, 370 F.2d 713 (1st Cir.1966), a constructive dividend was found where payments were made by one corporation to a sister corporation for services which were never in fact performed. See also Sparks Nugget, Inc. v. Commissioner, 458 F.2d 631 (9th Cir.1972) (constructive dividend found where excessive rentals were paid in a transaction between related corporations). Contra, White Tool and Machine Co. v. Commissioner, 41 T.C.M. 116 (1980) (no constructive dividend to common shareholder where corporation paid excessive rent to related corporation: reallocation of income under section 482 was adequate remedy).

In Rev.Rul. 69–630, supra, there was an express finding that the bargain sale had a tax avoidance purpose. However, Rev.Rul. 78–83, 1978–1 Cum. Bull. 79, involving a diversion of funds from one sister corporation to another to avoid foreign exchange control restrictions, indicated that the "constructive distribution-contribution to capital" analysis would be applied even though there was no motive to allocate income or deductions improperly.

H. REFERENCES

Davis and McGill, Corporate Charitable Contributions and the Constructive Dividend Problem, 8 J.Corp.Tax'n 323 (1982); Teschner, "Hidden Dividends"—The Paper Tiger of Constructive Corporate Distributions, 43

Taxes 644 (1965); Worthy, Accidental Dividends, 51 Taxes 724 (1973); Sneed, A Defense of the Tax Court's Result in *Prunier* and *Casale,* 43 Cornell L.Q. 339 (1958); Lawthers, Sixth Circuit in *Ducros* Departs from Basic Corporate Insurance Cases, 12 J.Tax. 92 (1960).

SECTION 5. INTERCORPORATE DIVIDENDS

INTERNAL REVENUE CODE: Sections 243(a)–(c); 246(c); 246A; 1059.

ILLUSTRATIVE MATERIAL

A. PARTIAL ELIMINATION OF DOUBLE TAX AT CORPORATE LEVEL

1. *General*

Corporate shareholders of domestic corporations may in effect exclude all or a portion of dividend income they receive. Without some exclusion, successive taxation of a dividend as it passed from corporation to corporation in a chain of corporations would result in multiple taxation of the dividend and leave very little for the ultimate individual shareholder. However, if the corporate shareholder has an insubstantial degree of ownership or control of the distributing corporation the argument in favor of relief from corporate taxation of dividend income is not as strong. For example, if a corporation has excess cash to invest on a short-term basis, it can be argued that the tax treatment of the corporation's investment return should not depend on whether the short-term investment is in portfolio stock or certificates of deposit. On the other hand, interest is deductible by the payor and dividends are not, so that if one believes that there should be only one tax imposed as long as earnings remain in corporate solution, the dividends received deduction is appropriate even in short-term investment situations.

2. *Statutory Structure*

If one corporation owns 80 percent or more of the voting stock and 80 percent or more in value of the stock of another corporation, these affiliated corporations may file a consolidated return which eliminates dividends paid by the subsidiary to the parent in computing their consolidated taxable income. See sections 1501–1505 (discussed infra, page 1042). If affiliated corporations choose not to file consolidated returns, the parent may still deduct in full dividends received from the subsidiary, subject to the conditions and limitations of section 243(b). See Regulations, section 1.243–4.

Prior to 1936 all intercorporate dividends were excluded in full. Taxation of a portion of intercorporate dividends was introduced in that year, reflecting the general policy pushed in the early 1930's of discouraging complicated corporate structures. Under current law, however, the tax on intercorporate dividends affects primarily investments in public corporations by other corporations. These investments generally have little to do with corporate operating structures. Intercorporate dividends for qualifying corporations (based on 80 percent control) are wholly excluded through a 100 percent deduction under current law, thus, in no way effectuating the goal of the 1936 legislation. For many years prior to the 1986 Act, section 243(a) granted a deduction equal to 85 percent of intercorporate dividends received by any corporation which either did not qualify for, or elect to take advantage of, section 243(b) or the consolidated return option. The 1986 Act reduced this intercorporate dividend received deduction to 80 percent in order to offset the effect of lower corporate tax rates introduced by the 1986 Act. The 1987 Act further amended section 243(a) and added section 243(c), thereby reducing the intercorporate dividend deduction to 70 percent for corporations that do not own 20 percent or more (in value and voting power) of the distributing corporation's stock, i.e., a higher rate of tax is imposed on dividends received on what might be broadly viewed as "portfolio" investments.

The maximum rate of tax on intercorporate dividends after the 1987 Act is 10.2 percent (34 percent times the 30 percent of the dividend included in income). However the dividend received deduction creates a difference between earnings and profits and taxable income, thus potentially bringing the alternative minimum tax (AMT) into play even for corporations qualifying for a 100 percent dividend received deduction. See sections 55 and 56(c), discussed supra, page 276. If the AMT applies, the maximum tax rate on intercorporate dividends is somewhat higher than under the regular tax.

B. TAX ARBITRAGE PROBLEMS

1. *Debt Financed Portfolio Stock*

The availability of the intercorporate dividend deduction creates tax arbitrage opportunities for corporations. One situation involves debt-financed acquisitions of dividend-paying stock. For example, X Corporation borrows $1,000,000, agreeing to pay 10 percent interest, and purchases, at par, $1,000,000 of preferred stock paying annual dividends of 10 percent. X Corporation will realize no pretax gain or loss because the interest expense equals the dividend income. However, if the interest paid to finance the acquisition and 70 percent of the dividends received from the debt-financed portfolio stock are both deductible, then the corporation will have an after-tax profit, even if the stock does not increase in value, because it will recognize income of $100,000, but claim $170,000 of deductions. For example, if X Corporation were in the 34 percent marginal tax bracket, the excess deductions would yield tax savings of $23,800 (34 percent × $70,000).

Section 246A, added by the 1984 Act, reduces the intercorporate dividend received deduction by the percentage of the corporation's portfolio stock which was debt financed during the applicable measuring period. Thus, for example, if the acquisition is three-quarters debt financed, the dividends received deduction is reduced by 75 percent. The dividends received deduction is never reduced, however, by an amount in excess of the interest deduction attributable to the debt that financed the portfolio stock. Section 246A(c)(2) defines "portfolio stock" in such a way that the provision generally does not apply to dividends received by a corporation which owns stock representing at least 50 percent of the total value and the total voting power of the outstanding stock of the distributing corporation. Section 246A also does not apply to dividends paid by certain closely-held corporations.

Is the problem addressed by section 246A created by the dividends received deduction or by the interest deduction? Compare the approach adopted in section 279, discussed infra, page 740, which disallows the interest deduction for certain acquisition indebtedness.

2. *Dividend–Related Losses*

(a) *Section 246(c)*

A corporation's basis in stock generally is unaffected by the receipt of an intercorporate dividend. Section 301(c)(2) requires a reduction in basis for the portion of a distribution which is not a dividend and, therefore, is treated as a return of capital. However, section 301(c)(2) does not apply to the untaxed portion of intercorporate dividends. The intercorporate dividend exclusion is intended to prevent double taxation at the corporate level, and reducing basis by the amount of the exclusion would only postpone the exaction of such double tax.

Arguably, however, the intercorporate dividend deduction coupled with short-term holding of stock purchased in anticipation of receiving a dividend, creates inappropriate tax arbitrage benefits. For example, suppose X Corporation realized a $500,000 capital gain and no offsetting capital loss during its current tax year. Shortly before the end of its taxable year, X Corporation purchases 10,000 shares of Z Corporation stock for $1,000,000. Before the close of its taxable year, X Corporation (1) receives a $200,000 dividend on its Z Corporation shares, and (2) sells its Z Corporation shares for $800,000 (the value of the shares having declined as a result of the dividend). X Corporation realizes a $200,000 loss on disposition of the Z Corporation shares, because its basis in the stock was not reduced by the intercorporate dividend received. This transaction is uneconomic because the dividend income is offset by the resulting capital loss. However, X Corporation pays tax at an effective rate of 10.2 percent on the $200,000 intercorporate dividend received (resulting in a tax of $20,400), while using the loss to offset a $200,000 capital gain that otherwise would have been taxed at the rate of 34 percent (saving a tax of $68,000). Thus, the transaction produces an after-tax benefit of $47,600.

Section 246(c) is aimed at such transactions and requires in general that stock be held for more than 45 days in order to receive the benefit of the dividend received deduction. For preferred stock the requisite holding period is extended by section 246(c)(2) to more than 90 days if the dividends received are attributable to a period in excess of 366 days.

Would it be preferable to approach the problem by denying the loss deduction where the purchase and sale are closely related in time to a dividend payment?

(b) *Section 1059*

(i) *General*

Congress considered section 246(c) to be inadequate to deal with the tax avoidance possibilities created by the availability of the dividends received deduction for extraordinarily large dividends. If an extraordinary dividend was expected to be paid on stock of another corporation, the corporation owning the stock would be willing to hold the stock for the period required to avoid the limitation in section 246(c). In response, Congress enacted section 1059, which it justified as follows:

"When a stock pays an extraordinary dividend, the acquisition of the stock often may be viewed as the acquisition of two assets: the right to the distributions to be made with respect to the stock and the underlying stock itself. In instances in which the acquisition of stock is the acquisition of two assets, the committee concludes that it is appropriate to reduce the basis of the underlying stock to reflect the value of the distribution not taxed to the corporate distributee. In the committee's view, the failure of [prior] law to apply a two-asset analysis in cases of extraordinary distributions when the taxpayer's holding period in the stock is short, leads to tax arbitrage opportunities * * *." H.Rep. No. 98–342, 98th Cong., 2d Sess. 1186 (1984).

Section 1059 requires that a corporate shareholder which receives an "extraordinary dividend" on stock which it has not held for more than two years *before* the dividend announcement date must, in computing the gain or loss realized upon a sale of the stock, reduce the basis of the stock (but not below zero) by the amount of the untaxed portion of the dividend. To the extent that the untaxed portion of any extraordinary dividend exceeds the shareholder's basis for the stock, the excess is taxed as gain on the sale of the stock (in addition to gain otherwise recognized). The amount by which the basis of the stock is reduced is intended to represent the portion of the cost of the "two assets" allocated to the extraordinary dividend. The "basis" of the extraordinary dividend is never recovered because the dividends received deduction is allowed in its place. Because there is no untaxed portion of the dividend if section 246(c) applies, section 1059 operates only where the holding period requirement of section 246(c) has been met.

Section 1059(c) defines an extraordinary dividend in terms of the size of the dividend in relation to the shareholder's adjusted basis in its stock, subject to an alternative test using fair market value instead of basis at the taxpayer's election. (For the application of the alternative test, see Rev.Rul. 88–49, 1988–1 Cum.Bull. 297.) A dividend is extraordinary if aggregate dividends received in any 85 day period exceed 10 percent of the basis of common stock, or 5 percent of the basis of preferred stock, with respect to which the dividends were paid. (Because the basis adjustment under section 1059 is made only when the stock is sold, basis adjustments required by prior extraordinary dividends are not taken into account for this purpose.) Furthermore, if aggregate dividends paid with respect to stock in any one year period exceed 20 percent of the corporate shareholder's basis for the stock, then all such dividends are aggregated and considered to be an extraordinary dividend.

Section 1059(e)(1) treats certain distributions as *per se* extraordinary dividends. This rule applies to any distribution (without regard to the holding period for the stock or the relative magnitude of the distribution) to a corporate shareholder in partial liquidation of the distributing corporation (as defined in section 302(e), discussed infra, page 579). Also, any redemption of stock that is non-pro rata (irrespective of the holding period of the stock or the relative size of the distribution) is treated as an extraordinary distribution. Finally, section 1059(f) treats as extraordinary all dividends on preferred stock if according to the terms of the stock the dividend rate declines over time or the issue price exceeds the liquidation or redemption value.

(ii) *Exceptions*

There are a few exceptions to section 1059. Section 1059(d)(7) generally exempts from the rules of section 1059 distributions to a corporate shareholder which has held the stock of the distributing corporation for the entire period the distributing corporation (and any predecessor corporation) has been in existence. It is unclear, however, whether this exception applies to extraordinary dividends arising from partial liquidations and nonprorata redemptions. Section 1059(e)(2) provides that the basis reduction rules do not apply to distributions between members of an affiliated group filing consolidated returns or to distributions that constitute qualifying dividends within the meaning of section 243(b)(1), except to the extent the dividends are attributable to pre-affiliation earnings or appreciation of the payor corporation. In addition, section 1059(e)(3) provides a special rule for dividends on certain preferred stock where there is no potential for effectively purchasing a dividend that accrued prior to the date of purchase ("dividend-stripping").

(iii) *Section 1059(c) Exception for Preferred Stock*

Because under the general rule a preferred stock that pays a greater than 5–percent dividend within any period of 85 days or less is paying an extraordinary dividend, a 6–percent preferred stock dividend that is paid once annually would be extraordinary. On the other hand, a preferred stock which paid four quarterly 5–percent dividends, which on an annual basis is a substantially higher percentage, would not be subject to a basis adjustment under the general rule. To provide relief for preferred stock like the 6–percent preferred stock in the above example, a special rule applies to preferred stock that pays dividends at a fixed rate not less often than annually, provided it was not purchased when dividends were in arrears. If the taxpayer has held the stock for more than 5 years, no dividends received by the shareholder will be treated as extraordinary dividends, and therefore no basis reduction will be required, if during the period the shareholder held the stock the dividend rate did not exceed an annualized rate of 15 percent of the lower of (a) the taxpayer's adjusted basis or (b) the liquidation preference of the stock. However, if the actual rate of return from dividends on qualifying preferred stock during this period exceeds 15 percent, no relief is available and all of the dividends are extraordinary dividends.

If the taxpayer has not held the stock for 5 years, dividends are extraordinary to the extent they exceed the dividends "earned" by the taxpayer. To determine whether the taxpayer's dividends exceed the dividends it earned, the taxpayer's "actual dividend rate" is computed. The actual dividend rate is the average annual amount of dividends received (or deemed received under section 305 or any other provision) during the period the taxpayer owned the stock, computed as a return on the taxpayer's adjusted basis or, if less, the stock's liquidation preference. This is then compared to the stock's "stated dividend rate," which is the return represented by the annual fixed preferred dividends payable on the stock. If the actual dividend rate exceeds the stated dividend rate, a portion of each dividend received or deemed received will be an extraordinary dividend, and basis will be reduced by the untaxed portion of such dividend. The Conference Committee Report, Tax Reform Act of 1986, H.Rep. No. 99–841, 99th Cong., 2d Sess., Vol. II, 165 (1986) provides the following example of this determination:

"[A]ssume that on January 1, 1987, a corporation purchases for $1,000 ten shares of preferred stock having a liquidation preference of $100 per share and paying fixed preferred dividends of $6 per share to shareholders of record on March 31 and September 30 of each year. If the taxpayer does not elect to have the special rule apply, the basic rule would generally require the taxpayer to reduce the basis in the stock by the untaxed portion of each dividend received prior to the expiration of the two-year holding period. This is because a dividend exceeding 5 percent of adjusted basis (or fair market value, if shown to the satisfaction of the Secretary) paid semi-annually is an extraordinary dividend under the general rule. However, special rule will apply to the preferred stock. Under this provision, the taxpayer's stated dividend rate is 12 percent ($12/$100). If the taxpayer sells the stock on October 1, 1988, (after holding the stock for 1.75 years) and no dividends in excess of the fixed preferred dividends have been paid, its factual dividend rate will be 13.7 percent ($240/$1,000 divided by 1.75). This 13.7 percent exceeds the 12 percent stated dividend rate by 1.7. This excess, as a fraction of the actual dividend rate, is 12.4 percent (1.7 divided by 13.7). Accordingly, each of the dividends will be treated as an extraordinary dividend described in section 1059(a) to the extent of 0.74 per share ($6 × 12.4 percent). However, if the corporation does not sell the stock until January 1, 1989, and no dividends in excess of the fixed preferred dividends have been paid, its 'actual dividend rate' will be 12 percent ($240/$1000 divided by 2.0). This does not exceed the stated dividend rate; accordingly, no portion of any dividend will be treated as an extraordinary dividend."

C. EARNINGS AND PROFITS RECALCULATION FOR DISTRIBUTIONS TO TWENTY PERCENT CORPORATE SHAREHOLDER

Section 301(e) provides that in determining the portion of any distribution to a corporate shareholder holding at least 20 percent of the stock of the distributing corporation, by both voting power and value, that is not a dividend, earnings and profits of the distributing corporation are computed without regard to section 312(n), discussed supra, page 465, (except the adjustments described in section 312(n)(7), relating to redemptions of corporate stock are taken into account). Section 312(n), in general, requires that certain income items that are deferred for purposes of computing taxable income be taken into account in an earlier year in computing earnings and profits. Thus, the effect of section 301(e) is to convert a distribution which otherwise might have been wholly a dividend, subject to the intercorporate dividend deduction, into a return of capital under section 301(c)(2), reducing the distributee's basis in its stock, or a gain under section 301(c)(3). This narrow provision is aimed at certain manipulative devices involving the distribution of an extraordinary dividend followed by the sale of subsidiary stock after the subsidiary has realized an economic gain but before the subsidiary corresponding taxable gain has been recognized, such as in the case of an installment sale under section 453. See H.Rep. No. 98–861, 98th Cong., 1st Sess. 842 (1984).

D. DIVIDENDS DISTRIBUTED IN CONNECTION WITH THE SALE OF A CORPORATE BUSINESS

When a subsidiary corporation pays a dividend to its parent shortly before the sale of the stock of the subsidiary by the parent, the issue arises whether the distribution is a dividend eligible for the dividends received deduction under section 243 or is to be treated as a portion of the amount realized on the sale of the stock, and, therefore, ineligible for the deduction. The result can differ depending on the facts and circumstances surrounding the distribution. This matter is discussed in detail infra, page 728.

E. REFERENCE

Note: Taxation of Intercorporate Dividends: A Missed Opportunity for Tax Reform, 7 Va.Tax Rev. 777 (1988).

CHAPTER 12

STOCK DIVIDENDS

SECTION 1. DISTRIBUTIONS IN GENERAL

A. JUDICIAL AND STATUTORY BACKGROUND

EISNER v. MACOMBER

Supreme Court of the United States, 1920.
252 U.S. 189.

[The taxpayer was the owner of 2,200 shares of common stock in the Standard Oil Company of California. The corporation declared a 50 percent stock dividend and the taxpayer received 1,100 additional shares of which 198.77 shares represented surplus of the corporation earned between March 1, 1913 and January 1, 1916, the latter date being the date of the stock dividend. The shares representing the post–March 1, 1913 surplus had a par value of $19,877 and the Commissioner treated the stock dividend as taxable income to the extent of the par value of such shares. Cash dividends in such an amount would have constituted taxable income. The applicable statute expressly included stock dividends in income. The taxpayer asserted that the stock dividend was not income within the meaning of the Sixteenth Amendment. The District Court rendered judgment against the Government.]

MR. JUSTICE PITNEY delivered the opinion of the Court. * * *

In Towne v. Eisner, [245 U.S. 418, 38 S.Ct. 158], the question was whether a stock dividend made in 1914 against surplus earned prior to January 1, 1913, was taxable against the stockholder under the Act of October 3, 1913, which provided that net income should include "dividends," and also "gains or profits and income derived from any source whatever." * * * When the case came here, after overruling a motion to dismiss made by the government upon the ground that the only question involved was the construction of the statute and not its constitutionality, we dealt upon the merits with the question of construction only, but disposed of it upon consideration of the essential nature of a stock dividend disregarding the fact that the one in question was based upon surplus earnings that accrued before the Sixteenth Amendment took effect. Not only so, but we rejected the reasoning of the District Court, saying (245 U.S. 426, 38 S.Ct. 159):

"Notwithstanding the thoughtful discussion that the case received below we cannot doubt that the dividend was capital as well for the purposes of the Income Tax Law as for distribution between tenant for life and remainderman. What was said by this court upon the latter question is equally true for the former. 'A stock dividend really takes nothing from the property of the corporation, and adds nothing to the interests of the shareholders. Its property is not diminished, and their interests are not increased. * * * The proportional interest of each shareholder remains the same. The only change is in the evidence which represents that interest, the new shares and the original shares together representing the same proportional interest that the original shares represented before the issue of the new ones.' Gibbons v. Mahon, 136 U.S. 549, 559, 560 [10 S.Ct. 1057]. In short, the corporation is no poorer and the stockholder is no richer than they were before. Logan County v. United States, 169 U.S. 255, 261 [18 S.Ct. 361]. If the plaintiff gained any small advantage by the change, it certainly was not an advantage of $417,450, the sum upon which he was taxed. * * * What has happened is that the plaintiff's old certificates have been split up in effect and have diminished in value to the extent of the value of the new."

This language aptly answered not only the reasoning of the District Court but the argument of the Solicitor General in this court, which discussed the essential nature of a stock dividend. And if, for the reasons thus expressed, such a dividend is not to be regarded as "income" or "dividends" within the meaning of the act of 1913, we are unable to see how it can be brought within the meaning of "incomes" in the Sixteenth Amendment; it being very clear that Congress intended in that act to exert its power to the extent permitted by the amendment. In Towne v. Eisner it was not contended that any construction of the statute could make it narrower than the constitutional grant; rather the contrary. * * * We adhere to the view then expressed, and might rest the present case there, not because that case in terms decided the constitutional question, for it did not, but because the conclusion there reached as to the essential nature of a stock dividend necessarily prevents its being regarded as income in any true sense.

Nevertheless, in view of the importance of the matter, and the fact that Congress in the Revenue Act of 1916 declared that a "stock dividend shall be considered income, to the amount of its cash value," we will deal at length with the constitutional question, incidentally testing the soundness of our previous conclusion.

* * *

[I]t becomes essential to distinguish between what is and what is not "income," as the term is there used, and to apply the distinction, as cases arise, according to truth and substance, without regard to form. Congress cannot by any definition it may adopt conclude the matter, since it cannot by legislation alter the Constitution, from which alone it derives its power to legislate, and within whose limitations alone that power can be lawfully exercised.

The fundamental relation of "capital" to "income" has been much discussed by economists, the former being likened to the tree or the land, the latter to the fruit or the crop; the former depicted as a reservoir supplied from springs, the latter as the outlet stream, to be measured by its flow during a period of time. For the present purpose we require only a clear definition of the term "income," as used in common speech, in order to determine its meaning in the amendment, and having formed also a correct judgment as to the nature of a stock dividend, we shall find it easy to decide the matter at issue.

After examining dictionaries in common use (Bouv.L.D.; Standard Dict.; Webster's Internat. Dict.; Century Dict.), we find little to add to the succinct definition adopted in two cases arising under the Corporation Tax Act of 1909 (Stratton's Independence v. Howbert, 231 U.S. 399, 415, 34 S.Ct. 136, 140; Doyle v. Mitchell Bros. Co., 247 U.S. 179, 185, 38 S.Ct. 467, 469)—"Income may be defined as the gain derived from capital, from labor, or from both combined," provided it be understood to include profit gained through a sale or conversion of capital assets, to which it was applied in the Doyle Case, 247 U.S. 183, 185, 38 S.Ct. 467, 469.

Brief as it is, it indicates the characteristic and distinguishing attribute of income essential for a correct solution of the present controversy. The government, although basing its argument upon the definition as quoted, placed chief emphasis upon the word "gain," which was extended to include a variety of meanings; while the significance of the next three words was either overlooked or misconceived. "*Derived—from—capital* "; "the *gain—derived—from—capital,* " etc. Here we have the essential matter: *not* a gain *accruing to* capital; not a *growth* or *increment* of value *in* the investment; but a gain, a profit, something of exchangeable value, *proceeding from* the property, *severed from* the capital, however invested or employed, and *coming in,* being "*dervied* "—that is, *received* or *drawn by* the recipient (the taxpayer) for his *separate* use, benefit and disposal—*that* is income derived from property. Nothing else answers the description.

The same fundamental conception is clearly set forth in the Sixteenth Amendment—"incomes, *from* whatever *source derived* "—the essential thought being expressed with a conciseness and lucidity entirely in harmony with the form and style of the Constitution.

Can a stock dividend, considering its essential character, be brought within the definition? To answer this, regard must be had to the nature of a corporation and the stockholder's relation to it. * * *

In the present case, the corporation had surplus and undivided profits invested in plant, property, and business, and required for the purposes of the corporation, amounting to about $45,000,000, in addition to outstanding capital stock of $50,000,000. In this the case is not extraordinary. The profits of a corporation, as they appear upon the balance sheet at the end of the year, need not be in the form of money on hand in excess of what is required to meet current liabilities and finance current operations of the company. Often, especially in a growing business, only a part, sometimes a small part, of the year's profits is in property capable of division; the remainder having been absorbed in the acquisition of increased plant, equipment, stock in trade, or accounts receivable, or in decrease of outstanding liabilities.

When only a part is available for dividends, the balance of the year's profits is carried to the credit of undivided profits, or surplus, or some other account having like significance. If thereafter the company finds itself in funds beyond current needs it may declare dividends out of such surplus or undivided profits; otherwise it may go on for years conducting a successful business, but requiring more and more working capital because of the extension of its operations, and therefore unable to declare dividends approximating the amount of its profits. Thus the surplus may increase until it equals or even exceeds the par value of the outstanding capital stock. This may be adjusted upon the books in the mode adopted in the case at bar—by declaring a "stock dividend." This, however, is no more than a book adjustment, in essence not a dividend but rather the opposite; no part of the assets of the company is separated from the common fund, nothing distributed except paper certificates that evidence an antecedent increase in the value of the stockholder's capital interest resulting from an accumulation of profits by the company, but profits so far absorbed in the business as to render it impracticable to separate them for withdrawal and distribution. In order to make the adjustment, a charge is made against surplus account with corresponding credit to capital stock account, equal to the proposed "dividend"; the new stock is issued against this and the certificates delivered to the existing stockholders in proportion to their previous holdings. This, however, is merely bookkeeping that does not affect the aggregate assets of the corporation or its outstanding liabilities; it affects only the form, not the essence, of the "liability" acknowledged by the corporation to its own shareholders, and this through a readjustment of accounts on one side of the balance sheet only, increasing "capital stock" at the expense of "surplus"; it does not alter the preexisting proportionate interest of any stockholder or increase the intrinsic value of his holding or of the aggregate holdings of the other stockholders as they stood before. The new certificates simply increase the number of the shares, with consequent dilution of the value of each share.

A "stock dividend" shows that the company's accumulated profits have been capitalized, instead of distributed to the stockholders or retained as surplus available for distribution in money or in kind should opportunity offer. Far from being a realization of profits of the stockholder, it tends rather to postpone such realization, in that the fund represented by the new stock has been transferred from surplus to capital, and no longer is available for actual distribution.

The essential and controlling fact is that the stockholder has received nothing out of the company's assets for his separate use and benefit; on the contrary, every dollar of his original investment, together with whatever accretions and accumulations have resulted from employment of his money and that of the other stockholders in the business of the company, still remains the property of the company, and subject to business risks which may result in wiping out the entire investment. Having regard to the very truth of the matter, to substance and not to form, he has received nothing that answers the definition of income within the meaning of the Sixteenth Amendment. * * *

We are clear that not only does a stock dividend really take nothing from the property of the corporation and add nothing to that of the shareholder, but that the antecedent accumulation of profits evidenced thereby, while indicating that the shareholder is the richer because of an increase of his capital, at the same time shows he has not realized or received any income in the transaction.

It is said that a stockholder may sell the new shares acquired in the stock dividend; and so he may, if he can find a buyer. It is equally true that if he does sell, and in doing so realizes a profit, such profit, like any other, is income, and so far as it may have arisen since the Sixteenth Amendment is taxable by Congress without apportionment. The same would be true were he to sell some of his original shares at a profit. But if a shareholder sells dividend stock he necessarily disposes of a part of his capital interest, just as if he should sell a part of his old stock, either before or after the dividend. What he retains no longer entitles him to the same proportion of future dividends as before the sale. His part in the control of the company likewise is diminished. Thus, if one holding $60,000 out of a total $100,000 of the capital stock of a corporation should receive in common with other stockholders a 50 per cent. stock dividend, and should sell his part, he thereby would be reduced from a majority to a minority stockholder, having six-fifteenths instead of six-tenths of the total stock outstanding. A corresponding and proportionate decrease in capital interest and in voting power would befall a minority holder should he sell dividend stock; it being in the nature of things impossible for one to dispose of any part of such an issue without a proportionate disturbance of the distribution of the entire capital stock, and a like diminution of the seller's comparative voting power—that "right preservative of rights" in the control of a corporation. Yet, without selling, the shareholder, unless possessed of other resources, has not the withdrawal to pay an income tax upon the dividend stock. Nothing could more clearly show that to tax a stock dividend is to tax a capital increase, and not income, than this demonstration that in the nature of things it requires conversion of capital in order to pay the tax.

* * *

Conceding that the mere issue of a stock dividend makes the recipient no richer than before, the government nevertheless contends that the new certificates measure the extent to which the gains accumulated by the corporation have made him the richer. There are two insuperable difficulties with this: In the first place, it would depend upon how long he had held the stock whether the stock dividend indicated the extent to which he had been enriched by the operations of the company; unless he had held it throughout such operations the measure would not hold true. Secondly, and more important for present purposes, enrichment through increase in value of capital investment is not income in any proper meaning of the term. * * *

It is said there is no difference in principle between a simple stock dividend and a case where stockholders use money received as cash dividends to purchase additional stock contemporaneously issued by the corporation. But an actual cash dividend, with a real option to the stockholder either to keep the money for his own or to reinvest it in new shares, would be as far removed as possible from a true stock dividend, such as the one we have under consideration, where nothing of value is taken from the company's assets and transferred to the individual ownership of the several stockholders and thereby subjected to their disposal.

* * *

Thus, from every point of view we are brought irresistibly to the conclusion that neither under the Sixteenth Amendment nor otherwise has Congress power to tax without apportionment a true stock dividend made lawfully and in good faith, or the accumulated profits behind it, as income of the stockholder. The Revenue Act of 1916, in so far as it imposes a tax upon the stockholder because of such dividend, contravenes the provisions of article 1, § 2, cl. 3, and article 1, § 9, cl. 4, of the Constitution, and to this extent is invalid, notwithstanding the Sixteenth Amendment.

Judgment affirmed.

MR. JUSTICE HOLMES, dissenting.

I think that Towne v. Eisner, 245 U.S. 418, 38 S.Ct. 158, was right in its reasoning and result and that on sound principles the stock dividend was not income. But it was clearly intimated in that case that the construction of the statute then before the Court might be different from that of the Constitution.* 245 U.S. 425, 38 S.Ct. 158. I think that the word "incomes" in the Sixteenth Amendment should be read in "a sense most obvious to the common understanding at the time of its adoption." * * * For it was for public adoption that it was proposed. McCulloch v. Maryland, 4 Wheat. 316, 407. The known purpose of this Amendment was to get rid of nice questions as to what might be direct taxes, and I cannot doubt that most people not lawyers would suppose when they voted for it that they put a question like the present to rest. I am of opinion that the Amendment justifies the tax. See Tax Commissioner v. Putnam, 227 Mass. 522, 532, 533, 116 N.E. 904.

MR. JUSTICE DAY concurs in this opinion.

MR. JUSTICE BRANDEIS, dissenting, delivered the following opinion, in which MR. JUSTICE CLARKE concurred.

* [Ed.: Justice Holmes put it this way in Towne v. Eisner: "But it is not necessarily true that income means the same thing in the Constitution and the act. A word is not a crystal, transparent and unchanged, it is the skin of a living thought and may vary greatly in color and content according to the circumstances and the time in which it is used." 245 U.S. 418, 425 (1918).]

Financiers, with the aid of lawyers, devised long ago two different methods by which a corporation can, without increasing its indebtedness, keep for corporate purposes accumulated profits, and yet, in effect, distribute these profits among its stockholders. One method is a simple one. The capital stock is increased; the new stock is paid up with the accumulated profits; and the new shares of paid-up stock are then distributed among the stockholders pro rata as a dividend. If the stockholder prefers ready money to increasing his holding of the stock in the company, he sells the new stock received as a dividend. The other method is slightly more complicated. Arrangements are made for an increase of stock to be offered to stockholders pro rata at par, and, at the same time, for the payment of a cash dividend equal to the amount which the stockholder will be required to pay to the company, if he avails himself of the right to subscribe for his pro rata of the new stock. If the stockholder takes the new stock, as is expected, he may endorse the dividend check received to the corporation and thus pay for the new stock. In order to ensure that all the new stock so offered will be taken, the price at which it is offered is fixed far below what it is believed will be its market value. If the stockholder prefers ready money to an increase of his holdings of stock, he may sell his right to take new stock pro rata, which is evidenced by an assignable instrument. In that event the purchaser of the rights repays to the corporation, as the subscription price of the new stock, an amount equal to that which it had paid as a cash dividend to the stockholder.

Both of these methods of retaining accumulated profits while in effect distributing them as a dividend had been in common use in the United States for many years prior to the adoption of the Sixteenth Amendment. They were recognized equivalents. Whether a particular corporation employed one or the other method was determined sometimes by requirements of the law under which the corporation was organized; sometimes it was determined by preferences of the individual officials of the corporation; and sometimes by stock market conditions. Whichever method was employed the resultant distribution of the new stock was commonly referred to as a stock dividend. * * *

It is conceded that if the stock dividend paid to Mrs. Macomber had been made by the more complicated method * * *; that is, issuing rights to take new stock pro rata and paying to each stockholder simultaneously a dividend in cash sufficient in amount to enable him to pay for this pro rata of new stock to be purchased—the dividend so paid to him would have been taxable as income, whether he retained the cash or whether he returned it to the corporation in payment for his pro rata of new stock. But it is contended that, because the simple method was adopted of having the new stock issued direct to the stockholders as paid-up stock, the new stock is not to be deemed income, whether she retained it or converted it into cash by sale. If such a different result can flow merely from the difference in the method pursued, it must be because Congress is without power to tax as income of the stockholder either the stock received under the latter method or the proceeds of its sale; for Congress has, by the provisions in the Revenue Act of 1916, expressly declared its purpose to make stock dividends, by whichever method paid, taxable as income. * * *

First. The term "income," when applied to the investment of the stockholder in a corporation, had, before the adoption of the Sixteenth Amendment, been commonly understood to mean the returns from time to time received by the stockholder from gains or earnings of the corporation. * * *

[W]hether a dividend declared payable from profits shall be paid in cash or in some other medium is wholly a matter of financial management. If some other medium is decided upon, it is also wholly a question of financial management whether the distribution shall be, for instance, in bonds, scrip or stock of another corporation or in issues of its own. And if the dividend is paid in its own issues, why should there be a difference in result dependent upon whether the distribution was made from such securities then in the treasury or from others to be created and issued by the company expressly for that purpose? So far as the distribution may be made from its own issues of bonds, or preferred stock created expressly for the purpose, it clearly would make no difference in the decision of the question whether the dividend was a distribution of profits, that the securities had to be created expressly for the purpose of distribution. If a dividend paid in securities of that nature represents a distribution of profits Congress may, of course, tax it as income of the stockholder. Is the result different where the security distributed is common stock? * * *

Second. It has been said that a dividend payable in bonds or preferred stock created for the purpose of distributing profits may be income and taxable as such, but that the case is different where the distribution is in common stock created for that purpose. Various reasons are assigned for making this distinction. One is that the proportion of the stockholder's ownership to the aggregate number of the shares of the company is not changed by the distribution. But that is equally true where the dividend is paid in its bonds or in its preferred stock. Furthermore, neither maintenance nor change in the proportionate ownership of a stockholder in a corporation has any bearing upon the question here involved. Another reason assigned is that the value of the old stock held is reduced approximately by the value of the new stock received, so that the stockholder after receipt of the stock dividend has no more than he had before it was paid. That is equally true whether the dividend be paid in cash or in other property, for instance, bonds, scrip or preferred stock of the company. The payment from profits of a large cash dividend, and even a small one, customarily lowers the then market value of stock because the undivided property represented by each share has been correspondingly reduced. The argument which appears to be most strongly urged for the stockholders is, that when a stock dividend is made, no portion of the assets of the company is thereby segregated for the stockholder. But does the issue of new bonds or of preferred stock created for use as a dividend result in any segregation of assets for the stockholder? In each case he receives a piece of paper which entitles him to certain rights in the undivided property. Clearly segregation of assets in a physical sense is not an essential of income. The year's gains of a partner is taxable as income, although there, likewise, no segregation of his share in the gains from that of his partners is had.

The objection that there has been no segregation is presented also in another form. It is argued that until there is a segregation, the stockholder cannot know whether he has really received gains; since the gains may be invested in plant or merchandise or other property and perhaps be later lost. But is not this equally true of the share of a partner in the year's profits of the firm or, indeed, of the profits of the individual who is engaged in business alone? And is it not true, also, when dividends are paid in cash? The gains of a business, whether conducted by an individual, by a firm or by a corporation, are ordinarily reinvested in large part. Many a cash dividend honestly declared as a distribution of profits, proves later to have been paid out of capital, because errors in forecast prevent correct ascertainment of values. Until a business adventure has been completely liquidated, it can never be determined with certainty whether there have been profits unless the returns at least exceeded the capital originally invested. Business men, dealing with the problem practically, fix necessarily periods and rules for determining whether there have been net profits—that is, income or gains. They protect themselves from being seriously misled by adopting a system of depreciation charges and reserves. Then, they act upon their own determination, whether profits have been made. Congress in legislating has wisely adopted their practices as its own rules of action.

Third. The Government urges that it would have been within the power of Congress to have taxed as income of the stockholder his pro rata share of undistributed profits earned, even if no stock dividend representing it had been paid. Strong reasons may be assigned for such a view. See The Collector v. Hubbard, 12 Wall. 1. The undivided share of a partner in the year's undistributed profits of his firm is taxable as income of the partner, although the share in the gain is not evidenced by any action taken by the firm. Why may not the stockholder's interest in the gains of the company? The law finds no difficulty in disregarding the corporate fiction whenever that is deemed necessary to attain a just result. * * * But we have no occasion to decide the question whether Congress might have taxed to the stockholder his undivided share of the corporation's earnings. For Congress has in this act limited the income tax to that share of the stockholder in the earnings which is, in effect, distributed by means of the stock dividend paid. In other words to render the stockholder taxable there must be both earnings made and a dividend paid. Neither earnings without dividend—nor a dividend without earnings—subjects the stockholder to taxation under the Revenue Act of 1916. * * *

MR. JUSTICE CLARKE concurs in this opinion.

ILLUSTRATIVE MATERIAL

A. SUBSEQUENT DEVELOPMENTS

1. *Statutory Exemption, 1921–1936*

Starting with the Revenue Act of 1921, Congress for many years provided that "a stock dividend shall not be subject to tax." In Koshland v. Helvering, 298 U.S. 441 (1936), the Supreme Court was faced with a taxpayer who had owned cumulative non-voting preferred stock, had received a dividend in common voting stock, and who then had her preferred stock redeemed. The Commissioner, following the Regulations, divided the cost of the preferred stock between that stock and the dividend stock, and then used the reduced cost allocated to the preferred to compute the gain on the redemption of the preferred. The taxpayer argued that she was entitled to her full cost as respects the preferred, and the Court agreed. It held that since the stock dividend could have been taxed because the shareholder received an interest different from her original stockholdings, its receipt represented "income" even though it was not taxed and there was therefore no statutory authority for the allocation formula of the Regulations.

Helvering v. Gowran, 302 U.S. 238 (1937), involved a preferred stock dividend to holders of common stock, there being like preferred stock also outstanding, but not held pro rata by the holders of the common. The preferred had a $100 par value, with a 7 percent cumulative dividend rate. A stockholder then sold his dividend stock. The Court held that the dividend constitutionally could have been taxed, under the authority of *Koshland,* but that it was exempt by statute. Being so exempt, it had a zero cost and hence a zero basis on sale.

2. *Statutory Inclusion and Judicial Exclusion, 1936–1954*

Commencing with 1936, and continued in the 1939 Code, Congress changed the statutory rule to provide "a distribution made by a corporation to its shareholders in its stock or in rights to acquire its stock shall not be treated as a dividend to the extent that it does not constitute income to the shareholder within the meaning of the Sixteenth Amendment to the Constitution." In 1939, the statute was amended to provide that in the case of exempt stock dividends, whenever issued, the basis of the old stock would be allocated between the old stock and the new stock, thus providing statutory authority for the Regulations rule held unauthorized in Koshland v. Helvering.

The first case decided by the Supreme Court under the amended statute was Helvering v. Griffiths, 318 U.S. 371 (1943), involving a common stock dividend on common stock in 1939. The Commissioner included in income the value of the dividend, $109.01, asserting a deficiency of $9.06. Mrs. Griffiths objected and the Supreme Court agreed. It pointed out that in 1939 the existing Treasury Regulations were in terms of a test of proportionate change in rights or interest and expressly stated that a distribution of common on common was not taxable.

Shortly thereafter the court decided Helvering v. Sprouse and Strassburger v. Commissioner, 318 U.S. 604 (1943), arising under the same statutory provision. In the *Sprouse* case (No. 22) the corporation had distributed a non-voting common stock dividend to holders of voting and nonvoting common. The Commissioner included the value of the dividend in the income of the taxpayer, who held some voting common stock. In the *Strassburger* case (No. 66), the taxpayer owned all of the common stock and received a dividend of preferred stock, which the Commissioner included in income. The Court held against inclusion in both cases, relying on Helvering v. Griffiths.

3. *Statutory Exemption 1954–1969*

Excerpt from SENATE FINANCE COMMITTEE REPORT, INTERNAL REVENUE CODE OF 1954, S.Rep. No. 83–1622, 83rd Cong., 2d Sess. (1954):

"Your committee has followed the policy of the House bill allowing the distribution of equity interests in a corporation as a dividend to the greatest extent possible. As long as a shareholder's interest remains in corporate solution, there is no appropriate occasion for the imposition of a tax. Accordingly, the general rule is that no tax is imposed upon the distribution of stock rights and stock dividends whether or not a particular shareholder's proportionate interest in the corporation is varied, but rather is postponed through the application of the pertinent basis provisions. [The bill] provides certain exceptions to this basic rule in cases where a distribution of stock [is] in lieu of arrearages on preferred stock. * * * Your committee continues the rule of the House bill and of existing law that where a shareholder has an election to take a dividend in stock or in cash, the election to take a stock dividend will not prevent the stock being subject to tax.

"[T]he problems involved in the line of court decisions such as Koshland v. Helvering (298 U.S. 441); Helvering v. Gowran (302 U.S. 238); Wiegand v. Commissioner (194 F.2d 479), etc., wherein the taxability of a stock distribution is dependent upon whether the proportionate interest of the shareholder in the corporation has been altered, are eliminated." (44, 241).

The 1954 Code revision also provided that the receipt of the preferred stock dividends paid on common stock continued to be nontaxable but special rules applied to the disposition of the preferred stock. This problem is discussed, infra, page 537.

B. REFERENCES

Lowndes, The Taxation of Stock Dividends and Stock Rights, 96 U.Pa.L. Rev. 147 (1947); Cohen, Surrey, Tarleau and Warren, A Technical Revision of the Federal Income Tax Treatment of Corporate Distributions to Shareholders, 52 Col.L.Rev. 1 (1952).

B. THE TAX REFORM ACT OF 1969

INTERNAL REVENUE CODE: Sections 305; 307(a).

REGULATIONS: Sections 1.305–1(a), (b); 1.305–3(a)–(c), Ex. (1)–(6).

The rules governing the treatment of stock dividends were substantially revised in 1969, and the 1969 amendments to section 305 have been carried forward in the 1986 Code.

SENATE FINANCE COMMITTEE REPORT, TAX REFORM ACT OF 1969

S.Rep. No. 91–552, 91st Cong., 1st Sess. 150–53 (1969).

[*Pre–1969*] law.—In its simplest form, a stock dividend is commonly thought of as a mere readjustment of the stockholder's interest, and not as income. For example, if a corporation with only common stock outstanding issues more common stock as a dividend, no basic change is made in the position of the corporation and its stockholders. No corporate assets are paid out, and the distribution merely gives each stockholder more pieces of paper to represent the same interest in the corporation.

On the other hand, stock dividends may also be used in a way that alters the interests of the stockholders. For example, if a corporation, with only common stock outstanding declares a dividend payable at the election of each stockholder, either in additional common stock or in cash, the stockholder, who receives a stock dividend is in the same position as if he received a taxable cash dividend and purchased additional stock with the proceeds. His interest in the corporation is increased relative to the interests of stockholders who took dividends in cash.

[Pre–1969] law (sec. 305(a)) provides that if a corporation pays a dividend to its shareholders in its own stock (or in rights to acquire its stock), the shareholders are not required to include the value of the dividend in income. There are two exceptions to this general rule. First, stock dividends paid in discharge of preference dividends for the current or immediately preceding taxable year are taxable. Second, a stock dividend is taxable if any shareholder may elect to receive his dividend in cash or other property instead of stock.

These provisions were enacted as part of the Internal Revenue Code of 1954. Before 1954 the taxability of stock dividends was determined under the "proportionate interest test," which developed out of a series of Supreme Court cases, beginning with Eisner v. Macomber, 252 U.S. 189 (1920). In these cases the Court held, in general, that a stock dividend was taxable if it increased any shareholder's proportionate interest in the corporation. The lower courts often had difficulty in applying the test as formulated in these cases, particularly where unusual corporate capital structures were involved.

Soon after the proportionate interest test was eliminated in the 1954 Code, corporations began to develop methods by which shareholders could, in effect, be given a choice between receiving cash dividends or increasing their proportionate interests in the corporation in much the same way as if they had received cash dividends and reinvested them in the corporation. The earliest of these methods involves dividing the common stock of the corporation into two classes, A and B. The two classes share equally in earnings and profits and in assets on liquidation. Thc only difference is that the class A stock pays only stock dividends and class B stock pays only cash dividends. The market value of the stock dividends paid on the class A stock is equated annually to the cash dividends paid on the class B stock. Class A stock may be converted into class B stock at any time. The stockholders can choose, either when the classes are established, when they purchase new stock, or through the convertibility option whether to own class A stock or class B stock.

In 1956, the Treasury Department issued proposed regulations which treated such arrangements as taxable (under sec. 305(b)(2)) as distributions subject to an election by the stockholder to receive cash instead of stock. In recent years, however, increasingly complex and sophisticated variations of this basic arrangement have been created. In some of these arrangements, the proportionate interest of one class of shareholders is increased even though no actual distribution of stock is made. This effect may be achieved, for example, by paying cash dividends on common stock and increasing by a corresponding amount the ratio at which convertible preferred stock or convertible debentures may be converted into common stock. Another method of achieving this result is a systematic periodic redemption plan, under which a small percentage, such as 5 percent, of each shareholder's stock may be redeemed annually at his election. Shareholders who do not choose to have their stock redeemed automatically increase their proportionate interest in the corporation.

On January 10, 1969, the Internal Revenue Service issued final regulations (T.D.6990) under which a number of methods of achieving the effect of a cash dividend to some shareholders and a corresponding increase in the proportionate interest of other shareholders are brought under the exceptions in section 305(b), with the result that shareholders who receive increases in proportionate interest are treated as receiving taxable distributions.

General reasons for change.—The final regulations issued on January 10, 1969, do not cover all of the arrangements by which cash dividends can be paid to some shareholders and other shareholders can be given corresponding increases in proportionate interest. For example, the periodic redemption plan described above is not covered by the regulations, and the committee believes it is not covered by the present statutory language (of sec. 305(b)(2)).

Methods have also been devised to give preferred stockholders the equivalent of dividends on preferred stock which are not taxable as such under present law. For example, a corporation may issue preferred stock for $100 per share which pays no dividends, but which may be redeemed in 20 years for $200. The effect is the same as if the corporation distributed preferred stock equal to 5 percent of the original stock each year during the 20–year period in lieu of cash dividends. The committee believes that dividends paid on preferred stock should be taxed whether they are received in cash or in another form, such as stock, rights to receive stock, or rights to receive an increased amount on redemption. Moreover, the committee believes that dividends on preferred stock should be taxed to the recipients whether they are attributable to the current or immediately preceding taxable year or to earlier taxable years.

Explanation of [section 305].—The bill continues (in sec. 305(b)(1)) the provision of present law that a stock dividend is taxable if it is payable at the election of any shareholder in property instead of stock.

The bill provides (in sec. 305(b)(2)) that if there is a distribution or series of distributions of stock which has the result of the receipt of cash or other property by some shareholders and an increase in the proportionate interests of other shareholders in the assets or earnings and profits of the corporation, the shareholders receiving stock are to be taxable (under sec. 301).

For example, if a corporation has two classes of common stock, one paying regular cash dividends and the other paying corresponding stock dividends (whether in common or preferred stock), the stock dividends are to be taxable.

On the other hand, if a corporation has a single class of common stock and a class of preferred stock which pays cash dividends and is not convertible, and it distributes a pro rata common stock dividend with respect to its common stock, the stock distribution is not taxable because the distribution does not have the result of increasing the proportionate interests of any of the stockholders.

In determining whether there is a disproportionate distribution, any security convertible into stock or any right to acquire stock is to be treated as outstanding stock. For example, if a corporation has common stock and convertible debentures outstanding, and it pays interest on the convertible debentures and stock dividends on the common stock, there is a disproportionate distribution, and the stock dividends are to be taxable (under section 301). In addition, in determining whether there is a disproportionate distribution with respect to a shareholder, each class of stock is to be considered separately.

The committee has added two provisions to the House bill (secs. 305(b)(3) and (4)) which carry out more explicitly the intention of the House with regard to distributions of common and preferred stock on common stock, and stock distributions on preferred stock. The first of these provides that if a distribution or series of distributions has the result of the receipt of preferred stock by some common shareholders and the receipt of common stock by other common shareholders, all of the shareholders are taxable (under sec. 301) on the receipt of the stock.

The second of the provisions added by the committee (sec. 305(b)(4)) provides that distributions of stock with respect to preferred stock are taxable (under sec. 301). This provision applies to all distributions on preferred stock except increases in the conversion ratio of convertible preferred stock made solely to take account of stock dividends or stock splits with respect to the stock into which the convertible stock is convertible. * * *

The bill provides (in sec. 305(c)) that under regulations prescribed by the Secretary or his delegate, a change in conversion ratio, a change in redemption price, a difference between redemption price and issue price, a redemption treated as a section 301 distribution, or any transaction (including a recapitalization) having a similar effect on the interest of any shareholder is to be treated as a distribution with respect to each shareholder whose proportionate interest is thereby increased. The purpose of this provision is to give the Secretary authority to deal with transactions that have the effect of distributions, but in which stock is not actually distributed.

The proportionate interest of a shareholder can be increased not only by the payment of a stock dividend not paid to other shareholders, but by such methods as increasing the ratio at which his stock, convertible securities, or rights to stock may be converted into other stock, by decreasing the ratio at which other stock, convertible securities, or rights to stock can be converted into stock of the class he owns, or by the periodic redemption of stock owned by other shareholders. It is not clear under present law to what extent increases of this kind would be considered distributions of stock or rights to stock. In order to eliminate uncertainty, the committee has authorized the Secretary or his delegate to prescribe regulations governing the extent to which such transactions shall be treated as taxable distributions. * * *

ILLUSTRATIVE MATERIAL

A. SCOPE OF SECTION 305

1. *General*

The blanket exclusion afforded stock dividends by section 305 prior to 1969 led to some difficulties as taxpayers probed for favorable tax techniques based on that exclusion. There arose a variety of sophisticated schemes which in effect allowed shareholders to choose, sometimes on a year-to-year basis, whether to receive cash dividends or instead to obtain an increase in their equity participation in the corporation. These plans had the effect of allowing shareholders who chose the second course to substitute potential capital gain income for current ordinary income cash dividends. The Internal Revenue Service attempted to reach some of these arrangements under Regulations, but as the Senate Finance Committee Report indicates, the existing statutory structure was not sufficiently broad to cover all of the situations. As a result, the 1969 legislation made some fundamental changes in the theory on which the taxation of stock dividends is based. Several related policies seem to lie behind the 1969 changes.

One of these policies was to limit the possibility of converting ordinary income into capital gain. With the elimination of the differential between ordinary income and capital gain rates after 1986, the role section 305 plays by requiring the current recognition of ordinary income with respect to transactions which otherwise are designed to achieve capital gain is of diminished importance with respect to this policy issue. However, the provision continues to play an important role in the timing of income inclusion. Furthermore, basis recovery and capital loss offset considerations are still relevant.

In the twenty years since the enactment of section 305, only two significant stock dividend cases governed by its provisions have been decided, and both cases involved the same issue. See infra, page 532. The Internal Revenue Service, however, has issued a number of significant Revenue Rulings clarifying the application of section 305. This dearth of litigation may indicate that section 305 has had a significant prophylactic effect with respect to the stock dividend transactions that it is designed to tax.

2. *Stock in Lieu of Cash*

From the beginning, Congress wished to prevent a shareholder from having an obvious choice on a year-by-year basis whether to receive cash dividends or an increase in his proportionate interest in the corporation. Thus, section 305(b)(1) provides that where the shareholder has an explicit election to receive stock or cash the stock distribution will be taxable. This is in effect a specific application of the general principle of constructive receipt, i.e., the shareholder cannot avoid taxation by simply turning his back on the possible cash dividend and taking a stock dividend instead.

3. *Disproportionate Distributions*

Even if the shareholders do not have an obvious choice to receive stock or cash, a stock distribution will be taxable under section 305(b)(2) if it has the result of (1) an increase in the proportionate interest of some shareholders coupled with (2) a receipt of property (including cash) by other shareholders in a distribution subject to section 301 or 356(a)(2).[1] See Regulations, section 1.305–3(b)(3). For example, suppose the corporation has two classes of common stock, one class paying quarterly cash dividends and the other class paying quarterly stock dividends, with the amount of the stock dividend adjusted to correspond to the amount of the cash dividend distribution. Under section 305(b)(2), the stock dividend would be treated as a taxable dividend, since some shareholders receive cash distributions while others receive an increase in their proportionate interest in the corporation's earnings and assets by virtue of the stock dividends. See Regulations, section 1.305–3(b)(2).

Section 305(b)(3), which taxes stock distributions when some shareholders receive common stock while others receive preferred, is in effect a variation on the disproportionate distributions treated by section 305(b)(2). Under section 305(b)(3), the shareholders receiving common stock are increasing their equity interests while other shareholders receive preferred stock, which is analogous to the receipt of cash or other property in the section 305(b)(2) situation. Paragraph (b)(3) is necessary to cover the situation described because section 317 excludes the distributed stock described in paragraph (b)(3) from "property" and hence it is not "other property" under paragraph (b)(2).

Section 305(b)(5), dealing with distributions of convertible preferred stock, is likewise related to the problem of disproportionate distributions and amplifies section 305(b)(2). Suppose a corporation makes a pro rata distribution on its common stock of preferred stock convertible into common stock. If all of the convertible preferred stock is converted into common the effect of the distribution will be the same as a distribution of common on

1. For section 356(a)(2), which deals with distributions in corporate reorganizations, see infra, page 800.

common, which would not affect the shareholder's proportionate interest in the corporation. On the other hand, if some of the recipients of the convertible preferred exercise the conversion privilege while others do not exercise but sell the preferred, the net effect will be an increase in the proportionate interest in the corporation by the converting shareholders and a corresponding receipt of cash by the selling shareholders, thus having the result which section 305(b)(2) was intended to prevent. Accordingly, section 305(b)(5) makes the distribution of convertible preferred taxable unless the distribution is not likely to result in an increase in the proportionate interest. See Regulations, section 1.305–6(a); compare Regulations, sections 1.305–4(b), Ex. (2), and 1.305–6(b), Ex. (2).

Section 305(b)(2), as reinforced by sections 305(b)(3) and 305(b)(5), thus appears to express a Congressional judgment that the same corporation should not be allowed to arrange its dividend policies to attract simultaneously both the investor who desires current cash distributions and the investor who seeks an increase in the value of her stock investment through corporate growth (and thus future capital gain rather than currently taxable cash distributions). This policy thus goes beyond the problems with which section 305(b)(1) is concerned, i.e., the year-to-year option to receive stock dividends rather than cash, and seems to express a general view that the investor must choose at the time of making a particular investment whether she wished to stress capital appreciation or current cash dividends; the same corporation cannot simultaneously offer both alternatives to the investing community. To reach this result, the statute in some way returns to the judicially developed proportionate interest test of the pre–1954 law discussed, supra, page 523, by making increases in proportionate interests an element in the tax pattern imposed on stock dividends. However, in keeping with the policy discussed above, the increases in the proportionate interests of some of the shareholders must be accompanied by a property distribution to other shareholders. Hence, section 305 does not fully mirror the pre–1954 case law, and its basic policy stands on a somewhat different footing.

4. *Distributions on Preferred Stock*

Section 305(b)(4) responds to a different problem than those considered above. While the 1954 version of section 305 dealt to a limited extent with stock dividends on preferred stock issued in lieu of cash distributions, it was generally possible under the 1954 provision to give preferred stockholders "the equivalent, of dividends" through devices which allowed them to obtain capital gain treatment. For example, convertible preferred stock might pay no cash dividends but the ratio at which it was converted into common might increase annually by a specified percentage. On conversion, the shareholder would sell the shares which in effect were issued in lieu of cash dividend distributions at capital gain rates. Or the preferred might have a redemption price substantially in excess of the issue price, with the redemption generating capital gain which substituted for current dividend distributions. Section 305(b)(4) prevents this result by currently taxing all stock distributions on preferred, either actual or constructive.

5. *Constructive Distributions*

Under section 305(c), the Treasury is given broad discretionary authority to issue Regulations dealing with situations which result in an increase in a shareholder's proportionate interest in the corporation. This authority was intended to forestall taxpayer attempts to probe the limits of nontaxability under the section 305 stock distribution rules and to prevent disputes as to the authority of the Treasury to deal with the ingenious arrangements which would and do inevitably develop. Under section 305(c), a number of devices such as a change in conversion ratio or redemption price, a recapitalization, etc., which have the effect of an increase in a shareholder's proportionate interest are treated as falling under section 305(b), thus making the constructive stock distribution potentially taxable. For example, the increase in proportionate interest of some shareholders caused by the redemption of the share of other shareholders can, in the appropriate circumstances, be treated as a constructive distribution under section 305(c). See infra, page 535.

B. TECHNICAL AND INTERPRETIVE PROBLEMS UNDER SECTION 305

1. *Manner of Taxation*

When a stock distribution is taxable under section 305(b), it is treated as a distribution of property to which section 301 applies, and a dividend results under section 301(b)(1)(A) in the amount of the fair market value of the stock dividend (either actual or constructive) if the distributing corporation has sufficient earnings and profits. See Regulations, section 1.305–2(b), Ex. (1).

In situations to which section 305(b)(1) applies, the amount which is taxable is the fair market value of the stock dividend itself and not the cash dividend which was foregone in lieu of the stock dividend should these two amounts for any reason not be equivalent. See Regulations, section 1.301–1(d)(ii). For example, Rev.Rul. 76–53, 1976–1 Cum.Bull. 87, involved a dividend reinvestment plan where the shareholder could elect to have the cash dividend reinvested in shares of the distributing company at a price 5 percent below the market price. The Ruling held that the amount taxable under section 305(b)(1) was the full fair market value of the stock received and not the cash dividend. On the other hand, if the corporation merely acts as the shareholder's agent to reinvest the cash dividend in shares of the distributing corporation purchased in the market then the cash dividend is taxable as a distribution under section 301 and section 305 does not apply. Rev.Rul. 77–149, 1977–1 Cum.Bull. 82. For another variation on a dividend reinvestment plan covered by section 305(b)(1) and 305(b)(2), see Rev.Rul. 78–375, 1978–2 Cum.Bull. 130.

2. *Impact on Earnings and Profits*

If the stock distribution is nontaxable under section 305(a), no reduction is made in earnings and profits. Section 312(d)(1). On the other hand, if the distribution is taxable under section 305(b), the earnings and profits are reduced by the fair market value of the stock dividend, both in the case of individual and corporate distributees. Regulations, section 1.312–1(d).

3. *Basis of Stock Dividend Shares*

If the stock distribution is taxable under section 305(b), its basis in the hand of the distributee is its fair market value at the time of the distribution. Regulations, section 1.301–1(h). If the stock distribution is not taxable by virtue of section 305(a), then the basis of the stock with respect to which the stock distribution is issued is allocated between the old stock and the new stock in accordance with the fair market value of each on the date of the distribution. Regulations, section 1.307–1(a). The rules with respect to the effect on earnings and profits and basis of a taxable stock dividend under section 305 apply equally when the taxable amount involved is a deemed distribution on convertible debentures under section 305(b)(2). Rev.Rul. 76–186, 1976–1 Cum.Bull. 86.

4. *The "Option" in Section 305(b)(1)*

One of the most common examples of the application of section 305(b)(1) is a dividend reinvestment plan under which shareholders may elect either to take cash dividends or to apply the dividends which they would have received to the purchase (frequently at a discount from market price) of new stock from the corporation. See Rev.Rul. 78–375, 1978–2 Cum.Bull. 130. Section 305(b)(1) also applies where the same effect is achieved by issuing a stock dividend to all shareholders and giving the shareholders an option to have the stock immediately redeemed by the corporation. Rev. Rul. 76–258, 1976–2 Cum.Bull. 295. This same result occurs even though not all of the shareholders have the option. Regulations, section 1.305–2(a)(5). See Rev.Rul. 83–68, 1983–1 Cum.Bull. 75. Conversely, a purported cash dividend which the shareholder *must* apply to the purchase of additional stock from the corporation is a tax free stock dividend under section 305(a). Rev.Rul. 80–154, 1980–1 Cum.Bull. 68.

In Frontier Savings and Loan Association v. Commissioner, 87 T.C. 665 (1986), aff'd sub nom. Colonial Savings and Loan Ass'n v. Commissioner, 854 F.2d 1001 (7th Cir.1988), the Federal Home Loan Bank of Chicago (FHLB), all of whose shareholders were banks, declared a stock dividend in December of each of several successive years. At the same time that it notified shareholders of the dividend, it also notified them that they could request the FHLB to redeem those shares held by any shareholder which exceeded the minimum shareholdings required under federal banking laws. Although the FHLB was not required to honor the requests for redemption, in both years before the court it granted all shareholder requests for redemption. The Commissioner asserted that the taxpayer, which had not requested redemption of any of its shares, received a taxable stock dividend under section 305(b)(1). Emphasizing that the FHLB did not surrender its discretionary authority to redeem or not to redeem the shares as it saw fit, the Tax Court held that the stock dividend was not taxable. The court rejected the Commissioner's argument that, because the authority was exercised so consistently in favor of redemption, the shareholders had the option to redeem their shares. An additional factor was that while the dividend was distributed in December, the shareholders generally would be unable to calculate their minimum required shareholdings in the FHLB, and thus would not be able to submit their redemption requests, until the following year. While acknowledging that the form of the transaction was admittedly motivated in part by tax considerations—to permit those shareholders of FHLB which were required to increase their shareholdings to do so through the receipt of a nontaxable stock dividend—the court concluded that the stock dividends were not a "mere subterfuge for cash distributions." A concurring opinion, joined in by four judges, noted that if discretionary redemptions of stock dividends were to become a "routine matter," the transaction should be treated differently. Nevertheless, the concurring opinion considered the redemptions in this case to be "isolated" rather than "periodic." (see

Regulations, section 1.301–3(b)(3). The Court of Appeals affirmed based on the reasoning of the Tax Court. Accord Western Federal Savings and Loan Ass'n v. Commissioner, 880 F.2d 1005 (8th Cir.1989).

Suppose that a corporation with ten equal shareholders issued a 1–for–1 stock dividend and simultaneously notified the shareholders that they could request redemption of any number of their shares received in the stock dividend distribution. Is the distribution nontaxable under *Frontier Savings and Loan* as long as the corporation does not "offer" to redeem the shares, but invites shareholders to "offer" their shares for redemption which offer the corporation formally would accept or reject? Should an "option" be found in the "circumstances of the distribution" pursuant to Regulations, section 1.305–2(a)(4)? Even though the Commissioner's "circumstances of the distribution" argument was rejected by the court in *Frontier Savings and Loan,* the peculiar bank regulatory aspects of the case may have played a role in the decision and, in the case of a closely held corporation, particularly where the shareholders are related, it would appear that the "circumstances of the distribution" argument should carry more weight.

5. *The Proscribed "Result" in Section 305(b)(2)*

Under section 305(b)(2), the stock distribution is taxable if it "has the result" of an increase in the proportionate interest of some shareholders in the corporation and the receipt of property by other shareholders in a section 301 distribution. See Regulations, section 1.305–3(b)(3). Under the Regulations, if the stock distribution and the property distribution are more than 36 months apart, they will be presumed not to have the proscribed statutory result unless made pursuant to a "plan." Regulations, section 1.305–3(b)(4). The negative implication of the Regulation is that if the property distribution and the stock distribution do take place within a 36 month period, then the stock dividend will be taxable even though there is no other connection between the two distributions. See also Regulations, section 1.305–3(b).

Section 305(b)(2) does not describe as a taxable stock dividend a stock dividend (either preferred or common) on one class of common stock where no property is distributed to another class of common stock within three years of the stock dividend, even though the proportionate interest of one class of common has been increased at the expense of the other. Presumably the drafters of section 305 considered such a provision unnecessary because due to the economic inequality of such a transaction it is unlikely that it would occur. But in Hagen v. Commissioner, 57 T.C.M. 1489 (1989), a shareholder of a closely held corporation increased his proportionate interest in a closely held corporation through stock dividends from which other shareholders were fraudulently excluded. Because the stock dividend was not accompanied by a distribution of property to the other shareholders, the Tax Court held that it was not taxable under section 305. The court specifically rejected the Commissioner's argument that an increase in the taxpayer's equity interest, standing alone, was taxable.

6. *Increase in Proportionate Interest*

The Regulations take the position that the determination of an increase in proportionate interest is to be made in terms of the class of stock taken as a whole. If the class of stock has an increase in proportionate interest, the individual shareholders of the class of stock will be deemed to have increased their respective interests. Regulations, section 1.305–3(b)(6). Suppose an individual owns two classes of stock pro rata and there is a distribution of additional shares on one class of stock without a distribution on the other class of stock. Or suppose the taxpayer is the sole shareholder of both classes of stock. Under the class-by-class approach, the individual might be taxed in both these situations when the stock distribution was coupled with a subsequent property distribution, as, for example, a cash dividend on the other class of stock within the 36 month period, even though viewed individually, there was no change in his proportionate interest. Compare the *Strassburger* case, discussed, supra, page 523.

The above analysis is limited, however, by the requirement that the increased interest in the assets or earnings and profits must be at the expense of another class of stock. See Regulations, section 1.305–3(e), Ex. (3). Thus, if a corporation has only one class of common stock outstanding and issues a stock dividend in shares of preferred stock, the distribution is tax free under section 305(a) (although the preferred stock would be section 306 stock, see infra, page 546). However, if at a time when preferred stock was outstanding, a stock dividend in preferred shares was issued to the holders of the common stock, section 305(b)(2) could be applicable since the class of common shareholders would increase its proportionate interest in the earnings and assets by virtue of their receipt of additional preferred stock while the preferred shareholders, on the subsequent payment of dividends, would receive the necessary cash distribution. But, a distribution of new junior preferred stock on common stock, coupled with payment of cash dividends on the senior preferred, does not invoke section 305(b)(2) since the subordination of the junior preferred prevents the required increase in proportionate interest. On the other hand, a distribution of new preferred stock on one class of common, coupled with a cash dividend on a different class of common stock, is subject to section 305(b)(2). If a corporation has outstanding both common stock and preferred stock convertible into common stock, a distribution of a common stock dividend on the common stock with no change in the conversion ratio of the convertible preferred, would, if coupled with a cash payment on the convertible preferred, make the common stock dividend taxable. See Regulations, section 1.305–3(e), Ex. (4).

7. *Distributions on Preferred Stock*

Preferred stock does not commonly pay stock dividends except in the event of default in the payment of cash dividends or to prevent dilution. Rev.Rul. 84–141, 1984–2 Cum.Bull. 80, involved cumulative preferred stock which gave the holders the option to elect to receive an amount of common stock equal in value to accrued past due dividends, increased by an interest factor, whenever dividends were past due for two or more successive quarters. The Ruling held that the preferred shareholders constructively received a stock dividend taxable under section 305(b)(4) upon the passage of two successive quarters without the payment of cash dividends. The stock attributable to the interest factor was treated as a distribution, not as interest.

Regulations, section 1.305–5, elaborate on the statutory exception for distributions in the form of an increase in the conversion ratio of convertible preferred stock to take into account a stock dividend on or a split in the common stock into which the preferred is convertible. Rev.Rul 83–42, 1983–1 Cum.Bull. 76, held that an actual distribution of common stock on convertible preferred stock to compensate for dilution as a result of a split of the common stock was taxable. The exception is limited to changes in the conversion ratio.

For the definition of preferred stock for purposes of section 305(b)(4), see Regulations, section 1.305–5(a).

8. *Constructive Distributions Under Section 305(c)*

A stock redemption can bring section 305 into play. Section 305(c). The redemption involves an increase in the proportionate interest in the corporation for those shareholders whose stock is not redeemed, and because the redeemed shareholders are receiving cash in the redemption, the "receipt of property" required by section 305(b)(2) is present. Regulations, section 1.305–3(b), state that the redemption transaction will not generate a taxable deemed distribution to the remaining shareholders under section 305(c) if the redemption itself is entitled to capital gains treatment by the redeemed shareholders. However, if the redemption distribution is treated as a dividend under section 302(d) and section 301, see infra, page 554, the increase in proportionate interest on the part of the other shareholders can be taxable under section 305(b)(2) and section 305(c). See Regulations, section 1.305–7.

Rev.Rul. 78–60, 1978–1 Cum.Bull. 81, involved a corporation that adopted a plan whereby each shareholder was entitled to have the corporation redeem two-thirds of one percent of the shareholder's stock annually. Pursuant to the plan, in a particular year the corporation redeemed shares from 8 of the 24 shareholders. All of the redemption distributions were treated as distributions subject to section 301. The Ruling held that the shareholders whose shares were not redeemed received a taxable stock dividend, the amount of which was to be computed under Regulations, section 1.305–3(e). On the other hand, Regulations, section 1.305–3(b)(3), provide that redemptions which are "isolated" are not covered by section 305(c). The exact scope of this exception is unclear. See Rev.Rul. 77–19, 1977–1 Cum.Bull. 83 (section 305(c) did not apply where over a three year period a publicly held corporation redeemed shares from 20 different retiring and deceased shareholders; the redemptions fell under the "isolated" redemption exception in Regulations, section 1.305–3(b)(3)).

Suppose a publicly held corporation purchases its own shares in the market. Viewed as redemptions, such purchases technically could result in constructive stock dividends to the other shareholders in the corporation. However, Regulations, section 1.305–3(e), Ex. (13), exempt such transactions from the application of section 305(b)(2) where the shares are purchased for use in connection with employee stock investment plans, for future acquisitions, etc., and there is no plan to increase the proportionate interests of some shareholders and distribute property to other shareholders.

Section 305(c) also provides that a difference between the redemption price of stock and its issue price can be treated as a constructive stock distribution to the shareholder. The provision is aimed at a technique by which the corporation issues preferred stock with an excessive redemption price on which it pays no dividends and which it subsequently redeems in a transaction qualifying for capital gain treatment under section 302(b). The transaction in effect converts what otherwise would have been current dividend income into deferred capital gain. Section 305(c) prevents this result by treating the excess redemption premium as a constructive distribution on the preferred stock, taxable under section 305(b)(4). This constructive stock dividend is received ratably over the period between the issue date of the stock and the expected redemption date. See Rev.Rul. 83–119, 1983–2 Cum.Bull. 57 (preferred stock issued for $600 was redeemable for $1,000 on death of holder, who had actual life expectancy of 24 years). However, no constructive distribution on the stock will be deemed to occur if the redemption premium is "reasonable." A 10 percent "safe haven" is provided in Regulations, section 1.305–5(b)(2). Where the redemption price exceeds a reasonable premium, the Internal Revenue Service treats only the excess of the issue price over a reasonable redemption premium, not the excess over the issue price, as a taxable stock dividend. Rev.Rul. 83–119, supra. See also Rev.Rul. 81–190, 1981–2 Cum.Bull. 84; Rev.Rul. 75–465, 1975–2 Cum.Bull. 486; and Rev.Rul. 75–179, 1975–1 Cum.Bull. 103, finding redemption premiums in excess of 10 percent of issue price nevertheless reasonable.

For discussions of the above issues, see Bacon, Share Redemptions By Publicly Held Companies: A New Look At Dividend Equivalence, 26 Tax L.Rev. 283 (1970); Chirelstein, Optional Redemptions And Optional Dividends: Taxing The Repurchase of Common Shares, 78 Yale L.J. 739 (1969).

Section 305(c) can also be relevant where the redemption provisions are being used to effect a sale of the corporate business, see infra, page 725, or in the case of a corporate recapitalization, see infra, page 873.

9. *De Minimis Aspects*

The Senate version of the 1969 bill contained a de minimis provision but it was eliminated by the Conference Committee. As a consequence it was feared for a time that the distribution of cash in lieu of fractional shares in a stock dividend distribution might trigger the application of section 305(b)(2) since the literal terms of the statute would apply: some shareholders would receive a dividend solely in stock, increasing their proportionate interest in the corporation, while other shareholders would receive cash in lieu of their fractional shares, thus providing the necessary property distribution for purposes of section 305(b)(2). But Regulations, section 1.305–3(c), take the position that section 305(b)(2) will not apply in such situations if "[t]he purpose in distributing the cash is to save the distributing corporation the trouble, expense, and inconvenience of issuing and transferring fraction shares * * * and not to give any particular group of shareholders an increased interest in the assets or earnings and profits of the corporation."

10. *Situations To Which Section 305 Does Not Apply*

Though section 305 has a wide scope, the Regulations explicitly exempt some transactions which otherwise might fall within the terms of the section. Thus, a change in conversion ratio or redemption price of stock which is in effect an adjustment in the purchase price of assets acquired in exchange for the stock will not fall within section 305. Regulations, section 1.305–1(c). Similarly, where stock is issued in what is in effect a security arrangement and it is anticipated that the bulk of the corporation's earnings will be used to redeem the stock the redemptions will not be treated as subject to section 305(b)(2). Regulations, section 1.305–3, Ex. (14); Rev.Rul. 78–115, 1978–1 Cum.Bull. 85.

C. STOCK OPTIONS

The general rules respecting stock options or stock rights issued on outstanding stock follow those for stock dividends. There is no income inclusion on issuance of the options, except for the cases in section 305(b). On a sale of the options, the proceeds would be capital gain, with the holding period of the rights being that of the stock, section 1223(5), unless the stock rights were classified as section 306 stock in which event ordinary income could result. If the value is 15 percent or more of the value of the old stock *and* the rights are either sold or exercised, the basis of the rights is an allocable portion of the basis of the old stock. Section 307(a); Regulations, section 1.307–1. If the value of the rights is less than 15 percent of the value of the old stock, the basis of the rights is zero unless an election is made under section 307(b) to allocate the stock basis between the rights and the stock. If the rights are allowed to lapse, no loss arises (regardless of the value of the rights) since for this purpose no part of the basis of the old stock is allocated to them, and the basis of the old stock is not reduced.

If the stock rights involve the option to purchase stock of another corporation, the distribution cannot be subject to section 305. The shareholders receive a distribution subject to section 301, and the distributing corporation may be required to recognize gain under section 311. See supra, page 477.

D. REFERENCES

Metzer, The "New" Section 305, 27 Tax L.Rev. 93 (1971); Del Cotto and Wolf, The Proportionate Interest Test of Section 305 and the Supreme Court, 27 Tax L.Rev. 49 (1971); Rustigan, Stock Distributions–Section 305, 49 Taxes 787 (1971); Committee on Corporate Taxation, New York State Bar Association Tax Section, Comments on Proposed Regulations Under Section 305 of the Internal Revenue Code of 1954, as Amended by Section 421 of the Tax Reform Act of 1969, 49 Taxes 460 (1971); Eustice, Corporations and Corporate Investors, 25 Tax.L.Rev. 509, 537–52 (1970); Andrews and Wilson, Stock Dividend Taxation under the Tax Reform Act of 1969: Expansion of an Ominous Past, 13 Ariz.L.Rev. 751 (1971); Chirelstein, Optional Redemptions and Optional Dividends: Taxing the Repurchase of Common Shares. 78 Yale L.J. 739 (1969); Bashian, Stock Dividends and Section 305: Realization and the Constitution, 1971 Duke L.J. 1105; de Kosmian, Taxable Stock Dividends under New Section 305, 28 Tax. Lawyer 57 (1974); Cohen, Taxing Stock Dividends and Economic Theory, 1974 Wisc.L.Rev. 142.

SECTION 2. THE SPECIAL ASPECT OF THE PREFERRED STOCK BAILOUT

A. THE SOURCE OF THE PROBLEM

Suppose that Z Corporation has outstanding only common stock, which is held equally by individuals A and B. At a time when Z Corporation has accumulated earnings and profits in excess of $100,000, the corporation declares a dividend payable in 100 shares of $1,000 par value 9 percent cumulative preferred stock which is subject to mandatory redemption in 5 years. A and B each receive 50 shares of preferred stock, having an aggregate par value of $50,000 and a fair market value that would in all likelihood be close to par value. This stock dividend would be tax free under section 305(a). Suppose further that before the distribution A and B each had a basis in their common stock of $60,000 and that after the distribution the fair market value of the common stock held by each shareholder was $25,000. Under section 307, A and B would each allocate a basis of $40,000 to their preferred stock. Suppose now that A and B each sell their preferred stock to X Corporation for $50,000. If the transaction is treated as an ordinary sale of stock, A and B each would recognize a capital gain of $10,000. X Corporation will have a basis in the preferred stock of $100,000 and when the stock is redeemed in 5 years, it will recognize neither gain nor loss. Even though Z Corporation effectively has distributed $100,000 of its earnings and profits to A and B, without diminishing their voting rights or percentage ownership in the assets or residual profits of the corporation (except as necessary to pay dividends on and redeem the preferred stock), they would not be required to recognize that amount as ordinary income.

Chamberlin v. Commissioner, 207 F.2d 462 (6th Cir.1953), involved just such a transaction. The taxpayers in that case asserted that the stock dividend, which was distributed in 1946, was a nontaxable distribution under the principles of *Strassberger,* discussed supra, page 523, which governed stock dividends under the 1939 Code. The Commissioner argued that under the circumstances there was not a true stock dividend, that in effect the taxpayers had received a cash distribution even though the corporation had not distributed the cash in 1946. The court held that the distribution was a stock dividend in substance as well as form, even though the taxpayer conceded that the form of the transaction was motivated by tax avoidance. Because the insurance company which purchased the stock acquired a bona fide investment in the corporation and the redemption features of the stock were not unreasonable, the court refused to treat the otherwise nontaxable stock dividend as taxable solely because the stock was sold soon after its receipt. Thus, the shareholders in *Chamberlin* were able not only to treat a portion of the sales proceeds as a recovery of basis, but also were able to report the gain as taxable at the preferential rate which then applied to long-term capital gains. If the principle of the *Chamberlin* case prevailed, closely held corporations in effect could have avoided ever paying taxable cash dividends.

Expressly responding to the *Chamberlin* decision, in the 1954 Code Congress foreclosed this tax avoidance route with the enactment of section 306. Rather than adopting the Commissioner's position in *Chamberlin* that the stock distribution itself was taxable, however, Congress chose to "taint" with ordinary income treatment any future disposition of the stock as explained in the following excerpt from SENATE FINANCE COMMITTEE REPORT, INTERNAL REVENUE CODE OF 1954, S.Rep. No. 83–1622, 83d Cong., 2d Sess 46 (1954):

"Your committee has * * * acted to close a possible loophole of existing law known as the 'preferred stock bail-out'. * * * Your committee's approach to this problem imposes a tax on the recipient of the dividend stock at the time of its sale. This dividend stock would be called 'section 306 stock' and any stock received as a dividend would be section 306 stock to the extent of its allocable share of corporate earnings at the time of issuance, except common stock issued with respect to common stock.

"The tax imposed at the time of the sale of the stock is at ordinary income rates to the extent of its allocable share of earnings and profits of the corporation at the time the stock dividend was declared. Any amount received for the section 306 stock which exceeds the earnings and profits attributable to it will be taxed as capital gain. If, instead of selling the section 306 stock, the shareholder redeems it, the proceeds received will be taxed as a dividend to the extent of corporate earnings at the time of redemption. * * * [C]ertain exceptions to this basic rule of ordinary income treatment with respect to dispositions of section 306 stock are provided."

With the repeal of the preferential tax rates for capital gains by the Tax Reform Act of 1986, one aspect of the potential tax avoidance at which section 306 is directed was eliminated. Nevertheless, section 306 continues to serve one function. When preferred stock is received as a tax-free stock dividend, a portion of the basis of the stock on which the dividend was issued is allocated to the preferred stock pursuant to section 307. In the case of a sale or redemption of the preferred stock, section 306 requires a portion of the amount received to be treated as income before any basis recovery is allowed.

B. OPERATION OF SECTION 306

INTERNAL REVENUE CODE: Section 306.

REGULATIONS: Section 1.306–1; –2; –3(a)–(c); (e).

PESCOSOLIDO v. COMMISSIONER *

United States Tax Court, 1988.
91 T.C. 52.

COHEN, JUDGE:

* * *

The sole issue for decision is whether petitioners' deductions for charitable contributions of section 306 stock are allowable at fair market value or limited to cost basis in the stock.

* * *

Petitioner graduated from Deerfield Academy and, in 1934, from Harvard College. He went to work for an oil company because other jobs were not available. In 1949, petitioner invested his savings in the

* The Tax Court decision was affirmed, 883 F.2d 187 (1st Cir.1989).

formation of Valley Oil Co. Through this closely held corporation, petitioner distributed fuel oil and gasoline. As petitioner's business grew, petitioner bought out several other small oil companies. Petitioner also established corporations in Maine and other parts of Massachusetts to carry out various aspects of his business.

The growth of petitioner's business was haphazard and unplanned. In 1976, petitioner decided to consolidate his enterprise into one efficient and cost-effective organization. He also planned to effect a "freeze" of the value of his stock for estate tax purposes. In a tax-free reorganization, petitioner merged his six controlled corporations into the Lido Corp. of New England, Inc. (Lido). Through counsel, petitioner obtained a ruling letter from the Internal Revenue Service with respect to the reorganization. The application for a ruling represented, among other things, that nonvoting preferred stock to be issued by Lido would not be redeemed for 5 years. Among other things, the ruling stated: "The Corp. A Preferred to be received by [petitioner] and [William Pescosolido] will constitute 'section 306 stock' within the meaning of section 306(c)."

Immediately after the reorganization, petitioner held all of the 2,500 shares of Lido class A voting stock and 11,708 shares of nonvoting preferred stock. Petitioner's sons, daughter, and brother received nonvoting common stock. The cost basis of petitioner's preferred stock was $16.32 per share.

By receiving all of the Lido voting stock, petitioner retained control over Lido's growth and development. Petitioner's children, who were employed by the company, were given an interest in Lido's welfare through their nonvoting shares. Petitioner's preferred stock also advanced the interests of petitioner's family by serving petitioner's estate planning needs. Petitioner did not plan at that time to sell or otherwise dispose of the preferred stock.

Petitioner had long been an ardent supporter of Deerfield Academy and Harvard College. As petitioner built his business, he contributed small amounts of cash and donated his time to the Harvard College Schools Committee.

* * *

As the energy crises of the early 1970's came to an end, petitioner's fortunes markedly improved. Petitioner felt that he was now in a position to make more substantial donations to Deerfield and Harvard. In 1978 and 1979, petitioner made the following donations of Lido preferred stock:

Years	*Number of preferred shares*	*Fair market value dollar amount*	*Recipient*
1978	500	$50,000	Harvard University
1979	500	50,000	Harvard University
1979	500	50,000	Deerfield Academy

Deerfield and Harvard were at all material times educational institutions described in section 501(c)(3). In each of the years in issue, the donees of the shares received 7-percent dividends.

At the time of the gifts, petitioner did not seek professional advice concerning the tax consequences of his gifts of preferred stock.

* * *

On their tax returns, petitioners deducted the contributions to Harvard and Deerfield calculated at $100 per share as follows:

Tax year	*Contributions deduction dollar amount*
1978	$50,000
1979	78,601
1980	21,399

* * *

In a notice of deficiency, respondent disallowed petitioners' charitable contribution deductions in their entirety. Respondent now concedes that petitioners are entitled to deduct their cost basis of $16.32 per share.

OPINION

Section 170(a) allows a deduction for any charitable contribution. Section 1.170–1(c), Income Tax Regs., provides that if the charitable contribution is made in property other than money, the amount of the deduction allowed under section 170(b) is the fair market value of the property on the date of the contribution. In such a case, section 170(e) imposes a significant limitation on the amount of an otherwise allowable deduction. That section provides, in pertinent part, as follows:

> SEC. 170(e). CERTAIN CONTRIBUTIONS OF ORDINARY INCOME AND CAPITAL GAIN PROPERTY.—
>
> (1) GENERAL RULE.—The amount of any charitable contribution of property otherwise taken into account under this section shall be reduced by the sum of—
>
> (A) the amount of gain which would not have been long-term capital gain if the property contributed had been sold by the taxpayer at its fair market value (determined at the time of such contribution) * * *

The property to which section 170(e)(1)(A) applies includes stock described in section 306(a). Sec. 1.170A–4(b)(1), Income Tax Regs.

Section 306 is designed to prevent "preferred stock bailouts," in which shareholders extract corporate earnings and profits as capital gain, rather than ordinary income, while retaining ownership of a corporation. Fireoved v. United States, 462 F.2d 1281, 1284–1286 (3d Cir.1972); Bialo v. Commissioner, 88 T.C. 1132, 1138–1139 (1987). Section 306(a) generally provides that if a shareholder sells or otherwise disposes of "section 306 stock," the amount realized on the disposition of the stock will be treated as ordinary income. The parties agree that the stock given by petitioner to Deerfield and Harvard was "section 306 stock." Petitioner argues, however, that his "tainted" stock was "purged" by section 306(b)(4), which provides, in pertinent part, as follows:

> SEC. 306(b). EXCEPTIONS.—Subsection (a) shall not apply—
>
> * * *
>
> (4) TRANSACTIONS NOT IN AVOIDANCE.—If it is established to the satisfaction of the Secretary—
>
> (A) that the distribution, and the disposition or redemption * * *
>
> * * *
>
> was not in pursuance of a plan having as one of its principal purposes the avoidance of Federal income tax.

Petitioner has the burden of proving that neither the distribution nor the disposition of section 306 stock was part of a plan of tax avoidance; that burden is a heavy one. Bialo v. Commissioner, 88 T.C. at 1138; Roebling v. Commissioner, 77 T.C. 30, 59 (1981).[2]

Petitioner testified, without contradiction, that he received Lido preferred stock in an attempt to "freeze" the value of his equity in the company for estate planning purposes. See Northern Trust Co., Transferee v. Commissioner, 87 T.C. 349 (1986), affd. sub nom. Citizens Bank & Trust Co. v. Commissioner, 839 F.2d 1259 (7th Cir.1988). There is no evidence that petitioner planned at the time of the distribution to sell or otherwise dispose of the preferred stock. Petitioner further testified that he was an ardent supporter of Deerfield Academy and Harvard College, institutions that he believes changed his life. Petitioner struggled for many years to build a prosperous family business. After years of effort he found himself in a position to repay his alma maters. Petitioner argues that he has thus negated a tax avoidance purpose for disposition of the stock and brought himself within the exception of section 306(b)(4)(A).

According to respondent, section 306(b)(4)(A) will generally apply *only* to minority shareholders who are not in control of the distributing corporation. Thus, he argues, petitioner cannot bring himself within this exception.

Respondent's argument is based on the following language in section 1.306–2(b)(3), Income Tax Regs.:

2. Respondent does not argue that the language in sec. 306(b)(4), "If it is established to the satisfaction of the Secretary," creates a special standard of review. See Fireoved v. United States, 318 F.Supp. 133 (E.D.Pa.1970), affd. in part and revd. in part 462 F.2d 1281, 1287 n. 10 (3d Cir. 1972); 3B J. Mertens, Law of Federal Income Taxation, sec. 22:90 (1980): "it is questionable whether this [language] confers any greater prerogative or discretion on the Commissioner than normally resides in him with respect to the usual kind of determination which first is made on the administrative level and which receives a presumption of correctness." See also sec. 3B J. Mertens, supra at 38D.35 n. 20.

(b) Section 306(a) does not apply to—

* * *

(3) A disposition or redemption, if it is established to the satisfaction of the Commissioner that the distribution, and the disposition or redemption, was not in pursuance of a plan having as one of its principal purposes the avoidance of Federal income tax. * * * For example, in the absence of such a plan and of any other facts the first sentence of this subparagraph would be applicable to the case of dividends and isolated dispositions of section 306 stock by minority shareholders. * * *

The regulatory language pertaining to minority shareholders is prefaced by the words "For example." Thus, an isolated disposition of section 306 stock by a minority shareholder is but one instance in which disposition of "tainted" stock is not part of a tax-avoidance plan. The regulation does not purport to set forth an exhaustive list of all situations that fall within section 306(b)(4). Certainly the statute contains no reference to the taxpayer's percentage of ownership or degree of control of the corporation. Respondent's argument, therefore, is overstated.

Respondent also cites the report of the Senate Finance Committee, S.Rept. 1622, 83d Cong., 2d Sess. 243–244 (1954), which states:

Paragraph (4) of subsection (b) excepts from the general rule of subsection (a) those transactions not in avoidance of this section where it is established to the satisfaction of the Secretary that the transaction was not in pursuance of a plan having as one of its principal purposes the avoidance of Federal income tax. Subparagraph (A) of this paragraph applies to cases where the distribution itself, coupled with the disposition or redemption was not in pursuance of such a plan. This subparagraph is intended to apply to the case of dividends and isolated dispositions of section 306 stock by minority shareholders who do not in the aggregate have control of the distributing corporation. In such a case it would seem to your committee to be inappropriate to impute to such shareholders an intention to remove corporate earnings at the tax rates applicable only to capital gains.

This legislative history was given persuasive effect in Fireoved v. United States, supra, and Bialo v. Commissioner, supra, the cases relied on by respondent. In Fireoved, the taxpayer contended that distribution and disposition of certain stock received by him as a stock dividend and later redeemed by the corporation fell within the exception of section 306(b)(4)(A). The taxpayer argued that the purpose of the stock dividend was business related, to wit, to obtain additional capital for the corporation from third parties. The Court of Appeals stated that the existence of a business purpose was not inconsistent with a conclusion in the statutory language that "one of [the] principal purposes" of the stock dividend was "the avoidance of Federal income tax." The Court of Appeals stated:

> In a situation such as the one presented in this case, where the facts necessary to determine the motives for the issuance of a stock dividend are peculiarly within the control of the taxpayer, it is reasonable to require the taxpayer to come forward with the facts that would relieve him of his liability. Here the stipulation was equivocal in determining the purpose of the dividend and is quite compatible with the thought that "one of the principal purposes" was motivated by "tax avoidance." We hold then that the district court did not err in refusing to apply the exception created by section 306(b)(4)(A). [462 F.2d at 1287; fn. ref. omitted.]

With respect to the redemption of the corporate stock by the corporation, the taxpayer argued that he had sold 24 percent of his underlying common stock in the corporation in order to give greater control to another investor and that the subsequent redemption of a part of his section 306 stock related to that business purpose. The Court of Appeals concluded:

> More important, however, is that an examination of the relevant legislative history indicates that Congress did not intend to give capital gains treatment to a portion of the preferred stock redeemed on the facts presented here. [462 F.2d at 1288.]

After quoting S.Rept. 1622, supra, the Court of Appeals continued:

> Thus, it is reasonable to assume that Congress realized the general lack of a tax avoidance purpose when a person sells *all* of his control in a corporation and then either simultaneously or subsequently disposes of his section 306 stock. However, when *only a portion* of the underlying common stock is sold, and the taxpayer retains essentially all the control he had previously, it would be unrealistic to conclude that Congress meant to give that taxpayer the advantage of section 306(b)(4)(B) when he ultimately sells his section 306 stock. Cf. United States v. Davis, 397 U.S. 301, 90 S.Ct. 1041, 25 L.Ed.2d 323 (1970).
>
> * * * although Mr. Fireoved did sell a portion of his voting stock prior to his disposition of the section 306 stock, he retained as much control in the corporation following the sale of his common stock as he had prior to the sale. Under these circumstances it is not consonant with the history of the legislation to conclude that Congress intended such a sale of underlying common stock to exempt the proceeds of the disposition of section 306 stock from treatment as ordinary income. Accordingly, the district court erred when it held that any of the preferred shares Mr. Fireoved redeemed were not subject to section 306(a) by virtue of section 306(b)(4)(B). [462 F.2d at 1289–1290; fn. refs. omitted; emphasis in original.]

Bialo v. Commissioner, supra, presented an easier case than Fireoved v. United States, supra, or the instant case. In Bialo, the taxpayers' closely held corporation issued a pro rata dividend of preferred stock on common stock. The preferred stock was contributed to a charitable trust and then redeemed by the corporation. The evidence did not establish the business purpose of the donation argued by the taxpayers on brief, and:

> The only document admitted into evidence, however, which was prepared prior to the distribution of stock and subsequent contribution to the Trust discusses only the tax advantages of the transaction. * * * The memorandum also notes that a contribution of stock in a privately held corporation is likely to result in quick redemption by the charitable organization. The majority shareholder who contributed such stock would thereby be restored to the status of a 100–percent shareholder. [88 T.C. at 1141.]

Thus we held that the amount of the charitable contribution deduction must be reduced under section 170(e)(1)(A).

In this case, there is evidence of the taxpayer's bona fide charitable intent in the disposition of the stock. Evidence of tax motivation is not as clear as it was in *Bialo.* The reasoning of *Fireoved,* however, is persuasive and applies to the facts of this case. Here, as in other areas of the law, the ultimate purpose of a transaction must be inferred from the objective facts rather than from the taxpayer's mere denial of tax motivation. Petitioner was a sophisticated businessman, making deliberate decisions and advised of the nature of section 306 stock at the time that he received it. We must assume that the potential tax consequences of future disposition of the section 306 stock were explained to petitioner by counsel who requested and received the ruling from the Internal Revenue Service in relation to the reorganization. That ruling specifically stated that the stock would be section 306 stock. See Roebling v. Commissioner, 77 T.C. at 60.

On his 1978 tax return, petitioner claimed a deduction for the fair market value of the stock as if he had made a $50,000 cash contribution. We are not persuaded that he was unaware that the consequence of such a deduction would be the avoidance of ordinary income tax on the bailout of corporate earnings. His testimony that he did not have tax advice at the time of the gifts does not mean that he was ignorant of the tax benefits that he was claiming.

Petitioners have presented a credible purpose other than income tax avoidance for both the distribution and the disposition of Lido stock. The statutory language and purpose and petitioner's control of the corporation, however, require that the evidence clearly negate an income-tax-avoidance plan to satisfy petitioner's burden. His control of the corporation permits an inference of unity of purpose and plan between the corporate issuer and the shareholder,[3] and the substantial tax savings that would result from the bailout and contribution of appreciated stock permit an inference of income-tax-avoidance purpose. Unlike those of a minority shareholder, petitioner's circumstances do

3. See Schneider, "Internal Revenue Code Section 306 and Tax Avoidance," 4 Va.Tax.Rev. 287, 317–319 (1985).

not require an exception to section 306 to avoid the trap for the unwary in section 306 or invoke the relief anticipated by Congress in limited circumstances. See generally B. Bittker & J. Eustice, Federal Income Taxation of Corporations and Shareholders, par. 10.05 (5th ed. 1987).

Petitioners' deduction for contributions of section 306 stock to Harvard and Deerfield are therefore limited to his cost basis in the stock, pursuant to section 170(e)(1)(A).

ILLUSTRATIVE MATERIAL

A. DEFINITION OF SECTION 306 STOCK

1. *Stock Other Than Common Stock Received As a Tax Free Stock Dividend*

Section 306(c) defines section 306 stock with reference to the potential for "bailing out" earnings and profits inherent in stock received in a tax free distribution. The basic rule, in section 306(c)(1)(A) defines section 306 stock to include any stock *other than common stock* received as a tax free stock dividend under section 305(a) by the shareholder disposing of the stock. This basic rule is limited by section 306(c)(2), which provides that stock which would otherwise have been section 306 stock will not be treated as such if the corporation had no current or accumulated earnings and profits at the time the stock dividend was issued.

2. *Definition of "Common Stock"*

Neither the Code nor the Regulations provide much assistance in defining the term "common stock" beyond the rule of section 306(e)(2) that common stock which is convertible into other than common stock is not "common stock." See Regulations, section 1.306–3. The scope of the term "common stock" has been clarified by a series of Revenue Rulings which illustrate that not all preferred stock is section 306 stock and that stock which is not traditional preferred stock may be section 306 stock. For example, Rev.Rul. 81–91, 1981–1 Cum.Bull. 123, involved "Class B" voting stock entitled to a preferential liquidation distribution equal to par value and an annual dividend equal to 6 percent of par value prior to dividends being paid on the Class A stock. After satisfaction of the Class B preference, the Class A and Class B stock shared equally in liquidation and dividend rights. In holding that the Class B stock was "common stock" and therefore not section 306 stock, the Ruling stated: "[S]tock is other than 'common stock' for purposes of section 306 not because of its preferred position as such, but because the preferred position is limited and the stock does not participate in corporate growth to any significant extent." Rev.Rul. 82–191, 1982–2 Cum.Bull. 78, expanded on this explanation as follows: "[T]he factors used to determine whether the stock in question was other than common stock were whether it could be disposed of without a loss in voting control and without a loss in an interest in the unrestricted equitable growth of the corporation. In other words, if a stock in question is nonvoting and is limited in either the right to dividends or the right to assets upon liquidation then it is considered to be other than common stock * * *." Rev.Rul. 82–191 held that *voting* preferred stock was section 306 stock because it was limited as to dividends and had a fixed liquidation preference. On the other hand, non-voting common stock presumably is still "common stock."

See also Rev.Rul. 79–163, 1979–1 Cum.Bull. 131 (limitations on either dividend or liquidation rights will cause stock to be classified as section 306 stock); Rev.Rul. 76–386, 1976–2 Cum.Bull. 95 (the fact that voting common stock is subject to a right of first refusal by the corporation in the case of sale does not prevent it from being classified as "common stock"); Rev.Rul. 57–132, 1957–1 Cum.Bull. 115 (common stock redeemable at the option of the corporation at a price in excess of its book value is not "common stock").

3. *Stock Received in Section 351 Transaction*

Prior to 1982, the rule that preferred stock issued when the corporation has no earnings and profits does not constitute section 306 stock left open the possibility of bailout-motivated transaction. For example, a taxpayer could create a holding company and, in a section 351 transaction, transfer to it stock of a controlled operating corporation which had earnings and profits in exchange for holding company common and preferred stock. The preferred stock would not constitute section 306 stock, due to the absence of earnings and profits in the newly formed holding company, and gain on the sale of the preferred stock would thus be capital gain. Section 306(c)(3) was added in 1982 to block this technique by providing, in effect, that any stock other than common stock issued in a section 351 transaction will be section 306 stock if it is issued in exchange for stock of another controlled corporation which has earnings and profits. The technical rules for determining the available earnings and profits are discussed in connection with section 304, infra, page 600.

Section 306(c)(2) extends the section 306 taint to stock other than common stock received in a corporate reorganization (as defined in section 368) or a corporate division (as defined in section 355) if either (a) the effect of the transaction was substantially the same as the receipt of a stock dividend, or (b) the stock was received in exchange for section 306 stock. This provision is discussed in detail infra, pages 813, and 882.

4. *Miscellaneous Definitional Issues*

(a) *Stock Having Transferred or Substituted Basis*

Section 306(c)(1)(C) brings within the meaning of section 306 stock any stock having a transferred or substituted basis determined with reference to the basis of section 306 stock. One of the principal effects of this rule is that the taint of section 306 stock carries over from a donor to a donee of such stock. However, if section 306 stock receives a fair market value basis under section 1014 when it is transferred at death, the section 306 "taint" is purged and the stock can be disposed of without ordinary income consequences. See Regulations, section 1.306–3(e).

(b) *Stock Rights and Convertible Stock*

Section 306(d) applies the section 306 taint to stock rights to purchase stock which would have been section 306 stock if the stock had been issued directly as a stock dividend. Stock purchased pursuant to such rights also is tainted. See Regulations, section 1.306–2(b).

Section 306(e) provides that if section 306 stock is converted into common stock, either through a conversion privilege or otherwise, the section 306 taint is purged. This rule will apply even though the common stock has an exchanged basis. Section 306(e) also provides that common stock convertible into other than common stock is not treated as common stock. Thus, such stock may be section 306 stock. Does such stock present the bailout potential at which section 306 is directed?

B. TAXATION OF DISPOSITIONS OF SECTION 306 STOCK

1. *Sales*

Section 306(a)(1) treats the entire amount realized on the sale of section 306 stock as ordinary income to the extent of the stock's ratable share of earnings and profits of the issuing corporation at the time of the distribution of the stock, i.e., the amount which would have been a taxable dividend if the original stock distribution had been a taxable distribution of money rather than a tax free stock dividend under section 305. The excess of any amount realized over the dividend amount is treated first as a return of capital which reduces the basis of the stock, and after the basis of the stock has been reduced to zero, any further excess is treated as capital gain on the sale of the stock. These rules are illustrated in the following example.

Suppose that X Corporation has outstanding 100 shares of common stock having a basis of $6 per share and a fair market value of $30 per share. Assume further that the X Corporation common stock is held in equal shares by A and B. At a time when X Corporation has no accumulated earnings and profits and $500 of current earnings and profits, it distributes a stock dividend of 50 shares of $10 par value preferred stock (which is section 306 stock) to each shareholder. The dividend is tax free under section 305. Assuming that after the distribution the fair market value of the common stock is $20 per share and the fair market value of the preferred stock is $10 per share, under section 307, discussed supra, page 531, the basis of the preferred stock is $2 per share. After five years A sells for $500 the 50 shares of preferred stock received in the distribution. Absent section 306, A would recognize a $400 capital gain. Under section 306(a)(1), however, A realizes ordinary income of $250 (50 percent of the $500 earnings and profits at the time the stock was issued), receives a return of capital of $100, and recognizes a capital gain of $150.

Note that while the *sale* of section 306 stock may result in ordinary income, the income is not dividend income. Thus, the amount of the corporation's current and accumulated earnings and profits in the year of the sale is irrelevant; and the earnings and profits of the issuing corporation are not reduced by the amount taxed to the shareholder as ordinary income. Regulations, section 1.306–1(b)(1). In the same vein, a corporate shareholder may not claim the section 243 deduction with respect to ordinary income realized on the sale of section 306 stock.

The amount which "would have been a dividend at the time of distribution" of the stock is a ceiling on the amount of ordinary income realized on the sale. Thus, in the above example, if the earnings and profits of X Corporation at the time of the distribution were $2,000 and A sold the preferred stock for $600, A would realize $500 of ordinary income and have a return of capital of $100. See Regulations, section 1.306–1(b)(2), Ex. (1).

No loss is allowed on the sale of section 306 stock. Section 306(a)(1)(C). Thus, in the above example, if A sold the 50 shares of preferred stock for only $310, A would realize $250 of ordinary income and recover $60 of basis. The remaining $40 of the basis of the preferred stock is reallocated to common stock on which the section 306 stock originally was issued. See Regulations, section 1.306–1(b)(2), Ex. (2).

2. *Redemptions*

When section 306 stock is redeemed by the issuing corporation, the amount realized is treated by section 306(a)(2) as a distribution subject to section 301. The corporation's current and accumulated earnings and profits for the year of the redemption determine the portion of the distribution which will be taxed as ordinary income. Thus, even though the corporation may have had sufficient earnings and profits at the time of the distribution of the stock to support dividend treatment of a cash distribution of equal value, if the corporation has no earnings and profits at the time of the redemption, no part of the distribution is ordinary income. If the corporation has earnings and profits at the time of the redemption, however, the "ratable share" of earnings and profits rule of section 306(a)(1)(A)(ii), which applies to limit ordinary income treatment in the case of sales, does not apply to redemptions of section 306 stock (although the proration of current earnings and profits rules of Regulations, section 1.316–2(b) may apply). But, if at the time of the stock distribution the corporation had no earnings and profits, no part of the amount distributed in redemption of the stock will be subject to section 306. See section 306(c)(2).

Application of these rules is illustrated in the following example. Suppose that Y Corporation has outstanding 100 shares of common stock which have a fair market value of $45 per share. Assume further that the Y Corporation common stock is held in equal shares by C and D who each have a basis of $9 per share. At a time when Y Corporation has no accumulated earnings and profits and $600 of current earnings and profits, it distributes a stock dividend of 50 shares of $15 par value preferred stock (which is section 306 stock) to each shareholder. Assuming that after the distribution the fair market value of the common stock is $30 per share and the fair market value of the preferred stock is $15 per share, the basis of the preferred stock is $3 per share. After five years Y Corporation has $700 of accumulated earnings and profits and no current earnings and profits. Y Corporation then distributes $750 to C in redemption of all 50 of C's shares of preferred stock; none of D's shares are redeemed. C is treated as receiving a $700 dividend and a $50 return of capital. The remaining $100 of C's basis for the preferred stock is reallocated to C's common stock. Y Corporation reduces its accumulated earnings and profits by $700. If D's 50 shares were redeemed the following year, if Y Corporation had no current earnings and profits, no portion of the distribution would be ordinary income.

Section 306 operates independently and overrides the rules of section 302(a) and (b), discussed infra, page 554, under which redemption distributions may be accorded capital gain treatment.

3. *Other Dispositions*

Note that section 306(a) applies if a shareholder "sells or otherwise *disposes*" of section 306 stock. Regulations, section 1.306–1(a), indicate that other dispositions may include a pledge of the stock if the lender can look only to the stock to satisfy the loan (i.e., a nonrecourse loan secured by section 306 stock). Such a transaction, however, usually is not viewed as a recognition event. As is implicit in the *Pescosolido* case, supra, a gift of section

306 stock is not a disposition that results in recognition of ordinary income to the donor.

At one time, the tax disadvantages inherent in section 306 preferred stock could be avoided by a contribution of the stock to a charitable organization. The shareholder would escape tax with respect to the section 306 stock, there being no sale, and could also treat its fair market value as a charitable contribution. See Rev.Rul. 57–328, 1957–2 Cum.Bull. 229. The Tax Reform Act of 1969 eliminated this tax advantage by adding section 170(e)(1)(A), which was applied in *Pescoslido,* requiring the charitable deduction to be reduced by the amount of potential ordinary income gain in the property. See also Bialo v. Commissioner, 88 T.C. 63 (1987). For an example of the computations involved when section 306 stock is donated to a charity, see Rev.Rul. 76–396, 1976–2 Cum.Bull. 55. A transfer by gift to a noncharitable donee of the section 306 stock is not a realization event, however, and hence section 306 income can be shifted from one member of the family group to another by means of a donative transfer. But in such a case pursuant to section 306(c)(1)(C), the stock retains its section 306 "taint" in the hands of the donee. See Regulations, section 1.306–3(e).

C. EXCEPTIONS TO ORDINARY INCOME TREATMENT

Section 306(b) provides a number of exceptions to the ordinary income treatment generally accorded to section 306 stock. Two of the exceptions are straightforward in their application: section 306(b)(2) exempts redemptions in complete liquidation of the corporation; section 306(b)(3) provides that the various nonrecognition provisions of the Code take precedence over the recognition rules of section 306. In the latter case, however, sections 306(c)(1)(B) and (c)(1)(C) assure that the section 306 taint will attach to any stock of a corporation acquired in such a transaction, even though that stock would not otherwise be section 306 stock. See Regulations, section 1.306–3(e).

Section 306(b)(1) provides an exception when the shareholder disposes (other than by redemption) of his entire interest in the corporation (taking into account the section 318 attribution rules) to a person not related to the shareholder within the section 318 attribution rules. (Section 318 is discussed infra, page 556.) A redemption in complete termination of the shareholder's interest in the corporation under section 302(b)(3) or in partial liquidation under section 302(b)(4) is excepted by section 306(b)(2).

Section 306(b)(4) provides two additional exceptions. Applicability of the exception in section 306(b)(4)(A) was at issue in the *Pescosolido* case, supra, page 539. The exception in section 306(b)(4)(B) is explained in the following excerpt from the 1954 Senate Finance Committee Report:

"Subparagraph (B) of subsection (b)(4) applies to a case where the shareholder has made a prior or simultaneous disposition (or redemption) of the underlying stock with respect to which the section 306 stock was issued. Thus if a shareholder received a distribution of 100 shares of section 306 stock on his holdings of 100 shares of voting common stock in a corporation and sells his voting common stock before he disposes of his section 306 stock, the subsequent disposition of his section 306 stock ordinarily would not be considered a tax avoidance disposition since the shareholder has previously parted with the stock which allows him to participate in the ownership of the business. However, variations of the above example may give rise to tax avoidance possibilities which are not within the exception of subparagraph (B). Thus if a corporation has only one class of common stock outstanding and it issues stock under circumstances that characterize it as section 306 stock, a subsequent issue of a different class of common having greater voting rights than the original common will not permit a simultaneous disposition of the section 306 stock together with the original common to escape the rules of subsection (a) of section 306." S.Rep. No. 83–1622, 83d Cong., 2d Sess. 244 (1954).

Rev.Rul. 75–247, 1975–1 Cum.Bull. 104, held that a disposition of both a portion of the shareholder's common stock and a corresponding portion of section 306 stock which had been issued with respect to the common stock did not of itself establish the non-tax avoidance purpose required by section 306(b)(4). See also Fireoved v. United States, 462 F.2d 1281 (3d Cir. 1972), where the taxpayer failed to qualify for Section 306(b)(4) relief, even though he sold a portion of his common stock prior to a redemption of section 306 stock, because he retained sufficient common stock to avoid any effective diminution in voting power and failed to prove that one of the principal purposes of the stock dividend was not tax avoidance.

Regulations, section 1.306–2(b)(3), give illustrations of non-tax avoidance transactions falling outside section 306 by reason of section 306(b)(4). In Rev.Rul. 81–81, 1981–1 Cum.Bull. 122, the Internal Revenue Service held that the exception in section 306(b)(4)(A) applied to cash received by minority shareholders in lieu of fractional shares in connection with a distribution of a dividend payable in preferred stock. Rev.Rul. 89–63, 1989–1 Cum.Bull. 90, held that the fact that section 306 stock was issued by a corporation whose stock is widely held is not sufficient grounds, standing alone, to apply the section 306(b)(4)(A) exception to a sale of the stock. See also Roebling v. Commissioner, 77 T.C. 30 (1981) (section 306(b)(4) (A) did not apply to a redemption of section 306 stock which represented capitalized dividend arrearages); Rev.Rul. 77–445, 1977–2 Cum.Bull. 93 (section 306(b)(4)(B) exception available where shareholder's entire *actual* interest was terminated; attributed ownership under section 318 was not fatal); Rev.Rul. 80–33, 1980–1 Cum.Bull. 69 (reaching same result as in *Pescosolido*).

Rev.Proc. 77–37, section 5, 1977–2 Cum.Bull. 568, sets forth the conditions under which the Service would rule favorably to the taxpayer on the section 306(b)(4) issue. Somewhat surprisingly, given the inherently factual nature of the issue, rulings were issued with some frequency. In Rev. Proc. 89–31, 1989–1 Cum.Bull. 895, the Service revoked Rev.Proc. 77–37, section 5, but indicated that it would continue to consider ruling requests regarding the applicability of section 306(b)(4).

D. POLICY ASPECTS OF THE TREATMENT OF PREFERRED STOCK DIVIDENDS

Why did Congress choose to address the preferred stock bailout problem by "tainting" preferred stock issued as a tax-free stock dividend rather than taxing the shareholders upon receipt of the stock dividend? First, unlike the situations which prompted Congress immediately to tax disproportionate and optional stock dividends under section 305(b), see supra, page 526, a dividend of preferred stock on common stock does not effect any tax avoidance until the shareholder disposes of the preferred stock. As long as all of the shareholders retain the preferred stock, the effect of the preferred stock dividend is not substantially different than a common on common stock dividend; none of the shareholders have changed their proportionate interest in the corporation. Thus, it may be inappropriate to tax the dividend upon receipt.

The argument that it is inappropriate to tax preferred stock dividends upon receipt is stronger if nontax business planning objectives of closely held corporations, which are not dependent on the sale of the stock, are served by the use of preferred stock dividends. One such situation occurs, for example, when a parent owns all the common stock of a family corporation and desires on retirement or death to transfer the ownership to his children, and in addition wants to have a child who has worked in the business with him run the business while other children receive a more certain income interest which does not participate in management. After a preferred stock dividend the parent would be in a position to leave the common stock to the participating child and the preferred stock to the other children. This rearrangement of family ownership does not appear to give rise to any tax avoidance. But if preferred stock dividends were taxable upon receipt, in all likelihood, the tax cost probably would deter the corporation from distributing a preferred stock dividend and the estate planning objectives of the shareholder could not be so easily achieved. By taxing preferred stock dividends only upon disposition, section 306 eliminates their income tax avoidance potential while permitting their use for estate planning purposes.

The preceding situation is not totally devoid of tax avoidance potential. For many years preferred stock dividends were useful in planning what was known as an "estate tax freeze." These transactions were designed to limit the appreciation to be realized in stock retained by members of the older generation holding stock in a family corporation, thus reducing the federal estate taxes which would be due upon their deaths, by transferring the growth potential to stock held by, or to be transferred to, the younger generation. For example, assume that the A, who is the parent of B and C, owns all 100 shares of common stock of X Corporation and the stock has an aggregate value of $1,000,000. The corporation declares a dividend of 1,000 shares of $1,000 par cumulative preferred stock, paying a dividend sufficient to justify valuing the stock at par (typically, as a matter of practice, it appeared that this condition was seldom if ever met; tax advisors instead relied on the fact that the preferred could be redeemed for no more than its par value to "freeze" the value of the preferred stock). As a result, the common stock has a very low value (applying a liquidation value theory) immediately after the distribution. A then transfers the common stock to B and C with little or no gift tax consequences. As the corporation grows in value, all of the increased value arguably inures to the common stock. Thus, even if the aggregate value of the corporation is $10,000,000 at the time of A's death, only the $1,000,000 value of the preferred stock would be included in A's taxable estate. Section 2036(c), added in 1987, forecloses this planning device by including in A's taxable estate the value of the common stock as well as the preferred stock.

E. REFERENCES

Rowland, Section 306: Its History and Function as a Bailout Preventer (Including Bailouts That May Never Occur), 39 Tax Lawyer 121 (1985); Schneider, Internal Revenue Code Section 306 and Tax Avoidance, 4 Va.Tax Rev. 287 (1985); Levmore, Identifying Section 306 Stock: The Sleeping

Beauty of Revenue Ruling 66–332, 2 Va.Tax Rev. 59 (1982); Walter, "Preferred Stock" and "Common Stock": The Meaning of the Terms and the Importance of the Distinction for Tax Purposes, 5 J.Corp.Tax. 211 (1978); Lowe, Bailouts: Their Role In Corporate Planning, 30 Tax L.Rev. 357 (1975); Alexander and Landis, Bail–Outs and the Internal Revenue Code of 1954, 65 Yale L.J. 909 (1956).

CHAPTER 13

STOCK REDEMPTIONS

SECTION 1. INTRODUCTION

INTERNAL REVENUE CODE: Sections 302(a), (b)(1)–(4), (c)(1), (d); 311; 317; 318.

REGULATIONS: Sections 1.302–1(a), –2.

When a shareholder sells stock back to the issuing corporation it is necessary to determine whether the transaction more nearly resembles a sale of stock or a dividend distribution. If the transaction is thought more nearly to resemble a sale, the shareholder should be entitled to a recovery of basis with respect to the surrendered shares and capital gain treatment for the profits (or capital loss treatment). Since liquidating distributions generally are entitled to capital gain treatment (see infra, page 609), similar treatment clearly would be appropriate where all of a shareholder's shares are sold back to the issuing corporation. Such treatment likewise appears to be appropriate where the shareholder's voting power and right to earnings are substantially reduced. But if there is no significant change in the voting rights or the share of earnings of the corporation to which a shareholder is entitled, the distribution is more like a normal dividend distribution and ordinary income treatment for the entire amount received, with no return of capital aspect, is appropriate.

Section 302(a) distinguishes those sales of stock back to the issuing corporation which are entitled to capital gain treatment from those that more nearly resemble dividends. That section provides that a redemption is a capital gain or loss transaction as respects the shareholder if the transaction meets one of the tests of section 302(b). This capital treatment is the effect of the language in section 302(a) which treats the redemption proceeds as "payment in exchange for the stock." If the transaction does not meet one of those tests, then the amounts distributed by the corporation in redemption of the stock are treated by section 302(d) as distributions of property under section 301, and, if earnings and profits are present, constitute dividend distributions.[1]

When capital gains were taxed at a preferential rate, the stakes turning on the classification of a redemption under these rules were high as far as individual shareholders were concerned. Dividend treatment swept the entire distribution under the higher rates applicable to ordinary income; preferential capital gain treatment applied only to the gain present (the excess of the amount of the distribution over the basis of the stock redeemed). Under current law, as far as an individual is concerned, the only advantages to exchange treatment under section 302(a) are the recovery of basis and the ability to offset capital losses with capital gains.

1. Redemption treatment may be available under section 303 with respect to certain stock held by a deceased shareholder's estate even though section 302(b) is inapplicable. See infra, page 575.

Where a corporation is the redeemed shareholder, the consequences turning on characterization under section 302 can be important because dividend characterization qualifies the distribution for the intercorporate dividends received deduction under section 243 (see supra, page 507).[2]

Subsections (b)(2) and (3) furnish two reasonably specific rules: the section 302(b)(2) test of a substantially disproportionate redemption applicable where the particular shareholder retains some stock after the redemption, with the degree of disproportion specified in mathematical terms; and the section 302(b)(3) termination test applicable where all of the stock of the particular shareholder is redeemed. If these tests are not met, resort must be made to the vague generality of section 302(b)(1)—a redemption is treated as a capital transaction if it is not essentially equivalent to a dividend. This test was employed under the 1939 Code and the earlier case law is still relevant under section 302(b)(1) except insofar as the factor of "business purpose" was utilized in evaluating the tax status of the distributions. See the cases cited in footnote 2 of the *Davis* opinion, infra, page 564. In applying all three of these tests, shareholders are treated as owning not only those shares of stock actually owned by them, but also any shares in the corporation owned by certain family members and related entities. See Section 318; Regulations, section 1.301–1(a).

In addition, section 302(b)(4) provides that a redemption of stock held by an individual shareholder in partial liquidation of the corporation will be entitled to exchange treatment. This provision differs from sections 302(b)(1) through (b)(3) in that, while those provisions are applied by examining the effect of the distribution at the shareholder level, section 302(b)(4) examines the distribution from the perspective of the distributing corporation to determine whether exchange treatment is appropriate for the shareholders.

SECTION 2. SUBSTANTIALLY DISPROPORTIONATE REDEMPTIONS

INTERNAL REVENUE CODE: Sections 302(a), (b)(2); 318.

REGULATIONS: Section 1.302–3.

ILLUSTRATIVE MATERIAL

A. GENERAL

Section 302(b)(2) provides a mathematical test of disproportion involving two ingredients: one, the shareholder's percentage ownership of voting stock after the redemption must be less than 80 percent of his percentage ownership before the reduction (and also a like reduction in ownership of common stock if some of the common stock is non-voting); and two, after the redemption the shareholder must own less than 50 percent of the voting stock of the corporation. Even without this 50 percent requirement, the reduction in size of the shareholding in the corporation required under the 80 percent rule can be quite large. Because the 80 percent test is based on comparing the percentage of outstanding shares of the corporation owned by

2. A disproportionage redemption which does not qualify for sale or exchange treatment under section 302(b), and which therefore is eligible for a section 243 dividends received deduction, is an extraordinary dividend with respect to which the basis of any remaining stock must be reduced under section 1059, discussed supra, page 509.

the shareholder after the redemption to the percentage of outstanding shares of the corporation owned by the shareholder before the redemption, a redemption of merely a fraction of a percent more than 20 percent of the shareholder's stock does not qualify. For example, a shareholder owning 60 shares of stock of a corporation having 100 shares outstanding must have at least 24 shares redeemed to meet the 80 percent test—a 40 percent reduction in the number of shares held by the redeemed shareholder. In order to qualify under section 302(b)(2), after the redemption the shareholder's percentage ownership must have been reduced to below 48 percent (80 percent of 60 percent), taking into account the reduced number of shares outstanding as a result of the redemption.

Under Regulations, section 1.302–3, a redemption of either common or preferred non-voting stock may qualify under section 302(b)(2) if there is a simultaneous redemption of voting stock. But a redemption of non-voting stock (preferred or common) alone may not qualify under this subsection; such a transaction is governed by section 302(b)(1), discussed infra, page 564.

The last two sentences of section 302(b)(2)(C) require that a shareholder's ownership of all common stock, measured by value, as well as the shareholder's voting power, must be reduced to less than 80 percent of what it was prior to the redemption. Note that there is no requirement that after the redemption the shareholder hold less than 50 percent of the *value* of the common stock. Rev.Rul. 87–88, 1987–2 Cum.Bull. 81, held that the reduction in value test is applied on an aggregate basis rather than a class-by-class basis. Suppose that prior to a redemption a shareholder held 90 percent of the voting common stock and all of the non-voting common stock of a corporation. As a result of the redemption of a portion of the shareholder's voting common stock the shareholder held 43 percent of the voting stock and 60 percent of the aggregate value of all common stock. Under the Ruling, the redemption qualifies under section 302(b)(2), even though none of the shareholder's nonvoting common stock was redeemed.

The next to last sentence of section 302(b)(2)(C) does not impose a requirement that common stock be redeemed in all cases. Rev.Rul. 81–41, 1981–1 Cum.Bull. 121, held that section 302(b)(2) could apply to a redemption solely of voting preferred stock where the shareholder did not own any common stock before or after the redemption.

B. CONSTRUCTIVE STOCK OWNERSHIP

Under section 302(c)(1), the attribution of stock ownership rules of section 318(a) respecting closely related family members and entities are applicable in the determining whether the section 302(b)(2) tests have been met; the proportionate or disproportionate character of the distribution is tested by reference to the entire group of related parties. The network of attributed ownership can be quite wide under section 318(a). The attribution rules primarily deal with four situations:

(1) Under section 318(a)(1), stock is attributed between *family members* standing in the specified familial relationships;

(2) Section 318(a)(2) attributes the ownership of stock held by *entities*—partnerships, estates, trusts, and corporations respectively—to the partners, beneficiaries, and shareholders owning more than 50 percent of the stock of a corporation;

(3) Section 318(a)(3) attributes stock owned by a partner, beneficiary, or shareholder owning more than 50 percent of the stock of a corporation to the "entity" where the stipulated relationships are present;

(4) Section 318(a)(4) treats a taxpayer as owning any stock which the taxpayer has an option to purchase.

In applying these rules, section 318(a)(5)(A) treats stock which is *constructively* owned by virtue of the application of the attribution rules as if it were *actually owned* for the purpose of reattribution. Thus, for example, if A is the beneficiary of a trust, stock owned by the trust would be attributed to A under section 318(a)(2)(B). Under section 318(a)(5)(A) that stock would then be considered as actually owned by A for "reattributing" the stock to A's parents under section 318(a)(1).

There are, however, some limits to the reattribution of constructively owned stock. Section 318(a)(5)(B) provides that the stock constructively owned by virtue of the application of the family attribution rules will not be considered as actually owned for purposes of its reattribution under those rules. Thus, stock owned by A which is attributed to A's parents under section 318(a)(1) will not be reattributed through A's parents to A's brother or sister (there is no direct attribution between siblings). Similarly, where stock is attributed to a partnership, estate, etc., under section 318(a)(3), it will not then be reattributed to another partner, beneficiary, etc., under section 318(a)(2). These limitations on reattribution eliminate so-called "sidewise" attribution.

Application of the attribution rules sometimes may help a taxpayer. Suppose that the husband owns voting common stock and the wife owns non-voting preferred stock. Some of the wife's preferred stock is redeemed in connection with a transaction in which part of the husband's common stock is redeemed and the husband's redemption meets the requirements of section 302(b)(2). Section 302(b)(2) applies to qualify the wife's redemption. Rev.Rul. 77–237, 1977–2 Cum.Bull. 88. On the other hand, where the attribution rules make another the constructive owner of stock actually held by the taxpayer, the attribution does not reduce the taxpayer's "real" ownership for purposes of testing the disproportionality of the distribution. Northwestern Steel and Supply Co. v. Commissioner, 60 T.C. 356 (1973). For example if A, who owns 50 shares of stock, and B, who owns 40 shares of stock, are parent and child, A is deemed to own B's 40 shares in addition to her own 50 shares; correspondingly B is deemed to own A's 50 shares. Thus, in testing a redemption of shares from either or both of A and B under section 302(b)(2), both A and B are deemed to own 90 shares before the transaction.

In applying the option attribution rules, Regulations, section 1.302–3(a), provide that options to purchase unissued stock from the corporation are disregarded. However, Rev.Rul. 68–601, 1968–2 Cum.Bull. 124, held that the holder of warrants and convertible debentures was deemed to hold the option shares, but that such shares were not to be counted in determining the percentage of stock owned by other shareholders. Henry T. Patterson Trust v. United States, 729 F.2d 1089 (6th Cir.1984), is to the contrary. In that case, a shareholder other than the shareholder whose stock was redeemed was treated as owning stock which he had an option to purchase from the corporation for purposes of determining the percentage of stock owned by the redeemed shareholder. See also Sorem v. Commissioner, 334 F.2d 275

(10th Cir.1964) (employees holding stock options on unissued stock treated as owning stock). Rev.Rul. 89–64, 1989–1 Cum.Bull. 91, held that the holder of an option to purchase shares from the corporation was deemed to hold the option shares even though the option was by its terms not exercisable until a future date.

C. SERIES OF DISTRIBUTIONS

Section 302(b)(2)(D) requires the taxpayer to treat a series of redemptions made pursuant to a plan as a single redemption in testing the disproportionality of the redemption. See Blount v. Commissioner, 425 F.2d 921 (2d Cir.1969). Rev.Rul. 85–14, 1985–1 Cum.Bull. 92, held that the existence of a "plan" does not require an agreement between two or more shareholders, but may be satisfied by "a design by a single redeemed shareholder to arrange a redemption as part of a sequence of events that ultimately restores to such shareholder the control that was apparently reduced in the redemption." In the Ruling, A held 1,466 out of 2,031 shares of the corporation, or 72.18 percent. On January 1, B, who held 210 shares which were to be repurchased by the corporation upon his retirement pursuant to a stock repurchase agreement, announced that he would retire on March 22. A then caused the corporation to redeem 902 of his shares on March 15, reducing his interest to 49.96 percent. One week later, when B's shares were redeemed, A's interest was increased to 61.37 percent (564 out of 919 shares). The Ruling held that the reduction in A's interest was not to be measured immediately following the redemption of his shares, but only after the redemption of B's shares. But Glacier State Electric Supply Co. v. Commissioner, 80 T.C. 1047 (1983), held that a possible future redemption upon the death of a shareholder pursuant to a buy-sell agreement should not be considered as part of a "plan" in testing whether a current redemption met the test of section 302(b)(2).

Because of the availability of the section 243 intercorporate dividend received deduction, a corporate shareholder frequently prefers to characterize a distribution as a dividend rather than as a section 302 redemption. In Bleily & Collishaw, Inc. v. Commissioner, 72 T.C. 751 (1979), aff'd by order, 647 F.2d 169 (9th Cir.1981), all of the shares of stock of another corporation held by a corporate shareholder were redeemed in seven installments over a six month period. Each of the first six installments left the shareholder with slightly more than 80 percent of the percentage ownership of stock that it held before that redemption. The shareholder claimed that each of the six distributions was a distribution under section 301 rather than section 302(a). Finding that there was a firm and fixed plan to eliminate the shareholder from the corporation, the Tax Court treated all of the installments as part of a single distribution in redemption of all of the taxpayer's shares under section 302(b)(3).

D. BASIS CONSIDERATIONS

If a redemptions fails to qualify for exchange treatment under section 302(a) and the distribution is a dividend, the basis of the redeemed stock is not relevant. Under Regulations, section 1.302–2(c), the basis of the redeemed stock is added to the basis of the other stock held by the taxpayer.

E. REFERENCE

Keller, Revamping the Tax Treatment of Stock Redemptions: A Two Transaction Approach, 20 Ariz.St.L.J. 989 (1988).

SECTION 3. TERMINATION OF A SHAREHOLDER'S INTEREST

INTERNAL REVENUE CODE: Section 302(b)(3), (c); 318.

REGULATIONS: Section 1.302–4.

ILLUSTRATIVE MATERIAL

A. GENERAL

Since the termination of a shareholder's interest is an example of a substantially disproportionate distribution, section 302(b)(3), treating a redemption in complete termination of a shareholder's interest as an exchange, initially appears to add little to the operation of section 302(b). It does, however, serve two major functions. First, it permits the redemption of nonvoting stock to qualify for capital gain treatment without resort to the vague "not essentially equivalent to a dividend" test of section 302(b)(1). Second, if all of the stock actually owned by a shareholder is redeemed, section 302(c) permits the family attribution rules of section 318(a)(1) to be disregarded in determining if the shareholder's interest has been completely terminated. This waiver of the family attribution rules is not available under section 302(b)(2).

A frequent issue under section 302(b)(3) is the treatment of redemptions of less than all of a shareholder's stock in each of a series of redemptions the ultimate result of which is the complete termination of the shareholder's interest. Where there is a firm and fixed plan to eliminate the shareholder from the corporation, the component redemptions will be treated as a single redemption of the shareholder's entire interest. The plan does not need to be enforceable or in writing, but it must be more than a "gentleman's agreement." Bleily & Collishaw, Inc. v. Commissioner, supra, page 558. Where the time frame for the redemption is vague and the redeemed shareholder retains control over corporate affairs in the interim, however, the individual transactions will not be aggregated; the preliminary redemptions will be treated as section 301 distributions. Benjamin v. Commissioner, 592 F.2d 1259 (5th Cir.1979); Johnston v. Commissioner, 77 T.C. 679 (1981) (individual redemptions were essentially equivalent to dividends where redemption plan not consistently followed).

Where all of a shareholder's stock is redeemed for the corporation's promissory note, the question arises of whether the note is debt or equity. See Lisle v. Commissioner, 35 T.C.M. 627 (1976) (finding twenty year notes secured by escrow of stock to be true debt). If the note is found to be equity rather than a debt instrument, the "complete termination" required by section 301(b)(3) is not present, and each principal payment must be tested separately against the various section 302(b) tests to determine whether redemption treatment is available.

B. WAIVER OF FAMILY ATTRIBUTION

1. *General*

Whether a shareholder's interest has been completely terminated as required by section 302(c)(1) is tested after applying the attribution rules of section 318(a). However, section 302(c)(2)(A) provides that the *family* attribution rules do not apply if the distributee has no further interest other than as a creditor and if the distributee files an agreement to notify the Internal Revenue Service of any subsequent acquisition of such an interest (which would retroactively disqualify the redemption if acquired within ten years from the distribution).

Under section 302(c)(2)(B), the waiver of family attribution rules may not be available if the redeemed stock was acquired by the distributee within the preceding 10–year period from a related person (a person whose stock would be attributable to the distributee). Thus, a complete termination under section 302(b)(3) is not available to a husband-distributee who received the redeemed stock from his wife within the 10–year period. Waiver of family attribution also is unavailable where within the 10–year period the distributee gave stock to a related person (as where the wife above is the distributee). The limitation of section 302(c)(3)(B), however, does not apply unless one of the principal purposes of the acquisition or disposition was tax avoidance. See section 302(c)(3)(B) (flush language) and Regulations, section 1.302–4(g), last sentence.

2. *Tax Avoidance Transactions*

The Internal Revenue Service has issued a number of rulings dealing with the question of whether transfers of stock between related parties within ten years of the redemption were tax avoidance transactions. Rev.Rul. 77–293, 1977–2 Cum.Bull. 91, held that tax avoidance was not present where a father made a gift of a part of his stock to his son concurrently with a redemption of the remainder of the stock from the father. The purpose of the gift was to give the son control of the corporation in connection with the transfer to him of management responsibility. Rev.Rul. 85–19, 1985–1 Cum.Bull. 94, held that there was no tax avoidance motive where a minority shareholder first sold to his father, the controlling shareholder, a number of shares received from the father by gift two years earlier, and the corporation then immediately redeemed the son's remaining shares, which he acquired by bequest. This Ruling suggests that tax avoidance exists only where the transferor seeks to retain indirect control, such as by transferring stock to a spouse prior to a redemption of all of the shares actually owned, or when the transfer is in contemplation of a redemption of the shares from the transferee. See also Rev.Rul. 79–67, 1979–1 Cum.Bull. 128 (distribution of stock from estate to beneficiary to qualify redemption from beneficiary under section 302(b)(3) is not tax avoidance); Rev.Rul. 82–129, 1982–2 Cum.Bull. 76 (partition of stock held as community property is not a transfer).

3. *Waiver of Family Attribution By Entities*

Prior to 1982, when section 302(c)(2)(C) was enacted, there was significant controversy regarding the type of taxpayer entitled to take advantage of the waiver of the family attribution rules. For example, suppose A owns 50 percent of the stock of X Corporation and Trust T, created by a deceased aunt for the benefit of A's children, owns 50 percent. Under

Section 318, A's children are deemed to own A's stock and the trust is deemed to own the stock of the children. If all of the stock actually owned by the trust is redeemed, can the trust take advantage of the waiver of the family attribution rules provided in section 302(c)(2) and treat the redemption as a complete termination under section 302(b)(3)? Rev.Rul. 59–233, 1959–2 Cum.Bull. 106, held that the waiver of the family attribution rules applied only where the distributee in the redemption was deemed to own stock under the family attribution rules. Since the last step in the attribution involved in the Ruling was not a "*family*" attribution, the exception did not apply. See also Rev.Rul. 68–388, 1968–2 Cum.Bull. 122. (In contrast, a redemption from A would have qualified because in that case, the family attribution was the last link in the chain and the waiver of attribution in section 302(c)(2) would have been effective).

The Tax Court rejected the Internal Revenue Service's narrow interpretation of the waiver of family attribution rules. See, e.g., Crawford v. Commissioner, 59 T.C. 830 (1973) (NA), (estate permitted to waive family attribution rules); Rodgers P. Johnson Trust v. Commissioner, 71 T.C. 941 (1979) (trust permitted to waive family attribution). In Rickey v. United States, 592 F.2d 1251 (5th Cir.1979), the court went a step further and held that an estate could waive the *entity* attribution rules where all of the stock owned by the estate was redeemed but the beneficiary continued to be an actual shareholder. David Metzger Trust v. Commissioner, 76 T.C. 42 (1981), aff'd, 693 F.2d 459 (5th Cir.1982), held to the contrary.

Section 302(c)(2)(C) permits waiver of the family attribution rules in situations like *Crawford* and *Johnson* Trust. The attribution rules may be waived if after the redemption neither the entity (trust, estate, partnership or corporation) nor the beneficiaries, partners or shareholders hold an interest in the redeeming corporation and if both agree not to acquire such an interest in the stipulated ten-year period. Under section 302(c)(2)(C), only the *family* attribution rules may be waived; the attribution rules between entity and beneficiary may not be waived. The Conference Committee Report accompanying the 1982 Act stated that the amendment to section 302(c) was intended to overrule *Rickey.* H.Rep. No. 97–760, 97th Cong., 2d Sess. 546 (1982).

4. *Timely Filing of Waiver Agreement*

Regulations, section 1.302–4(a)(1), state that the agreement required by section 302(c)(2) must be filed with the tax return reporting the redemption distribution but the courts have been much more lenient in their interpretation of the requirement. See, e.g., United States v. Van Keppel, 321 F.2d 717 (10th Cir.1963) (agreement filed over one year after the tax return was due, but not before issuance of a notice of deficiency, was timely); Fehrs v. United States, 556 F.2d 1019 (Ct.Cl.1977) (agreement filed seven years after redemption held timely). But Robin Haft Trust v. Commissioner, 62 T.C. 145 (1974), vacated on other grounds, 510 F.2d 43 (1st Cir.1975), held that agreements filed after an adverse Tax Court decision were not timely.

5. *Retention of Prohibited Interest*

Section 302(c)(2)(A) conditions the availability of the waiver of family attribution rules on the redeemed shareholder retaining no interest in the corporation, including an interest as an officer, director, or employee, other than an interest as a creditor. The Internal Revenue Service has been strict in its interpretation of what constitutes a prohibited "interest" in the corporation on the part of the redeemed shareholder, and the courts have generally upheld the Commissioner's position.

Whether post-redemption employment of a former shareholder by the corporation precludes availability of the waiver may depend on the nature of the employment. Service as a common law employee invariably has been found to be a prohibited interest even though the former shareholder's compensation was not contingent on corporate profits and he did not manage the corporation. See Cerone v. Commissioner, 87 T.C. 1 (1986) (employment at significantly reduced salary as bar tender and cashier in restaurant/bar); Seda v. Commissioner, 82 T.C. 484 (1984) (employment at fixed salary where no fact finding as to role in management). Where the employment is in the capacity of independent contractor, however, the Tax Court applies a facts and circumstances test based on "whether the former stockholder has either retained a financial stake in the corporation or continued to control the corporation and benefit by its operations." Lynch v. Commissioner, 83 T.C. 597, 605 (1984), rev'd, 801 F.2d 1176 (9th Cir. 1986). Compare Chertkof v. Commissioner, 72 T.C. 1113 (1979), aff'd, 649 F.2d 264 (4th Cir.1981), in which the Tax Court found a prohibited interest where the former shareholder had provided management services as an independent contractor, with Estate of Lennard v. Commissioner, 61 T.C. 554 (1974), where the court held that rendering accounting services as an independent contractor was not a prohibited interest. See also Rev.Rul. 70–104, 1970–1 Cum.Bull. 66.

In *Lynch,* supra, the Ninth Circuit rejected the Tax Court's facts and circumstances test in favor of a *per se* prohibition on post-redemption provision of services to the corporation. This *per se* rule was then applied to deny waiver of family attribution where the former shareholder provided nonmanagement services as an independent contractor for $500 per month. The Ninth Circuit expressly rejected the Tax Court's *Lennard* decision, and held that no qualitative judgments regarding the value of the retained interest are permissible. See also the concurring opinion in *Seda,* supra, in which eight Tax Court judges supported application of a *per se* rule.

Suppose that the redeemed shareholder retains or reacquires voting power in a fidiciary capacity. Rev.Rul. 81–233, 1981–2 Cum.Bull. 83, held that a redeemed shareholder who within ten years became a custodian under the Uniform Gift to Minors Act with respect to stock given to his children by the shareholder's parents had acquired a prohibited interest because he had the power to vote the stock. See also Rev.Rul. 71–426, 1971–2 Cum.Bull. 173 (where stock of the corporation was owned by a mother and her four children, with the childrens' stock held by a voting trust, retention by the mother of the position as voting trustee was a prohibited interest). Where the fiduciary position is as an executor or testamentary trustee, however, the Service has ruled that the exception for interests acquired by bequest or inheritance applies. Rev.Rul. 79–334, 1979–2 Cum.Bull. 127 (testamentary trustee); Rev.Rul. 72–380, 1972–2 Cum.Bull. 201 (executor of estate).

The statute allows the redeemed shareholder to remain as a "creditor" of the corporation, thus raising the issue whether obligations issued in the redemption constitute debt or equity. Regulations, section 1.302–4(d), specify conditions that must be met for the redeemed shareholder's interest as a creditor to be respected as such. See, e.g., Dunn v. Commissioner, 615 F.2d 578 (2d Cir.1980) (interest was as a "creditor" despite restrictions pursuant to automobile dealers franchise agreement on the payment of the obligations issued in the redemption if payment would leave inadequate working capital); *Estate of Lennard,* supra (subordination of the obligation to bank loans did not prevent "creditor" status notwithstanding Regulations, section 1.302–4(d)). For the Internal Revenue Service guidelines on issuing advance rulings where stock is redeemed with notes, see Rev.Proc. 83–22, 1983–1 Cum.Bull. 680. See also Regulations, section 1.302–4(e) (acquisition of assets of corporation to enforce creditor's rights is not prohibited interest; reacquisition of stock in enforcing creditor's rights is prohibited interest). Rev.Rul. 59–119, 1959–1 Cum.Bull. 68, held that where the shareholder retained the right to have a member of the law firm representing him serve on the board of directors of the corporation to protect his interests as a creditor and to determine that the conditions of the stock redemption agreement were being observed, the "limited" directorship by an agent prevented the application of section 302(c)(2)(A). Compare Rev.Rul. 76–524, 1976–2 Cum.Bull. 94 (continuing as director and officer does not prevent redemption from qualifying under section 302(b)(3) where waiver of family attribution is not necessary for complete termination).

Rev.Rul. 77–467, 1977–2 Cum.Bull. 92, held that a redeemed shareholder could lease real estate to the corporation and the lease would not be a prohibited interest where the rent was not dependent on corporate earnings. Rev.Rul. 84–135, 1984–2 Cum.Bull. 80, held that the right to receive a lifetime pension under an unfunded nonqualified pension plan was not a prohibited interest. Are these interests any less a continuing interest in the corporation than employment in a nonmanagerial capacity for a fixed salary?

C. BASIS OF STOCK

When a redemption is treated as a section 301 distribution under section 302(d), the basis of the redeemed shares is allocated to the shareholder's remaining shares. If the shareholder's actual interest is completely terminated but, due to the family attribution rules, the shareholder's entire interest has not been terminated, the basis of the redeemed shares should be added to the basis of the related person whose shares were attributed to the redeemed shareholder. Regulations, section 1.302–2(c); see also, Levin v. Commissioner, 385 F.2d 521 (2d Cir.1967) (basis of parent's redeemed shares added to basis of son's shares).

D. REFERENCES

Marusic, The Prohibited Interest of I.R.C. Section 302(c)(2)(A) After *Seda* and *Lynch,* 65 Neb.L.Rev. 486 (1986); Nuzum, Waiver of Family Ownership Rules Under Section 302(c)(2)(A): Retention or Reacquisition of A Prohibited Interest, 11 J. Corp. Tax'n 19 (1984); Owen, Waivers of the Family Attribution By Entities May Present Problems Despite TEFRA, 58 J. Tax'n 202 (1983); Rose, The Prohibited Interest of Section 302(c)(2)(A), 36 Tax L.Rev. 131 (1981); Kuntz, Stock Redemptions Following Stock Transfers—An Expanding "Safe Harbor" Under Section 302(c)(2)(B) 58 Taxes 29 (1980); Randall and Benson, Eliminating Family Attribution by Expanding the Definition of Distributee, 3 J. Corp. Tax. 176 (1976).

SECTION 4. DISTRIBUTIONS NOT "ESSENTIALLY EQUIVALENT TO A DIVIDEND"

INTERNAL REVENUE CODE: Section 302(b)(1); 318.

REGULATIONS: Section 1.302–2.

UNITED STATES v. DAVIS

Supreme Court of the United States, 1970.
397 U.S. 301.

MR. JUSTICE MARSHALL delivered the opinion of the Court.

In 1945, taxpayer and E.B. Bradley organized a corporation. In exchange for property transferred to the new company, Bradley received 500 shares of common stock, and taxpayer and his wife similarly each received 250 such shares. Shortly thereafter, taxpayer made an additional contribution to the corporation, purchasing 1,000 shares of preferred stock at a par value of $25 per share.

The purpose of this latter transaction was to increase the company's working capital and thereby to qualify for a loan previously negotiated through the Reconstruction Finance Corporation. It was understood that the corporation would redeem the preferred stock when the RFC loan had been repaid. Although in the interim taxpayer bought Bradley's 500 shares and divided them between his son and daughter, the total capitalization of the company remained the same until 1963. That year, after the loan was fully repaid and in accordance with the original understanding, the company redeemed taxpayer's preferred stock.

In his 1963 personal income tax return taxpayer did not report the $25,000 received by him upon the redemption of his preferred stock as income. Rather, taxpayer considered the redemption as a sale of his preferred stock to the company—a capital gains transaction under § 302 of the Internal Revenue Code of 1954 resulting in no tax since taxpayer's basis in the stock equaled the amount he received for it. The Commissioner of Internal Revenue, however, did not approve this tax treatment. According to the Commissioner, the redemption of taxpayer's stock was essentially equivalent to a dividend and was thus taxable as ordinary income under §§ 301 and 316 of the Code. Taxpayer paid the resulting deficiency and brought this suit for a refund. The District Court ruled in his favor, 274 F.Supp. 466 (D.C.M.D.Tenn.1967), and on appeal the Court of Appeals affirmed. 408 F.2d 1139 (C.A.6th Cir.1969).

The Court of Appeals held that the $25,000 received by taxpayer was "not essentially equivalent to a dividend" within the meaning of that phrase in § 302(b)(1) of the Code because the redemption was the final step in a course of action that had a legitimate business (as opposed to a tax avoidance) purpose. That holding represents only one of a variety of treatments accorded similar transactions under § 302(b)(1) in the circuit courts of appeals.[2] We granted certiorari, 396 U.S. 815, 90 S.Ct. 88 (1969), in order to resolve this recurring tax question involving stock redemptions by closely held corporations. We reverse.

I

The Internal Revenue Code of 1954 provides generally in §§ 301 and 316 for the tax treatment of distributions by a corporation to its shareholders; under those provisions, a distribution is includable in a taxpayer's gross income as a dividend out of earnings and profits to the extent such earnings exist.[3] There are exceptions to the application of these general provisions, however, and among them are those found in § 302 involving certain distributions for redeemed stock. The basic question in this case is whether the $25,000 distribution by the corporation to taxpayer falls under that section—more specifically, whether its legitimate business motivation qualifies the distribution under § 302(b)(1) of the Code. Preliminarily, however, we must consider the relationship between § 302(b)(1) and the rules regarding the attribution of stock ownership found in § 318(a) of the Code.

Under subsection (a) of § 302, a distribution is treated as "payment in exchange for the stock," thus qualifying for capital gains rather than ordinary income treatment, if the conditions contained in any one of the four paragraphs of subsection (b) are met. In addition to paragraph (1)'s "not essentially equivalent to a dividend" test, capital gains treatment is available where (2) the taxpayer's voting strength is substantially diminished, (3) his interest in the company is completely terminated, or (4) certain railroad stock is redeemed. Paragraph (4) is not involved here, and taxpayer admits that paragraphs (2) and (3) do not apply. Moreover, taxpayer agrees that for the purposes of §§ 302(b)(2) and (3) the attribution rules of § 318(a) apply and he is considered to own the 750 outstanding shares of common stock held by his wife and children in addition to the 250 shares in his own name.

2. Only the Second Circuit has unequivocally adopted the Commissioner's view and held irrelevant the motivation of the redemption. See Levin v. Commissioner, 385 F.2d 521 (1967); Hasbrook v. United States, 343 F.2d 811 (1965). The First Circuit however, seems almost to have come to that conclusion, too. Compare Wiseman v. United States, 371 F.2d 816 (1967), with Bradbury v. Commissioner, 298 F.2d 111 (1962).

The other courts of appeals that have passed on the question are apparently willing to give at least some weight under § 302(b)(1) to the business motivation of a distribution and redemption. See, e.g., Commissioner v. Berenbaum, 369 F.2d 337 (C.A.10th Cir.1966); Kerr v. Commissioner, 326 F.2d 225 (C.A.9th Cir.1964); Ballenger v. United States, 301 F.2d 192 (C.A.4th Cir. 1962); Heman v. Commissioner, 283 F.2d 227 (C.A.8th Cir.1960); United States v. Fewell, 255 F.2d 496 (C.A.5th Cir.1958). See also Neff v. United States, 157 Ct.Cl. 322, 305 F.2d 455 (1962). Even among those courts that consider business purpose, however, it is generally required that the business purpose be related, not to the issuance of the stock, but to the redemption of it. See Commissioner v. Berenbaum, supra; Ballenger v. United States, supra.

3. See, e.g., Commissioner v. Gordon, 391 U.S. 83, 88–89, 88 S.Ct. 1517 (1968). Taxpayer makes no contention that the corporation did not have $25,000 in accumulated earnings and profits.

Taxpayer, however, argues that the attribution rules do not apply in considering whether a distribution is essentially equivalent to a dividend under § 302(b)(1). According to taxpayer, he should thus be considered to own only 25 percent of the corporation's common stock, and the distribution would then qualify under § 302(b)(1) since it was not pro rata or proportionate to his stock interest, the fundamental test of dividend equivalency. See Treas.Reg. 1.302–2(b). However, the plain language of the statute compels rejection of the argument. In subsection (c) of § 302, the attribution rules are made specifically applicable "in determining the ownership of stock for purposes of this section." Applying this language, both courts below held that § 318(a) applies to all of § 302, including § 302(b)(1)—a view in accord with the decisions of the other courts of appeals,[5] a longstanding treasury regulation,[6] and the opinion of the leading commentators.[7]

Against this weight of authority, taxpayer argues that the result under paragraph (1) should be different because there is no explicit reference to stock ownership as there is in paragraphs (2) and (3). Neither that fact, however, nor the purpose and history of § 302(b)(1) support taxpayer's argument. The attribution rules—designed to provide a clear answer to what would otherwise be a difficult tax question—formed part of the tax bill that was subsequently enacted as the 1954 Code. As is discussed further, infra, the bill as passed by the House of Representatives contained no provision comparable to § 302(b)(1). When that provision was added in the Senate, no purpose was evidenced to restrict the applicability of § 318(a). Rather, the attribution rules continued to be made specifically applicable to the entire section, and we believe that Congress intended that they be taken into account wherever ownership of stock was relevant.

Indeed, it was necessary that the attribution rules apply to § 302(b)(1) unless they were to be effectively eliminated from consideration with regard to §§ 302(b)(2) and (3) also. For if a transaction failed to qualify under one of those sections solely because of the attribution rules, it would according to taxpayer's argument nonetheless qualify under § 302(b)(1). We cannot agree that Congress intended so to nullify its explicit directive. We conclude, therefore, that the attribution rules of § 318(a) do apply; and, for the purposes of deciding whether a distribution is "not essentially equivalent to a dividend" under § 302(b)(1), taxpayer must be deemed the owner of all 1,000 shares of the company's common stock.

5. See Levin v. Commissioner, 385 F.2d 521, 526–527 (C.A.2d Cir.1967); Commissioner v. Berenbaum, 369 F.2d 337, 342 (C.A.10th Cir.1966); Ballenger v. United States, 301 F.2d 192, 199 (C.A.4th Cir. 1962); Bradbury v. Commissioner, 298 F.2d 111, 116–117 (C.A.1st Cir.1962).

6. See Treas.Reg. 1.302–2(b).

7. See B. Bittker & J. Eustice, Federal Income Taxation of Corporations and Shareholders 292 n. 32 (2d ed. 1966).

II

After application of the stock ownership attribution rules, this case viewed most simply involves a sole stockholder who causes part of his shares to be redeemed by the corporation. We conclude that such a redemption is always "essentially equivalent to a dividend" within the meaning of that phrase in § 302(b)(1)[8] and therefore do not reach the Government's alternative argument that in any event the distribution should not on the facts of this case qualify for capital gains treatment.[9]

The predecessor of § 302(b)(1) came into the tax law as § 201(d) of the Revenue Act of 1921, 42 Stat. 228:

> "A stock dividend shall not be subject to tax but if after the distribution of any such dividend the corporation proceeds to cancel or redeem its stock at such time and in such manner as to make the distribution and cancellation or redemption essentially equivalent to the distribution of a taxable dividend, the amount received in redemption or cancellation of the stock shall be treated as a taxable dividend. * * *"

Enacted in response to this Court's decision that pro rata stock dividends do not constitute taxable income, Eisner v. Macomber, 252 U.S. 189, 40 S.Ct. 189 (1920), the provision had the obvious purpose of preventing a corporation from avoiding dividend tax treatment by distributing earnings to its shareholders in two transactions—a pro rata stock dividend followed by a pro rata redemption—that would have the same economic consequences as a simple dividend. Congress, however, soon recognized that even without a prior stock dividend essentially the same result could be effected whereby any corporation, "especially one which has only a few stockholders, might be able to make a distribution to its stockholders which would have the same effect as a taxable dividend." H.R.Rep. No. 1, 69th Cong., 1st Sess., 5. In order to cover this situation, the law was amended to apply "(whether or not such stock was issued as a stock dividend)" whenever a distribution in redemption of stock was made "at such time and in such manner" that it was essentially equivalent to a taxable dividend. Revenue Act of 1926, § 201(g), 44 Stat. 11.

This provision of the 1926 Act was carried forward in each subsequent revenue act and finally became § 115(g)(1) of the Internal Revenue Code of 1939. Unfortunately, however, the policies encompassed within the general language of § 115(g)(1) and its predecessors were not clear, and there resulted much confusion in the tax law. At first,

8. Of course, this just means that a distribution in redemption to a sole shareholder will be treated under the general provisions of § 301, and it will only be taxed as a dividend under § 316 to the extent that there are earnings and profits.

9. The Government argues that even if business purpose were relevant under § 302(b)(1), the business purpose present here related only to the original investment and not at all to the necessity for redemption. See cases cited, n. 2, supra. Under either view, taxpayer does not lose his basis in the preferred stock. Under Treas.Reg. 1.302–2(c) that basis is applied to taxpayer's common stock.

courts assumed that the provision was aimed at tax avoidance schemes and sought only to determine whether such a scheme existed. See, e.g., Commissioner v. Quackenbos, 78 F.2d 156 (C.A.2d Cir.1935). Although later the emphasis changed and the focus was more on the effect of the distribution, many courts continued to find that distributions otherwise like a dividend were not "essentially equivalent" if, for example, they were motivated by a sufficiently strong nontax business purpose. See cases cited n. 2, supra. There was general disagreement, however, about what would qualify as such a purpose, and the result was a case-by-case determination with each case decided "on the basis of the particular facts of the transaction in question." Bains v. United States, 153 Ct.Cl. 599, 603, 289 F.2d 644, 646 (1961).

By the time of the general revision resulting in the Internal Revenue Code of 1954, the draftsmen were faced with what has aptly been described as "the morass created by the decisions." Ballenger v. United States, 301 F.2d 192, 196 (C.A.4th Cir.1962). In an effort to eliminate "the considerable confusion which exists in this area" and thereby to facilitate tax planning, H.R.Rep. No. 1337, 83d Cong., 2d Sess., 35, the authors of the new Code sought to provide objective tests to govern the tax consequences of stock redemptions. Thus, the tax bill passed by the House of Representatives contained no "essentially equivalent" language. Rather, it provided for "safe harbors" where capital gains treatment would be accorded to corporate redemptions that met the conditions now found in §§ 302(b)(2) and (3) of the Code.

It was in the Senate Finance Committee's consideration of the tax bill that § 302(b)(1) was added, and Congress thereby provided that capital gains treatment should be available "if the redemption is not essentially equivalent to a dividend." Taxpayer argues that the purpose was to continue "existing law," and there is support in the legislative history that § 302(b)(1) reverted "in part" or "in general" to the "essentially equivalent" provision of § 115(g)(1) of the 1939 Code. According to the Government, even under the old law it would have been improper for the Court of Appeals to rely on "a business purpose for the redemption" and "an absence of the proscribed tax avoidance purpose to bail out dividends at favorable tax rates." See Northup v. United States, 240 F.2d 304, 307 (C.A.2d Cir.1957); Smith v. United States, 121 F.2d 692, 695 (C.A.3d Cir.1941); cf. Commissioner v. Estate of Bedford, 325 U.S. 283 (1945). However, we need not decide that question, for we find from the history of the 1954 revisions and the purpose of § 302(b)(1) that Congress intended more than merely to re-enact the prior law.

In explaining the reason for adding the "essentially equivalent" test, the Senate Committee stated that the House provisions "appeared unnecessarily restrictive, particularly, in the case of redemptions of preferred stock which might be called by the corporation without the shareholder having any control over when the redemption may take place." S.Rep. No. 1622, 83d Cong., 2d Sess., 44. This explanation gives no indication that the purpose behind the redemption should affect the result.[10] Rather, in its more detailed technical evaluation of § 302(b)(1), the Senate Committee reported as follows:

"The test intended to be incorporated in the interpretation of paragraph (1) is in general that currently employed under section 115(g)(1) of the 1939 Code. Your committee further intends that in applying this test for the future * * * the inquiry will be devoted solely to the question of whether or not the transaction by its nature may properly be characterized as a sale of stock by the redeeming shareholder to the corporation. For this purpose the presence or absence of earnings and profits of the corporation is not material. Example: X, the sole shareholder of a corporation having no earnings or profits causes the corporation to redeem half of its stock. Paragraph (1) does not apply to such redemption notwithstanding the absence of earnings and profits." S.Rep. No. 1622, supra, at 234.

The intended scope of § 302(b)(1) as revealed by this legislative history is certainly not free from doubt. However, we agree with the Government that by making the sole inquiry relevant for the future the narrow one whether the redemption could be characterized as a sale, Congress was apparently rejecting past court decisions that had also considered factors indicating the presence or absence of a tax-avoidance motive.[11] At least that is the implication of the example given. Congress clearly mandated that pro rata distributions be treated under the general rules laid down in §§ 301 and 316 rather than under § 302, and nothing suggests that there should be a different result if there were a "business purpose" for the redemption. Indeed, just the opposite inference must be drawn since there would not likely be a tax-avoidance purpose in a situation where there were no earnings or profits. We conclude that the Court of Appeals was therefore wrong in looking for a business purpose and considering it in deciding whether the redemption was equivalent to a dividend. Rather, we agree with the Court of Appeals for the Second Circuit that "the business purpose of a transaction is irrelevant in determining dividend equivalence" under § 302(b)(1). Hasbrook v. United States, 343 F.2d 811, 814 (1965).

Taxpayer strongly argues that to treat the redemption involved here as essentially equivalent to a dividend is to elevate form over

10. See Bittker & Eustice, supra, n. 7 at 291: "It is not easy to give § 302(b)(1) an expansive construction in view of this indication that its major function was the narrow one of immunizing redemptions of minority holdings of preferred stock."

11. This rejection is confirmed by the Committee's acceptance of the House treatment of distributions involving corporate contractions—a factor present in many of the earlier "business purpose" redemptions. In describing its action, the Committee stated as follows:

"Your committee, as did the House bill, separates into their significant elements the kind of transactions now incoherently aggregated in the definition of a partial liquidation. Those distributions which may have capital-gain characteristics *because they are not made pro rata* among the various shareholders, would be subjected, at the shareholder level, to the separate tests described in [§§ 301 to 318]. On the other hand, those distributions characterized by what happens solely at the corporate level by reason of the assets distributed would be included as within the concept of a partial liquidation." S.Rep. No. 1622, supra, at 49. (Emphasis added.)

substance. Thus, taxpayer argues, had he not bought Bradley's shares or had he made a subordinated loan to the company instead of buying preferred stock, he could have gotten back his $25,000 with favorable tax treatment. However, the difference between form and substance in the tax law is largely problematical, and taxpayer's complaints have little to do with whether a business purpose is relevant under § 302(b)(1). It was clearly proper for Congress to treat distributions generally as taxable dividends when made out of earnings and profits and then to prevent avoidance of that result without regard to motivation where the distribution is in exchange for redeemed stock.

We conclude that that is what Congress did when enacting § 302(b)(1). If a corporation distributes property as a simple dividend, the effect is to transfer the property from the company to its shareholders without a change in the relative economic interests or rights of the stockholders. Where a redemption has that same effect, it cannot be said to have satisfied the "not essentially equivalent to a dividend" requirement of § 302(b)(1). Rather, to qualify for preferred treatment under that section, a redemption must result in a meaningful reduction of the shareholder's proportionate interest in the corporation. Clearly, taxpayer here, who (after application of the attribution rules) was the sole shareholder of the corporation both before and after the redemption, did not qualify under this test. The decision of the Court of Appeals must therefore be reversed and the case remanded to the District Court for dismissal of the complaint.

It is so ordered.

MR. JUSTICE DOUGLAS, with whom THE CHIEF JUSTICE and MR. JUSTICE BRENNAN concur, dissenting.

I agree with the District Court, 274 F.Supp. 466, and with the Court of Appeals, 408 F.2d 1139, that respondent's contribution of working capital in the amount of $25,000 in exchange for 1,000 shares of preferred stock with a par value of $25 was made in order for the corporation to obtain a loan from the RFC and that the preferred stock was to be redeemed when the loan was repaid. For the reasons stated by the two lower courts, this redemption was not "essentially equivalent to a dividend," for the bona fide business purpose of the redemption belies the payment of a dividend. As stated by the Court of Appeals:

"Although closely-held corporations call for close scrutiny under the tax law, we will not, under the facts and circumstances of this case, allow mechanical attribution rules to transform a legitimate corporate transaction into a tax avoidance scheme." 408 F.2d, at 1143–1144.

When the Court holds it was a dividend, it effectively cancels § 302(b)(1) from the Code. This result is not a matter of conjecture, for the Court says that in the case of closely held or one-man corporations a redemption of stock is "always" equivalent to a dividend. I would leave such revision to the Congress.

ILLUSTRATIVE MATERIAL

A. GENERAL

If a shareholder is unable to meet the "safe haven" requirements of section 302(b)(2) or section 302(b)(3), the shareholder still may fall back on the general language of section 302(b)(1), allowing capital gain treatment to distributions found to be not essentially equivalent to a dividend. But the *Davis* case makes the task of the shareholder attempting to fit the transaction under section 302(b)(1) very difficult. First, the Court's holding that the attribution rules of section 318 apply to section 302(b)(1) situations means that the shareholder in a closely-held corporate context will almost invariably be deemed to own a higher percentage of stock than is actually owned, and hence the distribution to the shareholder will more likely have or approach the pro rata character of a dividend distribution. See, e.g., Title Insurance and Trust Co. v. United States, 484 F.2d 462 (9th Cir.1973), Johnson v. United States, 434 F.2d 340 (8th Cir.1970), and Rev.Rul. 71–261, 1971–1 Cum.Bull. 108, all situations in which, by virtue of the application of the attribution rules, the shareholder was deemed to own 100 percent of the stock of the corporation and hence the distribution was treated as a dividend. Indeed, in some cases the interaction of the attribution rules and the redemption can actually *increase* the redeemed shareholder's interest after the redemption, see, e.g., Sawelson v. Commissioner, 61 T.C. 109 (1973). Second, the Court's clear elimination of the "business purpose" factor in determining dividend equivalence under section 302(b)(1) removes from consideration any argument based on the reasons for the redemption (presumably including "shareholder" purposes, see Nicholson v. Commissioner, 17 T.C. 1399 (1952)), and focuses attention solely on the "effect" of the distribution. Here the factors discussed below, some of which were developed in the prior case law dealing with dividend equivalence, will be relevant after *Davis,* with the exception of those cases whose result turned on a finding of "business purpose" for the redemption.

B. "MEANINGFUL REDUCTION" IN THE SHAREHOLDER'S INTEREST

1. *Voting Stock*

(a) *Effect on Control*

In attempting to give some content to the "meaningful reduction" standard set forth by the Supreme Court in *Davis,* subsequent cases and Rulings have focused principally on the effect that the redemption has on the shareholder's voting control of the corporation. Thus in Rev.Rul. 75–502, 1975–2 Cum.Bull. 111, a redemption, which reduced the shareholder's voting stock interest in the corporation from 57 percent to 50 percent where the other 50 percent was held by unrelated shareholders, qualified as a meaningful reduction. The Ruling indicated that if the redemption had not reduced the shareholder's interest in the voting stock to 50 percent or less, then section 302(b)(1) would not have been applicable. See Rev.Rul. 77–218, 1977–1 Cum.Bull. 81 (8 percent reduction in actual and constructive ownership which left the shareholder with more than 50 percent of the voting stock because of the attribution rules was not a meaningful reduction even though all of the shares actually owned by the taxpayer were redeemed). Benjamin v. Commissioner, 66 T.C. 1084 (1976), aff'd, 592 F.2d

1259 (5th Cir.1979), involving a redemption of voting preferred stock, found that the redemption did not qualify under section 302(b)(1) because of the shareholder's continuing voting control over the corporation after the redemption. The facts that the shareholder's interest in the net worth of the corporation and the right to participate in its earnings were reduced were not sufficient since "the retention of absolute voting control in the present case outweighs any other considerations". (66 T.C. at 1111).

Roebling v. Commissioner, 77 T.C. 30 (1981), involved the redemption of voting preferred stock pursuant to a plan of the corporation to redeem all of its outstanding preferred stock over a number of years. Before the series of redemptions commenced, the shareholder held 91.94 percent of the preferred stock and 39.6 percent of the common stock, which gave her 57.12 percent of the total voting shares. If the plan had been carried out in full, the shareholder would have been left with less than forty percent of the voting stock of the corporation, which had approximately 500 shareholders. For the years in question, however, the shareholder's voting power was only reduced to 43.28 percent. Because the shareholder's voting power was reduced from majority control to less than 50 percent, the court concluded that the reduction was meaningful. This conclusion was reenforced by the reduction in the percentage of total dividend distributions that would be receivable by the taxpayer as a result of the redemption.

Rickey v. United States, 427 F.Supp. 484 (W.D.La.1976), aff'd on other grounds, 592 F.2d 1251 (5th Cir.1979), held that a reduction in voting stock from 72 percent to 58 percent was a qualifying redemption where the shareholder lost the ability to control the two-thirds vote necessary for certain corporate actions under the state corporation law. Henry T. Patterson Trust v. United States, 729 F.2d 1089 (6th Cir.1984), reached the same result where the shareholder's interest was reduced from 80 percent to 60 percent. This analysis was rejected in Rev.Rul. 78–401, 1978–2 Cum.Bull. 127, which held that a reduction from 90 percent to 60 percent did not qualify under section 302(b)(1); the shareholder still had the right to control the day-to-day operations of the corporation and the fact that he gave up the right to control actions requiring a two-thirds vote under state corporation law was not sufficient.

A similar analysis is applied in situations involving redemptions of voting stock held by minority shareholders. Thus, in Rev.Rul. 76–364, 1976–2 Cum.Bull. 91, the shareholder held 27 percent of the voting stock of the corporation and three other unrelated shareholders each had a 24.3 percent interest. A redemption which reduced the shareholder's 27 percent interest to 22.27 percent was held to be a meaningful reduction since through the redemption the shareholder lost the ability to control the corporation by acting in conjunction with only one of the other shareholders. See also Rev. Rul. 75–512, 1975–2 Cum.Bull. 112 (a reduction from 30 percent actual and constructive ownership to 24.3 percent constructive ownership, where all of the shares actually owned were redeemed, qualified under section 302(b)(1)). Compare Rev.Rul. 76–385, 1976–2 Cum.Bull. 92 (where the shareholder had a .0001118 percent interest in a publicly held corporation, and thus effectively no control at all with respect to the operation of the corporation, a 3.3 percent reduction in share ownership was meaningful); Rev.Rul. 81–289, 1981–2 Cum.Bull. 82 (redemption of 2 percent of stock of shareholder holding less than 1 percent of publicly traded corporation's outstanding stock was essentially equivalent to a dividend where simultaneous redemptions from other shareholders resulted in total redemption of 2 percent of corporation's outstanding stock).

(b) *Effect of "Family Hostility" on Application of Constructive Stock Ownership Rules*

If, after the redemption, the shareholder's directly owned stock is insufficient to provide control but the shareholder is deemed to own over 50 percent of the voting stock because of the attribution rules, she is still treated as the controlling shareholder for purposes of testing the meaningful reduction in the shareholder's interest. See, e.g., Fehrs Finance Co. v. Commissioner, 487 F.2d 184 (8th Cir.1973); Rev.Rul. 77–218, supra. While *Davis* indicates that the attribution rules apply in such a situation, *Davis* could be viewed as permitting this shareholder to argue that where the related parties in fact were in disagreement, the attribution rules should not be applied in testing control. Several pre-*Davis* cases had adopted this approach. See, e.g., Estate of Squier v. Commissioner, 35 T.C. 950 (1961). In the first case to raise the issue following *Davis,* however, the Tax Court held that the *Davis* view of the attribution rules precluded applying a "family fight" exception. Robin Haft Trust v. Commissioner, 61 T.C. 398 (1973). The Court of Appeals reversed (510 F.2d 43 (1st Cir.1975)) and remanded the case for consideration of whether "the existence of family discord [tended] to negate the presumption that taxpayers would exert continuing control over the corporation despite the redemption." In Rev.Rul. 80–26, 1980–1 Cum.Bull. 66, the Internal Revenue Service announced that it would not follow the Court of Appeals decision in *Robin Haft Trust* on the theory that a "family hostility" exception to the attribution rules is inconsistent with both *Davis* and the legislative history of section 301(b)(1)(a). Likewise, the Fifth Circuit, in David Metzger Trust v. Commissioner, 693 F.2d 459 (5th Cir.1982), held that there is no family hostility exception to the attribution rules. In Cerone v. Commissioner, 87 T.C. 1, 22 (1987), the Tax Court described relevance of family hostility as follows:

"First, the attribution rules are plainly and straightforwardly applied. Second, a determination is made whether there has been a reduction in the stockholder's proportionate interest in the corporation. If not, the inquiry ends because, if there is no change in the stockholder's interest, dividend equivalency results. If there has been a reduction, then all of the facts and circumstances must be examined to see if the reduction was meaningful under *United States v. Davis,* supra. It is at this point, *and only then,* that family hostility becomes an appropriate factor for consideration." Since the shareholder's interest in *Cerone* was not reduced, this version of the family hostility doctrine was, on the facts, inapplicable.

The circumscribed family hostility doctrine of *Cerone* could lead to unusual results. Suppose the stock of X Corp. is held as follows: A, 41 shares; B, 34 shares; C, 17 shares; and D, 8 shares. A and B are parent and child, but the shareholders are otherwise unrelated. If there was "bad blood" between A and B, a redemption of as few as one of B's shares might qualify under section 301(b)(1). But if ten shares were redeemed from each of B and C, the redemption never could qualify because, taking into account the attribution rules, B's ownership increased from 75 percent to 81.25 percent, even though actual ownership was reduced from 34 percent to 24 percent and A alone now holds actual voting control of the corporation. See Henry T. Patterson Trust v. United States, 729 F.2d 1089 (6th Cir.1984), where all of the stock actually owned by the taxpayer was redeemed; in an alternative holding the court concluded that due to family hostility there was a meaningful reduction even though after applying the attribution rules, the taxpayer's interest was reduced only from 97 percent to 93 percent.

2. *Non–voting Stock*

Where a redemption of non-voting stock is involved, the "meaningful reduction" is tested in terms of the change in the shareholder's rights with respect to the corporation's earnings and profits and assets on liquidation. See Himmel v. Commissioner, 338 F.2d 815 (2d Cir.1964), analyzing the "complex of shareholder rights" in a situation involving a multi-class capitalization. Rev.Rul. 77–426, 1977–2 Cum.Bull. 87, held that any redemption of non-voting preferred stock where the stockholder did not hold directly or indirectly any voting common stock would constitute a meaningful reduction for purposes of section 302(b)(1). The rights given up in the redemption were permanently lost and not retained through continuing common stock ownership.

On the other hand, where a preferred shareholder continues to own common stock, achieving a meaningful reduction with respect to a redemption of nonvoting preferred stock is much more difficult. For example in Hays v. Commissioner, 30 T.C.M. 378 (1971), the taxpayer owned 80 percent of the common stock of the corporation and all of the preferred stock. A redemption of 10 percent of the preferred stock was found to result in a dividend to the shareholder: "The redemption of 300 out of 3,000 shares of preferred stock held by Hays could not be termed 'meaningful.' Also, whatever significance the reduction might have standing alone, its importance is diminished upon consideration of the fact that Hays remained owner of 80 percent of the common stock in [the corporation]. Thus while his right to earnings and profits via the preferred stock was reduced * * *, he continued to have access to 80 percent of that amount via his common stock. Since Hays owned the overwhelming majority of the common, the only voting stock, his ability to declare dividends was assured." (382)

See also Rev.Rul. 85–106, 1985–2 Cum.Bull. 116 (redemption of two-thirds of non-voting preferred stock from shareholder who held 18 percent of non-voting preferred stock, and who by attribution also held approximately 18 percent of each class of voting common and non-voting common stock, was substantially equivalent to dividend because, after taking into account attribution, the redeemed shareholder's potential for participating in a control group by aligning himself with two other stockholders, who together held 38 percent of the voting common stock, was not reduced).

3. *Comparative Dividend Analysis*

Another approach to the problem of dividend equivalence is to compare the distribution on redemption with the distribution of a similar amount as a hypothetical dividend. See Himmel v. Commissioner, 338 F.2d 815 (2d Cir. 1964) (receipt of substantially larger distribution than would have been received as dividend indicates that redemption is not essentially equivalent to a dividend). While the *Davis* opinion does not discuss this so-called "comparative dividend" method, it is not necessarily inconsistent with the Court's focus on the effect rather than the purpose of the distribution. However, the cases decided since *Davis* do not use comparative dividend analysis of redemptions. Brown v. United States, 477 F.2d 599 (6th Cir.1973), held the approach inconsistent with *Davis,* and in Rev.Rul. 85–106, 1985–2 Cum. Bull. 116, the Internal Revenue Service rejected the use of comparative dividend analysis. But see Grabowski Trust v. Commissioner, 58 T.C. 650 (1972), finding comparative dividend analysis relevant after *Davis.*

Do the developments and litigation since Davis indicate that in the redemption area Congress should rely exclusively on mechanical tests such as that in section 302(b)(2)?

C. REFERENCES

Postlewaite and Finneran, Section 302(b)(1): The Expanding Minnow, 64 Va.L.Rev. 561 (1978); Zinn and Silverman, Redemptions of Stock Under Section 302(b)(1), 32 Tax Lawyer 91 (1978); Blum, Drawing the Line Between Dividends and Investment Adjustments: A Proposal For More Consistency, 55 Taxes 30 (1977); Chirelstein, Optional Redemptions and Optional Dividends: Taxing the Repurchase of Common Shares, 78 Yale L.J. 739 (1969).

SECTION 5. STOCK REDEMPTION DISTRIBUTIONS TO PAY DEATH TAX

INTERNAL REVENUE CODE: Section 303(a), –(c).

REVENUE RULING 87–132.

1987–2 Cumulative Bulletin 82.

ISSUE

Whether the application of section 303 of the Internal Revenue Code to a stock redemption is precluded when the stock redeemed was newly distributed as part of the same transaction.

FACTS

X corporation had outstanding 300 shares of voting common stock that were owned equally by an estate and by *A,* an individual, who had no interest in the estate under section 318 of the Code. The value of the *X* stock held by the estate exceeded the amount specified in section 303(b)(2)(A). The estate wanted to effect a redemption pursuant to section 303 to pay death taxes.

In order to maintain relative voting power and to preserve continuity of management, *X* undertook the following two steps. First, *X* issued 10 shares of a new class of nonvoting common stock on each share of common stock outstanding. Thus, the estate and *A* each received 1,500 shares of this stock. Immediately thereafter, 1,000 shares of the non-voting common stock were redeemed by *X* from the estate in exchange for cash. The overall result of these two steps was that the estate obtained the cash it needed while giving up only nonvoting stock.

The redemption of the *X* nonvoting common stock occurred within the time limits prescribed by section 303(b)(1)(A) of the Code and did not exceed the amount permitted by section 303(a).

LAW AND ANALYSIS

Section 303(a) of the Code provides that a distribution of property to a shareholder by a corporation in redemption of stock of the corporation, which (for federal estate tax purposes) is included in determining the gross estate of a decedent, is treated as a distribution in full payment in exchange for the stock redeemed to the extent of the sum of certain taxes and expenses. These taxes and expenses are the estate, inheritance, legacy and succession taxes plus the amount of funeral and administrative expenses allowable as deductions for federal estate tax purposes.

Section 303(c) of the Code provides that if a shareholder owns stock of a corporation (new stock) the basis of which is determined by reference to the basis of stock of a corporation (old stock) that was included in determining the gross estate of a decedent, and section 303(a) would apply to a distribution in redemption of the old stock, then section 303(a) applies to a distribution in redemption of the new stock. Section 1.303–2(d) of the Income Tax Regulations specifically provides that section 303 applies to a distribution in redemption of stock received by an estate in a distribution to which section 305(a) applies.

Section 305(a) of the Code provides that, generally, gross income does not include the amount of any distribution of the stock of a corporation made by the corporation to its shareholders with respect to its stock. Section 305(b)(1), however, provides that if the distribution is, at the election of any of the shareholders (whether exercised before or after the declaration of the distribution), payable either in its stock or in property, then the distribution of stock is treated as a distribution to which section 301 applies. Section 305(b)(2) provides that if the distribution has the result of the receipt of property by some shareholders and an increase in the proportionate interest of other shareholders in the assets or earnings and profits of the corporation, then the distribution of stock is treated as a distribution to which section 301 applies.

Section 307(a) of the Code provides that if a shareholder already owning stock in a corporation ("old stock") receives additional stock ("new stock") in a distribution to which section 305(a) applies, then the basis of the old stock prior to the distribution is allocated between the old stock and new stock subsequent to the distribution.

Here, 3,000 shares of nonvoting common stock were distributed and 1,000 shares were subsequently redeemed by *X* as part of a plan designed to allow the estate to avail itself of the benefits of section 303 of the Code. The intent of Congress in enacting the statutory predecessor of section 303 was to provide an effective means whereby the estate of a decedent owning an interest in a family enterprise could finance the estate tax without being required to dispose of its entire interest in the family business in order to avoid the imposition of an ordinary dividend tax. H.R.Rep. No. 2319, 81st Cong., 2d Sess. 63–64 (1950). Given this intent, it follows that the estate should be able to obtain the benefits of section 303 without a substantially adverse effect on the estate's ownership of the family business.

Moreover, section 303(c) of the Code is a remedial provision that was added to expand the application of section 303 to the redemption of stock which, despite a technical change in the form of ownership, represents the same stock as that owned at death. S.Rep. No. 1622, 83rd Cong., 2nd Sess. 239 (1954). The sole requirement for application of section 303 to the redemption, under section 303(c), is that the basis of the stock redeemed ("new stock") be determined by reference to the basis of the "old stock" included in the estate. Section 1.303–2(d) of the regulations provides that stock received by an estate in a section 305(a) distribution is entitled to section 303 treatment. Rev.Rul. 83–68, 1983–1 C.B. 75, holds that a distribution of stock that is immediately redeemable at the option of a shareholder gives the shareholder an election to receive either stock or property within the meaning of section 305(b)(1) and, therefore, is a distribution to which section 301 applies. See also Rev.Rul. 76–258, 1976–2 C.B. 95.

The nature of section 303 of the Code and the limited time period for redemption provided in section 303(b)(1) are generally indicative of a Congressional intent that section 303 be applicable to stock issued as part of the same plan as the redemption. Consequently, for purposes of section 303 only, section 305 should be applied prior to, and without reference to, the subsequent redemption.

HOLDING

The exclusion from gross income provision of section 305(a) of the Code, and the carryover of basis provisions of section 307(a), apply to *X*'s distribution of its new nonvoting common stock to *A* and the estate. Section 303(a) applies to *X*'s distribution of cash to the estate in redemption of the 1,000 shares of its new nonvoting common stock. For the tax consequences to *A* (the nonredeeming shareholder) as a result of this transaction, see section 305.

* * *

ILLUSTRATIVE MATERIAL

A. GENERAL

Section 303, whose provisions were first adopted in 1951, has a significant effect upon estate planning, since it permits certain redemptions for the purpose of paying estate taxes to qualify for sale or exchange treatment, even though the redemption does not meet any of the tests of section 302. In order to qualify under section 303 the stock must (1) have been included in the decedent's gross estate for Federal estate tax purposes; (2) have comprised the specified percentage of the gross estate (less certain expenses); (3) be redeemed from a person who bears the burden of the estate tax; and (4) be redeemed within a specified period of time after the decedent's death. A redemption which qualifies under section 303 generally produces limited tax consequences to the distributee as regards gain recognition because section 1014 provides the deceased shareholder's successor in interest with a basis in the stock equal to its value on the decedent's date of death. On the other hand, if section 303 is not satisfied, dividend treatment, which would generally be the case, would not allow tax-free basis recovery so the section in this regard gives the taxpayer a substantial advantage.

B. POLICY BASIS FOR SECTION 303

By making the treasury of a closely-held corporation available as a source of funds at the death of a principal shareholder, the problem of meeting estate taxes may be substantially eased. The enactment of this provision was justified as follows:

> "It has been brought to the attention of your committee that the problem of financing the estate tax is acute in the case of estates consisting largely of shares in a family corporation. The market for such shares is usually very limited, and it is frequently difficult, if not impossible, to dispose of a minority interest. If, therefore, the estate tax cannot be financed through the sale of the other assets in the estate, the executors will be forced to dispose of the family business. In many cases the result will be the absorption of a family enterprise by larger competitors, thus tending to accentuate the degree of concentration of industry in this country." S.Rep. No. 81–2375, 81st Cong., 2d Sess. 54 (1951).

In fact, section 303 largely was inserted to meet the problem of an estate holding all of the stock of a Boston newspaper. It is interesting that several years after some of the stock was redeemed to meet estate taxes, the estate then sold all of the remaining stock to an outside party.

Since the enactment of section 303, the Code has been amended by the addition of sections 6166 and 6166A which provide an extension of time for payment of the estate tax where the estate consists largely of an interest in a closely held business. It would seem that the availability of relief under these provisions should be sufficient to mitigate any hardship in paying estate taxes attributable to stock in closely held corporations and section 303 is, in fact, largely unnecessary.

C. TECHNICAL ASPECTS OF SECTION 303

Suppose the stock redeemed to pay death taxes is "section 306" preferred stock. See supra, page 537. Since the section 306 stock was included in the decedent's estate and its basis was determined under section 1014, it would lose its section 306 "taint" and can be redeemed under section 303 so as to receive exchange treatment at the shareholder level. See section 306(a)(1)(C).

Section 2035(d)(3)(a) includes in a decedent's gross estate for purposes of computing the section 303(b)(2) percentages (but not for purposes of computing Federal estate taxes) the value of any stock transferred by the decedent for less than adequate consideration within three years prior to death. Such transferred shares, however, may not be redeemed under section 303. Rev.Rul. 84–76, 1984–1 Cum.Bull. 91.

D. REFERENCE

Kahn, Closely Held Stocks—Deferral and Financing of Estate Tax Costs Through Sections 303 and 6166, 35 Tax Lawyer 639 (1982).

SECTION 6. PARTIAL LIQUIDATIONS

INTERNAL REVENUE CODE: Sections 302(b)(4), (e).

REGULATIONS: Section 1.346–1, –2, –3.

ESTATE OF CHANDLER v. COMMISSIONER *

Tax Court of the United States, 1954.
22 T.C. 1158.

[All of the petitioners were stockholders of Chandler–Singleton Company (hereinafter referred to as the Company), a Tennessee corporation organized on May 9, 1923. The capital stock of the Company consisted of 500 shares of common stock of $100 par value, all of which was outstanding until November 7, 1946. The stock was essentially all held by the Chandler family group. From its organization until February 28, 1946, the Company was engaged in the operation of a general department store in Maryville, Tennessee. It had a ladies' ready-to-wear department, men's department, children's department, piece goods department, and a bargain basement.

Chandler was the president and manager of the Company. At the beginning of 1944 he was in very poor health. John W. Bush was the secretary of the Company, but until 1944 he had not been particularly active in its affairs. On January 1, 1944, he became assistant manager of the Company. By profession he was a civil engineer, but at that time he was unemployed due to a change in the administration of the City of Knoxville, Tennessee. During 1944 and 1945 Chandler was sick most of the time. In his absence John W. Bush managed the department store.

John W. Bush did not like being a merchant and decided to return to engineering. In November 1945 he informed Chandler that he was resigning as manager at the end of the year. Chandler, feeling unable to manage the department store himself, decided to sell.

At a stockholders' meeting held on February 20, 1946, it was unanimously agreed that the Company should accept an offer to purchase its merchandise, furniture and fixtures, and lease. The sale was consummated and the Company ceased operating the department store on February 28, 1946. The purchaser, Arthur's Incorporated, moved in that night and began operating the store the following day.

Chandler had worked hard in the department store and had no outside interest. He wanted something to do and did not want to get out of business entirely. It was planned that a ladies' ready-to-wear store would be opened by the Company to be managed by Clara T. McConnell (now Clara M. Register) who had managed the ladies' ready-to-wear department of the department store. Thirty shares of stock in

* [Ed.: The Tax Court's decision was affirmed, 228 F.2d 909 (6th Cir.1955), the court stating that the finding as to divided equivalence was a finding of fact sustained by the evidence. Some courts, however, would call this a conclusion of law.]

the Company owned by Chandler's wife were cancelled on April 5, 1946. Ten of these shares were issued to Clara McConnell on April 13, 1946, in order that she might have an interest in the Company whose store she was going to manage. A men's store, to be eventually taken over by the eldest son of John and Margaret Bush, was also contemplated. It was thought that approximately half of the assets of the Company would be needed for each of the two stores.

About the first of June, 1946, the Company obtained space for the ladies' ready-to-wear store about one-half block from the old department store and the store was opened on September 23, 1946.

The ladies' ready-to-wear store was about the same size as that department in the former department store. The department store had occupied 8,000 to 9,000 square feet of floor space, had employed 10 to 20 persons, and had carried fire insurance in the amount of $65,000 on its stock and fixtures. The new store had approximately 1,800 square feet of floor space, employed four to six persons, and carried fire insurance in the amount of $10,000.

A special meeting of the stockholders was held on September 28, 1946, the minutes of which read in part as follows:

"The Chairman explained that the purpose of the meeting was to authorize partial liquidation for the following reasons:

"The old business was sold and plans were developed to go back into business, operating two stores, a ladies' ready-to-wear business and a men's store. The ladies' ready-to-wear store has been opened and is now operating. Up to now, we have been unable to negotiate a lease for a suitable location, and, after considerable thought, it has been decided to abandon the idea of operating an exclusive men's shop and operate only the one store at the present time. It appears that requirements of the one store will be approximately one-half the capital now invested in Chandler's, Inc.

"Upon motion of Margaret Chandler Bush, seconded by J.W. Bush, and unanimously carried, the officials were authorized and instructed to redeem from each shareholder one-half of his stock, paying therefor the book value, which is approximately $269.00 per share."

On November 7, 1946, each stockholder turned in one-half of his stock in return for cash, the total distributed being $67,250.

The amount of cash and United States Bonds possessed by the Company at the beginning of 1946 exceeded the amount required for the current operation of the business by approximately $45,000. Between January 1 and February 28, 1946, the Company's earned surplus increased by $39,460.44 out of which the Company paid dividends in the amount of $12,500. To the extent of at least $58,027.91, the excess cash possessed by the Company prior to the November 7 distribution was not created by a reduction in the amount of capital needed to operate the Company's business.

Petitioners reported the excess of the payments received over the cost of the stock in their individual income tax returns as capital gain. Respondent treated the payments, to the extent of the earned surplus of $58,027.91, as dividends and taxed them to the petitioners as ordinary income.

The acquisition and cancellation of one-half the Company's stock in 1946 was done at such a time and in such a manner as to make the distribution and cancellation essentially equivalent to the distribution of a taxable dividend to the extent of $58,027.91.]

OPINION

BRUCE, JUDGE: Respondent contends that the Company's pro rata distribution in redemption of half its capital stock at book value was made at such a time and in such a manner as to make the distribution essentially equivalent to the distribution of a taxable dividend to the extent of earnings and profits. If respondent's contention is correct the distribution to the extent of earnings and profits loses [its capital gain status and is treated as a taxable dividend].

A cancellation or redemption by a corporation of all of the stock of a particular shareholder has been held not to be essentially equivalent to the distribution of a taxable dividend. Cf. Carter Tiffany, 16 T.C. 1443; Zenz v. Quinlivan, (C.A.6), 213 F.2d 914; Regs. 111, sec. 29.115–9. However, "A cancellation or redemption by a corporation of its stock pro rata among all the shareholders will generally be considered as effecting a distribution essentially equivalent to a dividend distribution to the extent of the earnings and profits accumulated after February 28, 1913." Regs. 111, sec. 29.115–9. * * * But, as pointed out by the regulations, a pro rata distribution is not always "essentially equivalent to the distribution of a taxable dividend" and each case depends upon its own particular circumstances. Commissioner v. Sullivan, (C.A.5), 210 F.2d 607, affirming John L. Sullivan, 17 T.C. 1420. The circumstances in the instant case, however, do not warrant a finding that to the extent of earnings and profits the pro rata distribution was not essentially equivalent to a taxable dividend.

Being a question of fact, the decided cases are not controlling. However, in Joseph W. Imler, 11 T.C. 836, 840, we listed some of the factors which have been considered important, viz., "the presence or absence of a real business purpose, the motives of the corporation at the time of the distribution, the size of the corporate surplus, the past dividend policy, and the presence of any special circumstances relating to the distribution." * * *

An examination of the facts reveals that the Company had a large earned surplus and an unnecessary accumulation of cash from the standpoint of business requirement, both of which could have been reduced to the extent of earnings and profits by the declaration of a true dividend. The only suggested benefit accruing to the business by the distribution in cancellation of half the stock was the elimination of a substantial amount of this excess cash. Ordinarily such cash would be disposed of by the payment of a dividend. Coupled with the fact that the stockholders' proportionate interests in the enterprise remained unchanged, these factors indicate that [section 115(a) of the 1939 Code respecting distributions essentially equivalent to a dividend, the predecessor of sections 302 and 346] is applicable.

Petitioners seek to avoid application of [that section] by contending that the cash distribution and redemption of stock did not represent an artifice to disguise the payment of a dividend but was occasioned by a bona fide contraction of business with a resulting decrease in the need for capital. While important, the absence of a plan to avoid taxation is not controlling. A distribution in redemption of stock may be essentially equivalent to a taxable dividend although it does not represent an attempt to camouflage such a dividend. * * * Commissioner v. Cordingley, (C.A.1), 78 F.2d 118; and Commissioner v. Quackenbos, (C.A.2), 78 F.2d 156, both of which adopted a "bad faith" test as controlling, have either been overruled or rejected by later opinions. * * * Whether a cancellation or redemption of stock is "essentially equivalent" to a taxable dividend depends primarily upon the net effect of the distribution rather than the motives and plans of the shareholders or the corporation. * * * Moreover, we cannot find from the present record that the reduction of taxes was not the motivating factor causing the stockholders to make a distribution in redemption of stock rather than to declare a dividend to the extent of earnings and profits.

Petitioners' primary contention is that the sale of the department store and the opening of the smaller ladies' ready-to-wear store resulted in a contraction of corporate business. This is a vital factor to be considered, but a contraction of business per se does not render [the section in question] inapplicable. L.M. Lockhart, 8 T.C. 436. Furthermore, even though it is clear that there was a diminution in the size of the Company's business, there was no contraction such as was present in Commissioner v. Sullivan, Joseph W. Imler, and L.M. Lockhart, all supra. In those cases there was a contraction of business with a corresponding reduction in the amount of capital used. Here, although the business was smaller, the amount of capital actually committed to the corporate business was not reduced accordingly. On December 31, 1945, before the sale of the department store to McArthur's Incorporated, the Company had $32,736.53 tied up in fixed assets and inventories. On December 31, 1946, after the ladies' ready-to-wear store was opened, it had $31,504.67 invested in those items. Undoubtedly the department store required larger reserves than the ladies' ready-to-wear store for purchasing inventories and carrying accounts receivable. But to the extent of earnings and profits the excess cash distributed was not created by a reduction in the amount of capital required for the operation of the business. Most of the excess cash had existed since prior to the sale of the department store and did not arise from fortuitous circumstances, as petitioners contend, but from an accumulation of earnings beyond the needs of the business. This excess could have been eliminated by the payment of a taxable dividend, and its distribution in redemption of stock was essentially equivalent to a taxable dividend.

It is true that the entire $67,250 distribution could not have been made in the form of an ordinary dividend and to some extent a redemption of stock was required. But [the section] applies if the distribution is only "in part" essentially equivalent to a taxable dividend, and here the distribution was essentially equivalent to a taxable dividend to the extent of earnings and profits.

Decisions will be entered for the respondent.

ILLUSTRATIVE MATERIAL

A. PARTIAL LIQUIDATIONS IN GENERAL

1. *Non-Dividend Equivalence Test—"Contraction"*

Section 304(b)(4) extends sale or exchange treatment to redemptions of stock from *individual* shareholders in "partial liquidation" of the distributing corporation. The term "partial liquidation" is defined in section 302(e), and that definition makes clear that unlike the redemptions described in sections 302(b)(1) through (b)(3), which focus upon the effect of the distribution to the shareholder, whether a distribution qualifies as a partial liquidation is determined with reference to its effect on the corporation. Although the statutory language of section 302(e)(1) refers to a distribution "not essentially equivalent to a dividend (determined at the corporate level rather than at the shareholder level)," section 302(e) is in fact concerned primarily, perhaps exclusively, with the concept of a distribution in connection with a "corporate contraction." The partial liquidation provisions were amended in the 1982 Act, but section 302(e)(1) was described in the Conference Committee Report as "continuing" the law under former section 346(a)(2), which (as did the case law under the 1939 Code from which the language of section 302(e)(1) is drawn) focused on corporate contraction as the test for a partial liquidation. See S.Rep. No. 83–1622, 83rd Cong., 2d Sess. 49, 261–2 (1954); Regulations, section 1.346–1(a) ("genuine contraction of the corporate business"); Blaschka v. United States, 393 F.2d 983 (Ct.Cl.1968) (distribution was essentially equivalent to a dividend "in that there was no contraction of [the corporation's] business"); *Estate of Chandler,* supra; Imler v. Commissioner, 11 T.C. 836 (1948) (A); Lockhart v. Commissioner, 8 T.C. 436 (1947); Commissioner v. Sullivan, 210 F.2d 607 (5th Cir.1954). While there is relatively little case law since 1954 with respect to the "contraction" doctrine, the Internal Revenue Service has issued a number of rulings which provide guidelines in the area and this case law under the 1939 Code continues to be relevant under section 302(e)(1), at least as far as the "contraction" doctrine is concerned. See H.Rep. No. 97–760, 97th Cong, 2d Sess. 530 (1982). However, the mechanical test of section 304(e)(2), discussed below, may tend to restrict the judicial concept of a "contraction."

To qualify a distribution as a partial liquidation under section 302(e), the proceeds from the sale of the assets meeting either the safe harbor of section 302(e)(2) or the general "contraction" test must be distributed as soon as possible. See Regulations, section 1.346–1(c)(2). The distribution need not be immediate; the proceeds may be invested in portfolio securities pending distribution, but investment profits are not treated as distributions in partial liquidation. Rev.Rul. 76–279, 1976–2 Cum.Bull. 99; Rev.Rul. 71–250, 1971–1 Cum.Bull. 112. Investment of the proceeds in additional assets for use in the corporation's remaining business, however, precludes a subsequent distribution of an amount equal to the proceeds from qualifying as a partial liquidation. Rev.Rul. 67–299, 1967–2 Cum.Bull. 138. See also Rev.Rul. 58–565, 1958–2 Cum.Bull. 140 (use of proceeds to pay debts precludes treatment of subsequent distribution of equivalent amount as partial liquidation).

As in the other redemption situations, classification of a transaction as a partial liquidation is important to the shareholders to permit a recovery of basis and to absorb otherwise realized capital losses.

2. *Requirements of "Plan" and "Redemption"*

Section 302(e)(1)(B) limits partial liquidation treatment to redemption distributions which (1) are "pursuant to a plan," and (2) occur within the taxable year in which the plan is adopted or in the succeeding taxable year. A formal plan is not required, Fowler Hosiery Co. Inc. v. Commissioner, 301 F.2d 394 (7th Cir.1962), Rev.Rul. 79–287, 1979–2 Cum.Bull. 130, but the total absence of a plan can be fatal, Blaschka v. United States, 393 F.2d 983 (Ct.Cl. 1968). Adherence to the time limitations for distributions, however, is crucial. This strict enforcement of the two year window for distributions can be turned to the taxpayer's advantage where partial liquidation treatment is not desired. Section 302(e) is elective in the sense that its consequences may be avoided by failing to comply with the time requirements in section 302(e)(1)(B). See Rev.Rul. 77–468, 1977–2 Cum.Bull. 109. In some cases it may be important to determine precisely when the "plan" was adopted, a determination which may be difficult when the plan was not formally adopted. A number of cases and Revenue Rulings dealing with complete liquidations dealt with determining the date of adoption of an informal plan. See, e.g., Mountain Water Co. v. Commissioner, 35 T.C. 418 (1960); Rev.Rul. 65–235, 1965–2 Cum.Bull. 88.

An actual surrender of the shares is not required in the case of a pro rata distribution. *Fowler Hosiery Co.,* supra; H.Rep. No. 97–760, 97th Cong., 2d Sess. 530 (1982). Rev.Rul. 81–3, 1981–1 Cum.Bull. 125, held that where there was a genuine contraction of corporate business in partial liquidation, a surrender of shares would have been meaningless, and the shareholders would be deemed to have surrendered the number of shares the total fair market value of which equaled the amount of the distribution. See also Rev. Rul. 77–245, 1977–2 Cum.Bull. 105. But where the partial liquidation distribution was not pro rata, cases decided under the predecessor of section 302(e) have disqualified transactions where there was no actual redemption of the shares. Gordon v. Commissioner, 424 F.2d 378 (2d Cir.1970); Goodling v. United States, 267 F.Supp. 724 (S.D.Miss.1966), aff'd per curiam, 393 F.2d 933 (5th Cir.1968); Honigman v. Commissioner, 55 T.C. 1067 (1971), aff'd on this issue, 466 F.2d 69 (6th Cir.1972).

B. FIVE-YEAR SEPARATE BUSINESS SAFE HARBOR

Section 302(e)(2) provides a mechanical safe harbor rule for determining whether a distribution is not essentially equivalent to a dividend under section 302(e)(1). If the distribution consists of *all* of the assets, or the proceeds from the sale, of an *active* trade or business conducted for at least five years (which was not acquired by the corporation within the five year period in a taxable transaction) and after the distribution the corporation continues to conduct an *active* trade or business with a similar five year history, the distribution will not be essentially equivalent to a dividend. See Rev.Rul. 79–275, 1979–2 Cum.Bull. 137 (distribution of unrelated assets rather than promissory notes received on sale of terminated business did not qualify). Whether the distribution is pro rata or not is immaterial under this test. Section 302(e)(4). It is equally clear that a pro rata distribution can qualify under the "not essentially equivalent to a dividend" test of section 304(e)(1) if "contraction" is present, even though the transaction does not come within the safe harbor. Thus, although technically the attribution of ownership rules apply, as a practical matter they are not a factor under section 304(e).

Satisfaction of the mechanical test of section 302(e)(2) relates only to the "not essentially equivalent to a dividend" test of section 302(e)(1). It does not *per se* qualify the transaction under section 302(e)(1); the other tests of that section must be met even after satisfaction of section 302(e)(2). Rev. Rul. 77–468. 1977–2 Cum.Bull. 109; Baan v. Commissioner, 51 T.C. 1032 (1969) (alternative holding), aff'd on other grounds, *sub nom.* Gordon v. Commissioner, 424 F.2d 378 (2d Cir.1970), and Baan v. Commissioner, 450 F.2d 198 (9th Cir.1971).

The concept of an active business separately conducted for five years also is utilized with respect to corporate divisions under section 355 and will be considered more fully in relation to that section, infra, page 914. The Regulations under section 355 provide some detailed examples as to what constitutes the *active* conduct of a trade or business and are relevant for purposes of section 302(e). See Regulations, section 1.346–1(c)(2); Regulations, section 1.355–3(c). There is, however, a significant difference between the test under section 355 and the test under section 302(e)(2). While the division of a single business may be accomplished under section 355, section 302(e)(2) requires the existence of two distinct, separate trades or businesses prior to the partial liquidation. Kenton Meadows, Inc. v. Commissioner, 766 F.2d 142 (4th Cir.1985); Krauskopf v. Commissioner, 48 T.C.M. 620 (1984). In Bilar Tool & Die Corp. v. Commissioner, 530 F.2d 708 (6th Cir.1976), the court held that the division of a single business because of shareholder disputes, carried out by the transfer of one-half the assets and liabilities of the business to a newly created corporation for its stock followed by redemption of one of the shareholders' stock in the old corporation in exchange for stock of the new subsidiary, did not constitute a partial liquidation. (Such a transaction is a type (D) reorganization coupled with a split-off, discussed infra, Chapter 19.) In determining whether the terminated activity constituted a separate trade or business, the inquiry focuses on (1) whether the activity produced a substantial part of the combined corporate income, and (2) whether there was separate supervision and control. Blaschka v. Commissioner, 393 F.2d 983 (Ct.Cl.1968); Mains v. United States, 508 F.2d 1251 (6th Cir.1975).

The distributing corporation is not required to have conducted the terminated business throughout the five year predistribution period, as long as someone conducted the business and it was not acquired in a taxable transaction. Basically, this rule disqualifies acquisitions by purchase within the five year period but permits termination of a trade or business acquired in a tax free reorganization to qualify as a partial liquidation. The provision is designed to prevent the distributing corporation from temporarily "parking" excess funds in a trade or business for a short period prior to "termination" of the newly acquired business. Since tax free reorganizations entail acquisitions in exchange for stock of the acquiring corporation rather than cash, the same considerations do not apply.

C. CONTRACTION OF THE CORPORATE BUSINESS

As noted above, contraction of the corporate enterprise as the standard for testing nondividend equivalence originated under the 1939 Code, and that test has been carried forward through successive statutory revisions. It is available with respect to transactions which fail to come within the safe harbor of section 304(e)(2).

The leading case finding sufficient corporate contraction to constitute a partial liquidation is Imler v. Commissioner, 11 T.C. 836 (1948)(A). A corporation, whose stock was held by three stockholders, owned a seven story building and several smaller buildings and was engaged in retinning and soldering metals and in the rental of its excess space. A fire destroyed the upper two floors of the seven story building in 1941. Because of the shortage of building materials, the corporation did not rebuild the two floors but reduced the building to a five-story building. Finding its facilities inadequate to store materials for the retinning and soldering activities and also that a scarcity of materials made those operations unprofitable, it then discontinued those operations. The corporation then distributed $15,000 pro rata in redemption of part of its stock, the cash in part representing the excess of insurance proceeds over repair costs. The redemption was held not to be a dividend, the court stressing the bona fide contraction of business operations, the consequent reduction in capital needed, and the fact that except for the fire no distribution would have been made.

In Lockhart v. Commissioner, 8 T.C. 436 (1947), the sole stockholder of a corporation in the business of oil production, drilling, and operation of a recycling plant desired to operate the business as an individual. He could not completely liquidate as some of the shares were pledged to secure an obligation; in addition, he desired to retain the corporate name and to obtain limited liability respecting the drilling business. The stockholder also needed about $220,000 to pay pending income tax liabilities. Accordingly, net assets of about one million dollars, including about $250,000 in cash, were transferred to him in exchange for 16,245 out of his 17,000 shares, so that the corporation retained only the drilling assets, worth about $34,000. The court held that the reasons for and the results of the redemption did not render it essentially equivalent to a dividend.

Where a corporation did not want to incur the risks of developing certain oil leases, a pro rata distribution of the leases in cancellation of some of its stock was held not a dividend. Commissioner v. Sullivan, 210 F.2d 607 (5th Cir.1954); a dissent stressed the pro rata aspect as being almost conclusive and the lack of a business purpose for the redemption of the stock instead of a mere distribution.

The Internal Revenue Service has carried the principles of the above cases forward in Revenue Rulings issued after the 1954 Code revision. Rev. Rul. 74–296, 1974–1 Cum.Bull. 80, held that there was a genuine corporate contraction where a corporation changed from operating a large department store to a small discount clothing store. But where a corporation distributed only a small parcel of land adjacent to its place of business, which it had acquired in contemplation of expansion and leased out in the interim, there was not a contraction where the rentals represented only 2 percent of the corporation's gross receipts. Rev.Rul. 57–333, 1957–2 Cum.Bull. 239. Similarly, where a corporation in the quarrying business distributed a portion of a condemnation award received with respect to a taking of a portion of its mineral reserves, there was no contraction where the current operations of the corporation were unaffected. Rev.Rul. 67–16, 1967–1 Cum.Bull. 77.

The contraction must be represented by the disposition of all or part of the property used by the corporation in a trade or business. Rev.Rul. 56–512, 1956–2 Cum.Bull. 173 (distribution by corporation engaged in paper business of mineral land leased for royalties did not qualify because the corporation was not engaged in a trade or business with respect to the distributed property); Rev.Rul. 76–526, 1976–2 Cum.Bull. 101 (same as to distribution of parcel of land subject to net lease); Rev.Rul. 56–513, 1956–2 Cum.Bull. 191 (distribution of one-quarter of proceeds of contraction).

In Viereck v. United States, 3 Cl.Ct. 745 (1983), a corporation distributed to its sole shareholder real estate used in its flower business. Although the real estate constituted 80 percent of the net worth of the corporation before the distribution, the court found no partial liquidation because the corporation continued to conduct its flower business on the same scale as it had done previously. See also Rev.Proc. 88–3, 1988–1 Cum.Bull. 579 (I.R.S. will not issue ruling that redemption is a partial liquidation unless corporation reduces net fair market value of assets, gross revenues, and number of employees by 20 percent).

When the contraction of corporate business test is met, the partial liquidation distribution may include the working capital attributable to the discontinued activity. Rev.Rul. 60–232, 1960–2 Cum.Bull. 115. But funds transferred from another business into the terminated business shortly before the distribution may not constitute part of the working capital of the terminated business. Rev.Rul. 76–289, 1976–2 Cum.Bull. 100. Similarly, distribution of cash reserves for future acquisitions of equipment which are no longer needed because of a change of business operations does not qualify as a contraction. Rev.Rul. 78–55, 1978–1 Cum.Bull. 88. In determining the amount of the distribution which will be considered attributable to a contraction, the proceeds from the sale of assets and the working capital must be reduced by corporate liabilities attributable to the discontinued activity (including taxes on the sale of the assets). Rev.Rul. 77–166, 1977–1 Cum. Bull. 90.

Rev.Proc. 81–42, 1981–2 Cum.Bull. 611, provides a checklist of information required by the Internal Revenue Service to obtain an advance ruling as to the qualification of a transaction as a partial liquidation.

D. EFFECT OF OPERATION THROUGH A SUBSIDIARY

If a parent corporation operating a business also owns the stock of a subsidiary operating a five-year active business, a sale of the stock and distribution of the proceeds does not satisfy section 302(e)). Rev.Rul. 79–184, 1979–1 Cum.Bull. 143. Nor would a direct distribution of the stock of the subsidiary qualify under section 302(e), section 355 being the controlling section in these situations. On the other hand, the parent could liquidate the subsidiary, sell its assets, and then make a qualifying distribution of the proceeds under section 302(e). Alternatively, the subsidiary could sell the assets prior to its liquidation with the parent in turn distributing the proceeds under section 302(e). Rev.Rul. 75–223, 1975–1 Cum.Bull. 109; Rev.Rul. 77–376, 1977–2 Cum.Bull. 107.

In Rev.Rul. 77–375, 1977–2 Cum.Bull. 106, a subsidiary was indebted to its parent. The subsidiary sold all its assets for cash, liquidated, and the proceeds were distributed to the shareholders of the parent corporation in redemption of part of their stock. In the liquidation, the debt of the subsidiary to the parent was cancelled. The Ruling held that the assets the parent received in satisfaction of its debt were not received as a liquidation distribution even though no gain or loss was recognized by the subsidiary under the predecessor of section 337(b)(1). As a result, such assets, if distributed by the parent to its shareholders, would not be part of the distribution in partial liquidation of the parent corporation. Rev.Rul. 75–223 was distinguished on the ground that assets of the subsidiary used to satisfy its indebtedness reduced the amount available for distribution in partial liquidation of the parent.

If a parent corporation does not operate any active business itself but is a holding company, the holding of the stock of two operating subsidiaries presumably would not satisfy section 302(e)(2). See Blaschka v. United States, 393 F.2d 983 (Ct.Cl.1968) (management of a subsidiary did not establish a separate viable business for purposes of the two-business rule); Morgenstern v. Commissioner, 56 T.C. 44 (1971) (majority control of a corporation engaged in a business does not qualify the holder as engaged in that business for purposes of the two-active-businesses rule). The parent could, however, liquidate its operating subsidiaries and retain the assets of one while distributing the assets of the other to provide qualification under section 302(e)(2).

E. DISTRIBUTIONS TO CORPORATIONS

A distribution described in section 302(e) does not qualify as a partial liquidation under section 302(b)(4) if received by a corporate shareholder. Thus, unless the redemption also is described in any of sections 302(b)(1) through (3) with respect to the corporate shareholder, the redemption will be treated as a section 301 distribution. In determining whether the distributee is a corporation or an individual, section 302(e)(5) requires that stock owned by a trust or a partnership be treated as owned proportionately by the beneficiaries or partners.

Because a corporate distributee will be entitled to a section 243 dividends received deduction with respect to the distribution, denying partial liquidation treatment is not necessarily disadvantageous. The benefit of the dividends received deduction will be "recaptured," however, when the corporate shareholder later sells the stock with respect to which the partial liquidation distribution was received. Section 1059(e)(1) provides that a partial liquidation distribution is an "extraordinary dividend" regardless of the period for which the stock was held. Thus under section 1059(a), discussed supra, page 509, the corporate shareholder must reduce the basis of the stock by an amount equal to the dividends received deduction claimed with respect to the partial liquidation distribution. As a result, the gain on a taxable disposition will increase or the loss will be reduced. If the basis would have been reduced below zero if the full amount of the dividends received deduction had been subtracted from basis, the excess deduction, which did not reduce basis, is recaptured upon disposition of the stock.

Thus, the section 243 deduction operates only to defer taxes when it is claimed with respect to partial liquidation distributions.

F. OTHER ASPECTS OF PARTIAL LIQUIDATIONS

1. *Effect on Distributing Corporation*

If the corporation distributes appreciated property in a partial liquidation, gain will be recognized under section 311(b). No loss may be recognized on the distribution of depreciated property. Section 311(a). This result is in contrast to the treatment of distributions in complete liquidation, discussed infra, Chapter 14, in which losses are generally allowed by section 336.

Section 312(n)(7) governs the effect on earnings and profits of any redemption subject to section 302(a), including partial liquidations. These rules are discussed, infra, page 590.

2. *Qualification Under Section 302(b)(4) or Sections 302(b)(1)–(3)*

If a distribution fails to qualify as a redemption under section 302(b)(4), it still may qualify under one of sections 302(b)(1) through (3) and vice versa. Whether a distribution qualifies as a redemption in partial liquidation under section 302(b)(4) or under one of the tests in sections 302(b) through (3), the basic result to an individual shareholder is the same—capital gain or loss. Under section 302(b)(4), however, in determining the basis of the stock redeemed, the number of shares deemed surrendered is considered to be the same ratio of total shares as the amount of the distribution bears to the value of all corporate assets prior to the distribution, regardless of actual shares surrendered. Rev.Rul. 56–513, 1956–2 Cum.Bull. 191; Rev.Rul. 77–245, supra. Under sections 302(b)(1) through (3), the actual shares surrendered usually would govern. Also, a section 302(b)(1), (2), or (3) distribution apparently does not fall under section 341, relating to collapsible corporations, discussed infra, page 1079, while a section 302(b)(4) distribution is subject to section 341. Thus, it may be important to determine which subsection of section 302(b) controls. Regulations, section 1.302–1(a), indicate that a distribution which may be treated either as a partial liquidation or as a redemption under section 302(b) other than a partial liquidation should be treated as a partial liquidation. See also Rev.Rul. 82–187, 1982–2 Cum.Bull. 80 (section 346(a)(2), statutory predecessor of sections 302(b)(4) and (e), takes precedence over section 302); Regulations, section 1.346–2. Also, where a distribution may be either a complete termination under section 302(b)(3) only by virtue of the waiver of family attribution or a partial liquidation, section 302(b)(5) provides that the prohibition on acquisition of a prohibited interest within ten years does not apply.

3. *Partial Liquidation Versus Section 304 Transaction*

For the relationship of the partial liquidation rules to section 304, see infra, page 605.

4. *Partial Liquidation Under Section 302(e) Versus Serial Installment in Complete Liquidation*

Distributions which are one of a series leading to complete liquidation are treated as distributions in complete liquidation under section 331, discussed infra, Chapter 14, rather than as distributions in partial liquidation.

Characterization of a distribution in this regard may be important as respects the shareholder for two reasons. First, a loss may be realized and recognized on a distribution in partial liquidation. See Rev.Rul. 56–513, 1956–2 Cum. Bull. 191. But in a complete liquidation, no loss may be claimed until the series of distributions is completed, infra, page 612. Second, corporate distributees never qualify for exchange treatment under section 302(b)(4), but always will be accorded exchange treatment if the distribution is pursuant to a plan of complete liquidation. From the perspective of the distributing corporation the difference is significant because the corporation under section 311 recognizes only gains (with realized losses being disallowed) on the distribution of property in a partial liquidation, but recognizes both gains and losses on the distribution of property in complete liquidation, section 336.

5. *Other Recharacterizations*

Where the shareholder, following the receipt of assets in a partial liquidation, transfers the assets to a new corporation, the liquidation-reincorporation issue, discussed, infra, page 887, may be encountered; see, e.g., Rev.Rul. 76–429, 1976–2 Cum.Bull. 97 (subsidiary sold assets of one of two businesses liquidated and parent placed assets of the other business in a newly created subsidiary; the liquidation and reincorporation were ignored and the transaction was treated as a partial liquidation).

G. REFERENCES

Henderson, Redemptions and Partial Liquidations After TEFRA, 42 N.Y.U.Fed.Tax.Inst. 11 (1984); deKosmian, Partial Liquidations, Section 311(d) Redemptions and Section 304 Under TEFRA, 61 Taxes 918 (1983); Rose, Representations Required by IRS for Rulings on a Partial Liquidation of a Subsidiary's Business Go Further Than Necessary, 9 J. Corp. Tax'n 151 (1982); Burke and Parker, Partial Liquidations Under Section 346: Planning, Problems and Procedures, 24 Baylor L.Rev. 1 (1972); Chommie, Section 346(a)(2): The Contraction Theory, 11 Tax L.Rev. 407 (1956).

SECTION 7. OTHER ASPECTS OF REDEMPTIONS

ILLUSTRATIVE MATERIAL

A. EARNINGS AND PROFITS

1. *Reduction of Earnings and Profits*

The impact of a redemption distribution on earnings and profits is important, since any reduction in earnings and profits caused by the distribution will reduce the potential "pool" of earnings and profits available to make subsequent distributions taxable as dividends under sections 301 and 316. If a redemption fails to qualify under section 302(a) and is treated as a section 301 distribution, earnings and profits generally would be reduced under the rules of section 312(a) by the amount of the distribution. However, if the redemption qualifies for exchange treatment under section 302(a) or section 303, section 312(n)(7) provides that the portion of the distribution chargeable to earnings and profits shall not exceed the ratable share of the earnings and profits attributable to the redeemed stock.

Prior to the 1984 Act, former section 312(e) provided for the reduction of earnings and profits by the amount not properly chargeable to the "capital account," a term not defined in the Code or Regulations. Helvering v. Jarvis, 123 F.2d 742 (4th Cir.1941), held that a redemption distribution was chargeable to the capital account to the extent of the redeemed shares' pro rata portion of total par value plus paid-in surplus, and that the remainder of the distribution reduced the corporation's earnings and profits. Under this rule, the corporation's earnings and profits could be reduced by an amount substantially in excess of the pro rata share of earnings and profits allocable to the redeemed stock. Section 312(n)(7) prevents this result.

The legislative history of section 312(n)(7) provides some guidelines for dealing with situations where the statute is unclear. First, no amount of earnings and profits generally should be attributable to nonconvertible preferred stock, unless the distribution includes dividend arrearages. H.Rep. No. 98–861, 98th Cong., 2d Sess. 840 (1984). Presumably, however, the amount of any redemption premium also should reduce earnings and profits. Second, the Senate Committee Report indicates that earnings and profits are not to be reduced by more than the amount distributed. S.Rep. No. 98–169, 98th Cong., 2d Sess. 202 (1984). Thus, for example, if a corporation with $100,000 of accumulated earnings and profits redeemed 10 percent of its stock for $9,500, the *maximum* charge to earnings and profits is $9,500. And unless there is no paid-in capital attributable to the redeemed stock, the actual charge will be less. However, if the stock were redeemed in exchange for property having a basis of $12,000 and a fair market value of $9,500, section 312(a)(3) appears to permit earnings and profits to be reduced by $12,000.

In regard to another problem in this area, Baker v. United States, 460 F.2d 827 (8th Cir.1972), held that where current earnings and profits were not sufficient to cover both ordinary dividend distributions and redemptions made in the same year, the ordinary dividend distributions were to be treated as the first distributions out of earnings and profits. One opinion based this result on the legislative history of section 312; a second opinion reached the same conclusion on the ground that section 316(a) does not apply to redemption distributions which qualify under section 302; a lengthy dissent would have treated the ordinary dividends and the redemption distributions on a pro rata basis as far as earnings and profits were concerned. See Rev. Rul. 74–339, 1974–2 Cum.Bull. 103, following *Baker.*

2. *Insufficient Earnings and Profits*

Suppose a distribution in redemption of stock is made under circumstances which would make it essentially equivalent to a dividend, but there are no current or accumulated earnings and profits. Regulations, section 1.302–2(a), state that, despite the verbal difficulty of calling the distribution "essentially equivalent to a dividend," it should nevertheless be placed under sections 302(d) and 301(c) rather than section 302(a). The distribution would thus be applied against the basis of *all* of the distributee's stock, rather than only the redeemed stock, and taxable gain results only if his entire basis is exceeded.

B. REDEMPTION WITH PROPERTY

A distribution of appreciated property by a corporation to a shareholder results in taxable gain at the corporate level, whether or not the distribution is treated as a redemption or as a distribution to which section 301 applies.

Section 311(b), discussed supra, page 477. If stock is redeemed in exchange for depreciated property, however, section 311(a) disallows any loss.

C. REDEMPTION OF SECURITIES OTHER THAN STOCK

Section 301(a) refers to a distribution to a shareholder with "respect to its stock." Regulations, section 1.301–1(c), state that section 302 is not applicable unless the distribution is to the shareholder in his capacity as a shareholder. Hence the redemption of a debt instrument from a stockholder is not governed by either sections 301 or 302, but instead falls under the general rules governing the disposition of debt instruments. As a consequence, the rules, supra, page 384, relating to the classification of corporate obligations as stock or debt are important here. Could the taxpayer in *Davis,* supra, page 564, have avoided the dividend result if, instead of receiving the preferred stock, he had made a subordinated loan to the corporation of $25,000?

D. SECTION 305 ASPECTS OF STOCK REDEMPTIONS

A stock redemption can bring section 305 into play since it involves an increase in the proportionate interest in the corporation for those shareholders whose stock is not redeemed. See supra, page 535.

Section 305 can also be relevant where the redemption provisions are being used to effect a sale of the corporate business, see infra, page 725.

E. "GREENMAIL"

Due to Congressional concern that corporations might deduct expenses incurred to redeem stock in order to fight hostile takeover attempts, the 1986 Act added section 162(k), denying any deduction for all expenses incurred with respect to any redemption, not only the amount distributed to the shareholder. This provision applies to all redemptions, not only those which are made in the course of fighting a hostile takeover. See S.Rep. No. 99–426, 99th Cong., 2d Sess. 248–49 (1987); H.Rep. No. 99–841, 99th Cong., 2d Sess. II–168–69 (1987).

SECTION 8. REDEMPTIONS THROUGH THE USE OF RELATED CORPORATIONS

INTERNAL REVENUE CODE: Section 304 (omitting sections 304(b)(3)(C) and (D)).

REGULATIONS: Section 1.304–2.

FEHRS FINANCE CO. v. COMMISSIONER

United States Tax Court, 1972.
58 T.C. 174.

SIMPSON, JUDGE. [Mr. and Mrs. Fehrs owned all of the stock of Fehrs Rental Corporation (Rental). In December, 1964, Mr. Fehrs made gifts of the Rental stock to members of his family and after the gifts Mr. Fehrs owned 982 shares, Mrs. Fehrs 177 shares and 221 shares were owned by his son-in-law, his daughters and his grandchildren. Approximately two months later, Fehrs Finance Company (Finance) was incorporated with two of the Fehrs daughters as its sole shareholders. Immediately thereafter Mr. and Mrs. Fehrs transferred all of the remaining Rental stock which they held to Finance in return for Finance's promise to pay them annuities totaling $70,000 per year for the rest of their lives. Finance immediately resold the Rental stock to Rental in exchange for $100,000 cash and an unsecured promissory note of $625,000. The Commissioner asserted a deficiency against Finance based on the gain it allegedly recognized on the disposition of the Rental stock.]

The issue ultimately to be decided in this case appears to be simple: Did the petitioner realize a capital gain on the sale of the Rental stock in 1965? However, to reach that ultimate issue, we must work our way through an amazing maze of preliminary issues. At no time has the respondent taken the position that Rental's acquisition of its stock constituted a redemption under section 302 and that the payments received by the petitioner should be treated as dividends; at all times, he has treated such payments as a capital gain. The controversy revolves about the petitioner's basis in the stock. The respondent contends that section 304 is applicable to the petitioner's acquisition of stock from Mr. and Mrs. Fehrs and that its basis in such stock is therefore determined under sections 304 and 362(a). He concedes that if section 304 is applicable to the petitioner's acquisition of such stock, the gain which it realized on the transfer of such stock to Rental is taxable as a long-term capital gain. Thus, the initial issue for us to consider is whether section 304 is applicable to the petitioner's acquisition of the stock.

Section 304(a)(1) provides in relevant part that, if one or more persons are in "control" of each of two corporations, and if one of those corporations acquires stock in the other corporation from the person or persons in control, then the transaction shall be treated as a redemption under section 302. The stock shall be treated by the acquiring corporation as having been received as a contribution to its capital. The term "control" is defined in section 304(c)(1) as "the ownership of stock possessing at least 50 percent of the total combined voting power of all classes of stock entitled to vote, or at least 50 percent of the total value of shares of all classes of stock." Furthermore, section 304(c)(2) states that the rules contained in section 318(a) with respect to the constructive ownership of stock shall apply for the purpose of determining "control," except that the 50–percent limitations of sections 318(a)(2)(C) and 318(a)(3)(C) shall be disregarded for such purpose. Section 318(a) provides that an individual shall be considered as actually owning the stock which is owned by his spouse, his children, and his grandchildren.

Section 304(a)(1) applies to what is commonly referred to as a "redemption by related or brother-sister corporations." It is clear that by its terms, such section applies to the factual situation in this case. Immediately prior to the transactions here in issue, Mr. and Mrs. Fehrs actually owned 1,159 of the 1,380 outstanding shares of Rental and their daughters and grandchildren owned 196 shares; thus, a total of

1,355 shares, or 98.2 percent of the outstanding stock, was actually or constructively owned by either Mr. Fehrs or Mrs. Fehrs. Only the 25 shares owned by Mr. Vlcek were not attributed to either of the Fehrses under section 318(a). All of the outstanding shares of the petitioner were owned by the daughters of the Fehrses, and were, therefore, similarly attributable to Mr. Fehrs or Mrs. Fehrs. Thus, either Mr. Fehrs or Mrs. Fehrs, or both, were regarded as the person or persons in control of both the petitioner and Rental prior to the transactions in issue. The transaction in which the petitioner acquired stock in Rental from Mr. and Mrs. Fehrs in return for the annuities must be treated as a redemption, and the stock of Rental so acquired must be treated as having been transferred by Mr. and Mrs. Fehrs to the petitioner as a contribution to its capital, under the express mandate of section 304(a)(1). See Rose Ann Coates Trust, 55 T.C. 501 (1970), on appeal (C.A.9, June 17, 1971); Ray A. Maher, 55 T.C. 441 (1970), on appeal (C.A.8, Oct. 12, 1971); Ralph L. Humphrey, 39 T.C. 199 (1962). * * *

[W]e now reach the question as to what was the petitioner's basis for the Rental stock under section 304. The petitioner must treat the stock as if it received the stock from the Fehrses as a contribution to its capital; therefore, the petitioner's basis equals the basis of the transferred stock in the hands of Mr. and Mrs. Fehrs plus the amount of gain, if any, which was recognized by Mr. and Mrs. Fehrs upon the transfer. Secs. 304(a)(1)(B) and 362(a)(2); sec. 1.304–2(a), Income Tax Regs. It has been stipulated that the basis of the transferred stock in the hands of the Fehrses was zero, so the only remaining question in computing the petitioner's basis in such stock is with respect to the amount of the gain, if any, which Mr. and Mrs. Fehrs recognized upon the transfer. According to the income tax regulations, there is no step-up in the petitioner's basis if the redemption is treated as essentially equivalent to a dividend under section 302 and if the payments to Mr. and Mrs. Fehrs are taxable as a dividend under sections 302(d) and 301, but if the redemption qualifies as an exchange under section 302(b), the petitioner's basis is increased by the gain recognized by Mr. and Mrs. Fehrs. Sec. 1.304–2(c), examples (1) and (3), Income Tax Regs. The validity of such rules has not been challenged. Thus, to determine whether there is any step-up in the petitioner's basis in the stock, it becomes necessary to determine first whether the redemption is essentially equivalent to a dividend under section 302 or whether it qualifies as an exchange under such section.

Section 302 sets forth in subsection (b) the conditions under which a redemption of stock shall be treated as an exchange, and provides in subsection (d) that if those conditions are not met, then the distribution is one to which section 301 applies. If the redemption meets any one of the four tests set forth in section 302(b), it is treated as an exchange, and the amount of the distribution is treated as payment for the stock. Neither party argues the applicability of section 302(b)(2) or 302(b)(4) in this case, but the petitioner argues that the redemption should be treated as an exchange because it meets the test of either section 302(b)(1) or 302(b)(3). We shall consider each such test.

Section 302(b)(1) states, in effect, that the redemption shall be treated as an exchange if it "is not essentially equivalent to a dividend." To meet this test, a redemption must result in a meaningful reduction of the shareholder's proportionate interest in the corporation, after applying the attribution rules of section 318(a) to the stock ownership interests as they existed both before and after the redemption. Secs. 1.302–1(a), 1.302–2(b), Income Tax Regs.; United States v. Davis, 397 U.S. 301, 90 S.Ct. 1041 (1970). * * *

After applying the attribution rules, Mr. and Mrs. Fehrs are considered as owning 98.2 percent of the outstanding shares of Rental—1,355 out of 1,380—both immediately before and immediately after the redemption by the petitioner. We discussed previously the method of computing the preredemption figure; the postredemption figure is reached by attributing to the Fehrses the shares owned by the petitioner as well as those owned by their descendants. The latter result obtains from attributing the petitioner's 1,159 shares to Mmes. Vlcek and May by virtue of section 318(a)(2)(C), the 50–percent requirement of which is not applicable here by reason of section 304(b)(1), and then attributing those shares in turn to the Fehrses under section 318(a)(1)(A)(ii).

The respondent contends that the correct comparison of the Fehrses' stock ownership before and after the redemption is to measure the percentage of the shares owned by them *immediately* before and *immediately* after the redemption; if such contention is accurate, it is clear that the Fehrses' stock ownership (as viewed through the prism of the attribution rules) was not changed at all by the redemption, and thus the redemption clearly fails to meet the test of section 302(b)(1) as articulated by the Supreme Court in United States v. Davis, supra, and as followed by this Court in the decisions previously cited.

On the other hand, the petitioner contends that the Fehrses' postredemption stock ownership should be measured as of the end of the series of transactions—that is, after the transfer of the stock by the petitioner to Rental, and after the cancellation of such stock by Rental. * * * However, even when measured in this way, the Fehrses are still considered to own 196 out of the 221 outstanding shares of Rental, or 88.69 percent of the total.

We need not pass upon the question of at which point in time the Fehrses' postredemption stock ownership should be measured, because we think that even if we adopt the view urged by the petitioner, and assume for the sake of argument that the redemption reduced the Fehrses' ownership interest from 98.2 percent to 88.69 percent, there still has not been "a *meaningful* reduction of the shareholder's proportionate interest in the corporation," as required by United States v. Davis, supra at 313. (Emphasis added.) A reduction in stock ownership from 98.2 to 88.69 percent does not deprive such a dominant shareholder of his ability to control the corporate activities; such a reduction does not affect the shareholder's relationship to the corporation in any significant way. * * * Moreover, the reduction that did occur resulted from a transfer of stock to the son-in-law of Mr. and Mrs. Fehrs, hardly a stranger to the family, and such transfer of ownership occurred because Mr. Fehrs made a gift of the stock to his son-in-law. * * *

The petitioner also argues that the attribution rules should be considered only for the purpose of "determining the ownership of stock," as prescribed by section 302(c)(1), but not for the purpose of determining control as part of a dividend equivalency test under section 302(b)(1); thus, the petitioner argues, we should take cognizance of the alleged fact that the redemption "eliminated the actual control of Edward J. Fehrs over the affairs of Fehrs Rental Co." However, in section 304, Congress expressly indicated that the attribution rules are to be applied in determining control. Section 304(a)(1) applies when one or more persons "control" each of two corporations; section 304(c)(1) defines control by stating that "control means the ownership" of stock possessing a specified percentage of voting rights or value; and section 304(c)(2) expressly provides, with one exception not here relevant, "Section 318(a) (relating to the constructive ownership of stock) shall apply for purposes of determining control under paragraph (1) [of section 304(c)]." The application of the attribution rules of section 318 to a redemption under section 304(a) can operate in such a way as to cause a person who actually owns no shares in a corporation to be treated as having 100–percent *control* of it. Coyle v. United States, 415 F.2d 488, 490 (C.A.4, 1968), reversing 268 F.Supp. 233 (S.D.W.Va.1967). In *Coyle,* there is no indication that the taxpayer exercised actual control over the affairs of such corporation; the Fourth Circuit regarded the attribution rules alone as sufficient to impute complete control to him. This Court, too, has applied the attribution rules to determine who controlled a corporation involved in a redemption under section 304. Ralph L. Humphrey, supra at 205.

* * * We hold that the redemption cannot be treated as an exchange under section 302(b)(1).

The next question is whether section 302(b)(3) is applicable. Such section provides that the redemption is to be treated as an exchange "if the redemption is in complete redemption of all of the stock of the corporation owned by the shareholder." However, under section 302(c)(1), the attribution rules of section 318 are applicable in determining whether a redemption has resulted in the complete termination of a shareholder's interest under section 302(b)(3), but section 302(c)(2) sets forth certain conditions under which the attribution rules are not applicable for such purposes. Obviously, Mr. and Mrs. Fehrs did actually transfer all of their stock in Rental, but whether the redemption can qualify under section 302(b)(3) depends upon whether the conditions of section 302(c)(2) have been met so that the attribution rules are not applicable.

[The court then held that section 302(b)(3) did not apply because the Fehrs had failed to file the agreements required by section 302(c)(2), discussed supra, page 561.]

For the foregoing reasons, the redemption in which the petitioner acquired the Rental stock from Mr. and Mrs. Fehrs does not qualify for treatment as an exchange under any of the provisions of section 302(b), and therefore, under section 302(d), the redemption shall be treated as a distribution of property governed by section 301.

Section 301(c)(1) provides in effect that, to the extent that it is made out of the corporation's earnings and profits, the distribution is treated as a dividend and is taxed as ordinary income to the recipient. Section 301(c)(2) goes on to provide that, to the extent that the distribution is not a dividend, it is first applied against the recipient's adjusted basis in the stock, and then, according to section 301(c)(3), the amount which exceeds such adjusted basis is treated as gain from the sale or exchange of property. The petitioner argues that, because it had no earnings and profits during its 1965 taxable year, the tax consequences to Mr. and Mrs. Fehrs of the annuity payments are governed by section 301(c)(2) and (3) and that the petitioner's basis in the stock acquired in the redemption should include, for purposes of computing its gain on the sale of the stock in 1965, the gains to be recognized in subsequent years by Mr. and Mrs. Fehrs as a result of the receipt of the annuity payments.

Initially, the respondent contends that there should be no increase in the petitioner's basis by reason of any gain recognized by the Fehrses under section 301. The respondent argues that section 362(a) provides for an increase in basis by reason of a gain recognized on the transfer and that such language does not apply to gains recognized under section 301(c)(3). There is nothing in the statute or the legislative history to support such contention. The words of section 362(a) are clearly broad enough to apply to a gain recognized under section 301(c)(3), and accordingly, we reject such contention of the respondent.

The petitioner's argument that the annuity payments to Mr. and Mrs. Fehrs will be taxable, after recovery of basis, as a gain under section 301(c)(3) rests on the propositions that it had no earnings and profits in its 1965 taxable year and that the tax treatment of the payments that Mr. and Mrs. Fehrs will receive in later years is determined by its earnings and profits, or lack thereof, in 1965. The petitioner showed no earnings and profits in its books and records for 1965, but the respondent contends that its computations were incorrect for the reason that it recognized a gain on the sale of the Rental stock in that year and that such gain was erroneously omitted from its computation of earnings and profits. However, we would be required to determine the amount of the petitioner's earnings and profits in 1965 only if we conclude that the amount of, or the lack of, such earnings and profits governs the tax treatment of the property distributed to Mr. and Mrs. Fehrs. Thus, we must first decide what constituted the property distributed to the Fehrses, when the distribution or distributions occurred, and for what year or years the earnings and profits of the petitioner are determinative of the tax treatment of such property.

The petitioner argues that the making of the annuity contracts in 1965 constituted distributions of property under section 301, but we do not agree. The annuity agreements were simply promises to make payments to the Fehrses at a later time, contingent, of course, upon their surviving. The agreements provided unequivocally that they, and the payments to be made under them, could not be negotiated, assigned, or anticipated by the Fehrses, and that if the Fehrses did purport to make any such negotiation, assignment, or anticipation, the petitioner would be in no way obliged to recognize or give effect to it. Moreover, the petitioner, which was the obligor under the annuity agreements, was a new corporation with no substantial assets and no history indicating its financial reliability; the Fehrses' right to receive payments was no better secured than if the obligor were a private individual. Whatever the Fehrses may have considered the agreements to be worth to them, the agreements were in no way the equivalent of cash. Unlike the recipient of an ordinary promise to make a payment at a certain time in the future, the Fehrses did not receive anything in 1965 which they could have disposed of even at a substantial discount.

Leaving aside the question of the petitioner's ability to make the payments as they come due, it is true that a so-called actuarial value could be computed for the annuity agreements, but such value could not be realized by the Fehrses in 1965. No amount was recognizable by them in that year as a result of the receipt of the annuity agreements. * * * The annuity agreements are similar in certain significant respects to the contract involved in Allan S. Vinnell, 52 T.C. 934 (1969), in which we held that the making of the contract did not constitute a distribution of property because of its contingent nature, so that the payment of each sum due under the contract constituted a separate distribution. In *Vinnell,* the shareholder's rights to the payments were subject to certain business contingencies, and his rights were expressly subordinated to the claims of a bank with which the corporation dealt. The occurrence of one of the contingencies would have resulted in the deferral or postponement or subordination of the payments, but in the present case, the occurrence of one certain contingency—the death of Mr. or Mrs. Fehrs—would terminate the obligation completely. Moreover, the corporate obligor in *Vinnell* had proven its viability as a business entity over a 14–year period, whereas the fledgling nature of the present petitioner created an additional contingency to undermine the certainty of the Fehrses' receiving the payments in the future. In Thomas Kerr, 38 T.C. 723 (1962), affd. 326 F.2d 225 (C.A.9, 1964), certiorari denied 377 U.S. 963, 84 S.Ct. 1644 (1964); and Rose Ann Coates Trust, 55 T.C. 501 (1970), on appeal (C.A.9, June 17, 1971), we held that the distribution of a corporate obligation constituted a distribution of property; but in those cases, the obligations were to pay fixed amounts over fixed periods of time, and those obligations had ascertainable fair market values. Thus, in this case, we reach the conclusion that no property distribution within the meaning of sections 301 and 317 was made in 1965. * * *

Since no annuity payments were made to Mr. and Mrs. Fehrs in 1965, and since we have concluded that the making of the annuity contracts did not constitute a distribution of property to them in that year, no amount of gain was recognized by them in 1965 as a result of the transfer of their stock to the petitioner. The petitioner argues that its basis should include the amount of gains to be recognized by Mr. and Mrs. Fehrs in subsequent years. Although there may be circumstances in which the acquiring corporation's basis in property should take into consideration the gains to be recognized by the transferors in later years—a question which we need not and do not decide—it seems clear that such a prediction of future gains could be appropriate only when there is a reasonably reliable method for ascertaining the amount of such gains. Here, it is utterly impossible to anticipate the amount of gains to be recognized in the future. By use of actuarial tables, the amounts of the annuity payments that Mr. and Mrs. Fehrs will receive, if they live out their life expectancies, can be estimated, but it is impossible to forecast whether such payments will be treated as dividends under section 301(c)(1) or as gains under section 301(c)(3). According to its books and records, the petitioner showed substantial deficits for the years 1966, 1967, and 1968, but the respondent has raised several serious objections to the petitioner's method of computing its earnings and profits for those years. Irrespective of who is right as to those years, there is no certainty that the petitioner will operate at a loss in subsequent years during the lifetimes of Mr. and Mrs. Fehrs. In any year in which it earns profits, the payments to Mr. and Mrs. Fehrs would probably be considered as dividends under section 301(c)(1). In view of this uncertainty, there is no satisfactory method of anticipating the amounts that will be recognized as gains under section 301(c)(3) by Mr. and Mrs. Fehrs. Thus, we conclude that the petitioner's basis in 1965 must be limited to any gain recognized by the transferors in that year; that is, zero. It will be necessary to postpone to 1966 and subsequent years any adjustment in the petitioner's basis in the Rental stock to reflect any gains recognized under section 301(c)(3) by Mr. and Mrs. Fehrs. Accordingly, we hold that in 1965, the petitioner's basis for the purpose of computing its gain on the sale of the Rental stock must be zero, and it must recognize as a gain the entire payment which it received in that year. * * *

Decision will be entered under Rule [155].*

Reviewed by the Court. [Five judges concurred.]

* [Ed.: The decision of the Tax Court was affirmed in an opinion that essentially followed the reasoning of the Tax Court, 487 F.2d 184 (8th Cir.1973).].

ILLUSTRATIVE MATERIAL

A. GENERAL

Section 304 is designed to prevent a shareholder from escaping dividend treatment in a transaction involving the sale of shares in one controlled corporation to another controlled corporation. Though such a transaction formally is structured as a sale, it obviously has similarities to a redemption since it involves a distribution of cash by a corporation to the shareholder in a situation in which, because of the controlled nature of the corporations involved, there may be no real economic change in the shareholder's overall position. Section 304 requires that the sales proceeds received in such a transaction be treated as a corporate distribution which, to qualify for sale or exchange treatment, must meet the tests of sections 302 or 303.[3] Section 304 deals with two basic factual patterns, sales between brother-sister corporations and sales involving parent-subsidiary corporations.

B. BROTHER–SISTER TRANSACTIONS

1. *General*

Suppose that the shareholder owns all the stock of X Corporation and all of the stock of Y Corporation. If Y Corporation buys some of the X Corporation stock, section 304 restructures the transaction as a redemption of the Y Corporation stock. Dividend equivalence under section 302, however, is tested in terms of the shareholder's change in ownership in the corporation whose stock is sold, i.e., X Corporation. The amount actually taxed as a dividend is a function of the earnings and profits of *both* corporations, although section 304(b)(2) specifies that the earnings and profits of the purchasing corporation, i.e., Y Corporation are attributed to the distribution before the earnings and profits of the corporation whose stock is sold. The X Corporation stock which was actually transferred to Y Corporation is treated as a contribution to capital.

2. *"Control"*

Section 304(a)(1) applies to sales of stock in the brother-sister context only where "one or more persons are in control" of each corporation. "Control" for this purpose is defined in section 304(c)(1) as ownership of 50 percent or more of either combined voting power or value of all classes of stock. See Rev.Rul. 89–57, 1989–1 Cum.Bull. 90 (an individual who owned less than 50 percent of the voting stock, but more than 50 percent of the total value of the outstanding stock of a corporation, controlled the corporation).

Related sales transactions involving a number of shareholders can be subject to section 304 using a control group concept. See Regulations, section 1.304–2(b). In Bhada v. Commissioner, 89 T.C. 959 (1987), aff'd sub nom Caamano v. Commissioner, 879 F.2d 156 (5th Cir.1989), an exchange of shares of a publicly traded corporation was, in part, subject to section 304. In determining whether the 50 percent threshold has been met, the attribution rules of Section 318 apply, with certain modifications. Thus, as was the case in *Fehrs Finance Co.,* if A owns all of the stock of X

3. For qualification for sale or exchange treatment under section 303 of a sale of stock subject to section 304, see Webb v. Commissioner, 67 T.C. 293 (1976), aff'd per curiam, 572 F.2d 135 (5th Cir.1978). Section 303 is discussed supra, page 575.

Corporation, and A sells that stock to Y corporation, all of the stock of which is owned by A's child B, section 304 applies to the transaction. However, where the selling shareholder's entire *actual* interest in the corporation has been terminated, waiver of family attribution under section 304(c) may be available to avoid dividend treatment. In Fehrs v. United States, 556 F.2d 1019 (Ct.Cl.1977), the individual shareholders in *Fehrs Finance Co.,* who were not parties to the Tax Court litigation and thus not collaterally estopped, argued in the Court of Claims that the section 302(c)(2) agreement was timely filed, thus qualifying the section 304(a)(1) constructive redemption for capital gain treatment under section 302(b)(3). The Court of Claims, refusing to follow the case involving the corporate taxpayer, found the filing of the agreements in "substantial compliance" with section 302(c)(2). It left open, however, the question whether a tax avoidance motive was present in the gifts of the stock by Fehrs to his family members which, if so, would prevent qualification under section 302(b)(3).

In Niedermeyer v. Commissioner, 62 T.C. 280 (1974), aff'd per curiam 535 F.2d 500 (9th Cir.1976), the taxpayers sold all of their common stock in a corporation controlled by two of their sons to another corporation, in which they actually owned no stock, controlled by three other sons. Although the selling shareholders filed a section 302(c) waiver agreement, the court held it invalid because they retained some preferred stock in the first corporation. In requiring dividend treatment, the Tax Court rejected the taxpayer's argument that due to hostility between the brothers controlling the two different corporations the attribution rules should not have been applied to determine control.

Suppose that A owned 50 percent of the stock of X Corporation and A's child B owned the other 50 percent and all of A's stock in X Corporation was redeemed in a transaction which qualified under section 302(b)(3) by virtue of a waiver of family attribution under section 302(c)(3). Subsequently, A sold all of the stock of Y Corporation to X Corporation. Rev.Rul. 88–55, 1988–2 Cum.Bull. 45, held that the prior waiver of attribution for purposes of section 302(b)(3) did not affect application of the attribution rules in determining ownership of the Y stock held by X Corporation when applying section 304 to the sale of stock by A. Thus, since A continued to own by attribution 100 percent of Y Corporation after the sale, the transaction was treated as a redemption by X Corporation which was substantially equivalent to a dividend. The Ruling also held, however, that treatment of A as receiving a distribution with respect to X Corporation stock was not a prohibited interest in X Corporation in violation of the waiver of family attribution rules.

3. *Basis Issues*

(a) *Shareholder's Basis*

When a sale is treated as a section 301 distribution by virtue of section 304(a)(1), the stock sold to the acquiring corporation is treated as a contribution to capital. Thus, the basis of the stock which was sold is added to the basis of the shareholder's stock in the purchasing corporation. Regulations, section 1.304–2(a). What happens if the selling shareholder does not actually own any stock of the purchasing corporation after the transaction, but due to attribution rules constructively controls the purchasing corporation, for example, because the selling shareholder's child controls the purchasing corporation? Rev.Rul. 71–563, 1971–2 Cum.Bull. 175 holds that the basis of the sold stock should be added to the selling shareholder's basis for any remaining stock of the issuer.

What is the effect on basis if, as in *Fehrs Finance Co.,* the selling shareholder actually owns no stock of the issuer after the transaction? Coyle v. United States, 415 F.2d 488 (4th Cir.1968), suggests that in such a case the basis of the selling shareholder's stock could be added to the basis of the stock in the purchasing corporation held by the related person actually owning stock of the purchasing corporation. But Rev.Rul. 70–496, 1970–2 Cum.Bull. 74, holds that the basis of the stock simply disappears. In that Ruling, Y Corporation sold its wholly owned subsidiary, S Corporation, to Z Corporation. Both Y Corporation and Z Corporation were controlled by X Corporation. Due to the section 318 attribution rules, Y Corporation continued to own 100 percent of S Corporation after the sale and section 304(a)(1) recharacterized the transaction as a dividend. Because Y Corporation had no actual interest in Z Corporation, it had no basis to adjust, and X Corporation was denied a basis adjustment with respect to either Y Corporation or Z Corporation.

Although section 304(b)(1) directs that the determination of whether the transaction is entitled to redemption treatment is made with respect to the stock of the issuing corporation, i.e., the corporation the stock of which was sold, the treatment of the transaction by section 304(a)(1) as a redemption by the *purchasing* corporation is not unimportant. If the combined earnings and profits of the issuing and the purchasing corporations are not sufficient to support dividend treatment of the entire distribution, the excess distribution is applied against the basis of the purchasing corporation and, when that basis has been reduced to zero, the balance is taxable gain. The basis of the selling shareholder in any remaining shares of the issuer may not be applied against the distribution to avoid gain recognition.

(b) *Purchasing Corporation's Basis in Stock*

The Tax Court's holding in *Fehrs Finance Co.* that the annuity contracts transferred in the constructive redemption did not constitute a distribution of property for purposes of section 301 avoided some difficult problems with respect to the calculation of the earnings and profits of Fehrs Finance Co., which in turn would have affected both the treatment of the distributions in the hands of the selling shareholders and Fehrs Finance Co.'s basis in the stock of Fehrs Realty Corporation as well. If the annuity contracts had been considered as a distribution under section 301 (or if cash had been distributed) the question whether the distribution should be treated as a dividend or as a capital gain transaction under section 301(c)(3)(A) would have depended on the presence or absence of earnings and profits in Fehrs Finance Co. Fehrs Finance Co. had no earnings and profits except those generated by the disposition of the Rental stock. That amount, however, was determined in part by Fehrs Finance Co.'s basis in the Rental stock which, under section 362(a)(2), would be increased to the extent that the Fehrs recognized capital gain on the distribution, thus completing the circle. In effect, the amount of gain is a function of the earnings and profits and the earnings and profits are simultaneously a function of the amount of gain.

Note the importance of timing here. If Fehrs Finance had distributed cash or property prior to its disposition of the Rental stock, the distributions would have generated capital gain to the Fehrs which would have increased

Fehrs Finance's basis in the Rental stock and reduced or eliminated gain on its subsequent disposition.

4. *Effect of Sale of Stock for Promissory Notes*

Fehrs Finance Co. concluded that no gain was recognized under section 301(c)(3) in the year the annuity contracts were received because they could not be valued. Suppose that A controls both X Corporation and Y Corporation and sells all of the stock of X Corporation to Y Corporation for a $100,000 promissory note, bearing adequate interest, due in ten years. Suppose further, that the corporations' combined earnings and profits are only $20,000 and A's basis in the Y Corporation stock is zero. May A report the $80,000 section 301(c)(3) gain using the installment method under section 453? Cox v. Commissioner, 78 T.C. 1021 (1982), held that section 453 installment reporting of gains is not available for section 301(c)(3) gain because no "sale" occurs as a result of the distribution.

See also Schaefers v. Commissioner, 49 T.C.M. 228 (1984) (forgiveness of shareholder's debt to acquiring corporation is distribution in year stock transferred).

5. *Interaction With Section 351*

Suppose that A owns more than 50 percent of the stock of X Corporation and transfers the stock to Y Corporation, in which A owns 80 percent of the stock, in exchange for additional stock and cash. The transaction would fall within the literal language of section 351 and, on this approach, the cash received would be boot entitled to capital gain treatment. On the other hand, if section 304, which by its terms also applies, is controlling, the cash distribution would be subject to section 301 unless it met one of the tests of section 302(b). Commissioner v. Stickney, 399 F.2d 828 (6th Cir.1968), held that in situations of overlap between section 351 and section 304, section 351 controlled. Coates Trust v. Commissioner, 480 F.2d 468 (9th Cir.1973), reached the opposite conclusion.

The 1982 Act resolved the conflict between sections 351 and 304 by providing in section 304(b)(3) that section 304 controls in cases of overlap. Generally, if a shareholder transfers stock in a controlled corporation subject to liability to a second controlled corporation, section 357 is not applicable to allow the assumption of the liability by the transferee corporation without adverse tax consequences. See Rev.Rul. 78–422, 1978–2 Cum.Bull. 129. However, section 304(b)(3)(B) provides an exception for certain debt incurred to acquire the stock of a corporation which is assumed by a controlled corporation acquiring the stock; assumption of such debt is an alternative to a debt-financed direct acquisition by the acquiring company. In applying these rules, indebtedness includes debt to which the stock is subject as well as debt assumed by the acquiring company. Citizens Bank & Trust Co. v. United States, 580 F.2d 442 (Cl.Ct.1978), reached the same result as is provided in section 304(b)(3)(B) for a tax year before the enactment of that provision.

C. PARENT–SUBSIDIARY SITUATIONS

1. *General*

The second situation with which section 304 is concerned involves the purchase by a subsidiary of its parent's stock from the shareholders of its parent corporation (subsidiary being defined in terms of 50 percent or greater stock ownership). Under section 304(a)(2) the shareholders are treated as if the parent redeemed its stock from them. In testing for dividend equivalence under section 302, stock of the parent owned by the subsidiary after the transaction is attributed under section 318(a)(2)(C) first to the parent corporation and then, in turn, to the shareholder. Assume, for example, that A owns 80 percent (80 out of 100 shares) of the stock of X Corporation, which in turn owns 70 percent (70 out of 100 shares) of Y Corporation. If A sells 40 shares of X Corporation stock to Y Corporation, A now actually owns only 40 of 100 shares, or 40 percent. But 70 percent of the 40 shares of X Corporation owned by Y (28 shares) are attributed to X Corporation under section 318(a)(3)(A) and 40 percent of the 28 X Corporation shares thus constructively owned by X are attributed to A, with the result that A constructively owns 11.2 shares of X Corporation. A's total ownership of X has therefor been reduced only from 80 percent to 51.2 percent, and dividend treatment is likely. Because section 304(b)(2) permits the earnings and profits of both the issuer and the acquiring corporation to support dividend treatment, a dividend may result even though the parent corporation has no earnings and profits.

2. *Parent–Subsidiary Relationships and the Attribution Rules*

The attribution rules raise special problems under section 304(a) since two corporations which, absent these rules, are in a brother-sister relationship can be viewed by virtue of the attribution rules as being in a parent-subsidiary relationship. Similarly, in the converse situation a real parent-subsidiary relationship can constructively become a brother-sister arrangement. Regulations, section 1.304–2(c), without discussion, appear to take the position that "real" brother-sister corporations will not be characterized as parent-subsidiary for purposes of section 304. Broadview Lumber Co. v. United States, 561 F.2d 698 (7th Cir.1977), held in the converse situation that two corporations in a "real" parent-subsidiary relationship would not be recharacterized for purposes of section 304 as brother-sister corporations.

The application of the attribution rules in the section 304 context can create some unusual results. In Continental Bankers Life Insurance Co. v. Commissioner, 93 T.C. 52 (1989), P Corporation owned 100 percent of the stock of X Corporation and Y Corporation. P Corporation owned 56 percent of Z Corporation and Y Corporation owned 20 percent of the stock of Z Corporation. X Corporation purchased all of the stock of Z Corporation held by Y. Although Y Corporation held no X stock directly, by attribution through P Corporation, Y controlled both X and Z. Thus, the acquisition was a redemption of X stock pursuant to section 304(a)(1).

See also Rev.Rul. 74–605, 1974–2 Cum.Bull. 97, holding that the attribution rules did not cause section 304 to apply to situations involving a purchase by the parent of stock of a second tier subsidiary.

3. *Meaning of "Property" in Section 304(a)(2)*

Suppose that A controls P Corporation, which in turn owns all of the stock of S Corporation. To reverse the parent subsidiary relationship, A transfers to S Corporation more than 50 percent of the stock of P Corporation in exchange for newly issued shares constituting more than 50 percent (but less than 80 percent) of the stock of S Corporation. Does section 304(a)(2) apply to the transaction? Section 317(b) defines property so as to include all corporate stock other than "stock in the corporation making the distribution." Section 304(a)(2) recharacterizes transfers of stock to a subsidiary as a redemption by the issuer, i.e., the issuer is the distributing corporation. In the example, since P Corporation is the issuing corporation which was deemed to make the distribution and S Corporation stock was distributed, it is arguable that the S Corporation stock would be "property" as defined. However, Bhada v. Commissioner, 89 T.C. 959 (1987), aff'd sub nom Caamano v. Commissioner, 879 F.2d 156 (5th Cir.1989), held that the "distribution" in section 304(a) is not the deemed redemption, *but the actual transaction.* Thus, in the example, the distribution by S Corporation to A was a distribution of its own stock, which under section 317(a) is not property. The court reenforced its conclusion that the exchange was not subject to section 304 by noting that in receiving stock of the subsidiary, the shareholders of the parent did not withdraw assets from either the parent or the subsidiary. Rather, "[t]he transaction resulted in a change in the ownership structure of the two corporations. Congress did not intend to prevent such a change in corporate ownership by enacting section 304." (970)

D. RELATIONSHIP OF SECTION 304 TO PARTIAL LIQUIDATION RULES

Assume that A owns all of the stock of X Corporation, which in turn owns all of the stock of Y Corporation, and A transfers a portion of his shares in X Corporation to Y Corporation in exchange for all of the assets of one of its two operating divisions. This transaction is described by both 304 and section 302(b)(4), discussed supra, page 579. Can the distribution be treated as a partial liquidation of Y Corporation and avoid section 301 treatment under section 304? Based upon a technical analysis of the language of a prior version of section 304 and the statutory predecessor of section 302(e), Blaschka v. United States, 393 F.2d 983 (Ct.Cl.1968), concluded as follows:

"The function of 304, then is to complement 302. To that end, 304(b)(1) provides that such a sale is defined as a redemption of the stock of the acquiring corporation, and that for purposes of 302(b), whether such stock acquisition is to be treated as a distribution in exchange for the stock is determined by reference to the stock of the issuing corporation. * * * The essential question is whether the distribution has affected the stockholder's proportionate interest and control in the issuing corporation, and for that reason the special rule of 304(b)(1) points to the issuing corporation to apply 304(a) to 302. * * * [N]o mention is made of * * * any provision in 304 or elsewhere in the 1954 Code, as to which corporation is to be tested to determine whether there has been a partial liquidation in a stock redemption through use of related corporations. * * * [H]owever, * * * the considerations underlying the tax treatment of partial liquidations requires that a 304 stock redemption, involving the question of a partial liquidation under [302(b)(4) and 302(e)], be tested on the level of the acquiring corporation. * * * The very nature of a partial liquidation, at least as purportedly involved in this case, is a curtailment or contraction of the activities of the acquiring corporation, and the distribution to a stockholder of unneeded funds in exchange for stock in a related corporation. It is concluded that the purported partial liquidation is not to be measured by 302[(b)(1)–(3)], but that a general rule of 304(a)—that the stock sale is to be treated as a redemption by the acquiring corporation—applies subject, however, to the statutory definition as to what constitutes a partial liquidation under [302(b)(4)] and [302(e)] * * *, applied to the acquiring corporation." (986–87)

E. REFERENCES

Tiger, Redemptions Through Use of Related Corporations: New and Old Problems Under Section 304, 39 Tax Law Rev. 77 (1984); Royal, Recovery of Basis in Non–Qualifying Stock Redemptions Under Sections 302 and 304, 4 Va.Tax Rev. 85 (1984); Stewart & Randall, A Proposed Solution to the Statutory Overlap of Sections 304(a)(1) and 304(a)(2), 9 J. of Corp. Tax'n 125 (1982); Cohen, Receipts Related to Corporate Equity: Return on Investment or Exchange?, 53 Taxes 824, 833 (1975); Tiger, Sales of Stock to Related Corporations: Current Problems Under 304, 40 J.Tax. 86 (1974); Marans, Section 304: The Shadowy World of Redemptions Through Related Corporations, 22 Tax L.Rev. 161 (1967).

CHAPTER 14

CORPORATE LIQUIDATIONS

SECTION 1. INTRODUCTION

The termination of an activity conducted in the corporate form through liquidation of the corporation raises a number of important structural issues for the income tax. One issue is similar to that encountered in the redemption area: Is the corporate liquidating distribution analogous to an ongoing dividend distribution and thus to the extent of earnings and profits taxable as ordinary income in the hands of the shareholder; or is the controlling analogy a sale of the shares of stock, in which case the shareholder would receive capital gain treatment. Note, however, that since the corporation is disappearing, even if ordinary income treatment is considered to be more appropriate to the extent of earnings and profits, the shareholder logically should be allowed a tax free recovery of basis either through a cash distribution or a loss deduction; this consideration is not present in the case of redemption distributions taxed as ordinary income (except in the case of termination of interests). Alternatively, liquidation of the corporation might be likened to the tax-free incorporation transaction under section 351. If this analogy were followed, nonrecognition would be appropriate; and a mechanism for providing the shareholders with an exchanged or transferred basis in the distributed property would be necessary. In addition, if this model were applied rules for dealing with cash distributions, which cannot be accorded nonrecognition if the distribution exceeds the shareholder's basis for his stock, would be necessary. From the corporation's perspective, the primary issue is whether gains and losses should be recognized with respect to the distribution to the shareholders of appreciated and depreciated assets.

Unlike Subchapter K, which accords nonrecognition to liquidation of a partnership, Subchapter C long has treated a corporate liquidation as a recognition event from the shareholder's perspective.[1] As for characterization of the income, the sale of stock model generally has been accepted, and shareholders are taxed on capital gains to the extent that the distribution exceeds the basis for their stock;[2] if the amount of the distribution is less than the basis of a shareholder's

1. Former section 333, repealed by the Tax Reform Act of 1986, provided for limited nonrecognition at the shareholder level for liquidating distributions if certain conditions were met. The conditions were such that section 333 was not widely used except in the real estate area. When it was used it presented numerous pitfalls for the taxpayer. Compare Meyer's Estate v. Commissioner, 200 F.2d 592 (5th Cir.1952), with Cohen v. Commissioner, 63 T.C. 527 (1975). For a discussion of section 333, see McGaffey, The Deferral of Gain in One–Month Liquidations, 19 Tax L.Rev. 327 (1964).

2. Section 341, discussed infra, page 1079, treats gain on a corporate liquidation as ordinary income in certain instances.

stock, a capital loss is realized. See section 331. This characterization was of great importance prior to the repeal of the preferential rate for capital gains in the Tax Reform Act of 1986 because, unlike in the redemption situation, the corporate accumulated earnings and profits disappear at the termination of the corporation's existence. Thus as a result of the liquidation the accumulated earnings and profits permanently escape treatment as ordinary income to the shareholders.

As to the corporation, prior to the Tax Reform Act of 1986, the general rule was that neither gain nor loss was recognized as a result of liquidating distributions of appreciated or depreciated property. This treatment was a branch of the *General Utilities* rule, discussed supra, page 472, which accorded nonrecognition to the corporation on all distributions of property. As a result of this corporate nonrecognition treatment, the corporation's economic profits in the form of asset appreciation permanently escaped double taxation. This gap in the double taxation system was filled by the repeal of the *General Utilities* doctrine in 1986, and under section 336 the liquidating corporation now must recognize gains and losses on distributed assets.

Liquidation of the corporation may occur in a number of contexts. In some cases the shareholders may use the distributed assets to continue the corporation's trade or business or another trade or business, either separately or as partners. Even though in this case some plausible arguments may be made for nonrecognition based on continuity of the business enterprise, gain and loss nevertheless always have been recognized to the shareholder. In other cases, the sale of the business may be the objective. Under one selling method, the corporation sells its assets and distributes the cash proceeds to the shareholders as a liquidating distribution. As a policy matter, in a system that adopts double taxation of corporate profits, recognition of gain and loss at both the corporate and shareholder level is appropriate in this case. On the other hand, a sale of stock results in only a single level tax to the selling shareholder. Since, under pre–1986 law, the appreciation in corporate assets was not taxed if the assets were distributed in kind, from a tax planning perspective it was preferable to distribute the corporation's appreciated assets to the shareholders for a sale by them, rather than have the corporation sell its assets and then distribute the proceeds to the shareholders. To provide comparable tax treatment for the sale of stock situation, the distribution of assets situation, and the sale of assets situation, former section 337 allowed a corporation to sell its assets and liquidate without the recognition of gain or loss at the corporate level, if certain qualifying conditions were met; only a shareholder level tax was imposed as in the other two forms of sale transactions. Currently, however, gain and loss are recognized by both the corporation and its shareholders in all situations (except that corporate level tax may be deferred by sale of stock).

The nature of the shareholder also may affect issues involved in corporate liquidation. Thus, suppose the shareholder is another corporation rather than an individual. Should there be any analogy drawn to the exclusion of intercorporate dividends allowed under section 243, discussed supra, page 507? If so, it could be argued that a corporation which receives a liquidating distribution should be able to exclude a portion of the distribution attributable to the liquidating corporation's earnings and profits (with an appropriate basis adjustment). Nevertheless, except in the case of liquidations of controlled (80 percent or more) subsidiary corporations, the rules governing corporate liquidations generally are applied in the same manner to both individual and corporate shareholders. In the case of liquidations of controlled subsidiaries, sections 332, and 337 generally provide for nonrecognition of gains and losses to both the liquidating corporation and the distributing corporation. As is usual in nonrecognition transactions, the transferee must take an exchanged or transferred basis. In this case section 334(b) requires that the parent corporation take the subsidiary's basis as its basis for the assets received in the liquidating distribution.

The materials in this chapter are concerned both with the rules that govern corporate liquidations in general and with the special rules governing subsidiary liquidations. Chapter 16 contrasts the problems encountered when a liquidation occurs in the context of a sale of the assets of the corporation with these encountered when the shareholders choose to dispose of the corporate business by selling the stock of the corporation. In these cases the tax treatment accorded to the purchaser may influence the form of the transaction. Chapter 17 examines the treatment of those "tax free" reorganizations which involve the disposition of either corporate stock or all of the corporation's assets in exchange for stock of another corporation.

SECTION 2. TREATMENT OF SHAREHOLDERS

INTERNAL REVENUE CODE: Sections 331; 334(a); 346(a); 453(h)(1)(A)–(C).

REGULATIONS: Section 1.331–1.

ILLUSTRATIVE MATERIAL

A. LIQUIDATING DISTRIBUTIONS

1. *Existence of a "Liquidation"*

A distribution in complete liquidation is treated as a capital transaction under section 331(a)(1), producing capital gain or loss. While this rule generally is not difficult to apply, certain situations may cause problems. Not all liquidations are accomplished by a single distribution following a formal vote of the shareholders. Where a liquidation is accomplished through a series of distributions, section 346(a) provides that all distributions in the series pursuant to a plan to liquidate the corporation will be treated as liquidating distributions. Neither the Code nor the Regulations under section 331 define a "liquidation", and thus the existence of a distribution in "liquidation" may be an issue. Compare Regulations, section 1.332–2(c), defining the term "liquidation" in the context of liquidation of a corporate subsidiary. The status of liquidation may be important to the tax treatment of the shareholder, since capital gain and recovery of basis with respect to the liquidating distribution result only if a "liquidation" exists; otherwise, the shareholder will generally be treated as having received an ordinary dividend.

In Estate of Maguire v. Commissioner, 50 T.C. 130 (1968), the court formulated the test for determining whether a liquidation has in fact occurred as follows: "[T]here are three basic tests: (1) There must be a manifest intention to liquidate; (2) there must be a continuing purpose to terminate corporate affairs; and (3) the corporation's activities must be directed to such termination." (142). Under these tests, distributions received in 1960 were held to be dividends and not liquidating distributions; although a plan of liquidation had been adopted in 1944, the corporation after the 1960 distributions still had assets of over $48 million and annual income of over $1.5 million, and liquidation had not been completed by 1964.

The factual nature of this inquiry is illustrated by contrasting *Estate of Maguire* with Olmsted v. Commissioner, 48 T.C.M. 594 (1984). During 1969 and 1970 the shareholders entered into contractual agreements to wind up corporation's affairs and liquidate it. The board of directors began selling properties in 1970, but shareholders did not approve a plan of liquidation until December, 1973. Due to difficulties in selling mineral and timber properties, the corporation leased the properties to others and received almost $1,200,000 of income from mineral royalties, timber sales, and rents during the period 1973 through 1981. It distributed over $1,900,000 to shareholders over the same period. The Tax Court held that a status of liquidation existed during 1974 and 1975. Because the corporation would have had difficulty selling its properties, the leasing and royalty arrangements were substitutes for sales and were not inconsistent with the status of liquidation; the fact that the corporation ceased exploration and development of new mineral properties evidenced intent to wind up business.

Formal action by the directors or shareholders is not necessarily required to effect a complete liquidation for tax purposes. See, e.g., Silverman v. Commissioner, 30 T.C.M. 617 (1971) (withdrawal of all funds of the corporation in 1958 entitled to capital gain treatment since action constituted a de facto liquidation of the corporation); Rev.Rul. 69–534, 1969–2 Cum. Bull. 48 (corporation liquidated and business conducted as a partnership by the three shareholders of the corporation who had the same relative interests in the partnership; no amounts were actually distributed to the shareholders, each shareholder's partnership account being credited with his share of the equity of the corporation; held, the transaction constituted the equivalent of a distribution in liquidation and section 331 controlled); Shore v. Commissioner, 286 F.2d 742 (5th Cir.1961) ("loans" to shareholders of a Cuban corporation which were intended to be liquidating distributions were so treated, even though no formal plan of liquidation was ever adopted in order to avoid a Cuban law requiring completion of liquidation within 30 days after adoption of a formal plan).

See also Messer v. Commissioner, 438 F.2d 774 (3d Cir.1971) (corporation adopted plan of liquidation in September, 1960, but retained interest-bearing notes and an anti-trust claim which were distributed in July, 1961; held, the corporation continued in existence for tax purposes up to the distribution and was taxable on income received prior to the distribution, even though the 1960 action may have constituted a valid liquidation under state law); Hersloff v. United States, 310 F.2d 947 (Ct.Cl.1962) (corporations continued in existence until 1954 by virtue of activities of trustees in dissolution even though one corporation had adopted a plan of liquidation in 1928 and the charter of the other had expired in 1937; income realized by the corporations subject to corporate income tax until 1954); Ochs v. United States, 305 F.2d 844 (Ct.Cl.1962) (corporate charter expired in 1944, although shareholders did not become aware of this fact until December, 1947; business was continued until 1948 when the stock was surrendered and cancelled; held, no liquidation until 1948 and corporation liable for corporate income taxes until then).

2. *"Distribution in Complete Liquidation"*

Only distributions in complete liquidation are accorded sale or exchange treatment under section 331. Generally a distribution other than one in liquidation will be subject to section 301 and will be taxed as ordinary income to its full extent if the corporation has sufficient earnings and profits. Section 346(a) provides that all distributions which are part of a series in a plan of complete liquidation are treated as liquidating distributions, thus eliminating any necessity to distinguish between dividend distributions and liquidating distributions once the liquidation process begins. Furthermore, as indicated by the cases in A.1., supra, the "plan" need not be formal as long as the corporation is in the "status" of liquidation.

Payments of debts to shareholders are not treated as liquidating distributions. See, e.g., Braddock Land Co., Inc. v. Commissioner, 75 T.C. 324 (1980). Thus, a cash method shareholder generally will recognize ordinary income when in the course of liquidation, the corporation pays an account payable due to the shareholder. Suppose that a cash method shareholder forgives a corporate indebtedness on a book account prior to adoption of a plan of liquidation, but shortly thereafter the corporation liquidates. What will be the consequences of the two transactions? In *Braddock Land Co., Inc.*, the shareholder's forgiveness of indebtedness after the corporation had adopted a plan of liquidation was ignored because the court determined that there was no "business purpose" for the forgiveness. See also Dwyer v. United States, 622 F.2d 460 (9th Cir.1980) (shareholder who purportedly forgave accrued interest on debt owed to him by corporation realized ordinary income equal to "forgiven" interest upon liquidation). Why does section 108(e)(6) not require the corporation to recognize income?

B. TREATMENT OF DISTRIBUTIONS

1. *Allocation of Liquidating Distributions*

Where the shareholder of a liquidating corporation owns a single block of stock acquired at the same time and at the same cost, and receives a single liquidating distribution, the distribution is applied first to the basis of the stock. Gain is recognized to the extent the fair market value of the assets received exceeds the basis of the stock. However, where a series of liquidating distributions are received or where the shareholder owns different blocks of stock acquired at different times and at different costs, each distribution must be allocated to each block of stock and gain or loss is computed separately for each block of stock. Regulations, section 1.331–1(e). Rev.Rul. 68–348, 1968–2 Cum.Bull. 141, amplified in Rev.Rul. 85–

48, 1985–1 Cum.Bull. 126, provides examples of how to make the required allocations.

Computation of gain and loss on a block-by-block basis when the shareholder receives a single liquidating distribution generally is relevant either if long term capital gains are taxed differently than short term capital gains or if liquidating distributions are made over the course of two or more years. Thus, block-by-block computations often are unnecessary. A block-by-block computation may have an impact, however, where the taxpayer holds a block of stock as a capital asset which has depreciated in value and holds an appreciated block as an ordinary income asset, as may be the case with a dealer in securities.

Where the shareholder receives a series of distributions with respect to two or more blocks of stock, significant timing differences may occur as a result of the block-by-block computation. After each distribution has been allocated among the blocks of stock, gain is recognized with respect to a block of stock after its basis has been recovered. This treatment, ratified by Rev.Rul. 85–48, supra, reflects the "open transaction" doctrine of Burnet v. Logan, 283 U.S. 404 (1931), even though such treatment generally is not available for installment sales. See Regulations, section 15A.453–1(c). However, no loss is recognized in a section 331 liquidation until after the corporation has made its final distribution. Rev.Rul. 68–348, 1968–2 Cum-Bull. 141; Schmidt v. Commissioner, 55 T.C. 335 (1970). Thus, gain may be recognized on a particular block before basis has been completely recovered on another block. Furthermore, where the series of distributions spans two or more years, it is possible for a shareholder with no overall gain to realize capital gain in one year and a capital loss in a subsequent year, without being able to offset the two.

2. *Problems Raised by Character of Distribution*

(a) *Distributions Subject to Liabilities*

Where property is distributed in liquidation and the shareholder assumes liabilities of the corporation in connection therewith, the shareholder's gain is computed by subtracting the basis of his stock from the fair market value of the property received less any liabilities assumed. For purposes of computing gain on a subsequent sale, the shareholder's basis for the property under section 334(a) is the fair market value of the property distributed at the time of liquidation; there is no increase to reflect the assumed liabilities. Ford v. United States, 311 F.2d 951 (Ct.Cl.1963). This failure to take liabilities directly into account in computing basis is appropriate because the liabilities were subtracted from the fair market value of the distributed property in computing the shareholder's amount realized on the liquidation.

If the amount of a liability is contingent at the time of the distribution and the shareholder later repays an amount in excess of the liability taken into account in computing his gain or loss on the distribution, the repayment will give rise to a capital loss, not an ordinary deduction. See Arrowsmith v. Commissioner, 344 U.S. 6 (1952).

(b) *Distribution of Installment Notes*

Where the corporation makes a liquidating distribution of an installment note, the corporation must include any remaining deferred gain in income, see section 453B, and the shareholders generally are not entitled to treat the note on an installment basis under section 453. Instead, they must treat the fair market value of the note as an amount realized with respect to the stock. Any gain recognized is capital gain; and the note takes a basis in the hands of the shareholders equal to its fair market value at the time of the distribution. Rev.Rul. 66–280, 1966–2 Cum.Bull. 304. If the principal amount of the note exceeds the fair market value, the excess, when collected, is ordinary income. See Weiss v. Commissioner, 24 T.C.M. 79 (1965).

Section 453(h) provides an exception to the shareholder recognition rule when the shareholders receive installment obligations arising from a sale or exchange of corporate assets occurring after the adoption of a plan of complete liquidation, if the liquidation is completed within twelve months following adoption of the plan. If this requirement is met, shareholders recognize gain on the liquidation with respect to the notes under the installment method of section 453 as they receive payments on the obligations. If an installment obligation arises from the sale of inventory, however, deferred recognition is available only if substantially all of the inventory attributable to a particular trade or business of the corporation was sold in bulk to a single purchaser. Furthermore, if the property sold for an installment obligation is depreciable property and the purchaser is related to the shareholder (i.e., the shareholder's spouse, a trust of which the shareholder or the shareholder's spouse is a beneficiary, or a corporation or partnership under more than 50 percent control of the shareholder of the selling corporation), installment reporting is not available to the shareholder. Where a corporation distributes cash or property (other than qualifying installment obligations) in one tax year and then in a subsequent tax year (but within 12 months) distributes installment obligations qualifying under section 453(h), the gain included in the first year must be recomputed—usually on an amended return—to reflect treatment of the earlier cash distribution as an installment payment. In turn, a portion of the basis for the stock originally used to offset the cash distribution must be allocated to the installment obligation, thereby increasing the gain recognized in the first year. See S.Rep. No. 96–1000, 96th Cong., 2d Sess. 20–22 (1980).

Section 453(h) is a vestige of the pre–1987 rules under which a corporation did not recognize gain or loss on the sale or exchange of certain assets if the assets were sold after the adoption of a plan of liquidation and the liquidation was completed within twelve months. (For these rules see infra, page 692.) Although those rules were repealed by the Tax Reform Act of 1986, installment reporting of shareholder gain was continued. Section 453(k)(2), denying installment sale treatment for sales of marketable stock and securities, might render section 453(h) unavailable in the liquidation of a publicly traded corporation.

(c) *Goodwill and Assets With Unascertainable Values*

Where goodwill is distributed in a liquidation, the value of the goodwill is includible for purposes of determining shareholder gain. Cf. Carty v. Commissioner, 38 T.C. 46 (1962). The valuation of goodwill and other intangible assets distributed in liquidation historically has presented difficult problems. See Jack Daniel Distillery v. United States, 379 F.2d 569 (Ct.Cl. 1967) (approving "residual" method of valuing goodwill, whereby the excess of the purchase price over the fair market value of tangible assets determines the value of goodwill); Rev.Rul. 68–609, 1968–2 Cum.Bull. 327 (capitalization of earnings method of valuing goodwill). The Tax Reform

Act of 1986 added section 1060, which requires that in any "applicable asset acquisition," the value of acquired goodwill be determined by the "residual" method. See Temporary Regulations, section 1.1060–1T. The definition of "applicable asset acquisition" in section 1060(c), if read literally, includes corporate liquidations in which the shareholders acquire the assets of a trade or business of the corporation. In the context of liquidations of closely held corporations, application of the "residual" method to distributed goodwill is problematical because that valuation method contemplates that the consideration for the transferred assets is susceptible to valuation without reference to the assets themselves. In the case of a closely held corporation, the stock usually is valued with reference to the value of the assets, including the value of goodwill determined under a capitalization of earnings method. But see Temporary Regulations, section 1.1060–1T, requiring the application of section 1060 when assets are acquired from the corporation in a stock redemption transaction.

Suppose that a corporation liquidates and distributes to the shareholders a contractual right to receive royalties with respect to sales by a licensee of a product on which the corporation holds the patent. At the time of liquidation, there is no reasonable basis for estimating future sales. May the shareholders treat the liquidation as an open transaction, applying distributions and royalty payments against the basis of the stock and reporting gain only when the basis of the stock has been recovered fully? A number of cases allowed open transaction treatment for liquidating distributions of rights with a speculative or unascertainable value which occurred in years prior to the enactment of section 453(j)(2), which limited the use of the open transaction approach generally. See, e.g., Likins–Foster Honolulu Corp. v. Commissioner, 840 F.2d 642 (9th Cir.1988) (open transaction doctrine applied at Commissioner's behest to claims for condemnation of liquidated subsidiary's property); Cloward Instruments Corp. v. Commissioner, 52 T.C.M. 34 (1986) (royalty contract). In other cases, income-producing intangibles were valued and the liquidation was taxed as a closed transaction. See, e.g., Waring v. Commissioner, 412 F.2d 800 (3d Cir.1969) (patent royalty contract). Whether section 453(j)(2), applies to liquidating distributions is unclear; literally a liquidation may fall within the definition of "installment" sale in section 453(b)(1). If this section is applicable, open transaction reporting of a liquidating distribution generally will be foreclosed, and the shareholder will recover the basis of the stock ratably over fifteen years, unless a different basis recovery period can be established. See Temporary Regulations, section 15A.453–1(c)(4).

C. "RECEIPT" OF DISTRIBUTION

A distribution need not actually be received for a shareholder to be taxed on the gain realized on the liquidation. Rev.Rul. 80–177, 1980–2 Cum.Bull. 109, held that a cash method shareholder had constructively received a liquidating distribution on the date announced by the corporation as the date on which it would make a liquidating distribution to any shareholder presenting a stock certificate for surrender. If a shareholder makes a gift of stock in a liquidating corporation after a plan of liquidation has been adopted but prior to receiving the liquidating distribution, the gain generally will be taxed to the donor, even though the distribution is received by the donee. See Kinsey v. Commissioner, 477 F.2d 1058 (2d Cir.1973) (charitable contribution of stock following adoption of plan of liquidation);

Dayton Hydraulic Co. v. United States, 592 F.2d 937 (6th Cir.1979) (corporation taxed on gain of stock of another corporation distributed to shareholder).

Typically, distributions in complete liquidation of a corporation are pro rata to the shareholders. If, however, a non-pro rata distribution occurs in a section 331 liquidation, a shareholder who receives less than a pro rata share of the liquidating distribution is treated as having received a pro rata share and then, in a separate transaction, having conveyed a portion of the liquidating distribution (equal to the difference between a pro rata share and the share actually received) to the other shareholders as compensation, gifts, in satisfaction of obligations, or the like, as the facts indicate. Rev.Rul. 79–10, 1979–1 Cum.Bull. 140.

In some cases a liquidating distribution may be made to a trust for the benefit of the shareholders rather than directly to the shareholders. A liquidation often is structured in this manner to facilitate a post-liquidation sale of assets that are not readily divisible where there are numerous shareholders. Generally, the shareholders will be treated as receiving a liquidating distribution when the assets are transferred to the trust. See Rev. Rul. 72–137, 1972–1 C.B. 101. The trust is then treated as a grantor trust for income tax purposes. However, if a liquidation involving a liquidating trust is unreasonably prolonged or the business activities of the trust are significant enough to obscure its stated purpose of facilitating an orderly liquidation, the trust may be reclassified as an association taxable as a corporation or as a partnership. Regulations, section 301.7701–4(d). See also Rev.Proc. 82–58, 1982–2 Cum.Bull. 847 (requirements for advance ruling on classification of liquidating trust).

D. LOSSES

A shareholder may realize a loss on liquidation of a corporation. Suppose the stock of the corporation has become worthless prior to the liquidation and the shareholder receives nothing in the liquidation. Since there is no sale or exchange of the stock because there has been no liquidating distribution, see Aldrich v. Commissioner, 1 T.C. 602 (1943), it would appear that the loss would be an ordinary rather than capital loss. This result is foreclosed by section 165(g), which provides capital loss treatment upon the worthlessness of corporate stock and securities. Contrast this result with section 1244, discussed supra, page 427, which provides for ordinary loss treatment on the sale or exchange or worthlessness of certain common stock.

Section 267(a)(1) generally disallows loss deductions on the sale or exchange of property between a shareholder and a corporation of which the shareholder directly or through attribution owns more than 50 percent of the stock. Losses incurred on the complete liquidation of a corporation, however, are exempted from this disallowance provision.

E. REFERENCES

Brod, Liquidations Involving Shareholders–Creditors—Tax Traps For the Unwary, 7 J.Corp.Tax. 352 (1981); Schenk, *Arrowsmith* and its Progeny: Tax Characterization by Reference to Past Events, 33 Rutgers L.Rev. 317 (1981); Bittker and Eustice, Complete Liquidations and Related Problems, 26 Tax L.Rev. 191 (1971); Gordon, Winding up the Close or Family

Corporation: Liquidations and Related Problems, 23 N.Y.U. Tax Inst. 643 (1965).

SECTION 3. TREATMENT OF THE CORPORATION

INTERNAL REVENUE CODE: Sections 336(a), (b), (c), (d)(1).

ILLUSTRATIVE MATERIAL

A. GAIN SITUATIONS UNDER SECTION 336

1. *General*

Extending the policies discussed in connection with section 311, supra, page 477, as part of the repeal of the *General Utilities* doctrine, Congress in 1986 amended section 336(a) to require recognition of gain or loss as if the property distributed in liquidation had been sold to the distributee for its fair market value. Gain and loss are computed separately on each asset. As a result, in some cases the liquidating corporation may find itself with ordinary income and capital losses which may not be deducted against that income. See section 1211(a).

The distribution of appreciated property may result in a tax to both the corporation and the shareholder. However, because there is generally no relationship between the corporation's basis for its assets and the basis of a shareholder's stock, one may recognize gain while the other recognizes a loss. For example, assume that a corporation with a single asset having a basis of $100 and a fair market value of $400 distributes the asset in a liquidating distribution to its shareholder, who has a $500 basis for the stock. The corporation recognizes a gain of $300 while the shareholder recognizes a loss of $100. Given the potential for two taxes on liquidating distributions, including a corporate tax on gain that accrued prior to the formation of the corporation, taxpayers must be very sure that the corporate form is, and for the foreseeable future will be, the form in which they wish to carry on business. Undoing a decision to operate in corporate form can be very expensive.

2. *Character of Gain*

Section 336(a) provides that gain is recognized "as if such property were sold to the distributee." Generally the gain will be characterized with reference to the purpose for which the corporation held the property. Thus ordinary income will be recognized if inventory is distributed, capital gain will be recognized with respect to capital assets, section 1231 gain will be recognized with respect to depreciable property and land used in the corporation's business, and recapture income will be recognized where appropriate.

Presumably section 1239 will treat as ordinary income any gain recognized with respect to property distributed to a related party who holds the property as depreciable property. Thus, for example, if a corporation distributes to its sole shareholder a building held for rental purposes, having an adjusted basis of $100,000 and a fair market value of $1,000,000, the entire $900,000 gain is ordinary income to the corporation, without regard to any applicable depreciation recapture.

3. *Distributions of Encumbered Property*

If any distributed property is subject to a liability, section 336(b) deems the value of the property to be not less than the amount of the liability. This provision extends the principle of Commissioner v. Tufts, 461 U.S. 300 (1983), which applies only to nonrecourse liabilities, to recourse liabilities. Compare Regulations, section 1.1001–2(a)(1), which generally treat as discharge of indebtedness income the amount by which a recourse debt exceeds the fair market value of the encumbered property when the property is transferred subject to the debt. Because the nonrecognition rules of section 108 generally will not apply to debt discharged in the liquidation of a solvent corporation, the primary effect of the application of section 336(b) to recourse debt is to convert ordinary income into capital gain.

Where a liability does not specifically encumber a particular property but a shareholder assumes the liability in connection with the distribution, the liability will be allocated among the distributed properties relative to their respective fair market values. See Rev.Rul. 80–283, 1980–2 Cum.Bull. 108 (applying now repealed version of former section 311(c), which was analogous to present section 336(b)).

4. *Other Income Recognition Rules*

A number of rules outside of Subchapter C may also require income recognition by a liquidating corporation. Thus, the Commissioner can exercise his power under section 446(b) to require a liquidating corporation to include in its final year income which had been earned but was not yet received at the time of liquidation. See, e.g., Commissioner v. Kuckenberg, 309 F.2d 202 (9th Cir.1962) (cash method corporation required to accrue income on completed construction contracts); Jud Plumbing & Heating, Inc. v. Commissioner, 153 F.2d 681 (5th Cir.1946) (corporation using completed contract method required to report on percentage of completion method in year of liquidation). Section 482 also can be invoked to reallocate income and deduction items between the liquidating corporation and its shareholders. See *Jud Plumbing & Heating, Inc.,* supra.

In other cases, the Commissioner has relied on the judicially developed assignment of income doctrine to allocate to the liquidated corporation income not recognized until after the liquidation. See, e.g., Wood Harmon Corp. v. United States, 311 F.2d 918 (2d Cir.1963) (corporation assigned to shareholders the right to receive proceeds from condemnation of corporate property).

For taxable years prior to 1987, the "tax benefit" doctrine was invoked to include in income for the corporation's final year an amount equal to a previously claimed deduction in cases where the corporation had treated the cost of acquiring property as a deductible business expense and the property remained on hand and was distributed in the liquidation. Hillsboro National Bank v. Commissioner, 460 U.S. 370 (1983) (previously expensed unconsumed grain supplies distributed by liquidating farming corporation). The tax benefit doctrine also applied when a liquidating corporation distributed debts owed to it against which a bad debt deduction under section 166 had been claimed, if the value of the debts at the time of the liquidation exceeded the face amount reduced by the prior bad debt deduction. Rev.Rul. 78–278, 1978–2 Cum.Bull. 134.

After 1986, it generally is no longer necessary to apply the above income recognition rules to a liquidating corporation because gain is recognized under section 336. But if application of one of these rules would require the corporation to recognize a greater amount of income than would section 336, there remains a possibility that one of them might be applied. For example, suppose that a corporation in the trucking business expensed a supply of spare tires for which it paid $1,000, but at the time the still unused tires are distributed in liquidation, they are worth only $900. The tax benefit rule may require inclusion by the corporation of the full $1,000 deduction, not merely the $900 fair market value of the tires. However, if the tax benefit rule is applied, the corporation might then have an offsetting $100 loss deduction under section 336 on the distribution of the "depreciated" property, unless the deduction is disallowed under one of the specialized loss disallowance provisions discussed in B., infra. But see Rojas v. Commissioner, 90 T.C. 1090 (1988), aff'd 901 F.2d 810 (9th Cir.1990) (tax benefit rule does not apply to previously expensed farm supplies expended to produce farm crops distributed in liquidation).

B. LOSS SITUATIONS UNDER SECTION 336

1. *General*

Unlike current distributions in kind, which under section 311, discussed supra page 477, give rise to gain but not loss, liquidating distributions cause recognition to the corporation of loss as well as gain. The legislative history of sections 311 and 336 does not explain the reason for this differing treatment. Perhaps the answer is that Congress was concerned that allowing losses to be recognized on current distributions would have presented too much opportunity for manipulation, for example, by distributing of an asset, such as portfolio securities, which had temporarily fallen in value but which was expected to regain its value. On the other hand, a liquidation terminates the corporate existence, and even though depreciated assets may regain value after the liquidation, the distribution is not a selective distribution subject to manipulation. Thus, it is appropriate to permit the corporation to recognize losses on liquidating distributions. Furthermore, section 267(a), which generally disallows deductions for losses incurred on sales and exchanges between certain related taxpayers, by its terms does not apply to losses recognized under section 336. However, Congress has provided for disallowance of losses that it considered to be artificial or duplicative of shareholder losses.

2. *Distributions of Recently Contributed Property*

Section 336(d)(1)(A)(ii) disallows any loss deduction with respect to a distribution to a person who is related to the corporation within the meaning of section 267 if the property was acquired in a section 351 transaction or as a contribution to capital within the five year period ending on the date of the distribution. The purpose of this rule is to prevent "stuffing" property with built-in losses into the corporation in anticipation of the liquidation. In the absence of this rule the corporation could recognize losses to offset gains on property held by the corporation; the shareholder also would recognize an additional loss on the liquidation because the basis of the stock would be increased under section 358 by the basis of the appreciated asset. At the same time, only the fair market value of the asset would be taken into account as an amount realized in computing gain or loss on the liquidation.

This "double loss" situation is a corollary of the double taxation of gains and is normally the appropriate result. Congress has limited the availability of double losses in this situation because of the tax avoidance potential. See H.Rep. No. 99–841, 99th Cong., 2d Sess. II–200 (1986).

In operation, however, section 336(d)(1)(A)(ii) is mechanical and applies without regard to whether the property was appreciated or depreciated at the time it was contributed to the corporation. Suppose, for example, that for a valid business purpose A contributes two items of property to X Corporation in exchange for all of its stock. The first asset has a basis of $500 and a fair market value of $1,000; the second has a basis of $1,000 and a fair market value of $1,600. Four years later X Corporation is liquidated and both properties are distributed to A. At the time of the liquidation, the first property has appreciated in value to $2,000 and its basis remains $500; the second property has depreciated in value to $600 and its basis remains $1,000. X Corporation must recognize the $1,500 gain on the first property, but may not recognize the $400 loss on the second property.

If 336(d)(1) is not applicable, section 336(d)(2) may disallow losses at the corporate level without regard to whether the distribution is to a related shareholder. Section 336(d)(2) applies to property acquired by the corporation in a section 351 transaction or as a contribution to capital if "the acquisition of such property by the liquidating corporation was part of a plan a principal purpose of which was to recognize loss by the liquidating corporation with respect to such property in connection with the liquidation." Section 336(d)(2)(B)(i)(II). Section 336(d)(2), which also is intended to disallow built-in double losses, is more accurately targeted than section 336(d)(1)(A)(ii). Section 336(d)(2) disallows only that portion of the loss that is attributable to the excess of the adjusted basis of the property immediately before the acquisition over the fair market value of the property at that time. In other words, only the built-in loss is disallowed; any loss accruing while the property was owned by the corporation is allowed. Mechanically, this result is accomplished by reducing the basis of the contributed property in an amount equal to the built-in loss.

The basis reduction under section 336(d)(2) applies only for purposes of computing losses. For example, if an asset was contributed to the corporation at a time when its basis was $500 and its fair market value was $400 and the asset was distributed when its adjusted basis, without regard to section 336(d)(2), was $450 and its fair market value was $150, the adjusted basis would be reduced to $350, reflecting the $100 built-in loss, and only a $200 loss would be allowed, assuming that section 336(d)(1) does not also apply. However, because the basis reduction rule does not apply when computing gain, if the property had a fair market value of at least $350 but not more than $450 at the time it was distributed, the corporation would recognize neither a gain nor a loss.

Although the general applicability of the loss disallowance rule of section 336(d)(2) is based on intent, a timing element is introduced by section 336(d)(2)(b)(ii), which conclusively deems property contributed to the corporation within two years prior to adoption of the plan of liquidation to have been contributed as part of the proscribed plan, except as otherwise provided in regulations. However, the Conference Committee Report indicates that the regulations should provide that the presumption "will be disregarded *unless* there is no clear and substantial relationship between the contributed property and the conduct of the corporation's current or future business enterprises." H.Rep. No. 99–841, 99th Cong., 2d Sess. II–201 (1986). Stated affirmatively, the presumption does not apply to assets used in the corporation's trade or business and the question reverts to one of intent. Thus, contributions of portfolio securities will be presumed to have been made for the prohibited purpose. Furthermore, the Conference Report indicates that the loss disallowance rule should not apply at all if a plan of liquidation is adopted within two years of formation of the corporation. Id.

Technically, the loss disallowance rule of section 336(d)(2) applies to property transferred to the corporation more than two years prior to adoption of the plan of liquidation if the acquisition by the corporation was pursuant to a plan having the prohibited purpose. However, the Conference Committee Report indicates that section 336(d)(2) should be applied to property contributed more than two years prior to adoption of the plan of liquidation "only in the most rare and unusual cases." Id. at II–200.

The flush material of section 336(d)(2)(B)(i) includes within property subject to the basis adjustment any property the basis of which is determined with reference to property contributed pursuant to the proscribed plan. Thus, if contributed property is subject to a basis adjustment under section 336(d)(2), the taint cannot be purged by exchanging the property for other property which takes an exchanged basis (such as in a section 351 transaction or a section 1031 like-kind exchange).

3. *Non-pro Rata Distributions to Related Persons*

Another nonrecognition rule of section 336(d)(1) applies to non-pro rata distributions of property to a related shareholder, generally a more than 50 percent shareholder. If loss property is distributed among the shareholders other than in proportion to their shareholdings, the loss attributable to the portion distributed to a related person is disallowed. Section 336(d)(1)(A)(i). Assume, for example, that 60 percent of the stock of Y Corporation is held by B and 40 percent is held by C, who is unrelated to B. The corporation makes a liquidating distribution as follows: B receives Asset # 1, having a fair market value of $60 and a basis of $70; C receives Asset # 2, having a fair market value of $40 and a basis of $50. Y Corporation may recognize the loss on the distribution of Asset # 2 to C because C is not a related person. But because B is a related person and B received 100 percent of the asset, none of the loss on Asset # 1 may be recognized. However, if Y Corporation had distributed an undivided 6/10th's of each asset to B and an undivided 4/10th's of each asset to C, it would have been allowed to recognize the loss with respect to both assets. Like the rule disallowing losses on distributions to related persons of property contributed within five years of the distribution, this rule applies without regard to whether there was a valid business purpose for distributing the property non-pro rata. Furthermore, the disallowance rule applies regardless of how the corporation acquired the property.

The purpose of section 336(d)(1)(A)(i) is puzzling. If Y Corporation distributed Asset # 1 and Asset # 2 to B and C pro rata, under section 334(a) B and C each would have a basis in their respective interests in the property equal to fair market value. Thus, immediately after the distribution they could exchange the undivided interests received in the liquidating distribution without realization of gain. (An undivided 4/10th's of Asset # 1 is equal in value to an undivided 6/10th's of Asset # 2.) It would appear that B could end up with all of Asset # 1 and C could receive all of Asset # 2, and the corporation could recognize its losses. Could the Commissioner successfully apply the "sham transaction" doctrine to treat the distribution as being made by the corporation non-pro rata? What if it made good business sense for B to own all of Asset # 1 and C to own all of Asset # 2?

C. EXCEPTIONS TO SECTION 336

Section 336 does not apply to distributions which are part of a corporate reorganization. Section 336(c). However, section 361(c) may require recognition of gain, but not loss, with respect to property other than stock or securities of the acquiring corporation distributed in liquidations pursuant to a corporate reorganization. Corporate reorganizations are discussed, infra Chapter 17.

Section 337, discussed infra, page 629, displaces section 336 and provides nonrecognition in the case of liquidating distributions by an 80 percent controlled corporate subsidiary.

D. POLICY ISSUES ON TREATMENT OF BUILT–IN GAINS AND LOSSES

In section 336(d)(2) Congress has demonstrated that it is possible to construct a formula to deny the corporation a deduction for built-in losses. Presumably, Congress did not provide an exclusion for built-in gains with respect to distributed property because the opportunity for manipulation in loss situations is so much greater.

E. REFERENCES

Zolt, Corporate Taxation After the Tax Reform Act of 1986: A State of Disequilibrium, 66 N.C.L.Rev. 839 (1988); Kahn, Should *General Utilities* Be Reinstated to Provide Partial Integration of Corporate and Personal Income—Is Half a Loaf Better Than None?, 13 J.Corp.L. 953 (1988); Yin, Taxing Corporate Liquidations (and Related Matters) After the Tax Reform Act of 1986, 42 Tax L.Rev. 573 (1987); Battle, Filler and Schultz, New Section 336; Selected Issues in the Taxation of Complete Liquidations, 65 Taxes 775 (1987): Nolan, Taxing Corporate Distributions of Appreciated Property: Repeal of the *General Utilities* Doctrine and Relief Measures, 22 San Diego L.Rev. 97 (1985); Lyons, Corporate Liquidations and the "*General Utilities*" Rule, 38 Southwestern L.J. 1081 (1985); Block, Liquidations Before and After the Repeal of *General Utilities,* 21 Harv.J. on Leg. 307 (1984): Byrne, The Tax Benefit Rule as Applied to Corporate Liquidations and Contributions to Capital: Recent Developments, 56 Notre Dame L.Rev. 215 (1980).

SECTION 4. LIQUIDATION OF SUBSIDIARY CORPORATIONS—SECTION 332

INTERNAL REVENUE CODE: Sections 332; 334(b); 337(a), (b)(1), (c), (d); 381(a); 453B(d).

REGULATIONS: Section 1.332–2, –5, –7.

H.K. PORTER COMPANY, INC. v. COMMISSIONER

United States Tax Court, 1986.
87 T.C. 689.

OPINION

CLAPP, JUDGE: Respondent determined deficiencies in petitioner's 1978 and 1979 Federal income tax in the amounts of $105,281 and $745,161, respectively. After concessions, the issue for decision is whether section 332 applies to bar the recognition of gain or loss on the liquidation of H.K. Porter Australia, Pty., Ltd., petitioner's subsidiary.

* * *

In 1962, petitioner paid $219,336 for all of the outstanding stock of an Australian business corporation which manufactured saws, brake linings, and clutch facings. Petitioner changed the name of the corporation to H.K. Porter Australia, Pty., Ltd. (Porter Australia), and loaned Porter Australia the funds it needed to operate. At all relevant times, petitioner owned all of Porter Australia's outstanding stock.

In 1966, Porter Australia authorized 400,000 shares of $1 par common stock and 1 million shares of $1 par preferred stock. In 1968, it authorized 2 million additional shares of preferred stock.

The preferred stock only had voting rights at meetings convened to wind up the business, reduce its capital, sanction the sale of a business, or consider any question affecting the rights and privileges of the preferred stock. It had a 5–percent, noncumulative dividend, was redeemable, and had a $2,452,000 liquidation preference over the common stock.

In September 1966, and again in December 1968, Porter Australia capitalized loans from petitioner of $1 million and issued to petitioner 896,861 shares of preferred stock on each occasion. In November 1969, it capitalized loans from petitioner totalling $452,000 and issued petitioner 405,380 shares of preferred stock. Porter Australia capitalized the loans because it was unable to "satisfy" the loans in the short term and it wanted to avoid any further claim by respondent that income should be allocated to petitioner by reason of those loans.

* * *

In October 1978, petitioner's board of directors voted to terminate Porter Australia's operations because they were unprofitable, and dispose of all its assets. In May 1979, pursuant to Australian law, a certified liquidator was appointed to liquidate Porter Australia. In December 1979, petitioner surrendered all of its common and preferred stock in Porter Australia in exchange for a $477,876 liquidating distribution which included $10,288 to satisfy an intercompany receivable. Said distribution was not enough to cover the $2,452,000 liquidation preference of the preferred stock.

As of December 31, 1978, petitioner's adjusted basis in its 182,664 shares of Porter Australia's common stock was $249,981. As of January 1, 1979, petitioner's adjusted basis in its 2,199,102 shares of Porter Australia's preferred stock was $2,425,358.

On its 1978 and 1979 Federal income tax returns, petitioner claimed losses with respect to its Porter Australia stock. In his notice of deficiency, respondent disallowed said losses because "under I.R.C. Sec. 332, no gain or loss is recognized on the receipt of property distributed in complete liquidation of a subsidiary corporation."

* * *

Respondent contends that section 332 bars the recognition of petitioner's losses. Petitioner contends that section 332 is inapplicable and cites Spaulding Bakeries, Inc. v. Commissioner, 27 T.C. 684 (1957), affd. 252 F.2d 693 (2d Cir.1958).

In *Spaulding Bakeries,* the taxpayer purchased all the outstanding common and preferred stock of Hazleton Bakeries, Inc. between 1930 and 1946. In 1950, Hazleton Bakeries was liquidated and the taxpayer received the assets distributed in the liquidation. The distributed assets failed to cover the preferred stock's liquidation preference. No assets were distributed with respect to the common stock. On its 1950 Federal income tax return, the taxpayer claimed a worthless stock deduction with respect to the common stock. Respondent disallowed the deduction because of section 112(b)(6),[4] the predecessor of section 332. The sole issue for decision was whether section 112(b)(6) barred the recognition of the taxpayer's claimed losses. Specifically, the issue focused on whether Hazleton Bakeries distributed its assets in complete cancellation or redemption of "all its stock."

In a Court-reviewed opinion, we held that the phrase "all its stock" did not include "nonvoting stock which is limited and preferred as to dividends." 27 T.C. at 688. Thus, Hazleton Bakeries' distribution, which was in respect of only the nonvoting preferred stock, was not a distribution in complete cancellation or redemption of all its stock.

The Second Circuit, in affirming this Court, stated:

> The [taxpayer], it seems to us, argues with convincing force that the two classes of stock of Hazleton cannot be treated as

4. Sec. 112(b)(6) of the Internal Revenue Code of 1939 provided that no gain or loss shall be recognized upon the receipt by a corporation of property distributed in complete liquidation of another corporation if—

(A) the corporation receiving such property was * * * the owner of at least 80 per centum of the total number of shares of all other classes of stock (except nonvoting stock which is limited and preferred as to dividends) * * *; and

* * *

(C) the distribution is by such other corporation in complete cancellation or redemption of *all its stock,* * * * [Emphasis added.]

> though they were but one class, nor can the distribution in respect to the preferred stock be treated as though it were a distribution by Hazleton in respect to *all* its stock, all classes. It is convincingly argued as a matter of law, that there could be no distribution in respect to the common stock until the prior claim of the preferred stock had been satisfied. [252 F.2d at 697; emphasis in original.]

Respondent, in essence, advances two arguments: (1) *Spaulding Bakeries* was erroneously decided and the decision should be reconsidered; and (2) even under the rationale of *Spaulding Bakeries,* section 332 applies.

Spaulding Bakeries Reconsidered

Respondent contends that *Spaulding Bakeries* was erroneously decided because: (1) The phrase "all its stock" was misread as referring to only voting or common stock and not to nonvoting preferred stock; (2) an inappropriate analogy was constructed between preferred stock and indebtedness; and (3) the legislative history suggests that section 332 applies when a liquidating distribution is made on preferred stock only.

"all its stock"

In *Spaulding Bakeries* we stated:

> The statute is specific in that there must be a "distribution" in liquidation and the distribution must be "in complete cancellation or redemption of *all its [parent's] stock.*" What does the phrase "all its stock" mean? Clearly it means at least 80 per cent of the common or voting stock. Does it also mean to include nonvoting stock which is limited and preferred as to dividends? We think not. The statute specifically excepts such preferred stock from the classes of stock which the parent should own—it could be owned by the parent or outsiders. * * * This means the payment in liquidation, in satisfaction of the preferred stock claim, whether to the parent or outsiders, will be immaterial. * * * Here there was no payment or distribution to the parent after the payment of the preferred stock claim in liquidation. The preferred stock claim captured all of the assets. There was nothing left to distribute to the parent as a common stockholder in the subsidiary. We hold the parent received no distribution in liquidation on its common stock within the intendment of the statute. Petitioner merely received in liquidation, payment of a part of its preferred stock claim—a fact which the statute, in effect, states will be immaterial. [27 T.C. at 688; emphasis added.]

In summary, we held that "its" referred to the parent's stock, i.e., the distribution had to be in complete cancellation or redemption of all the stock the parent owned in the subsidiary. Furthermore, because the parent had to own only 80 percent of each class of stock except nonvoting stock which was limited and preferred as to dividends, any distribution with respect to only the nonvoting preferred stock was "immaterial," i.e., not with respect to all the stock.

We agree with respondent that the phrase "all its stock" might be better interpreted as all *the subsidiary's* stock. Our decision, however, was not based on this analysis alone, and, as discussed below, we are not required to reach a different result.

Analogy Between Preferred Stock and Indebtedness

In *Spaulding Bakeries,* we cited cases which set forth the proposition that where the parent was the sole stockholder and also a creditor of the subsidiary, and the liquidating distribution to the parent was insufficient to satisfy the debt, the parent has both a deductible bad debt and a deductible stock loss. We analogized those cases to the facts in *Spaulding Bakeries.* We concluded that those cases were "authority for the conclusion that nothing was or could be 'distributed' on dissolution to the common stockholders until the full liquidation preference of the preferred stockholders was satisfied." 27 T.C. at 689.

Respondent contends that it was illogical to analogize preferred stock to indebtedness rather than to common stock. We disagree. We previously thought the analogy appropriate; the Second Circuit cited our analogy with approval; and we again find said analogy logical.

We further find that the Second Circuit aptly focused on the importance of priorities on dissolution. It stated, and we hold, that "the respective priorities of indebtedness over preferred and common stock and of preferred stock over common stock must be given full force and effect." 252 F.2d at 697. Here the assets were distributed with respect to the preferred stock. No assets were distributed with respect to the common. Consequently, the distribution was not a distribution with respect to all the subsidiary's stock.

Legislative History

Respondent contends that Congress originally passed section 112(b)(6) because (1) the nonrecognition of gain or loss on the liquidation of a controlled subsidiary would encourage simplification of corporate structures, thereby destroying unnecessary holding companies, and (2) in actuality, the parent and subsidiary represent one unitary business venture and unification of such closely connected businesses should not be subject to tax consequences. Respondent further contends that the second reason, the unitary theory, supports him in the present case and cites the dissenting opinion in *Spaulding Bakeries.*

The majority opinion did not adopt the unitary theory in *Spaulding Bakeries.* The dissenting opinion adopted the theory. The Second Circuit concluded that "no help was afforded by a reading of the legislative reports." Commissioner v. Spaulding Bakeries, 252 F.2d 693, 697 (2d Cir.1958).

Respondent gives us no new reason as to why the unitary theory, a theory implicitly rejected or accorded little weight by the Second Circuit and our majority opinion, should control the disposition of this case. He simply points to the dissenting opinion in *Spaulding Bakeries.* Suffice it to say that we are not persuaded. See *Commissioner v. Spaulding Bakeries,* supra.

Respondent also contends that the Senate Finance Committee report accompanying the enactment of the Internal Revenue Code of 1954 reflects congressional intent to minimize the elective features, and hence taxpayer manipulation, of section 332. Specifically, respondent cites a Finance Committee report which stated "Your committee has removed this provision with the view to limiting the elective features of the section." S.Rept. 1622, 83d Cong., 2d Sess. 255 (1954).

The provision referred to above prohibited the parent from selling any part of the subsidiary's stock between the time of adoption of the plan of liquidation and the time of distribution. See sec. 112(b)(6)(A), I.R.C. 1939. If a sale was effected, section 112(b)(6) would not apply. This provision, however, was deleted in 1954 upon the enactment of the Internal Revenue Code of 1954.

We cannot infer from the quoted excerpt, or respondent's purported fear of taxpayer manipulation, that Congress intended the result respondent seeks. See Granite Trust Co. v. United States, 238 F.2d 670, 679 (1st Cir.1956), revg. 150 F.Supp. 276 (D.Mass.1955). First, we decided Spaulding Bakeries in 1957. The Second Circuit affirmed in 1958. Congress has had ample opportunity to address any perceived taxpayer abuse spawned by Spaulding Bakeries.

Secondly, a manipulating taxpayer need not rely on Spaulding Bakeries. Section 332 has several requirements which can easily be avoided. See, e.g., Commissioner v. Day & Zimmerman, Inc., 151 F.2d 517 (3d Cir.1945), affg. a Memorandum Opinion of this Court (taxpayer sold stock to avoid 80–percent requirement); Granite Trust Co. v. United States, supra (taxpayer made gift and sale of stock to avoid 80–percent requirement).

Notwithstanding Spaulding Bakeries, Does Section 332 Apply?

Respondent alternatively argues that section 332 applies, even under the rationale of *Spaulding Bakeries,* because: (1) Porter Australia's preferred stock had voting rights and, therefore, the distribution in the present case cannot be considered "immaterial;" and (2) substance prevails over form and, here, petitioner in substance held only one class of stock.

Porter Australia's Preferred Stock

Respondent focuses on the voting rights of Porter Australia's preferred stock.[5] We need not. We agree that the Second Circuit's analysis was correct in that priorities on dissolution cannot be disregarded. In the instant case, Porter Australia's preferred stock had a liquidation preference. In satisfying that preference, no assets remained to distribute with respect to the common stock. Thus, the distribution was not in cancellation or redemption of *all* its stock.

Substance Over Form

Respondent contends that the substance of the transaction indicates that petitioner held only one class of stock which, when so viewed, would render Porter Australia's liquidating distribution subject to section 332 even under the rationale of *Spaulding Bakeries.* In support of his position, he states that Porter Australia's preferred stock did not grant petitioner any benefits or privileges that it did not already possess as the only stockholder in Porter Australia.

In Weiss v. Stearn, 265 U.S. 242, 254, 44 S.Ct. 490, 492 (1924), the Supreme Court stated:

> Questions of taxation must be determined by viewing what was actually done, rather than the declared purpose of the participants; and when applying the provisions of the Sixteenth Amendment and income laws enacted thereunder we must regard matters of substance and not mere form.

In the instant case, petitioner loaned Porter Australia money which Porter Australia needed to operate. Porter Australia capitalized the loans and issued preferred stock in 1966, 1968, and 1969 because it was unable to satisfy the loans in the short term and it wanted to avoid any further claim by respondent that income should be allocated to petitioner by reason of those loans. In 1979, petitioner received the liquidating distribution with respect to its preferred stock.

The preferred stock issued in 1966, 1968, and 1969, approximately 10 years before Porter Australia liquidated, was not "illusory" or part of a financial facade constructed of shuffled papers. Cf. Gregory v. Helvering, 293 U.S. 465, 55 S.Ct. 266 (1935) (transaction in form of corporate reorganization was just an elaborate conveyance). Significant consequences attached to petitioner's decision to capitalize the loans. Petitioner capitalized the loans with preferred stock, not common. We need not know why petitioner issued preferred stock instead of common. See Granite Trust Co. v. United States, supra. What is important here is that Porter Australia authorized and issued preferred stock with specific rights and privileges. Respondent has not argued that those rights and privileges have been ignored and the record does

5. The preferred stock in *Spaulding Bakeries* was treated as nonvoting even though, as in this case, it had certain limited voting rights on matters which affected it.

not suggest such a finding. We find that the preferred stock was exactly what it purported to be—preferred stock.

* * *

Finally, because we have held that section 332 does not bar the recognition of petitioner's losses, we hold that, based on the record, petitioner is entitled to an ordinary loss of $249,981 in 1978 with respect to the worthlessness of its common stock and a long-term capital loss of $1,957,770 in 1979 with respect to its preferred stock. See sec. 165(a) and (g).

* * *

ILLUSTRATIVE MATERIAL

A. TREATMENT OF THE PARENT CORPORATION

1. *General*

Where a parent corporation completely liquidates a subsidiary corporation which it controls, under section 332 no gain or loss is recognized to the parent. Under section 334(b) the basis of the assets in the parent corporation's hands remains the same as the basis of the assets to the subsidiary corporation. "Control" is defined in section 332(b)(1), through a cross reference to section 1504(a)(2), as at least 80 percent of the total combined voting power of all classes of voting stock and 80 percent of the total number of shares of all nonvoting stock; except that pursuant to section 1504(a)(4) nonvoting, nonparticipating nonconvertible preferred stock is not counted in determining control. When the nonrecognition rule of section 332 applies, the parent's investment in the stock of the subsidiary is irrelevant, and any potential gain or loss inherent in the stock disappears. This treatment differs from the exchanged basis rule which is more commonly encountered in tax free transactions and is the same as the transferred basis rule generally applied to the transferee corporation in a section 351 exchange or a corporate reorganization. Elimination of the potential gain inherent in the subsidiary's stock prevents double taxation of corporate profits which have not been distributed out of corporate solution. In this regard, section 332 serves a purpose analogous to the dividends received deduction under section 243, discussed supra page 507. The theory behind section 332 also is related to the consolidated return provisions of sections 1501 through 1504, discussed infra page 1042, which permit affiliated corporations (defined with reference to the 80 percent control test) to file a single income tax return reflecting their combined incomes. The results under section 332, however, are not the same as the results of filing a consolidated return.

As a corollary to the transferred basis provisions of section 334(b), section 381(a), discussed infra, Chapter 20, provides that the tax attributes of the subsidiary carry over to the parent. The most notable of these attributes are net operating loss carryovers, capital loss carryovers, and the earnings and profits accumulations or deficits.[3]

3. Under section 381(c)(2), if either the parent or the subsidiary has a deficit in its earnings and profits accounts, after a section 332 liquidation the parent must maintain separate earnings and profits accounts; the deficit of one corporation cannot be used to offset the surplus in the earnings and profits account of the other. Luckman v. Commissioner, 56 T.C. 1216 (1971). Earnings and profits accumulated by the parent after the liquidation are used to exhaust the deficit account before the accumulated earnings and profits account

2. *Cash Distributions*

Under section 332, the term "property" includes money. Rev.Rul. 69–379, 1969–2 Cum.Bull. 48. Thus the parent corporation recognizes neither gain nor loss even though only cash is received on the liquidation. International Investment Corp. v. Commissioner, 11 T.C. 678 (1948), aff'd per curiam, 175 F.2d 772 (3d Cir.1949). Taxable gain or loss would have been recognized previously by the subsidiary on the conversion of its assets to cash. Similarly, in Rev.Rul. 74–54, 1974–1 Cum.Bull. 76, in a section 332 liquidation, a note of the parent corporation held by the subsidiary was cancelled in the liquidation; the note was held to constitute property received by the parent corporation in the liquidation and it therefore did not realize cancellation of indebtedness income under either section 61(a)(12) or Regulations, section 1.301–1(m).

B. TREATMENT OF THE LIQUIDATED SUBSIDIARY IN GENERAL

When section 332 applies to the parent of a liquidating corporation, section 337, as amended in 1986, provides a general exception to the basic rule of section 336 that a liquidating corporation recognizes gain or loss on liquidating distributions. Under section 337(a), no gain or loss is recognized on a distribution to an "80 percent distributee", defined in section 337(c) as a corporation which meets the stock ownership requirements of section 332(b). The final sentence of section 337(c), referring to the consolidated return regulations, requires that a single corporation meet the 80 percent requirement: it is not sufficient for two or more affiliated corporations to have aggregate holdings meeting the 80 percent test. In concert, sections 332 and 337 provide for complete nonrecognition of gain or loss at the corporate level on the liquidation of a wholly owned subsidiary.

To prevent the complete avoidance of tax on appreciation in the subsidiary's assets, subject to certain exceptions, section 337 does not apply to a liquidation of a subsidiary of a tax-exempt organization. Section 337(b)(2). This provision is necessary because notwithstanding a carryover basis under section 334(b), a subsequent sale of the former subsidiary's assets would not be taxable.

C. CONTINUITY OF BUSINESS REQUIREMENT

The liquidation of a subsidiary clearly qualifies under section 332 where the parent continues to conduct the same business as, for example, operation of the assets as a division following the liquidation. Rev.Rul. 70–105, 1970–1 Cum.Bull. 70. But is continuation of the same business of the subsidiary required? Rev.Rul. 70–357, 1970–2 Cum.Bull. 79, ruled that it was sufficient if the parent used the assets of the subsidiary in the parent's business even though the business of the subsidiary was discontinued. What if the parent does not continue in any business, but itself liquidates following the liquidation of the subsidiary? In Fairfield S.S. Corp. v. Commissioner, 157 F.2d 321 (2d Cir.1946), Judge Learned Hand stated that the predecessor of section 332 did not apply where, following the liquidation of the subsidiary into the parent, the parent is then itself liquidated. Similarly, in Kamis Engineering Co. v. Commissioner, 60 T.C. 763 (1973), the Tax Court accepted the taxpayer's argument that section 332 did not apply where both

of the parent is increased. See Regulations, section 1.312–11(b)(2), (c).

the subsidiary and the parent were liquidated according to a single plan. However, Rev.Rul. 69–172, 1969–1 Cum.Bull. 99, seemed to assume that section 332 applied even in the situation where the parent was liquidated following the liquidation of the subsidiary.

The problem may be avoided by first liquidating the parent under section 331. Since under section 334(a) the shareholders would receive a fair market value basis for the stock of the subsidiary as the result of the section 331 liquidation of the parent, little if any gain would be realized by the shareholders upon the subsequent liquidation of the subsidiary. Where the parent is liquidated first, section 337 does not shield the subsidiary from recognizing gain or loss under section 336 on its subsequent liquidation, but this result is the same as if the subsidiary were liquidated first pursuant to section 332; the transferred basis that the parent took in the subsidiary's assets would have caused an identical gain to have been recognized to the parent corporation on the liquidating distribution by it of the former subsidiary's assets.

D. TRANSFERS TO SATISFY INDEBTEDNESS TO PARENT CORPORATION

If the subsidiary is indebted to the parent corporation and pursuant to a plan of liquidation to which section 332 applies the subsidiary distributes property in satisfaction of the debt, under section 337(b)(1) the distributing corporation recognizes no gain or loss, and the parenthetical clause in section 334(b)(1) provides the parent corporation with a transferred basis in the assets used to satisfy the debt. Thus, at least insofar as concerns liquidation of a solvent subsidiary, no distinction is made between distributions to satisfy an indebtedness to the parent and distributions in exchange for surrender of the parent's stock in the subsidiary. This rule prevents any attempt selectively to recognize losses by satisfying indebtedness with depreciated property while distributing appreciated property in a nonrecognition distribution.

E. INSOLVENT SUBSIDIARIES

As illustrated in *H.K. Porter Co.,* supra, for section 332 to apply there must be some distribution applicable to the common stock, so as to supply the "cancellation or redemption of *all* [the] stock" required by section 332(b)(2). Thus, if the assets of the subsidiary are insufficient to pay its debts or satisfy its preferred shares, including those held by the parent, the common stock simply becomes worthless rather than being cancelled or redeemed and section 332 is therefore inapplicable. In such a case, a section 165(g)(3) ordinary loss deduction may be recognized by the parent on the common stock, assuming the requirements of that section are met. See Northern Coal & Dock Co. v. Commissioner, 12 T.C. 42 (1949)(A); Commissioner v. Spaulding Bakeries, Inc., 252 F.2d 693 (2d Cir.1958); Waterman Steamship Corp. v. United States, 203 F.Supp. 915 (S.D.Ala.1962); Textron, Inc. v. United States, 561 F.2d 1023 (1st Cir.1977) (loss allowed even though subsidiary was subsequently reactivated). Capital gain or loss may be recognized with respect to the preferred stock when there are no distributions on the common stock. Any assets received by the parent corporation in exchange for the preferred stock in this situation take a fair market value basis under section 334(a). In such cases, there is no carryover of the tax attributes of the subsidiary under section 381. Rev.Rul. 68–359, 1968–2 Cum.Bull. 161; Rev.Rul. 59–296, 1959–2 Cum.Bull. 87; Rev.Rul. 70–489,

1970–2 Cum.Bull. 53 (where the parent continued to operate the subsidiary's business as a division).

Since nonrecognition of gain or loss to the subsidiary is conditioned on the liquidation qualifying under section 332, gain or loss will be recognized by the subsidiary with respect to transfers of property to satisfy indebtedness. Gain recognition is appropriate where the parent receives no distribution on any class of stock because the corporation is insolvent and all assets are used to retire debts. But the appropriateness of recognition of gain or loss is not as clear in cases such as *H.K. Porter Co.* where the parent receives a distribution with respect to preferred stock, but none with respect to common stock, particularly when the parent owns all (or at least 80 percent) of the preferred stock. Even though the taxpayer's argument to this effect was rejected by the court in *H.K. Porter Co.,* the preferred stock represents all of the equity interest in the corporation at the time of the liquidation and is therefore tantamount to common stock. Furthermore, for all other purposes, unless the preferred stock is reclassified as debt under the general debt-equity principles, discussed supra, page 384, the preferred stock will be treated as stock rather than as debt. This analysis cannot be applied, however, if the parent owns less than 80 percent of any class of preferred stock which actually receives a liquidating distribution.

Where a subsidiary's insolvency is due to indebtedness to the parent, cancellation of the debt by the parent to make the subsidiary solvent followed by liquidation of the subsidiary might enable the liquidation to qualify under section 332, and hence, for example, make available to the parent a net operating loss carryover of the subsidiary; but such a cancellation of indebtedness will be ignored if it was an integral part of the liquidation. Rev.Rul. 68–602, 1968–2 Cum.Bull. 135. See also Braddock Land Co. v. Commissioner, 75 T.C. 324 (1980). Often, however, this will not be a desirable planning technique because under section 108(e)(6), the subsidiary will recognize income as a result of the cancellation of indebtedness, even if the cancellation is classified as a contribution to capital.

For purposes of section 332, insolvency exists when the fair market value of the subsidiary's assets is less than the sum of its debts plus the liquidation preference of the preferred stock. Difficult valuation problems may exist where the subsidiary is potentially insolvent, especially where intangible assets, such as patents, copyrights, and goodwill, are involved. See, e.g., Swiss Colony, Inc. v. Commissioner, 52 T.C. 25 (1969) (judicial determination of fair market value of patents), aff'd on other issues in 428 F.2d 49 (7th Cir.1970); Continental Grain Co. v. Commissioner, 57 T.C.M. 57 (1989) (in determining that subsidiary was insolvent court took into account imputed interest on book account debt to parent). In addition, problems arise in determining whether advances to the subsidiary by the parent in fact constituted equity. Inductotherm Industries, Inc. v. Commissioner, 48 T.C.M. 167 (1984), reclassified as equity a subsidiary's purported indebtedness to the parent, thereby eliminating an insolvency situation and bringing the liquidation within the nonrecognition rule of section 332. See Development Corp. of America v. Commissioner, 55 T.C.M. 455 (1988) (same); see also Byerlite Corp. v. Williams, 286 F.2d 285 (6th Cir.1960).

F. TIMING PROBLEMS

A liquidation qualifies under section 332 if it is completed within single taxable year or if the plan requires completion of the liquidation within three years from the close of the year in which the plan is adopted *and* the liquidation is in fact completed within that period. No formal plan is required if a liquidation actually is completed within a single year. Burnside Veneer Co. v. Commissioner, 167 F.2d 214 (6th Cir.1948). Where a subsidiary for valid business reasons did not make a liquidating distribution until February, 1966, pursuant to a plan of liquidation adopted on July 1, 1963, section 332 treatment was upheld; the phrase "within the taxable year" in section 332(c)(2) refers to the year in which liquidating distributions are made and not to the year of the adoption of the plan of liquidation. Rev. Rul. 71–326, 1971–2 Cum.Bull. 177. See also Rev.Rul. 76–317, 1976–2 Cum.Bull. 98, which held that the "taxable year" referred to in section 332(b)(2) and (3) is the taxable year of the subsidiary corporation. If the liquidation takes more than a year to complete, the Commissioner may require the corporation to post a bond. See Regulations, section 1.332–4. The statute provides that if the liquidation is not completed within the required period, none of the distributions are treated as liquidating distributions within the meaning of section 332(a). However, the distributions presumably remain liquidating distributions within the meaning of sections 331 and 336. Thus, if the conditions of section 332 are not met, both the liquidating subsidiary corporation and the parent corporation will recognize gain or loss on the liquidation. The property received by the parent would take a fair market value basis under section 334(a) rather than a transferred basis.

In general, retention of any property by a subsidiary, regardless of amount, for the purpose of continuing the operation of a business or of engaging in a new business will prevent the application of section 332. Rev. Rul. 76–525, 1976–2 Cum.Bull. 98. But Rev.Rul. 84–2, 1984–1 Cum.Bull. 92, held that the transfer to a new subsidiary by the parent of a nominal amount of the liquidated subsidiary's assets for the purpose of protecting the corporate name of the subsidiary did not disqualify the liquidation.

Suppose that both the parent and the subsidiary will recognize losses if the liquidation is taxable. Can sections 332 and 337 be avoided by intentionally spreading liquidating distributions out over a four year period? In Cherry–Burrell Corp. v. United States, 367 F.2d 669 (8th Cir.1966), a U.S. parent received the first liquidating distribution from its British subsidiary in 1952. However, because claims were pending against the subsidiary and British law prohibited further distributions until the claims were finally settled in 1968, the court held that section 332 applied because all assets were converted to cash in 1952, only an amount necessary for a reasonable reserve for the claims asserted was retained as required by British law, no commercial activity was engaged in during the interim period, and the final liquidating distribution was made immediately after the settlement of claims.

G. EIGHTY PERCENT CONTROL REQUIREMENT AND TAX PLANNING

Section 332 is not by its terms elective. But if the taxpayer desires to avoid sections 332 and 337 to obtain loss deductions on the parent's stock investment and the subsidiary's liquidating distributions, it may do so by a sale of stock, prior to the adoption of the plan of liquidation, which reduces the parent's stock ownership below the 80 percent control line. Commissioner v. Day & Zimmermann Inc., 151 F.2d 517 (3d Cir.1945) (sale at public auction to corporation's treasurer who purchased stock with his own funds). See also Granite Trust Co. v. United States, 238 F.2d 670 (1st Cir.1956) (Commissioner was not allowed to use the step transaction doctrine to bring a liquidation under the predecessor of section 332 where, after the plan of liquidation was adopted, certain sales and gifts were made so as to come within the provision disqualifying liquidation if the amount of stock ownership dropped during liquidation). In the opposite situation, in Estate of Glass v. Commissioner, 55 T.C. 543 (1970), aff'd per curiam, 453 F.2d 1375 (5th Cir.1972), a parent corporation was unable to utilize the step transaction doctrine to come within section 332, where it owned only 75 percent of the stock of the subsidiary at the time of adoption of the plan of liquidation and thereafter acquired the balance of the stock. The difference in result between *Day & Zimmerman Inc.* and *Estate of Glass* can be explained by the statutory requirement of section 332(b)(1) that the parent meet the 80 percent control test at the time of adoption of the plan and at all times until receipt of the distribution. Thus, although control may be broken after adoption of the plan, control acquired after adoption of the plan does not meet the statutory prerequisite.

Because control acquired after adoption of a plan of liquidation does not bring the liquidation under section 332, it sometimes is important to determine when the plan was adopted. In Rev.Rul. 70–106, 1970–1 Cum.Bull. 70, the parent corporation owned 75 percent of the stock of its subsidiary and desired to liquidate the subsidiary under section 332. Pursuant to an agreement with the minority shareholders, their stock was redeemed and the subsidiary corporation was then liquidated. The Ruling held that the plan of liquidation was adopted at the time the agreement was reached with the minority shareholders and the transaction therefore did not qualify under section 332, since at that time the parent corporation owned only 75 percent of the stock of the subsidiary. All shareholders thus were taxed under Section 331. On the other hand, where the parent corporation first purchased the stock of the minority shareholders and then liquidated the subsidiary, section 332 treatment was allowed. Rev.Rul. 75–521, 1975–2 Cum.Bull. 120. The later Ruling distinguished Rev.Rul. 70–106 on the grounds that in the earlier Ruling the entire distribution was a distribution in liquidation; in Rev.Rul. 75–521, however, the purchase by the parent corporation was not a part of a distribution in liquidation and the mere sale between shareholders did not constitute the adoption of a plan of liquidation.

In George L. Riggs, Inc. v. Commissioner, 64 T.C. 474 (1975) (A), a corporation, during the time that it owned less than 80 percent of the stock of its subsidiary, voted in favor of selling substantially all of the assets of the subsidiary and took various other steps evidencing an intention to liquidate the subsidiary. Subsequently, by virtue of a redemption by the subsidiary, the parent corporation obtained 80 percent control of the subsidiary. Thereafter the subsidiary formally adopted a plan of liquidation. The Commissioner asserted that a plan of liquidation had been adopted prior to obtaining 80 percent control and thus section 332 was inapplicable. The court held, however, that although the actions taken prior to formal adoption of the plan of liquidation may have evidenced an intention to liquidate the subsidiary, the intent to liquidate is not tantamount to adoption of a plan of liquidation. The date of adoption of the plan of liquidation controlled and section 332 therefore provided nonrecognition treatment to the liquidation. The court stated that "section 332 is elective in the sense that with advance planning and properly structured transaction, a corporation should be able to render section 332 applicable or inapplicable". (489) Rev.Rul. 70–106 was distinguished on the basis that the plan of liquidation there was adopted when the agreement regarding the redemption was reached with the minority shareholders.

Thus, if liquidation of a subsidiary is contemplated, the tax advisor has a choice of recommending a taxable or tax-free liquidation of the subsidiary. In choosing between the alternatives, the effect of sections 336 and 337 often will be more important than the effect of section 332. Because the parent's basis in the stock of the subsidiary is unaffected by the subsidiary's earnings and profits history (unless a consolidated return has been filed), the parent may realize little or no gain on the liquidation while the subsidiary realizes a substantial gain or loss on the liquidating distribution. In general, a taxable liquidation will be advisable where the subsidiary has depreciated assets and both the subsidiary and the parent will realize a loss or the subsidiary's loss exceeds the parent's gain, or where the parent's loss exceeds the subsidiary's gain. On the other hand, the tax-free route of section 332 ordinarily will be advisable where the subsidiary's gain exceeds the parent's loss or both corporations realize a gain. Where the subsidiary has a net operating loss carryover that would be available to the parent, the determination is more complex. If the net operating loss carryover is large enough, the tax benefit to the parent of acquiring the carryover may compensate for denial of otherwise available losses, but in other cases, current loss recognition may yield a greater benefit.

H. DISTRIBUTIONS TO MINORITY SHAREHOLDERS

Section 332 applies only to the controlling corporate parent. Minority shareholders cannot take advantage of its provisions. Therefore, the liquidating distribution received by a minority shareholder will be taxable under section 331; and a minority shareholder will hold the distributed property with a basis determined under section 334(a).

Furthermore, even though section 337 shields the subsidiary from recognition of gain or loss on liquidating distributions to the parent in a section 332 liquidation, section 337(a) limits nonrecognition to gain or loss inherent in property distributed to the parent. If property is distributed to minority shareholders, section 336 applies as to gains, but section 336(d)(3) requires nonrecognition of losses with respect to property distributed to minority shareholders. This asymmetrical treatment presumably is grounded on concerns that a liquidating subsidiary with minority shareholders would selectively distribute depreciated assets to the minority shareholders in order to recognize the loss while distributing appreciated assets to the parent subject to section 332 nonrecognition. Nonrecognition of losses, however, extends to pro rata liquidating distributions to minority shareholders as well as to non-pro rata liquidations. Thus the nonrecognition rule with respect to losses appears to be overbroad.

I. RELATED MATTERS

The liquidation of a subsidiary may closely resemble one of the forms of corporate reorganizations specified in section 368, discussed, infra, Chapters 17 and 18. For example, the merger of a controlled subsidiary into its parent is treated as a section 332 liquidation pursuant to Regulations, section 1.332–2(d). In this case, if minority shareholders receive stock of the parent, they might be required to recognize gain on the liquidation, even though the receipt of the parent's stock would have been tax free if the corporate reorganization rules governed. Must the subsidiary also recognize gain on a constructive distribution of the parent's stock? This issue is explored further infra, page 798. For problems involved in liquidating a partially owned subsidiary, see infra, page 849. Regulations, section 1.1502–32, specify the treatment where a parent and subsidiary have been filing a consolidated return prior to the liquidation of the subsidiary.

J. REFERENCES

Grainer, Affiliated Groups: Liquidating an Insolvent Subsidiary, 14 J.Corp.Tax. 251 (1987); Burke, Complete Liquidation of the Corporate Subsidiary: The Questions, Some Answers and Some Observations, 22 Me.L. Rev. 363 (1970); Niswander, Techniques for Liquidation of a Subsidiary: Taxable vs. Tax–Free: Wholly or Partially Owned: Problems of Minority Stockholders, Including Section 334(b)(2), 28 N.Y.U. Tax Inst. 667 (1970); Halperin, Carryovers of Earnings and Profits, 18 Tax L.Rev. 289, 305 (1963); Seplow, Acquisition of Assets of a Subsidiary: Liquidation or Reorganization?, 73 Harv.L.Rev. 484 (1960).

PART III

ELECTIVE TAX TREATMENT

CHAPTER 15

S CORPORATIONS

INTERNAL REVENUE CODE: Sections 1361–1378.

SECTION 1. BACKGROUND

The Pre-1982 Version of Subchapter S. Subchapter S was enacted in 1958 to make it possible for "businesses to select the form of business organization desired, without the necessity of taking into account major differences in tax consequence." [1] As originally enacted, Subchapter S status was elective for corporations which had no more than ten individual stockholders, but over the years the number of permissible stockholders has been increased [2] and grantor trusts, voting trusts, and certain trusts with a single current income beneficiary have been added to the list of permissible stockholders.[3]

Despite references in the early legislative history to partnerships,[4] the original version of Subchapter S did not adopt the pass-through treatment of items in the partnership model. Only corporate level capital gains and losses were given pure conduit treatment, retaining their character when included in the stockholder's gross income. Stockholders were taxable on actual dividend distributions from the corporation plus their share of the corporation's "undistributed taxable income." The corporation's net operating losses also passed through to stockholders, each of whom was allowed to deduct the corporate losses to the extent of the stockholder's total investment in the corporation, measured by the aggregate bases of corporate stock and debt instruments held by the stockholder. A stockholder's stock basis was increased by undistributed taxable income and decreased by pass-through net operating losses. Undistributed taxable income that was taxed to the stockholder for the taxable year could be distributed to the stockholder as a return of basis during the two and one-half month period following the close of the taxable year. Distributions after the two and

1. S.Rep. No. 85–1983, 85th Cong., 2d Sess. 87 (1958).

2. Fifteen stockholders were approved for electing corporations in existence for more than five years by the Tax Reform Act of 1976 and all electing corporations by the Revenue Act of 1978. The number was increased to 25 in 1981 and to 35 in 1982.

3. The 1976 Act also permitted an estate of a deceased stockholder to continue as a qualified stockholder, but only for a period of 60 days.

4. S.Rep. No. 83–1622, 83d Cong., 2d Sess. 118 (1954).

one-half month period were treated as a return of basis only if the corporation had no earnings and profits.

An electing corporation was not subject to tax unless it realized extraordinary capital gains. The corporate level tax was designed to discourage a "one-shot" election by a corporation anticipating gain on the disposition of capital (or section 1231) assets.[5]

Use of a Subchapter S corporation as a vehicle for passive investment activities and real estate investments was restricted by a provision that terminated a Subchapter S election if more than 20 percent of the corporation's gross receipts were derived from passive investments such as interest, dividends, rents and royalties. Prior to 1982, only a relatively small number of corporations elected Subchapter S status because of the restriction on passive income coupled with the fact that most small businesses could achieve close to a single level of taxation in a C corporation through a combination of deductible salaries and interest payments to stockholders, without the additional tax and accounting complexity imposed by Subchapter S. The election was mostly valuable during the early years of a venture when the corporation produced losses which could be passed through to the stockholders. Often the election would be terminated when the enterprise became profitable.[6]

The Subchapter S Revision Act of 1982. In 1969 the Treasury Department, in conjunction with the Tax Section of the American Bar Association, proposed revising Subchapter S to conform more closely to the complete pass-through model of the partnership rules.[7] The Treasury study pointed out that the hybrid nature of the S corporation, "not quite a corporation and not quite a partnership," led to misunderstandings of the workings of the rules which in turn created complexities and unintended hardships. To alleviate these problems the Treasury study recommended adoption of complete pass-through taxation of the entity's tax-significant items under the partnership rules plus a number of other changes to simplify Subchapter S. After many years the 1969 proposal was adopted, generally intact, in 1982.[8] As amended in 1982, Subchapter S allows an electing corporation, referred to as an "S corporation," to have 35 stockholders. Section 1361(b)(1)(A). Qualified stockholders include only individuals, grantor trusts, voting trusts, and "qualified Subchapter S trusts." Section 1361(d). A qualified trust is a trust that has a single income beneficiary who is currently taxed on the

5. From 1966 through 1986, section 1374 imposed a tax on capital gains in excess of $25,000. The tax applied only if capital gains exceeded 50 percent of taxable income for the year and the corporation's Subchapter S election had been in effect for less than three years.

6. In 1973, for example, some 313,800 corporations filed returns as S corporations. Of these, about 190,000 showed net income. The total number of corporations, electing and nonelecting, filing returns in 1973 was 1,905,000. U.S. Treas. Dept., Internal Revenue Service, Statistics of Income, 1973—Corporation Income Tax Returns, 117–123, 148–150 (1977).

7. U.S. Treasury Dept. Tax Reform Studies and Proposals, House Ways and Means Committee and Senate Finance Committee, 91st Cong., 1st Sess. (1969).

8. The revisions were effective for taxable years beginning after December 31, 1982.

pass-through income of the S corporation. As under prior law, an S corporation must be a domestic corporation, it cannot have a stockholder who is a nonresident alien individual, a corporation or a partnership, and it may issue only one class of stock (although there is an exception for stock that varies in voting rights). See section 1361(b) and (c). S corporation status may be elected only with the consent of all stockholders at the time the election is filed. An election is effective on the first day of the taxable year following the filing of the election, except that an election filed within the first two and one-half months of the taxable year may be retroactive to the first day of the taxable year. Section 1362(b). Once made, an election continues in effect until it is revoked by a majority of the stockholders, the corporation ceases to meet the qualifications as an S corporation, or the corporation has accumulated earnings and profits [9] and earns passive investment income in excess of 25 percent of gross receipts for three consecutive taxable years. Section 1362(d).

Generally an S corporation is not subject to corporate tax. Section 1363(a). There are two exceptions. Under section 1374, enacted in the Tax Reform Act of 1986 as a backstop to repeal of the *General Utilities* doctrine, see supra, page 477, some S corporations are taxable on gain recognized on disposition of appreciated assets or income items acquired while the corporation was a C corporation, or acquired from a C corporation in a nonrecognition transaction. In addition, under section 1375, an S corporation with accumulated earnings and profits is taxable at regular corporate rates to the extent that passive investment income exceeds 25 percent of its gross receipts.

S corporation items of income, loss or deduction are passed through the entity to the stockholders, and retain their character in the stockholder's hands, in the same manner that partnership items are passed through to partners under Subchapter K. Section 1366. Thus each item of income or deduction that may affect stockholders differently must be separately stated and reported to the stockholders. For example, tax exempt interest income retains its exemption under section 103, and interest expense must be categorized under the complex interest allocation rules to determine its deductibility by the individual stockholders. Each stockholder reports the item on his return as if the item were derived by the stockholder directly. The character of items, such as capital gain, is based on the character of income at the corporate level. The stockholder's basis in S corporation stock is increased for income items and decreased for deduction or loss items passed through to the stockholder from the corporation. Section 1367. As under the pre–1982 provisions, the stockholder's deductible loss is limited to the stockholder's basis in stock and debt of the S corporation. Section 1366(d)(1).

9. A corporation will accumulate earnings and profits only in years it is a C corporation. Thus, this restriction does not apply to a corporation that has no tax history as a C corporation.

Since S corporation income is taxed to the stockholders when realized by the corporation, subsequent distributions of the previously taxed income are received by stockholders without additional tax. Section 1368. Distributions reduce the stockholder's basis in stock of the corporation. Distributions in excess of basis result in recognition of capital gain.

A second tier of distribution rules applies to an S corporation that has accumulated earnings and profits from taxable years in which it was a C corporation. The corporation must maintain an "accumulated adjustments account" which reflects net corporate income items that have been passed through to stockholders. Distributions to the extent of this accumulated adjustments account are received by the stockholders without tax. Section 1368(b). To the extent that distributions exceed the accumulated adjustments account, the distributions are treated as distributions of earnings and profits, to the extent thereof, and are taxed to the stockholders as dividends. Thus a "double" tax pattern is preserved for earnings originally generated in a C corporation. Any further distributions are received by the stockholders as a reduction of basis, then capital gain to the extent that a distribution exceeds the recipient stockholder's basis. Discussion of the problems of an S corporation with a prior history as a C corporation is deferred to Section 4, infra, page 672.

Although the 1982 Act in general adopted the partnership model for taxing S corporations, there are significant differences between the taxation of S corporations and partnerships which affect a taxpayer's choice between the two entities. Beneficial ownership of an S corporation is limited to 35 stockholders, while there is no limit on the number of persons who may be partners in a partnership. Nor is there any restriction upon the types of entities that may be partners. The partnership form provides a significant advantage in the case of leveraged investment where losses are anticipated. Partners are allowed to include their shares of partnership debt in the bases of their partnership interests which in turn allows partners to deduct partnership losses attributable to partnership level debt. In contrast, the stockholder's basis in Subchapter S stock or debt is limited to the stockholder's actual investment in the corporation. This limitation also means that while untaxed entity level cash, e.g., from a refinancing, can be distributed by a partnership free of tax, the same distribution by an S corporation may trigger gain recognition. For these reasons, S corporations have not been used as a viable form for leveraged investments such as real estate.

Subchapter S also differs from Subchapter K in its treatment of distributions of appreciated property. An S corporation is required to recognize gain on a distribution of appreciated property to stockholders. The recognized gain is passed through to the stockholders. The distributee stockholder obtains a fair market value basis in the distributed property. Subject to some exceptions, distributions of appreciated property by a partnership generally do not trigger recognition of gain.

Instead, the distributee partner takes the partnership's basis in the partnership and recognition of gain is deferred until the distributee disposes of the property. The Code is thus not completely neutral as to the choice between a Subchapter S corporation and a partnership.

The Tax Reform Act of 1986. Two significant changes to the taxation of C corporations in the 1986 Tax Reform Act made S corporation status more attractive to many taxpayers. As a result of the present rate structure, taking into account the double taxation of distributed earnings of a C corporation, the maximum effective rate of taxation of distributed C corporation income is 52.4 percent, compared to a top effective rate of 28 percent on S corporation income. For C corporations the 1986 Act also ensured double taxation of corporate level appreciation on corporate assets by requiring corporate level recognition of gain on liquidation and distribution of assets. This potential tax is avoided if Subchapter S status is used. These two changes, coupled with the repeal of preferential treatment of long-term capital gains have resulted in the pass-through entity being the preferred form of business organization, from a tax perspective, after 1986. Whether a partnership or an S corporation is more desirable than a C corporation, however, depends on a broad range of factors. It is clear, however, that after 1986, S corporation status is the preferred form of business for most corporations that qualify for its benefits.[10]

The tax treatment of S corporations that have always been S corporations is relatively straight-forward. Technical complexities, of course, are encountered. But for such corporations, the governing provisions are not particularly difficult either in concept or in practice. Section 3 discusses Subchapter S in the context of a corporation which was formed as an S corporation and never changed that status.

A corporation which has a C corporation history can elect S corporation status. The rules governing such corporations are much more complex than those applicable to S corporations with no C corporation history. These rules are discussed in Section 4.

Subchapter S represents one way of integrating the corporate and personal income taxes. At the end of Section 3, consider whether the S corporation regime can be applied to corporations such as General Motors or Polaroid. At the end of Section 4, consider whether the rules adopted for corporations with a C corporation history can or should be used as transition rules to a fully integrated corporate and individual tax system.

References: Yelen, Choosing the S Corporation as the Preferred Entity, 42 N.Y.U.Inst. on Fed.Tax. 13–1 (1984); Starr, The S Corporation: Is it the Right Choice?, N.Y.U. 43d Ann.Inst. on Fed.Tax. 5–1

10. In calendar year 1987, 892,376 out of 3,828,613 corporations filed S corporation returns. For 1988 the Internal Revenue Service estimates that the number of S corporation returns will increase to 1,071,600. Int. Rev. Service, Statistics of Income Bull. Spring 1988, 87.

(1984); Eustice & J. Kuntz, Federal Income Taxation of S Corporations (1985).

SECTION 2. ELIGIBILITY, ELECTION AND TERMINATION

A. STOCKHOLDER RULES

INTERNAL REVENUE CODE: Section 1361(b)(1), (c)(1)–(3), (d).

Almost every tax provision enacted for small business has its own concept of "small business." In Subchapter S, this concept is embodied in the requirements of section 1361(b)(1) that the electing corporation have no more than thirty-five stockholders, and that it have no stockholder who is not an individual, an estate, a grantor trust or a "qualified Subchapter S trust." [11]

Section 1361(c)(2) permits four types of domestic trusts as stockholders of an S corporation; trusts treated as owned by a United States citizen or resident (grantor trusts), grantor trusts that survive the death of the grantor (but only for a limited period), testamentary trusts (again only for a limited period), and voting trusts. Section 1361(d) further provides for a "qualified Subchapter S trust", which is a trust with a single income beneficiary who has elected to be treated as the owner of S corporation stock held by the trust so that, for purposes of the beneficiary's tax liability, S corporation items of income and loss pass through the trust directly to the beneficiary.

ILLUSTRATIVE MATERIAL

A. NUMBER OF STOCKHOLDERS

1. *Policy Aspects*

The legislative history of the Subchapter S Revision Act of 1982 indicates that the 35 stockholder limit is intended to correspond to the private placement exemption of federal securities law.[12] There is, however, no inherent tax policy rationale for limiting pass through tax treatment to 35 stockholders, although if there are too many stockholders administrative problems may arise because tax deficiencies must be assessed and collected at the shareholder level. (Audits, however, are conducted on the corporate level. See sections 6241–6245.) Although limiting the number of stockholders allowed to an S corporation reduces the complexity of accounting for allocations of corporate items to the stockholders, experience with Subchapter K demonstrates that pass-through accounting on a large scale is possible. It has been suggested that the principal purpose of restrictions on S corporation ownership is budgetary. "An elective system of complete integration—such as we would have in Subchapter S without this limitation—would be expen-

11. Compare section 1244, which, for purposes of allowing ordinary loss treatment rather than capital loss treatment upon the worthlessness of certain common stock, defines a "small business corporation" as a corporation having no more than $1,000,000 of paid-in capital.

12. S.Rep. No. 97–640, 97th Cong. 2d Sess. 7 (1982).

sive, more expensive than a mandatory system because the election would not be made where the substitution of the stockholder for the corporate tax would yield more to the Treasury. In an era of mega deficits, such a change is probably not feasible." [13]

2. *Some Technical Issues*

As to identifying the number of stockholders, a husband and wife (and their respective estates) are treated as a single stockholder regardless of the form of ownership in which the stock is held. Section 1361(c)(1).[14] Aside from this one case, each family member owning shares is counted separately.

In Rev.Rul. 77–220, 1977–1 Cum.Bull. 263, promulgated when the statute allowed only 10 stockholders, 30 unrelated individuals attempted to enter into the joint operation of a single business using S corporations. Three corporations were organized with 10 stockholders each. Each corporation became a partner in a partnership which operated the business. The Ruling held that "solely for the purpose of making the [S corporation] election," three corporations would be considered as a single corporation with 30 stockholders, thus disqualifying it for S corporation treatment. The three separate corporations had been formed for the principal purpose of making the S corporation election which the Ruling treated as a tax avoidance purpose citing Gregory v. Helvering, 293 U.S. 465 (1935).

Under section 1361(b)(1)(C) an S corporation may not have a nonresident alien stockholder. In Ward v. United States, 661 F.2d 226 (Ct.Cl. 1981), a corporation's Subchapter S election was held invalid because the taxpayer's nonresident alien wife was the beneficial owner of the corporation's stock under community property laws.

B. ESTATES AND TRUSTS AS ELIGIBLE STOCKHOLDERS

1. *General*

Section 1361 permits the estate of a deceased stockholder, the estate of an individual in bankruptcy, and certain trusts, including "grantor trusts" if the grantor is a United States citizen or resident, voting trusts, and, for a limited period of time, testamentary trusts to be S corporation stockholders. In the case of a grantor trust, the grantor is treated as the stockholder and in the case of voting trusts, each beneficiary of the trust is treated as a stockholder.

Under section 1361(c)(2)(A), a grantor trust may continue as an S corporation stockholder for 60 days following the death of the grantor, or, if the corpus of the trust is includable in the gross estate of the grantor for estate tax purposes, the trust may continue as a stockholder for two years. If grantor trust status terminates for some reason other than the death of the grantor—for example if the grantor relinquishes the powers that make the trust a grantor trust—the trust becomes an ineligible stockholder and the corporation's S corporation status is terminated immediately.

13. Eustice, Subchapter S Corporations and Partnerships: A Search for the Pass Through Paradigm (Some Preliminary Proposals), 39 Tax L.Rev. 345, 356–357 (1984).

14. Before January 1, 1979, a husband and wife who owned some shares jointly and other shares individually counted as two stockholders. See Hicks Nurseries, Inc. v. Commissioner, 517 F.2d 437 (2d Cir. 1975).

A testamentary trust to which stock of an S corporation has been transferred is an eligible S corporation stockholder for only 60 days following the day on which the stock is transferred. Section 1361(c)(2)(A)(iii).

There is no statutory limit on the length of time that an estate may remain a qualified stockholder. However, Old Virginia Brick Co. v. Commissioner, 367 F.2d 276 (4th Cir.1966), held that where an estate which was one of the stockholders of an S corporation was kept open substantially beyond the period necessary for the performance of administrative duties, it became in effect an ineligible testamentary trust and the corporation was disqualified from S corporation status. But Rev.Rul. 76–23, 1976–1 Cum. Bull. 264, allows retention of S corporation stock by an estate for purposes of the ten year installment payment of estate taxes in section 6166.[15]

2. *Qualified Subchapter S Trusts*

Section 1361(d) permits a "qualified Subchapter S trust," to be an S corporation stockholder. A qualified Subchapter S trust is one which, by its terms, has only one current income beneficiary who will be the sole income beneficiary during the beneficiary's life or for the term of the trust. Section 1361(d)(3). To avoid any possibility of splitting S corporation income and deductions between the trust and the beneficiary, a qualified Subchapter S trust is an eligible stockholder only if the beneficiary elects in effect to treat the trust as a grantor trust with respect to the S corporation stock. Thus the income beneficiary is treated as the owner of the portion of the trust which consists of S corporation stock. The beneficiary is taxed on the income and receives the deductions allocable to the S corporation stock without regard to the normal rules of trust taxation. Section 1361(d)(1)(B). These requirements are designed to prevent use of trusts to avoid the 35 stockholder limitation and to facilitate pass-through taxation of the trust beneficiary as the ultimate recipient of the S corporation income.

A trust is a qualified Subchapter S trust only if a timely election is filed with the Internal Revenue Service by the beneficiary (or the beneficiary's legal representative or parent if there is no legal representative appointed). A separate election is required with respect to the stock of each S corporation owned by a qualified Subchapter S trust. Failure to file the election for a trust that becomes an S corporation stockholder will result in revocation of the corporation's status as an S corporation.

Section 1361(d)(2)(D) provides that an election is retroactively effective for the two month and fifteen day period preceding the filing of the election. See Proposed Regulations, section 1.1361–1A(i)(3), as to timing matters.

B. ELIGIBILITY

INTERNAL REVENUE CODE: Section 1361(a), (b)(1)(D), (b)(2), (c)(4).

Only a domestic corporation which is not a member of an affiliated group of corporations may elect to be an S corporation. This means that an S corporation cannot own the stock of an 80 percent controlled subsidiary. However, section 1361(c)(6) permits ownership of control-

15. See also Regulations, section 1.641(b)–3(a) (an estate is deemed terminated for federal tax purposes after the expiration of a reasonable period for the performance by the executor of the duties of administration).

ling stock of an inactive subsidiary which has neither begun business nor derived gross income. Certain other corporations also are ineligible for S corporation status. These include banks, insurance companies, and other corporations subject to a special tax regime. Section 1362(b)(2).

Under section 1361(b)(1)(D), an S corporation is allowed to have only one class of stock. The purpose of this requirement is to avoid accounting difficulties which would arise if the corporation were permitted to create different interests in income and loss in different classes of stock. Thus, unlike partnerships, S corporations are not allowed to make special allocations of income and loss among S corporation stockholders.

Section 1361(c)(4) allows differences in voting rights without violating the one-class-of-stock rule so long as the outstanding shares are identical with respect to the rights of the holders in the profits and in the assets of the corporation.

The existence of debt of an S corporation that might be classified as equity creates a risk that the re-classified equity interests will be treated as a prohibited second class of stock. To reduce this risk, section 1361(c)(5) provides a safe-harbor in which certain "straight debt" will not be considered a second class of stock.

ILLUSTRATIVE MATERIAL

A. ONE CLASS OF STOCK

1. *Debt Reclassified as Equity*

Before the Subchapter S Revision Act of 1982, the one class of stock requirement was the cause of considerable litigation. Regulations, section 1.1371–1(g), promulgated under the pre–1983 version of Subchapter S, provided that prorata debt obligations reclassified as equity would not be treated as a second class of stock. The Commissioner litigated, without success, a string of cases attempting to treat as a second class of stock nonprorata debt that was classified as equity. See Stinnett v. Commissioner, 54 T.C. 221 (1970); Amory Cotton Oil Co. v. United States, 468 F.2d 1046 (5th Cir.1972); Shores Realty Co., Inc. v. United States, 468 F.2d 572 (5th Cir.1972); Portage Plastics Co., Inc. v. United States, 486 F.2d 632 (7th Cir. 1973). The debt versus equity arguments of the taxpayer and the Commissioner were presented in reverse of the usual posture in Brutsche v. Commissioner, 65 T.C. 1034 (1976), where the taxpayers in 1969 sought to avoid subchapter S status elected in 1961 by arguing that a stockholder loan was really equity rather than debt and constituted a second class of stock thereby terminating the prior election. The Commissioner argued that there was a true loan and was sustained by the Tax Court.

The straight debt safe harbor of section 1361(c)(5) eases somewhat the tension in this area. The Senate Finance Committee Report explained the provision as follows:

"In order to insure that the corporation's election will not terminate in certain situations where the existence of a purported debt instrument (that otherwise would be classified as stock) may not lead to tax avoidance and does not cause undue complexity, the bill provides that an instrument which is straight debt will not be treated as a second class of stock (within the meaning of sec. 1361(b)(1)(D)), and therefore cannot disqualify a Subchapter S election. For this purpose, a straight debt instrument means a written unconditional promise to pay on demand or on a specified date a sum certain in money so long as the interest rate, and payment date are fixed. For this purpose these factors are fixed if they are not contingent on the profits of the corporation, the discretion of the corporation, or other similar factors. However, the fact that the interest rate is dependent upon the prime rate or a similar factor not related to the debtor corporation will not disqualify the instrument from being treated under the safe harbor. In order for the 'safe harbor' to apply, the instrument must not be convertible into stock, and must be held by a person eligible to hold Subchapter S stock." [16]

The potential classification of purported debt instruments as a second class of stock remains a problem where debt is convertible, held by a corporation related to a shareholder, or otherwise falls outside of the safe harbor. However, even if debt which falls outside of the safe harbor of section 1361(c)(5) is classified as equity, if it is held pro-rata, under Regulations, section 1.1371–1(g), it may not be treated as a second class of stock. The Internal Revenue Service may re-examine this position when it promulgates Regulations under section 1361(c)(5).

2. *Voting Rights*

Section 1361(c)(4) allows variations in voting rights among the shares of common stock without creating a second class of stock. This provision settled an issue that also gave rise to litigation under the pre–1983 Subchapter S provisions. See e.g. Parker Oil Co. v. Commissioner, 58 T.C. 985 (1972) (unpublished case) (stockholders' agreement providing that the right to vote certain shares was irrevocably granted by proxy to an unrelated third party did not create a second class of stock); Rev.Rul. 73–611, 1973–2 Cum. Bull. 312 (agrees with *Parker Oil,* but stated that if differences in voting rights, etc., arise from the articles of incorporation as such, rather than from agreements between stockholders and third parties, a second class of stock would result).

In Paige v. United States, 580 F.2d 960 (9th Cir.1978), a second class of stock was created as a result of conditions imposed by the California Department of Corporations on stock held by stockholders transferring property to the corporation. Similar conditions were not imposed on stockholders who had transferred cash to the corporation. Among the conditions were restrictions on dividend and liquidation distributions preventing distributions to the property stockholders until the cash stockholders received cumulative dividends equal to 5 percent of the purchase price. The result in *Paige* is unaffected by the enactment of section 1361(c)(4).

In Rev.Rul. 85–161, 1985–2 Cum.Bull. 191, the stock of an S corporation was held by A, B and C who were related, and D, an unrelated individual who was an officer of the corporation. D's stock was subject to restrictions on transfer which required D to obtain the consent of A and B before disposing of the stock to an outsider. If consent were denied, D could sell the stock only to the corporation or the other stockholders at book

16. S.Rep. No. 97–640, 97th Cong., 2d Sess. 8 (1982).

value. The Internal Revenue Service concluded that the stock purchase agreement did not affect D's rights in the corporation's profits and assets and, therefore, did not create a prohibited second class of stock.

Regulations, section 1.1371–1(g), also provide that stock is counted only if it is issued and outstanding. Thus unissued or treasury stock of a different class than the issued stock will not create a second class of stock.

B. AFFILIATED GROUPS

Following section 1361(c)(6), Proposed Regulations, section 1.1361–1A(d)(2) (1986), allow an S corporation to own stock in an inactive subsidiary, i.e., one which has not begun business or derived gross income, without being considered to be a member of an affiliated group; but otherwise the existence of an 80 percent controlled subsidiary precludes S corporation treatment. The Proposed Regulations indicate that the date on which a corporation has begun business is a question of facts and circumstances. Mere organizational activities are not business operations for this purpose, but the Proposed Regulations state that "if the activities of the corporation have advanced to the extent necessary to define the nature of the business * * * the corporation will be deemed to have begun business."

Transitory ownership of an active subsidiary may not disqualify the election of an S corporation if the transitory ownership is a part of an integrated transaction. In Revenue Ruling 72–320, 1972–1 Cum.Bull. 270, X Corporation, which had an S election in effect, distributed some of its operating assets to a newly formed subsidiary in order to split-off that business to a group of X stockholders. These stockholders immediately exchanged their X stock for the stock of the subsidiary in a split-off transaction qualified as a reorganization under sections 368(a)(1)(D) and 355, discussed infra, Chapter 19. The Ruling held that X Corporation's transitory ownership of the newly created subsidiary did not terminate its S corporation status. Rev.Rul. 73–496, 1973–2 Cum.Bull. 312, reached the same conclusion with respect to the brief ownership (30 days) of the stock of a newly acquired controlled subsidiary that was liquidated under section 332. The Ruling states that control by the S corporation was merely momentary control since it was the initial step of a plan to acquire assets. However, in Haley Brothers Construction Corp. v. Commissioner, 87 T.C. 498 (1986), acquisition of 100 percent of the stock of another corporation was held to disqualify the S election of the acquiring corporation where the separate legal existence of the subsidiary was continued even though the subsidiary was operated as a division of the acquiring S corporation. The court refused to disregard the separate corporate existence of the controlled subsidiary. In May v. United States, 644 F.2d 578 (6th Cir.1981), a newly organized S corporation purchased all of the assets of another corporation including a horse racing track and the stock of a subsidiary. The subsidiary owned land which it had leased to its parent corporation for use as a parking lot for the race track. After the acquisition, the subsidiary was inactive and received no income from the S corporation, although it did continue to hold title to the land. Because the subsidiary had conducted business after its incorporation, it could not be treated as an inactive corporation under the predecessor to section 1361(c)(6).

C. S CORPORATION ELECTION PROCEDURES

INTERNAL REVENUE CODE: Section 1362(a), (b) and (c).

TEMPORARY REGULATIONS: Sections 18.1362–1(a) and (b), –2(b) and (c).

A Subchapter S election is made by the corporation, but the election is valid only if all of the stockholders file consent to this election. Section 1362(a). After an election has been made, new stockholders are not required to consent. A stockholder individually cannot directly revoke or terminate an election, but undertaking a transaction which causes the corporation no longer to qualify for S corporation status may have that effect. See infra, page 284.

An election made any time during the taxable year will be effective for the corporation's next succeeding taxable year. Section 1362(b)(1)(A). Section 1362(b)(1)(B) provides for an election retroactive to the first day of the taxable year if the election is made on or before the fifteenth day of the third month of the taxable year. However, a retroactive election is effective for the taxable year in which made only if the corporation meets all of the requirements for S corporation status during the portion of the taxable year preceding the filing of the election and all of the stockholders consent to the election, including stockholders who were stockholders before the election was filed but who are no longer stockholders at the time of the election. Section 1362(b)(2). See also Proposed Regulations, sections 1.1362–1(c)(2)(ii) and 1.1362–2(b)(1) (1988). The legislative history indicates that this requirement is intended to avoid an allocation of income and loss to pre-election stockholders who were either ineligible to hold S corporation stock or who did not consent to the election.[17] If the corporation and its stockholders were not qualified to elect S corporation status during each day of the portion of the taxable year preceding a retroactive election, the election will be effective on the first day of the next taxable year. Section 1362(b)(3).

ILLUSTRATIVE MATERIAL

A. STOCKHOLDER CONSENTS

Section 1362(a)(2) requires the consent of all stockholders of the corporation as of the day of the election. See Kean v. Commissioner, 469 F.2d 1183 (9th Cir.1972) (consent was required from the beneficial owner of stock of an electing corporation even though the person was not included on the corporate books as a stockholder of record). See Temporary Regulations, section 18.1362–2(c), and Proposed Regulations, section 1.1362–2(c) (1988), for procedural aspects of shareholder consents and extensions of time for filing consents. Regulations, section 1.1372–2(c), regarding stockholder consents, provides for a waiver of the timely consent requirement in certain circumstances.

17. S.Rep. No. 97–640, 97th Cong., 2d Sess. 11 (1982).

Although husband and wife are treated as a single stockholder, Temporary Regulations, section 18.1362–2(b)(2), and Proposed Regulations, section 1.1362–2(b)(2) (1986), require that both husband and wife consent to the election if they own the stock as community property, tenants in common, joint tenants, or as tenants by the entirety. In Wilson v. Commissioner, 560 F.2d 687 (5th Cir.1977), the record owner of a single share of stock who held the stock as an accommodation to other stockholders filed a consent to the corporation's S election but his wife did not. The court held that the husband had no beneficial interest in the stock and was therefore not required to consent to the corporation's S election. Thus his wife's consent was also unnecessary.

B. CORPORATE ELECTION

There is no provision for waiver of a late filed corporate election and the requirement has been strictly enforced. Thus an election filed after the two month and 15 day period for a retroactive election will not be effective until the first day of the succeeding taxable year regardless of the cause for the late filing. See e.g. Pestcoe v. Commissioner, 40 T.C. 195 (1963) (election not timely when the accountant who was responsible for filing suffered a heart attack and filed the election 27 days late); Feldman v. Commissioner, 47 T.C. 329 (1966) (election deposited in mail slot of U.S. post office on due date but not postmarked until the following day, was not timely).[18]

With respect to a newly formed corporation, it is necessary to identify the date on which the taxable year begins in order to determine whether an election has been filed on or before the fifteenth day of the third month of the taxable year. Proposed Regulations, section 1.1362–1(c)(3) (1988), provide that the taxable year of a new corporation begins on the date the corporation has stockholders, acquires assets, or begins doing business, whichever is the first to occur. See Bone v. Commissioner, 52 T.C. 913 (1969) (first taxable year had begun when the corporation acquired assets and engaged in business even though no stock had been issued to stockholders; under state law the issuance of stock was not a prerequisite to corporate existence.

Proposed Regulations, section 1.1362–1(c)(3) (1988), provide that a month is measured from the first day of the corporation's taxable year to the day preceding the same numerical date of the following month, or the last day of the month if there is no corresponding date in the succeeding month. Proposed Regulations, section 1.1362–1(e), Ex. (1) (1988), indicates that an election filed before the corporation begins its first taxable year will not be valid.

D. REVOCATION OR TERMINATION OF S CORPORATION STATUS

INTERNAL REVENUE CODE: Section 1362(d), (e), (f) and (g).

An S corporation election is effective for the taxable year to which it first applies and all succeeding taxable years until revoked or

18. Before the 1982 Act, failure to make a timely election voided the attempted election completely. After 1983, a late election of an otherwise qualified corporation is effective for the next succeeding taxable year without further action.

terminated. S corporation status may be ended in three ways: voluntary revocation by stockholders holding a majority of the S corporation stock, failure to comply with the requirements for S corporation status, or receipt of passive investment income in excess of 25 percent of gross income for three consecutive years if the corporation has Subchapter C previously accumulated and undistributed earnings and profits in those years.[19] Section 1362(d)(1) provides that a voluntary revocation of S corporation status by stockholders can be effective on the date specified by the revocation. Termination of S corporation status because the corporation or its stockholders subsequently fail to meet the initial requirements for eligibility is effective on the date the corporation ceases to qualify as an S corporation. Section 1362(d)(2). The S corporation's taxable year ends on the day preceding the effective date of a revocation or termination and a new taxable year begins for the corporation as a C corporation on the following day. Section 1362(e). Items of income and deduction must be allocated between the corporation's short Subchapter S and Subchapter C taxable years.

ILLUSTRATIVE MATERIAL

A. TERMINATION BY VOLUNTARY REVOCATION

Section 1362(d)(1) allows revocation of an S election by stockholders owning a majority of outstanding stock. A revocation made on or before the fifteenth day of the third month of the taxable year will be retroactively effective as of the first day of the taxable year. Otherwise, a revocation is effective on the first day of the next taxable year. Alternatively, the revocation may specify an effective date as long as the date specified is subsequent to the date of the revocation. Proposed Regulations, section 1.1362–3(b)(3) (1988), require that the date be specified in terms of a day, month and year, rather than in terms of a particular event. Proposed Regulations, section 1.1362–3(b)(5) (1988), also allow rescission of a voluntary prospective revocation at any time before the revocation becomes effective. Rescission requires the consent of any person who consented to the revocation and any person who became a stockholder of the corporation after the revocation as filed.

B. INADVERTENT TERMINATION

A corporation's S election terminates immediately upon an event which disqualifies the corporation or one of its stockholders under the initial requirements for S corporation status. Section 1361(d)(2). However, the savings clause of section 1362(f) allows the Commissioner to overlook an inadvertent termination if the Commissioner determines that disqualification was inadvertent, the corporation and/or its stockholders take steps to remedy the disqualifying event within a reasonable period after discovery, and the corporation and each stockholder agree to such adjustments as the Commissioner may prescribe. The Senate Finance Committee indicated that it "intends that the Internal Revenue Service be reasonable in granting waivers, so that corporations whose Subchapter S eligibility requirements have been

19. The rules governing an S corporation with a prior history as a C corporation are discussed infra, page 672.

inadvertently violated do not suffer the tax consequences of a termination if no tax avoidance would result from the continued Subchapter S treatment." [20] Proposed Regulations, section 1.1362–5(b) (1988), state that the burden of establishing that termination is inadvertent under the facts and circumstances is on the corporation. The Proposed Regulations add: "The fact that the terminating event was not reasonably within the control of the corporation and was not part of a plan to terminate the election, or the fact that the event took place without the knowledge of the corporation notwithstanding its due diligence in the course of its business to safeguard itself against such an event, tends to establish that the termination was inadvertent."

Rev.Rul. 86–110, 1986–2 Cum.Bull. 150, granted inadvertent termination relief to an S corporation which lost its eligibility because the majority stockholders transferred stock to trusts for the stockholder's children. The stockholder acted on the advice of counsel that the transfer would not disqualify the corporation's S election and would not have made the transfer but for the advice of counsel. Private letter rulings issued by the Internal Revenue Service indicate that it is quite lenient in applying the authority granted under section 1362(f).

C. INTENTIONAL TERMINATION

May a stockholder intentionally terminate an S election by transferring stock to a disqualified person or by otherwise taking action to fail the initial requirements for S corporation status? In T.J. Henry Associates, Inc. v. Commissioner, 80 T.C. 886 (1983) (A), the controlling stockholder of a Subchapter S corporation transferred a single share of stock to himself as custodian for his children under a Uniform Gifts to Minors statute. The transfer was intended to terminate the corporation's S election.[21] The Tax Court rejected the Commissioner's assertion that the transfer was not a bona fide transfer of beneficial ownership of the stock and that the stockholder acted as a custodian for his children merely as an accommodation. The Tax Court further held that, so long as there is a bona fide transfer of beneficial ownership, a transfer deliberately made to disqualify an S election should be recognized and the Internal Revenue Service has acquiesced in this result. 1984–1 Cum.Bull. 1.

The result in *T.J. Henry Associates, Inc.* permits a single shareholder to terminate an S election without the consent of majority stockholders which otherwise is required for voluntary revocation under section 1361(d)(1). Provisions in corporate documents and shareholder agreements often seek to limit the shareholder's ability to make a stock transfer which would terminate the corporation's S election.

D. SHORT SUBCHAPTER S AND SUBCHAPTER C TAXABLE YEARS ON TERMINATION

Section 1362(e) requires that in any taxable year in which the S corporation election terminates effective on a date other than the first day of the taxable year, income and deduction items must be allocated between the portion of the year the corporation is qualified as an S corporation and the

20. S.Rep. No. 97–640, 97th Cong., 2d Sess. 12 (1982).

21. With respect to the taxable year involved, section 1372(e)(1) required an affirmative consent to the election by a new stockholder in order to maintain S corporation status. The stockholder in *T.J. Henry Assoc., Inc.* did not file the requisite consent.

portion of the year the corporation is treated as a C corporation.[22] The Senate Finance Committee Report explained the allocation rule as follows:

"The day before the day on which the terminating event occurs will be treated as the last day of a short Subchapter S taxable year, and the day on which the terminating event occurs will be treated as the first day of a short regular (i.e., subchapter C) taxable year. There will be no requirement that the books of a corporation be closed as of the termination date. Instead the corporation will allocate the income or loss for the entire year (i.e., both short years) on a proration basis."[23]

Each separately stated item of the corporation's income and loss during the short Subchapter S year must be allocated to each day of the short taxable year and taken into account by the stockholders. Section 1362(e)(2). The remaining taxable income for the taxable year is allocated to the short C corporation year. Taxable income for the short Subchapter C year is then annualized for purposes of computing the tax under section 11. First, the corporation's tax for the short Subchapter C year is determined as if it had earned a proportionate amount of taxable income for a full taxable year; then the corporation pays only the proportionate amount of the tax that corresponds to the portion of a full taxable year that it is deemed a C corporation. See Proposed Regulations, section 1.1362–4(d)(1) (1988). For example, suppose S Corporation has taxable income of $100,000 in 1989. Its Subchapter S election terminates effective April 1, 1989. There have been 90 days in S Corporation's short taxable year ending on March 31, 1989, and there are 275 days in S Corporation's short Subchapter C year beginning on April 1, 1989. As a result, $25,000 of S Corporation's $100,000 taxable income is allocated to the short S corporation year ($100,000×90/365) and the remaining $75,000 of taxable income is allocated to S Corporation's Subchapter C year. The $75,000 of taxable income is annualized so that S Corp. is deemed to have $100,000 of taxable income for purposes of determining its corporate tax for the short Subchapter C year ($75,000×365/275). The tax under section 11 on $100,000 of taxable income is $22,250. S Corporation's actual tax liability for the short Subchapter C year then is calculated to be $16,763.70 ($22,250 × 275/365).

In lieu of a pro rata allocation of income between the short Subchapter S and C years, the corporation may elect, with the consent of *all* stockholders, to report income and deductions on the basis of actual amounts shown on the corporate books. Section 1362(e)(3). Allocation of amounts based on the corporate books is required if there is a sale or exchange of more than 50 percent of the corporation's stock during the year the S election is terminated, or the corporation's stock is acquired by a corporation that elects to treat the acquisition as an asset purchase under section 338, infra, page 701. Section 1362(e)(6)(C) and (D). The "closing of the books" method may be desirable where the parties do not want events occurring after termination to affect income determination for the S corporation portion of the year. Note, however, that a single shareholder, who may be adversely affected, can prevent the use of the closing of the books method.

22. Section 1362(e)(6)(A) provides that the short taxable years required by section 1362(e) shall be treated as only one year for purposes of the carryback and carryforward of corporate items such as net operating losses.

23. S.Rep. No. 97–640, 97th Cong., 2d Sess. 11 (1982).

E. ELECTION FOLLOWING REVOCATION OR TERMINATION OF S CORPORATION STATUS

Under section 1362(g), if an S corporation election is revoked or terminated the corporation or its successor is not eligible to make a new election for five years unless the Commissioner consents to an earlier election. Proposed Regulations, section 1.1362–6(a) (1988), provide that consent ordinarily will be denied unless it can be shown that the event causing termination was not reasonably within the control of the corporation or stockholders having a substantial interest in the corporation and was not part of a plan to terminate the election. The Proposed Regulations also state that consent should be granted if more than 50 percent of the corporation's stock is owned by persons who were not stockholders at the time the election was terminated. Private letter rulings reflect a rather relaxed approach on the part of the Commissioner in granting the requisite consent.

See Lederman, Many Options Available to Avoid Excess Passive Investment Income Tax and S Termination, 69 J.Tax. 4 (1988).

SECTION 3. EFFECT OF THE SUBCHAPTER S ELECTION BY A CORPORATION WITH NO C CORPORATION HISTORY

A. PASS THROUGH OF INCOME AND LOSS

INTERNAL REVENUE CODE: Sections 1363(b) and (c), 1366, 1367.

SENATE FINANCE COMMITTEE REPORT, SUBCHAPTER S REVISION ACT OF 1982

S.Rep. No. 97–640, 97th Cong., 2d Sess. 15–18 (1982).

In general

The bill sets forth new rules for the taxation of income earned by, and the allowance of losses incurred by, subchapter S corporations. These rules generally follow the [pre–1983] law rules governing the taxation of partners with respect to items of partnership income and loss.

Computation of corporate items

A subchapter S corporation's taxable income will be computed under the same rules presently applicable to partnerships under section 703, except that the amortization of organization expenditures under section 248 will be an allowable deduction. As in the case of partnerships, deductions generally allowable to individuals will be allowed to subchapter S corporations, but provisions of the Code governing the computation of taxable income which are applicable only to corporations, such as the dividends received deduction (sec. 243) or the special rules relating to corporate tax preferences (sec. 291), will not apply.

Items, the separate treatment which could affect the liability of any shareholder (such as investment interest) will be treated separately. Elections will generally be made at the corporate level, except for those elections which the partners of a partnership may make separately (such as the election to claim the foreign tax credit).

Generally subchapter C will apply, except that a subchapter S corporation will be treated in the same manner as an individual in transactions, such as the treatment of dividends received under section 301, where the corporation is a shareholder in a regular corporation. Provisions relating to transactions by a subchapter S corporation with respect to its own stock will be treated as if the S corporation were a regular corporation. However, the subchapter C rules are not to apply where the result would be inconsistent with the purpose of the subchapter S rules which treat the corporation as a passthrough entity.

Passthrough of items

The following examples illustrate the operation of the bill's passthrough rules:

a. *Capital gains and losses.*—Gains or losses from sales or exchanges of capital assets will pass through to the shareholders as capital gains or losses. Net capital gains will no longer be offset by ordinary losses at the corporate level.

b. *Section 1231 gains and losses.*—The gains and losses on certain property used in a trade or business will be passed through separately and will be aggregated with the shareholder's other section 1231 gains and losses. Thus, section 1231 gains will no longer be aggregated with capital gains at the corporate level and passed through as capital gains.

c. *Charitable contributions.*—The corporate 10–percent limitation will no longer apply to contributions by the corporation. As in the case of partnerships, the contributions will pass through to the shareholders, at which level they will be subject to the individual limitations on deductibility.

d. *Tax-exempt interest.*—Tax-exempt interest will pass through to the shareholders as such and will increase the shareholders' basis in their subchapter S stock. Subsequent distributions by a corporation will not result in taxation of the tax-exempt income. (See discussion below for rules relating to corporate distributions.)

* * *

f. *Credits.*—As with partnerships, items involved in the determination of credits, * * * will pass through to the subchapter S corporation's shareholders.

g. *Depletion.*—The present rules governing depletion with regard to partnership interests in minerals will apply to depletion of properties of a subchapter S corporation (see discussion below for special rules in the case of oil and gas properties).

* * *

i. *Other items.*—Limitations on the * * * expensing of certain depreciable business assets (sec. 179), and the amortization of reforestation expenditures (sec. 194) will apply at both the corporate level and shareholder level, as in the case of partnerships. Exclusions of income from discharge of indebtedness will be determined at the shareholder level (sec. 108). The election to capitalize intangible costs by a shareholder who does not actively participate in the management of the corporation will be the same as the election by a limited partner, i.e. 10 year amortization (sec. [59(e)]). The subchapter S corporation will be treated as a middleman with respect to the withholding on payment of interest and dividends it receives (sec. 3453).

Carryovers from years in which the corporation was not a subchapter S corporation will not be allowed to the corporation while in subchapter S status.

Shareholders treatment of items

In general.—As with the partners of a partnership, each shareholder of a subchapter S corporation will take into account separately his or her pro rata share of items of income, deduction, credit, etc., of the corporation. These rules parallel the partnership rules under section 702.

Each shareholder's share of the items will be taken into account in the shareholder's taxable year in which the corporation's year ends. In the case of the death of a shareholder, the shareholder's portion of subchapter S items will be taken into account on the shareholder's final income tax return. Items from the portion of the corporation's taxable year after the shareholder's death will be taken into account by the estate or other person acquiring the stock.

For these purposes, a shareholder's pro rata share generally will be determined in the same manner as the [pre–1983] law rule for passing through net operating losses. In cases of transfers of subchapter S stock during the taxable year, income, losses, and credits will be allocated in essentially the same manner as when the election terminates during the year. Thus, the allocation generally will be made on a per-share, per-day basis unless the corporation, with the consent of its shareholders, elected to allocate according to its permanent records (including work papers).

A "conduit" rule for determining the character of items realized by the corporation and included in the shareholder's pro rata share will be the same as the partnership rule (sec. 702(b)). Under the partnership rules, this has generally resulted in an entity level characterization. Also, the "gross income" determinations made by a shareholder will parallel the partnership rule (sec. 702(c)).

Worthless stock.—If the corporation's stock becomes worthless in any taxable year of the corporation or shareholder, the corporate items for that year will be taken into account by the shareholders and the adjustments to the stock's basis will be made before the stock's worthlessness is taken into account under section 165(g).

Family members.—Under [section 1366(e)], items taken into account by members of the family (whether or not themselves shareholders) wherever it is necessary to reflect reasonable compensation to the shareholder for services rendered or capital furnished to the corporation may be properly adjusted. Both the amount of compensation and the timing of the compensation can be so adjusted.

Loss limitations.—As under [pre–1983] law, a shareholder's allowable pro rata share of the corporation's loss will be limited to the sum of the shareholder's adjusted basis in the stock of the corporation plus the shareholder's adjusted basis of any indebtedness of the corporation to the shareholder. However, unlike [pre–1983] law, disallowed losses can be carried forward or allowed in any subsequent year in which the shareholder has adequate basis in such stock or debt.

* * *

Terminated election.—Subsequent to a termination of a subchapter S election, these disallowed losses will be allowed if the shareholder's basis in his stock in the corporation is restored by the later of the following dates:

(1) One year after the effective date of the termination, or the due date for the last subchapter S return, whichever is later; or

(2) 120 days after a determination that the corporation's subchapter S election had terminated for a previous year. (A determination will be defined as a court decision which becomes final, a closing agreement, or an agreement between the corporation and the Internal Revenue Service that the corporation failed to qualify.)

3. Basis adjustment (sec. 1367)

Under [section 1367(a)], both taxable and nontaxable income and deductible and nondeductible expenses will serve, respectively, to increase and decrease a subchapter S shareholder's basis in the stock of the corporation. These rules generally will be analogous to those provided for partnerships under section 705. Under these rules, income and loss for any corporate taxable year will apply to adjust basis before the distribution rules apply for that year. Unlike the partnership rules, however, to the extent property distributions are treated as a return of basis, basis will be reduced by the fair market value of these properties (see below). Any passthrough of income for a particular year (allocated according to the proportion of stock held in the corporation) will first increase the shareholder's basis in loans to the corporation to the extent the basis was previously reduced by the passthrough of losses.

ESTATE OF LEAVITT v. COMMISSIONER

Court of Appeals, United States, Fourth Circuit, 1989.
875 F.2d 420.

MURNAGHAN, CIRCUIT JUDGE:

The appellants, Anthony D. and Marjorie F. Cuzzocrea and the Estate of Daniel Leavitt, Deceased, et al., appeal the Tax Court's decision holding them liable for tax deficiencies for the tax years 1979, 1980 and 1981. Finding the appellants' arguments unpersuasive, we affirm the Tax Court.

I.

As shareholders of VAFLA Corporation,[1] a subchapter S corporation during the years at issue, the appellants claimed deductions under § 1374 of the Internal Revenue Code of 1954 to reflect the corporation's operating losses during the three years in question. The Commissioner disallowed deductions above the $10,000 bases each appellant had from their original investments.

The appellants contend, however, that the adjusted bases in their stock should be increased to reflect a $300,000 loan which VAFLA obtained from the Bank of Virginia ("Bank") on September 12, 1979, after the appellants, along with five other shareholders ("Shareholders–Guarantors"), had signed guarantee agreements whereby each agreed to be jointly and severally liable for all indebtedness of the corporation to the Bank.[5] At the time of the loan, VAFLA's liability exceeded its assets, it could not meet its cash flow requirements and it had virtually no assets to use as collateral. The appellants assert that the Bank would not have lent the $300,000 without their personal guarantees.

VAFLA's financial statements and tax returns indicated that the bank loan was a loan from the Shareholders–Guarantors. Despite the representation to that effect, VAFLA made all of the loan payments, principal and interest, to the Bank. The appellants made no such payments. In addition, neither VAFLA nor the Shareholders–Guarantors treated the corporate payments on the loan as constructive income taxable to the Shareholders–Guarantors.

The appellants present the question whether the $300,000 bank loan is really, despite its form as a borrowing from the Bank, a capital contribution from the appellants to VAFLA. They contend that if the bank loan is characterized as equity, they are entitled to add a *pro rata*

1. VAFLA is a Virginia corporation incorporated in February 1979 to acquire and operate the Six–Gun Territory Amusement Park near Tampa, Florida. At that time, both Cuzzocrea and Leavitt each paid $10,000 for their respective shares of VAFLA. Therefore, the adjusted bases of their stock amounted to $10,000 each, the cost of the stock.

5. All the guarantees to the Bank were unlimited except the guarantee of Cuzzocrea which was limited to $300,000. The Shareholders–Guarantors had an aggregate net worth of $3,407,286 and immediate liquidity of $382,542.

share of the $300,000 bank loan to their adjusted bases, thereby increasing the size of their operating loss deductions.[7] Implicit in the appellants' characterization of the bank loan as equity in VAFLA is a determination that the Bank lent the $300,000 to the Shareholders–Guarantors who then contributed the funds to the corporation. The appellants' approach fails to realize that the $300,000 transaction, regardless of whether it is equity or debt, would permit them to adjust the bases in their stock if, indeed, the appellants, and not the Bank, had advanced VAFLA the money. The more precise question, which the appellants fail initially to ask, is whether the guaranteed loan from the Bank to VAFLA is an economic outlay of any kind by the Shareholders–Guarantors. To decide this question, we must determine whether the transaction involving the $300,000 was a loan from the Bank to VAFLA or was it instead a loan to the Shareholders–Guarantors who then gave it to VAFLA, as either a loan or a capital contribution.

Finding no economic outlay, we need not address the question, which is extensively addressed in the briefs, of whether the characterization of the $300,000 was debt or equity.

II.

To increase the basis in the stock of a subchapter S corporation, there must be an economic outlay on the part of the shareholder. See Brown v. Commissioner, 706 F.2d 755, 756 (6th Cir.1983), affg. T.C. Memo 1981–608 (1981) ("In similar cases, the courts have consistently required some economic outlay by the guarantor in order to convert a mere loan guarantee into an investment."); Blum v. Commissioner, 59 T.C. 436, 440 (1972) (bank expected repayment of its loan from the corporation and not the taxpayers, i.e., no economic outlay from taxpayers).[8] A guarantee, in and of itself, cannot fulfill that requirement. The guarantee is merely a promise to pay in the future if certain unfortunate events should occur. At the present time, the appellants have experienced no such call as guarantors, have engaged in no economic outlay, and have suffered no cost.

The situation would be different if VAFLA had defaulted on the loan payments and the Shareholders–Guarantors had made actual disbursements on the corporate indebtedness. Those payments would represent corporate indebtedness to the shareholders which would increase their bases for the purpose of deducting net operating losses

7. Former § 1374 of the 1954 tax code which was in effect during the years in issue provides that a shareholder of an electing small business corporation may deduct from gross income an amount equal to his or her portion of the corporation's net operating loss to the extent provided for in § 1374(c)(2). Such deduction is limited, however, to the sum of (a) the adjusted basis of the shareholder's stock in the corporation, and (b) the adjusted basis of any indebtedness of the corporation to the shareholder, as determined as of the close of the corporation's taxable year.

8. Even the Eleventh Circuit case on which the appellants heavily rely applies this first step. See Selfe v. United States, 778 F.2d 769, 772 (11th Cir.1985) ("We agree with *Brown* inasmuch as that court reaffirms that economic outlay is required before a stockholder in a Subchapter S corporation may increase her basis.").

under § 1374(c)(2)(B). Brown, 706 F.2d at 757. See also Raynor v. Commissioner, 50 T.C. 762, 770–71 (1968) ("No form of indirect borrowing, be it guaranty, surety, accommodation, co-making or otherwise, gives rise to indebtedness from the corporation to the shareholders until and unless the shareholders pay part or all of the obligation.").

The appellants accuse the Tax Court of not recognizing the critical distinction between § [1366(d)(1)(A)] (adjusted basis in stock) and § [1366(d)(1)(B)] (adjusted basis in indebtedness of corporation to shareholder). They argue that the "loan" is not really a loan, but is a capital contribution (equity). Therefore, they conclude, § [1366(d)(1)(A)] applies and § [1366(d)(1)(B)] is irrelevant. However, the appellants once again fail to distinguish between the initial question of economic outlay and the secondary issue of debt or equity. Only if the first question had an affirmative answer, would the second arise.

The majority opinion of the Tax Court, focusing on the first issue of economic outlay, determined that a guarantee, in and of itself, is not an event for which basis can be adjusted. It distinguished the situation presented to it from one where the guarantee is triggered *and actual payments are made.* In the latter scenario, the first question of economic outlay is answered affirmatively (and the second issue is apparent on its face, i.e., the payments represent indebtedness from the corporation to the shareholder as opposed to capital contribution from the shareholder to the corporation). To the contrary is the situation presented here. The Tax Court, far from confusing the issue by discussing irrelevant matters, was comprehensively explaining why the transaction before it could not represent any kind of economic outlay by the appellants.

The Tax Court correctly determined that the appellants' guarantees, unaccompanied by further acts, in and of themselves, have not constituted contributions of cash or other property which might increase the bases of the appellants' stock in the corporation.

The appellants, while they do not disagree with the Tax Court that the guarantees, standing alone, cannot adjust their bases in the stock, nevertheless argue that the "loan" to VAFLA was in its "true sense" a loan to the Shareholders–Guarantors who then theoretically advanced the $300,000 to the corporation as a capital contribution. The Tax Court declined the invitation to treat a loan and its uncalled-on security, the guarantee, as identical and to adopt the appellants' view of the "substance" of the transaction over the "form" of the transaction they took. The Tax Court did not err in doing so.

Generally, taxpayers are liable for the tax consequences of the transaction they actually execute and may not reap the benefit of recasting the transaction into another one substantially different in economic effect that they might have made. They are bound by the "form" of their transaction and may not argue that the "substance" of their transaction triggers different tax consequences. Don E. Williams Co. v. Commissioner, 429 U.S. 569, 579–80, 97 S.Ct. 850, 856–57, 51

L.Ed.2d 48 (1977); Commissioner v. National Alfalfa Dehydrating & Milling Co., 417 U.S. 134, 149, 94 S.Ct. 2129, 2137, 40 L.Ed.2d 717 (1974).[10] In the situation of guaranteed corporate debt, where the form of the transaction may not be so clear, courts have permitted the taxpayer to argue that the substance of the transaction was in actuality a loan to the shareholder. See Blum, 59 T.C. at 440. However, the burden is on the taxpayer and it has been a difficult one to meet. That is especially so where, as here, the transaction is cast in sufficiently ambiguous terms to permit an argument either way depending on which is subsequently advantageous from a tax point of view.

In the case before us, the Tax Court found that the "form" and "substance" of the transaction was a loan from the Bank to VAFLA and not to the appellants:

> The Bank of Virginia loaned the money to the corporation and not to petitioners. The proceeds of the loan were to be used in the operation of the corporation's business. Petitioners submitted no evidence that they were free to dispose of the proceeds of the loan as they wished. Nor were the payments on the loan reported as constructive dividends on the corporation's Federal income tax returns or on the petitioners' Federal income tax returns during the years in issue. Accordingly, we find that the transaction was in fact a loan by the bank to the corporation guaranteed by the shareholders.

Whether the $300,000 was lent to the corporation or to the Shareholders/Guarantors is a factual issue which should not be disturbed unless clearly erroneous. Finding no error, we affirm.

It must be borne in mind that we do not merely encounter naive taxpayers caught in a complex trap for the unwary. They sought to claim deductions because the corporation lost money. If, however, VAFLA had been profitable, they would be arguing that the loan was in reality from the Bank to the corporation, and not to them, for that would then lessen their taxes. Under that description of the transaction, the loan repayments made by VAFLA would not be on the appellants' behalf, and, consequently, would not be taxed as construc-

10. On the other hand, the Commissioner is not so bound and may recharacterize the nature of the transaction according to its substance while overlooking the form selected by the taxpayer. Higgins v. Smith, 308 U.S. 473, 477, 60 S.Ct. 355, 357, 84 L.Ed. 406 (1940). In doing so, the Commissioner usually applies debt-equity principles to determine the true *nature* of the transaction. As the *Selfe* court noted:

> This principle is particularly evident where characterization of capital as debt or equity will have different tax consequences. Thus in Plantation Patterns [462 F.2d 712 (5th Cir.1972)] the court held that interest payments by a corporation on debentures were constructive stockholder dividends and could not be deducted by the corporation as interest payments. There, the former Fifth Circuit recharacterized debt as equity at the insistence of the Commissioner.

Selfe, 778 F.2d at 773.

It is important to note that those cases did not involve the question posed here of whether an economic outlay existed because it clearly did. Actual payments were made. The only question was what was the nature of the payments, debt or equity.

tive income to them. See Old Colony Trust Co. v. Commissioner, 279 U.S. 716, 49 S.Ct. 499, 73 L.Ed. 918 (1929) (payment by a corporation of a personal expense or debt of a shareholder is considered as the receipt of a taxable benefit). It came down in effect to an ambiguity as to which way the appellants would jump, an effort to play both ends against the middle, until it should be determined whether VAFLA was a profitable or money-losing proposition. At that point, the appellants attempted to treat the transaction as cloaked in the guise having the more beneficial tax consequences for them.

Finally, the appellants complain that the Tax Court erred by failing to apply debt-equity principles to determine the "form" of the loan. We believe that the Tax Court correctly refused to apply debt-equity principles here, a methodology which is only relevant, if at all,[12] to resolution of the second inquiry—what is the nature of the economic outlay. Of course, the second inquiry cannot be reached unless the first question concerning whether an economic outlay exists is answered affirmatively. Here it is not.

The appellants, in effect, attempt to collapse a two-step analysis into a one-step inquiry which would eliminate the initial determination of economic outlay by first concluding that the proceeds were a capital contribution (equity). Obviously, a capital contribution is an economic outlay so the basis in the stock would be adjusted accordingly. But such an approach simply ignores the factual determination by the Tax Court that the Bank lent the $300,000 to the corporation and not to the Shareholders–Guarantors.

The appellants rely on Blum v. Commissioner, 59 T.C. 436 (1972), and Selfe v. United States, 778 F.2d 769 (11th Cir.1985), to support their position. However, the appellants have misread those cases. In *Blum,* the Tax Court declined to apply debt-equity principles to determine whether the taxpayer's guarantee of a loan from a bank to a corporation was an indirect capital contribution.[13] The Tax Court held that

12. In a § [1366(d)] subchapter S corporation case, the inquiry whether or not the economic outlay, assuming there is one, is debt or equity appears not to matter since the economic outlay, regardless of its characterization as debt or equity, will increase the adjusted basis. * * * There are no different tax consequences from the point of view of the taxpayer on the narrow issue of what amount of net operating losses may be deducted. Therefore, application of debt-equity principles in a case such as this one appears to be a red herring. However, we do not reach that issue because the Tax Court's factual finding that the appellants have shown no economic outlay on their part is not clearly erroneous.

13. The *Blum* court stated:

The respondent [Commissioner] has argued that the entire equity-contribution argument espoused by petitioner is inimical to the subch. S area. Because of our holding that the facts do not warrant the applicability of this doctrine to the present case we will not consider this rather fascinating question.

Blum, 59 T.C. at 439 n. 4. In other words, the *Blum* court never reached the second step of the analysis, if there is a second step, because it found that there was no economic outlay. The Tax Court focused on the first inquiry: "we must find that the bank in substance loaned the sums to petitioner, not the corporation, and that petitioner then proceeded to advance such funds to the corporation." Id. at 440. The court found that "there is no evidence to refute the fact that the bank expected repayment of its loan from the corporation and not the petitioner." Id.

Similarly, in *Brown,* the Sixth Circuit refused to "accept petitioners' contorted

the taxpayer had failed to carry his burden of proving that the transaction was in "substance" a loan from the bank to the shareholder rather than a loan to the corporation. The *Blum* court found dispositive the fact that "the bank expected repayment of its loan from the corporation and not the petitioner." Blum, 59 T.C. at 440.[14]

With regard to *Selfe,* the Tax Court stated:

> the Eleventh Circuit applied a debt-equity analysis and held that a shareholder's guarantee of a loan made to a subchapter S corporation may be treated for tax purposes as an equity investment in the corporation where the lender looks to the shareholder as the primary obligor. We respectfully disagree with the Eleventh Circuit and hold that a shareholder's guarantee of a loan to a subchapter S corporation may not be treated as an equity investment in the corporation absent an economic outlay by the shareholder.[15]

The Tax Court then distinguished Plantation Patterns, 462 F.2d 712 (5th Cir.1972), relied on by *Selfe,* because that case involved a C corporation, reasoning that the application of debt-equity principles to subchapter S corporations would defeat Congress' intent to limit a shareholder's passthrough deduction to the amount he or she has actually invested in the corporation.[16]

view of the transaction in furtherance of their 'substance over form' argument when, as the court below observed, 'the substance matched the form.'" *Brown,* 706 F.2d at 756. In other words, the loan to the corporation was, indeed, a loan to the corporation. See also In re Breit, 460 F.Supp. 873 (E.D.Va.1978).

14. The appellants and Judge Fay, in his dissent, content that the Tax Court has misread its earlier opinion. Indeed, Judge Fay was the author of *Blum.* However, the Tax Court, sitting *en banc,* has now had the opportunity to interpret more precisely the language of *Blum* in light of subsequent cases and arguments. Leavitt v. Commissioner, 90 T.C. 206 (1988) (court reviewed). We agree with the amplification the Tax Court has given *Blum.*

The confusion may be explained to some degree because the test applied in *Blum* to determine whether the bank lent the money to the corporation or to the shareholders sounds similar to one of the debt-equity factors, i.e., the source of the payments. When focusing on the proper question, however, it becomes clear that the debt-equity principles are simply irrelevant to the determination of whether the $300,000, unquestionably a loan when it left the Bank, went to VAFLA or to the appellants. In *Blum,* the fact that the bank expected repayment from the corporation indicated that it actually lent the funds to the corporation and not the shareholder. Similarly, in the case before us, the fact that VAFLA paid the principal and interest on the $300,000 loan and did not treat the payments as constructive income taxable to the Shareholders–Guarantors, indicated that the Bank actually lent the money to VAFLA and not the appellants.

15. Our reading of the *Selfe* opinion, as explained below, does not require us to reject the case completely. In this respect we disagree with the Tax Court's interpretation of Selfe in the present case and in Erwin v. Commissioner, 56 T.C.M. (CCH) 1343 (1989).

16. The Committee on Finance of the Senate stated in its report:

> The amount of the net operating loss apportioned to any shareholder pursuant to the above rule is limited under § [1366(d)(1)] to the adjusted basis of the shareholder's investment in the corporation; that is, to the adjusted basis of the stock in the corporation owned by the shareholder and the adjusted basis of any indebtedness of the corporation to the shareholder.

S.Rep. No. 1983, 85th Cong., 2d Sess. at 220, (1958–3 Cum.Bull. at 1141). The word "investment" was construed to mean the actual economic outlay of the shareholder in question. Perry v. Commissioner, 54 T.C. 1293, 1296 (1970).

In other words, the economic outlay must be found to exist first.

The Tax Court also distinguished In re Lane, 742 F.2d 1311 (11th Cir.1984), relied on by the *Selfe* court, on the basis that the shareholder had actually paid the amounts he had guaranteed, i.e., there was an economic outlay. In Lane, which involved a subchapter S corporation, the issue was "whether advances made by a shareholder to a corporation constitute debt or equity * * *." Id. at 1313. If the advances were debt, then Lane could deduct them as bad debts. On the other hand, if the advances were capital, no bad debt deduction would be permitted. Thus, the issue of adjusted basis for purposes of flow-through deductions from net operating losses of the corporation was not at issue. There was no question of whether there had been an economic outlay.

Although *Selfe* does refer to debt-equity principles, the specific issue before it was whether any material facts existed making summary judgment inappropriate. The Eleventh Circuit said:

> At issue here, however, is not whether the taxpayer's contribution was either a loan to or an equity investment in Jane Simon, Inc. The issue is whether the taxpayer's guarantee of the corporate loan was in itself a contribution to the corporation [as opposed to a loan from the bank] sufficient to increase the taxpayer's basis in the corporation.

The *Selfe* court found that there was evidence that the bank primarily looked to the taxpayer and not the corporation for repayment of the loan.[17] Therefore, it remanded for "a determination of whether or not the bank primarily looked to Jane Selfe [taxpayer] for repayment [the first inquiry] and for the court to apply the factors set out in In re Lane and I.R.C. section 385 to determine if the taxpayer's guarantee amounted to either an equity investment in or shareholder loan to Jane Simon, Inc. [the second inquiry]." Id. at 775. The implications are that there is still a two-step analysis and that the debt-equity principles apply only to the determination of the characterization of the economic outlay, once one is found.

Granted, that conclusion is clouded by the next and final statement of the *Selfe* court: "In short, we remand for the district court to apply Plantation Patterns and determine if the bank loan to Jane Simon, Inc.

17. The loan officer so stated during deposition testimony. Furthermore, the bank originally extended a credit line to the taxpayer in consideration of her pledge of 4500 shares of stock in another corporation. When her business was later incorporated, the bank converted the loans made on the existing credit line to corporate loans, accompanied by taxpayer's agreement guaranteeing the corporation's indebtedness to the bank. The Eleventh Circuit noted that "a guarantor who has pledged stock to secure a loan has experienced an economic outlay to the extent that the pledged stock is not available as collateral for other investments." Id. at 772 n. 7. Thus, upon remand, the district court could determine that there was an economic outlay on that basis alone, before deciding whether the form of the loan was to the taxpayer or to the corporation.

This particular situation is not before us and we decline to address the question of whether a guarantee can be an economic outlay when accompanied by pledged collateral.

was in reality a loan to the taxpayer." Id.[18] To the degree that the *Selfe* court agreed with Brown that an economic outlay is required before a shareholder may increase her basis in a subchapter S corporation, *Selfe* does not contradict current law or our resolution of the case before us. Furthermore, to the extent that the *Selfe* court remanded because material facts existed by which the taxpayer could show that the bank actually lent the money to her rather than the corporation, we are still able to agree.[19] It is because of the *Selfe* court's suggestion that debt-equity principles must be applied to resolve the question of whether the bank actually lent the money to the taxpayer/shareholder or the corporation, that we must part company with the Eleventh Circuit for the reasons stated above.

In conclusion, the Tax Court correctly focused on the initial inquiry of whether an economic outlay existed. Finding none, the issue of whether debt-equity principles ought to apply to determine the nature of the economic outlay was not before the Tax Court. The Tax Court is

Affirmed.

ILLUSTRATIVE MATERIAL

A. STOCKHOLDER BASIS

1. *General*

The stockholder's basis in S corporation stock initially is determined in the same manner as the basis of any other stock or security. Thereafter, in general, the stockholder's basis is increased by items included in the stockholder's income and reduced by deductions allocated and distributions made to the stockholder. Section 1367.

When net losses have reduced a stockholder's basis to zero, additional allocations of deduction and loss items reduce the basis of any indebtedness of the S corporation to the stockholder. Section 1367(b)(2)(a). When the basis of both the stockholder's stock and corporate indebtedness have been reduced to zero, pass through losses no longer can be deducted by the stockholder. The losses are suspended and may be deducted in a later year in which the stockholder acquires basis. Section 1366(d).

After a stockholder has reduced basis in her stock and debt to zero, any increase in basis in a subsequent year will be applied first to restore the basis of indebtedness before there is any increase in the basis of stock. Section 1367(b)(2)(B). This provision can produce an unexpected conse-

18. It is unclear whether the reference to *Plantation Patterns* means that debt-equity principles should be applied or refers back to an earlier statement in the *Selfe* court's opinion which related to the initial inquiry:

> In Plantation Patterns, the Fifth Circuit held that a loan is deemed to be made to a stockholder who has guaranteed a corporate note when the facts indicate that the lender is looking primarily to the stockholder for repayment.

Selfe, 778 F.2d at 771.

19. We note, however, that under the circumstances presented here, the Tax Court resolved that factual determination against the appellants because they could not overcome the uncontradicted fact that they did not treat the loan repayments made by VAFLA as constructive income to them. Such a position was inconsistent with their claim that the transaction was in actuality a loan from the Bank to them followed by their contribution of the $300,000 to the corporation.

quence to the stockholder. To the extent that corporate earnings passed-through to the stockholder under section 1366 are allocated to increase the basis of stockholder debt, the stockholder's stock basis will not be adjusted to reflect income previously taxed to the stockholder. Distributions of these earnings will be taxed to the stockholder to the extent distributions exceed the stockholder's stock basis even though the stockholder has basis in the debt. As a consequence, the stockholder appears to be taxed twice on the same income; once as the stockholder is allocated a proportionate share of the income under section 1366, and a second time to the extent the distribution of that income exceeds the stockholder's stock basis. The "second" tax, however, can be viewed as a consequence of the pass through of losses in excess of stock basis which has reduced the basis in the debt; the statute in effect requires those losses to be "recaptured" when distributions are made on the stock before the full basis of the debt has been accounted for.

In Cornelius v. Commissioner, 494 F.2d 465 (5th Cir.1974), stockholders of an S corporation that was engaged in farming advanced funds to the corporation in the fall of 1966 to enable the corporation to finance its next year's crops. A net operating loss incurred in 1966 was deducted by the stockholders, eliminating basis in their stock and reducing basis in the debt. In the spring of 1967, the corporation repaid the face amount of the loans and this amount exceeded the debt basis. In the fall of 1967, the taxpayers made new advances to the corporation for financing of the next year's crop. The court held that the taxpayers realized ordinary income to the extent that the loan repayments exceeded basis in the debt. The court rejected the taxpayers' argument that the stock and debt should be treated as a composite investment so that the 1967 undistributed earnings of the corporation increased the basis in the investment and hence there was no gain or loss on the cash distributions—the statute provides an increase in basis for undistributed taxable income only for stock, not debt. In addition, the court held that the debt was really debt and not equity as asserted by the taxpayer; hence undistributed taxable income stepped-up the basis of the equity. Finally, the taxpayers were not allowed to net the 1966 and 1967 transactions.

In Rev.Rul. 81–187, 1981–2 Cum.Bull. 167, the stockholder of an S corporation attempted to increase basis for purposes of deducting a net operating loss by transferring the stockholder's own promissory note to the corporation. The Internal Revenue Service ruled that the note did not increase the stockholder's basis because the stockholder incurred no cost in executing the note, the stockholder's basis in the note was zero. But see Lessinger v. Commissioner, 872 F.2d 519 (2d Cir.1989), supra, page 357.

In Wiebusch v. Commissioner, 59 T.C. 777 (1973), aff'd per curiam, 487 F.2d 515 (8th Cir.1973), the taxpayer transferred assets to an existing S corporation which also assumed certain of the transferor's liabilities. The liabilities exceeded the taxpayer's basis for the assets, which resulted in gain to the taxpayer under section 357(c), and, as a result of section 358(d)(1), the taxpayer's basis in the stock was reduced to zero. Accordingly, the corporation's current losses could not be deducted by the taxpayer. As a result of incorporation, the taxpayer recognized gain and lost the benefit of a current loss deduction, neither of which would have occurred had the business continued to be operated in a sole proprietorship form.

2. *Determining "Actual" Investment*

As *Leavitt* indicates, the form in which an investment in a Subchapter S corporation is made can be crucially important. The taxpayers in *Leavitt* could have increased their stock bases by borrowing directly from the bank and contributing or lending the proceeds to the corporation, transactions which are economically essentially the same as the one which was actually carried out. The *Selfe* case, discussed in the *Leavitt* opinion, represented a rare taxpayer victory in the guaranty context. See also Harrington v. United States, 605 F.Supp. 53 (D.Del.1985) (stockholders and S corporation were co-makers of a note originally executed by the stockholders only; the corporation was added at the request of the lender to perfect a pledge of corporate assets as security; the corporation was treated as a principal debtor on the note to the lender under state law and, therefore, did not receive the proceeds as a loan from stockholders; the stockholders were not allowed to include the note in basis).

If a stockholder is required to satisfy a corporate liability pursuant to a guaranty of the corporation's note, an obligation from the corporation to the stockholder is created as a result of the subrogation doctrine[24] with a basis equal to the amount paid on the guaranty. Rev.Rul. 70–50, 1970–1 Cum. Bull. 178 (holding that basis arises only in the year of payment under the guaranty); Rev.Rul. 75–144, 1975–1 Cum.Bull. 277 (same result where the stockholder executes a personal note which the creditor accepts in satisfaction of the corporate obligation); but see Underwood v. Commissioner, 535 F.2d 309 (5th Cir.1976) (substitution of stockholder note for note of S corporation to another corporation controlled by the stockholder merely amounted to a guaranty since, unlike Rev.Rul. 75–144, the creditor was not an independent third party and there was no likelihood the payment would ever be required under the note; as a result no basis was acquired in the indebtedness of the S corporation until payments were actually made on the note to the creditor corporation); Brown v. Commissioner, 706 F.2d 755 (6th Cir.1983) (guaranteeing stockholders must make actual disbursements on the corporate indebtedness before they can increase basis).

In Frankel v. Commissioner, 61 T.C. 343 (1973) (unpublished case), taxpayers were stockholders of an S corporation that operated a restaurant located in a building owned by a partnership in which the taxpayers were partners. The taxpayers' interests in the corporation and the partnership were identical. The partnership loaned funds to the corporation and the taxpayers asserted that their bases for purposes of passing through a net operating loss should include the partnership loans on the theory that loans from the partnership constituted loans made by the individual partners. The court held, however, that the debt ran to the partnership and the stockholders were not entitled to reflect the loans in their bases.

3. *Subchapter S and Partnership Treatment of Entity–Level Debt*

The requirement that only actual investment in the corporation, however determined, is included in the S corporation stockholder's stock and debt basis precludes the kind of pass-through treatment provided to debt incurred by a partnership. In the case of a partnership, each partner is deemed to

24. See Putnam v. Commissioner, 352 U.S. 82 (1956), holding that the bad debt of a C corporation paid by a stockholder is deductible as a bad debt because the stockholder steps into the shoes of the original creditor and becomes a creditor of the corporation.

contribute money to the partnership to the extent of the partner's share of partnership liabilities. This deemed contribution increases the partner's basis in the partner's partnership interest. Sections 752(a) and 722, supra, page 122. In this sense, a partnership is treated as an aggregate of the partners' interests with each partner sharing in the partnership's liabilities. The S corporation is treated as an entity separate from the stockholders, who do not share corporate debt as a pass-through attribute. Why should the S corporation be treated differently? One possible answer is that, unlike general partners, S corporation stockholders are not responsible for corporate debt by virtue of their corporate limited liability. However, this protection is often eliminated by stockholder guarantees, as in *Leavitt.* In addition, nonrecourse partnership debt for which no partner is subject to an economic risk of loss is allocated to the partners and increases their basis in their partnership interests. However, the partnership rules also require a matching allocation of partnership income to partners who receive credit for nonrecourse partnership debt so that, as the debt is repaid, the partner whose basis was increased by the debt is charged with partnership income equivalent to the debt principal. See supra, page 105. The same matching of income allocations with payments of debt may occur in a partnership with respect to partner guarantees of partnership debt and partnership debt for which a partner is personally liable. In addition, a partner who personally assumes a non-pro rata share of partnership debt may be specially allocated the partnership income used to satisfy debt principal (as long as the allocation satisfies the substantial economic effect requirement of section 704(b)) so that the partner's basis increase and deductions claimed by the partner based on the debt are matched with an offsetting income allocation. There is no equivalent vehicle for such an allocation of S corporation income, which is shared pro rata among stockholders in proportion to stock ownership. An allocation of corporate debt to stockholders of an S corporation could be unsatisfactory because the allocation would not be adjusted to account for a particular stockholder's secondary liability through guarantees or other devices. Although these problems can be resolved with provisions similar to the partnership rules providing for adjustable allocations to S corporation stockholders, the change would add substantial complexity to Subchapter S.

B. DISALLOWED LOSS

1. *Subchapter S*

The loss limitation of section 1366(d)(1) prevents a stockholder from claiming losses in excess of the stockholder's investment in the S corporation. Losses disallowed by section 1366(d)(1) may be carried over indefinitely to future years and deducted whenever the stockholder has sufficient basis to support the deduction. Section 1366(d)(2). A stockholder may have losses carried into the last taxable year of the S corporation. In such a case, the loss is treated as a loss incurred by the stockholder on the last day of a "post-termination transition period", the period beginning on the last day of the corporation's taxable year as an S corporation and ending on the later of (a) one year after the last day of the S corporation taxable year, (b) the due date for the tax return for the last taxable year as an S corporation (including extensions), or, (c) if there is a judicial determination or administrative agreement that the corporation's S election terminated in an earlier taxable year, 120 days after the date of the determination. Section 1377(b). The loss carryover is personal to each individual stockholder. Section 1366(d)

(2). Disposition of S corporation stock by the stockholder thus terminates the loss carryforward attributable to that stock.

2. *Interaction With At Risk Rules and Passive Activity Loss Limitation*

The at risk rules of section 465, discussed supra, page 147, apply to the stockholder of an S corporation. As a result, a loss that is passed through to a stockholder may be deducted only to the extent that the stockholder is at risk with respect to the activities that generated the loss. Under the aggregation rules of section 465(c)(3)(B), an S corporation may be treated as engaged in a single activity if its activities constitute a trade or business and 65 percent or more of the losses are allocable to persons who actively participate in the management of the trade or business.

The passive activity loss limitation of section 469 also applies to losses passed through to S corporation stockholders in the same manner as to partners. See supra, page 155. Thus net losses of an activity operated by an S corporation in which the stockholder does not materially participate are deductible by the stockholder only to the extent of the stockholder's passive activity income. Disallowed losses are carried forward and treated as passive activity deductions in the next succeeding year until offset by the taxpayer's passive activity income. Complete disposition of the activity of the S corporation allows the taxpayer to deduct the unused loss attributable to the specific activity.

C. ALLOCATIONS AMONG FAMILY GROUPS

The Commissioner is given authority to allocate items described in section 1366 among those stockholders who are members of the stockholder's family (spouse, ancestors, and lineal descendants) if he determines that reallocation is necessary to reflect the value of services rendered by any of those persons. Section 1366(e). Thus, if a parent works for a low salary in an effort to shift income to the parent's stockholder-children, the Commissioner may allocate additional income to the parent or reduce the deduction for salary allocable to the parent. Unlike section 704(e)(3), discussed supra at page 111, which reallocates partnership income in the case of an interest purchased from a related person, section 1366(e) permits reallocation of S corporation income among family members who purchased their stock from an outsider in an arm's length transaction. On the other hand, section 1366(e) is more restrictive than section 704(e)(1) and (2) (which provide for reallocation of partnership income in the case of transfers by gift) in the sense that it permits reallocation only among family members.

In Davis v. Commissioner, 64 T.C. 1034 (1975), the Tax Court held that the Commissioner abused this discretion under the predecessor to section 1366(e) by allocating 100 percent of the income of two S corporations to the taxpayer. The taxpayer was an orthopedic surgeon who organized two corporations to perform X-ray and physical therapy services related to his medical practice. Ninety percent of the stock of each corporation was owned by the taxpayer's three minor children. The Tax Court indicated that the value of the taxpayer's services depended upon factors such as the nature of the services, the responsibilities involved, the time spent, the size and complexity of the business, economic conditions, compensation paid by others for comparable services and salary paid to company officers in prior years. The court held that 20 or so hours per year that the taxpayer spent directly performing services for the corporations was minimal and rejected the Commissioner's argument that the taxpayer's referral of patients to the corporations was personal service rendered by him to the corporations. Thus, the fees earned by the corporations were the result of the use of equipment owned by the corporations and the services of corporate employees, and not the result of services rendered by the taxpayer. The Tax Court also rejected the Commissioner's claim that income was allocable to the taxpayer under section 482 and assignment of income principles. See supra, page 330.

As indicated in the family partnership context, supra, page 111, the significance of these assignment of income issues has been greatly reduced for years after 1986 by the flattening of the rate structure.

D. REFERENCES

Powell, Will Stockholder Guarantees Ever Increase Basis? 69 J.Tax. 12 (1988); Comment, Subchapter S Loss Limitation: The Effect of Stockholder Loan Guarantees on Basis, 40 S.W.L.J. 1241 (1987); Bogdanski, Closely Held Corporations, Shareholder Guarantees, Interest Deductions, and S Corporation Stock Basis: The Problems with *Putnam,* 13 J.Corp.Tax. 264 (1986).

B. THE CORPORATION'S TAXABLE YEAR

INTERNAL REVENUE CODE: Sections 1378; 444.

ILLUSTRATIVE MATERIAL

A. PERMITTED TAXABLE YEAR

Before enactment of section 1378 in the 1982 Act, calendar year stockholders of a profitable S corporation generally preferred a taxable year for the corporation ending on January 31. Under section 1366(a), stockholders account for their share of an S corporation's items in the taxable year of the stockholder in which the taxable year of the S corporation ends. A January 31 year-end permitted calendar year stockholders to defer income for up to eleven months. If, on the other hand, the S corporation was passing through losses to the stockholders, the stockholders preferred a calendar year so as to avoid any deferral of deductions.

The Tax Reform Act of 1986 added the last sentence of 1378(b) to prohibit stockholder deferral from being treated as a business purpose for adopting a fiscal year. Section 444, added in 1987, allows for a limited deferral but at the price of a corporate level payment to the government. The rules governing use of a taxable year other than a calendar year are the same as those for partnerships, discussed supra, page 84.

C. DISTRIBUTIONS

INTERNAL REVENUE CODE: Sections 1368, 1371(c) and (e); 453B(h).

SENATE FINANCE COMMITTEE REPORT, SUBCHAPTER S REVISION ACT OF 1982

S.Rep.No. 97–640, 97th Cong., 2d Sess. 20 (1982).

Explanation of Provisions

1. Taxation of shareholders (secs. 1368 and 1371(c))

Under [section 1368(a)], the amount of any distribution to a shareholder will equal the amount of cash distributed plus the fair market value of any property distributed, as under [pre–1983] law.

The amount of a distribution by a corporation without accumulated earnings and profits will be tax-free to the extent of the shareholder's basis in the stock. The distribution will be applied to reduce the shareholder's basis in his stock. To the extent the amount of the distribution exceeds basis, capital gains generally will result.

No post–1982 earnings of a subchapter S corporation will be considered earnings and profits for this purpose. Thus, under [section 1371(c) (1)], a corporation will not have earnings and profits attributable to any taxable year beginning after 1982 if a subchapter S election was in effect for that year.

* * *

The rules described above will apply to the transferee of stock in a subchapter S corporation regardless of the manner in which the transferee acquires the stock.

2. Treatment of corporation (sec. 1363(d))

Gain will be recognized by a subchapter S corporation on a distribution of appreciated property, other than distributions [of property permitted to be received without recognition of gain under sections 354, 355 or 356], in the same manner as if the property had been sold to the shareholder as its fair market value. Like other corporate gain, it will pass-thru to the shareholders.

Without this rule, assets could be distributed tax-free (except for recapture in certain instances) and subsequently sold without income recognition to the selling shareholder because of the stepped-up fair market value basis.

ILLUSTRATIVE MATERIAL

A. DISTRIBUTIONS OF APPRECIATED PROPERTY

In a significant departure from the partnership provisions on which treatment of S corporation distributions is generally based, Subchapter S requires recognition of gain at the corporate level on the distribution of appreciated property to stockholders. In the corresponding partnership situation, gain recognition is postponed through the rules on basis adjustments.[25] Presumably, Congress believed that the partnership approach would have been too complex to apply in a corporate context. Technically, this result is reached under section 1371(a), which provides that, except when specifically displaced, the normal Subchapter C rules, including the rules governing corporate distributions, are applicable to Subchapter S corporations. Thus, section 311(b) requires recognition of corporate level gain on the distribution of appreciated property as if the property were sold for its fair market value.[26] The recognized gain is passed through to stockholders who report the gain as income under section 1366. Under section 1368, the distribution of the property itself is taxfree to the stockholder to the extent of the stockholders' basis in his stock. The stockholder's basis in the property received is fair market value. Section 301(d).

Liquidating distributions by an S corporation also are subject to the liquidation rules of Subchapter C. Section 336 requires recognition of gain at the corporate level as if the property were sold for its fair market value. The gain is passed through to stockholders under section 1366 and their bases in their stock are adjusted accordingly pursuant to section 1367. Under section 331 liquidating distributions are treated as received by the stockholders in exchange for their stock; gain is recognized to the extent the distribution exceeds basis, or loss is recognized if the distribution is less than the stockholder's basis. Stock gain or loss is recognized in situations where the stockholder's stock basis is not the same as the stockholder's ratable share of the corporation's asset bases, e.g., where the stockholder acquired the stock by purchase or bequest.

Section 453B(h) provides that distribution of an installment obligation acquired by an S corporation on sale of its assets within twelve months preceding complete liquidation of the corporation generally does not trigger recognition of corporate level gain on disposition of the installment obligation.[27] The receipt of each installment payment by the stockholder, but not receipt of the installment obligation itself, is treated as a payment in exchange for the stockholder's stock in complete liquidation of the corporation. Section 453(h). In effect, S corporation stockholders are permitted to defer recognition of liquidation gain in the same manner that section 453(h) permits deferral of recognition by C corporation stockholders. See supra, 613. But section 453B(h) requires that the character of the stockholder's gain be determined as if the corporation had recognized the gain and the gain had passed through to the stockholders under section 1366.

B. DISTRIBUTIONS FOLLOWING TERMINATION OF S CORPORATION STATUS

Following termination of an S election, distributions of money may be received by stockholders as a tax-free reduction in basis to the extent of the

25. As discussed in Chapter 5, supra, page 212, except to the extent required by section 751, no gain is recognized by a partnership on distribution of appreciated property. The partnership basis carries over to the distributee partner to the extent of the partner's basis in the partner's partnership interest.

26. H.Rep.No. 100–795, 100th Cong., 2d Sess. 64 (1988).

27. Section 453B(h) does not apply for purposes of determining the corporation's tax liability under Subchapter S. Thus the corporation is not relieved from recognition of gain on the distribution of an installment obligation that triggers the built-in gain tax of section 1374, discussed infra, page 676, or the tax on passive investment income of section 1375, discussed infra at page 674.

undistributed taxable income of the S corporation which has been passed through to the stockholders. Section 1371(e)(1). The distribution must be made within the "post termination transition period" as defined in section 1377(b). If the stockholders fail to withdraw previously taxed income from the corporation within the applicable period, the privilege of tax-free distribution under section 1368 is lost and subsequent corporate distributions are taxable under section 301, i.e., subsequent distributions are taxable dividends if supported by sufficient earnings and profits. (If the corporation has always been an S corporation, earnings and profits will arise only in the period following termination of the election.)

Tax-free distributions during the post-termination transition period must be in money. Under a requirement of the pre–1983 Subchapter S rules, distributions of money during the first two and one-half months of the taxable year were received tax-free by the stockholders as distributions of previously taxed income of the prior taxable year.[28] Taxpayers attempted various devices to circumvent this "money" distribution requirement, but with a marked lack of success. This case law remains relevant under section 1371(e)(1). See Roesel v. Commissioner, 56 T.C. 14 (1971) (cash distribution and subsequent loan to corporation by stockholders were disregarded and the transaction was treated as a taxable distribution of the debt obligations); Detreville v. United States, 445 F.2d 1306 (4th Cir.1971) (two transactions treated as one where the stockholders purported to receive cash distributions of previously taxed income and then purchased property from the corporation; the court found the transactions were in substance a distribution of property which did not carry out previously taxed income from the corporation but constituted a taxable dividend to the stockholders); McWhorter's Estate v. Commissioner, 69 T.C. 650 (1978) (distribution of notes within the period allowed from distribution of previously taxed income, but in year in which corporation was no longer an S corporation, did not constitute a constructive distribution of the undistributed taxable income for the previous year followed by a bank loan back to the corporation; the notes constituted a dividend in the year of distribution); Stein v. Commissioner, 65 T.C. 336 (1975) (fact that stockholders were in constructive receipt of amounts credited to their accounts on the books of the corporation within the period allowed for distribution of previously taxed income did not satisfy the money requirement); McKelvy v. United States, 478 F.2d 1217 (Ct.Cl.1973) (same). In Fountain v. Commissioner, 59 T.C. 696 (1973), the corporation distributed checks within the period allowed for distribution of previously taxed income. The corporation did not have enough cash to cover the checks. The stockholders never cashed the checks but endorsed them back to the corporation as "loans" some two years later. The checks were held to constitute promissory notes, not "money," and, because the corporation had terminated its S corporation status in the year of distribution of the checks, the face amount of the checks constituted dividends to the stockholders to the extent of earnings and profits in that year. As a result, the amount of the checks was taxed under Subchapter S in the earlier year and as an actual dividend in the year of distribution.

28. Otherwise, distributions during the taxable year were taxed as dividends to the extent of the current year's earnings and profits. After current earnings were distributed, distributions of prior years' undistributed taxable income were also received tax-free by stockholders.

C. SHAREHOLDER–EMPLOYEE FRINGE BENEFITS

For purposes of employee fringe benefit provisions, section 1372 treats an S corporation as a partnership and each 2 percent stockholder as a partner. As a result, S corporation stockholders holding 2 percent or more of the stock are not eligible for employee fringe benefits. An S corporation may not maintain a qualified pension or profit sharing plan for employees who are 2 percent or greater stockholders, but may maintain such a plan for other employees. However, S corporation stockholders may maintain qualified plans as self employed individuals (H.R. 10 Plan). The distinctions are relatively insignificant after 1984 because the Deficit Reduction Act of 1984 harmonized the benefits and contribution restrictions applicable to self-employed individuals with those available under regular corporation pension and profit sharing plans.

SECTION 4. S CORPORATIONS WHICH HAVE A C CORPORATION HISTORY

A. DISTRIBUTIONS FROM AN S CORPORATION WITH EARNINGS AND PROFITS ACCUMULATED FROM SUBCHAPTER C YEARS

INTERNAL REVENUE CODE: Section 1368(c), (e).

The conversion of an existing C corporation to S corporation status raises several problems which are related to the double tax regime of Subchapter C. The Subchapter S rules are structured to maintain the possibility of a second layer of tax on income earned or appreciation in assets occurring while the Subchapter S corporation was subject to Subchapter C. Thus, under section 1368(c)(1), distributions by an S corporation that has accumulated earnings and profits from its C corporation years are tax-free to stockholders only to the extent of an "accumulated adjustments account". The accumulated adjustments account, as defined in section 1368(e)(1), reflects the S corporation's taxable income which has been passed through and taxed to shareholders under section 1368, i.e., while the corporation has been subject to Subchapter S. Distributions in excess of the accumulated adjustments account are treated as taxable dividends to the stockholders to the extent of the corporation's accumulated earnings and profits. Section 1368(c)(2). Distributions in excess of both the accumulated adjustments account and accumulated earnings and profits are treated the same as distributions from a corporation with no earnings and profits; distributions are not included in the stockholders' gross income to the extent of the stockholder's basis in the S corporation's stock, and any excess is capital gain.

ILLUSTRATIVE MATERIAL

A. GENERAL

Generally, corporate activities during the period of Subchapter S election is in effect have no impact on the corporation's earnings and profits. Section

1371(c)(1). An S corporation will have earnings and profits only (1) if it has accumulated earnings from a period before its S election during which it was a C corporation, (2) under certain provisions applicable to pre–1983 S corporations, or (3) if it inherited the earnings and profits account of a C corporation which was acquired in a merger or other transaction to which section 381 applies. (For Section 381, see infra, Chapter 20.)

Distributions to stockholders from an S corporation with earnings and profits are not included in the stockholders' gross incomes to the extent of the corporation's accumulated adjustments account. Section 1368(c)(1). The accumulated adjustments account is basically a running total of the corporation's net taxable income while operating as an S corporation. The account is based on adjustments to the stockholders' basis under section 1367 except that the accumulated adjustments account does not include tax-exempt income, nor is it reduced by deductions not allowed in computing the corporation's taxable income. Section 1368(e)(1). The exclusion of tax-exempt items from the accumulated adjustment account means that tax-exempt income of the S corporation may not be distributed tax-free to stockholders until after the taxable distributions of accumulated earnings and profits from the Subchapter C period have been made.

If a distribution is received by a stockholder as a redemption in exchange for stock under section 302(a) or 303, a pro rata portion of the distribution is deemed to reduce the accumulated adjustments account. Section 1368(e)(1)(B).[29] Section 1368(e)(3) provides an election, with the consent of all stockholders, to treat distributions as dividends from accumulated earnings and profits before reducing the accumulated adjustments account. The election may be used to prevent termination for excess passive investment income, see infra, page 674, or to avoid the section 1375 tax on passive investment income of an S corporation with the accumulated earnings and profits, discussed infra at page 674. Operation of the stacking principle used in section 1368(e) is illustrated as follows: As of January 1, 1990, the effective date of its Subchapter S election, Y Corporation had $50,000 of Subchapter C accumulated earnings and profits. Y Corporation's sole shareholder, A, had a basis in her stock of $6,000. For 1990, Y Corporation had taxable income of $30,000 and made a cash distribution to A of $100,000. Before taking into account the effect of the distribution, the $30,000 of current taxable income generates an increase in the basis of A's stock in Y Corporation from $6,000 to $36,000 and the balance in the accumulated adjustments account is increased from zero to $30,000. The distribution is treated as follows: The first $30,000, attributable to the accumulated adjustments account, is applied against the basis of the stock, reducing A's basis in the stock to $6,000; and the balance in the accumulated adjustments account is reduced to zero. The next $50,000, attributable to the accumulated earnings and profits, is taxed as a dividend. The next $6,000 is applied against basis, reducing A's basis in the stock to zero. The final $4,000 is treated as gain from the sale or exchange of the stock.

29. Section 1371(c)(2) requires adjustments to the earnings and profits account in the case of redemptions, liquidations, reorganizations and other transactions to which Subchapter C is applicable. Section 1371(c)(3) provides for an adjustment to earnings and profits in the case of distributions treated as dividends under section 1368(c)(2).

B. PASSIVE INVESTMENT INCOME OF AN S CORPORATION WITH ACCUMULATED EARNINGS AND PROFITS

INTERNAL REVENUE CODE: Sections 1362(d)(3); 1375.

PROPOSED REGULATIONS: Section 1.1362–3(d).

There are no limitations on the type of income, e.g., passive versus active, that can be earned by an S corporation with no C corporation history. On the other hand, Section 1375 imposes a tax on an S corporation with accumulated Subchapter C earnings and profits in any year in which the corporation has passive investment income in excess of 25 percent of gross receipts. The tax is imposed at the highest rate under section 11(b) on "excess net passive income", which is defined in section 1375(b) as an amount which bears the same ratio to net passive income as the passive investment income in excess of 25 percent of gross receipts bears to the passive investment income for the taxable year. In other words, the taxable amount is determined from the formula—

$$\text{Net Passive Investment Income} \times \frac{\text{Investment Income minus 25 percent of Gross Receipts}}{\text{Passive Investment Income}}$$

"Net passive investment income" is defined as passive income (defined below) less deductible expenses incurred to produce the passive investment income. By virtue of this definition, the apportionment formula automatically allocates expenses between the passive investment income in excess of 25 percent of gross receipts, which is subject to the tax, and the passive investment income that is less than 25 percent of gross receipts, which is not taxed. Finally, the amount subject to tax as net passive investment income is limited to the corporation's regular taxable income for the year. Section 1375(b)(1)(B).

The Commissioner may waive imposition of the passive investment income tax if the corporation establishes it determined in good faith that it had no Subchapter C earnings and profits and within a reasonable period of time the corporation distributed its earnings and profits to stockholders. Section 1375(d).

In addition, an S election is terminated if the corporation has Subchapter C earnings and profits at the close of each of three consecutive taxable years following the election and during each of the three years more than 25 percent of the corporation's gross receipts are passive investment income. Section 1362(d)(3).[30] The provision is in-

30. The termination rule does not apply with respect to earnings and profits accumulated before the effective date of the 1982 Act. Prior to 1983 it was possible for an S corporation to accumulate earnings and profits because earnings and profits could exceed pass-through taxable income.

tended to prevent an S corporation from utilizing accumulated C corporation earnings for passive investment purposes.

The tax on passive investment income and termination of S status both can be avoided by distributing accumulated earnings and profits to stockholders as a taxable dividend prior to making the S election.

A termination because of excess passive investment income is effective on the first day of the taxable year following the third consecutive year in which the corporation has disqualifying earnings and profits and investment income. Termination may be avoided if the Internal Revenue Service determines that the termination is inadvertent under the standards of section 1362(f), supra, page 649.

ILLUSTRATIVE MATERIAL

A. BACKGROUND

Before the Subchapter S Revision Act of 1982, section 1375(e)(5) provided for termination of an S election for any corporation if more than 20 percent of its gross receipts constituted passive investment income, without regard to whether the corporation also had Subchapter C earnings and profits. The definition of passive investment income under this now repealed provision raised interpretive issues which continue to be important under current law.

B. PASSIVE INVESTMENT INCOME

Passive investment income for purposes of sections 1362(d)(3) and 1375 is defined as income from royalties, rents, dividends, interest, annuities and sales or exchanges of stock or securities (but only to the extent of gains). Passive investment income does not include interest on notes acquired in the ordinary course of business on the sale of inventory, or gross receipts from the regular conduct of a lending or finance business. Section 1362(d)(3)(D).

As did their pre–1983 predecessors, Proposed Regulations, section 1.1362–3(d)(5)(iv) (1988), provide that the term "rent" does not include payments for the use or occupancy of rooms where significant services are also rendered. Thus, for example the income from hotel and motel operations is not rent. However, Feingold v. Commissioner, 49 T.C. 461 (1968), held under the predecessor to the Proposed Regulations that rental income from summer bungalows did not fall within the "significant services" exception and constituted disqualifying income.

The list of passive interest income items in section 1372(e)(5)(C), the predecessor to section 1362(d)(3)(D)(i), was held to be exclusive, so that gains from the sale of unimproved real estate did not constitute passive investment income for purposes of the limitation. Howell v. Commissioner, 57 T.C. 546 (1972) (A); Rev.Rul. 75–188, 1975–1, Cum.Bull. 276.

If an S corporation is in receipt of one of the items of income specified in the statute, the fact that it is an active operating company with respect to such income does not prevent application of the disqualification rule. See Zychinski v. Commissioner, 506 F.2d 637 (8th Cir.1974), in which a corporation's Subchapter S status was terminated where over 20 percent of the corporation's income was from gains on sales of stocks or securities; the fact that the corporation was a dealer did not change the result and Regulations, section 1.1372–4(b)(5), to that effect, were upheld. This result is mitigated by the 1982 addition of sections 1362(d)(3)(D)(i) and (ii), which permit the interest received by certain S corporations in the ordinary course of a trade or business to be excluded from investment income. Also section 1362(d)(3)(E) provides that gains or losses on certain futures contracts and options derived by commodities and options dealers will not be taken into account in determining passive investment income. There is no corresponding relief for rental income derived in the ordinary course of a business. Thus a corporation with Subchapter C earnings and profits still cannot conduct rental operations for more than three years and retain S corporation status.

C. GROSS RECEIPTS

Proposed Regulations, section 1.1362–3(d)(4) (1988), provide that gross receipts are not the same as gross income. A corporation operating at a loss because its cost of goods sold exceeds its receipts will still have gross receipts. In contrast, proceeds from the sale or exchange of capital assets (except for stocks or securities) are taken into account in computing gross receipts only to the extent that gains from the sale or exchange of capital assets exceed losses from the sale or exchange of capital assets. Section 1362(d)(3)(C). Gross receipts from the sale of stock or securities are taken into account only to the extent of gains. Losses from the sale of stock or securities do not offset the gains for this purpose. See Proposed Regulations, section 1.1362–3(d)(4)(B) (1988). This rule prevents the corporation from acquiring and selling stocks to enhance artificially the amount of its gross receipts.

C. BUILT–IN GAINS TAX

INTERNAL REVENUE CODE: Section 1374.

TECHNICAL AND MISCELLANEOUS REVENUE ACT OF 1988, REPORT OF THE COMMITTEE ON WAYS AND MEANS HOUSE OF REPRESENTATIVES

H.Rep. No. 100–795, 100th Cong., 2d Sess. 62–64 (1988).

A corporate level tax is imposed [by section 1374] on gain that arose prior to the conversion of a C corporation to an S corporation ("built-in gain") that is recognized by the S corporation through sale, distribution, or other disposition within 10 years after the date on which the S election took effect. The total amount of gain that must be recognized by the corporation, however, is limited to the aggregate net built-in gain of the corporation at the time of conversion to S status.

The 1986 Act provided that the amount of recognized built-in gains taken into account for any taxable year shall not exceed the excess (if any) of 1) the net unrealized built-in gain, over 2) the recognized built-in gains for prior years beginning in the 10–year recognition period. Also, recognized built-in gain is not taxed in a year to the extent that it exceeds the taxable income of the corporation for the year computed as if the corporation were a C corporation.

Under the [1986] Act, the corporation may take into account certain subchapter C tax attributes in computing the amount of tax on recognized built-in gains. Thus, for example, it may use unexpired net operating losses to offset the gain and may use business credit carryforwards to offset the tax.

The [1988 Act] modifies the operation of the built-in gains tax. [Section 1374(d)(2)(A)(ii)] retains the net income limitation of the [1986] Act by providing that a net recognized built-in gain for a year will not be taxed to the extent the corporation would not otherwise have taxable income for the year if it were a C corporation (determined in accordance with section 1375(b)(1)(B)). Under [Section 1374(d)(2)(A)(ii)], therefore, recognized built-in gain in any post-conversion year is reduced for purposes of the built-in gains tax by any recognized built-in loss for that year, and also by any other post-conversion losses for that year.

Although the committee believes it is appropriate not to impose the built-in gains tax in a year in which the taxpayer experiences losses, the committee also believes it is appropriate to reduce the potential for taxpayers to manipulate the timing of post-conversion losses in a manner that might entirely avoid the built-in gains tax on the net unrealized built-in gain of the former C corporation. Accordingly, [section 1374(d)(2)(B)] provides that any net recognized built-in gain that is not subject to the built-in gains tax due to the net income limitation will be carried forward.

Thus, an amount equal to any net recognized built-in gain that is not subject to the built-in gains tax because of the net income limitation will be carried forward and will be subject to the built-in gains tax to the extent the corporation subsequently has other taxable income (that is not already otherwise subject to the built-in gains tax) for any taxable year within the 10 year recognition period. [Section 1374(d)(2)(B)] applies only in the case of subchapter S elections made on or after March 31, 1988.

The provision is illustrated by the following example: Corporation A elects S status on March 31, 1988. The corporation has two assets, one with a value of $200 and an adjusted basis of $0 and the other with a value of $0 and an adjusted basis of $100. It has no other items of built-in gain or loss. The corporation thus has a net unrealized built-in gain of $100. In its first taxable year for which it is an S corporation, the corporation sells both assets for their fair market value and has a net recognized built-in gain of $100. It also has an additional $100 loss from other post-conversion activities. The corporation is not subject to any built-in gains tax in that year because its net recognized built-in gain ($100) exceeds its net income determined in accordance with section 1375(b)(1)(B) ($0). In its next taxable year, the corporation has $200 of taxable income. $100 is subject to the built-in gains tax in that year, because of the carryforward of the $100 of net unrecognized built-in gain that had been untaxed due to the net income limitation.

[Section 1374(d)(8)] clarifies that the built-in gain provision applies not only when a C corporation converts to S status but also in any case in which an S corporation acquires an asset and the basis of such asset in the hands of the S corporation is determined (in whole or in part) by reference to the basis of such asset (or any other property) in the hands of the C corporation. In such cases, each acquisition of assets from a C corporation is subject to a separate determination of the amount of net built-in gain, and is subject to the provision for a separate 10–year recognition period. [Section 1374(e)] clarifies that the Treasury Department has authority to prescribe regulations providing for the appropriate treatment of successor corporations—for example, in situations in which an S corporation engages in a transaction that results in carryover basis of assets to a successor corporation pursuant to subchapter C of the Code.

[Section 1374(d)(5)(A)] clarifies that, for purposes of this built-in gains tax under section 1374, any item of income which is properly taken into account for any taxable year in the recognition period but which is attributable to periods before the first taxable year for which the corporation was an S corporation is treated as a recognized built-in gain for the taxable year in which it is properly taken into account. Thus, the term "disposition of any asset" includes not only sales or exchanges but other income recognition events that effectively dispose of or relinquish a taxpayer's right to claim or receive income. For example, the term "disposition of any asset" for purposes of this provision also includes the collection of accounts receivable by a cash method taxpayer and the completion of a long-term contract performed by a taxpayer using the completed contract method of accounting.

Similarly, [Section 1374(d)(5)(B)] clarifies that amounts that are allowable as a deduction during the recognition period but that are attributable to periods before the first S corporation taxable year are thus treated as recognized built-in losses in the year of the deduction.

As an example of these built-in gain and loss provisions, in the case of a cash basis personal service corporation that converts to S status and that has receivables at the time of the conversion, the receivables, when received, are built-in gain items. At the same time, built-in losses would include otherwise deductible compensation paid after the conversion to the persons who performed the services that produced the receivables, to the extent such compensation is attributable to such pre-conversion services. To the extent such built-in loss items offset the built-in gains from the receivables, there would be no amount subject to the built-in gains tax.

[Section 1374(b)(2)] clarifies that capital loss carryforwards may also be used to offset recognized built-in gains.

ILLUSTRATIVE MATERIAL

A. OPERATION OF THE BUILT-IN GAINS TAX

Section 1374 was amended by the Tax Reform Act of 1986 and by the Technical and Miscellaneous Revenue Act of 1988 to ensure double taxation of appreciation that occurred while assets were held by a C corporation which subsequently made an S election. Section 1374 imposes a corporate level tax on recognized built-in gain with respect to assets held by the corporation at the time of conversion from C to S corporation status. The tax also applies to built-in gain recognized on disposition of assets acquired from a C corporation in a nonrecognition transaction with transferred basis to the acquiring S corporation. Section 1374 is not applicable to a corporation that never was a C corporation or that has no assets acquired from a C corporation in a nonrecognition transaction. Section 1374(c)(1). Nor is section 1374 applicable to assets purchased by the corporation or contributed to it during the period an S election is in effect.

Built-in gain recognized by an S corporation is subject to tax at the highest corporate tax rate under section 11(b). Recognized built-in gain is then subject to a second tax at the stockholder level as the recognized gain is passed through to stockholders under section 1366. Each stockholder's proportionate share of recognized built-in gain is reduced by the stockholder's proportionate share of the section 1374 tax. Section 1366(f)(2). For example, if S Corporation sells a built-in gain asset with a basis of $10 for $110, the corporation's recognized gain of $100 is subject to tax of 34 percent. Stockholders are allocated their proportionate share of the $100 of gain, less the tax of $34, or a net taxable gain of $66. Then the stockholders pay a tax equal to 28 percent of $66. The total taxes of $52.48 are the same as would be imposed on a C corporation selling its assets and distributing the after-tax proceeds.

The Tax Reform Act of 1986 granted broad authority to the Secretary to promulgate regulations to ensure that the double tax regime is not circumvented.[31] In Announcement 86–128, I.R.B. 1986–51, 22, the Internal Revenue Service indicated that it intended to promulgate regulations filling gaps in the statutory language. Some of the items described in the Announcement, such as provisions expanding the definition of "dispositions" of appreciated assets to include realization of pre-conversion income items and an "anti-stuffing" rule to prevent contribution of loss assets to the corporation to reduce recognized built-in gains, were enacted in the 1988 Technical and Miscellaneous Revenue Act.[32] The Announcement indicated that the inventory method maintained by a corporation will be used to determine whether goods required to be included in inventory were on hand with built-in gain at the time of conversion to S corporation status.

B. PRE–1987 TAX ON EXCESS CAPITAL GAINS

Corporations which are not subject to the built-in gains tax of section 1374, i.e., corporations which filed an S election before the applicable effective date,[33] are instead subject to a tax under the pre–1987 version of

31. The initial authority is in section 337(d). The 1988 Act also added section 1374(e) providing specific regulatory authority under section 1374.

32. See H.Rep. No. 100–795, 100th Cong., 2d Sess. 62–64 (1988).

33. The capital gains tax of former section 1374 also applied to recognized capital

section 1374 on certain dispositions of assets producing long term capital gain. Former section 1374 was enacted to prevent "one-shot" elections of S corporation status which avoided double taxation. Without the tax, a corporation contemplating the disposition of appreciated assets might have elected S corporation status and disposed of appreciated capital assets subject to a single tax on the capital gain at the stockholder level. The alternative was recognition of gain at the corporate level followed by a taxable dividend on distribution of the proceeds to the stockholders.

Former section 1374 imposed a tax on capital gain in excess of $25,000 at regular corporate rates. The tax was imposed only if the net capital gain of an S corporation exceeded $25,000, the capital gain was in excess of 50 percent of the corporation's tax income, and total taxable income was in excess of $25,000. Thus the tax was intended to apply only if recognition of capital gains was a major part of the corporation's income for the year. In addition, the tax was not imposed on any corporation that had been an S corporation for the three taxable years preceding the year in which the capital gain was recognized, or which had been an S corporation for its whole existence if the corporation was less than three years old.

C. REFERENCES

August, Corporate–Level Taxes on S Corporation After the Tax Reform Act of 1986, 4 J. Partnership Tax. 91 (1987).

D. COORDINATION WITH SUBCHAPTER C

INTERNAL REVENUE CODE: Section 1371.

ILLUSTRATIVE MATERIAL

A. GENERAL

Section 1371 contains rules coordinating the treatment of items which affect both Subchapter S and Subchapter C years when a former C corporation elects S corporation status or an S corporation revokes or terminates its Subchapter S election.

There are no carrybacks or carryovers of loss or other items from Subchapter C years to Subchapter S years and vice versa. Section 1371(b). Thus a carryover of net operating losses incurred in a Subchapter C year will not be available to reduce S corporation income taxable to the stockholders. There is an exception for built-in gains that are required to be recognized and taxed to the S corporation under section 1374. See supra, page 311. The period during which the S election is in effect will be counted in determining the number of years during which a carryforward or carryback is available. Section 1371(b)(3). In the case of a former S corporation, however, losses will have passed through to stockholders who may carryover losses on their individual returns to a year following revocation of the S election.

gain on disposition of property acquired by the S corporation within the 3 year period preceding the disposition if the basis of the property in the hands of the S corporation was determined in whole or in part by reference to the basis of the property in the hands of another corporation that was a C corporation during the three year period preceding sale. This provision prevented the transfer of capital or section 1231 assets to a newly formed or existing S corporation in a nonrecognition transaction as a device to avoid the capital gains tax.

E. POLICY ASPECTS OF THE TREATMENT OF SUBCHAPTER S CORPORATIONS WITH A SUBCHAPTER C HISTORY

The policy basis of the various rules dealing with Subchapter S corporations which have previously operated as C corporations is not clearly articulated in the legislative history of the provisions. With respect to the built in gain rules, the provisions can perhaps best be understood as a variation on the *General Utilities* problem. The conversion from C status to S status and the consequent move to a single tax regime is in many ways like a liquidation of the corporation and a transfer of the assets out of corporate solution. If this change in taxing pattern had been achieved through a liquidation, section 336 would have required recognition of gain at the corporate level, followed by a shareholder level gain. In the Subchapter S situation, rather than impose an immediate tax at the time of conversion, the statute defers the tax until a sale of the assets and in effect turns that deferral into an exemption if the assets are held for ten years.

As to the passive income limitations, if the liquidation model is continued, on a liquidation, the accumulated but undistributed corporate level earnings would not be subject to dividend taxation when distributed in liquidation, but would incur a shareholder level capital gains tax, the size of which would depend on the stock basis. Since the conversion to S status does not result in any shareholder level tax, Congress apparently felt that it was inappropriate to allow those earnings, unreduced by any second level tax, to be reinvested in assets generating passive income unrelated to the basic business operations of the corporation. Initially the sanction is an additional level of tax, with the corporation ultimately losing its S status if the situation goes on for too long.

Which of the other Subchapter S rules could be eliminated if the conversion from C to S status was treated as a liquidation?

SECTION 5. POLICY ASPECTS OF SUBCHAPTER S

Subchapter S raises significant questions both in theory and in practice. Given the fundamental decision to have a separate corporation income tax, the question is whether there are situations that justify departure from that model. The argument in favor of Subchapter S is that taxes should be as neutral as possible as respects the form of doing business for a closely held enterprise. That argument may justify the special pass-through treatment of S corporations. On the other hand, Subchapter S contains significant differences from the other major form of pass-through enterprise, the partnership, which create significant advantages and disadvantages depending upon particular circumstances. Compared to partnerships, Subchapter S provides a less complex device for pass-through taxation of a joint enterprise. The differences between Subchapters K and S are substantial, however, and require tax motivated choices between the forms of doing business. Does the reduced complexity of Subchapter S justify its variations from the partnership model?

While the partnership rules of Subchapter K adopt an aggregate approach to many issues, with attendant complexity attributable to the aggregate treatment of liabilities and the partner's aggregate shares of the partnership's inside basis if they so elect, the S corporation can be characterized as an entity with a specific pass-through of designated income and loss items. The aggregate versus entity distinction is apparent in the divergent treatment of distributions of appreciated property; distributions by partnerships do not trigger recognition by the partnership and the partners take a carryover basis; distributions of appreciated property by an S corporation require recognition of gain by all the stockholders and the recipient stockholder receives a set-up in basis to fair market value. Entity level recognition by the S corporation avoids the partnership problems addressed in section 751(b) and the need for adjustments to aggregate bases provided for in Section 734, both highly complex provisions. On the other hand, the entity level recognition operates as a disincentive to non-pro rata distributions since the nonrecipient shareholders recognize current gain and the tax effect of that recognition may not be reversible until liquidation (by means of a capital loss deduction).

These disparate distribution rules also affect liquidations. Subject to the exceptions of section 751(b), a partnership can be liquidated and assets distributed to the partners without current taxation. The partners substitute their outside basis in their partnership interests for the partnership's basis in the assets distributed to them. The liquidation of an S corporation is subject to the normal rules of Subchapter C (sections 331 and 336) which require recognition of gain at the corporate level. In tandem these provisions require recognition of at least corporate level gain on distributed appreciated assets, and perhaps additional gain at the stockholder level depending upon the relationship between the stockholders' stock bases and the value of distributed property. As a result of the taxable nature of the transaction, the stockholders take a fair market value basis in the distributed assets.

Similar disparities exist in comparing the redemption (under section 302) of an S corporation stockholder with the retirement of a partner. A distribution of appreciated property to an S corporation stockholder in a stock redemption will result in recognition of gain by the corporation. The gain is passed-through to all shareholders in proportion to stockholdings, while only the redeemed stockholder receives the distributed property. The redeemed stockholder may or may not recognize gain depending on the basis of redeemed stock. A distribution of appreciated property in retirement of a partner's partnership interest will not trigger partnership level recognition of gain or loss, unless section 751 assets are involved. The distributee partner will recognize gain, loss, or in some cases (if section 736(a) is involved) both ordinary gain and a capital loss.

The entity approach to Subchapter S also affects the potential for shifting income from one stockholder to another as a result of a contribution of appreciated property to the corporation. Section 704(c) operates in Subchapter K to prevent a shift of pre-contribution appreciation or losses to the non-contributing partners by requiring that the difference between basis and fair market value at the time of contribution be reflected in allocations to the partners. There is no provision for equivalent adjustments under Subchapter S where each stockholder is required to report the stockholder's proportionate share of corporate income and loss items.

The restrictions of Subchapter S on the number and types of S corporation stockholders may also be analyzed as a response to perceived problems of complexity. Although Subchapter K demonstrates that pass-through accounting on a large scale is a possible alternative for income tax purposes, the limited number of permissible stockholders of an S corporation and the restrictions on the types of permissible stockholders, excluding other pass-through entities and corporations, substantially reduces the burden of accounting of the pass-through of S corporation income.

However, the goal of simplicity in Subchapter S creates its own complexity. Differences in the pass-through treatment under Subchapters K and S require careful planning choices regarding the choice of entity. The flexibility permitted by Subchapter K with respect to allocations of income and loss items, can be contrasted with the rather rigid requirements of a single class of stock under Subchapter S. Stockholder attempts to create preferential interest in an S corporation through the use of purported debt instruments have been a source of considerable litigation. Additional difficulty is created by the detailed requirements for election S corporation status. Failure to comply with the statutory requirements regarding timing and form can defeat the attempts of well-intentioned taxpayers to elect S corporation status. No such requirements are imposed on operation as a partnership, an entity also requiring participants to report their share of entity level income and loss, though the question of entity classification represents a somewhat similar problem. Although provisions for notifying the Internal Revenue Service of an intent to operate a corporation as a pass-through entity and requiring stockholders to consent to the pass-through of tax significant items are warranted, perhaps Subchapter S should provide liberal remedial steps to correct defective filings.

Beyond the question of the relationship between Subchapter S and partnership taxation, the Subchapter S provisions raise the more fundamental issue of the extent to which operation in corporate form should be coupled with a double level of tax on distributions. Absent a decision to adopt some general form of integration of corporate and individual taxes, why should, roughly speaking, closely held corporations without subsidiaries be subject to a single level of tax while all other corporate entities operate in a two tax world? Do these characteristics have any bearing on whether double tax or single tax is appropriate?

For a detailed discussion of these issues see Eustice, Subchapter S Corporations and Partnerships: A Search for the Pass Through Paradigm (some Preliminary Proposals), 39 Tax L.Rev. 345 (1984). See also Coven, Subchapter S Distributions and Pseudo Distributions: Proposals for Revising the Defective Blend of Entity and Conduit Concepts, 42 Tax L.Rev. 381 (1987).

SECTION 6. CHOICE OF METHODS OF DOING BUSINESS

For federal income tax purposes, taxpayers who associate to carry on a business have the choice of operating as a partnership or as a corporation (including an S corporation). As the materials in Parts I and II have indicated, the tax rules governing each of these forms of business differ. From the standpoint of the tax advisor, it is important to identify the points at which different tax treatment occur and provide the client with an evaluation of the significance of those differences in the context of the business operation being conducted, or to be conducted, by the client.

The following table summarizes the principal points of tax difference that can affect the choice of the business form. The list is not exhaustive, but is rather intended to provide in a summary way an indication of the major considerations that should be taken into account in deciding what form of business organization is most appropriate from a tax standpoint. The descriptions of the tax consequences are in very general terms and do not attempt to reflect the fine points of the rules that have been discussed in Parts I and II. Reference should be made back to the earlier discussions to make a more precise evaluation of the various provisions summarized in the following table.

Item	Partnership	S Corporation *	C Corporation
1. Taxable year	Generally must conform to year of majority of partners, unless business purpose for different year; may elect certain fiscal years without business purpose if make additional tax deposit	Generally must use calendar year, unless business purpose for different year; may elect certain fiscal years without business purpose if make additional tax deposit	May select fiscal year—in general no effect on shareholders; personal service corporations subject to limitations similar to partnerships and S corporations
2. Compensation			
a. Fringe benefits	Partners not "employees" and provisions such as health plans, group term life insurance, etc., not available	More than 2% shareholders cannot qualify for employee fringe benefits	Officer-shareholders can qualify for employee fringe benefits

Item	Partnership	S Corporation *	C Corporation
b. Retirement benefits	Partners subject to limitations applicable to self-employed individuals	Shareholder-employees subject to limitations applicable to self-employed individuals	Shareholder-employees may be included in qualified employee retirement plans
c. Reasonable compensation limitations	Apply to partnerships where capital is material factor; otherwise not applicable	Apply to employee-shareholders	Apply to employee-shareholders
3. Character of income and deductions	Determined at partnership level and flow through to partners	Generally determined at corporate level and flow through to shareholders	Determined at corporate level and do not flow through to shareholders
4. Capital gains	Character and amounts flow through to partners	Except as to certain built-in gains taxed at the corporate level, character and amounts flow through to shareholders	No flow through to shareholders
5. Net Capital Losses	Flow through to partners; unlimited carryovers	Flow through to shareholders; unlimited carryovers	Can only be carried forward five years by corporation
6. Contributions of appreciated or depreciated property	No gain or loss; carryover basis; adjustments can be made among partners to compensate for differences between fair market value and basis of property contributed	No gain or loss; carryover basis; shareholders share ratably in subsequent depreciation, gain, loss, etc., without possibility for adjustment for differences in fair market value and basis of property contributed	Same as Subchapter S
7. Allocation of income, deductions, etc.	May be determined by partnership agreement if reflects economic realty	No allocation permitted	Allocation possible to limited extent through different classes of stock or securities
8. Treatment of statutory limitations, e.g., charitable contributions, percentage limits on soil and water conservation costs	Imposed at individual partner level	Imposed at individual shareholder level	Imposed at corporate level
a. Investment interest limit	Imposed at partner level	Imposed at shareholder level	Not applicable
b. $3,000 limit on deduction for net capital losses against ordinary income	Imposed on and available to partners for partnership capital losses	Imposed on and available to shareholders for corporate capital losses	Not applicable
9. Net operating loss	Flow through to extent of basis; suspense account for excess	Flow through to extent of basis; suspense account for excess	No flow through to shareholders; carryback and carryover at corporate level
a. At risk rules	Apply to partnership and partners	Apply to corporation and shareholders	Apply only to corporations with five or fewer shareholders

Item	Partnership	S Corporation *	C Corporation
b. Passive Activity loss limitation	Imposed at partner level	Imposed at shareholder level	Applicable only to closely held C corporations and personal service corporations
10. Gain on sales to entity by owner	Ordinary income to seller if property not a capital asset in hands of partnership and seller is 50% partner, actual or constructive	Ordinary income to seller if property is depreciable and selling shareholder is owner of 50% of stock, actual or constructive	Same as Subchapter S
11. Distribution in kind			
a. Current	No gain or loss to partnership or distributee-partner; carryover or substituted basis, exception for section 751 items	Tax-free to extent of basis in stock, then capital gain; corporation recognizes gain on distribution; shareholder gets basis in property equal to fair market value	Shareholder taxed as dividend equal to fair market value of property to extent of current and accumulated earnings and profits; then section 301(a) applies; section 311 applies to corporation
b. Liquidating	Substituted basis in assets equal to basis in partnership interest	Capital gain on excess of value over basis; section 336 applies to corporation	Same as Subchapter S as to shareholder; section 336 applies to corporation
c. Collapsible items	Ordinary income to partners under section 751	Ordinary income under section 341; but definitions differ from section 751	Same as Subchapter S
12. Distribution of cash representing previously taxed income	Tax-free to extent of basis; capital gain to extent of excess (subject to section 751); treatment applies whether recipient was partner at time of previous taxation	Tax-free to extent of basis; capital gain on excess (subject to section 341); treatment applies whether or not recipient was shareholder at time of previous taxation	Taxable as dividend to extent of earnings and profits, then reduces basis in stock, and excess is capital gain
13. Purchase by entity of owner's entire interest	Capital gain to extent of interest in partnership tangible assets; capital gain or ordinary income for excess depending on whether transaction constitutes "purchase" or "distributive share" under section 736; section 751 applies	Distribution first applied against basis in stock; excess is capital gain; collapsible rules under section 341 apply	Possible capital gain under section 302; subject to attribution rules of section 318 and collapsible rules under section 341 which may produce ordinary dividend; section 303 may apply
14. Death	Generally, taxable year of partnership does not close; income for year of death taxed to estate and section 691(c) applies; any heir or legatee can continue as partner if agreement permits	Taxable year of corporation does not close; income for year of death taxed pro rata in decedent's final return and in estate's return; estate can continue as shareholder	No effect on corporation; estate taxed on post-death dividends

Item	Partnership	S Corporation *	C Corporation
15. Sale of ownership interests	Capital gain subject to section 751; optional adjustment to basis of partnership assets permitted	Capital gain subject to section 341; no effect on basis of corporation's assets	Same as Subchapter S
16. Qualified owners	No limitations	Only individuals, estates and certain trusts may be shareholders	No limitations
17. Income shifting within family	Family partnership rules impose substantial restrictions	Family rules similar to partnerships apply	Bona fide transfer of stock shifts tax on actual dividend distributions
18. Types of ownership interests	More than one class of partner permitted	Only one class of stock permitted (though differences in voting rights allowed)	More than one class of stock permitted

* The table assumes that the S corporation has never operated as a C corporation.

Having taken the foregoing tax factors into account, the choice from a tax point of view among the possible business forms is to a large extent a matter of tax arithmetic. What is required is a detailed comparison of the tax rates which would be incurred if the operation is conducted in regular corporate form with the individual tax rates of the investors that would govern if the operation is to be in partnership or S corporation form. In addition, the choice depends on the special features of each individual situation. Are initial losses anticipated? What are the projected levels of income? Are any assets involved which would generate special tax credits or deductions? What are the cash flow needs of the parties?

Finally, nontax considerations can and should play an important role in the decision whether to operate as a partnership, an S corporation or a C corporation. The sophistication of the clients must be taken into account even when the tax considerations point in a given direction.

PART IV

THE PURCHASE AND SALE OF A CORPORATE BUSINESS: TAXABLE AND TAX FREE

CHAPTER 16

TAXABLE ACQUISITIONS

SECTION 1. INTRODUCTORY NOTE

The material considered up to this point has focused on the provisions of Subchapter C from the perspective of their function in the statutory structure provided for the taxation of corporations and shareholders. The material in this Part changes from this structural focus to concentrate on the application of the corporate rules to a specific transaction, the purchase and sale of a corporate business. This chapter deals with the tax aspects of a taxable purchase and sale of the corporate business; the various techniques for tax free acquisitions are considered in Chapter 17.

In some cases a taxable purchase and sale of a business involves a fairly straightforward application of the general principles which have previously been considered. In other situations, however, issues peculiar to the sale of a corporate business have arisen and rules have been fashioned, either by the Congress or by the courts, to deal with these problems. The materials in Section 2 deal with the sale of a business which takes the form of a sale of corporate assets and explore the problems which this form of transaction historically has generated and the currently applicable rules. Section 3 focuses on the other basic alternative form for the sale of a corporate business, the sale of the shares of stock of the corporation and again focuses on the corporate tax rules designed for this form of transaction. Section 4 examines the problems which arise when corporate distributions are made in connection with the sale of a corporate business.

In examining these materials keep in mind that the manner in which the parties structured transactions involving the sale of a corporate business historically has been influenced by three major tax factors: the seller's desire to maximize the portion of the gain that would be taxed as capital gain rather than as ordinary income; the buyer's desire to obtain as high a basis as possible for the corporation's assets, particularly inventory and depreciable property; and, finally, the ability to avoid recognition of gain at the corporate level under the *General Utilities* doctrine. Consider first how the repeal of the *General*

Utilities rule and the elimination of preferential rate of tax for capital gains have altered the manner in which the parties are likely to structure transactions. Then consider the extent to which portions of the current statutory rules may be vestiges of the era in which there was a capital gains preference and the *General Utilities* doctrine applied. Should these provisions be repealed as "deadwood" or is there still some useful purpose, albeit a less central one, served by them?

Tax results are not the only factors which influence the form of a sale and purchase of a corporate business. Indeed, tax results in many cases are of lesser importance than nontax factors. For example, a purchaser may be absolutely unwilling to acquire the stock of a corporation because of concerns regarding contingent or unascertained liabilities. On the other hand, an asset purchase may be ruled out if the acquired business owns contract rights which may not be assignable; in such a case the acquisition must be structured as a sale and purchase of stock. Other important factors to be considered include state law rights of dissenting shareholders, federal and state securities laws, and the authority of state and federal regulatory agencies to approve or disapprove a transaction.

SECTION 2. THE PURCHASE AND SALE OF CORPORATE ASSETS

A. INTRODUCTION

Several theoretical models exist for taxing the corporation and its shareholders on the disposition of the corporate business. These are best examined through application to a simple example. Suppose that A owns all of the stock of X Corporation, which operates a business consisting of two assets, Asset # 1, having a basis of $50 and a fair market value of $500, and Asset # 2, having a basis of $250 and a fair market value of $200. Also assume that the basis of A's stock is $200. If Y Corporation desires to acquire the business of X Corporation it might purchase the assets of X Corporation for $700. X Corporation would realize a net gain of $400 on the sale of its assets. If this gain were taxed at the maximum corporate rate of 34 percent, X Corporation would pay taxes of $136 and make a $564 liquidating distribution to A, who would recognize a gain of $364. A would pay a tax, at 28 percent, of $102 and would receive net proceeds of $462. Y Corporation would take a basis of $500 for Asset # 1 and $200 for Asset # 2. On a subsequent sale of the assets, assuming that their fair market values were unchanged, Y Corporation would realize neither gain nor loss.

Alternatively, Y Corporation might purchase the stock of X Corporation from A. If Y Corporation paid $700 for the stock, A would recognize a gain of $500. The basis of the assets in X Corporation's hands would be unaffected by the sale of the stock, and on a subsequent sale of the assets, X Corporation would recognize an aggregate gain of $400. Since the economic burden of the tax on this gain would be borne by Y Corporation, presumably it would offer A less than $700 for the stock of X Corporation to reflect this inherent tax burden. If the gain were to be realized and taxed contemporaneously with the purchase, it could be expected that Y Corporation would offer A only $564 for the stock, the same amount that he would receive in a liquidating distribution following a taxable sale of its assets by X Corporation. But if the gain was not expected to be realized until sometime in the future, Y Corporation could be expected to be willing to pay somewhat more for the stock.

Suppose, however, as was the case prior to 1986, that X Corporation could distribute its assets to A in a liquidating distribution without recognition of gain. A would receive a liquidating distribution of $700, recognizing a $500 gain. He would take the assets with a fair market value basis and could turn around and immediately sell them to Y Corporation for no gain or loss. In this case the assets would have been transferred to Y Corporation with a fair market value basis in its hands, but only a single tax of $140 would have been paid at the shareholder level, leaving A with net proceeds of $560.

The availability of this third possibility at first caused corporations and their shareholders to attempt to avoid preliquidation asset sales by the corporation, instead structuring the sale of the corporate business, at least in form, as an in-kind liquidation followed by a shareholder sale of assets. The form versus substance aspects of this planning technique inevitably led to litigation, which in turn spawned the enactment in 1954 of a statutory provision to equalize substantially the taxation of the sale regardless of whether the liquidation or the asset sale came first.

B. ASSET SALES BEFORE 1987

(1) The Case Law Before 1954

The importance of tax planning and the form versus substance tension in asset sale transactions that existed under prior law is illustrated by comparing the decisions in Commissioner v. Court Holding Co, 324 U.S. 331 (1945) and United States v. Cumberland Public Service Co., 338 U.S. 451 (1950).

In *Court Holding Co.* a corporation owned an apartment building as its sole operating asset. An oral agreement for the sale and purchase of the building was reached between the corporation and a potential purchaser, who paid the corporation a $1,000 deposit against the purchase price. When the parties met to reduce the agreement to writing, the corporation's attorney advised the purchaser that the transaction could not be consummated as agreed upon because the corporation would be taxable on the gain realized on the sale. Accordingly, execution of a written contract was delayed. The following day the corporation was liquidated and the apartment building distributed to its two shareholders, a husband and wife, in a liquidating distribution. The former shareholders then executed a contract of purchase and sale with the potential buyer, and three days later title to the property was transferred, with the purchaser being credited for the $1,000 deposit.

On these facts the Tax Court held that the corporation never had abandoned the sale. Rather the various steps by which the transaction was consummated "were mere formalities designed 'to make the transaction appear to be other than what it was', in order to avoid tax liability." (333) Drawing different inferences from the facts, the Court of Appeals reversed, holding that the corporation had called off the sale and that the subsequent sale by the shareholders was unrelated.

The Supreme Court held that there were sufficient facts to support the Tax Court's conclusion and that, accordingly, it should have been sustained. The Court observed as follows: "[T]he transaction must be viewed as a whole, and each step from the commencement of negotiations to the consummation of the sale is relevant. A sale by one person cannot be transformed for tax purposes into a sale by another by using the latter as a conduit through which to pass title. To permit the true nature of a transaction to be disguised by mere formalisms, which exist solely to alter tax liabilities, would seriously impair the effective administration of the tax policies of Congress." (334). Thus the transaction was taxed as a sale followed by a liquidation, and two levels of tax were imposed.

Over the next five years the lower courts reacted with diverse approaches to the basic problem presented in the *Court Holding Co.* case. See Guinness v. United States, 73 F.Supp. 119 (Ct.Cl.1947) (gain to the corporation always resulted if the sale by the stockholder followed after the distribution in accordance with a previous plan); Howell Turpentine Co. v. Commissioner, 162 F.2d 319 (5th Cir.1947) (automatic rule that even though the stockholder-officers negotiate the sale prior to the liquidation, a liquidation followed by the conveyance to the purchaser should not be treated as a sale by the corporation); Kaufmann v. Commissioner, 175 F.2d 28 (3d Cir.1949) (specific facts pointed to a sale by the corporation); Beaty & Co. v. Commissioner, 14 T.C. 52 (1950) (A) (specific facts indicated that sale was not by the corporation).

Then the Supreme Court revisited the issue in *Cumberland Public Service Co.* In that case the shareholders of a closely held corporation in the business of generating electric power decided that the corporation no longer could be competitive and offered their stock for sale to an electric power cooperative. The cooperative refused to buy the stock, but offered to buy the assets. The corporation declined to sell its assets because it would have been required to pay tax on its gain, but the shareholders offered to liquidate the corporation and sell the assets to the cooperative. This offer was accepted.[1] The Commissioner asserted

1. Although not noted by the Supreme Court in its opinion, the persons who were the corporate officers negotiating on behalf of the corporation were the shareholders.

that the corporation properly was taxable on the sale of the corporate assets under the *Court Holding Co.* doctrine, but the Court of Claims held that the sale was in fact made by the shareholders. Once again, the Supreme Court upheld the trial court's decision as follows:

"Here, on the basis of adequate subsidiary findings, the Court of Claims has found that the sale in question was made by the stockholders rather than the corporation. The Government's argument that the shareholders acted as a mere 'conduit' for a sale by respondent corporation must fall before this finding. The subsidiary finding that a major motive of the shareholders was to reduce taxes does not bar this conclusion. Whatever the motive and however relevant it may be in determining whether the transaction was real or a sham, sales of physical properties by shareholders following a genuine liquidation distribution cannot be attributed to the corporation for tax purposes." (455).

Lower court decisions after the *Cumberland Public Service Co.* opinion favored the taxpayer. Courts frequently did not ascribe the sale to the corporation even though negotiations occurred prior to liquidation and were conducted by stockholder-officers, as long as the contract to sell was entered into by the stockholders and not the corporation. See, e.g., St. Louis Union Trust Co. v. Finnegan, 197 F.2d 565 (8th Cir.1952); Gensinger v. Commissioner, 208 F.2d 576 (9th Cir. 1953); Merkra Holding Co. v. Commissioner, 27 T.C. 82 (1956)(A). But see Donner v. Commissioner, 227 F.2d 381 (2d Cir.1955) (liquidation following contract of sale but before conveyance of title governed by *Court Holding Co.*) If the necessary formalities were observed, the parties were able to prevent a gain from arising to the liquidated corporation on a sale of its assets. The situation was not a satisfactory one, however, since substantially similar cases led to sharply different tax results.

(2) THE 1954 CODE SOLUTION

In 1954 Congress enacted the prior version of section 337 in an attempt to resolve the *Court Holding Company* problem by imposing only a single tax on the sale of corporate business carried out as a sale of assets. The general rule of former section 337 was that a corporation recognized neither gain nor loss on the sale or exchange of assets after the adoption of a plan of liquidation, if all of the assets (including proceeds from the sale of assets) were distributed in liquidation within twelve months of adoption of the plan.[2] Elimination of the corporate tax through nonrecognition of gain depended, however, on following mechanical formulae involving time intervals, bulk inventory sales of a

See 83 F.Supp. 843 (Ct.Cl.1949). Neither the Court of Claims nor the Supreme Court attached any importance to their dual roles, however.

2. The version of section 337 enacted in 1954 was repealed by the Tax Reform Act of 1986, which enacted a different provision using the same section number. Current section 337 is discussed supra, page 629.

certain nature, and the like. Taxpayers seeking nonrecognition of gain generally were able to satisfy these formulae, except for special situations, bad planning, or lack of knowledge. Taxpayers desiring recognition of loss, of course, attempted to plan their transactions to avoid satisfaction of the formulae.

ILLUSTRATIVE MATERIAL

A. QUALIFICATION UNDER SECTION 337

The Internal Revenue Service recognized the essentially mechanical nature of the tests under former section 337 and ruled that the taxpayer intentionally could avoid the application of the section when it was to his advantage. Rev.Rul. 77–150, 1977–1 Cum.Bull. 88 (intentional failure to distribute assets within the 12–month period prevented application of section 337). Section 337 thus became an elective device for the informed taxpayer. Both City Bank of Washington v. Commissioner, 38 T.C. 713 (1962), and Virginia Ice and Freezing Corp. v. Commissioner, 30 T.C. 1251 (1958), allowed the corporation to "straddle" the date of adoption of the plan of liquidation, selling its loss assets prior to that date to obtain a loss deduction and its gain assets after that date, thereby shielding the gain from recognition.

B. REFERENCES

Ratliff, Equalizing Tax Treatment of Liquidations Under Section 337, 54 Texas L.Rev. 151 (1975); Morrison, Assignment of Income and Tax Benefit Principles in Corporate Liquidations 54 Taxes 902 (1976).

C. ASSET SALES AFTER 1986

INTERNAL REVENUE CODE: Section 1060.

REGULATIONS: Section 1.1060–1T(a)(1), (b)(1), (c), (d), (e)(1), (h)(1)–(2).

With the repeal of the *General Utilities* doctrine by the Tax Reform Act of 1986, the rationale for former section 337 was eliminated and it was repealed. Asset sales by a liquidating corporation are fully taxable transactions. If a corporation sells its business by selling its assets to the purchaser, it recognizes gain or loss as would a partnership or sole proprietorship selling its business. On liquidation the shareholders recognize capital gain or loss under the rules governing complete liquidations considered previously, subject to the exception under section 332 for liquidations of controlled subsidiaries. Thus, gain or loss generally results to both the corporation and the shareholders. The same tax results follow if the corporation liquidates first, recognizing gain or loss under section 336, with the shareholders again taxable under section 331.

In an asset sale, both buyer and seller must allocate the purchase price to the various assets transferred: the seller in order to determine the amount of gain or loss on each asset and the buyer to establish the tax basis for the newly acquired assets. These allocations generally present no problem if the parties have bargained on an asset-by-asset basis, but that is rarely the case. More commonly the parties have bargained for the sale and purchase based on a lump sum price. Historically, after the total purchase price had been determined the parties often then bargained as to the allocation among all of the assets. The parties objectives in this *ex post* allocation were to a large extent determined by tax considerations. The seller sought to attribute as much of the purchase price as possible to assets that produced capital gain or gain entitled to nonrecognition under former section 337, while the purchaser sought to allocate as much of the price as possible to depreciable and ordinary income assets, which often required recognition of gain by the seller even if former section 337 applied to the transaction. Generally, allocations of the purchase price by the parties were respected by the Internal Revenue Service and the courts on the theory that the parties had adverse interests and that a bargained-for allocation was therefore presumptively correct.

However, there is some danger that the Treasury may be "whipsawed" by inconsistent allocations, that is, each party will allocate the purchase price in the manner most advantageous to that party and differently from the other party. In addition, the purchaser may attempt to allocate all or part of a "premium" payment in excess of the value of the assets among all of the assets, rather than allocating the premium solely to nondepreciable goodwill or going concern value.[3] Congress responded to these problems with the enactment in 1986 of section 1060, requiring the use by both the buyer and the seller of the "residual method" of valuing goodwill.[4] This provision is intended not only to prevent the allocation of purchase price premium to depreciable assets, but to help insure that the seller and purchaser allocate the price consistently. Pursuant to its statutory authority, the Treasury Department has promulgated Regulations requiring both parties to file information returns with respect to the purchase price allocation thus allowing the Internal Revenue Service to identify situations where allocations have been made on an inconsistent basis.

ILLUSTRATIVE MATERIAL

A. ALLOCATION OF PURCHASE PRICE

1. *General*

Section 1060 refers to preexisting Regulations under section 338(b)(5), discussed infra, page 711, which contain a detailed set of rules for the allocation of purchase price to acquired assets.

Temporary Regulations, section 1.1060–1T(d), set forth the allocation rules, which divide all assets into four classes. Class I assets include cash, bank deposits, and similar assets; Class II includes certificates of deposit, United States Government securities, and readily marketable stock or securities; Class III includes all other assets except goodwill and going concern value; and Class IV includes goodwill and going concern value. The purchase price is allocated first to Class I assets based on their aggregate fair market value, then to Class II assets, and so on. Within each class, the price is allocated among assets relative to their respective fair market values. Since each asset in Classes I–III should be allocated a portion of the purchase price equal to its fair market value, the entire premium is allocated to Class IV.

3. See United States v. Cornish, 348 F.2d 175 (9th Cir.1965) (allowing premium paid for partnership interest to be allocated among partnership assets in making basis adjustment under section 743).

4. For earlier judicial application of the residual method of valuing goodwill, see Carty v. Commissioner, 38 T.C. 46 (1962); compare Rev.Rul. 68–609, 1968–2 Cum. Bull. 327 (capitalization of earnings method).

Conversely, if a going business is purchased for less than its liquidation value, the Class III assets are allocated an amount less than their individual fair market values. Prior to the enactment of section 1060, purchasers had sometimes applied a so-called "proportional allocation method" in determining purchase price premiums. Under this approach, an independent value was established for goodwill, often by a capitalization of earnings method, and then the premium was allocated proportionately to all assets, including goodwill. Section 1060 requires that the "residual" method be used which allocates all premium to goodwill.

There is still room for controversy involving purchase price allocations. Class III includes intangible assets such as patents, copyrights, trademarks, tradenames, secret processes, customer lists and the like, which may be depreciable or with respect to which an abandonment loss might be claimed even though the business remains a going concern. In some cases it is difficult to distinguish between the value of these items and the value of goodwill, and purchasers are likely to attempt to establish a high fair market value for these items, while sellers rarely will care how the purchase price is allocated among goodwill and these intangibles. Furthermore, Class III itself contains both depreciable and nondepreciable assets, such as land and trademarks. Purchasers will want to establish as high a fair market value as is possible for depreciable assets. While this allocation may give rise to section 1245 recapture income for the seller instead of capital gain, in a system without a capital gains preference this result generally will not be of consequence to the seller.

In addition, the repeal of the capital gains preference has caused purchasers to revise the form of their offer, especially where the selling corporation is closely held. In such cases, the purchaser will seek to allocate a significant part of the "purchase" price to covenants not to compete, long-term employment contracts, "signing bonuses," or the like which are entered into with the shareholders of the corporation whose assets are being acquired. The purchaser seeks immediate deduction or short-term amortization of the payments while the sellers are indifferent to the tax characterization of the payments. In such cases, the Service may seek to challenge the payments as made for nondepreciable goodwill. But there is a significant body of case law developed under prior law (in part at the instigation of the Service where it sought ordinary income treatment as to the sellers) which could prove an obstacle to such characterization. The extent to which section 1060 applies in this situation is unclear.

Even in cases where the seller and purchaser might desire different allocations, nothing in section 1060 or the Regulations requires that the parties agree upon an allocation or that they file consistent information returns with respect to the allocation. The existence of this information return requirement, however, will help insure more consistent filing, particularly since it requires a statement whether the parties have agreed on the allocation. In addition, where the parties do agree on an allocation, they generally will be bound to it for tax purposes. See, e.g., Commissioner v. Danielson, 378 F.2d 771 (3d Cir.1967); Landry v. Commissioner, 86 T.C. 1284 (1986). The Internal Revenue Service, however, is not restricted from challenging the taxpayers' allocations. S.Rep. No. 99–313, 99th Cong., 2d Sess. 255 (1986).

2. *Applicable Asset Acquisition*

The legislative history indicates that section 1060 applies to any sale and purchase of assets that constitute an active trade or business under section 355, discussed infra, page 914, or to which "goodwill or going concern value could under any circumstances attach." S.Rep. No. 99–313, 99th Cong., 2d Sess. 255 (1986). Temporary Regulations, section 1.1060–1T(b)(2) and (3), Ex. (1)–(4), indicate that the term "applicable asset acquisition" will be broadly construed. Thus, if a liquidating corporation sells a portion of its assets to each of several purchasers, several applicable asset acquisitions may have occurred. Conversely, if a purchasing corporation acquires assets of a seller that constituted a trade or business of the seller, an applicable asset acquisition has occurred even though the purchaser discontinues the seller's trade or business and uses the assets in a different trade or business conducted by it.

B. OTHER ASPECTS OF ASSET SALES

1. *Liabilities*

Assumption by the buyer of the seller's liabilities is, of course, treated as a payment received by the seller. Regulations, section 1.1001–2. However, if those liabilities would have given rise to a deduction when paid, then the seller is entitled to an offsetting deduction. See Commercial Security Bank v. Commissioner, 77 T.C. 145 (1981).

Assignment of income and clear reflection of income issues, discussed supra, page 371, also are of continuing importance.

2. *Installment Reporting by Acquired Corporation's Shareholders*

Where publicly held companies are not involved, the shareholders of the acquired corporation may be eligible to report gain using the installment method under section 453 in either an asset sale followed by a liquidation or a taxable merger. Only installment obligations arising from sales qualifying under section 453(h), discussed supra, page 613, are eligible for installment reporting upon receipt by the shareholders in a liquidation or taxable merger.

Suppose that under the terms of the merger agreement, the shareholders of T Corporation may elect to receive either cash or installment obligations of A Corporation. Will those shareholders electing to receive the installment obligations nonetheless be found to be in constructive receipt of cash and thus currently taxable? See Rev.Rul. 73–396, 1973–2 Cum.Bull. 160 (no constructive receipt where purchaser willing to pay cash but buyer insisted on deferred payments).

C. TAXABLE "CASH" MERGERS

The use of a statutory merger under state law allows an acquisition to take place on a tax-free basis if the various requirements of section 368, discussed infra, Chapter 17, are met. The statutory merger technique frequently has been used instead of a direct asset sale to carry out a taxable acquisition in which the acquiring corporation pays the shareholders of the target corporation cash, corporate bonds (installment obligations), or a combination of cash and installment obligations in connection with the merger. One of the reasons for using a "cash" merger is to effect a transfer of the properties of the acquired corporation directly to the acquiring corporation as a matter of state law, avoiding the need to document separately each transfer. In addition, a merger forces out any minority shareholders in the acquired corporation who dissented from the merger. Furthermore, if the acquisition takes the form of a "reverse" merger in which the acquired corporation is the surviving corporation, problems can be avoided with regard to assets which cannot be assigned or transferred, for example, assets subject to a restriction on transferability in connection with a loan agreement.

To take the simplest case, suppose T Corporation is merged into A Corporation in a transaction in which the T Corporation shareholders all receive cash or debt instruments of A Corporation. For tax purposes, the transaction is treated as a sale of assets followed by the liquidation of T Corporation. See West Shore Fuel, Inc. v. United States, 598 F.2d 1236 (2d Cir.1979) (all debt merger treated as corporate assets sale); Rev.Rul. 69–6, 1969–1 Cum.Bull. 104. (merger of mutual savings banks). Thus, both the acquired corporation and its shareholders recognize gain or loss on the transaction. This double tax treatment of cash mergers may be avoided through the use of a "reverse" triangular merger, the merger of a subsidiary of the acquiring corporation in the target corporation, with the shareholders of the target receiving cash from the parent. Rev.Rul. 79–273, 1979–2 Cum.Bull. 125, indicates that this transaction will be treated as a sale and purchase of shares of the target corporation.

D. REFERENCES

Coven, Taxing Corporate Acquisitions: A Proposal for Mandatory Uniform Rules, 44 Tax L.Rev. 145 (1989); Swirsky, Purchase Price Allocations in Taxable Asset Acquisitions, 67 Taxes 252 (1989); Bogdanski, Contractual Allocations of Price in Sales of Businesses, 15 J.Corp.Tax. 99 (1988); Unger, Gain Recognition and Basis in Acquisitions, 45 N.Y.Fed.Tax.Inst. 3–1 (1987); Yin, Taxing Corporate Liquidations After the Tax Reform Act of 1986, 42 Tax L.Rev. 573 (1987); Tufts, The Taxable Merger, 7 J.Corp.Tax. 342 (1981).

SECTION 3. THE SALE AND PURCHASE OF STOCK

A. THE SITUATION PRIOR TO 1983

In the transactions considered in Section 2, the purchaser of the corporate business desired to acquire assets and the seller agreed to this form of the transaction. Very often, however, the seller desires to structure the transaction as a sale of corporate stock. Historically, one of the prime motivations for a stock sale was that the preferential tax rate previously accorded to capital gains would apply to the entire recognized gain. Many of the tax motivations for a seller to prefer a sale of stock rather than assets were removed with the repeal in 1986 of the *General Utilities* doctrine and the capital gains preference, but sellers still may have reasons for preferring a stock sale in certain cases.

Often, however, for a variety of reasons the purchaser does not want to purchase the stock but prefers to purchase the assets directly. First, the corporation may have liabilities which the purchaser does not wish to assume indirectly. Second, if the assets have a basis lower than their market value, and hence lower than the price to be paid for the business, the assets will retain that low basis when the ownership of the corporation changes hands. This basis result may be unsatisfactory to the purchaser, especially with respect to inventory or depreciable property. Third, a stock purchase involves taking over other tax attributes such as accumulated earnings and profits.

Suppose the purchaser, desiring to buy the assets but unable to persuade the seller to agree, buys the stock and then proceeds to liquidate the corporation to obtain the assets, thereby making it clear that the purchase of the stock was but a step in the direction of an asset purchase. This was the problem presented in the *Kimbell–Diamond Milling Company* case, infra, where the Commissioner contended that the stock purchase should be disregarded. In that case, and cases following it, the courts took the view that where the liquidation was part of an overall plan for the acquisition of assets, the liquidation would in effect be disregarded, no gain or loss would result to the purchaser, and the purchaser's basis for the assets would be the price paid for the stock. The cases regarded the transaction as basically a purchase of assets by the purchaser (even though it remained a sale of stock by the seller) and hence treated the temporary stock acquisition and the liquidation as not significant for tax purposes. Prior to the repeal of the *General Utilities* doctrine, if the purchaser was an individual, the result would have been the same whether the liquidation was held to have substance or not, since the price paid for the stock would generally reflect the value of the assets and thus there would be no additional gain in the liquidation transaction. But where a corporation was the purchaser, if section 332(a) governed the liquidation, the basis of the assets would remain the same under section 334(b) and would be unaffected by the amount paid for the stock; hence the need for the step-transaction approach of *Kimbell–Diamond.* Congress responded to this situation by in effect codifying the *Kimbell–Diamond* approach in former section 334(b)(2).

KIMBELL–DIAMOND MILLING COMPANY v. COMMISSIONER

Tax Court of the United States, 1950.
14 T.C. 74.

[In August, 1942, the taxpayer's milling plant was destroyed by fire and in November, 1942, it collected insurance as reimbursement for its loss. On December 26, 1942, it used the insurance proceeds and other cash to acquire all of the stock of Whaley Mill and Elevator Co., its sole intention in purchasing that stock being to acquire the milling plant of Whaley by liquidating Whaley as soon as possible. On December 31, 1942, Whaley was liquidated. The basis of the milling plant in Whaley's hands was $139,521.62. The taxpayer's basis for the stock of Whaley was the cost of its destroyed milling plant, $18,921.90, plus $91,799.84, the cash outlay for the stock in excess of the insurance proceeds, oil $110,721.74. The issue is the taxpayer's basis for depreciation of the Whaley plant, as respects the years 1945 and 1946.]

OPINION

BLACK, JUDGE. * * * Petitioner argues that the acquisition of Whaley's assets and the subsequent liquidation of Whaley brings petitioner within the provisions of [the former version of section 332(a)] and, therefore, by reason of [the former version of section 334(b)(1)], petitioner's basis in these assets is the same as the basis in Whaley's hands. In so contending, petitioner asks that we treat the acquisition of Whaley's stock and the subsequent liquidation of Whaley as separate transactions. It is well settled that the incidence of taxation depends upon the substance of a transaction. Commissioner v. Court Holding Company, 324 U.S. 331, 65 S.Ct. 707. It is inescapable from petitioner's minutes set out above and from the "Agreement and Program of Complete Liquidation" entered into between petitioner and Whaley, that the only intention petitioner ever had was to acquire Whaley's assets.

We think that this proceeding is governed by the principles of Commissioner v. Ashland Oil and Refining Co., 99 F.2d 588, certiorari denied 306 U.S. 661, 59 S.Ct. 786. In that case the stock was retained for almost a year before liquidation. Ruling on the question of whether the stock or the assets of the corporation were purchased, the court stated:

"The question remains, however whether if the entire transaction, whatever its form, was essentially in intent, purpose and result, a purchase by Swiss of property, its several steps may be treated separately and each be given an effect for tax purposes as though each constituted a distinct transaction. * * * And without regard to whether the result is imposition or relief from taxation, the courts have recognized that where the essential nature of a transaction is the acquisition of property, it will be viewed as a whole, and closely related steps will not be separated either at the instance of the taxpayer or the taxing authority. Prairie Oil and Gas Co. v. Motter, 10 Cir., 66 F.2d 309; Tulsa Tribune Co. v. Commissioner, 10 Cir., 58 F.2d 937, 940; Ahles Realty Corp. v. Commissioner, 2 Cir., 71 F.2d 150; Helvering v. Security Savings Bank, 4 Cir., 72 F.2d 874. * * * " See also Koppers Coal Co., 6 T.C. 1209 and cases there cited.

We hold that the purchase of Whaley's stock and its subsequent liquidation must be considered as one transaction, namely, the purchase of Whaley's assets which was petitioner's sole intention. This was not a reorganization within [the former version of section 332(a)], and petitioner's basis in these assets, both depreciable and nondepreciable, is, therefore, its cost, or $110,721.74 ($18,921.90, the basis of petitioner's assets destroyed by fire, plus $91,799.84, the amount expended over the insurance proceeds). Since petitioner does not controvert respondent's allocation of cost to the individual assets acquired from Whaley, both depreciable and nondepreciable, respondent's allocation is sustained. * * *

Decision will be entered for the respondent.* Reviewed by the Court.

ILLUSTRATIVE MATERIAL

A. JUDICIAL APPLICATION OF *KIMBELL–DIAMOND* DOCTRINE

In *Kimbell–Diamond,* the Commissioner successfully contended that where the basis of the stock was less than the basis of the assets, section 332(a) did not govern, the court agreeing that there was not a liquidation within section 332(a) but a purchase of assets. Tennessee, Alabama & Georgia Railway Co. v. Commissioner, 187 F.2d 826 (6th Cir.1951), similarly refused to apply section 332(a). In Texas Bank and Trust Company of Dallas v. Commissioner, 12 T.C.M. 588 (1953), the *Kimbell–Diamond* case was followed in the taxpayer's favor, since stock cost was higher than asset basis. The courts thus held that while the purchaser really bought assets through temporarily buying stock, it did not follow that on the seller's side the sale was to be regarded as a sale of assets. Instead, the courts rested on the intent of the selling stockholders to sell stock and not assets and the formal sale of the stock.

B. FORMER SECTION 334(b)(2)

1. *General*

The *Kimbell–Diamond* approach proved to be unsatisfactory because it relied on the intent of a corporate purchaser to acquire assets. This subjective approach was difficult to administer, and it was replaced in 1954 by an objective standard codified in former section 334(b)(2). That section replaced the subjective intent test of *Kimbell–Diamond* with a set of objective standards to determine when a stock purchase would be treated as a purchase of assets for tax purposes. In general terms, under section 334(b)(2), if a corporation "purchased" 80 percent or more of the stock of another corporation and then liquidated it within two years, the basis of the assets acquired in the liquidation would be determined by the purchase price of the stock, i.e., in the same manner as if the assets had been purchased directly.

However, the "purchase" requirement, and the computations of asset basis if the liquidation was delayed raised problems of their own.

2. *The "Purchase" Requirement*

The requisite 80 percent of stock ownership had to be acquired by purchase, as defined in the statute. A "purchase" was not present where the basis of the stock in the hands of the acquiring corporation was determined in whole or in part by reference to the basis of the stock in the hands of the person from whom the stock was acquired. See Chrome Plate, Inc. v. District Director of the Internal Revenue Service, 614 F.2d 990 (5th Cir. 1980) (liquidation of subsidiary acquired from parent in section 351 transaction). The "purchase" requirement has been carried forward in section 338, which has replaced section 334(b)(2).

* [Ed. The Tax Court decision was affirmed per curiam, 187 F.2d 718 (5th Cir. 1951).]

3. *Tax Treatment of the Acquired Corporation on Liquidation*

During the entire period that former section 334(b)(2) was in effect, the *General Utilities* doctrine prevailed generally to provide nonrecognition of gain to the liquidating subsidiary, subject to the various recapture rules. The tax benefit rule, however, required recognition of income in a number of instances. See Tennessee–Carolina Transportation, Inc. v. Commissioner, 582 F.2d 378 (6th Cir.1978) (restoration to income of previously expensed supplies).

C. REPEAL OF SECTION 334(b)(2)

Although nominally nonelective, section 334(b)(2) in fact provided significant flexibility to the purchasing corporation to obtain a purchase price basis for only selected assets, particularly where the acquired corporation was the parent of an affiliated group. Largely for this reason, the 1982 Act substantially revised the tax treatment of stock acquisitions. Section 334(b)(2) was repealed and replaced by section 338, discussed infra. The provisions of section 338 are aimed in particular at preventing the purchaser from achieving a step-up in basis for "selected" assets.

D. REFERENCES

Bruce, Liquidations and Reorganizations: Madison Square Garden and Kass, 30 Tax L. Rev. 303 (1975); Mopsick, Yoc Heating Corp. and Two–Step Asset Acquisitions, 1 J. Corp. Tax. 235 (1974); Seplow, Acquisition of Assets of a Subsidiary: Liquidation or Reorganization?, 73 Harv.L.Rev. 484 (1960); Cohen, Gelberg, Surrey, Tarleau and Warren, Corporate Liquidations under the Internal Revenue Code of 1954, 55 Col.L.Rev. 37 (1955); Semmell and Stern, Tax Effect of Form in the Acquisition of Assets, 63 Yale L.J. 765 (1954).

B. STOCK SALES AND ACQUISITIONS UNDER SECTION 338

INTERNAL REVENUE CODE: Section 338.

REGULATIONS: Section 1.338–4T(f)(6)(i)(A).

(1) SALES AND ACQUISITIONS OUTSIDE THE CONSOLIDATED RETURN CONTEXT

GENERAL EXPLANATION, TAX EQUITY AND FISCAL RESPONSIBILITY ACT OF 1982

Staff of the Joint Committee on Taxation, 131–139 (1982).*

[Pre–TEFRA] Law

Upon the complete liquidation of a subsidiary corporation, 80 percent of the voting power and 80 percent of the total number of shares of all other classes of stock (other than nonvoting preferred stock) of which is owned by the parent corporation, gain or loss is

* [Ed. The bracketed material reflects changes made by the Deficit Reduction Act of 1984 and the Tax Reform Act of 1986.]

generally not recognized and the basis of the subsidiary's assets and its other tax attributes are carried over (secs. 332, 334(b)(1), and 381(a)).

Under [pre-TEFRA] law, however, if the controlling stock interest was acquired by purchase within a 12-month period and the subsidiary was liquidated pursuant to a plan of liquidation adopted within 2 years after the qualifying stock purchase was completed, the transaction was treated as in substance a purchase of the subsidiary's assets (sec. 334(b)(2)). The acquiring corporation's basis in the "purchased" assets was the cost of the stock purchased as adjusted for items such as liabilities assumed, certain cash or dividend distributions to the acquiring corporation, and postacquisition earnings and profits of the subsidiary. The liquidating distributions could be made over a 3-year period beginning with the close of the taxable year during which the first of a series of distributions occurs (sec. 332(b)(3)). Thus, this treatment applied even though the liquidation could extend over a 5-year period after control had been acquired.

In these cases, when the assets were treated as purchased by the acquiring corporation, recapture income was taxed to the liquidating corporation, the investment tax credit recapture provisions were applicable, and tax attributes, including carryovers, of the liquidated corporation were terminated.

Cases interpreting the law applicable before the rules in section 334(b)(2) were adopted, treated the purchase of stock and prompt liquidation in some cases as a purchase of assets (Kimbell–Diamond Milling Co. v. Commissioner, 14 T.C. 74, aff'd per curiam, 187 F.2d 718 (5th Cir.), cert. denied, 342 U.S. 827 (1951)). It is not clear whether such treatment still applied after the enactment of section 334(b)(2) in cases where the requirements of that provision were not met.

A stock purchase and liquidation was treated as a purchase of all the assets of the acquired corporation under [pre-TEFRA] law if section 334(b)(2) applied. Revision of the special treatment of partial liquidations under [TEFRA] restricts the options of a corporate purchaser seeking to treat a purchase of a corporation as a purchase of assets in part combined with a continuation of the tax attributes of the acquired entity. Neither [pre-TEFRA] law nor [TEFRA's] revision of the treatment of partial liquidations restrict a corporate purchaser from achieving such selectivity by purchasing assets directly from a corporation while concurrently purchasing the corporation's stock. Selectivity could also be achieved if an acquired corporation, prior to the acquisition, dispersed its assets in tax-free transactions among several corporations which could be separately purchased. The corporate purchaser then through selective qualifying liquidations could obtain asset purchase treatment for one or more acquired corporations while preserving the tax attributes of one or more other corporations.

Reasons for Change

While section 334(b)(2) did not permit selectivity within the context of a single corporation in that the transaction was treated as wholly an asset purchase or wholly a stock purchase, inconsistency was inherent in permitting a continuation of the acquired corporation's tax attributes for up to 5 years after a stock purchase while also treating the transaction as though assets had been purchased.

* * *

[T]he extended period that could elapse between stock purchase and liquidation required complex adjustments for earnings or deficits of the acquired corporation during the intervening period as well as for sales of assets and other items during such period in order to properly allocate the cost of the stock to the assets upon their ultimate distribution. Existing case law permitted a stepped-up basis for assets distributed in liquidation that in some cases exceeded the cost basis that would be applicable if the assets were purchased directly by the controlling corporation. See, R.M. Smith, Inc., 69 T.C. 317 (1977).

[Pre–TEFRA] law also provided unwarranted tax motivations for structuring a corporate acquisition as in part a purchase of assets and in part a purchase of stock or as a purchase of several corporations historically operated as a unit in order to preserve selectivity of tax treatment. These motivations included the ability to achieve a stepped-up basis for some assets while avoiding recapture tax and other unfavorable tax attributes with respect to other assets.

Explanation of Provisions

General treatment of stock purchase as asset purchase

[TEFRA] repeals the provision of prior law (sec. 334(b)(2)) that treated a purchase and liquidation of a subsidiary as an asset purchase. The amendments made by the Act were also intended to replace any nonstatutory treatment of a stock purchase as an asset purchase under the *Kimbell–Diamond* doctrine. Instead, an acquiring corporation, within [8½ months] after a qualified stock purchase, except as regulations may provide for a later election, may elect to treat an acquired subsidiary (target corporation) as if it sold all its assets pursuant to a plan of complete liquidation at the close of the stock acquisition date. The target corporation will be treated as a new corporation that purchased the assets on the day following such date. Gain or loss will not be recognized to the target corporation, except for gain or loss attributable to stock held by minority shareholders as described below, to the same extent gain or loss is not recognized (sec. 337) when a corporation sells all its assets in the course of a complete liquidation. This provision was intended to provide nonrecognition of gain or loss to the same extent that gain or loss would not be recognized under section 336 if there were an actual liquidation of the target corporation on the acquisition date to which prior law section 334(b)(2) applied.

* * *

A qualified stock purchase occurs if 80 percent or more of the voting power and 80 percent of the total number of shares of other classes of stock (except nonvoting, preferred stock) is acquired by purchase during a 12–month period (the acquisition period). The acquisition date is the date within such acquisition period on which the 80–percent purchase requirement (the qualified stock purchase) is satisfied. Generally, the 80–percent purchase requirement may be satisfied through the combination of stock purchases and [certain qualifying] redemptions. * * *

The election is to be made in the manner prescribed by regulations and, once made, will be irrevocable.

Treatment of target corporation as new corporation

[The assets of the target company will be treated as sold for an amount equal to their fair market value as of the acquisition date. The basis of the assets in the hands of the target corporation will equal the grossed-up basis of the purchasing corporation's stock in the target corporation acquired during the acquisition period and the basis of any other stock in the target corporation which was not acquired during the acquisition period (so-called non-recently purchased stock). The amount is to be adjusted under regulations for liabilities of the target corporation and other relevant items.]

Under the gross-up formula, if the acquiring corporation owns less than 100 percent by value of the target corporation's stock on the acquisition date, the deemed purchase price is grossed up to equal 100–percent ownership by the acquiring corporation. It was not intended that minority shareholders in the target corporation be treated as having exchanged their shares for stock in the new corporation. However, nonrecognition of gain or loss to the target corporation is limited, unless the target corporation is liquidated within one year after the acquisition date, to the highest actual percentage by value of target corporation stock held by the acquiring corporation during the one-year period beginning on the acquisition date.

[The acquiring corporation can also elect to recognize the gain attributable to appreciation in the nonrecently purchased stock and add that amount to its deemed purchase price. Section 338(b)(3). The gross-up formula is adjusted in section 338(b)(3)(B)(ii) to take into account the fact that the nonrecently purchased stock is accounted for separately.]

* * *

The Act provides that the deemed sale (and purchase) of all its assets by the target corporation applies for purposes of subtitle A of the Internal Revenue Code and is deemed to occur at the close of the acquisition date in a single transaction. Under these rules, the provisions of subtitle F of the Code relating to assessment, collection, refunds, statutes of limitations, and other procedural matters apply without regard to the status of the target corporation as a new corporation. The target corporation thus remains liable for any tax liabilities incurred by it for any period prior to the election.

* * *

Definition of purchase

The term "purchase" is defined as it was under [pre-TEFRA] law (sec. 334(b)(3)) to exclude acquisitions of stock with a carryover basis or from a decedent, acquisitions in an exchange to which section 351 applies, and acquisitions from a person whose ownership is attributed to the acquiring person under section 318(a). Attribution under section 318(a)(4) relating to options will be disregarded for this purpose. [If the target corporation owns stock in a third corporation and the acquiring corporation makes a section 338 election, the acquisition by the "new" target corporation of the third corporation's stock in the section 338 deemed sale will itself qualify as a "purchase" for purposes of section 338. Section 338(h)(3)(B). If the target corporation owns at least 80% of the stock in the third corporation, it would then qualify as a purchaser of that stock within the acquisition period and the section 338 election would apply to its acquisition. Section 338(f).]

Consistency requirement

The rules require consistency where the purchasing corporation makes qualified stock purchases of two or more corporations that are members of the same affiliated group. For this purpose, purchases by a member of the purchasing corporation's affiliated group, except as regulations provide otherwise, are treated as purchases by the purchasing corporation.[2] The consistency requirement applies as well to a combination of a direct asset acquisition and qualified stock purchase.

The consistency requirement applies with respect to purchases over a defined "consistency period" determined by reference to the acquisition date applicable to the target corporation. The "consistency period" is the one-year period preceding the target corporation acquisition period plus the portion of the acquisition period up to and including the acquisition date, and the one-year period following the acquisition date. Thus, if all the target corporation's stock is purchased on the same day by the purchasing corporation, the one-year period immediately preceding and the one-year period immediately following such date are included in the consistency period. If, within such period, there is a direct purchase of assets from the target corporation or a target affiliated by the purchasing corporation, the rules require that the acquisition of the target corporation be treated as an asset purchase.

The consistency period may be expanded in appropriate cases by the Secretary where there is in effect a plan to make several qualified

2. Transfers of target corporation stock within the purchasing corporation's affiliated group will not disqualify a section 338 election (cf. Chrome Plate Inc. v. U.S., 614 F.2d 990 (5th Cir.1980)).

stock purchases or any such purchase and asset acquisition with respect to a target corporation and its target affiliates.

The consistency requirement is applied to an affiliated group with reference to a target corporation and any "target affiliate." A corporation is defined as a "target affiliate" of the target corporation if each was, at any time during that portion of the consistency period ending on the acquisition date of the target corporation, a member of an affiliated group that had the same common parent. An affiliated group has the same meaning given to such term by section 1504(a) (without regard to the exceptions in sec. 1504(b)). This definition also applies in determining whether a purchase is made by a member of the same affiliated group as the purchasing corporation.

* * *

In applying these rules, acquisitions of assets pursuant to sales by the target corporation or a target affiliate in the ordinary course of its trade or business and acquisitions in which the basis of assets is carried over will not cause the consistency requirement to apply. The sale by a target corporation will be considered as a sale in the ordinary course of business for this purpose even though it is not customary in the course of the selling corporation's business provided it is a transaction that is a normal incident to the conduct of a trade or business, such as a sale of used machinery that was employed in the seller's trade or business.

Where there are, within a consistency period, only qualified stock purchases of the target corporation and one or more target affiliates by the purchasing corporation, an election with respect to the first purchase will apply to the later purchases. A failure to make the election for the first purchase will preclude any election for later purchases.

To prevent avoidance of the consistency requirements, the Act authorizes the Secretary to treat stock acquisitions which are pursuant to a plan and which satisfy the 80–percent requirement to be treated as qualified stock purchases even though they are not otherwise so defined. For example, an acquiring corporation may acquire 79 percent of the stock of a target corporation and, within a year, purchase assets from such corporation or a target affiliate planning to purchase the remaining target corporation stock more than one year after the original stock purchase. The Secretary may under these circumstances treat the purchase of the target corporation's stock as a deemed sale of its assets by the target corporation. [Section 338(i)] also authorizes such regulations as may be necessary to ensure that the requirements of consistency of treatment of stock and asset purchases with respect to a target corporation and its target affiliates are not circumvented through the use of other provisions of the law or regulations, including the consolidated return regulations.

* * *

The Act provides regulatory authority pursuant to which the Secretary may determine that the deemed election will not apply as the result of a *de minimis* acquisition of assets and may also preclude the application of the deemed election rule if it is determined that the taxpayer has acquired assets in order to avoid the [8½ month] limit on the period after the acquisition date within which the election must be made.

The application of the consistency requirements is illustrated in the following examples. * * *

Example 1

The acquiring corporation makes a qualified stock purchase of T's stock and within a one-year period purchases assets from T or a target affiliate of T. The acquiring corporation is deemed to have made an election with respect to T as of the acquisition date applicable to T.

* * *

Example 3

P, an acquiring corporation, makes a qualified stock purchase of all the stock of corporation T on February 1, 1983. No election is made. On December 1, 1983, P makes a qualified stock purchase of all the stock of corporation U, a target affiliate of corporation T. No election may be made with respect to corporation U.

ILLUSTRATIVE MATERIAL

A. GENERAL

In many important respects section 338 eliminated or resolved the problems and discontinuities which arose under former section 334(b)(2). An acquiring corporation may obtain a step-up in basis without liquidating a newly acquired subsidiary which for independent business reasons the acquiring corporation wishes to continue to operate as a subsidiary. Conversely, a newly acquired subsidiary may be liquidated for independent business reasons either with or without a step-up (or step-down) in the basis of its assets. Inevitably, section 338 has given rise to its own complexity: new interpretive issues have been raised and different avenues for manipulation of the rules governing taxable acquisitions have been created.

One by-product of section 338 has been to create a form of corporate acquisition which was not previously possible: the purchase of the stock in the target corporation followed by immediate liquidation of the target in which all tax attributes of the target corporation are preserved. Under the mechanical rules of former section 334(b)(2), the transaction resulted in a step-up in basis of the acquired assets, but elimination of all the tax attributes of the target corporation. If no section 338 election is made, the liquidation of the target will be governed by section 332, the acquired corporation's basis in the assets will be carried over under section 334(b), and all corporate attributes such as earnings and profits, net operating loss carryovers, etc., will be preserved under section 381(a). Such a procedure might be preferable to the section 338 route where, for example, the target corporation's basis in its assets is high relative to the stock purchase price and the target has net operating loss carryovers that could be utilized by the acquiring corporation. (See infra, Chapter 21, for limitations that are applicable to the use of such carryover items following a corporate acquisition.)

B. IMPACT OF *GENERAL UTILITIES* REPEAL

1. *General*

When section 338 originally was enacted, the codification of the *General Utilities* doctrine in the pre–1987 version of section 337, discussed supra, page 692, provided nonrecognition to the target corporation on the deemed sale of its assets under section 338(a) when a section 338 election was made. Thus, except to the extent that one of the exceptions to former section 337 required that gain be recognized on the sale of a liquidating corporation's assets, the effect of a section 338 election was to secure a step-up in basis without an attendant gain. Because of this highly advantageous treatment, section 338 elections frequently were made when the qualifying conditions were satisfied. Section 338 was amended by the 1986 Act to bring it in line with the repeal of the *General Utilities* doctrine.

Section 338(a)(1) now provides that if an election is made under section 338, the target corporation will be treated as having sold all of its assets in a transaction in which gain or loss is fully recognized. This corresponds to the treatment which the target corporation would have received if it had distributed all of its assets in liquidation or had made a direct sale of the assets. Thus, in all circumstances in which the purchaser obtains, directly or indirectly, a step-up in basis for the target corporation's assets, the target corporation will be required to recognize gain currently. This change substantially reduces the advantage of a section 338 election. The tax benefit of increased future depreciation or amortization deductions generated by the step-up in basis must be "purchased" at the price of a present tax liability with respect to any appreciation in the acquired corporation's assets. And with the elimination of the preferential treatment for capital gains, the tax price is at full rates. Thus, only in very unusual circumstances, for example, where the target corporation has a net operating loss which would shield the gain required to be recognized under section 338, would an election make economic sense from the point of view of the purchaser. See section 382(h), permitting the net operating loss of an acquired corporation to be used to offset recognized built-in gain without regard to the limitations otherwise imposed by section 382, discussed infra, Chapter 21.

2. *Example*

Generally, as long as the parties take into account tax burdens in negotiating the price and the seller does not otherwise have unusable capital loss deductions, from a tax perspective it makes no difference to either the seller or the buyer whether a purchase and sale is structured as an asset sale or as a stock sale followed by a section 338 election and a section 332 liquidation.

Suppose that individual C owns all of the stock of T Corporation. C's basis for the stock is $200. T Corporation's sole asset has a basis of $100 and a fair market value of $400. If T Corporation sold the asset to A Corporation (assuming that T Corporation was subject to a flat corporate tax of 34 percent), it would owe taxes of $102 on its $300 gain and would distribute $298 to C in a liquidating distribution. C would pay taxes of $27 (assuming a 28 percent rate) on the $98 gain, leaving C with $271 of net proceeds.

Alternatively, A Corporation could pay C $298 in cash for the stock, again leaving C with $271 after taxes. A Corporation could make a section

338 election, which would give rise to a $102 tax liability on the deemed sale of T Corporation's asset. The asset would acquire a $400 basis, see infra, page 711, which under section 334 would carryover to A corporation if it liquidated T Corporation. Again, A Corporation has paid a total of $400 to acquire T Corporation's asset with a basis of $400.

In actual practice, however, things will work somewhat differently. Although the two levels of tax theoretically cannot be avoided, the corporate level tax can be deferred through a sale and purchase of stock without a section 338 election. Alternatively, one level of tax can be deferred through an installment purchase of assets coupled either with continuation of the selling corporation (perhaps as an S corporation) or the use of section 453(h), discussed, supra, page 613. If the acquiring corporation is willing to buy stock, it will not likely be willing to make the section 338 election; hence it will not pay the shareholders of the target corporation the full net asset value (including goodwill and going concern value) of the target corporation, but will discount the offset for the corporate level tax to reflect the deferral of that tax. Thus, in the preceding example, A Corporation likely would pay C more than $298 but less than $400 for the stock of T Corporation. Thus section 338 is something of an anachronism after 1986, providing a complex solution to a situation which seldom arises.

3. *Policy Issues*

Recall that the broad purpose of section 338 and its statutory predecessor, former section 334(b)(2), is to equalize the treatment of stock and asset acquisitions by providing a stepped-up basis in either case, albeit at the price of an immediate corporate level tax on asset appreciation. The treatment of the two transactions is not always equalized, however, because of the elective aspects of the transaction. Should the tax treatment of stock and asset acquisitions be fully equalized by amending the Code to apply section 338 to every "qualified stock purchase" on a mandatory basis?

C. QUALIFYING CONDITIONS

1. *General*

An election under section 338 is available only to a corporation which makes a "qualified stock purchase" of stock of another corporation. A "qualified stock purchase" is defined in section 338(d)(3) as the acquisition by purchase within a twelve month period of 80 percent or more of the voting stock and 80 percent or more of each class of nonvoting stock (other than nonvoting stock which is limited as to dividends and liquidation rights). Stock of the target corporation already owned by the acquiring corporation is not counted toward the 80 percent requirement. Thus, for example, if A Corporation has owned 21 percent of the stock of T Corporation for one year or more, A Corporation cannot thereafter complete a "qualified stock purchase." Note that section 338(h)(8) provides that all acquisitions by corporations which are part of an affiliated group are treated as made by one corporation. Thus, if A Corporation purchases 40 percent of the stock of T Corporation and A Corporation's controlled subsidiary, S Corporation, purchases an additional 40 percent of the T Corporation stock, a qualified stock purchase has been made, presumably by A Corporation.

2. *The "Purchase" Requirement*

In general, the "purchase" requirement under section 338(h)(3) tracks the same requirement in former section 334(b)(2), discussed supra, page 700. The term "purchase" includes any "acquisition" which is not specifically excluded. Thus, for example, stock acquired in a section 301 distribution is "purchased" (unless received from a corporation of which the shareholder owns 50 percent or more of the stock). See Rev.Rul. 74–211, 1974–1 Cum. Bull. 76.

In Madison Square Garden Corp. v. Commissioner, 500 F.2d 611 (2d Cir.1974), the taxpayer purchased 52 percent of the stock of another corporation. The acquired corporation then redeemed some of its stock. Following the redemption, the taxpayer owned approximately 79 percent of the stock of the acquired corporation, and it then acquired by purchase additional stock sufficient to give it 80.22 percent ownership. The acquired corporation was then merged into the taxpayer. Under Regulations, section 1.332–2(d) and (e), the merger was treated as a liquidation for tax purposes, and the taxpayer argued that section 334(b)(2) was applicable. The Commissioner asserted that the 80 percent requirement applied to the shares of stock outstanding at the time the purchase of the stock began, and thus former section 334(b)(2) was not satisfied. The Court of Appeals, affirming the Tax Court, held that the taxpayer had acquired the requisite 80 percent by "purchase".

The issues posed by *Madison Square Garden* continue to be present in determining whether a redemption constitutes a "purchase" under section 338. See Temporary Regulations, section 1.338–4T(c)(4). See also Yoc Heating Corp. v. Commissioner, 61 T.C. 168 (1973).

3. *The Timetable*

The statutory twelve month period within which a "qualified stock purchase" must be made begins to run on the date of the first "purchase" of stock by the acquiring corporation, but each purchase starts a new twelve month period running. For example, if A Corporation purchases 10 percent of the stock of T Corporation on January 1, 1990, and another 10 percent on February 1, 1990, the purchase of an additional 70 percent of the stock of T Corporation anytime before February 2, 1991 will constitute a "qualified stock purchase. Section 338(g) gives the acquiring corporation 8½ months after the completion of a qualified stock purchase in which to make the election to obtain a step-up in basis. For example, if A Corporation acquires 70 percent of the stock of T Corporation on March 1, 1990, 10 percent on April 1, 1990, and 20 percent on May 1, 1990, the period for making the election begins to run on April 2, and the election must be made by February 15, 1991. The deadline will not be extended by A Corporation's purchase of additional T Corporation stock on May 1.

4. *The Consistency Requirement*

Section 338(f) requires that the acquiring corporation make consistent elections with respect to all "qualified stock purchases" of target corporations which are members of the same affiliated group that are made within the consistency period defined in section 338(h)(4). See Temporary Regulations, section 1.338–4T(e). Generally, the consistency period begins one year before the first stock purchase of a series which culminates in a qualified stock acquisition and extends until one year after the stock acquisition transaction by which control has been obtained, i.e., a "qualified stock acquisition" has been completed. Thus, for example, the consistency rules apply if A Corporation purchases at least 80 percent of the stock of S Corporation from T Corporation on July 1, 1990 and then also purchases at least 80 percent of the stock of R Corporation from T Corporation anytime on or before July 2, 1991. If A Corporation made a section 338 election with respect to S Corporation, it is deemed to have made one with respect to R Corporation; if a section 338 election was not made with respect to S Corporation, no election may be made with respect to R Corporation. See section 338(h)(4)(B) for extension of the consistency period.

D. DEEMED ELECTIONS

Section 338(e) provides for a deemed election if the acquiring corporation or any of its affiliates purchases any assets (other than in the ordinary course of business) from the target corporation or any of its affiliates during the period beginning one year before the first stock acquisition which is part of a qualified stock purchase and ending one year after the date of the transaction by which the acquiring corporation acquired 80 percent control of the target corporation. See Temporary Regulations, section 1.338–4T(f).

For example, if the acquiring corporation, A Corporation, acquires assets from T Corporation or any corporation affiliated with T Corporation (a controlled subsidiary or a controlling parent corporation) and within twelve months thereafter A makes a qualified purchase of the stock of T Corporation, then A Corporation is deemed to have made a section 338 election with respect to the stock of T Corporation, despite the fact that no actual election was made and a step-up in basis presumably was not desired. The same result would occur, for example, if A Corporation purchased the stock of T Corporation from T Corporation's former parent, P Corporation, and within twelve months thereafter A Corporation purchased an asset from P Corporation or any of its affiliates. As a result of the deemed election, T Corporation would be required to recognize all of the gain inherent in its appreciated assets as if it had sold them at fair market value. To prevent an inadvertent deemed election under section 338(e), Temporary Regulations, section 1.338–4T(f)(6)(i)(A), permit A Corporation to make a "protective carryover basis election" requiring T Corporation to continue to use its historic basis in its assets. Such an election should be made anytime a corporate purchaser makes a qualified stock acquisition, unless the purchaser intends to make an affirmative section 338 election.

E. DETERMINATION OF ASSET BASIS

1. *General*

In general, section 338 is intended to produce the same tax consequences as a direct asset acquisition. However, section 338 does not directly assign to each asset of the target corporation a fair market value basis. Instead, under section 338(b) the aggregate basis of the assets, term "adjusted grossed-up basis" (AGUB) by Temporary Regulations, section 1.338–4T(j)(1), is first determined according to a formula based on the acquiring corporation's basis for all of the stock of the target corporation which it owns, adjusted for liabilities assumed, and the aggregate basis then is allocated among the assets as provided in Regulations, section 1.338(b)–2T. The basis allocation rules are substantially the same as the allocation rules under section 1060, discussed supra, page 694, and many of the same valuation issues arise.

2. *Adjusted Grossed–Up Basis*

Section 338(b)(1) provides that the starting point for determining the AGUB, the deemed purchase price of the target corporation's assets, is the sum of (1) the "grossed-up basis" of the "recently purchased stock" of the target, plus (2) the basis of the "nonrecently purchased stock." Recently purchased stock generally is defined as stock acquired in the "qualified stock purchase." Nonrecently purchased stock is stock owned by the acquiring corporation prior to commencement of the acquisition period, which is not counted toward the "qualified stock purchase." Section 338(b)(6). The grossed-up basis of the recently purchased stock is the basis of that stock multiplied by a fraction, the numerator of which is 100 minus the percentage of target corporation stock owned by the acquiring corporation which is not recently purchased stock and the denominator of which is the percentage of stock of the target which is recently purchased stock. Section 338(b)(4).

The purpose of the "grossed-up basis" concept is to assign to the target's assets a basis equal to the aggregate fair market value of the target corporation's stock where the acquiring corporation purchases more than 80 percent but less than all of the target corporation's stock. For example, assume that A Corporation, which previously owned none of the stock of T Corporation, purchases 85 percent of the T Corporation stock for $850. The grossed-up basis of the stock is $1,000, computed as follows: $850 × (100 – 0) / 85.

Section 338(b)(2) provides for an adjustment to the deemed purchase price in computing AGUB to reflect the acquired corporation's liabilities which would have been included in the purchaser's basis if the transaction had been an asset sale. Temporary Regulations, section 1.338(b)–1T(f). Included among these liabilities is the target corporation's tax liability arising from the deemed sale of its assets under section 338(a)(1). Temporary Regulations, section 1.338–4T(j)(2), Q & A 1.

F. OTHER ASPECTS OF SECTION 338

1. *Acquisition of Target With Subsidiaries*

Special rules apply if the target corporation in turn has subsidiary corporations. Assume that A Corporation purchases 100 percent of the stock of T Corporation, which owns 100 percent of the stock of S Corporation and 75 percent of the stock of R Corporation, and A Corporation makes a section 338 election with respect to T Corporation. Under section 338(h)(3)(B) the deemed sale and repurchase of the stock of S Corporation and R Corporation by T Corporation constitutes a "purchase" of that stock for purposes of section 338. Since A Corporation has made an election with respect to T Corporation, and since section 338(h)(3)(A)(iii) treats the deemed purchase of the S Corporation stock by T Corporation as a qualified stock purchase, the section 338(f) consistency requirement causes the election to apply to S Corporation as well. The election does not apply to R Corporation, since the stock ownership does not reach the 80 percent threshold. See Temporary Regulations, section 1.338–4T(c)(3).

2. *Allocation of Tax Liability*

The target corporation nominally bears the liability for any taxes generated by the section 338 deemed sale. Economically the burden is borne by the purchasing corporation, except to the extent that the purchase price is reduced to reflect the tax burden. Where the target was not a member of a group filing a consolidated return, then the deemed sale is reported on a final short-year return for the year ending with the acquisition date.

G. REFERENCES

Yin, Taxing Corporate Liquidations After the Tax Reform Act of 1986, 42 Tax L.Rev. 573 (1989); Lewis, A Proposal For A Corporate Level Tax on Major Stock Sales, 37 Tax Notes 1041 (1987); Roche, Meyers and Zucker, Price Allocation on Acquisitions and Basis Step-up: Tilting at Windmills?, 65 Taxes 833 (1987); Yancy, Section 338: The Result of the Legal Evolution of the Tax Treatment of Two Step Asset Acquisitions, 61 Tex.L.Rev. 1109 (1983).

(2) SALES AND ACQUISITIONS IN THE CONSOLIDATED RETURN CONTEXT: A FUTURE FOR SECTION 338?

ILLUSTRATIVE MATERIAL

A. GENERAL

As a general rule, if the target corporation otherwise would have been included in a consolidated return, it is required to file a special "deemed sale return" reporting the items from the section 338 sale. Temporary Regulations, section 1.338–1T(f)(3). Section 338(h)(9) requires that the target not be treated as a member of a affiliated group for purposes of reporting the sale, thereby precluding the use of net operating losses or capital losses of the purchaser (or its consolidated group) to offset the gain recognized on the deemed sale. However, if the acquiring corporation on the same acquisition date made qualified stock purchases with respect to two or more corporations which were members of the same consolidated group prior to the purchases, a consolidated deemed sale return covering all of such corporations may be filed. Section 338(h)(15).

B. ACQUISITION OF SUBSIDIARY FROM CONSOLIDATED GROUP: SECTION 338(h)(10)

A special rule applies when a corporation makes a qualified stock purchase of the stock of a controlled subsidiary of another corporation and the target corporation and the selling parent corporation filed a consolidated return.[5] Section 338(h)(10) allows a joint election by the acquiring corporation and the former consolidated group of the target corporation by which the gain or loss on the sale of the stock will not be recognized by the selling parent, but the selling group will include on its consolidated tax return the gain and loss recognized under section 338(a)(1) by virtue of the section 338 election. In essence, this election permits the selling corporation to treat the sale as if its subsidiary had first made a taxable sale of its assets followed by a section 332 liquidation. See Temporary Regulations, section 1.338(h)(10)–1T. As a result, the selling shareholder will bear the tax liability for any gain recognized with respect to the section 338 election. The existence of section 338(h)(10) allows the parties to keep the form of the transaction as a sale of stock but have the tax results of an asset sale. Since this situation does not involve a double tax on the sale of the stock and the deemed liquidating sale of assets, a section 338 election remains a viable tax planning technique when

5. For consolidated returns, see infra, Chapter 24.

section 338(h)(10) is available, despite the repeal of the *General Utilities* doctrine. It is a particularly attractive planning device when the selling group has losses from other activities which will offset the gains on the consolidated return, since section 338(h)(9) does not apply where a section 338(h)(10) election has been made.

Where the section 338(h)(10) route is followed there is another difference worth noting. Unlike the case in a normal section 338 election, in the case of a section 338(h)(10) election, the tax attributes of the target corporation are inherited by the selling parent corporation. See Temporary Regulations, section 1.338(h)(10)–1T(9).

The statute expressly authorizes, but does not require, the Treasury to promulgate regulations extending the approach of section 338(h)(10) to situations where the target is not a member of a group which files a consolidated return.

C. EXTENSION OF SECTION 338(h)(10) PRINCIPLES

Section 336(e) authorizes Regulations under which a sale of all of the stock of a controlled subsidiary may be treated as a sale of assets coupled with nonrecognition of the gain or loss on the sale of the stock. This is analogous to section 338(h)(10), but the statute does not limit the application of the Regulations, which have not yet been promulgated, to corporate purchasers from consolidated groups.

Thus, for example, section 336(e) may apply where individual A owns all of the stock of P Corporation, which in turn owns all of the stock of T Corporation, and B, who may be either an individual or a corporation, purchases all of the T Corporation stock from P Corporation. In some cases treatment of this transaction as an asset sale with nonrecognition of the gain or loss on the stock is necessary to prevent "triple" taxation as a result of the repeal of *General Utilities.* If this transaction were taxed under the normal rules, P Corporation would recognize a taxable gain on the sale of the stock of T Corporation; if A were to liquidate P Corporation to acquire the proceeds from the sale of T Corporation, A would recognize a taxable gain on the liquidation (assuming that P Corporation's sole asset was the cash proceeds from the sale of T Corporation, it would recognize no gain on the liquidation). In addition, if B were an individual, T Corporation would recognize gain under section 336 if B liquidated T Corporation to acquire its assets (assuming that the purchase price equalled the value of the assets, A would not realize any gain on the liquidation). Thus, a triple tax would have resulted from the removal of both the assets and the sale proceeds from corporate solution.

By treating the transaction as an asset sale, however, the bases of the assets to T Corporation presumably are increased to the stock purchase price when B acquires T Corporation, and thus the corporation does not realize any gain on its liquidation. The legislative history does not indicate whether P Corporation or T Corporation reports the taxable gain on the deemed asset sale. See H.Rep. No. 99–841, 99th Cong., 2d Sess. II–204 (1986). By analogy to section 338(h)(10), the gain and tax liability ought to be on P Corporation's tax return. Otherwise, the purchaser would bear the direct corporate tax burden with respect to appreciation of assets occurring prior to the purchase, and the burden could be shifted to the seller only through a price adjustment. This conclusion is further supported by the analogy of section 336(e) treatment to the results which would have occurred if P Corporation had liquidated T Corporation in a section 332 liquidation and then sold the assets directly to B.

D. REFERENCES

Bartlett, The Joint Election Under Section 338(h)(10), 42 Tax Lawyer 235 (1989); Schler, Sales of Assets After Tax Reform: Section 1060, Section 338(h)(10), and More, 43 Tax L.Rev. 605 (1988).

SECTION 4. DISTRIBUTIONS MADE IN CONNECTION WITH THE SALE OF A CORPORATE BUSINESS: "BOOTSTRAP" ACQUISITIONS

INTRODUCTORY NOTE

Where the sale of a corporate business is accomplished by the sale of stock, the parties may at the same time desire to reduce the size of the corporation prior to the sale. There can be a variety of motivations for structuring of the transaction in this manner. The corporation may have assets which the purchaser does not wish to acquire. Or the purchaser may not be able to afford the "full" corporation and may wish to have it reduced in size prior to the acquisition, thus acquiring a smaller corporation for a correspondingly smaller purchase price. Finally, tax planning to maximize the after-tax proceeds to the seller sometimes may be a principal purpose for the structure of the sale and purchase.

The reduction in size of the corporation can take place either through a redemption of some of the shares of an existing shareholder or through a dividend distribution to the shareholder. Which technique is preferable may depend in part on the status of the shareholder. Prior to the repeal of the preferential tax rate for capital gains, a redemption distribution taxed as a capital gain under section 302 was more advantageous to an individual shareholder than the ordinary income treatment which a normal dividend distribution would receive. After 1986, however, much less is at stake for a selling individual shareholder; unless the shareholder has otherwise unusable capital losses, tax liability will be unaffected by the characterization of the distribution, since full basis recovery will be allowed in any event. On the other hand, if the shareholder is a corporation, dividend treatment, with a corresponding intercorporate dividend deduction under section 243, may be preferable to recognizing capital gain on the sale of the stock depending on the basis of the stock. In addition, the timing of the distribution is important because the redemption or dividend distribution may be deemed to have taken place after the actual ownership of the stock has been transferred to the purchaser by the seller. In some cases whether the distribution is characterized as a redemption or as a dividend turns on when the distribution is considered to have been made. The following materials in A and B below are concerned with various aspects of the issues created by distributions in connection with the sale of corporate stock.

In other situations, the bootstrap acquisition may utilize the deduction for interest expense to finance the acquisition out of tax sheltered future earnings of the acquired corporation. The "leveraged buy out" mania of the 1980s in large part was fueled by this technique. The materials in C discuss the statutory responses to such transactions.

A. BOOTSTRAP TRANSACTIONS INVOLVING INDIVIDUALS

HOLSEY v. COMMISSIONER

United States Court of Appeals, Third Circuit, 1958.
258 F.2d 865.

MARIS, CIRCUIT JUDGE. This is a petition to review a decision of the Tax Court. The petitioners, husband and wife, filed a joint return and the case involves their income tax liability for the year 1951. The income in controversy is that of the husband alone, however, and he will accordingly be referred to as the taxpayer. The facts as found by the Tax Court, some of which were stipulated, may be summarized as follows:

J.R. Holsey Sales Company, a New Jersey corporation, was organized on April 28, 1936, as an Oldsmobile dealership. Taxpayer has been president and a director of the company since its organization. Only 20 shares were issued out of the 2,500 shares of no par value stock authorized; these 20 shares were issued to Greenville Auto Sales Company, a Chevrolet dealership, in exchange for all of the latter's right, title, and interest to the Oldsmobile franchise and other assets with respect to the franchise which had been owned and operated by the Greenville Company. The 20 shares issued were assigned a value of $11,000. Taxpayer's father, Charles V. Holsey, in 1936, owned more than two-thirds of the outstanding stock of the Greenville Company, and taxpayer was vice-president and a director of that corporation.

On April 30, 1936, taxpayer acquired from the Greenville Company an option to purchase 50% of the outstanding shares of the Holsey Company for $11,000, and a further option to purchase, within ten years after the exercise of the first option, all the remaining shares for a sum to be agreed upon. The Greenville Company owned all of the outstanding stock of the Holsey Company from its organization in 1936 until November, 1939, when taxpayer exercised his first option and purchased 50% of the outstanding stock of the Holsey Company for $11,000.

On June 28, 1946, the further option in favor of taxpayer was revised. Under the terms of the revised option, taxpayer was granted the right to purchase the remaining outstanding shares of the Holsey Company at any time up to and including June 28, 1951, for $80,000. The revised option was in favor of taxpayer individually and was not assignable by him to anyone other than a corporation in which he owned not less than 50% of the voting stock. On the date of the revision of this option, taxpayer's father owned 76% of the stock of the Greenville Company and taxpayer was a vice-president and director of that corporation. On April 28, 1948, the Holsey Company declared a 3–for–1 stock dividend and the common stock was allocated a value of $750 per share. This stock dividend increased the outstanding stock to 80 shares which was held in equal amounts by taxpayer and the Greenville Company.

On January 19, 1951, taxpayer assigned his revised option to the Holsey Company; on the same date the Holsey Company exercised the option and paid the Greenville Company $80,000 for the stock held by it. This transaction resulted in taxpayer becoming the owner of 100% of the outstanding stock of the Holsey Company. In his income tax return for the year 1951, taxpayer gave no effect to this transaction.

The principal officers and only directors of the Holsey Company from April 28, 1936, to December 31, 1951, were taxpayer, his brother, Charles D. Holsey, and their father, Charles V. Holsey. On January 19, 1951, when the revised option was exercised, the earned surplus of the Holsey Company was in excess of $300,000.

The Oldsmobile franchise, under which the Holsey Company operated, was a yearly contract entered into by the Corporation and the manufacturer in reliance upon the personal qualifications and representations of taxpayer as an individual. It was the manufacturer's policy to have its dealers own all of the stock in dealership organizations.

The Commissioner determined that the effect of the transaction of January 19, 1951, wherein the Holsey Company paid $80,000 to the Greenville Company for 50% of the outstanding stock of the Holsey Company, constituted a dividend to taxpayer, the remaining stockholder. The Commissioner therefore asserted a deficiency against taxpayer in the sum of $41,385.34. The Tax Court sustained the Commissioner. 28 T.C. 962.

The question presented for decision in this case is whether the Tax Court erred in holding that the payment by the Holsey Company of $80,000 to the Greenville Company for the purchase from that company of its stock in the Holsey Company was essentially equivalent to the distribution of a taxable dividend to the taxpayer, the remaining stockholder of the Holsey Company. To determine that question we must begin with the applicable statute [reference is made to the predecessors of sections 316(a) and 302].

It will be observed that [section 316(a)] defines a dividend as a distribution made by a corporation "to its shareholders". Accordingly unless a distribution which is sought to be taxed to a stockholder as a dividend is made to him or for his benefit it may not be regarded as either a dividend or the legal equivalent of a dividend. Here the distribution was made to the Greenville Company, not to the taxpayer.

This the Government, of course, concedes but urges that it was made for the benefit of the taxpayer. It is true that it has been held that a distribution by a corporation in redemption of stock which the taxpayer stockholder has a contractual obligation to purchase is essentially the equivalent of a dividend to him since it operates to discharge his obligation. Wall v. United States, 4 Cir., 1947, 164 F.2d 462; Ferro v. Commissioner of Internal Revenue, 3 Cir., 1957, 242 F.2d 838; Zipp v. Commissioner of Internal Revenue, 6 Cir., 1958, 259 F.2d 119. But where, as here, the taxpayer was never under any legal obligation to purchase the stock held by the other stockholder, the Greenville Company, having merely an option to purchase which he did not exercise but instead assigned to the Holsey Company, the distribution did not discharge any obligation of his and did not benefit him in any direct sense.

It is, of course, true that the taxpayer was benefited indirectly by the distribution. The value of his own stock was increased, since the redemption was for less than book value, and he became sole stockholder. But these benefits operated only to increase the value of the taxpayer's stock holdings; they could not give rise to taxable income within the meaning of the Sixteenth Amendment until the corporation makes a distribution to the taxpayer or his stock is sold. Eisner v. Macomber, 1920, 252 U.S. 189, 40 S.Ct. 189, 64 L.Ed. 521; Schmitt v. Commissioner of Internal Revenue, 3 Cir., 1954, 208 F.2d 819. In the latter case in a somewhat similar connection this court said (at page 821):

"During these years when Wolverine was buying its own shares it, of course, was subject to income tax as a corporation. Mrs. Green was subject to tax on whatever profit she made by the sale of these shares to the corporation. But what happened to warrant imposing a tax upon Schmitt and Lehren? [These two and Mrs. Green, the majority shareholder, had been the three shareholders of Wolverine. Mrs. Green's shares had been purchased by Wolverine and later distributed to the other two shareholders. The Commissioner asserted tax on the latter for the year of the distribution of the shares.] If one owns a piece of real estate and, because of its favorable location in a city, the land becomes increasingly valuable over a period of years, the owner is not subject to income taxation upon the annual increase in value. In the same way, if a man owns shares in a corporation which gradually become more valuable through the years he is not taxed because of the increase in value even though he is richer at the end of each year than he was at the end of the year before. If he disposes of that which has increased, of course he must pay tax upon his profit. All of this is hornbook law of taxation; nobody denies it."

We think that the principle thus stated is equally applicable here. Indeed the Tax Court itself has so held in essentially similar cases. S.K. Ames, Inc., v. Commissioner, 1942, 46 B.T.A. 1020; Fred F. Fischer v. Commissioner, 1947, 6 T.C.M. 520.

The question whether payments made by a corporation in the acquisition and redemption of its stock are essentially equivalent to the distribution of a taxable dividend has been often before the courts and certain criteria have been enunciated. The most significant of these is said to be whether the distribution leaves the proportionate interests of the stockholders unchanged as occurs when a true dividend is paid. Ferro v. Commissioner of Internal Revenue, 3 Cir., 1957, 242 F.2d 838, 841. The application of that criterion to the facts of this case compels the conclusion that in the absence of a direct pecuniary benefit to the taxpayer the Tax Court erred in holding the distribution in question taxable to him. For in his case prior to the distribution the taxpayer and the Greenville Company each had a 50% interest in the Holsey Company whereas after it was over the taxpayer had 100% of the outstanding stock and the Greenville Company none.

The Government urges the lack of a corporate purpose for the distribution and the taxpayer seeks to establish one. But we do not consider this point for, as we have recently held, "It is the effect of the redemption, rather than the purpose which actuated it, which controls the determination of dividend equivalence." Kessner v. Commissioner of Internal Revenue, 3 Cir., 1957, 248 F.2d 943, 944. Nor need we discuss the present position of the Government that the transaction must be treated as a sham and the purchase of the stock as having been made by the taxpayer through his alter ego, the Holsey Company. For the Tax Court made no such finding, doubtless in view of the fact that at the time the taxpayer owned only 50% of the stock and was in a minority on the board of directors. On the contrary that court based its decision on the benefit which the distribution by the corporation to the Greenville Company conferred upon the taxpayer, which it thought gave rise to taxable income in his hands.

For the reasons stated we think that the Tax Court erred in its decision. The decision will accordingly be reversed and the cause remanded for further proceedings not inconsistent with this opinion.

MCLAUGHLIN, CIRCUIT JUDGE (dissenting). I think that the net effect of the facile operation disclosed in this case amounts to the distribution of a taxable dividend to the taxpayer. I do not think that the Schmitt decision controls here. Quite the contrary to the Schmitt facts, this taxpayer himself acquired a valuable option to buy the shares and solely on the theory of a gift of the option rights would make the corporation the true purchaser. I agree with the Tax Court that "The assignment of the option contract to J.R. Holsey Sales Co. was clearly for the purpose of having that company pay the $80,000 in exercise of the option that was executed for petitioner's personal benefit. The payment was intended to secure and did secure for petitioner exactly what it was always intended he should get if he made the payment personally, namely, all of the stock in J.R. Holsey Sales Co."

I would affirm the Tax Court decision.

ILLUSTRATIVE MATERIAL

A. *HOLSEY* SITUATION IN GENERAL

Suppose A and B each own 50 percent of the stock of a corporation. A desires to end his participation and B buys A's stock for its fair market value, $150,000. In effect, B has decided to invest $150,000 more in the corporation, and now owns 100 percent of a $300,000 corporation. Alternatively, suppose that B did not have sufficient funds or never contemplated buying A's stock. Instead of the above arrangement, therefore, the corporation redeems A's stock for $150,000. B now owns 100 percent of a corporation worth $150,000. Was the Tax Court, which was reversed by the Court of Appeals in the *Holsey* opinion, supra, saying that in this latter case B has a dividend of $150,000? How has B benefitted? While he is now the sole owner, he is the sole owner of a corporation half as large. Another possible view of the Tax Court decision, which does not rest on a dividend distribution, is that the redemption and consequent change in the interests of the shareholders may be treated as an appropriate occasion to tax any increase in the value of the shares of the remaining shareholders over the tax basis for their shares. But to treat this event as a realization of that gain would be a departure from existing rules. These questions are related to the problem of the proper treatment of the increase in the shareholder's proportionate interest in the corporation caused by a stock dividend, either actual or constructive, see supra, page 535 and infra, page 725.

Going back to the first situation, suppose that B first had agreed to buy A's stock and then, after B had received the stock and undertaken this obligation, the obligation was assumed by the corporation and it paid A. Here in form and legal effect an obligation of B has been discharged by the corporation and he should have dividend income. The relief from a $150,000 debt is the receipt of income. This was the situation in Zipp v. Commissioner, referred to in the *Holsey* opinion. Suppose then, as the next case, A and B are about to conclude a contract for the purchase by B, and B's lawyer, thinking of taxes, suddenly says the corporation should buy A's stock. The contract is hastily redrawn and the corporation acquires A's stock. Is the case to fall on the dividend side or on the nondividend side? In effect, this is a facet of the *Court Holding Company–Cumberland Public Service Company* issue, supra, page 690—did the parties proceed so far along the "purchase" by B that the taking over of B's obligation by the corporation came too late?

Where does the *Holsey* case itself fall? Certainly the parties were moving along the "purchase by B" route and then changed. Also, the option was a favorable one, since $80,000 was less than the value of 50 percent of the stock. Let us assume that value was $200,000. To gain this $120,000 benefit, the taxpayer B had to have $80,000. By taking over this option and providing the $80,000, the corporation produced a benefit for the taxpayer B. Is this what the Tax Court had in mind? If so, is the dividend $80,000 or $120,000?

Rev.Rul. 58–614, 1958–2 Cum.Bull. 920, states that the Service will follow the *Holsey* case where the stock was not in reality purchased by the continuing shareholder.

B. ASPECTS AS RESPECTS THE CONTINUING SHAREHOLDER

1. *Was the Corporation or the Continuing Shareholder the Purchaser of the Stock?*

(a) *Conditional Versus Unconditional Obligation to Purchase Shares*

As noted above, the cases dealing with this issue turn on the factual question whether the continuing shareholder is regarded as the purchaser, so that the corporation in either paying funds to the selling shareholder as in the *Zipp* and *Wall* cases referred to in the *Holsey* opinion, or in taking the stock from the continuing shareholder and paying him for it, as in Lowenthal v. Commissioner, 169 F.2d 694 (7th Cir.1948), is in effect paying a dividend to the continuing shareholder. Here the primary issue is whether the continuing shareholder has a "personal, unconditional, primary obligation" to purchase the stock which is discharged by the corporation. In Sullivan v. United States, 363 F.2d 724 (8th Cir.1966), the majority shareholder in a corporation was obligated personally to purchase stock from a minority shareholder on the latter's leaving the employ of the corporation. When the minority shareholder left the employ of the corporation, however, instead of purchasing it himself, the majority shareholder caused the corporation to redeem the minority shareholder's stock. The redemption of the employee's shares in lieu of purchase by the majority shareholder under the agreement resulted in a dividend.

In general, however, both the cases and the Rulings in this area have been quite favorable to taxpayers. Thus, for example, in Priester v. Commissioner, 38 T.C. 316 (1962), a minority shareholder agreed to purchase the majority interest in a corporation but was financially unable to meet his commitment under the agreement. He then assigned the contract of sale to a third party with an understanding that the shares to be purchased by the third party would be redeemed by the corporation within a short period of time. Seven months following the purchase the shares were redeemed. The court found no dividend to the continuing shareholder since his obligation to the original owner of the stock was extinguished by the third party's purchase of the shares and not by the corporate distribution; the court refused to view the third party as a "straw man" through whom the taxpayer indirectly received the benefit of the corporate distribution. In addition, the Tax Court indicated that it would follow the Court of Appeals holding in *Holsey* that the benefit derived by the shareholder in becoming the sole shareholder of the corporation as a result of the redemption was not a taxable event.

Rev.Rul. 69–608, 1969–2 Cum.Bull. 42, discussed a number of commonly recurring situations in which the redemption of stock from retiring shareholders will not result in a constructive dividend to the continuing shareholder. In general, the Ruling allows the continuing shareholder to avoid dividend consequences as long as at the time of the redemption there is no existing primary and unconditional obligation on his part to purchase the redeemed shares. Thus, in one situation, A and B owned all of the outstanding stock of a corporation and had an agreement that, on the death of either, the survivor would purchase the decedent's shares from his estate. The cancellation of the agreement prior to the death of either shareholder, in favor of a new contract under which the corporation would redeem the shares of the decedent was held not to result in a constructive dividend since at the time of the revision of the agreement there was no unconditional obligation to purchase the shares. In another situation dealt with by the Ruling, an individual entered into a contract for the purchase of the stock of a corporation. The contract provided that it could be assigned to another corporation, thereby releasing the purchaser from his obligations under the contract. The individual organized a corporation and assigned the stock purchase contract to it, the corporation borrowing funds to consummate the transaction. The purchasing corporation was subsequently merged into the acquired corporation, which then satisfied the loan liabilities. The Ruling, following Kobacker v. Commissioner, 37 T.C. 882 (1962), found no dividend on the repayment of the loan since the shareholder was not unconditionally obligated to purchase the stock. See also Smith v. Commissioner, 70 T.C. 651 (1978) (taxpayer was found to be unconditionally obligated to purchase stock under a stock purchase agreement with one shareholder but not so obligated with respect to another shareholder who only had an option to sell the stock to the taxpayer; consequently only redemptions in connection with the binding stock purchase agreement constituted dividends to the taxpayer).

On the other hand, Rev.Rul. 69–608 makes clear that where the continuing shareholder has become unconditionally bound to purchase the retiring or deceased shareholder's stock, a redemption by the corporation will give rise to a constructive dividend to the continuing shareholder. Thus, a constructive dividend was found where A and B agreed that upon the death of either the survivor would purchase the decedent's stock, and after the death of B, A caused the corporation to redeem the stock from B's estate. But, if the obligation is not unconditional, constructive dividend treatment may be avoided. Thus, the Ruling holds that no constructive dividend occurred where A and B and the corporation agreed that upon the death of either A or B, the corporation would redeem the decedent's shares and, to the extent that the corporation did not so redeem the shares, the survivor would purchase them. The same result follows where A agrees that if B desires to sell his shares, A will purchase the shares or cause another person to purchase the shares, and A causes the corporation to purchase the shares.

The results in individual cases turn on whether under state contract law the continuing shareholder has a contractual obligation. For example, in Apschnikat v. United States, 421 F.2d 910 (6th Cir.1970), the court found that the negotiations and correspondence between the purchaser and the sellers resulted in a binding obligation on the purchaser to purchase the stock and were not simply pre-contract dealings. Accordingly, payments for the stock by a corporation to which the purchaser had transferred the sales contract resulted in dividends to him. See also Gerson v. Commissioner, 56 T.C.M. 1202 (1989) (surviving shareholder's obligation to purchase deceased shareholder's stock established by state court decision ordering specific performance of buy-sell agreement).

If a shareholder of X Corporation is obligated to purchase stock of Y Corporation and, rather than purchasing the Y Corporation stock directly, the shareholder assigns the contractual obligation to X Corporation, which purchases the stock, there is no dividend to the shareholder. In this case X Corporation has not redeemed its own stock. Rather it has received fair value for the amount paid and thus it is not a distribution. See Citizens Bank & Trust Co. v. United States, 580 F.2d 442 (Ct.Cl.1978).

(b) *Continuing Shareholder as Agent of Corporation*

Sometimes where the shares first pass through the continuing shareholder, the court may regard him as an agent acquiring the stock on behalf of the corporation, which was the real purchaser, so that no dividend results. Thus in Bennett v. Commissioner, 58 T.C. 381 (1972), the majority shareholder in the corporation wished to terminate his interest. The taxpayer, a minority shareholder, suggested that the corporation redeem the shares but the retiring shareholder (in order not to incur a possible liability to creditors of the corporation because of a depletion of corporate assets) insisted that the taxpayer appear as the purchaser of the shares. It was agreed that the corporation would borrow money to advance to the taxpayer; the latter would then purchase the shares from the retiring shareholder and the corporation would immediately redeem. The transaction was consummated in this manner and the Tax Court found no dividend, distinguishing the *Wall* case, relied on by the Government, as follows:

"In *Wall,* the taxpayer in one transaction acquired stock, paid an amount of cash, and obligated himself personally to pay additional amounts; in a subsequent, separate transaction the corporation paid the notes. In contrast, [the taxpayer here] never intended to acquire personal ownership of the Jones stock and never incurred any personal obligation to do so; at all times, he was serving as a conduit or agent for the Corporation in a single, integrated transaction in which it acquired the stock." (388)

A similar result was reached in Ciaio v. Commissioner, 47 T.C. 447 (1967), where, as a result of disagreements, two shareholders agreed to sell their stock to the corporation, leaving the taxpayer as the sole shareholder. To finance the transaction, the corporation obtained a bank loan. The bank, as a condition of the loan (imposed under banking law), required that the stock be deposited with it as security and that the documents reflect the continuing shareholder and not the corporation as the buyer of the stock. The continuing shareholder was also required to guarantee the bank loan. The loan proceeds were used to redeem the shares of the two retiring shareholders. The court found no dividend to the continuing shareholder on account of the redemption since he was at all times acting as an agent for the corporation. See also, Fox v. Harrison, 145 F.2d 521 (7th Cir.1944), and Bunton v. Commissioner, 27 T.C.M. 9 (1968), reaching similar results. Compare Deutsch v. Commissioner, 38 T.C. 118 (1962), rejecting the agency argument where the contract for the purchase of the stock was at all times between the individual taxpayer and the seller, and Glacier State Electric Supply Co. v. Commissioner, 80 T.C. 1047 (1983), holding that a parent corporation was the true owner of redeemed stock of its wholly owned subsidiary, rather than an agent of the parent corporation's shareholders who were asserted to be the beneficial owners of the stock of the subsidiary.

In Schroeder v. Commissioner, 831 F.2d 856 (9th Cir.1987), the selling shareholder, after initially agreeing to cause the corporation to redeem 90 percent of her stock and to sell 10 percent of her stock to the purchaser, on the advice of counsel changed her mind and insisted on selling all of the stock to the purchaser. The bank which was financing the acquisition, however, required that the permanent loan be made to the corporation as primary obligor and be guaranteed by the purchaser. In order to effect the acquisition of all of the stock directly by the purchaser a "bridge" loan was made directly to the purchaser, subject to an agreement between the purchaser and the bank that immediately after the acquisition, the corporation would assume primary responsibility for the loan in consideration of a redemption of a proportionate amount of its stock. In fact, the corporation assumed approximately two-thirds of the loan two months after the acquisition, and it redeemed a proportionate amount of stock. The taxpayer argued that the purchase and the redemption were part of a single transaction which should have been treated as a redemption from the seller. The court rejected this argument as follows:

"The Tax Court found that 'there was no common or mutually agreed plan of action between the estate of Fred Collins [the seller], Schroeder [the buyer], and Skyline [the corporation] whose object was the ultimate redemption by Skyline of a part of its stock. * * * ' We agree with the Tax Court. The record confirms Schroeder's stated intentions, but also shows that this intention was particular to him. Donna Collins, as the personal representative of her husband's estate and as the seller of Skyline's stock, made it clear to Schroeder by April 13, 1976, that she would not agree to Skyline redeeming its stock as part of a bootstrap acquisition of Skyline proposed by Schroeder. Instead, she insisted that Schroeder buy the stock personally, which Schroeder undertook to do. In addition, Skyline cannot have had any intention different from Donna's, since she controlled 100 percent of Skyline's stock.

"Schroeder, because of Donna's insistence, could not undertake a bootstrap acquisition and had to buy the Skyline stock himself. He had business reasons for choosing the form of the transaction that he did. He cannot now argue that he is immunized from tax because the transaction was really something that never occurred. * * *

"Schroeder's contention that he acted as an agent or conduit of the corporation pursuant to a prearranged plan is without merit. First, as noted above, there was no mutually agreed plan between Collins and Schroeder or between Schroeder and Skyline. The intention to have the corporation redeem its own stock was Schroeder's intention alone. Second, when he acquired the stock on April 30, 1976, 'Schroeder was neither an officer, director nor a shareholder of Skyline, and he had no apparent authority to bind or commit Skyline to acquire its own stock or to borrow $600,000 from the bank in Skyline's name.' * * * It was not until he acquired sole ownership of the Skyline stock, on July 1, 1976, when the debt to State Bank was restructured, and on August 1, 1976, when Skyline redeemed his stock, that Schroeder caused his intention to become Skyline's as well. Schroeder was not Skyline's agent or conduit on April 30, 1976." (859)

Can *Schroeder* be distinguished from *Bennett* and *Ciaio?*

(c) *Post–Acquisition Redemption From Purchaser*

While a well-tailored plan for the purchase of a corporate business can use part of the corporation's assets to finance the transaction, the formalities generally must be observed. Where an agency argument fails, a distribution to the purchaser following the acquisition of all of the stock, for the purpose of reducing the net out-of-pocket purchase price paid for the corporate business, will be a dividend to the purchaser. In Television Industries, Inc. v. Commissioner, 284 F.2d 322 (2d Cir.1960), the purchasing shareholder borrowed money to complete the purchase of all the shares then had some of the shares redeemed to obtain funds to repay the loan; a dividend resulted. Accord, Adams v. Commissioner, 594 F.2d 657 (8th Cir.1979) (pro-rata redemption of shares following purchase taxed as dividend even though pursuant to prearranged plan of which seller's had knowledge). Even though in economic effect and intent this transaction may not differ from a pre-acquisition redemption from the seller, the form of the transaction will control for tax purposes. See Jacobs v. Commissioner, 41 T.C.M. 951 (1981), aff'd, 698 F.2d 850 (6th Cir.1983), where upon finding that the corporation acted as the continuing shareholders' agent in acquiring the seller's shares, the Tax Court observed as follows: "Petitioners could very easily have avoided dividend treatment of this transaction had they obtained tax advice from the start. * * * Unfortunately, this is another area of the law in which 'the formalities of handling a particular transaction assume a disproportionate importance and * * * a premium is placed upon consulting one's lawyer early enough in the game.' * * * Petitioners have chosen the wrong form and consequently must suffer the consequences." (953). Is the agency theory employed in *Bennett* and *Ciaio* inconsistent with the "form controls" theory of *Jacobs?*

2. *Section 305 Aspects*

While the case law after *Holsey* was unanimous in rejecting the Government's argument that the continuing shareholder's increase in his proportionate interest in the corporation as a result of the redemption of other shareholders constituted a taxable dividend to him, increase in proportionate interest again became relevant with the amendments to section 305 in 1969, see supra, page 524. Under section 305(b)(2) the increase in the proportionate interests of some shareholders in the earnings or assets of the corporation caused by a stock dividend, when coupled with the receipt of property by other shareholders, can result in a taxable distribution to the former group. Under section 305(c), the increase in proportionate interest caused by a redemption can be treated as a constructive stock dividend for purposes of section 305(b)(2). However, the Regulations take the position that in a situation like *Holsey,* where the redemption distribution is entitled to capital gains treatment under section 302(b), no constructive dividend will result to the continuing shareholders under the "isolated transaction" rule. Regulations, section 1.305–7(a). See Regulations, section 1.305–3(b), (e) Ex. (10) (no constructive dividend as a result of isolated redemption even though redemption was treated as a section 301 distribution). For an example of a redemption situation in which section 305(b)(2) was applicable by virtue of section 305(c), see Rev.Rul. 78–60, 1978–1 Cum.Bull. 81.

C. REDEMPTION AS PART OF THE SALE OF THE CORPORATION TO NEW SHAREHOLDERS

Where a prospective purchaser of the stock is unwilling to pay for all the stock at its present value and the parties arrange for the corporation to redeem some of the shares of the existing shareholders contemporaneously with the sale of the balance of their stock to the purchaser, who thus is required to pay a lesser figure (but who also receives a corporation with fewer assets), the courts have held that the redemption does not constitute a dividend to the selling shareholders. Zenz v. Quinlivan, 213 F.2d 914 (6th Cir.1954); Rev.Rul. 55–745, 1955–2 Cum.Bull. 223 (Service will follow *Zenz*); Auto Finance Co. v. Commissioner, 24 T.C. 416 (1955), aff'd per curiam, 229 F.2d 318 (4th Cir.1956); In re Lukens' Estate, 246 F.2d 403 (3d Cir.1957) (father had part of his stock redeemed at book value and gave the balance to his adult children, who also were shareholders and who managed the corporation). The Internal Revenue Service has ruled that the actual sequence of the redemption and the sale will be ignored in a *Zenz*-type corporate sale as long as the two steps are both part of an integrated plan to reduce the outgoing shareholders' interest. Thus, the fact that the redemption precedes the sale of the shares will not cause the outgoing shareholders to receive dividend treatment; the formal order of the steps in the transaction is not crucial. Rev.Rul. 75–447, 1975–2 Cum.Bull. 113; accord Monson v. Commissioner, 79 T.C. 827 (1982). See also Rev.Rul. 77–226, 1977–2 Cum.Bull. 90 (corporate shareholder tendered part of its shares for redemption and sold the remaining shares of stock on the market; it treated the redemption as a section 301 distribution under section 302(d) qualifying for the intercorporate dividends deduction and claimed a capital loss on the disposition of the remaining shares which were attributed the basis of the shares which were redeemed; held, the entire transaction resulted in a termination of the corporate shareholders interest and hence a taxable capital gain).

It is not necessary for the selling shareholder's interest to be completely terminated in order for the *Zenz* principle to apply. Rev.Rul. 75–447, 1975–2 Cum.Bull. 113, held that the reduction in interest effected through a combined sale and redemption should be aggregated to determine whether the redemption qualified for sale or exchange treatment under section 302(b)(2), discussed supra, page 555. Furthermore, in private letter rulings the Internal Revenue Service has applied *Zenz* to qualify a redemption under section 301(b)(1). See Ltr.Rul. 8540074.

A variation on Zenz v. Quinlivan was involved in McDonald v. Commissioner, 52 T.C. 82 (1969). There the shareholder, who owned all of the preferred stock and most of the common stock in a corporation, had the preferred stock redeemed and, as part of a prior arrangement, exchanged his common stock for the common stock of a public corporation in a tax-free exchange. The Commissioner argued that the preferred stock redemption constituted a dividend, distinguishing *Zenz,* since in this situation the shareholder retained a continuing interest in the assets of old corporation by virtue of his stock ownership in the acquiring corporation. The court found the redemption and subsequent reorganization effected a "substantial change" in the shareholder's interest and refused to treat the redemption as a dividend. For the reorganization aspects of *McDonald* see infra, page 837.

Assuming the selling shareholder can avoid dividend treatment, what about incoming shareholders? In Edenfield v. Commissioner, 19 T.C. 13 (1952) (A), because the purchaser was willing to buy only part of the stock, the corporation redeemed the balance of the shares from the former shareholder with notes. The court stated that the payments on the notes by the corporation were not dividends to the new shareholder since the notes were not his indebtedness. On the other hand, as the cases in B.1., supra, indicate, if the redemption is in discharge of the incoming shareholder's purchase obligation, dividend treatment can result. Why should there be any difference in the treatment of "new" and "old" shareholders?

D. DIVIDENDS DISTRIBUTED IN CONNECTION WITH THE SALE OF A CORPORATE BUSINESS

While the treatment of redemptions made as part of the sale of a corporate business is fairly well established since the initial decisions in *Holsey* and *Zenz,* the appropriate treatment of dividend distributions in similar situations is a matter of continuing controversy.

In Casner v. Commissioner, 450 F.2d 379 (5th Cir.1971), substantial shareholders in the corporation wished to withdraw by selling their stock to the remaining shareholders. The buyers did not have enough cash to finance the transaction. It was agreed that a distribution of some of the cash of the corporation would be made pro rata to all the shareholders, thus reducing the value of the corporation and giving the remaining shareholders some cash to pay a portion of the purchase price. Accordingly, the corporation made a cash distribution and contemporaneously the retiring shareholders sold their shares. The selling shareholders treated all the payments as sales proceeds; the buying shareholders regarded themselves as conduits. The Tax Court treated the corporate distributions to both the selling and buying shareholders as dividends (28 T.C.M. 535 (1969)). The Court of Appeals reversed, finding that the distributions to the *selling* shareholders were in fact part of the payment of the purchase price and as such resulted in dividends to the *buying* shareholders (in addition to the latter's own direct dividends). The court found alternatively that the buying stockholders were the beneficial owners of the stock at the time of the dividend distribution.

The *Casner* treatment of the distributions to the selling shareholders as dividends to the buying shareholders followed by a payment of the purchase price to the sellers is clearly inconsistent with the redemption line of cases dealing with a similar factual pattern. The Internal Revenue Service will not apply *Casner* to tax the buyer where the payment of the dividend to the selling shareholder does not reduce the buyer's obligation to pay an agreed upon purchase price, Rev.Rul. 75–493, 1975–2 Cum.Bull. 108. This position is consistent with the redemption cases which likewise focus on the question of whether the distribution by the corporation discharges the buying shareholder's personal obligation. It similarly places a premium on the careful timing of the transactions since very different tax consequences result depending on whether the distribution is made before or after entering into a binding purchase agreement.

Even where the dividend does not reduce the buying shareholder's obligation under the purchase agreement, a dividend to the buyer may still be found on the theory that the buyer had become the beneficial owner of the stock at the time the dividend was declared. See Steel Improvement and Forge Co. v. Commissioner, 314 F.2d 96 (6th Cir.1963); Walker v. Commissioner, 544 F.2d 419 (9th Cir.1976).

E. REFERENCES

Lang, Dividends Essentially Equivalent to Redemptions: The Taxation of Bootstrap Stock Acquisitions, 41 Tax L.Rev. 309 (1986); Coven, The Relevance of Fresh Investment to the Characterization of Corporate Distributions and Adjustments, 38 Tax L.Rev. 419 (1983); Jassy, The Tax Treatment of Bootstrap Stock Acquisitions: The Redemption Route Versus The Dividend Route, 87 Harv.L.Rev. 1459 (1974); Kingson, The Deep Structure of Taxation: Dividend Distributions, 85 Yale L.J. 861 (1976).

B. BOOTSTRAP TRANSACTIONS INVOLVING CORPORATIONS

INTRODUCTORY NOTE

Special problems arise where a dividend in connection with a sale is paid to a selling shareholder which is itself a corporation and thus able to take advantage of the reduction or elimination of tax on intercorporate dividends under section 243. Suppose that X Corporation owns 100 percent of the stock of Y Corporation, which has a basis of $200 and a fair market value of $500. If X Corporation sold the stock of Y Corporation to Z Corporation for $500, after paying taxes (at 34 percent) on its $300 gain, X Corporation would have net after-tax proceeds of $398. Now suppose that prior to the sale Y Corporation declared a dividend of $200, which was eligible for 100 percent exclusion under section 243(a)(3), following which X Corporation sold the stock of Y Corporation for $300. In this case, X Corporation would pay taxes on only a $100 gain, and after taxes it would receive $466.

The Commissioner generally argues that such a dividend payment was in fact additional purchase price, and therefore constituted capital gain which was not eligible for the section 243 deduction. See Rev.Rul. 75–493, supra, page 727, characterizing such a transaction as a "sham designed to disguise the true substance of the transaction." The Commissioner has had mixed success with this argument in the courts.

LITTON INDUSTRIES, INC. v. COMMISSIONER

Tax Court of the United States, 1987.
89 T.C. 1086.

[The taxpayer's board of director's began to consider a sale of its subsidiary, Stouffer, in July of 1972. In late August, Stouffer declared a $30 million dividend, which was paid in the form of a negotiable promissory note for $30 million; and on September 7, Litton announced that it was interested in selling Stouffer. After considering making a public offering of the Stouffer stock in late 1972, on March 1, 1973, Litton sold its Stouffer stock to Nestle for $75 million; simultaneously, it sold the promissory note to Nestle for $30 million. The Commissioner contended that the $30 million "dividend" was in fact part of the purchase price and disallowed Litton's dividends received deduction.]

OPINION

* * *

The instant case is substantially governed by Waterman Steamship Corp. v. Commissioner, 50 T.C. 650 (1968), revd. 430 F.2d 1185 (5th Cir. 1970), cert. denied 401 U.S. 939 (1971). [The Commissioner] urges us to follow the opinion of the Fifth Circuit * * *. [Taxpayer] contends that the reasoning of the Fifth Circuit in *Waterman Steamship* should not apply since the facts here are more favorable to petitioner. Additionally, petitioner points out that several business purposes were served by the distribution here which provide additional support for recognition of the distribution as a dividend. For the reasons set forth below, we conclude that the $30 million distribution constituted a dividend which should be recognized as such for tax purposes. * * *

In many respects, the facts of this case and those of *Waterman Steamship* are parallel. The principal difference, and the one which we find to be most significant, is the timing of the dividend action. In *Waterman Steamship,* the taxpayer corporation received an offer to purchase the stock of two of its wholly owned subsidiary corporations, Pan–Atlantic and Gulf Florida, for $3,500,000. The board of directors of Waterman Steamship rejected that offer but countered with an offer to sell the two subsidiaries for $700,000 after the subsidiaries declared and arranged for payments of dividends to Waterman Steamship amounting in the aggregate to $2,800,000. Negotiations between the parties ensued, and the agreements which resulted therefrom included, in specific detail, provisions for the declaration of a dividend by Pan–Atlantic to Waterman Steamship prior to the signing of the sales agreement and the closing of that transaction. Furthermore, the agreements called for the purchaser to loan or otherwise advance funds to Pan–Atlantic promptly in order to pay off the promissory note by which the dividend had been paid. Once the agreement was reached, the entire transaction was carried out by a series of meetings commencing at 12 noon on January 21, 1955, and ending at 1:30 p.m. the same day. * * *

As the Fifth Circuit pointed out, "By the end of the day and within a ninety minute period, the financial cycle had been completed. Waterman had $3,500,000, hopefully tax-free, all of which came from Securities and McLean, the buyers of the stock." 430 F.2d at 1190. This Court concluded that the distribution from Pan–Atlantic to Waterman was a dividend. The Fifth Circuit reversed, concluding that the dividend and sale were one transaction. 430 F.2d at 1192.

The timing in the instant case was markedly different. The dividend was declared by Stouffer on August 23, 1972, at which time the promissory note in payment of the dividend was issued to Litton. There had been some general preliminary discussions about the sale of Stouffer, and it was expected that Stouffer would be a very marketable company which would sell quickly. However, at the time the dividend was declared, no formal action had been taken to initiate the sale of Stouffer. It was not until 2 weeks later that Litton publicly announced that Stouffer was for sale. There ensued over the next 6 months many discussions with various corporations, investment banking houses, business brokers, and underwriters regarding Litton's disposition of Stouffer through sale of all or part of the business to a particular buyer, or through full or partial public offerings of the Stouffer stock. All of this culminated on March 1, 1973, over 6 months after the dividend was declared, with the purchase by Nestle of all of Stouffer's stock. * * *

In the instant case, the declaration of the dividend and the sale of the stock were substantially separated in time in contrast to *Waterman Steamship* where the different transactions occurred essentially simultaneously. In *Waterman Steamship,* it seems quite clear that no dividend would have been declared if all of the remaining steps in the transaction had not been lined up in order on the closing table and did not in fact take place. Here, however, Stouffer declared the dividend, issued the promissory note, and definitely committed itself to the dividend before even making a public announcement that Stouffer was for sale. Respondent argues that the only way petitioner could ever receive the dividend was by raising revenue through a sale of Stouffer. Therefore, respondent asserts the two events (the declaration of the dividend and then the sale of the company) were inextricably tied together and should be treated as one transaction for tax purposes. In our view, respondent ignores the fact that Stouffer could have raised sufficient revenue for the dividend from other avenues, such as a partial public offering or borrowing. Admittedly, there had been discussions at Litton about the sale of Stouffer which was considered to be a very salable company. However, there are many slips between the cup and the lip, and it does not take much of a stretch of the imagination to picture a variety of circumstances under which Stouffer might have been taken off the market and no sale consummated. Under these circumstances, it is unlikely that respondent would have considered the dividend to be a nullity. On the contrary, it would seem quite clear that petitioner would be charged with a dividend on which it would have to pay a substantial tax. Petitioner committed itself to the dividend and, thereby, accepted the consequences regardless of the outcome of the proposed sale of Stouffer stock. See Crellin v. Commissioner, 17 T.C. 781, 785 (1951), affd. 203 F.2d 812 (9th Cir.1953), cert. denied 346 U.S. 873, 74 S.Ct. 123 (1953).

Since the facts here are distinguishable in important respects and are so much stronger in petitioner's favor, we do not consider it necessary to consider further the opinion of the Fifth Circuit in *Waterman Steamship.*

* * * [T]he $30 million distribution by Stouffer would clearly constitute a dividend if the sale of Stouffer had not occurred. We are not persuaded that the subsequent sale of Stouffer to Nestle changes that result merely because it was more advantageous to Litton from a tax perspective.

It is well established that a taxpayer is entitled to structure his affairs and transactions in order to minimize his taxes. This proposition does not give a taxpayer carte blanche to set up a transaction in any form which will avoid tax consequences, regardless of whether the transaction has substance. Gregory v. Helvering, 293 U.S. 465, 55 S.Ct. 266 (1935). A variety of factors present here preclude a finding of sham or subterfuge. Although the record in this case clearly shows that Litton intended at the time the dividend was declared to sell Stouffer, no formal action had been taken and no announcement had been made.

There was no definite purchaser waiting in the wings with the terms and conditions of sale already agreed upon. At that time, Litton had not even decided upon the form of sale of Stouffer. Nothing in the record here suggests that there was any prearranged sale agreement, formal or informal, at the time the dividend was declared.

Petitioner further supports its argument that the transaction was not a sham by pointing out Litton's legitimate business purposes in declaring the dividend. Although the Code and case law do not require a dividend to have a business purpose, it is a factor to be considered in determining whether the overall transaction was a sham. T.S.N. Liquidating Corp. v. United States, 624 F.2d 1328 (5th Cir.1980). Petitioner argues that * * * since Litton was considering disposing of all or part of Stouffer through a public or private offering, the payment of a dividend by a promissory note prior to any sale had two advantages. First, Litton hoped to avoid materially diminishing the market value of the Stouffer stock. At that time, one of the factors considered in valuing a stock, and in determining the market value of a stock was the "multiple of earnings" criterion. Payment of the dividend by issuance of a promissory note would not substantially alter Stouffer's earnings. Since many investors were relatively unsophisticated, Litton may have been quite right that it could increase its investment in Stouffer by at least some portion of the $30 million dividend. Second, by declaring a dividend and paying it by a promissory note prior to an anticipated public offering, Litton could avoid sharing the earnings with future additional shareholders while not diminishing to the full extent of the pro rata dividend, the amount received for the stock. Whether Litton could have come out ahead after Stouffer paid the promissory note is at this point merely speculation about a public offering which never occurred. The point, however, is that Litton hoped to achieve some business purpose, and not just tax benefits, in structuring the transaction as it did.

Under these facts, where the dividend was declared 6 months prior to the sale of Stouffer, where the sale was not pre-arranged, and since Stouffer had earnings and profits exceeding $30 million at the time the dividend was declared, we cannot conclude that the distribution was merely a device designed to give the appearance of a dividend to a part of the sales proceeds. In this case, the form and substance of the transaction coincide; it was not a transaction entered into solely for tax reasons, and it should be recognized as structured by petitioner.

ILLUSTRATIVE MATERIAL

A. CASE DEVELOPMENTS

As in *Waterman Steamship,* discussed in the excerpt from *Litton Industries,* supra, the Commissioner met with success in the District Court in TSN Liquidating Corp. v. United States, 77–2 U.S.T.C. ¶ 9741 (N.D.Tex.1977), but on appeal the decision was reversed, 624 F.2d 1328 (5th Cir.1980). In that case, Union Mutual agreed to purchase from TSN the stock of TSN's subsidiary, CLIC, but Union Mutual insisted that prior to the acquisition

CLIC distribute to TSN certain securities, primarily stock of closely held corporations, constituting some 78 percent of CLIC's total assets. Although Union Mutual did not desire CLIC to hold the particular securities distributed pursuant to the agreement, neither did it desire to own a "smaller" corporation. To the contrary, for reasons having to do with state law it desired to maintain the net assets of CLIC, and shortly after the closing, Union Mutual contributed to CLIC cash and marketable securities slightly in excess of the amount distributed to TSN.

Emphasizing that the distribution of investment assets immediately prior to the sale of the stock was matched by a post acquisition infusion of investment assets, the Commissioner argued that the conduit rationale of *Waterman Steamship* applied. Although it agreed with the District Court that "the substance of the transaction controls over the form," the Court of Appeals found *Waterman Steamship,* upon which the District Court had relied, to be distinguishable. The earlier case involved a "sham transaction," which even the Commissioner did not argue was the case in *TSN Liquidating.* Instead, the Commissioner argued, successfully in the District Court, that from CLIC's perspective there was no business purpose for the distribution which could not have occurred other than in the context of the sale. The Court of Appeals, however, concluded as follows:

"We agree that the transaction must be viewed as a whole and we accept the district court's finding of fact that the dividend of the unwanted assets was 'part and parcel of the purchase arrangement with Union Mutual,' motivated specifically by Union Mutual's unwillingness to take and pay for such assets. That being the case, we decline to focus on the business purpose of one participant in the transaction—a corporation controlled by the taxpayer—and instead find that the business purpose for the transaction as a whole, viewed from the standpoint of the taxpayer, controls. The facts found by the district court clearly demonstrate a business purpose for the presale dividend of the unwanted assets which fully explains that dividend. We note that there is no suggestion in the district court's opinion of any tax avoidance motivation on the part of the taxpayer TSN. The fact that the dividend may have had incidential tax benefit to the taxpayer, without more, does not necessitate the disallowance of dividend treatment." (1336)

In Basic, Inc. v. United States, 549 F.2d 740 (Ct.Cl.1977), the court refused to respect the taxpayers' structure of the transaction even though payment of an intercorporate dividend was not in effect a conduit device to transfer funds from the purchaser to the seller. Basic owned all the shares of Falls which in turn owned all the shares of Carbon. A corporate purchaser was interested in buying the shares of Falls and Carbon but, in order to take advantage of a now repealed provision governing a subsequent liquidation of the subsidiaries, it desired to purchase the stock of both Falls and Carbon directly rather than simply purchasing the Falls stock and obtaining the Carbon stock on a liquidation of Falls. After an irrevocable offer by the purchaser to purchase the Falls and Carbon stock, Falls distributed the Carbon stock to Basic as a dividend. The dividend of the stock was entitled to the dividends received deduction under section 243(a)(1) but because under section 301(d) the basis of the Carbon stock was not reduced to reflect the dividends received deduction, Basic acquired an essentially "cost free" basis in the Carbon stock against which to offset the sales price to be paid for the stock of the two corporations. The Court of Claims held that the transfer of the Carbon stock to Basic did not qualify as a dividend. The court rested its decision on general notions of tax avoidance, citing Gregory v. Helvering, and took the position that for a corporate distribution to qualify as a dividend it must have an independent "business purpose":

"These facts leave no room for a conclusion that a business interest was served by the claimed dividend. From all that appears, the case is plain that Falls, through its controlling parent, was caused to transfer the property whose sale the parent had decided upon for its own separate purposes. Nothing therefore remains save the obvious: the transaction reduced the tax that Basic would otherwise have incurred in the sale of its own property, i.e., the shares of Falls. * * *

"Under the facts and circumstances presented here, plaintiff has not shown that there was a reason for the transfer of the Carbon stock from Falls to Basic aside from the tax consequences attributable to that move. Accordingly, for purposes of taxation, the transfer was not a dividend within the meaning of Section 316(a)(1). Instead, it should be regarded as a transfer that avoided part of the gain to be expected from the sale of the business to Carborundum, and should, therefore, be now taxed accordingly. Such a treatment is in keeping with the results reached in like situations. Waterman Steamship Corp. v. Commissioner, supra; Steel Improvement & Forge Co. v. Commissioner, 314 F.2d 96, 98 (6th Cir.1963); Commissioner v. Transport Trading & Terminal Corp., supra." (746, 749).

The *Basic, Inc.* opinion cannot be reconciled with *Litton Industries* and *TSN Liquidating. Basic, Inc.* appears to require that the payor have a business purpose for paying the dividend totally apart from the business purpose of the parent. It will be difficult, if not impossible, ever to establish an independent business purpose for the payment of an extraordinary dividend by a controlled subsidiary.

The cases involving intercorporate dividends associated with a bootstrap acquisition requiring that a dividend distribution must have a "business purpose" are in marked contrast to the cases in the redemption area in which the form which the taxpayer has selected for the extraction of corporate assets prior to a sale of the corporation is in general respected without regard to any inquiry into purposes. Does the fact that intercorporate dividends are in general either tax free or subject to reduced taxation mean that special safeguards are required with respect to such distributions in the context of corporate acquisitions? If so is the introduction of a "business purpose" doctrine an appropriate response? Compare the treatment given intercorporate dividends in the consolidated return situation discussed infra, page 1042, where the parent corporation upon receipt of an excluded intercorporate dividend must reduce its basis in the stock of the subsidiary by an amount equal to the dividend. Thus, in a consolidated return context, the intercorporate dividend prior to the sale does not produce a tax advantage to the seller.

B. SECTION 1059

A further impediment to intercorporate dividends as part of a bootstrap acquisition strategy is presented by section 1059, which was enacted in 1984.

Section 1059 requires that a corporate shareholder which receives an "extraordinary dividend" under certain circumstances must, in computing the gain or loss realized upon the sale of the stock, reduce the basis of the stock by the amount of the untaxed portion of the dividend. See supra, page 509.

As long as the stock has been held for more than two years prior to the dividend announcement date, however, only a distribution in partial liquidation of the corporation (as defined in section 302(e), discussed supra, page 583) or a non-pro rata redemption distribution will be treated as an extraordinary distribution. Thus section 1059 is of limited application in this context, and it would not apply, for example, to a transaction identical to that in *Litton.*

Section 1059 was not enacted for the purpose of dealing with *Litton* type transactions, but the mechanical approach of section 1059 could be extended to apply to such transactions if Congress considered bootstrap acquisitions involving intercorporate dividends to involve inappropriate tax avoidance.

C. LEVERAGED BUYOUTS

INTERNAL REVENUE CODE: Sections 163(e)(5), (i), (j); 172(m); 279.

MENTZ, CARLISE, AND NEVAS, LEVERAGED BUYOUTS: A WASHINGTON PERSPECTIVE OF THE 1989 LEGISLATION AND PROSPECTS FOR 1990.

46 Tax Notes 1047 (1990).

I. WHAT IS A LEVERAGED BUYOUT?

In broad terms, a leveraged buyout (or "LBO") is one of the many procedures that are used to accomplish a transaction whereby a group of assets, and usually the employees who operate the assets, are transferred from one group of owners to another. In a leveraged buyout, however, the managers of the enterprise generally obtain some significant equity position in the enterprise, and thus have a material economic interest in the success or failure of the business. In most cases, such employees previously maintained little or no stake in the business.[3]

Leveraged buyouts may be structured in a number of ways. For example, the new management could form a new corporation ("Newco") to acquire the assets and employees of a private or publicly held company or a division or subsidiary of a larger corporation ("Target") for cash and/or securities. Alternatively, a purchase of the stock of Target could occur, either directly, through a tender offer, or by a reverse merger of a wholly owned subsidiary of the acquiring entity into Target. In addition, although not involving a purchase of assets or stock by the new owners, the recapitalization of a public company, with the public shareholders exchanging their shares for cash or securities while management and any LBO participating firm retain the equity interest, results in the economic equivalent of a "typical" LBO transaction.

3. Other equity owners may be the members of the leveraged buyout firm which arranges the transaction and the partners in the partnership that has been created by the buyout firm to participate in the transaction. For example, Clayton & Dubilier, a highly successful LBO firm, has raised about $1.2 billion for partnership investments in the equity of their leveraged buyout transactions.

The typical financing structure of a leveraged buyout in the United States is composed of senior bank debt, "mezzanine debt" and equity. The bank debt is generally secured and relatively traditional in its terms. The mezzanine debt is subordinate to the bank debt and may be subordinate to trade creditors and to other classes of mezzanine debt (e.g., junior mezzanine debt).

The bank debt is normally provided by the large money center banks, which frequently syndicate the bank debt to other banks. The mezzanine debt is commonly referred to as "junk bonds," because this indebtedness is usually not of investment grade. While there may be no public market for the mezzanine debt, in most instances the investment banking firm or firms that have facilitated the transaction act as market-makers in these securities to provide investors with some degree of liquidity.

Equity for leveraged buyouts in the United States has typically been raised through partnerships created by the major leveraged buyout firms. The productivity, employment, research and development expenditures and general performance of many, but not all, LBOs has been favorable, apparently reflecting the substantially greater effort expended by managers whose own investment is at stake. Accordingly, these investments, which generally have demonstrated significant positive performance records, have proven attractive to a variety of investors, including pension funds, insurance companies, tax-exempt U.S. institutions and foreign investors.

II. TAX CONSIDERATIONS IN STRUCTURING THE FINANCING OF AN LBO OF A U.S. CORPORATION UNDER CURRENT LAW

If the purchaser involved in an LBO is a United States taxpayer, the central tax issue in financing the LBO is whether indebtedness incurred is debt or equity. Due to the separate ownership of the debt and equity in the typical LBO transaction, counsel for leveraged buyout transactions have been relatively comfortable advising that under current law both the senior bank debt and the mezzanine debt are true debt for U.S. tax purposes.[8]

8. In certain cases some debt holders may be offered warrants as an encouragement to invest in the mezzanine debt. The warrants are not allocated pro rata and their allocation depends on a number of economic and business factors.

One pending Tax Court case could be relevant to interest deductibility in LBOs, even though it is not a typical LBO financing structure. In a Tax Court petition filed on November 3, 1989, interest deductions were disallowed by the IRS in a case where a foreign parent corporation capitalized its U.S. subsidiary with $210 million of equity and $419 million of 14%, 20-year, nonsubordinated debt. The capital was used to acquire the Howard Johnson franchise in the United States. The debt was paid off well in advance of the 20-year maturity. The IRS has taken the position that the interest is not deductible because the "debt" is really equity. The case is pending in the U.S. Tax Court. The Ground Round of Baltimore, Inc. v. Commissioner, Docket No. 31696–88. Although the ownership of the equity and debt were held by the same person in this case, in view of the low debt-to-equity ratio and normal debt features, any adverse decision to the taxpayer could have unfavorable

* * *

If a foreign purchaser is engaged in a leveraged buyout, the use of the interest deduction in the most advantageous jurisdiction becomes of paramount importance. Typically, the indebtedness would be placed with the U.S. assets being acquired, and thus the U.S. interest deduction would be taken. Nevertheless, for a taxpayer with other foreign operations, it may be possible to place the indebtedness in another high tax jurisdiction where the interest deduction is available.

III. LBO TAX LEGISLATIVE PROCESS IN 1989

A. "Stamp Out LBOs"

In late 1988 and early 1989, there seemed to be general agreement on Capitol Hill that leveraged buyouts should be discouraged. The Chairmen of both the Senate Finance Committee and the House Ways and Means Committee expressed concern about amounts of debt incurred in leveraged buyouts, such as the RJR–Nabisco transaction, and the effects of such debt on the economy. They stated their concern about erosion in the corporate tax base, and recommended that serious consideration be given to a change in the U.S. tax structure to discourage leveraged buyouts.[10] Indeed, proposals to eliminate completely the deductibility of interest on indebtedness used to finance LBOs were advanced.[11] Secretary of the Treasury Brady, while not proposing or supporting particular tax legislation, gave general support to this notion by decrying the activities of the best and brightest Americans in "financial engineering." [12]

In addition, much rhetoric was devoted to the disadvantage of equity as compared to debt and the desirability of integrating the U.S. corporate and individual income tax systems. Indeed, Secretary Brady implied that if the systems were integrated, the LBO phenomenon would disappear.

While it is difficult to predict the impact on LBOs of full integration, it seems unlikely that this will come to pass in the near future.

* * *

ramifications to the deductibility of interest in LBO transactions.

10. Address by Congressman Daniel Rostenkowski at Coopers & Lybrand tax symposium in New York City, December 6, 1988; Statement by Senator Lloyd Bentsen at Senate Finance Committee LBO Hearings (January 24, 1989), reprinted in Highlights & Documents (Tax Analysts) 821–22 (January 25, 1989).

11. See, e.g., Options B–1 and B–3, "House Ways and Means Committee Press Release Announcing Continuation of Hearings on Tax Policy Aspects of Mergers and Acquisitions," issued April 12, 1989" (hereinafter "4/12/89 Press Release"), reprinted in 70 Daily Tax Report (BNA) L–6, L–7 (April 13, 1989) (hereinafter "4/12/89 DTR"), discussed in note 22 below.

12. Testimony by Secretary of the Treasury Nicholas F. Brady before the Senate Finance Committee, January 24, 1989, reprinted in Highlights & Documents (Tax Analysts) 822, 826 (January 25, 1989) (hereinafter "1/24/89 Brady testimony").

* * *

B. LBO Means "Let's Back Off"

In the spring of 1989, both Congress and the Administration began to temper their views on LBOs. The Chairman of the Senate Finance Committee stated that he did not want a solution to the LBO problem that was "worse than the problem." * * * The Ways and Means Committee Chairman, after expressing his displeasure at the Treasury's position, was able to obtain a concession from Treasury that in the case of zero coupon or low coupon high-yield securities, an original issue discount deduction is inconsistent with sound tax policy because the payment may never be made. This testimony led to the provision which became section 7202 of the Revenue Reconciliation Act of 1989, dealing with high yield indebtedness issued at a substantial discount with a term of more than five years.

A primary concern with any proposal that would disallow interest in the U.S. acquisition context is the recognition that such a rule could put a U.S. buyer at a competitive disadvantage compared to a non-U.S. buyer which could obtain interest deductions in another jurisdiction. For example, a non-U.S. corporation with a significant overseas tax base could incur indebtedness in that jurisdiction on which interest would be deductible, and capitalize a U.S. affiliate with equity in order to make the U.S. acquisition. Thus, the interest expense in that situation would be fully deductible, albeit not in the United States, while a U.S. acquirer would be subject to whatever new interest limitation rule would be imposed by new legislation.

The * * * Ways and Means Committee * * * suggested that this problem could be solved by treating some of the foreign acquirer's worldwide debt as allocable to the U.S. acquisition. Accordingly, the amount of interest related to such allocated debt would be included as additional income subject to tax to the United States corporation. The Treasury Department correctly pointed out that such an approach would violate the antidiscrimination provisions in our major treaties. Moreover, such an approach would seem to involve hopeless audit issues for the IRS in attempting to analyze the worldwide financing of non-U.S. corporations. The lack of a solution to this problem clearly limits a broad disallowance of interest deductions in LBOs and other leveraged transactions.

C. The 1989 Congressional Action on LBOs

Congress included a number of provisions in the 1989 revenue reconciliation legislation [25] that clearly impact upon LBOs. Moreover, the legislative history of these provisions suggests that LBOs may again be the subject of Congressional scrutiny. The legislation enacted that most directly affects LBOs may be described as follows:

25. Revenue Reconciliation Act of 1989, Title VII of the Omnibus Budget Reconciliation Act of 1989, Pub.L. No. 101–239, 103 Stat. 2106 (1989) (hereinafter "Reconciliation Act").

1. Section 7202 of the Reconciliation Act—original issue discount ("OID") on certain high yield obligations. Section 7202 amends section 163(e) to limit the availability of OID deductions to issuers of any "applicable high yield discount obligation." An applicable high yield discount obligation is an obligation with a term in excess of five years, a yield to maturity equal to or in excess of the applicable Federal rate ("AFR") at the time of issuance plus five percentage points, and "significant OID." "Significant OID" exists if, at the end of any accrual period ending five years after the date of issuance, the cumulative accruals of interest and OID will exceed the cumulative interest payments by more than the product of the instrument's issue price and its yield to maturity (i.e., approximately the first year's yield on the debt).

The OID on an applicable high yield discount obligation issued after July 10, 1989, is bifurcated into a deferred portion and a disqualified portion. The issuer generally is not permitted a deduction for the disqualified portion, which is the portion that produces a yield in excess of 6% over the AFR. The issuer may deduct OID for the remaining, or deferred, portion only when such portion is paid in cash.

A corporate holder of an applicable high yield discount obligation will be permitted a dividend received deduction with respect to the disqualified portion of the OID to the extent that a dividend received deduction would have been permitted on a distribution on corporate stock. This feature of the new provision, like the separations of OID into deductible and nondeductible portions, reflects the House's proposal to bifurcate long-term high yield OID debt instruments into debt and preferred stock in certain cases.

The new rules are extremely complex and address only one type of high-yield debt obligation: that which is issued with "significant OID." The view has been expressed by senior Congressional staff members that in 1990 Congress may consider broader limitations on the deductibility of interest on "junk bonds," even if paid currently. Certain key members agree with this view. Thus, there is the risk that the 1990 legislative process may produce a result that would broaden and "simplify" this bifurcation approach by applying it, or a variation, to all high-yield debt.

2. Section 7208—"clarification" of the regulatory authority of the Treasury Department under section 385 and required information reporting. Section 7208 amends Code section 385 to "clarify" Treasury's authority to characterize instruments with significant debt and equity characteristics as part debt and part equity. Such authority is to apply on a prospective basis only, to instruments issued after the publication of a regulation, ruling, or other public guidance. The legislative history indicates that treatment of a debt instrument as part debt and part equity may be appropriate where payments on a debt instrument are dependent to a significant extent on corporate performance, as evidenced by equity kickers, contingent interest, significant deferral of payment, subordination, or an interest rate high enough to suggest a significant risk of default.

* * *

An instrument that would be considered part debt and part equity for tax purposes would essentially have no defined market. Investors seeking dividend income, with a dividend received deduction, would not find the instrument attractive, nor would debt purchasers because presumably the yield would be lower than that in a pure debt instrument. Nevertheless, creative bankers and lawyers would probably try to find a way of stripping such hybrid or bifurcated instruments into pure debt and pure equity pieces, and selling each to the appropriate market.[27]

It should be noted that the House Committee Report directs the Treasury Department to increase the issuance of published rulings on the debt/equity issue.[28] This could be a very important form of guidance. For example, if an adverse view is taken by the IRS in a situation where the debt and equity are separately owned by different taxpayers, as in the case of most LBOs, it is likely that the financing of LBOs will be affected, irrespective of whether the IRS position is ultimately upheld by a court.

3. Section 7210—earnings stripping. Section 7210 adds subsection (j) to Code section 163 in order to limit interest deductions of U.S. corporations attributable to interest payments and accruals to certain related persons who are wholly or partially exempt from U.S. income tax on such income. A deduction for interest paid (or accrued) to a 50 percent or greater owner (including a constructive owner) which pays no U.S. tax on such interest is disallowed up to the amount of the "excess interest expense" of a payor corporation with a debt-to-equity ratio in excess of 1.5 to 1 at the end of the tax year. Excess interest expense is defined as the amount by which the corporation's "net interest expense" exceeds 50 percent of its "adjusted taxable income" plus any excess limitation carryforward. Net interest expense is any excess of interest paid or accrued over interest income received. Adjusted taxable income is taxable income before deductions for interest expense, net operating losses, depreciation, depletion or amortization. A corporation will have an excess limitation amount to the extent that its net interest expense is less than 50 percent of its adjusted taxable income.

Section 7210 will affect those LBOs financed with debt from related foreign or tax-exempt lenders. Thus its application could affect the financing of some LBOs.

4. Section 7211—corporate equity reduction transactions ("CERTs"). Section 7211 amends Code section 172 to limit the car-

27. Under the fixed investment trust regulations, it is not clear that such targeted bifurcation can be accomplished without creating an association taxable as a corporation. See Reg. section 301.7701–4(c).

28. H.Rep. No. 247, 101st Cong., 1st Sess. 1236 (1989).

ryback of a net operating loss ("NOL") to the extent it is attributable to interest expense allocable to a CERT. Such portion of an NOL, which may occur as much as two years after the year in which the CERT occurs, cannot be carried back to a tax year before the CERT occurred.

A CERT is a "major stock acquisition" (generally an acquisition by a corporation of at least 50 percent by vote or value of the stock of another corporation) or an "excess distribution." An "excess distribution" generally is any excess of aggregate distributions with respect to a corporation's stock over the greater of (a) 150 percent of the average of distributions made by the corporation in the preceding three years, or (b) 10 percent of the fair market value of the stock of such corporation at the beginning of the tax year. Interest is allocated to a CERT to the extent that the corporation's debt could have been reduced absent expenditures on the CERT. Such allocated deductions may not exceed the increase in average interest expenditures incurred by the corporation. A corporation with less than $1 million of allocable interest deductions will be treated as having no allocable interest deductions.

In some cases, deferral of the benefit of an NOL carryback attributable to interest expense connected with a CERT will prevent an immediate refund of previously paid corporate taxes. The CERT provision was enacted to prohibit corporations from financing leveraged transactions in part through tax refunds generated by carrybacks of NOLs caused by the payment of interest expense on debt incurred to finance the transaction.

* * *

IV. WHERE DO WE GO FROM HERE?

The Revenue Reconciliation Act of 1989 did not seriously alter the tax treatment of the financing of most leveraged buyouts. Certainly a number of key members of Congress have the view that more should be done to limit the tax deductibility of interest, particularly in the LBO context. It is likely that this concern will continue to focus on the mezzanine indebtedness, particularly in situations where debt-to-equity ratios are relatively high. Indeed, section 7202 provides a natural base for expanding the bifurcation approach to cover all high yield subordinated debt—and Congress could even claim that "simplification" was achieved in the process if some of the intricacies of section 7202 could be expunged from the Code.

* * *

ILLUSTRATIVE MATERIAL

A. CORPORATE ACQUISITION INDEBTEDNESS

In the late 1960's Congress became concerned over acquisition activities which involved as the payment vehicle the use of various kinds of debt instruments, frequently convertible into the common stock of the acquiring corporation. This use of convertible debt had several advantages in the acquisition. Because interest on the debentures was deductible the corporation was willing to pay a much higher price for the acquired corporation; if the selling shareholders could report the gain under the installment method of section 453, taxation of the gain realized on the transaction could be deferred for many years; and the convertibility feature gave to the shareholders of the acquired corporation the opportunity to secure an equity interest in the acquiring corporation at a future date.

In the Tax Reform Act of 1969, Congress took several steps to restrict the use of convertible debentures by corporations engaged in aggressive acquisition programs. Installment payment treatment under section 453 was denied to selling shareholders who received readily marketable debentures. See section 453(f)(4). The original issue discount rules, discussed supra, page 432, required the debenture holders to include the discount in income over the life of the debentures. Finally, Congress added section 279, which disallows the interest deduction to the acquiring corporation on certain "corporate acquisition indebtedness".

In brief, section 279 disallows a deduction for interest on debt obligations issued by a corporation to acquire the stock or assets of another corporation (in the case of asset acquisitions only if such assets constitute at least two-thirds of the value of all of the assets used in the trades or businesses carried on by the acquired corporation) if all of the following conditions are met:

(1) The obligation is subordinated to the claims of trade creditors generally or expressly subordinated to any substantial amount of unsecured indebtedness, whether presently outstanding or subsequently issued, of the issuing corporation;

(2) The obligation is convertible into the stock of the issuing corporation or is part of an investment unit which includes an option to acquire stock in the issuing corporation (through warrants, rights, etc.);

(3) Either the ratio of debt to equity of the issuing corporation after the issuance of the obligation exceeds 2:1, or the "projected earnings" of the issuing corporation (or of the combined corporations, if "control" has been acquired), exceeds three times the annual interest to be paid or incurred with respect to the obligation.

In order to avoid the disallowance of the interest deduction under section 279, a corporation need only avoid conditions (1) or (2), or meet the conditions of (3). Thus, for example, a corporation's obligations will not be affected by section 279 if not subordinated to trade creditors generally, even though the obligations may be subordinated to a very substantial amount of secured debt. In addition, as another hurdle to the application of section 279 interest on "acquisition indebtedness" must exceed $5 million annually. For a corporation which pays 8 percent interest, this means that it can have outstanding $62.5 million dollars of debt without running afoul of section 279. There is also a de minimis rule which provides that section 279 will not apply where the issuing corporation after the transaction owns less than 5 percent of the voting stock of the corporation whose stock has been acquired with the debt. Finally, the provisions in section 279(d)(3) and (4) offer means for removing the section 279 "taint" once acquired.

The debt-equity principles discussed supra, page 384, take precedence over section 279, so that it would be possible for an obligation to fall outside the conditions of section 279 but for a deduction for the interest on the obligation still to be disallowed on the grounds that the instrument constituted an equity instrument. See Regulations, section 1.279–1, –7. Proposals have been made in Congress to disallow interest on all acquisition debt above a de minimus amount. Congress has not been willing to take such an extreme step.

B. ANOTHER VIEW OF THE LEVERAGED BUYOUT ISSUE

Professor Michael Graetz (who was appointed Deputy Assistant Secretary of the Treasury for Tax Policy in 1990) offered another perspective on the leverage buyout issue, which is discussed, in part, in the following excerpt from GRAETZ, THE TAX ASPECTS OF LEVERAGED BUYOUTS AND OTHER CORPORATE FINANCIAL RESTRUCTURINGS, 42 TAX NOTES 721 (1989):

"It is no small irony that this year marks the twentieth anniversary of two well-known "solutions" to the kinds of problems we are discussing here today. The first is section 385, added to the Internal Revenue Code in 1969, which, as every schoolchild knows, delegated to Treasury regulatory authority to resolve the question how to distinguish between debt and equity. The Treasury Department failed to produce as much as a whimper in this regard until it issued proposed regulations in 1980 that ultimately were withdrawn in 1983 when the enterprise attempting to distinguish debt from equity based on their economic substance once again returned to a moribund state.

"The 1969 Tax Reform Act also added section 279 to the Code in an effort to restrict deductibility of interest on acquisition indebtedness, apparently on the view that, like construction period interest, such interest is in the nature of a capital expenditure. Corporate financiers, however, apparently have not found section 279 to be even a tiny barrier to corporate financial restructurings or LBOs.

"The two decades of experience with these laws suggest great caution in attempting to enact solutions that require the recharacterization of debt as equity or that attempt to limit a disallowance of interest to indebtedness incurred for a particular purpose, such as a hostile (or even any) takeover. The past two decades also teach that there is little gain and no stability to be had from such marginal tinkering as opposed to beginning to address the underlying fundamental income tax problems. * * *

"In my view, the least propitious course for Congress to take now lies in proposals for legislation aimed at limiting deductions for interest on indebtedness incurred in connection with corporate acquisitions. If LBOs are the subject, the problem is the "L," not the BO. (It has not been an auspicious time for "L" words.) Erosion of the corporate tax base identical to that which occurs with a leveraged buyout may be accomplished, without any takeover at all, by a corporate recapitalization that substitutes debt for equity, for example, by a corporation using borrowed funds to purchase its own stock from its shareholders or by incurring debt to finance a large extraordinary dividend. Indeed, it is so obvious from the perspective of the corporate income tax that buyouts or takeovers are not the critical problem, that one cannot help but suspect that many of these proposals are being advanced either because members of Congress perceive political gains from corporate-takeover bashing or are acting in response to corporate managers who would applaud any legislation that would make hostile takeovers more difficult.

* * *

"Somewhat greater promise may lie in proposals of the sort recently put forward by Professor William Andrews of the Harvard Law School in connection with his study of the corporate income tax for the American Law Institute (ALI). * * * Professor Andrews regards corporate distributions rather than corporate debt as the culprit. This vision seems to be grounded in concerns that the taxes that are imposed on the distributee of corporate assets often are inadequate to compensate for the revenues lost due to the removal of cash or other assets from corporate solution. This problem certainly has been exacerbated in recent years by the trend to share repurchases and other nondividend distributions. The goal of Professor Andrews' most recent proposal—a new minimum tax of 28 percent on certain corporate distributions—seems to be to maintain the revenue potential of the currently existing corporate tax base, while simultaneously precluding immediate gains to existing shareholders from increased share prices due to the elimination of future corporate taxes on existing equity.

* * *

"Coupled with his earlier ALI proposal for allowing limited deductions for dividends on new equity and disallowing a related portion of interest deductions, Andrews' proposals seem to imply that the corporate income tax should be a tax on all income from existing equity, on no income from existing debt, and on income above a specified rate of return on both new equity and new debt. It is difficult to know why this is an appropriate vision of a corporate income tax.

"To be sure, most of the transactions that are now threatening the corporate income tax base involve both debt and distributions, and a law that successfully addresses either aspect of the problem may preserve corporate tax revenues. In addition, there is no consensus favoring comprehensive interest deduction limitations designed to solve the problem of debt-financed distributions, and the ability of corporations to uncouple their borrowing and their distributions makes such solutions elusive. A corporation, for example, might use accumulated cash reserves to buy back its own stock and then at a later date borrow to finance new investments in plant and equipment. If interest deductions on such subsequent borrowing are allowed in full and no tax is imposed due to the distribution, a result identical, from the perspective of the corporate tax, to a debt-financed share repurchase or even a leveraged buyout would be achieved. If this kind of corporate tax reduction is to be prevented, either the debt or the distribution must trigger additional taxes.

"I continue to believe, however, that the core of the tax problem lies in the age-old corporate tax distinction between debt and equity, rather than in the removal of assets from corporate solution. You may test your own intuitions about whether distributions or debt are the principal problem by evaluating two extreme versions of each transaction:

- a complete liquidation of corporate equity built up through retained earnings; and
- a purchase of a debt-financed corporate asset.

"The latter case provides the classic illustration of the bias of current law in favor of new debt rather than new equity as a source of corporate capital. To date, I fail to see any reason for a special corporate tax in the former case, and I would be inclined generally to distinguish the case of a genuine corporate contraction from the far more typical case where the equity distributed is either simultaneously or subsequently replaced by debt.

* * *

"Congress should reject gerrymandered ad hoc solutions designed to preserve the status quo, and, instead, seize this opportunity to move—slowly perhaps, but with a clear sense of direction—toward true corporate income tax reform by embarking on a path that ultimately would provide equal corporate income tax treatment for debt and equity—in other words, to move in the direction of an integrated corporate income tax." (723–724)

C. REFERENCES

Yin, A Proposed Tax on Corporate Distributions, 67 Taxes 962 (1989); Golub and Henderson, Tax Advantages and Pitfalls Facing Highly Leveraged Corporations, 67 Taxes 917 (1989); Warren, Recent Corporate Restructuring and the Corporate Tax System, 42 Tax Notes 715 (1989); Jensen, Effects of LBOs on Tax Revenues of the U.S. Treasury, 42 Tax Notes 727; Thompson, A Suggested Approach to Debt/Equity Issues and Leveraged Acquisitions, 42 Tax Notes 483 (1989); Bryan, Leveraged Buyouts and Tax Policy, 65 N.C.L.Rev. 1039 (1987); Canellos, The Over-Leveraged Acquisition, 39 Tax Lawyer 91 (1985).

CHAPTER 17

TAX FREE ACQUISITIVE REORGANIZATIONS

SECTION 1. EARLY JUDICIAL BACKGROUND

MARR v. UNITED STATES

Supreme Court of the United States, 1925.
268 U.S. 536.

MR. JUSTICE BRANDEIS delivered the opinion of the Court.

Prior to March 1, 1913, Marr and wife purchased 339 shares of the preferred and 425 shares of the common stock of the General Motors Company of New Jersey for $76,400. In 1916, they received in exchange for this stock 451 shares of the preferred and 2,125 shares of the common stock of the General Motors Corporation of Delaware which (including a small cash payment) had the aggregate market value of $400,866.57. The difference between the cost of their stock in the New Jersey corporation and the value of the stock in the Delaware corporation was $324,466.57. The Treasury Department ruled that this difference was gain or income under the Act of September 8, 1916, * * *

The exchange of securities was effected in this way. The New Jersey corporation had outstanding $15,000,000 of 7 per cent. preferred stock and $15,000,000 of the common stock; all shares being of the par value of $100. It had accumulated from profits a large surplus. The actual value of the common stock was then $842.50 a share. Its officers caused to be organized the Delaware corporation with an authorized capital of $20,000,000 in 6 per cent. nonvoting preferred stock and $82,600,000 in common stock; all shares being of the par value of $100. The Delaware corporation made to stockholders in the New Jersey corporation the following offer for exchange of securities: For every share of common stock of the New Jersey corporation, five shares of common stock of the Delaware corporation. For every share of the preferred stock of the New Jersey corporation, one and one-third shares of preferred stock of the Delaware corporation. In lieu of a certificate for fractional shares of stock in the Delaware corporation, payment was to be made in cash at the rate of $100 a share for its preferred and at the rate of $150 a share for its common stock. On this basis all the common stock of the New Jersey corporation was exchanged and all the preferred stock except a few shares. These few were redeemed in cash. For acquiring the stock of the New Jersey corporation only $75,000,000 of the common stock of the Delaware corporation was needed. The remaining $7,600,000 of the authorized common stock was either sold or held for sale as additional capital should be desired. The Delaware corporation, having thus become the owner of all the outstanding stock of the New Jersey corporation, took a transfer of its assets and assumed its liabilities. The latter was then dissolved.

It is clear that all new securities issued in excess of an amount equal to the capitalization of the New Jersey corporation represented income earned by it; that the new securities received by the Marrs in excess of the cost of the securities of the New Jersey corporation theretofore held were financially the equivalent of $324,466.51 in cash; and that Congress intended to tax as income of stockholders such gains when so distributed. The serious question for decision is whether it had power to do so. Marr contends that, since the new corporation was organized to take over the assets and continue the business of the old, and his capital remained invested in the same business enterprise, the additional securities distributed were in legal effect a stock dividend; and that under the rule of Eisner v. Macomber, 252 U.S. 189, 40 S.Ct. 189, applied in Weiss v. Stearn, 265 U.S. 242, 44 S.Ct. 490,[1] he was not taxable thereon as income, because he still held the whole investment. The government insists that identity of the business enterprise is not conclusive; that gain in value resulting from profits is taxable as income, not only when it is represented by an interest in a different business enterprise or property, but also when it is represented by an essentially different interest in the same business enterprise or property; that, in the case at bar, the gain actually made is represented by securities with essentially different characteristics in an essentially different corporation; and that, consequently, the additional value of the new securities, although they are still held by the Marrs, is income under the rule applied in United States v. Phellis, 257 U.S. 156, 42 S.Ct. 63;[2] Rockefeller v. United States, 257 U.S. 176, 42 S.Ct. 68;[3] and

1. [Ed.] Weiss v. Stearn (1924): Stockholders of an Ohio corporation deposited their stock, par $5,000,000, with a trust company. A banking group deposited $7,500,000 cash. A new Ohio corporation was then formed by the depositors with $25,000,000 authorized stock. The new corporation acquired the assets of the old corporation, and the latter dissolved. The bankers took one-half of the stock of the new company. The other half and the $7,500,000 cash were distributed pro rata to the shareholders of the old corporation, so that for each $100 par share they received five $50 par shares (actual value $30 per share) of new stock and $150 cash. The government contended there was a sale of stock for stock and cash. The Court held there was a sale of only half of the stock interest, so that one half of the former stock was exchanged for cash and a non-taxable stock dividend received on the balance.

2. [Ed.] United States v. Phellis (1921): The taxpayer held common stock in a New Jersey corporation. Its assets were transferred to a Delaware corporation for debentures and common stock. Some of the debentures and some cash retained by the New Jersey corporation were used to retire its bonds and preferred stock. The common stock of the Delaware corporation was then distributed as a dividend by the New Jersey corporation, so that the taxpayer received two Delaware shares for each New Jersey share, which he retained. The New Jersey company continued as a holding company, owning only debentures of the Delaware corporation. The market value of the combined Delaware and New Jersey shares equalled the market value of the New Jersey shares prior to the transaction. The Court upheld the Commissioner's treatment of the value of the Delaware shares as a taxable dividend.

3. [Ed.] Rockefeller v. United States (1921): The taxpayer was a share holder in a Kansas corporation producing and transporting oil. Another Kansas corporation was formed and the pipe line business transferred to it in exchange for its stock. These new shares were then distributed to stockholders of the old corporation, who retained their old shares. The Court sus-

Cullinan v. Walker, 262 U.S. 134, 43 S.Ct. 495.[4] In our opinion the government is right.

In each of the five cases named, as in the case at bar, the business enterprise actually conducted remained exactly the same. In United States v. Phellis, in Rockefeller v. United States, and in Cullinan v. Walker, where the additional value in new securities distributed was held to be taxable as income, there had been changes of corporate identity. That is, the corporate property, or a part thereof, was no longer held and operated by the same corporation; and, after the distribution, the stockholders no longer owned merely the same proportional interest of the same character in the same corporation. In Eisner v. Macomber and in Weiss v. Stearn, where the additional value in new securities was held not to be taxable, the identity was deemed to have been preserved. In Eisner v. Macomber the identity was literally maintained. There was no new corporate entity. The same interest in the same corporation was represented after the distribution by more shares of precisely the same character. It was as if the par value of the stock had been reduced, and three shares of reduced par value stock had been issued in place of every two old shares. That is, there was an exchange of certificates but not of interests. In Weiss v. Stearn a new corporation had, in fact, been organized to take over the assets and business of the old. Technically there was a new entity; but the corporate identity was deemed to have been substantially maintained because the new corporation was organized under the laws of the same state, with presumably the same powers as the old. There was also no change in the character of securities issued. By reason of these facts, the proportional interest of the stockholder after the distribution of the new securities was deemed to be exactly the same as if the par value of the stock in the old corporation had been reduced, and five shares of reduced par value stock had been issued in place of every two shares of the old stock. Thus, in Weiss v. Stearn, as in Eisner v. Macomber, the transaction was considered, in essence, an exchange of certificates representing the same interest, not an exchange of interests.

In the case at bar, the new corporation is essentially different from the old. A corporation organized under the laws of Delaware does not have the same rights and powers as one organized under the laws of New Jersey. Because of these inherent differences in rights and powers, both the preferred and the common stock of the old corporation is an essentially different thing from stock of the same general kind in

tained the Commissioner's treatment of the value of the pipe line shares as a taxable dividend.

4. [Ed.] Cullinan v. Walker (1923): The taxpayer was a shareholder in a Texas corporation producing and transporting oil. The corporation dissolved, and liquidating trustees transferred the producing business to a new Texas company and the pipe line business to a second new Texas company in exchange for stocks and bonds of each. The stock was transferred to a newly created Delaware corporation in return for the latter's stock. The stock of the Delaware corporation and the bonds of the new Texas companies were transferred to the shareholders of the old Texas corporation. The Court sustained a tax on the taxpayer's gain, determined by the difference between the value of the new stock and bonds and the cost of the old stock.

the new. But there are also adventitious differences, substantial in character. A 6 per cent. nonvoting preferred stock is an essentially different thing from a 7 per cent. voting preferred stock. A common stock subject to the priority of $20,000,000 preferred and a $1,200,000 annual dividend charge is an essentially different thing from a common stock subject only to $15,000,000 preferred and a $1,050,000 annual dividend charge. The case at bar is not one in which after the distribution the stockholders have the same proportional interest of the same kind in essentially the same corporation.

Affirmed.

The separate opinion of MR. JUSTICE VAN DEVANTER, MR. JUSTICE MCREYNOLDS, MR. JUSTICE SUTHERLAND, and MR. JUSTICE BUTLER.

We think this cause falls within the doctrine of Weiss v. Stearn, 265 U.S. 242, 44 S.Ct. 490, and that the judgment below should be reversed. The practical result of the things done was but the reorganization of a going concern. The business and assets were not materially changed, and the stockholder received nothing actually severed from his original capital interest—nothing differing in substance from what he already had.

Weiss v. Stearn did not turn upon the relatively unimportant circumstance that the new and old corporations were organized under the laws of the same state, but upon the approved definition of income from capital as something severed therefrom and received by the taxpayer for his separate use and benefit. Here stockholders got nothing from the old business or assets except new statements of their undivided interests, and this, as we carefully pointed out, is not enough to create taxable income.

ILLUSTRATIVE MATERIAL

A. STATUTORY NONRECOGNITION

By the time *Marr* was decided the Internal Revenue Code already contained rudimentary provisions for nonrecognition in certain corporate reorganizations. The first such provisions were enacted in 1918 (and thus did not apply to the transaction in *Marr,* which occurred in 1916), and these early statutes were exceedingly simplistic. For example, both the 1924 and 1928 Acts defined a tax-free reorganization as follows:

"[A] merger or consolidation (including the acquisition by one corporation of at least a majority of the voting stock and at least a majority of the total number of shares of all other classes of stock of another corporation, or substantially all the properties of another corporation)." The statutory definition of reorganization was expanded and refined through the 1930's. Most of the basic principles regarding nonrecognition, however, were in place by 1928. Further changes were made when the 1954 Code was adopted, and a number of refinements have been enacted since that time.

B. JUDICIAL LIMITATIONS

Because the statutory provisions governing a wide range of corporate reorganizations and acquisitions remained relatively simple until the mid–

1930's, the courts imposed a number of judicial limitations on the operation of the reorganization provisions. Although the current statutory provisions and regulations are much more detailed than their antecedents, these judicial limitations continue to be important. The most significant judicial doctrines limiting the application of the reorganization provisions are (1) the continuity of interest doctrine, (2) the business purpose doctrine, and (3) the step transaction doctrine. These judicial limitations on the applicability of the reorganization provisions are discussed in further detail infra, page 757.

C. REFERENCES

R. Paul, Studies in Federal Taxation, Third Series (1940) 3–42; Satterlee, The Income Tax Definition or Reorganization, 12 Tax Mag. 639 (1934); Miller, Hendricks and Everett, Reorganizations and Other Exchanges in Federal Income Taxation (1931); Hall, Exchange of Securities in Corporate Reorganization As Income, 20 Ill.L.Rev. 601 (1926).

SECTION 2. THE PRESENT STATUTORY SCHEME

INTERNAL REVENUE CODE: Sections 1001; 354(a), (b); 355; 356; 357; 358; 361; 362; 368.

REGULATIONS: Section 1.368–1(a)–(c).

A. INTRODUCTORY NOTE

The corporate reorganization sections cover a great variety of corporate transformations. In general these sections are designed to permit business transactions involving certain corporate acquisitions and readjustments to be carried out without a tax being incurred by the participating corporations or their shareholders at the time of the transaction. The policy rationale for according nonrecognition to these transactions is that while such acquisitions and readjustments may produce changes in the form of a business enterprise, these changes do not involve a change in the nature or character of the relation of the owners of the enterprise to that enterprise sufficient to warrant taxation of gain (generally it would have been as capital gain) or allowance of loss. Since the sections, like the other nonrecognition provisions, permit nonrecognition and hence postponement of gain, and as a corollary require nonrecognition and postponement of loss, special provisions are needed to reflect such nonrecognition in the basis of the corporate assets and stock involved.

In this Chapter, the sale and purchase of a corporate business are viewed from the standpoint of the provisions permitting deferral of gain recognition in such transactions (usually referred to as "tax free" reorganizations). The transactions covered are the same in form as those considered in Chapter 16, i.e., the sale may be effected by the transfer of stock or assets. But the purchasing medium is different. In general, the acquiring corporation utilizes its stock, rather than cash or notes, to make the acquisition. As a policy matter, consider whether this difference justifies such a radical difference in tax treatment, particularly where publicly traded corporations are involved. Further, within the tax free reorganization provisions themselves, small difference in form can produce significantly different tax results. Consider whether these differences are either justified or necessary. Perhaps in no other area of corporate taxation is Professor Eustice's dictum more apt: "In subchapter C, form *is* the substance."

In addition to "acquisitive" reorganizations, there are a number of other corporate readjustments which are governed by the reorganization provisions. Although the acquisition of one corporation by another may be furthered by one these types of reorganization, more frequently they involve a realignment of ownership of a single corporation. Such nonacquisitive reorganizations are considered in subsequent chapters.

B. DEFINITION OF REORGANIZATION

The essential nonrecognition sections are 354(a) and 361(a). But they operate only after it has been determined that a "reorganization", a term that is defined in the Code, has occurred. Thus, reference first must be made to the definition of that term in section 368(a). Seven basic situations are covered; and these are the only situations included within the term "reorganization." Section 368(a)(1) states that the term "reorganization" "*means* " rather than "*includes* ".

The reorganizations considered in this Chapter are defined as follows:

Type (A) Mergers. Section 368(a)(1)(A) describes a merger or consolidation in compliance with the state statutes permitting such transactions—as where X Corporation merges into Y Corporation or X Corporation and Y Corporation consolidate into new Z Corporation.[1] X Corporation and Y Corporation may be existing parent and subsidiary corporations, or may be corporations that have not previously been related. Where Y Corporation acquires the assets of X Corporation in a statutory merger, Y Corporation may then transfer part or all of the assets to to its controlled subsidiary,[2] S Corporation, without disqualifying the (A) reorganization. See section 368(a)(2)(C).

In addition, section 368(a)(2)(D) permits S Corporation, which may either be an existing or a newly-created subsidiary of Y Corporation, to acquire the assets of X Corporation in a statutory merger between S Corporation and X Corporation in which the shareholders of X Corporation receive the stock of Y Corporation, the parent corporation, for "substantially all" of the properties of X Corporation if (1) the transac-

1. See Regulations, section 1.368–2(b); Russell v. Commissioner, 40 T.C. 810, 822 (1963), aff'd per curiam, 345 F.2d 534 (5th Cir.1965) (failure to follow state merger laws prevented (A) reorganization).

2. "Control" is defined in section 368(c) as ownership of 80 percent of the total combined voting power of all classes of stock entitled to vote and 80 percent of the total number of shares of all other classes of stock. Rev.Rul. 59–259, 1959–2 Cum. Bull. 115, interpreted the statute to require ownership of 80 percent of each class of nonvoting stock.

tion would have qualified as an (A) reorganization if the merger had been directly into Y Corporation,[3] and (2) no stock of S Corporation is used in the transaction. If these conditions are met, the transaction will be treated as an (A) reorganization. The section 368(a)(2)(D) transaction frequently is referred to as a "forward" triangular reorganization.

Section 368(a)(2)(E) permits a "reverse" triangular merger to qualify under certain specified conditions.[4] Here, rather than a merger of X Corporation into S Corporation (using the stock of Y Corporation), S Corporation is merged into X Corporation, with the shareholders of X Corporation receiving stock of Y Corporation. This transaction qualifies if (1) after the transaction X Corporation holds substantially all of its properties and the properties of S Corporation (other than stock of Y Corporation which may have been issued to S Corporation to be distributed in the transaction to the shareholders of X Corporation), and (2) in the transaction, the former shareholders of X Corporation exchange for voting stock of Y Corporation an amount of stock in X Corporation which constitutes *control* of X Corporation. If these conditions are met, the transaction will qualify as an (A) reorganization.

Under section 368(a)(2)(E), X Corporation ends up as a subsidiary of Y Corporation, replacing S Corporation. In contrast, in a section 368(a)(2)(D) transaction, X Corporation ends up as a part of S Corporation. In both cases, however, the shareholders of X Corporation become shareholders of Y Corporation. The "triangular merger" leaves the shareholders of X Corporation in the same position as in the "two corporation" direct merger of X Corporation and Y Corporation, but with the assets of X Corporation transferred to a subsidiary of Y Corporation. The same result occurs under section 368(a)(2)(C). In effect, all of the subparagraphs are designed to qualify as tax-free the differing merger mechanics utilized to obtain the same end result. However, the statutory development has not been an orderly one and as outlined above, there are different technical requirements to be satisfied depending on the route chosen to reach the end result. These technical differences are of such a magnitude—for example the requirement in section 368(a)(2)(E) that the acquiring corporation use its voting stock as consideration as opposed to the allowance of the use of nonvoting stock in a section 368(a)(2)(D) transaction—that it is often more useful to think of section 369(a)(2)(D) and (E) transactions as representing two separate and independent forms of corporate reorganization.

Type (B) Stock-for-Stock Exchanges. The acquisition by one corporation of another corporation through the acquisition of the latter's

3. The restriction that the transaction "would have qualified" as an (A) reorganization if it had involved Y Corporation directly does not require that the hypothetical merger would have been permissible under state merger statutes; it has reference to qualification under judicially developed restrictions on tax-free reorganizations such as "business purpose," "continuity of interest," etc. discussed, infra, pages 757, et seq.; see Regulations, section 1.368–2(b)(2).

4. A reverse merger is one in which the corporation to be acquired is the surviving corporation.

stock from its shareholders—as where Y Corporation acquires the stock of X Corporation from the shareholders of X Corporation, so that Y Corporation now owns X Corporation—may qualify under section 368(a)(1)(B). The shareholders of X Corporation become shareholders in Y Corporation. They may be minority or majority shareholders, depending on the amount of stock issued by Y Corporation, which in turn would depend on the relative size of X Corporation and Y Corporation. If X Corporation is liquidated (which may be accomplished under section 332 without recognition of gain or loss), the end result is the same as either a statutory merger under (A) above or a stock-for-assets acquisition under (C), below.

In order to qualify as a (B) reorganization, after the stock-for-stock exchange, the acquiring corporation must have *control* of the acquired corporation, as defined by the 80 percent standard in section 368(c). In addition, the acquisition of stock of X Corporation, if it is to constitute a reorganization, must be *solely* in return for *voting stock* of Y Corporation.

There is no requirement that 80 percent or more of the stock of X Corporation be acquired in one transaction. Thus, any particular acquisition is a reorganization if after that acquisition Y Corporation has "control" of X Corporation. Hence, while a previous acquisition of some shares of X Corporation for cash or non-voting stock, or for voting stock but without "control", would not constitute a reorganization, the earlier acquisition would not prevent a later separate acquisition for voting stock from being a reorganization if after the latter acquisition the requisite 80 percent of the share of X Corporation were held by Y Corporation as a result of the several acquisitions. This acquisition of control over a period of time is called "creeping control." Even though this rule has been in the statute for over thirty years, its application is uncertain, in that an acquisition for cash related in time or by plan to an acquisition for stock could be treated as one transaction and prevent a reorganization, since the "acquisition" would not be solely for voting stock. Regulations, section 1.368–2(c).

A transaction is not disqualified as a (B) reorganization if, after the transaction, Y Corporation in turn transfers the stock of X Corporation to its subsidiary, S Corporation. Section 368(a)(2)(C). In addition, S Corporation may acquire the stock of X Corporation solely in return for the *voting* stock of Y Corporation, if S Corporation is a controlled subsidiary of Y Corporation.

Type (C) Stock-for-Assets Exchanges. The acquisition by one corporation of another corporation through the acquisition of substantially all its assets—as where Y Corporation acquires the assets rather than the stock (as in (B) above) of X Corporation, sometimes referred to as a "practical merger"—may qualify under section 368(a)(1)(C). Subject to a limited exception, the acquisition must be *solely* by means of the *voting* stock of Y Corporation. X Corporation need not end up with any specific percentage of the shares of Y Corporation. The important point is that Y Corporation has obtained all or substantially all of X Corporation's assets—thus paralleling the acquisition under (B) as far as quantity goes. As part of the overall transaction, X Corporation must be liquidated, distributing the Y Corporation stock it receives, as well as any other assets it has retained, to its shareholders. As for the "substantially all the assets" requirement, a transfer of 90 percent of the net assets and 70 percent of the gross assets is considered by the Internal Revenue Service clearly to qualify.[5] Depending on the circumstances, however, lower percentages may qualify, particularly if the retained assets are used to pay creditors.

While the acquisition in general must be solely for the voting stock of Y Corporation, there are several exceptions which allow the use of other consideration. First, the assumption by Y Corporation of the liabilities of X Corporation or the acquisition subject to its liabilities does not prevent the acquisition from being regarded as solely for voting stock. Second, cash or other property may be used if at least 80 percent of *all* of the assets of X Corporation are acquired for voting stock. See section 368(a)(2)(B). Any additional assets may be acquired for cash, other property, or other stock. However, in applying the 20 percent limitation, liabilities of X Corporation which are assumed are treated as cash. Finally, the assets of X Corporation may be acquired for the voting stock of a parent, Z Corporation, of which Y Corporation is a controlled subsidiary. Similarly, if the acquisition was made directly by Z Corporation, it may then transfer the assets to Y Corporation without destroying the reorganization. Or if the acquisition was by Y Corporation but for the voting stock of Z Corporation, Y Corporation may then transfer the assets to its controlled subsidiary S Corporation. See section 368(a)(2)(C).

Subparagraphs (A), (B) and (C) of section 368(a)(1), together with subparagraphs (D) and (E) of section 368(a)(2), thus cover various methods by which several corporations may be combined into one ownership. A chain store swallowing a corner grocery store (obtaining its assets directly under (C), or obtaining its stock under (B) and then liquidating it or keeping it alive as a subsidiary, or pursuing a statutory merger under (A)), so that the owners of the grocery are really "selling" their business for stock, is within these sections. So is the amalgamation of two industrial giants. While the various statutorily deferred reorganizations overlap to a considerable extent, there are differences among them which can influence the choice of the particular reorganization route to be utilized.

C. NONRECOGNITION AND BASIS: CORPORATE TRANSFERORS AND TRANSFEREES

As noted previously, section 368 does not govern the tax consequences of a reorganization; it merely defines a reorganization. The

5. See Rev.Proc. 77–37, 1977–2 Cum. Bull. 568.

operative provisions which provide for nonrecognition and the attendant basis consequences appear in other sections of the Code. Section 361(a) provides for nonrecognition of gain to the corporation transferring its assets, the acquired corporation (X Corporation in the above examples), in the situations constituting reorganizations under section 368(a). Thus, X Corporation above would have a tax-free exchange with respect to the assets transferred by it in type (A) and (C) reorganizations.[6] Section 361(a) is applicable only if the exchange is solely for stock or securities. Qualification as an (A) reorganization does not guarantee complete nonrecognition under section 361(a) since property other than stock or securities may form part of the consideration under the merger or consolidation (as long as some stock is present). If the reorganization qualifies as a type (C) reorganization, however, this condition usually is satisfied because in most cases only voting stock will be involved. An assumption of liabilities does not violate either the "solely for voting stock" or "solely for stock or securities" requirements under the express provisions of sections 368(a)(1)(C) and 357(a). However, because in type (C) reorganizations a limited amount of property other than voting stock may pass from the acquiring corporation to the acquired corporation under section 368(a)(2)(B), qualification as a type (C) reorganization does not automatically guarantee compliance with section 361(a).

If in any of the above situations, *boot* (money, property or obligations not qualifying as stock or securities) is received by the transferor corporation, section 361(a) does not apply. If boot is received, sections 361(b) and (c) determine the consequences to the acquired transferor corporation.[7] Under section 361(b), no gain is recognized to the acquired corporation as a result of the receipt of the boot if the boot is transferred to its shareholders or creditors pursuant to the plan of reorganization. In a type (A) reorganization, such transfer takes place automatically under the state law merger statute. In a type (C) reorganization, the requirement in section 368(a)(2)(G) that the acquired corporation be liquidated generally will insure the required distribution. If the boot is distributed, the acquired corporation recognizes no gain on receipt of the boot, but under section 361(c), it recognizes gain (but apparently not loss) upon the distribution of the boot if at the time of the distribution the boot property has a fair market value in excess of basis.

Section 358 prescribes the basis which the acquired transferor corporation in type (A) and (C) reorganizations, takes in the stock, securities, and boot received in the exchange. Section 362(b) prescribes

6. A merger under section 368(a)(1)(A) is regarded as involving such a transfer of property. See Rev.Rul. 69–6, 1969–1 Cum. Bull. 104. Triangular mergers under sections 368(a)(2)(D) and (E) raise some special problems, see infra, page 852.

7. Technically speaking, section 361(c)(2) permits the distribution of stock, rights to acquire stock, or "obligations" of "another corporation which is a party to the reorganization." The scope of the term "obligations" presumably is broader than the term "securities."

the basis for the acquiring transferee corporation in type (A) and (C) reorganizations. Both transferor and transferee end up with the original basis of the transferor (aside from adjustments where boot is involved), so that possibilities of two gains or two losses exist. While section 362(b), carrying over the transferor's basis to the transferee corporation, adds to that basis any gain recognized to the transferor, as indicated above, the reorganization provisions allow little room for gain to be recognized to the transferor corporation. If, however, a reorganization does not exist, then the general rule of "cost" applies to fix the basis for the transferee corporation. Regulations, section 1.1032–1(d).

ILLUSTRATIVE MATERIAL

A. REFERENCES

Posin, Taxing Corporate Reorganizations: Purging Penelope's Web, 133 U.Pa.L.Rev. 1335 (1985); Sapienza, Tax Considerations in Corporate Reorganizations and Mergers, 60 Nw.U.L.Rev. 765 (1966); Surrey, Income Tax Problems of Corporations and Shareholders: American Law Institute Tax Project, 14 Tax L.Rev. 1 (1958); American Law Institute, Income Tax Problems of Corporations and Shareholders (1958); Papers on Corporate Distributions and Adjustments in Tax Revision Compendium, House Committee on Ways and Means, 86th Cong., 1st Sess. (1959) Vol. 3, pages 1611–1652; Darrell, The Use of Reorganization Techniques in Corporate Acquisitions, 70 Harv.L.Rev. 1183 (1957); Cohen, Silverman, Jr., Surrey, Tarleau and Warren, The Internal Revenue Code of 1954: Corporate Distributions, Organizations and Reorganizations, 68 Harv.L.Rev. 393 (1955); Paul, Selected Studies in Federal Taxation: Second Series 200 (1938).

D. EXTENT OF NONRECOGNITION AND BASIS: SHAREHOLDERS AND SECURITY HOLDERS

Sections 354 and 356 control taxation of the shareholders in acquisitive reorganization transactions. Section 358(a) prescribes exchanged basis rules for the shareholders in sections 354 and 356 exchanges.

In type (A), (B), and (C) reorganizations, the shareholders of X Corporation are exchanging their X Corporation stock for stock of Y Corporation. In type (A) and (B) reorganizations, the exchange is made between the X shareholders and Y Corporation; in a type (C) reorganization, the exchange is made upon the liquidation of X Corporation. X and Y both are parties to the reorganization under section 368(b). In type (A) and (C) reorganizations, the X Corporation shareholders also may receive securities of Y Corporation (although the receipt of securities in a type (C) reorganization is limited by section 368(a)(2)(B)). These exchanges are covered by section 354 and generally any gain or loss realized by the shareholders will not be recognized.

Section 354(a) applies only to an exchange *solely* for stock or securities, so that the presence of boot prevents its application. Suppose, however, that X Corporation transfers its assets to Y Corporation for stock of Y Corporation and cash in a transaction which qualifies as a (C) reorganization by virtue of section 368(a)(2)(B). Pursuant to section 361(b), X Corporation avoids recognition of gain by distributing the cash. This distribution, however, constitutes boot to the distributee shareholders. When Corporation X liquidates, as is required to qualify the transaction as a (C) reorganization, the accompanying exchange by the shareholders of their X Corporation stock for Y Corporation stock is not accorded complete nonrecognition under section 354(a). Section 356(a)(1) operates to provide partial nonrecognition; any realized gain is recognized but only to the extent of the boot. Loss may be not recognized.

Determination of the gain which must be recognized under the rule of section 356(a)(1) is illustrated as follows. Suppose that in a type (A) reorganization (statutory merger) individual A, a shareholder of X Corporation, surrendered shares of stock of X Corporation having a basis to A of $100 in exchange for $40 of cash and shares of Y Corporation having a fair market value of $110. A realizes a gain of $50, but only $40, an amount equal to the cash boot, must be recognized. Under section 358(a), A's basis in the Y Corporation stock would be only $100, thus accounting for the $10 of realized but unrecognized gain. If A's basis for the X Corporation stock were $120, then A would realize a gain of only $30, all of which would be recognized. The receipt of the other $10 of cash "tax-free" would be taken into account by reducing the basis of the Y Corporation stock received in the exchange from $100 to $90 pursuant to section 358(a)(1)(A).

In all of these situations, the transfer of boot to shareholders of X Corporation constitutes a distribution by a corporation to its shareholders. A safeguard is necessary to insure that distributions which in substance are dividends rather than additional consideration for the exchange of stock will be appropriately taxed. Section 356(a)(2) provides generally that if the distribution of boot pursuant to the plan of reorganization has the *effect of the distribution of a dividend*, the amount of the gain shall be taxed as a dividend and not as part of the exchange transaction. The resemblance to section 302 is apparent, but there are some differences. This provision will be considered infra, page 800.

An exchange of securities other than stock gives rise to boot under section 354(a)(2) if the corporation distributes securities of a principal amount in excess of the securities received in return. In such a case the amount of the boot as determined under section 356(d) is not the excess principal amount, but rather the fair market value of the excess principal amount.[8] See infra, page 810.

Section 357 does not apply to section 356(a), so that if any liabilities of shareholders of the acquired corporation are assumed, boot has been distributed. If the initial corporate transaction had involved a situation which could qualify as a reorganization only if solely for voting

8. Note that application of the original issue discount rules can produce a principal amount that differs from the face amount of the bond.

stock, such as a type (B) reorganization, then the presence of boot would prevent a reorganization and sections 354(a) and 356 would not be applicable at all.

If sections 354 and 356 do not apply, then the distributions are considered under section 301, 302 and 331. Sections 354 and 356 thus operate as exceptions to these other sections respecting corporate distributions and exchanges, though those other sections do not contain any explicit references to the reorganization exceptions.

SECTION 3. JUDICIAL LIMITATIONS

Professor Stanley S. Surrey wrote in an earlier edition of this book:

"The reorganization sections are written against a background of many varied business transactions. They are stated in terms of specific rules which chart a tax-free corridor through which may flow the corporate transactions intended to be so favored. But the very breadth of the transactions to which the rules could extend and the mechanical terms in which they are written combine to make that corridor a tempting avenue of tax avoidance to persons who were not intended to be the recipients of such a safe-conduct pass. This is especially true in the case of closely-held family corporations where the corporation may be readily maneuvered by the shareholders. From the very beginning the courts, prompted by the Commissioner, have undertaken the task of policing this tax-free corridor. Their guarding has been vigorous and diligent, and many a corporation or shareholder who presented a pass carefully prepared to match the literal language of the sections has nevertheless been denied entrance. As a consequence, the literal language of the sections cannot be relied upon,[9] and safe passage depends upon knowledge of the rules of the judicial gendarmerie. An attorney who reads section 368(a)(1)(A) and believes that a statutory merger always constitutes a reorganization may be sadly mistaken—his particular statutory merger may be on the judicial proscribed list if it fails to possess the necessary continuity of interest. Some of these judicial rules have been incorporated in the statute; part of their flavor is in the Regulations.[10] But most of them still remain as they originated—judicial safeguards devised to protect the underlying statutory policy. Nor is the role of the judiciary confined to enforcing rules previously announced. Anyone applying for passage through the corridor runs the risk of the judicial policeman inventing a new rule on the spot if he thinks such action is demanded. And the Internal Revenue Service, in administering the statutory provisions, is alert to bring these situations before the courts. It must be remembered that most of the taxpayers who thus prompt administrative and judicial ingenuity

9. E.g., Helvering v. Alabama Asphaltic Limestone Co., 315 U.S. 179 (1942): "It has been recognized that a transaction may not qualify as a 'reorganization' under the various revenue acts though the literal language of the section is satisfied." (182).

10. See, e.g., Regulations, sections 1.368–1(b); 1.368–1(c), referring to "plan of reorganization"; 1.368–2(a); 1.368–2(g); 1.1002–1(b), (c).

have no real business in the corridor. But when such trespassers are in the throng, the barriers designed to separate them may catch an innocent, or may force the innocent to take added precautions to identify himself. The rules may also produce some uncertainty and confusion where the innocent too closely resembles a trespasser. Some have criticized the judicial vigilance on this score. Others believe that any effort to prescribe statutory rules covering all of the everyday transactions of the business world is bound to fail unless courts and administrators are able to cope with transactions that would otherwise involve a distorted application of those rules."

Professor Surrey's words apply with equal force today. The various judicial doctrines of which he spoke will be examined throughout this chapter in the context of specific acquisition transactions. But since they apply to all forms of reorganizations, a general discussion of the most important principles follows at this point.

A. BUSINESS PURPOSE

REGULATIONS: Section 1.368–1(a)–(c).

GREGORY v. HELVERING

Supreme Court of the United States, 1935.
293 U.S. 465.

[*The Facts.* Mrs. Gregory in 1928 owned all of the stock of United Mortgage Corporation. That corporation held among its assets 1000 shares of Monitor Securities Corporation. The value of the Monitor shares exceeded their basis. Mrs. Gregory's problem was to have the Monitor shares sold and to obtain in her hands the cash received on such sale. One method would be to have the Monitor shares distributed as a dividend and then sold by her. But this would result in a tax on the value of the shares as ordinary income, which she wished to avoid. She was willing to pay some capital gains tax. The key to Mrs. Gregory's maneuvers to achieve her goals was section 112(g) of the 1928 Act. That section provided for no gain to the shareholder on the distribution by a corporation, a party to a reorganization, of stock or securities of another corporation, also a party to the reorganization, even though the shareholder did not surrender any shares, so that it in effect exempted a dividend distribution of such stock or securities. It was thus similar to present section 355 but without the latter's conditions.

Mrs. Gregory proceeded to follow the statute in literal fashion. To that end, she caused the Averill Corporation to be organized under the laws of Delaware on September 18, 1928. Three days later, the United Mortgage Corporation transferred to the Averill Corporation the 1,000 shares of Monitor stock, for which all the shares of the Averill Corporation were issued to Mrs. Gregory. This was a short-cutting step, whose effect was the same as the issuance of the Averill shares to United and their distribution by United to Mrs. Gregory. On September 24, the

Averill Corporation was dissolved, and liquidated by distributing all its assets, namely the Monitor shares, to its sole shareholder, Mrs. Gregory. No other business was ever transacted, or intended to be transacted, by Averill. She immediately sold the Monitor shares for $133,333.33. She then contended that the transfer to Averill was a reorganization as United controlled Averill; the distribution to her of Averill shares was tax free under old section 112(g); the Averill shares took part ($57,325.45) of the basis of her United shares (originally $350,000) on an allocation of her United basis based on the market values of the United and Averill shares; the liquidation of Averill and her acquisition thereby of the Monitor shares worth $133,333.33 produced a capital gain (of $76,007.88) taxable at capital gain rates; the sale of the Monitor shares resulted in no gain since the taxable liquidation resulted in a basis in her hands equal to their market value.

The Commissioner argued that the creation of the Averill Corporation was without substance and must be disregarded; consequently, the entire transaction must be considered as a distribution of the Monitor shares as a dividend, producing ordinary income of $133,333.33, the value of such shares. The sale of the Monitor shares had no tax effect under his theory, since, once taxed as a dividend, they had a basis equal to their value.

The Decision of the Board of Tax Appeals, 27 B.T.A. 223 (1932). The Board held for Mrs. Gregory:

"A statute so meticulously drafted must be interpreted as a literal expression of the taxing policy, and leaves only the small interstices for judicial consideration. The general legislative plan apparently was to recognize the corporate entity and, in view of such recognition, to specify when the gains or losses would be recognized and upon what basis they should be measured. We may not destroy the effectiveness of this statutory plan by denying recognition to the corporation and thus preventing consideration of its transactions." (225–6)

The Decision of the Circuit Court of Appeals, Second Circuit, 69 F.2d 809 (1934). The Circuit Court held for the Commissioner, in an opinion by Judge Learned Hand:

"We agree with the Board and the taxpayer that a transaction, otherwise within an exception of the tax law, does not lose its immunity, because it is actuated by a desire to avoid, or, if one choose, to evade, taxation. Any one may so arrange his affairs that his taxes shall be as low as possible; he is not bound to choose that pattern which will best pay the Treasury; there is not even a patriotic duty to increase one's taxes. U.S. v. Isham, 17 Wall. 496, 506; Bullen v. Wisconsin, 240 U.S. 625, 630, 36 S.Ct. 473. Therefore, if what was done here, was what was intended by [the section corresponding to present 368(a)(1)(D), but without the present requirement of a distribution of the stock], it is of no consequence that it was all an elaborate scheme to get rid of income taxes, as it certainly was. Nevertheless, it does not follow that Congress meant to cover such a transaction, not even though the facts answer the dictionary definitions of each term used in the statutory definition. It is quite true, as the Board has very well said, that as the articulation of a statute increases, the room for interpretation must contract; but the meaning of a sentence may be more than that of the separate words, as a melody is more than the notes, and no degree of particularity can ever obviate recourse to the setting in which all appear, and which all collectively create. The purpose of the section is plain enough; men engaged in enterprises—industrial, commercial, financial, or any other—might wish to consolidate, or divide, to add to, or subtract from, their holdings. Such transactions were not to be considered as 'realizing' any profit, because the collective interests still remained in solution. But the underlying presupposition is plain that the readjustment shall be undertaken for reasons germane to the conduct of the venture in hand, not as an ephemeral incident, egregious to its prosecution. To dodge the shareholders' taxes is not one of the transactions contemplated as corporate 'reorganizations.'

"We do not indeed agree fully with the way in which the Commissioner treated the transaction; we cannot treat as inoperative the transfer of the Monitor shares by the United Mortgage Corporation, the issue by the Averill Corporation of its own shares to the taxpayer, and her acquisition of the Monitor shares by winding up that company. The Averill Corporation had a juristic personality, whatever the purpose of its organization; the transfer passed title to the Monitor shares and the taxpayer became a shareholder in the transferee. All these steps were real, and their only defect was that they were not what the statute means by a 'reorganization,' because the transactions were no part of the conduct of the business of either or both companies; so viewed they were a sham, though all the proceedings had their usual effect. But the result is the same whether the tax be calculated as the Commissioner calculated it, or upon the value of the Averill shares as a dividend." (810–811)

On this theory the value of the Averill shares, and hence the amount taxed as a dividend, would be $133,333.33, the value of the underlying Monitor shares. The later liquidation of Averill and sale of the Monitor shares would have no tax effect since the Averill shares, taxed as a dividend, thereby obtained a basis equal to the value of the Monitor shares.]

MR. JUSTICE SUTHERLAND delivered the opinion of the Court.
* * *

It is earnestly contended on behalf of the taxpayer that since every element required by [the section of the 1928 Act corresponding to present section 368(a)(1)(D), but without the present requirement of a distribution of the stock] is to be found in what was done, a statutory reorganization was effected; and that the motive of the taxpayer thereby to escape payment of a tax will not alter the result or make unlawful what the statute allows. It is quite true that if a reorganization in reality was effected within the meaning of [that provision], the ulterior purpose mentioned will be disregarded. The legal right of a taxpayer to decrease the amount of what otherwise would be his taxes, or altogether avoid them, by means which the law permits, cannot be doubted. United States v. Isham, 17 Wall. 496, 506; Superior Oil Co. v. Mississippi, 280 U.S. 390, 395, 396, 50 S.Ct. 169; Jones v. Helvering, 63 App.D.C. 204, 71 F.2d 214, 217. But the question for determination is whether what was done, apart from the tax motive, was the thing which the statute intended. The reasoning of the court below in justification of a negative answer leaves little to be said.

When [the statutory provision] speaks of a transfer of assets by one corporation to another, it means a transfer made "in pursuance of a plan of reorganization" * * * of corporate business; and not a transfer of assets by one corporation to another in pursuance of a plan having no relation to the business of either, as plainly is the case here. Putting aside, then, the question of motive in respect of taxation altogether, and fixing the character of the proceeding by what actually occurred, what do we find? Simply an operation having no business or corporate purpose—a mere device which put on the form of a corporate reorganization as a disguise for concealing its real character, and the sole object and accomplishment of which was the consummation of a preconceived plan, not to reorganize a business or any part of a business, but to transfer a parcel of corporate shares to the petitioner. No doubt, a new and valid corporation was created. But that corporation was nothing more than a contrivance to the end last described. It was brought into existence for no other purpose; it performed, as it was intended from the beginning it should perform, no other function. When that limited function had been exercised, it immediately was put to death.

In these circumstances, the facts speak for themselves and are susceptible of but one interpretation. The whole undertaking, though conducted according to the terms of [the statutory provision], was in fact an elaborate and devious form of conveyance masquerading as a corporate reorganization, and nothing else. The rule which excludes from consideration the motive of tax avoidance is not pertinent to the situation, because the transaction upon its face lies outside the plain intent of the statute. To hold otherwise would be to exalt artifice above reality and to deprive the statutory provision in question of all serious purpose.

Judgment affirmed.

ILLUSTRATIVE MATERIAL

A. REPEAL AND RESTORATION OF FORMER SECTION 112(g).

The tax avoidance potential of former section 112(g) had led to its elimination in 1934, prior to the Supreme Court's decision in *Gregory.* But in 1951 the provision was revived in altered form as the predecessor of section 355, discussed infra, page 902.

B. JUDGE HAND ON THE GREGORY DECISION

A year after *Gregory* was decided, in Chisholm v. Commissioner, 79 F.2d 14 (2d Cir.1935), Judge Learned Hand described the *Gregory* case as follows:

"It is important to observe just what the Supreme Court held in that case. It was solicitous to reaffirm the doctrine that a man's motive to avoid taxation will not establish his liability if the transaction does not do so without it. The question always is whether the transaction under scrutiny is in fact what it appears to be in form; a marriage may be a joke; a contract may be intended only to deceive others; an agreement may have a collateral defeasance. In such cases the transaction as a whole is different from its appearance. True, it is always the intent that controls; and we need not for this occasion press the difference between intent and purpose. We may assume that purpose may be the touchstone, but the purpose which counts is one which defeats or contradicts the apparent transaction, not the purpose to escape taxation which the apparent, but not the whole, transaction would realize. In Gregory v. Helvering, supra, 293 U.S. 465, 55 S.Ct. 266, the incorporators adopted the usual form for creating business corporations; but their intent, or purpose, was merely to draught the papers, in fact not to create corporations as the court understood that word. That was the purpose which defeated their exemption, not the accompanying purpose to escape taxation; that purpose was legally neutral. Had they really meant to conduct a business by means of the two reorganized companies, they would have escaped whatever other aid they might have had, whether to avoid taxes, or to regenerate the world." (15)

And in 1948, Judge Hand said in Commissioner v. National Carbide Corporation, 167 F.2d 304 (2d Cir.1948), aff'd, 336 U.S. 422 (1949):

"In Gregory v. Helvering the taxpayer had organized a corporation only to serve as a means of transfer; it was used once and only for that purpose, and was dissolved as soon as it had done so. The Court held that it was not a 'corporation' within the meaning of that term, as Congress must be understood to have used it, because in common speech, it means a jural person created to conduct industry, commerce, charity or some other commonly practiced activity, and not to serve merely as an escape from taxation. Such a corporation might be in some contexts a 'corporation'; but words are chameleons, which reflect the color of their environment, and in a tax statute 'corporation' could not have been so intended.

"This decision has at times been thought to trench upon the doctrine—which courts are never tired of repeating—that the rights resulting from a legal transaction otherwise valid, are not different, vis-a-vis taxation, because it has been undertaken to escape taxation. That is a doctrine essential to industry and commerce in a society like our own, in which, so far as possible, business is always shaped to the form best suited to keep down taxes. Gregory v. Helvering, supra, was no exception, in spite of the fact that it was the purpose for which the taxpayer created the corporation that determined the event; for it is not the presence of an accompanying motive to escape taxation that is ever decisive, but the absence of any motive which brings the corporation within the group of those enterprises which the word ordinarily includes. Indeed, a corporation may be a 'sham' and 'unreal,' when the only reason for its creation was 'to deter the creditors of one of the partners,' who organized it, for that is not an activity commonly understood to be corporate." (306–7)

C. OTHER ASPECTS OF *GREGORY*

As Randolph Paul stated: "Few cases have been the subject of such violent disagreement and confusion as the *Gregory* case. The case is all things to all men." [11] The disagreement is between those who follow the philosophy of the Board of Tax Appeals in that case and those who follow the view of Judge Hand and the Supreme Court. But while the dispute may be heated, every wise tax advisor realizes that the attitude of the *Gregory* decision is still alive today in the tax world. Tax avoidance schemes must reckon with that attitude and with judicial and administrative ingenuity in applying it. The principle of the decision is not limited to the reorganization provisions, but pervades the entire Code. The *Gregory* decision is expressed in many ways and words, all of which come to the pointed warning, "Beware—Proceed with Caution", that faces tax reduction plans having any element of artificiality or non-conformance with normal business or family conduct.

There are, as the quotations above from Judge Hand's opinions indicate, many facets to the *Gregory* "business purpose" doctrine. While the facets often overlap, there are some recognizable patterns. For example:

1. *Sham Situations.* The business purpose test is applied to disregard the existence of a particular entity or the effect of a particular status where its existence serves no function apart from its tax-saving function. This is the *Gregory* case itself.

2. *Step Transactions.* The business purpose test may be applied to disregard the separate existence of several steps and instead to judge the transaction by its end result with the intervening steps omitted. The step transaction doctrine is discussed in Part C, infra, page 775.

3. *Transactions Lacking Economic Reality.* Suppose that a transaction is entered into which involves binding legal obligations not of a transitory character, so it is not a "sham," and which in its arrangements and end result complies with the statutory requirements, so that it is not defeated by the end-result or step transaction argument. The transaction, however, lacks economic or business reality in the sense that it would not be entered into except for the benefit that results solely from the expected tax consequences. Here courts sometimes will apply the "business purpose" doctrine to defeat such plans on the ground that they represent a distortion of the function of the particular statutory provisions in question or will require that the transaction involve some "purposive" activity apart from the tax benefits to be derived. For example, Wortham Machinery Co. v. United States, 521 F.2d 160 (10th Cir.1975), denied a net operating loss carryover (otherwise available under sections 381 and 382, discussed infra, Chapters 20 and 21) to the acquiring corporation in a transaction that literally complied with the statutory requirements for a type (C) reorganization. In the transaction a corporation transferred its assets, which consisted primarily of a net operating loss carryover, to its sister corporation in exchange for that corporation's stock. The stock was distributed to the controlling shareholders of both corporations in a liquidating distribution. The court held that while the "questioned transaction was within the 'inert language' of section 368(a)(1)(C) the only attraction shown by the record for the acquisition of [the assets of the transferor] was the net operating loss carryover which [the acquiring

11. Paul, Studies in Federal Taxation, Third Series (1940) 125 and references cited.

corporation] used in its tax return to reduce its tax liability." (163) Hence, there was no business purpose for the transaction.

One or more of the above doctrines often are loosely applied by a court invoking the principles of "substance over form". As far as corporate reorganizations are concerned, the business purpose doctrine has been incorporated into Regulations, section 1.368–1(c) and –2(g), but the *Gregory* decision and the ramifications of the business purpose doctrine stand primarily as judicial warnings that *some* provisions are off limits in *some* situations. This combination of the existence of a rule permitting transactions to be disregarded but uncertainty as to when the rule will be applied has an *in terrorem* effect that dampens the enthusiasm of some would-be tax manipulators but prompts others to take a chance where little is at risk if the scheme fails. But it is difficult to see how the Internal Revenue Code could be applied successfully without the safeguards afforded by the *Gregory* doctrine and its various facets. It is a technique of statutory interpretation difficult to apply but essential to our tax system as it now operates.

B. CONTINUITY OF INTEREST

REGULATIONS: Section 1.368–2(a).

PAULSEN v. COMMISSIONER

Supreme Court of the United States, 1985.
469 U.S. 131.

JUSTICE REHNQUIST delivered the opinion of the Court.

Commerce Savings and Loan Association of Tacoma, Wash., merged into Citizens Federal Savings and Loan Association of Seattle in July 1976. Petitioners Harold and Marie Paulsen sought to treat their exchange of stock in Commerce for an interest in Citizens as a tax-free reorganization under 26 U.S.C. §§ 354(a)(1) and 368(a)(1)(A). * * *

At the time of the merger, petitioner Harold T. Paulsen was president and a director of Commerce. He and his wife, petitioner Marie B. Paulsen, held as community property 17,459 shares of "guaranty stock" in Commerce. In exchange for this stock petitioners received passbook savings accounts and time certificates of deposit in Citizens. Relying on 26 U.S.C. §§ 354(a)(1) and 368(a)(1)(A), they did not report the gain they realized on their 1976 federal income tax return because they considered the merger to be a tax-free reorganization.

Before it ceased to exist, Commerce was a state-chartered savings and loan association incorporated and operated under Washington State law. It was authorized to issue "guaranty stock," to offer various classes of savings accounts, and to make loans. Each stockholder, savings account holder, and borrower was a member of the association. Each share of stock and every $100, or fraction thereof, on deposit in a savings account carried with it one vote. Each borrower also had one vote.

The "guaranty stock" had all of the characteristics normally associated with common stock issued by a corporation. Under the bylaws, a certain amount of guaranty stock was required to be maintained as the fixed and nonwithdrawable capital of Commerce. In accordance with Wash.Rev.Code Ann. § 33.48.080 (Supp.1981), holders of guaranty stock, but no other members, had a proportionate proprietary interest in its assets and net earnings, subordinate to the claims of creditors. Dividends could not be declared or paid on the guaranty stock unless certain reserves had been accumulated and dividends had been declared and paid on withdrawable savings accounts.

Citizens is a federally chartered mutual savings and loan association under the jurisdiction of the Federal Home Loan Bank Board. 12 U.S.C. § 1461 et seq. It offers savings accounts and makes loans, but has no capital stock. Its members are its depositors and borrowers. Each savings account holder has one vote for each $100, or fraction thereof, of the withdrawal value of his savings account up to a maximum of 400 votes. Each borrower has one vote.

Citizens is owned by its depositors. Twice each year its net earnings and any surplus are to be distributed to its savings account holders pro rata to the amounts on deposit. Its net assets would similarly be distributed if liquidation or dissolution should occur. It is obligated to pay written withdrawal requests within 30 days, and may redeem any of its accounts at any time by paying the holder the withdrawal value.

The merger was effected pursuant to a "Plan of Merger," under which Commerce's stockholders exchanged all their stock for passbook savings accounts and certificates of deposit in Citizens. The plan was designed to conform to the requirements of Wash.Rev.Code § 33.40.010 (1983), which provides for mergers between business entities, and to qualify as a tax-free reorganization under the terms of §§ 354(a)(1) and 368(a)(1)(A). Under the plan, Commerce stockholders received for each share a $12 deposit in a Citizens passbook savings account, subject only to the restriction that such deposits could not be withdrawn for one year. They also had the alternative of receiving time certificates of deposit in Citizens with maturities ranging from 1 to 10 years at the same $12–per–share exchange rate. The plan further provided that former Commerce stockholders could borrow against their deposits resulting from the exchange at 1.5% above the passbook rate as opposed to a 2% differential for other depositors. Following the exchange, the merged entity continued to operate under the Citizens name.

Petitioners had a cost basis in their Commerce stock of $56,802; in the exchange they received passbook accounts and certificates of deposit worth $209,508.

* * *

Section 368(a)(1)(A) defines a "reorganization" to include "a statutory merger or consolidation," and §§ 7701(a)(3), 7701(a)(7), and 7701(a)(8) further define the terms "corporation" to include "associations," "stock" to include "shares in an association," and "shareholder" to include a "member in an association." There is no dispute that at the time of the merger Commerce and Citizens qualified as associations, petitioners qualified as shareholders, Commerce's guaranty stock and Citizens' passbook accounts and certificates of deposit qualified as stock, and the merger qualified as a statutory merger within these provisions of the Code. Accordingly, under the literal terms of the Code the transaction would qualify as a tax-free "reorganization" exchange rather than a sale or exchange on which gain must be recognized and taxes paid.

Satisfying the literal terms of the reorganization provisions, however, is not sufficient to qualify for nonrecognition of gain or loss. The purpose of these provisions is " 'to free from the imposition of an income tax purely "paper profits or losses" wherein there is no realization of gain or loss in the business sense but merely the recasting of the same interests in a different form.' " Southwest Natural Gas Co. v. Commissioner, 189 F.2d 332, 334 (CA5), cert. denied, 342 U.S. 860, 72 S.Ct. 88 (1951) (quoting Commissioner v. Gilmore's Estate, 130 F.2d 791, 794 (CA3 1942)). See Treas.Reg. § 1.368–1(b), 26 CFR § 1.368–1(b) (1984). In order to exclude sales structured to satisfy the literal terms of the reorganization provisions but not their purpose, this Court has construed the statute to also require that the taxpayer's ownership interest in the prior organization must continue in a meaningful fashion in the reorganized enterprise. Pinellas Ice & Cold Storage Co. v. Commissioner, 287 U.S. 462, 468–470, 53 S.Ct. 257, 259–260 (1933). In that case we held that "the seller must acquire an interest in the affairs of the purchasing company more definite than that incident to ownership of its short-term purchase-money notes." Id., at 470. We soon added the requirement that "this interest must be definite and material; it must represent a substantial part of the value of the thing transferred." Helvering v. Minnesota Tea Co., 296 U.S. 378, 385, 56 S.Ct. 269, 272 (1935). Compare LeTulle v. Scofield, 308 U.S. 415, 420–421, 60 S.Ct. 313, 315–316 (1940) (no retained property interest where transferor received transferee's bonds), with John A. Nelson Co. v. Helvering, 296 U.S. 374, 377, 56 S.Ct. 273, 274 (1935) (continuity of interest satisfied where nonvoting preferred stock received). Known as the "continuity-of-interest" doctrine, this requirement has been codified in Treas.Regs. §§ 1.368–1(b), 1.368–2(a).

The present case turns on whether petitioners' exchange of their guaranty stock in Commerce for their passbook savings accounts and certificates of deposit in Citizens satisfies this continuity-of-interest requirement. More generally, we must decide whether a merger of a stock savings and loan association into a mutual savings and loan association qualifies as a tax-free reorganization. Following his ruling in Rev.Rul. 69–6, 1969–1 Cum.Bull. 104, which itself apparently was at odds with his earlier policy expressed in Rev.Rul. 54–624, 1954–2 Cum. Bull. 16, the Commissioner rejected petitioners' treatment of the Commerce–Citizens merger as a tax-free reorganization under §§ 354(a)(1) and 368(a)(1)(A) and issued a statutory notice of deficiency finding petitioners liable for tax on their entire $152,706 gain.

* * *

Citizens is organized pursuant to Charter K (Rev.), 12 CFR § 544.1(b) (as of July 1, 1976), which provides for raising capital "by accepting payments on savings accounts representing share interests in the association." These shares are the association's only means of raising capital. Here they are divided into passbook accounts and certificates of deposit. In reality, these shares are hybrid instruments having both equity and debt characteristics. They combine in one instrument the separate characteristics of the guaranty stock and the savings accounts of stock associations like Commerce.

The Citizens shares have several equity characteristics. The most important is the fact that they are the only ownership instrument of the association. Each share carries in addition to its deposit value a part ownership interest in the bricks and mortar, the goodwill, and all the other assets of Citizens. Another equity characteristic is the right to vote on matters for which the association's management must obtain shareholder approval. The shareholders also receive dividends rather than interest on their accounts; the dividends are paid out of net earnings, and the shareholders have no legal right to have a dividend declared or to have a fixed return on their investment. The shareholders further have a right to a pro rata distribution of any remaining assets after a solvent dissolution.

These equity characteristics, however, are not as substantial as they appear on the surface. Unlike a stock association where the ownership of the assets is concentrated in the stockholders, the ownership interests here are spread over all of the depositors. The equity interest of each shareholder in relation to the total value of the share, therefore, is that much smaller than in a stock association. The right to vote is also not very significant. A shareholder is limited to 400 votes; thus any funds deposited in excess of $40,000 do not confer any additional votes. The vote is also diluted each time a loan is made, as each borrower is entitled to one vote. In addition the Commissioner asserts, and petitioners do not contest, that in practice, when depositors open their accounts, they usually sign proxies giving management their votes.

The fact that dividends rather than interest are paid is by no means controlling. Petitioners have not disputed the Commissioner's assertion that in practice Citizens pays a fixed, preannounced rate on all accounts. As the Court of Appeals observed, Citizens would not be able to compete with stock savings and loan associations and commercial banks if it did not follow this practice. Potential depositors are motivated only by the rate of return on their accounts and the security of their deposits. In this latter respect, the Citizens accounts are insured by the Federal Savings and Loan Insurance Corporation (FSLIC), up to $40,000 in 1976 and now up to $100,000. 12 U.S.C.

§ 1728(a). The Code treats these dividends just like interest on bank accounts rather than like dividends on stock in a corporation. The dividends are deductible to Citizens, 26 U.S.C. § 591, and they do not qualify for dividend exclusion by the Citizens shareholders under § 116.

The right to participate in the net proceeds of a solvent liquidation is also not a significant part of the value of the shares. Referring to the possibility of a solvent liquidation of a mutual savings association, this Court observed: "It stretches the imagination very far to attribute any real value to such a remote contingency, and when coupled with the fact that it represents nothing which the depositor can readily transfer, any theoretical value reduces almost to the vanishing point." Society for Savings v. Bowers, 349 U.S. 143, 150, 75 S.Ct. 607, 611 (1955).

In contrast, there are substantial debt characteristics to the Citizens shares that predominate. Petitioners' passbook accounts and certificates of deposit are not subordinated to the claims of creditors, and their deposits are not considered permanent contributions to capital. Shareholders have a right on 30 days' notice to withdraw their deposits, which right Citizens is obligated to respect. While petitioners were unable to withdraw their funds for one year following the merger, this restriction can be viewed as akin to a delayed payment rather than a material alteration in the nature of the instruments received as payment. In this case petitioners were immediately able to borrow against their deposits at a more favorable rate than Citizens' depositors generally. As noted above, petitioners were also in effect guaranteed a fixed, preannounced rate of return on their deposits competitive with stock savings and loan associations and commercial banks.

In our view, the debt characteristics of Citizens' shares greatly outweigh the equity characteristics. The face value of petitioners' passbook accounts and certificates of deposit was $210,000. Petitioners have stipulated that they had a right to withdraw the face amount of the deposits in cash, on demand after one year or at stated intervals thereafter. Their investment was virtually risk free and the dividends received were equivalent to prevailing interest rates for savings accounts in other types of savings institutions. The debt value of the shares was the same as the face value, $210,000; because no one would pay more than this for the shares, the incremental value attributable to the equity features was, practically, zero. Accordingly, we hold that petitioners' passbook accounts and certificates of deposit were cash equivalents.

Petitioners have failed to satisfy the continuity-of-interest requirement to qualify for a tax-free reorganization. In exchange for their guaranty stock in Commerce, they received essentially cash with an insubstantial equity interest. Under *Minnesota Tea Co.,* their equity interest in Citizens would have to be "a substantial part of the value of the thing transferred." 296 U.S., at 385, 56 S.Ct., at 272. Assuming an arm's-length transaction in which what petitioners gave up and what they received were of equivalent worth, their Commerce stock was worth $210,000 in withdrawable deposits and an unquantifiably small incremental equity interest. This retained equity interest in the reorganized enterprise, therefore, is not a "substantial" part of the value of the Commerce stock which was given up. We agree with the Commissioner that the equity interests attached to the Citizens shares are too insubstantial to satisfy *Minnesota Tea Co.* The Citizens shares are not significantly different from the notes that this Court found to be the mere "equivalent of cash" in Pinellas & Cold Storage Ice Co., 287 U.S., at 468–469, 53 S.Ct., at 259–260. The ownership interest of the Citizens shareholders is closer to that of the secured bondholders in LeTulle v. Scofield, 308 U.S., at 420–421, 60 S.Ct., at 315–316, than to that of the preferred stockholders in John A. Nelson Co. v. Helvering, 296 U.S., at 377, 56 S.Ct., at 274. The latter case involved a classic ownership instrument—preferred stock carrying voting rights only in the event of a dividend default—which we held to represent "a definite and substantial interest in the affairs of the purchasing corporation." Ibid.

Petitioners argue that the decision below erroneously turned on the relative change in the nature and extent of the equity interest, contrary to the holding in *Minnesota Tea Co.* that "the relationship of the taxpayer to the assets conveyed [could] substantially chang[e]," and only a "material part of the value of the transferred assets" need be retained as an equity interest. 296 U.S., at 386, 56 S.Ct., at 272. In that case, taxpayers received voting trust certificates representing $540,000 of common stock and $425,000 cash; 56% of the value of the assets given up was retained as an equity interest in the transferee. In *John A. Nelson Co.,* supra, the taxpayer received consideration consisting of 38% preferred stock and 62% cash. Here, in contrast, the retained equity interest had almost no value. It did not amount to a "material part" of the value of the Commerce stock formerly held by petitioners. See Southwest Natural Gas Co. v. Commissioner, 189 F.2d, at 335 (insufficient continuity of interest where stock received represented less than 1% of the consideration).

Petitioners' real complaint seems to be our willingness to consider the equity and debt aspects of their shares separately. Clearly, if these interests were represented by separate pieces of paper—savings accounts on the one hand and equity instruments of some kind on the other—the value of the latter would be so small that we would not find a continuity of proprietary interest. In order not "to exalt artifice above reality and to deprive the statutory provision in question of all serious purpose," Gregory v. Helvering, 293 U.S. 465, 469–470, 55 S.Ct. 266, 267–268 (1935), it is necessary in the present case to consider the debt and equity aspects of a single instrument separately. See Rev.Rul. 69–265, 1969–1 Cum.Bull. 109, 109–110, which treats the conversion rights incorporated in convertible preferred stock as "property other than voting stock" for purposes of § 368(a)(1)(C).

Petitioners also complain that the result reached by the court below is inconsistent with the Commissioner's position that a merger of one mutual savings and loan institution into another mutual association or into a stock association would still qualify as a tax-free reorganization. See Rev.Rul. 69–3, 1969–1 Cum.Bull. 103. If the continuity-of-interest test turns on the nature of the thing received, and not on the relative change in proprietary interest, argue petitioners, the interest received in the merger of two mutual associations is no different from the interest received in the instant case.

As already indicated, shares in a mutual association have a predominant cash-equivalent component and an insubstantial equity component. When two mutual associations merge, the shares received are essentially identical to the shares given up. As long as the cash value of the shares on each side of the exchange is the same, the equity interest represented by the shares received—though small—is equivalent to the equity interest represented by the shares given up. Therefore, to the extent that a mutual association share reflects an equity interest, the continuity-of-interest requirement, as defined in *Minnesota Tea Co.,* is satisfied in an exchange of this kind. The fact that identical cash deposits are also exchanged does not affect the equity aspect of the exchange. In the case of a merger of a mutual association into a stock association, the continuity-of-interest requirement is even more clearly satisfied because the equity position of the exchanging shareholders is not only equivalent before and after the exchange, but it is enhanced.

* * *

The judgment of the Court of Appeals is

Affirmed.

JUSTICE POWELL took no part in the decision of the case.

JUSTICE O'CONNOR, with whom THE CHIEF JUSTICE joins, dissenting.

* * *

I agree that a mutual share account is a hybrid security, and that it has substantial debt characteristics. The opportunity to withdraw from the account after one year cloaks the account holder with some of the attributes of a creditor, and the account with some of the attributes of debt. I nevertheless believe that the equity interest represented in a mutual share account is substantial, and thus satisfies the continuity-of-proprietary-interest requirement.

The taxpayers in this case received mutual share accounts and certificates of deposit from Citizens which gave them the same proprietary features of equity ownership which they previously had as stockholders in Commerce, plus the right after a stated interval to withdraw their cash deposits.

* * *

The petitioners possess not only the primary voting interest in the continuing enterprise, but also the only interests in existence with proprietary and equity rights in the mutual association. To the extent there is any equity at all in a mutual association, it is represented by the share accounts obtained by the petitioners.

To find that the equity of a mutual association is insubstantial, the Court today looks to each equitable power or attribute of mutual share account ownership to determine its value and the extent to which it is actually exercised. The Court values the debt characteristics separately from the equity characteristics of the same instrument to determine whether the equity interest is a substantial part of the value of the property transferred. * * *

The Court's opinion also has ramifications beyond mutual associations. This case presents the first opportunity for the Court to consider the use of hybrid instruments in reorganizations. Previously, the Court has held that the receipt of stock, whether common, voting, or nonvoting preferred, satisfies the continuity-of-interest test. If the Court is to now examine the actual exercise of the proprietary rights conferred by ownership of a particular security, it will inevitably reach conflicting results in similar cases. Predicting the tax consequences of reorganizations undertaken for a valid business purpose will become increasingly difficult. I would adhere to precedent and to a clear test and hold that a hybrid instrument which has the principal characteristics of equity ownership should be treated as equity for purposes of the continuity-of-proprietary-interest requirement. If the value of that instrument considered as a whole represents a substantial part of the value of the property transferred, in my view the continuity-of-interest requirement is satisfied and the transaction should qualify as a tax-deferred reorganization. I, therefore, dissent.

ILLUSTRATIVE MATERIAL

A. HISTORICAL BACKGROUND

Paulsen is the most recent of a long line of Supreme Court decisions developing the "continuity of interest" doctrine. The first pronouncement by the Supreme Court regarding the requisite consideration in a reorganization was in Pinellas Ice & Cold Storage Co. v. Commissioner, 287 U.S. 462 (1933). In that case, on December 15, 1926 the taxpayer corporation transferred all of its assets to the acquiring corporation in consideration of $400,000 cash (which was used to pay off debts) and promissory notes for $500,000, due on January 31, 1927, $250,000, due on March 1, 1927, and $250,000, due on April 1, 1927. As the notes were paid, the taxpayer distributed the proceeds to its shareholders in liquidation.

The Commissioner asserted that the taxpayer was required to recognize a gain on the sale of its assets, but the taxpayer contended that the transaction was a "reorganization" as defined in the Revenue Act of 1926, and that, accordingly, the predecessor of section 361 provided for nonrecognition of the gain. Notwithstanding that the statutory provision imposed no requirements or limits on the nature of the consideration required to qualify the transaction as a reorganization, the Court rejected the taxpayer's argument. "[T]he mere purchase for money of the assets of one company by another is beyond the evident purpose of the provision, and has no real semblance to a merger or consolidation. Certainly, we think that to be within the exemption the seller must acquire an interest in the affairs of the purchasing company more definite than that incident to ownership of its short-term purchase-money notes." (470).

In Helvering v. Minnesota Tea Co., 296 U.S. 378 (1935), a transfer of assets for common stock (value, $712,195.90, amounting to 7½ percent of the transferee's outstanding stock) and cash ($426,842.52) was considered a reorganization. After referring to the *Pinellas* statement that an "interest" must be acquired in the transferee, the Court said:

"And we now add that this interest must be definite and material; it must represent a substantial part of the value of the thing transferred. This much is necessary in order that the result accomplished may genuinely partake of the nature of merger or consolidation. * * *

"The transaction here was no sale, but partook of the nature of a reorganization, in that the seller acquired a definite and substantial interest in the purchaser.

"True it is that the relationship of the taxpayer to the assets conveyed was substantially changed, but this is not inhibited by the statute. Also, a large part of the consideration was cash. This, we think, is permissible so long as the taxpayer received an interest in the affairs of the transferee which represented a material part of the value of the transferred assets." (385–6)

John A. Nelson Co. v. Helvering, 296 U.S. 374 (1935), found the requisite continuity of interest where assets were transferred .$2,000,000 in cash and preferred stock worth approximately $1,250,000. The preferred stock was non-voting in the absence of a default in dividends and presumably non-participating. The Court stated:

"The owner of preferred stock is not without substantial interest in the affairs of the issuing corporation, although denied voting rights. The statute does not require participation in the management of the purchaser; nor does it demand that the conveying corporation be dissolved." (377)

In LeTulle v. Scofield, 308 U.S. 415 (1940), the Court refused to allow bonds to qualify as a "proprietary interest." Here the transfer of assets was for cash and ten-year bonds secured by a mortgage. The Court said:

"As the court below properly stated, the section is not to be read literally, as denominating the transfer of all the assets of one company for what amounts to a cash consideration given by the other a reorganization. We have held that where the consideration consists of cash and short term notes the transfer does not amount to a reorganization within the true meaning of the statute, but is a sale upon which gain or loss must be reckoned. We have said that the statute was not satisfied unless the transferor retained a substantial stake in the enterprise and such a stake was thought to be retained where a large proportion of the consideration was in common stock of the transferee,[12] or where the transferor took cash and the entire issue of preferred stock of the transferee corporation.[13] * * *

"In applying our decision in the *Pinellas* case, supra, the courts have generally held that receipt of long term bonds as distinguished from short term notes constitutes the retention of an interest in the purchasing corporation. There has naturally been some difficulty in classifying the securities involved in various cases.

12. Helvering v. Minnesota Tea Co., 296 U.S. 378, 56 S.Ct. 269.

13. John A. Nelson Co. v. Helvering, 296 U.S. 374, 56 S.Ct. 273.

"We are of opinion that the term of the obligations is not material. Where the consideration is wholly in the transferee's bonds, or part cash and part such bonds, we think it cannot be said that the transferor retains any proprietary interest in the enterprise. On the contrary, he becomes a creditor of the transferee; and we do not think that the fact referred to by the Circuit Court of Appeals, that the bonds were secured solely by the assets transferred and that, upon default, the bondholder would retake only the property sold, changes his status from that of a creditor to one having a proprietary stake, within the purview of the statute." (420–21)

As a result of these opinions, an ownership interest cannot be turned into a creditor interest, though long-term in nature, and still have the exchange qualify as a reorganization. A fortiori, the ownership interest cannot be turned into cash or its equivalent in the form of notes or other evidences of a short-lived creditor status. An equity interest in the transferee thus has to be obtained by the transferor of the property. The equity interest obtained, moreover, has to be substantial, so that a non-equity interest which is too extensive might disqualify the exchange. But the nature of the equity interest can be either that of a common stockholder or that of a preferred stockholder, whether voting or non-voting. Obviously, the line drawn between preferred stock and bonds may in some instances come very close to one of form since the participation in earnings and assets and effective control can be drafted nearly alike for both types of instruments.

For further judicial and administrative development of the continuity of interest doctrine, see infra, page 795.

B. SPECIAL ASPECTS OF MERGERS OF MUTUAL FINANCIAL INSTITUTIONS

As is illustrated by *Paulsen,* supra, page 764, mergers involving mutual savings and loans associations and mutual savings banks present particularly difficult problems in applying the continuity of interest rules. The Internal Revenue Service has ruled that continuity of interest exists where two mutual savings banks merge and depositors of the acquired bank receive deposits in the surviving bank because the deposits represent the only equity interests in either corporation. Rev.Rul. 78–286, 1978–2 Cum.Bull. 145.

C. "CONTINUITY OF INTEREST" AND "PARTY TO A REORGANIZATION"

In Groman v. Commissioner, 302 U.S. 82 (1937), X Corporation desired to acquire Y Corporation. Accordingly, X Corporation organized Z Corporation, and held all of its common stock. The shareholders of Y Corporation transferred their Y stock to Z Corporation in return for preferred stock of Z Corporation, preferred stock of X Corporation, and cash. Z Corporation then liquidated Y Corporation. In effect, the assets of Y Corporation went to a newly-formed subsidiary of X Corporation. The Court held that the preferred stock of X Corporation was not stock in a "party to a reorganization" and hence was boot received by the Y Corporation shareholders. The Court relied on the continuity of interest doctrine and stated that since X Corporation had not received the Y Corporation assets, the possession of the X stock by the Y shareholders did not represent a continuing interest in those assets. This case was followed in Helvering v. Bashford, 302 U.S. 454 (1938), where there was a transitory ownership of the Y Corporation stock by X Corporation but it was then immediately transferred by X Corporation to its subsidiary Z Corporation. The Y Corporation shareholders received some common stock of Z Corporation and some preferred and common stock of X Corporation. Since the ownership of the Y stock by X Corporation was only transitory and the transfer to Z Corporation was part of a plan, the transitory ownership did not serve to distinguish the *Groman* case.

In the *Groman* and *Bashford* cases the former stockholders had divided their ownership—they now owned some stock (preferred stock in the *Groman* case, minority common stock in the *Bashford* case) in the corporation to which the assets had been transferred and also some stock (preferred in the *Groman* case, preferred and minority common in the *Bashford* case) in the parent corporation of the corporation to which the assets had been transferred. They were thus free to dispose of one interest without the other. Suppose, however, that the assets had gone to a wholly-owned subsidiary of the parent and the former owners had received only stock in the parent? The courts held that the results were the same: stock of the parent does not provide continuity of interest and make the parent a party to the reorganization where the assets go to another corporation even though it is a wholly owned subsidiary of the parent and even though a reorganization would obviously be present if the assets had gone to the parent. This was also the result under some decisions where the assets were first transferred to the parent and then by it transferred to the subsidiary if the latter step was contemplated as part of the plan of reorganization. Anheuser–Busch, Inc. v. Helvering, 115 F.2d 662 (8th Cir.1940); Hedden v. Commissioner, 105 F.2d 311 (3d Cir. 1939); Mellon v. Commissioner, 12 T.C. 90 (1949) (NA), other issues aff'd 184 F.2d 157 (3d Cir.1950); Campbell v. Commissioner, 15 T.C. 312 (1950)(A).

Subsequent statutory developments have changed these results to some extent. Section 368(a)(2)(C) permits the acquiring corporation to drop assets of the acquired corporation down to a controlled subsidiary following the merger. As long as there is no splitting of interests, as was present in the *Groman* and *Bashford* cases themselves, section 368(a)(2)(D) defines as a reorganization a "triangular merger," a merger in which the shareholders of the acquired corporation receive stock of the acquiring corporation's parent; and section 368(a)(2)(E) permits "reverse triangular mergers" subject to several restrictive conditions. Triangular acquisitions are considered in detail infra, page 852.

D. REFERENCES

Kovey, Characterizing Reorganizations By Reference to the Historic Shareholder, 5 J. Corp. Tax. 115 (1978); Turnier, Continuity of Interest—Its Application to Shareholders of the Acquiring Corporation, 64 Calif.L.Rev. 902 (1976): Hellerstein, Mergers, Taxes, and Realism, 71 Harv.L.Rev. 254 (1957).

C. STEP TRANSACTION DOCTRINE

McDONALD'S RESTAURANTS OF ILLINOIS v. COMMISSIONER

United States Court of Appeals, Seventh Circuit, 1982.
688 F.2d 520.

CUMMINGS, CHIEF JUDGE.

* * *

The pertinent facts as found by the Tax Court and supplemented by the record are not in dispute. In June 1977, when they filed their petitions in the Tax Court to review the deficiency assessments, taxpayers were 27 wholly-owned subsidiaries of McDonald's Corporation (McDonald's), the Delaware corporation that franchises and operates fast-food restaurants.

* * *

On the opposite end of the transaction at issue here were Melvin Garb, Harold Stern and Lewis Imerman (known collectively as the Garb–Stern group). The group had begun with a single McDonald's franchise in Saginaw, Michigan, in the late 1950's and expanded its holdings to include McDonald's restaurants elsewhere in Michigan and in Oklahoma, Wisconsin, Nevada and California. After 1968 relations between the Garb–Stern group and McDonald's deteriorated. In 1971 McDonald's considered buying some of the group's restaurants in Oklahoma, but abandoned the idea when it became clear that the acquisition could not be treated as a "pooling of interests" for accounting purposes [2] unless all of the Garb–Stern group's restaurants were acquired simultaneously. In November 1972, however, negotiations resumed, McDonald's having decided that total acquisition was necessary to eliminate the Garb–Stern group's friction.

The sticking point in the negotiations was that the Garb–Stern group wanted cash for its operations, while McDonald's wanted to acquire the Garb–Stern group's holdings for stock, consistent with its earlier expressed preference for treating the transaction as a "pooling of interests" for accounting purposes. McDonald's proposed a plan to satisfy both sides: it would acquire the Garb–Stern companies for McDonald's common stock, but it would include the common stock in a

2. The Tax Court's opinion describes "pooling of interests" as follows:

> The pooling of interests method accounts for a business combination as the uniting of the ownership interests of two or more companies by exchange of equity securities. No acquisition is recognized because the combination is accomplished without disbursing resources of the constituents. Ownership interests continue and the former bases of accounting are retained. The recorded assets and liabilities of the constituents are carried forward to the combined corporation at their recorded amounts. Income of the combined corporation includes income of the constituents for the entire fiscal period in which the combination occurs. The reported income of the constituents for prior periods is combined and restated as income of the combined corporation.

76 T.C. at 976, n. 4. See also note 6 infra.

planned June 1973 registration so that the Garb–Stern group could sell it promptly.[3]

Final agreement was not reached until March 1973. Negotiations then were hectic; for a variety of accounting and securities-law reasons, the acquisition had to be consummated not before and not after April 1, 1973. The final deal was substantially what had been proposed earlier. The Garb–Stern companies would be merged in stages into McDonald's, which would in turn transfer the restaurant assets to the 27 subsidiaries that are the taxpayers here. In return the Garb–Stern group would receive 361,235 shares of unregistered common stock. The agreement provided that the Garb–Stern group could participate in McDonald's planned June 1973 registration and underwriting or in any other registration and underwriting McDonald's might undertake within six years (Art. 7.4); the group also had a one-time right to demand registration in the event that McDonald's did not seek registration within the first year (Art. 7.5). The Garb–Stern group was not obligated by contract to sell its McDonald's stock but fully intended to do so.

After the April 1 closing, both parties proceeded on the assumption that the Garb–Stern group's shares would be included in the June 1973 "piggyback" registration. In mid-June a widely publicized negative report about McDonald's stock caused the price to drop from $60 to $52 a share in two weeks, and McDonald's therefore decided to postpone the registration and sale of additional stock. The Garb–Stern group acquiesced, although it had made no effort to withdraw from the registration before McDonald's decided to cancel it.

Through the rest of the summer, the price of McDonald's stock staged a recovery. In late August McDonald's decided to proceed with the registration, and the Garb–Stern group asked to have its shares included. The registration was announced on September 17 and completed on October 3, 1973. The Garb–Stern group thereupon sold virtually all of the stock it had acquired in the transaction at a price of more than $71 per share.

In its financial statements McDonald's treated the transaction as a "pooling of interests". In its tax returns for 1973, however, it treated it as a purchase.[6] Consistent with that characterization, McDonald's gave itself a stepped-up basis in the assets acquired from the Garb–Stern

3. The stock the Garb–Stern group received was unregistered. It could not be sold until it was registered or until the Garb–Stern group met the conditions of S.E.C. Rule 144 (2–year holding period and limitation on number of shares sold within a 6–month period thereafter). 76 T.C. at 982 and n. 17. Sale rather than retention was attractive to the Garb–Stern group, because McDonald's stock had paid no cash dividends from 1968 to the time of this transaction. Id. at 985, n. 18.

6. The Commissioner's brief makes much of the differences between the accounting and the tax treatment (Br. 9, 20), characterizing McDonald's strategies as "disingenuous" and "bordering on the duplicitous." The short answer to this argument is found in McDonald's Reply Br. at 9–10: such variations are common and accepted. The service has a special form (Schedule M) for corporations to file in order to reconcile their financial and tax records. McDonald's duly filed such a form. Suppl.App.G.

group to reflect their cost ($29,029,000, representing the value of the common stock transferred and a $1–2 million "nuisance premium" paid to eliminate the Garb–Stern group from the McDonald's organization). It allocated that basis among various Garb–Stern assets, then dropped the restaurant assets to the 27 taxpayer subsidiaries pursuant to Section 351 of the Internal Revenue Code governing transfers to corporations controlled by the transferor. The subsidiaries used the stepped-up basis allocable to them to compute depreciation and amortization deductions in their own 1973 tax returns.

It is those deductions by the subsidiary taxpayers that the Commissioner reduced. He ruled that the transfer of the Garb–Stern group's assets to McDonald's was not a taxable acquisition but a statutory merger or consolidation under Section 368(a)(1)(A) of the Code, and that under Section 362(b) McDonald's was required to assume the Garb–Stern group's basis in the assets acquired. In turn, the subsidiaries were required to compute depreciation and amortization deductions on this lower, carryover basis. With properly computed deductions, the subsidiary taxpayers owed an additional $566,403 in 1973 income taxes. The Tax Court upheld the Commissioner's deficiency assessments, and this appeal is the result.

The Code distinguishes between taxable acquisitions and nontaxable (or more accurately tax-deferrable) acquisitive reorganizations under Sections 368(a)(1)(A)–(C) and 354(a)(1) for the following common-sense reason: If acquired shareholders exchange stock in the acquired company for stock in the acquiring company, they have simply readjusted the form of their equity holdings. They have continued an investment rather than liquidating one, and the response of the tax system is to adjust their basis to reflect the transaction but postpone tax liability until they have more tangible gain or loss.

To ensure that the tax treatment of acquisitive reorganizations corresponds to the rationale that justifies it, the courts have engrafted a "continuity of interest" requirement onto the Code's provisions. See, e.g., Helvering v. Alabama Asphaltic Limestone Co., 315 U.S. 179, 62 S.Ct. 540, 86 L.Ed. 775; LeTulle v. Scofield, 308 U.S. 415, 60 S.Ct. 313, 84 L.Ed. 355. That test examines the acquired shareholders' proprietary interest before and after the reorganization to see if "the acquired shareholders' investment remains sufficiently 'at risk' after the merger to justify the nonrecognition tax treatment," 76 T.C. at 997.

The taxpayers, the Commissioner, and the Tax Court all agree that the Garb–Stern group holdings were acquired by statutory merger. They also all agree that the "continuity of interest" test is determinative of the tax treatment of the transaction of which the statutory merger was a part. But the taxpayers on the one hand, and the Commissioner and the Tax Court on the other, part company over how the test is to be applied, and what result it should have produced. In affirming the Commissioner, the Tax Court recognized that the Garb–Stern group had a settled and firm determination to sell their McDonald's shares at the first possible opportunity rather than continue as investors, 76 T.C. at 989. It nonetheless concluded that because the Garb–Stern group was not contractually bound to sell, the merger and the sale could be treated as entirely separate transactions and the continuity-of-interest test applied in the narrow time-frame of the April transaction only. Thus tested, the transaction was in Judge Hall's view a nontaxable reorganization, and the taxpayer subsidiaries were therefore saddled with the Garb–Stern group's basis in taking depreciation and amortization deductions. The taxpayers by contrast argue that the step-transaction doctrine should have been applied to treat the April merger and stock transfer and the October sale as one taxable transaction. They also argue that the Tax Court's extremely narrow view of both the step-transaction doctrine and the continuity-of-interest test in this case is not consonant with appellate court case law, the Tax Court's own precedents, or the Service's practices hitherto. We agree with the taxpayers.

The Step–Transaction Doctrine

The step-transaction doctrine is a particular manifestation of the more general tax law principle that purely formal distinctions cannot obscure the substance of a transaction. See e.g., Redding v. Commissioner, 630 F.2d 1169, 1175 (7th Cir.1980), certiorari denied, 450 U.S. 913, 101 S.Ct. 1353, 67 L.Ed.2d 388. * * *

Nonetheless, under any of the tests devised—including the intermediate one nominally adopted by the Tax Court and the most restrictive one actually applied in its decision—the transactions here would be stepped together. For example, under the "end result test," "purportedly separate transactions will be amalgamated with a single transaction when it appears that they were really component parts of a single transaction intended from the outset to be taken for the purpose of reaching the ultimate result." 76 T.C. at 994, citing King Enterprises, Inc. v. United States, 418 F.2d 511, 516 (Ct.Cl.1969) and referring to *Redding,* supra, 630 F.2d at 1175. Here there can be little doubt that all the steps were taken to cash out the Garb–Stern group, although McDonald's sought to do so in a way that would enable it to use certain accounting procedures. Admittedly, not every transaction would be as pellucid as this one, but here the history of the parties' relationships, the abortive attempt to buy some of the group's holdings, the final comprehensive deal, and the Garb–Stern group's determination to sell out even in the face of falling prices in the stock all are consistent and probative.

A second test is the "interdependence" test, which focuses on whether "the steps are so interdependent that the legal relations created by one transaction would have been fruitless without a completion of the series." *Redding,* supra, at 1177, quoting with approval Paul, Selected Studies in Federal Taxation (2d Series 1938) 200, 254. This is the test the Tax Court purported to apply, 76 T.C. at 997–999, although its version of the test is indistinguishable from yet another formulation, the "binding commitment" test. That is, the Tax Court would have found interdependence only if the Garb–Stern group had itself been legally bound to sell its stock. In fact, the "interdependence" test is more practical and less legalistic than that. It concentrates on the relationship between the steps, rather than on the "end result" (cf. p. 524, supra). Here it would ask whether the merger would have taken place without the guarantees of saleability [sic], and the answer is certainly no. The Garb–Stern group's insistence on this point is demonstrated both by its historic stance in these negotiations and by the hammered-out terms of the agreement. Although the Tax Court emphasized the permissive terms about "piggyback" registration, it glossed over the Garb–Stern group's one-time right to force registration—and hence sale—under the agreement. The very detail of the provisions about how McDonald's would ensure free transferability of the Garb–Stern group's McDonald's stock shows that they were the *quid pro quo* of the merger agreement.

Finally the "binding commitment" test most restricts the application of the step-transaction doctrine, and is the test the Tax Court actually applied, despite its statements otherwise. The "binding commitment" test forbids use of the step-transaction doctrine unless "if one transaction is to be characterized as a 'first step' there [is] a binding commitment to take the later steps." *Redding,* supra, at 1178, quoting Commissioner v. Gordon, 391 U.S. 83, 96, 88 S.Ct. 1517, 1524, 20 L.Ed. 2d 448. The Tax Court found the test unsatisfied because the Garb–Stern group was not legally obliged to sell its McDonald's stock. We think it misconceived the purpose of the test and misapplied it to the facts of this case.

In the first place, the "binding commitment" test is the most rigorous limitation on the step-transaction doctrine because it was formulated to deal with the characterization of a transaction that in fact spanned several tax years and could have remained "not only indeterminable but unfixed for an indefinite and unlimited period in the future, awaiting events that might or might not happen." *Gordon,* supra, 391 U.S. at 96, 88 S.Ct. at 1524. By contrast this transaction was complete in six months and fell entirely within a single tax year. The degree of uncertainty that worried the *Gordon* court is absent here, and a strong antidote for uncertainty is accordingly not needed.

In the second place, the Tax Court underestimated the extent to which the parties were bound to take the later steps. The registration and underwriting provisions in the parties' agreement did not just enhance salability; they were essential to it. Unless and until McDonald's registered the stock, it was essentially untransferable. 76 T.C. at 981–982; see note 3 supra. Second, although McDonald's had the choice of when during the first year after the merger it would seek registration, if it did nothing the Garb–Stern group could make a legally enforceable demand for registration in either year two or year three. On the other hand, if McDonald's did register stock during the first year but the Garb–Stern group chose not to "piggyback," the group's demand registration rights would be lost. These limitations made it extremely likely that the sale would—as it did—take place promptly. They are enough to satisfy the spirit, if not the letter, of the "binding commitment" test.

Under any of the three applicable criteria, then, the merger and subsequent sale should have been stepped together. Substance over form is the key (Kuper v. Commissioner, 533 F.2d 152, 155 (5th Cir. 1976)). Had the Tax Court taken a pragmatic view of the actions of the Garb–Stern group, it would have found that they clearly failed to satisfy the continuity-of-interest requirement that has been engrafted onto the Code provisions governing nonrecognition treatment for acquisitive reorganizations.

Statutory Merger Precedents

Quite apart from the proper application of the step-transaction doctrine, the available precedents dealing with statutory mergers and the effect of post-merger sales by acquired shareholders—though scanty—strongly support the taxpayers. No case supports the myopic position adopted below that although "the crux of the continuity-of-interest test lies in the *continuation* of the acquired shareholders' proprietary interest" (76 T.C. at 997), the test "by itself does not require *any length* of postmerger retention," (id.) (emphasis supplied).

The taxpayers rely on, and the Tax Court was unsuccessful in distinguishing, Heintz v. Commissioner, 25 T.C. 132 (1955). The *Heintz* case differs from this case only in focusing on the tax liability of the acquired shareholders rather than the acquiring corporation. The facts of the case, somewhat simplified, are as follows.

Heintz and Jack (taxpayers) formed a company (Jack & Heintz, Inc.) to manufacture arms and ammunition during World War II. At the war's end, they determined to sell it rather than try to reorganize its production for peacetime. The buyer was the Precision Corporation, which had been formed to acquire Jack & Heintz. On March 5, 1946, Precision acquired almost all the outstanding shares of Jack & Heintz from the taxpayers for $5 million cash and 50,000 preferred shares of Precision, with a par value of $50 each. On March 6 Precision merged its newly acquired subsidiary with itself. At the time the deal was being negotiated, two of the parties representing the buyer assured the taxpayers that the Precision shares they had received as part payment would be sold in a public offering planned for thirty days after the merger (25 T.C. at 135), but this promise was nowhere reflected in the thirty-five page written agreement covering the whole transaction (id. at 137). Owing to unforeseen delays, the contemplated registration and sale did not take place, but the buyers helped arrange a private sale at $30 per share in August 1946. In their 1946 returns, the taxpayers reported long-term capital gain computed on a figure arrived at by deducting from the sale proceeds ($5 million in cash + $2,500,000 worth of Precision stock) their $112,000 basis in the Jack & Heintz stock. They also reported short-term capital losses of $1 million on the August private sale of the Precision stock.

The Commissioner assessed deficiencies, using exactly the reasoning the Tax Court has adopted in McDonald's case. He treated the transaction as a statutory reorganization, which had no immediate tax consequences (except that the cash component of the price was ordinary income). He then gave the taxpayers a carry-over basis of $112,000, rather than a cost basis, in the Precision stock. Finally he treated the August sale as producing sizable capital gains ($1,500,000 less $112,000) rather than capital losses. Although the Commissioner's position is sketchily presented in the Tax Court's opinion, his treatment must have involved a conviction that neither the promise to sell the Precision stock nor the actual sale changed the character of the reorganization.

The Tax Court rejected the Commissioner's position unequivocally.

* * *

As in the present case, the taxpayers' wishes to sell were clear and the transaction was designed to accommodate them. As in the present case, the acquiring corporation's promise was to facilitate the sale, not to guarantee it. As in the present case, the acquiring corporation did not require a reciprocal commitment from the acquired shareholders—for all that appears, Heintz and Jack were free to retain their equity interest in Precision. As in the present case, these understandings of the parties were not reflected in the written agreement. There is no principled way to distinguish the two cases, and the Tax Court's efforts to do so here (76 T.C. at 1001) are unsuccessful.

* * *

The Commissioner's usual position in this context is not the one adopted by the Tax Court, namely, that the intent of the acquired shareholders is irrelevant and no period of post-merger retention is required. 76 T.C. at 990, 992, 997. See, for example, Rev.Proc. 77–37, 1977–2 C.B. 568, 569:

* * *

PENROD v. COMMISSIONER

United States Tax Court, 1987.
88 T.C. 1415.

SIMPSON, JUDGE: * * *

The issue for our decision [is] [w]hether the exchange of stock of corporations owned by the petitioners for stock of McDonald's Corp. (McDonald's) qualifies as a tax-deferred reorganization under section 368 * * *.

FINDINGS OF FACT

* * *

Prior to May 15, 1975, petitioners Robert A. Penrod (Bob), Charles E. Penrod (Chuck), and Ronald L. Peeples (Ron), together with Jack

Penrod (Jack), owned stock in a number of corporations which operated McDonald's fast-food restaurants in South Florida. * * *

* * *

By May 1975, the Penrods had acquired franchises for 16 McDonald's restaurants in South Florida. In all cases but one, a separate corporation was formed to hold each franchise and to operate each restaurant. * * * On May 15, 1975, the Penrods had interests in such corporations as follows:

Corporation	*Jack Penrod*	*Bob Penrod (acquisition date)*	*Chuck Penrod (acquisition date)*	*Ron Peeples (acquisition date)*
Dania Foods, Inc.	900 shares	100 shares (01/01/75)	0	0
Davie Foods, Inc.	600 shares	200 shares (01/01/75)	200 shares (01/01/75)	0
Inverrary Foods, Inc.	800 shares	200 shares (01/01/75)	200 shares (01/01/75)	0
441 Hollywood Foods, Inc.	600 shares	200 shares (01/01/75)	200 shares (01/01/75)	0
Davie I–95 Foods, Inc.	600 shares	200 shares (01/01/75)	200 shares (01/01/75)	0
Hallandale Foods Inc.	600 shares	200 shares (01/01/75)	200 shares (01/01/75)	0
Cutler Ridge Foods Inc.	600 shares	200 shares (01/01/75)	0	200 shares (01/01/75)
Margate Foods Inc.	889 shares	111 shares [1]	0	0
Sunrise Foods Inc.	100 shares	0	0	0
Coral Ridge Foods Inc.	800 shares	100 shares (01/01/75)	100 shares (01/01/75)	0
Ft. Lauderdale Foods, Inc.	600 shares	100 shares [1]	0	0
No. 1167 Foods, Inc.	41 shares	17 shares [1]	0	10 shares [1]
Homestead Foods, Inc.	48 shares	16 shares [1]	0	16 shares [1]
Dade Foods, Inc.	408 shares	[unknown] [1]	136 shares [1]	136 shares [1]
P.M.C., Inc.	56 shares	12 shares [1]	12 shares [1]	0

[1] Sometime prior to May 15, 1974.

* * *

* * * On February 20, 1975, Jack was visiting McDonald's corporate headquarters near Chicago, Illinois, when McDonald's president, Fred Turner, told Jack that he wished to acquire the restaurants owned by the Penrods. In subsequent discussions, McDonald's management indicated that the company wanted to use the pooling of interest method of accounting for the acquisition on its financial statements. Accounting rules then in effect prevented McDonald's from using the pooling of interest method if McDonald's purchased the Penrod corporations for cash. For such reason, McDonald's management contemplated the acquisition would be achieved through an exchange of the stock owned by the Penrods for McDonald's common stock. At no time did

Jack request cash for the Penrod stock; at all times, he agreed to the acquisition in exchange for McDonald's stock.

In March 1975, Jack met with McDonald's controller, Gerald Newman, and agreed upon the approximate value of the Penrod restaurants and the method to be used in computing the number of McDonald's shares to be issued in the exchange. The remaining terms of the acquisition were negotiated by the Penrods' attorney, J. Bradbury Reed.

* * * Bob, Chuck, and Ron were not involved in the negotiations with the McDonald's organization. Jack acted as the group's leader in such negotiations.

The final agreement and plan of reorganization (the agreement) called for McDonald's to issue its unregistered common stock in exchange for the stock in the Penrod corporations. Since SEC rules required that stock such as that received by the Penrods be registered before it could be sold in the first 2 years, Mr. Reed insisted on provisions in the agreement giving the Penrods incidental and demand registration rights with respect to their stock. The incidental rights * * * required McDonald's to give written notice to the Penrods of any proposed registration of stock and to include any of the Penrod stock in such registration if requested to do so. The demand registration rights * * * provided that a majority of the Penrod stockholders could inquire whether McDonald's proposed a registration of stock and, if McDonald's did not, could demand that McDonald's register their stock. The demand registration rights could first be exercised in mid-August 1975 and expired on May 15, 1976. * * * It was Mr. Reed's practice to negotiate for such registration rights on behalf of his clients each time he represented shareholders in a corporate acquisition. The Penrods made no express request that he negotiate for registration rights.

* * *

After Jack and McDonald's agreed on the basis for the acquisition, the Penrods' attorneys drafted a proposed ruling request to be submitted to the IRS, in which the Penrods requested a determination that the acquisition would be treated as a reorganization under section 368. Representatives of McDonald's informed the Penrods' attorneys that McDonald's was anxious to close the acquisition quickly and that there was not sufficient time to wait for a ruling from the IRS; therefore, no ruling request was ever submitted to the IRS. Instead, the Penrods obtained an opinion from their attorneys that the merger qualified as a reorganization under section 368. The opinion included the statement that:

> Our understanding of the circumstances under which the reorganizations will be accomplished is as follows:
>
> * * *
>
> 12. * * * McDonald's has no claims or agreements to reacquire any of the McDonald's shares issued to the shareholders of the Companies, and the shareholders have no present intention to sell

> or otherwise dispose of the McDonald's stock to be received in the reorganizations.

Mr. Newman, McDonald's controller, indicated that McDonald's would try to structure the merger as a tax-deferred reorganization. However, McDonald's provided no guarantee to the Penrods as to the tax consequences of the transaction.

On May 15, 1975, McDonald's and the Penrods executed the agreement, which transferred ownership and management of the Penrod corporations to McDonald's. In exchange for the stock of such corporations, the Penrods received 106,464 shares of McDonald's unregistered common stock. * * * As required by the agreement, 10 percent of the shares received by the Penrods, or 10,646 shares, were held in escrow to cover any claims or liabilities of the acquired corporations which arose after the closing.

* * *

Sometime in 1974, Jack began to plan the development of a chain of restaurants to be known as "Wuv's." Jack intended Wuv's to compete in the fast-food market and expected his competition to be other fast-food restaurants such as McDonald's, Burger King, and Wendy's. In August 1974, Jack engaged a Washington, D.C., attorney to conduct a trademark search to determine whether the name "Wuv's" was available for use as a fast-food service mark.

On May 16, 1975, Jack and Bob, as officers, directors, and incorporators, executed a certificate of incorporation for Wuv's, Inc. (Wuv's). Such certificate showed Wuv's corporate purpose to be to "engage in the business of selling food and beverages at retail, [and the] operation of a restaurant." Jack served as the president of Wuv's. * * *

In connection with his plans for Wuv's, Jack * * * concluded that he could have in operation 30 restaurants by the end of 1976 requiring not more than $1,500,000 of funds supplied by him.

On October 7, 1975, the Dania Bank sent Jack a commitment letter which stated the terms of a negotiated loan agreement between Jack, Wuv's, and the bank. The bank agreed to offer a credit line not to exceed $2 million, with $1,500,000 extended to Jack personally and $500,000 to Wuv's. On October 8, 1975, the controller of Penrod Management, Peter N. Bonitatibus, sent a letter to the Dania Bank accepting the loan commitment. In such letter, Mr. Bonitatibus indicated that Jack planned to sell enough McDonald's stock to pay existing debts of $1 million and to satisfy an estimated Federal income tax liability of 25 percent on such sale. In addition, he indicated that Jack agreed to retain approximately $2 million worth of McDonald's stock to serve as collateral for the loan.

In mid-August 1975, * * * Mr. Reed sent a letter to McDonald's management * * * inquiring as to whether McDonald's intended within 60 days to file a registration statement with the SEC which would allow the Penrods to register their McDonald's stock for sale. Such letter further stated that, if McDonald's did not intend to file such registration statement, the Penrods as a group desired to sell approximately 60,000 shares received from McDonald's pursuant to the acquisition. By reply letter dated December 3, 1975, McDonald's informed the Penrods that it did not plan to file a regular registration statement and that it was preparing to file a registration statement on the Penrods' behalf to be effective after January 1, 1976. Such letter further reflected McDonald's understanding that the Penrods had decided, subsequent to Mr. Reed's November 11 letter, to sell all of the shares received by them in the acquisition, except for those held in escrow. * * * When the registration statement for the Penrods was filed with the SEC, the number of shares to be sold by them had increased to 96,554.

McDonald's stock covered by the registration statement for the Penrods was sold on January 12, 1976, for approximately $60 per share. Bob, Chuck, and Ron appointed Jack as their agent in negotiating for such sale. As of January 14, 1976, the Penrods owned 10,646 shares of McDonald's stock, all of which was held in escrow by McDonald's pursuant to the agreement. * * *

* * * By December 31, 1975, Jack had opened three Wuv's restaurants. One such restaurant was in Boca Raton, Florida, and another was in Deland, Florida. By December 31, 1976, approximately 20 Wuv's restaurants were opened. Ordinarily, it takes a minimum of 12 months to plan, obtain zoning variances and building permits, and actually construct a fast-food restaurant such as Wuv's. * * *

OPINION

* * * The parties agree that the transaction constituted a statutory merger that was in form eligible for reorganization treatment under section 368(a)(1)(A). However, the Commissioner determined that such exchange of stock did not qualify as a reorganization because the petitioners failed to maintain a sufficient equity interest in McDonald's after the exchange. * * *

It is well settled that, in addition to meeting specific statutory requirements, a reorganization under section 368(a)(1)(A) must also satisfy the continuity of interest doctrine. See sec. 1.368–1(b), Income Tax Regs. * * * Because the reorganization provisions are based on the premise that the shareholders of an acquired corporation have not terminated their economic investment, but have merely altered its form, the continuity of interest doctrine limits the favorable nonrecognition treatment enjoyed by reorganizations to those situations in which (1) the nature of the consideration received by the acquired corporation or its shareholders confers a proprietary stake in the ongoing enterprise, and (2) the proprietary interest received is definite and material and represents a substantial part of the value of the property transferred. * * *

The entire consideration received by the Penrods pursuant to the May 15, 1975, merger consisted of McDonald's common stock. Thus, the parties agree that, in form, the nature and amount of such consideration satisfied the continuity of interest test. However, they do not agree on the effect of the Penrods' subsequent actions.

The Commissioner argues that the acquisition and the subsequent sale of McDonald's stock by the Penrods was part of an overall plan to "cash out" their investment in the acquired corporations and that, therefore, the two events should be considered to be, in substance, one transaction. The consequence of his position would be to treat the petitioners as having received all cash on the date of the acquisition, and therefore, the acquisition would fail the continuity of interest test. On the other hand, the petitioners argue that their decision to sell their McDonald's stock was based only upon events which occurred after the acquisition and that the acquisition and subsequent sale should therefore be treated as separate transactions.

The resolution of this issue turns on the application of the so-called step transaction doctrine. The step transaction doctrine is in effect another rule of substance over form; it treats a series of formally separate "steps" as a single transaction if such steps are in substance integrated, interdependent, and focused toward a particular result. * * * There is no universally accepted test as to when and how the step transaction doctrine should be applied to a given set of facts. Courts have applied three alternative tests in deciding whether to invoke the step transaction doctrine in a particular situation.

The narrowest alternative is the "binding commitment" test, under which a series of transactions are collapsed if, at the time the first step is entered into, there was a binding commitment to undertake the later step. See Commissioner v. Gordon, 391 U.S. 83, 96 (1968) * * *. The binding commitment test has the advantage of promoting certainty in the tax planning of shareholders. Under such test, a court must make an objective determination as to whether the acquired shareholders were bound by an obligation to sell the shares received in an acquisition. Other factors, such as intent by such shareholders to sell their shares, are not considered. However, there have been objections to that test on the ground that the result is easily manipulable by taxpayers. * * *

At the other extreme, the most far-reaching alternative is the "end result" test. Under this test, the step transaction doctrine will be invoked if it appears that a series of formally separate steps are really prearranged parts of a single transaction intended from the outset to reach the ultimate result. See King Enterprises, Inc. v. United States, 418 F.2d at 516 * * *. The end result test is based upon the actual intent of the parties as of the time of the merger. It can be argued that any test which requires a court to make a factual determination as to a party's intent promotes uncertainty and therefore impedes effective tax planning. However, in contrast to the binding commitment test, the end result test is flexible and bases tax consequences on the real substance of the transactions, not on the formalisms chosen by the participants.

The third test is the "interdependence" test, which focuses on whether "the steps are so interdependent that the legal relations created by one transaction would have been fruitless without a completion of the series." Redding v. Commissioner, 630 F.2d at 1177 * * * American Bantam Car Co. v. Commissioner, 11 T.C. 397 (1948), affd. 177 F.2d 513 (3d Cir.1949). This test concentrates on the relationship between the steps, rather than on their "end result." See Security Industrial Insurance Co. v. United States, 702 F.2d 1234, 1245 (5th Cir. 1983). However, since the interdependence test requires a court to find whether the individual steps had independent significance or whether they had meaning only as part of the larger transaction, the court may be called upon to determine the result the participants hoped to achieve. Thus, the interdependence test is a variation of the end result test.

Courts have applied each of these three alternatives to a variety of transactions to determine whether the transactions should be "stepped." In Heintz v. Commissioner, 25 T.C. 132 (1955), * * * the Court placed little weight on the absence of a binding commitment on the part of the taxpayers to sell the preferred shares received by them in the acquisition. Instead, the Court focused on the facts that the taxpayers wished to "cash out" their investment * * * and that the acquisition was a step toward that goal.

More recently, the Court considered the step transaction doctrine in connection with an acquisition by McDonald's of a number of franchised restaurants in a statutory merger similar in form to the transaction in the present case. McDonald's of Zion v. Commissioner, 76 T.C. 972 (1981).

* * * The Court first found that the facts "when viewed in a realistic and objective manner, portray the direct and unwavering intent of the Garb–Stern group to sell virtually all of the McDonald's stock they received pursuant to the merger." 76 T.C. at 990. The Court also found that "the two transactions were independent. The merger transaction did not require or commit the Garb–Stern group to sell their McDonald's stock." 76 T.C. at 998; fn. ref. omitted. Consequently, this Court held that there was no binding commitment by the Garb–Stern group to sell their stock when it was acquired, that the steps were not mutually interdependent, that the step transaction doctrine was not applicable, that the Garb–Stern group did intend to continue to hold a proprietary interest in McDonald's, and that the acquisition constituted a reorganization within the meaning of section 368(a)(1)(A).

The Seventh Circuit reversed, holding that the merger and subsequent sale should have been stepped together. McDonald's Restaurants of Illinois v. Commissioner, 688 F.2d 520, 524 (7th Cir.1982). * * *

* * *

The Circuit Court * * * believed that the facts "are enough to satisfy the spirit, if not the letter, of the 'binding commitment' test." 688 F.2d at 525. Finally, the Seventh Circuit held that the result in the case was controlled by *Heintz v. Commissioner,* supra, and viewed this Court's attempt to distinguish *Heintz* as unpersuasive. See 688 F.2d at 527.

In the present case, there was no binding commitment by the Penrods at the time of the acquisition to sell their stock. However, we need not decide whether the absence of a binding commitment, standing alone, is sufficient to prevent the application of the step transaction doctrine; after carefully examining and evaluating all the circumstances surrounding the acquisition and subsequent sale of the McDonald's stock received by the Penrods, we have concluded that, at the time of the acquisition, the Penrods did not intend to sell their McDonald's stock and that therefore the step transaction doctrine is not applicable under either the interdependence test or the end result test. * * *.

In this case, Jack was unquestionably the leader of the Penrod group. He owned not less than 60 percent of the outstanding stock of each of the Penrod corporations at the time of the acquisition. Further, Jack was solely responsible for negotiating the terms of the agreement with McDonald's, and the petitioners appointed him as their agent to negotiate the terms of the sale of their McDonald's shares. Thus, we shall focus our analysis on the intention of Jack at the time of the acquisition and subsequent sale of McDonald's stock.

The Commissioner argued vigorously that Jack intended to sell his McDonald's stock when he acquired it because he planned to organize Wuv's, a competing fast-food restaurant chain. The evidence shows that Jack began thinking about a fast-food restaurant to be named Wuv's in 1974. * * *. Yet, he was then engaged in operating 16 McDonald's restaurants, and there is absolutely no evidence that he planned to sell or otherwise terminate his interest in those McDonald's restaurants at that time. In fact, Jack testified that it was the president of McDonald's who first mentioned the possibility of McDonald's acquiring the restaurants in February 1975. Jack did not initiate the proposal to exchange the stock of the Penrod corporations for McDonald's stock; it was McDonald's that took the initiative. Moreover, Jack never asked for cash for his restaurants. McDonald's proposed to issue unregistered common stock in exchange for the stock of the Penrod corporations, and Jack never questioned that proposal. This evidence shows that, at the outset, Jack expected to operate his Wuv's restaurants without any liquidation of his interest in McDonald's.

* * *

In August 1975, the Penrods could have demanded registration of their McDonald's stock, but they did not. * * * [The] evidence reveals that by October 1975, Jack had decided to sell some of his McDonald's stock; yet, if the evidence correctly reflects his intention at the time, he would have retained enough of the McDonald's stock to constitute a substantial interest in McDonald's, and the continuity of interest requirement would have been satisfied. * * *

We do not know why the Penrods did not demand registration of their McDonald's stock at the earliest opportunity * * *. It may be that by the fall of 1975, Jack decided to sell his McDonald's stock in part because he wanted the funds to open the Wuv's restaurants and in part because the market for the stock was favorable. Yet, a review of the record of events that occurred in 1975 supports Jack's testimony that he did not intend to sell his McDonald's stock when he acquired it and that he expected to be able to continue to hold that stock and to operate the Wuv's restaurants simultaneously.

* * *

For these reasons, we have concluded that Jack and the other Penrods intended to continue to hold the McDonald's stock acquired by them in the acquisition. Accordingly, in our judgment, the acquisition of the stock and its subsequent sale were not interdependent steps, nor were they steps in a plan the end result of which was to cash out their interests in the restaurants. Under such circumstances, we hold that such transactions should not be stepped together, that the Penrods' ownership of the McDonald's stock satisfied the continuity of interest requirement, and that the acquisition of such stock constituted a reorganization within the meaning of section 368(a)(1)(A). Thus, we hold here (as did this Court in *McDonald's,* but on a different factual record) that there was a continuity of interest. In addition, since we have found as a fact that the acquired shareholders intended to continue to hold the stock acquired by them, and since the record fully supports that factual conclusion, we believe that our opinion here is factually distinguishable from that of the Seventh Circuit in the *McDonald's* case.

* * *

ILLUSTRATIVE MATERIAL

A. OTHER APPLICATIONS OF THE STEP TRANSACTION DOCTRINE

The step transaction doctrine, like the business purpose doctrine, is especially important in the area of corporate reorganizations. When this judicial doctrine is applied, the tax treatment of several transactions is determined by examining their overall effect rather than giving effect to each of the several transactions in sequence. In some cases, however, the form of a transaction will be allowed to control. Predicting when the step transaction doctrine will be applied is difficult.

The step transaction doctrine may be applied to produce a tax-free reorganization where following the form of the several steps would have produced a taxable transaction. In Heller v. Commissioner, 2 T.C. 371 (1943), aff'd, 147 F.2d 376 (9th Cir.1945), the shareholders of a Delaware corporation organized a California corporation, contributing borrowed cash for the stock of the California corporation. The California corporation then borrowed additional cash and purchased the assets of the Delaware corporation, which paid its existing indebtedness and distributed the balance of the cash to its shareholders in liquidation. The taxpayer claimed a deductible loss on the liquidation of the Delaware corporation because his basis for his stock in that corporation exceeded the amount of the liquidating distribution. The Commissioner disallowed the loss, asserting that the series of steps was in fact a single transaction which was a reorganization under the predecessors of section 368(a)(1)(C) or section 368(a)(1)(E) and that, accordingly, pursuant to the predecessor of section 354(a)(1), no loss was recognizable. In response, the taxpayer argued that even if the transaction had the same result as a reorganization, no exchange of stock for stock as required by the predecessor of section 354(a)(1), had occurred.

The Tax Court held for the Commissioner, reasoning as follows:

"In determining the substance of a transaction it is proper to consider the situation as it existed at the beginning and end of the series of steps as well as the object sought to be accomplished, the means employed, and the relation between the various steps. * * *

"Petitioner and two others, the stockholders and directors of the Delaware corporation, decided to have the business, assets, and liabilities of that company taken over by a new California corporation. The desired end was accomplished by a series of steps, all of which were planned in advance. * * * The net result was that petitioner and the other two stockholders had substituted their interest in the Delaware corporation for substantially the same interest in the California corporation. The nonrecognition of gain or loss provisions of the statute are 'intended to apply to cases where a corporation in form transfers its property, but in substance it or its stockholders retain the same or practically the same interest after the transfer.' * * *

"The result achieved under the plan could have been accomplished by having the California corporation acquire the assets of the Delaware corporation for its stock, and by having the latter distribute the stock to its stockholders in complete liquidation. Petitioner and his associates apparently chose the longer route, hoping that they might thereby become entitled to a loss deduction. However, as the Supreme Court pointed out in Minnesota Tea Co. v. Helvering, 302 U.S. 609, 613, 58 S.Ct. 393, 'a given result at the end of a straight path is not made a different result because reached by following a devious path.' The effect of all the steps taken was that petitioner made an exchange of stock of one corporation for stock of another pursuant to a plan of reorganization." (383–84)

In Rev.Rul. 67–448, 1967–2 Cum.Bull. 144, P Corporation formed a subsidiary, S Corporation, and contributed P's stock to the subsidiary. S Corporation was then merged into unrelated corporation Y with shareholders of Y receiving P Corporation stock in the merger. The Ruling treated the series of transactions as the direct acquisition by P of the Y stock in exchange of its own shares, thereby qualifying the transaction as a type (B) reorganization. "It is evident that the shortest route to the end result described above would have been achieved by a transfer of P voting stock directly to the shareholders of Y in exchange for their stock. This result is not negated because the transaction was cast in the form of a series of interrelated steps. The transitory existence of the new subsidiary, S, will be disregarded. The effect of all the steps taken in the series is that Y became a wholly owned subsidiary of P, and P transferred solely its voting stock to the former shareholders of Y." (145) The Ruling dealt with a situation arising before the enactment of section 368(a)(2)(E).

Despite the existence of the step transaction doctrine, in some situations, the tax result may in the end become one turning purely on form alone, with one route leading to one tax consequence and another route leading to a different tax consequence, though the non-tax end result is the same. In Granite Trust Co. v. United States, 238 F.2d 670 (1st Cir.1956), supra, page 633, the court gave effect to sales and a gift of stock designed to take a corporate taxpayer out of the conditions of section 332(b) to avoid nonrecognition of loss. The court stated:

"As for the Commissioner's 'end-result' argument, the very terms of [section 332(b)] make it evident that it is not an 'end-result' provision, but rather one which prescribes specific conditions for the nonrecognition of realized gains or losses, conditions which if not strictly met, make the section inapplicable. * * *

"In the present case the question is whether or not there actually were sales. Why the parties may wish to enter into a sale is one thing, but that is irrelevant under the *Gregory* case so long as the consummated agreement was no different from what it purported to be.

"Even the Commissioner concedes that '[l]egal title' passed to the several transferees on December 13, 1943, but he asserts that 'beneficial ownership' never passed. We find no basis on which to vitiate the purported sales, for the record is absolutely devoid of any evidence indicating an understanding by the parties to the transfers that any interest in the stock transferred was to be retained by the taxpayer. * * *

"In addition to what we have said, there are persuasive reasons of a general nature which lend weight to the taxpayer's position. To strike down these sales on the alleged defect that they took place between friends and for tax motives would only tend to promote duplicity and result in extensive litigation as taxpayers led courts into hair-splitting investigations to decide when a sale was not a sale. It is no answer to argue that, under Gregory v. Helvering, there is an inescapable judicial duty to examine into the actuality of purported corporate reorganizations, for that was a special sort of transaction whose bona fides could readily be ascertained by inquiring whether the ephemeral new corporation was in fact transacting business, or whether there was in fact a continuance of the proprietary interests under an altered corporate form. * * *

"In short, though the facts in this case show a tax avoidance, they also show legal transactions not fictitious or so lacking in substance as to be anything different from what they purported to be, and we believe they must be given effect in the administration of [section 332(b)] as well as for all other purposes." (675–78)

For a controversial recent case involving the step transaction doctrine, see Esmark, Inc. and Affiliated Cos. v. Commissioner, 90 T.C. 171 (1988) (the substantive issue involved in the case no longer arises). See also the discussion of American Bantam Car Co. v. Commissioner, supra, page 360.

In the end, determining when the form of a particular transaction will be respected and when a step transaction approach will be applied is a complex process which resists a simple verbal formulation. Nonetheless, it is central to understanding the reorganization provisions and corporate taxation generally.

B. REFERENCES

Blum, The Importance of Form in the Taxation of Corporate Transactions, 54 Taxes 613 (1976); Mintz and Plumb, Step Transactions In Corporate Reorganizations, 12 N.Y.U. Tax Inst. 247 (1954); Rice, Judicial Techniques in Combating Tax Avoidance, 51 Mich.L.Rev. 1021 (1953).

D. CONTINUITY OF BUSINESS ENTERPRISE

REGULATIONS: Section 1.368–1(d).

REVENUE RULING 81–92

1981–1 Cumulative Bulletin 133.

ISSUE

Does the acquisition by one corporation of all of the stock of another corporation solely in exchange for voting stock of the acquiring corporation qualify as a tax-free reorganization under section 368(a)(1)(B) if the acquired corporation's assets consist solely of cash that it realized from the sale of assets it previously used in its manufacturing business?

FACTS

T, a corporation engaged in manufacturing, sold all of its assets for cash to *Z*, an unrelated corporation. The sale was made as part of a plan of reorganization in which *P*, a corporation engaged in the manufacture of products different than those previously manufactured by *T*, acquired all of the outstanding stock in *T* from *T*'s shareholders, in exchange solely for *P* voting stock. *T*, as a wholly owned subsidiary of *P*, then used the cash realized on the sale of its manufacturing assets to engage in a business entirely unrelated to its previous manufacturing business.

LAW AND ANALYSIS

Section 368(a)(1)(B) of the Code provides, in pertinent part, that the term "reorganization" means the acquisition by one corporation, in exchange solely for shares of its voting stock, of the outstanding stock of another corporation if, immediately after the transaction, the acquiring corporation has control of such other corporation.

Section 1.368–1(b) of the Income Tax Regulations states that in order for a reorganization to qualify under section 368(a)(1) of the Code there must be a continuity of the business enterprise under the modified corporate form.

Section 1.368–1(d) of the regulations provides, in general, that the continuity of business enterprise requirement of section 1.368–1(b) is satisfied if the transferee in a corporate reorganization either (i) continues the transferor's historic business or (ii) uses a significant portion of the transferor's historic business assets in a business. Because the continuity of business enterprise requirement must be met for a transaction to qualify as a reorganization, section 1.368–1(d) is applicable to a transaction intended to qualify as a tax free reorganization under section 368(a)(1)(B) of the Code. See section 1.368–1(d)(1)(iii). Therefore, the transferee corporation must continue the transferor's historic business, or continue to use a significant portion of the transferor's historic business assets, in modified corporate form as a subsidiary of the transferee corporation for the transaction to qualify under section 368(a)(1)(B).

HOLDING

In the instant transaction, the acquisition by *P* of the *T* stock solely for *P*'s voting stock does not qualify as a tax-free reorganization under section 368(a)(1)(B) since *P* did not continue *T*'s historic (the manufacturing) business or use a significant portion of *T*'s historic business assets (those used in the manufacturing business) in a business conducted as a subsidiary of *P* after the transaction.

Accordingly, gain or loss is realized and recognized to the former shareholders of *T* upon the receipt by them from *P* of the *P* voting stock in exchange for their *T* stock under section 1001 of the Code.

ILLUSTRATIVE MATERIAL

A. BACKGROUND

Regulations, section 1.368–1(b), state that one prerequisite to a "reorganization" is "a continuity of the business enterprise under the modified corporate form." Prior to 1981, establishing the scope of this requirement was left to case law and Revenue Rulings. In general, the requirement was not particularly difficult to satisfy; as long as the acquiring corporation used the assets of the acquired corporation in some business, even though different than the historic business of the acquired corporation, the continuity of business enterprise test was met. See, e.g., Bensten v. Phinney, 199 F.Supp. 363 (S.D.Tex.1961) (merger of land development business into insurance company, which thereafter conducted only an insurance business); Atlas Tool Co. v. Commissioner, 614 F.2d 860 (3d Cir.1980) (continuity of business enterprise existed where acquired corporation's business was discontinued and its assets were held in reserve for future use in acquiring corporation's business; assets were restored to use within three months following acquisition). The requirement also was satisfied where the acquiring corporation discontinued its own historic business and continued the business of the acquired corporation. Rev.Rul. 63–29, 1963–1 Cum.Bull. 77 (corporation which had discontinued its toy business acquired the property of a steel distributor in a (C) reorganization and continued the steel business; held, continuity of business enterprise established). However, Wortham Machinery Co. v. United States, 521 F.2d 160 (10th Cir.1975), found no continuity of business enterprise where the transferor corporation in a purported (C) reorganization was engaged in no business activity at the time of the transfer and the acquiring corporation merely tried to dispose of the acquired assets; there was more than a "temporary suspension" of business activities. Consequently there was no reorganization: "Liquidation of assets is not continuation of a business enterprise." (163)

B. REGULATIONS

Regulations, section 1.368–1(d), issued in 1981, expand substantially the continuity of business enterprise requirement applicable to post–1981 acquisitions. These Regulations require that the acquiring corporation either (1) continue at least one of the acquired corporation's historic businesses, or (2) use a significant portion of the acquired corporation's historic assets in a business. Thus, as under prior law, the historic business of either corporation may be discontinued as long as some business is conducted after the acquisition. Examples in the Regulations indicate that continuity of business enterprise does not exist where the historic assets of the acquired corporation are sold either before the acquisition (thereby rendering it an investment company) or shortly after the acquisition. See also Rev.Rul. 81–25, 1981–1 Cum.Bull. 132 (Rev.Rul. 63–29. supra applies to post–1981 acquisitions).

Laure v. Commissioner, 653 F.2d 253 (6th Cir.1981), involved a tax year prior to the 1981 Regulations. But the court noted that the Regulations supported its conclusion that the retention of 27 percent of the acquired corporation's operating assets for use in the acquiring corporation's business satisfied the continuity of business requirement. Prior to the merger the acquired corporation had operated an air charter service, using leased aircraft. After the merger all of the air charter business assets, other than land and an airport hangar on the land, were sold. The hangar was leased to the purchaser of the bulk of the assets, who in turn provided air charter services to the taxpayer. The Court of Appeals held the Tax Court's finding of a lack of continuity of business enterprise was clearly erroneous because the retained assets were "substantial both in relation to the other assets transferred and in importance to the acquiring corporation."

Where a holding company is merged into its operating subsidiary, the continuity of business interest requirement is satisfied by looking through the holding company to treat the operating subsidiary's business as the business of the holding company. Rev.Rul. 85–197, 1985–2 Cum.Bull. 120. Where X Corporation acquires Y Corporation, which is a holding company, the continuity of business requirement is satisfied as long as a significant business of one of Y's subsidiary corporations is conducted directly or indirectly by X, for example by a second tier subsidiary of X. Rev.Rul. 85–198, 1985–2 Cum.Bull. 120.

Suppose that, following the acquisition, the acquiring corporation drops all or part of the assets of the acquired corporation into one or more of its subsidiaries, as is permitted under section 368(a)(2)(C). Rev.Rul. 81–247, 1981–2 Cum.Bull. 87, held that as long as the assets of the acquired corporation held by the acquiring corporation and any of its controlled subsidiaries, taken in the aggregate, constituted a significant portion of the acquired corporation's historic business assets, the continuity of business enterprise requirement was satisfied even if no one corporation held a significant portion of the assets.

Suppose that a corporation which is a personal holding company whose historic business is that of purchasing, holding, and selling marketable securities is acquired by a mutual fund in a transaction which literally qualifies as a reorganization. Rev.Rul. 74–155, 1974–1 Cum.Bull. 86, held that the acquisition of a personal holding company by a regulated investment company in a (C) reorganization met the "continuity of business enterprise" test where the personal holding company had been engaged in purchasing, selling and managing securities for a number of years before the reorganization.[14] Compare Rev.Rul. 87–86, 1987–2 Cum.Bull. 252 (no continuity of business enterprise where an investment company in the business of investing in stocks and corporate bonds sold its portfolio and invested the proceeds in municipal bonds prior to its acquisition by another investment company in a transaction which otherwise qualified as a type (C) reorganization). See also Regulations, section 1.368–1(d)(5), Ex. (3).

C. REFERENCES

Faber, Continuity of Interest and Business Enterprise: Is It Time to Bury Some Sacred Cows?, 34 Tax.Law. 239 (1981); Libin, Continuity of Business Enterprise: The New Regulations, 39 N.Y.U. Fed.Tax Inst. 4–1 (1981); Brown, An Approach to Subchapter C, in Tax Revision Compendium, House Committee on Ways and Means, 86th Cong., 1st Sess. Vol. 3, p. 1619 (1959).

SECTION 4. STATUTORY MERGERS: (A) REORGANIZATIONS

A. DEFINITIONAL ASPECTS

INTERNAL REVENUE CODE: Sections 368(a)(1)(A), (a)(2)(C).

REGULATIONS: Sections 1.368–2(b).

In terms of Code requirements, the (A) reorganization represents the simplest type of acquisitive reorganization. Section 368(a)(1)(A) defines an (A) reorganization as a "statutory merger or consolidation." Thus, generally speaking, any type of amalgamation or consolidation of corporate entities under state law would meet the statutory definition. The assets and liabilities of the acquired corporation are transferred to the acquiring corporation by operation of state law; the shareholders of the acquiring corporation receive the consideration agreed upon in the merger agreement in exchange for their stock. State corporate law typically requires the approval of the shareholders of both the acquiring and acquired corporations in a statutory merger.[15] While the statutory definition of an (A) reorganization does not contain any explicit requirement of continuity of shareholder interest, the courts uniformly have applied the requirement.

ILLUSTRATIVE MATERIAL

A. APPLICATION OF THE CONTINUITY OF INTEREST DOCTRINE TO (A) REORGANIZATIONS

1. *Qualitative and Quantitative Aspects*

Unlike the type (B) and type (C) reorganizations, discussed infra, pages 817 and 844, there are no specific statutory requirements concerning con-

14. The Tax Reform Act of 1976 added section 368(a)(2)(F), denying reorganization treatment to such acquisitions where the transaction has the effect of diversifying the investments of the holding company.

15. The difficulties involved in obtaining shareholder approval on the part of the acquiring corporation's shareholders, as well as other factors, have led to the development of so-called "triangular" statutory mergers discussed, infra, page 852.

tinuity of interest in an (A) reorganization. Thus the required continuity is tested under court developed standards.

In Southwest Natural Gas Company v. Commissioner, 189 F.2d 332 (5th Cir.1951), continuity of interest was held to be lacking in a statutory merger where those shareholders of the transferor who chose to receive some stock in the merger had received about 16 percent of the common stock of the transferee, but such interest was worth only about $5,500 out of a total consideration of about $660,000 in bonds, cash, assumptions of liabilities, and stock. However, prior to the merger the group that owned 35 percent of the common stock of the transferor also held 85 percent of the transferee's common stock and after the merger this group owned 88 percent of the transferee's stock. Thus, an underlying equity interest in the transferee actually existed, as a dissent pointed out, though "control" did not exist because 80 percent of the preferred stock was not held by the group.

The *Southwest Natural Gas* opinion phrased the continuity of interest test as follows:

"Where no precise formula has been expressed for determining whether there has been retention of the requisite interest, it seems clear that the requirement of continuity of interest consistent with the statutory intent is not fulfilled in the absence of a showing: (1) that the transferor corporation or its shareholders retained a substantial proprietary stake in the enterprise represented by a material interest in the affairs of the transferee corporation, and, (2) that such retained interest represents a substantial part of the value of the property transferred." (334)

Taken literally, the first requirement would in general depend on the relative size of the two corporations that are merged. This measure of the *quantitative* aspect is not stressed in the cases and does not appear to be a significant factor in Internal Revenue Service policy.

The focus instead is primarily on the second factor, the relation between the value of the stock received and the value of the equity interest in the acquired corporation. Although the case law has not established a specific minimum percentage of the total consideration which must be received in the form of stock of the acquiring corporation, the Service will grant advance rulings in (A) reorganizations under the following conditions:

"The 'continuity of interest' requirement of section 1.368–1(b) of the Income Tax Regulations is satisfied if there is a continuing interest through stock ownership in the acquiring or transferee corporation (or a corporation in 'control' thereof within the meaning of section 368(c) of the Code) on the part of the former shareholders of the acquired or transferor corporation which is equal in value, as of the effective date of the reorganization, to at least 50 percent of the value of all of the formerly outstanding stock of the acquired or transferor corporation as of the same date. It is not necessary that each shareholder of the acquired or transferor corporation receive in the exchange stock of the acquiring or transferee corporation in 'control' thereof, which is equal in value to at least 50 percent of the value of his former stock interest in the acquired or transferor corporation, so long as one or more of the shareholders of the acquired or transferor corporation have a continuing interest through stock ownership in the acquiring or transferee corporation (or a corporation in 'control' thereof) which is, in the aggregate, equal in value to at least 50 percent of the value of all of the formerly outstanding stock of the acquired or transferor corporation." Rev.Proc. 77–37, 1977–2 Cum.Bull. 568 (section 3.2).

Note, however, that in John A. Nelson Co. v. Helvering, 296 U.S. 374 (1935), supra, page 772, the Supreme Court found the continuity of interest requirement to have been satisfied where only 38.46 percent of the consideration was stock of the acquiring corporation. See also Kass v. Commissioner, 60 T.C. 218 (1973), aff'd by order, 491 F.2d 749 (3d Cir.1974) (16 percent insufficient); Yoc Heating Corp. v. Commissioner, 61 T.C. 168 (1973) (15 percent insufficient); Civic Center Finance Co. v. Kuhl, 83 F.Supp. 251 (E.D.Wisc.1948), aff'd per curiam, 177 F.2d 706 (7th Cir.1949) (participation by 40 percent of the former stockholders was held insufficient to provide continuity of interest); Western Mass. Theatres, Inc. v. Commissioner, 236 F.2d 186 (1st Cir.1956) (67 percent participation was held sufficient in a bankruptcy reorganization).

Rev.Rul. 66–224, 1966–2 Cum.Bull. 114, held that the continuity of interest requirement is to be applied with reference to the aggregate consideration received by the entire group of the shareholders of the acquired corporation. Thus, for example, if A, B, C, and D each own 25 percent of the stock of X Corporation, and X Corporation is merged into Y Corporation in consideration of $100,000 cash and $100,000 worth of Y Corporation stock, the transaction will qualify as a type (A) reorganization regardless of how the consideration is distributed among A, B, C, and D; thus A and B could receive only cash while C and D received only stock. The gain attributable to the cash boot that must be recognized by each shareholder, however, will be determined individually.

In Roebling v. Commissioner, 143 F.2d 810 (3d Cir.1944), the acquired corporation had leased all its properties to the acquiring corporation for 900 years. As a result of a merger, the former shareholders of the acquired corporation received 100 year bonds of the acquiring corporation which paid annual interest equal to the amount previously paid as rent. The court rejected the taxpayer's argument that the former shareholders' interests after the merger were substantially equivalent to their interests before the merger and applied LeTulle v. Scofield, 308 U.S. 415 (1940), supra, page 772, to find that there was not a reorganization.

Suppose that the acquired corporation is insolvent so that the shareholders receive little or no equity interest in the acquiring corporation, while the creditors of the insolvent acquired corporation receive an equity interest in the acquiring corporation. Has the continuity of interest requirement been satisfied? In Helvering v. Alabama Asphaltic Limestone Co., 315 U.S. 179 (1942), the Supreme Court held that a transfer of assets pursuant to which creditors of a bankrupt concern became the controlling stockholders of a new corporation, provided the requisite continuity of interest. Although the old continuity of proprietary interest was broken when the creditors took steps to enforce their demands against the insolvent concern, by such action they stepped into the shoes of the stockholders and hence continuity was present on the subsequent exchange. See also Norman Scott, Inc. v. Commissioner, 48 T.C. 598 (1967) (statutory merger between the surviving corporation and its insolvent sister corporation qualified as an (A) reorganization; the continuity of interest test was satisfied since the principal shareholder-creditors of the insolvent corporation received stock in the surviving corporation). The special aspects of reorganizations involving insolvent corporations are considered in Chapter 22.

2. *Historic Shareholders Requirement*

A number of decisions have imposed the requirement that continuity of interest be tested with respect to the "historic" shareholders of the acquired corporation, not those persons who owned the stock of the acquired corporation immediately before the merger. In Superior Coach of Florida, Inc. v. Commissioner, 80 T.C. 895 (1983), individuals A and B, the majority shareholders of P Corporation, purchased all of the stock of T Corporation from its shareholders, who were unrelated to A or B. Immediately thereafter, T Corporation was merged into P Corporation. To prevent P Corporation from utilizing T Corporation's net operating loss carryovers under section 381 and a prior version of section 382, the Commissioner argued that the merger was not a reorganization under section 368(a)(1)(A) because there was no continuity of interest. The court held for the Commissioner, stating that in order for shareholders to be considered historic shareholders the acquired corporation's shares must be "old and cold" in their hands.

In Kass v. Commissioner, 60 T.C. 218 (1973), aff'd by order, 491 F.2d 749 (3d Cir.1974), individuals A and B, minority shareholders in X Corporation, desired to obtain control of X Corporation. To accomplish this goal, A and B organized Y Corporation and contributed their X Corporation stock to Y Corporation. As a result, Y Corporation held 10.23 percent of the stock of X Corporation. Shortly thereafter, Y Corporation purchased for cash an additional 83.95 percent of the stock of X Corporation. Finally, X Corporation was merged into Y Corporation, with the remaining shareholders of X Corporation stock, who held 5.82 percent of the X Corporation stock, receiving Y Corporation stock. The taxpayer was one of the minority shareholders who received Y Corporation stock in the merger and claimed that the transaction was a type (A) reorganization. The court agreed with the Commissioner's argument that as far as the shareholders were concerned the transaction was a taxable sale because shareholders of Y Corporation had held only 16 percent of the stock of X Corporation prior to the commencement of the series of transactions culminating in the merger. Thus the continuity of interest requirement was not satisfied. See also Security Industrial Insurance Co. v. United States, 702 F.2d 1234 (5th Cir.1983) (applying "historic" shareholder test to defeat taxpayer's assertion of (F) reorganization status); Yoc Heating Corp. v. Commissioner, 61 T.C. 168 (1973) (same); Russell v. Commissioner, 832 F.2d 349 (6th Cir.1987) (merger of subsidiary into parent after purchase of 98 percent of subsidiary stock was not a reorganization).

3. *Temporal Aspects*

While the continuity of interest requirement is literally satisfied by the transferor's receipt of stock consideration in the reorganization, the continued participation in the acquiring corporation must be more than transitory. In Rev.Rul. 66–23, 1966–1 Cum.Bull. 67, the shareholder was required under the terms of an antitrust decree to divest itself of stock received in an (A) reorganization within seven years. The Ruling held that the continuity of interest test was met:

"It is the position of the Internal Revenue Service that the continuity of interest requirements of a reorganization can be satisfied where the shareholder of the transferor corporation receives stock of the transferee corporation without any preconceived plan or arrangement for disposing of any of the stock and with unrestricted rights of ownership for a period of time sufficient to warrant the conclusion that such ownership is definite and substantial, notwithstanding that at the time of the reorganization the shareholder is required by a court decree to dispose of the stock before the end of such period. Ordinarily, the Service will treat five years of unrestricted rights of ownership as a sufficient period for the purpose of satisfying the continuity of interest requirements of a reorganization.

"Further if in fact [the shareholder] does sell some or all of [the shares] within 5 years of the date of the reorganization, the status of the reorganization will not be affected, since at the time of the reorganization [the shareholder] had no preconceived plan or arrangement for such sales." (68).

Rev.Proc. 77–37, 1977–2 Cum.Bull. 568 (section 3.02), indicates that for purposes of issuing advance rulings "sales, redemptions, and other dispositions of stock occurring prior or subsequent to the exchange which are part of the plan of reorganization" will be considered in determining whether the continuity of interest test has been met.

United States v. Adkins–Phelps, Inc., 400 F.2d 737 (8th Cir.1968), found the continuity of interest test satisfied where the principal shareholder and creditor received a one-sixth stock interest in the surviving corporation; the court rejected the Government's argument that the stock interest obtained did not provide the requisite continuity of interest where it was subject to a right of first refusal in the corporation to purchase the stock for $997 should the shareholder wish to dispose of the interest.

Why should the shareholder's intention to dispose of the stock of the acquiring corporation received in the merger be taken into account in determining whether the continuity of interest test has been met as long as the shareholder has not entered into a binding commitment to dispose of the shares? Recall that in determining whether the transferors of property to a corporation have "control" as is required for nonrecognition under section 351, post incorporation transfers of stock which the original transferor was not obligated to make at the time of the transfer of property to the corporation generally are not considered to defeat the control requirement. See supra, page 367. If this standard had been applied in *McDonald's of Illinois,* supra, the transaction would have been found to be a reorganization.

4. *Regulations*

Regulations, section 1.368–1(b), impose the continuity of interest requirement on all types of acquisitive reorganizations and further require continuity on the part of those persons who "directly or indirectly" owned the acquired corporation prior to the transaction. Rev.Rul. 84–30, 1984–1 Cum.Bull. 114, held that the continuity of interest requirement was satisfied where X Corporation owned all of the stock of Y Corporation and Z Corporation; Z Corporation in turn owned all of the stock of N Corporation; N Corporation was merged into Y Corporation, and Z Corporation immediately distributed the Y Corporation stock received in the merger to X Corporation. X Corporation was considered to be an indirect owner of N Corporation prior to the merger.

B. CONTINUITY OF BUSINESS ENTERPRISE

See supra, page 792.

B. TAX RESULTS TO THE PARTIES TO AN (A) REORGANIZATION

(1) Shareholders and Security Holders

INTERNAL REVENUE CODE: Sections 354(a); 356(a), (c), (d), (e); 358(a), (b); 368(b).

REGULATIONS: Sections 1.354–1(a), (b), (e); 1.356–1, –3, –4; 1.358–1, –2; 1.368–2(f), (g).

COMMISSIONER v. CLARK

Supreme Court of the United States, 1989.
489 U.S. 726.

Justice Stevens delivered the opinion of the Court.

This is the third case in which the Government has asked us to decide that a shareholder's receipt of a cash payment in exchange for a portion of his stock was taxable as a dividend. In the two earlier cases, Commissioner v. Estate of Bedford, 325 U.S. 283, 65 S.Ct. 1157, 89 L.Ed. 1611 (1945), and United States v. Davis, 397 U.S. 301, 90 S.Ct. 1041, 25 L.Ed.2d 323 (1970), we agreed with the Government largely because the transactions involved redemptions of stock by single corporations that did not "result in a meaningful reduction of the shareholder's proportionate interest in the corporation." Id., at 313, 90 S.Ct. at 1048. In the case we decide today, however, the taxpayer in an arm's length transaction exchanged his interest in the acquired corporation for less than one percent of the stock of the acquiring corporation and a substantial cash payment. The taxpayer held no interest in the acquiring corporation prior to the reorganization. Viewing the exchange as a whole, we conclude that the cash payment is not appropriately characterized as a dividend. We accordingly agree with the Tax Court and with the Court of Appeals that the taxpayer is entitled to capital gains treatment of the cash payment.

I

In determining tax liability under the Internal Revenue Code, gain resulting from the sale or exchange of property is generally treated as capital gain, whereas the receipt of cash dividends is treated as ordinary income.[2] The Code, however, imposes no current tax on certain stock-for-stock exchanges. In particular, § 354(a)(1) provides, subject to

2. In 1979, the tax year in question, the distinction between long-term capital gain and ordinary income was of considerable importance. Most significantly, § 1202(a) of the Code allowed individual taxpayers to deduct 60% of their net capital gain from gross income. Although the importance of the distinction declined dramatically in 1986 with the repeal of § 1202(a), see Tax Reform Act of 1986, Pub.L. 99–514, § 301(a), 100 Stat. 2216, the distinction is still significant in a number of respects. For example, § 1211(b) allows individual taxpayers to deduct capital losses to the full extent of their capital gains, but only allows them to offset up to $3000 of ordinary income insofar as their capital losses exceed their capital gains.

various limitations, for nonrecognition of gain resulting from the exchange of stock or securities solely for other stock or securities, provided that the exchange is pursuant to a plan of corporate reorganization and that the stock or securities are those of a party to the reorganization. 26 U.S.C. § 354(a)(1).

Under § 356(a)(1) of the Code, if such a stock-for-stock exchange is accompanied by additional consideration in the form of a cash payment or other property—something that tax practitioners refer to as "boot"—"then the gain, if any, to the recipient shall be recognized, but in an amount not in excess of the sum of such money and the fair market value of such other property." 26 U.S.C. § 356(a)(1). That is, if the shareholder receives boot, he or she must recognize the gain on the exchange up to the value of the boot. Boot is accordingly generally treated as a gain from the sale or exchange of property and is recognized in the current tax-year.

Section 356(a)(2), which controls the decision in this case, creates an exception to that general rule. * * * [If] the "exchange * * * has the effect of the distribution of a dividend," the boot must be treated as a dividend and is therefore appropriately taxed as ordinary income to the extent that gain is realized. In contrast, if the exchange does not have "the effect of the distribution of a dividend," the boot must be treated as a payment in exchange for property and, insofar as gain is realized, accorded capital gains treatment. The question in this case is thus whether the exchange between the taxpayer and the acquiring corporation had "the effect of the distribution of a dividend" within the meaning of § 356(a)(2).

The relevant facts are easily summarized. For approximately 15 years prior to April 1979, the taxpayer was the sole shareholder and president of Basin Surveys, Inc. (Basin), a company in which he had invested approximately $85,000. The corporation operated a successful business providing various technical services to the petroleum industry. In 1978, N.L. Industries, Inc. (NL), a publicly owned corporation engaged in the manufacture and supply of petroleum equipment and services, initiated negotiations with the taxpayer regarding the possible acquisition of Basin. On April 3, 1979, after months of negotiations, the taxpayer and NL entered into a contract.

The agreement provided for a "triangular merger," whereby Basin was merged into a wholly owned subsidiary of NL. In exchange for transferring all of the outstanding shares in Basin to NL's subsidiary, the taxpayer elected to receive 300,000 shares of NL common stock and cash boot of $3,250,000, passing up an alternative offer of 425,000 shares of NL common stock. The 300,000 shares of NL issued to the taxpayer amounted to approximately 0.92% of the outstanding common shares of NL. If the taxpayer had instead accepted the pure stock-for-stock offer, he would have held approximately 1.3% of the outstanding common shares. The Commissioner and the taxpayer agree that the merger at issue qualifies as a reorganization under § 368(a)(1)(A) and (a)(2)(D).

Respondents filed a joint federal income tax return for 1979. As required by § 356(a)(1), they reported the cash boot as taxable gain. In calculating the tax owed, respondents characterized the payment as long-term capital gain. The Commissioner on audit disagreed with this characterization. In his view, the payment had "the effect of the distribution of a dividend" and was thus taxable as ordinary income up to $2,319,611, the amount of Basin's accumulated earnings and profits at the time of the merger. The Commissioner assessed a deficiency of $972,504.74.

Respondents petitioned for review in the Tax Court, which, in a reviewed decision, held in their favor. 86 T.C. 138 (1986). The court started from the premise that the question whether the boot payment had "the effect of the distribution of a dividend" turns on the choice between "two judicially articulated tests." Id., at 140. Under the test advocated by the Commissioner and given voice in Shimberg v. United States, 577 F.2d 283 (CA5 1978), cert. denied, 439 U.S. 1115, 99 S.Ct. 1019, 59 L.Ed.2d 73 (1979), the boot payment is treated as though it were made in a hypothetical redemption by the acquired corporation (Basin) immediately *prior* to the reorganization. Under this test, the cash payment received by the taxpayer indisputably would have been treated as a dividend.[6] The second test, urged by the taxpayer and finding support in Wright v. United States, 482 F.2d 600 (CA8 1973), proposes an alternative hypothetical redemption. Rather than concentrating on the taxpayer's pre-reorganization interest in the acquired corporation, this test requires that one imagine a pure stock-for-stock exchange, followed immediately by a post-reorganization redemption of a portion of the taxpayer's shares in the acquiring corporation (NL) in return for a payment in an amount equal to the boot. Under § 302 of the Code, which defines when a redemption of stock should be treated

6. The parties do not agree as to whether dividend equivalence for the purposes of § 356(a)(2) should be determined with reference to § 302 of the Code, which concerns dividend treatment of redemptions of stock by a single corporation outside the context of a reorganization. Compare Brief for the United States 28–30 with Brief for Respondent 18–24. They are in essential agreement, however, about the characteristics of a dividend. Thus, the Government correctly argues that the "basic attribute of a dividend, derived from Sections 301 and 316 of the Code, is a pro rata distribution to shareholders out of corporate earnings and profits. When a distribution is made that is not a formal dividend, 'the fundamental test of dividend equivalency' is whether the distribution is proportionate to the shareholders' stock interests (United States v. Davis, 397 U.S. 301, 306 [90 S.Ct. 1041, 1044, 25 L.Ed.2d 323] (1970))." Brief for Petitioner 7. Citing the same authority, but with different emphasis, the taxpayer argues that "the hallmark of a non-dividend distribution is a 'meaningful reduction of the shareholder's proportionate interest in the corporation.' United States v. Davis, 397 U.S. 301, 313 [90 S.Ct. 1041, 1048, 25 L.Ed.2d 323] (1970)." Brief for Respondents 5.

Under either test, a pre-reorganization distribution by Basin to the taxpayer would have qualified as a dividend. Because the taxpayer was Basin's sole shareholder, any distribution necessarily would have been pro rata and would not have resulted in a "meaningful reduction of the [taxpayer's] proportionate interest in [Basin]."

as a distribution of dividend, NL's redemption of 125,000 shares of its stock from the taxpayer in exchange for the $3,250,000 boot payment would have been treated as capital gain.[7]

The Tax Court rejected the pre-reorganization test favored by the Commissioner because it considered it improper "to view the cash payment as an isolated event totally separate from the reorganization." 86 T.C., at 151. Indeed, it suggested that this test requires that courts make the "determination of dividend equivalency fantasizing that the reorganization does not exist." Id., at 150 (footnote omitted). The court then acknowledged that a similar criticism could be made of the taxpayer's contention that the cash payment should be viewed as a post-reorganization redemption. It concluded, however, that since it was perfectly clear that the cash payment would not have taken place without the reorganization, it was better to treat the boot "as the equivalent of a redemption *in the course of implementing the reorganization,*" than "as having occurred *prior to and separate from the reorganization.*" Id., at 152 (emphasis in original).[8]

The Court of Appeals for the Fourth Circuit affirmed. 828 F.2d 221 (1987). Like the Tax Court, it concluded that although "[s]ection 302 does not explicitly apply in the reorganization context," id., at 223, and although § 302 differs from § 356 in important respects, id., at 224, it nonetheless provides "the appropriate test for determining whether boot is ordinary income or a capital gain," id., at 223. Thus, as explicated in § 302(b)(2), if the taxpayer relinquished more than 20% of his corporate control and retained less than 50% of the voting shares

7. * * *

As the Tax Court explained, receipt of the cash boot reduced the taxpayer's potential holdings in NL from 1.3% to 0.92%. 86 T.C., at 153. The taxpayer's holdings were thus approximately 71% of what they would have been absent the payment. Ibid. This fact, combined with the fact that the taxpayer held less than 50% of the voting stock of NL after the hypothetical redemption, would have qualified the "distribution" as "substantially disproportionate" under § 302(b)(2).

8. The Tax Court stressed that to adopt the pre-reorganization view "would in effect resurrect the now discredited 'automatic dividend rule' * * *, at least with respect to pro rata distributions made to an acquired corporation's shareholders pursuant to a plan of reorganization." 86 T.C., at 152. On appeal, the Court of Appeals agreed. 828 F.2d 221, 226–227 (CA4 1987).

The "automatic dividend rule" developed as a result of some imprecise language in our decision in Commissioner v. Estate of Bedford, 325 U.S. 283, 65 S.Ct. 1157, 89 L.Ed. 1611 (1945). Although *Estate of Bedford* involved the recapitalization of a single corporation, the opinion employed broad language, asserting that "a distribution, pursuant to a reorganization, of earnings and profits 'has the effect of a distribution of a taxable dividend' within [§ 356(a)(2)]." Id., at 292, 65 S.Ct., at 1161. The Commissioner read this language as establishing as a matter of law that all payments of boot are to be treated as dividends to the extent of undistributed earnings and profits. See Rev.Rul. 56–220, 1956–1 Cum.Bull. 191. Commentators, see, e.g., Darrel, The Scope of Commissioner v. Bedford Estate, 24 Taxes 266 (1946); Shoulson, Boot Taxation: The Blunt Toe of the Automatic Rule, 20 Tax L.Rev. 573 (1965), and courts, see, e.g., Hawkinson v. Commissioner, 235 F.2d 747 (CA2 1956), however, soon came to criticize this rule. The courts have long since retreated from the "automatic dividend rule," see, e.g., Idaho Power Co. v. United States, 161 F.Supp. 807, 142 Ct.Cl. 534, cert. denied, 358 U.S. 832, 79 S.Ct. 53, 3 L.Ed.2d 70 (1958), and the Commissioner has followed suit, see Rev.Rul. 74–515, 1974–2 Cum.Bull. 118. As our decision in this case makes plain, we agree that *Estate of Bedford* should not be read to require that all payments of boot be treated as dividends.

after the distribution, the boot would be treated as capital gain. However, as the Court of Appeals recognized, "[b]ecause § 302 was designed to deal with a stock redemption by a single corporation, rather than a reorganization involving two companies, the section does not indicate which corporation [the taxpayer] lost interest in." Id., at 224. Thus, like the Tax Court, the Court of Appeals was left to consider whether the hypothetical redemption should be treated as a pre-reorganization distribution coming from the acquired corporation or as a post-reorganization distribution coming from the acquiring corporation. It concluded:

> "Based on the language and legislative history of § 356, the change-in-ownership principle of § 302, and the need to review the reorganization as an integrated transaction, we conclude that the boot should be characterized as a post-reorganization stock redemption by N.L. that affected [the taxpayer's] interest in the new corporation. Because this redemption reduced [the taxpayer's] N.L. holdings by more than 20%, the boot should be taxed as a capital gain." Id., at 224–225.

This decision by the Court of Appeals for the Fourth Circuit is in conflict with the decision of the Fifth Circuit in *Shimberg,* 577 F.2d 283 (1978), in two important respects. In *Shimberg,* the court concluded that it was inappropriate to apply stock redemption principles in reorganization cases "on a wholesale basis." Id., at 287; see also ibid, n. 13. In addition, the court adopted the pre-reorganization test, holding that "§ 356(a)(2) requires a determination of whether the distribution would have been taxed as a dividend if made prior to the reorganization or if no reorganization had occurred." Id., at 288.

* * *

II

We agree with the Tax Court and the Court of Appeals for the Fourth Circuit that the question under § 356(a)(2) of whether an "exchange . . . has the effect of the distribution of a dividend" should be answered by examining the effect of the exchange as a whole. We think the language and history of the statute, as well as a commonsense understanding of the economic substance of the transaction at issue, support this approach.

The language of § 356(a) strongly supports our understanding that the transaction should be treated as an integrated whole. Section 356(a)(2) asks whether "*an exchange* is described in paragraph (1)" that "has the effect of the distribution of a dividend." (Emphasis supplied.) The statute does not provide that boot shall be treated as a dividend if its payment has the effect of the distribution of a dividend. Rather, the inquiry turns on whether the "exchange" has that effect. Moreover, paragraph (1), in turn, looks to whether "the property received in *the exchange* consists not only of property permitted by section 354 or 355 to be received without the recognition of gain but also of other property or money." (Emphasis supplied.) Again, the statute plainly refers to one integrated transaction and, again, makes clear that we are to look to the character of the exchange as a whole and not simply its component parts. Finally, it is significant that § 356 expressly limits the extent to which boot may be taxed to the amount of gain realized in the reorganization. This limitation suggests that Congress intended that boot not be treated in isolation from the overall reorganization.

* * *

Our reading of the statute as requiring that the transaction be treated as a unified whole is reinforced by the well-established "step-transaction" doctrine, * * *.

Viewing the exchange in this case as an integrated whole, we are unable to accept the Commissioner's pre-reorganization analogy. The analogy severs the payment of boot from the context of the reorganization. Indeed, only by straining to abstract the payment of boot from the context of the overall exchange, and thus imagining that Basin made a distribution to the taxpayer independently of NL's planned acquisition, can we reach the rather counterintuitive conclusion urged by the Commissioner—that the taxpayer suffered no meaningful reduction in his ownership interest as a result of the cash payment. We conclude that such a limited view of the transaction is plainly inconsistent with the statute's direction that we look to the effect of the entire exchange.

The pre-reorganization analogy is further flawed in that it adopts an overly expansive reading of § 356(a)(2). As the Court of Appeals recognized, adoption of the pre-reorganization approach would "result in ordinary income treatment in most reorganizations because corporate boot is usually distributed pro rata to the shareholders of the target corporation." 828 F.2d, at 227. * * * Such a reading of the statute would not simply constitute a return to the widely criticized "automatic dividend rule" (at least as to cases involving a pro rata payment to the shareholders of the acquired corporation), see n. 8, supra, but also would be contrary to our standard approach to construing such provisions. The requirement of § 356(a)(2) that boot be treated as dividend in some circumstances is an exception from the general rule authorizing capital gains treatment for boot. In construing provisions such as § 356, in which a general statement of policy is qualified by an exception, we usually read the exception narrowly in order to preserve the primary operation of the provision. See Phillips, Inc. v. Walling, 324 U.S. 490, 493, 65 S.Ct. 807, 808, 89 L.Ed. 1095 (1945) ("To extend an exemption to other than those plainly and unmistakably within its terms and spirit is to abuse the interpretative process and to frustrate the announced will of the people"). Given that Congress has enacted a general rule that treats boot as capital gain, we should not eviscerate that legislative judgment through an expansive reading of a somewhat ambiguous exception.

The post-reorganization approach adopted by the Tax Court and the Court of Appeals is, in our view, preferable to the Commissioner's approach. Most significantly, this approach does a far better job of treating the payment of boot as a component of the overall exchange. Unlike the pre-reorganization view, this approach acknowledges that there would have been no cash payment absent the exchange and also that, by accepting the cash payment, the taxpayer experienced a meaningful reduction in his potential ownership interest.

Once the post-reorganization approach is adopted, the result in this case is pellucidly clear. Section 302(a) of the Code provides that if a redemption fits within any one of the four categories set out in § 302(b), the redemption "shall be treated as a distribution in part or full payment in exchange for the stock," and thus not regarded as a dividend. As the Tax Court and the Court of Appeals correctly determined, the hypothetical post-reorganization redemption by NL of a portion of the taxpayer's shares satisfies at least one of the subsections of § 302(b). In particular, the safe harbor provisions of subsection (b)(2) provide that redemptions in which the taxpayer relinquishes more than 20% of his or her share of the corporation's voting stock and retains less than 50% of the voting of stock after the redemption, shall not be treated as distributions of a dividend. See n. 7, supra. Here, we treat the transaction as though NL redeemed 125,000 shares of its common stock (i.e., the number of shares of NL common stock foregone in favor of the boot) in return for a cash payment to the taxpayer of $3,250,000 (i.e., the amount of the boot). As a result of this redemption, the taxpayer's interest in NL was reduced from 1.3% of the outstanding common stock to 0.9%. See 86 T.C., at 153. Thus, the taxpayer relinquished approximately 29% of his interest in NL and retained less than a 1% voting interest in the corporation after the transaction, easily satisfying the "substantially disproportionate" standards of § 302(b)(2). We accordingly conclude that the boot payment did not have the effect of a dividend and that the payment was properly treated as capital gain.

III

The Commissioner objects to this "recasting [of] the merger transaction into a form different from that entered into by the parties," Brief for the United States 11, and argues that the Court of Appeals' formal adherence to the principles embodied in § 302 forced the court to stretch to "find a redemption to which to apply them, since the merger transaction entered into by the parties did not involve a redemption," id., at 28. There are a number of sufficient responses to this argument. We think it first worth emphasizing that the Commissioner overstates the extent to which the redemption is imagined. As the Court of Appeals for the Fifth Circuit noted in *Shimberg,* "[t]he theory behind tax-free corporate reorganizations is that the transaction is merely 'a continuance of the proprietary interests in the continuing enterprise under modified corporate form.' * * * As a result, the boot-for-stock transaction can be viewed as a partial repurchase of stock by the continuing corporate enterprise—i.e., as a redemption. It is of course true that both the pre- and post-reorganization analogies are somewhat artificial in that they imagine that the redemption occurred outside the confines of the actual reorganization. However, if forced to choose between the two analogies, the post-reorganization view is the less artificial. Although both analogies "recast the merger transaction," the post-reorganization view recognizes that a reorganization has taken place, while the pre-reorganization approach recasts the transaction to the exclusion of the overall exchange.

Moreover, we doubt that abandoning the pre- and post-reorganization analogies and the principles of § 302 in favor of a less artificial understanding of the transaction would lead to a result different from that reached by the Court of Appeals. Although the statute is admittedly ambiguous and the legislative history sparse, we are persuaded—even without relying on § 302—that Congress did not intend to except reorganizations such as that at issue here from the general rule allowing capital gains treatment for cash boot. 26 U.S.C. § 356(a)(1). The legislative history of § 356(a)(2), although perhaps generally "not illuminating," Estate of Bedford, 325 U.S., at 290, 65 S.Ct., at 1160, suggests that Congress was primarily concerned with preventing corporations from "siphon[ing] off" accumulated earnings and profits at a capital gains rate through the ruse of a reorganization. * * * This purpose is not served by denying capital gains treatment in a case such as this in which the taxpayer entered into an arm's length transaction with a corporation in which he had no prior interest, exchanging his stock in the acquired corporation for less than a one percent interest in the acquiring corporation and a substantial cash boot.

* * *

Moreover, the legislative history of § 302 supports this reading of § 356(a)(2) as well. In explaining the "essentially equivalent to a dividend" language of § 302(b)(1)—language that is certainly similar to the "has the effect * * * of a dividend" language of § 356(a)(2)—the Senate Finance Committee made clear that the relevant inquiry is "whether or not the transaction by its nature may properly be characterized as a sale of stock. * * *" S.Rep. No. 1622, 83d Cong., 2d Sess., 234 (1954); cf. United States v. Davis, 397 U.S., at 311, 90 S.Ct., at 1047.

Examining the instant transaction in light of the purpose of § 356(a)(2), the boot-for-stock exchange in this case "may properly be characterized as a sale of stock." Significantly, unlike traditional single corporation redemptions and unlike reorganizations involving commonly owned corporations, there is little risk that the reorganization at issue was used as a ruse to distribute dividend. Rather, the transaction appears in all respects relevant to the narrow issue before us to have been comparable to an arm's length sale by the taxpayer to NL. This conclusion, moreover, is supported by the findings of the Tax Court. The court found that "[t]here is not the slightest evidence that the cash payment was a concealed distribution from BASIN." 86 T.C., at 155. As the Tax Court further noted, Basin lacked the funds to make such a distribution:

> "Indeed, it is hard to conceive that such a possibility could even have been considered, for a distribution of that amount was not only far in excess of the accumulated earnings and profits ($2,319,611), but also of the total assets of BASIN ($2,758,069). In fact, only if one takes into account unrealized appreciation in the value of BASIN's assets, including good will and/or going-concern value, can one possibly arrive at $3,250,000. Such a distribution could only be considered as the equivalent of a complete liquidation of BASIN. * * *" Ibid.

In this context, even without relying on § 302 and the post-reorganization analogy, we conclude that the boot is better characterized as a part of the proceeds of a sale of stock than as a proxy for a dividend. As such, the payment qualifies for capital gains treatment.

The judgment of the Court of Appeals is accordingly

AFFIRMED.

JUSTICE WHITE, dissenting.

* * *

[T]he question today is whether the cash payment to Clark had the *effect* of a distribution of a dividend. We supplied the straightforward answer in United States v. Davis, 397 U.S. 301, 306, 312, 90 S.Ct. 1041, 1044, 1047, 25 L.Ed.2d 323 (1970), when we explained that a pro rata redemption of stock by a corporation is "essentially equivalent" to a dividend. A pro rata distribution of stock, with no alteration of basic shareholder relationships, is the hallmark of a dividend. This was precisely Clark's gain. As sole shareholder of Basin, Clark necessarily received a pro rata distribution of monies that exceeded Basin's undistributed earnings and profits of $2,319,611. Because the merger and cash obligation occurred simultaneously on April 18, 1979, and because the statutory merger approved here assumes that Clark's proprietary interests continue in the restructured NLAC, the exact source of the pro rata boot payment is immaterial, which truth Congress acknowledged by requiring only that an exchange have the *effect* of a dividend distribution.

To avoid this conclusion, the Court of Appeals—approved by the majority today—recast the transaction as though the relevant distribution involved a single corporation's (NL's) stock redemption, which dividend equivalency is determined according to § 302 of the Code. Section 302 shields distributions from dividend taxation if the cash redemption is accompanied by sufficient loss of a shareholder's percentage interest in the corporation. The Court of Appeals hypothesized that Clark completed a pure stock-for-stock reorganization, receiving 425,000 NL shares, and thereafter redeemed 125,000 of these shares for his cash earnings of $3,250,000. The sum escapes dividend taxation because Clark's interest in NL theoretically declined from 1.3% to

0.92%, adequate to trigger § 302(b)(2) protection. Transporting § 302 from its purpose to frustrate shareholder sales of equity back to their own corporation, to § 356(a)(2)'s reorganization context, however, is problematic. Neither the majority nor the Court of Appeals explains why § 302 should obscure the core attribute of a dividend as a pro rata distribution to a corporation's shareholders,[1] nor offers insight into the mechanics of valuing hypothetical stock transfers and equity reductions; nor answers the Commissioner's observations that the sole shareholder of an acquired corporation will always have a smaller interest in the continuing enterprise when cash payments combine with a stock exchange. Last, the majority and the Court of Appeals' recharacterization of market happenings describes the exact stock-for-stock exchange, without a cash supplement, that Clark refused when he agreed to the merger.

Because the parties chose to structure the exchange as a tax-free reorganization under § 354(a)(1), and because the pro rata distribution to Clark of $3,250,000. during this reorganization had the *effect* of a dividend under § 356(a)(2), I dissent.

ILLUSTRATIVE MATERIAL

A. NONRECOGNITION OF GAIN

Section 354 protects the shareholders from gain recognition to the extent they receive stock of the acquiring corporation. Where cash or other non-qualifying property, including debt securities, is received in addition to stock, the shareholders will recognize gain under section 356, but only to the extent of the amount of cash or the fair market value of the other property received. If a shareholder exchanges more than one block of stock in exchange for stock and boot, the gain must be computed separately on each block; gain may be recognized on one block of stock while an unrecognized loss is realized on the other. Rev.Rul. 68–23, 1968–1 Cum.Bull. 144. If a loss has been realized, it may not be recognized even though boot has been received. Section 356(c). Section 356(a)(2) provides that gain recognized under section 356(a) sometimes may be treated as a dividend, although after *Clark* there is little room to characterize boot as a dividend in the context of acquisitive mergers. Problems also can arise if shareholders of the acquired corporation receive the right to obtain additional stock conditioned, for example, on the earnings level of the corporation. See infra, page 838.

For the nonrecognition protection of section 354 to apply the stock must be received as part of the reorganization exchange. Thus, where minority shareholders in a merger refused to vote in favor of the merger unless they

1. The Court of Appeals' zeal to excoriate the "automatic dividend rule" leads to an opposite rigidity—an automatic non-dividend rule, even for pro rata boot payments. Any significant cash payment in a stock-for-stock exchange distributed to a sole shareholder of an acquired corporation will automatically receive capital gains treatment. Section 356(a)(2)'s exception for such payments that have attributes of a dividend disappears. Congress did not intend to handicap the Commissioner and courts with either absolute; instead, § 356(a)(1) instructs courts to make fact-specific inquiries into whether boot distributions accompanying corporate reorganizations occur on a pro rata basis to shareholders of the acquired corporation, and thus threaten a bailout of the transferor corporation's earnings and profits escaping a proper dividend tax treatment.

received a disproportionate amount of stock in the acquiring corporation, the amount of stock received in excess of their proportionate interest was taxable under section 61. A contribution to capital by the majority shareholder was disregarded and the transaction was treated as if all of the parties had received their proportionate shares of stock in the acquiring corporation with the majority shareholder then transferring to the minority shareholders additional shares of stock as consideration for their voting in favor of the merger. Rev.Rul. 73–233, 1973–1 Cum.Bull. 179.

B. RECEIPT OF SECURITIES

1. *Amount of Boot*

Although section 354(a) extends nonrecognition to an exchange of "stock or securities * * * for stock or securities," section 354(b) excludes from the nonrecognition rule the receipt of securities in exchange for stock or the receipt of securities in a principal amount greater than the principal amount of any securities surrendered. In such a case, section 356(d) applies. Where securities are received in exchange for stock, the entire fair market value of the securities is treated as boot. Regulations, section 1.356–3(b), Ex. (1). Where securities are received in exchange for other securities, only the fair market value of the excess principal amount constitutes boot. The value of the excess principal amount is determined by the following formula:

$$\text{Fair Market Value of Securities Received} \times \frac{\text{Principal Amount of Securities Received} - \text{Principal Amount of Securities Surrendered}}{\text{Principal Amount of Securities Received}}$$

In determining the "principal amount" of securities received in the reorganization, the original issue discount rules of sections 1272 and 1274, discussed supra, page 432, must be taken into account. If the OID rules do not apply, generally speaking, the amount of any excess face value of a security received also will be its value. However, if the OID rules apply because the securities do not bear adequate interest, the principal amount of the securities received must be reduced as required by those rules to an amount less than their face value when computing gain under section 356. Thus, receipt of a security having a *face* value in excess of the principal amount of the security surrendered will not give rise to boot under section 356 if under the OID rules the imputed principal amount of the security received does not exceed the principal amount of the security surrendered. Section 1273(b) applies to the determination of the amount of OID if either the securities surrendered or the securities received are publicly traded. In such a case, the "issue price" and thus the "principal amount" of the securities received will be equal to their fair market value if they are publicly traded. If the securities received are not publicly traded, but the securities surrendered are so traded, then the issue price is the value of the securities surrendered. Section 1274 controls if the securities involved in the exchange are not publicly traded.

See also Regulations, section 1.356–3(d), Ex. (2)–(6).

In some cases where the face value of the security received exceeds the principal amount of the security surrendered, both boot and OID may be present, even though the fair market value of the old and new securities is equal. For example, assume that pursuant to the merger of X Corporation into Y Corporation, individual A exchanges an X Corporation 10 percent, $1,000 principal bond, having a fair market value of $1,060 (but which is not an OID instrument) for a Y Corporation 9 percent, $1,100 face amount bond, which also has a fair market value of $1,060. Assuming that the Y bond is publicly traded, its issue price under section 1273(b) is $1,060. This should be treated as its principal amount for purposes of section 356. Thus, the excess principal amount is $60, and its value is $60.00 ($1,060 × ($1,060 − $1,000) / $1,060). The $40 difference between the $1,060 principal amount and the $1,100 face amount is OID.

Section 1275(a)(4) has special rules limiting the amount of new OID attributable to securities received in exchange for debt instruments in a reorganization. Generally speaking, this provision prevents the creation of OID where the redemption value of the new securities issued in the reorganization does not exceed the redemption value plus any OID accrued on the surrendered securities prior to the exchange.

2. *Installment Reporting*

Gain recognized on the receipt of securities in a reorganization may be reported using the installment method under section 453 unless either the stock or securities surrendered were readily tradable on an established securities market (section 453(h)(1)) or the securities received are readily tradable (section 453(f)(4)). See Proposed Regulations, section 1.453–1(f)(2) (1984).

C. BASIS CONSIDERATIONS

The basis for the stock of the acquiring corporation received by the shareholders of the acquired corporation without recognition of gain under section 354 is determined under section 358(a). That section provides that the basis of the stock will be the same as the stock in the acquired corporation which was given up in the reorganization transaction. If, in addition to stock or securities of the acquiring corporation, nonqualifying "boot" is received, the aggregate basis of all property received in the exchange, including both qualified stock and securities and boot, first is increased by the sum of the gain recognized and the amount treated as a dividend under section 356(b). Section 358(a)(1)(B). Then the amount of cash received is subtracted, and the boot is assigned a basis equal to its fair market value. The remaining basis is allocated among the qualified stock and securities, as provided in Regulations, section 1.358–2. If the boot is in the form of debt obligations of the acquiring corporation for which installment reporting under section 453 is available, the basis of the stock received in the reorganization is computed under Proposed Regulations, section 1.453–1(f)(2) (1984), in the same manner as the basis of stock received in a section 351 transaction is computed if an installment note is received as boot. See supra, page 348.

Generally speaking, Regulations, section 1.358–2, require that the basis be allocated among the stock or securities received in proportion to their fair market values. Where a single class of stock or securities has been surrendered, the Regulations permit the aggregate basis of the stock or securities to be used as the starting point in a single computation. Regulations, section 1.358–2(a)(2) and (3), (c), Ex. (2). But where multiple blocks of stock or both stock and securities have been exchanged, the basis for each class of stock or securities surrendered must be assigned to the particular stock and securities received in exchange therefor. Regulations, section 1.358–2(a)(4), (c), Ex. (3) and (4).

D. STOCK RIGHTS AND WARRANTS

Regulations, section 1.354–1(e), state that warrants to acquire stock do not constitute either "stock or securities" for purposes of section 354. Bateman v. Commissioner, 40 T.C. 408 (1963), found that warrants were not "stock" but did not resolve the issue whether they were securities or "other property," since in the situation involved the tax result would have been the same by virtue of section 354(a)(2)(A)(ii). See Estate of Smith v. Commissioner, 63 T.C. 722 (1975) (*Bateman* followed). Baan v. Commissioner, 51 T.C. 1032 (1969), aff'd on other grounds sub nom. Gordon v. Commissioner, 424 F.2d 378 (2d Cir.1970), held that stock rights were neither stock nor securities. The court distinguished Carlberg v. United States, 281 F.2d 507 (8th Cir.1960), and Hamrick v. Commissioner, 43 T.C. 21 (1964), discussed infra, page 838, in which contingent stock rights were held to be the equivalent of stock, on the ground that in those situations no additional payment was required by the shareholder to obtain the additional shares of stock. See also Rev.Rul. 69–264, 1969–2 Cum.Bull. 102 (option received by a corporate shareholder in a statutory merger allowing the corporation to call its preferred stock held by the acquiring corporation was "boot").

If warrants are found to be "securities" for purposes of section 354, how is the "principal amount" limitation in 354(a)(2) to be applied? In *Bateman* the problem was avoided since the exchange fell within section 354(a)(2) (A)(ii). But suppose the exchange involved stock and bonds for stock and warrants?

E. CHARACTERIZATION OF GAIN

The decision in *Clark,* supra, page 800, settled a long standing dispute regarding the manner in which dividend equivalency under section 356(b) is to be tested. The rule announced in *Clark* rejected the position taken by the Internal Revenue Service, reflected in Rev.Rul. 75–83, 1975–1 Cum.Bull. 112, that the transaction was to be treated as if there had been a pre-reorganization redemption of shares of the acquired corporation. See, Shimberg v. United States, 577 F.2d 283 (5th Cir.1978) (adopting IRS pre-reorganization distribution analysis to tax pro rata cash boot as dividend). The pre-reorganization redemption analysis urged by the Internal Revenue Service in effect leads to a dividend in all cases where the boot is paid pro rata to the shareholders of the acquired corporation.

Conversely, the post-reorganization constructive redemption analysis adopted in *Clark* generally will lead to capital gain treatment if the principles of section 302 are applied to determine dividend equivalency. Whenever the acquiring corporation is publicly traded, section 302(b)(1) in all likelihood will apply to most of the shareholders. See Rev.Rul. 76–385, 1976–2 Cum.Bull. 92. But see Rev.Rul. 81–289, 1981–2 Cum.Bull. 82 (section 302(b)(1) does not apply where other shareholders of a publicly-traded corporation also had shares redeemed and taxpayer's proportionate interest was not reduced). See also the discussion, supra, page 571. Furthermore, as was the case in *Clark,* where the cash represents a significant part of the value received by the shareholders of the acquired corporation, section 302(b)(2) principles should provide capital gain treatment.

F. SECTION 306 ASPECTS

If pursuant to the reorganization the shareholders of the acquired corporation surrender common stock and receive both common stock and preferred stock, the preferred stock may be characterized as section 306 stock pursuant to section 306(c)(1)(B) if "the effect of the transaction was substantially the same as the receipt of a stock dividend." See Regulations, section 1.306–3(d). The Regulations and Rev.Rul. 56–586, 1956–2 Cum. Bull. 214, indicate that unless a cash distribution in lieu of the preferred stock would have been a dividend under section 356(a)(2), the stock will not be section 306 stock. (For section 306 generally, see supra, page 537.) However, as a result of the Supreme Court's decision in *Clark,* which makes it much less likely that a dividend will be found, classification of preferred stock received in an acquisitive reorganization as section 306 stock probably will be rare. Nevertheless, Rev.Rul. 89–63, 1989–1 Cum. Bull. 90, held that where both common and preferred stock of a publicly held acquiring corporation were issued to the former holders of the common stock of a publicly held acquired corporation in a type (A) statutory merger, the preferred stock was section 306 stock. Furthermore, the fact that the corporations were publicly held, standing alone, was not sufficient to bring the preferred stock within the section 306(b)(4) exception for transactions not involving tax avoidance. The Ruling did not provide any rationale for its conclusion that the stock was section 306 stock, and if cash had been distributed in lieu of the preferred stock, under *Clark* the cash would not have been substantially equivalent to a dividend.

Preferred stock received for preferred stock in acquisitive reorganizations will not be section 306 stock if it is of equal value to the preferred stock surrendered, the terms of the new preferred stock are not substantially different from the terms of the old preferred stock, and the preferred stock surrendered in the exchange was not itself section 306 stock. Rev.Rul. 88–100, 1988–2 Cum.Bull. 46 (holding that Regulations, section 1.306–3(d), Ex. (2), apply to acquisitive reorganizations); Rev.Rul. 82–118, 1982–1 Cum.Bull. 56. The Rulings emphasize that in such cases the new preferred stock is merely a substitute for the old preferred stock, and the distribution therefore does not have the effect of a distribution of earnings and profits. However, if the surrendered preferred stock was section 306 stock, then any preferred stock (or common stock) received in exchange for the tainted preferred stock will be section 306 stock. Section 306(c)(1)(C).

For the application of section 306(c)(1)(B) to recapitalizations, see infra, page 882.

G. REFERENCES

Posin, The Time Value of Money in Corporate Takeovers, 21 Conn.L. Rev. 49 (1988); Knotts, The Characterization of Boot Distributions in Corporate Reorganizations After 1986, 66 Taxes 387 (1988); Kayser, The Long and Winding Road: Characteristics of Boot Under Section 356(a)(2), 39 Tax L.Rev. 297 (1984); Corry, Preferred Stock Issued in Tax Free Exchanges: Does Section 306 Apply?, 35 Tax L.Rev. 113 (1979); Kohl, The Fundamentals of Debt Swaps, 48 Tax Notes 1037 (1990).

(2) TREATMENT OF THE CORPORATIONS PARTICIPATING IN AN (A) REORGANIZATION

INTERNAL REVENUE CODE: Sections 357(a), (b); 358(a), (b)(1), (e), (f); 361; 362(b); 368(b).

ILLUSTRATIVE MATERIAL

A. ACQUIRING CORPORATION

1. *Nonrecognition of Gain*

The acquiring corporation in an (A) reorganization is protected from gain recognition by section 1032. However, if the acquiring corporation also transfers non-qualifying "boot" (other than its own securities) which has appreciated in value, none of the reorganization nonrecognition provisions apply and gain must be recognized on the transfer. Rev.Rul. 72–327, 1972–2 Cum.Bull. 197. See also Proposed Regulations, section 1.1032–2(c), Ex. (1) (1981). Loss is similarly recognized if the basis of the boot property is less than its fair market value.

2. *Basis of Assets*

Under section 362(b), the acquiring corporation takes as its basis in the acquired assets the basis which the assets had in the hands of the transferor corporation. The statute provides that the basis of the assets in the hands of the acquiring corporation is increased by any gain recognized by the acquired-transferor corporation in the reorganization transaction, but since gain is only recognized if the property received is not distributed (see B below) in a type (A) reorganization the acquiring corporation always takes a transferred basis in the assets without any increase for gain recognized to the transferor.

B. ACQUIRED CORPORATION

Section 361 protects the acquired corporation from gain recognition in the reorganization transaction regardless of the nature of the consideration received from the acquiring corporation. If only stock or securities of the acquiring corporation is received in the reorganization, section 361(a) provides nonrecognition upon receipt of the stock or securities. (Section 361(a)(2) bars the recognition of any loss.) No gain or loss is recognized by the acquired corporation on the distribution of the acquiring corporation's stock or securities. Section 361(c)(1), (2)(B). If boot is received, section 361(b)(1) requires that the acquired corporation recognize gain upon receipt only if that boot is not distributed to either its shareholders or creditors pursuant to the plan of reorganization. See also section 361(c). Since in an (A) reorganization the acquired corporation disappears by operation of law, all of the boot must be distributed and no gain can be recognized under section 361(b).

Section 361(c)(2) provides for recognition of gain to the acquired corporation upon the distribution of appreciated boot. However, because section 358(a)(2) provides the acquired corporation with a fair market value basis in any boot received in the reorganization transaction, no gain will be realized.

C. CAPITAL EXPENDITURE ASPECTS

Costs involved in acquisition transactions must generally be capitalized rather than deducted currently under section 162 or 212. United States v. Hilton Hotels Corp., 397 U.S. 580 (1970), so held with respect to the expenses of an appraisal proceeding involving payments to dissenting shareholders in a merger transaction. National Starch and Chemical Corp. v. Commissioner, 93 T.C. 67 (1989), held that legal, investment banking, and other expenses incurred by the acquired corporation in a friendly merger to evaluate the offer and make recommendations to its shareholders must be capitalized, rather than deducted under section 162(a). Rev.Rul. 73–580, 1973–2 Cum.Bull. 86, requires that the salary of corporate employees who spend a "substantial" amount of time on acquisition work, e.g., legal accounting and other such activities in connection with mergers and acquisitions, must similarly be capitalized. If a proposed reorganization is abandoned a capital loss under section 165 is permitted. Obviously difficult allocation questions arise in the application of the Ruling.

D. MERGER OF CONTROLLED SUBSIDIARY INTO PARENT

Where an 80 percent controlled subsidiary is merged into its parent, Regulations, section 1.332–2(d) and (e) provide that the transaction will be taxed as if the subsidiary had been liquidated. Does this mean that minority shareholders of the subsidiary who receive parent corporation stock in the merger must recognize gain or loss on the exchange of shares? If the reasoning of Kass v. Commissioner, supra, page 798, were applied, they would be required to recognize gain or loss.

In *Kass* the Government conceded that "theoretically" it would be possible for the same transaction to be treated as a liquidation under section 332 and section 334(b) at the corporate level and as a reorganization from the point of view of minority shareholders. While no case has expressly so held, such treatment was implicit in several earlier decisions. In King Enterprises, Inc. v. United States, 418 F.2d 511 (Ct.Cl.1969), the taxpayer and ten other corporate shareholders owned Tenco. Minute Maid acquired Tenco stock for cash, notes, and Minute Maid stock (the stock constituting more than 50% of the total consideration received by the Tenco shareholders and about 15% of the total Minute Maid stock). Minute Maid through a statutory merger then merged four subsidiaries, including Tenco, into itself and received an Internal Revenue Service ruling that this transaction was covered by former section 334(b)(2), discussed supra, page 700, thus in effect treating the transactions as a "purchase." The taxpayer corporate shareholder, however, treated the Minute Maid stock as having been received tax-free in an (A) reorganization, with the cash and notes constituting "boot" under section 356 (and a dividend subject to the section 243 dividends received deduction), arguing that the exchange and the subsequent merger were steps in an integrated transaction. The Internal Revenue Service asserted that the exchange for Tenco stock was a separate sale transaction, resulting in capital gain to the taxpayer. The court held that the merger of Tenco into Minute Maid was intended by Minute Maid from the outset (the court does not indicate that this intent was revealed to the Tenco shareholders) and, treating the acquisition and merger as a unified transaction, an (A) reorganization existed. See also Kansas Sand & Concrete, Inc. v. Commissioner, 462 F.2d 805 (10th Cir.1972). Regulations, section 1.332–2(d), also seem to imply that the same transaction can be both a liquidation under section 332 and a reorganization as far as minority shareholders are concerned.

In Rev.Rul. 69–617, 1969–2 Cum.Bull. 57, a parent corporation owned more than 80 percent of the stock of its subsidiary. In order to operate its subsidiary as a wholly-owned subsidiary, it merged the subsidiary into itself and the minority shareholders of the subsidiary received the parent's stock. The parent then transferred all of the assets acquired from the subsidiary to a newly created wholly-owned subsidiary. The Ruling held that the transaction constituted an (A) reorganization; section 332 was not applicable because the immediate transfer of the subsidiary's assets to the newly created subsidiary meant that there was not a complete liquidation of the former subsidiary. Thus the minority shareholders of the former subsidiary received tax-free reorganization treatment, whereas under liquidation treatment, gain would have resulted to them.

See also FEC Liquidating Corp. v. United States, 548 F.2d 924 (Ct.Cl. 1977), holding that the reorganization provisions preempted the pre–1986 Act liquidation provisions. Compare General Housewares v. United States, 615 F.2d 1056 (5th Cir.1980) (rejecting the approach of *FEC Liquidating Corp*).

E. REFERENCES

Levin and Bowen, Taxable and Tax–Free Two–Step Acquisitions and Minority Squeeze–Outs, 33 Tax L.Rev. 425 (1978); Seplow, Acquisitions of Assets of A Subsidiary: Liquidation or Reorganization?, 73 Harv.L.Rev. 484 (1960).

(3) Summary of Tax Results to Parties to an (A) Reorganization

Acquired Corporation and Shareholders. No gain or loss is recognized by the acquired corporation on the exchange with the acquiring corporation regardless of the nature of the property received from the acquiring corporation. Because the acquired corporation disappears by operation of state law, any nonqualifying boot is deemed to have been distributed to its shareholder or creditors, and thus no gain can be recognized under section 361(b).

As to the shareholders of the transferor corporation, no gain or loss will be recognized if they receive solely the stock of the acquiring corporation in exchange for their stock in the transferor corporation. Section 354(a). If "boot" is involved, the shareholders may recognized gain under section 356, either as capital gain or as a dividend, depending on the circumstances, although after the decision in *Clark,* supra, page 800, the gain usually will be capital gain. Section 358 provides an exchanged basis for the acquiring corporation's stock. If any boot is received, however, the basis is determined by first increasing the basis by the amount of any gain recognized by the shareholders as the result of the receipt of boot, and then decreasing it by the amount of cash or the fair market value of any other property received.

Acquiring Corporation. The acquiring corporation recognizes no gain or loss on the transfer of its share in an (A) reorganization. Section 1032. If the acquiring corporation transfers any boot other than cash or its own securities, it must recognize gain or loss with respect to the boot transferred. Under section 362(b), the acquiring corporation's basis in the assets is equal to the acquired corporation's basis in those assets. Under section 381, the tax attributes of the acquired corporation, e.g., net operating loss carryovers, earnings and profits accounts, etc., carryover to the acquiring corporation. The limitations of section 382(b) are, however, applicable. See infra, Chapters 20 and 21.

SECTION 5. STOCK FOR STOCK ACQUISITIONS: (B) REORGANIZATIONS

INTERNAL REVENUE CODE: Sections 354; 362(b); 368(a)(1)(B), (a)(2)(C), (c).

REGULATIONS: Section 1.368–2(c).

CHAPMAN v. COMMISSIONER

United States Court of Appeals, First Circuit, 1980.
618 F.2d 856.

LEVIN H. CAMPBELL, CIRCUIT JUDGE.

* * * We must decide whether the requirement of Section 368(a)(1)(B) that the acquisition of stock in one corporation by another be solely in exchange for voting stock of the acquiring corporation is met where, in related transactions, the acquiring corporation first acquires 8 percent of the acquiree's stock for cash and then acquires more than 80 percent of the acquiree in an exchange for voting stock. The Tax Court agreed with the taxpayers that the latter exchange constituted a valid tax-free reorganization. Reeves v. Commissioner, 71 T.C. 727 (1979).

THE FACTS

Appellees were among the more than 17,000 shareholders of the Hartford Fire Insurance Company who exchanged their Hartford stock for shares of the voting stock of International Telephone and Telegraph Corporation pursuant to a formal exchange offer from ITT dated May 26, 1970. On their 1970 tax returns, appellees did not report any gain or loss from these exchanges. Subsequently, the Internal Revenue Service assessed deficiencies * * *. Appellees petitioned the Tax Court for redetermination of these deficiencies, and their cases were consolidated with those of twelve other former Hartford shareholders. The Tax Court, with five judges dissenting, granted appellees' motion for summary judgment, and the Commissioner of Internal Revenue filed this appeal.

* * * In October 1968, ITT executives approached Hartford about the possibility of merging the two corporations. This proposal was spurned by Hartford, which at the time was considering acquisitions of its own. In November 1968, ITT learned that approximately 1.3 million shares of Hartford, representing some 6 percent of Hartford's voting stock, were available for purchase from a mutual fund. After assuring Hartford's directors that ITT would not attempt to acquire Hartford against its will, ITT consummated the $63.7 million purchase from the mutual fund with Hartford's blessing. From November 13, 1968 to January 10, 1969, ITT also made a series of purchases on the open market totalling 458,000 shares which it acquired for approximately $24.4 million. A further purchase of 400 shares from an ITT subsidiary in March 1969 brought ITT's holdings to about 8 percent of Hartford's outstanding stock, all of which had been bought for cash.

In the midst of this flurry of stock-buying, ITT submitted a written proposal to the Hartford Board of Directors for the merger of Hartford into an ITT subsidiary, based on an exchange of Hartford stock for ITT's $2 cumulative convertible voting preferred stock. Received by Hartford in December of 1968, the proposal was rejected in February of 1969. A counterproposal by Hartford's directors led to further negotiations, and on April 9, 1969 a provisional plan and agreement of merger was executed by the two corporations. * * *

[On] April 15, 1969, attorneys for the parties sought a ruling from the IRS that the proposed transaction would constitute a reorganization under Section 368(a)(1)(B) of the Internal Revenue Code of 1954, so that, among other things, gain realized on the exchange by Hartford shareholders would not be recognized, see 26 U.S.C. § 354(a)(1). By private letter ruling, the Service notified the parties on October 13, 1969 that the proposed merger would constitute a nontaxable reorganization, provided ITT unconditionally sold its 8 percent interest in Hartford to a third party before Hartford's shareholders voted to approve or disapprove the proposal. On October 21, the Service ruled that a proposed sale of the stock to Mediobanca, an Italian bank, would satisfy this condition, and such a sale was made on November 9.

On November 10, 1969, the shareholders of Hartford approved the merger, which had already won the support of ITT's shareholders in June. On December 13, 1969, however, the merger plan ground to a halt, as the Connecticut Insurance Commissioner refused to endorse the arrangement. ITT then proposed to proceed with a voluntary exchange offer to the shareholders of Hartford on essentially the same terms they would have obtained under the merger plan. After public hearings and the imposition of certain requirements on the post-acquisition operation of Hartford, the insurance commissioner approved the exchange offer on May 23, 1970, and three days later ITT submitted the exchange offer to all Hartford shareholders. More than 95 percent of Hartford's outstanding stock was exchanged for shares of ITT's $2.25 cumulative convertible voting preferred stock. The Italian bank to which ITT had conveyed its original 8 percent interest was among those tendering shares, as were the taxpayers in this case.

In March 1974, the Internal Revenue Service retroactively revoked its ruling approving the sale of Hartford stock to Mediobanca, on the ground that the request on which the ruling was based had misrepresented the nature of the proposed sale. Concluding that the entire transaction no longer constituted a nontaxable reorganization, the Service assessed tax deficiencies against a number of former Hartford shareholders who had accepted the exchange offer. Appellees, along with other taxpayers, contested this action in the Tax Court, where the case was decided on appellees' motion for summary judgment. For purposes of this motion, the taxpayers conceded that questions of the merits of the revocation of the IRS rulings were not to be considered; the facts were to be viewed as though ITT had not sold the shares previously acquired for cash to Mediobanca. The taxpayers also conceded, solely for purposes of their motion for summary judgment, that the initial cash purchases of Hartford stock had been made for the purpose of furthering ITT's efforts to acquire Hartford.

The Issue

Taxpayers advanced two arguments in support of their motion for summary judgment. Their first argument related to the severability of the cash purchases from the 1970 exchange offer. Because 14 months had elapsed between the last of the cash purchases and the effective date of the exchange offer, and because the cash purchases were not part of the formal plan of reorganization entered into by ITT and Hartford, the taxpayers argued that the 1970 exchange offer should be examined in isolation to determine whether it satisfied the terms of Section 368(a)(1)(B) of the 1954 Code. The Service countered that the two sets of transactions—the cash purchases and the exchange offer—were linked by a common acquisitive purpose, and that they should be considered together for the purpose of determining whether the arrangement met the statutory requirement that the stock of the acquired corporation be exchanged "solely for * * * voting stock" of the acquiring corporation. The Tax Court did not reach this argument; in granting summary judgment it relied entirely on the taxpayers' second argument.

For purposes of the second argument, the taxpayers conceded arguendo that the 1968 and 1969 cash purchases should be considered "parts of the 1970 exchange offer reorganization." Even so, they insisted upon a right to judgment on the basis that the 1970 exchange of stock for stock satisfied the statutory requirements for a reorganization without regard to the presence of related cash purchases. The Tax Court agreed with the taxpayers, holding that the 1970 exchange in which ITT acquired more than 80 percent of Hartford's single class of stock for ITT voting stock satisfied the requirements of Section 368(a)(1)(B), so that no gain or loss need be recognized on the exchange under section 354(a)(1). The sole issue on appeal is whether the Tax Court was correct in so holding.

I.

* * *

The single issue raised on this appeal is whether "the acquisition" in this case complied with the requirement that it be "solely for * * * voting stock." It is well settled that the "solely" requirement is mandatory; if any part of "the acquisition" includes a form of consideration other than voting stock, the transaction will not qualify as a (B) reorganization. See Helvering v. Southwest Consolidated Corp., 315 U.S. 194, 198, 62 S.Ct. 546, 550 (1942) ("'Solely' leaves no leeway. Voting stock plus some other consideration does not meet the statutory requirement"). The precise issue before us is thus how broadly to read the term "acquisition." The Internal Revenue Service argues that "the acquisition * * * of stock of another corporation" must be understood to encompass the 1968–69 cash purchases as well as the 1970 exchange offer. If the IRS is correct, "the acquisition" here fails as a (B) reorganization. The taxpayers, on the other hand, would limit "the acquisition" to the part of a sequential transaction of this nature which meets the requirements of subsection (B). They argue that the 1970 exchange of stock for stock was itself an "acquisition" by ITT of stock in Hartford solely in exchange for ITT's voting stock, such that after the exchange took place ITT controlled Hartford. Taxpayers contend that the earlier cash purchases of 8 percent, even if conceded to be part of the same acquisitive plan, are essentially irrelevant to the tax-free reorganization otherwise effected.

The Tax Court accepted the taxpayers' reading of the statute, effectively overruling its own prior decision in Howard v. Commissioner, 24 T.C. 792 (1955), rev'd on other grounds, 238 F.2d 943 (7th Cir. 1956). The plurality opinion stated its "narrow" holding as follows:

> "We hold that where, as is the case herein, 80 percent or more of the stock of a corporation is acquired in one transaction,[18] in exchange for which only voting stock is furnished as consideration, the 'solely for voting stock' requirement of section 368(a)(1)(B) is satisfied.
>
> 18. In determining what constitutes 'one transaction,' we include all the acquisitions from shareholders which were clearly part of the same transaction."

71 T.C. at 741. The plurality treated as "irrelevant" the 8 percent of Hartford's stock purchased for cash, although the opinion left somewhat ambiguous the question whether the 8 percent was irrelevant because of the 14–month time interval separating the transactions or because the statute was not concerned with transactions over and above those mathematically necessary to the acquiring corporation's attainment of control.[15]

15. If the holding rested on the former basis, it would be difficult to credit the Tax Court's repeated assertions that it was not reaching or deciding the severability issue.

II.

For reasons set forth extensively in section III of this opinion, we do not accept the position adopted by the Tax Court.[16] Instead we side with the Commissioner on the narrow issue presented in this appeal, that is, the correctness of taxpayers' so-called "second" argument premised on an assumed relationship between the cash and stock transactions. As explained below, we find a strong implication in the language of the statute, in the legislative history, in the regulations, and in the decisions of other courts that cash purchases which are concededly "parts of" a stock-for-stock exchange must be considered constituent elements of the "acquisition" for purposes of applying the "solely for * * * voting stock" requirement of Section 368(a)(1)(B). We believe the presence of non-stock consideration in such an acquisition, regardless of whether such consideration is necessary to the gaining of control, is inconsistent with treatment of the acquisition as a nontaxable reorganization. It follows for purposes of taxpayers' second argument—which was premised on the assumption that the cash transactions were part of the 1970 exchange offer reorganization—that the stock transfers in question would not qualify for nonrecognition of gain or loss.

Our decision will not, unfortunately, end this case. The Tax Court has yet to rule on taxpayers' "first" argument. * * * The question

As the taxpayers conceded their cash purchases were "parts of the 1970 exchange offer reorganization," the Tax Court had no reason to consider the actual lapse of time which occurred as a factor in treating the cash purchases as legally irrelevant. We assume, therefore, that any indications in the Tax Court's opinion that the separation in time was necessary to its holding were inadvertent, and that the holding actually rests on the Tax Court's reading of the statute. If the Tax Court wishes explicitly to articulate a rule regarding the time period which will suffice to separate two transactions for purposes of Section 368(a)(1)(B), we think it will have an adequate opportunity to do so in considering on remand the issue of severability raised by taxpayers' first argument.

16. Taxpayers in this case have also argued that we should adopt the reasoning of the district court in Pierson v. United States, 472 F.Supp. 957 (D.Del.1979), another case arising on these same facts. The plaintiff in *Pierson* paid the tax assessed by the IRS after it revoked its private letter ruling, and then sued in district court for a refund, advancing substantially the same arguments presented to the Tax Court. The *Pierson* court reached a result similar to the Tax Court's, although it seemed less concerned with attempts to distinguish prior case law on this point. The district court appears to have assumed, for example, that the Tax Court's decision in *Reeves* overruled Howard v. Commissioner, 24 T.C. 792 (1955). 472 F.Supp. at 966. The *Pierson* court also assumed, for purposes of taxpayer's motion for summary judgment, that the taxpayer was conceding that the cash purchases were part of the "same transaction" as the 1970 exchange offer. The district court therefore stated its holding as follows:

> "I conclude that at least where eighty percent of the stock of an acquired corporation is exchanged in a single transaction for voting stock in the acquiring corporation, the payment within the same transaction of cash or other nonstock consideration for additional shares in the acquired corporation will not preclude the transaction's qualification as a tax-free reorganization under Section 368(a)(1)(B) of the Internal Revenue Code."

472 F.Supp. at 975. We are given to understand by the parties to this appeal that the *Pierson* case is being appealed in the Third Circuit. [Ed.: The Third Circuit reversed *Pierson* sub nom. Heverly v. Commissioner, 621 F.2d 1227 (3d Cir.1980)].

of what factors should determine, for purposes of Section 368(a)(1)(B), whether a given cash purchase is truly "related" to a later exchange of stock requires further consideration by the Tax Court, as does the question of the application of those factors in the present case. We therefore will remand this case to the Tax Court for further proceedings on the question raised by the taxpayers' first argument in support of their motion for summary judgment.

We view the Tax Court's options on remand as threefold. It can hold that the cash and stock transactions here in question are related as a matter of law—the position urged by the Commissioner—in which case, under our present holding, there would not be a valid (B) reorganization. On the other hand, the Tax Court may find that the transactions are as a matter of law unrelated, so that the 1970 exchange offer was simply the final, nontaxable step in a permissible creeping acquisition. Finally, the court may decide that, under the legal standard it adopts, material factual issues remain to be decided, so that a grant of summary judgment would be inappropriate at this time.[17]

III.

A.

* * * We begin with the words of the statute itself. The reorganization definitions contained in Section 368(a)(1) are precise, technical,

17. We do not intend to dictate to the Tax Court what legal standard it should apply in determining whether these transactions are related. We would suggest, however, that the possibilities should include at least the following; perhaps others may be developed by counsel or by the Tax Court itself.

One possibility—advanced by the taxpayers—is that the only transactions which should be considered related, and so parts of "the acquisition," are those which are included in the formal plan of reorganization adopted by the two corporations. The virtues of this approach—simplicity and clarity—may be outweighed by the considerable scope it would grant the parties to a reorganization to control the tax treatment of their formal plan of reorganization by arbitrarily including or excluding certain transactions. A second possibility—urged by the Commissioner—is that all transactions sharing a single acquisitive purpose should be considered related for purposes of Section 368(a)(1)(B). Relying on an example given in the legislative history, see S.Rep. No. 1622, 83d Cong., 2d Sess. 273, reprinted in [1954] U.S.Code Cong. & Admin.News, pp. 4621, 4911 [hereinafter cited as *1954 Senate Report*], the Commissioner would require a complete and thoroughgoing separation, both in time and purpose, between cash and stock acquisitions before the latter would qualify for reorganization treatment under subsection (B).

A third possible approach, lying somewhere between the other two, would be to focus on the mutual knowledge and intent of the corporate parties, so that one party could not suffer adverse tax consequences from unilateral activities of the other of which the former had no notice. Cf. Manning, *"In Pursuance of the Plan of Reorganization": The Scope of the Reorganization Provisions of the Internal Revenue Code,* 72 Harv.L.Rev. 881, 912–13 (1959). Such a rule would prevent, for example, the situation where the acquiree's shareholders expect to receive favorable tax treatment on an exchange offer, only to learn later that an apparently valid (B) reorganization has been nullified by anonymous cash purchases on the part of the acquiring corporation. See Bruce v. Helvering, 64 App.D.C. 192, 76 F.2d 442 (D.C.Cir.1935), rev'g, 30 B.T.A. 80 (1934).

Difficulties suggest themselves with each of these rules, and without benefit of thorough briefing and argument, as well as an informed decision by the lower court, we are reluctant to proceed further in exploring this issue. We leave to the Tax Court the task of breaking ground here.

and comprehensive. They were intended to define the exclusive means by which nontaxable corporate reorganizations could be effected. See Treas.Reg. § 1.368–1 (1960) * * *. In examining the language of the (B) provision, we discern two possible meanings. On the one hand, the statute could be read to say that a successful reorganization occurs whenever Corporation X exchanges its own voting stock for stock in Corporation Y, and, immediately after the transaction, Corporation X controls more than 80 percent of Y's stock. On this reading, purchases of shares for which any part of the consideration takes the form of "boot" should be ignored, since the definition is only concerned with transactions which meet the statutory requirements as to consideration and control. To take an example, if Corporation X bought 50 percent of the shares of Y, and then almost immediately exchanged part of its voting stock for the remaining 50 percent of Y's stock, the question would arise whether the second transaction was a (B) reorganization. Arguably, the statute can be read to support such a finding. In the second transaction, X exchanged only stock for stock (meeting the "solely" requirement), and after the transaction was completed X owned Y (meeting the "control" requirement).

The alternative reading of the statute—the one which we are persuaded to adopt—treat the (B) definition as prescriptive, rather than merely descriptive. We read the statute to mean that the entire transaction which constitutes "the acquisition" must not contain any nonstock consideration if the transaction is to qualify as a (B) reorganization. In the example given above, where X acquired 100 percent of Y's stock, half for cash and half for voting stock, we would interpret "the acquisition" as referring to the entire transaction, so that the "solely for * * * voting stock" requirement would not be met. We believe if Congress had intended the statute to be read as merely descriptive, this intent would have been more clearly spelled out in the statutory language.[18]

We recognize that the Tax Court adopted neither of these two readings. For reasons to be discussed in connection with the legislative history which follows, the Tax Court purported to limit its holding to cases, such as this one, where more than 80 percent of the stock of Corporation Y passes to Corporation X in exchange solely for voting stock. The Tax Court presumably would assert that the 50/50 hypothetical posited above can be distinguished from this case, and that its holding implies no view as to the hypothetical. See 71 T.C. at 742. The plurality opinion recognized that the position it adopted creates no small problem with respect to the proper reading of "the acquisition" in the statutory definition. See 71 T.C. at 739, 741. In order to distinguish the 80 percent case from the 50 percent case, it is necessary to

18. For example, Congress could have used the word "any" rather than the word "the" before "acquisition" in the first line of the (B) definition. This would have tended to negate the implication that this definition prescribes the conditions a transaction *must* meet to qualify, rather than simply describing that part of a transaction which is entitled to the statutory tax deferral.

read "the acquisition" as referring to at least the amount of stock constituting "control" (80 percent) where related cash purchases are present. Yet the Tax Court recognized that "the acquisition" cannot always refer to the conveyance of an 80 percent bloc of stock in one transaction, since to do so would frustrate the intent of the 1954 amendments to permit so-called "creeping acquisitions."

The Tax Court's interpretation of the statute suffers from a more fundamental defect, as well. In order to justify the limitation of its holding to transactions involving 80 percent or more of the acquiree's stock, the Tax Court focused on the *passage* of control as the primary requirement of the (B) provision. This focus is misplaced. Under the present version of the statute, the *passage* of control is entirely irrelevant; the only material requirement is that the acquiring corporation *have* control immediately after the acquisition. As the statute explicitly states, it does not matter if the acquiring corporation already has control before the transaction begins, so long as such control exists at the completion of the reorganization. * * * In our view, the statute should be read to mean that the related transactions that constitute "the acquisition," whatever percentage of stock they may represent, must meet both the "solely for voting stock" and the "control immediately after" requirements of Section 368(a)(1)(B). Neither the reading given the statute by the Tax Court, nor that proposed as the first alternative above, adequately corresponds to the careful language Congress employed in this section of the Code.

B.

The 1924 Code defined reorganization, in part, as "a merger or consolidation (including the acquisition by one corporation of at least a majority of the voting stock and at least a majority of the total number of shares of all other classes of stock of another corporation, or substantially all the properties of another corporation)." Pub.L. No. 68–176, c. 234, § 203(h)(1), 43 Stat. 257. Although the statute did not specifically limit the consideration that could be given in exchange for stock or assets, courts eventually developed the so-called "continuity of interest" doctrine, which held that exchanges that did not include some quantum of stock as consideration were ineligible for reorganization treatment for lack of a continuing property interest on the part of the acquiree's shareholders. See, e.g., Cortland Specialty Co. v. Commissioner, 60 F.2d 937, 939–40 (2d Cir.1932), cert. denied, 288 U.S. 599, 53 S.Ct. 316 (1933); Pinellas Ice Co. v. Commissioner, 287 U.S. 462, 470, 53 S.Ct. 257, 260 (1933).

Despite this judicial development, sentiment was widespread in Congress that the reorganization provisions lent themselves to abuse, particularly in the form of so-called "disguised sales." See, e.g., "Prevention of Tax Avoidance," Report of Subcomm. of House Comm. on Ways and Means, 73d Cong., 2d Sess. (Dec. 4, 1933). In 1934, the House Ways and Means Committee proposed abolition of the stock-acquisition and asset-acquisition reorganizations which had appeared in the parenthetical section of the 1924 Act quoted above. See H.R.Rep. No. 704, 73d Cong., 2d Sess. 12–14 (1939–1 Cum.Bull. (Part 2) 554, 563–65). The Senate Finance Committee countered with a proposal to retain these provisions, but with "restrictions designed to prevent tax avoidance." S.Rep. No. 558, 73d Cong., 2d Sess. 15 (1939–1 Cum.Bull. (Part 2) 586, 598).[20] One of these restrictions was the requirement that the acquiring corporation obtain at least 80 percent, rather than a bare majority, of the stock of the acquiree. The second requirement was stated in the Senate Report as follows: "the acquisition, whether of stock or of substantially all the properties, must be in exchange solely for the voting stock of the acquiring corporation." Id. at 17. The Senate amendments were enacted as Section 112(g)(1) of the Revenue Act of 1934, 48 Stat. 680, which provided in pertinent part:

> "(1) The term 'reorganization' means (A) a statutory merger or consolidation, or (B) the acquisition by one corporation in exchange solely for all or a part of its voting stock: of at least 80 per centum of the voting stock and at least 80 per centum of the total number of shares of all other classes of stock of another corporation; or of substantially all the properties of another corporation * * *."

Congress revised this definition in 1939 in response to the Supreme Court's decision in United States v. Hendler, 303 U.S. 564, 58 S.Ct. 655 (1938), which held that an acquiring corporation's assumption of the acquiree's liabilities in an asset-acquisition was equivalent to the receipt of "boot" by the acquiree. Since virtually all asset-acquisition reorganizations necessarily involve the assumption of the acquiree's liabilities, a literal application of the "solely for * * * voting stock" requirement would have effectively abolished this form of tax-free reorganization. In the Revenue Act of 1939, Congress separated the stock-acquisition and asset-acquisition provisions in order to exempt the assumption of liabilities in the latter category of cases from the "solely for * * * voting stock" requirement.

* * *

The next major change in this provision occurred in 1954. In that year, the House Bill, H.R. 8300, would have drastically altered the corporate reorganization sections of the Tax Code, permitting, for example, both stock and "boot" as consideration in a corporate acquisition, with gain recognized only to the extent of the "boot." See H.R. Rep. No. 1337, 83d Cong., 2d Sess. A118–A119, A132–A134, reprinted in [1954] U.S.Code Cong. & Admin.News, pp. 4017, 4256–4257, 4269–4271. The Senate Finance Committee, in order to preserve the familiar terminology and structure of the 1939 Code, proposed a new version of Section 112(g)(1), which would retain the "solely for * * * voting stock" requirement, but alter the existing control requirement to per-

20. The Senate's purpose in retaining these provisions was apparently to make available an alternative to statutory merger or consolidation in those states where merger statutes were overly restrictive or nonexistent. See Howard v. Commissioner, 238 F.2d 943, 946 (7th Cir.1956).

mit so-called "creeping acquisitions." Under the Senate Bill, it would no longer be necessary for the acquiring corporation to obtain 80 percent or more of the acquiree's stock in one "reorganization." The Senate's proposal permitted an acquisition to occur in stages; a bloc of shares representing less than 80 percent could be added to earlier acquisitions, regardless of the consideration given earlier, to meet the control requirement. The Report of the Senate Finance Committee gave this example of the operation of the creeping acquisition amendment:

> "[C]orporation A purchased 30 percent of the common stock of corporation W (the only class of stock outstanding) for cash in 1939. On March 1, 1955, corporation A offers to exchange its own voting stock, for all the stock of corporation W tendered within 6 months from the date of the offer. Within the 6 months period corporation A acquires an additional 60 percent of the stock of W for its own voting stock. As a result of the 1955 transactions, corporation A will own 90 percent of all of corporation W's stock. No gain or loss is recognized with respect to the exchanges of the A stock for the W stock."

1954 Senate Report, supra note 17, at 273, U.S.Code Cong. & Admin. News 1954, p. 4911. See also Treas.Reg. § 1.368–2(c) (1960).

At the same time the Senate was revising the (B) provision, (while leaving intact the "solely for * * * voting stock" requirement), it was also rewriting the (C) provision to explicitly permit up to 20 percent of the consideration in an asset acquisition to take the form of money or other nonstock property. See 26 U.S.C. § 368(a)(2)(B). The Senate revisions of subsections (B) and (C) were ultimately passed, and have remained largely unchanged since 1954. * * * Proposals for altering the (B) provision to allow "boot" as consideration have been made, but none has been enacted.[22]

As this history shows, Congress has had conflicting aims in this complex and difficult area. On the one hand, the 1934 Act evidences a strong intention to limit the reorganization provisions to permit forms of tax avoidance that had proliferated under the earlier revenue acts. This intention arguably has been carried forward in the current versions through retention of the "solely for * * * voting stock" requirement in (B), even while the (C) provision was being loosened. On the other hand, both the 1939 and 1954 revisions represented attempts to make the reorganization procedures more accessible and practical in both the (B) and (C) areas. In light of the conflicting purposes, we can

22. See, e.g., H.R.Rep. No. 4459, 86th Cong., 1st Sess. § 26 (1959). * * *

Furthermore, the legislative report accompanying a later revision of Section 368(a)(1) explicitly stated that cash is not permitted in a (B) reorganization:

"[I]n order to qualify as a tax-free stock-for-stock [B] reorganization it is necessary that the acquisition be *solely* for voting stock and that no stock be acquired for cash or other consideration." (Emphasis in original.)

S.Rep. No. 1533, 91st Cong., 2d Sess. 2–3, reprinted in [1970] U.S.Code Cong. & Admin.News, pp. 6123, 6123–24.

discern no clear Congressional mandate in the present structure of the (B) provision, either in terms of the abuses sought to be remedied or the beneficial transactions sought to be facilitated. At best, we think Congress has drawn somewhat arbitrary lines separating those transactions that resemble mere changes in form of ownership and those that contain elements of a sale or purchase arrangement. In such circumstances we believe it is more appropriate to examine the specific rules and requirements Congress enacted, rather than some questionably delineated "purpose" or "policy," to determine whether a particular transaction qualifies for favorable tax treatment.

To the extent there is any indication in the legislative history of Congress' intent with respect to the meaning of "acquisition" in the (B) provision, we believe the intent plainly was to apply the "solely" requirement to all related transactions. In those statutes where Congress intended to permit cash or other property to be used as consideration, it made explicit provision therefor. See, e.g., 26 U.S.C. § 368(a)(2)(B). It is argued that in a (B) reorganization the statute can be satisfied where only 80 percent of the acquiree's stock is obtained solely for voting stock, so that additional acquisitions are irrelevant and need not be considered. In light of Congress' repeated, and increasingly sophisticated, enactments in this area, we are unpersuaded that such an important question would have been left unaddressed had Congress intended to leave open such a possibility. We are not prepared to believe that Congress intended—either when it enacted the 1934, the 1939, or the 1954 statutes—to permit a corporation to exchange stock tax-free for 80 percent of the stock of another and in a related transaction to purchase the remaining 20 percent for cash. The only question we see clearly left open by the legislative history is the degree of separation required between the two transactions before they can qualify as a creeping acquisition under the 1954 amendments. This is precisely the issue the Tax Court chose not to address, and it is the issue we now remand to the Tax Court for consideration.

C.

Besides finding support for the IRS position both in the design of the statute and in the legislative history, we find support in the regulations adopted by the Treasury Department construing these statutory provisions.

* * *

Appellees point to language appearing in the regulations under the 1934 Act which seems to them to suggest that only the 80 percent of stock essential for control must meet the "solely" requirement:

> "In order to qualify as a 'reorganization' under section 112(g)(1)(B), the acquisition by the acquiring corporation of the *required amount* of the stock of the other corporation must be in exchange solely for all or a part of the voting stock of the acquiring corporation. If for example Corporation X exchanges nonvoting preferred stock or

> bonds in addition to all or part of its voting stock in the acquisition of the *required amount* of stock in Corporation Y, the transaction is not a 'reorganization' under section 112(g)(1)(B)."

Reg. 111, § 29.112(g)–2 (emphasis supplied). While it is possible to read the "required amount" language as equivalent to the "80 per centum" requirement of the 1934 Act, we find it equally plausible to read the language as simply reiterating the "*at least* 80 per centum" notion. In other words, the "required amount" does not mean that only 80 percent of the exchange need be for stock, but rather means that the bloc of shares constituting no less than 80 percent—and possibly more—must *all* be exchanged for stock only. See Howard v. Commissioner, 238 F.2d 943, 945 (7th Cir.1956).

When we turn to the regulations under the 1954 Act, the implication that the entire transaction must be judged under the "solely" test is stronger still.

> "In order to qualify as a 'reorganization' under section 368(a)(1)(B), the *acquisition* by the acquiring corporation of stock of another corporation must be in exchange solely for all or a part of the voting stock of the acquiring corporation * * * and the acquiring corporation must be in control of the other corporation immediately after *the transaction.* If, for example, Corporation X in one transaction exchanges nonvoting preferred stock or bonds *in addition to* all or a part of its voting stock in the acquisition of stock of Corporation Y, the transaction is not a reorganization under section 368(a)(1)(B)." (Emphasis supplied.)

Treas.Reg. § 1.368–2(c) (1960). The equation of "transaction" and "acquisition" in the above-quoted passage is particularly significant, since it seems to imply a functional test of what constitutes "the acquisition" as opposed to a view of "the acquisition" as simply that part of a transaction which otherwise satisfies the statutory requisites.[23] The regulation also goes on to say, in explaining the treatment of creeping acquisitions:

> "The acquisition of stock of another corporation by the acquiring corporation solely for its voting stock * * * is permitted tax-free even though the acquiring corporation already owns some of the stock of the other corporation. Such an acquisition is permitted

23. Furthermore, the regulation explicitly states that the presence of "boot" in addition to stock as consideration would prevent treatment of the transaction as a (B) reorganization. This language is not wholly dispositive, however; it could be read as reaching only cases where "boot" was present in the consideration given for each share exchanged. It is clear that the "solely for * * * voting stock" requirement prevents stock acquired for such "mixed" consideration from qualifying for reorganization treatment. The "in addition to" language in the regulation could be construed as reaching only this situation, and not the contrasting case where Corporation X acquires 80 percent of Y's stock solely for voting stock and another separate 20 percent for some other consideration. The *Reeves* case is, of course, of the latter type; with respect to every single share transferred, the consideration was either wholly in stock or wholly in cash.

tax-free in a single transaction or in a series of transactions taking place over a relatively short period of time such as 12 months."

Treas.Reg. § 1.368–2(c).[24] This regulation spells out the treatment afforded related acquisitions, some of which occur before and some after the acquiring corporation obtains the necessary 80 percent of stock in the acquiree. It would be incongruous, to say the least, if a series of stock-for-stock transactions could be combined so that the tax-free treatment of later acquisitions applied to earlier ones as well, yet a related cash purchase would be ignored as irrelevant. This section reinforces our view that all related transactions must be considered part of "the acquisition" for purposes of applying the statute.

D.

Finally, we turn to the body of case law that has developed concerning (B) reorganizations to determine how previous courts have dealt with this question. Of the seven prior cases in this area, all to a greater or lesser degree support the result we have reached, and none supports the result reached by the Tax Court. We recognize that the Tax Court purported to distinguish these precedents from the case before it, and that reasonable persons may differ on the extent to which some of these cases directly control the question raised here. Nevertheless, after carefully reviewing the precedents, we are satisfied that the decision of the Tax Court represents a sharp break with the previous judicial constructions of this statute, and a departure from the usual rule of stare decisis, which applies with special force in the tax field where uncertainty and variety are ordinarily to be avoided.

Of the seven precedents, the most significant would seem to be Howard v. Commissioner, 238 F.2d 943 (7th Cir.1956), rev'g, 24 T.C. 792 (1955), which stands out as the one case prior to *Reeves* that specifically addressed the issue raised herein. In *Howard,* the Truax–Traer Coal Company acquired 80.19 percent of the outstanding stock of Binkley Coal Company solely in exchange for Truax–Traer voting stock. At the same time and as part of the same plan of acquisition, Truax–Traer purchased the other 19.81 percent of Binkley's stock for cash. The taxpayers, former shareholders of Binkley who had exchanged their shares solely for voting stock, sold some of the Truax–Traer stock they had received in August 1950, the same year as the exchange. The Commissioner, treating the exchange as a taxable event and not a reorganization, employed a new holding period, beginning with the effective date of the exchange, and treated the taxpayers' gain on their sale of the Truax–Traer stock as a short-term capital gain. The Tax Court sustained the Commissioner, concluding the exchange had not been made "solely for * * * voting stock," as required by the 1939 Act, even though the cash purchases were not essential to Truax–Traer's acquisition of control. 24 T.C. at 804.

24. Compare Commissioner v. Gordon, 391 U.S. 83, 88 S.Ct. 1517 (1968).

The Seventh Circuit, after reviewing the legislative history of Section 112(g)(1)(B) of the 1939 Code, agreed with the Tax Court's conclusion that the presence of cash purchases prevented the transaction from meeting the "solely" requirement of the statute. Like the Tax Court, the court of appeals relied heavily on two prior decisions arising in slightly different contexts. The principal linchpin of the Seventh Circuit's decision was Helvering v. Southwest Consolidated Corp., 315 U.S. 194, 62 S.Ct. 546 (1942), in which the Supreme Court denied tax-free treatment to an asset acquisition under the 1934 Act because a substantial amount of the consideration was given in the form of stock warrants and cash. The Court first noted that under the law existing before 1934, this transaction would have been a perfectly valid tax-free reorganization. The revised statute, see text at notes 20–21 supra, had made the continuity of interest test much stricter, however:

> "Congress has provided that the assets of the transferor corporation must be acquired in exchange 'solely' for 'voting stock' of the transferee. 'Solely' leaves no leeway. Voting stock plus some other consideration does not meet the statutory requirement."

315 U.S. at 198, 62 S.Ct. at 550. The Seventh Circuit noted that in the 1934 Act the asset and stock acquisition reorganizations were dealt with in the same clause both in the statutory language and in the legislative history. It therefore seemed reasonable to the Seventh Circuit to conclude that the Supreme Court's "no leeway" rule for asset acquisitions applied with equal force to stock acquisitions.

Appellees argue that *Southwest Consolidated* is distinguishable from the present facts, and implicitly, that it should not have been relied on by the *Howard* court. This argument rests, in our view, on a strained reading of *Southwest Consolidated.* The taxpayers point out that the nonstock consideration in that case amounted to 37 percent of the total consideration, by the Tax Court's reckoning. Further, they say that the stock and nonstock consideration could not be separated where one bundle of assets was exchanged for one bundle of consideration, so that *Southwest Consolidated* was essentially a mixed consideration case. We disagree. Had the Supreme Court chosen to decide the issue of whether "substantially all" the assets of one corporation were obtained solely for voting stock, it could have allocated the consideration on a proportional basis, much as the Tax Court did in making its calculations. The Supreme Court did not consider, however, whether the voting stock consideration was sufficient to cover "substantially all" the assets, so that Section 112(g)(1)(B) would be satisfied. The Court determined rather that the presence of *any* nonstock consideration in the acquisition negated the possibility of a valid tax-free reorganization. While the facts were such that the Court could have reached the same result on another rationale, this does not detract from the weight of its words. The Seventh Circuit was, in our opinion, justified in resting its holding by analogy on the decision in *Southwest Consolidated.*

* * *

[T]he Tax Court plurality made three attempts to distinguish the *Howard* case or undercut its holding. First, the Tax Court argued that *Howard* was a case in which "some stockholders involved in the one exchange transaction * * * received cash." 71 T.C. at 737. The impact of this distinction is less than clear. There was no finding in *Howard* that any stockholder received both cash and stock for the *same* shares. In both *Howard* and this case, more than 80 percent of the shares were exchanged for stock only, and additional shares were purchased for cash. The only possible meaning of the Tax Court's statement is that it did not consider the 1968–69 cash purchases and the 1970 exchange offer part of "one exchange transaction." Yet the taxpayers' specific concession on motion for summary judgment was that the two events should be assumed to constitute "parts of the 1970 exchange offer reorganization." * * * We do not see how *Howard* can be distinguished from the present case other than on a finding that the cash and stock transactions here were unrelated as a matter of law, a finding the Tax Court specifically declined to make. (As we are remanding this latter issue to the Tax Court, we take no position on it now.)

The Tax Court's second attack on *Howard* * * * is equally unpersuasive. The fact that one shareholder of Binkley (the acquiree) received voting stock for some of its shares and cash for other shares, so that the 80 percent necessary for control was not acquired from shareholders receiving only stock, was not relied on by the Seventh Circuit. Furthermore, the focus of the statute is on the consideration furnished in the exchange, not on the consideration received by a particular shareholder. Any rule premised on the consideration each shareholder received would quickly founder on the realities of the stock market. Corporations could rarely assure themselves that an exchange for more than 80 percent of one corporation's stock would not be tainted by some stockholder's withholding of shares to sell to the acquiring corporation through the relative anonymity of market transactions. Indeed, in this case there is no proof that some of ITT's earlier market purchases were not made from shareholders of Hartford who later exchanged other shares for ITT's voting stock. Compare Pulfer v. Commissioner, 43 B.T.A. 677, 681 (1941). * * *

In short, we find *Howard* factually and legally indistinguishable from *Reeves,* and see no reason to question its continuing vitality. Even were we doubtful as to the correctness of the result reached in *Howard* (and we are not), we would nonetheless be reluctant to see a rule of tax law which has stood virtually unchallenged by courts for 25 years discarded so unceremoniously. As the dissenting judges of the Tax Court noted, much tax planning must proceed on the basis of settled rules. Avoidance of risk and uncertainty are often the keys to a successful transaction. Transactions may have been structured on the basis of *Howard,* with cash intentionally introduced to prevent reorganization treatment. Where a long standing tax rule of this sort is not clearly contrary to Congressional intent or markedly inconsistent with some generally accepted understanding of correct doctrine, we think the proper body to make changes aimed at improving the law is Congress, and not the courts. The complex and delicate judgments as to proper tax policy, and the balancing of interests between corporations, their shareholders, and the public, required to formulate appropriate rules in this area are not the proper province of courts. Our role is to interpret the mandate of Congress as best we can, and to adhere to the reasonable standards supplied by our predecessors where possible. Our role is emphatically not to read into the tax law our own notions of "a well-ordered universe." Compare Pierson v. United States, 472 F.Supp. 957, 974 (D.Del.1979).

Our reading of the statute is reinforced by another more recent circuit decision as well. In Mills v. Commissioner, 331 F.2d 321 (5th Cir.1964), *rev'g,* 39 T.C. 393 (1962), the issue was whether cash payments for fractional shares in an exchange prevented a nontaxable reorganization. General Gas Corporation, the acquiror, offered the three taxpayers, sole stockholders in three small gas corporations, shares of General common stock in exchange for all of their stock. The number of General shares to be exchanged—at a value of $14 per share—was to be determined by measuring the net book value of the three small corporations. In the event the purchase price was not evenly divisible by 14, cash was to be paid in lieu of fractional shares. As a result, each taxpayer received 1,595 shares of General Stock and $27.36 in cash. The Tax Court held this transaction invalid as a tax-free reorganization, declining to adopt a *de minimis* rule. 39 T.C. at 400.[36] The Fifth Circuit agreed that cash could not form any part of the consideration in a (B) reorganization, but concluded in reversing the Tax Court that the fractional-share arrangement was merely a bookkeeping convenience and not an independent part of the consideration. 331 F.2d at 324–25.

Taxpayers, and the Tax Court argued that *Mills* was distinguishable, despite its sweeping language, because each shareholder of the acquired corporations received both stock and cash in the exchange. We have discussed earlier our reasons for rejecting any rule premised on the consideration received by the acquiree's shareholders. If *Mills* were distinguishable at all, it would be only because the consideration for some of the *shares* in *Mills* consisted of both stock and cash. But even this distinction evaporates when one notes that the one share in each exchange for which a fractional share would have been necessary never constituted more than 20 percent of the stock of any one of the acquiree corporations (since each shareholder held at least six shares in each corporation). In every exchange it was theoretically possible to

36. The Tax Court in *Mills* stated:

"We construe the word 'solely' as meaning precisely what it purports to mean, namely that the receipt by the stockholders of an acquired corporation of any consideration whatsoever other than voting stock forbids a transaction from being a reorganization as defined under section 368(a)(1)(B) * * *. We cannot assume that Congress was incapable of expressing a grant of leeway when that was its purpose."

39 T.C. at 400.

identify a bloc of more than 80 percent of the stock of the acquiree which was exchanged solely for the voting stock of the acquiring corporation. Thus, in the only case raising the issue now before us under the 1954 Code, the Tax Court accepted as a premise that no cash was permissible as consideration in a (B) reorganization, even where the facts showed that control had passed solely for voting stock.

IV.

We have stated our ruling, and the reasons that support it. In conclusion, we would like to respond briefly to the arguments raised by the Tax Court, the District Court of Delaware, and the taxpayers in this case against the rule we have reaffirmed today. The principal argument, repeated again and again, concerns the supposed lack of policy behind the rule forbidding cash in a (B) reorganization where the control requirement is met solely for voting stock. It is true that the Service has not pointed to tax loopholes that would be opened were the rule to be relaxed as appellees request. We also recognize, as the Tax Court and others have highlighted, that the rule may produce results which some would view as anomalous. For example, if Corporation X acquires 80 percent of Corporation Y's stock solely for voting stock, and is content to leave the remaining 20 percent outstanding, no one would question that a valid (B) reorganization has taken place. If Corporation X then decides to purchase stock from the remaining shareholders, the *Howard* rule might result in loss of nontaxable treatment for the stock acquisition if the two transactions were found to be related. See 71 T.C. at 740–41. The Tax Court asserted that there is no conceivable Congressional policy that would justify such a result. Further, it argued, Congress could not have felt that prior cash purchases would forever ban a later successful (B) reorganization since the 1954 amendments, as the legislative history makes clear, specifically provided that prior cash purchases would not prevent a creeping acquisition.[37]

While not without force, this line of argument does not in the end persuade us. First of all, as already discussed, the language of the statute, and the longstanding interpretation given it by the courts, are persuasive reasons for our holding even in the absence of any clear policy behind Congress' expression of its will. Furthermore, we perceive statutory anomalies of another sort which the Tax Court's rule would only magnify. It is clear from the regulations, for example, that a corporation which already owned as much as 80 percent of another's stock, acquired solely for cash, could in some circumstances acquire all or a part of the remainder solely for voting stock as a valid (B) reorganization.[38] Why, then, could not as little as 10 percent of an acquisition constitute a (B) reorganization, if made solely for voting stock, even though the remaining transactions—totaling more than 80 percent—were made for nonstock consideration? If it is true that

37. See *1954 Senate Report,* supra note 17, at 273.

38. See Treas.Reg. § 1.368–2(c).

Congress did not view related cash transactions as tainting a stock-acquisition reorganization, why would it enact a "solely for * * * voting stock" requirement at all, except to the extent necessary to prevent mixed consideration of the sort employed in the "disguised sales" of the twenties?

Possibly, Congress' insertion of the "solely for * * * voting stock" requirement into the 1934 Act was, as one commentator has suggested, an overreaction to a problem which could have been dealt with through more precise and discriminating measures.[39] But we do not think it appropriate for a court to tell Congress how to do its job in an area such as this. If a more refined statutory scheme would be appropriate, such changes should be sought from the body empowered to make them. While we adhere to the general practice of construing statutes so as to further their demonstrated policies, we have no license to rework whole statutory schemes in pursuit of policy goals which Congress has nowhere articulated. Appellees have not shown us any reason to believe that reaffirmation of the settled rule in this area will frustrate the Congressional purpose of making the (B) reorganization provision generally available to those who comply with the statutory requirements.[40]

* * *

Finally, we see no merit at all in the suggestion that we should permit "boot" in a (B) reorganization simply because "boot" is permitted in some instances in (A) and (C) reorganizations. Congress has never indicated that these three distinct categories of transactions are to be interpreted *in pari materia.* In fact, striking differences in the treatment of the three subsections have been evident in the history of the reorganization statutes.[42] We see no reason to believe a difference in the treatment of "boot" in these transactions is impermissible or irrational.

Accordingly, we vacate the judgment of the Tax Court insofar as it rests on a holding that taxpayers were entitled to summary judgment irrespective of whether the cash purchases in this case were related by purpose or timing to the stock exchange offer of 1970. The case will be remanded to the Tax Court for further proceedings consistent with this opinion.

Vacated and remanded.

39. See Dailey, *The Voting Stock Requirement of B and C Reorganizations,* 26 Tax L.Rev. 725, 731 (1971); Pierson v. United States, 472 F.Supp. 957, 968 n. 37 (D.Del.1979).

40. We do not see how the argument that cash purchases are necessary to buy out the interests of "dissenting shareholders" who decline to take part in the exchange advances taxpayers' cause. One of the purposes of stock-acquisition arrangements, as opposed to statutory mergers, is to provide the option to minority shareholders not to take part. In this case, had such protection not been afforded, the Connecticut Insurance Commissioner evidently would not have approved the acquisition.

42. For example, under the 1954 version of the (C) reorganization, voting stock of a parent corporation could be used to acquire assets for a subsidiary. A similar provision was not added to the (B) section until 1964. Revenue Act of 1964, Pub.L. No. 88–272, § 218(a), 78 Stat. 57.

ILLUSTRATIVE MATERIAL

A. DEFINITIONAL ASPECTS

1. *The Solely for Voting Stock Requirement*

(a) *General*

Heverly v. Commissioner, 621 F.2d 1227 (3d Cir.1980), reached the same result as *Chapman* in a case involving other taxpayers involved in the Hartford–ITT acquisition.

The taxpayers in *Chapman* and *Heverly* petitioned for writ of certiorari but the petitions were dismissed pursuant to agreement of the parties. 451 U.S. 1012 (1981). Under the agreement, ITT paid $18.5 million in taxes and the IRS agreed not to contest the tax-free treatment of the former Hartford shareholders on the exchange for ITT stock so long as the shareholders did not attempt to claim a stepped-up basis in the ITT shares. IR 81–53 (1981). If the case had not been settled, on remand the Tax Court would have had to decide whether the two acquisition transactions constituted a single transaction and, if so, whether the "sale" of the stock acquired for cash to the Italian bank in fact transferred the burdens and benefits of ownership so that the subsequent stock exchange could qualify as a (B) reorganization.

Prior to the decision of the Tax Court in the Reeves v. Commissioner, 71 T.C. 727 (1979), which was reversed in *Chapman,* it was generally accepted that the presence of nonqualifying consideration would defeat a (B) reorganization even though the requisite 80 percent control had been acquired solely for voting stock. See, e.g., Rev.Rul. 75–123, 1975–1 Cum. Bull. 115. Most of the prior case law and rulings in situations similar to *Chapman* were concerned with the taxpayer's alternative argument in *Chapman,* that the nonqualifying consideration was not part of the "plan of reorganization" and therefore should not be taken into account in determining if the solely for voting stock requirement was met. After *Chapman,* the focus of attention in the (B) reorganization area will continue to be on whether any nonqualifying consideration was received pursuant to the plan of reorganization. See A.2., infra.

The material below deals with various aspects of the "solely for voting stock" requirement.

(b) *The "Voting" Stock Requirement*

In Rev.Rul. 72–72, 1972–1 Cum.Bull. 104, a corporation acquired all the outstanding shares of a second corporation in exchange for its voting stock. The shareholders of the acquired corporation agreed that the former sole shareholder of the acquiring corporation would have the irrevocable right to vote their new shares for five years, after which time they would receive their right to vote without restriction. The Ruling held that the transaction did not qualify as a (B) reorganization; it was in effect an acquisition for non-voting common stock which would be converted to voting common stock in five years, and thus did not meet the voting stock test. Compare Federal Grain Corp. v. Commissioner, 18 B.T.A. 242 (1929), in which the fact that voting shares received by the transferors of property were immediately placed in a voting trust was ignored in determining whether the transferors had "control" for purposes of the predecessor of section 351.

Rev.Rul. 63–234, 1963–2 Cum.Bull. 148, indicates that to qualify as "voting stock" the shares must confer "upon the holders * * * the right to significant participation in the management of the affairs of the corporation." (149) See also Rev.Rul. 70–108, 1970–1 Cum.Bull. 78 (exchange involving voting convertible preferred stock under the terms of which the shareholder had an option upon conversion to purchase an additional share of stock at a stipulated price did not satisfy the "solely for voting stock" requirement; the right to purchase the additional stock constituted property other than voting stock).

(c) *The "Solely" for Voting Stock Requirement: "Boot" Problems*

(i) *The Presence of Cash Payments*

Rev.Rul. 85–139, 1985–2 Cum.Bull. 123, held that the "solely for voting stock" requirement had been violated where X Corporation acquired 90 percent of the stock of Y Corporation for X Corporation voting stock and pursuant to the overall plan X Corporation caused its wholly owned subsidiary, S Corporation, to purchase the remaining 10 percent of the Y Corporation stock for cash.

If the cash transaction is separate from the stock transaction, however, the solely for voting stock requirement is not violated. See, e.g., Rev.Rul. 69–91, 1969–1, Cum.Bull. 106 (separate purchase for cash of convertible debentures); Rev.Rul. 68–562, 1968–2 Cum.Bull. 157 (unrelated purchase of shares by majority shareholder of acquiring corporation); Rev.Rul. 72–522, 1972–2 Cum.Bull. 215 (cash paid by the acquiring corporation to the acquired corporation in a (B) reorganization to provide it with working capital did not affect the solely for voting stock exchange at the shareholder level); Rev.Rul. 75–33, 1975–1 Cum.Bull. 115 (provision for payment of additional dividend on convertible preferred stock of acquiring corporation to insure that the shareholders of the acquired corporation would receive as large a dividend as they would have received had they accepted a competing offer from another corporation did not constitute "other property"; the right to the additional dividend inhered in the stock itself, since the right was lost if the conversion privilege was exercised and purchasers of the preferred stock also obtained the right to the extra dividend).

As *Chapman* indicates, the Internal Revenue Service originally took the position that cash issued in lieu of fractional shares violated the solely for voting stock requirement, but this position was rejected in Mills v. Commissioner, 331 F.2d 321 (5th Cir.1964). The Service subsequently indicated that it would follow *Mills* unless the cash received for the fractional shares was "separately bargained-for consideration," Rev.Rul. 66–365, 1966–2 Cum.Bull. 116. The cash received is not treated as "boot" but as a payment in redemption of the taxpayer's stock, the transaction thus being viewed as in effect the transfer of voting stock to the shareholder followed by a redemption.

If the acquiring corporation agrees to pay expenses of transferor shareholders incurred in connection with the (B) reorganization, does disqualification result? Rev.Rul. 73–54, 1973–1 Cum.Bull. 187, held that the solely for voting stock requirement is not violated in such a case if the expenses were "solely and directly related to the reorganization." But the Ruling cautions that payment of shareholders' expenses "for legal, accounting or investment advice or counsel pertaining to participation in, or action with respect to, the reorganization" will result in disqualification. See also infra, page 845. Payment of shareholders' transfer taxes similarly results in disqualification. However, the Service has ruled that the acquiring corporation may pay the costs necessary to register with the Securities and Exchange Commission the voting shares used in the acquisition without violating the "solely for voting stock" requirement, on the theory that such costs are properly costs of the acquiring corporation and not of the transferor shareholders. Rev.Rul. 67–275, 1967–2 Cum.Bull. 142.

If the payment of cash or other property is made by the *acquired* corporation rather than the acquiring corporation, the solely for voting stock requirement is not violated. See e.g., Rev.Rul. 68–435, 1968–2 Cum.Bull. 155 (dividend paid by the acquired corporation based on the dividend its shareholders would have received from the acquiring corporation had the final transaction been consummated as originally planned held not to violate the solely for voting stock requirement); Rev.Rul. 75–421, 1975–2 Cum. Bull. 108 ((B) reorganization upheld where the acquired corporation paid the fees of a financial consultant and accountant employed by its sole shareholder to determine the value of the acquiring company's stock; the fees were paid before the reorganization was consummated and constituted a dividend to the shareholder). Similarly, the acquired corporation can make cash payments to shareholders who dissent without endangering the reorganization as long as the funds for the payment do not come from the acquiring corporation. See Rev.Rul. 68–285, 1968–1 Cum.Bull. 147. Compare Rev. Rul. 75–360, 1975–2 Cum.Bull. 110 (in the *McDonald* case, supra page 726, stock of the acquired corporation was redeemed prior to the (B) reorganization exchange with funds provided indirectly by the acquiring corporation; the Ruling stated that the case had been wrongly argued solely as a redemption case (with a separate valid (B) reorganization conceded); the redemption and stock exchange were steps in a single transaction and the receipt of cash thus prevented (B) reorganization treatment).

(ii) *The Presence of Non–Cash Consideration*

Where shareholders of the acquired corporation are also debenture holders and exchange their shares and debentures for voting stock and new debentures of the acquiring corporation, disqualification as a (B) reorganization can result if some of the new debentures are determined to be part of the consideration attributable to the shares transferred. See Rev.Rul. 69–142, 1969–1 Cum.Bull. 107; Rev.Rul. 78–408, 1978–2 Cum.Bull. 203 (dealing with warrants). Rev.Rul. 70–269, 1970–1 Cum.Bull. 82, held that the acquiring corporation may substitute its stock options for options of the acquired corporation without affecting qualification as a (B) reorganization; the acquiring corporation's options were not given in consideration of stock of the acquired corporation.

See also, Fisher v. Commissioner, 62 T.C. 73 (1974) (additional shares of stock paid by the acquiring corporation in lieu of cash dividend held to constitute a separate transaction from otherwise valid (B) reorganization; the additional stock constituted a taxable stock dividend under the former version of section 305(b)(2)).

An assumption of indebtedness of the shareholders of the acquired corporation in connection with the acquisition of their stock can prevent the qualification of the transaction as a (B) reorganization. See, e.g., Rev.Rul. 79–4, 1979–1 Cum.Bull. 150 (where corporation was thinly capitalized and shareholder-guaranteed loan was treated as direct loan by shareholder, assumption of the obligation as a condition of the reorganization exchange was disqualifying consideration); Rev.Rul. 70–65, 1970–1 Cum.Bull. 77 (60% of stock of Y Corporation was owned by Z Corporation and the balance by unrelated parties; X Corporation obtained the Y stock from Z along with the remaining Z assets in exchange for X voting stock and the assumption of Z's liabilities; X then exchanged X voting stock for the additional outstanding shares of Y; the acquisition of Y stock from Z qualified as a (C) reorganization, but neither of the acquisitions of the Y stock qualified as a (B) reorganization because of the assumption of Z's liabilities, the two transactions being treated as one for purposes of testing the transaction as a (B) reorganization). However, in most stock for stock acquisitions, the liabilities of the acquired corporation simply stay with the corporation. Dealings between the acquiring corporation and the acquired corporation's creditors which are separate from the "plan of reorganization" do not disqualify an otherwise valid (B) reorganization. See Rev.Rul. 79–89, 1979–1 Cum.Bull. 152 (contribution of cash to the acquired corporation used to pay debt of the corporation guaranteed by a shareholder was not disqualifying additional consideration where the payment of the debt was not a condition of the exchange of stock).

(iii) *Compensation Arrangements*

The shareholders of the acquired corporation may enter into employment contracts in connection with the reorganization. If part of the alleged compensation for services is in fact paid for stock of the acquired corporation the solely for voting stock requirement would not be met. However, in Rev. Rul. 77–271, 1977–2 Cum.Bull. 116, where the president of the acquired corporation, as part of the plan of reorganization entered into an employment contract with the acquired corporation and received additional stock of the acquiring corporation as consideration for entering into the contract, the Service treated the employment arrangement as a transaction separate from the otherwise valid (B) reorganization; the additional stock received by the president constituted ordinary income to him.

(iv) *Contingent Stock Payouts*

The shareholders of acquired corporation also may receive the right to obtain additional voting shares in the future if specified conditions are met, e.g., the earnings of the acquired corporation reaching a certain level. Generally, such contingent stock payout agreements are utilized in situations in which the parties to the reorganization are unable to agree on the fair market value of the acquired corporation's stock. The right to receive voting shares in the future is not the same as the present receipt of voting shares as such and hence arguably could violate the solely for voting stock restriction.

Carlberg v. United States, 281 F.2d 507 (8th Cir.1960), held that certificates representing a contingent interest in shares in the acquiring corporation should be treated as "stock" for purposes of nonrecognition under section 354 (a result disputed by the Service because the certificates in question were negotiable). In Hamrick v. Commissioner, 43 T.C. 21 (1964), the court treated a nonnegotiable contingent right to receive additional shares of stock as the equivalent of stock for purposes of section 351. Neither case had to decide whether the contingent interest represented "voting stock," a somewhat more difficult question. That question was resolved, however, in Rev.Rul. 66–112, 1966–1 Cum.Bull. 68, which held that the receipt of a contingent contractual right to additional voting shares which was not assignable and could only ripen into additional voting shares did not violate the solely for voting stock requirement in a (B) reorganization.

After the issuance of Rev.Rul. 66–112, the following transactions were held not to violate the solely for voting stock requirement: Rev.Rul. 73–205, 1973–1 Cum.Bull. 188 (the conversion ratio of convertible preferred stock received in a (B) reorganization was subject to upward adjustment after five years based on the acquired corporation's earnings performance; the right to additional shares, if any, was forfeited by those shareholders who converted within the 5–year period); Rev.Rul. 75–456, 1975–2 Cum.Bull. 128 (subsequent to a (B) reorganization in which a contingent stock payout provision was employed, the acquiring corporation changed its place of incorporation by means of an (F) reorganization in which a new corporation was formed in another state and the acquiring corporation merged into it; the fact that the new corporation assumed the acquiring corporation's contingent stock payout obligation and agreed to issue its own additional shares of stock in lieu of the acquiring corporation's stock did not affect the status of the prior (B) reorganization); Rev.Rul. 75–237, 1975–1 Cum.Bull. 116 (acceleration of contingent stock payout agreement by acquiring corporation in a (B) reorganization prior to the transfer of all of its assets to a third corporation in a (C) reorganization did not affect the validity of the earlier (B) reorganization; same result if the earlier reorganization had itself been a (C) reorganization).

Rev.Proc. 77–37, 1977–2 Cum.Bull. 568 (section 3.03), amplified by Rev.Proc. 84–42, 1984–1 Cum.Bull. 521, sets forth nine conditions under which a favorable ruling will be issued on the solely for voting stock issue in a contingent stock payout situation. The principal requirements are that all the additional stock must be issued within five years from the date of the original reorganization transaction, there must be a valid business reason for not issuing all the stock immediately, such as the difficulty of valuing the stock of one or both of the corporations, the maximum number of shares which may be issued is stated, and at least one half of the total number of shares to be issued must be issued in the initial distribution.

In contingent stock payout situations, Regulations, sections 1.483–1(b), Ex. (7), and 1.483–1(e)(3), Ex. (2), provide that a portion of the additional stock received constitutes interest under section 483. These Regulations predate the expansion of coverage of the original issue discount rules in 1984; and in most cases, sections 1272 through 1275 now govern the imputation of interest. See Proposed Regulations, section 1.1275–1(b)(1) (1986). Taxpayers challenged the validity of the section 483 Regulations, arguing that treatment of the receipt of additional stock as a "payment" under section 483 is inconsistent with the conclusion that the receipt of the right to additional stock does not violate the solely for voting stock requirements in the reorganization provisions. The position taken in the Regulations, however, has been upheld by the courts. See Kingsley v. Commissioner, 72 T.C. 1095 (1979); Catterall v. Commissioner, 68 T.C. 413 (1977), aff'd sub nom., Vorbleski v. Commissioner, 589 F.2d 123 (3d Cir.1978); Jeffers v. United States, 556 F.2d 986 (Ct.Cl.1977) ((A) reorganization); Solomon v. Commissioner, 570 F.2d 28 (2d Cir.1977); Katkin v. Commissioner, 570 F.2d 139 (6th Cir.1978) ((A) reorganization).

For a variation on a contingent stock payout situation, consider Rev.Rul. 75–94, 1975–1 Cum.Bull. 111. In 1973, a type (B) reorganization took place. In the following year it was discovered that the acquiring corporation had misrepresented its earnings because of an improper accounting practice. Upon correction of the improper practice, the earnings were reduced and the acquired corporation's shareholders asserted that they were entitled to additional stock of the acquiring corporation to satisfy the negotiated acquisition price. After discussions between the parties, the acquiring corporation did issue additional stock. The Ruling concluded that the additional shares received were part of the original "plan of reorganization" and hence qualified as part of the (B) reorganization.

Another technique that is employed where the parties cannot agree upon the value of the corporations is the "escrowed stock" arrangement. Under such an arrangement, the acquiring corporation issues its stock to the shareholders of the acquired corporation, but part of the stock is placed in escrow to be returned to the acquiring corporation upon the occurrence of a specified event, for example, the failure of the acquired corporation to reach a specified earnings level. If the earnings level is reached, the stock is transferred out of escrow to the shareholders of the acquired corporation. Since the stock is actually issued, subject to subsequent forfeiture, some problems of contingent stock payouts are avoided. For example, interest will not be imputed under either section 483 or the original issue discount rules if the transaction is properly structured. Regulations, section 1.483–2(b)(6), Ex. (8); Rev.Rul. 70–120, 1970–1 Cum.Bull. 124 (shareholders entitled to unrestricted voting rights and received dividends on stock); Feifer v. United States, 500 F.Supp. 102 (N.D.Ga.1980) (same even though voting rights were restricted); see also Development Corporation of America v. Commissioner, 55 T.C.M. 455 (1988).

Rev.Rul. 76–42, 1976–1 Cum.Bull. 102, held that no gain or loss is recognized by the shareholders of the acquired corporation if the escrowed stock is returned to the acquiring corporation where the number of shares to be returned was based on their initially negotiated value. The adjusted basis of the returned shares is added to the basis of those received by the shareholders of the acquired corporation. Compare Rev.Rul. 78–376, 1978–2 Cum.Bull. 149 (where the number of shares to be returned from the escrow to discharge an indemnity obligation was based on the value of the shares on the date of the return from escrow and not on the initially negotiated price, the taxpayer was required to realize gain since he received a benefit from the appreciation in value which was used to discharge his obligations).

Rev.Proc. 77–37, supra (section 3.06), amplified by Rev.Proc. 84–42, supra, sets forth nine conditions under which a favorable ruling will be issued in escrowed stock transactions. The principal requirements are that there must be a valid reason for establishing the arrangement, the stock subject to the escrow agreement must be treated as issued and outstanding stock of the acquiring corporation for all purposes, voting rights must be exercisable by the shareholders or their agent, all shares must be released from the escrow within five years, and not more than 50 percent of the total number of shares to be issued may be subject to the escrow.

Contingent stock and escrowed stock arrangements are not unique to type (B) reorganizations. They may be used in connection with any type acquisition, but different problems may arise with respect to qualifying the transaction under different provisions of section 368. For example, Rev.Rul. 76–334, 1976–2 Cum.Bull. 108, involved the use of an escrow arrangement in a type (C) reorganization in which the transferor corporation liquidated and distributed all rights in the escrowed stock to its shareholders. The purpose of the escrow was to protect the acquiring corporation from a breach of representations and warranties made by the transferor corporation as a part of the reorganization transaction. The acquiring corporation asserted a breach and the escrow agent returned part of the escrowed stock to the acquiring corporation, with the balance being distributed to the transferor corporation's shareholders. However, those shareholders disputed the validity of the acquiring corporation's claim to a return of part of the escrowed stock. Negotiations between the parties resulted in a settlement pursuant to which the acquiring corporation paid cash equal to one-half the value of the escrowed shares distributed to the shareholders and the shareholders returned the balance of the escrowed shares to the acquiring corporation. The Ruling held that the cash payment was separate from, and did not violate the solely for voting stock requirement of, the (C) reorganization. There was a redemption of one-half the escrowed stock under section 302 and the other one-half was simply returned pursuant to the escrow arrangement with no gain or loss being recognized by the acquired corporation's shareholders under the principles of Rev.Rul. 76–42.

2. *Multi–Step Acquisitions*

The taxpayer's alternative argument in *Chapman* was that the cash purchases of the stock and the exchange of stock for voting stock were separate transactions. If the cash acquisitions were separated from the stock exchange, the exchange by itself would have qualified as a (B) reorganization. The Tax Court did not face the factual issue of whether the stock purchases were "old and cold" and thus did not taint the share exchange because of its holding that in any event a (B) reorganization was present. The Court of Appeals remanded for consideration of the factual question whether the cash purchase and the exchange were connected. However, because the case was settled prior to consideration of this issue by the Tax Court, there remains only sparse authority regarding the extent to which prior or subsequent acquisitions for nonqualifying consideration will defeat the (B) reorganization. Regulations, section 1.368–2(c), give as an example of a qualifying reorganization a situation where the corporation purchased 30 percent of the stock for cash and then 16 years later acquired an additional 60 percent in exchange for its voting stock. Whether the various steps in the acquisition will be considered together or separately depends in part on the time interval between the steps and in part on other circumstances which indicate that the various steps in the acquisition are part of the "same transaction". See Rev.Rul. 75–123, 1975–1 Cum.Bull. 115 (cash acquisition and stock exchange pursuant to the "same plan" resulted in a taxable exchange and not a (B) reorganization). The step transaction cases discussed supra, page 775, are relevant in this determination.

A similar question is involved when the acquisition is made solely in exchange for voting stock but the stock of the acquired company is obtained in a series of transactions. Regulations, section 1.368–2(c), seem to require that the requisite 80 percent control be acquired within a 12–month period. If this time limitation is satisfied, the series of acquisitions is in effect treated as a single transaction and all shares acquired in the 12–month period will qualify for tax free treatment. If the 12-month time limitation in the Regulations is not met, then possibly only those shares acquired for stock that provide or exceed the 80 percent control requirement qualify for (B) reorganization treatment and the other exchanges would be treated as taxable transactions. However, in American Potash & Chemical Corp. v. United States, 402 F.2d 1000 (Ct.Cl.1968), the Government took the position that a transaction qualified as a (B) reorganization even though the series of acquisitions to obtain control of the target corporation occurred over a 14-month period, asserting that the 12-month rule in Regulations, section 1.368-2(c), "is merely a guideline to determine which exchanges of a series of exchanges of stock for stock qualify as tax-free under the B reorganization provisions." (1001) In *American Potash,* the Government unsuccessfully sought reorganization treatment to prevent a step-up in basis on the subsequent liquidation of the acquired corporation; it seems doubtful that the Commissioner would accept a similar argument by a taxpayer seeking to qualify for reorganization treatment.

See also Rev.Rul. 69-585, 1969-2 Cum.Bull. 56 (subsidiary distributed its previously acquired 25% of the stock of the acquired corporation to its parent as a dividend and the parent then acquired the remaining 75% of the stock of the corporation from the latter's shareholders; parent's acquisitions held to constitute a valid (B) reorganization); Rev.Rul. 69-294, 1969-1 Cum.Bull. 110 (parent liquidated subsidiary to obtain 80% stock interest in target corporation and then acquired the balance of the stock in a stock-for-stock exchange; parent's acquisition held not to constitute a valid (B) reorganization since part of the acquired corporation's stock was obtained in exchange for the subsidiary's stock in the liquidation).

3. *The "Control" Requirement*

In Rev.Rul. 76-223, 1976-1 Cum.Bull. 103, X Corporation had outstanding 81 shares of voting common stock and 19 shares of non-voting preferred stock. Y Corporation wished to obtain all of the common, but none of the preferred in exchange for its voting stock. This transaction, however, would not have qualified as a (B) reorganization, since the "control" test is expressed in terms of each class of voting and non-voting stock. Accordingly, prior to the reorganization, X Corporation amended its charter to grant voting rights to the preferred stock. Voting stock of Y Corporation was then exchanged for the common stock of X Corporation. The Ruling held that the control requirement was met since Y Corporation received over 80 percent of all the classes of stock entitled to vote at the time of the acquisition, there being at that time no non-voting classes of stock outstanding in X Corporation.

4. *Parties to the Reorganization*

Section 368(a)(2)(C) provides that the acquiring corporation in a (B) reorganization may transfer the stock of the acquired corporation to a subsidiary without disqualifying the reorganization. The acquired corporation, as a result, becomes a second tier subsidiary of the acquiring corporation. Moreover, by virtue of the first parenthetical provision in section 368(a)(1)(B) itself, a valid (B) reorganization can occur where an 80 percent controlled subsidiary is the acquiring corporation, using the stock of its parent in the reorganization. Again, as a result, the acquired corporation becomes a second tier subsidiary in the corporate group.

5. *Relationship of (B) and (C) Reorganizations*

A valid (B) reorganization followed by the immediate liquidation of the acquired corporation may be treated by the Internal Revenue Service as a (C) reorganization. See Rev.Rul. 67–274, 1967–2 Cum.Bull. 141. See, infra, page 849.

B. TAX TREATMENT OF PARTIES TO A TYPE (B) REORGANIZATION

1. *Acquiring Corporation*

No gain or loss will be recognized by the acquiring corporation in a valid (B) reorganization. Section 1032. If the acquiring corporation uses stock of its parent as is permitted by the parenthetical in section 368(a)(1)(B), section 1032 does not apply on its face, but Proposed Regulations, section 1.1032–2(a) (1981), would provide nonrecognition.

The acquiring corporation's basis in the stock of the acquired corporation is the aggregate of the bases of the transferring shareholders. Section 362(b). If the acquiring corporation is widely held, this information may be difficult to obtain. Rev.Proc 81–70, 1981–2 Cum.Bull. 729, provides guidelines for estimating the transferor shareholders' bases, including, where appropriate, the use of standard statistical methods using a probability sample.

The assets of the acquired corporation are unaffected by the reorganization exchange and thus keep the same basis.

2. *Shareholders of Acquired Corporation*

In a (B) reorganization the shareholders of the acquired corporation will recognize no gain or loss. Section 354(a). Section 356 does not come into play since receipt of "other property" disqualifies the transaction as a "reorganization" under section 368(a)(1)(B). The shareholders of the acquired corporation take as their basis in the acquiring corporation's shares received, the basis of their stock in the acquired corporation. Section 358(a).

C. REFERENCES

McMahon, Defining the "Acquisition" in B Reorganizations Through the Step Transaction Doctrine, 67 Iowa L.Rev. 31 (1981); Steines, Policy Considerations in the Taxation of B Reorganizations, 31 Hastings L.J. 993 (1980); Dailey, The Voting Stock Requirement of B and C Reorganizations, 26 Tax L.Rev. 725 (1971); Tillinghast, Contingent Stock Payouts in Tax–Free Reorganizations, 22 Tax Law. 467 (1969); Davis, Tax Problems of Modification of Previously Entered–Into Tax–Free Reorganizations on Account of Breach of Warranties, 32 N.Y.U.Tax Inst. 593 (1974).

SECTION 6. STOCK FOR ASSETS ACQUISITIONS: (C) REORGANIZATIONS

INTERNAL REVENUE CODE: Sections 354; 356(a), (c); 357(a), (b); 358(a); 361; 362(b); 368(a)(1)(C), (a)(2)(B), (C), and (G).

REGULATIONS: Section 1.368–2(d).

The (C) reorganization resembles an (A) reorganization in that a transfer of assets is involved. Indeed, the (C) reorganization is often referred to as a "practical merger." But requirements are imposed which are not present in an (A) reorganization: "Substantially all" the assets of the transferor corporation must be exchanged in the transaction and, since the transferor corporation in a (C) reorganization does not automatically disappear as in an (A) reorganization, section 368(a)(2)(G) requires the transferor corporation to liquidate. Moreover, the (C) reorganization has elements in common with a (B) reorganization which are not present in an (A) reorganization, notably the requirement that the consideration for the acquired assets be "solely" voting stock of the acquiring corporation. But, in turn, the solely for voting stock requirement is less stringently applied in the (C) reorganization context. Thus, a number of the issues considered in connection with (A) and (B) reorganizations are also present in (C) reorganizations.

ILLUSTRATIVE MATERIAL

A. DEFINITIONAL ASPECTS

1. *Solely for Voting Stock Requirement*

(a) *General*

As in the case of a (B) reorganization, section 368(a)(1)(C) imposes the requirement that the acquisition be "solely for voting stock". The phrase has the same meaning as in the context of a (B) reorganization and the materials discussed supra, page 817, are equally applicable in interpreting the requirement in a (C) reorganization. The rigors of the solely for voting stock requirement are, however, relaxed to some extent where a (C) reorganization is involved. The (C) reorganization definition allows 20 percent non-voting stock consideration to be used in the acquisition. Section 368(a)(2)(B). The 20 percent leeway for (C) reorganizations is of limited scope, however, since liabilities of the transferor which are assumed or to which its property are subject are applied against the permissible 20 percent consideration that may be in a form other than voting stock. Moreover, the 80 percent voting stock consideration is tested by reference to "all" and not "substantially all" of the transferor's assets and presents significant valuation problems with regard to the assets involved.

(b) *Assumption of Liabilities*

Where assets are acquired for voting stock in a (C) reorganization, the additional presence of an assumption of indebtedness by the acquiring corporation does not prevent qualification as a reorganization (except as to the effect on the operation of section 368(a)(2)(B)). Consequently in a (C) reorganization, the transferee may, in addition to issuing voting stock, issue debt securities to the creditors of the transferor. Southland Ice Co. v.

Commissioner, 5 T.C. 842, 850 (1945) (A). If all of the consideration consists of voting stock and assumption of liabilities, there is no specific limitation on the portion of the consideration which may be in the form of assumption of liabilities, although if too high a percentage of the total consideration is debt assumption there is some possibility that the "substantially all the assets" requirement may be violated. See infra, page 846. But if any portion of the consideration is boot as permitted by section 368(a)(2)(B), then the total amount of boot plus the liabilities assumed may not exceed 20 percent of the value of *all* of the acquired corporation's assets. This requirement effectively eliminates the possibility of using any boot in a (C) reorganization whenever the acquired corporation's net assets are not more than 80 percent of its gross assets. See Rev.Rul. 85–138, 1985–2 Cum.Bull. 122.

Even where boot is not present, not all debt assumptions are permitted. In Helvering v. Southwest Consolidated Corp., 315 U.S. 194 (1942), the transferee had assumed a bank loan entered into by the bondholders' committee to obtain cash to pay nonparticipating security holders. The Court held that the bank loan did not fall within the assumption of liabilities clause, since the requirement to pay cash arose out of the reorganization plan itself and could not therefore be regarded as an obligation of the "other corporation". Subsequent cases, however, limited the scope of *Southwest Consolidated.* See Claridge Apartments Co. v. Commissioner, 1 T.C. 163 (1942) (assumption of expenses of bankruptcy reorganization did not disqualify transaction); Alcazar Hotel, Inc. v. Commissioner, 1 T.C. 872 (1943) (same); Roosevelt Hotel Co. v. Commissioner, 13 T.C. 399 (1949) (loans used to pay preexisting liabilities did not disqualify transaction). In Rev.Rul. 73–54, 1973–1 Cum.Bull. 187, the Service declined to apply the holding of *Southwest Consolidated* to the fullest extent possible by ruling that the payment by the acquiring corporation of valid reorganization expenses of the transferor corporation is not a violation of the solely for voting stock requirement: "Although the acquired corporation and its shareholders are relieved of the reorganization expenses otherwise attributable to them, nevertheless they will be receiving solely voting stock of the acquiring corporation." On the other hand, in Rev.Rul. 73–102, 1973–1 Cum.Bull. 186, where the acquiring corporation assumed the obligation of the acquired corporation to pay the claims of dissenting shareholders, the assumption was treated as in substance a payment of cash (and thus not within the exception of section 368(a)(1)(C) for liability assumptions) and also did not fall within the exception for reorganization expenses set out in Rev.Rul 73–54. Reorganization treatment was still possible, however, as the cash payment fell within the leeway allowed under section 368(a)(2)(B).

In Rev.Rul. 76–365, 1976–2 Cum.Bull. 110, prior to a (C) reorganization, the transferor corporation had employed an accountant and a financial consultant to value the stock of each of six prospective acquiring corporations, including the stock of the corporation with which the transaction was ultimately consummated. As part of the reorganization, the acquiring corporation paid the fees of the consultants. The Ruling held that the expenses of valuing the stock of the acquiring corporation itself were covered by Rev. Rul. 73–54 and did not violate the solely for voting stock requirement. The expenses of evaluating the other five potential acquiring corporations were treated as liabilities of the transferor corporation assumed by the acquiring corporation. Hence, such assumption of liabilities fell within the exception in section 368(a)(1)(C) and the solely for voting stock requirement was satisfied.

Care must be taken that only existing liabilities are assumed and that new liabilities of the acquiring corporation are not created. In Stoddard v. Commissioner, 141 F.2d 76 (2d Cir.1944), the issuance of mortgage bonds to replace unsecured indebtedness of the acquired corporation was held to go beyond assumption of the acquired corporation's debts and to constitute additional impermissible consideration. But where new bonds issued by the acquiring corporation to replace outstanding bonds of the transferor vary only somewhat from the terms of the old bonds the courts have tended to treat the replacement as an assumption. See, e.g. Southland Ice Co. v. Commissioner, supra, page 844, and the Service likewise allows some leeway here. See Rev.Rul. 79–155, 1979–1 Cum.Bull. 153 (replacement of 8% nonconvertible bonds due in 1995 with 9% convertible bonds due in 1990 was treated as "assumption").

The relaxation of the solely for voting stock requirement in section 368(a)(1)(C) applies only to the assumption of liabilities by "the acquiring corporation." Thus the Service has ruled that where a subsidiary acquires by means of its parent's stock the assets of a third corporation as is permitted under section 368(a)(1)(C), the assumption by the parent of liabilities of the acquired corporation violated the solely for voting stock requirement since the subsidiary is technically the acquiring corporation. Rev.Rul. 70–107, 1970–1 Cum.Bull. 78. However, if the parent retains the right to direct the transfer of the assets to the subsidiary, the parent is then considered the acquiring corporation and its assumption of liabilities falls within the exception. Rev.Rul. 70–224, 1970–1 Cum.Bull. 79.

Section 357(b), discussed supra, page 354, will treat all of the acquired corporation's debts assumed by the acquiring corporation as boot if a tax avoidance motive is present with respect to any of the assumed indebtedness. See Rev.Rul. 79–258, 1979–2 Cum.Bull. 143 (on facts, declining to apply section 357(b) to assumption of liabilities in a type (D) reorganization).

2. *The "Substantially All of the Properties" Requirement*

The "substantially all of the properties" requirement in section 368(a)(1)(C) appears to reflect the view that reorganization treatment should be allowed only if there is a continuation of the business enterprise. Perhaps too, the requirement may reflect elements of the continuity of interest requirement, i.e., that the shareholders of the transferor corporation retain a continuing interest in the assets which had comprised their pre-transfer investment.

In Smith v. Commissioner, 34 B.T.A. 702 (1936) (A), the Board of Tax Appeals permitted 71 percent of the gross assets to qualify where the balance was retained for the sole purpose of liquidating liabilities. The Board, in distinguishing other cases, stressed the purpose of the retention and emphasized it was not to engage in business or to distribute assets to shareholders. Referring to this decision, the Tax Court in Southland Ice Company v. Commissioner, 5 T.C. 842 (1945), said "Even this [the 'substantially all'] provision has been subjected to a construction which in effect applies a continuity test rather than mere blind percentages." Rev.Rul. 57–518, 1957–2 Cum.Bull. 253, following the *Smith* case, stressed that a transaction will not qualify as a (C) reorganization if the net assets transferred are too low a percentage of gross assets. The Ruling held that a transfer of all of the corporation's net assets, equalling 70 percent of its gross assets, satisfied the substantially all requirement. However, the Ruling stated that where net assets equal only 10 percent of gross assets, the requirement clearly could not be satisfied if assets in excess of those sufficient to discharge liabilities were retained. In National Bank of Commerce of Norfolk v. United States, 158 F.Supp. 887 (E.D.Va.1958), a transfer of 81 percent of the assets was held not "substantially all" where the remaining assets were not retained to meet liabilities but were to be distributed to shareholders.

In Rev.Proc. 77–37, 1977–2 Cum.Bull. 568 (Sec. 3.01), the Service stated that it would issue advance rulings on the "substantially all" issue where the transferred assets represent at least 90 percent of the fair market value of the net assets and at least 70 percent of the fair market value of the gross assets of the corporation immediately prior to the transfer; this test, as with the continuity of interest test, supra, page 796, is only an "operating rule" and does not "define, as a matter of law, the lower limits of 'continuity of interest' or 'substantially all of the properties'." Rev.Proc. 77–37 also stated that payments to dissenters and pre-acquisition redemptions and extraordinary dividends which are part of the plan of reorganization are considered assets held immediately prior to the transfer for purposes of determining whether substantially all the assets are transferred to the acquiring corporation. See also Rev.Rul. 74–457, 1974–2 Cum.Bull. 122 (cash used in payment of regular cash dividend prior to the reorganization by the transferor corporation is not taken into account in applying the "substantially all" test; however, if the payment occurred after the reorganization, the cash required to pay the dividend and the liability for payment of the dividend are taken into account).

Rev.Rul. 88–48, 1988–1 Cum.Bull. 117, found the "substantially all" requirement to have been met where X Corporation sold for cash one of its two historic businesses which represented 50 percent of its historic business assets and then transferred the cash and all its remaining assets to Y Corporation for Y voting stock and assumption of X's liabilities. The sale of the assets was pursuant to the overall plan because Y did not wish to acquire the business which was sold. The Ruling stressed that the Service views the purpose of the "substantially all" requirement as preventing the use of section 368(a)(1)(C) to effect a divisive reorganization. Since the sale was to unrelated persons and no part of the proceeds was directly or indirectly retained by the shareholders of Y, the test was met.

In Helvering v. Elkhorn Coal Co., 95 F.2d 732 (4th Cir.1937), the Elkhorn Coal and Coke Co. desired to transfer a part of its mining property to Mill Creek Company for stock. To qualify as a reorganization since Mill Creek would not obtain control of Elkhorn Coal Co., Elkhorn would have had to transfer substantially all its assets. To accomplish this, Elkhorn first formed a new company, transferred the other Elkhorn properties to it for its stock, and distributed such stock to its shareholders, this distribution being nontaxable under the predecessors of sections 368(a)(1)(D) and 355. It then transferred the mining properties, now "all its properties," to Mill Creek for stock, technically a reorganization. The new company then acquired the Elkhorn stock for its stock and dissolved Elkhorn so that the old Elkhorn stockholder ended up as the stockholders of a corporation which owned the remaining Elkhorn properties and stock of Mill Creek. The transaction predated the enactment of the liquidation requirement in section

368(a)(2)(G). Applying *Gregory* principles, the court disregarded the distribution of the stock of the new company and held that Elkhorn had not transferred substantially all of its assets to Mill Creek. Hence no reorganization had occurred and the transaction was taxable. Compare Rev.Rul. 70–434, 1970–2 Cum.Bull. 83 (preacquisition spin off of assets does not preclude (B) reorganization treatment).

3. *Liquidation Requirement*

Section 368(a)(2)(G) requires that the acquired corporation liquidate and distribute the stock and securities it receives in the reorganization as well as its other properties to its shareholders in pursuance of the plan of reorganization. This requirement was added in 1984 to forestall tax avoidance effected by keeping the acquired corporation in existence as an investment company following the acquisition. This tax avoidance potential arose because under section 381 all of the acquired corporation's tax attributes are transferred to the acquiring corporation as a result of the reorganization. See infra, Chapter 20. Thus if not required to liquidate, the acquired corporation would have substantial assets, against which it might borrow to make distributions, but would have no earnings and profits to support dividend treatment. See H.Rep. No. 98–861, 98th Cong., 2d Sess. 205 (1984).

The distribution requirement may be waived by the Internal Revenue Service in circumstances in which an actual distribution would result in substantial hardship. However, the waiver will be granted only on the condition that the acquired corporation and its shareholders be treated as if the retained assets were distributed and then recontributed to a new corporation. See H.Rep. No. 98–861, 98th Cong., 2d Sess. 845–46 (1984). This constructive liquidation and contribution will trigger recognition of gain and loss to the acquired corporation under section 361(c)(2)(A) as well as recognition of gain to the shareholders of the acquired corporation under section 356(a).

As a further safeguard, the 1984 Act also amended section 312(h)(2) to authorize the Treasury to promulgate regulations requiring that the earnings and profits of the acquired corporation be allocated between the acquiring and the acquired corporations.

In Rev.Rul. 84–30, 1984–1 Cum.Bull. 114, X Corporation owned all the stock of Y Corporation and Z Corporation; Z Corporation, in turn, owned all of the stock of N Corporation. Y acquired substantially all the assets of N for its voting stock. N was liquidated and Z received the Y stock, which it immediately distributed to X. The Ruling held that the continuity of interest requirement of Regulations, section 1.368–1(b), is satisfied where the stock of the acquiring corporation exchanged for the assets of the acquired corporation is distributed through the acquiring corporation's 100 percent parent to that corporation's 100 percent parent. It does not appear to have been crucial to the result in the Ruling that X Corporation was the common parent of both Y and Z. Furthermore, there is no obvious reason why the holding should apply only if the ultimate distributee is a 100 percent parent corporation, rather than individual shareholders. Note, however, that the distribution from the acquiring corporation's parent to its own shareholders should be treated as a dividend, which may result in recognition to both the distributing corporation and the shareholders.

See also the discussion, infra, pages 887 and 898, of the "liquidation-reincorporation" doctrine which treats shareholder-inspired liquidations followed by a reincorporation as reorganizations under section 368(a)(1)(D) or (F), accompanied by a dividend distribution if any property is retained by the shareholders.

4. *Multi–Step Acquisitions*

(a) *Treated as a Single Transaction*

The Internal Revenue Service may regard a stock for stock type (B) acquisition followed by liquidation of the acquired corporation as a (C) reorganization. Rev.Rul. 67–274, 1967–2 Cum.Bull. 141; Resorts International, Inc. v. Commissioner, 60 T.C. 778 (1973), aff'd on this issue, 511 F.2d 107 (5th Cir.1975) (no intention to operate acquired corporations as subsidiaries; the liquidations were part of a series of continuing transactions that constituted a (C) reorganization); American Potash & Chemical Corp. v. United States, 399 F.2d 194 (Ct.Cl.1968). One result of this treatment, is that, if the acquiring corporation had previously owned stock of the acquired corporation, the *Bausch & Lomb* doctrine, discussed infra, may be applicable.

The Service recharacterization of a (B) reorganization-liquidation as a (C) reorganization rests on a *Kimbell–Diamond* type of analysis, i.e., the transaction is actually an asset acquisition (see supra, page 697). See Rev. Rul. 74–35, 1974–1 Cum.Bull. 85 (holding that *Kimbell–Diamond* reasoning and Rev.Rul. 67–254 do not apply to recast a (B) reorganization where the acquired corporation does not transfer substantially all its assets to the acquiring corporation); Rev.Rul. 72–405, 1972–2 Cum.Bull. 217 ((C) reorganization upheld where a newly-created subsidiary acquired the assets of another corporation in a merger utilizing the parent corporation's stock, followed by a liquidation of the subsidiary).

Where one of the steps in a multi-step acquisition is a cash purchase of stock of the acquired corporation, which is followed by an asset acquisition using voting stock, the transaction may fail to qualify as a (C) reorganization because the "solely for voting stock" requirement has been violated. In Rev. Rul. 85–138, 1985–2 Cum.Bull. 122, P Corporation owned all of the stock of S1 and S2. Pursuant to a plan by which S1 would acquire substantially all the properties of X Corporation in consideration of P voting stock and the assumption by S1 of X's liabilities, S2 purchased some of the outstanding stock of X Corporation for cash in order to eliminate any possible adverse minority interest in X. The liabilities of X assumed by S1 exceeded 20 percent of the value of X's assets. Because the cash purchases of stock by S2 were part of a prearranged plan, the cash was treated as additional consideration provided by S1 and, since the cash and liabilities together exceeded the 20 percent limit in section 368(a)(2)(B), the acquisition did not qualify as a (C) reorganization.

(b) *Treated as Separate Transactions*

The problems of "creeping acquisitions," as in the case of a (B) reorganization, discussed supra, page 891, also are encountered in the (C) reorganization context.

Bausch & Lomb Optical Co. v. Commissioner, 267 F.2d 75 (2d Cir. 1959), and Rev.Rul. 54–396, 1954–2 Cum.Bull. 147, denied (C) reorganization status under the 1939 Code where Y Corporation, which earlier had acquired 79 percent of the stock of X Corporation for cash, issued its stock for the assets of X Corporation and then liquidated it. The Ruling stated that only 21 percent of the assets had been acquired solely for voting stock, since the balance had been in effect acquired because of the stock previously acquired. Grede Foundries, Inc. v. United States, 202 F.Supp. 263 (E.D. Wis.1962), followed *Bausch & Lomb* on similar facts. However, Rev.Rul. 57–278, 1957–1 Cum.Bull. 124, would permit the above transaction to be accomplished by Y Corporation forming Z Corporation by exchanging new Y stock for Z stock, Z Corporation then acquiring the assets of X Corporation with the new Y stock, and X Corporation then liquidating. The minority shareholders of X Corporation have become minority shareholders of Y Corporation which was intended, though Z Corporation remains as a subsidiary. The Ruling stresses the fact that Y Corporation could have acquired the minority shares of X Corporation in a (B) reorganization and the above route ends the same way. See also Rev.Rul. 58–93, 1958–1 Cum. Bull. 188 (upholding the foregoing transaction as an (A) or (C) reorganization, even though, in order to satisfy a requirement of state law, the transfer to Z Corporation occurred prior to the merger). Rev.Rul. 57–278 was held not to apply in a transaction in which Y Corporation acquired part of the stock of X Corporation for cash, followed by the acquisition by Z Corporation of the assets of X Corporation, where the cash purchase was an integral step in a pre-conceived plan to acquire substantially all of the properties of X Corporation; the acquisition of the assets of X Corporation was for cash plus voting stock, and the solely for voting stock requirement of a (C) reorganization was not met. Rev.Rul. 69–48, 1969–1 Cum.Bull. 106.

Other means are available to avoid the adverse tax consequences of *Bausch & Lomb* where a corporation finds itself in the predicament of owning part, but not all, of the stock of a subsidiary as to which it desires 100 percent ownership. Corporations X and Y could each transfer their assets to new W Corporation in return for its stock in (C) reorganizations and then liquidate. Rev.Rul. 68–526, 1968–2 Cum.Bull. 156; George v. Commissioner, 26 T.C. 396 (1956). This technique, however, assumes that Y Corporation is willing to be liquidated. In Rev.Rul. 69–413, 1969–2 Cum.Bull. 55, (C) reorganization treatment was upheld where Y Corporation, owning 99 percent of the stock of X Corporation, created a new subsidiary, W Corporation, which then exchanged Y Corporation stock for X Corporation assets and X then liquidated.

5. *Parties to the Reorganization*

Section 368(a)(2)(C) allows the acquiring corporation in a (C) reorganization to transfer the acquired assets to a controlled subsidiary. See Rev.Rul. 68–261, 1968–1 Cum.Bull. 147 (where X Corporation operated through six divisions and merged into Y Corporation, which then transferred each division to six wholly-owned subsidiaries, section 368(a)(2)(C) applied). See also Rev.Rul. 81–247, 1981–2 Cum.Bull. 87 (drop down of assets acquired in merger does not violate continuity of business enterprise requirement of Regulations, section 1.368–1(d)). The transfer down can also be made to a "second tier" subsidiary controlled indirectly by the parent. Rev.Rul. 64–73, 1964–1 Cum.Bull. 142.

In addition, by virtue of the parenthetical clause in section 368(a)(1)(C) a subsidiary can be utilized as the acquiring corporation, exchanging voting stock of its parent for substantially all the assets of the transferor corporation.

6. *Relationship of (C) Reorganizations to Other Provisions*

Section 368(a)(2)(A) provides that if a (C) reorganization also constitutes a (D) reorganization it will be treated only as a (D) reorganization, thus insuring that the (C) reorganization provisions cannot be used to accomplish a disguised tax-free division of a corporation that does not comply with the requirements of section 355. See Chapter 19.

Rev.Rul. 76–188, 1976–1 Cum.Bull. 99, involved a transaction in which a parent corporation transferred all its assets to its wholly-owned subsidiary and the subsidiary assumed all of the parent corporation's liabilities. The liabilities assumed exceeded the basis of the assets transferred to the subsidiary. Section 357(c) was held to be applicable, since the transaction was one "described in" section 351 (a provision to which section 357(c) applies); the fact that it also constituted a (C) reorganization did not prevent the application of section 357(c), and the parent corporation accordingly recognized a gain on the transaction. If brother-sister corporations are involved, it is possible for a (C) reorganization to overlap with section 304, supra, page 592. It is not clear which provision will control.

B. TAX TREATMENT OF PARTIES TO A TYPE (C) REORGANIZATION

1. *Acquiring Corporation*

Pursuant to section 1032, the acquiring corporation recognizes no gain or loss on the transfer of its shares in a (C) reorganization. If, however, the acquiring corporation transfers any boot other than cash or its own stock or securities, it must recognize gain or loss with respect to the boot transferred.

Under section 362(b) the acquiring corporation's basis in the assets is equal to the acquired transferor corporation's basis in those assets. Although section 362(b) provides that the acquiring corporation's basis in the assets is to be increased by any gain recognized under section 361(b) by the acquired corporation on the transfer by its assets to the acquiring corporation, it is not possible for the acquired corporation to recognize any gain as a result of the transfer of its assets to the acquiring corporation. See infra, B.2.

Under section 381, the tax attributes of the transferor corporation, e.g., net operating loss carryovers, earnings and profits accounts, etc., carry over to the acquiring corporation. The limitations of section 382(b) are, however, applicable. See infra, Chapters 20 and 21.

2. *Acquired Corporation and Shareholders*

No gain or loss is recognized by the acquired corporation on the exchange with the acquiring corporation regardless of the nature of the property received from the acquiring corporation. If only stock or securities of the acquiring corporation is received in the reorganization, section 361(a) provides nonrecognition. If nonqualifying boot is received, section 361(b) requires that the acquired corporation recognize gain upon receipt only if that boot is not distributed to either its shareholders or creditors pursuant to the plan of reorganization. Because section 368(a)(2)(G) requires the acquired corporation to liquidate, all of the boot must be distributed and, in general, no gain can be recognized under section 361(b). However, if boot is received and expended, for example to pay ongoing expenses, so that it is not distributed, then gain recognition will result.

As for the liquidating distributions, no gain or loss is recognized by the acquired corporation on the distribution of qualified stock or securities. Section 361(c)(1), (2)(B). Distribution of appreciated boot in the liquidation results in recognition of gain (but not loss) under section 361(c)(2), but because section 358(a)(2) provides the acquired corporation with a fair market value basis in any boot received in the reorganization transaction, no gain will be realized unless there is a change in value between the receipt and the liquidating distribution. If any property was retained by the acquired corporation, gain may be recognized by the corporation as a result of distributing such property in the liquidation.

The operative rules of section 361 leave little room for the acquired corporation to recognize gain in a (C) reorganization. However, although section 361(b)(3) accords tax free treatment to the receipt and distribution of stock in satisfaction of creditors' claims, if stock of the acquiring corporation received in the reorganization is *sold* by the acquired corporation and the proceeds used to pay creditors' claims, the acquired corporation must recognize gain on the sale; the receipt of the stock remains nontaxable.

For the shareholders of the transferor corporation, the tax results are similar to those in an (A) reorganization. No gain or loss will be recognized if they receive solely the stock of the acquiring corporation in exchange for their stock in the transferor corporation. Section 354(a). If the permissible amount of "boot" is involved and it is distributed to the shareholders, they may recognize gain under section 356, either as capital gain or as a dividend, depending on the circumstances, as discussed supra, page 800. Section 358 then provides an exchanged basis for the acquiring corporation's stock. If any boot is received, however, the basis is determined by first increasing the basis by the amount of any gain recognized by the shareholders as the result of the receipt of boot, and then decreasing it by the amount of cash or the fair market value of any other property received.

SECTION 7. TRIANGULAR REORGANIZATIONS

INTERNAL REVENUE CODE: Sections 368(a)(2)(D), (E); 368(c).

REGULATIONS: Section 1.368–2(b)(2), (j).

SENATE FINANCE COMMITTEE REPORT, PUBLIC LAW 91–693

S.Rep. No. 91–1533, 91st Cong., 2d Sess. 622–23 (1971).

[H.R. 19562] amends the tax law to permit a tax-free statutory merger when stock of a parent corporation is used in a merger between a controlled subsidiary of the parent and another corporation, and the other corporation survives—here called a "reverse merger."

In 1968 Congress added a provision to the tax laws permitting statutory mergers where the stock of the parent of the corporation making the acquisition was used in the acquisition (sec. 368(a)(2)(D)). At the time that statute was enacted, the use of stock of a parent corporation was permitted in the type of reorganization involving the acquisition of stock (subparagraph (B)) and in the type of reorganization involving the acquisition of assets (subparagraph (C)) but was not permitted in the case of a statutory merger of a subsidiary. After noting this fact, the House committee report went on to explain the reasons for the amendment as follows:

> Apparently the use of a parent's stock in statutory mergers was not initially provided for because there was no special concern with the problem at the time of the adoption of the 1954 code. However, this is no longer true. A case has been called to the attention of your committee in which it is desired to have an operating company merged into an operating subsidiary in exchange for the stock of the parent holding company. Your committee sees no reason why tax-free treatment should be denied in cases of this type where for any reason the parent cannot or, for business or legal reasons, does not want to acquire the assets (even temporarily) through a merger.
>
> For the reasons set forth above your committee concluded that it was desirable to permit the use of the stock of the parent corporation in a statutory merger in acquiring a corporation in essentially the same manner as presently is available in the case of other tax-free acquisitions. (House report on H.R. 18942 (90th Cong.).)

Thus, under existing law, corporation X (an unrelated corporation) may be merged into corporation S (a subsidiary) in exchange for the stock in corporation P (the parent of S) in a tax-free statutory merger. However, if for business and legal reasons (wholly unrelated to Federal income taxation) it is considered more desirable to merge S into X (rather than merging X into S), so that X is the surviving corporation—a "reverse merger"—the transaction is not a tax-free statutory merger.

Although the reverse merger does not qualify as a tax-free statutory merger, it may, in appropriate circumstances, be treated as tax-free as a stock-for-stock reorganization (subparagraph (B)). However, in order to qualify as a tax-free stock-for-stock reorganization it is necessary that the acquisition be *solely* for voting stock and that no stock be acquired for cash or other consideration. Thus, if a small amount of the stock of X (the unrelated corporation) is acquired for cash before the merger of S into X, there often may be doubt as to whether or not the transaction will meet the statutory requirements of a stock-for-stock reorganization.

The committee agrees with the House, that there is no reason why a merger in one direction (S into X in the above example) should be taxable, when the merger in the other direction (X into S), under identical circumstances, is tax-free. Moreover, it sees no reason why in cases of this type the acquisition needs to be made solely for stock. For these reasons the amendment makes statutory mergers tax-free in the circumstances described above.

In discussions on this bill, the Treasury Department has expressed concern that the corporate reorganization provisions need review and modification. The committee in agreeing to this amendment does not intend to foreclose consideration of any substantive changes which the Treasury may propose in the corporate reorganization provisions in any future presentations.

ILLUSTRATIVE MATERIAL

A. BACKGROUND

As long as the division of interest present in the *Groman* and *Bashford* situations, discussed supra, page 773, is absent, there is no obvious policy objection to allowing acquisitions involving the use of a subsidiary corporation to be tax-free. As discussed in the preceding materials, a series of amendments to the reorganization definitions made it possible to transfer assets or stock acquired in a reorganization transaction to a controlled subsidiary or to employ the subsidiary itself as the acquiring vehicle, using stock of the parent company as consideration for the acquisition. However, the amendments did not cover two situations which were important in practice. In the first place, a direct acquisition by the subsidiary of the acquired company's assets in an (A) reorganization in exchange for the parent stock was not possible since the parent was not considered to be a party to the reorganization under section 368(b). In addition, though the subsidiary could acquire assets in a (C) reorganization for the parent stock, the parent could not assume liabilities of the acquired corporation directly since section 368(a)(1)(C) applies only to liabilities assumed by the "acquiring" corporation, in this case the subsidiary. The desired results could have been obtained through other somewhat complicated means, such as the acquisition by the parent of the assets in a (C) reorganization and the subsequent transfer of the acquired assets to a newly formed subsidiary under section 368(a)(2)(C), with the parent assuming the liabilities of the acquired corporation.

As discussed in the Senate Finance Committee Report, Congress made such arrangements unnecessary by enacting section 368(a)(2)(D), which, together with a corresponding amendment to the section 368(b) definition of "party to a reorganization," permits the direct use of the parent's stock by the subsidiary in an (A) reorganization. See Regulations, section 1.368–2(b)(2). The prohibition against a splitting of interests, reflected in the *Groman* and *Bashford* decisions, is present in the requirement that no stock of the subsidiary corporation be used in the transaction, although other non-stock securities of both the parent and the subsidiary may be used.

As the Senate Finance Committee Report indicates, section 368(a)(2)(E) covers the so-called "reverse triangular merger" situation by allowing the subsidiary to be merged into the acquired corporation using stock of the parent in an (A) reorganization. As to the relation between section 368(a)(2)(D) and (E) and the preexisting reorganization forms, compare Rev.Rul. 67–448, 1967–2 Cum.Bull. 144 (treating reverse triangular merger into corporate shell in consideration solely for parent's voting stock as a type (B) reorganization) with Bercy Industries, Inc. v. Commissioner, 70 T.C. 29 (1978) (disallowing reorganization treatment for forward triangular merger), rev'd on other grounds, 640 F.2d 1058 (9th Cir.1981).

B. DEFINITIONAL ASPECTS

1. *Permissible Consideration*

Since section 368(a)(2)(D) is grafted onto the basic type (A) reorganization definition, there is no restriction on the consideration which may be used by the subsidiary in the acquisition other than the general continuity of interest limitation in an (A) reorganization (see supra, page 795) and the express statutory restriction that no stock of the subsidiary be used. Thus, for example, the requirements of an (A) reorganization can be met where the subsidiary uses as consideration non-voting stock of the parent and other securities of either the subsidiary or the parent corporation. Regulations, section 1.368–2(b)(2). In addition, the assumption of liabilities of the acquired corporation by the parent will not prevent the transaction from qualifying as a reorganization, nor will the assumption be treated as "boot" under section 361(b). See Rev.Rul. 73–257, 1973–1 Cum.Bull. 189 (both parent and subsidiary may assume acquired corporation's debts). In Rev.Rul. 79–155, 1979–1 Cum.Bull. 153, the holders of convertible securities of the acquired corporation in a forward triangular merger received securities on which the parent and the subsidiary were jointly and severally liable and which were convertible into stock of the parent, unless the parent sold the subsidiary, in which case the securities were convertible into stock of the subsidiary. The Ruling held that the exchange of securities, which had identical principal amounts, was tax-free under section 354; in addition, conversion of the securities into stock of the parent was not a realization event. Would the result have differed if the securities were convertible into stock of the subsidiary from the outset?

The continuity of interest doctrine appears in section 368(a)(2)(E) in the requirement that former shareholders of the surviving corporation exchange a controlling interest in the acquired corporation for voting stock of the parent. While this requirement is reminiscent of the (B) reorganization, it also has aspects of a (C) reorganization in that a 20 percent leeway for other consideration is permissible. Within this exception there are no limits on the character of the boot that may be exchanged; stock of the subsidiary is permissible. See also Regulations, section 1.368–2(j)(5), permitting the acquiring parent to assume the acquired corporation's liabilities.

2. *Substantially all of the Properties*

In a section 368(a)(2)(D) acquisition, the acquiring subsidiary must *acquire* substantially all of the properties of the acquired corporation. Regulations, section 1.368–2(b)(2), indicate that the "substantially all" criteria developed in the context of (C) reorganizations (supra, page 846) are to be applied.

In the case of a section 368(a)(2)(E) acquisition, the surviving corporation must *hold* substantially all of its properties and the properties of the merged corporation (other than the stock of the parent distributed in the acquisition). Regulations, section 1.368–2(j)(3)(iii), indicate that the "substantially all" criteria developed in the context of (C) reorganizations are to be applied, but assets transferred from the controlling corporation to the merged corporation pursuant to the plan of reorganization are not taken into account. Thus, for example, cash transferred from the controlling corporation to the merged corporation to pay dissenting shareholders of the surviving corporation pursuant to state law or to pay reorganization expenses would not be considered in determining whether the resulting corporation held "substantially all" the assets of the two corporations involved in the acquisition transaction. See also Rev.Rul. 77–307, 1977–2 Cum.Bull. 117 (same result prior to issuance of Regulations).

3. *Hypothetical Merger Requirement*

The requirement in section 368(a)(2)(D) that the merger "would have qualified" as an (A) reorganization if the transaction had taken place between the acquired corporation and the parent is not interpreted literally. It need not be established that the merger actually could have taken place under state or federal law; it is sufficient that the "general requirements of a reorganization (such as a business purpose, continuity of business enterprise and continuity of interest)" are met. Regulations, section 1.368–2(b)(2). See also Rev.Rul. 84–104, 1984–2 Cum.Bull. 94 (section 368(a)(2)(E) applies only to state law mergers, not to "consolidations" involving a subsidiary).

C. SPECIAL PROBLEMS UNDER SECTIONS 368(a)(2)(D) AND (a)(2)(E)

1. *Cash Payments to Dissenting Shareholders*

In the case of a reverse triangular merger, Regulations, section 1.368–2(j)(3)(i), provide that stock of the acquired corporation which is redeemed for cash or property of the acquired corporation (in contrast to cash or property provided by the acquiring parent or its subsidiary) is not counted as outstanding immediately prior to the reorganization. Thus, for example, if the holders of 100 out of 1000 shares of the acquired corporation dissent from the merger, the acquired corporation may redeem those shares, and to qualify under section 368(a)(2)(E) the acquiring parent's stock need be exchanged only for 80 percent of the remaining 900 shares, or 720 shares; the remaining 120 shares may be acquired for cash. But if the funds to redeem the stock are provided by the acquiring parent or subsidiary, then all 1000 shares are taken into account and 800 shares must be acquired for parent's voting stock. Furthermore, although a redemption of stock by the acquired corporation does not prevent compliance with the continuity of interest requirement, cash and property of the acquired corporation used to redeem the stock of its own dissenting shareholders are taken into account in determining whether the "substantially all the properties" test has been met. Regulations, section 1.368–2(j)(7), Ex. (3). If the cash or property distributed in redemption of the dissenting stockholder's shares constitutes too high a percentage of the acquired corporation's assets, the transaction may fail to meet the "substantially all the properties" test.

In a forward triangular merger under section 368(a)(2)(D) treatment of payments to dissenting shareholders is governed by the same continuity of interest rules that apply to type (A) reorganizations.

2. *The Parent Corporation's Basis for the Stock of the Subsidiary*

In a reorganization under Section 368(a)(2)(D), what is the basis of the parent in the stock of its acquiring subsidiary? Likewise, what is the basis to the subsidiary of the parent corporation's shares used in the acquisition? Since the basis to the parent in its own shares presumably would be zero, it might be argued that there is a zero basis in both cases. See Rev.Rul. 74–503, 1974–2 Cum.Bull. 117, so holding, though the Ruling explicitly stated that the transfer of the parent shares to the subsidiary "was not for the purpose of enabling [the subsidiary] to acquire property by the use of such stock." On the other hand, if the transaction is viewed as in substance the acquisition by the parent of the acquired corporation's assets followed by a transfer of those assets to the subsidiary, a basis for the subsidiary stock equal to the transferor corporation's basis for its assets would be the result. See Rev.Rul. 64–73, 1964–1 Cum.Bull. 142, suggesting this approach.

A similar problem is present in the case of a section 368(a)(2)(E) "reverse" acquisition. Should the acquiring parent corporation have a basis for the shares it holds in the surviving corporation of zero (under the above analysis) or a basis equal to the basis of the acquired corporation's shareholders (following the (B) reorganization analogy)?

These questions arose because of the grafting of sections 368(a)(2)(D) and (E) onto the preexisting reorganization structure without adequate analysis of the implications of the change in structure. Proposed Regulations, sections 1.358–6(a) and (c) (1980), dealing with forward triangular mergers and reverse triangular mergers respectively, would give the parent a basis in the subsidiary's stock equal to the sum of (1) the parent's basis in the subsidiary's stock prior to the reorganization, (2) the net basis of property transferred from the parent to the subsidiary and *not distributed* to the acquired corporation's shareholders pursuant to the reorganization, and (3) the net basis of the surviving subsidiary's property (other than property described in (2) above) after the reorganization. There is a *downward* adjustment for any consideration not furnished by the parent, for example if the subsidiary pays cash to the acquired corporation's dissenting shareholders. This formula adopts the model based on a hypothetical (C) reorganization followed by a drop-down of the assets.

On a related point, Proposed Regulations, section 1.1032–2 (1981), would provide express authority for nonrecognition of gain to the subsidiary on the exchange of the parent's stock in which the subsidiary has a zero basis under section 362(a). (The Proposed Regulations would reach the same result in a type (C) reorganization involving a subsidiary corporation.)

3. *"Creeping" Acquisitions*

As in the (B) and (C) reorganization situations, discussed supra, pages 841, and 849, prior ownership by the parent corporation of stock in the corporation which is to be acquired can present problems in the (a)(2)(E) context. There is no such thing as a "creeping" reverse triangular merger under section 368(a)(2)(E). If the parent corporation already owns over 20 percent of the stock of the to be acquired corporation, an (a)(2)(E) reorganization is not possible because of the statutory requirement that an amount of stock constituting "control" in the corporation be exchanged in the reorganization transaction. Rev.Rul. 74–564, 1974–2 Cum.Bull. 124. However, a failed section 368(a)(2)(E) reverse triangular merger may be recharacterized as a (B) reorganization under the principles of Rev.Rul. 67–448, supra, page 854, if the requirements for a (B) reorganization have been met. See Regulations, section 1.368–2(j)(7), Ex. (4) and (5). This recharacterization will save the reorganization only if the sole consideration used is voting stock of the parent. The 20 percent leeway granted by section 368(a)(2)(E) is not available. Compare the *Bausch & Lomb* situation discussed, supra, page 849.

4. *"Remote" Continuity*

While the statutory amendments to section 368 permit the use by a first tier subsidiary of its parent's stock in a reorganization acquisition, the problem of "remote" continuity of interest still exists where stock of a corporation further removed in the chain of ownership is used in the acquisition transaction. Thus, Rev.Rul. 74–565, 1974–1 Cum.Bull. 125, held that an acquisition made by a second tier subsidiary using the stock of its "grandparent" did not qualify under section 368(a)(2)(E). However, since the second tier subsidiary which formally made the acquisition was formed solely for the purpose of the acquisition and disappeared as a result of the "reverse" merger, its existence could be ignored; because the sole consideration was now parent's voting stock the transaction was viewed as an acquisition by the now first tier subsidiary of the stock of the acquired company in exchange for its parent's stock which qualified as a (B) reorganization under the principles of Rev.Rul. 67–448, supra, page 854.

On a different, but related point, Rev.Rul. 79–250, 1979–2 Cum.Bull. 156, held that an (F) reorganization entered into for the purpose of changing the state of incorporation of a subsidiary immediately following the merger of an acquired corporation into the subsidiary in a forward triangular merger under section 368(a)(2)(D) did not cause the acquisition transaction to fail to be tax-free, even though the two reorganizations were part of a single overall plan.

E. TAX TREATMENT OF PARTIES TO A TRIANGULAR REORGANIZATION

1. *Section 368(a)(2)(D) Forward Triangular Merger*

(a) *Acquired Corporation and Shareholders*

No gain or loss is recognized by the acquired corporation on the exchange with the acquiring corporation regardless of the nature of the property received from the acquiring corporation. Because the acquired corporation disappears by operation of state law, any nonqualifying boot not directly distributed to its shareholders or creditors is deemed to have been distributed to its shareholders or creditors, and thus no gain can be recognized under section 361(b).

As to the shareholders of the acquired corporation, no gain or loss will be recognized if they received solely the stock of the parent acquiring corporation in exchange for their stock in the acquired corporation. Section 354(a). If "boot" is involved, the shareholders may recognize gain under section 356, either as capital gain or as a dividend, depending on the circumstances, although after the decision in *Clark,* supra, page 800, the gain usually will be capital gain. Section 358 provides an exchanged basis for the acquiring parent corporation's stock. If any boot is received, however, the basis is determined by first increasing the basis by the amount of any gain recognized by the shareholders as the result of the receipt of boot, and then decreased it by the amount of cash and the fair market value of any other property received.

(b) *Acquiring Corporation*

Neither the acquiring subsidiary nor its parent recognizes any gain or loss on the transfer of the parent's shares in a forward triangular merger. If the acquiring subsidiary or its parent transfers any boot other than cash or its own securities, gain or loss must be recognized with respect to the boot transferred. Under section 362(b) the acquiring corporation's basis in the assets is equal to the acquired transferor corporation's basis in those assets. The acquiring parent corporation's basis in its subsidiary's stock after the reorganization equals the sum of (1) its basis in the subsidiary stock prior to the reorganization, (2) the net basis of any property transferred to the subsidiary by the parent and not distributed pursuant to the reorganization, and (3) the net basis of the acquired corporation's assets.

Under section 381, the tax attributes of the acquired corporation e.g., net operating loss carryovers, earnings and profits accounts, etc., carryover to the acquiring subsidiary corporation. The limitations of section 382(b) are applicable, however. See infra, Chapters 20 and 21.

2. *Section 368(a)(2)(E) Reverse Triangular Merger*

(a) *Acquired Corporation and Shareholders*

Generally, no gain or loss is recognized by the acquired corporation on the exchange with the acquiring corporation because boot, if any is involved, will be distributed to the shareholders. Section 361(b).

The shareholders of the acquired corporation recognize no gain or loss if they receive solely the stock of the parent of the acquiring corporation in exchange for their stock in the transferor corporation. Section 354(a). If "boot" is involved, the shareholders may recognize gain under section 356, as in the case of a forward triangular merger. Section 358 provides an exchanged basis of the stock received in the reorganization, subject to the same adjustments as are made in a forward triangular merger if boot is involved.

(b) *Acquiring Corporation*

Neither the acquiring corporation nor its parent recognizes any gain or loss on the transfer of the parent's shares in a section 368(a)(2)(E) reorganization. If the acquiring corporation or its parent transfers any boot other than cash or its own securities, gain or loss must be recognized with respect to the boot transferred. Because the acquired corporation remains in existence, its basis for its assets is unchanged. The acquiring parent corporation's basis in the stock of the surviving subsidiary is determined in the same manner as in a forward triangular merger.

Under section 381, the acquired corporation retains its tax attributes, but the section 382(b) limitations are applicable. See infra, Chapters 20 and 21.

D. POSSIBLE STATUTORY REVISION

As the last paragraph of the Senate Finance Committee Report indicates, the addition of layers of statutory complexity to the already convoluted reorganization provisions has been a source of concern. What is needed is a thorough-going review of the technical issues in the reorganization area. See infra, page 865.

F. REFERENCES

Cook and Coalson, The "Substantially All of the Properties" Requirement in Triangular Reorganizations–A Current Review, 35 Tax Law. 303 (1982); New York State Bar Association Tax Section Committee on Reorganizations, Report on Reverse Triangular Mergers and Basis–Nonrecognition

Rules in Triangular Reorganizations, 36 Tax L.Rev. 395 (1981); Blanchard, The Effect of the Step–Transaction Doctrine on Reverse Subsidiary Mergers: An Analysis, 55 J.Tax'n 72 (1981); Ferguson and Ginsburg, Triangular Reorganizations, 1972 So.Calif.Tax Inst. 1; Freling, Current Problems in Subsidiary Mergers and Other Triangular Reorganizations, 29 N.Y.U.Tax Inst. 347 (1971); Levin, The New Subsidiary–Merger Statute and Other Current Tax Problems in Acquisitions, 47 Taxes 779 (1969).

SECTION 8. ACCOUNTING ASPECTS OF ACQUISITION TRANSACTIONS

ILLUSTRATIVE MATERIAL

A. BACKGROUND

Determining the proper treatment of an acquisition by a corporation of the business of another corporation has been as difficult for the accounting profession as for tax technicians. From a financial reporting standpoint, important differences in accounting treatment result depending on whether the transaction is treated as a purchase of one company by another or as a uniting of the ownership of the two companies. The problem is especially difficult where debt obligations are involved that are convertible into equity interests. From an accounting standpoint, a "pooling of interests" approximately corresponds to the tax-free treatment accorded under the Internal Revenue Code. See *McDonald's of Illinois,* supra page 775, where the structure of the acquisition was designed to permit the acquiring corporation to treat the acquisition as a pooling even though the shareholders of the acquired corporation sought a cash sale. Correspondingly, a "purchase" for accounting purposes in many respects resembles taxable acquisition for tax purposes. However, in some instances, it is possible for a tax-free reorganization to be treated as a purchase for accounting purposes and for a taxable acquisition to be treated as a pooling for accounting purposes. In 1970 the treatment of the two methods of accounting for business combinations was substantially revised. The following material sets forth the two methods and situations in which the tax and financial reporting results are different.

B. ACCOUNTING METHODS

Excerpt from PODOLIN, NEW PROBLEMS IN TAX ACCOUNTING FOR MERGERS AND ACQUISITIONS: POOLING OF INTERESTS AND GENERALLY ACCEPTED ACCOUNTING PRINCIPLES, 29 N.Y.U.Fed.Tax Inst. 499 (1971):

[Accounting Principles Board Opinions No. 16 and 17 promulgated in 1970, modified the two methods of accounting for business combinations, the "purchase" and "pooling of interests" methods.]

Purchase Method

The purchase method accounted for a combination as the acquisition of one company by another. The acquiring corporation recorded the acquired net assets at its "cost" which was the "fair market value" of the consideration paid. The difference between that "cost" and the previous carrying value of the acquired assets was generally recorded as goodwill.

Goodwill was written off as an extraordinary charge to income only when there was a "diminution in the value of the investment." Few businessmen would admit to this, and goodwill writeoffs were an understandably rare occurrence.

The income of the acquired company was reflected in the parent's consolidated income statement from the date of acquisition forward.

Pooling of Interests Method

The pooling of interests method accounted for a business combination as the retroactive "marriage" of the ownership interests of two or more companies. Accordingly, no new basis of accountability arose and the assets were carried forward at their old book values.

Income of the combined companies included income of the constituents for the entire year in which the combination occurred, and the income for prior years was reported as if the combined companies had always been one. Earnings per share were then recomputed for all years on the basis of the new capitalization. The retained earnings of the constituents were combined and reported as retained earnings of the combined companies. Accounting Principles Board Opinion No. 16

* * * All of the following criteria must be met in order for a combination to be treated as a pooling of interests. If they are met, the pooling treatment is mandatory, not optional:

Companies Must Be Independent

1. Each of the combining companies must be autonomous and independent, and may not have been a subsidiary or division of another corporation within two years before the plan of combination is initiated. Therefore, a subsidiary which effects a business combination may not use pooling accounting.

However, a wholly-owned subsidiary which effects a combination by issuance of its parent company's shares may use pooling accounting providing all the other criteria are met. * * *

Single Transaction

2. The combination must be effected in a single transaction or completed according to a specific plan within one year after the plan is initiated, unless the delay in completing the combination results from proceedings of a governmental authority or litigation.

Only Common Stock

3. A corporation may issue only common stock with rights identical to those of the majority of its outstanding voting common stock in exchange for substantially all of the voting common stock interest of another company. "Substantially all" of the voting common stock means 90 percent or more. The remaining 10 percent, including fractional shares or shares held by dissenting stockholders, may remain outstanding as a minority interest or may be obtained for cash or other consideration. But no pro rata distribution of cash or other consideration may be made.

In other words, if each shareholder were to receive his price 90 percent in cash and 10 percent in stock there would be no pooling. But if 90 percent of the shareholders receive stock and 10 percent get cash there would be a pooling.

Common Stock Interest to Be Maintained

4. Each of the combining companies must maintain substantially the same voting common stock interest, both before and after the plan of combination is initiated. They may not change those interests by exchanges, retirements, or unusual distributions in contemplation of effecting the combination.

Limitation on Acquisition of Own Stock

5. Each of the combining companies may acquire its own voting common stock (treasury stock) only for purposes other than business combinations. No more than a normal number of shares may be acquired after the date the plan of combination is initiated.

Stock Must Be Issued Pro Rata

6. The exchange of stock in the combination cannot alter the interest of an individual common stockholder relative to any other common stockholder in a combining company. In other words, the stock must be issued pro rata to each selling stockholder.

Voting Rights Preserved

7. Only the stockholders themselves (not voting trusts, for example) may exercise the voting rights of the common stock ownership interest in the resulting corporation, and no stockholder may be deprived of nor restricted in exercising those rights.

No Contingencies

8. The plan of combination may not provide for issuance of securities or other consideration on a contingent basis (or for the contingent return of shares issued), with some minor exceptions. But a price based on current year earnings would qualify so long as the rule of completing the transaction in one year is not violated.

This would preclude most so-called "earn-outs" and stock price guarantees from being treated as poolings, but would not preclude stock options and deferred compensation plans.

Common Stock to Remain Issued

9. The combined corporation may not agree directly or indirectly to retire or reacquire all or part of the common stock issued in the combination.

No Arrangements for Former Stockholders

10. The combined corporation may make no financial arrangement for the benefit of the former stockholders of a combining company, such as a guaranty of loans secured by the stock issued. This does not preclude granting of stock options and deferred compensation plans.

Limitation on Disposition of Assets

11. No plan or intention may exist to dispose of a significant part of the assets of the combining companies within two years after the combination except to eliminate duplicate facilities, excess capacity, or those assets that would have been disposed of in the ordinary course of business of the separate company. * * *

No Partial Pooling

14. The practice of accounting for a business combination as a partial pooling of interests is no longer acceptable. * * *

Continuity of Ownership

The opinion does not require continuity of ownership or management. Yet, there is little apparent substantive difference between the immediate sale of the stock received by the sellers in a pooling transaction, and a company's issuance of stock for cash which it then uses to acquire another company in a purchase transaction.

The former rules limiting sales of stock of the acquiring company by the sellers no longer exist. However, the spirit and intent of the Opinion would be violated if an intent to sell existed at the date of the pooling. * * *

Accounting Principles Board Opinion No. 17

Opinion 17 covers the treatment of goodwill in business combinations which do not meet the pooling criteria and must therefore be accounted for as a "purchase." The most significant requirement imposed by the opinion is the mandatory amortization of goodwill over a period not to exceed forty years.

* * *

Tax Accounting Problems

Until very recently acquisitions which were tax-free were permitted to be accounted for as poolings of interests, and taxable acquisitions were required to be treated as purchases. This generalization can no longer be made.

The following are some of the specific situations where a tax-free reorganization is not allowed to be treated as a pooling:

1. The use of voting preferred stock to acquire a company's common;

2. The tax-free acquisition of a subsidiary in ordinary circumstances;

3. The existence of contingently issuable or contingently returnable shares;

4. An acquisition which takes more than a year from initiation to consummation;

5. An acquisition using treasury stock bought for use in the acquisition;

6. An acquisition where shares are temporarily put into a voting trust;

7. An acquisition involving a planned disposition of significant assets, with some exceptions; and

8. An acquisition following a redemption of the stock of some stockholders in contemplation of the acquisition.

On the other hand, there may be some taxable acquisitions which must be treated as poolings, such as:

1. A stock-for-stock or stock-for-assets acquisition where some minor amount of cash is part of the consideration;

2. An acquisition which violates the continuity of interest test of a tax-free reorganization, where an intention to sell stock received in a pooling is not specifically a bar to the pooling method, although the spirit of the Opinion probably requires no intention to dispose.

Basis Differences

In poolings which are taxable, and in purchases which are tax-free, some very material differences in tax basis as compared to book values of assets will exist. These are not differences in the timing of the tax, and therefore, they are not to be accounted for as deferred taxes.

In the purchase method, these differences in tax basis are to be considered in setting the values assigned to various assets. For example, an asset whose tax basis is less than its value would presumably be assigned a somewhat lower value to cover this factor.

The situation of a pooling which is taxable presents a somewhat different problem, since assets are not revalued in a pooling. Yet, they may have substantially higher tax bases, producing much lower taxes payable.

Miscellaneous Problems

While the examples mentioned are problem enough, perhaps more frequent will be cases where goodwill must be amortized and is not tax-deductible. The new rules also require that expenses of a pooling, such as registration fees, proxy expenses, finders' fees, and legal and accounting fees, must be charged to earnings, although they are generally not tax-deductible. On the other hand, the tax reductions arising out of imputed interest may not be used to increase reported earnings.

Effect Upon Taxes

* * * Where large amounts of non-deductible goodwill are being amortized, the effective tax rate will increase. * * * Where a taxable acquisition is treated as a pooling, the effective tax rate will probably decrease in most situations. (501–10)

C. REFERENCES

Fiflis, Accounting for Mergers Acquisitions and Investments in a Nutshell: the Interrelationships of, and Criteria for, Purchase or Pooling, the Equity Method, and Parent–Company–Only and Consolidated Statements, 37 Bus.Law. 89 (1981); Perlmutter, Comparison of Tax, Accounting, and Securities Aspects of Business Combinations, 2 J.Corp.Tax 305 (1976); Lippman, Comparison of Financial and Tax Accounting Rules for Business Combinations, 1974 So.Calif.Tax Inst. 943.

SECTION 9. TAX POLICY: ACQUISITION TRANSACTIONS

REPORT BY THE STAFF OF THE SENATE FINANCE COMMITTEE, THE SUBCHAPTER C REVISION ACT OF 1985 *

S.Prt. 99–47, 99th Cong., 1st Sess. 50–53 (1985).

IV. SUMMARY OF PROPOSALS

The principal proposals contained in the bill are described below. A more detailed description of the proposals is set forth in the Technical Explanation accompanying the bill.

A. Definition of qualified acquisition (new section 364 of the Code)

In general, the bill consolidates, simplifies, and makes uniform the rules classifying corporate mergers and acquisitions, whether treated under current law as a "reorganization", a liquidating sale * * *, or a section 338 stock acquisition.

New section 364 defines "qualified acquisition" as meaning any "qualified stock acquisition" or any "qualified asset acquisition." A qualified stock acquisition is defined as any transaction or series of transactions during the 12–month acquisition period in which one corporation acquires stock representing control of another corporation. A qualified asset acquisition means (1) any statutory merger or consolidation, or (2) any other transaction in which one corporation acquires at least 70 percent of the gross fair market value and at least 90 percent of the net fair market value of the assets of another corporation held immediately before the acquisition, and the transferor corporation distributes, within 12 months of the acquisition date, all of its assets (other than assets retained to meet claims) to its shareholders or creditors.

For these purposes, the definition of "control" is conformed to that contained in section 1504(a)(2) of the Code.

Where an acquiring corporation makes a qualified stock acquisition of a target corporation and the target corporation owns stock in a subsidiary, a special rule would treat the acquiring corporation as having also acquired the stock of the subsidiary, for purposes of determining whether the acquiring corporation has made a qualified stock acquisition of the subsidiary.

A special rule is also provided where an acquisition might qualify as both a qualified asset acquisition and a qualified stock acquisition. For example, where an acquiring corporation acquires all of the assets of a target corporation, and certain of those assets consist of all of the stock of a subsidiary, the transaction is treated as a qualified stock

* [Ed.: The Suchapter C Revision Act of 1985 was not enacted into law.]

acquisition of the subsidiary and a qualified asset acquisition of all of the other assets of the target corporation.

The common-law doctrines of continuity of interest, continuity of business enterprise, and business purpose would have no applicability in determining whether a transaction qualifies as a qualified acquisition.

The bill repeals section 368. Acquisitive reorganizations ("A" "B" and "C" reorganizations and subsidiary mergers) under current law would be replaced by the rules for qualified acquisitions. The "D" reorganization rules would be replaced by special rules (described below) relating to qualified acquisitions between related parties. Transactions qualifying under current law as an "E" reorganization (a recapitalization) and an "F" reorganization (a mere change in identity, form, or place of organization of one corporation) are conformed to the definition of qualified acquisitions. Finally, the "G" reorganization rules (bankruptcy reorganizations), developed largely in response to continuity of interest problems in those types of transactions, are no longer needed and therefore are repealed.

B. Elective tax treatment of qualified acquisitions (new section 365 of the Code)

The corporate level tax consequences of a qualified acquisition are explicitly made elective. Under new section 365, all qualified acquisitions are treated as "carryover basis acquisitions" unless an election to be treated as a "cost basis acquisition" is made.

In general, elections may be made on a corporation-by-corporation basis. Thus, for example, if an acquiring corporation makes a qualified stock acquisition of both a target corporation and a target subsidiary, a cost basis election may be made for the target corporation but, if desired, no such election need be made for the target subsidiary.

Within a single corporation, the same election must generally apply for all of the assets of the corporation. A consistency rule would provide that assets that are acquired which were held by a single corporation during the consistency period must be treated consistently, either as all cost basis or all carryover basis.

Notwithstanding the consistency rule, an inconsistent carryover basis election may be made with respect to goodwill and certain other unamortizable intangibles. For example, a separate carryover basis election may be made with respect to such property even though a cost basis election is made for all of the other assets of the target corporation.

In general, no cost basis election may be made with respect to any qualified acquisition between related parties. These generally refer to transactions where, after application of the attribution rules, there is 50 percent or greater common ownership between the target and acquiring corporations. In addition, no cost basis election may be made with respect to a transaction qualifying as an "E" or "F" reorganization under current law. Finally, a mandatory cost basis election generally applies to a qualified asset acquisition where the acquiring corporation is a non-taxable entity (such as a tax-exempt entity, a regulated investment company, or a foreign corporation).

An election must be made before the later of (1) the 15th day of the 9th month following the month in which the acquisition date occurs, or (2) the date prescribed in regulations. Once made, an election is irrevocable.

C. Corporate level tax consequences of qualified acquisitions (sections 361, 362 and 381 of the Code)

The corporate level tax consequences of a qualified acquisition result directly from the election made at the corporate level. For example, in the case of a carryover basis acquisition, no gain or loss is recognized by the target corporation and the acquiring corporation obtains a carryover basis in any assets acquired. Attributes carry over under section 381.

In the case of a cost basis acquisition, the target corporation recognizes gain or loss and the acquiring corporation obtains a basis in any assets acquired determined under section 1012. Attributes do not carry over. Where the cost basis acquisition is a qualified stock acquisition, the target corporation is deemed to have sold all of its assets for fair market value at the close of the acquisition date in a transaction in which gain or loss is recognized, and then is treated as a new corporation which purchased all of such assets as of the beginning of the day after the acquisition date.

A special rule is provided in the case where a target corporation is a member of an affiliated group and a cost basis election is made. In general, unless the parties elect otherwise, a target corporation in that situation shall not be treated as a member of such group with respect to the gain or loss recognized in the transaction.

The basis of any property received by a target corporation in a qualified asset acquisition is the fair market value of such property on the acquisition date. The basis of stock acquired by an acquiring corporation in a qualified stock acquisition is determined under new section 1020 of the Code (see description below for rules concerning basis of stock of controlled subsidiaries).

Under the bill, section * * * 338 of current law [is] repealed.

D. Shareholder level tax consequences of qualified acquisitions (sections 354, 356, and 358 of the Code)

In general, shareholder level tax consequences of a qualified acquisition are determined independent of the corporate level tax consequences and independent of the election made at the corporate level. Thus, even if a transaction is treated as a cost basis acquisition at the corporate level, it may be wholly or partly taxfree at the shareholder level. In addition, shareholder level consequences are generally determined shareholder-by-shareholder, and the consequences to one shareholder do not affect the tax treatment of other shareholders or investors of the target corporation.

As a general rule, nonrecognition treatment is provided to shareholders or security holders of the target corporation upon receipt of "qualifying consideration," i.e., stock or securities of the acquiring corporation and, where the acquiring corporation is a member of an affiliated group, of the common parent of such group and any other member of such group specified in regulations. The nonrecognition rule applies to the receipt of securities only to the extent the issue price of any securities received does not exceed the adjusted basis of any securities surrendered.

A special rule is provided in the case of investment company stock. In general, stock or securities of an investment company does not qualify as qualifying consideration. An exception applies, however, and such stock or securities will qualify as qualifying consideration, if the target corporation is a diversified investment company. The term "investment company" and "diversified investment company" generally have the same meaning as under current law. In short, the existence of an investment company as the acquiring corporation may affect the tax treatment of the transaction at the shareholder level, but does not affect the corporate level tax consequences.

Receipt of "nonqualifying consideration" (i.e., any consideration other than qualifying consideration) generally results in recognition of gain to the shareholder or security holder. Such gain is treated as gain from the sale or exchange of property unless the receipt of nonqualifying consideration has the effect of a distribution of a dividend. The determination of dividend effect is made by treating the shareholder as having received only qualifying consideration in the exchange, and then as being redeemed of all or a portion of such qualifying consideration (to the extent of the nonqualifying consideration received). For these purposes, earnings and profits of both the target and acquiring corporations are generally taken into account.

Special rules are provided where there is a controlling corporate shareholder of the target corporation. In general, these rules are designed to avoid a second corporate level tax where the target corporation is acquired in a cost basis acquisition. In addition, where the target corporation is acquired in a carryover basis acquisition and all or part of the consideration is nonqualifying consideration, these rules are designed to insure that the controlling corporate shareholder or a distributee of such shareholder will recognize gain on the receipt of the nonqualifying consideration.

In general, shareholders or security holders obtain a substitute basis in any [qualifying] consideration received, and a fair market value basis in any nonqualifying consideration received. Controlling corporate shareholders of the target corporation generally obtain a basis in any qualifying consideration received equal to the lesser of substitute basis or fair market value basis.

ILLUSTRATIVE MATERIAL

A. AMERICAN LAW INSTITUTE PROPOSALS

The 1985 proposals of the Staff of the Senate Finance Committee were based in part on proposals in the American Law Institute Federal Income Tax Project—Subchapter C (1980). The following excerpt explains the reasons for the ALI proposals:

"[The] search for substantive differences among acquisitions by which to determine their tax classification has been essentially fruitless. * * * So are many of the criteria for reorganization treatment. In the context of a complete acquisition of all shareholders' interests in all corporate assets, even the distinction between a stock and an asset acquisition is one of corporate procedure rather than financial import. Indeed, for financial reporting purposes, no distinction is drawn between a stock purchase and an asset purchase, or between a pooling of interests effected by an acquisition of stock and one effected by an acquisition of assets.

"A better approach would begin by acknowledging that the choice between carryover and cost-basis treatment is essentially elective.

* * *

"E. *Recommended Revisions*

"1) *Making electivity explicit and independent of corporate procedural choices.* The trouble with present law, in this view, is not that tax classification of acquisitions is effectively elective, but that the election is tied unnecessarily to matters of corporate procedure. The solution to the trouble is to make tax classification explicitly elective and as independent as possible of corporate procedural considerations. * * *

"2) *Classification in the absence of election.* In the absence of effective election, acquisitions should be classified as simply and as consistently as possible with the likely expectations of those who are most apt to neglect to make a specific election. These criteria suggest that any stock acquisition should be a carryover-basis acquisition and any asset purchase should be a cost-basis acquisition, unless there is a specific election to the contrary. * * *" (35–42)

B. REFERENCES

Posin, Taxing Corporate Reorganizations: Purging Penelope's Web, 133 U.Pa.L.Rev. 1335 (1985); Ginsburg, Special Topics in the Acquisitions Area, 22 San Diego L.Rev. 159 (1985); LeDuc, Current Proposals to Restructure the Taxation of Corporate Acquisitions and Dispositions: Substance and Process, 22 San Diego L.Rev. 17 (1985); Thompson, A Comparison of the Merger and Acquisition Provisions of Present Law with the Provisions in the Senate Finance Committee's Draft Bill, 22 San Diego L.Rev. 171 (1985); ABA Committee on Corporate Stockholder Relations, Tax Section Recommendations No. 1981–5, 34 Tax Law. 1386 (1981); Faber, Continuity of Interest and Continuity of Business Enterprise: Is It Time To Bury Some Sacred Cows 34 Tax L.Rev. 239 (1981); Beghe, The American Law Institute Subchapter C Study: Acquisitions and Distributions, 33 Tax Law. 743 (1980); Jacobs, Reorganizing the Reorganization Provisions, 35 Tax L.Rev. 415 (1980); Pugh, Combining Acquired and Acquiring Corporations and Their Subsidiaries Following a Purchase of Stock: Some Anomalies of Form and Substance, 35 Tax L.Rev. 359 (1980); Crockett, Federal Taxation of Corporate Unifications: A Review of Legislative Policy, 15 Duq.L.Rev. 1 (1976); Lovett, Tax Subsidies for Merger: Should Mergers Be Made To Meet a Market Test for Efficiency?, 45 N.Y.U.L.Rev. 844 (1970).

PART V

NONACQUISITIVE REORGANIZATIONS

CHAPTER 18

SINGLE CORPORATION REORGANIZATIONS

SECTION 1. STATUTORY STRUCTURE

While the reorganization provisions historically have been most important in the context of acquisition transactions, there are also several forms of reorganizations which involve changes or adjustments in the form or capital structure of an existing corporation. Here the reorganization provisions allow a modification of some aspects of the corporate capital structure without requiring the current recognition of gain (or allowing the recognition of loss) on the exchanges involved in the restructuring. The controversies involving nonacquisitive reorganizations have revolved primarily around attempts by taxpayers to avoid dividend treatment on cash or other property extracted from the corporation. In some situations, the issue has been whether the reorganization rules themselves, as properly applied, should result in the receipt of a dividend when, in the context of an admitted reorganization, a shareholder receives property. In other cases, the question is whether the transaction is in fact a reorganization at all or is more appropriately characterized as some form of sale or liquidation transaction qualifying for capital gain treatment. In these latter cases, it has often been the Internal Revenue Service which was arguing for characterization as a reorganization in order to apply the reorganization rules requiring dividend treatment.

The elimination of the preferential treatment for capital gains and the requirement of gain recognition at the corporate level on the distribution of appreciated property have reduced substantially taxpayer attempts to convert potential dividend income into capital gains by extracting property from the corporation. There remains, however, the fundamental question of whether an otherwise taxable transaction should be given nonrecognition treatment when it takes place in the context of a corporate adjustment or restructuring. Here the present statutory structure provides for reorganization treatment in three specific situations. Section 368(a)(1)(E) deals with corporate "recapitalizations", i.e., adjustments to the corporation's capital structure, as when a bondholder exchanges his bonds for stock in the corporation. Section 368(a)(1)(F) deals with another type of change in corporate structure, a change in place of incorporation or form of organization, as when a

New York corporation reincorporates in California. Finally, section 368(a)(1)(D) describes reorganizations involving a transfer of assets by a corporation to a subsidiary corporation and the distribution of the stock of the subsidiary corporation to the corporation's shareholders. These three types of reorganization transactions are considered in this Part. In addition, since the (D) reorganization is often the first step in a corporate division, additional aspects of (D) reorganizations are considered in Chapter 19.

Section 368 provides the following definitions of the reorganizations considered in this Part:

Type (E) Recapitalizations. Section 368(a)(1)(E) covers the recapitalization of an existing corporation, such as the exchange of one type of common stock for another, or of one type of preferred stock for another, or of new preferred stock for old bonds, of new preferred stock for old stock or of new common stock for old preferred stock, or of new bonds for old bonds. Here only one corporation and its shareholders (or bondholders) are involved. These same transactions, however, can be implemented under sections 368(a)(1)(A), (B) or (C), for example, by creating a new corporation and having the new corporation issue to the parent, in return for the parent's assets, stock and securities of the nature desired which the parent will then distribute to its shareholders on its liquidation. Type (E) reorganizations are considered in Section 2.

Type (F) Change of Identity, Form, or Place of Organization. A mere change in identity form, or place of organization of one corporation, however effected, is governed by section 368(a)(1)(F). For example, X Corporation may change its state of incorporation from New Jersey to Delaware by forming Y Corporation, a Delaware subsidiary into which X Corporation merges with the shareholders (and bondholders) of X Corporation receiving identical securities of Y Corporation in exchange for their interests in X Corporation. But if X Corporation simultaneously effects a recapitalization, for example, by exchanging both common and preferred shares of Y Corporation for X Corporation common stock (as was the case in Marr v. United States, 268 U.S. 536 (1925), supra, page 745), then the transaction is not an (F) reorganization. Furthermore, it probably is not an (E) reorganization either. In this case the transaction will be a reorganization only if it fits within the definition of one of the other subparagraphs, such as type (A). Type (F) reorganizations are considered in Section 3.

Type (D) Transfer of Assets to New Corporation. The transfer of some or all of the parent's assets to a newly created or existing subsidiary—as where X Corporation transfers some of its assets to new or existing Y Corporation—is governed by section 368(a)(1)(D) if following the transfer to the subsidiary the parent, X Corporation, distributes a controlling amount of the stock of the subsidiary, Y Corporation, to its shareholders. The nature of the securities received, if any (a contribution to capital without additional stock may be involved), is immaterial as long as immediately after the transfer either X Corporation, its shareholders, or a combination of the two, control Y Corporation. Thus, unless Y Corporation is a newly formed corporation, the use of voting stock is not an essential factor in the reorganization. The quantity of assets transferred, however, can be material. Although a type (D) reorganization generally involves the division of an enterprise, in contrast to the amalgamation or acquisition transactions of the first three subparagraphs of section 368(a)(1), subsection (D) also can describe a single corporation reorganization where all of the assets of X Corporation are transferred to Y Corporation. The inclusion of these two substantially different transactions under one definitional paragraph of the reorganization provisions complicates matters.

Where X Corporation desires to create controlled subsidiary Y Corporation or to transfer assets to existing Y Corporation without recognition of gain but wishes to retain Y Corporation as a subsidiary, a (D) reorganization would not be the statutory vehicle. This type of transfer falls under section 351. Where there is no distribution of Y Corporation stock to the shareholders of X Corporation, there is no division in the sense considered under a (D) situation. Instead, the shareholders through their ownership of X Corporation have become the owners of a corporate chain of parent and subsidiary corporations. If X Corporation does distribute some or all of the Y Corporation stock, which it may do under section 351(c) without distributing the tax-free character of the initial transfer of the assets, the situation begins to resemble a divisive (D) situation. Divisive type (D) reorganizations are considered in Chapter 19.

SECTION 2. RECAPITALIZATIONS

INTERNAL REVENUE CODE: Sections 368(a)(1)(E); 354(a); 356(a), (c)–(e); 306(c)(1)(B), (C).

REGULATIONS: Sections 1.354–1(d), (e); 1.356–1, –3, –4, –5; 1.368–2(e); 1.306–3(d), (e); 1.301–1(l).

BAZLEY v. COMMISSIONER *

Supreme Court of the United States, 1947.
331 U.S. 737.

MR. JUSTICE FRANKFURTER delivered the opinion of the Court.

The proper construction of provisions of the Internal Revenue Code relating to corporate reorganizations is involved in both these cases. Their importance to the Treasury as well as to corporate enterprise led us to grant certiorari, 329 U.S. 695, 67 S.Ct. 62; 329 U.S. 701, 67 S.Ct. 77. While there are differences in detail to which we shall refer, the two cases may be disposed of in one opinion.

In the Bazley case, No. 287, the Commissioner of Internal Revenue assessed an income tax deficiency against the taxpayer for the year

* Together with No. 209, Adams v. Commissioner of Internal Revenue.

1939. Its validity depends on the legal significance of the recapitalization in that year of a family corporation in which the taxpayer and his wife owned all but one of the Company's one thousand shares. These had a par value of $100. Under the plan of reorganization the taxpayer, his wife, and the holder of the additional share were to turn in their old shares and receive in exchange for each old share five new shares of no par value, but of a stated value of $60, and new debenture bonds, having a total face value of $400,000, payable in ten years but callable at any time. Accordingly, the taxpayer received 3,990 shares of the new stock for the 798 shares of his old holding and debentures in the amount of $319,200. At the time of these transactions the earned surplus of the corporation was $855,783.82.

The Commissioner charged to the taxpayer as income the full value of the debentures. The Tax Court affirmed the Commissioner's determination, against the taxpayer's contention that as a "recapitalization" the transaction was a tax-free "reorganization" and that the debentures were "securities in a corporation a party to a reorganization," "exchanged solely for stock or securities in such corporation" "in pursuance of a plan of reorganization," and as such no gain is recognized for income tax purposes. [The court cites the predecessors of sections 368(a)(1)(E) and 354(a)(1)].** The Tax Court found that the recapitalization had "no legitimate corporate business purpose" and was therefore not a "reorganization" within the statute. The distribution of debentures, it concluded, was a disguised dividend, taxable as earned income under [the predecessors of sections 61(a), 301, 302 and 318(a)]. 4 T.C. 897. The Circuit Court of Appeals for the Third Circuit, sitting en banc, affirmed, two judges dissenting. 155 F.2d 237.

Unless a transaction is a reorganization contemplated by [the predecessor of section 368(a)(1)], any exchange of "stock or securities" in connection with such transaction, cannot be "in pursuance of the plan of reorganization" under [the predecessor of section 354(a)(1)]. While [§ 368(a)(1)] informs us that "reorganization" means, among other things, "a recapitalization," it does not inform us what "recapitalization" means. "Recapitalization" in connection with the income tax has been part of the revenue laws since 1921. Congress has never defined it and the Treasury Regulations shed only limited light. [Citing the predecessor of Regulations, section 1.368–2(e).] One thing is certain. Congress did not incorporate some technical concept, whether that of accountants or of other specialists, into [§ 368(a)(1)], assuming that there is agreement among specialists as to the meaning of recapitalization. And so, recapitalization as used in [§ 368(a)(1)] must draw its meaning from its function in that section. It is one of the forms of reorganization which obtains the privileges afforded by [§ 368(a)(1)]. Therefore, "recapitalization" must be construed with reference to the presuppositions and purpose of [§ 368(a)(1)]. It was not the purpose of

** [Ed.: The case arose under the 1939 Code which did not contain provisions corresponding to sections 354(a)(2) and 356(d).]

the reorganization provision to exempt from payment of a tax what as a practical matter is realized gain. Normally, a distribution by a corporation, whatever form it takes, is a definite and rather unambiguous event. It furnishes the proper occasion for the determination and taxation of gain. But there are circumstances where a formal distribution, directly or through exchange of securities, represents merely a new form of the previous participation in an enterprise, involving no change of substance in the rights and relations of the interested parties one to another or to the corporate assets. As to these, Congress has said that they are not to be deemed significant occasions for determining taxable gain.

These considerations underlie [§ 368(a)(1)] and they should dominate the scope to be given to the various sections, all of which converge toward a common purpose. Application of the language of such a revenue provision is not an exercise in framing abstract definitions. In a series of cases this Court has withheld the benefits of the reorganization provision in situations which might have satisfied provisions of the section treated as inert language, because they were not reorganizations of the kind with which [section 368] in its purpose and particulars, concerns itself. See Pinellas Ice & Cold Storage Co. v. Commissioner, 287 U.S. 462, 53 S.Ct. 257; Gregory v. Helvering, 293 U.S. 465, 55 S.Ct. 266; Le Tulle v. Scofield, 308 U.S. 415, 60 S.Ct. 313.

Congress has not attempted a definition of what is recapitalization and we shall follow its example. The search for relevant meaning is often satisfied not by a futile attempt at abstract definition but by pricking a line through concrete applications. Meaning frequently is built up by assured recognition of what does not come within a concept the content of which is in controversy. Since a recapitalization within the scope of [§ 368(a)(1)] is an aspect of reorganization nothing can be a recapitalization for this purpose unless it partakes of those characteristics of a reorganization which underlie the purpose of Congress in postponing the tax liability.

No doubt there was a recapitalization of the Bazley corporation in the sense that the symbols that represented its capital were changed, so that the fiscal basis of its operations would appear very differently on its books. But the form of a transaction as reflected by correct corporate accounting opens questions as to the proper application of a taxing statute; it does not close them. Corporate accounting may represent that correspondence between change in the form of capital structure and essential identity in fact which is of the essence of a transaction relieved from taxation as a reorganization. What is controlling is that a new arrangement intrinsically partake of the elements of reorganization which underlie the Congressional exemption and not merely give the appearance of it to accomplish a distribution of earnings. In the case of a corporation which has undistributed earnings, the creation of new corporate obligations which are transferred to stockholders in relation to their former holdings, so as to produce, for all practical purposes, the same result as a distribution of cash earnings of equivalent value, cannot obtain tax immunity because cast in the form of a recapitalization-reorganization. The governing legal rule can hardly be stated more narrowly. To attempt to do so would only challenge astuteness in evading it. And so it is hard to escape the conclusion that whether in a particular case a paper recapitalization is no more than an admissible attempt to avoid the consequences of an outright distribution of earnings turns on details of corporate affairs, judgment on which must be left to the Tax Court. See Dobson v. Commissioner, 320 U.S. 489, 64 S.Ct. 239.

What have we here? No doubt, if the Bazley corporation had issued the debentures to Bazley and his wife without any recapitalization, it would have made a taxable distribution. Instead, these debentures were issued as part of a family arrangement, the only additional ingredient being an unrelated modification of the capital account. The debentures were found to be worth at least their principal amount, and they were virtually cash because they were callable at the will of the corporation which in this case was the will of the taxpayer. One does not have to pursue the motives behind actions, even in the more acertainable forms of purpose, to find, as did the Tax Court, that the whole arrangement took this form instead of an outright distribution of cash or debentures, because the latter would undoubtedly have been taxable income whereas what was done could, with a show of reason, claim the shelter of the immunity of a recapitalization-reorganization.

The Commissioner, the Tax Court and the Circuit Court of Appeals agree that nothing was accomplished that would not have been accomplished by an outright debenture dividend. And since we find no misconception of law on the part of the Tax Court and the Circuit Court of Appeals, whatever may have been their choice of phrasing, their application of the law to the facts of this case must stand. A "reorganization" which is merely a vehicle, however elaborate or elegant, for conveying earnings from accumulations to the stockholders is not a reorganization under [§ 368(a)(1)]. This disposes of the case as a matter of law, since the facts as found by the Tax Court bring them within it. And even if this transaction were deemed a reorganization, the facts would equally sustain the imposition of the tax on the debentures under [the predecessors of § 356(a)(1) and (2)]. Commissioner v. Estate of Bedford, 325 U.S. 283, 65 S.Ct. 1157.

In the Adams case, No. 209, the taxpayer owned all but a few of the 5914 shares of stock outstanding out of an authorized 6000, par value $100. By a plan of reorganization, the authorized capital was reduced by half, to $295,700, divided into 5914 shares of no par value but having a stated value of $50 per share. The 5914 old shares were cancelled and the corporation issued in exchange therefor 5914 shares of the new no-par common stock and 6 per cent 20 year debenture bonds in the principal amount of $295,700. The exchange was made on the basis of one new share of stock and one $50 bond for each old share. The old capital account was debited in the sum of $591,400, a new no-par capital account was credited with $295,700, and the balance of $295,700 was credited to a "Debenture Payable" account. The corporation at this time had accumulated earnings available for distribution in a sum not less than $164,514.82, and this account was left unchanged. At the time of the exchange, the debentures had a value not less than $164,208.82.

The Commissioner determined an income tax deficiency by treating the debenture bonds as a distribution of the corporation's accumulated earnings. The Tax Court sustained the Commissioner's determination, 5 T.C. 351, and the Circuit Court of Appeals affirmed. 155 F.2d 246. The case is governed by our treatment of the Bazley case. The finding by the Tax Court that the reorganization had no purpose other than to achieve the distribution of the earnings, is unaffected by the bookkeeping detail of leaving the surplus account unaffected. See [the predecessor to section 316(a), second sentence], and Commissioner v. Wheeler, 324 U.S. 542, 546, 65 S.Ct. 799.

Other claims raised have been considered but their rejection does not call for discussion.

Judgments affirmed.

MR. JUSTICE DOUGLAS and MR. JUSTICE BURTON dissent in both cases for the reasons stated in the joint dissent of Judges Maris and Goodrich in the court below. Bazley v. Commissioner, 3 Cir., 155 F.2d 237, 244.

ILLUSTRATIVE MATERIAL

A. DEFINITION OF "RECAPITALIZATION" IN GENERAL

Section 368(a)(1)(E) includes within the definition of a reorganization a "recapitalization". The term "recapitalization" is not defined in either the Code or Regulations, however, and its scope and contours have been left to judicial development. Speaking generally, a recapitalization involves a "reshuffling of a capital structure within the framework of an existing corporation," Helvering v. Southwest Consolidated Corporation, 315 U.S. 194, 202 (1942), and encompasses transactions involving exchanges of one class of stock or securities in a corporation for another class issued by the same corporation. Regulations, section 1.368–2(e), provide examples of five different recapitalization exchanges, but those examples are not exhaustive.[1]

The following material discusses the most common types of recapitalizations.

B. EXCHANGE OF DEBT SECURITIES FOR DEBT SECURITIES

1. *Court Decisions*

Commissioner v. Neustadt's Trust, 131 F.2d 528 (2d Cir.1942), involved the exchange of outstanding 20 year, 6 percent debentures for a like face amount of 10 year, $3^{1}/_{4}$ percent convertible debentures of the corpora-

1. In Rev.Proc. 87–3, 1987–1 Cum.Bull. 523, the Service announced that it would not ordinarily rule on whether a transaction constitutes a recapitalization. For prior ruling practice, see Rev.Proc. 81–60, 1981–2 Cum.Bull. 680 (check list of information to be included in a request for an advance ruling that a transaction constitutes a reorganization under section 368(a)(1)(E)).

tion. The Commissioner contended that a taxable gain resulted, but the court disagreed and applied the reorganization provisions:

"The first question is whether the debentures are 'securities' within the meaning of [the predecessor of section 354(a)(1)]. The word is used in contrast to 'stock'; it necessarily refers to bonds of some sort, since bonds are the most usual, if not the only, form of corporate securities to contrast with stock. * * * [It] is usual financial practice to speak of debentures as 'securities' and the term should be given its ordinary meaning. In Helvering v. Watts, 296 U.S. 387, 56 S.Ct. 275, bonds with a maximum maturity of seven years were held to be 'securities' within the corresponding provision of the Revenue Act of 1924. We do not understand that the authority of this case has been destroyed by the subsequent decision in LeTulle v. Scofield, 308 U.S. 415, 60 S.Ct. 313. There it was held that continuity of proprietary interest must be found if the transaction is to be deemed within the definition of reorganization, and that a transfer of all the assets of one corporation to another in exchange for cash and bonds of the latter did not fall within such a definition. It was not held that an exchange of bonds for bonds pursuant to a plan of reorganization is not an exchange of 'securities' within the meaning of [the predecessor of section 354(a)(1)]. * * * We think the debentures involved in the case at bar are 'securities' within that section.

"It remains to determine whether they were exchanged pursuant to a plan of reorganization and this turns on whether the exchange amounts to a 'recapitalization,' as that word is used in [the predecessor of section 368(a)(1)(E)]. * * * The Commissioner contends that only a change in authorized or outstanding capital stock of a corporation can properly be denominated a recapitalization or a reshuffling of the capital structure. He describes an exchange of old debentures for new debentures in the same corporation as a mere refinancing operation. * * * But in common financial parlance the long term funded debt of a corporation is usually regarded as forming part of its capital structure. * * * The Security and Exchange Commission has required the funded debt of a corporation to be listed under the caption of 'capital securities.' The Interstate Commerce Commission treats funded debt as part of the corporate capital structure. St. Louis, San Francisco Ry. Co., Reorganization, 240 I.C.C. 383, 406 * * *. [T]he purpose of the statutory nonrecognition of gain or loss from reorganization transactions, favors ascribing to the word 'recapitalization' a broad rather than a restricted meaning. Such purpose, as indicated by the Congressional reports * * * was apparently twofold: To encourage legitimate reorganizations required to strengthen the financial condition of a corporation, and to prevent losses being established by bondholders, as well as stockholders, who have received the new securities without substantially changing their original investment. The transaction in the case at bar meets both of these tests. By changing the interest rate and date of maturity of its old bonds and adding a conversion option to the holders of the new, the corporation could strengthen its financial condition, while the bondholders would not substantially change their original investments by making the exchange. 'Recapitalization' seems a most appropriate word to describe that type of reorganization and it is the very kind of transaction where Congress meant the recognition of gain or loss to be held in suspense until a more substantial change in the taxpayer's original investment should occur. We hold that the exchange of securities was made pursuant to a plan of 'recapitalization.'" (529–530)

2. *Current Statutory Provisions*

(a) *General*

While the examples of recapitalizations in Regulations, section 1.368–2(e), do not include an exchange only of debt securities, the Committee Reports under the 1954 Act approve the *Neustadt* rule. Senate Finance Committee Report, S.Rep. No. 83–1622, 83rd Cong., 2d Sess. 51 (1954). Rev.Rul. 77–415, 1977–2 Cum.Bull. 311, accepted the principle that continued equity interest is not required in an otherwise qualifying (E) reorganization. Thus, the exchange of new ten-year, 10 percent debentures for outstanding 20–year, 8 percent debentures did not result in gain or loss to the exchanging debenture holders since the principal amounts of the two issues were the same.

Sections 354(a)(2) and 356(d), however, combine to find boot in an exchange of debt securities where the principal amounts differ. See supra, page 810. If the excess principal amount is in satisfaction of accrued interest, section 354(a)(2)(B) requires that the entire amount of the excess so attributable be recognized as ordinary income. To the extent the excess is not attributable to accrued interest, the value of the excess principal amount is treated as boot taxable under section 356(a). In a bond for bond exchange, none of the boot gain should be treated as a dividend under section 356(a)(2). Boot can result under section 354(a)(2) and give rise to taxable gain under section 356(d) even where the value of the securities given up is the same as the value of those received. For example, if a 9½ percent, $100 face amount bond with basis of $100 is exchanged for a new 6 percent, $120 face amount publicly traded bond and the value of each is $120, the value of the excess $20 in principal amount is i.e., $120 × 20/120, is boot. See Regulations, section 1.356–3. The new bond has a basis under section 358 of $120 ($100 basis of old bond + $20 gain).

(b) *Interaction With Original Issue Discount Rules*

If either the securities received or the securities surrendered are publicly traded and the face amount of the securities received exceeds the fair market value of the securities surrendered, the original issue discount (OID) provisions must be considered in addition to sections 354 and 356. Under section 1273(b), the issue price, and thus the principal amount, of the securities received, will be equal to the fair market value of the securities surrendered. Suppose a publicly traded 9½ percent, $100 face amount bond with a basis of $90 is exchanged for a new 6 percent, $130 face amount publicly traded bond and the values of both are $120. The issue price, and thus the principal amount of the new bond is $120. The value of the excess $20 of principal amount, i.e., $20 ($120 × ($20/$120)), is boot. Because the face amount of the security received, $130, exceeds the fair market value of the security surrendered, $120, the excess amount, $10, is OID. The new bond has a basis under section 358 of $110 ($90 basis of the old bond plus $20 gain), and upon redemption at maturity the holder will recognize gain of $10. This gain will be ordinary income under section 1276 because it is market discount. See section 1278(a)(1)(C)(iii).

Where neither security is publicly traded, whether a security issued in a recapitalization is an OID instrument is determined by treating the instrument as issued for property. Section 1275(a)(5). Thus, the issue price (and principal amount) are determined by discounting to net present value the payments due on the instrument (including both principal and interest), using the proper "applicable federal rate". See section 1274, discussed supra, page 439.

Under Rev.Rul. 60–37, 1960–1 Cum.Bull. 309, if the old bonds had an original issue discount element, the new bonds were to be similarly treated. This rule is, in effect, carried forward by the "issue price" rules in section 1273(b)(3) where either security is publicly traded. Thus, for example, a 10 percent, $100 face value bond received in exchange for a zero interest $150 face value OID bond, with a fair market value of $100, will be an OID instrument. However, if the adjusted issue price of the old bond exceeds its fair market value, section 1275(a)(4) limits the maximum amount of OID to be attributed to the new bond to the excess of the face value of the new bond over the adjusted issue price of the old bond. Thus if the adjusted issue price of the zero interest bond were $105 at the time of the exchange, the OID inherent in the new bond would be $45.

(c) *Treatment of the Corporation*

If a corporation issues new bonds in exchange for outstanding bonds having a higher principal amount, an (E) reorganization exists but the corporation realizes cancellation of indebtedness income since neither section 361(a) nor section 1032 applies to relieve the corporation from tax. Rev. Rul. 77–437, 1977–2 Cum.Bull. 28. On the other hand, where the new bonds have a higher principal amount than the old bonds and the new bonds are not OID instruments, the corporation may deduct the retirement premium as an additional cost of borrowing, unless a portion of the premium is attributable to extinguishment of a conversion feature in the old bonds. See section 249.

C. EXCHANGE OF OUTSTANDING BONDS FOR NEW STOCK

Regulations, section 1.368–2(e)(1), provide that the issuance by a corporation of new preferred stock in exchange for existing bonds is a recapitalization. See also Commissioner v. Capento Securities Corporation, 140 F.2d 382 (1st Cir.1944). An exchange of outstanding bonds for new common stock would likewise be a recapitalization. In either case, the former security owners are accorded nonrecognition under section 354 (subject to recognition under section 354(a)(2)(B) to the extent that the stock is attributable to interest arrearages). From the corporation's perspective, however, if the corporation is solvent the transaction gives rise to taxable discharge of indebtedness income to the extent that the sum of the principal amount of the securities plus accrued but unpaid interest exceeds the fair market value of the stock issued in the transaction. Section 108(e)(10). To the extent of the fair market value of the stock, section 1032 provides nonrecognition to the corporation.

If the holder of a security which is an OID instrument receives stock in exchange for the instrument in a recapitalization, the balance of the original issue discount will not be included in the income of the exchanging bondholder. See Rev.Rul. 75–39, 1975–1 Cum.Bull. 272. The stock will take a basis under section 358 equal to the basis of the debt instrument, and any remaining unrecognized OID income is thereby converted into unrealized appreciation.

On a related point, the exercise of a conversion privilege of a bond convertible into stock of the same corporation is not an "exchange" and hence the recapitalization provision and section 354 are not involved, Rev. Rul. 72–265, 1972–1 Cum.Bull. 222. See also Rev.Rul. 79–155, 1979–1 Cum.Bull. 153 (parent of subsidiary which issued debt obligations convertible into stock of parent was treated as a joint obligor on debt, thereby resulting in conversion not being a taxable event).

D. EXCHANGE OF OUTSTANDING STOCK FOR NEW STOCK OR NEW BONDS

1. *General*

The exchange of outstanding preferred stock for new preferred stock or of outstanding common stock for new common stock will constitute a recapitalization. The exchange of outstanding preferred stock for common stock is likewise a recapitalization as is an exchange of common stock for common and preferred stock. Regulations, section 1.368–2(e). In the latter situation, however, special rules apply to limit the "bailout" potential of the transaction. See infra, page 882.

It is not necessary that all shareholders in a recapitalization exchange their stock. Thus, a valid (E) reorganization results where only one of three shareholders exchanges common stock for preferred stock and the fair market value of the preferred equals the fair market value of the common stock exchanged. If there is a difference in value between the common and the preferred stock, the difference may constitute a gift, compensation, etc. Rev. Rul. 74–269, 1974–1 Cum.Bull. 87. See also Rev.Rul. 89–3, 1989–1 Cum. Bull. 278 (recapitalization whereby shareholder who had acquired shares by gift from controlling shareholder exchanged common stock for new voting common and donor shareholder exchanged common stock for new common stock with restricted voting rights resulted in taxable gift).

Where the exchange is of stock for stock, the effect of section 1036 must also be considered. That section applies both to an exchange between shareholders and one between the shareholder and the issuing corporation, so that it in part overlaps the recapitalization sections. See Rev.Rul. 72–57, 1972–1 Cum.Bull. 103 (exchange of outstanding stock for stock and cash as part of a transaction to eliminate minority shareholders was a recapitalization and therefore under Regulations, section 1.1031(b)–1(a)(3) (which apply to section 1036 transactions), was not a section 1036 exchange coupled with the receipt of nonqualifying property by the majority shareholder under section 1031(b)); Rev.Rul. 78–351, 1978–2 Cum.Bull. 148, modifying Rev.Rul. 72–57, held the cash was a section 356(a)(2) dividend to the majority shareholder.

2. *Security Bailouts*

Sections 354(a)(2) and 356(d) extend the rationale of the *Bazley* case to all recapitalization and other reorganization exchanges since the value of the excess in principal amount of securities received by the shareholder over the principal amount of securities given up is considered "other property" or "boot". Hence if a shareholder exchanges stock, whether common or preferred, for new stock, whether common or preferred, and debt securities, the securities will be boot and governed by section 356(a). If stock is exchanged for securities alone, section 354(a)(2) renders section 354(a)(1) inapplicable entirely, section 356(a)(1)(B) does not come into play, and the treatment of the exchange is determined under sections 301, 302, and 331. Regulations, section 1.354–1(d), Ex. (3); Rev.Rul. 77–415, 1977–2 Cum. Bull. 311.

As discussed infra, page 884, the lack of continuity of equity interest does not destroy the validity of a type (E) reorganization. However section 354(a)(2) in effect applies a continuity of interest concept on a shareholder by shareholder basis, in that the pro tanto loss of proprietary status will result in recognition of gain or in dividend treatment.

3. *Preferred Stock Bailouts—Exchange of Outstanding Common Stock for New Preferred Stock*

Suppose holders of common stock exchange some common stock for new preferred, or exchange all of their common stock for new common stock and new preferred, so that after the exchange they own both common stock and preferred stock. This is of course a recapitalization variant of the preferred stock dividend bailout, dealt with by section 306. Section 306(c)(1)(B) extends the section 306 solution to the recapitalization exchange if "the effect of the transaction was substantially the same as the receipt of a stock dividend." Regulations, section 1.306–3(d), refer to section 356(a)(2) and state that if any cash received in lieu of the stock would have been a dividend under section 356(a)(2), then the stock is section 306 stock.

In applying this test, Revenue Rulings appear to treat as section 306 stock any preferred stock received by a shareholder whose proportionate common stock interest is at least substantially as large as before the transaction. Rev.Rul. 56–116, 1956–1 Cum.Bull. 164; Rev.Rul. 59–84, 1959–1 Cum.Bull. 71; Rev.Rul. 59–197, 1959–1 Cum.Bull. 77; Rev.Rul. 75–236, 1975–1 Cum.Bull. 106 (same result even though preferred was voting and common was non-voting). Rev.Rul. 81–186, 1981–2 CumBull. 85, held that where a sole shareholder exchanged some of has common stock for preferred stock in a recapitalization and gave his remaining common stock to his children, the preferred stock was not section 306 stock because if the shareholder had received cash it would not have been a dividend since he would have terminated his entire interest in the corporation (see Zenz v. Quinlivan, supra, page 725).

Do the attribution of ownership rules apply in determining whether preferred stock received in a recapitalization is section 306 stock? For example, if a husband retains his common stock but his wife receives preferred stock in a recapitalization, is the preferred stock section 306 stock? Or suppose that a cash distribution would not have been taxable under section 356(a)(2) because of the "dividend within the gain" limitation; would the stock distributed in such a situation be section 306 stock? See Rev.Rul. 56–586, 1956–2 Cum.Bull. 214 (indicating that section 356(a)(2) is relevant).

Where, in a reorganization, boot is distributed for section 306 stock, section 356(e) applies to treat the boot under section 301. In Rev.Rul. 76–14, 1976–1 Cum.Bull. 97, the majority shareholder desired to transfer control of the business to an employee-minority shareholder. Under a recapitalization plan, the majority shareholder turned in his common stock for cash and his preferred stock (which was section 306 stock) for a new class of nonvoting common stock. The Ruling held section 356(e) applied; thus the cash received was applied first to the section 306 stock, with a resulting dividend. But if cash is distributed to minority shareholders in lieu of fractional shares, the exception in section 306(b)(4)(A) applies, and the cash will be treated as received in a redemption subject to section 302. Rev.Rul. 81–81, 1981–1 Cum.Bull. 123. If in the reorganization, stock which is other than common stock is issued for section 306 stock under section 306(c)(1)(B), the new stock is section 306 stock.

A recapitalization exchange can occur without a direct exchange of stock. Thus, in Rev.Rul. 56–654, 1956–2 Cum.Bull. 216, a corporation with outstanding common and preferred stock amended its charter to increase the liquidation value of the preferred stock. The Ruling states that this represented an exchange of all preferred stock and a portion of the common stock for new preferred stock; presumably the increase in value of the preferred stock is section 306 stock. See also Rev.Rul. 66–332, 1966–2 Cum.Bull. 108, holding that a "reclassification" of outstanding common stock together with the issuance of additional classes of stock could result in the reclassified stock being treated as section 306 stock.

4. *Relation of Security Bailout to Preferred Stock Bailout*

The Service's view of *Bazley* type recapitalizations prior to the 1954 Code was that the vice lay in splitting a common stockholder's interest into common stock which could be retained and another interest, preferred stock or debt, which could be sold, thereby obtaining capital gain treatment for a part of the accumulated earnings without reducing the shareholder's common stock interest. The current Code embodies the view that an exchange of outstanding stock for debt must meet the tests of the dividend sections. It is akin to the policy of section 306 respecting preferred stock bailouts, in that it seeks to block the efforts to convert situations having potential dividend taxation into situations involving capital gain potential only. The solution for the "security bailout," however, is that of an immediate tax, while under section 306 the solution for the "preferred stock bailout" is that of "tainting" by giving the preferred stock an ordinary income status on future disposition.

E. OTHER ASPECTS OF RECAPITALIZATIONS

1. *Applicability of "Business Purpose" Doctrine*

The Court of Appeals and the Tax Court had held in the *Bazley* and *Adams* cases that no corporate business purpose existed and that the business purpose test must be viewed in terms of the corporation qua corporation and apart from the shareholders. Dissenting opinions in both courts contended that the shareholders had persuasive business reasons for the transaction (obtaining a more marketable security and one that could be sold without reducing stock control of the corporation, an equal footing with creditors to the extent of the debentures, and a more permanent dedication of the accumulated profits to the business). They rejected the view that shareholder business purposes do not supply the necessary corporate business purpose, stating that such a distinction between "corporate" and "shareholder" purpose lacked substance since a corporation did not have purposes apart from its shareholders. The Government's brief stressed the argument that the transaction was not actuated by a purpose germane to the corporation's business, relied strongly on the *Gregory* case, and stated in effect that the stockholders' purposes were not relevant. In the light of this background, note the Supreme Court's avoidance of direct "business purpose" terminology. For a similar issue in the context of divisive reorganizations, see infra, page 927.

Rev.Rul. 77–238, 1977–2 Cum.Bull. 115, found an (E) reorganization existed where the certificate of incorporation required retiring employees owning common stock to exchange that stock for preferred. The purpose of the provision was to eliminate common stockholdings by employees no longer with the corporation, thus supplying the business purpose necessary to support the reorganization.

2. *Applicability of Continuity of Interest Doctrine*

In Hickock v. Commissioner, 32 T.C. 80 (1959) (A), the Tax Court held that the continuity of interest doctrine, discussed supra, page 764, does not apply to recapitalizations. The Service has followed this principle in Revenue Rulings. See Rev.Rul. 77–415, 1977–2 Cum.Bull. 311. Thus, for example, if A, B, C, and D each held 25 percent of the stock of X Corporation, a transaction whereby A exchanged common stock for new common stock and new preferred stock, while B, C, and D exchanged their stock for debentures could qualify as a recapitalization. B, C, and D would recognize gain, but A would be entitled to nonrecognition. Likewise, a prearranged sale of newly issued stock received in an (E) reorganization does not impair the validity of the reorganization. Rev.Rul. 77–479, 1977–2 Cum.Bull. 119.

3. *Applicability of Continuity of Business Enterprise Doctrine.*

Rev.Rul. 82–34, 1982–1 Cum.Bull. 59, held that the continuity of business enterprise doctrine embodied in Regulations, section 1.368–1(b), does not apply to a recapitalization. Thus, incident to a recapitalization a corporation may sell all of its assets and purchase new assets to engage in a different line of business. Presumably, the corporation also could sell its assets and acquire investment assets, thereby becoming a holding company.

4. *Treatment of Boot as Capital Gain or Dividend*

Where the recapitalization exchange "has the effect" of a dividend distribution, dividend income is recognized to the extent of the gain realized on the exchange. See Commissioner v. Estate of Bedford, 325 U.S. 283 (1945). Dividend equivalency of boot distributions made in connection with a recapitalization is determined by applying the principles of section 302, which governs redemptions (discussed supra, page 554). Johnson v. Commissioner, 78 T.C. 564 (1982) ($850 per share boot in recapitalization which converted nonvoting common stock into voting common stock was a dividend because it was pro rata and compensated nonvoting shareholders for dividends previously withheld). The reasoning in *Clark,* supra, page 800, which significantly limits the application of section 356(a)(2) in the case of acquisitive reorganizations, should not affect the application of that section to recapitalizations because only a single corporation is involved. In addition, in the appropriate circumstances, the Internal Revenue Service might argue that under the approach of *Bazley,* the full amount of the boot was a dividend. Regulations, section 1.301–1(1), preserve this contention.

On the face of the statute, there is an overlap of section 368(a)(1)(E) and section 1036 in these various situations and, where boot is involved, section 1031(b). Regulations, section 1.1031(b)–1(a)(3), defer to the reorganization provisions, at least where boot is involved. See Rev.Rul. 72–57, 1972–1 Cum.Bd. 103.

5. *Section 305 Aspects*

A recapitalization, which would be tax-free under the reorganization provisions, is one of the transactions which can result in a constructive stock dividend under section 305(c). See supra, page 535. For example, in a recapitalization in which a shareholder exchanges preferred stock with dividend arrearages for new common and preferred stock, the exchange would be a tax-free recapitalization under section 368. See e.g., Kaufman v. Commissioner, 55 T.C. 1046 (1971). When viewed from the perspective of section 305, however, the recapitalization has the effect of a distribution of additional shares of stock to the preferred stockholder which would result in a taxable dividend under sections 305(c) and 305(b)(4). Regulations, section 1.305–5(d), Ex. (1) (taxable stock dividend if arrearages are eliminated).

In Rev.Rul. 83–119, 1983–2 Cum.Bull. 57, pursuant to a recapitalization a corporation issued preferred stock with an issue price of $600, which was according to its terms required to be redeemed for $1,000 upon the holder's death. The Ruling held that under sections 305(c) and 305(b)(4), $340 of the redemption premium was a taxable stock dividend which was includable ratably over the holder's life expectancy. Upon the holder's death, any portion of the $340 not yet included in income would be includable. For valuation of preferred stock issued in a recapitalization, see Rev.Rul. 83–120, 1983–2 Cum.Bull. 170.

See also Regulations, section 1.305–3(e), Ex. (12), illustrating that section 305 is inapplicable to a "single and isolated" recapitalization transaction.

6. *Taxable Recapitalizations*

In Microdot, Inc. v. United States, 728 F.2d 593 (2d Cir.1984), the corporation issued 25 year debentures with an aggregate principal amount of $6,064,400 in exchange for 404,298 shares of its outstanding common stock. Because the fair market value of the debentures was only $4,548,300, the corporation claimed an interest deduction under the then applicable original issue discount rules, on the theory that the debentures were issued in a transaction which was not a recapitalization. The corporation's conclusion was based on two lines of argument. First, the corporation argued that the transaction was not a recapitalization because section 354(a)(2)(B) denies nonrecognition to the shareholder when debt securities are received and none are surrendered. The court held that section 354 has no bearing on whether a transaction meets the statutory definition of a reorganization. Second, the corporation argued that under *Bazley* a transaction which is essentially a redemption at the shareholder level—which was undoubtedly true in *Microdot*—could not be a recapitalization to the corporation because it was not intended to be accorded tax-free treatment. The court concluded that *Bazley* was not intended to so restrict the definition of a recapitalization in all cases. Rather, the court characterized *Bazley* as limiting the definition of recapitalizations only insofar as application of the nonrecognition provisions is concerned. See also Golden Nugget, Inc. v. Commissioner, 83 T.C. 28 (1984).

F. REFERENCES

Hariton, Recapitalizations: The Issuer's Treatment, 40 Tax Law. 873 (1987); Hanna, A Recapitalization: The E Reorganization of the Internal Revenue Code, 27 Tax Lawyer 447 (1974); Cohen, The E and F Reorganizations: Use and Abuse; Use As Part Of A Major Reorganization Plan, 31 N.Y.U.Tax Inst. 333, 354 (1973); Metzer, The Impact of Section 306 upon Convertible Preferred Stock Issued in a Corporate Reorganization, 116 U.Pa. L.Rev. 755 (1968).

SECTION 3. CHANGES IN IDENTITY, FORM, OR PLACE OF ORGANIZATION: TYPE (F) REORGANIZATIONS

INTERNAL REVENUE CODE: Section 368(a)(1)(F).

ILLUSTRATIVE MATERIAL

A. GENERAL

1. *Definition*

Section 368(a)(1)(F) treats as a reorganization a change in "identity, form or place of organization." The statute was amended in 1982 to make it clear that the provision was not intended to apply to a transaction which involved what was in effect the merger of two or more pre-existing operating companies. See H.Rep. No. 97–760, 97th Cong., 2d Sess. 540–541 (1982). Prior to the amendment, some courts had permitted (F) reorganization treatment in such circumstances. See, e.g., Home Construction Corp. v. United States, 439 F.2d 1165 (5th Cir.1971).

The (F) reorganization definition may overlap with other forms of reorganization. For example, in order to change its state of incorporation, X Corporation might form a new Y Corporation in another jurisdiction and then merge into it. The transaction is both an (A) and an (F) reorganization and the Internal Revenue Service has indicated that in these circumstances the transaction will be characterized as an (F) reorganization. Rev.Rul. 57–276, 1957–Cum.Bull. 126. See also Rev.Rul. 88–25, 1988–1 Cum.Bull. 116 (conversion of foreign corporation to domestic corporation by filing domestication certificate under state law); Rev.Rul. 87–27, 1987–1 Cum. Bull. 134 (reincorporation of domestic corporation in foreign country is a type (F) reorganization); Rev.Rul. 87–66, 1987–2 Cum.Bull. 168 (reincorporation of foreign corporation in U.S. is a type (F) reorganization); Rev.Rul. 80–105 (conversion of federal mutual savings and loan association to state stock savings and loan association was a type (F) reorganization).

Type (F) reorganizations appear to be subject to a stricter "continuity of business enterprise" test than that which applies to acquisitive reorganizations under Regulations, section 1.368–1(d), discussed supra, page 792. Rev.Rul. 75–561, supra, required that the transferor's business continue unchanged after the transaction. In Mariani Frozen Foods, Inc. v. Commissioner, 81 T.C. 448 (1983), the court declined to find an (F) reorganization because most of the assets of the old corporation had been sold.

2. *Effects*

Classifying a transaction as a type (F) reorganization has two principal effects: (1) the old corporation's taxable year does not end; and, (2) the new corporation is entitled under section 172 to carry back to taxable years of the old corporation post-reorganization net operating losses. See section 381(b). These results reflect the fact that the reorganized corporation is "really" unchanged by the reorganizing transaction. In other respects, the new (or acquiring) corporation succeeds to the old (or acquired) corporation's tax attributes under section 381, discussed infra, Chapter 20, in the same manner as in any other reorganization.

Type (F) reorganizations also differ from other types of reorganizations in that section 357(c) does not apply to (F) reorganizations. Rev.Rul. 79–289, 1979–2 Cum.Bull. 145 (section 357(c) does not apply to reorganization meeting requirement for both (D) and (F)). For example, if X Corporation, whose sole asset is land and a building which has a basis of $50,000 and is subject to a $70,000 mortgage, reincorporates in a different state by merging into Y Corporation, a wholly owned subsidiary formed solely for the reincorporation transaction, no gain is recognized to X Corporation and Y Corporation takes a $50,000 basis in the land and building.

B. CONTINUITY OF INTEREST

1. *Background—"Liquidation–Reincorporation" Transactions and the (F) Reorganization Provisions*

Prior to the 1986 Act elimination of the capital gains preference and repeal of the *General Utilities* doctrine, shareholders often attempted to extract property from corporate solution at capital gains rates while continuing to operate the business in corporate form. In a typical transaction, the corporation would be liquidated and simultaneously or within a short period the operating assets of the corporation would be reincorporated in a new corporation with the shareholders retaining the liquid assets. If the form of the transaction was respected, the liquidation would generate capital gains to the shareholders under section 331 and the incorporation would be tax free under section 351.

In attacking such transactions, the Commissioner often argued that the overall effect of the transaction was an (F) reorganization with the retained assets representing "boot" in the reorganization taxable as a dividend. This argument was generally successful where the shareholders in the "old" and "new" corporations were substantially identical. See, e.g., Pridemark v. Commissioner, 42 T.C. 510 (1964), aff'd in part and rev'd in part, 345 F.2d 35 (4th Cir.1965). However, where some shareholders were eliminated in the transaction, it was harder to characterize the transaction as a "mere" change of form. Here the Commissioner argued that the aspect of the transaction which resulted in the change in share ownership was "unrelated" to the (F) reorganization transaction. See, e.g., Rev.Rul. 61–156, 1961–2 Cum.Bull. 62 (stock issued to new shareholders in a liquidation-reincorporation transaction was "functionally unrelated" to the reorganization and did not prevent the finding of an (F) reorganization.) The Commissioner's approach had only mixed success in the courts with the Tax Court insisting on complete identity of share ownership as a precondition for finding an (F) reorganization. See, e.g., Gallagher v. Commissioner, 39 T.C. 144 (1962); Reef Corp. v. Commissioner, 24 T.C.M. 379 (1965), rev'd, 368 F.2d 125

(5th Cir.1966). Type (D) reorganization aspects of the liquidation-reincorporation transaction are discussed, infra, page 898.

After the 1986 Act elimination of capital gains preference coupled with the requirement of corporate level gain recognition on the distribution of appreciated assets in liquidation, intentionally structured transactions of this sort no longer occur. However, the case law developed in connection with liquidation-reincorporation transactions has had some effect on the case law involving "normal" (F) reorganizations. Compare Romy Hammes v. Commissioner, 68 T.C. 900, 906 note 8 (1977) ("The (F) reorganization received relatively little judicial or administrative attention until [the government] began to use the (F) reorganization as a weapon in the liquidation-reincorporation area. * * * Although the litigating positions of the Service and the taxpayer are reversed when the scope of the (F) reorganization is to be determined for purposes of section 381(b)(3) loss carryback, the judicial interpretation of section 368(a)(1)(F) must obviously be consistent."); The Aetna Casualty and Surety Co. v. United States, 568 F.2d 811, 823 (2d Cir.1977) ("We specifically declin[e] to decide whether classifying a reorganization as an (F) reorganization for purposes of section 381(b)(3) will necessarily mean it is an (F) reorganization for purposes of other provisions of the Code.").

2. *Current Continuity of Interest Issues*

(a) *"Functionally Unrelated" Transactions*

Suppose that X Corporation, which is incorporated in California, wishes to reincorporate in Delaware and simultaneously to redeem the stock of A, a 20 percent shareholder. To this end, X Corporation forms Y Corporation (a Delaware corporation) and then merges into Y Corporation with A receiving cash and all of the other X shareholders receiving Y Corporation stock. Does the transaction qualify as an (F) reorganization or does it qualify only as an (A) reorganization? This will be an important issue if, for example, Y Corporation incurs a net operating loss, which can be carried back to an X Corporation year only if the transaction qualifies as an (F) reorganization.

If the "functionally unrelated" analysis adopted by the Internal Revenue Service in Rev.Rul. 61–156, supra, page 887, is applicable, then the transaction can be divided into a redemption and an (F) reorganization. There is some support in the case law for application of the "functionally unrelated" analysis. In Reef Corp. v. Commissioner, 368 F.2d 125 (5th Cir.1966), two groups of shareholders controlled a corporation. One group desired to buy out the other and a plan was developed whereby a new corporation was formed which issued stock in exchange for a portion of the stock in the old corporation held by the shareholders desiring to continue in the business. Both groups then sold the remaining stock in the old corporation to a third party with the outgoing shareholders receiving cash and notes. The old corporation then sold its assets to the new corporation in exchange for notes of the new corporation. Those notes were then distributed to the old shareholders in discharge of the third party's obligation for the purchase price. The outgoing group was thus left with notes of the new corporation and cash while the continuing group now controlled the new corporation and held its notes as well. The court found that an (F) reorganization had occurred:

"Distilled to their pure substance, two distinct and unrelated events transpired. First, the holders of 48 percent of the stock in Reef Fields had their stockholdings completely redeemed. Second, new Reef was formed and the assets of Reef Fields were transferred to new Reef. The business enterprise continued without interruption during both the redemption and the change in corporate vehicles.

"Much confusion flows from the fact that the corporate reorganization took place simultaneously with the stock redemption. But taking the Code as a standard, these two elements were functionally unrelated. Reef Fields could have completely redeemed the stock of 48 percent of its shareholders without changing the state of its incorporation. A complete redemption is not a characteristic of a reorganization. Congress clearly indicated this when it defined reorganization in section 368. Section 368(a)(1)(A) speaks of a 'merger or consolidation' which looks to the joining of two or more corporations. Section 368(a)(1)(B) and (C) look to one corporation acquiring the assets of another or control of another corporation solely for its voting stock. Section 368(a)(1)(D) looks to the consolidation of two or more corporations or the division of two or more going businesses into separate corporations. Only sections 368(a)(1)(E) and (F) look to adjustments within a corporation. But none of these provisions focuses on a complete redemption as a characteristic of a reorganization. Congress did not have redemption of stock as a primary purpose of any of the forms of a reorganization. That subject came under consideration when it undertook to enact specific legislation on complete and partial redemptions, section 302.

"The boot provision, section 356, is adequate to cover a complete redemption when it occurs incident to a reorganization * * *. When the primary characteristics of the reorganization conform to those described by 368(a)(1)(F), we should parse the occurrences into their functional elements. * * * To effectuate the intention of Congress manifested in the Code, we must separate this transaction into its two distinctly separate functional parts. The test of whether events should be viewed separately or together as part of a single plan is not temporal but is functional.

"Applying this test to the instant case, it is clear that the redemption and the change of corporate vehicles must be viewed as separate and distinct occurrences. Cf. Bazley v. Commissioner, 1947, 331 U.S. 737, 67 S.Ct. 1489." (134)

In The Aetna Casualty and Surety Co. v. United States, 568 F.2d 811 (2d Cir.1976), Aetna Life, which held 61 percent of the stock of Old Aetna, formed a new corporation, New Aetna, to which it transferred its stock of Old Aetna. Old Aetna was then merged into New Aetna with the minority shareholders in Old Aetna receiving shares of Aetna Life. The minority shareholders of Old Aetna thus became shareholders of Aetna Life and New Aetna became a wholly owned subsidiary of Aetna Life. Subsequent to the reorganization, New Aetna operated at a loss and attempted to carry that loss back against part of Old Aetna's taxable income, arguing that the transaction constituted an (F) reorganization and that the carryback was thus permitted under section 381(b)(3). The court held that the transaction constituted an (F) reorganization despite the fact that the minority shareholders in Old Aetna emerged from the transaction with a substantially changed interest in the reorganized corporate structure. The court treated the transaction as if the minority shareholders' interests in Old Aetna had been redeemed (i.e., by exchanging their Old Aetna shares for shares in Aetna Life) in the course of an (F) reorganization: "Clearly a corporation which merely redeems its minority shareholders' stock has not undergone a reorganization at all under section 368(a)(1) and is entitled to carryback its losses under § 172. We see no reason why the result should be different simply because the redemption occurs in the course of merging one corporation into a different shell. * * * If the redemption, reorganization and carryback provisions were not intended to preclude carrybacks where there has been a simple redemption, we do not believe those provisions should be construed to preclude the carryback here involved." (822)

In Casco Products Corp. v. Commissioner, 49 T.C. 32 (1967), "New Casco" corporation acquired 91 percent of the stock of "Old Casco" by means of a public tender. Solely to acquire 100 percent ownership of Old Casco, the New Casco formed a subsidiary and Old Casco was merged into it, with the dissenting shareholders receiving cash. The Tax Court treated the overall transaction, including the merger, as a "reorganization in form" only, and regarded the subsidiary as "merely a meaningless detour" to accomplish the effect of a redemption of the remaining 9 percent of the shares. Thus a net operating loss of the now wholly owned subsidiary was allowed to be carried back to the taxable years of Old Casco.

(b) *(F) Reorganization Following an Acquisition*

Suppose that X Corporation purchases all of the stock of Y Corporation and immediately thereafter merges Y Corporation into Z Corporation, a subsidiary of X Corporation with no assets which was formed solely for the purpose of changing the state of incorporation of Y Corporation. Does the merger qualify as an (F) reorganization? In Security Industrial Insurance Co. v. United States, 702 F.2d 1234 (5th Cir.1983), OIC, a holding company, purchased all of the stock of Southern, following which OIC liquidated Southern and then contributed OIC's operating assets to Security, another subsidiary of OIC. The taxpayer argued that the transaction was an (F) reorganization. Applying the step transaction doctrine, the court held that no (F) reorganization had occurred because the intended result of the transaction was an acquisition of the assets of OIC. The court tested shareholder continuity of interest by comparing ownership of Southern before the acquisition with ownership of OIC after the entire transaction had been completed. Since the historic shareholders of Y corporation have been eliminated, the transaction failed to meet the continuity of interest requirement. A key element in the reasoning of Security Industrial Insurance Co., however, was the application of the step transaction doctrine.

See also Cannonsburg Skiing Corporation v. Commissioner, 51 T.C.M. 844 (1986), aff'd sub nom. Russell v. Commissioner, 832 F.2d 349 (6th Cir. 1987) (step transaction doctrine applied to treat the overall transaction as an asset acquisition, and concluded that no (F) reorganization had occurred because there was a 98 percent shift in ownership "which clearly violates the identity of shareholders and their proprietary interests as required for an F reorganization").

If the merger fails to qualify as an F reorganization because all of the historical shareholders of Y Corporation have been cashed out, it likewise should fail the continuity of interest test for treatment as a type (A) reorganization. Unless the transaction is a reorganization, however, section 336 would require the transferor corporation to recognize gain as a result of the merger. Should the "functionally unrelated" analysis of Rev.Rul. 61–

156, supra, page 887, be applied to avoid recognition in such a case? Rev. Rul. 79–250, 1979–2 Cum.Bull. 156, indicates that such analysis may be applied in some cases. In that Ruling, W Corporation, for business reasons, dropped its operating assets into two subsidiaries, X Corporation and Y Corporation, in transactions subject to section 351. Thereafter, Z Corporation, which was unrelated to W Corporation was merged into Y Corporation in a triangular merger in which the former Z Corporation shareholders received stock of W Corporation. Finally, immediately following the merger, W Corporation changed its state of incorporation by merging into N Corporation, which had been organized for this purpose. The Ruling concluded that the reincorporation of W Corporation was a valid (F) reorganization: "Although the overall plan comprehends both the acquisition and the reincorporation transactions, the economic motivation supporting each transaction is sufficiently meaningful on its own account, and is not dependent upon the other transaction for its substantiation, to warrant the conclusion that the overall plan presents two separate and independent reorganizations." (157)

See also Dunlap & Associates, Inc. v. Commissioner, 47 T.C. 542 (1967) (merger of a New York corporation into its Delaware subsidiary as part of an overall plan subsequently to acquire stock of two other corporations in type (B) reorganizations prior to making a public offering of stock in the Delaware corporation, was held to be an (F) reorganization).

C. REFERENCES

Barbosa, An Analysis of "F" Reorganizations Involving a Single Operating Company After TEFRA, 11 J.Corp.Tax. 3 (1984); Metzer, An Effective Use of Plain English—The Evolution and Impact of Section 368(a)(1)(F), 32 Tax Law. 703 (1979): Pugh, The (F) Reorganization: Reveille for a Sleeping Giant?, 24 Tax L.Rev. 437 (1969); Hutton, Musings on Continuity of Interest–Recent Developments, 56 Taxes 904 (1978).

SECTION 4. NONDIVISIVE TYPE (D) REORGANIZATIONS

INTERNAL REVENUE CODE: Section 354(b); 368(a)(1)(D), (a)(2)(A), (c); 312(h)(2).

WARSAW PHOTOGRAPHIC ASSOCIATES, INC. v. COMMISSIONER

Tax Court of the United States, 1985.
84 T.C. 21.

CHABOT, JUDGE:

[Warsaw Studios, Inc. (Studios) conducted a photography business in leased premises on Madison Avenue and East 34th Street in New York City. Warsaw & Co., Inc, which was wholly owned by J.J. Warsaw, owned all the preferred stock and 7,549 shares of common stock of Studios. Approximately 2,000 shares of Studio's common stock were owned by ten employees of Studios. For a number of years Studios incurred significant net operating losses, due in part to unfavorable terms of the 34th Street lease. Shawn, one of the employee-shareholders, thought the corporation could be made profitable if the corporation could rid itself of the burden of the lease. Shawn and the nine other employee-shareholders of Studios formed Warsaw Photographic Studios, Inc. (Photographic) which issued 100 shares of common stock to each of the ten shareholders. At the same time, Studios transferred its operating assets (but not the adverse lease) to Photographic for $21,000. The employee-shareholders surrendered their stock in Studios. No Photographic stock was transferred to Studios or to Warsaw & Co. Photographic took the position that the transaction constituted a (D) reorganization, claiming depreciation deductions on the operating assets based on a transferred basis from Studios and utilizing Studios' net operating loss carryover deductions.]

OPINION

I. D Reorganization

Ordinarily, a corporation is a separate entity for Federal income tax purposes; its tax attributes are not combined with those of its shareholders or other corporations. One of the major exceptions to this normal rule is part of the complex of provisions relating to corporate reorganizations, in particular that part of the complex that allows a corporation to use for income tax purposes certain parts of the income tax history of another corporation.

Corporate reorganizations, as defined in one or another of the subparagraphs of section 368(a)(1), qualify for special treatment for Federal income tax purposes under certain rules. The dispute in the instant case is as to whether petitioner is entitled to the special treatment provided under two of these rules. One of these rules gives a transferee corporation a carryover basis (subject to certain adjustments) in the assets acquired from the transferor corporation. Sec. 362(b). The other of these rules allows the transferee corporation to "succeed to and take into account" certain tax attributes of the transferor, including net operating loss carryovers (the tax attribute in issue in the instant case). Secs. 381(a), 381(c).

Of the various definitions of corporate reorganization, the parties have apparently limited the controversy to whether the transaction qualifies as nondivisive D reorganization (sec. 368(a)(1)(D)); we have chosen in the instant case to adhere to the parties' view of the parameters of the controversy. See Estate of Fusz v. Commissioner, 46 T.C. 214, 215 n. 2 (1966).

In order to qualify as a nondivisive D reorganization (and thus, permit petitioner to (1) use Studios' bases for calculating depreciation, and (2) under sections 368(a)(1)(D) and 354, deduct Studios' net operating losses), the transaction in the instant case must satisfy a series of statutory requirements and also a series of judicial requirements.

Respondent contends that the transfer from Studios to petitioner does not qualify as a nondivisive D reorganization because it does not satisfy certain of the statutory and judicial requirements. Instead, respondent contends, the transfer of assets from Studios to petitioner is a sale. Respondent maintains that the transaction does not satisfy the statutory requirement that stock of the transferee corporation (i.e., petitioner) be issued and distributed in the purported reorganization. * * *

Petitioner contends that the transaction between Studios and petitioner qualifies as a nondivisive D reorganization because it satisfies all the statutory and judicial requirements. In particular, petitioner contends that the 100 shares were given as consideration for Studios' assets and that the 100 shares were worth at least $42,727, far more than the $21,000 of cash and other property transferred by petitioner to Studios. Petitioner further contends that the fact that the 100 shares were issued directly to the 10 shareholders, rather than first to Studios and then distributed from Studios to the 10 shareholders, does not mean that petitioner's stock was not distributed within the meaning of section 354(b)(1)(B). * * *

We agree with respondent that the transaction is not a D reorganization because of the failure to satisfy the statutory requirement that petitioner's stock be transferred to Studios and distributed in a transaction which qualifies under sec. 354.

In order for a transaction to be a D reorganization, the transaction must be one "which qualifies under section 354." (Sec. 368(a)(1)(D); Baan v. Commissioner, 51 T.C. 1032, 1040 (1969), affd. sub nom. Gordon v. Commissioner, 424 F.2d 378 (2d Cir.1970), affd. 450 F.2d 198 (9th Cir.1971).) In order for petitioner to succeed to Studios' net operating losses under a D reorganization, Studios must have received stock of petitioner, and Studios must have distributed the stock it thus received (secs. 354(a)(1) and 354(b)(1)(B)). The July 2, 1973, agreement between petitioner and Studios provides * * * that, as part of the consideration flowing from petitioner to Studios, "The Buyer is hereby issuing 10 shares of Common Stock, $.05 par value, of the Buyer to each of the shareholders of the Seller other than Warsaw & Co., Inc. who are the only shareholders of the Buyer." There was not literally a transfer of petitioner's stock from petitioner to Studios and a distribution of this stock by Studios to Studios' shareholders. Accordingly, we conclude that the statute's formal requirements have not been met in this regard.

It is true that "we have repeatedly held that, when the stock ownership of transferor and transferee is identical, the actual distribution would be a mere formality and the statute [sec. 368(a)(1)(D)] may be satisfied without it. See American Manufacturing Co. v. Commissioner, 55 T.C. 204, 221 (1970); James Armour, Inc. v. Commissioner, 43 T.C. 295, 307 (1964)." Atlas Tool Co. v. Commissioner, 70 T.C. 86, 97 (1978), affd. 614 F.2d 860, 865 (3d Cir.1980). See also Rose v. United States, 640 F.2d 1030, 1034 (9th Cir.1981). However, in the instant case, the stock ownerships of petitioner and Studios were not identical.

Warsaw & Co., Inc., which owned about 80 percent of Studios' common stock and all of Studios' preferred stock, was not a shareholder in petitioner. The 10 shareholders, each holding 10 percent of petitioner's shares, had differing holdings in Studios. These holdings ranged from Zad's 375 shares down to Sinn's 92 shares. Indeed, apart from Shawn and Neil (each holding 250 shares), none of the 10 shareholders held the same number of Studios' shares as any of the others among the 10 shareholders * * * even though all were equal shareholders in petitioner.

Thus, the instant case does not qualify for the one exception that the courts have created regarding the stock transfer and distribution rule. Compliance with this rule is essential for the net operating loss carryover benefit sought by petitioner (secs. 381(a)(2) and 354(b)(1)(B)) and the carryover basis benefit sought by petitioner (secs. 362(b), 368(a)(1)(D), 354(b)(1)(B)). Accordingly, we conclude that petitioner is entitled to use neither of the tax benefits it seeks to carry over from Studios.

On brief, petitioner makes the following contention regarding the stock transfer and distribution requirement:

> Code section 354(b)(1)(B) requires that all properties of the transferor corporation must be distributed in pursuance of the plan of reorganization. This provision is satisfied whenever, pursuant to the plan of reorganization, the shareholders of the transferor receive shares of the transferee sufficient to satisfy the control requirements of Code section 368(a)(1)(D). A direct issuance of shares of the transferee corporation to shareholders of the transferor corporation will suffice. An actual exchange of the transferor corporation's assets for shares of the transferee corporation, followed by a distribution of those shares to the transferor corporation's shareholders is not required. See Commissioner v. Morgan, 288 F.2d 676 (3d Cir.[1961]), cert. denied, 368 U.S. 836 (1961). Accord, South Texas Rice Warehouse Co., 43 T.C. 540 (1965), aff'd sub nom., Davant v. Commissioner, 366 F.2d 874 (5th Cir.1966). * * *.
>
> * * *. Where as in the case at bar the acquiring corporation issues stock directly to the shareholders of the transferor corporation in consideration of the assets received from the transferor corporation, the transfer is treated as if the shares were first issued to the transferor corporation and then distributed in redemption of the outstanding shares of the transferor corporation.

We believe petitioner's reliance on the cases it cites is misplaced.

In Commissioner v. Morgan, 288 F.2d 676 (3d Cir.1961), the Court of Appeals for the Third Circuit reversed this Court (Morgan v. Commissioner, 33 T.C. 30 (1959)), holding that an actual transfer and distribution of the transferee corporation's stock "would have been a meaningless gesture" in that case, since one individual held all the stock in both the transferor corporation and the transferee corporation (288 F.2d at 680, see 33 T.C. at 32). In South Texas Rice Warehouse Co.

v. Commissioner, 43 T.C. 540 (1965), we rejected the taxpayers' contention that a transaction did not qualify as a D reorganization because no stock was transferred and distributed. In that case, each of the 14 individuals who were the shareholders held the same percentage of the transferor corporation's stock as he or she held in the transferee corporation. (43 T.C. at 544.) The Court of Appeals for the Fifth Circuit noted the identity of ownership, followed the rationale of *Morgan,* and affirmed on this point. (Davant v. Commissioner, 366 F.2d 874, 886–887.) * * *

All of these authorities on which petitioner relies are distinguishable from the instant case in that the transferors and transferees in those instances had identical ownership, while in the instant case, the ownership interests in petitioner and Studios differed widely. Further, in each of these cases in which a court has held that the requirement of an actual stock transfer and distribution may be ignored, it was respondent who urged on the court that the realities of the situation belied the form chosen by the taxpayer. In those situations where the courts have departed from the literal language of the statute, it was to counter a perceived abuse by the taxpayer, these courts having concluded that the taxpayer should not be permitted to shape the form of the transaction so as to secure an unwarranted benefit. See B. Bittker & J. Eustice, Federal Income Taxation of Corporations and Shareholders, par. 14.54, at 14–159—14–160. We have not found, and petitioner has not cited us to, any case in this area in which the court has acceded to a taxpayer's urging that the taxpayer be permitted to obtain a D reorganization tax benefit even though the form of the transaction which the taxpayer shaped did not meet the literal requirements of the statute.

Petitioner contends that the "transaction in form and in substance qualified as a reorganization described in Code section 368(a)(1)(D)". * * *

When we examine the substance of what was done, we conclude that it points toward "sale" at least as much as toward "reorganization". Ten people put up an aggregate of $100,000 to acquire and bankroll a going business. The business had suffered substantial losses. The 10 shareholders trimmed the work force and avoided the burdens of an unfavorable lease, and apparently succeeded in reviving the business. The 10 shareholders had owned about 20 percent of the old corporation's common stock and none of its preferred. If they had purchased the remaining common stock or a controlling interest, then (as petitioner notes on brief) the corporation's tax characteristics would not be affected by the substance of the change in ownership and control. Apparently, for a legitimate business reason (escaping from the burdens of the 34th Street lease), the 10 shareholders specifically turned down an opportunity to buy the old corporation, thus turning down the simple route toward retention of the old corporation's tax attributes.

If the 10 shareholders (or petitioner, their new corporation) had merely purchased Studios' assets, then the transaction would be a sale, the normal tax rules would apply (i.e., petitioner would not be entitled to use Studios' tax attributes) even though petitioner carried on the business that Studios had carried on and did so with essentially the same work force at the "same old stand."

What, in these circumstances, is the matter of substance that distinguishes the transaction from a sale? Petitioner contends that the issuance of the 100 shares is an element of substance that (1) enables the transaction to satisfy the statutory requirement of stock distribution, (2) enables the transaction to satisfy the judicial requirement that its stock be a substantial part of the consideration given by it * * *. In connection with the latter [point], petitioner contends that the 100 shares were worth $349,000.

After examining the transaction with care in light of petitioner's contentions, we note the following:

Firstly, the 100 shares effected no change, not even a subtle one, in the positions of the 10 shareholders. Each of the 10 shareholders merely had one extra piece of paper. See Eisner v. Macomber, 252 U.S. 189 (1920). None involved in the transaction—not petitioner, Studios, the 10 shareholders, Warsaw & Co., Inc., or J.J. Warsaw—were any richer or any poorer on account of the issuance of the 100 shares, than they would have been if no shares were issued or if 1 million shares were issued.

Secondly, care was taken to be sure that the 100 shares were not held by Studios at any time. This element is of some significance because Studios made a general assignment for the benefit of creditors only 3 weeks after the transaction in dispute, and the assignee was not able to find assets to make any payments to the creditors.

Thirdly, although the 100 shares were supposed to be issued to the 10 shareholders in their capacities as Studios' shareholders, they were issued * * * in proportion to the 10 shareholders' ownership of petitioner and not in proportion to the 10 shareholders' ownership of Studios.

Fourthly, petitioner contends that the 100 shares were worth a total of $349,000, while at the same time the initial 1,000 shares were worth a total of $100,000. The contentions, as to identical shares issued virtually simultaneously, are manifestly inconsistent. We are not given any hint as to why the 100 shares would be worth $3,490, each, while the 1,000 shares were worth $100, each.

On answering brief, petitioner tells us that "Taxation is a practical art; labels will not replace or substitute for judgment as to the roles played by the parties and whether or not those roles were acted out in such a way as to effect a reorganization described by the Internal Revenue Code". We agree. We conclude that, as a practical matter, the appearance of the 100 shares in the transaction provides only a smell of reorganization. We will not speculate as to why the July 2,

1973, agreement provided for the issuance of the 100 shares in such a manner that their issuance satisfies neither the form nor the substance of section 368(a)(1)(D). We conclude that the 100 shares did not constitute any part of petitioner's consideration for the assets, tangible or intangible, that petitioner received from Studios. * * *

To sum up: petitioner is not entitled to use Studios' bases for depreciation of assets and is not entitled to deduct Studios' net operating losses unless petitioner shows that it has complied with the requirements of a D reorganization. Baan v. Commissioner, supra. See also Corn Products Co. v. Commissioner, 350 U.S. 46, 52 (1955), where, in another context, the Supreme Court stated that "an exception from the normal tax requirements of the Internal Revenue Code, * * * must be narrowly applied and its exclusions interpreted broadly." Petitioner acknowledges that the transaction failed to comply with one of the requirements of the statute, but seeks to excuse this failure by citing certain authorities. Those authorities rest on circumstances (identical ownership of the corporations that are parties to the reorganization) which are materially different from the facts of the instant case. Atlas Tool Co. v. Commissioner, supra; Baan v. Commissioner, 51 T.C. at 1038–1039. There was no substance to the issuance of the 100 shares. Petitioner cannot escape from the failure of the transaction to comply with the statute. Petitioner is not entitled to the tax benefits of another corporation's bases and net operating losses.

We hold for respondent on this issue.

ILLUSTRATIVE MATERIAL

A. DEFINITIONAL ASPECTS

The transfer of some or all of a corporation's assets to a newly created or existing subsidiary—as where X Corporation transfers some of its assets to new or existing Y Corporation—is a type (D) reorganization if following the transfer X Corporation, distributes a controlling amount of the stock of Y Corporation to its shareholders in a distribution which meets the requirements of sections 354, 355, or, if boot also is distributed, 356. A type (D) reorganization usually is the first step in dividing a corporate enterprise into two separate corporations by a distribution of stock of the subsidiary to the parent's shareholders in a transaction subject to section 355. See Chapter 19. However, subsection (D) also can describe a single corporation reorganization. In this case, the stock distribution must qualify under section 354. That section requires that (1) X Corporation transfer *substantially all* of its assets to Y Corporation and (2) all of the properties of X Corporation, including the stock of Y Corporation, be distributed to the X Corporation shareholders. The purpose of the "substantially all the assets" requirement in section 354(b) is to insure that the provisions of section 355 be met in any transaction which potentially would involve the division of a corporation. Rev. Rul. 74–545, 1974–2 Cum.Bull. 122, held that the distribution requirement means that the transferor corporation must liquidate. As a result of these two overlapping rules, a nondivisive (D) reorganization generally occurs when X Corporation transmutes itself into Y Corporation through an asset transfer and a liquidation. A nondivisive (D) reorganization also may occur, however, when X Corporation transfers all of its assets Y Corporation, which is owned by the same shareholders as owned X Corporation.

The first step of a nondivisive (D) reorganization—the asset transfer—usually overlaps with a section 351 incorporation transfer, which, like a reorganization, is a nonrecognition event. The second step, overlaps with the liquidation provisions, which require corporate and shareholder gain or loss recognition. However, when the liquidation is pursuant to a plan of reorganization, sections 354 and 356 provide nonrecognition to the shareholders, except to the extent of boot. Section 361 displaces section 336 to provide nonrecognition to the liquidating corporation, X Corporation in the proceedings example, with respect to the distribution of the Y Corporation stock. However, section 361(c) requires that the liquidating corporation recognize gain (but not loss) with respect to all other property distributed in the liquidation.

A transaction meeting the definition of a type (D) reorganization also may meet the definition of a type (C) reorganization, discussed supra, page 844. Suppose that X Corporation owns all of the stock of both Y Corporation and Z Corporation. If Z Corporation transfers all of its assets to Y Corporation for Y stock and then liquidates, the transaction meets the definitions of both a (C) and a (D) reorganization. In such a case, section 368(a)(2)(A) requires that the transaction be treated as a type (D) reorganization. As discussed in *Warsaw Photographic,* the asset transfer from Z to Y would be classified as a (D) reorganization even if no additional Y Corporation stock were issued since X would own 100 percent of Y in any event. As a consequence, Y succeeds to Z's tax attributes under section 381. An overlap between a type (D) and type (F) reorganization results in classification as a type (F). Rev.Rul. 57–276, 1957–1 Cum.Bull. 126; Rev.Rul. 87–27, 1987–1 Cum.Bull. 134 (reincorporation of domestic corporation in foreign country which is both a type (F) and type (D) reorganization is treated as type (F)); Rev.Rul. 87–66, 1987–2 Cum.Bull. 168 (reincorporation of foreign corporation in U.S. which is both a type (D) and a type (F) reorganization treated as a type (F)).

Suppose that X Corporation owns 50 percent of the stock of Y Corporation and 100 percent of the stock of Z Corporation, and that Z Corporation owns the other 50 percent of the stock of Y Corporation. If Y Corporation transfers all of its assets to Z Corporation in exchange for Z stock, which is distributed equally to X Corporation and Z Corporation in liquidation of Y, is the transaction a (D) reorganization or does the *Bausch & Lomb* doctrine, which applies in type (C) reorganizations, see supra, page 849, apply to treat Z as having received 50 percent of Y's assets in liquidation rather than in exchange for its stock, thereby violating the "substantially all" requirement. Rev.Rul. 85–107, 1985–2 Cum.Bull. 121, holds that the *Bausch & Lomb* doctrine will not be applied to a reorganization which otherwise qualifies as a type (D) reorganization because there is no "solely for voting stock" requirement applicable to type (D) reorganizations.

B. LIQUIDATION–REINCORPORATION TRANSACTIONS AND THE (D) REORGANIZATION PROVISIONS

1. *Background*

Prior to 1986, the nondivisive (D) reorganization provisions were used principally by the Commissioner as a weapon to attack the liquidation-reincorporation transactions described supra, page 887, in connection with (F) reorganizations. Indeed, the definition of "control" for purposes of (D) reorganizations subject to section 354 was reduced from the 80 percent benchmark in section 368(c) to 50 percent (section 368(a)(2)(H)) to make it easier to fit liquidation-reincorporation transactions under the (D) reorganization definition when there was a change in the shareholder ownership between the "new" and "old" corporations. See S.Rep. No. 98–169, 98th Cong., 2d Sess. 207–209 (1984)

In general, the courts were quite liberal in interpreting the (D) reorganization requirements in order to find a reorganization with an accompanying dividend to block the tax avoidance possibilities in the liquidation-reincorporation situations. In testing whether "substantially all" the assets have been transferred, as is required by section 354(b)(1)(A), the focus has been on the operating assets of the corporation. See, e.g., Smothers v. United States, 642 F.2d 894 (5th Cir.1981):

"To maintain the integrity of the dividend provisions of the Code, 'substantially all assets' in this context must be interpreted as an inartistic way of expressing the concept of 'transfer of a continuing business.' * * * Properly interpreted, therefore, the assets looked to when making the 'substantially all assets' determination should be all the assets, and only the assets, necessary to operate the corporate business—whether or not those assets would appear on a corporate balance sheet. * * * Inclusion of assets unnecessary to the operation of the business in the 'substantially all assets' assessment would open the way for the shareholders of any enterprise to turn dividends into capital gains at will. * * * [E]xclusion of assets not shown on a balance sheet * * * would offer an unjustified windfall to owners of service businesses conducted in the corporate form. The most important assets of such a business may be its reputation and the availability of skilled management and trained employees * * *. [F]or example a sole legal practitioner who owns nothing but a desk and chair could incorporate himself, accumulate earnings, and then set up a new corporation and liquidate the old at capital gain rates—as long as he is careful to buy a new desk and chair for the new corporation, rather than transferring the old." (901)

2. *Control and Continuity of Interest*

Even in the liquidating-reincorporation cases, the requirement that the transferor corporation or its shareholders be in control of the transferee corporation after the transfer has been strictly construed. For example, in Breech v. United States, 439 F.2d 409 (9th Cir.1971), a corporation sold all of its assets to a second corporation the stock of which was owned 20 percent by one of its shareholders and 80 percent by a third corporation in which its shareholders had a 75 percent interest. The court refused to ignore the separate existence of the third corporation or to apply the attribution rules in section 318 (which by their terms did not then apply) to find control of the transferee in the shareholders of the transferor. Hence a (D) reorganization was not present. Similar results were reached in Commissioner v. Berghash 361 F.2d 257 (2d Cir.1966), and Turner Advertising, Inc. v. Commissioner. 25 T.C.M. 532 (1966) (where the continuing direct stock ownership was less than the amount required for control). However, in Ringwalt v. United States, 549 F.2d 89 (8th Cir.1977), the court found that the "control" test was satisfied where the corporation was controlled before the reorganization by a ten-year trust for the benefit of the taxpayer's children with the taxpayer as trustee, and after the liquidation-reincorporation transaction by the taxpayer directly. Section 368(a)(2)(H) now incorporates the attribution rules of section 318 for purposes of determining controlling stock ownership.

Can the "functionally unrelated" concept be applied to "disaggregate" a transaction in order to create a reorganization provision in which the continuity of interest requirement has been met? Suppose for example that X Corporation transfers its operating assets to Y Corporation, which is controlled by a group of X Corporation shareholders who own less than 50 percent of the X stock, and Y Corporation then liquidates, distributing the Y Corporation stock to its shareholders who control Y and liquid assets to its shareholders who do not own Y stock. Could this be treated as a (D) reorganization and a separate redemption of the stock owned by the shareholders who received the liquid assets. A type (D) (or an (F)) reorganization could be present since, under this analysis, there would be no change in the continuing shareholders of the corporation.

As in the (F) reorganization area, the Commissioner attempted to fit liquidation-reorganization transactions into the (D) reorganization definition by considering pieces of the transaction which might defeat reorganization treatment as "functionally unrelated" to the reorganization. Reef Corporation v. Commissioner, 368 F.2d 125 (5th Cir.1966), discussed supra, page 888, upheld the Commissioner in finding a (D) reorganization (as well as an (F) reorganization) coupled with a redemption in a series of transactions having substantially the same result as described above, where the continuing shareholders held only 48 percent of the old corporation's stock. Other cases hesitated to separate related transactions in order to find a reorganization. Thus, in Commissioner v. Berghash, 361 F.2d 257 (2d Cir.1966), the sole shareholder of a corporation agreed to transfer to a corporate employee a 50 percent ownership in the business which the employee demanded as a condition of his continued employment. The employee was willing to invest $25,000 in the business but, because of the size of the business, this would not have entitled him to a 50 percent interest. Accordingly, the corporation was liquidated and its operating assets transferred to a new corporation in exchange for notes and 50 percent of the stock. The additional 50 percent of the stock was issued to the employee for cash. The old shareholder treated the transaction as a liquidation entitled to capital gain treatment under section 331. The Government argued that the sale of stock to the employee should be disregarded as an "unrelated step" and thus the transaction would fit the pattern of a (D) or an (F) reorganization and an accompanying boot distribution under section 356. The Tax Court, however, finding the sale a "critical fact" in evaluating the transaction, refused to find a reorganization and a boot distribution, and the Court of Appeals affirmed.

In Estate of Lammerts v. Commissioner, 54 T.C. 420 (1970), 90 percent of the stock of the corporation was held by the estate of the deceased president and 10 percent by his son. The son and widow were the principal beneficiaries of the estate. Under the terms of the will, the executor was directed to dissolve the corporation and distribute its assets. Subsequently, the son and the widow reincorporated the business with the son receiving 100 percent of the common stock and the widow a new class of preferred stock. The Tax Court refused to treat the transaction as involving a "functionally unrelated" redemption and an (F) reorganization with a boot distribution or as a section 301 dividend distribution. The taxpayers were entitled to liquidation treatment under section 331. On appeal, however, the taxpayers conceded that the transaction constituted a (D) reorganization and the boot distribution was taxable as ordinary income to the extent of gain. 456 F.2d 681 (2d Cir.1972).

CHAPTER 19

CORPORATE DIVISIONS: SPIN-OFFS, SPLIT-OFFS, AND SPLIT-UPS

SECTION 1. CORPORATE DIVISIONS: STATUTORY PATTERN

A. GENERAL RULES

INTERNAL REVENUE CODE: Sections 355; 368(a)(1)(D), (2)(A); 354(b); 356(b); 358; 312(h).

REGULATIONS: Sections 1.355–1 to –4.

In a divisive type (D) reorganization the corporation divides by transferring some assets to a subsidiary corporation and distributing the subsidiary's stock to its stockholders. To qualify as a reorganization under section 368(a)(1)(D), the distribution to stockholders must comply with section 355, the pivotal section in the treatment of transactions seeking to accomplish a corporate division. Under section 355, X Corporation conducting businesses A and B may divide by placing business B in a new Y Corporation and then distributing the stock of Y Corporation to the shareholders of X Corporation. The same division may be undertaken by a corporation operating a single business which is capable of division into two separate independently functioning trades or businesses. X Corporation divides its single business into two parts transferring assets to Y Corporation which, following the transaction, is also actively engaged in the conduct of a trade or business. X Corporation then distributes all of the stock of Y Corporation to the X Corporation stockholders.

Not all divisive transactions covered by section 355 involve type (D) reorganizations. An existing patent-subsidiary group may divide with a distribution of the stock of subsidiary's stock to stockholders of the parent. For example, X Corporation conducting business A owns the stock of Y Corporation which conducts business B. X Corporation divides by distributing the stock of Y Corporation to the stockholders of X Corporation. The transaction does not involve a reorganization of either X or Y. Nonetheless, section 355(a)(1) may provide nonrecognition treatment to both the distributing corporation and the recipient stockholders with respect to the distribution of Y stock provided the requirements of that section are met.

A divisive transaction under section 355 may take one of three forms. A "spin-off" occurs when, as in the examples above, a corporation transfers assets to a subsidiary and distributes the stock of the subsidiary pro rata to its stockholders (a type (D) reorganization), or distributes the stock of an existing subsidiary to its stockholders pro rata. In a "split-off", the distributing corporation distributes the stock of the subsidiary to its stockholders in exchange for some of the stock of the distributing corporation. A split-off distribution which results in a pro rata exchange of stock among the stockholders of the distributing corporation is functionally equivalent to a "spin-off". A non-pro rata split-off, however, results in a change in proportionate ownership of both businesses. The third transaction is a "split-up" in which the original corporation transfers a separate trade or business to each of two or more subsidiaries. The distributing corporation then transfers the stock of the subsidiaries to its stockholders and liquidates. In a split-up, each separate trade or business, still in corporate solution, may be distributed to different stockholders. Thus, X Corporation which owns businesses A and B transfers business A to a new Y Corporation and business B to a new Z Corporation. X Corporation is liquidated distributing the stock of Y to one group of X stockholders, and the stock of Z to the other group of X stockholders.

The essence of a section 355 division is the separate ownership at the stockholder level of the corporate businesses. In many cases the businesses already were divided or separated prior to the distribution to the stockholders. In the first example above, they could have been conducted as separate branches or divisions of X Corporation; in the third example they were conducted separately through parent-subsidiary operation. Thus, X Corporation in the first example could in effect further separate the businesses by placing business B in new Y Corporation and operating it as a subsidiary. If the desired separation is a degree of insulation of one business from the other, it will have been accomplished through parent-subsidiary operation. But section 355 looks to a different type of separation, that of separate ownership at the stockholder level.

As noted, the separate ownership at the stockholder level may be pro rata or non-pro rata. Thus, section 355 applies to very different divisions of corporate ownership. Suppose X Corporation is owned by individuals R and S. If X Corporation distributes the stock of its subsidiary Y Corporation pro rata, each individual stockholder now owns what the stockholder owned before—a one-half interest in each business—but the stockholders have separated the form of ownership. Corporations which are each owned pro rata by the same individual stockholders or group are called "brother-sister corporations," to distinguish such common ownership at the stockholder level from the "parent-subsidiary corporations" where the common ownership of the activities is at the corporate level through the stockholder ownership possessed by the single corporate parent. If the distribution of the Y Corporation stock is completely non-pro rata, as where stockholder S surrenders his stock in X Corporation for all the stock of Y Corporation, then a complete division of ownership has been accomplished at the stockholder level in addition to the division at the corporate level. The corporations are no longer related in any way, assuming there is no family or other special relationship between R and S.

Prior to the 1986 Act, the pro rata corporate division into brother-sister corporations presented the potential for a bail-out of corporate profits taxable to the stockholders at capital gains rates. Thus, in the above transfer, if the stockholders of X and Y Corporations sold the stock of Y Corporation, they ended up with stock of X Corporation and cash taxed at capital gain rates. This situation, it will be recalled, is also the end result of a "preferred stock bail-out" or a "security bail-out." Section 355 imposed limitations intended to insure that the tax-free corporate division privilege was not abused. Of course, after the 1986 Act, with individual capital gain rates being the same as ordinary income rates, the incentive to "bail-out" earnings and profits by means of a corporate division is seldom present.

On the other hand, after the 1986 Act, the limitations of section 355 may play a role in ensuring that a corporate division is not used to avoid corporate level tax on appreciated assets which would be otherwise recognized under section 311 or 336. Whether the present limitations are appropriate to achieve that objective is a matter that needs further attention by tax policymakers.

After 1986, therefore, the tax stakes for the distributee shareholders in a corporate division are whether they receive a current taxable dividend equal to the fair market value of the stock received or a distribution of stock on which tax is deferred until a subsequent sale. While the rate of tax may be the same in both cases, deferral of tax can be a great financial benefit. In addition, the gain realized on the sale would be reduced by some portion of original basis in the stock of the distributing corporation. With respect to the distributing corporation, the tax issue is whether the spun-off stock can be distributed without recognition of gain by the corporation under section 311.

The statutory pattern for qualifying a division as a tax-free transaction is as follows:

With respect to section 355:

a. To prevent the isolation of cash or passive investments into a separate corporation with its potential for ready sale, each corporation after the division must be operating an active trade or business. In addition, to prevent either the distributing corporation or the controlled corporation from utilizing accumulated earnings to acquire the active business, the active businesses must have a prior five-year history and must not have been acquired in a taxable transaction within the five year period. Section 355(a)(1)(C), (b).

b. The transaction must not be used principally as a *device* for the distribution of the earnings and profits of either of the corporations. Section 355(a)(1)(B).

c. All of the stock and securities which the parent owns in the controlled corporation being separated must be distributed to the stockholders (or at least 80 percent of the stock of the controlled corporation if retention of the balance of stock and securities can be justified). Section 355(a)(1)(D). This requirement was originally designed to differentiate between genuine separations and incidental distributions of a controlled corporation's stock which took the place of current cash dividends. If, in addition, boot is distributed, section 356 applies and the distribution may be taxed as a dividend to the extent of the boot under the principles discussed supra, page 800. The distributing corporation also must recognize gain with respect to appreciated property distributed as boot. Section 355(c).

d. A "security bail-out" is not permitted as part of a corporate division, and rules similar to section 354(a)(2), supra, page 810, are utilized to treat the excess principal amount of securities received over the principal amount of securities surrendered as boot. Sections 355(a)(3), (a)(4)(A); 356(b), (d)(2)(C).

With respect to the reorganization provisions generally:

A reorganization transaction which has the potential of a corporate division, must, if reorganization status is desired, either:

a. comply with the requirement of section 354(b)(1)(A) that substantially all of the assets of the distributing corporation be transferred to the controlled corporation so as to eliminate the effect of a division (see supra, page 897), or

b. be channeled into section 355 so that the resulting division is tested by the rules of that section.

Thus, the attempt is to provide unified treatment of corporate divisions regardless of the form of the transaction.

This plan explains the addition of the last clause in section 368(a)(1)(D), which requires that a corporation forming a controlled subsidiary must, to qualify as a reorganization, distribute the stock of the subsidiary to its stockholders in a transaction qualifying under sections 354 or 355 (and 356). The reference to section 355 thus brings into play the tests for qualifying corporate divisions. The reference to section 354 brings into play section 354(b), which makes section 354 inapplicable unless substantially all the assets are transferred and the transferor liquidates. As a result, the transfer cannot create the result of a corporate division. If the requirements of section 354(b) are not met, as where only some of the assets are transferred or where the transferor does not liquidate, then a corporate division is present since the stockholders will now own stock in the old and the new corporations. Section 354(a) is not applicable, and the exchange with the stockholders is thrown into section 355 to see if it meets the corporate division tests.

Further, section 368(a)(2)(A), discussed supra, page 851, is intended to prevent a transaction which otherwise would fit the definition of both a type (C) and a type (D) reorganization, as the transfer of substantially all the assets to a controlled subsidiary, from escaping the above requirements regarding corporate divisions by being treated as a type (C) reorganization. This overlap possibility is intended to be eliminated by exclusively regarding the transaction as a type (D) reorganization, so that the mechanisms described above to channel the reorganization into section 355 are operative.[1] If a corporation desires to transfer some of its assets in a tax-free transaction to a controlled subsidiary and retain the stock of the latter, it therefore cannot proceed under the reorganization provisions. But it can proceed under section 351, which does not require distribution of the transferee's stock to the stockholders of the transferor.

The "device" restriction of section 355 is aimed solely at a bail-out of corporate earnings at capital gains rates rather than as a dividend. In a tax world which lacks preferential treatment for capital gains, the potential for earnings bail-out is generally not present and the device restriction focused on this problem seems outmoded. However, a corporate division also

1. Technically, the statute speaks in terms of transactions "described in" sections 368(a)(1)(C) and (D). Rev.Rul. 74–545, 1974–2 Cum.Bull. 122, held that for a reorganization to be "described in" section 368(a)(1)(D) it did not have to "qualify" as a (D) reorganization for the (D) provisions to control. In that situation, the corporation transferred substantially all of its assets to a new subsidiary in exchange for voting stock of the subsidiary and distributed the subsidiary's stock to its stockholder. The transferor corporation however, remained in existence. The transaction otherwise would have qualified as a (C) reorganization (under the statute as it was then written), but was held to be "described in" section 368(a)(1)(D) despite the fact that the distribution did not meet the requirements of section 354(b) or 355. Thus, the transaction was prevented from qualifying as a reorganization and was treated as a section 351 transfer followed by a dividend to the stockholder.

permits the transfer of stock to the distributee stockholders without recognition of gain by either the distributing corporation or the stockholders. The business purpose test and continuity of interest requirements inherent in the "device" clause may serve to identify corporate reorganizations which are appropriate transactions for this nonrecognition treatment. In this connection, compare the direct distribution of a corporate trade or business in partial liquidation under sections 302(b)(4) and (e), discussed supra, page 579. These sections require recognition of gain by the corporation on distribution of appreciated assets under section 311 and a second level recognition by the distributee stockholders of capital gain on the distribution. However, an economically similar transaction which meets the requirements of section 355 can be completed on a tax free basis. The requirements of section 355 were developed in the context of preventing a "bail-out" of earnings and profits and they fit somewhat awkwardly in a post-*General Utilities* world with no capital gains preference. As is the case with acquisitive reorganizations, nonrecognition and carryover basis are justified, if at all, by the stockholder's continued ownership of assets in corporate solution.

ILLUSTRATIVE MATERIAL

A. SCOPE OF SECTION 355

Under Regulations, section 1.355–4, section 355 does not apply to transactions which are in effect exchanges of interests between stockholders of brother-sister corporations. Thus, assume that A and B each own 50 percent of the stock of X and Y Corporations. A and B transfer their stock to a newly created Z Corporation. Z Corporation then distributes the stock of X Corporation to A and the stock of Y Corporation to B. As a result, A owns all the stock of X Corporation and B owns all the stock of Y Corporation. In effect, A and B have made a taxable exchange of their 50 percent interests in X and Y Corporations and the transaction will not qualify under section 355.

In Portland Mfg. Co. v. Commissioner, 56 T.C. 58 (1971), aff'd by order, 75–1 U.S.T.C. ¶ 9449 (9th Cir.1975), two corporations each owned 50 percent of a third corporation and 50 percent of a joint venture. Because of disagreements between the two corporations, the mechanics of a tax-free split-off under section 355 were implemented at the conclusion of which one corporation owned all the stock of the third corporation. The court upheld the Commissioner's treatment of the transaction as a taxable exchange. A similar result was reached in Atlee v. Commissioner, 67 T.C. 395 (1976), where the taxpayers sought to avoid having the transaction characterized as a taxable exchange by making pre-spin-off contributions to capital.

B. THE "CONTROL" REQUIREMENT OF SECTION 355(a)(1)(A)

Immediately prior to the distribution, the distributing corporation must have "control" (as defined in section 368(c)) of the corporation whose stock is being distributed. Section 355(a)(1)(A). Transfers solely for the purpose of giving the distributing corporation the requisite 80 percent stock ownership under section 368(c) may be disregarded. See Rev.Rul. 63–260, 1963–2 Cum.Bull. 147, where the sole stockholder of a corporation, which owned 70 percent of the stock of a subsidiary, transferred an additional 10 percent of the subsidiary stock to the parent corporation which then spun off the subsidiary shares to the sole stockholder. The Ruling held that section 355 was inapplicable because the distributing corporation did not have "control" except in a "transitory and illusory sense."

But where there is greater economic reality to the transaction in which the distributing corporation obtains control, then section 355 treatment is allowed. Rev.Rul. 69–407, 1969–2 Cum.Bull. 50, involved a situation in which X Corporation owned 70 percent of the stock of Y Corporation and A and B, two individuals, owned the remaining 30 percent. In an (E) recapitalization, two classes of voting stock were created, A and B receiving shares of one class and X Corporation receiving the other class. The relative values of the interests of X Corporation, A, and B did not change, but after the recapitalization, X Corporation held over 80 percent of the total voting power. X Corporation then distributed the Y Corporation stock to its stockholders. The Ruling held that the transaction constituted a valid (E) recapitalization followed by a section 355 distribution; the recapitalization resulted in a permanent realignment of voting control and hence Rev.Rul. 63–260 was distinguishable. See also Rev.Rul. 71–593, 1971–2 Cum.Bull. 181, where a transfer of additional assets to a 75 percent owned subsidiary in exchange for sufficient stock to give the parent 90 percent control, followed by a spin-off of the subsidiary's stock, was held to constitute a "meaningful exchange" and section 355 was applicable. In Rev.Rul. 70–18, 1970–1 Cum.Bull, 74, A, an individual, owned 100 percent of the stock of X and Y Corporations. In turn Y Corporation owned 60 percent of Z Corporation and X Corporation owned 40 percent of Z Corporation. X Corporation was required by a regulatory agency to divest itself of its Z stock. Y Corporation merged into X Corporation and X Corporation then distributed all of the Z stock to A. The Ruling held that there were substantial business reasons for the merger other than giving X Corporation control of Z Corporation for the purposes of a spin-off and the transaction qualified under section 355.

In Rev.Rul. 77–11, 1977–1 Cum.Bull. 93, A and B each owned 50 percent of the stock of X and Y Corporations, each of which was engaged in the construction business. The parties desired B to be the sole owner of a corporation engaged in the construction business. X and Y Corporations each distributed one-half of their assets to Z Corporation in exchange for Z stock, with X receiving 84 percent of the Z stock and Y 16 percent. X then distributed all the Z stock to B for B's X stock and Y distributed all its Z stock to B for B's Y stock. As a result, A owned all the stock of X and Y, and B owned all the stock of Z. The Ruling held: (1) The transfers by X and Y to Z followed by the distribution of the Z stock constituted a valid section 351 transaction and a good (D) reorganization; (2) the distribution of Z stock by X to B qualified under section 355 because before the distribution X had the requisite control over Z (the predecessor to Regulations, section 1.355–4, did not require treatment of the transaction as a taxable exchange because Z received operating assets and A remained as a stockholder in X and Y); and (3) the distribution of Z stock by Y to B did not qualify under section 355 because Y owned less than 80 percent of the Z stock before the distribution; this aspect of the transaction was treated as a redemption under section 302 which qualified for capital gain treatment under section 302(b)(3).

C. TREATMENT OF CORPORATE ATTRIBUTES

Section 381, which provides for the carryover of corporate attributes (including earnings and profits) in certain reorganizations and liquidations, discussed infra, Chapter 20, is not applicable to a corporate division under section 355. Section 312(h) provides that the earnings and profits of the two corporations must be allocated as provided in Regulations. In the case of a newly created controlled corporation, earnings are allocated between the distributing corporation and the controlled corporation in proportion to the fair market value of assets transferred to the controlled corporation. In other cases, earnings are allocated on the basis of the relative net bases of assets transferred to the controlled corporation and assets retained by the distributing corporation, or by some other appropriate method. Regulations, section 1.312–10.

The treatment of net operating loss carryovers in a section 355 transaction is discussed in Rev.Rul. 77–133, 1977–1 Cum.Bull. 96. In a split-off under section 355, M Corporation transferred assets constituting a business to S, a newly formed corporation, and distributed all of the S stock to one of M's two stockholders in exchange for all of stockholder's M stock. The Internal Revenue Service held that no part of M's net operating loss carryforward was transferred to S in the split-off but that M could continue to use its loss carryover. However, where the transaction is a split-up under section 355 in which the loss corporation transfers separate businesses to each of two new corporations and distributes the stock of each corporation to different stockholders in complete liquidation, Rev.Rul. 56–373, 1956–2 Cum.Bull. 217, holds that neither of the successor corporations can take advantage of the distributing corporation's unused net operating loss carryover. The Ruling concludes that because all of the assets of the distributing corporation are transferred to two corporations, the type (D) reorganization is not a transaction described by section 354(b)(1) and is therefore not subject to attribute carryover under section 381(a)(2). Thus the survival of net operating loss carryovers in a divisive type (D) reorganization depends upon whether the transaction is structured as a split-off or a split-up, even though the economic result of the two transactions may be identical.

The limitations on net operating loss carryforwards of section 382, discussed infra, Chapter 21, will apply to unused losses which survive a split-off as described in Rev.Rul. 77–133 if the continuing stockholders of the loss corporation increase their ownership interest by more than 50 percent.

D. REFERENCES

Whitman, Draining the Serbonian Bog: A New Approach to Corporate Separations under the 1954 Code, 81 Harv.L.Rev. 1194 (1968); Brosnan, Spin-Offs Before and After the Tax Reform Act, 38 Buff.L.Rev. 157 (1988).

B. "ACTIVE CONDUCT OF A TRADE OR BUSINESS" AND "DEVICE" LIMITATIONS

INTERNAL REVENUE CODE: Section 355(a)(1)(B) and (C), (b).

REGULATIONS: Section 1.355-2(d), -3.

RAFFERTY v. COMMISSIONER

United States Court of Appeals, First Circuit, 1971.
452 F.2d 767.

McENTEE, CIRCUIT JUDGE. Taxpayers, Joseph V. Rafferty and wife, appeal from a decision of the Tax Court, 55 T.C. 491, which held that a distribution to them of all the outstanding stock of a real estate holding corporation did not meet the requirements of § 355 of the Internal Revenue Code of 1954 and therefore was taxable as a dividend. Our opinion requires a construction of § 355 and the regulations thereunder.

The facts, some of which have been stipulated, are relatively simple. The taxpayers own all the outstanding shares of Rafferty Brown Steel Co., Inc. (hereinafter RBS), a Massachusetts corporation engaged in the processing and distribution of cold rolled sheet and strip steel in Longmeadow, Massachusetts. In May 1960, at the suggestion of his accountant, Rafferty organized Teragram Realty Co., Inc., also a Massachusetts corporation. In June of that year RBS transferred its Longmeadow real estate to Teragram in exchange for all of the latter's outstanding stock. Thereupon Teragram leased back this real estate to RBS for ten years at an annual rent of $42,000. In 1962 the taxpayers also organized Rafferty Brown Steel Co., Inc., of Connecticut (RBS Conn.), which corporation acquired the assets of Hawkridge Brothers, a general steel products warehouse in Waterbury, Connecticut. Since its inception the taxpayers have owned all of the outstanding stock in RBS Conn. From 1962 to 1965 Hawkridge leased its real estate in Waterbury to RBS Conn. In 1965 Teragram purchased some unimproved real estate in Waterbury and built a plant there.[2] In the same year it leased this plant to RBS Conn. for a term of fourteen years. Teragram has continued to own and lease the Waterbury real estate to RBS Conn. and the Longmeadow realty to RBS, which companies have continued up to the present time to operate their businesses at these locations.[3]

During the period from 1960 through 1965 Teragram derived all of its income from rent paid by RBS and RBS Conn. Its earned surplus increased from $4,119.05 as of March 31, 1961, to $46,743.35 as of

2. Teragram contracted for the construction of the plant, arranged mortgage financing by using the Longmeadow and Waterbury properties as security, and became solely obligated on the mortgage.

3. Both properties are also suitable for use by other companies in other types of business.

March 31, 1965. The earned surplus of RBS increased from $331,117.97 as of June 30, 1959, to $535,395.77 as of June 30, 1965. In August 1965, RBS distributed its Teragram stock to the taxpayers. Other than this distribution, neither RBS nor Teragram has paid any dividends.

Joseph V. Rafferty has been the guiding force behind all three corporations, RBS, RBS Conn., and Teragram. He is the president and treasurer of Teragram which, while it has no office or employees, keeps separate books and records and filed separate tax returns for the years in question.

On various occasions Rafferty consulted his accountant about estate planning, particularly about the orderly disposition of RBS.[5] While he anticipated that his sons would join him at RBS, he wanted to exclude his daughters (and/or his future sons-in-law) from the active management of the steel business. He wished, however, to provide them with property which would produce a steady income. The accountant recommended the formation of Teragram, the distribution of its stock, and the eventual use of this stock as future gifts to the Rafferty daughters. The taxpayers acted on this advice and also on the accountant's opinion that the distribution of Teragram stock would meet the requirements of § 355.

In their 1965 return the taxpayers treated the distribution of Teragram stock as a nontaxable transaction under § 355. The Commissioner viewed it, however, as a taxable dividend and assessed a deficiency. He claimed (a) that the distribution was used primarily as a device for the distribution of the earnings and profits of RBS or Teragram or both, and (b) that Teragram did not meet the active business requirements of § 355.

We turn first, to the Tax Court's finding that there was no device because there was an adequate business purpose for the separation and distribution of Teragram stock. In examining this finding we are guided by the rule that the taxpayer has the burden of proving that the transaction was not used principally as a device. Wilson v. Commissioner of Internal Revenue, 42 T.C. 914, 922 (1964), rev'd on other grounds, 353 F.2d 184 (9th Cir.1965). Initially, we are disturbed by the somewhat uncritical nature of the Tax Court's finding of a business purpose. Viewing the transaction from the standpoint of RBS, RBS Conn., or Teragram, no immediate business reason existed for the distribution of Teragram's stock to the taxpayers. Over the years the businesses had been profitable, as witnessed by the substantial increase of the earned surplus of every component, yet none had paid dividends. The primary purpose for the distribution found by the Tax Court was to facilitate Rafferty's desire to make bequests to his children in accordance with an estate plan.[6] This was a personal motive. Taxpayers

5. Rafferty's concern is understandable in view of the fact that he had nine children.

6. This plan incorporated two objectives: (1) the exclusion of daughters and sons-in-law from active management of the

seek to put it in terms relevant to the corporation by speaking of avoidance of possible interference with the operation of the steel business by future sons-in-law, pointing to Coady v. Commissioner of Internal Revenue, 33 T.C. 771 (1960), aff'd per curiam 289 F.2d 490 (6th Cir.1961).

In *Coady,* however, the separation was in response to a seemingly irreconcilable falling-out between the owners of a business. This falling-out had already occurred and, manifestly, the separation was designed to save the business from a substantial, present problem. See also Olson v. Commissioner of Internal Revenue, 48 T.C. 855, 867 modified, 49 T.C. 84 (1967). In the case at bar there was, at best, only an envisaged possibility of future debilitating nepotism. If avoidance of this danger could be thought a viable business purpose at all, it was so remote and so completely under the taxpayers' control that if, in other respects the transaction was a "device," that purpose could not satisfy the taxpayers' burden of proving that it was not being used "principally as a device" within the meaning of the statute.

Our question, therefore, must be whether taxpayers' desire to put their stockholdings into such form as would facilitate their estate planning, viewed in the circumstances of the case, was a sufficient personal business purpose to prevent the transaction at bar from being a device for the distribution of earnings and profits. While we remain of the view, which we first expressed in Lewis v. Commissioner of Internal Revenue, 176 F.2d 646 (1st Cir.1949), that a purpose of a shareholder, qua shareholder, may in some cases save a transaction from condemnation as a device, we do not agree with the putative suggestion in Estate of Parshelsky v. Commissioner of Internal Revenue, 303 F.2d 14, 19 (2d Cir.1962), that any investment purpose of the shareholders is sufficient. Indeed, in *Lewis,* although we deprecated the distinction between shareholder and corporate purpose, we were careful to limit that observation to the facts of that case, and to caution that the business purpose formula "must not become a substitute for independent analysis." 176 F.2d at 650. For that reason we based our decision on the Tax Court's finding that the transaction was "undertaken for reasons germane to the continuance of the corporate business." Id. at 647.

This is not to say that a taxpayer's personal motives cannot be considered, but only that a distribution which has considerable potential for use as a device for distributing earnings and profits should not qualify for tax-free treatment on the basis of personal motives unless those motives are germane to the continuance of the corporate business. Cf. Commissioner of Internal Revenue v. Wilson, 353 F.2d 184 (9th Cir.1965); Treas.Reg. § 1.355–2(c). We prefer this approach over reliance upon formulations such as "business purpose," and "active business." See generally Whitman, Draining the Serbonian Bog: A

steel business and (2) providing his daughters with investment assets, safe and independent from the fluctuations of the steel business.

New Approach to Corporate Separations Under the 1954 Code, 81 Harv. L.Rev. 1194 (1968). The facts of the instant case illustrate the reason for considering substance. Dividends are normally taxable to shareholders upon receipt. Had the taxpayers received cash dividends and made investments to provide for their female descendants, an income tax would, of course, have resulted. Accordingly, once the stock was distributed, if it could potentially be converted into cash without thereby impairing taxpayers' equity interest in RBS, the transaction could easily be used to avoid taxes. The business purpose here alleged, which could be fully satisfied by a bail-out of dividends, is not sufficient to prove that the transaction was not being principally so used.

Given such a purpose, the only question remaining is whether the substance of the transaction is such as to leave the taxpayer in a position to distribute the earnings and profits of the corporation away from, or out of the business. The first factor to be considered is how easily the taxpayer would be able, were he so to choose, to liquidate or sell the spun-off corporation. Even if both corporations are actively engaged in their respective trades, if one of them is a business based principally on highly liquid investment-type, passive assets, the potential for a bail-out is real. The question here is whether the property transferred to the newly organized corporation had a readily realizable value, so that the distributee-shareholders could, if they ever wished, "obtain such cash or property or the cash equivalent thereof, either by selling the distributed stock or liquidating the corporation, thereby converting what would otherwise be dividends taxable as ordinary income into capital gain. * * *" Wilson v. Commissioner, supra, 42 T.C. at 923. In this connection we note that the Tax Court found that a sale of Teragram's real estate properties could be "easily arranged." 55 T.C. at 353. Indeed, taxpayers themselves stressed the fact that the buildings were capable of multiple use.

There must, however, be a further question. If the taxpayers could not effect a bail-out without thereby impairing their control over the on-going business, the fact that a bail-out is theoretically possible should not be enough to demonstrate a device because the likelihood of it ever being so used is slight. "[A] bail-out ordinarily means that earnings and profits have been drawn off without impairing the shareholder's residual equity interest in the corporation's earning power, growth potential, or voting control." B. Bittker & J. Eustice, Federal Income Taxation of Corporations and Shareholders (3d ed. 1971) § 13.06. If sale would adversely affect the shareholders of the on-going company, the assets cannot be said to be sufficiently separated from the corporate solution and the gain sufficiently crystallized as to be taxable. See Lewis v. Commissioner of Internal Revenue, supra, 176 F.2d 650. In this case, there was no evidence that the land and buildings at which RBS carried on its steel operations were so distinctive that the sale of Teragram stock would impair the continued operation of RBS, or that the sale of those buildings would in any other way impair Rafferty's control and other equity interests in RBS.[7]

In the absence of any direct benefit to the business of the original company, and on a showing that the spin-off put saleable assets in the hands of the taxpayers, the continued retention of which was not needed to continue the business enterprise, or to accomplish taxpayers' purposes, we find no sufficient factor to overcome the Commissioner's determination that the distribution was principally a device to distribute earnings and profits.

The taxpayers fail for a further reason. The Tax Court found that Teragram was not an active business within the meaning of § 355(b). The Commissioner contends that this result is mandated by Treas.Reg. § 1.355–1(c) and the examples in Treas.Reg. § 1.355–1(d). The correctness of these regulations is questionable in view of the rejection of the separate business requirement of § 1.355–1(a) in United States v. Marett, 325 F.2d 28 (5th Cir.1963) and Coady v. Commissioner of Internal Revenue, supra.[10] In fact, Revenue Ruling 64–147, 1964–1 Cum.Bull. pt. I, at 136, indicates that the Commissioner recognized a need to modify the § 355 regulations. Moreover, we find that the regulations in this area are so broadly drawn that they may in some instances defeat the congressional purpose behind the enactment of § 355,[12] and we decline to rest our decision on so tenuous a foundation.

It is our view that in order to be an active trade or business under § 355 a corporation must engage in entrepreneurial endeavors of such a nature and to such an extent as to qualitatively distinguish its operations from mere investments. Moreover, there should be objective indicia of such corporate operations. Prior to 1965 Teragram's sole venture was the leasing back to its parent of its only asset for a fixed return, an activity, in economic terms, almost indistinguishable from an investment in securities. Standing by itself this activity is the type of "passive investment" which Congress intended to exclude from § 355 treatment. Furthermore, there are hardly any indicia of corporate operations. Prior to 1965 Teragram paid neither salaries nor rent. It

7. Our conclusion is reinforced by the fact that RBS and RBS Conn. were guaranteed occupancy of Teragram property under long term leases at fixed rents.

10. Treas.Reg. § 1.355–1(a) (1955) states: "Section 355 does not apply to the division of a single business." The Commissioner has since acquiesced in the decisions holding this regulation invalid. * * * At argument the Commissioner contended for a broad reading of the phrase in Treas.Reg. § 1.355–1(c)(3) which excludes from the active business definition those activities not themselves independently producing income. We find that these regulations are largely a restatement of the rejected separate business requirement of § 1.355–1(a), and we believe the Coady rationale is also applicable to functional divisions of existing businesses. See B. Bittker & J. Eustice, Federal Income Taxation of Corporations and Shareholders, supra at § 13.04. We therefore reject the Commissioner's broad contention.

12. For example, the regulations could be construed to deny § 355 treatment to a large hotel chain which spun-off its land purchasing, hotel construction, and leasing activities from its hotel management operations if the spun-off corporation leased the completed hotels exclusively to the management corporation. We are reluctant to approve such regulations which appear to fly in the face of congressional intent.

did not employ independent contractors, and its only activity appears to have been collecting rent, paying taxes, and keeping separate books. Prior to 1965 it failed to meet either set of criteria for an active trade or business. We need not reach the more difficult question of whether its activities in 1965 constituted an active trade or business.

Affirmed.

ILLUSTRATIVE MATERIAL

A. BACKGROUND

As the discussion in *Rafferty* indicates, the scope and interpretation of the tests specified in section 355 have been the object of considerable dispute and continued development. Much of the uncertainty is created by the statutory structure itself, which raises a number of questions. What is the role of the "active trade or business" requirement? What is the nature and degree of activity required before an "active" trade or business is present? What is the relationship of the active business requirement to the "device" prohibition? How do the business purpose and continuity of interest requirements of the Regulations relate to those issues?

Prior to 1973, the Internal Revenue Service relied primarily on the "active trade or business" requirement to police divisive reorganizations. The Service seemed to exclude absolutely from the active trade or business category investment activities and transactions involving owner-occupied real estate. Moreover, it was the Service position that two separate pre-division businesses were required before section 355 could be employed by a taxpayer. The *Coady* case discussed in *Rafferty,* rejected the second position and the *Rafferty* court articulated an entirely different standard to test for "active" business operations.

Beginning in 1973, the Internal Revenue Service appeared to shift its position to conform more closely to the approach adopted in *Rafferty.* Thus, in its published rulings, the Service seemed to rely to a greater extent upon the "device" limitation and adopted a view of the active trade or business requirement patterned on the *Rafferty* test. Regulations proposed in 1977 and finally adopted in 1989, confirmed these developments. The Regulations place greater emphasis on the "device" limitation as the principal technique for insuring that spin-off transactions do not involve bail-outs of earnings and profits. The Regulations also elevate the business purpose requirement discussed in *Rafferty* to the level of an independent test and add a specific continuity of interest requirement which theretofore had played only a subsidiary role. After 1986, these latter two requirements are important with respect to a divisive transaction designed to avoid double tax on appreciated corporate assets but which may not involve any attempt to bail-out accumulated earnings. The active trade or business requirement is substantially modified by the Regulations, and its close interaction with the device requirement is more clearly spelled out. In addition, the Regulations relax the prior requirements concerning the types of business activities which may be split up.[2]

2. See Rev.Proc. 86–41, 1986–2 Cum. Bull. 716, for a check list of information that must be submitted to obtain an advance ruling under section 355.

B. ACTIVE CONDUCT OF A TRADE OR BUSINESS

1. *General*

The "active business" requirements of section 355(a)(1)(C) and (b) are directed at several different, though related, aspects of divisive transactions and raise a number of interpretive problems. The technical rules of section 355(a)(1)(C) and (b) require each of the surviving corporations following a division to be actively engaged in the conduct of a trade or business. In addition, the business in each corporation must have been actively conducted for the five year period preceding the distribution to stockholders. These rules require not only the classification of assets in each of the corporations surviving a divisive reorganization as an active trade or business, but also identification of the scope of the trade or business conducted during the five year qualifying period.

At the first level, the provisions are designed to prevent the tax-free separation of liquid assets from operating assets because of the once substantial bail-out potential involved in such transactions. Here the principle interpretive problems concern the classification of owner-occupied real estate (and real estate leased by a subsidiary to its parent) as an active trade or business or as property that constitutes investment assets. In such situations, the question is whether the nature and extent of the taxpayer's activities are sufficient to qualify as an "active business."

A second set of issues arises when the plan is to divide a single business, to divide a business along geographical lines, to separate different lines of business (e.g., wholesaling from retailing), or to separate a particular function (e.g., research). Here the issues are whether there are separate businesses following division, each of which consists of an individual profit-making enterprise, and whether each of the separated businesses may inherit the five-year operating history of the original business.

The purpose of the five-year rule originally was to prevent the use of corporate earnings generated by one business—and otherwise available for dividend distribution to its stockholders—to establish or acquire another business which could be spun-off and sold creating capital gains. The difficult questions in this area involve a determination of the point at which simple expansion of a single existing business becomes the acquisition of a new business which must then establish its own five-year history. As a backstop to the basic five-year rule, sections 355(b)(2)(C) and (D) preclude tax-free distribution of a business acquired in a taxable transaction during the five years preceding the spin-off.

Occasionally a question arises as to whether the business has been conducted for the requisite five-year period. An unusual case is W.E. Gabriel Fabrication Co. v. Commissioner, 42 T.C. 545 (1964). There two brothers, who owned a corporation which was actively engaged in three businesses, decided to divide up the corporation because of disputes between them. The taxpayer-brother was to receive two of the businesses. Pursuant to an agreement entered into in 1955, the corporation loaned the assets of the two businesses to the taxpayer who operated the businesses as a sole proprietor for about 14 months. In 1956 a new corporation was formed to which the assets of the businesses were formally transferred and this corporation was spun-off to the taxpayer. The taxpayer then transferred his sole proprietorship interest (in which the "loaned" assets had been used) to the new corporation. Under the facts, the distributing corporation had ceased to engage in the spun-off businesses for the 14–month period prior to the distribution and the new corporation itself had not engaged in the business until after the distribution. The court upheld the taxpayer's argument that section 355 nonetheless applied since it concluded that there was no requirement that the business in the five-year period preceding the distribution be conducted by either the distributing corporation or the distributee corporation. It was sufficient that the business itself was conducted during the five-year period, and the taxpayer was permitted to add on the 14–month operation as a sole proprietorship to the time when the businesses had been conducted by the distributing corporation for the purpose of satisfying the five-year requirement.

In Rev.Rul. 82–219, 1982–2 Cum.Bull. 82, a subsidiary corporation which manufactured pollution control equipment for a single unrelated automobile manufacturer was required to cease its production activities for a year when the automobile manufacturer unexpectedly filed for bankruptcy. During the year in which it was shut down, the subsidiary pursued new customers for its products. The subsidiary was spun-off by its parent corporation for valid business reasons. The fact that the subsidiary had income in only four of the five years preceding the distribution of its stock to its parent's stockholders did not defeat the five-year active conduct of business requirement.

2. *Rental Property as an Active Trade or Business or Investment*

The operation and maintenance of rental real estate, as well as other rental property, readily may be classified as the operation of a trade or business. The principal question which arises in the case of dividing off the rental business is whether the relationship of the distributing corporation to the rental activity is the *active* conduct of that business. The problem is further complicated when the distributing corporation occupies the rental property.

Another question is whether the form in which property is held should matter in the analysis of the active trade or business requirement. Suppose in *Rafferty* the property had been owned directly by the parent and managed and operated as a real estate division, with the real estate division "charging" rent to the operating division for internal accounting purposes. The Internal Revenue Service appears to regard the parent-subsidiary rental situation as a variation on the owner-occupied real estate situation and uses the same tests in each to determine whether the requisite level of business activity is present.

The pre–1989 Regulations refused to find an active trade or business where owner occupied real estate was involved unless the rental activities with respect to, and the rental income from, third parties were substantial. See pre–1989 Regulations, section 1.355–1(c)(1) and (d), Ex. (2), (3), and (4). Some cases used a similar approach; see, e.g. Appleby v. Commissioner, 35 T.C. 755 (1961), aff'd per curiam, 296 F.2d 925 (3d Cir.1962) (rental of less than 50 percent of space in building occupied by insurance agency where rentals were small part of total income did not constitute an active trade or business); Bonsall v. Commissioner, 317 F.2d 61 (2d Cir.1963) (lease of small part of owner occupied building as an accommodation to a supplier and rental of another building not a trade or business where rental income small). See also Spheeris v. Commissioner, 461 F.2d 271 (7th Cir. 1972) (no active trade or business where a fire-damaged building was not rented after its distribution because the stockholder hoped to include it in a new construction project which never materialized).

Further, the Service held the view that if "investment" property was involved, no amount of activity with respect to the investment would constitute an active trade or business. See Rev.Rul. 66–204, 1966–2 Cum. Bull. 113 (substantial activity in managing an investment portfolio of a broker-dealer not an active trade or business).

But *Rafferty* signaled a new approach to the treatment of investment property and property used in the trade or business of the owner under the active trade or business test of section 355. Under *Rafferty,* the satisfaction of the active trade or business test turns on the question whether the corporation engaged "in entrepreneurial endeavors of such a nature and to such an extent as to qualitatively distinguish its operations from mere investments." Thus under the *Rafferty* approach, it is possible for the operation of owner occupied real estate to constitute an active trade or business under section 355, even though no renting of the property to third parties is present.

King v. Commissioner, 458 F.2d 245 (6th Cir.1972), applied the *Rafferty* approach in a transaction where a transportation company owned three subsidiaries formed earlier to acquire real estate, erect terminals, and lease the terminals on a net lease basis to the parent company. To facilitate a merger with another operating company, the transportation company decided to put all of the transportation operations in one corporate group and the nonoperating corporations in a separate corporate group. The stock of the real estate subsidiaries was distributed to the stockholders of the transportation company who then transferred the stock to a sister corporation and the business activities were operated as before. The court concluded, reversing the Tax Court, that the financing and construction activities of the real estate group constituted an active trade or business, even though performed by the identical persons who were employees of the operational group and no third party leasing was involved.

Rev.Rul. 73–234, 1973–1 Cum.Bull. 180, reflected a shift in the Internal Revenue Service interpretation of the active conduct of a trade or business requirement. The Ruling stated that an actively conducted business denoted "substantial management and operational activities directly carried on by the corporation itself." There a farm corporation which utilized tenant farmers (independent contractors) was held to be engaged in an active trade or business where it did perform substantial activities with respect to the farm business. Rev.Rul. 89–27, 1989–1 Cum.Bull. 106, discussed the role of services performed by outside contractors:

> "[I]n order for a trade or business to be actively conducted, substantial management and operational activities generally must be directly carried on by the corporation itself and such activities generally do not include the activities of others outside the corporation, including independent contractors. However, the fact that a portion of a corporation's business activities is performed by others will not preclude the corporation from being engaged in the active conduct of a trade or business if the corporation itself directly performs active and substantial management and operational functions."

The Ruling held that the owner of a working interest in an oil lease was actively engaged in the conduct of a business despite outside work by independent contractors. See also Rev.Rul. 73–237, 1973–1 Cum.Bull. 184 (construction corporation acting as a general contractor was in an active trade or business even though it utilized independent subcontractors for actual construction work where the general contractor's activities were substantial); Rev.Rul. 79–394, 1979–2 Cum.Bull. 141 (corporation engaged in an active business even though it had no paid employees of its own; all of the corporation's operational and management activity was performed by employees of its parent corporation which was reimbursed by the controlled corporation); Rev.Rul. 80–181, 1980–2 Cum.Bull. 121 (clarifying Rev.Rul. 79–394 and indicating that the controlled corporation would be actively engaged in the conduct of a business if the parent had not been reimbursed for the services provided by its employees). However, in Rev.Rul. 86–125, 1986–2 Cum.Bull. 57, the Service held that a subsidiary's ownership of an office building which was operated and managed by an independent real estate management company was not the active conduct of a business. The subsidiary's limited managerial and operational activities were compared to those of a prudent investor.

The 1989 Regulations, section 1.355–3(b)(2)(iii), incorporate the requirement that to satisfy the "active conduct" test the corporation must "perform active and substantial management and operational functions." The Regulations modify the prior strict rule with respect to investment property by stating that the holding of real or personal property used in a trade or business can satisfy the active conduct test if the owner performs significant services with respect to the operation and management of the property. Regulations, section 1.355–3(b)(2)(iv)(B). Despite the modification in principle of the Internal Revenue Service's prior strict rule regarding investment property and owner-occupied real estate, however, Examples (1)–(3), (12) and (13), in Regulations, section 1.355–3(c), indicate that the Service will continue to scrutinize closely divisive transactions involving investment assets and owner-occupied real estate. Indeed, only one of the examples, Example (12), concludes that an active trade or business is involved. In that Example, the owner of a building occupied only one of eleven floors and the spun-off corporation continued the prior practice of renting the other ten floors to unrelated tenants. Example (13) indicates that if the controlled corporation leases the property it owns back to the distributing corporation, it will be difficult to establish, that an active trade or business is present. See also Regulations, section 1.355–2(d)(2)(iv)(C), discussed infra, page 927, which indicate that the functional relationship between the active trade or businesses of the distributing and controlled corporations may be evidence of a "device."

3. *Vertical Division of a Single Business Activity*

As noted by the court in *Rafferty,* the Internal Revenue Service position for many years was that section 355 could not be applied to divide a single business, which did have the requisite five-year active trade or business history, into two separate corporations. The Service position was rejected in Coady v. Commissioner, 33 T.C. 771 (1960), the court holding invalid Regulations which provided that section 355 did not apply to the separation of a single business. The Tax Court's decision was affirmed per curiam, 289 F.2d 490 (6th Cir.1961).

The *Coady* principle, allowing the vertical division of a single business enterprise, was applied in Badanes v. Commissioner, 39 T.C. 410 (1962), and Lester v. Commissioner, 40 T.C. 947 (1963)(A). The Fifth Circuit followed *Coady* in United States v. Marett, 325 F.2d 28 (5th Cir.1963), and in Rev.Rul. 64–147, 1964–1 Cum.Bull. 136, the Service announced that it would follow *Marett* and *Coady.* See also Rev.Rul. 75–160, 1975–1 Cum. Bull. 112 (indicating also that the Service would apply *Rafferty*).

Regulations, section 1.355–3(c), Ex. (4) and (5), now specifically sanction the use of section 355 to divide a single business with the requisite five-year pre-distribution history. See also Regulations, section 1.355–1(b) and –3(c), Ex. (6) and (7).

4. *Single Business Versus Two Separate Businesses*

As a result of the *Coady* and *Marett* cases, the Commissioner and taxpayers tended to shift sides in the single business versus separate businesses controversy. The Commissioner contended that an activity involved two separate businesses, and one of the two did not satisfy the five-year rule; the taxpayer argued that the activities constituted a single business, which could be divided under *Coady.* The question of whether an activity constituted a single business, or two separate businesses may arise in several different contexts.

(a) *Geographical Division*

Suppose that a multi-state business operated through branches in each of its market states. Is each branch a separate business, or is there but a single business? In Burke v. Commissioner, 42 T.C. 1021 (1964), the Commissioner asserted that establishing a second retail store in another town constituted the creation of a separate trade or business as to which the five-year rule was not satisfied. The court upheld the taxpayer' assertion that under the *Coady* rule the second store constituted a branch of a single retail business which satisfied the five-year rule. In Estate of Lockwood v. Commissioner, 350 F.2d 712 (8th Cir.1965), a corporation operated in the Midwest through branches that were ultimately separately incorporated and spun-off. In 1949 it began to make sales in New England and in 1954 established a branch office in Maine. In 1956, the branch was incorporated separately and the stock distributed. No sales activity was present in Maine from 1951 to 1953 and the Commissioner asserted that the business had not been actively conducted in the Maine location for the five years preceding the division in 1956. The court rejected the Commissioner's reliance on its "geographical area" test:

"Nothing in the language of section 355 suggests that prior business activity is only to be measured by looking at the business performed in a geographical area where the controlled corporation is eventually formed. In this case, when the entire Lockwood market is viewed, it can be seen that Lockwood was engaged in active business as required by section 355 for the five years prior to the incorporation of Maine, Inc. Since its incorporation Maine, Inc. has carried on the same kind of manufacturing and selling business previously and concurrently performed by Lockwood. Thus all section 355 prerequisites are met. * * *

"Since there is no Congressional intent evidenced to the contrary, the test, restated, is not whether active business had been carried out in the geographic area later served by the controlled corporation. But, simply, whether the distributing corporation, for five years prior to distribution, had been actively conducting the type of business now performed by the controlled corporation without reference to the geographic area." (715, 717).

Regulations, section 1.355–3(c), Ex. (7), follow the *Burke* and *Estate of Lockwood* cases. Example (6) likewise approves the separation of the downtown and suburban branches of a retail clothing store.

(b) *Separate Lines of Business*

In Rev.Rul. 56–451, 1956–2 Cum.Bull. 208, the Service ruled that the publication of a trade magazine for one industry was a business separate from the publication of three magazines for another industry, and the former could be spun-off since the requirements of section 355 were met. See also Lester v. Commissioner, 40 T.C. 947 (1963) (A), where a corporation was both a warehouse distributor (in which capacity it sold to "jobbers") and a "jobber" (in which capacity it sold to retailers). Jobber customers objected to purchasing from a corporation which was also a competitor, and the warehouse activity was spun-off. The court reaffirmed *Coady,* but in any event found that the activities constituted two separate businesses, each with its own five-year history. See also Wilson v. Commissioner, 42 T.C. 914 (1964), rev'd on other grounds, 353 F.2d 184 (9th Cir.1965) (furniture business and its financing activities were two separate businesses).

The problems in this area are closely related to the "functional division" situations discussed below, and the position in the Regulations that there can be a valid functional division of a single business under section 355 will presumably have an impact in the single business-two separate businesses context as well. As discussed below, Regulations, section 1.355–2(d)(2)(iv)(C), focus on the device test in this context.

5. *Functional Division of a Single Business*

Regulations, section 1.355–1(b)(2)(ii), define a "business" for purposes of 355 as a specific group of activities consisting of the operations necessary to the process of earning income or profit. The 1989 Regulations reverse the position of the prior Regulations and provide that activities which merely contributed to the process of earning income before the distribution may themselves constitute a business. Regulations, section 1.355–3(c), Ex. (9), take the position that a research department of a manufacturing activity may be spun-off as a separate business. The Example states that the status of the research department as a separate business is independent of whether it furnishes services solely to the distributing corporation or undertakes to contract with others. The Example cautions, however, that if the research department continues to function as a secondary business providing service solely to the distribution corporation, that fact is evidence of a "device" under the Regulations, section 1.355–2(d)(2)(iv), discussed infra, page 927. See also Examples (10) (sales function separated from manufacturing function), and (11) (captive coal mine separated from steel products manufacturing).

6. *Diversification and Expansion of an Existing Business With a Five-Year History*

There is also the problem of determining whether the business conducted earlier is the same as that now conducted so that the current business inherits the history of the original operation. What about changes in product, location, or methods? What about growth itself? Is a small rental business started in 1985 the same business as a large rental activity with many more properties in 1990; is the operation of a single retail store in 1985 the same business as the operation in 1990 of a chain of 50 stores? See Regulations, section 1.355–3(b)(3)(d)(ii).

The Internal Revenue Service addressed the expansion issue in Rev.Rul. 59–400, 1959–2 Cum.Bull. 114:

"M corporation was engaged in two businesses, operating a hotel and renting improved real estate (both commercial and residential). The hotel business was started upon organization in 1920 and has been actively conducted up to the present time. In 1934, M corporation also entered into the rental real estate business when it purchased property, constructed a garage and automobile agency facilities thereon and rented it to a dealer. In the intervening years, it acquired other rental properties which it has continued to operate. In 1954 the hotel had a fair market value of 550x dollars and a net book value of 167x dollars.

"During the five-year period commencing with 1954, the operation of the hotel business resulted in earnings, after taxes, of 240x dollars, and the operation of the real estate business resulted in earnings of approximately 75x dollars. In 1958, a new rental office building was built for 400x dollars, some 175x dollars thereof being provided by loans from banks. At the beginning of 1959, the hotel business was placed in a new corporation N, and the stock thereof distributed to the stockholders of M on a pro rata basis. N corporation received the hotel, plus certain receivables and other hotel business assets. M corporation retained the real estate liabilities and assets, which at that time had a net book value of 372x dollars and a fair market value of 705x dollars.

* * *

"The purpose behind the five-year limitation of section 355 is to prevent the corporate earnings of one business from being drawn off for such a period and put into a new business and thereby, through the creation of a marketable enterprise, convert what would normally have been dividends into capital assets that are readily saleable by the stockholders.

"It is the position of the Internal Revenue Service that where a corporation which is devoted to one type of business also engages in the rental business, and substantial acquisitions of new rental property are made within the five-year period preceding the separation of these businesses, a spin-off transaction will not qualify under section 355 unless it can be shown that the property acquisitions were substantially financed out of the earnings of the rental business and not out of the earnings of the other business.

"From the facts presented herein, it is readily apparent that there has been a very substantial increase in the rental properties subsequent to 1954, primarily as a result of the addition of the large office building in 1958. Further, it is also apparent that, viewing the transaction most favorably to the taxpayer, earnings properly attributable to the hotel business, in the amount of approximately 150x dollars, have been employed in increasing the real estate business. In view of this substantial financing out of the earnings of the hotel business, it is held that the distribution of the stock of N corporation to the stockholders of M corporation will not qualify as a nontaxable distribution under section 355 of the Code."

What is the basis for the Ruling? Is it that the infusion of funds into the real estate business so changed its character that it became a "new" business which required a five-year aging period? Or was the transaction struck down by the "device" language of section 355(a)(1)(B)? The Ruling is unclear on these questions, but stands as a warning that substantial infusions of funds into a going business may create problems where a spin-off is contemplated.

In a related fashion, the parent corporation in a parent subsidiary group already conducting separate businesses may use its earnings to make a capital contribution to the subsidiary prior to distribution of the subsidiary's stock. The expansion of the subsidiary's business with the parent's earnings does not affect the presence of the group's historic business, but may be evidence of a "device" as discussed infra, page 926.

7. *Taxable Acquisitions Within the Five–Year Period*

Similar problems are involved where the business expands by acquiring a business similar to its own from third parties. Here the provisions of section 355(b)(2)(C) and (D) stand as barriers. In Boettger v. Commissioner, 51 T.C. 324 (1968), a corporation had operated a hospital since 1956. In 1961 it acquired another hospital in a separate location by means of a taxable purchase. Because of disagreement between the two groups of stockholders, a split-up was effected in 1964. The taxpayers who received the 1956 hospital argued that the acquisition in 1961 simply represented an expansion of a single business and Coady applied. The Tax Court did not reach the question of whether there was one or two businesses. It held that the word "such" in section 355(b)(2)(C) referred to the business engaged in by the distributed corporation after the distribution and since this business, viewed alone, was acquired in a taxable transaction within five years preceding the distribution, section 355 was inapplicable. Subsequently, the Tax Court in Nielsen v. Commissioner, 61 T.C. 311 (1973), a case involving the stockholders who received the 1961 hospital, concluded that two separate businesses were involved, only one of which had the requisite five-year history. Each hospital had been run separately, there was not shared staff or patients, and each was a separate income-producing activity. On this factual basis, the Court distinguished the *Burke* and *Estate of Lockwood* cases, supra, page 919. See also Russell v. Commissioner, 40 T.C. 810 (1963), aff'd per curiam, 345 F.2d 534 (5th Cir.1965) (taxable acquisition within five-year period preceding distribution disqualified transaction under section 355); Rev.Rul. 78–442, 1978–2 Cum.Bull. 143 (corporation transferred assets and liabilities of one business to a newly formed corporation and then distributed the stock; gain was recognized in the transaction under section 357(c) because liabilities exceeded the bases of the assets transferred; despite the fact that gain was recognized on the transfer section 355(b)(2)(C) was held not applicable because it was not intended to apply to an acquisition of a trade or business by a controlled corporation from the distributing corporation).

8. *Holding Companies*

Section 355(b)(2)(A) provides that a holding company will be engaged in the active conduct of a trade or business if "substantially all" of its assets consists of stock or securities of controlled corporations that are actively engaged in the conduct of a business. For advance Ruling purposes, the "substantially all" requirement is met if at least 90 percent of the fair market value of the *gross* corporate assets consist of stock and securities in controlled corporations that have actively been engaged in a trade or business for the requisite five-year period. Rev.Proc. 86–41, 1986–2 Cum.Bull. 716, 719 (section 3.03 1(b)4); Rev.Proc. 77–37 1977–2 Cum.Bull. 568, 570 (section 3.04). See also Rev.Rul. 74–382, 1974–2 Cum.Bull. 120 (same result where first tier subsidiary is a holding company but all the second tier subsidiaries are actively engaged in a trade or business); Rev.Rul. 74–79, 1974–1 Cum.Bull. 81 (operating subsidiaries acquired in taxable transactions within five-year period are treated as stock in corporations not actively engaged in a trade or business).

9. *Acquisition of Control by the Distributee Corporation*

Following repeal of the *General Utilities* doctrine by the 1986 Act, there was concern that a section 355 division could be used to thwart recognition of corporate level gain in a corporate acquisition followed by a disposition of unwanted assets. For example, T Corporation operates two separate businesses. X Corporation wishes to acquire business number 1, but not business number 2. T is not willing to dispose of the businesses separately. To accomplish the transaction, T transfers each business into separate subsidiaries, S1 and S2, in a nontaxable transaction under section 351. X acquires the T stock from the T stockholders. X causes T to distribute the stock of S1, the wanted subsidiary, to it in a section 355 distribution. Subsequently, X sells the T stock thereby disposing of the unwanted assets of business number 2 (held in S2) without corporate level recognition of unrealized gain in the assets of business number 2.[3] Section 355(b)(2)(D) was amended in 1987 to apply the five-year rule to the acquisition of control by the distributee corporation of a corporation conducting a trade or business. Thus, in the example, because X, the distributee of the S1 stock, indirectly acquired control of S1 and S2 within the five-year period preceding the distribution, section 355 would not apply to the distribution of S1 stock to X. T will be required to recognize gain on the distribution of S1 stock to X under section 311.

Note that the transaction as described above would have difficulty satisfying both the business purpose and continuity of interests requirements, discussed infra, pages 927 and 930. Section 355(b)(2)(D) was amended to avoid the need to rely on these general subjective tests.

C. THE "DEVICE" LIMITATION

1. *General*

The "device" language of section 355 is aimed at preventing a division from being merely a step in a bail-out of earnings and profits through the sale of the stock of one of the corporations or its liquidation. The elimination of preferential treatment of capital gains by the 1986 Act eliminates the need for avoidance measures to prevent conversion of ordinary income into capital gains. Thus the role of the "device" restriction in section 355 is substantially diminished. However, the business purpose and continuity of interest requirements, discussed infra, pages 927 and 930, which were originally

3. This transaction was thought to have been approved by Rev.Rul. 74–5, 1974–1 Cum.Bull. 82, in which P Corporation in 1969 acquired all of the stock of X Corporation for cash. X Corporation in turn owned all of the stock of Y Corporation which it had acquired in 1965. In 1971, X distributed the Y stock to P and in 1972 P distributed the Y stock to its stockholders. The Ruling held that the 1971 distribution satisfied section 355(b)(2)(D), since P was neither the distributing nor the controlled corporation but simply the stockholder of the distributing corporation. On the other hand, the 1972 distribution did not satisfy section 355(b)(2)(D), since the business of controlled Corporation Y was acquired indirectly by P through another Corporation (X) in a transaction within five years in which gain or loss had been recognized. See also Rev.Rul. 69–461, 1969–2 Cum.Bull. 52.

derived in part from the device restriction, continue to limit nonrecognition treatment in divisive transactions.

What constitutes a "device" is far from clear, especially after 1986. Is it akin to a distribution essentially equivalent to a dividend? Or does it refer to tax avoidance of the Gregory v. Helvering type? Regulations, section 1.355–2(d)(1), state: "Section 355 recognizes that a tax-free distribution of the stock of a controlled corporation presents a potential for tax avoidance by facilitating the avoidance of the dividend provisions of the Code through the subsequent sale or exchange of stock of one corporation and the retention of the stock of another corporation." The presence of the "device" test in section 355 focuses the inquiry on the circumstances under which the corporate division has taken place. Since every corporate division carries with it the potential for extracting earnings from the corporation with no dividend consequences, the problem is how to identify those situations in which dividend treatment is nonetheless proper. Compare, however, the treatment of partial liquidations under section 302(b)(4) and (e)(2), supra page 579, where a corporate "division" is involved, but no "device" limitation is imposed.

2. *Non-pro Rata Distributions*

Pro rata divisions represent a clear situation in which there is a bail-out potential in a divisive distribution. Regulations, section 1.355–2(d)(2)(ii), therefore, treat the fact that a distribution is pro rata, or substantially pro rata, as evidence that the transaction is used as a device to effect a distribution of earnings and profits. At the other extreme, however, Regulations, section 1.355–2(d)(5), provide that a non-pro rata distribution which qualifies as a redemption under section 302(a), supra, page 554, ordinarily will not be considered to be a device. There is no "bail-out" potential in a transaction which would produce capital gains in any event. See also Rev.Rul. 64–102, 1964–1 Cum.Bull. 136 (transfer to a previously existing subsidiary of assets representing more than 50 percent of the value of the subsidiary to equalize the value of the subsidiary stock with the value of the parent company stock owned by a minority stockholder, followed by a distribution of the subsidiary stock in exchange for the minority stockholder's parent stock, did not amount to a "device" since the transaction as to the minority stockholder would have entitled him to capital gain treatment under section 302(b)(3)); Rev.Rul. 71–383, 1971–2 Cum.Bull. 180 (a distribution which was substantially disproportionate under section 302(b)(2) did not constitute a "device" since under that section the taxpayer was entitled to capital gain treatment). For the same reason, Regulations, section 1.355–2(d)(5)(ii), provide that there is ordinarily no device present where neither the distributing nor controlled corporations have earnings and profits (including built-in gain property that would create earnings if distributed) which would cause taxable dividend treatment on a distribution to stockholders. Rev.Rul. 71–384, 1971–2 Cum. Bull. 181, is to the same effect. In such situations, the "business purpose" and "continuity of interest" requirements of the Regulations still must be met.

3. *Post–Distribution Sale or Exchange*

Regulations, section 1.355–2(d)(2)(iii), provide that a sale or exchange of the stock of either the distributing or the spun-off corporation following a division is evidence that the transaction was used principally as a device for distribution of the earnings and profits of either or both of the corporations. The percentage of stock sold and the period of time before the stock sale affect the strength of this evidence of a "device." If the stock sale is negotiated or agreed upon before the section 355 division occurs, the evidence of "device" is elevated by the Regulations to the level of "substantial evidence", while a sale or exchange arranged only after the division is merely "evidence" of a "device." Regulations, section 1.355–2(d)(2)(iii)(B) and (C).

Regulations, section 1.355–2(d)(2)(iii)(E), also provide that a post distribution exchange of stock of either the distributing or the controlled corporation in a reorganization in which no more than an insubstantial amount of gain is recognized will not be treated as a subsequent sale or exchange constituting evidence of a "device." This portion of the Regulations adopts the holding of Commissioner v. Morris Trust, 367 F.2d 794 (4th Cir.1966). In *Morris Trust,* a state bank desired to merge into a national bank. However, the state bank operated an insurance department, an operation which could not be continued by the national bank. To avoid a violation of the national banking laws, the state bank organized a new corporation to which it transferred the insurance business assets and then distributed the stock in the insurance corporation to its stockholders. Following the distribution, the state bank was merged into the national bank. The Commissioner argued that the active business requirements of section 355(b)(1)(A) were not met since the state bank's business was not continued in unaltered corporate form and because there was "an inherent incompatibility in substantially simultaneous divisive and amalgamating reorganizations." The court rejected both arguments and upheld the validity of the section 355 transaction.[4] See also Rev.Rul. 70–434, 1970–2 Cum.Bull. 83, where the stockholders of the distributing corporation, after receiving the stock of the spun-off corporation, then exchanged their stock in the distributing corporation in a (B) reorganization. *Elkhorn Coal Company,* supra, page 847, indicates, however, that a (C) reorganization is not available following a spin-off because of the requirement that the acquired corporation transfer "substantially all" its assets in the (C) reorganization. Rev.Rul. 70–18, 1970–1 Cum.Bull. 74, upheld section 355 treatment where there was a pre-distribution merger involving the distributing corporation.

In Rev.Rul. 77–377, 1977–2 Cum.Bull. 111, an estate owned 80 percent of the stock of X Corporation. In a split-up transaction, X transferred its assets to new Y and Z Corporations, and then liquidated. Prior to the split-up, the estate had contemplated a section 303 redemption of a part of its X stock to pay estate taxes. The section 303 redemption could not be completed before the split-up. Therefore, after the split-up, new Y and Z Corporations redeemed part of the estate's stock in each under section 303. The Ruling held that no "device" was involved since the dividend provisions

4. Curtis v. United States, 336 F.2d 714 (6th Cir.1964), was to the contrary, holding that section 355 did not apply where following the distribution of the stock of the corporation holding the unwanted assets, the distributing corporation merged into another corporation. It construed section 355 to require the distributing corporation to stay in existence. In Rev.Rul. 68–603, 1968–2 Cum.Bull. 148, the Service announced that it would follow the *Morris Trust* decision to the extent that it held (1) the active trade or business requirement is met even though the distributing corporation merges following the distribution; (2) the control requirement of a (D) reorganization implies no limits on the reorganization of the distributing corporation after the spin-off; and (3) there is a business purpose for the spin-off and the merger.

of the Code had not been avoided. See Regulations, section 1.355–2(d)(5)(iii) (a transaction is generally not considered to be a device if the distribution would have been treated as a redemption under section 303).

Apart from providing evidence of a "device", a post-distribution change in stock ownership of the controlled corporation may defeat nonrecognition treatment for failure to satisfy the control requirement of a (D) reorganization, discussed infra, page 932. In addition, post-distribution ownership changes may cause the transaction to fail the continuity of interest requirement, discussed infra, page 930.

4. *Nature and Use of Assets*

Regulations, section 1.355–2(d)(2)(iv)(A), provide that in determining whether a transaction is principally a device for the distribution of earnings and profits, consideration will be given to the "nature, kind, amount, and use" of the assets of both corporations immediately after the transactions. There are two aspects to this consideration.

(a) *Nonbusiness Assets*

The presence of assets not related to the trade or business of one of the corporations, such as cash and other liquid assets, is evidence of a device. Regulations, section 1.355–2(d)(2)(iv)(B). The presence of unrelated assets is particularly damaging where the amount of unrelated assets transferred to or retained by one corporation is disproportionate to the relative value of the business assets in that corporation. See Regulations, section 1.355–2(d)(4), Ex. (3). In Rev.Rul. 86–4, 1986–1 Cum.Bull. 174, the Internal Revenue Service held that the transfer of investment assets to the controlled corporation in a spin-off is a factor to be considered in determining whether the transaction is a device regardless of the percentage of the investment assets relative to the total amount of assets transferred to the controlled corporation.

In Rev.Rul. 73–44, 1973–1 Cum.Bull. 182, clarified by Rev.Rul. 76–54, 1976–1 Cum.Bull. 96, the distributing corporation conducted three businesses: (1) A manufacturing and distribution business which it had conducted for more than five years and which constituted over one-half the value of the corporation's total business assets; (2) a newspaper business, acquired in a taxable transaction within the preceding five years, which had been transferred to a newly created subsidiary in a nontaxable transaction; and (3) a separate manufacturing business conducted for more than five years. The distributing corporation transferred business (3) to the subsidiary and then distributed all the stock of the subsidiary to its shareholders. Business (3) represented a "substantial portion" of the value of the spun-off corporation, but less than one-half. The Ruling held that a "device" was not present since the newspaper business acquired in the taxable transaction represented "operating businesses and not assets that would be used" as a device. Compare also the "expansion" situations discussed supra, page 920.

A contribution to the capital of the controlled corporation preceding a spin-off of the subsidiary's stock also may provide an opportunity for the distribution of earnings to stockholders. In Rev.Rul. 83–114, 1983–2 Cum. Bull. 66, the Service held that a predistribution capital contribution to the controlled corporation was not per se a device. P was required by an antitrust decree to divest itself of its subsidiary S. In order to improve S's capital and expand S's business opportunities, P discharged S's indebtedness to it. The debt discharge increased S's net worth by more than 100 percent. A distributed S stock to P stockholders. The Ruling concluded that there was no device since both the distribution of S stock and the discharge of S's indebtedness were undertaken for valid business reasons.

(b) *Related Business Activities*

The second part of the inquiry into the nature of transferred assets concerns the relationship of the businesses of the two corporations. Although the Regulations now recognize that section 355 can be employed to divide a single business or to effect a functional division of the business, there is evidence of a device where the businesses of the distributing and controlled corporations are functionally related in the sense that one of the businesses is a secondary business of the other, and the secondary business can be sold without adversely affecting the other. Regulations, section 1.355–2(d)(2)(iv)(C). Example (10) of Regulations, section 1.355–3(c), illustrates this concept. A corporation engaged in the manufacture of steel products spins off a subsidiary which owns a coal mine supplying the steel plant. Evidence of a device exists if the principal function of the coal mine is to satisfy the requirements of the steel business for coal and the stock of the coal mine could be sold without adversely affecting the steel business.

The related function test of the Regulations, section 1.355–2(d)(2)(iv)(C), is closely related to the situations involved in *Rafferty* supra, page 909, and *King,* supra, page 917, and is not wholly inconsistent with those cases. Under the approach in those cases, however, it would appear possible for a spun-off corporation to satisfy the "entrepreneurial activities" test even though those activities were undertaken solely for related parties.

The *Rafferty* court's reliance on the factor of "readily realizable value" to determine the bail-out potential refers to the division of liquid from illiquid assets; even if the spun-off corporation is in an active trade or business, the bail-out potential may be high because of the nature of the assets (as would be the case with real estate). But further, if the sale or liquidation of the spun-off corporation would seriously impair the ability of the distributing corporation to operate, then a "device" is not likely to be present. In contrast, the court in *King* upheld section 355 treatment for the spin-off of real estate leased solely to the distributing corporation on the ground that, while the real estate operations were highly liquid (net leases were involved), the properties were uniquely suited to the distributing company's needs and a sale would have impaired the company's ability to obtain financing. Under the *Rafferty* approach, transactions involving real estate must be closely scrutinized. For example, long-term leases on the real estate may make possible a sale of the stock of the distributed corporation without impairing in any way the operating functions of the distributing corporation. In such a case, the transaction should constitute a "device" under the *Rafferty* test.

D. THE "BUSINESS PURPOSE" REQUIREMENT

The role of "business purpose" in the section 355 framework is important and has several aspects. Under Regulations, section 1.355–2(d)(3)(ii), the presence of a corporate business purpose for the transaction is evidence that a "device" is not present. The stronger the device factors, the stronger the evidence of business purpose necessary to overcome the presence of a device. In addition, Regulations, section 1.355–2(b), independently require a corporate business purpose for nonrecognition treatment in order to limit nonrecognition to "distributions that are incident to readjustments of corporate structures required by business exigencies and that effect only readjustments of continuing interests in property under modified corporate forms." This business purpose test is independent of the "device" language, so that even upon a finding of no "device", the transaction nonetheless fails to qualify for want of a "business purpose." The Regulations are consistent with the decision in Commissioner v. Wilson, 353 F.2d 184 (9th Cir.1965), holding that section 355 was inapplicable where, although the transaction was not a "device" because there was no tax avoidance motive, no affirmative business purpose was demonstrated for the transaction, and that under the *Gregory* doctrine "business purpose" is an essential ingredient of the law. *Rafferty,* on the other hand, appears to deal with "business purpose" only as a factor under the "device" prohibition.

Regulations, section 1.355–2(b)(3), indicate that the "business purpose" must relate not only to the need for separate operations in corporate form of the two businesses, but that the corporate business purpose must extend also to the distribution of the stock to the stockholders. There may be business reasons for separate corporate operation, but these usually can be satisfied by parent-subsidiary operation. Thus, a distribution will not qualify for nonrecognition treatment under section 355 if the corporate business purpose can be achieved through a nontaxable separation of the businesses into two corporations without a distribution to stockholders. To illustrate, in Regulations, section 1.355–2(b)(5), Ex. (3), X Corporation is engaged in the manufacture and sale of toys and candy. The stockholders of X wish to protect the candy business from the risks of the toy business. To achieve this business purpose X transfers the assets of the toy business to a new corporation Y, and distributes the Y stock to X stockholders. The Regulations conclude that since the purpose of protecting the candy business from the risks of the toy business is accomplished at the moment the separate businesses are divided into separate corporations, the distribution of Y stock to X's stockholders is not carried out for a corporate business purpose.

The requisite business purpose must be a nontax business purpose of one or both of the corporations involved in a division. Regulations, section 1.355–2(b)(2). The Regulations provide expressly that a shareholder purpose such as personal planning is not a corporate business purpose. The Regulations recognize, however, that a stockholder purpose may be "so nearly coextensive" with the corporation's business purpose as to preclude any distinction between them. Compare the decision in *Rafferty,* which employed the business purpose test as one factor relevant to a determination of the "device" issue, with the taxpayer having the burden of proving that no device was involved. The court stated that where the only purpose for the distribution is a "stockholder" purpose, the bail-out potential of the transaction is to be closely scrutinized. See also Rev.Rul. 75–337, 1975–2 Cum. Bull, 124, which concluded that a stockholder's purpose could supply the requisite "business purpose", where the estate planning problem faced by the stockholder was immediate and was directly related to the ability of the corporation to carry on its business without interruption or loss. X Corporation held an automobile sales franchise and its subsidiary Y was in the automobile rental business. Fifty-three percent of the X Corporation stock was held by A and the remainder was held by A's five daughters. Three of the daughters were active in X's automobile sales business. To facilitate A's estate planning, Y Corporation stock was distributed pro-rata to the X

Corporation stockholders. The spin-off was justified by the fact that the franchise policy of the automobile manufacturer required that the stockholders of a corporation owning a franchise be actively involved in the business. On A's death, the inactive stockholders would receive their inheritance in Y stock and assets and no interest in X. The Ruling distinguished *Rafferty* on the basis that the stockholder problem involved there had only a "remote and conjectural" impact on the business.

Regulations, section 1.355–2(b)(2), stress that the requisite business purpose must be a purpose unrelated to federal taxes and germane to the business of the corporations involved. A corporate separation to save state taxes satisfies the business purpose requirement only if there is no corresponding federal income tax savings which is greater than or substantially coextensive with the state tax savings. Under this provision, a parent corporation cannot justify distribution of the stock of a subsidiary with a claim that the distribution is necessary to qualify for elective status under a state pass-through taxation provision similar to Subchapter S of the Code, which bars the election by affiliated groups, where the distribution also would allow qualification for federal subchapter S status. See Regulations, section 1.355–2(b)(5), Ex. (7). See also Rev.Rul. 76–187, 1976–1 Cum.Bull. 97 (valid business purpose to distribute stock of subsidiary to reduce state and local taxes on the capital value of the subsidiary); Rev.Rul. 89–101, 1989–2 Cum. Bull 67 (distribution to domestic parent corporation by foreign first tier subsidiary of all of the stock of second tier foreign subsidiary for purposes of reducing foreign taxes satisfied business purpose requirement).

The adequacy of business purpose for nonrecognition under section 355 is generally a question which depends upon the facts and circumstances of particular cases. Regulations, section 1.355–2(b)(1), provide that potential for tax avoidance is relevant in determining the extent to which the distribution is motivated by a bona fide corporate business purpose. There are numerous authorities identifying valid business purposes for a distribution under section 355. See Lester v. Commissioner, 40 T.C. 947 (1963) (A) (corporation was both warehouse distributor and jobber of auto parts; valid business purpose to separate the two businesses where warehouse business sold to other jobbers who objected to doing business with a company that was a competitor insofar as its jobber business was concerned); Olson v. Commissioner, 48 T.C. 855 (1967) (desire to confine union difficulties to one corporation was valid business purpose for spin-off distribution); Rev. Rul. 69–460, 1969–2 Cum.Bull. 51 (valid business purpose for distribution of a subsidiary corporation was upheld where necessary to permit key employees to buy into the parent corporation at a price which they could afford; but where the key employees desired to buy into the subsidiary corporation, there was no business purpose for distribution of the subsidiary); Rev.Rul. 85–127, 1985–2 Cum.Bull. 119, and Rev.Rul. 88–34, 1988–1 Cum.Bull. 115 (same conclusions); Rev.Rul. 72–530, 1972–2 Cum.Bull. 212 (valid business purpose to distribute stock of subsidiary to facilitate a merger involving the parent corporation, where state law restrictions imposed serious disadvantages on handling transaction through creation of a new corporation); Rev.Rul. 76–527, 1976–2 Cum.Bull. 103 (valid business purpose to distribute stock of subsidiary to enable subsidiary to acquire an unrelated corporation, where the acquired corporation would not accept the subsidiary stock if it were controlled by the distributing corporation); Rev. Rul. 77–22, 1977–1 Cum.Bull. 91 (valid business purpose to distribute stock of subsidiary to enable each corporation to obtain separate borrowing limits from a bank, the aggregate borrowing limits of the two separate corporations being greater than that of the parent-subsidiary); Rev.Rul. 82–130, 1982–2 Cum.Bull. 83 (valid business purpose to distribute stock of real estate subsidiary with long-term indebtedness to facilitate financing by parent in high-technology business; underwriters stated that subsidiary's long-term debt would make it difficult for the parent to raise equity in a public offering and that significant commitment to subsidiary's real estate activities made the parent corporation less attractive to investors; also notes that a holding company with parent and subsidiary as subsidiaries would raise the same problems); Rev.Rul. 82–131, 1982–2 Cum.Bull. 83 (valid business purpose to distribute stock of unregulated subsidiary by regulated parent to justify parent's rate increase for its regulated business; regulatory agency included subsidiary's earnings in rate base to deny rate increase to parent); Rev.Rul. 83–23, 1983–1 Cum.Bull. 82 (valid business purpose for spin-off to satisfy foreign decree requiring 60 percent direct ownership of local business by nationals); Rev.Rul. 85–122, 1985–2 Cum.Bull. 118 (valid business purpose for the separation of an unprofitable ski resort from profitable golf and tennis resort in order to meet the recommendation of securities underwriter on marketing of debentures); Rev.Rul. 88–33, 1988–1 Cum.Bull. 115 (valid business purpose to distribute stock of subsidiary to allow parent to escape burdensome administrative compliance costs imposed on it because of subsidiary's business; subsidiary was subject to state regulatory scheme which also required burdensome registration and compliance by the parent; stock of the subsidiary spun-off pro rata to the parent's stockholders in order to free the parent of the registration requirement).

E. THE "CONTINUITY OF INTEREST" REQUIREMENT

Regulations, section 1.355–2(c), impose a "continuity of interest" requirement in section 355 transactions. This requirement is closely related to the "device" provision in terms of preventing post-distribution sales. See Rev.Rul. 59–197, 1959–1 Cum.Bull. 77, treating a pre-distribution sale of stock in the distributing corporation as in effect a binding contract to sell stock in the newly-created corporation after the distribution; but the transaction did not constitute a "device" in view of the valid business purpose for the spin-off, i.e., to permit a key employee to obtain a proprietary interest in the spun-off business. Nonetheless, continuity of interest is an independent requirement aimed at limiting nonrecognition in corporate separations to transactions where shareholders of the original corporation maintain a continuing interest in each of the corporations surviving a division.

The continuity of interest doctrine in the divisive distribution area does not require that every stockholder in the distributing corporation maintain a continuing interest in each corporation surviving the division. A non-pro rata division may result in some of the stockholders of the divided corporation owning no interest at all in a business in which they were stockholders prior to the divisive reorganization.

The continuity of interest requirement is satisfied in a divisive reorganization as long as one or more of the stockholders of the original corporation retain sufficient continuing interest in each of the divided corporations, but not necessarily in both. Thus, the Regulations indicate that the continuity of interest requirement is satisfied in the following example: A and B own all of the stock of X Corporation. X in turn owns the stock of S Corporation. C acquires 50 percent of A's stock in X. Immediately thereafter, and as part of a prearranged plan, X distributes its S stock to B in exchange for B's stock in X. There is sufficient continuity of interest for nonrecognition treatment under section 355 since the former stockholders of X have a continuing interest in one of the businesses formerly undertaken by X. A has a 50 percent continuing interest in X, B has 100 percent continuing interest in S. Regulations, section 1.355–2(c)(2), Ex. (2). If C purchased all of A's X stock before the division continuity would not exist because the original stockholders of X would have a continuing interest in only one of the two corporations following division. Regulations, section 1.355–2(c)(2), Ex. (3). The Regulations, section 1.355–2(c)(2), Ex. (4), indicate further that a 20 percent continuing interest is not enough.

Some Rulings, issued mostly before the current Regulations were proposed in 1977, also illustrate the application of the continuity of interest requirement under section 355. Rev.Rul. 69–293, 1969–1 Cum.Bull. 102, disqualified a section 355 transaction for want of continuity of interest where two stockholders who owned all of the stock of a private university spun off a subsidiary trade school and then converted the distributing corporation into a section 501(c)(3) organization in order to qualify for federal financial aid; the stockholder proprietary interests were converted into non-proprietary interests and the requisite continuity of interests was therefore lacking. In Rev.Rul. 79–273, 1979–2 Cum.Bull. 125, continuity of interest was found lacking where P Corporation distributed the stock of its subsidiary to P stockholders as part of a reverse cash merger in which P was acquired by an unrelated corporation. Since the former P stockholders had no continuing interest in P, the distribution of S stock to the P stockholders did not qualify for nonrecognition treatment under section 355. The required continuity of interest was found in Rev.Rul. 62–138, 1962–2 Cum.Bull. 95, where a bank subsidiary owned two apartment buildings which banking regulatory authorities required the bank to divest. The subsidiary transferred the two apartment buildings to a new corporation and distributed the stock of that corporation to the bank, which in turn distributed the stock to its stockholders. See also Rev.Rul. 70–18, 1970–1 Cum.Bull. 74 (A, an individual, owned 100 percent of the stock of X and Y Corporations; Y Corporation owned 60 percent and X Corporation owned 40 percent of Z Corporation; Y Corporation was required to divest itself of its interest in Z Corporation; Y Corporation merged into X Corporation, which then distributed all of the Z stock to A; continuity of interest was satisfied under these circumstances); Rev.Rul. 76–528, 1976–2 Cum.Bull. 103 (continuity of interest requirement satisfied despite pre-split-up dissolution of partnership that owned 60 percent of the stock of the distributing corporation); Rev.Rul. 75–406, 1975–2 Cum. Bull. 125 (continuity of interest requirement satisfied despite post-distribution merger of spun-off corporation into unrelated third corporation by virtue of the continuing interest of the stockholders in the assets of the merged corporation).

F. REFERENCES

Posin, Once More Into the Serbonian Bog: Corporate Divisions After the 1986 Tax Reform Act, 13 J.Corp. Tax 635 (1988); Schneider, Internal Revenue Code § 355 Before and After the Tax Reform Act of 1986: A Study in the Regulation of Corporate Tax Bailouts, 39 Okla.L.Rev. 567 (1986).

Lee, Functional Divisions and Other Corporate Separations under Section 355 after *Rafferty,* 27 Tax L.Rev. 453 (1972); Lee, "Active Conduct" Distinguished from "Conduct" of a Rental Real Estate Business, 25 Tax Lawyer 317 (1972); Lee, The "Active Business" Test of Section 355: Implications of a Trilogy of Revenue Rulings, 31 Wash. & Lee L.Rev. 251 (1974); Jacobs, Spin-offs: The Pre-distribution Two Business Rule—Edmund P. Coady and Beyond, 19 Tax L.Rev. 155 (1964).

Crocker, the Business Purpose Test in Section 355 Distributions: Major Pitfalls for Close Corporation Planning, 15 Rich.L.Rev. 757 (1981); Cordes, The Device of Divisive Reorganizations: An Analysis of Section 355(a)(1)(B) and Its Relation to Section 368(a)(1)(D) and the Doctrines of "Continuity of Interest" and "Business Purpose," 10 Kan.L.Rev. 21 (1961); Cohen, Reconciling Business Purpose With Bail–Out Prevention: Federal Tax Policy and Corporate Divisions, 21 Stan.L.Rev. 1077 (1976).

Canellos, Using Spin–Offs in Planning: Spin–Offs in Combination With an Acquisition, 39 N.Y.U. Tax Inst. 9–1 (1981); Bugg, When the Party's Over: Use of Divisive Reorganizations for a Tax–Free Division of the Professional Service Corporation, 13 St. Mary's L.J. 113 (1981); Cohen, Tax–Free Acquisition of Part of a Corporation's Assets by Combining a Spin-off with a Unifying Reorganization, 26 N.Y.U. Tax Inst. 849 (1968); Massee, Section 355: Disposal of Unwanted Assets in Connection with a Reorganization, 22 Tax L.Rev. 439 (1967).

For materials on the Regulations as proposed in 1977, see New York State Bar Association Tax Section, Committee on Reorganizations, Report on Proposed Section 355 Regulations, 55 Taxes 656 (1977); Lee, Proposed Regs. Under Section 355 Overhaul Device Test and Single-business Divisions, 46 J.Tax 194 (1977); Helfand and Lafving, Filling the Serbonian Bog With Quicksand—Proposed Section 355 Regulations Further Obscure Corporate Separations, 5 J.Corp.Tax. 345 and 6 J.Corp.Tax. 53, 133 (1979).

C. DISTRIBUTION OF "CONTROL" REQUIREMENT

COMMISSIONER v. GORDON

Supreme Court of the United States, 1968.
391 U.S. 83.

MR. JUSTICE HARLAN delivered the opinion of the Court.

These cases, involving the interpretation of § 355 of the Internal Revenue Code of 1954, have an appropriately complex history.

American Telephone and Telegraph Company (hereafter A.T. & T.) conducts its local communications business through corporate subsidiaries. Prior to July 1, 1961, communications services in California, Oregon, Washington, and Idaho were provided by Pacific Telephone and Telegraph Company (hereafter Pacific). A.T. & T. held about 90% of the common stock of Pacific at all relevant times. The remainder was widely distributed.

Early in 1961, it was decided to divide Pacific into two separate corporate subsidiaries of A.T. & T. The plan was to create a new corporation, Pacific Northwest Bell Telephone Company (hereafter

Northwest) to conduct telephone business in Oregon, Washington, and Idaho, leaving the conduct of the California business in the hands of Pacific. To this end, Pacific would transfer all its assets and liabilities in the first three States to Northwest, in return for Northwest common stock and debt paper. Then, Pacific would transfer sufficient Northwest stock to Pacific shareholders to pass control of Northwest to the parent company, A.T. & T.

Pacific had, however, objectives other than fission. It wanted to generate cash to pay off existing liabilities and meet needs for capital, but not to have excess cash left over. It also feared that a simple distribution of the Northwest stock would encounter obstacles under California corporation law.[1] Consequently, the "Plan for Reorganization" submitted to Pacific's shareholders on February 27, 1961, had two special features. It provided that only about 56% of the Northwest common stock would be offered to Pacific shareholders immediately after the creation of Northwest. It also provided that, instead of simply distributing Northwest stock pro rata to shareholders, Pacific would distribute to its shareholders transferable rights entitling their holders to purchase Northwest common from Pacific at an amount to be specified by Pacific's Board of Directors, but expected to be below the fair market value of the Northwest common.

In its February 27 statement to shareholders, Pacific said that it was seeking a ruling from the Internal Revenue Service

"with respect to the tax status of the rights to purchase which will be issued in connection with the offerings of capital stock of the New Company to shareholders of the Company * * *."

The statement warned, however, that "[t]axable income to the holders of such shares may result with respect to such rights."

The plan was approved by Pacific's shareholders on March 24, 1961. Pacific transferred its assets and liabilities in Oregon, Washington, and Idaho to Northwest, and ceased business in those States on June 30, 1961. On September 29, 1961, Pacific issued to its common stockholders one right for each outstanding share of Pacific stock. These rights were exercisable until October 20, 1961. Six rights plus a payment of $16 were required to purchase one share of Northwest common. The rights issued in 1961 were sufficient to transfer about 57% of the Northwest stock.

By September 29, 1961, the Internal Revenue Service had ruled that shareholders who sold rights would realize ordinary income in the amount of the sales price, and that shareholders who exercised rights would realize ordinary income in the amount of the difference between

1. The record indicates that Pacific's attorneys had advised that if Pacific distributed the Northwest shares without payment of consideration by Pacific's shareholders, the distribution would have to be charged to earned surplus; the attorneys further advised that Pacific had insufficient earned surplus for this purpose, and that if this difficulty were avoided by creation of a reduction surplus, the reduction surplus would, under California law, have to be used first to redeem Pacific's preferred shares.

$16 paid in and the fair market value, measured as of the date of exercise, of the Northwest common received. The prospectus accompanying the distributed rights informed Pacific shareholders of this ruling.

On June 12, 1963, the remaining 43% of the Northwest stock was offered to Pacific shareholders. This second offering was structured much as the first had been, except that eight rights plus $16 were required to purchase one share of Northwest.

The Gordons, respondents in No. 760, and the Baans, petitioners in No. 781, were minority shareholders of Pacific as of September 29, 1961. In the rights distribution that occurred that day the Gordons received 1,540 rights under the plan. They exercised 1,536 of the rights on October 5, 1961, paying $4,096 to obtain 256 shares of Northwest, at a price of $16 plus six rights per share. The average price of Northwest stock on the American Stock Exchange was $26 per share on October 5. On the same day, the Gordons sold the four odd rights for $6.36. The Baans received 600 rights on September 29, 1961. They exercised them all on October 11, 1961, receiving 100 shares of Northwest in return for their 600 rights and $1,600. On October 11, the agreed fair market value of one Northwest share was $26.94.

In their federal income tax returns for 1961, neither the Gordons nor the Baans reported any income upon the receipt of the rights or upon exercising them to obtain Northwest stock at less than its fair market value. The Gordons also did not report any income on the sale of the four rights. The Commissioner asserted deficiencies against both sets of taxpayers. He contended, in a joint proceeding in the Tax Court, that the taxpayers received ordinary income in the amount of the difference between the sum they paid in exercising their rights and the fair market value of the Northwest stock received. He contended further that the Gordons realized ordinary income in the amount of $6.36, the sales price, upon the sale of their four odd rights.

The Tax Court upheld the taxpayers' contention that the 1961 distribution of Northwest stock met the requirements of § 355 of the Code, with the result that no gain or loss should be recognized on the receipt by them or their exercise of the rights. The Tax Court held, however, that the Gordons' sale of the four odd rights resulted in ordinary income to them. The Commissioner appealed the *Baan* case to the Court of Appeals for the Ninth Circuit, and the *Gordon* case to the Court of Appeals for the Second Circuit; in the latter, the Gordons cross-appealed. The Ninth Circuit reversed the Tax Court, holding that the spread between $16 and fair market value was taxable as ordinary income to the Baans. The Second Circuit disagreed, sustaining the Tax Court on this point in the *Gordon* case, Judge Friendly dissenting. The Second Circuit went on to hold that the amount received by the Gordons for the four odd rights was taxable as a capital gain rather than as ordinary income, reversing the Tax Court on this point.

Because of the conflict, we granted certiorari. 389 U.S. 1033, 1034. We affirm the decision of the Court of Appeals for the Ninth Circuit, and reverse the decision of the Court of Appeals for the Second Circuit on both points.

Under §§ 301 and 316 of the Code, subject to specific exceptions and qualifications provided in the Code, any distribution of property by a corporation to its shareholders out of accumulated earnings and profits is a dividend taxable to the shareholders as ordinary income. Every distribution of corporate property, again except as otherwise specifically provided, "is made out of earnings and profits to the extent thereof." It is here agreed that on September 28, 1961, Pacific's accumulated earnings and profits were larger in extent than the total amount the Commissioner here contends was a dividend—the difference between the fair market value of all Northwest stock sold in 1961 and the total amount, at $16 per share, paid in by purchasers.

Whether the actual dividend occurs at the moment when valuable rights are distributed or at the moment when their value is realized through sale or exercise, it is clear that when a corporation sells corporate property to stockholders or their assignees at less than its fair market value, thus diminishing the net worth of the corporation, it is engaging in a "distribution of property" as that term is used in § 316.[4] Such a sale thus results in a dividend to shareholders unless some specific exception or qualification applies. In particular, it is here agreed that the spread was taxable to the present taxpayers unless the distribution of Northwest stock by Pacific met the requirements for nonrecognition stated in § 355, or § 354, or § 346(b) of the Code.[5]

4. See, e.g., Choate v. Commissioner, 129 F.2d 684 (C.A.2d Cir.). In Palmer v. Commissioner, 302 U.S. 63, 69, 58 S.Ct. 67, 70 this Court said:

"While a sale of corporate assets to stockholders is, in a literal sense, a distribution of its property, such a transaction does not necessarily fall within the statutory definition of a dividend. For a sale to stockholders may not result in any diminution of its net worth and in that case cannot result in any distribution of its profits.

"On the other hand such a sale, if for substantially less than the value of the property sold, may be as effective a means of distributing profits among stockholders as the formal declaration of a dividend."

In *Palmer,* rights were distributed entitling shareholders to purchase from the corporation shares of stock in another corporation. Finding that the sales price represented the reasonable value of the shares at the time the corporation committed itself to sell them, this Court found no dividend. It held that the mere issue of rights was not a dividend. It has not, however, been authoritatively settled whether an issue of rights to purchase at less than fair market value itself constitutes a dividend, or the dividend occurs only on the actual purchase. In the present case this need not be decided. [Ed.: See also supra, page 480.]

5. It is important to begin from this premise. In our view, the Court of Appeals for the Second Circuit erred in its approach to the § 355 problem because it assumed, at the outset, that the Commissioner essentially sought to tax a transaction that brought no "income" to Pacific shareholders. Whether the shareholders received income, however, cannot in practice be determined in the abstract, before looking at § 355.

Any common shareholder in some sense "owns" a fraction of the assets of the corporation in which he holds stock, including those assets that reflect accumulated corporate earnings. Earnings are not taxed to the shareholder when they accrue to the corporation, but instead when they are passed to shareholders individually through dividends. Consequently it does

Since the Tax Court concluded that the requirements of § 355 had been met, it did not reach taxpayers' alternative contentions. Under the disposition that we make here upon the § 355 question, these alternative contentions remain open for further proceedings in the Tax Court.

Section 355 provides that certain distributions of securities of corporations controlled by the distributing corporation do not result in recognized gain or loss to the distributee shareholders. The requirements of the section are detailed and specific, and must be applied with precision. It is no doubt true, as the Second Circuit emphasized, that the general purpose of the section was to distinguish corporate fission from the distribution of earnings and profits. However, although a court may have reference to this purpose when there is a genuine question as to the meaning of one of the requirements Congress has imposed, a court is not free to disregard requirements simply because it considers them redundant or unsuited to achieving the general purpose in a particular case. Congress has abundant power to provide that a corporation wishing to spin off a subsidiary must, however bona fide its intentions, conform the details of a distribution to a particular set of rules.

The Commissioner contends that the 1961 distribution of Northwest stock failed to qualify under § 355 in several respects.[7] We need, however, reach only one. Section 355(a)(1)(D) requires that, in order to qualify for nonrecognition of gain or loss to shareholders, the distribution must be such that

"as part of the distribution, the distributing corporation distributes—

"(i) all of the stock and securities in the controlled corporation held by it immediately before the distribution, or

not help to note, as the Second Circuit here did, that the distribution of Northwest stock merely changed the form of ownership that Pacific's shareholders enjoyed and did not increase their wealth. This is only very roughly true at best, but in the rough sense in which it is here true, it is true of any dividend. The question is not whether a shareholder ends up with "more" but whether the change in the form of his ownership represents a transfer to him, by the corporation, of assets reflecting its accumulated earnings and profits.

There may be a genuine theoretical difference between a change in form representing a mere corporate fission, separating what the shareholder owns into two smaller but essentially similar parts, and a change in form representing a dividend, separating what a shareholder owns *qua* shareholder from what he owns as an individual. This difference, however, must be defined by objectively workable tests, such as Congress supplied in § 355. Neither the Second Circuit nor the taxpayers have suggested any other way of identifying a true fission.

7. The Commissioner contends, first, that Pacific did not distribute "solely stock or securities" as required by § 355(a)(1)(A), because it distributed rights rather than stock. He contends, second, that Pacific did not distribute the Northwest stock "to a shareholder, with respect to its stock" as required by § 355(a)(1)(A)(i), because it did not distribute the stock to shareholders but sold it to holders of transferable rights, for cash consideration. He contends, third, that Northwest did not meet the quantity requirements of § 355(a)(1)(D) because it parted with only 57% of the stock in 1961.

Any one of these arguments, if established, would support the result the Commissioner seeks. The Court of Appeals for the Second Circuit perforce rejected all three. The Court of Appeals for the Ninth Circuit accepted all three. We reach only the last.

"(ii) an amount of stock in the controlled corporation constituting control within the meaning of section 368(c), and * * *"

Section 368(c) provides in relevant part that

"the term 'control' means the ownership of stock possessing at least 80 percent of the total combined voting power of all classes of stock entitled to vote and at least 80 percent of the total number of shares of all other classes of stock of the corporation." [8]

On September 28, 1961, the day before the first rights distribution, Pacific owned all of the common stock of Northwest, the only class of securities that company had issued. The 1961 rights offering contemplated transferring, and succeeded in transferring, about 57% of the Northwest common to Pacific shareholders. It therefore could not be clearer that this 1961 distribution did not transfer "all" of the stock of Northwest held by Pacific prior to it, and did not transfer "control" as that term is defined in § 368(c).

Nevertheless, taxpayers contend, and the Second Circuit agreed, that the requirements of subsection (a)(1)(D) were here met because Pacific distributed the remaining 43% of the Northwest stock in 1963. The court said that the purpose of the subsection "in no way requires a single distribution." [9] The court apparently concluded that so long as it appears, at the time the issue arises, that the parent corporation has in fact distributed all of the stock of the subsidiary, the requirements of § (a)(1)(D)(i) have been satisfied.

We are forced to disagree. The Code requires that "the distribution" divest the controlling corporation of all of, or 80% control of, the controlled corporation. Clearly, if an initial transfer of less than a controlling interest in the controlled corporation is to be treated for tax purposes as a mere first step in the divestiture of control, it must at least be identifiable as such at the time it is made. Absent other specific directions from Congress, Code provisions must be interpreted so as to conform to the basic premise of annual tax accounting.[10] It would be wholly inconsistent with this premise to hold that the essential character of a transaction, and its tax impact, should remain not only undeterminable but unfixed for an indefinite and unlimited period in the future, awaiting events that might or might not happen. This requirement that the character of a transaction be determinable does not mean that the entire divestiture must necessarily occur within a

8. In the Tax Court, the Commissioner did not argue that Pacific had failed to meet the requirement that it distribute at least 80% of the Northwest stock, but rested upon his other arguments against applying § 355. When the Tax Court rejected these arguments, the Commissioner raised the 80% question, as well as his other arguments in both Courts of Appeals. Both considered the point on the merits, dividing on it as on the others. Since the general issue of the applicability of § 355 has been in the case since its inception, taxpayers do not contend that the 80% question is not properly before this Court. Since the record leaves no disputed issue of fact with respect to this question, we find it proper to decide it here without reference to a trier of fact.

9. 382 F.2d 499, 507.

10. See Burnet v. Sanford & Brooks Co., 282 U.S. 359–363–365, 51 S.Ct. 150, 151–152.

single tax year. It does, however, mean that if one transaction is to be characterized as a "first step" there must be a binding commitment to take the later steps.[11]

Here, it was little more than a fortuity that, by the time suit was brought alleging a deficiency in taxpayers' 1961 returns, Pacific had distributed the remainder of the stock. The plan for reorganization submitted to shareholders in 1961 promised that 56% of that stock would be distributed immediately. The plan went on,

"It is expected that within about three years after acquiring the stock of the New Company, the Company by one or more offerings will offer for sale the balance of such stock, following the procedures described in the preceding paragraph. The proceeds from such sales will be used by the Company to repay advances then outstanding and for general corporate purposes including expenditures for extensions, additions and improvements to its telephone plant.

"The prices at which the shares of the New Company will be offered pursuant to the offerings referred to * * * will be determined by the Board of Directors of the Company at the time of each offering."

It was further stated that such subsequent distributions would occur "[a]t a time or times related to its [Pacific's] need for new capital." Although there is other language in the plan that might be interpreted as preventing Pacific management from dealing with the Northwest stock in any way inconsistent with eventual sale to Pacific shareholders, there is obviously no promise to sell any particular amount of stock, at any particular time, at any particular price. If the 1961 distribution played a part in what later proved to be a total divestiture of the Northwest stock, it was not, in 1961, either a total divestiture or a step in a plan of total divestiture.

Accordingly, we hold that the taxpayers, having exercised rights to purchase shares of Northwest from Pacific in 1961, must recognize ordinary income in that year in the amount of the difference between $16 per share and the fair market value of a share of Northwest common at the moment the rights were exercised.

The second question presented by the petition in No. 760, whether the $6.36 received by taxpayers Gordon upon the sale of four rights was taxable as ordinary income, as a capital gain, or not at all, does not

11. The Commissioner contends that a multistep divestiture presents special problems in preventing bailouts of earnings and profits. The Second Circuit, recognizing such potential problems, held that they can be dealt with under § (a)(1)(B), which provides that nonrecognition shall result only when it appears that

"the transaction was not used principally as a device for the distribution of the earnings and profits of the distributing corporation or the controlled corporation or both. * * *"

Congress may, of course, have chosen not to leave problems created by multistep divestitures to specific adjudication under this "device" subsection, but to require *both* a unitary divestiture *and* satisfaction of the "device" requirement. Whether § (a)(1)(D) would prohibit or limit a divestiture of control committed from the outset but spread over a series of steps is a problem we need not reach.

require extended discussion in light of our view upon the first question. Since receipt and exercise of the rights would have produced ordinary income, receipt and sale of the rights, constituting merely an alternative route to realization, also produced income taxable at ordinary rates. Helvering v. Horst, 311 U.S. 112, 61 S.Ct. 144; Gibson v. Commissioner, 133 F.2d 308 (C.A.2d Cir.).

The judgment of the Court of Appeals for the Second Circuit is reversed. The judgment of the Court of Appeals for the Ninth Circuit is affirmed.

It is so ordered.

MR. JUSTICE MARSHALL took no part in the consideration or decision of these cases.

ILLUSTRATIVE MATERIAL

A. SUBSEQUENT DEVELOPMENTS IN *GORDON*

Following the Supreme Court decision in *Gordon,* the case went back to the Tax Court for consideration of the taxpayer's alternative arguments. The Tax Court held, 51 T.C. 1032 (1969), that the taxpayer could not prevail, either under section 354 or the predecessor to section 302(e). As to the applicability of section 302(e) to the transaction, see supra, page 587. The taxpayer also argued that an acquisitive type (D) reorganization was involved and the distribution was covered under section 354. The Tax Court held that the stock rights did not constitute "securities" and therefore section 354(a)(1) did not apply. In addition, the Tax Court held that section 354(b)(1) was not applicable since, if the transaction were tested as a type (D) reorganization, Pacific did not transfer substantially all its assets to Northwest and did not distribute all the stock and securities it received from Northwest in return, as section 354(b)(1) requires. The Court of Appeals affirmed the Tax Court, 424 F.2d 378 (2d Cir.1970) on these grounds.

B. THE DISTRIBUTION REQUIREMENT

In Redding v. Commissioner, 630 F.2d 1169 (7th Cir.1980), the courts again were presented with a transaction similar to that before the Supreme Court in *Gordon.* In *Redding,* the parent corporation distributed transferable rights to its stockholders which enabled the stockholders to subscribe to shares of stock of the parent corporation's wholly owned subsidiary. The rights could be exercised only for a two-week period. A stockholder could receive one share of the subsidiary's stock for two rights plus $5. During the two-week period the fair market value of the subsidiary's stock ranged from $5.70 per share to $7 per share. An over-the-counter market for the warrants developed during this subscription period. After the two-week period, the warrants became worthless. The Commissioner and the taxpayers stipulated that, as the result of the exercise of the stock rights, more than 80 percent of the subsidiary's stock was distributed in the offering. The parties stipulated further that there was a good business purpose for the distribution of the subsidiary stock, the distribution was not a device for the distribution of earnings and profits, and the 20 percent of the subsidiary's stock retained by the parent corporation was not held for tax avoidance purposes under section 355(a)(1)(D)(ii).

The Commissioner asserted that the rights distribution constituted a taxable dividend under section 301, relying on Rev.Rul. 70–521, 1970–2 Cum.Bull. 72, to that effect. The taxpayers, on the other hand, asserted that the transaction was an integrated transaction and qualified under section 355. The Tax Court, 71 T.C. 597 (1979), following its initial decision in Baan v. Commissioner, 45 T.C. 71 (1965), held that the requirements of section 355(a)(1)(A) and (D) were met. The issuance of the rights by the distributing corporation "was merely a procedural device to give [the distributing corporation] stockholders the opportunity to be included or excluded from the [subsidiary] stock distribution." Having found that the distribution of the stock rights was "merely a brief transitory phase of the corporate separation", the Tax Court concluded that the requirements of section 355(a)(1)(A) and (D) were met. The requisite 80 percent of the subsidiary stock was in fact distributed and after the transaction the stockholders held only stock of the subsidiary.

The Court of Appeals disagreed with the Tax Court's finding that the issuance of the warrants was only a procedural step. The Court of Appeals concluded that the warrants had independent economic significance in light of their readily ascertainable market value and transferability on an open market. The issuance of the warrants could not, therefore, be disregarded as a mere transitory step in the distribution of the stock of the subsidiary to stockholders of the distribution corporation. The Court of Appeals concluded further that the distribution of the stock of the subsidiary failed the requirement of section 355(a)(1)(A) that the stock of the controlled corporation be distributed with respect to the stock of the distributing corporation. Since the warrants had independent significance, the distribution of the subsidiary's stock was made with respect to the warrants rather than the stock of the distributing corporation. The court held that the distribution of warrants was a dividend to the stockholders.[5]

Although it felt bound by the parties' stipulation that 80 percent control of the subsidiary was distributed to the stockholders of the distributing corporation, the Court of Appeal in *Redding* questioned whether the control requirement of section 355(a)(1)(D) was in fact satisfied. For valid business reasons the distributing corporation retained 1 share less than 20 percent of the subsidiary's stock. Fifty thousand shares of the subsidiary's stock were distributed to underwriters. The remaining shares distributed with respect to exercised warrants represented approximately 76 percent of the subsidiary's stock. Following the dissent of Judge Sterrett in the Tax Court, 71 T.C. at 617, the Court of Appeals read section 355(a)(1)(D) in conjunction with section 355(a)(1)(A) to require the distribution of control to persons who were the stockholders of the distributing corporation before the division. That requirement was not satisfied in *Redding* because of the distribution of stock to the underwriters.

The Internal Revenue Service has indicated that it will use the step transaction doctrine to find a distribution in a section 355 transaction in appropriate cases. In Rev.Rul. 83–142, 1983–2 Cum.Bull. 68, a foreign subsidiary of a United States parent corporation distributed assets to a new subsidiary, the controlled corporation, in exchange for stock. To satisfy a requirement of the foreign country in which it was incorporated, the subsidia-

5. Receipt of the warrants was not sheltered from dividend treatment under section 305 because the warrants did not represent rights to acquire the stock of the distributing corporation. 630 F.2d at 1181.

ry sold the stock of the controlled corporation to its parent for cash. The subsidiary thereupon redistributed the cash to its parent as a dividend. The Service held that the transfer of stock of the controlled corporation to the parent was a section 355 distribution by the subsidiary. The subsidiary's sale of stock and subsequent return of cash as a dividend were disregarded for Federal tax purposes as transitory steps taken for the purpose of complying with local law.

Although Commissioner v. Morris Trust, 367 F.2d 794 (4th Cir.1966), discussed supra, page 925, held that a post-distribution tax-free reorganization of the distributing corporation does not invalidate a section 355 transaction, the Service held in Rev.Rul. 70–225, 1970–1 Cum.Bull. 80, that an attempted post-distribution (B) reorganization involving the stock of the controlled subsidiary defeated nonrecognition treatment because of the control requirement of section 368(a)(1)(D). T Corporation desired to acquire one of two businesses of R Corporation. Pursuant to a prearranged plan, R Corporation transferred the assets of the desired business to a newly created subsidiary and then distributed the stock of the subsidiary to its sole stockholder. The stockholder then immediately exchanged the stock of the subsidiary for stock of T Corporation in an attempted (B) reorganization. The spin-off failed because the stockholder failed to acquire control of the distributed corporation. The transaction was treated in effect as a transfer by R Corporation of part of its assets in exchange for stock of T Corporation, followed by a distribution of the T Corporation stock as a dividend to the sole stockholder of R Corporation. Rev.Rul. 75–406, 1975–2 Cum.Bull. 125, upheld a section 355 transaction where a post-distribution merger of the spun-off corporation into an unrelated corporation was not pursuant to a prearranged plan. Likewise, Rev.Rul. 73–246, 1973–1 Cum.Bull. 181, approved a post-distribution section 351 transfer in which a stockholder transferred all of the stock in the distributed corporation to another wholly owned corporation.

C. RETENTION OF STOCK OR SECURITIES

Section 355(A)(1)(D) permits the distributing corporation to retain up to 20 percent of the stock of the spun-off corporation if it is established that the retention of the stock was not motivated by tax avoidance purposes. Regulations, section 1.355–2(e)(2), warn, however, that ordinarily the corporate business purpose for a divisive reorganization will require the distribution of all the stock and securities of the controlled corporation. The Internal Revenue Service, in addition to examining whether there is a good business purpose for retention of any stock or securities, also looks to whether the retained stock gives the distributing corporation "practical control" over the spun-off corporation. See Rev.Rul. 75–321, 1975–2 Cum. Bull. 123 (pursuant to federal banking laws, distributing corporation was required to divest itself of at least 95 percent of the stock of a bank subsidiary; retention of a percent of the bank stock to use as collateral for short-term financing for the distributing corporation's remaining business enterprises was for a valid business purpose and the retained interest did not give the distributing corporation practical control); Rev.Rul. 75–469, 1975–2 Cum.Bull. 126 (stock of controlled corporation was pledged as collateral for bank loan; to eliminate dissident stockholders, the distributing corporation desired to spin-off the subsidiary's stock, but the bank required substitute collateral for the loan; debenture issued by the subsidiary to the parent, which was pledged to the bank to secure the loan, could be retained since it gave the distributing corporation no practical control over the spun-off corporation).

D. STOCK OF THE CONTROLLED CORPORATION AS BOOT

Section 355(a)(3)(B) provides that stock of the controlled corporation which had been acquired by the distributing corporation in a taxable transaction within the five year period preceding distribution to stockholders will be treated as other property taxable to the stockholders as boot.

Trust of E.L. Dunn v. Commissioner, 86 T.C. 745 (1986), narrowly interpreted the meaning of "acquired" in a taxable transaction. In a taxable reverse triangular merger consummated on May 12, 1982, AT&T acquired all of the stock of Pacific Telephone and Telegraph with the exception of nonvoting preferred stock held by institutional investors. Following this transaction, AT&T owned the only share of Pacific common stock outstanding. The reverse triangular merger was a taxable transaction because, by virtue of the outstanding nonvoting preferred stock, AT&T did not meet the control requirement of section 368(c). On August 24, 1982, a long standing antitrust action between AT&T and the United States government was settled with a judicially approved agreement that AT&T would divest itself of each of its regional telephone operating companies, including Pacific. At that time, AT&T was the common parent of a group of corporations known as the Bell System. The divestiture plan required AT&T to group its 22 operating companies into seven regional holding companies. The stock of the regional holding companies was distributed to AT&T stockholders pro rata. As part of this plan, Pacific was reorganized under section 368(a)(1)(E) to convert the single share of Pacific Stock held by AT&T into 224,504,982 shares of voting common stock (the number of shares outstanding before AT&T's taxable reorganization of Pacific) and to convert the nonvoting preferred stock into voting preferred stock. By virtue of this transaction the holding company to which Pacific was transferred, the PacTel Group, would acquire control of Pacific within the meaning of section 368(c). AT&T transferred its Pacific stock along with other assets to the PacTel Group in exchange for all of the stock of the PacTel Group which was then distributed to AT&T stockholders in the divestiture.

The Commissioner asserted that the receipt of PacTel Group stock was taxable in part to the AT&T stockholders as a dividend under section 355(a)(3)(B) because a portion of the value of the PacTel Group stock represented the stock of Pacific acquired by AT&T in a taxable merger within five years of the distribution. The Tax Court rejected the Commissioner's argument and held that the distribution was completely tax free to the AT&T stockholders. The court read section 355(a)(3)(B) literally, concluding that the provision applied only to the stock of the controlled corporation which is distributed to the stockholders of the distributing corporation. The controlled corporation is the corporation which the distributing corporation controls immediately before the distribution. The Tax Court refused to look through the controlled corporation, in this case the PacTel Group, to examine the stock of its subsidiaries for purposes of applying the boot rule of section 355(a)(3)(B). The court reasoned in part that since Congress carefully provided a look-through rule for purposes of identifying under section 355(b)(2)(D) whether a trade or business had been acquired "directly (or through 1 or more corporations)" in a taxable transaction by the controlled corporation, Congress would have specifically provided a similar look-through rule in subdivision (a)(3)(B) if it had intended such a rule to be applied.

SECTION 2. POLICY ANALYSIS OF SECTION 355

SIMON AND SIMMONS, THE FUTURE OF SECTION 355.

40 Tax Notes 291 (1988).

It is apparent from the history of section 355 that the focus of its cumulative and overlapping restrictions is on the bailout potential of corporate divisions. The statute requires continuity of business enterprise and continuity of shareholder interest in order to prevent the shareholder from converting an interest in corporate assets into cash at capital gain rates. The separated actively conducted businesses must be continued in corporate solution by the same owners. Not incidentally, of course, compliance with the shareholder-tax-focused requirements of section 355 permits the deferral of whatever corporate level tax might otherwise be imposed on the distribution.

In the two-tier tax structure that exists after the 1986 Act, without a capital gain preference but with tax at the corporate level on asset appreciation in corporate redemptions and liquidations, the importance of section 355 as a defense against an earnings bailout is significantly diminished. Bailout *per se* is no longer a relevant concern. What is of more significance is the fact that section 355 permits corporate level tax deferral in transactions that fit its requirements. Thus, despite the focus of section 355 prior to the 1986 Act on the shareholder tax, Congress clearly expressed the view with its 1987 revisions to section 355 that the provision has a role in plugging the dike of complete double taxation erected by the 1986 Act.

In this environment, any analysis of section 355 must consider initially whether a divisive restructuring of a corporate organization justifies nonrecognition treatment at the corporate level, shareholder level, or both. If it is determined that some divisive restructurings should continue to be permitted, the issue is which ones are appropriately deserving of nonrecognition treatment. In the current tax environment, therefore, the principal question is whether stock acquisitions and dispositions that fit within the literal language of section 355 ought to be permitted when their principal purpose is avoidance of the corporate tax on asset appreciation.

The first of these questions borders on the metaphysical, at least insofar as tax issues can be so described. Nonrecognition treatment for both the corporate parties to an acquisitive corporate reorganization and their shareholders is generally justified by the underlying assumption that stock or securities received in the exchange represent a continuation of the old investment in a revised corporate form. Other justifications for nonrecognition include suggestions that the exchange of stock and securities is just a paper transaction, taxing such gains would impede legitimate business transactions, the transaction yields no cash, and the shareholder is at the mercy of actions undertaken by the corporation. All of these rationalizations fall short to some extent when applied to a transaction in which the shareholders of a closely held target corporation receive the stock of a large publicly held entity in exchange for their target stock. In spite of significant changes in the nature of the shareholder's investment, however, the shareholder's continued interest in assets in corporate form provides the basic underpinnings for nonrecognition with carryover basis. Acquisitive reorganizations—even those that involve significant dilution of shareholder interests in the corporate assets—are thus favored under current law.

While the conclusion is not entirely free from doubt, it is arguable that the degree to which the shareholder's relationship to corporate assets is changed in a corporate divorce does not differ significantly from the change in the shareholder's relationship to corporate assets in a corporate marriage. As a result, the logic supporting nonrecognition treatment in acquisitive reorganizations should apply with equal force to divisive transactions. Thus, the basic theory underlying the favorable tax treatment of divisive restructurings is that they are closely analogous to acquisitive reorganizations. What this suggests, then, is that the basic reorganization requirements are inherent in section 355 and have been since its inception.

Taking this view, the [current] regulations under section 355 provide that nonrecognition treatment is appropriate only in an exchange of stock or securities which is "incident to such readjustment of corporate structures as is required by business exigencies and which effected only a readjustment of continuing interest in property under modified corporate forms." If one accepts the premise that nonrecognition is appropriate in a corporate division because of the shareholders' continued interest in corporate assets, then section 355 occupies an important place in the Code by providing a description of divisive restructurings of corporate interests entitled to nonrecognition. It is also the vehicle for imposing appropriate limitations to ensure the existence of sufficient continuity of shareholder interest. As is the case with acquisitive reorganizations, nonrecognition is justified by continued interests in assets in corporate solution at both the shareholder and corporate levels. Further, the notion of shareholder continuity of interest in assets remaining in corporate solution provides a framework for assessing the post–1986 Act role of section 355.

* * *

A. Anti–Bailout Provisions

Without a capital gain preference, the underlying historic purpose behind the "device" restriction and the active trade or business requirements of section 355 largely disappears. Looking back at the checkered history of section 355 prior to the adoption of the 1954 Code, the principal concern with respect to the propriety of permitting tax-free spin-offs was that taxpayers such as Mrs. Gregory would subvert the substance of any spin-off provision by converting an ordinary dividend result into a capital gain transaction. When section 355 came into being in the 1954 Code, it was designed to encourage legitimate corporate divisions. It was also structured to prevent bailouts, and its anti-bailout role was reinforced by numerous overlapping tests.

While the portions of section 355 that are designed to prevent bailouts are not a model of statutory clarity and precision, the general focus of section 355 on the shareholder level tax should be preserved for the foreseeable future. Perhaps we proceed from an excess of caution, but in the not unlikely event that Congress enacts a new capital gain preference, it seems appropriate to be prepared for it. In addition, section 355 continues to distinguish between ordinary dividends and nontaxable distributions. If the latter are followed by stock sales, the difference between a dividend and a sale producing capital gain is still of some importance, particularly where the taxpayer's basis in her stock is high. Finally, as interpreted by the [current] regulations, the device clause requires a degree of shareholder continuity in divisive reorganizations. * * * Thus, it is useful to retain section 355 in the statute to serve legitimate goals related to the shareholder level tax.

That does not, however, suggest that the current statute and the 1977 proposed regulations thereunder should simply be left as is. Some changes in the current scheme may be appropriate, either to better tailor section 355 to accomplish its intended purpose with respect to shareholder level conversion or to make its application fairer. * * *

Section 355(a)(2)(A) currently provides that distributions of stock or securities are to be treated as tax-free to the stock—or security—holder regardless of whether they are pro rata. One possible objection to this is the theory that pro rata spin-offs are really dividends and ought to be taxed as such both for shareholder and for corporate level tax purposes. Under an approach that would treat spin-offs as dividends, split-offs would also receive dividend treatment unless they satisfied one of the exceptions to dividend treatment under section 302(b).

If section 355 were amended to remove pro rata distributions from its ambit, nonrecognition of gain or loss at the corporate and shareholder levels would be available under section 355 only in situations in which there was a complete division of the original corporation, with the owners of its separate parts going their separate ways. If this approach were followed, the result would be that the device and active trade or business requirements of the current section 355 would be of importance mainly to prevent the use of a split-up to accomplish a bailout.

Alternatively, it is thought by some that non pro rata distributions are the ones treated inappropriately under section 355. This thinking is reinforced by the recent Tax Court decision in Esmark v. Commissioner,[33] which was not decided under section 355, but which considered

33. 90 T.C. No. 171 (1988).

a transaction that is the functional equivalent of a classical split-off.[34] The theory behind the position that non prorata distributions should be removed from section 355 is that it permits nonrecognition of gain due to asset appreciation in transactions in which shareholder interests in various corporate assets are revised in an exchange. The basic approach would be to amend section 355 to eliminate the theoretical inconsistency in its application to transactions that are the functional equivalent of transactions in which asset gain is taxed under sections 311 and 336.

Addressing the first point with respect to the equivalence of spin-offs and dividends, we think it is appropriate to continue to permit spin-offs to be tax-free as long as the requirements that prevent bailouts are met. The logic of current section 355's approach to corporate divisions has two general underpinnings. First, what is distributed is stock of a corporation and not its assets. The assets remain in corporate solution. Thus, the justification for immediate double taxation is reduced.

Second, the continuity of interest requirement implicit in the device requirement (and explicit in the current * * * regulations) supplies the theoretical justification for nonrecognition at the shareholder level. Shareholders who retain their shares following a pro rata spin-off are in essentially the same tax and economic position before and after the distribution except that the form of their ownership of assets formerly in a single corporation or in a parent/subsidiary group is changed to ownership of separate entities. By requiring continuity, the statute provides nonrecognition only to real corporate readjustments closely akin to acquisitive corporate reorganizations. We note here, as we did previously, that the theoretical legitimacy of nonrecognition treatment under section 355 largely depends on the extent to which the continuity of interest requirement is strictly applied.

* * *

In the case of a non pro rata distribution, a split-up, or split-off, the focus of inquiry is not on the potential for an earnings and profits bailout. * * *

Despite the lack of bailout potential, however, a transaction in which a shareholder's interest in corporate assets is revised as in a split-up or a split-off also raises the question whether nonrecognition is appropriate in those cases. In a non pro rata distribution in the form of a split-up or split-off, the shareholders exchange all or a portion of their interest in the distributing corporation for an increased interest in the corporate assets of the distributed corporation. There is clearly

34. Esmark intended to restructure its business by disposing of its energy subsidiaries and redeeming its shares. Pursuant to an agreement, Mobil acquired over 50 percent of Esmark's shares in a public tender offer, and Esmark then distributed shares of Vickers, its wholly owned subsidiary, in redemption of the shares acquired by Mobil. Rejecting the government's argument that the transaction was merely a sale of Vickers to Mobil, the Tax Court held that Esmark's distribution of Vickers stock in exchange for its own stock was a redemption qualified for nonrecognition under pre-1986 sections 311(a) and 311(d)(2)(B). * * *

less continuity of interest here than in a pro rata spin-off.[37a] Nonetheless, it appears that nonrecognition treatment is generally appropriate in these transactions. The shareholders' revised interests in assets in corporate solution are not dissimilar from revisions that occur in acquisitive reorganizations. In both cases the shareholders continue an ownership interest in some original assets, but in different percentages and in a different form. The common thread to all of these transactions is the shareholders' continued ownership of assets in corporate solution.

It is appropriate to compare the results under section 355 with the vastly different tax treatment of partial liquidations under section 302(b)(4). Both transactions involve the distribution to shareholders of an active trade or business undertaken by the distributing corporation for the five-year period preceding the distribution. Where a trade or business is distributed directly to shareholders in kind in a partial liquidation, whether or not pro rata, gain or loss is recognized at both the corporate and shareholder levels. Under section 355, if the trade or business distributed to shareholders is housed in a corporation, no gain or loss is recognized at either level. The distinction is justified only by the shareholders' continued interest in corporate assets retained in corporate solution. In the nonrecognition transaction double tax is deferred to be recognized on the shareholder's disposition of the distributed stock, as well as on the corporation's disposition of its assets. In a partial liquidation, immediate recognition of gain or loss on distribution of a trade or business to individual shareholders is justified because the business assets leave the corporate fold entirely. There is no future opportunity to tax the corporate level gain in the case of the partial liquidation distribution.

Noting this distinction between partial liquidations and divisive restructurings under section 355 makes it amply clear that the role of section 355 in the tax law after the repeal of *General Utilities* is an important one because the section permits transactions to be accomplished without corporate level tax. * * * [T]he question becomes whether section 355 should be changed in any way so as to deny its application to transactions that are fundamentally asset acquisitions rather than divisive restructurings of ongoing corporate organizations.

Example: * * * *T* Corp operates stores in two locations, Los Angeles and San Diego. The two businesses are not functionally integrated with each other except to the extent that warehouse and trucking operations are shared. The values of the two businesses are approximately equal. *P* Corp desires to buy the assets of *T* that are devoted to the operation of its San Diego store and the delivery trucks used by the two stores. *T* Corp may organize a new subsidiary, contributing to it the assets related to the San Diego store and the delivery trucks, and it may distribute the stock of the new subsidiary to

37a. See Case v. Commissioner, 103 F.2d 283 (9th Cir.1939) for the recognition of this lack of continuity of interest under prior law.

its shareholders, avoiding recognition of corporate level gain under section 355. The shareholders may sometime thereafter sell the stock of the newly formed corporation to *P* Corp. Thus, only a single level of tax will be paid if *T* is successful in its assertion that section 355 applies to the transaction.[40]

Whether or not the statute should now be amended to prevent the application of section 355 to the * * * transaction and to similar transactions that produce the same economic result is an important question. * * *

Although the radical approach to eliminating end-runs around *General Utilities* repeal through the use of section 355 would be to eliminate section 355 from the Code, it is not necessary to go that far. * * * What should not be continued is the use of section 355 to circumvent the clear intent of Congress to require gain recognition in asset acquisitions and their functional equivalents.

* * * One alternative that has been discussed would have Treasury simply amend its treatment of the device restriction in the regulations to prevent the use of section 355 to avoid recognition of corporate level gain in acquisitive transactions. While that approach has a certain seductive appeal, we do not agree with it. The historical function of the device clause is to deal with shareholder tax issues, and we think it should be left that way.

There are, however, other alternatives that should be explored in more detail. * * * One method of dealing with the avoidance of the corporate level tax on asset appreciation would be to require the distributees of the stock of the controlled corporation to hold the stock for some period (five years, for example) after the distribution. This alternative was suggested by the staff of the Joint Committee on Taxation in a list of revenue options it published in June 1987.[44] With a holding period of this sort, the statute would continue its focus on the shareholder tax, but with an added requirement for qualification under section 355 that would stifle attempts to use it to avoid the corporate level tax * * *. This requirement would tend to reinforce the device restriction in the statute and the continuity of interest and business purpose requirements * * *. It would make the transaction described in our Example * * * a taxable distribution both for the corporation and the shareholders.

However, this solution has a fundamental flaw. It would essentially make section 355 inapplicable to public corporations unless aggregation and segregation rules similar to those under section 382 were to be

40. While it is clear that a prearranged sale implicates the device clause, a sale that is not prearranged will not necessarily oust section 355 from application. The step transaction doctrine may, of course, cause this transaction to flunk section 355. But that requires that subjective tests be applied. In addition, it should be noted that a post-distribution acquisition that is nontaxable will presumably qualify the distribution under section 355. See Commissioner v. Morris Trust, 367 F.2d 794 (4th Cir.1966) * * *.

44. Joint Committee on Taxation, Description of Possible Options to Increase Revenues Prepared for the Committee on Ways and Means, 172 (Comm.Print 1987).

applied.[47] The proposal could, of course, be modified by providing, for example, that a business purpose would suffice to make section 355 apply despite a sale of a large percentage of the distributed stock during the holding period, which would have the effect of permitting the use of the subjective step transaction doctrine to such instances. Alternatively, the holding period requirement could be applied only to five percent or greater shareholders, with the public aggregated as under section 382.

If such a post-distribution holding period were hedged about by special rules regarding the purpose of the sale of the stock, rebuttable presumptions, etc., the proposed rule would no longer be simple. While we are not entirely comfortable with a rule that would make a *de facto* distinction between large and small corporations, it is preferable to save section 355 treatment for a limited number of legitimate transactions than to abandon it altogether. Thus, this proposal has merit even if there are problems with its application.

Other possibilities for dealing with the *General Utilities* repeal avoidance problem abound. * * * One would be to amend section 355 by removing the entire parenthetical clause in section 355(a)(1)(B) so that any sales after distribution would not be given favorable treatment. This would have the same result as the holding period in the first option we discussed, but would test the transaction on the basis of more subjective continuity of interest and step transaction principles with variable application. It would have the virtue of making the application of section 355 to publicly traded corporations a possibility as long as the business purpose test of the regulations is satisfied, which would tend to make this solution preferable to the one advanced by the JCT staff. This proposal has the additional benefit of refocusing the inquiry under section 355 on the shareholders' retention of a continuing interest in the distributed corporate stock. The proposal relies on the shareholder-oriented device clause, however, to solve the corporate level recognition issue in acquisitive transactions. Because continuing a subjective approach to the shareholder holding period is desirable, an alternative to this proposal would be to adopt a separate requirement that section 355 not be used as a device to avoid *General Utilities* repeal.

Other possible solutions to the perceived problem would remove non pro rata distributions from section 355's ambit, at least to the extent that corporate level tax treatment is at issue. While that would clearly achieve the desired effect, it also seems overly complicated because it would set up additional tests for section 355's application in only limited circumstances. Alternatively, it would be possible to amend section 355 so that it applied to non pro rata distributions only to historic common shareholders.[48] This solution does not differ much

47. See I.R.C. section 382(g)(4) and the proposed regulations issued thereunder.

48. This would take care of *Esmark* and related problems. See, e.g., Rev.Rul. 83–38, 1983–1 C.B. 77; Idol v. Commissioner, 38 T.C. 444, *aff'd*, 319 F.2d 647 (8th Cir. 1963); and Standard Linen Service, Inc. v. Commissioner, 33 T.C. 1 (1959).

from the others and shares their virtues and their defects. Further, as we have discussed above, application of section 355 to non pro rata distributions seems to be appropriate as long as shareholders maintain sufficient continuity of interest in assets held in corporate solution. Thus, the real issue with respect to trying to resolve section 355's role after *General Utilities* repeal is essentially how to apply the requirement of continuity of shareholder interest. * * *

* * *

There is more than one aspect to the continuity of interest requirement in the context of the corporate level tax. On the one hand, what seems to be suggested by the proposed holding period discussed above is that there should be shareholder continuity after the distribution so that raiders could not sell off stock or unwanted assets as it suited them. On the other hand, the application of section 355's non pro rata distribution rule to historic common shareholders suggests that continuity of interest might be tested at some time prior to the distribution. The distributee shareholders' predistribution holding period would thus be relevant in determining whether there is a tax on the corporate level asset gain in what are fundamentally asset acquisitions.

* * *

It seems clear that a continuity of interest requirement focused on the corporate level tax in order to determine whether or not it is properly deferred under section 355 would bolster the business purpose test of the current and proposed regulations under section 355. Limiting section 355 to historic shareholders' continued participation would prevent a distribution for the purpose of an asset acquisition by an outsider. Thus, where the acquisition of stock is motivated solely by the desire on the part of the acquiror to obtain assets more cheaply (e.g., without the tax at the corporate level on asset appreciation) by virtue of the fact that they are acquired in a corporate shell rather than directly, there would presumably be no business purpose for the acquisition and distribution.

In analyzing the scope of the continuity of interest doctrine as it applies to determining whether the corporate level tax should be collected in circumstances that formally fit within section 355, it is important to keep in mind that the economic position of a recent purchaser of stock in the distributing corporation is not much different from the position of an historic shareholder. In each instance, the shareholder would have an interest before the distribution that differed little from her interest in altered corporate form after the distribution. The major difference between the two situations is that the recent purchaser had, only a short time before, acquired an interest that entitled her to the distribution and had done so in a transaction in which gain was recognized. Requiring predistribution continuity of interest in all circumstances would thus extend the rule in section

A further alternative would be to expand the application of section 346(b) (transactions that reach the same result as partial liquidations (e.g., split-offs and split-ups)) to ensure that *General Utilities* repeal is not avoided.

355(a)(2)(D) to its logical limits, and it would do so in the context of strengthening the underlying business purpose requirement of section 355.

It is apparent, then, that a predistribution holding period for the stock, either stated explicitly or as a limitation on section 355's non pro rata distribution rule to historic common shareholders, would have the same function as the requirement for a post-distribution holding period would have. It would help to limit section 355's application to legitimate restructurings of the corporate form in which the original parties' intent is to continue a business investment in assets held in corporate solution for some extended period of time. In addition, it would bolster the device clause with respect to the shareholder level tax by recognizing that a predistribution sale of stock can have much the same effect as a prearranged post-distribution sale.[50]

In the section 355 context, continuity of shareholder interest has overarching importance in ensuring that the statutory purposes are served. Thus, it appears appropriate to impose a requirement that would test continuity of shareholder interest both before and after the purported section 355 stock distribution. Although such a test might be thought to be somewhat stricter than the test for continuity of interest in an acquisitive reorganization, * * * [s]ection 355 currently requires five-year continuity of business enterprise and five-year continuity of shareholder interest (through the distributing corporation) where a subsidiary is acquired in a taxable transaction prior to its distribution to shareholders of the distributing corporation. Thus, it does not seem inappropriate to suggest that a five-year before and after rule would accomplish the intended result and would have the further virtue of using the same time period currently used in the statute a number of times.

While this test may appear to be harsh and to disqualify a number of legitimate transactions, the same can be said of any arbitrary rule.

50. See Rev.Rul. 59–196, 1959–1 C.B. 641.

PART VI

CARRYOVER OF CORPORATE ATTRIBUTES IN REORGANIZATIONS AND OTHER TRANSACTIONS

CHAPTER 20

CARRYOVER OF TAX ATTRIBUTES

INTERNAL REVENUE CODE: Section 381

COMMISSIONER v. SANSOME

United States Court of Appeals, Second Circuit, 1932.
60 F.2d 931.

[Corporation A in 1921 transferred all its assets to newly-formed Corporation B in return for all of the latter's stock, which went to the Corporation A shareholders. Corporation A had a large amount of earnings and profits. Corporation B did not earn profits after its formation but instead suffered some losses. Corporation B then made cash distributions in 1923 which under the applicable statute, section 201 of the 1921 Act, were taxable if those distributions were out of "its earnings and profits." If the earnings and profits of Corporation A were taken into account, then the distributions would be taxable. The 1921 transaction was a reorganization under the applicable statute, section 202(c)(2).]

L. HAND, CIRCUIT JUDGE. * * * It seems to us that [§ 202(c)(2) of the 1921 Act] should be read as a gloss upon [§ 201 of the 1921 Act]. That section provides for cases of corporate "reorganization" which shall not result in any "gain or loss" to the shareholder participating in them, and it defines them with some particularity. He must wait until he has disposed of the new shares, and use his original cost as the "base" to subtract from what he gets upon the sale. Such a change in the form of the shares is "an exchange of property," not a "sale or other disposition" of them * * *. It appears to us extremely unlikely that what was not "recognized" as a sale or disposition for the purpose of fixing gain or loss, should be "recognized" as changing accumulated profits into capital in a section which so far overlapped the latter. That in substance declared that some corporate transactions should not break the continuity of the corporate life, a troublesome question that the courts had beclouded by recourse to such vague alternatives as "form" and "substance," anodynes for the pains of reasoning. The effort was at least to narrow the limits of judicial inspiration, and we cannot think that the same issue was left at large in the earlier section. Hence we hold that a corporate reorganization which results in no "gain or loss" under [§ 202(c)(2) of the 1921 Act], does not toll the company's life as a continued venture under [§ 201 of the 1921 Act], and that what were "earnings or profits" of the original * * * company remain, for purposes of distribution, "earnings and profits" of the successor * * *.

Order reversed; cause remanded for further proceedings in accord with the foregoing.

ILLUSTRATIVE MATERIAL

A. GENERAL

The *Sansome* doctrine respecting earnings and profits is but one facet of a larger problem—to what extent is the transferee corporation to be regarded as succeeding to the tax characteristics, benefits and obligations possessed by the transferor corporation, where both were parties to a tax-free reorganization. Prior to 1954, the rules regarding carryover of corporate attributes were found mainly in court decisions. The 1939 Code contained only one provision, the predecessor to section 269 (discussed infra, page 993), which was intended to restrict the transfer of tax benefits in transactions motivated by thoughts of tax avoidance.

Section 381, enacted in 1954, contains detailed but non-exclusive statutory rules regarding the carryover of items in corporate liquidations and reorganizations in which the successor corporation steps into the shoes of the predecessor corporation. Under section 381(a), corporate attributes carryover on the liquidation of a controlled subsidiary in which the parent takes the basis of the subsidiary's assets pursuant to sections 332 and 334(b), discussed supra, page 622, and in type (A), (C), and (F) reorganizations and nondivisive type (D) and (G) reorganizations. In general, section 381 applies to transactions in which the transferor corporation is absorbed by the transferee.

B. CARRYOVER OF EARNINGS AND PROFITS

Sections 381(a) and 381(c)(2) provide in general that in the transactions covered under section 381(a) the earnings and profits, or deficit in earnings and profits, of the transferor or distributor corporation carry over to the acquiring corporation, but that any deficit of the corporations involved shall be used only to offset earnings and profits accumulated after the date of transfer or distribution. See Regulations, section 1.381(c)(2)–1(a)(5). Thus, a deficit earnings account of one corporation cannot be used to offset pre-transfer accumulated earnings of the other. See Regulations, section 1.381(c)(2)–1(a)(2). If both corporations either have accumulated earnings, or a deficit in accumulated earnings, the earnings and profits accounts are consolidated into a single account in the surviving corporation. Regulations, section 1.381(c)(2)–1(a)(4). Regulations, section 1.381(c)(2)–1(a)(2), also provide that earnings and profits inherited by the acquiring corporation become part of its accumulated earnings and profits, but not part of current earnings and profits for purposes of section 316(a)(2).

The rule that a deficit in accumulated earnings can offset only profits accumulated after the date of transfer requires identification of the transfer date. Regulations, section 1.381(b)–1(b)(1), provide that the relevant date is the date on which the transfer is finally completed. Regulations, section

1.381(b)–1(b)(2) and (3), also allow the taxpayer to specify a transfer date by filing a statement indicating the date on which substantially all of the assets of the transferor are transferred and the transferor has ceased business operations. The Regulations allow the transferor to retain reasonable assets to pay the corporation's debts and to preserve its corporate existence.

Regulations, section 1.381(c)(2)–1(c), require an adjustment to the earnings and profits of the acquired corporation to reflect distributions. In the case of a reorganization, the earnings and profits of the transferor corporation as of the transfer date are reduced for distributions of property to the stockholders of the transferor corporation. The adjustment applies to distributions of both stock and securities received by the stockholders without recognition of gain under the reorganization provisions, and property received as boot. In the case of a liquidation of the transferor corporation under section 332, the earnings and profits of the transferor must be adjusted to account for distributions of property to minority stockholders. In both cases, the adjustments are required whether the distributions are made before or after the transfer date.

C. CARRYOVER OF NET OPERATING LOSSES

1. *General*

The carryover of net operating losses is probably the most significant corporate tax attribute affected by section 381. Normally a corporation with a net operating loss for the taxable year is entitled to carryback its loss to the three taxable years preceding the loss year, and then forward for the next fifteen taxable years. Section 172(b)(1)(A), (B). Section 381(c)(1) allows the carryover of the transferor's net operating loss to the acquiring corporation in a transaction covered by section 381(a), but limits the carryover to taxable income of the acquiring corporation attributable to the period following the transfer date. If the transfer date is any day other than the last day of the acquiring corporation's taxable year, the taxable year of the acquiring corporation is divided into two periods and taxable income is allocated to each period on a daily basis. An inherited loss carryover may be deducted by the acquiring corporation in the year of the transfer only against income allocated to the period subsequent to the transfer date.[1] If the acquiring corporation acquires several loss corporations during a taxable year, the taxable year of the acquiring corporation will be divided into several short periods, one for the transfer date of each acquisition. Regulations, section 1.381(c)(1)–2(b)(2). If the transfer occurs on the last day of the acquiring corporation's taxable year, the inherited loss carryover may be used only in subsequent taxable years. Examples of the operation of these rules can be found in Regulations, section 1.381(c)(2)–1(a)(7).

Even though section 381 provides for the carryover of net operating losses to the acquiring corporation, section 382, discussed infra, Chapter 21, restricts the rate at which those losses may be claimed against post-acquisition income, even if that income is derived from the business of the acquired corporation.

The taxable year of the transferor corporation ends on the transfer date. Section 381(b)(1). Under section 381(b)(3), net operating losses of the

1. This results in the creation of two counting periods for carryover purposes; one carryover year for the transferor corporation ending on the transfer date, and a second period ending on the last day of the acquiring corporation's taxable year.

acquiring corporation may not be carried back to taxable years of the transferor corporation preceding the transfer date, except in an (F) reorganization. See supra, page 886. Thus, for example, if X Corporation acquires the assets of Y Corporation in a statutory merger, and following the transfer date the combined enterprise incurs a net operating loss, the loss cannot be carried back to pre-acquisition profitable years of Y, even if the loss is attributable entirely to a trade of business acquired from Y. The loss may, however, be carried back and deducted from pre-acquisition taxable income of X, the acquiring corporation.

The exception from the carryback limitation of section 381(b)(3) for type (F) reorganizations gave that transaction a heightened significance for a period of time. The use of an (F) reorganization to avoid the carryback limitation of section 381(b)(3) was curtailed by Congress in 1982, however, with an amendment to section 368(a)(1)(F) which limits the (F) reorganization to a change involving a single operating company. See H.Rep. No. 97–760, 97th Cong., 2d Sess. 541 (1982),[2] discussed supra, page 886.

2. *Liquidation of a Worthless Subsidiary*

In the case of a parent-subsidiary relationship, there is an interplay between sections 381 and 165(g)(3). If section 332 applies to the liquidation of a controlled subsidiary, see supra, page 622, section 381 provides for the carryover to the parent of the subsidiary's tax attributes. But section 332 does not apply to the liquidation of an 80 percent controlled subsidiary unless some assets of the liquidating subsidiary are allocable to the common stock, after payment of all creditors and preferred stockholders including the parent. If the common stock of the subsidiary is worthless, then section 332 is not applicable and section 381(a) does not permit a carryover of net operating losses. See Rev.Rul. 68–359, 1968–2 Cum.Bull. 161; Rev.Rul. 68–602, 1968–2 Cum.Bull. 135. However, if the parent owns 80 percent of the subsidiary stock (and the subsidiary was operating a business), then section 165(g)(3) applies to give the parent an ordinary loss on its stock and security investment in the subsidiary. "Securities" here means any debt obligation that is in registered form or with interest coupons. If the debt obligation is not a security, an ordinary loss still results under section 166. These ordinary losses in turn can create both loss carrybacks and carryovers for the parent, the duration of which starts with the year of worthlessness. If section 165(g)(3) does not apply, the parent's worthless stock and security losses are capital losses, with other worthless debt losses being ordinary.

In Marwais Steel Co. v. Commissioner, 354 F.2d 997 (9th Cir.1965), a subsidiary corporation borrowed operating capital from its parent and incurred net operating losses. The parent claimed bad debt deductions with respect to loans made to the subsidiary. The subsidiary was subsequently liquidated and the parent attempted to use the subsidiary's net operating losses under section 381. Despite the literal satisfaction of section 381, the court denied the carryover since the net operating losses had formed the rationale for the previous bad debt deductions, and double deduction was not

2. Before 1982, a number of cases held that the combination into a single entity of more than one corporation under common control could constitute an (F) reorganization thereby allowing a carryback of post transfer losses from the combined entity to pre-transfer years of one or more of the corporate parties to the reorganization. See e.g., Estate of Stauffer v. Commissioner, 403 F.2d 611 (9th Cir.1968); Home Construction Corporation of America v. United States, 439 F.2d 1165 (5th Cir.1971); Movielab, Inc. v. United States, 494 F.2d 693 (Ct.Cl.1974).

permitted. But in Textron Inc. v. United States, 561 F.2d 1023 (1st Cir. 1977), discussed infra, page 988, a parent corporation was allowed to claim a deduction for the worthless stock of its subsidiary despite the fact that the subsidiary was subsequently able to acquire a new profitable business and use its net operating loss carryovers to offset the income from the new business. Section 382(g)(4)(D) now limits the use of net operating losses by the parent in a *Textron* type situation.

D. CAPITAL LOSS CARRYOVERS

Under section 381(c)(3), the transferor's excess capital losses carryover to the acquiring corporation on much the same terms as net operating losses. The inherited capital loss carryover becomes a capital loss carryover of the acquiring corporation for purposes of section 1212, the capital loss carryover provision. The transferor's capital losses are available to the acquiring corporation in the acquiring corporation's first taxable year ending after the transfer date, section 381(c)(3)(A), but the amount of the transferor's capital loss that can be utilized by the acquiring corporation in the year of the transfer is limited to the proportion of the acquiring corporation's capital gain net income that is allocable on a daily basis to the portion of the acquiring corporation's taxable year remaining after the transfer date. Section 381(c)(3)(B). In addition, under section 381(b)(3), any net capital loss of the acquiring corporation incurred after the transfer date cannot be carried back to offset capital gain net income of the transferor derived in a taxable year ending on or prior to the transfer date.

E. OTHER ATTRIBUTE CARRYOVER ITEMS

In addition to earnings and profits and loss carryovers, section 381(c) lists a number of separate corporate attributes which carryover in a transaction described by section 381(a). Several of these provisions deal with accounting issues. In general, section 381(c)(4) provides for continuation of the transferor's method of accounting, but authorizes Regulations to prescribe the method to be used if the parties to the transfer use different methods. Under Regulations, section 1.381(c)(4)–1(b)(2), if the acquiring corporation maintains the assets of the transferor as a separate and distinct trade or business, the acquiring corporation must continue to use the accounting method of the transferor with respect to that trade or business. If the assets of the transferor are integrated into a trade or business of the acquiring corporation, the acquiring corporation must adopt whichever accounting method is determined to be the "principal method of accounting" based on a comparison of the relative asset bases and gross receipts of the component businesses immediately preceding the transfer date. Regulations, section 1.381(c)(4)–1(b)(2), (c). In any event, the method adopted must clearly reflect income of the acquiring corporation and the acquiring corporation may apply for permission from the Commissioner to adopt a different method of accounting. Any change in a method of accounting under these provisions may require adjustments under section 481, which is intended to avoid double counting of income and deduction items. A method of accounting for purposes of section 381(c)(4) includes, under section 446, the accounting treatment of any material item of income or deduction in addition to the taxpayer's overall method of accounting. Regulations, section 1.382(c)(4)–1(a)(2). Thus, section 381(c)(4) applies broadly to numerous items not specifically enumerated in section 381(c).

Several accounting matters are specifically described in section 381(c): inventory accounting carries over under rules similar to accounting methods, section 381(c)(5); the acquiring corporation inherits the transferor's depreciation and capital recovery elections and methods, sections 381(c)(6) and (24); the transferor's installment sales reporting continues without change, section 381(c)(8); amortization of premium and discount on the transferor's bonds for which the acquiring corporation becomes liable are reported by acquiring corporation as they would have been by the transferor, section 381(c)(9); and the acquiring corporation is entitled to the benefits of section 111 with respect to the recovery of items previously deducted by the transferor, section 381(c)(12).

The acquiring corporation steps directly into the shoes of the transferor with respect to some deduction and credit items: the acquiring corporation may deduct contributions to employee benefit plans under section 404, section 381(c)(11); the acquiring corporation inherits an obligation to replace property involuntarily converted if nonrecognition treatment was claimed by the transferor under section 1033, section 381(c)(13); the acquiring corporation becomes entitled to general business credit carryovers and is potentially liable for credit recapture, section 381(c)(25); and the acquiring corporation becomes entitled to the transferor's section 53 credit for prior year alternative minimum tax liability, section 381(c)(27).

Section 381(c)(16) allows the acquiring corporation to deduct payments of liabilities which result from obligations of the transferor assumed by the acquiring corporation if the liability would have been deductible by the transferor if paid by it. This provision permits the acquiring corporation to avoid capitalization of such liabilities as part of the cost of the acquired assets. Section 381(c)(16) provides, however, that deductibility is available only if the assumed obligation is not reflected in the amount of stock or securities transferred by the acquiring corporation for the assets of the transferor. Regulations, section 1.381(c)(16)–1(b)(5), provide that if the liability is known at the time of transfer, and the amount of consideration transferred by the acquiring corporation is reduced to account for the liability, the liability will be treated as reflected in the stock transfer. Otherwise, it is presumed that a liability is not reflected in the consideration transferred. Regulations, section 1.381(c)(16)–1(a)(1), provide that a liability not subject to section 381(c)(16) is subject to the general accounting provision of section 381(c)(4). Although this reference may be read to require that a liability assumed as part of the consideration for the acquisition must be capitalized, that is not necessarily the case. In Rev.Rul. 83–73, 1983–1 Cum.Bull. 84, the taxpayer acquired the assets of Y Corporation in a type (A) reorganization. The assets were subject to an outstanding contingent claim against Y which the taxpayer settled for $700x. Pursuant to an agreement entered into at the time of the reorganization, the former stockholders of Y reimbursed the taxpayer for $500x. The $500x reimbursement was based on the taxpayer's cost of settling the claim, taking into account the taxpayer's section 162 deduction for the payment. The Internal Revenue Service held that, because of the former stockholders' indemnity agreement, the contingent liability was reflected in the consideration given for the transfer of the assets. Thus, payment of the liability was not covered by section 381(c)(16). The Ruling further held, however, that the $500x reimbursement from Y's former stockholders was to be deemed a nontaxable contribution by them to Y's capital, and that the taxpayer's satisfaction of the claim was deductible under

Y's accounting method which carried over to the taxpayer under section 381(c)(4) and Regulations, section 1.381(c)(4)–1(a)(1).

F. REFERENCES

Nesson Earnings and Profits Discontinuities under the 1954 Code, 77 Harv.L.Rev. 450 (1964); Halperin, Carryovers of Earnings and Profits, 18 Tax L.Rev. 289 (1963); Zarky and Biblin, The Role of Earnings and Profits in the Tax Law, 18 So.Cal.Tax Inst. 145, 174 (1966); Petri, Handling E & P in Corporate Mergers, Liquidations and Reorganizations, 40 J. Tax 48 (1974); LaRue, A Case for Neutrality in the Design and Implementation of the Merger and Acquisition Statutes: The Post–Acquisition Net Operating Loss Carryback Limitations, 43 Tax L.Rev. 85 (1987).

CHAPTER 21

LIMITATIONS ON NET OPERATING LOSS CARRYOVERS

INTERNAL REVENUE CODE: Sections 382; 383; 384.

GENERAL EXPLANATION OF THE TAX REFORM ACT OF 1986

Staff of the Joint Committee on Taxation 288–299 (1987).

Overview

In general, a corporate taxpayer is allowed to carry a net operating loss ("NOL(s)") forward for deduction in a future taxable year, as long as the corporation's legal identity is maintained. After certain nontaxable asset acquisitions in which the acquired corporation goes out of existence, the acquired corporation's NOL carryforwards are inherited by the acquiring corporation. Similar rules apply to tax attributes other than NOLs, such as net capital losses and unused tax credits. Historically, the use of NOL and other carryforwards has been subject to special limitations after specified transactions involving the corporation in which the carryforwards arose (referred to as the "loss corporation"). [Pre–1986] law also provided other rules that were intended to limit tax-motivated acquisitions of loss corporations.

The operation of the special limitations on the use of carryforwards turned on whether the transaction that caused the limitations to apply took the form of a taxable sale or exchange of stock in the loss corporation or one of certain specified tax-free reorganizations in which the loss corporation's tax attributes carried over to a corporate successor. After a purchase (or other taxable acquisition) of a controlling stock interest in a loss corporation, NOL and other carryforwards were disallowed unless the loss corporation continued to conduct its historical trade or business. In the case of a tax-free reorganization, NOL and other carryforwards were generally allowed in full if the loss corporation's shareholders received stock representing at least 20 percent of the value of the acquiring corporation.

NOL and other carryforwards

Although the Federal income tax system generally requires an annual accounting, a corporate taxpayer was allowed to carry NOLs back to the three taxable years preceding the loss and then forward to each of the 15 taxable years following the loss year (sec. 172). The rationale for allowing the deduction of NOL carryforwards (and carrybacks) was that a taxpayer should be able to average income and losses over a period of years to reduce the disparity between the taxation of businesses that have stable income and businesses that experience fluctuations in income.

In addition to NOLs, other tax attributes eligible to be carried back or forward include unused investment tax credits (secs. 30 and 39), excess foreign tax credits (sec. 904(c)), and net capital losses (sec. 1212). Like NOLs, unused investment tax credits were allowed a three-year carryback and a 15-year carryforward. Subject to an overall limitation based on a taxpayer's U.S. tax attributable to foreign-source income, excess foreign tax credits were allowed a two-year carryback and a five-year carryforward. For net capital losses, generally, corporations had a three-year carryback (but only to the extent the carrybacks did not increase or create a NOL) and a five-year carryforward.

NOL and other carryforwards that were not used before the end of a carryforward period expired.

Carryovers to corporate successors

In general, a corporation's tax history (e.g., carryforwards and asset basis) was preserved as long as the corporation's legal identity was continued. Thus, under the general rules of prior law, changes in the stock ownership of a corporation did not affect the corporation's tax attributes. Following are examples of transactions that effected ownership changes without altering the legal identity of a corporation:

(1) A taxable purchase of a corporation's stock from its shareholders (a "purchase"),

(2) A type "B" reorganization, in which stock representing control of the acquired corporation is acquired solely in exchange for voting stock of the acquiring corporation (or a corporation in control of the acquiring corporation) (sec. 368(a)(1)(B)),

(3) A transfer of property to a corporation after which the transferors own 80 percent or more of the corporation's stock (a "section 351 exchange"),

(4) A contribution to the capital of a corporation, in exchange for the issuance of stock, and

(5) A type "E" reorganization, in which interests of investors (shareholders and bondholders) are restructured (sec. 368(a)(1)(E)).

Statutory rules also provided for the carryover of tax attributes (including NOL and other carryforwards) from one corporation to another in certain tax-free acquisitions in which the acquired corporation went out of existence (sec. 381). These rules applied if a corporation's assets were acquired by another corporation in one of the following transactions:

(1) The liquidation of an 80-percent owned subsidiary (sec. 332),

(2) A statutory merger or consolidation, or type "A" reorganization (sec. 368(a)(1)(A)),

(3) A type "C" reorganization, in which substantially all of the assets of one corporation is transferred to another corporation in exchange for voting stock, and the transferor completely liquidates (sec. 368(a)(1)(C)),

(4) A "nondivisive D reorganization," in which substantially all of a corporation's assets are transferred to a controlled corporation, and the transferor completely liquidates (secs. 368(a)(1)(D) and 354(b)(1)),

(5) A mere change in identity, form, or place of organization of a single corporation, or type "F" reorganization (sec. 368(a)(1)(F)), and

(6) A type "G" reorganization, in which substantially all of a corporation's assets are transferred to another corporation pursuant to a court approved insolvency or bankruptcy reorganization plan, and stock or securities of the transferee are distributed pursuant to the plan (sec. 368(a)(1)(G)).

In general, to qualify an acquisitive transaction (including a B reorganization) as a tax-free reorganization, the shareholders of the acquired corporation had to retain "continuity of interest." Thus, a principal part of the consideration used by the acquiring corporation had to consist of stock, and the holdings of all shareholders had to be traced. Further, a tax-free reorganization was required to satisfy a "continuity of business enterprise" test. Generally, continuity of business enterprise requires that a significant portion of an acquired corporation's assets be used in a business activity (see Treas. reg. sec. 1.368–1(d)).

Acquisitions to evade or avoid income tax

The Secretary of the Treasury was authorized to disallow deductions, credits, or other allowances following an acquisition of control of a corporation or a tax-free acquisition of a corporation's assets if the principal purpose of the acquisition was tax avoidance (sec. 269). This provision applied in the following cases:

(1) where any person or persons acquired (by purchase or in a tax-free transaction) at least 50 percent of a corporation's voting stock, or stock representing 50 percent of the value of the corporation's outstanding stock;

(2) where a corporation acquired property from a previously unrelated corporation and the acquiring corporation's basis for the property was determined by reference to the transferor's basis; and

(3) where a corporation purchased the stock of another corporation in a transaction that qualified for elective treatment as a direct asset purchase (sec. 338), a section 338 election was not made, and the acquired corporation was liquidated into the acquiring corporation (under sec. 332).

Treasury regulations under section 269 provided that the acquisition of assets with an aggregate basis that is materially greater than their value (i.e., assets with built-in losses), coupled with the utilization of the basis to create tax-reducing losses, is indicative of a tax-avoidance motive (Treas.reg. sec. 1.269–3(c)(1)).

* * *

1954 Code special limitations

The application of the special limitations on NOL carryforwards was triggered under the 1954 Code by specified changes in stock ownership of the loss corporation (sec. 382). In measuring changes in stock ownership, section 382(c) specifically excluded "nonvoting stock which is limited and preferred as to dividends." Different rules were provided for the application of special limitations on the use of carryovers after a purchase and after a tax-free reorganization. Section 382 did not address the treatment of built-in losses.

If the principal purpose of the acquisition of a loss corporation was tax avoidance, section 269 would apply to disallow NOL carryforwards even if section 382 was inapplicable.

* * *

Special limitations on other tax attributes

Section 383 incorporated by reference the same limitations contained in section 382 for carryforwards of investment credits, foreign tax credits, and capital losses.

* * *

Reasons for Change

* * *

Preservation of the averaging function of carryovers

The primary purpose of the special limitations is the preservation of the integrity of the carryover provisions. The carryover provisions perform a needed averaging function by reducing the distortions caused by the annual accounting system. If, on the other hand, carryovers can be transferred in a way that permits a loss to offset unrelated income, no legitimate averaging function is performed. With completely free transferability of tax losses, the carryover provisions become a mechanism for partial recoupment of losses through the tax system. Under such a system, the Federal Government would effectively be required to reimburse a portion of all corporate tax losses. Regardless of the merits of such a reimbursement program, the carryover rules appear to be an inappropriate and inefficient mechanism for delivery of the reimbursement.

Appropriate matching of loss to income

[Amendments to section 382 enacted in 1976 which never became effective] reflect the view that the relationship of one year's loss to another year's income should be largely a function of whether and how much the stock ownership changed in the interim, while the *Libson Shops* business continuation rule [Ed.: See infra, page 991] measures the relationship according to whether the loss and the income were generated by the same business. The Act acknowledges the merit in both approaches, while seeking to avoid the economic distortions and administrative problems that a strict application of either approach would entail.

A limitation based strictly on ownership would create a tax bias against sales of corporate businesses, and could prevent sales that would increase economic efficiency. For example, if a prospective buyer could increase the income from a corporate business to a moderate extent, but not enough to overcome the loss of all carryovers, no sale would take place because the business would be worth more to the less-efficient current owner than the prospective buyer would reasonably pay. A strict ownership limitation also would distort the measurement of taxable income generated by capital assets purchased before the corporation was acquired, if the tax deductions for capital costs economically allocable to post-acquisition years were accelerated into pre-acquisition years, creating carryovers that would be lost as a result of the acquisition.

Strict application of a business continuation rule would also be undesirable, because it would discourage efforts to rehabilitate troubled businesses. Such a rule would create an incentive to maintain obsolete and inefficient business practices if the needed changes would create the risk of discontinuing the old business for tax purposes, thus losing the benefit of the carryovers.

Permitting the carryover of all losses following an acquisition, as is permitted under the 1954 Code if the loss business is continued following a purchase, provides an improper matching of income and loss. Income generated under different corporate owners, from capital over and above the capital used in the loss business, is related to a pre-acquisition loss only in the formal sense that it is housed in the same corporate entity. Furthermore, the ability to use acquired losses against such unrelated income creates a tax bias in favor of acquisitions. For example, a prospective buyer of a loss corporation might be a less efficient operator of the business than the current owner, but the ability to use acquired losses could make the loss corporation more valuable to the less efficient user and thereby encourage a sale.

Reflecting the policies described above, the Act addresses three general concerns: (1) the approach of prior law (viz., the disallowance or reduction of NOL and other carryforwards), which is criticized as being too harsh where there are continuing loss-corporation shareholders, and ineffective to the extent that NOL carryforwards may be available for use without limitation after substantial ownership changes, (2) the discontinuities in the prior law treatment of taxable purchases and tax-free reorganizations, and (3) defects in the prior law rules that presented opportunities for tax avoidance.

General approach

After reviewing various options for identifying events that present the opportunity for a tax benefit transfer (e.g., changes in a loss corporation's business), it was concluded that changes in a loss corporation's stock ownership continue to be the best indicator of a potentially abusive transaction. Under the Act, the special limitations generally apply when shareholders who bore the economic burden of a corporation's NOLs no longer hold a controlling interest in the corporation. In such a case, the possibility arises that new shareholders will contribute income-producing assets (or divert income opportunities) to the loss corporation, and the corporation will obtain greater utilization of carryforwards than it could have had there been no change in ownership.

To address the concerns described above, the Act adopts the following approach: After a substantial ownership change, rather than reducing the NOL carryforward itself, the earnings against which an NOL carryforward can be deducted are limited. This general approach has received wide acceptance among tax scholars and practitioners. This "limitation on earnings" approach is intended to permit the survival of NOL carryforwards after an acquisition, while limiting the ability to utilize the carryforwards against unrelated income.

The limitation on earnings approach is intended to approximate the results that would occur if a loss corporation's assets were combined with those of a profitable corporation in a partnership. This treatment can be justified on the ground that the option of contributing assets to a partnership is available to a loss corporation. In such a case, only the loss corporation's share of the partnership's income could be offset by the corporation's NOL carryforward. Presumably, except in the case of tax-motivated partnership agreements, the loss corporation's share of the partnership's income would be limited to earnings generated by the assets contributed by the loss corporation.

For purposes of determining the income attributable to a loss corporation's assets, the Act prescribes an objective rate of return on the value of the corporation's equity. Consideration was given to the arguments made in favor of computing the prescribed rate of return by reference to the gross value of a loss corporation's assets, without regard to outstanding debt. It was concluded that it would be inappropriate to permit the use of NOL carryforwards to shelter earnings that are used (or would be used in the absence of an acquisition) to service a loss corporation's debt. The effect of taking a loss corporation's gross value into account would be to accelerate the rate at which NOL carryforwards would be used had there been no change in ownership, because interest paid on indebtedness is deductible in its own right (thereby deferring the use of a corresponding amount of NOLs). There is a fundamental difference between debt capitalization and equity capitalization: true debt represents a claim against a loss corporation's assets.

Annual limitation

The annual limitation on the use of pre-acquisition NOL carryforwards is the product of the prescribed rate and the value of the loss corporation's equity immediately before a proscribed ownership change. The average yield for long-term marketable obligations of the U.S. government was selected as the measure of a loss corporation's expected return on its assets.

The rate prescribed by the Act is higher than the average rate at which loss corporations actually absorb NOL carryforwards. Indeed, many loss corporations continue to experience NOLs, thereby increasing—rather than absorbing—NOL carryforwards. On the other hand, the adoption of the average absorption rate may be too restrictive for loss corporations that out-perform the average. Therefore, it would be inappropriate to set a rate at the lowest rate that is theoretically justified. The use of the long-term rate for Federal obligations was justified as a reasonable risk-free rate of return a loss corporation could obtain in the absence of a change in ownership.

Anti-abuse rules

The mechanical rules described above could present unintended tax-planning opportunities and might foster certain transactions that many would perceive to be violative of the legislative intent. Therefore, the Act includes several rules that are designed to prevent taxpayers from circumventing the special limitations or otherwise appearing to traffic in loss corporations by (1) reducing a loss corporation's assets to cash or other passive assets and then selling off a corporate shell consisting primarily of NOLs and cash or other passive assets, or (2) making pre-acquisition infusions of assets to inflate artificially a loss corporation's value (and thereby accelerate the use of NOL carryforwards). In addition, the Act retains the prior law principles that are intended to limit tax-motivated acquisitions of loss corporations (e.g., section 269, relating to acquisitions to evade or avoid taxes, * * *.

* * *

Continuity-of-business enterprise

The requirement under the 1954 Code rules that a loss corporation continue substantially the same business after a purchase presented potentially difficult definitional issues. Specifically, taxpayers and the courts were required to determine at what point a change in merchandise, location, size, or the use of assets should be treated as a change in the loss corporation's business. It was also difficult to identify a particular business where assets and activities were constantly combined, separated, or rearranged. Further, there was a concern that the prior law requirement induced taxpayers to continue uneconomic businesses.

The Act eliminates the business-continuation rule. The continuity-of-business-enterprise rule generally applicable to tax-free reorganizations also applies to taxable transactions.

* * *

Built-in gains and losses

Built-in losses should be subject to special limitations because they are economically equivalent to pre-acquisition NOL carryforwards. If built-in losses were not subject to limitations, taxpayers could reduce or eliminate the impact of the general rules by causing a loss corporation (following an ownership change) to recognize its built-in losses free of the special limitations (and then invest the proceeds in assets similar to the assets sold).

The Act also provides relief for loss corporations with built-in gain assets. Built-in gains are often the product of special tax provisions that accelerate deductions or defer income (e.g., accelerated depreciation or installment sales reporting). Absent a special rule, the use of NOL carryforwards to offset built-in gains recognized after an acquisition would be limited, even though the carryforwards would have been fully available to offset such gains had the gains been recognized before the change in ownership occurred. (Similarly, a partnership is required to allocate built-in gain or loss to the contributing partner.)

Although the special treatment of built-in gains and losses may require valuations of a loss corporation's assets, the Act limits the circumstances in which valuations will be required by providing a generous de minimis rule.

* * *

Explanation of Provisions

Overview

The Act alters the character of the special limitations on the use of NOL carryforwards. After an ownership change, as described below, the taxable income of a loss corporation available for offset by pre-acquisition NOL carryforwards is limited annually to a prescribed rate times the value of the loss corporation's stock immediately before the ownership change. In addition, NOL carryforwards are disallowed entirely unless the loss corporation satisfies continuity-of-business enterprise requirements for the two-year period following any ownership change. The Act also expands the scope of the special limitations to include built-in losses and allows loss corporations to take into account built-in gains. The Act includes numerous technical changes and several anti-avoidance rules. Finally, the Act applies similar rules to carryforwards other than NOLs, such as net capital losses and excess foreign tax credits.

Ownership change

The special limitations apply after any ownership change. An ownership change occurs, in general, if the percentage of stock of the new loss corporation owned by any one or more 5-percent shareholders (described below) has increased by more than 50 percentage points relative to the lowest percentage of stock of the old loss corporation owned by those 5-percent shareholders at any time during the testing period (generally a three-year period) (new sec. 382(g)(1)).[27] The determination of whether an ownership change has occurred is made by aggregating the increases in percentage ownership for each 5-percent shareholder whose percentage ownership has increased during the testing period. For this purpose, all stock owned by persons who own less than five percent of a corporation's stock generally is treated as stock owned by a single 5-percent shareholder (new sec. 382(g)(4)(A)). The determination of whether an ownership change has occurred is made after any owner shift involving a 5-percent shareholder or any equity structure shift.

Determinations of the percentage of stock in a loss corporation owned by any person are made on the basis of value. Except as provided in regulations to be prescribed by the Secretary, changes in proportionate ownership attributable solely to fluctuations in the relative fair market values of different classes of stock are not taken into account (new sec. 382(1)(3)(D)).

In determining whether an ownership change has occurred, changes in the holdings of certain preferred stock are disregarded. Except as provided in regulations, all "stock" (not including stock described in section 1504(a)(4)) is taken into account (new sec. 382(k)(6)(A)). Under this standard, the term stock does not include stock that (1) is not entitled to vote, (2) is limited and preferred as to dividends and does not participate in corporate growth to any significant extent, (3) has redemption and liquidation rights that do not exceed the stock's issue price upon issuance (except for a reasonable redemption premium), and (4) is not convertible to any other class of stock. If preferred stock carries a dividend rate materially in excess of a market rate, this may indicate that it would not be disregarded.

Under grants of regulatory authority, the Treasury Department is expected to publish regulations disregarding, in appropriate cases, certain stock that would otherwise be counted in determining whether an ownership change has occurred, when necessary to prevent avoidance of the special limitations (new sec. 382(k)(6)(B)). For example, it may be appropriate to disregard preferred stock (even though voting) or common stock where the likely percentage participation of such stock in future corporate growth is disproportionately small compared to the percentage value of the stock as a proportion of total stock value, at the time of the issuance or transfer. Similarly, there is a concern that the inclusion of voting preferred stock (which is not described in section 1504(a)(4) solely because it carries the right to vote) in the definition of stock presents the potential for avoidance of section 382. * * *

27. Unless specifically identified as a taxable year, all references to any period constituting a year (or multiple thereof) means a 365-day period (or multiple thereof).

In addition, the Treasury Department will promulgate regulations regarding the extent to which stock that is not described in section 1504(a)(4) should nevertheless not be considered stock. For example, the Treasury Department may issue regulations providing that preferred stock otherwise described in section 1504(a)(4) will not be considered stock simply because the dividends are in arrears and the preferred shareholders thus become entitled to vote.

Owner shift involving a 5-percent shareholder

An owner shift involving a 5-percent shareholder is defined as any change in the respective ownership of stock of a corporation that affects the percentage of stock held by any person who holds five percent or more of the stock of the corporation (a "5-percent shareholder") before or after the change (new sec. 382(g)(2)). For purposes of this rule, all less-than-5-percent shareholders are aggregated and treated as one 5-percent shareholder. Thus, an owner shift involving a 5-percent shareholder includes (but is not limited to) the following transactions:

(1) A taxable purchase of loss corporation stock by a person who holds at least five percent of the stock before the purchase;

(2) A disposition of stock by a person who holds at least five percent of stock of the loss corporation either before or after the disposition;

(3) A taxable purchase of loss corporation stock by a person who becomes a 5-percent shareholder as a result of the purchase;

(4) A section 351 exchange that affects the percentage of stock ownership of a loss corporation by one or more 5-percent shareholders;

(5) A decrease in the outstanding stock of a loss corporation (e.g., by virtue of a redemption) that affects the percentage of stock ownership of the loss corporation by one or more 5-percent shareholders;

(6) A conversion of debt (or pure preferred stock that is excluded from the definition of stock) to stock where the percentage of stock ownership of the loss corporation by one or more 5-percent shareholders is affected; and

(7) An issuance of stock by a loss corporation that affects the percentage of stock ownership by one or more 5-percent shareholders.

* * *

Equity structure shift

An equity structure shift is defined as any tax-free reorganization within the meaning of section 368, other than a divisive "D" or "G" reorganization or an "F" reorganization (new sec. 382(g)(3)(A)). In addition, to the extent provided in regulations, the term equity structure shift may include other transactions, such as public offerings not involving a 5-percent shareholder or taxable reorganization-type transactions (e.g., mergers or other reorganization-type transactions that do not qualify for tax-free treatment due to the nature of the consideration or the failure to satisfy any of the other requirements for a tax-free transaction) (new secs. 382(g)(3)(B), (g)(4), and [(m)(4)]. A purpose of the provision that considers only owner shifts involving a 5–percent shareholder is to relieve widely held companies from the burden of keeping track of trades among less–than–5–percent shareholders. For example, a publicly traded company that is 60 percent owned by less–than–5–percent shareholders would not experience an ownership change merely because, within a three-year period, every one of such shareholders sold his stock to a person who was not a 5–percent shareholder. There are situations involving transfers of stock involving less–than–5–percent shareholders, other than tax-free reorganizations (for example, public offerings), in which it will be feasible to identify changes in ownership involving such shareholders, because, unlike public trading, the changes occur as part of a single, integrated transaction. Where identification is reasonably feasible or a reasonable presumption can be applied, the Treasury Department is expected to treat such transactions under the rules applicable to equity structure shifts.

For purposes of determining whether an ownership change has occurred following an equity structure shift, the less–than–5–percent shareholders of each corporation that was a party to the reorganization will be segregated and treated as a single, separate 5–percent shareholder (new sec. 382(g)(4)(B)(i)). The Act contemplates that this segregation rule will similarly apply to acquisitions by groups of less–than–5–percent shareholders through corporations as well as other entities (e.g., partnerships) and in transactions that do not constitute equity structure shifts (new sec. 382(g)(4)(C)). Moreover, the Act provides regulatory authority to apply similar segregation rules to segregate groups of less than 5–percent shareholders in cases that involve only a single corporation, (for example, a public offering or a recapitalization). (new sec. [382(m)(4)]).

* * *

To the extent provided in regulations that will apply prospectively from the date the regulations are issued, a public offering can be treated, in effect, as an equity structure shift with the result that the offering is a measuring event, even if there is otherwise no change in ownership of a person who owns 5–percent of the stock before or after the transaction. Rules also would be provided to segregate the group of less–than–5–percent shareholders prior to the offering and the new group of less than–5–percent shareholders that acquire stock pursuant to the offering. Under such regulations, therefore, the less–than–5–percent shareholders who receive stock in the public offering could be segregated and treated as a separate 5–percent shareholder. * * * The Act contemplates that the regulations may provide rules to allow the corporation to establish the extent, if any, to which existing shareholders acquire stock in the public offering.

Attribution and aggregation of stock ownership

Attribution from entities.—In determining whether an ownership change has occurred, the constructive ownership rules of section 318, with several modifications, are applied (new sec. 382(1)(3)). Except to the extent provided in regulations, the rules for attributing ownership of stock (within the meaning of new section 382(k)(6)) from corporations to their shareholders are applied without regard to the extent of the shareholders' ownership in the corporation. Thus, any stock owned by a corporation is treated as being owned proportionately by its shareholders. Moreover, except as provided in regulations, any stock attributed to a corporation's shareholders is not treated as being held by such corporation. Stock attributed from a partnership, estate or trust similarly shall not be treated as being held by such entity. The effect of the attribution rules is to prevent application of the special limitations after an acquisition that does not result in a more than 50 percent change in the ultimate beneficial ownership of a loss corporation. Conversely, the attribution rules result in an ownership change where more than 50 percent of a loss corporation's stock is acquired indirectly through an acquisition of stock in the corporation's parent corporation.

* * *

3–year testing period

In general, the relevant testing period for determining whether an ownership change has occurred is the three-year period preceding any owner shift involving a 5–percent shareholder or any equity structure shift (new sec. 382(i)(1)). Thus, a series of unrelated transactions occurring during a three-year period may constitute an ownership change. A shorter period, however, may be applicable following any ownership change. In such a case, the testing period for determining whether a second ownership change has occurred does not begin before the day following the first ownership change (new sec. 382(i)(2)).

In addition, the testing period does not begin before the first day of the first taxable year from which there is a loss carryforward (including a current NOL that is defined as a pre-change loss) or excess credit (new sec. 382(i)(3)). Thus, transactions that occur prior to the creation of any attribute subject to limitation under section 382 or section 383 are disregarded. Except as provided in regulations, the special rule described above does not apply to any corporation with a net unrealized built-in loss. The Act contemplates, however, that the regulations will permit such corporations to disregard transactions that occur before the year for which such a corporation establishes that a net unrealized built-in loss first arose.

Effect of ownership change

Section 382 limitation

For any taxable year ending after the change date (i.e., the date on which an owner shift resulting in an ownership change occurs or the date of the reorganization in the case of an equity structure shift resulting in an ownership change), the amount of a loss corporation's (or a successor corporation's) taxable income that can be offset by a pre-change loss (described below) cannot exceed the section 382 limitation for such year (new sec. 382(a)). The section 382 limitation for any taxable year is generally the amount equal to the value of the loss corporation immediately before the ownership change multiplied by the long-term tax-exempt rate (described below) (new sec. 382(b)(1)).

The Treasury Department is required to prescribe regulations regarding the application of the section 382 limitation in the case of a short taxable year. These regulations will generally provide that the section 382 limitation applicable in a short taxable year will be determined by multiplying the full section 382 limitation by the ratio of the number of days in the year to 365. Thus, taxable income realized by a new loss corporation during a short taxable year may be offset by pre-change losses not exceeding a ratable portion of the full section 382 limitation.

If there is a net unrealized built-in gain, the section 382 limitation for any taxable year is increased by the amount of any recognized built-in gains (determined under rules described below). Also, the section 382 limitation is increased by built-in gain recognized by virtue of a section 338 election (to the extent such gain is not otherwise taken into account as a built-in gain). Finally, if the section 382 limitation for a taxable year exceeds the taxable income for the year, the section 382 limitation for the next taxable year is increased by such excess.

If two or more loss corporations are merged or otherwise reorganized into a single entity, separate section 382 limitations are determined and applied to each loss corporation that experiences an ownership change.

* * *

Special rule for post-change year that includes the change date.—In general, the section 382 limitation with respect to an ownership change that occurs during a taxable year does not apply to the utilization of losses against the portion of the loss corporation's taxable income, if any, allocable to the period before the change. For this purpose, except as provided in regulations, taxable income (not including built-in gains or losses, if there is a net unrealized built-in gain or loss) realized during the change year is allocated ratably to each day in the year. The regulations may provide that income realized before the change date from discrete sales of assets would be excluded from the ratable allocation and could be offset without limit by pre-change losses. Moreover, these regulations may provide a loss corporation with an option to determine the taxable income allocable to the period before the change by closing its books on the change date and thus forgoing the ratable allocation.

Value of loss corporation

The value of a loss corporation is generally the fair market value of the corporation's stock (including preferred stock described in section

1504(a)(4)) immediately before the ownership change (new sec. 382(e)(1)). If a redemption occurs in connection with an ownership change—either before or after the change—the value of the loss corporation is determined after taking the redemption into account (new sec. 382(e)(2)). The Treasury Department is given regulatory authority to treat other corporate contractions in the same manner as redemptions for purposes of determining the loss corporation's value. The Treasury Department also is required to prescribe such regulations as are necessary to treat warrants, options, contracts to acquire stock, convertible debt, and similar interests as stock for purposes of determining the value of the loss corporation (new sec. 382(k)(6)(B)(i)).

In determining value, the price at which loss corporation stock changes hands in an arms-length transaction would be evidence, but not conclusive evidence, of the value of the stock. Assume, for example, that an acquiring corporation purchased 40 percent of loss corporation stock over a 12–month period. Six months following this 40 percent acquisition, the acquiring corporation purchased an additional 20 percent of loss corporation stock at a price that reflected a premium over the stock's proportionate amount of the value of all the loss corporation stock; the premium is paid because the 20–percent block carries with it effective control of the loss corporation. Based on these facts, it would be inappropriate to simply gross-up the amount paid for the 20–percent interest to determine the value of the corporation's stock. Under regulations, it is anticipated that the Treasury Department will permit the loss corporation to be valued based upon a formula that grosses up the purchase price of all of the acquired loss corporation stock if a control block of such stock is acquired within a 12–month period.

* * *

Long-term tax-exempt rate

The long-term tax-exempt rate is defined as the highest of the Federal long-term rates determined under section 1274(d), as adjusted to reflect differences between rates on long-term taxable and tax-exempt obligations, in effect for the month in which the change date occurs or the two prior months (new sec. 382(f)). The Treasury Department will publish the long-term tax-exempt rate by revenue ruling within 30 days after the date of enactment and monthly thereafter. The long-term tax-exempt rate will be computed as the yield on a diversified pool of prime, general obligation tax-exempt bonds with remaining periods to maturity of more than nine years.

The use of a rate lower than the long-term Federal rate is necessary to ensure that the value of NOL carryforwards to the buying corporation is not more than their value to the loss corporation. Otherwise there would be a tax incentive to acquire loss corporations. If the loss corporation were to sell its assets and invest in long-term Treasury obligations, it could absorb its NOL carryforwards at a rate equal to the yield on long-term government obligations. Since the price paid by the buyer is larger than the value of the loss company's assets (because the value of NOL carryforwards are taken into account), applying the long-term Treasury rate to the purchase price would result in faster utilization of NOL carryforwards by the buying corporation. The long-term tax-exempt rate normally will fall between 66 (1 minus the maximum corporate tax rate of 34 percent) and 100 percent of the long-term Federal rate.

* * *

Continuity of business enterprise requirements

Following an ownership change, a loss corporation's NOL carryforwards (including any recognized built-in losses, described below) are subject to complete disallowance (except to the extent of any recognized built-in gains or section 338 gain, described below), unless the loss corporation's business enterprise is continued at all times during the two-year period following the ownership change. If a loss corporation fails to satisfy the continuity of business enterprise requirements, no NOL carryforwards would be allowed to the new loss corporation for any post-change year. This continuity of business enterprise requirement is the same requirement that must be satisfied to qualify a transaction as a tax-free reorganization under section 368. (See Treasury regulation section 1.368–1(d)). Under these continuity of business enterprise requirements, a loss corporation (or a successor corporation) must either continue the old loss corporation's historic business or use a significant portion of the old loss corporation's assets in a business. Thus, the requirements may be satisfied even though the old loss corporation discontinues more than a minor portion of its historic business. Changes in the location of a loss corporation's business or the loss corporation's key employees, in contrast to the results under the business-continuation rule in the 1954 Code version of section 382(a), will not constitute a failure to satisfy the continuity of business enterprise requirements under the conference agreement.

Reduction in loss corporation's value for certain capital contributions

Any capital contribution (including a section 351 transfer) that is made to a loss corporation as part of a plan a principal purpose of which is to avoid any of the special limitations under section 382 shall not be taken into account for any purpose under section 382. For purposes of this rule, except as provided in regulations, a capital contribution made during the two-year period ending on the change date is irrebuttably presumed to be part of a plan to avoid the limitations. The application of this rule will result in a reduction of a loss corporation's value for purposes of determining the section 382 limitation. The term "capital contribution" is to be interpreted broadly to encompass any direct or indirect infusion of capital into a loss corporation (e.g., the merger of one corporation into a commonly owned loss corporation). Regulations generally will except (i) capital contributions received on the formation of a loss corporation (not accompanied by the incorporation of assets with a net unrealized built-in loss) where an ownership change occurs within two years of incorporation, (ii) capital contributions received before the first year from which there is an NOL or excess credit carryforward (or in which a net unrealized built-in loss arose), and (iii) capital contributions made to continue basic operations of the corporation's business (e.g., to meet the monthly payroll or fund other operating expenses of the loss corporation). The regulations also may take into account, under appropriate circumstances, the existence of substantial nonbusiness assets on the change date (as described below) and distributions made to shareholders subsequent to capital contributions, as offsets to such contributions.

* * *

Losses subject to limitation

The term "pre-change loss" includes (i) for the taxable year in which an ownership change occurs, the portion of the loss corporation's NOL that is allocable (determined on a daily pro rata basis, without regard to recognized built-in gains or losses, as described below) to the period in such year before the change date, (ii) NOL carryforwards that arose in a taxable year preceding the taxable year of the ownership change and (iii) certain recognized built-in losses and deductions (described below).

For any taxable year in which a corporation has income that, under section 172, may be offset by both a pre-change loss (i.e., an NOL subject to limitation) and an NOL that is not subject to limitation, taxable income is treated as having been first offset by the pre-change loss (new sec. 382(*l*)(2)(B)). This rule minimizes the NOLs that are subject to the special limitations. For purposes of determining the amount of a pre-change loss that may be carried to a taxable year (under section 172(b)), taxable income for a taxable year is treated as not greater than the section 382 limitation for such year reduced by the unused pre-change losses for prior taxable years. (New sec. 382(*l*)(2)(A)).

Built-in losses

If a loss corporation has a net unrealized built-in loss, the recognized built-in loss for any taxable year ending within the five-year period ending at the close of the fifth post-change year (the "recognition period") is treated as a pre-change loss (new sec. 382(h)(1)(B)).

Net unrealized built-in losses.—The term "net unrealized built-in loss" is defined as the amount by which the fair market value of the loss corporation's assets immediately before the ownership change is less than the aggregate adjusted bases of a corporation's assets at that time. Under a *de minimis* exception, the special rule for built-in losses is not applied if the amount of a net unrealized built-in loss does not exceed 25 percent of the value of the corporation's assets immediately before the ownership change. For purposes of the *de minimis* exception, the value of a corporation's assets is determined by excluding any

(1) cash, (2) cash items (as determined for purposes of section 368(a)(2)(F)(iv)), or (3) marketable securities that have a value that does not substantially differ from adjusted basis.

* * *

Recognized built-in losses.—The term "recognized built-in loss" is defined as any loss that is recognized on the disposition of an asset during the recognition period, except to the extent that the new loss corporation establishes that (1) the asset was not held by the loss corporation immediately before the change date, or (2) the loss (or a portion of such loss) is greater than the excess of the adjusted basis of the asset on the change date over the asset's fair market value on that date. The recognized built-in loss for a taxable year cannot exceed the net unrealized built-in loss reduced by recognized built-in losses for prior taxable years ending in the recognition period.

The amount of any recognized built-in loss that exceeds the section 382 limitation for any post-change year must be carried forward (not carried back) under rules similar to the rules applicable to net operating loss carryforwards and will be subject to the special limitations in the same manner as a pre-change loss.

* * *

Built-in gains

If a loss corporation has a net unrealized built-in gain, the section 382 limitation for any taxable year ending within the five-year recognition period is increased by the recognized built-in gain for the taxable year (new sec. 382(h)(1)(A)).

Net unrealized built-in gains.—The term "net unrealized built-in gain" is defined as the amount by which the value of a corporation's assets exceeds the aggregate bases of such assets immediately before the ownership change. Under the *de minimis* exception described above, the special rule for built-in gains is not applied if the amount of a net unrealized built-in gain does not exceed 25 percent of the value of a loss corporation's assets.

Recognized built-in gains.—The term "recognized built-in gain" is defined as any gain recognized on the disposition of an asset during the recognition period, if the taxpayer establishes that the asset was held by the loss corporation immediately before the change date, to the extent the gain does not exceed the excess of the fair market value of such asset on the change date over the adjusted basis of the asset on that date. The recognized built-in gain for a taxable year cannot exceed the net unrealized built-in gain reduced by the recognized built-in gains for prior years in the recognition period.

* * *

Carryforwards other than NOLs

The Act also amends section 383, relating to special limitations on unused business credits and research credits, excess foreign tax credits, and capital loss carryforwards. Under regulations to be prescribed by the Secretary, capital loss carryforwards will be limited to an amount determined on the basis of the tax liability that is attributable to so much of the taxable income as does not exceed the section 382 limitation for the taxable year, with the same ordering rules that apply under present law. Thus, any capital loss carryforward used in a post-change year will reduce the section 382 limitation that is applied to pre-change losses. In addition, the amount of any excess credit that may be used following an ownership change will be limited, under regulations, on the basis of the tax liability attributable to an amount of taxable income that does not exceed the applicable section 382 limitation, after any NOL carryforwards, capital loss carryforwards, or foreign tax credits are taken into account. The Act also expands the scope of section 383 to include passive activity losses and credits and minimum tax credits.

* * *

ILLUSTRATIVE MATERIAL

A. GENERAL

The *General Explanation* indicates that net operating loss carryovers are provided to average the loss years of a business with a fluctuating income against its profitable years. The averaging rationale is not applicable to the new owners of a loss business who have not borne the burden of pre-acquisition losses. The existence of a net operating loss carryover which is transferable to new owners, however, allows the previous owners to recoup a portion of their loss from the new owners who are willing to pay for the future tax savings available from an acquired net operating carryover. The *General Explanation* indicates that eliminating net operating loss carryovers completely following a substantial ownership change would discourage the sale of a loss corporation and hence the partial recoupment of the losses by the historic shareholders who have borne the losses. Thus, the "limitation of earnings" approach was adopted which focuses on the market value of the loss to the loss corporation.

In general terms, the market value of a net operating loss carryover to a loss corporation is the present value of its anticipated tax savings on future earnings. The present value of a loss carryover is dependent on the net return the loss corporation can expect to derive from its invested capital. The value of a loss carryover to a purchaser is likewise the present value of anticipated tax savings on the future earnings which will be offset by acquired losses. Since a profitable enterprise may be expected to achieve a higher rate of return on its investment than a loss corporation (whose rate of return may be negative), an unlimited loss carryover will be more valuable to a profitable purchaser than to the loss corporation. The difference in value may result in a sale of loss carryovers for a price substantially less than the value of the carryover to the purchaser or, in any event, at a price somewhere between the value to the purchaser and the value to the loss corporation. Thus, an unlimited loss carryover not only provides a form of recoupment of prior losses for the seller of a loss corporation, but also provides a windfall profit for the purchaser financed by the Treasury. Section 382 is intended to eliminate this windfall potential by limiting the value of a loss carryover following a substantial ownership change to an approximation of the value of the carryover to the loss corporation. So limited, the carryover has the same value to both seller and purchaser. The cost of this limitation falls, in part, on the loss corporation which is limited in the amount it can receive for the transfer of loss carryovers.

Theoretically, because the loss carryover has the same value to each, the seller and the purchaser should be neutral with respect to the presence of a loss carryover as part of an asset transfer. This neutrality principle works only if the limitation on the use of acquired loss carryovers does not reduce the value of loss carryovers to an amount less than the present value of the losses to the loss corporation. An overly restrictive limitation will inhibit the transfer of assets to more efficient operators. A limitation that is too generous, however, will provide a windfall profit to one of the parties. Section 382 attempts to strike a balance by limiting the annual recovery of a net operating loss carryover following an ownership change to the fair market value of the equity interests in the loss corporation multiplied by a federal tax exempt rate. This formula is focused on the possibility that a loss corporation could dispose of its assets and invest the proceeds in risk-free taxable government bonds thereby earning an annual rate of return at least equal to the rate on long-term federal instruments. Senate Finance Committee, Final Report on Subchapter C, The Subchapter C Revision Act of 1985 (Staff Report), S. Prt. 99–47, 99th Cong., 1st Sess. 71 (1985). The Conference Report on the 1986 Act indicates that the rate is reduced to a tax-exempt rate, in part, because Congress believed that the fair market value of the loss corporation includes the value of the loss carryover itself. The loss carryover is an asset which could not be individually sold and the proceeds reinvested. See H. Rep. No. 99–841, 99th Cong., 2d Sess. II–188 (1986). In addition, Congressional studies have indicated that loss corporations typically have absorbed net operating losses the rate of 4.4 percent of book net worth.[1] Senate Finance Committee, Final Report on Subchapter C, The Subchapter C Revision Act of 1985 (Staff Report), S. Prt. 99–47, 99th Cong., 1st Sess. 71 (1985). The federal tax-exempt rate, which has varied between approximately 7 percent and 8 percent since section 382 was enacted,[2] is generous when compared with actual experience. Some commentators argue, however, that the limitation based on the federal exempt rate is too low thereby undervaluing the loss corporation's loss carryovers. See, e.g., N.Y. State Bar Ass'n Tax Section, Comm. on Net Operating Losses, The Net Operating Loss and Excess Credit Carryforwards Under H.R. 3838, 31 Tax Notes 725, 729 (1986).

B. OWNERSHIP CHANGE

1. *In General*

The disposition of a corporate business by investors who suffered the burden of losses terminates the averaging function of loss carryovers as to those investors and thus eliminates this particular justification for further loss carryovers. The only remaining justification for allowing loss carryovers to the new owners of a loss corporation is to provide the former investors with some recoupment of a portion of their loss in the form of consideration paid for the carryover. Thus, the limitation on loss carryovers in section 382 is

1. This rate will itself overstate the true rate of recovery on the fair market value of assets if book values are less than fair market value.

2. The federal tax-exempt rate is determined monthly by the Internal Revenue Service and announced in Revenue Rulings.

triggered by an "ownership change", in general, a 50 percent increase in the ownership of the stock of a loss corporation by one or more five percent stockholders over a three year testing period. Section 382(g)(1).

Under the statutory language, an ownership change may occur after an "owner shift", any change in ownership of a loss corporation's stock involving a five percent stockholder, or an "equity structure shift", a reorganization of a loss corporation (with the exception of divisive (D) and (G) reorganizations, and (F) reorganizations). Under the statutory definitions, an equity structure shift which results in an ownership change also will qualify as an owner shift. This is true even for a publicly held corporation with no single five percent stockholder because of rules which aggregate the stock ownership of non-five percent stockholders. Section 382(g)(4)(B) and (C), discussed infra, page 985. The preamble to the section 382 Temporary Regulations states that there are no substantive differences (except for some transitional rule purposes) between classifying a transaction as an owner shift or an equity structure shift. T.D. 8149, 52 Fed. Reg. 29,668, 29,670 (1987); See also Temporary Regulations, section 1.382–2T(e)(2)(iii) (an equity structure shift which affects the stock ownership of a five percent stockholder is also an owner shift). There is no apparent reason for the distinction. It appears that the distinction is attributable to an early version of the statute which was changed during the drafting process.

The recipient of stock by reason of death, as a gift, or in a transfer from a spouse by reason of divorce or separation, is treated as the owner of the stock for the period the stock was held by the transferor. Section 382(l)(3)(B). These transfers, therefore, are not counted in testing for an ownership change.

Technically, the section 382 limitation applies to losses carried over to any "post change year" of a "new loss corporation". Section 382(a). A new loss corporation is defined as a corporation entitled to a net operating loss carryover following an ownership change. Section 382(k)(1) and (3). The "post change year" is any taxable year ending after the date of an ownership change. Section 382(d)(2). A loss corporation to which the limitation applies following an ownership change is any corporation entitled to a net operating loss carryover or which incurred a net operating loss in the year of an ownership change. Section 382(k)(1). The term "loss corporation" also includes a corporation with built-in losses, discussed infra, page 990, which are also subject to the section 382 limitation. A corporation which is a loss corporation before the date of an ownership change is referred to as an "old loss corporation." Section 382(k)(2).

2. *Counting Owner Shifts During the Testing Period*

An ownership change occurs if the percentage stock ownership of five percent stockholders on the date of any owner shift or equity structure shift (the "testing date") has increased by more than 50 percentage points over the lowest percentage of stock ownership of five percent stockholders at any time within the three-year period preceding the testing date. Section 382(g)(1). An ownership change may result from the sum of unrelated stock transfers by 5 percent stockholders and transfers from less than five percent stockholders to persons who become 5 percent stockholders. A loss corporation is thus required during a rolling three-year period to keep track of all stock transfers from or to persons who are or become five percent stockholders.

A full three year look-back is not necessary in all cases. The testing period does not begin until the first day of a taxable year in which a loss corporation incurs a net operating loss which is carried over into a taxable year ending after the testing date. Section 382(i)(3). Thus, stock transfers occurring in a year in which a corporation has neither a net operating loss nor loss carryover do not count towards an ownership change. In addition, a new testing period begins following an ownership change. Section 382(i)(2). Stock transfers predating an ownership change will not be counted again towards a subsequent ownership change.

The basic operation of these rules is illustrated by the following example. As of January 1, 1990, A, B, C, D, and E each owned 20 of the 100 outstanding shares of L Corporation. L Corporation had no net operating loss carryovers as of that date and did not incur a net operating loss in 1990. On July 1, 1990, A sold her 20 shares of L Corporation stock to P Corporation, which previously owned no L Corporation stock. In 1991, L Corporation incurred a net operating loss which is carried forward. On January 1, 1991, B sold his 20 shares to P Corporation, and on June 30, 1993, C sold her 20 shares to P Corporation. Although P has increased its stock ownership of L from zero percent to 60 percent during the three-year period ending on June 30, 1993, because L Corporation will not have any net operating loss carryovers from 1990 or earlier years, the ownership shift effected by the July 1, 1990 purchase from A is not counted in determining whether there has been an ownership change. On December 31, 1993, D sold his 20 shares to P Corporation. Looking backwards from December 31, 1993, P has increased its stock ownership by 60 percentage points, from 20 percent to 80 percent. Because L had a net operating loss in 1991 which was carried forward to subsequent years, all the purchases from B, C, and D are taken into account and an ownership change has occurred. Because the ownership change starts a new testing period, if E sold her stock to F on June 30, 1996, there would be no ownership change, even though in the three-year period ending June 30, 1996, P Corporation would have increased its stock ownership by 40 percentage points (from 40 percent to 80 percent) and F would have increased his stock ownership by 20 percentage points, for a total shift of 60 percentage points.

In some circumstances, the requirement of section 382(g)(1)(B) that an ownership change be tested with the lowest percentage of stock owned by a five percent stockholder during the testing period can have a surprising result. For example, L has 200 shares of stock outstanding of which A owns 100 shares and B and C each own 50 shares. On January 2, 1988, A sells 60 shares of L stock to B. B's ownership interest increases by 30 percentage points, from 25 percent of L stock to 55 percent. A's interest drops to 20 percent. On January 1, 1989, A acquires all of C's L stock. A and B have in the aggregate increased their percentage ownership of L by only 25 percentage points during the testing period; B's interest has increased by 30 percentage points and A's percentage interest has declined by five percentage points. Nonetheless, Temporary Regulations, section 1.382–2T(c)(4), Ex. (i), treat A's acquisition of C's stock as an ownership change. The Temporary Regulations conclude that, as a result of A's purchase of C's stock, A's percentage interest increased from a low of 20 percent, the lowest percentage of A's ownership interest during the testing period, to 45 percent. A's 25 percentage points increase plus B's 30 percentage points increase within the testing period are sufficient to trigger an ownership change despite the fact that their aggregate overall increase in stock ownership during the testing period is only 25 percentage points. The Temporary Regulations reach this result even if A's sale to B and purchase from C are part of an integrated plan. Temporary Regulations, section 1.382–2T(c)(3). Arguably, the Temporary Regulations misread section 382(g)(1) and reach an unduly harsh result. Section 382(g)(1) can be interpreted as requiring that the increased interests of A and B be aggregated for purposes of both subsections (A) and (B). To paraphrase the statutory language, A and B's stock ownership of L has increased by only 25 percentage points over the lowest percentage of stock owned by A and B together ("such shareholders") at any time during the testing period (from a low of 75% [20% plus 55%] to 100%). Given the Treasury's broad regulatory authority under section 382(m) to interpret section 382, however, it is not likely that its interpretation of section 382(g)(1) will be challenged successfully.

3. *Stock Ownership and Five Percent Stockholders*

(a) *Identifying Five Percent Stockholders*

The section 382 trigger focuses on stock transfers to or by persons who own five percent or more of the loss corporation stock. Proportionate stock ownership is determined by the value of stock held by the stockholder. Section 382(k)(6)(C). A person is treated as a five percent stockholder if the person was a five percent stockholder at any time during the testing period, even though the person may not own five percent of the loss corporation stock on the testing date. Temporary Regulations, section 1.382–2T(g)(1)(iv). The five percent figure was chosen to relieve companies from the burden of keeping track of trades among stockholders with a minor interest. H.Rep. No. 99–841, 99th Cong., 2d Sess. II–176 (1986).[3] Thus stock transfers between less than five percent stockholders are not counted in testing for an ownership change. Temporary Regulations, section 1.382–2T(e)(1)(ii). The less than five percent stockholders as a group, however, are treated as a single five percent stockholder regardless of the percentage interest held by such persons. Section 382(g)(4)(A). Temporary Regulations, section 1.382–2T(f)(13), refer to the group of less than five percent stockholders as a "public group". As a single five percent stockholder, transfers to or by a public group can trigger an ownership change. Thus, for example, a public issue of more than 50 percent of the stock of a closely held loss corporation to less than five percent stockholders will trigger an ownership change because the public group of new stockholders increases its ownership interest from zero preceding the public offering to more than 50 percent following the public offering. See Temporary Regulations, section 1.382–2T(e)(1)(iii), Ex. (5). Various groups of less than five percent stockholders separately may represent five percent stockholders and transfers between those groups can be an ownership change. See (e) below.

(b) *Attribution Rules*

The attribution rules of section 318 apply, with certain modifications, to identify proportionate stock ownership. Section 382(1)(3). In general, the modifications to section 318 have two effects. First, members of a family who are subject to stock attribution under section 318(a)(1) are treated as a

3. In general, any person who acquires five percent or more of the stock of a publicly traded corporation is required to register the acquisition with the Securities and Exchange Commission.

single individual. Thus, stock transfers among family members will not trigger an ownership change. If an individual is a member of more than one family group under the attribution rules, that individual will be treated as a member of the family which results in the smallest increase in stock held by five percent stockholders on a testing date. Temporary Regulations, section 1.382–2T(h)(6)(iv). The Temporary Regulations also provide that an individual who is not otherwise a five percent stockholder will not be treated as a five percent stockholder as a result of family attribution. Second, stock of a loss corporation owned by any entity (corporation, partnership or trust) which has a five percent or greater interest is attributed up the ownership chain to the last person from whom no further attribution is possible. Section 382(1)(3)(A)(ii)(II); Temporary Regulations, sections 1.382–2T(g)(2) and (h)(2)(i). Intermediate entities are disregarded. Temporary Regulations, section 1.382–2T(h)(2)(A). Temporary Regulations, section 1.382–2T(g)(4), Ex. (1), illustrate application of these attribution rules as follows:

The stock of L, a loss corporation is owned 20 percent by A, 10 percent by corporation P1, and 20 percent by E, a joint venture. The remaining 50 percent of L stock is publicly held ("Public Group L"). B owns 15 percent of the stock of P1 corporation. The remaining 85 percent of the shares of P1 are publicly held ("Public Group P1"). E, the joint venture, is owned 30 percent by corporation P2 and 70 percent by corporation P3. Both P2 and P3 are publicly held ("Public Group P2" and "Public Group P3"). L's ownership structure is illustrated as follows:

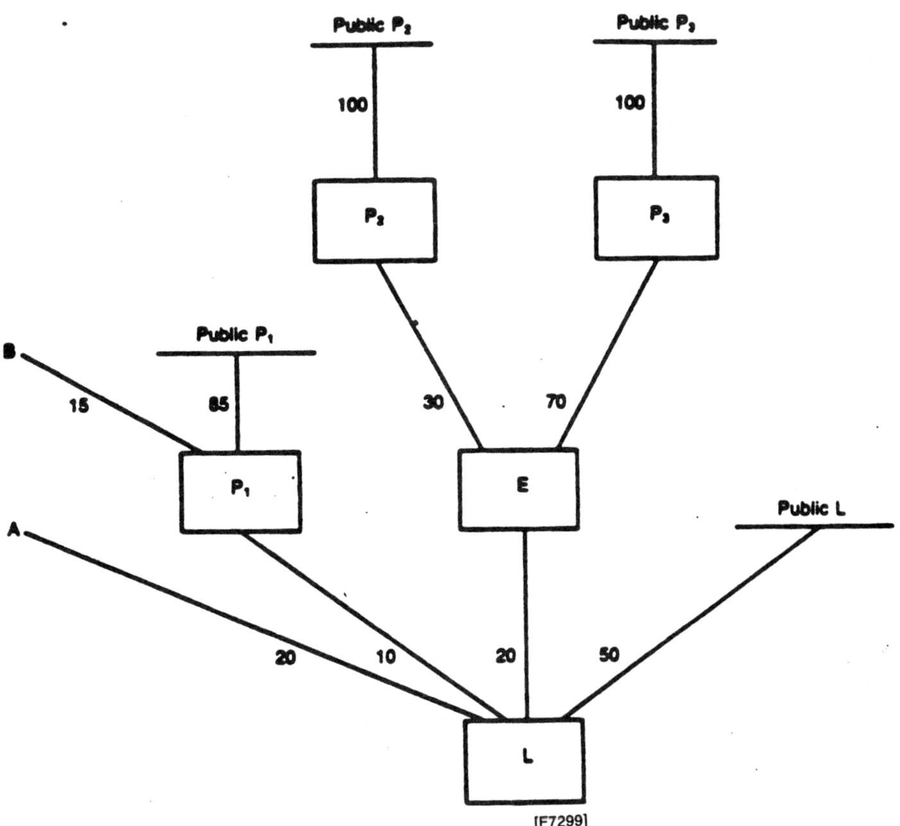

A is a five percent stockholder of L because of A's direct ownership of 20 percent of L stock. Public Group L is a single five percent stockholder by virtue of its collective 50 percent interest in L.

B is not a five percent stockholder. Although B is a five percent stockholder of P1, and thereby indirectly owns the L stock owned by P1, Temporary Regulations, section 1.382–2T(g)(2), B's ownership interest in L is only 1.5 percent (15% of P1's 10%). Because B is not a five percent stockholder of L, B is treated as a member of the Public Group P1. See Temporary Regulations, section 1.382–2T(j)(iv). P1 is not a five percent stockholder because its interest is attributable to its stockholders. P1's public stockholders, Public P1, are treated as a single five percent stockholder of L owning 8.5 percent plus B's 1.5 percent.

Public Group P2 is also a five percent stockholder. P2 has a six percent interest attributed from P2's 30 percent interest in E, which in turn owns 20 percent of L (30% × 20% = 6%). P2's five percent interest is attributed to the P2 public group which owns 100 percent of P2. Public Group P3 is also a five percent stockholder with a 14 percent interest attributed to it ([20% × 70%] × 100%).

(c) *Option Attribution*

Outstanding options and other rights to acquire stock (including convertible debt) may trigger an ownership change, even in the absence of direct stock transfers. Options to acquire stock and any warrants, contingent purchase rights or other contract rights to acquire stock (whether or not contingent) are attributable to the owner of the option or other right and are treated as exercised on the date issued and on any other testing date, but only if the deemed exercise results in an ownership change. Sections 382(1)(3)(A)(iv) and 382(1)(3)(A) flush language; Temporary Regulations, section 1.382–2T(a)(2)(i)(B) and (h)(4)(i). Because options are treated as exercised on any testing date when the deemed exercise will trigger an ownership change, the Temporary Regulations effectively extend the testing period for the term of an option. Thus, for example, on January 1, 1987, B, who owns all 100 shares of the stock of L Corporation, issues an option to A to acquire 25 shares. January 1, 1987, is a testing date. Since acquisition of 25 shares by A would not trigger an ownership change, the option is not deemed exercised. However, if on July 1, 1991, with A's option still outstanding, B sells 31 shares of L stock to C, the sale will trigger an ownership change. Treating A's option as exercised on the testing date, the date of B's sale to C, means that A has increased A's deemed interest in L from 0 to 25 percent. C's interest is increased from 0 to 31 percent. Together, A and C have increased their interest in L by more than 50 percent.

Once an ownership change has occurred, options outstanding both before and after the ownership change, whether or not deemed exercised, will not be counted again as long as the option or other right is held by the same five percent stockholder. Temporary Regulations, section 1.382–2T(h)(4)(x)(F). Thus, in the example, a sale by B and C of 50 shares or less within a testing period will not trigger a second ownership change. The actual exercise of an option will also be disregarded following an ownership change subsequent to creation of the option, but only if the option is exercised by the original holder. Temporary Regulations, section 1.382–2T(h)(4)(vi). However, exercise of an option held during a period in which there was no ownership change will not be disregarded and the actual exercise of the option can be an owner shift. Temporary Regulations, section 1.382–2T(h)(4)(xii).

Although the option attribution provisions refer directly only to options to acquire the stock of a loss corporation, options with respect to the stock of a corporation owning, directly or indirectly, the stock of a loss corporation are also subject to the deemed exercise provision if its application would trigger an ownership change of the loss corporation. Temporary Regulations, section 1.382–2T(f)(18)(iv). This rule is consistent with the general purpose of the attribution provisions which attribute ownership interests to the end of an ownership chain of five percent interests.

Temporary Regulations, section 1.382–2T(h)(4)(i), provide that the option attribution rule is to be applied separately to each class of options outstanding and separately to each five percent stockholder or each optionholder who would be a five percent stockholder if the option were deemed exercised. This means that some options may be treated as exercised and some not so treated in order to construct an ownership change. Temporary Regulations, section 1.382–2T(h)(4)(ii), Ex. (2), illustrate the impact of this rule as follows:

"(*i*) A owns all of the outstanding 100 shares of the stock of L. On July 22, 1988, the value of A's stock in L is $500 and the following agreements are entered into: (i) A sells 40 shares of his L stock to B for $200, (ii) in exchange for $10, A grants B an option to acquire the balance of his L stock for $305 at any time before July 22, 1992, and (iii) L grants A an option to acquire 100 shares of L stock at a price of $600 exercisable until such time as B's option is no longer outstanding.

"(*ii*) If the stock subject to the options owned by both A and B were treated as acquired on the July 22, 1988 testing date, B would have increased his ownership interest in L only 50 percentage points to 50 percent ([40 shares purchased + 60 shares acquired pursuant to the option]/200 outstanding shares of L stock, including 100 shares deemed outstanding pursuant to the option issued to A by L) as compared with 0 percent prior to July 22, 1988. In determining whether the options with respect to the stock of L would, if exercised, result in an ownership change, paragraph (h)(4)(i)(B) of this section requires that such options be treated as exercised separately with respect to each five percent stockholder, each person who would be a five percent stockholder if the option were treated as exercised or each combination of such persons. Therefore, by treating the options owned by A as not having been exercised and the option owned by B as having been exercised, B's interest in L increases by 100 percentage points during the testing period. An ownership change with respect to L therefore results from the transactions occurring on July 22, 1988."

If an option that has been deemed to have been exercised lapses or is forfeited, the option is treated as if it had never existed. Temporary Regulations, section 1.382–2T(h)(4)(viii). Any ownership change that had occurred as a result of the option is disregarded and the loss corporation may, subject to the statute of limitations, file an amended return for prior years to deduct its net operating loss carryover under section 172 without regard to the limitation of section 382.

Temporary Regulations, section 1.382–2T(h)(4)(ix), contain a de minimis rule which provides that options to acquire stock of a loss corporation will not be attributed to the holder if the losses of the corporation before the date of an ownership change are no greater than twice the annual limitation (two times the value of the loss corporation multiplied by the applicable tax-exempt rate). Temporary Regulations, section 1.382–2T(h)(4)(x), also list a number of options which are not subject to the attribution rule. These include, among others, options to acquire stock of a loss corporation which is publicly traded if the option holder has held the option for at least three years (but only until such time as the exercise price exceeds the fair market value of the stock on a testing date) (subdivision (A)), the right to receive stock in satisfaction of an obligation if the amount of stock is based upon a fixed dollar figure as of the date the stock is to be transferred (subdivision (B)), any right or obligation of the loss corporation to redeem its stock, but only if the stock was issued to less than five percent stockholders (subdivision (C)), options exercisable only on death, disability or mental incompetency (subdivision (D)), a right to acquire stock held by a bank, insurance company or qualified employee benefit trust on default under a loan agreement entered into in the ordinary course of the business of such bank, insurance company or trust (subdivision (G)), and buy-out agreements to sell stock on retirement (subdivision (H)).

(d) *The Definition of Stock*

By reference to section 1504(a)(4), section 382(k)(6)(A) defines stock for section 382 purposes as excluding nonvoting, nonconvertible stock interests which are limited as to dividends and which do not participate in corporate growth "to any significant extent." This provision prevents a loss corporation from increasing the amount of its outstanding stock with insignificant equity interests in order to avoid an ownership change. In addition, section 382(k)(6)(B) directs the Treasury to promulgate regulations treating certain stock which is stock under section 1504(a)(4) (such as voting stock with no significant participation in growth) as nonstock for section 382 purposes. Temporary Regulations, section 1.382–2T(f)(18)(ii), contain a three part test for the identification of nonstock stock: (A) the likely participation of the interest of a five percent stockholder at the time of the stock's issue is disproportionately small compared to the fair market value of outstanding stock of the corporation, (B) treating the interest as nonstock would result in an ownership change, and (C) net operating losses and built-in losses are at least twice the annual limitation (two times the value of the loss corporation times the tax-exempt rate).

To cover the field completely, under the authority of section 382(k)(6)(B)(ii), Temporary Regulations, section 1.382–2T(f)(18)(iii), treat certain interests which are not normally classified as stock (potential equity disguised as debt) as constituting stock for section 382 purposes if (A) at the time of issue, a nonstock interest issued to a five percent stockholder offers the potential for significant participation in corporate growth, (B) treating the interest as stock would result in an ownership change, and (C) the loss corporation's net operating losses and built-in losses are at least twice the annual limitation. This provision is designed to prevent the issuance of equity-flavored instruments which are not equity in form to avoid the ownership change rules. However, since, under the option attribution rules of section 382(*l*)(3)(A)(iv), any instrument which allows participation in future growth through conversion into stock is counted as transferred stock, the rules treating nonstock interests as stock are applicable to only a narrow range of nonconvertible nonstock instruments such as a debt instrument with a contingent payout large enough to constitute a significant participation in future growth. Such an instrument likely would be classified as stock under debt/equity rules, but the drafters of the Regulations were not willing to leave the question open to the vagaries of litigation. Identifying instruments that provide a significant participation in future growth may prove to be no less difficult, however.

In Notice 88–67, 1988–1, Cum.Bull. 555, the Internal Revenue Service indicated that it intended to promulgate Regulations treating preferred stock which is classified as nonstock under the section 1504(a)(4) rules, but which is convertible into stock, as not constituting stock. The conversion feature is to be treated as an option, however, subject to the option attribution rules, discussed supra, page 982. The Notice indicates further that other convertible stock, stock which is not excluded from the definition of stock by section 1504(a)(4), will be classified as stock for section 382 purposes and not subject to the option rules.

(e) *Aggregation and Segregation of Less Than Five Percent Stockholders*

All stockholders of a corporation who individually own less than five percent of the stock are aggregated into a group (a "public group") and treated as a single five percent stockholder regardless of the percentage of stock held by less than five percent stockholders either individually or as a group. Section 382(g)(4)(A). Sections 382(g)(4)(B) and (C) provide for the segregation of identifiable groups of less than five percent stockholders for purposes of determining whether an ownership change has occurred following either an equity structure shift or an owner shift. In certain transactions, particularly equity structure shifts, it is possible to trace the changes in ownership of separate identifiable public groups. For example, on the merger of a publicly held loss corporation into another publicly held corporation, there are two identifiable groups of less than five percent stockholders, the public group of the loss corporation and the public group of the acquiring corporation. The transfer of ownership of the loss corporation from its pre-merger public stockholders to the public stockholders of the acquiring corporation may be treated as a stock transfer from the loss corporation public group to the pre-merger public group of the acquiring corporation. Similar transfers by or to a public group can be identified with respect to other reorganizations (whether taxable or nonrecognition transactions), a public offering (the new stockholders are a separate five percent stockholder), or a redemption (stockholders whose interests are increased are a separate five percent stockholder).

Temporary Regulations, section 1.382–2T(j), first aggregate groups of less than five percent stockholders of a loss corporation into different public groups depending upon direct and indirect ownership of stock in a loss corporation. The Temporary Regulations then segregate public groups that are separated following a reorganization, a stock issue covered by section 1032, or a redemption. The same aggregation and segregation rules apply to stockholders who are less than five percent stockholders of a loss corporation by attribution from an entity which directly or indirectly owns five percent or more of the loss corporation stock. Temporary Regulations, section 1.382–2T(j)(3). The operation of these rules may be illustrated by the following example:

L, a loss corporation, P1, and P2 each have 1000 shares of stock outstanding. The stock of L is owned 600 shares by P1, 200 shares by P2, and 170 shares by a public group, none of whom owns more than five percent of the L stock, and A who owns 30 shares. A owns 50 shares of the P1 stock. The remaining 950 shares of P1 stock are owned by public stockholders none of whom owns more than five percent of P1 stock. A owns 100 shares of P2 stock. The remaining 950 shares of P2 stock are held by public stockholders none of whom owns more than five percent of P2 stock. The ownership structure of L is as follows:

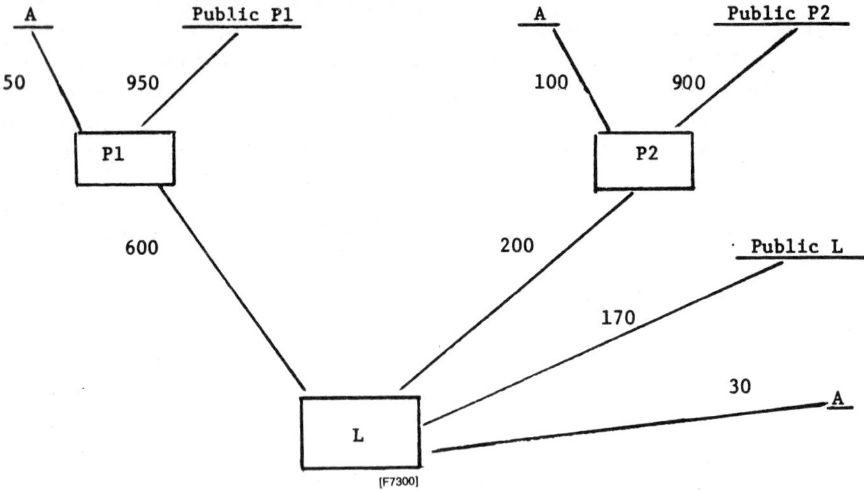

L's stock is held by three separate public groups, each of which is treated as a single five percent stockholder: the public group that directly holds L stock, the public group of P1 stockholders which by attribution holds 60 percent of L stock, and the public group of P2 stockholders which by attribution holds 20 percent of L stock.

Although A directly and indirectly owns more than five percent of L stock, A is not a five percent stockholder of L. A owns 3 percent of L directly. As a five percent owner of P1, A is attributed a proportionate share of P1's L stock, an interest of 3 percent (5% × 60%). Since A's interest is less than five percent, A is treated as a member of the P1 public group. Temporary Regulations, section 1.382–2T(j)(1)(iv)(A). As a 10 percent owner of P2, A indirectly owns an additional 2 percent of L, but again A's stock interest is included as part of the interest of the P2 public group. Temporary Regulations, section 1.382–2T(j)(1)(iii), contain a presumption that stockholders, including five percent owners of a higher tier entity which owns stock in a loss corporation, who are not five percent stockholders of a loss corporation, are not members of more than one public group. Thus, A's direct interest of 3 percent is not added to A's indirect 6 percent interest by attribution through P1 and P2 to make A a five percent stockholder. Because L is required to keep track of only five percent stockholders who can be traced through a chain of at least five percent ownership interests, L is presumed not to have knowledge of A's existence as a five percent stockholder. However, A will be treated as a five percent stockholder if L has actual knowledge of A's ownership interests. Temporary Regulations, section 1.382–2T(j)(1)(iii), (k)(2).

On April 1, 1989, L issues 111 shares of new stock to the public. The stock is not purchased by any person who owns five percent of L stock. The issue of L stock to less than five percent stockholders creates a new public group which is treated as a five percent stockholder. This new group ("new public L") increased its interest in L during the testing period from 0 percent before the stock offering to 10 percent (111/1,111) afterwards. The Temporary Regulations, section 1.382–2T(j)(1)(iii), presume that there is no cross-ownership between the old public stockholders of L and the new public stockholders. Thus, absent actual knowledge by L, any acquisition of the newly issued L stock by existing stockholders will be ignored. The stock issue is, therefore, a 10 percent owner shift.

On April 1, 1990, all of the assets of P1, including the L stock, are acquired by P2 in a statutory merger. The P1 stockholders receive 1 share of P2 stock for every four shares of P1 stock. A receives 12.5 shares of P2 stock, the remaining P1 stockholders receive 237.5 shares of P2 stock. P2 now owns 72 percent (800/1111 shares) L. The transaction is tested for an ownership change by segregating the post-merger stockholders of P2 into two public groups, the original P2 stockholders, who now own 72 percent of P1 ("old public P2"), and the pre-merger P1 stockholders ("new public P2"). (As will be discussed below, A has become a five percent stockholder of L and is therefore no longer included in a P2 public group.) Before the reorganization, the original P2 public group owned 16.2 percent of L by attribution from P2 ([200/1111] × 90%). After the reorganization, the original P2 public group owns 51.8 percent of L ([800/1111] × [900/1250]). Thus old public P2 has increased its ownership interest in L by 35.6 percent.

Within the testing period, the 35.6 percent owner shift in L from new public P2 to old public P2, plus the 10 percent owner shift from old public L to new public L, are not sufficient to trigger an ownership change of L. However, A's interest in the transaction causes an ownership change to be triggered. Before the merger of P1 into P2, A's cross-ownership was disregarded under the presumption of Temporary Regulations, section 1.382–2T(j)(1)(iii), and A was treated as a less than five percent stockholder whose stock interests are part of public groups. A becomes a distinct five percent stockholder as a result of the merger, however. After the merger A owns 112.5 shares of P2 stock, 9 percent of P2. A is, therefore, deemed to own 6.5 percent of L by attribution from P2. Even though A is now identified as a five percent stockholder, A's ownership interest is presumed to include only A's five percent interest through P2. A's 2.7 percent direct interest in L is still treated as part of the old public L group. Temporary Regulations, section 1.382–2T(j)(1)(vi), Ex. (5). As a result, A's interest as an identified five percent stockholder increased from zero before the transaction to 6.5 percent after the merger. A's 6.5 percent owner shift, when added to the increased interests of old public P2 and new public L, result in an increased interest by five percent stockholders of 52.1 percent, sufficient to trigger an ownership change.

Once an ownership change has occurred following a transaction that requires segregation of different groups of less than five percent stockholders, the groups are no longer treated as separate five percent stockholders. Temporary Regulations, section 1.382–2T(j)(2)(iii)(B), Ex. (3)(iv).

If L has actual knowledge of A's pre-merger stock ownership interest, L may overcome the presumption of Temporary Regulations, section 1.382–2T(j)(1)(iii), and avoid the ownership change. See Temporary Regulations, section 1.382–2T(k)(2). Before the merger, A's lowest actual percentage interest during the testing period was 7.5 percent, 2.7 percent direct interest in L stock, 2.7 percent attributed through P1, and 1.8 percent attributed through P2. A's percentage interest in L after the merger is 9.2, of which 6.5 percent is attributed from P2 and 2.7 percent is direct. The owner shift attributable to A is only 1.7 percent. That is not sufficient to trigger an ownership change on the merger of P1 into P2 (35.6% + 10% + 1.7% = 47.3%).

(f) *Reporting Requirements*

Temporary Regulations, section 1.382–2T(a)(2)(ii) and (iii), contain burdensome information reporting and record keeping requirements which require the corporation to monitor its status under section 382 even if there is only a remote possibility of an ownership change. In any taxable year in which a corporation is a loss corporation (see section 382(k)(1)), the corporation must file a statement with its tax return indicating whether there has been a testing date during the year, identifying any testing dates on which an ownership change occurred, identifying testing dates that occurred closest to the end of each calendar quarter of the taxable year, indicating the percentage stock ownership of each five percent stockholder on each testing date reported and the percentage increase of each five percent stockholder during the testing period, and identifying the extent to which the corporation relied on presumptions provided in Temporary Regulations, section 1.382–2T(k)(1). Temporary Regulations, section 1.382–2T(k)(1), allow a publicly held loss corporation to rely on filings with the Securities and Exchange Commission to disclose the existence of five percent stockholders. A loss corporation is also allowed to rely on statements by responsible persons (such as officers, trustees, partners, etc.), signed under penalties of perjury, which disclose the ownership interests and changes in interest of the owners of an upper-tier entity which owns an interest in the loss corporation. The Temporary Regulations also require a loss corporation to maintain records adequate to identify five percent stockholders and ascertain whether an ownership change has occurred. In many cases, it is possible that the cost of providing information returns will outweigh the value of loss carryovers.

4. *Worthless Stock Deduction by a 50 Percent Stockholder*

In Textron, Inc. v. United States, 561 F.2d 1023 (1st Cir.1977), a parent corporation claimed a worthless stock deduction for the stock of its controlled subsidiary. The court held that the net operating loss carryover of the subsidiary was unaffected by the parent's worthless stock deduction and thus the subsidiary was permitted to claim its loss carryover as a deduction against future income. In effect, *Textron, Inc.* allowed the same loss to be accounted for twice, once at the corporation level and once at the stockholder level. Section 382(g)(4)(D) was enacted in 1987 to overrule this result.

Section 382(g)(4)(D) treats a worthless stock *deduction* by a 50 percent stockholder, who continues to own the stock at the close of the taxable year, as an owner shift. The stockholder is treated as acquiring the stock on the first day of the taxable year following the year in which the stock is claimed to have become worthless, and as not having any stock ownership preceding that date. The consequence is an owner shift from zero percent to an ownership interest of 50 percent or greater. This owner shift triggers an ownership change thereby subjecting the corporation's loss carryovers to the section 382 limitation.

The legislative history regarding section 382(g)(4)(D) raises a question with respect to the scope of its application. Under the statutory language, it seems clear that the effect of the stockholder's worthless stock deduction is an ownership change which restricts, but does not entirely eliminate, the corporation's net operating loss carryover. Under section 382(a), income arising subsequent to an ownership change is offset by pre-change losses to the extent allowed by the annual limitation. The legislative history to section 382(g)(4)(D) states, however, that "if a worthless stock deduction is claimed during the testing period by persons holding more than 50-percent of a loss corporation's stock, net operating loss carryovers of the corporation arising prior to the change may not be used to offset the corporation's post change income." H.R.Rep. No. 100–391, 100th Cong., 1st Sess. 1096 (1987). See also H.R.Rep. No. 100–495 (Conf.Rep.), 100th Cong., 1st Sess. A–40 (1987).

C. COMPUTING THE SECTION 382 LIMITATION

1. *Valuing the Loss Corporation*

The annual limitation on income of a loss corporation that can be offset by net operating loss carryovers following an ownership change is computed by multiplying the value of the loss corporation by the federal long-term tax-exempt rate. Section 382(b)(1). Value is based on the value of the stock of the loss corporation on the date immediately preceding an ownership change. Section 382(e)(1). As noted in the *General Explanation*, the value of a loss corporation includes the value of interests that are not treated as stock under section 1504(a)(4). Presumably, valuation also includes stock which is declared to be nonstock under Temporary Regulations, section 1.382–2T(f)(18)(iii).

To prevent a loss corporation from artificially enhancing its value on the eve of an ownership change, section 382(1) provides that any capital contributed to the loss corporation as part of a plan to increase the limitation shall not be taken into account in determining value. Section 382(1)(2) provides that, except as otherwise provided in Regulations, any capital contribution within 2 years of the date of an ownership change shall be treated as part of a forbidden plan.

Additional anti-abuse rules are found in section 382(1)(4), which reduces the value of a loss corporation that has substantial nonbusiness assets. The value of the loss corporation is reduced by the fair market value of nonbusiness assets less liabilities attributable to such assets. A loss corporation has substantial nonbusiness assets if more than one-third of the total value of the loss corporation consists of investment assets. This limitation is intended to prevent the sale of carryovers by a loss corporation which has disposed of its operating assets. However, given the severity of the limitation imposed by section 382, a market for shell corporations with loss carryovers is not likely to exist in any event. The provision works ultimately only to reduce the sales price of a loss corporation with substantial investment assets.

Under section 382(e)(2), if an ownership change occurs in connection with a redemption or other corporate contraction, the value of the loss corporation immediately before the ownership change must be adjusted to account for assets distributed in the redemption.

2. *Built-in Gains and Losses*

Section 382 also deals with unrealized losses of a loss corporation which could be utilized by an acquiring corporation to offset future income in the same manner as a net operating loss carryforward. To prevent this result, net unrealized losses existing at the time of an ownership change are subject to the annual section 382 limitation in the taxable year the losses are recognized. Section 382(h)(1)(B). Recognized built-in losses that are not deductible in the taxable year because of the section 382 limitation are carried forward into subsequent taxable years (subject to the limitation in future years) in the same manner as a net operating loss which arose in the year of recognition. Section 382(h)(4).

With respect to built-in gains, section 382 takes into account the fact that at any time a loss corporation could absorb its loss carryovers by disposing of assets with unrealized appreciation. Section 382(h)(1)(A) thus allows a loss corporation to increase its annual limitation following an ownership change by built-in gain recognized during the taxable year.

The rules of section 382(h) apply only to unrealized gains or losses recognized by the loss corporation within five years of an ownership change.

Furthermore, the built-in gain or loss rules of section 382(h) apply only if the corporation has net unrealized gain or loss on the acquisition date. Net unrealized built-in gains and losses are based on the difference between the fair market value and adjusted bases of the assets of a loss corporation immediately before an ownership change. Section 382(h)(3)(A). Net unrealized loss also includes any depreciation or other capital recovery deductions attributable to the excess of the adjusted basis of an asset over its fair market value on the date of an ownership change. Thus, a valuation of the corporation's assets is required as of the acquisition date. Net unrealized built-in gain or loss is ignored, however, if the amount of unrealized gain or loss is not greater than the lesser of $10,000 or 15 percent of the fair market value of the loss corporation's assets (computed without regard to cash or marketable securities the value of which approximates cost) immediately prior to the date of an ownership change. Section 382(h)(3)(B). In the case of a corporation with respect to which a section 338 election is in effect following an ownership change, the section 382 limitation is increased by the lesser of gain recognized by reason of the section 338 election, or built-in gain determined without regard to the limitation of section 382(h)(3)(B). Section 382(h)(1)(C).

Section 382(h)(6) provides that income earned prior to the date of an ownership change, but which has not been taken into account by the loss corporation, will be treated as built-in gain recognized in the year the item is properly taken into account. Thus earned but unreported income items increase the annual limitation in the year the item is properly accounted for by the loss corporation. Conversely, deduction items attributable to periods predating the date of an ownership change, but which have not been deducted by the loss corporation, are treated as recognized built-in losses in the year the item is deducted. These items are thus subject to the section 382 limitation in the year deducted.

Temporary Regulations, section 1.382–2T(c)(3)(iii), contain a special rule for commencement of the three year testing period in the case of a corporation with built-in losses. As described supra, page 978, the testing period generally begins on the earlier of the first day of a taxable year from which there is a loss or excess tax credit carryforward, or the first day of a taxable year in which a testing date occurs. In the case of a corporation with a net unrealized built in loss, the testing date extends back a full three years from the date of an owner shift or equity structure shift which requires testing for an ownership change. The testing period may be shortened, however, if the corporation can show that unrealized built-in losses accrued at an earlier date, in which case the testing period will begin on the first day of the taxable year in which the losses accrued, from which there is a loss carryover, or the year the transaction being tested occurs, whichever is earlier.

D. CONTINUITY OF BUSINESS ENTERPRISE

Prior to the 1986 revision of section 382, loss carryovers survived a change in ownership of the loss corporation in a purchase transaction if the corporation continued to conduct business substantially the same as before the ownership change.[4] Section 382(c) retains a vestige of the business continuity requirements by disallowing loss carryovers following an ownership change if the corporation "does not continue the business enterprise" of the loss corporation for a period of at least 2 years. The legislative history indicates that section 382(c) is intended to adopt the continuity of business requirement applied to reorganizations by Regulations, section 1.368–1(d). See supra, page 792. Thus the continuity requirement is satisfied if the new loss corporation either continues the trade or business which existed before an ownership change, or uses a significant portion of the business assets of the old loss corporation in a business. The Conference Report makes it clear that loss carryovers survive an ownership change even if the new loss corporation discontinues more than a minor portion of the historic business of the old loss corporation. H.Rep. No. 99–841, 99th Cong., 2d Sess. II–189 (1986).

4. In Libson Shops, Inc. v. Koehler, 353 U.S. 382 (1957), the Court held that following a merger of seventeen separate entities (all of which were engaged in the same line of business and owned by the same stockholders) into a single corporation, the loss carryovers of three of the merged entities could not be deducted from the income of the combined enterprise. The Court held that the prior year's loss could be offset against the current year's income only to the extent that income was derived from the operation of substantially the same business which produced the loss. The Court stated that it could find no indication in the legislative history to the predecessor of section 172 that it was intended "to permit the averaging of the pre-merger losses of one business with the post-merger income of some other business which had been operated and taxed separately before the merger." (386–387)

Maxwell Hardware Company v. Commissioner, 343 F.2d 713 (9th Cir.1965), held that enactment of the predecessor to section 382 in the 1954 Code destroyed the precedential value of *Libson Shops*. *Maxwell Hardware* was followed in Frederick Steel Co. v. Commissioner, 375 F.2d 351 (6th Cir.1967); Euclid–Tennessee, Inc. v. Commissioner, 352 F.2d 991 (6th Cir.1965); United States v. Adkins–Phelps, Inc., 400 F.2d 737 (9th Cir.1968). However, the Internal Revenue Service announced that it would continue to apply the *Libson Shops* doctrine to any loss carryover case under the 1954 Code where there has been both a 50% or more shift in beneficial interests in a loss carryover and a change of business. T.I.R. No. 773, 657 CCH 6751 (1965). The legislative history of the 1986 Act states that the *Libson Shops* doctrine is to have no application to transactions covered by the carryover limitations of section 382. H.R.Rep. No. 841, 99th Cong., 2d Sess. II–194 (1986). There remains an argument, however, that the *Libson Shops* doctrine is applicable to the carryover of items not limited by section 382. See Bittker and Eustice, Federal Income Taxation of Corporations and Shareholders, 16.26 (5th Ed. 1985).

Does Congress' incorporation of the continuity standard applicable to reorganizations under Regulations, section 1.368–1(d), include case law weakening the standard to require only some minimal use of the acquired corporation's assets? For example, in Laure v. Commissioner, 653 F.2d 253 (6th Cir.1981), the taxpayer claimed a net operating loss carryover following a statutory merger of its insolvent subsidiary in which the taxpayer obtained all of the subsidiary's assets. The subsidiary operated an air charter business and an airport base operation which was important to the taxpayer's business. In a prearranged plan following the merger, the taxpayer sold all of the acquired assets, with the exception of a hanger and land representing 27 percent of the subsidiary's assets, to a former employee who would continue operation of the subsidiary's business. The hanger was leased to the former employee. The Commissioner asserted that the transaction failed to qualify as a reorganization under section 368 because of the continuity of business requirement, and thus disallowed the net operating loss carryover. The Court of Appeals, reversing the Tax Court, disagreed: "[A]dequate evidence shows that [the value of the land and hanger] was indeed substantial, both in relation to other assets transferred and in importance to [the taxpayer] due to its continuing need for air charter and repair services * * *" (261.)[5]

The insistence on continuity of business is to some extent inconsistent with the basic theory behind the limitation of section 382. The section 382 limitation is based, in part, on the assumption that the loss corporation could dispose of its assets, invest the proceeds in income generating securities, and absorb its loss carryover with interest income. There is no continuity of business restriction preventing use of loss carryovers following such a transaction. Why is it necessary to encourage continued investment in a loss operation following an ownership change? Perhaps the answer is that the continuity of business requirement is necessary to prevent the acquisition of a corporation to acquire only loss carryovers. However, the section 382 limitation itself is sufficiently restrictive to eliminate transactions motivated by only tax reduction. To the extent the continuity requirement inhibits the purchaser, it restrains the sale of the loss corporation, encourages continuation of an unprofitable business, and thereby violates the neutrality principle on which section 382 is based.

E. LIMITATIONS ON CARRYOVERS UNDER SECTION 383

Section 383 applies the limitation of section 382 following an ownership change to capital loss carryovers, general business credits, minimum tax credits under the alternative minimum tax, and foreign tax credits. Section 383(b) states that Regulations are to be issued to provide that capital losses carried forward from a year pre-dating an ownership change are limited under section 382 principles and shall reduce the section 382 limitation on net operating losses. Section 383(a) and (c) provide for Regulations to limit the use of tax credit carryforwards to tax liability computed on income up to the section 382 limitation. Tax credits are thereby converted into their taxable income equivalents for limitation purposes. See Temporary Regulations, 1.383–1T.

5. The reorganization in *Laure* predated the effective date of Regulations, section 1.368–1(d), but the court expressed its opinion that the transfer qualified under that provision in any event. (653 F.2d at 262, n. 9.).

F. APPLICATION OF SECTION 382 IN BANKRUPTCY AND INSOLVENCY PROCEEDINGS

See infra, page 1012.

G. ACQUISITION OF BUILT–IN GAIN PROPERTY BY A LOSS CORPORATION: SECTION 384

The section 382 limitation is not applied to restrict loss carryovers if, instead of being acquired by new owners, the loss corporation directly or indirectly acquires appreciated assets of a profitable enterprise in a carryover basis transaction and uses its loss carryover to avoid tax on gain recognized on disposition of the acquired assets. Section 384 was enacted in 1987 to deal with this situation. The legislative history explains the provision as follows:

"[Section 384] provides that loss corporations will be precluded from using their losses to shelter built-in gains of an acquired company recognized within five years of the acquisition. Built-in gains for this purpose includes any item of income which is attributable to periods before the acquisition date. For example, built-in gains for this purpose include so-called 'phantom' gains on property on which depreciation had been taken prior to the acquisition. It is likewise expected that built-in gains for this purpose will also include any income recognized after an acquisition in which the fair market value of the property acquired is less than the present value of the taxes that would be due on the income associated with the property (for example, in the case of a 'burnt-out' leasing subsidiary with built-in income transferred to a loss corporation). No inference is intended that such situations are not subject to section 269 of present law." H.Rep. No. 100–391, 100th Cong., 1st Sess. 1093–1094 (1987).

Section 384 applies to built-in gain recognized during the five-year period following the corporate acquisition of control of another corporation, or the acquisition of corporate assets in an (A), (C) or (D) reorganization, when either the acquiring corporation or the acquired corporation has a "net unrealized built-in gain" at the time of acquisition. By reference to section 382(h), net unrealized built-in gain exists if the aggregate value of transferred assets at the time of acquisition exceeds the aggregate adjusted bases of such assets. Section 384(c)(1) and (8). Section 384 prohibits the use of pre-acquisition losses (including recognized built-in losses) of one corporation to offset recognized built-in gain of the gain corporation. It does not prevent a loss corporation from acquiring an on-going profitable enterprise for the purpose of using its loss carryovers to offset future income (other than recognized built-in gain) of the acquired business. Such an acquisition may be subject to section 269, however.

H. SECTION 269 AND LOSS CARRYOVERS

Section 269 allows the Commissioner to deny the benefit of deductions made possible by an acquisition of control of another corporation or assets with a carryover basis when the principal purpose of the acquisition is tax avoidance. Before 1986, section 269 was a moderately important weapon for the Commissioner to prevent abusive acquisitions of shell corporations with loss carryovers. For example, in Scroll, Inc. v. Commissioner, 447 F.2d 612 (5th Cir.1971), the stock of the taxpayer which had a substantial net operating loss carryforward, was acquired by another corporation, Keller. Several months after the acquisition, Keller merged the operations of a profitable subsidiary into the loss corporation. As a result of the merger, the income of the profitable business was offset by the loss corporation's operating loss carryforward. The taxpayer asserted that the transaction enabled the profitable subsidiary to reduce state income taxes and provided the loss corporation with the benefit of the marketing skills of the profitable enterprise. The Court of Appeals affirmed the Tax Court's finding that the forbidden tax avoidance motive was present:

"Regardless of whether these non-tax motives were actual or illusory, however, the practical effect of the entire transaction was to enable the corporation to set off substantial pre-acquisition losses against subsequent earnings and thereby to obtain a tax benefit not otherwise available. According to the Treasury Regulations (section 1.269–3), such a result by itself indicates a tax-avoidance motive irrespective of whether any other evidence points to the proscribed principal purpose. And, contrary to Taxpayer's contention that the disallowance fails for want of verbal testimony linking (i) the initial acquisition of [the taxpayer] with (ii) the soon-to-follow merger of [the profitable subsidiary into the taxpayer], the Tax Court was entitled to treat both acquisition and merger as interrelated steps in a single transaction. [Citation omitted.]

"There is a good deal of practical wisdom in the regulation, whether its principle comes from the mind of Judge or the pen of a regulation redactor. A 269 problem is not one of torts in which the judicial inquiry artificially cuts off at the moment of wrong. What was intended by such a merger-acquisition can properly be ascertained both by initial actions and those taken shortly thereafter, especially when the subsequent steps are so obviously necessary that they must have been in the minds of the strategists. The record here is undisputed that Keller's top management—including a former practicing certified public accountant—was aware in detail of this $600,000 loss carryover. We think a court experienced in the affairs of Federal income taxation was entitled to believe that no businessman in his right mind would allow this plum to go unplucked. To do nothing was to forsake forever the hope of a tax savings. To try, the structural change had to be made. If it worked, all was well. If it didn't, the try was worth the risk—indeed, there was no risk at all because what is here 'lost' is what would have been paid had the game plan not been chosen. The burden of proof on the taxpayer is not an easy one, and when the disputed tax benefits are so disproportionate to the value of the other asserted advantages, that burden may be practically impossible to sustain. * * * " (617–618)

The legislative history of the 1986 Act indicates that section 382 does not alter the application of section 269 to acquisitions made to evade or avoid taxes. H.Rep. No. 99–841, 99th Cong., 2d Sess. II–194. However, after 1986, section 382 so severely discounts net operating loss carryforwards following an ownership change that there is no longer a significant tax avoidance potential in a transaction subject to the limitation. Nonetheless, because the 50 percent ownership change rules of section 382 and the acquisition of control provisions of section 269 are not identical, there is a possibility that an acquisition will fall within section 269 without triggering an ownership change under section 382. For example, P, which owns 49 percent of L, a loss corporation, acquires an additional 31 percent of the loss corporation stock. P then liquidates L under section 332 thereby inheriting L's loss carryover under section 381. If there have been no other owner shifts with respect to the L stock during the three year testing period, P has acquired control of L for section 269 purposes without triggering the section 382 limitation on L's loss carryovers. If P's acquisition of L, or its assets, is undertaken with the requisite tax avoidance purpose, section 269 may be invoked to deny P the benefit of L's loss carryforward even though the transaction escapes the reach of section 382.

The section 382 limitation is applicable only to an ownership change of the loss corporation itself. Although section 384 restricts the acquisition of assets with built-in gain by a loss corporation, there is nothing in the statutory scheme to prevent a loss corporation from acquiring a profitable business in a taxable or nontaxable transaction to generate income absorbing the corporation's loss carryforward. In Rev.Rul. 63–40, 1963–1 Cum.Bull. 46, the Internal Revenue Service indicated that it would not contend that an acquisition is undertaken for tax avoidance purposes under section 269 where a loss corporation acquires the stock of a profitable corporation, liquidates the profitable business, and discontinues the loss business. The Ruling does not apply, however, where the purchase price for the profitable business is paid over a long period of time or exceeds the fair market value of the acquired business. Could the Service ever successfully overcome a loss corporation's assertion that its acquisition of a profitable enterprise was undertaken for valid business purposes? Indeed, would imposition of section 269 restrictions on this transaction achieve a desirable policy goal? If the stockholders who suffered the losses are still in the picture, there is not the windfall that is present in the case when newcomers acquire a loss corporation, which is the typical "trafficking in loss corporation" case.

I. REFERENCES

Simmons, Net Operating Losses and Section 382: Searching for a Limitation on Loss Carryovers, 63 Tul.L.Rev. 1045 (1989); Glicklich, Section 384: Less Left for Loss Corporations, 16 J. of Corp.Tax. 23 (1989); Silverman and Keyes, An Analysis of the New Ownership Regs. Under Section 382, Part I, 68 J.Tax 72, Part II, 68 J.Tax 142, Part III, 68 J.Tax 300, Part IV, 69 J.Tax 42 (1988); Posin, Three Strikes Are We Out? Transfer of Loss Carryovers After the 1986 Act, 7 Va.Tax Rev. 697 (1988); Wooten, Section 382 After the Tax Reform Act of 1986, 64 Taxes 874 (1986).

For proposals leading to the 1986 amendments see American Law Inst., Federal Income Tax Project, Subchapter C, 212 et. seq. (W. Andrews Reporter) (1982); Staff of the Senate Comm. of Finance, 99th Cong., 1st Sess., The Subchapter C Revision Act of 1985, 69 et. seq. (Comm. Print 1985); Stone & Jacobs, An Analysis of the Net Operating Loss and Excess Credit Carryforwards Under H.R. 3838, 31 Tax Notes 725 (1986).

PART VII

BANKRUPTCY TAX ISSUES

CHAPTER 22

INSOLVENCY REORGANIZATIONS AND RELATED MATTERS

INTERNAL REVENUE CODE: Sections 61(a)(12); 108(a), (b), (d)(2), (3), (e); 354(b); 368(a)(1)(G), (a)(3); 1017.

A failing or bankrupt business encounters a number of tax issues as it seeks to work out its future, either inside or outside bankruptcy proceedings. In some cases, the issues are the same as those discussed at various points in prior Chapters, but additional tax issues are confronted by the financially distressed business. Several Code provisions directly address transactions engaged in by failing or bankrupt businesses and resolve some of the questions. There remain, however, significant areas where there is little or no guidance with respect to tax issues encountered by a financially troubled business.

SENATE FINANCE COMMITTEE REPORT, BANKRUPTCY TAX ACT OF 1980.

S.Rep. No. 96–1035, 96th Cong., 2d Sess. 8 (1980).

A. Tax Treatment of Discharge of Indebtedness

[Pre–1981] Law

In general.—Under [pre–1981] law, income is realized when indebtedness is forgiven or in other ways cancelled (sec. 61(a)(12) of the Internal Revenue Code). For example, if a corporation has issued a $1,000 bond at par which it later repurchases for only $900, thereby increasing its net worth by $100, the corporation realizes $100 of income in the year of repurchase (United States v. Kirby Lumber Co., 284 U.S. 1 (1931)).

There are several exceptions to the general rule of income realization. Under a judicially developed "insolvency exception," no income arises from discharge of indebtedness if the debtor is insolvent both before and after the transaction;[1] and if the transaction leaves the debtor with assets whose value exceeds remaining liabilities, income is realized only to the extent of the excess.[2] Treasury regulations provide that the gratuitous cancellation of a corporation's indebtedness by a shareholder-creditor does not give rise to debt discharge income to the

1. Treas.Regs. § 161–12(b)(1); Dallas Transfer & Terminal Warehouse Co. v. Comm'r, 70 F.2d 95 (5th Cir.1934).

2. Lakeland Grocery Co., 36 B.T.A. 289 (1937).

extent of the principal of the debt, since the cancellation amounts to a contribution to capital of the corporation.[3] Some courts have applied this exception even if the corporation has previously deducted the amount owed to the shareholder-creditor.[4] Under a related exception, cases have held that no income arises from discharge of indebtedness if stock is issued to a creditor in satisfaction of the debt, even if the creditor was previously a shareholder, and even if the stock is worth less than the face amount of the obligation satisfied.[5] Further, cancellation of a previously accrued and deducted expense does not give rise to income if the deduction did not result in a reduction of tax (Code sec. 111). * * *

A debtor which otherwise would be required to report current income from debt cancellation under the preceding rules instead may elect to reduce the basis of its assets in accordance with Treasury regulations (Code secs. 108 and 1017). This income exclusion is available if the discharged indebtedness was incurred by a corporation or by an individual in connection with property used in his trade or business. These provisions were intended to allow the tax on the debt discharge income to be deferred and collected through lower depreciation deductions for the reduced-basis assets, or greater taxable gains on sale of the assets.

* * *

Bankruptcy proceedings.—The Bankruptcy Act contains certain rules relating to the Federal income tax treatment of discharge of indebtedness in bankruptcy proceedings. However, these rules have been repealed by P.L. 95–598 effective for bankruptcy cases instituted on or after October 1, 1979.

Under the Bankruptcy Act provisions, no income is recognized on cancellation of indebtedness in an insolvency reorganization (under chapter X). The Act requires the debtor corporation to reduce the basis of its assets by the amount of indebtedness discharged, but not below the fair market value of such assets as of the date the bankruptcy court confirms the reorganization plan.[7] However, under section 372 of the Internal Revenue Code, no basis reduction is required if the corporation's property is transferred to a successor corporation as part of the bankruptcy reorganization.[8]

Similar rules apply in the case of an "arrangement" (under chapter XI) * * *. In addition, in the case of a Bankruptcy Act discharge other than under an insolvency reorganization or an arrangement

3. Treas. Regs. § 1.61–12(a).

4. Putoma Corp. v. Comm'r, 66 T.C. 652 (1978), aff'd, 604 F.2d 734 (5th Cir.1979).

5. Comm'r v. Motor Mart Trust, 156 F.2d 122 (1st Cir.1946).

7. Secs. 268 and 270 of the Bankruptcy Act.

8. While under [pre–1981] law no basis reduction is required if a successor corporation is used in the insolvency reorganization, the Code under present law does not permit the carryover of tax attributes, such as net operating losses, from the debtor to the successor corporation (except possibly in certain situations where the reorganization meets the requirements of secs. 368 and 381 of the Code, in which case net operating losses may be limited by section 382 of the Code).

described above, income is not realized to the extent the general "insolvency exception" applies.[10]

Reasons for Change

Overview.—In P.L. 95–598, Congress repealed provisions of the Bankruptcy Act governing Federal income tax treatment of debt discharge in bankruptcy, effective for cases instituted on or after October 1, 1979. The committee's bill provides tax rules in the Internal Revenue Code applicable to debt discharge in the case of bankrupt or insolvent debtors, and makes related changes to existing Code provisions applicable to debt discharge in the case of solvent debtors outside bankruptcy.

The rules of the bill concerning income tax treatment of debt discharge in bankruptcy are intended to accommodate bankruptcy policy and tax policy. To preserve the debtor's "fresh start" after bankruptcy, the bill provides that no income is recognized by reason of debt discharge in bankruptcy, so that a debtor coming out of bankruptcy (or an insolvent debtor outside bankruptcy) is not burdened with an immediate tax liability. The bill provides that the debt discharge amount thus excluded from income is applied to reduce the taxpayer's net operating losses and certain other tax attributes, unless the taxpayer elects to apply the debt discharge amount first to reduce basis in depreciable assets (or in realty held as inventory).

* * *

Debtors given flexibility.—The committee believes that these attribute-reduction provisions of the bill give flexibility to the debtor to account for a debt discharge amount in a manner most favorable to the debtor's tax situation. For example, a bankrupt or insolvent debtor which wishes to retain net operating losses and other carryovers will be able to elect to reduce asset basis in depreciable property (or in realty held as inventory). On the other hand, a debtor having an expiring net operating loss which otherwise would be "wasted" will be able (by not making the election) to apply the debt discharge amount first against the net operating loss. Similarly, a solvent debtor can continue to defer recognition of income by electing to reduce basis of depreciable assets (or in realty held as inventory), or (by not electing) can include all or part of the debt discharge amount in income (for example, in order to offset an expiring net operating loss).

At the same time, in developing the rules of the bill, the committee recognized that the basis-reduction mechanism of [pre–1981] law fails to effectuate the Congressional intent of deferring, but eventually collecting tax on, ordinary income realized from debt discharge.

Thus [pre–1981] law permits both solvent and insolvent taxpayers to apply the amount of their discharged debts to reduce the basis of nondepreciable assets which may never be sold, such as stock in a

10. Treas.Regs. § 1.61–12(b). See text accompanying notes 1 and 2.

subsidiary corporation or the land on which the company operates its business, thereby avoiding completely, rather than deferring, the tax consequences of debt discharge. Also under [pre–1981] law, a related party (such as the parent corporation of a debtor) can acquire the taxpayer's debt at a discount and effectively eliminate it as a real liability to outside interests, but the debtor thereby avoids the tax treatment which would apply if the debtor had directly retired the debt by repurchasing it. In other cases, the debtor may be able to convert ordinary income from discharge of indebtedness into capital gain, as where the debtor reduces basis in a nondepreciable capital asset.

* * *

Explanation of Provisions

Debt discharge in bankruptcy.—*In general.*—Under [section 108(a)(1)(A)], no amount is to be included in income for Federal income tax purposes by reason of a discharge of indebtedness in a bankruptcy case.[11] Instead, the amount of discharged debt which is excluded from gross income by virtue of the bill's provisions (the "debt discharge amount") is to be applied to reduce certain tax attributes.

Unless the taxpayer elects first to reduce basis in depreciable assets (or in real property held primarily for sale to customers in the ordinary course of a trade or business), the debt discharge amount is applied to reduce the taxpayer's tax attributes in the following order:

(1) net operating losses and carryovers;

(2) carryovers of the investment tax credit (other than the ESOP credit), * * * the new jobs credit, and the credit for alcohol used as a fuel;

(3) capital losses and carryovers;

(4) the basis of the taxpayer's assets (both depreciable and nondepreciable); and

(5) carryovers of the foreign tax credit.[12]

* * *

Any amount of debt discharge which is left after attribute reduction under these rules is disregarded, i.e., does not result in income or have other tax consequences.

Election to reduce basis in certain property.—[Sections 108(b)(5) and 1017(b)(3)(E) provide] that the taxpayer can elect, in accordance with

11. For purposes of these rules, the term "bankruptcy case" (referred to in the bill as a "title 11 case") means a case under new title 11 of the U.S. Code, but only if the taxpayer is under the jurisdiction of the court in the case and the discharge of indebtedness is granted by the court or is pursuant to a plan approved by the court.

12. For purposes of the attribute reduction rules, credits are reduced at the rate of 50 cents for each dollar of debt discharge amount. This flat-rate reduction avoids the complexity of determining a tax on the debt discharge amount and determining how much of the amount would be used up by the credits for purposes of determining other reductions. Except for reductions in credit carryovers, the specified tax attributes are reduced one dollar for each dollar of debt discharge amount.

Treasury regulations, to apply all or a portion of the debt discharge amount first to reduce basis (but not below zero) in depreciable property [14] or in real property held primarily for sale to customers in the ordinary course of a trade or business (within the meaning of Code sec. 1221(1)). Any remaining amount is then applied to reduce net operating losses and other tax attributes in the order described above. A debtor making this election can elect to reduce basis (but not below zero) in depreciable property or in realty held as inventory below the amount of remaining liabilities (i.e., where the debtor would rather reduce basis in such assets than reduce carryovers).

In addition, [section 1017(b)(3)(D)] provides that, for purposes of this election, stock held by a parent corporation in a subsidiary is treated as depreciable property (or as realty held as inventory) if the parent and subsidiary file a consolidated return for the taxable year in which the discharge occurs, and if the subsidiary agrees to reduce its basis in depreciable property (or in real property held as inventory) which the subsidiary holds.[15] Thus, if the debtor is a parent corporation which files a consolidated return with a subsidiary, the debtor can elect to apply the debt discharge amount, in accordance with Treasury regulations, to reduce the basis of stock it holds in the subsidiary to the extent the subsidiary consents to reduce the basis of depreciable property which it holds (or realty which it holds as inventory).

An election first to reduce basis in depreciable property [or] in realty held as inventory must be made on the taxpayer's return for the year in which the discharge occurs, or at such time as permitted by Treasury regulations. Once made, the election can be revoked by the taxpayer only with the consent of the Internal Revenue Service.

Recapture rule.—If the basis of property is reduced pursuant to the attribute reduction rules in [sections 108 and 1017], any gain on a subsequent disposition of the property is subject to "recapture" under section 1245 of the Code or, in the case of depreciable realty, under section 1250. (This recapture rule applies to any reduced-basis asset, whether depreciable or non-depreciable, and whether or not a disposition of such asset otherwise would be subject to recapture under Code section 1245 or 1250.) * * *

Basis reduction—general rule.—To the extent a debtor makes an election to reduce basis in depreciable property, or reduces basis in assets after reduction of other attributes, the particular properties the

14. For this purpose, the term "depreciable property" means any property of a character subject to the allowance for depreciation, but only if the basis reduction would reduce the amount of depreciation or amortization which otherwise would be allowable for the period immediately following such reduction. Thus, for example, a lessor could not reduce the basis of leased property where the lessee's obligation in respect of the property will restore to the lessor the loss due to depreciation during the term of the lease, since the lessor cannot take depreciation in respect of that property. See Harry H. Kem, Jr., 51 T.C. 455 (1968), aff'd, 432 F.2d 961 (9th Cir. 1970).

15. This rule can be applied successively through a chain of corporations so long as the lowest tier subsidiary reduces its basis in actual depreciable property (or realty which it holds as inventory).

bases of which are to be reduced will be determined pursuant to Treasury regulations. It is anticipated that the order of reduction prescribed in such regulations will generally accord with present Treasury regulations which apply in the case of basis reduction under section 270 of the (now repealed) Bankruptcy Act (Treas.Regs. §§ 1.1016–7 and 1.1016–8). If the debtor elects to reduce basis in realty held as inventory, the particular real properties the bases of which are to be reduced will be determined pursuant to Treasury regulations.

* * *

Debt discharge outside bankruptcy—insolvent debtors.—[Section 108(b)(1)(B)] provides that if a discharge of indebtedness occurs when the taxpayer is insolvent (but is not in a bankruptcy case), the amount of debt discharge is excluded from gross income up to the amount by which the taxpayer is insolvent.[16] The excluded amount is applied to reduce tax attributes in the same manner as if the discharge had occurred in a bankruptcy case. Any balance of the debt discharged which is not excluded from gross income (because it exceeds the insolvency amount) is treated in the same manner as debt cancellation in the case of a wholly solvent taxpayer.

* * *

Equity-for-debt rules.—*Issuance of stock.*—* * *

[[The provisions in sections 108(e)(10) and (8) treat] a corporation which issues stock in cancellation of its debt in the same manner as if it had satisfied the indebtedness with an amount of money equal to the fair market value of the stock. Thus, the corporation will have income from the discharge of indebtedness to the extent the principal of the debt exceeds the value of the stock (and other property transferred, if any). This rule applies where the principal amount of a corporate debt is discharged, including by reason of the exercise of a conversion right by the holder of the debt. It does not apply where payments are simply deferred. (Section 1032 does not prevent the recognition of this income from the discharge of indebtedness.)

The repeal of the stock-for-debt exception does not apply if the discharge occurs pursuant to a title 11 (bankruptcy) case or to the extent the debtor is insolvent; in these cases, prior law continues to apply.] *

Recapture on disposition of stock.—[Section 108(e)(7)] provides that if a creditor acquires stock of the debtor corporation in exchange for the corporation's indebtedness, then upon subsequent disposition of the stock, any deduction taken with respect to the debt either as a bad debt

16. [Section 108(d)(3)] defines "insolvent" as the excess of liabilities over the fair market value of assets, determined with respect to the taxpayer's assets and liabilities immediately before the debt discharge. [Section 108(e)(1)] provides that except pursuant to section 108(a)(1)(B) of the Code (as added by the bill), there is to be no insolvency exception from the general rule that gross income includes income from discharge of indebtedness.

* [Ed.: The material in brackets is from General Explanation of the Revenue Provisions of the Deficit Reduction Act of 1984, Staff of the Joint Committee on Taxation, at 168 (Comm.Print, 1984).]

deduction (under Code secs. 166(a) or (c)), reduced by any gain on the exchange, or as an ordinary loss on the exchange shall be subject to "recapture" under the rules of Code section 1245.[20a]

Thus, for example, assume that corporation A made a $1,000 short-term loan to corporation B on July 1, 1980, and that corporation A, for its taxable year 1982, takes an $800 deduction for partially worthless bad debt under Code section 166(a). Assume further that on March 1, 1983, B satisfies the principal of the debt with B stock worth $500, resulting in a gain to A of $300. If A later disposes of the B stock for $1,500, $500 of A's gain will be treated as ordinary income ($800 bad debt deduction less $300 gain on receipt of the stock). In addition, if the stock is disposed of in a tax-free transaction (for example, by reason of secs. 354 or 1306), the potential recapture will carry over to the stock received.

In the case of a cash-basis creditor, any amount not taken into account by reason of his method of accounting shall be treated the same as a deduction allowed with respect to the debt. * * *

Capital contributions.—[Section 108(e)(6)] provides that the discharge of indebtedness rules apply to the extent that the amount of debt transferred to a corporation as a contribution to capital exceeds the shareholder's basis in the debt.[21] Thus, the discharge of indebtedness rules apply when a cash-basis taxpayer contributes to the capital of an accrual-basis corporation a debt representing an accrued expense previously deducted by the corporation.[22]

20a. For purposes of these recapture rules, the bill provides that the term "debtor corporation" includes a successor corporation, and that stock of a corporation in control of the debtor corporation is treated as stock of the debtor. Also, the bill provides that similar recapture rules apply in the case of discharge of partnership indebtedness.

21. For example, assume a corporation accrues and deducts (but does not actually pay) a $1,000 liability to a shareholder-employee as salary, and the cash-basis employee does not include the $1,000 in income. In a later year, the shareholder-employee forgives the debt.

Under the bill, the corporation must account for a debt discharge amount of $1,000. If the corporation is insolvent or in bankruptcy, it must apply the $1,000 debt discharge amount to reduce tax attributes pursuant to the rules discussed in the text above. If the debtor is a solvent corporation outside bankruptcy, it can elect to reduce basis of depreciable assets (or of realty held as inventory) by $1,000 in lieu of recognizing $1,000 of income in the year of discharge.

On the other hand, if the shareholder-employee were on the accrual basis, had included the salary in income, and his or her basis in the debt was still $1,000 at the time of the contribution, there would be no debt discharge amount, and no attribute reduction would be required.

22. This contribution-to-capital rule reverses the result reached in Putoma Corp. v. Comm'r, 66 T.C. 652 (1976), aff'd, 601 F.2d (5th Cir.1979). Moreover, it is intended that the result reached in *Putoma* could not alternatively be sustained on the ground that the shareholder has made a "gift" to the corporation, since it is intended that there will not be any gift exception in a commercial context (such as a shareholder-corporation relationship) to the general rule that income is realized on discharge of indebtedness.

Whether a cancellation of indebtedness by a shareholder-creditor is a contribution to capital depends upon the facts of the particular case. In order for the contribution to capital rule to apply, the shareholder's action in cancelling the debt must be related to his status as a shareholder. If the shareholder-creditor acts merely as a creditor attempting to maximize the satisfaction of a claim, such as where the stock and bonds are publicly held and the creditor simply happens also to be a shareholder, the cancellation of the indebtedness on exchange of the bonds for stock is not to be treated as a contribution to capital by a shareholder for purposes of this rule.

Debt acquired by related party.—[Section 108(e)(4)] provides that, for purposes of determining income of the debtor from discharge of indebtedness, an outstanding debt acquired from an unrelated party by a party related to the debtor is treated as having been acquired by the debtor to the extent provided in regulations issued by the Treasury Department.

For purposes of this rule, a person is treated as related to the debtor if the person is (1) a member of a controlled group of corporations (as defined for purposes of Code sec. 414(b)) of which group the debtor is a member; (2) a trade or business treated as under common control with respect to the debtor (within the meaning of Code secs. 414(b) or 414(c)); (3) either a partner in a partnership treated as controlled by the debtor or a controlled partnership with respect to the debtor (within the meaning of Code sec. 707(b)(1); or (4) a member of the debtor's family or other person bearing a relationship to the debtor specified in Code section 267(b). * * *

This rule is intended to treat a debtor as having its debt discharged if a party related to the debtor purchases the debt at a discount (for example, where a parent corporation purchases at a discount debt issued by its subsidiary).[23]

Other rules concerning debt discharge.—* * *

Indebtedness of taxpayer.—The debt discharge rules of the bill apply with respect to discharge of any indebtedness for which the taxpayer is liable or subject to which the taxpayer holds property.

Unamortized premium and discount.—[Section 108(e)(3)] provides that the amount taken into account with respect to any discharge of

23. It is intended that the Treasury Department has authority to and will issue regulations providing for the following income tax consequences on repayment or capital contribution of debt which had been acquired by a related party subject to the rule of the bill treating the debtor as having acquired the debt.

If the debtor subsequently pays the debt to the related party, the entire transaction is to be treated generally the same as if the debtor had originally acquired the debt. For example, assume a parent corporation purchases for $900 on the open market a $1,000 bond issued at par by its wholly owned subsidiary. Under the bill, the debtor (the subsidiary) must account for a debt discharge amount of $100 for its taxable year during which the debt was so acquired. In the following year when the debt matures, assume the subsidiary pays its parent the full principal amount ($1,000). The Treasury regulations are to provide that the debtor is treated as having paid a dividend of $100 ($1,000 payment to the parent less the $900 paid by the parent to acquire the debt) to its parent corporation.

If a related party transfers to a corporation as a contribution to capital debt issued by the corporation and the debtor corporation thereby would otherwise have a debt discharge amount pursuant to the rules of the bill, the bill provides that no such income shall arise a second time. For example, assume a parent corporation purchases for $900 on the open market a $1,000 bond issued at par by its wholly owned subsidiary. Under the bill, the debtor (the subsidiary) must account for a debt discharge amount of $100 for its taxable year during which the debt was so acquired. In the following year, assume the parent transfers the debt to its subsidiary as a contribution to capital (i.e., forgives the debt). The Treasury regulations are to provide that the amount treated as a debt discharge amount under the capital contribution rules of the bill ($100 in the example given, assuming the parent's basis in the bond is still $900) is to be reduced by the debt discharge amount previously taken into account by the subsidiary ($100) and thus no additional amount is to be taken into income.

indebtedness is to be properly adjusted for unamortized premium and unamortized discount with respect to the indebtedness discharged.

"Lost" deductions.—[Section 108(e)(2)] provides that if the payment of a liability would have given rise to a deduction, the discharge of that liability does not give rise to income or require reduction of tax attributes. For example, assume a cash-basis taxpayer owes $1,000 to its cash-basis employee as salary and has not actually paid such amount. If later the employee forgives the debt (whether or not as a contribution to capital), then the discharge does not give rise to income or require any reduction of tax attributes.

Tax benefit rule.—[Section 111(c)] clarifies present law by providing that in applying the tax benefit rule of Code section 111 in order to determine if the recovery of an item is taxable, a deduction is treated as having produced a reduction in tax if the deduction increased a carryover that had not expired at the end of the taxable year in which the recovery occurs. Thus, if an accrual-basis taxpayer incurs a deductible obligation to pay rent in 1980, and that obligation is forgiven in 1981, the rent deduction is treated as having produced a reduction in tax even if it had entered into the calculation of a net operating loss that had not expired at the end of 1981 but had not been used as of that time.

* * *

C. Corporate Reorganization Provisions

[Pre–1981] Law

Definition of reorganization.—A transfer of all or part of a corporation's assets, pursuant to a court order in a proceeding under chapter X of the Bankruptcy Act (or in a receivership, foreclosure, or similar proceeding), to another corporation organized or utilized to effectuate a court-approved plan may qualify for tax-free reorganization treatment under special rules relating to "insolvency reorganizations" (secs. 371–374 of the Internal Revenue Code).

These special rules for insolvency reorganizations generally allow less flexibility in structuring tax-free transactions than the rules applicable to corporate reorganizations as defined in section 368 of the Code. Also, the special rules for insolvency reorganizations do not permit carryover of tax attributes to the transferee corporation, and otherwise differ in important respects from the general reorganization rules.[1] While some reorganizations under chapter X of the Bankruptcy Act

1. Under [pre–1981] law, it is not clear to what extent creditors of an insolvent corporation who receive stock in exchange for their claims may be considered to have "stepped into the shoes" of former shareholders for purposes of satisfying the nonstatutory "continuity of interest" rule, under which the owners of the acquired corporation must continue to have a proprietary interest in the acquiring corporation. Generally, the courts have found the "continuity of interest" test satisfied if the creditors' interests were transformed into proprietary interests prior to the reorganization (e.g., Helvering v. Alabama Asphaltic Limestone Co., 315 U.S. 179 (1942); Treas.Reg. § 1.371–1(a)(4)). It is unclear whether affirmative steps by the creditors are required or whether mere receipt of stock is sufficient.

may be able to qualify for nonrecognition treatment under Code section 368, other chapter X reorganizations may be able to qualify only under the special rules of sections 371–374 and not under the general reorganization rules of section 368.

Triangular reorganizations.—In the case of an insolvency reorganization which can qualify for nonrecognition treatment only under the special rules of Code sections 371–374, the stock or securities used to acquire the assets of the corporation in bankruptcy must be the acquiring corporation's own stock or securities. This limitation generally precludes corporations in bankruptcy from engaging in so-called triangular reorganizations, where the acquired corporation is acquired for stock of the parent of the acquiring corporation. By contrast, tax-free triangular reorganizations generally are permitted under the general rules of Code section 368.

Transfer to controlled subsidiary.—In the case of an insolvency reorganization which can qualify for nonrecognition treatment only under the special rules of Code sections 371–374, it is not clear under [pre–1981] law whether and to what extent the acquiring corporation may transfer assets received into a controlled subsidiary. In the case of other corporate reorganizations, the statute expressly defines the situations where transfers to subsidiaries are permitted (Code sec. 368(a)(2)(C)).

* * *

Reasons for Change.—The committee believes that the provisions of existing Federal income tax law which are generally applicable to tax-free corporate reorganizations should also apply to reorganizations of corporations in bankruptcy or similar proceedings, in order to facilitate the rehabilitation of financially troubled businesses.

Also, the committee believes that a creditor who exchanges securities in a corporate reorganization (including an insolvency reorganization) should be treated as receiving interest income on the exchange to the extent the creditor receives new securities, stock, or any other property for accrued but unpaid interest on the securities surrendered.

Explanation of Provisions.—[The Act] generally conforms the tax rules governing insolvency reorganizations with the existing rules applicable to other corporate reorganizations. * * *

Definition of reorganization.—*In general.*—The bill adds a new category—"G" reorganizations—to the general Code definition of tax-free reorganizations (sec. 368(a)(1)). The new category includes certain transfers of assets pursuant to a court-approved reorganization plan in a bankruptcy case under new title 11 of the U.S. Code, or in a receivership, foreclosure, or similar proceeding in a Federal or State court.

* * *

In order to facilitate the rehabilitation of corporate debtors in bankruptcy, etc., these provisions are designed to eliminate many requirements which have effectively precluded financially troubled companies from utilizing the generally applicable tax-free reorganization provisions of present law. To achieve this purpose, the new "G" reorganization provision does not require compliance with State merger laws (as in category "A" reorganizations), does not require that the financially distressed corporation receive solely stock of the acquiring corporation in exchange for its assets (category "C"), and does not require that the former shareholders of the financially distressed corporation control the corporation which receives the assets (category "D").

The "G" reorganization provision added by the bill requires the transfer of assets by a corporation in a bankruptcy or similar case, and the distribution (in pursuance of the court-approved reorganization plan) of stock or securities of the acquiring corporation in a transaction which qualifies under sections 354, 355, or 356 of the Code. This distribution requirement is designed to assure that either substantially all of the assets of the financially troubled corporation, or assets which consist of an active business under the tests of section 355, are transferred to the acquiring corporation.

"Substantially all" test.—The "substantially all" test in the "G" reorganization provision is to be interpreted in light of the underlying intent in adding the new "G" category, namely, to facilitate the reorganization of companies in bankruptcy or similar cases for rehabilitative purposes. Accordingly, it is intended that facts and circumstances relevant to this intent, such as the insolvent corporation's need to pay off creditors or to sell assets or divisions to raise cash, are to be taken into account in determining whether a transaction qualifies as a "G" reorganization. For example, a transaction is not precluded from satisfying the "substantially all" test for purposes of the new "G" category merely because, prior to a transfer to the acquiring corporation, payments to creditors and asset sales were made in order to leave the debtor with more manageable operating assets to continue in business.[5]

Relation to other provisions.—A transaction which qualifies as a "G" reorganization is not to be treated as also qualifying as a liquidation under section 332, an incorporation under section 351, or a reorganization under another category of section 368(a)(1) of the Code.[6]

A transaction in a bankruptcy or similar case which does not satisfy the requirements of new category "G" is not thereby precluded

5. Because the stated intent for adding the new "G" category is not relevant to interpreting the "substantially all" test in the case of other reorganization categories, the comments in the text as to the appropriate interpretation of the "substantially all" test in the context of a "G" reorganization are not intended to apply to, or in any way to affect interpretations under present law of, the "substantially all" test for other reorganization categories.

6. However, if a transfer qualifying as a "G" reorganization also meets the requirements of section 351 or qualifies as a reorganization under section 368(a)(1)(D) of the Code, the "excess liability" rule of section 357(c) applies if any former shareholder of the transferor corporation receives consideration for his stock, but does not apply if no former shareholder of the transferor corporation receives any consideration for his stock (i.e., if the corporation is insolvent). This rule parallels present law, under which insolvency reorganizations under sections 371 or 374 are excluded from the application of section 357(c).

from qualifying as a tax-free reorganization under one of the other categories of section 368(a)(1). For example, an acquisition of the stock of a company in bankruptcy, or a recapitalization of such a company, which transactions are not covered by the new "G" category, can qualify for nonrecognition treatment under sections 368(a)(1)(B) or (E), respectively.

Continuity of interest rules.—The "continuity of interest" requirement which the courts and the Treasury have long imposed as a prerequisite for nonrecognition treatment for a corporate reorganization must be met in order to satisfy the requirements of new category "G". Only reorganizations—as distinguished from liquidations in bankruptcy and sales of property to either new or old interests supplying new capital and discharging the obligations of the debtor corporation—can qualify for tax-free treatment.

It is expected that * * * shareholders or junior creditors, who might previously have been excluded, may now retain an interest in the reorganized corporation.

For example, if an insolvent corporation's assets are transferred to a second corporation in a bankruptcy case, the most senior class of creditor to receive stock, together with all equal and junior classes (including shareholders who receive any consideration for their stock), should generally be considered the proprietors of the insolvent corporation for "continuity" purposes. However, if the shareholders receive consideration other than stock of the acquiring corporation, the transaction should be examined to determine if it represents a purchase rather than a reorganization.

Thus, short-term creditors who receive stock for their claims may be counted toward satisfying the continuity of interest rule, although any gain or loss realized by such creditors will be recognized for income tax purposes.

Triangular reorganizations.—[Section 368(a)(1)(G)] permits a corporation to acquire a debtor corporation in a "G" reorganization in exchange for stock of the parent of the acquiring corporation rather than for its own stock.

In addition, [Section 368(a)(1)(G)] permits an acquisition in the form of a "reverse merger" of an insolvent corporation (i.e., where no former shareholder of the surviving corporation receives any consideration for his stock) in a bankruptcy or similar case if the former creditors of the surviving corporation exchange their claims for voting stock of the controlling corporation which has a value equal to at least 80 percent of the value of the debt of the surviving corporation.

Transfer to controlled subsidiary.—[Section 368(a)(1)(G)] permits a corporation which acquires substantially all the assets of a debtor corporation in a "G" reorganization to transfer the acquired assets to a controlled subsidiary without endangering the tax-free status of the reorganization. This provision places "G" reorganizations on a similar footing with other categories of reorganizations.

* * *

"Principal amount" rule; "boot" test.—* * * "G" reorganizations are subject to the rules governing the tax treatment of exchanging shareholders and security holders which apply to other corporate reorganizations.

Accordingly, an exchanging shareholder or security holder of the debtor company who receives securities with a principal amount exceeding the principal amount of securities surrendered is taxable on the excess, and an exchanging shareholder or security holder who surrenders no securities is taxed on the principal amount of any securities received. Also, any "boot" received is subject to the general dividend-equivalence test of Code section 356.

Treatment of accrued interest.—[Section 354(b)(2)(B) provides that] a creditor exchanging securities in any corporate reorganization described in section 368 of the Code (including a "G" reorganization) is treated as receiving interest income on the exchange to the extent the security holder receives new securities, stock, or any other property attributable to accrued but unpaid interest (including accrued original issue discount) on the securities surrendered. This provision, which reverses the so-called *Carman* rule, applies whether or not the exchanging security holder realizes gain on the exchange overall. Under this provision, a security holder which had previously accrued the interest (including original issue discount) as income recognizes a loss to the extent the interest is not paid in the exchange.

Example.—The reorganization provisions of the bill are illustrated in part by the following example.

Assume that Corporation A is in a bankruptcy case commenced after December 31, 1980. Immediately prior to a transfer under a plan of reorganization, A's assets have an adjusted basis of $75,000 and a fair market value of $100,000. A has a net operating loss carryover of $200,000. A has outstanding bonds of $100,000 (on which there is no accrued but unpaid interest) and trade debts of $100,000.

Under the plan of reorganization, A is to transfer all its assets to Corporation B in exchange for $100,000 of B stock. Corporation A will distribute the stock, in exchange for their claims against A, one-half to the security holders and one-half to the trade creditors. A's shareholders will receive nothing.

The transaction qualifies as a reorganization under new section 368(a)(1)(G) of the Code, since all the creditors are here treated as proprietors for continuity of interest purposes. Thus, A recognizes no gain or loss on the transfer of its assets to B (Code sec. 361). B's basis in the assets is: $75,000 (sec. 362), and B succeeds to A's net operating loss carryover (sec. 381).

* * * [T]he pro-rata distribution of B stock to A's creditors does not result in income from discharge of indebtedness or require attribute reduction.

Assume the same facts as above except that B also transfers $10,000 in cash, which is distributed by A to its creditors. Although A would otherwise recognize gain on the receipt of boot in an exchange involving appreciated property, the distribution by A of the $10,000 cash to those creditors having a proprietary interest in the corporation's assets for continuity of interest purposes prevents A from recognizing any gain (Code sec. 361(b)(1)(A)).

ILLUSTRATIVE MATERIAL

A. TRANSACTIONS OUTSIDE BANKRUPTCY

1. *General*

A corporation encountering financial difficulties in general has one of three options available to it. It can try to work with its creditors to reduce or restructure existing debt. It can issue stock for debt, thus replacing debt with equity on its balance sheet. Or it can seek to acquire or be acquired by another corporation. Each avenue presents different tax considerations. The following material summarizes the tax results of these various routes.

2. *Debt Restructuring*

If a *solvent* corporation is able to persuade its creditors simply to reduce the debt burden, the corporation generally will recognize cancellation of indebtedness income. Sections 61(a)(12) and 108(a). Limited exceptions are provided in section 108(e).

If an *insolvent* corporation (as defined in section 108(d)(3)) is relieved of debt, no cancellation of indebtedness income arises if the corporation is insolvent before and after the cancellation of the debt; income does arise to the extent the corporation is rendered solvent and is treated in the same manner as debt cancellation in the case of a solvent corporation. Section 108(a)(1)(B) and (3). The insolvent corporation, however, is required to reduce its tax attributes, such as net operating loss carryovers, by the amount of income excluded by the insolvency exception, and in the order specified in section 108(b)(2). A taxpayer can elect to reduce the basis of depreciable assets under section 1017 in lieu of the tax attribute reduction. Section 108(b)(5).

The debt restructuring may take the form of modification of the interest rate, payment schedule, maturity date, etc. of the existing debt. If the modification is material, the transaction may be treated as an exchange of the "old" debt for "new" debt. A taxable loss could then be recognized by the creditor under Regulations, section 1.1001–1(a). The transaction also must be tested under the original issue discount rules discussed, supra, page ___. If the "new" debt has an imputed principal amount under the OID computation which is less than the face amount of the "old" debt, the debtor will realize cancellation of indebtedness income. The regular OID rules apply to the OID component of the "new" debt. See Proposed Regulations, section 1.1274–1(c) (1986). On the other hand, if the old and new debt are "securities," then an (E) reorganization has taken place and section 1275(a)(4) discussed supra, page 880, may limit the amount of OID interest in the new securities.

3. *Issuance of Stock for Debt*

Under Section 108(e)(10), a corporation which issues stock in exchange for its own debt realizes and must recognize discharge of indebtedness income to the extent that the amount of the debt exceeds the fair market value of the stock (unless one of the exceptions is applicable). A creditor which receives stock for debt and which takes a bad debt or loss deduction with respect to the debt, must recapture under section 1245 the deduction upon a later sale of the stock. Section 108(e)(7).

4. *Two-Corporation Reorganizations*

The acquisition techniques discussed in Part IV are available in the case of a failing business not yet in bankruptcy. For true bankruptcy situations, see B. 4. below. However, if the corporation is sufficiently "under water," there may be little or no value to the corporation's stock. Absent special provisions, there would be several possible impediments to achieving tax-free reorganization treatment for the acquisition of an insolvent corporation. First, the shareholders of an insolvent corporation presumably would receive no consideration in the acquisition. Any stock or securities issued by the acquiring corporation would be received by the acquired corporation's creditors. Thus qualification as a tax-free reorganization in the first place might be questionable because the continuity of interest requirement has not been met. But see Helvering v. Alabama Asphaltic Limestone Co., 315 U.S. 179 (1942), infra, page 1011. Second, even if the creditors of the insolvent corporation are treated as its shareholders for purposes of applying the continuity of interest doctrine, the insolvency reorganization might not neatly fit within any particular type of reorganization. Third, even if the transaction met the definition of a reorganization under the Code, stock of securities received by unsecured creditors could be taxable because no securities would have been surrendered. Finally, the insolvent corporation itself might recognize income from the discharge of indebtedness if its creditors become shareholders.

B. TRANSACTIONS BY CORPORATIONS IN BANKRUPTCY

1. *General*

The three general approaches available to the financially troubled corporation outside bankruptcy are available in bankruptcy. In general, however, the tax rules are more favorable in bankruptcy situations.

2. *Debt Restructuring*

A bankrupt taxpayer is not required to recognize any cancellation of indebtedness income that might result from debt restructuring. Section 108(a)(1)(A). While tax attributes must be reduced, as in the case of the insolvent taxpayer, no income results even if the taxpayer is made solvent by the debt cancellation or if the amount of indebtedness forgiven exceeds the tax attributes available to be reduced.

3. *Stock for Debt*

A bankrupt taxpayer does not recognize cancellation of indebtedness income on the issuance of stock for debt, even if the fair-market value of the stock is less than the face amount of the debt. Section 108(e)(10) and (e)(8).

4. *Acquisition Reorganizations in Bankruptcy*

(a) *Section 368(a)(1)(G): General*

A transfer by X Corporation of all or part of its assets to Y Corporation in a bankruptcy reorganization or a receivership, foreclosure, or similar judicial proceeding in a federal or state court is a tax-free reorganization under section 368(a)(1)(G) if the stock or securities received from Y Corporation are distributed pursuant to the plan of reorganization in a transaction which qualifies under section 354, 355, or 356. X Corporation recognizes no gain or loss if any boot which is received by it is distributed. Section 361(b).

Section 368(a)(1)(G) applies only to judicially supervised insolvency proceedings. Thus a nonjudicial reorganization of an insolvent corporation must qualify under one of the other provisions of section 368 in order to achieve reorganization status, assuming the continuity of interest test can be met. But, where a transaction qualifies both as a type (G) and, as a result of its form, as another type of reorganization, for example a type (C), it will be classified solely as a type (G). Section 368(a)(3)(C).

When an insolvency reorganization qualifies as a type (G) reorganization, sections 354 and 356 continue to control taxation of the shareholders and creditors. Thus, e.g., short-term creditors who do not hold "securities" will have a taxable exchange; shareholders and other securities holders will be subject to the usual pattern of reorganization taxation.

(b) *Issues Under Section 368(a)(1)(G)*

(i) *Continuity of Interest*

In Helvering v. Alabama Asphaltic Limestone Co., 315 U.S. 179 (1942), a creditor's committee formed a new corporation to acquire the assets of an insolvent corporation. An involuntary bankruptcy proceeding was instituted in which the creditors' claims were satisfied by the transfer of assets to the new corporation pursuant to a judicial sale. Ninety-five percent of the stock of the new corporation was issued to noteholders and the balance was issued to unsecured creditors of the insolvent corporation. The new corporation claimed depreciation based on a transferred basis from the old corporation, arguing that a reorganization had taken place. The Commissioner contended that the assets were acquired by purchase because the continuity of shareholder interest requirement had not been satisfied. Citing LeTulle v. Scofield, 308 U.S. 415 (1940), supra, page 772, the Commissioner argued that for a transaction to qualify as a reorganization, a substantial ownership interest in the transferee company must be retained by the holders of the ownership interest in the transferor. In holding that the assets had been acquired in a tax-free reorganization, the Supreme Court explained the application of the continuity of interest rules to insolvent acquired corporations as follows:

"We conclude, however, that it is immaterial that the transfer shifted the ownership of the equity in the property from the stockholders to the creditors of the old corporation. Plainly, the old continuity of interest was broken. Technically, that did not occur in this proceeding until the judicial sale took place. For practical purposes, however, it took place not later than the time when the creditors took steps to enforce their demands against the insolvent debtor. In this case, that was the date of the institution of the bankruptcy proceedings. From that time on, they had effective command over the disposition of the property. The full priority rule * * * in bankruptcy

* * * gives creditors, whether secured or unsecured, the right to exclude the stockholders entirely from the reorganization plan when the debtor is insolvent. When the equity owners are excluded and the old creditors become the stockholders of the new corporation, it conforms to realities to date their equity ownership from the time when they invoked the process of the law to enforce their rights to full priority. At the time they stepped into the shoes of the old stockholders. * * *

"That conclusion involves no conflict with the principals of the *LeTulle* case. A bondholder interest in a solvent corporation plainly is not the equivalent of a proprietary interest * * *." (183–84)

This approach continues under the (G) reorganization provisions. In testing for continuity, all classes of creditors who receive stock in the reorganized corporation are considered the historic shareholders of the corporation. In addition if the shareholders receive anything for their shares, they too will be taken into account in the continuity test. Thus, for example, if all the stock in the reorganized company is received by junior creditors, with the secured creditors receiving cash and the shareholders receiving nothing, continuity of interest would be present. On the other hand, if the secured creditors also receive stock, they too would be counted in testing for continuity, which might be lacking if the amount of the cash payment is too large in relation to the stock. If shareholders receive cash, the Committee Report indicates that the transaction may be considered a purchase rather than a reorganization.

(ii) *Securities*

In Neville Coke & Chemical Co. v. Commissioner, 148 F.2d 599 (3d Cir.1945), the taxpayer held stock, bonds, three-, four-, and five-year notes, and accounts receivable of an insolvent corporation. Pursuant to a bankruptcy proceeding the debtor corporation was recapitalized and the taxpayer received new common stock for its stock, new debentures for its bonds, and new debentures and common stock for its notes and accounts receivable. The Commissioner asserted that the taxpayer recognized a gain on the exchange of the notes and accounts receivable for debentures and common stock. The taxpayer asserted that the notes and accounts receivable were "securities" within the meaning of the predecessor of section 354(a)(1) and that it had exchanged "securities" for "stock and securities," thereby entitling it to nonrecognition on the exchange. In holding for the Commissioner, the court held that "securities" has the same meaning in the context of the interest surrendered as it does in the context of the interest received, that a "security" entails having a "proprietary" interest in the corporation, and that the rights of the taxpayer as a noteholder were merely those of a creditor.

Under section 368(a)(1)(G), while short-term creditors who receive stock in the reorganization will be counted for continuity purposes, the exchange of their debt claims for stock presumably will be a taxable transaction, since the "securities" test has not been met.

5. *Net Operating Loss Carryovers*

Under section 382, a corporation's net operating loss carryover is limited if there has been a greater than 50 percent change in ownership over a three year testing period (an "ownership change"). See supra, Chapter 21. In the case of a bankruptcy or insolvency proceeding, the section 382 limitation is not applied if, following an ownership change, the creditors and former stockholders of the loss corporation own at least 50 percent of the loss corporation stock. Section 382(1)(5)(A). Under this provision, an exchange of debt for stock by creditors does not trigger the section 382 limitation. The relief of section 382(1)(5)(A) is available only with respect to an exchange of stock for indebtedness which has been held by the creditor for at least eighteen months preceding the date of filing of the bankruptcy or insolvency proceeding, or with respect to indebtedness incurred in the ordinary course of business of the old loss corporation which at all times has been held by the same person. Section 382(1)(5)(E).

There is a substantial cost imposed for avoiding the general section 382 limitation under the exception provided by section 382(1)(5)(A). Section 382(1)(5)(B) requires that loss carryovers be reduced by the amount of interest on indebtedness converted into stock which is paid or accrued during the taxable year of the ownership change and during the three year period preceding the taxable year of the ownership change. In addition, section 382(1)(5)(C) requires a reduction of tax attributes under section 108(b) (net operating loss carryovers, general business credits, capital loss carryovers, basis, and foreign tax credits, in that order) by 50 percent of the amount by which indebtedness coverted into stock exceeds the fair market value of the stock (but not including any discharged indebtedness for interest subtracted from loss carryovers by section 382(1)(5)(C)).

If there is a second ownership change within two years with respect to a corporation that avoided the section 382 limitation under section 382(1)(5)(A), the section 382 limitation following the second ownership change will be zero. Section 382(1)(5)(D).

C. PARTNERSHIP SITUATIONS

A failing business operating in partnership form can also encounter several tax issues as discussed in the following excerpt from the 1980 Senate Finance Committee Report, on the Bankruptcy Tax Act of 1980, S.Rep. No. 96–1035, 96th Cong., 2d Sess. (1980).

"**Partnerships.**—[Section 108(d)(6)] provides that the rules of exclusion from gross income and reduction of tax attributes in section 108 of the Code (as amended by the bill) are to be applied at the partner level and not at the partnership level.[26] Accordingly, income from discharge of a partnership debt is not excludable at the partnership level under amended section 108. Instead, such income is treated as an item of income which is allocated separately to each partner pursuant to section 702(a) of the Code.

"This allocation of an amount of debt discharge income to a partner results in that partner's basis in the partnership being increased by such amount (sec. 705). At the same time, the reduction in the partner's share of partnership liabilities caused by the debt discharge results in a deemed distribution (under sec. 752), in turn resulting in a reduction (under sec. 733) of the partner's basis in the partnership. The section 733 basis reduction, which offsets the section 705 basis increase, is separate from any basis reduction pursuant to the attribute-reduction rules of the bill.

"**26.** The effect of these provisions of the bill is to overturn the decision in Stackhouse v. U.S., 441 F.2d 465 (5th Cir. 1971).

"The tax treatment of the amount of discharged partnership debt which is allocated as an income item to a particular partner depends on whether that partner is in a bankruptcy case, is insolvent (but not in a bankruptcy case), or is solvent (and not in a bankruptcy case). For example, if the particular partner is bankrupt, the debt discharge amount is excluded from gross income pursuant to amended section 108 and is applied to reduce the partner's net operating losses and other tax attributes, unless the partner elects to apply the amount first to reduce basis in depreciable property.[27] If the particular partner is solvent (and not in a bankruptcy case), the amount allocated to the partner is included in that partner's gross income except to the extent the partner elects to reduce basis of depreciable assets.

"[Section 1017(b)(3)(C)] provides that, in connection with these attribute-reduction rules, a partner's interest in a partnership is to be treated as depreciable property to the extent of such partner's proportionate interest in the depreciable property held by the partnership if the partnership agrees to make a corresponding reduction in the basis of the partnership property with respect to such partner (in a manner similar to that which would be required if the partnership had made an election under Code section 754 to adjust basis in the case of a transfer of a partnership interest).[28] " (21–23)

D. REFERENCES

Jacobs, The Chapter 11 Corporate Tax Survival Kit or How to Succeed as Guardian Ad Litem of a Corporate Debtor's NOL's, 42 Tax Law. 3

"**27.** For purposes of this explanation of the partnership rules, the term "depreciable property" also refers to real property held for sale to customers in the ordinary course of business.

"**28.** For example, assume that a partnership is the debtor in a bankruptcy case which begins March 1, 1981, and that in the bankruptcy case a partnership liability in the amount of $30,000 is discharged. The partnership has three partners. The three partners have equal distributive shares of partnership income and loss items under section 702(a) of the Code. Partner A is the debtor in a bankruptcy case; partner B is insolvent (by more than $10,000), but is not a debtor in a bankruptcy case; and partner C is solvent, and is not a debtor in a bankruptcy case.

"Under section 705 of the Code, each partner's basis in the partnership is increased by $10,000, i.e., his distributive share of the income of the partnership. (The $30,000 debt discharge amount constitutes income of the partnership for this purpose, inasmuch as the income exclusion rules of amended sec. 108 do not apply at the partnership level.) However, also by virtue of present law, each partner's basis in the partnership is decreased by the same amount (Code secs. 752 and 733). Thus, there is no net change in each partner's basis in the partnership resulting from discharge of the partnership indebtedness except by operation at the partner level of the rules of sections 108 and 1017 of the Code (as amended by the bill).

"In the case of bankrupt partner A, the $10,000 debt discharge amount must be applied to reduce net operating losses and other tax attributes as specified in the bill, unless A elects first to reduce the basis of depreciable assets. The same tax treatment applies in the case of insolvent partner B. In the case of solvent partner C, such partner can elect to reduce basis in depreciable assets in lieu of recognizing $10,000 of income from discharge of indebtedness.

"If A, B, or C elects to reduce basis in depreciable assets, such partner may be permitted, under the Treasury regulations, to reduce his basis in his partnership interest (to the extent of his share of partnership depreciable property), because the bill treats that interest as depreciable property. However, a partner may reduce basis in his interest in the partnership only if the partnership makes a corresponding reduction in the basis of the partnership property with respect to such partner (in a manner similar to that which would be required if the partnership had made an election under section 754 to adjust basis in the case of a transfer of a partnership interest)."

* * *

(1988); Witt and Lyons, The Tax Consequences of Discharge of Indebtedness: An Examination of General Principles and an Analysis of Section 108, 10 Va.Tax Rev. 1 (1990); Rabinowitz and Jacobson, Reorganization of the Bankrupt Corporation Under Section 368(a)(1)(G): Panacea or Placebo? 42 N.Y.U.Tax Inst. 10–1 (1984); Scranton, Corporate Transactions Under the Bankruptcy Tax Act of 1980, 35 Tax Law. 49 (1981).

PART VIII

AFFILIATED CORPORATIONS

CHAPTER 23

TAX REDUCTION THROUGH MULTIPLE CORPORATIONS

SECTION 1. GENERAL

INTERNAL REVENUE CODE: Sections 1561; 1563(a)(1)–(3), (b)(1)–(3), (c)–(f).

TRIBUNE PUBLISHING COMPANY v. COMMISSIONER

United States Court of Appeals, Ninth Circuit, 1984.
731 F.2d 1401.

J. BLAINE ANDERSON, CIRCUIT JUDGE:

This is an appeal of a decision by the United States Tax Court, 79 T.C. 1029, affirming a determination by the Commissioner of Internal Revenue (Commissioner) that the appellants were deficient in their federal income taxes for the years 1976, 1977, and 1978.

I. BACKGROUND

Appellants Tribune Publishing Co. (Tribune) and News Review Publishing Co., Inc. (News) are two Idaho corporations which operate daily newspapers out of Lewiston, Idaho, and Moscow, Idaho, respectively. Both appellants filed federal corporate income tax returns for the years in question. Tribune publishes a morning newspaper in Lewiston, named the Lewiston Tribune. News publishes an afternoon newspaper in Moscow, about 30 miles away, named the Daily Idahonian. Both papers serve the same general area and there are a significant number of readers who subscribe to both.

During the years in issue, Tribune was owned primarily by the members of the Alford family, several of whom served as corporate officers. Prior to 1967, News was owned and operated by the Marineau family. William Marineau (William) was the president and publisher and A.J. Marineau (A.J.) was the vice-president and general manager.

The Alfords and Marineaus enjoyed cordial relations with one another. There was a long-established relationship of friendly competition between the two papers.

In 1967, the shareholders of News received an offer for their stock from a large national newspaper chain. All of the shareholders except the two Marineaus wished to accept the offer. William became concerned about the prospect of the control of the paper leaving the community. He contacted the Alford family at the offices of the Tribune, and expressed his concern. He pointed out that it would be to Tribune's disadvantage for a chain newspaper to be located only 30 miles away from Lewiston. William proposed that the Tribune might buy the stock of News that was up for sale to the national chain. The Alford family shared William's concern and agreed to purchase some of the shares. The remaining shares were purchased by E. Russell Short and Reta S. Tate. Following the sale, the outstanding News stock was owned as follows:

Stockholder	Number of Shares
Tribune Publishing Co.	100
A.J. Marineau	50
William T. Marineau	25
E. Russell Short and Reta S. Tate	75
Total	250

The day after the sale of stock, the shareholders of News entered into an agreement (the 1967 Agreement). A.L. Alford, Jr. and Charles Alford were also parties to the agreement even though they had not, as individuals, purchased any stock in News. The agreement provided that certain conditions were required to be met before a shareholder could sell his shares. Under the agreement, Tribune and the two Alfords were granted "the sole and exclusive first option to meet any bona fide offer of sale" to be received by any of the remaining shareholders for their stock. This is commonly known as a "right of first refusal," whereby one party has the first right to another's stock if he can match the offer made by a third party. If Tribune desired to sell its stock in News, the agreement similarly gave the remaining shareholders the right to "meet the terms" of the proposed sale. The terms of the agreement were never printed on the stock certificates themselves. Neither was the agreement ever incorporated into the Articles of Incorporation or the corporate by-laws.

In 1972, Russell Short and Reta S. Tate decided to sell their interest in News. William contacted A.L. Alford, Jr. and informed him of the proposed sale, and Tribune bought the shares. However, Tribune did not formally invoke its right of first refusal when it acquired the Short/Tate shares. Following the purchase of the Short/Tate shares, the stock of News was owned as follows:

Stockholder	Number of Shares
Tribune Publishing Co.	175
A.J. Marineau	50
William T. Marineau	25
Total	250

Tribune now owned 70% of the outstanding stock of News. However, the Alfords did not attempt to control the day-to-day operations of that company.

In 1976, the two Marineaus decided to transfer some of their stock to other members of their family. A.J. contacted A.L. Alford, Jr. to make sure that Tribune and the Alfords would agree to the proposed transfers within the Marineau family. Neither Tribune nor the Alfords had any desire to purchase the Marineau stock and the Marineaus were informed that they were free to dispose of it as they desired. Subsequently, at the meeting of the board of directors of News, it was resolved to allow the Marineaus to convey their stock in News to any member of their family, and that those members would, thereafter, hold the stock free of any restrictions. Then, in 1979, the Marineaus decided to offer their stock to Tribune and the Alfords under the terms of the 1967 agreement. However, they declined to purchase the stock and it was ultimately sold to an outside party.

During the years in question, every corporation was allowed one surtax exemption when filing yearly federal income tax returns, pursuant to section 11(d) of the Internal Revenue Code. 26 U.S.C. § 11(d) (1976), *amended by* 26 U.S.C. § 11 (Supp. II 1978) (imposing graduated surtax) (amended 1981). However, sections 1561–1563 of the Code placed a limitation on surtax exemptions when corporations were part of a "controlled group." 26 U.S.C. § 1561 (1976) (amended 1978 to limit benefits of graduated surtax; amended 1981, 1982); 26 U.S.C. § 1563 (1976). One type of controlled group of corporations is a "parent-subsidiary controlled group," which is defined in section 1563(a)(1) as:

> One or more chains of corporations connected through stock ownership with a common parent corporation if
>
> (A) stock possessing at least 80 percent of the total combined voting power of all classes of stock entitled to vote or at least 80 percent of the total value of shares of all classes of stock of each of the corporations, except the common parent corporation, is owned * * * by one or more of the other corporations; and
>
> (B) the common parent corporation owns * * * stock possessing at least 80 per cent of the total combined voting power of all classes of stock entitled to vote or at least 80 percent of the total value of shares of all classes of stock of at least one of the other corporations, excluding, in computing such voting power or value, stock owned directly by such other corporations.

In determining whether the stock ownership tests of section 1563(a)(1) are satisfied, some of the outstanding stock of the subsidiary corporations in the group is disregarded in certain circumstances. Section 1563(c), in pertinent part, provides as follows:

> (1) General Rule.—For purposes of this part, the term "stock" does not include—
>
> * * * * * * * * *
>
> (C) stock which is treated as "excluded stock" under paragraph (2).

(2) Stock Treated as Excluded Stock.—

(A) Parent-subsidiary controlled group.—

For purposes of subsection (a)(1), if a corporation * * * owns * * * 50 percent or more of the total combined voting power of all classes of stock entitled to vote or 50 percent or more of the total value of shares of all classes of stock in another corporation, * * * the following stock of the subsidiary corporation shall be treated as excluded stock

* * * * * * * * *

(iii) stock in the subsidiary corporation owned * * * by an employee of the subsidiary corporation if such stock is subject to conditions which run in favor of such parent * * * corporation and which substantially restrict or limit the employee's right * * * to dispose of such stock.

During 1976 through 1978, Tribune owned more than 50 percent of News' outstanding stock, satisfying the ownership requirement of section 1563(c)(2)(A). Because of the 1967 Agreement, the Commissioner determined that the Marineau stock was "excluded stock" within the meaning of section 1563(c)(2)(A)(iii) and, therefore, Tribune and News were a "controlled group" under the Code since Tribune owned more than 80 percent of News with the Marineau stock excluded from the calculation. Therefore, they were entitled to only one surtax exemption between them. Since they each took an exemption for the years in question, the Commissioner determined Tribune deficient in the amount of $18,392.00 and News deficient in the amount of $40,608.00 on their federal income taxes. The Tax Court entered a decision in accordance with this determination.

II. ANALYSIS

The appellants' first contention is that section 1563 was designed for circumstances other than those existing here. They cite the legislative history of section 1563 which states: "[T]he Internal Revenue Code contains several provisions designed to prevent taxpayers from using the multiple form of corporate organization, to avoid taxes." H.R.Rep. No. 749, 88th Cong. 1st Sess., *reprinted in* 1964 U.S.Code Cong. & Ad. News, 1313, 1425. But, "there are legitimate business reasons for the use of separate corporations and, therefore, the separate corporations should generally be recognized as separate taxpayers, retaining the benefit of the use of multiple surtax exemptions." Id. at 1426. Appellants argue that since News was already an existing business with outstanding stock when it was acquired by Tribune, there were no tax avoidance motives involved. Therefore, the legislative history of Section 1563 mandates that they be allowed multiple exemptions.

However, the legislative history of 1563 also states: "An example of a condition which substantially restricts or limits an employee's right to dispose of his stock within the meaning of subparagraph (A)(iii) [of section 1563(c)(2)] is a condition whereby the parent corporation is given a right of first refusal if such stock is offered for sale." Id. at 1630. The current tax regulations implement this example used in the House Report. Treas.Reg. § 1.1563–2(b)(2)(iii) (1983). This seems to imply that a more objective test is to be used in determining when to apply section 1563. In fact, this is what the United States Supreme Court determined recently, in U.S. v. Vogel Fertilizer Co., 455 U.S. 16, 27–28, 102 S.Ct. 821, 828–29, 70 L.Ed.2d 792 (1982). There, the court stated:

> Until 1964, the method prescribed by the Code to curb the abuse of multiple incorporation was subjective: Multiple exemptions or benefits were allowed or disallowed depending on the reasons for the taxpayer's actions. The Revenue Act of 1964 changed this approach, adding §§ 1561–1563 to the Code. * * * These sections prescribed the application of mechanical, objective tests for determining whether two corporations were a "controlled group" and thereby restricted to one surtax exemption.

Thus, Congress has changed its approach in determining the existence of "controlled groups" from subjective (i.e., tax avoidance motives) to "mechanical, objective tests." This supports the finding of the Tax Court, in this case, when it followed an earlier Tax Court decision, Barton Naphtha Co. v. Commissioner, 56 T.C. 107, 116 (1971).

Appellants further argue that since the 1967 Agreement was reciprocal (i.e. the Tribune was bound to the same conditions as were the Marineaus), it did not constitute a "substantial restriction" on the Marineau's [sic] right to freely dispose of their stock. Appellants cite section 1563(c)(2)(B)(ii) of the Code which defines "excluded stock" for purposes of determining whether a corporation is a member of a "brother-sister controlled group of corporations." It states that if a restriction on the stock of an employee also applies to the common owner, then it shall not be excluded.

Appellants' reliance on this section is misplaced. This section applies only to brother-sister controlled groups. The same exemption is not included under parent-subsidiary controlled groups, and this court will not rewrite the statute to include it.

In furtherance of their argument that the Marineau stock was not substantially restricted, appellants point to the resolution passed by the Board of Directors of News on April 26, 1976, which purportedly amended the 1967 Agreement to allow the Marineaus to convey their stock to family members who would, thereafter, hold it free of any restrictions.

We do not think that the Board of Directors of News had the authority to amend the 1967 Agreement since News was not even a party to that agreement. The Agreement was between Tribune and News' other shareholders. Tribune did not participate in the board's resolution. The resolution could not modify the original shareholders agreement.

Finally, appellants argue that the right of first refusal on the Marineau's [sic] stock was not a substantial restriction because it was not legally enforceable. Their argument is based largely on a repealed Idaho statute. Former Idaho Code § 30–415 provides:

> There shall be no lien in favor of a corporation upon the shares represented by certificates issued by such corporation and there shall be no restriction upon the transfer of shares so represented by virtue of any bylaws of such corporation, or otherwise, unless the right of the corporation to such lien or the restriction is stated upon the certificate.

Uniform Stock Transfer Act, ch. 88, § 15, 1927 Idaho Sess.Laws 107 (repealed 1967). This statute was part of the Uniform Stock Transfer Act (USTA) which was repealed, effective Dec. 31, 1967, after the 1967 Agreement was entered into. However, in adopting the Uniform Commercial Code, which replaced the USTA, the legislature addressed the problem of the effect of the Code on transactions entered into before its effective date, as in the present case. This is Idaho Code § 28–10–102(2), which states:

> Transactions validly entered into before the effective date [Dec. 31, 1967] and the rights, duties and interests flowing therefrom remain valid thereafter and may be terminated, completed, consummated or enforced as required or permitted by any statute or other law amended or repealed by this Act as though such repeal or amendment had not occurred.

Assuming the original Code section 30–415 still applies to this case, it is not dispositive. We are not faced here with the typical situation of a third party contesting the validity of a restriction on stock that is acquired from another. Rather, the 1967 Agreement was in the nature of a contract. The parties, possessing unrestricted stock, entered into a binding agreement to restrict that stock. Tribune and News are now simply denying the validity of that agreement for tax purposes.

Both Tribune and the Marineaus have acted according to the agreement up to the present. In 1976, the Marineaus found it necessary to attempt to modify the agreement, and in 1979 they abided by the terms of the agreement when they formally notified Tribune of their desire to sell their stock in News.

We believe the rationale of Baumohl v. Goldstein, 95 N.J.Eq. 597, 124 A. 118, is sound:

> [Section 15 of the Uniform Stock Transfer Act] was designed for the protection of innocent purchasers of stock in the open market or otherwise and not at all as a shield by one with knowledge of a condition to unconscionably protect himself from the consequences thereof.

124 A. at 121. Idaho's subsequent repeal of section 15 further supports our conclusion that Idaho courts would follow this rationale and enforce the agreement between the parties.

III. CONCLUSION

We conclude that there were substantial restrictions on the Marineau stock and, as between the parties to the 1967 Agreement, these restrictions are enforceable. Therefore, section 1563 clearly mandates that the Marineau stock must be excluded from total stock outstanding in determining whether there is a parent-subsidiary controlled group within the meaning of the statute.

The judgment of the tax court is

AFFIRMED.

ILLUSTRATIVE MATERIAL

A. GENERAL

For tax years before 1978, the corporate tax consisted of a normal tax plus a surtax on taxable income in excess of the "surtax exemption." Prior to enactment of the limitations of sections 1561–1563 by the Tax Reform Act of 1969, a principal tax motivation for utilizing multiple corporations was the possibility of obtaining multiple surtax exemptions and, to a lesser extent, multiple accumulated earnings tax credits. The Revenue Act of 1978 replaced the normal tax and surtax structure with a five-step graduated rate structure with rates ranging from 17 to 46 percent. The five-step graduated rate structure was in turn replaced by the 1986 Act with its three bracket rate structure plus a 5 percent surtax on taxable income in excess of $100,000 to phase out the benefit of lower brackets, as discussed supra, page 272. The restrictions on multiple surtax exemptions were modified to provide that a controlled group of corporations is collectively limited to one amount in each of the taxable income brackets of the corporate rate table of section 11(b). For example, if there are five members of a controlled group, and if no plan of unequal apportionment is adopted, each member would be subject to tax at a rate of 15 percent on its first $10,000 of taxable income (1/5 of $50,000), 25 percent on the next $5,000 of taxable income, and 34 percent on taxable income in excess of $15,000. In addition, the five percent surtax would apply to the income of each corporation in excess of $25,000 until each corporation paid $2,350 of additional tax. Section 1561(a) permits the members of a controlled group to consent to an unequal allocation of the amounts limited by the provision.

In addition to limiting a controlled group to a single amount of taxable income in each tax rate bracket, section 1561 limits the group to one exemption credit under the accumulated earnings tax, infra, page 1064, one $40,000 exemption for purposes of the alternative minimum tax, discussed supra, page 276, and one $2,000,000 exemption from the special environmental 0.12 percent superfund tax on alternative minimum taxable income of section 59A. Other provisions of the Code specifically treat a controlled group as a single corporation. See, for example, section 179(d)(6) (members of a controlled group are treated as one taxpayer for purposes of the $10,000 limit on the first year depreciation allowance of section 179); 414(b) (anti-discrimination rules and other provisions regarding qualified pension and employee benefit plans all applied to a controlled group as if it were a single employer).[1]

1. The dollar limitations on the general business credit of section 38, before its repeal in 1986, were applied to the controlled group as a single corporation.

Prior to the 1969 legislation, the Commissioner did have some weapons to attack multiple corporations, both statutory and judicially developed. Section 269 could be used by the Commissioner to disallow benefits of multiple corporations where tax avoidance was involved. See Coastal Oil Storage Company v. Commissioner, 242 F.2d 396 (5th Cir.1957). Similarly, section 1551 was also available. Section 1551 denies the multiple use of the lower corporate tax brackets in the event of a transfer of property to a controlled corporation by a group of five or fewer controlling stockholders, or by a controlling corporation, where the taxpayers are unable to establish by a preponderance of the evidence that securing the benefits of lower brackets was not a major purpose of the transfer. Control for purposes of section 1551 is defined the same as for purposes of section 1561. Thus, almost any affiliated group subject to section 1551 is also subject to the limitation of section 1561. Because the application of section 1561 is automatic, section 1551 is virtually an obsolete provision. The Commissioner could also invoke judicially developed doctrines to disregard the corporate entity, discussed supra, page 311. Section 482, discussed infra, page 1026, could also be employed. Assignment of income principles could be used to tax the true earner of the income (see e.g., Shaw Construction Co. v. Commissioner, 323 F.2d 316 (9th Cir.1963); but compare Rubin v. Commissioner, 429 F.2d 650 (2d Cir.1970)).

B. BROTHER–SISTER CONTROLLED GROUP

In United States v. Vogel Fertilizer Co., 455 U.S. 16 (1982), the Court held that a person's stock ownership may not be taken into account for purposes of the 80 percent requirement of section 1563(a)(2)(A) unless that person also owns stock in another member of the corporate group. Arthur Vogel owned 77.49 percent of the Vogel Fertilizer Company. The remaining 22.51 percent was owned by Richard Crain, who was unrelated to Vogel. Vogel also owned 87.5 percent of the voting stock and 93 percent of the value of Vogel Popcorn. Applying Regulations, section 1.1563–1(a)(3), the Commissioner took the position that Crain and Vogel's ownership of more than 80 percent of Vogel Fertilizer, and Vogel's ownership of more than 80 percent of Vogel Popcorn, satisfied the 80 percent test of section 1563(a)(2)(A), and that Vogel's ownership of more than 50 percent of each corporation satisfied the 50 percent test of section 1563(a)(2)(B). The Court concluded that the limitations of sections 1561–1563 are intended to apply to related corporations and held that the 50 percent limitation of section 1563(a)(2)(B) is a "safeguard" to "insure that the . . . definition is limited to cases where the brother-sister corporations are, in fact, *controlled* by the group of stockholders as one economic enterprise." (30) The Court also observed that 80 percent ownership by five or fewer persons indicates only that the two corporations are closely held. The Court thus declared the regulations invalid to the extent that they permitted a stockholder who owned stock in only one corporation to be taken into account for purposes of the 80 percent requirement. Regulations, section 1.1563–1(a)(3), were amended in 1988 to follow the result in *Vogel Fertilizer.*

In Complete Finance Corp. v. Commissioner, 766 F.2d 436 (10th Cir. 1985), the court rejected the taxpayers' argument that under *Vogel Fertilizer* persons must directly own stock in each brother-sister corporation to be counted as part of the five or fewer persons in control under section 1563(a)(2)(A). Thus, the stock attribution rules of section 1563(d)(2) are applied to determine whether the 80 percent and 50 percent tests of section 1563(a)(2) are satisfied.

C. TECHNICAL MATTERS UNDER SECTIONS 1561–1563

1. *Stock Ownership and Control*

Section 1563(c) excludes certain stock from consideration in determining whether corporations are members of a controlled group. These provisions result in a concentration of stock ownership which makes it easier to establish the existence of control. Stock which is limited and preferred as to dividends and treasury stock is not counted. In the case of a parent-subsidiary group in which the parent owns 50 percent or more of the voting power or value, control is determined without regard to, (a) restricted stock owned by an employee of a subsidiary, as discussed in *Tribune Publishing Company,* supra, page 1016, (b) stock held by an employee deferred compensation trust, (c) stock of the subsidiary which is owned by an individual stockholder who is also a 50 percent or greater stockholder in the parent corporation or an officer of the parent, and, (d) stock in a subsidiary corporation held by an organization exempt from tax under section 501 which is controlled by the parent corporation, a principal stockholder of the parent, or by an officer of the parent corporation.

Section 1563 has its own set of constructive ownership rules for determining control. Section 1563(e). An option holder is treated as the owner of optioned stock, stock owned by a partnership is attributed to five percent or greater partners, and stock owned by an estate or trust is attributed to beneficiaries with a five percent or greater interest in the trust, and to a person who is treated as the owner of trust property under the grantor trust rules. In the case of brother-sister corporations, stock owned by a corporation is attributed to five percent or greater stockholders in proportion to the value of stock held by the five percent stockholder, stock is attributed to a spouse (with an exception for a spouse who holds no direct interest and is not a director, employee or manager of the corporation, as long as not more than 50 percent of the corporation's income is derived from passive sources), and stock is attributed to minor children and the adult children and grandchildren of a more than 50 percent stockholder. Section 1563(d)(2). In Complete Finance Corp. v. Commissioner, 766 F.2d 436 (10th Cir.1985), the court held that under section 1563(e)(5), attribution of stock to a spouse does not dilute the interest of the direct stockholder and each spouse is counted as owning both all of the stock owned by the individual directly plus the stock attributed from his or her spouse.

2. *Component Members of a Controlled Group*

The limitations of section 1561 apply to the component members of a controlled group. Under section 1563(b), a corporation is a component member of a group if the corporation is a member of the controlled group on December 31 of the taxable year. However, a corporation which was not a member of the controlled group on December 31 will be included as a component member if it was a member of the group for one-half or more of the number of days in the taxable year preceding December 31. Conversely, a corporation which is a member of the controlled group on December 31 of the taxable year but was not a member of the group for one-half of the number of days preceding December 31 will be excluded from the controlled group. Component members of a controlled group do not include certain corporations subject to special tax provisions such as corporations exempt from tax under section 501, foreign corporations, insurance companies, and a franchise corporation which the parent corporation is obligated to sell (as defined in section 1563(f)(4)).

D. POLICY ISSUES UNDER SECTION 1561

It is still possible for a corporate enterprise to avoid the section 1561 limitations where its constituent corporations are not members of a "controlled group" as defined in section 1563(a). Thus 79 percent ownership of a subsidiary will allow use of multiple lower rate brackets under section 11 as will proper arrangement of stock ownership in a brother-sister group to avoid the more than 50 percent limitation applicable to such groups. Presumably the Commissioner still would utilize the approaches discussed in A. in such situations.

An interesting policy aspect of the multiple corporation legislation is the success with which multi-corporate groups were able to resist effective legislation for so long by invoking the argument that they had a "business purpose" for conducting their business operations in multiple rather than single corporate form. There may be valid "business reasons" to operate in multiple corporation form, but this factor hardly justifies a difference in tax liability from a single corporation conducting the same number of businesses through branches. But in this, as in other areas, Congress was willing to be persuaded for a considerable period of time that if there was a "business reason" for engaging in a certain kind of conduct, favorable tax consequences should also flow from that business decision. It appears difficult for Congress to apply consistently the principle that all businesses should be taxed on the same basis regardless of what genuine business decisions may be controlling as to their forms of operation where the forms do not change essentially the "similarity" of the businesses from the standpoint of the particular tax policy issue involved.

E. REFERENCES

Eustice, Tax Problems Arising from Transactions between Affiliated or Controlled Corporations, 23 Tax L.Rev. 451 (1968); Bonovitz, Brother–Sister Controlled Groups under Section 1563: The 80 Percent Ownership Test, 28 Tax Law. 511 (1975); Smith, *Fairfax* Revisited, 4 J.Corp.Tax. 347 (1978); Note, Proposed Revision of IRC § 1563(a)(2): A New Definition for Brother–Sister Controlled Groups, 34 Hast.L.J. 665 (1983).

SECTION 2. TRANSACTIONS BETWEEN AFFILIATED CORPORATIONS

INTERNAL REVENUE CODE: Section 482.

HOSPITAL CORPORATION OF AMERICA v. COMMISSIONER

Tax Court of the United States, 1983.
81 T.C. 520.

OPINION

Hospital Corp. of America (hereinafter HCA or petitioner) is in the business of owning and/or managing hospitals. During the years before the Court, petitioner generally had a separate domestic subsidiary corporation to operate and manage each hospital it owned and had another domestic subsidiary for all of the hospitals it managed under management contracts with the owners thereof. Until 1973, petitioner's organization operated exclusively in the United States.

In late 1972, after an initial contact by a certain finder, petitioner gave a "hunting license" to that finder to pursue an opportunity for a contract to manage a hospital in Saudi Arabia. In February of 1973, after introductions by that finder, petitioner was invited to send representatives to Saudi Arabia to discuss the possibility of contracting to manage the King Faisal Specialist Hospital (hereinafter KFSH or the King Faisal Hospital), which was then under construction in Riyadh, Saudi Arabia. The KFSH, owned by the Royal Cabinet of the Kingdom of Saudi Arabia, was intended to be equipped with the latest in sophisticated computers and medical equipment and to be a showcase or the "Mayo Clinic" of the Middle East. Petitioner made preliminary investigations as to the potential profit and prestige of contracting to manage the KFSH and decided to pursue the opportunity.

Petitioner decided at the outset that it would not become directly involved in international operations but would organize foreign subsidiaries for any foreign expansion. It therefore organized two corporations in the Cayman Islands. Tax consequences were considered in making the decision to incorporate in the Cayman Islands. These Cayman Islands corporations were organized as first- and second-tier subsidiaries of petitioner. The first-tier subsidiary was Hospital Corp. International, Ltd. (HCI One), and the second-tier subsidiary was Hospital Corp. of the Middle East, Ltd. (LTD). The names of these corporations were later changed to Hospital Development Co., Ltd. (HCI One), and Hospital Corp. of America, Ltd. (LTD). HCI One was formed to be an umbrella corporation for any expansion into foreign countries. LTD was formed specifically to obtain and perform the management contract for the King Faisal Hospital. On August 26, 1973, LTD and the Royal Cabinet of the Kingdom of Saudi Arabia executed that management contract. Petitioner did not include any of the income earned from the KFSH management contract on its 1973 tax return. This case involves only the adjustments for this foreign income for the year 1973.

In the statutory notice of deficiency, respondent determined that petitioner transferred property to LTD, its foreign subsidiary, without an advance ruling, as required by section 367. Therefore, respondent asserted that the value of the contract, which his expert valued at $34,985,626, was taxable income to petitioner in 1973. Alternatively, respondent determined that the income earned from the management contract in 1973 was taxable to petitioner under section 61 or allocable to petitioner under section 482. Under either of these alternatives, respondent determined that LTD's net income of $1,787,030 was taxable to petitioner in its entirety.

Respondent has since shifted his emphasis. His primary argument now is that LTD is a sham corporation and therefore all income derived from the KFSH management contract in 1973 was in fact earned by petitioner and taxable to it under section 61. Alternatively, * * * respondent argues that all of the income and expenses of LTD are allocable to petitioner under section 482. Thus, respondent has attacked the validity of LTD's existence, and consequently the income earned by LTD, from several different angles.

I. SHAM CORPORATION

Respondent's primary position is that LTD is a "sham" corporation that should not be recognized for Federal income tax purposes. Respondent asserts that LTD was "a mere skeleton; a sham corporation that existed in form only for the purpose of obtaining the tax benefits available to a foreign corporation."

* * *

Since LTD was organized for a business purpose and actually carried on some business activities in 1973, we hold that LTD was not a sham corporation and that it is to be recognized for tax purposes. Moline Properties, Inc. v. Commissioner, supra; Ross Glove Co. v. Commissioner, 60 T.C. at 590; V.H. Monette & Co. v. Commissioner, 45 T.C. 15, 35 (1965); Columbian Rope Co. v. Commissioner, 42 T.C. 800, 813 (1964); Nat Harrison Associates, Inc. v. Commissioner, 42 T.C. at 620; Bush Hog Manufacturing Co. v. Commissioner, supra. For the reasons recited above, we have been persuaded by a preponderance of the evidence that LTD is a separate corporate entity to be recognized for tax purposes in 1973. Therefore, we cannot find that all of the income of LTD is taxable to petitioner under section 61, as respondent contends. We are also persuaded, however, that petitioner itself performed substantial services for LTD for which it was not compensated. We therefore think it appropriate in this case to allocate substantial portions of LTD's 1973 income to petitioner pursuant to section 482. We will further consider this matter and determine below what portion of LTD's income is properly allocable to petitioner.

* * *

IV. Section 482 Allocation

Respondent's final argument is that all of LTD's taxable income for 1973 in the amount of $1,787,030 should be allocated to petitioner pursuant to section 482. Section 482 authorizes respondent to distribute, apportion, or allocate gross income, deductions, credits, or allowances between or among organizations owned or controlled by the same interests, if he determines that such is necessary in order to prevent the evasion of taxes or clearly to reflect the income of the organizations. As a logical shortcut to allocating gross income and deductions, respondent, in certain instances, may also allocate net income. Nat Harrison Associates, Inc. v. Commissioner, 42 T.C. at 621; Ach v. Commissioner, 42 T.C. 114, 126 (1964), affd. 358 F.2d 342 (6th Cir.1966); Hamburgers York Road, Inc. v. Commissioner, 41 T.C. 821, 834 (1964); Ballentine Motor Co. v. Commissioner, 39 T.C. 348, 358 (1962), affd. 321 F.2d 796 (4th Cir.1963). We think respondent properly may do so in this instance.

One of the reasons for the enactment of section 482 and its predecessors was to prevent the evasion of taxes by shifting income from a domestic business to a foreign corporation controlled by the same interests. Nat Harrison Associates, Inc. v. Commissioner, 42 T.C. at 621; Asiatic Petroleum Co. (Delaware) Ltd. v. Commissioner, 31 B.T.A. 1152, 1159 (1935), affd. 79 F.2d 234 (2d Cir.1935), cert. denied 296 U.S. 645 (1935). The regulations state that "The purpose of section 482 is to place a controlled taxpayer on a tax parity with an uncontrolled taxpayer, by determining, according to the standard of an uncontrolled taxpayer, the true taxable income from the property and business of a controlled taxpayer." Sec. 1.482–1(b)(1), Income Tax Regs.; Commissioner v. First Security Bank of Utah, N.A., 405 U.S. 394, 400 (1972).

Section 482 thus permits respondent to examine dealings between controlled corporations and make allocations so as to place these dealings on the same basis for tax purposes as if they had taken place between independent and uncontrolled taxpayers. Achiro v. Commissioner, 77 T.C. 881, 896–897 (1981). On the other hand, if the dealings between controlled organizations are fair and equivalent in result to arm's-length bargaining, no allocation is authorized. Hamburgers York Road, Inc. v. Commissioner, 41 T.C. at 835; Ballentine Motor Co. v. Commissioner, 39 T.C. at 357. The standard to be applied in every case is that of an uncontrolled taxpayer dealing at arm's length with another uncontrolled taxpayer. Sec. 1.482–1(b)(1), Income Tax Regs. The regulations also provide that "Transactions between one controlled taxpayer and another will be subjected to special scrutiny to ascertain whether the common control is being used to reduce, avoid, or escape taxes." Sec. 1.482–1(c), Income Tax Regs.

Petitioner and LTD were controlled by the same interests. Section 1.482–1(a)(3), Income Tax Regs., provides that the control may be direct or indirect, whether legally enforceable and however exercisable or exercised. Petitioner had control over LTD since LTD was a second-tier subsidiary of petitioner. Moreover, the same individuals who were officers and directors of LTD were also officers and directors of petitioner. The conclusion is inescapable that the requisite control was present.

Section 482, however, does not permit allocation merely because the common interests have the power to shift income. A reallocation under section 482 must be based on actual shifting of income. Your Host, Inc. v. Commissioner, 58 T.C. 10, 25 (1972), affd. 489 F.2d 957 (2d Cir.1973); V.H. Monette & Co. v. Commissioner, 45 T.C. at 37; Bush Hog Manufacturing Co. v. Commissioner, 42 T.C. at 725. We must therefore examine whether there has been a shifting of income between LTD and petitioner.

Respondent enjoys broad discretion in his application of section 482. Spicer Theatre, Inc. v. Commissioner, 346 F.2d 704, 706 (6th Cir. 1965); Foster v. Commissioner, 80 T.C. 34, 142, 143 (1983). Our review of his determination is limited. Hamburgers York Road, Inc. v. Commissioner, 41 T.C. at 833. Respondent's determination must be sustained unless we find an abuse of discretion—that his determination is unreasonable, arbitrary, or capricious. Your Host, Inc. v. Commissioner, 489 F.2d 957, 960 (2d Cir.1973); Foster v. Commissioner, 80 T.C. at 143, 144; Ach v. Commissioner, 42 T.C. at 125–127; Hamburgers York Road, Inc. v. Commissioner, 41 T.C. at 833; Grenada Industries, Inc. v. Commissioner, 17 T.C. 231, 255 (1951), affd. 202 F.2d 873 (5th Cir.1953). Whether respondent has abused his discretion is a question of fact. Ballentine Motor Co. v. Commissioner, 321 F.2d 796, 800 (4th Cir.1963); Foster v. Commissioner, 80 T.C. at 160, 178. We must examine all of the facts and circumstances to determine whether respondent has abused his discretion.

Respondent, both in his deficiency notice and on brief after the trial in this Court, allocated all of LTD's taxable income to petitioner. By allocating 100 percent of LTD's taxable income to petitioner, respondent has attempted in still another fashion to resurrect his argument that LTD is a "sham" corporation that should not be recognized for tax purposes. Respondent's argument under all of the theories that he has presented is that petitioner could as well have done the things that LTD did and therefore could have received all earnings from the King Faisal Hospital management contract. Since petitioner could have had these earnings, respondent would make it so by exercising his authority under section 482. We answer the argument as we did in Seminole Flavor Co. v. Commissioner, 4 T.C. 1215, 1235 (1945), and Koppers Co. v. Commissioner, 2 T.C. 152, 158 (1943): petitioner did not do this. Petitioner organized a separate corporation to contract with the Royal Cabinet of the Kingdom of Saudi Arabia to manage the King Faisal Hospital. We have held that LTD is a valid corporate entity that is to be recognized for tax purposes. In these circumstances, section 482 does not authorize an allocation that would in effect disregard the separate corporate existence of LTD. Keller v. Commissioner, 77 T.C.

1014, 1024 (1981), on appeal (10th Cir., Apr. 2, 1982). Moreover, section 1.482–1(b)(3), Income Tax Regs., states that section 482 is not intended to effect an allocation as would produce a result equivalent to a computation of consolidated taxable income. See also Seminole Flavor Co. v. Commissioner, 4 T.C. at 1232. We therefore hold that to the extent respondent attempted to shift all of LTD's taxable income to petitioner under section 482, his determination is arbitrary and capricious. Keller v. Commissioner, 77 T.C. at 1025.

Respondent has cited three cases in which a 100–percent allocation of income was sustained: Cobo Cleaners Co. v. United States, an unreported case (E.D. Mich. 1975, 36 AFTR2d 75–5147, 75–2 USTC par. 9592), affd. 535 F.2d 1253 (6th Cir.1976); Marc's Big Boy–Prospect, Inc. v. Commissioner, 52 T.C. 1073 (1969), affd. sub nom. Wisconsin Big Boy Corp. v. Commissioner, 452 F.2d 137 (7th Cir.1971), and Hamburgers York Road, Inc. v. Commissioner, supra. We find those cases distinguishable on their facts from this case.

Here, LTD, through Frayer, its employee and the executive director of the KFSH, had greater independence than the separate corporations in the three cases upon which respondent relies. In Cobo Cleaners Co. v. United States, supra, all operations of Cobo–Rumar, the department store dry cleaning corporation, were conducted daily under the direct supervision and control of Cobo Cleaners. All dry cleaning, pressing, pick-ups, and deliveries were conducted by Cobo Cleaners. Cobo–Rumar was not independent from Cobo Cleaners in any way. Thus, the District Court sustained the 100–percent allocation of Cobo–Rumar's net income to Cobo Cleaners.

Similarly, in Marc's Big Boy–Prospect, Inc. v. Commissioner, supra, we sustained a 100–percent allocation of the net income of several Big Boy Restaurants, which were set up as separate corporations to WBB, the dominant corporation. In that case, too, WBB exercised complete control over the daily operations of the other restaurant corporations.

In Hamburgers York Road, Inc. v. Commissioner, supra, we sustained a 100–percent allocation of all of the taxable income of a newly organized corporation operating a suburban clothing store to its sister corporation, which operated a well-established downtown clothing store. Here, too, all day-to-day operations of the suburban store corporation were directly controlled by the downtown store corporation.

Petitioner in Nashville, Tenn., did not exercise day-to-day control over LTD's operations at the King Faisal Hospital in Riyadh, Saudi Arabia. That control was exercised by LTD. We think that this factor is sufficient reason for us to reject respondent's 100–percent allocation under section 482.

Even though we have rejected respondent's 100–percent allocation of taxable income from LTD to petitioner, the evidence indicates overwhelmingly that an allocation is necessary and proper in this case. Nat Harrison Associates, Inc. v. Commissioner, 42 T.C. at 618; Ach v. Commissioner, 42 T.C. at 126. Unfortunately, there is little quantitative evidence in this record upon which we can determine what a reasonable allocation of profits would be. Neither party has been particularly helpful to the Court in this regard. However, we must do the best we can with what we have. See Nat Harrison Associates, Inc. v. Commissioner, 42 T.C. at 622.

The regulations provide as a general rule that where one member of a group of controlled entities performs services for the benefit of another member without charge or at a charge which is not at arm's length, appropriate allocations may be made to reflect an arm's-length charge for the services. Sec. 1.482–2(b), Income Tax Regs. The regulations also provide that where intangibles are made available in any manner by one member of a group of controlled entities to another member of the group for other than arm's-length consideration, an allocation can be made to reflect arm's-length consideration for the use of the intangibles. Sec. 1.482–2(d), Income Tax Regs.

Neither petitioner nor respondent has made any attempt to define specific services rendered by petitioner to LTD, to define LTD's use of intangibles belonging to petitioner, or to establish arm's-length charges for either. Petitioner argues that the only services that could arguably be said to have been performed by petitioner for LTD during 1973 were in the negotiations of the management contract and in the guarantee. Petitioner further argues that LTD reimbursed petitioner for all of the travel expenses of petitioner's personnel who went to London, Geneva, and Riyadh in 1973, and also reimbursed petitioner for the finder's fee that was paid to Joe Dini. Petitioner also argues that any services which it did perform were merely supervisory services of a parent with respect to a subsidiary that are not subject to allocation under section 482. Young & Rubicam, Inc. v. United States, 187 Ct.Cl. 635, 656, 410 F.2d 1233, 1245 (1969).

The evidence, however, indicates that in 1973, petitioner performed substantial services for LTD within the meaning of section 1.482–2(b), Income Tax Regs., and that it made available to LTD the use of its intangibles within the meaning of section 1.482–2(d)(3), Income Tax Regs. Petitioner played an active role in the contract negotiations. In formulating the contract proposal, some of petitioner's personnel, particularly hospital administrators and accountants, worked under the direction of Todd. These people were paid by petitioner but performed services for LTD. No payments were made to petitioner for these services. Once the contract had been executed, Frayer was notified of his appointment as executive director of the King Faisal Hospital. He began performing services for LTD after September 14, 1973, but he was not put on LTD's payroll until November 1, 1973. During this time, he worked on the staffing pattern to be presented to Dr. Rifat in November. He received assistance from employees at petitioner's Coliseum Park Hospital in formulating the staffing plan, and he also received their assistance in ordering supplies and equipment. There is no question that these services were performed for LTD, but LTD did not make any payments to petitioner for these services.

In 1973, petitioner sent Whitten, Oscar, and Carbone to London to meet with SCICON representatives concerning the King Faisal Hospital. These individuals received a total consulting fee of $75 per day plus reimbursement of their expenses. The hospitals that employed them were also reimbursed an amount equal to the employee's salary for the number of days the employee was unavailable. There is no evidence that these charges were equivalent to arm's-length charges.[41]

Petitioner also made available to LTD the use of intangibles. Section 1.482–2(d)(3), Income Tax Regs., defines intangibles as follows:

> (3) *Definition of intangible property.* (i) Solely for the purposes of this section, intangible property shall consist of the items described in subdivision (ii) of this subparagraph, provided that such items have substantial value independent of the services of individual persons.
>
> (ii) The items referred to in subdivision (i) of this subparagraph are as follows:
>
> (a) Patents, inventions, formulas, processes, designs, patterns, and other similar items;
>
> (b) Copyrights, literary, musical, or artistic compositions, and other similar items;
>
> (c) Trademarks, trade names, brand names, and other similar items;
>
> (d) Franchises, licenses, contracts, and other similar items;
>
> (e) Methods, programs, systems, procedures, campaigns, surveys, studies, forecasts, estimates, customer lists, technical data, and other similar items.

In contracting with LTD for the management of the King Faisal Hospital, the Royal Cabinet of the Kingdom of Saudi Arabia definitely

41. On the contrary, the evidence indicates that these charges were not at arm's length. A formal contract between LTD and petitioner was executed in 1975 purportedly to document an oral agreement under which the parties had allegedly been operating since Jan. 1, 1974. See note 30. Under the terms of this contract, LTD agreed to pay petitioner an amount equal to 3 times the daily salary of petitioner's employees for services performed outside the continental United States. These charges were allegedly equivalent to arm's-length charges. Even assuming that the amount is equivalent to those an arm's-length agreement would produce, and there is no evidence to so establish, LTD still did not pay that amount. Much of the confusion in this case arises from the multiple roles of the officers and directors of petitioner. For example, Neff, as president of both LTD and petitioner, was asked on cross-examination about the alleged oral agreements between LTD and petitioner:

> Q. You had oral agreements as—as—let me—now, here I don't try to trick you, but how do you make an oral agreement between yourself as president of Ltd. and president of HCA? Do you just make a decision? Or do you discuss it—
>
> A. I just make a decision.

While the identity of interest is not controlling, petitioner has not produced evidence of prices and terms which would have resulted had these services been performed for an unrelated party. See *Engineering Sales, Inc. v. United States,* 510 F.2d 565, 569 (5th Cir.1975). Even under the written intercompany agreements that were executed in 1975 (see note 30), there is no evidence in the record to establish that the prices in those intercompany agreements were reasonable and represented arm's-length charges.

looked to petitioner's experience and expertise. At the outset in the contract negotiations, petitioner was told to emphasize in its proposals HCA's experience and expertise. Later, LTD's name was changed from Hospital Corp. of the Middle East, Ltd., to Hospital Corp. of America, Ltd., because the Saudi Arabian officials wanted an "American flavor." The management contract itself is replete with references to and discussions of HCA's experience and expertise in the management of 51 hospitals in the United States. Also the KFSH management contract expressly required that petitioner guarantee LTD's performance of the contract.

As noted above, petitioner's expertise was specifically referenced in the contract. For example, the contract stated that petitioner had the capability to staff and assume management of operations of the hospital. The contract stated that LTD would make available to all personnel employed at the KFSH the full facilities of the U.S. hospitals owned and operated by petitioner for specialized continuing education programs. Representations in regard to Schedule A,3 of the contract stated that petitioner was well-managed financially and that it was able to forecast yearly operational costs within a 1–percent tolerance through use of its detailed computerized budget planning system. The contract stated that "Hospital Corporation of America, Ltd. has utilized the experience outlined above to estimate the operational supply costs of the King Faisal Specialist Hospital in a full operating year for the hospital, at present day values." These estimates were in part based on 1973 year-to-date operational costs from Los Robles Hospital, which was represented to be petitioner's most sophisticated hospital, but which did not equal the sophistication of the King Faisal Hospital. In estimating Schedule B variable expense items too, LTD used all of petitioner's experience, including estimates from the Los Robles Hospital. Moreover, it was because of petitioner's "acknowledged efficiency in hospital operations" that a lower inflationary factor was used for the price-escalation provisions of the contract. The contract contained statements that in carrying out the contract, LTD would use "the extensive experience of Hospital Corporation of America." We think that LTD used these intangibles and therefore an allocation is proper. Sec. 1.482–2(d), Income Tax Regs.

While petitioner has attempted to persuade us that it has no "system" that LTD could use, that attempt has not been successful. Indications of petitioner's system have permeated the entire record in this case. Petitioner's 1973 annual report gives a good indication of what petitioner saw as its management system. The "combination of medical-financial-administrative orientation and skills at all levels of the management structure provides the ideal combination for the effective management of hospitals. It is unique within the health care industry and is one of the company's most important competitive advantages." Petitioner's interim report for 9 months ended September 30, 1974, also refers to petitioner's system:

> Systems of monitoring and control have been perfected through the use of budgets, operating indicators and quality guidelines, which permit continuing evaluation of operating results at all facilities. Instant recognition of operating variances facilitates timely corrective action. These systems have resulted in dependable and predictable operating results through the hospital group.

We conclude that petitioner made its system available to LTD in both the negotiations for and the performance of the management contract for the King Faisal Hospital. There is no indication that LTD paid petitioner for the use of the system. Therefore an allocation is proper. Sec. 1.482–2(d), Income Tax Regs.

With undue modesty, petitioner has tried to suggest to this Court that its much-vaunted expertise and experience is a mere nothing: just setting up another corporation and installing an executive director or hospital administrator to run the hospital practically on his own. However, Frayer, the executive director of the King Faisal Hospital, candidly testified that while he was receiving a salary of $244,000 a year to run the hospital, he would not undertake to do the job on his own for $500,000 a year. Even discounting some of the sales puffery inherent in annual reports to stockholders or in sales pitches to secure hospital management contracts, we are persuaded that petitioner had a system involving considerable expertise and experience. While petitioner in 1973 admittedly did not have any prior experience in international operations, LTD at that time had no experience and no track record in either domestic or international hospital management. HCA's president, Mr. Neff, testified that "we felt that in the long run HCA had an enormous expertise that we could take into the foreign marketplace and if there was anybody who could be of help it was us." We are satisfied that what the Royal Cabinet of the Kingdom of Saudi Arabia contracted for and in large part received was HCA's expertise and experience, particularly during the year 1973.

Since petitioner performed substantial services for LTD and permitted LTD to use its system without compensation, there was a substantial distortion of income. We have found that LTD had an existence separate and apart from petitioner and that LTD's employees, Todd and Frayer, had the day-to-day responsibilities for preparing in 1973 to commence performing the KFSH management contract. Some of the 1973 profits are attributable to their efforts. However, the most important factor in earning those profits was petitioner's managerial expertise and experience which were readily available to and used by LTD. Using our best judgment on the lengthy but inconclusive record before us, we have concluded and found as a fact that 75 percent of the taxable income of LTD in 1973 was attributable to petitioner. Ach v. Commissioner, 42 T.C. at 126, 127. Cf. Cohan v. Commissioner, 39 F.2d 540, 544 (2d Cir.1930). We therefore hold that respondent erred in allocating the remaining 25 percent to petitioner.

Decisions will be entered under Rule 155.

ILLUSTRATIVE MATERIAL

A. SECTION 482 AND RELATED CORPORATIONS

The cases arising under section 482 discussed, supra, page 330, involved attempts by taxpayers to channel income between the corporation and its stockholder so as to take advantage of the differences between individual and corporate tax rates. The issues under section 482 as it applies to related corporations involve the same strategic goal of reduced taxation, though the situations are somewhat different. Prior to enactment of section 1561, there was an incentive to divide income artificially among related corporations to take advantage of the rate differential created by the surtax exemption. Section 482 was one of the weapons used by the Commissioner on that front. Though section 482 was not a direct basis for the denial of surtax exemptions, Challenger, Inc. v. Commissioner, 23 T.C.M. 2096 (1964), an allocation of the entire net income of the subsidiary to the parent had the same effect and the Commissioner had some success with this approach. See Hamburgers York Road, Inc. v. Commissioner, 41 T.C. 821 (1964); Wisconsin Big Boy Corp. v. Commissioner, 452 F.2d 137 (7th Cir.1971).

Enactment of section 1561 reduced the importance of section 482 as a regulator of transactions between related corporations in the *domestic context.* There is no longer much in the way of tax savings to be obtained by strategic arrangements of transactions among domestic corporations. However, special situations still exist which prompt such arrangements and in turn prompt the Commissioner to apply section 482. Thus, a tax advantage still can be obtained by the artificial shifting of income from a profitable corporation to a related corporation with a net operating loss which it would not otherwise be able to use. See, e.g., Ballentine Motor Co. v. Commissioner, 321 F.2d 796 (4th Cir.1963) (appreciated inventory was transferred by a parent to a subsidiary with a loss carryover, the subsidiary subsequently realizing the income; held, Commissioner properly allocated the income on the sale to the parent under section 482); Likins–Foster Honolulu Corp. v. Commissioner, 417 F.2d 285 (10th Cir.1969) (section 482 allocation prevented use of losses in a consolidated return). For other cases applying section 482 in a domestic context, see Engineering Sales, Inc. v. United States, 510 F.2d 565 (5th Cir. 1975); Liberty Loan Corp. v. United States, 498 F.2d 225 (8th Cir.1974).

As illustrated by *Hospital Corporation of America,* it is in the *international area* that section 482 is of greatest importance. Here the significance of transactions between related corporations arises because of the deferral of U.S. tax on the profits of foreign subsidiaries controlled by U.S. parent corporations which operate in countries with tax rates lower than the United States. If, for example, a U.S. parent corporation sells its products to its controlled foreign subsidiary at an artificially low price and the subsidiary then sells the products in the foreign market, there would be an understatement of the parent's portion of the profits on the transactions, and an overstatement of the subsidiary's portion. In addition, even if the foreign related corporation is taxed at rates comparable to U.S. rates, so that no overall tax saving is involved, section 482 is still necessary to insure that the U.S. obtains its appropriate share of revenues from international transactions. For representative cases see Eli Lilly & Co. v. Commissioner, 856 F.2d 855 (7th Cir.1988), and G.D. Searle & Co. v. Commissioner, 88 T.C. 252 (1987), discussed supra, page 376 (section 482 applied to reallocate income from the manufacture of pharmaceuticals in Puerto Rico based on patents and research developed by the United States parent corporation); Bausch & Lomb v. Commissioner, 92 T.C. 525 (1989) (Commissioner's increase of sales price of soft contact lenses from Irish manufacturing subsidiary to domestic parent corporation was an abuse of discretion, but 5% royalty for use of intangibles paid to parent was too low; the court rejected the Commissioner's assertion that a royalty in the range of 27% to 33% was proper and adopted a royalty of 20%).

The Commissioner has promulgated a complex set of Regulations under section 482 intended to insure that in general an "arms-length" change will be made between related corporations in order to insure a proper allocation of income between the United States parent and the foreign subsidiary, and then between the United States and the foreign country. The Regulations provide detailed methods for the pricing of intercompany transfers of property and services. See Regulations, sections 1.482–2(a) (loans); 1.482–2(b) (services); 1.482–2(c), (tangible property); 1.482–2(d) (intangible property); 1.482–2(e) (sales). The rules with respect to intangibles were modified by the 1986 Act. See section 482 (last sentence). The Regulations of course, also apply to the situation of a U.S. subsidiary and a foreign parent corporation, for the latter may be seeking because of the different level in the tax rates to keep the subsidiary profits as low as possible. See e.g. Ciba–Geigy Corp. v. Commissioner, 85 T.C. 172 (1985) (Commissioner abused his discretion finding that royalty payment from domestic subsidiary to its Swiss parent corporation was not arm's length consideration for license agreements for the manufacture of herbicides).

In the application of section 482, the Commissioner need not show a tax avoidance purpose to justify a reallocation of income among related corporations. See Regulations, section 1.482–1(c).

B. SECTION 482 AND THE CREATION OF INCOME

The Tax Court originally took the position that section 482 could not be used to "create" income in transactions between related parties. For example, in Huber Homes, Inc. v. Commissioner, 55 T.C. 598 (1971), the taxpayer sold rental property to its subsidiary at cost rather than at fair market value. The subsidiary then rented the property to unrelated third parties. The Commissioner, under section 482, attempted to allocate as income to the taxpayer the difference between the cost of the rental property and its fair market value at the time of the transfer. The Tax Court held for the taxpayer, finding section 482 inapplicable where the property transferred within the controlled group was not resold to a third party. Since it found section 482 not applicable, the court did not consider the taxpayer's alternative argument that the transfer should be treated as a tax-free contribution to capital.

In Central Bank of the South v. United States, 834 F.2d 990 (11th Cir. 1987), the taxpayer leased earthmoving equipment to a corporation owned by the taxpayer's wife and children. The Commissioner used section 482 to impose a higher rental charge for use of the equipment. The rental charge allocated by the Commissioner exceeded the corporation's net income. The District Court held, in part, that the allocation was an improper creation of income. The Court of Appeals reversed, holding that the question under section 482 in all cases is "whether unrelated parties could have enjoyed the same benefits of a transaction that the controlled parties enjoyed, i.e., whether the parties dealt at arm's length." (994)

The Court of Appeals decision in *Central Bank of the South* was based on cases involving interest-free loans between related corporations. Prior to the 1984 enactment of section 7872, which treats forgone interest on a below market loan between corporation and its stockholder as paid by the borrower and received by the lender, the Commissioner applied section 482 to create interest income for the lender on an interest free loan between related corporations. Relying on the *Huber Homes* line of reasoning, taxpayers argued that the Commissioner could not "create" interest income in such transactions. The Tax Court originally analyzed intercompany loan transactions by focusing on whether the borrower of the funds used the funds to realize income. If so, a portion of the income could be reallocated to the lender. See Kahler Corporation v. Commissioner, 58 T.C. 496 (1972). Reversing the Tax Court in *Kahler Corporation,* the Court of Appeals held that the proper standard to be applied is whether or not the loans from the taxpayer to other members of a controlled group would have been made on an interest free basis in arm's length dealings between uncontrolled taxpayers. Whether the borrowed funds actually produced income for the borrowing corporation was of no importance. "Money, and the use of money is an essential element in the profit making activities of most corporations, just as raw material is a necessary component in the manufacture of salable goods." Kahler Corporation v. Commissioner, 486 F.2d 1, 5 (8th Cir.1973). This approach was uniformly followed by the Courts of Appeals. B. Forman Co. v. Commissioner, 453 F.2d 1144 (2d Cir.1972); Kerry Investment Co. v. Commissioner, 500 F.2d 108 (9th Cir.1974); Fitzgerald Motor Co. v. Commissioner, 508 F.2d 1096 (5th Cir.1975). In the light of these adverse decisions the Tax Court modified its position and recognized the Commissioner's ability to find interest income in the case of interest-free loans between related corporations without regard to the use of the loan to produce income. Latham Park Manor, Inc. v. Commissioner, 69 T.C. 199 (1977), aff'd, 618 F.2d 100 (4th Cir.1980); see also Likins–Foster Honolulu Corp. v. Commissioner, 840 F.2d 642 (9th Cir.1988) (allocation of interest to parent on interest free loan to subsidiary created personal holding company income to the parent).

The treatment of intercompany transactions under section 482 should be compared with the approach in the consolidated return area, infra, page 1042. There a deferred accounting technique is used which postpones the recognition of gain on intercompany *sales* until the property is sold outside the group.

C. TECHNICAL ASPECTS OF SECTION 482 ALLOCATIONS

1. *Inability to Receive Income Directly*

In Commissioner v. First Security Bank of Utah, 405 U.S. 394 (1972), a holding company controlled a bank and a life insurance company. The bank would arrange credit life insurance for its borrowers with independent life insurance companies which reinsured the risks with the controlled insurance company. Under life insurance practices, because the bank originated the insurance, it was entitled to a commission based on a percentage of the premium charged to the customer by the initial insurance company. Federal banking law, however, prohibited the bank from receiving the sales commissions, and so the commissions were paid to the insurance company subsidiary.

The effective tax rate on insurance companies was lower than the rate on banks and, as a result, the total tax liability of the group was less than if the commissions had been received by the bank. The Commissioner allocated the commissions to the bank under section 482. The Supreme Court held that the Commissioner had no authority under section 482 to allocate the commission income to the bank where the direct receipt of that income would have been a violation of banking law. Does this decision make any tax sense at all? Is it consistent with James v. United States, 366 U.S. 213 (1961)? With the principles underlying section 482? With Lucas v. Earl, 281 U.S. 111 (1930)?

First Security Bank of Utah was followed in Salyersville National Bank v. United States, 613 F.2d 650 (6th Cir.1980), where, although the bank might have qualified under state law to issue credit life insurance had it undertaken to qualify as an insurance agent, the bank had no duty to qualify so that income the Commissioner attempted to allocate under section 482 could have been received legally. Since the taxpayer bank had not applied for an insurance license under state law, it was barred from legally receiving insurance commissions. Thus an allocation of commission income to it under section 482 was barred.

In Rev.Rul. 82–45, 1982–1 Cum.Bull. 89, the Internal Revenue Service held that the *First Security Bank of Utah* principle is not applicable to foreign law restrictions. The Ruling concludes that the laws of a foreign country do not limit the scope of the law of the United States.

2. *Constructive Dividends From Reallocation*

Suppose a sale between two commonly controlled brother-sister corporations is at less than an arm's length price and suppose further, to avoid the creation of income issue, that the property is then resold by the purchasing corporation outside the controlled group. Because of the bargain sale, under section 482 a portion of the income will be allocated from the purchasing corporation to the selling corporation for tax purposes though the actual proceeds of the ultimate sale remain with the purchasing corporation. Rev. Rul. 69–630, 1969–2 Cum.Bull. 112, takes the position that in such a situation the transaction will be treated as if the selling corporation had made a distribution of the reallocated income to its stockholders who in turn contributed that amount to the capital of the buying corporation. Under this approach any reallocation under section 482 resulting from a failure of the related parties to deal at arm's length would result in a constructive dividend distribution to the controlling stockholder. This approach has some support in the case law, though it has usually been applied when there was an intentional diversion of funds from one corporation to the other. In Worcester v. Commissioner, 370 F.2d 713 (1st Cir.1966), a constructive dividend was found where payments were made by one corporation to a sister corporation for services which were never in fact performed: "Since [taxpayer] was the controlling stockholder of both corporations, [the payments resulted in] income to him. * * * Any other rule would permit a stockholder to convert income into capital gain by transferring funds from one business to another then selling the latter company at a profit; or, if that were not permitted, at least to escape the strictures placed on accumulations of income by sections 531–37 * * * and thereby postpone at will the realization of taxable income." (715). See also Knipe v. Commissioner, 24 T.C.M. 668 (1965), aff'd per curiam, 356 F.2d 514 (3d Cir.1966) (a transfer of funds from one controlled corporation to another ostensibly for services, held to have been made without any independent business purpose; the court relied on Helvering v. Horst, 311 U.S. 112 (1940), to find income to the stockholder from the payments)); Sparks Nugget, Inc. v. Commissioner, 458 F.2d 631 (9th Cir.1972) (constructive dividend found where excessive rentals were paid in a transaction between related corporations). Contra, PPG Industries, Inc. v. Commissioner, 55 T.C. 928 (1970) (no constructive dividend on bargain sale between related corporations).

In Rev.Rul. 69–630, there was an express finding that the bargain sale had a tax avoidance purpose. However, Rev.Rul. 78–83, 1978–1 Cum.Bull. 79, involving a diversion of funds from one sister corporation to another to avoid foreign exchange control restrictions, indicated that the "constructive distribution-contribution to capital" analysis would be applied even though there was no motive to allocate income or deductions improperly. Should section 482 reallocation always result in a constructive dividend regardless of purpose? If not, under what theory can the presence of the "excess" assets in the corporation from which the allocation was made be accounted for?

In this connection compare the treatment of a *chain* of related corporations with a commonly controlled *brother-sister* group. In both situations, the group is limited to a single taxable income bracket, accumulated earnings tax credit, etc. And in both situations, if one of the constituent elements of the group is in a special tax rate bracket, section 482 would apply to prevent artificial income allocations from taking advantage of that rate differential. On the other hand, if a bargain purchase transaction takes place in a *chain,* while the income may have to be recognized currently, there is no constructive dividend to the stockholder. Thus the *chain* structure in effect allows the group to shift funds among corporations in the chain with no tax at the stockholder level. In contrast, on transactions between corporations standing in the *brother-sister* relationship, despite the fact that for purposes of the surtax exemption the group is treated as one corporation, intra-group transactions can generate constructive dividends under the approach of Rev.Rul. 69–630 and in a sense can increase the tax cost of operating in a brother-sister arrangement as compared to a chain. See Sammons v. Commissioner, 472 F.2d 449 (5th Cir.1972), for further discussion of the relationship between brother-sister and parent-subsidiary groups.

Some relief is available to taxpayers under Rev.Proc. 65–17, 1965–1 Cum.Bull. 833, which provides that, upon application to the Commissioner, payments between related taxpayers with respect to which the Commissioner has made a section 482 adjustment may be made without further tax consequences, provided that the taxpayer can show that the transaction subject to the section 482 adjustment was not entered into for the purpose of tax avoidance. If exclusion is permitted, a parent corporation to which income has been allocated from a subsidiary may receive a dividend in an equal amount without further tax consequences. Alternatively, subject to certain procedural requirements, the taxpayer (whether the parent, subsidiary, or sister corporation) may set up an account receivable, in an amount equal to the adjustment, from the related taxpayer with which it engaged in the transaction giving rise to the section 482 adjustment, and neither the creation nor payment of the account receivable will have any tax consequences. For application of this procedure, see Rev.Rul. 82–80, 1982–1 Cum.Bull. 89, holding that a bargain seller may receive payment, not in excess of taxable income allocated to it under section 482, without further tax consequences. Rev.Rul. 82–80 further provides that if an adjustment is allowed under Rev.Proc. 65–17, the price as adjusted under section 482 will be treated as the purchase price for all subsequent events and transactions. If payment to reflect a section 482 adjustment is made without following Rev. Proc. 65–17, the recipient recognizes taxable income. See Long v. Commissioner, 93 T.C. 5 (1989) (dividend to common shareholder of brother-sister corporations between which a section 482 adjustment had been made).

In Cappuccilli v. Commissioner, 668 F.2d 138 (2d Cir.1981), the taxpayer attempted to claim a bad debt deduction for rental income allocated to the taxpayer under section 482 which was not paid to the taxpayer. The court held that section 482 was designed accurately to reflect income and that allowing the taxpayer to claim a bad debt deduction would retroactively nullify the original allocation. See also Eisenberg v. Commissioner, 78 T.C. 336 (1982) (no bad debt deduction when the corporation failed to pay interest allocated to the stockholder under section 482).

3. *Section 482 and Property Dividend Distributions*

In Northwestern Nat'l Bank of Minneapolis v. United States, 556 F.2d 889 (8th Cir.1977), a subsidiary paid a dividend in-kind to its parent corporation. The parent corporation then donated the distributed property to a charity, taking a charitable contribution deduction. The transaction was structured in this form because the charitable deduction was worth substantially more to the parent than to the subsidiary. The Commissioner, under section 482, allocated the deduction to the subsidiary. The court upheld the Commissioner on the ground that the transaction was made possible solely because of the parent's control over the subsidiary. Suppose that after the dividend distribution the parent had sold the distributed property. Should section 482 apply to allocate the income on the sale to the subsidiary? Southern Bankcorp. v. Commissioner, 67 T.C. 1022 (1977), so held, where the sale by the parent resulted in a lower tax because of the peculiarities of the taxation of banks. One approach to cases such as these is to apply *Court Holding Company* principles and the *Horst* case in determining the taxpayer to which the income or deduction should be allocated. However, *Northwestern National Bank* appears to view section 482 as an independent basis for determining the taxpayer in situations in which a dividend distribution is involved. Is this an appropriate use of section 482, given that by definition a dividend can only occur between related parties and cannot be analyzed in terms of "arm's length" principles?

D. OTHER ASPECTS OF TRANSACTIONS BETWEEN BROTHER–SISTER CORPORATIONS

As amended in 1984, section 267(a)(1) applies to disallow a deduction for losses on sales of property between two members of a controlled group of corporations. Section 267(f)(1) defines a controlled group for this purpose as a controlled group under section 1563(a), discussed supra, page 1016, except that the 80 percent threshold for control of section 1563(a) is replaced by a 50 percent threshold. Losses disallowed to a controlled group under section 267 are deferred until the property is transferred outside of the controlled group. Section 267(f)(2). In this respect, losses incurred on inter-company sales within a controlled group are subject to deferred loss provisions similar to the deferred inter-company sales rules of the consolidated return regulations, discussed infra, page 1060.

Another issue in the context of affiliated corporations is raised by the case of captive insurance companies. In general, a taxpayer may not claim a deduction for amounts set aside as a reserve for future expenditures. In an attempt to avoid this limitation, taxpayers would form an affiliated insurance company to which deductible "insurance premiums" were paid in lieu of maintaining a self-insurance reserve. In general, the courts have denied deductions for payments to a captive insurance company on the ground that the arrangement lacks risk shifting from the affiliated group and is, therefore, not insurance. See Gulf Oil Corp. v. Commissioner, 89 T.C. 1010 (1987); Clougherty Packing Co. v. Commissioner, 811 F.2d 1297 (9th Cir.1987); Carnation Co. v. Commissioner, 640 F.2d 1010 (9th Cir.1981). In Humana, Inc. v. Commissioner, 881 F.2d 247 (6th Cir.1989), the court disallowed a deduction for premiums paid by the common parent of an affiliated group to its captive insurance subsidiary, but allowed deductions for premiums paid by other subsidiaries to its captive sister corporation. In the case of the parent there was no risk shifting in the event of loss because the parent's balance sheet would bear the burden of loss as its subsidiary paid a claim for the parent's liability. However, the balance sheets of the other subsidiaries were protected from loss as risk was shifted to the sister corporation. In so holding, the Court of Appeals rejected the Commissioner's argument that insurance cannot exist with respects to risks covered within the same economic corporate family.

E. REFERENCES

Note, Internal Revenue Code Section 482 Tax Implications for Closely–Held Domestic Business Associations, 9 Va.Tax Rev. 199 (1989); Cochran, The Infield Fly Rule and the Internal Revenue Code: An Even Further Aside, 29 Wm. & Mary L.Rev. 567 (1988); Wheeler, An Academic Look at Transfer Pricing in a Global Economy, 40 Tax Notes 88 (1988); Bohman & Bohman, Transfer Pricing Under the Tax Reform Act of 1986—Sections 482 and 1059A, 14 Int'l Tax J. 83 (1988); Higinbotham, Asper, Stoffregen & Wexler, Effective Application of the Section 482 Transfer Pricing Regulations, 42 Tax L.Rev. 293 (1987); Granwell & Hirsh, the Super Royalty: A New International Concept, 33 Tax Notes 1037 (1986); Cliff & Cohen, Collateral Fictions and Sections 482, 36 Tax Lawyer 37 (1982); Jenks, Section 482 and the Nonrecognition Provisions: The Transfer of Intangible Assets, 32 Tax Lawyer 775 (1979); Adess, The Role of Section 482 in Nonrecognition Transactions—The Outer Edges, 57 Taxes 946 (1979); King & Dinur, Tax Court Gives In on Creation-of-Income Issue under 482, 48 J.Tax'n 66 (1978); Fuller, Section 482 Revisited, 31 Tax L.Rev. 475 (1976); Nauheim, B. Forman & Co., Inc.—A Crucial Test of the Future of Section 482, 26 Tax Lawyer 107 (1972); Jenks, Constructive Dividends Resulting from Section 482 Adjustments, 24 Tax Lawyer 83 (1970); Eustice, Tax Problems Arising from Transactions between Affiliated or Controlled Corporations, 23 Tax L.Rev. 451 (1968).

With respect to captive insurance companies: Taylor, Taxing Captive Insurance: A New Solution for an Old Problem, 42 Tax Law. 859 (1989); Winslow, Tax Avoidance and the Definition of Insurance: The Continuing Examination of Captive Insurance Companies, 38 Case Western L.Rev. 79 (1989).

CHAPTER 24

CONSOLIDATED RETURNS

INTERNAL REVENUE CODE: Sections 243(b); 1501; 1503(b); 1504(a)–(b).

REGULATIONS: Sections 1.1502–1(f), (g), –2, –11, –12, –13(a) to (g), –13T, –14, –14T, –15, –19, –21, –31, –32(a)–(b), –75(d), –80.

TEMPORARY REGULATIONS: Section 1.1502–13T, –20T.

CAPS, WHAT EVERY BUSINESS LAWYER AND ACCOUNTANT MUST KNOW ABOUT THE LAW REGARDING CONSOLIDATED RETURNS

1969 Southern California Tax Institute 191.*

What is a consolidated return?

A consolidated return is a return filed by certain related corporations wherein the federal tax liability is computed as though such related corporations constituted a single entity. That is, the tax liability is computed substantially as though lower-tier corporations were operating divisions of a common parent corporation rather than distinct corporate entities. However, the mere filing of a consolidated return does not create a single corporate structure and there are significant differences between filing a consolidated return and filing a single return following a merger. Certain of these differences are hereinafter discussed in detail.

Statutory framework

The statutory authorization for consolidated return filing is set forth in Chapter 6 of Subtitle A of the Internal Revenue Code of 1954. Subchapter A of Chapter 6, Code Sections 1501–1505, pertains to filing consolidated returns and the payment of tax. Subchapter B, Sections 1551–1552 and 1561–1563, contains related rules for consolidated filing.

The Code provisions are brief and do little more than define who has the privilege of making consolidated returns and authorize the Secretary of the Treasury to

"prescribe such regulations as he may deem necessary in order that the tax liability of any affiliated group of corporations making a consolidated return * * * may be * * * determined * * * in such manner as clearly to reflect the income tax liability * * * and in order to prevent avoidance of such tax liability." [1]

1. I.R.C. § 1502.

In response to the foregoing congressional directive, consolidated return regulations have been copiously supplied by the Secretary. The current[2] Regulations under Section 1502 contain some thirty-four definitive subdivisions, most of which are replete with examples. These subdivisions are the heart of the consolidated filing requirements and have the force and effect of law.

Advantages and disadvantages of consolidated filing

Any determination of the desirability of filing a consolidated return necessarily will depend upon a critical analysis of the facts in each case. Therefore, an abstract listing of advantages and disadvantages to be obtained from consolidated filing is meaningless absent application to the unique characteristics of an eligible related group of corporations. However, the following are advantages and disadvantages which commonly may be found.

Advantages

Consolidated filing permits one member's current net operating losses ("NOLs"), capital losses and excess charitable contribution deductions to be offset against the income of other members of the group.[4] This may be of particular benefit when the loss member has no preceding profit years against which the NOLs may be applied to recover taxes previously paid. Similarly, one member's excess investment credits and foreign tax credits may be utilized to reduce the current tax liability of other members of the group.[5]

Absent separate return limitation years * * * one member's unused or unusable carryovers and carrybacks of NOLs, investment credits and foreign tax credits and carryovers of capital losses ("Tax Attributes") may be used to offset tax or income attributable to other members.[6]

Other advantages include the elimination of intercompany dividends[7] and the deferral of gain on certain types of intercompany transactions.[8] * * *

2. The current Regulations are applicable generally to consolidated taxable years beginning after December 31, 1965. The consolidated return Regulations applicable to years beginning before such date have been redesignated by adding a letter following the major division number (e.g., Reg. § 1.1502–30A).

4. Reg. § 1.1502–11.

5. Reg. § 1.1502–2. With high depreciation deductions, situations may well arise in which one member does not generate a sufficient tax liability to currently utilize its entire investment credit. Consolidated filing makes the entire consolidated tax paid by the group available for purposes of computing the limitation on the use of investment credits.

6. Reg. §§ 1.1502–3(b), 4(e), 21(b) and 22(b).

7. Reg. § 1.1502–14.

8. Reg. § 1.1502–13.

Disadvantages

Perhaps one of the principal disadvantages of consolidated filing is the loss of flexibility occasioned by the continuing requirement to file consolidated returns once such a filing has been made.[9] * * *

An additional disadvantage is that subsequent to consolidated filings, amounts in excess loss accounts, deferred inventory accounts and deferred intercompany profit accounts may be brought into income in the first year in which separate returns are filed.[16]

The decision of related corporations to file a consolidated return in lieu of separate returns may substantially affect the overall tax liability of the group in both current and future years. Therefore, before deciding to file a consolidated return, the group must consider carefully the effect of the consolidated return rules upon each member of the group and upon the group as a whole. Before analyzing the rules and determining their effect in given situations, it is necessary to determine the eligibility of a group to file a consolidated return and to obtain an understanding and working knowlege of certain terms and concepts utilized in the consolidated return Regulations.

Eligibility

Section 1501 of the Code provides that an *affiliated group* of corporations shall have the privilege of making a consolidated return. An affiliated group, defined in Section 1504, consists of a common parent corporation, which must be an includable corporation,[17] and at least one other includable corporation in which the parent owns at least 80 percent of the voting power of all classes of stock and 80 percent of each class of nonvoting stock. The affiliated group also consists of

9. An election to discontinue filing consolidated returns may be made with the permission of the Commissioner upon the parent's showing of good cause or upon blanket permission being granted by the Commissioner. Reg. § 1.1502–75(c). Under the old Regulations, a group could discontinue filing not only upon the showing of good cause but also upon the acquisition of a new member or upon a change in law which made consolidated returns substantially less advantageous. Reg. § 1.1502–11A(a). [Ed.: Rev.Proc. 70–4, 1970–1 Cum. Bull. 417, refused to apply the blanket permission to discontinue filing because of the changes made by the Tax Reform Act of 1969. The Regulations requirement that, once consolidated returns have been filed, consolidated filing must be continued until permission to change to separate returns has been obtained has been upheld as valid. Regal, Inc. v. Commissioner, 53 T.C. 261 (1969), aff'd per curiam, 435 F.2d 922 (2d Cir.1970); Orgill Brothers & Co. v. United States, 508 F.2d 1219 (6th Cir. 1975).]

16. Reg. §§ 1.1502–13, 18, and 19.

17. An *includable* corporation is defined in I.R.C. § 1504(b) as being any corporation except (1) exempt corporations; (2) insurance companies; (3) foreign corporations; (4) corporations entitled to special tax benefits under I.R.C. § [930] (i.e., corporations which receive substantial income from U.S. possessions); (5) China Trade Act corporations; (6) regulated investment companies and real estate investment trusts; and (7) [a DISC].

Although foreign corporations generally do not qualify as includable corporations, 100 percent owned Mexican or Canadian corporations organized and maintained solely for the purpose of complying with the laws of such country as to title and operation of property, *may* be treated as domestic corporations and included in the consolidated return of the group at the election of the domestic corporation which owns the stock. I.R.C. § 1504(d).

other includable corporations which are related to the parent or to each other under the same basic stock-ownership tests. In applying the stock-ownership tests, nonvoting stock which is limited and preferred as to dividends is not to be included. All includable corporations meeting the 80 percent requirement must be included in the consolidated return. * * *

[Ed.: Section 1504(a) was amended by the 1984 Act to require ownership of stock representing both 80 percent of the voting power and value of the stock of an included corporation.]

Effect on accounting year and accounting method

Accounting year

When filing a consolidated return, all members of the group must have the same taxable year as the parent.[27] Members on a different year must change their years to conform to the parent's year. A short-period return required by reason of the change in year of a member will constitute a taxable year of such member. The income of such member need not be annualized for the short period unless items of income or deduction cannot be clearly determined from the member's permanent records. A loss in the short period may be carried back despite the fact that on a separate-return basis, the member could not change its taxable year for this reason without permission.

Similarly, when a group acquires a new member or disposes of a member, such member's income or loss during the period of affiliation must be included in the consolidated return. However, if a corporation has been a member of the group for a period of thirty days or less during the [consolidated return year (CRY)], it may, at its option, be considered as not having been a member for such year. If, within thirty days after the beginning of a corporation's taxable year, it becomes a member of a group filing a consolidated return, it may, at its option, be considered to be a member from the first day of its taxable year.

Accounting method

There is no provision requiring or authorizing a member to change its overall method of accounting or method of accounting used for any particular item to conform to any principal method or to the parent's accounting method.[28] Therefore, under the current Regulations, a member's income is computed under the same method of accounting which it would use if filing a separate return.

27. Reg. § 1.1502–76(a)(1). However, if a member is on a 52–53 week taxable year ending within seven days of the taxable year of all members of the group and the Commissioner has given advance consent, the same taxable year rule will be deemed satisfied.

28. Reg. § 1.1502–17. In the event a member changes its method of accounting and the change is substantial as defined in I.R.C. § 481, the increase in tax for any prior year shall be computed on the basis of a consolidated return or a separate return, depending on which was filed for such prior year.

The common parent and each subsidiary which was a member of the group during *any part* of the CRY are *severally liable* for the tax imposed upon the group.[29] Agreements among members or with any other person are ineffectual to reduce or eliminate the several liabilities prescribed by the Regulations. * * *

The Regulations provide that the common parent, for all purposes other than consenting to the Regulations under Section 1502, is the *sole agent* for each member of the group and is duly authorized to act in its own name in all matters relating to the tax liability for the CRY.[30] The members, other than the parent, do not have authority to act for or to represent themselves in any such matter. * * *

Minority shareholder considerations

Many situations may arise wherein the requisite 80 percent control of a member is present but minority shareholders continue to have an equity interest in such member. Consideration should be given to possible liability which might arise if a consent to file a consolidated return is extracted by the parent from the member. It is possible that a cause of action might lie because of the sole agency given the common parent and the several liability tax exposure for each member of the consolidated group. The manner selected in allocating the consolidated tax liability could also give rise to objections by minority shareholders.

Net Operating Losses

[Ed.: Rules with respect to the treatment of net operating losses in consolidated returns are considered infra, page 1052.]

Intercompany transactions

Intercompany transactions are defined as transactions during a CRY between corporations which are members of the same group immediately after such transactions.[42] Such transactions would include a sale of property by one member to another, the performance of services by one member for another, or the payment of interest by one member to another during a CRY. However, intercompany transactions do not include distributions by one member to another with respect to the distributing member's stock, or a contribution to capital on which no gain is realized.

Intercompany transactions are generally classified into two separate groups: deferred and nondeferred. If a transaction consists of a sale or exchange of property, or the performance of services or the incurrence of other types of expenditures which are required to be capitalized, then such a transaction constitutes a *deferred* intercompany transaction. Any gain or loss realized in a deferred intercompany transaction is not reported in accordance with the seller's method of

29. Reg. § 1.1502–6.

30. Reg. § 1.1502–7.

42. Reg. § 1.1502–13(a)(1).

accounting but under the special rules prescribed in the consolidated return Regulations.[43]

Gain or loss on *nondeferred* intercompany transactions (i.e., transactions not involving property or capitalized expenditures) are not deferred or eliminated.[44] For example, if during a CRY a purchasing member makes an interest payment on an indebtedness to a selling member in an intercompany transaction, the purchasing member will take the deduction for interest into account and the selling member shall take the interest income into account. However, if the income and the corresponding deduction are not reportable in the same CRY, a special rule applies and both items must be reported in the later year.[45] Thus, if *P*, a cash-basis taxpayer paid interest accrued to December 31, 1967 to *S–1* in January of 1968 and *S–1* is an accrual-basis taxpayer, both the interest and expense must be reported in 1968. But for this special rule, *S–1* would report the accrued interest income in 1967 and *P* would claim the deduction in 1968. However, if a [separate return year] SRY earlier than the CRY is involved for the member first having to recognize the items of income or expense the normal accounting methods would be followed.[46]

To the extent gain or loss on a *deferred* intercompany transaction is recognized for a CRY such gain or loss is deferred by the selling member.[47] The amount of deferred gain or loss is determined on the basis of gross profit or loss rather than net profit or loss. Both direct costs and indirect costs which are properly includable in the cost of goods sold are included in the computations.[48] Other indirect expenses, however, including general administrative and selling expenses may be deducted in the year incurred and need not be deferred until the gain or loss on the transaction is reported.

Generally, the source and character of the deferred intercompany transaction is determined at the time of the transaction as though the members had filed separate returns.[49] However, part or all of the deferred gain or loss may be treated as ordinary income or loss if the acquiring member is entitled to a depreciation, amortization or depletion deduction, or an abandonment loss on the transferred property.[50]

The selling member annually restores to income gain or loss at the same percentage rate the purchasing member depreciates the asset.

* * *

43. Reg. § 1.1502–13(c).

44. Reg. § 1.1502–13(b)(1).

45. Reg. § 1502–13(b)(2).

46. Ibid.

47. Reg. § 1.1502–13(c). However, the selling member may not report gain on the installment method under I.R.C. § 453. Reg. § 1.1502–13(c)(1)(ii)(a).

48. Reg. § 1.1502–13(c)(2).

49. Reg. § 1.1502–13(c)(4) provides that the character and source of deferred gain or loss on a deferred intercompany transaction shall be determined at the time of the deferred intercompany transaction as if such transaction had not occurred during a CRY except when such gain or loss has been restored under Reg. § 1.1502–13(d)(1) or as the result of abandonment under (f) in which case it shall be treated as ordinary income or loss.

50. Reg. § 1.1502–13(d).

Any gain or loss realized on a deferred intercompany transfer of an installment obligation is not reported in the year of the transfer, but is reported ratably over the period the obligation is satisfied.[53] The amount of deferred gain or loss to be reported in each taxable year during such period is determined by multiplying the total deferred gain or loss arising at the time of the transfer by the amount of the obligation satisfied and dividing the resulting figure by the amount of the unpaid installment obligation at the time of transfer.

When property is sold or otherwise disposed of outside the group, the deferred gain or loss which has not previously been restored to income will [generally] be taken into account.[54] The character of the gain or loss recognized will remain the same as it was at the date of the original transaction, reduced by the interim amounts restored to income. If the deferred gains include any ordinary income, such as recapture of depreciation, periodic amounts taken into account are first to be applied against the ordinary income portions.[55]

If property acquired in a deferred intercompany transaction is subsequently disposed of outside the group and the member who sells outside the group elects to report the gain under the installment method, the amount of deferred gain or loss the original selling member must report in a taxable year is calculated by multiplying the remaining deferred gain at the time of the second disposition, by the installment payment received by the member selling outside the group, and dividing the resulting figure by the total contract price of the second disposition.[56] * * *

The basis of property acquired in a deferred intercompany transaction is the cost of the property to the purchasing member including the deferred profit or loss.[57] The acquiring member may continue to use one of the accelerated methods of depreciation.[58] The holding period of such property includes only the time the purchasing corporation held the property and the holding period of the selling member is not permitted to be tacked.[59]

The group may elect, with the consent of the Commissioner, not to defer any gain or loss recognized in an intercompany transaction with respect to all property or to any class or classes of property.[60] Such an election would permit the character of the gain or loss to be retained but at the expense of prepayment of the tax due on such gain. However, since the consent of the Commissioner is required, the "election" title is somewhat of a misnomer.

53. Reg. § 1.1502–13(e)(1), [(f)(2)].

54. Gain or loss on deferred intercompany transactions upon a disposition is taken into account by the selling member upon the earliest to occur of an event described in one of the eight subdivisions of Reg. § 1.1502–13(f).

55. Reg. §§ 1.1502–13(d)(3) and (e)(3).

56. Reg. § 1.1502–13(e)(2).

57. Reg. § 1.1502–31(a).

58. Reg. § 1.1502–12(g) * * *.

59. Reg. § 1.1502–13(g).

60. Reg. § 1.1502–13(c)(3).

Should the members merge into a single corporation and file a single return, property would be freely transferable from one division to another division without recognition of gain or loss. Holding periods would also be tacked.

With separate filings, the respective members would not be permitted to defer gain or loss. However, there would be no conversion of what would otherwise be capital gain into ordinary income.

Inventory adjustments

A member which sells goods at a profit to another member in a preconsolidation year and includes the profits in its gross income in the year of sale again may be subjected to tax on the profits if the goods are includable in inventory at the beginning of the first year in which the group files a consolidated return. Such preconsolidation inventory profits are referred to as "the initial inventory amount" [61] and are again [generally] includable as ordinary income by the selling member in the CRY in which the goods are disposed of outside the group or when the selling member leaves the group. * * *

Investment adjustments

Section 1.1502–32 of the Regulations provides for an investment adjustment designed to eliminate the dual tax consequences normally attributable to corporate profits and losses. A parent corporation filing a consolidated return with a subsidiary deducts currently its subsidiary's operating losses or includes its subsidiary's income thereby adjusting what otherwise would be its tax liability accordingly.[66] The consolidated return Regulations require an annual investment adjustment reducing or increasing the basis of a subsidiary's stock held by the parent.[67] This adjustment will either be a net positive adjustment or a net negative adjustment depending upon the operations and distributions, if any, of the subsidiary. The "net" adjustment is the difference between the positive adjustment and the negative adjustment.

If a subsidiary owns shares of one or more affiliates, adjustments must be made in the basis of such stock to reflect the operation of the affiliates, starting with the lowest tier subsidiary and working upward. Thus, if *P* owns 100 percent of the stock of *S–1* and *S–1* owns 80 percent of the stock of *S–2,* and if *S–2* has a net positive adjustment for the year of $100 of which $80 is allocable to *S–1, P* must also take into account the $80 positive adjustment in determining the annual adjustment to the stock of *S–1.*[68]

61. Reg. § 1.1502–18(b) defines the term "initial inventory amount" as the intercompany profit amount of a member for the immediately preceding taxable year in which such member filed a separate return. The term "intercompany profit amount" for a taxable year is defined in Reg. § 1.1502–18(a) as an amount equal to the profits of a member arising in transactions with other members with respect to goods which are included in the inventories of other members at the close of such member's taxable year.

66. Reg. § 1.1502–11.

67. Reg. § 1.1502–32(a).

68. See Example (2) of Reg. § 1.1502–32(j).

Separate annual adjustments are made for common stock and for preferred stock that is limited and preferred as to dividends. The preferred stock adjustments are made prior to adjustments to the common stock.

The positive adjustments to be made with respect to common stock are:

(1) An allocable part of the undistributed earnings and profits of the subsidiary for the taxable year;

(2) An allocable part of the portion of any consolidated NOL or consolidated net capital loss for the taxable year which is attributable to such subsidiary and which is not carried back and absorbed in a prior taxable year; and

(3) If the subsidiary owns stock in another subsidiary, an allocable part of the net positive adjustment made by the higher-tier subsidiary for the taxable year with respect to the stock in such other subsidiary.[69]

The negative adjustments to be made with respect to common stock are:

(1) An allocable part of the deficit in earnings and profits of the subsidiary for the taxable year;

(2) An allocable part of any NOL or net capital loss incurred by the subsidiary in a prior SRY and of any portion of the consolidated NOL or consolidated net capital loss incurred by the group in a prior CRY which is attributable to the subsidiary which is carried over and absorbed in the taxable year;

(3) Distributions by the subsidiary during the tax year out of earnings and profits accumulated in prior CRYs beginning after December 31, 1965 or in preaffiliation years of the subsidiary; and

(4) If a subsidiary owns stock in another subsidiary, an allocable part of the net negative adjustment made by the higher-tier subsidiary for the taxable year with respect to the stock in such other subsidiary.[70]

For preferred stock, a positive adjustment is required for current undistributed earnings and profits, and a negative adjustment is required only for distributions either from preaffiliation[71] earnings or from post–1965 prior CRY earnings.[72]

Should the net negative adjustments exceed the basis of stock of a subsidiary an "Excess Loss Account"[73] is created. The Excess Loss Account is a negative basis and is designed to insure that the ultimate measure of income gained or lost to each member of an affiliated group

69. Reg. § 1.1502–32(b)(1).

70. Reg. § 1.1502–32(b)(2).

71. A "preaffiliation year" is defined in Reg. § 1.1502–32(d)(9) as a "taxable year during which such subsidiary was not a member for each day."

72. Reg. § 1.1502–32(c).

73. Reg. § 1.1502–32(e)(1) defines an "excess loss account" as the excess of the net negative adjustment over the basis of the subsidiary's stock.

filing a consolidated return with a subsidiary is its investment in the subsidiary. An Excess Loss Account can also be created or increased by a distribution not out of earnings which exceeds the basis of the stock with respect to which the distribution is made.[74]

Disposition of the stock of a subsidiary [generally] requires the inclusion in income of the Excess Loss Account with respect to the stock disposed of. A disposition is deemed to have occurred on the day either the subsidiary or the member holding stock ceases to be a member or on the last day of the taxable year preceding the first taxable year for which a consolidated return is not filed. The subsidiary's stock is also deemed disposed of for this purpose on the last day of the taxable year in which it becomes worthless.[75]

If the subsidiary is not insolvent at the time of the disposition, the amounts required to be included in income are treated as gain from the sale of stock. Thus, the gain from the disposition will usually be capital gain. If the subsidiary is insolvent, the Excess Loss Account after being decreased by the portion thereof attributable to non-dividend distributions is treated as ordinary income to the extent of such insolvency. However, even with insolvency, if the Excess Loss Account reflects amounts that served only to reduce long-term capital gain of other members of the group, capital gain treatment is available.[76]

The treatment of excess losses is prescribed in order to prevent substantially the same loss from being deducted by two taxpayers. For example, assume that *P* owns 100 percent of the stock of *S–1* because of its $100 capital contribution to *S–1*. *S–1* borrows $1,000 from outsiders. If *S–1* proceeds to lose the entire $1,100 invested in it and other members are profitable, the $1,100 would be deducted by the group in CRYs. The Regulations require the creation of an Excess Loss Account when *P*'s investment in the stock of *S–1* is exhausted. Therefore, upon the worthlessness of *S–1*'s stock, the excess loss of $1,000 will come into the income of *P*.

The group may elect to treat a subsidiary as having distributed its entire accumulated earnings and profits on the first day of the taxable year, provided all of the stock of the subsidiary was owned by members of the group on each day of the taxable year. Each shareholder will be treated as having received its share of the dividend and immediately thereafter having contributed the same amount to the capital of the subsidiary. The result will generally be an increase in basis of the stock of the subsidiary and an increase in the earnings and profits of the affiliated shareholders. This rule is referred to as the "deemed dividend rule." [77]

74. Reg. § 1.1502–14(a)(2).

75. A member is deemed to have disposed of shares of stock in a subsidiary upon the occurrence of any of the events specified in Reg. § 1.1502–19(b). [Ed.: See Regulations, section 1.1502–19(a)(6), allowing deferral of recognition of the income attributable to the Excess Loss Account in certain situations.]

76. The rules for determining the character of income are set forth in Reg. § 1.1502–19(a)(2).

77. Reg. § 1.1502–32(f)(2).

The deemed-dividend rule accommodates certain groups that have subsidiaries with earnings and profits realized in separate return affiliation years or in pre–1966 consolidated return years. These earnings represent earnings already taxed to the group or one of its members during a period of affiliation. The deemed-dividend rule facilitates the inclusion of such earnings in the affiliated shareholders' stock basis.

Allocation of group's tax liability

Section 1552 authorizes three specific methods for allocating the tax liability of a group. The three methods for apportioning tax liability are:

(1) proportionately to a member's share of consolidated taxable income;

(2) proportionately to a member's tax, if separate returns had been filed, as opposed to the total tax for all members of the group if separate returns had been filed; and

(3) on the basis of each member's contribution to the consolidated taxable income, with increases in tax of members resulting from consolidation being allocated to members whose tax had been reduced because of filing consolidated returns.[78]

Section 1552 also authorizes such other method as may be selected by the group with the approval of the Secretary.[79] (192–220)

ILLUSTRATIVE MATERIAL

A. NET OPERATING LOSS ASPECTS

1. *General*

Regulations, section 1.1502–21(b)(1), allow the net operating losses of a member of an affiliated group to be carried over from a pre-consolidation return period against the consolidated income of the group. This general rule, is, however, subject to three limitations: (1) if the loss year was a "separate return limitation year" (SRLY), then the loss may be carried over only against the income of the member of the group that generated the loss, Regulations, section 1.1502–21(c); (2) if there has been a "consolidated return change of ownership" (CRCO), then losses may be carried over only against income of the original group, Regulations, section 1.1502–21(d); and (3) if section 382 is applicable, then the carryovers are limited accordingly, Regulations, section 1.1502–21(e).

2. *Separate Return Limitation Year*

Regulations, section 1.1502–1(f), provide the definition for "separate return limitation year." In general it is a year in which any member of the group filed a separate return. But there are exceptions. One important exception is that a SRLY does not include a separate return year for a subsidiary which was a member of the group at the time the loss was incurred, although no consolidated returns were filed in such year. See

78. The methods for allocating the consolidated tax liability are set forth in I.R.C. § 1552(a)(1), (2), and (3), respectively.

79. I.R.C. § 1552(a)(4).

Regulations, section 1.1502–1(f)(2)(ii). In addition, the exception in Regulations, section 1.1502–1(f)(2)(i), permits a loss corporation to acquire a profitable subsidiary and apply its own loss carryovers against the profits of the newly acquired subsidiary. Acquisition of a corporation with built-in gain, however, is subject to the limitations of section 384, supra, page 993, which restricts the use of preacquisition losses against recognized built-in gain of either the acquired or acquiring corporation.

Wolter Construction Co., Inc. v. Commissioner, 634 F.2d 1029 (6th Cir. 1980), upheld the validity of the SRLY Regulations. In that case, losses incurred by a subsidiary in separate return years could not be used by the consolidated group even though the corporations in the separate return years were commonly controlled as brother-sister corporations by individual stockholders. Since the stockholders were individuals and not corporations, the group did not fall within the "common parent" exception in Regulations, section 1.1502–1(f)(2)(1). The court in *Wolter Construction Co.* described the operation of the SRLY rule as follows:

"Reg. 1.1502–21(b)(1) is concerned with the use of net operating losses on a consolidated return. That regulation permits an affiliated group to use net operating losses sustained by any members of the group in 'separate return years' if the losses could be carried over pursuant to the general principles of § 172 of the Code. A 'separate return year' is defined as any year in which a company filed a separate return or in which it joined in the filing of a consolidated return by another group. Reg. 1.1502–1(e).

"As a general rule, then, net operating losses reported on a separate return can be carried over to and used on a consolidated return. An important exception to this rule is found in Reg. 1.1502–21(c). That section provides that the net operating loss of a member of an affiliated group arising in a 'separate return *limitation* year' which may be included in the consolidated net operating loss deduction of the group shall not exceed the amount of consolidated taxable income contributed by the loss-sustaining member for the taxable year at issue. The term 'separate return limitation year' is defined in Reg. 1.1502–1(f), in essence, as a separate return year in which the member of the group (except, with qualifications, the common parent) was either: 1) not a member of the group for its entire taxable year; or 2) a member of the group for its entire taxable year, that enjoyed the benefit of multiple surtax exemptions. In summary, losses incurred by a brother-sister corporation or by a corporation which is unrelated at the time of its losses to its subsequent affiliates, before it becomes a member of an affiliated group filing a consolidated return, can only be carried forward and used on the consolidated return to the extent that the corporation that incurred the losses has current income reflected on the consolidated return." (1032–1033)

In *Wolter Construction Co.,* the fact that the Regulations imposed a greater limitation on net operating loss carryovers in the context of the consolidated return than is contained in sections 381 and 382 did not invalidate the Regulations.

3. *Consolidated Return Change of Ownership*

The second limitation on the use of net operating loss carryovers in the consolidated return Regulations is the "consolidated return change of ownership" (CRCO) defined in Regulations 1.1502–1(g). A CRCO occurs when there is a more than 50 percent change of ownership during a taxable year by one or more of the ten persons who own the greatest percentage of the fair market value of the stock of the common parent. A CRCO will occur only if the increase in ownership is by taxable purchase or is the result of the liquidation or redemption of stock of the common parent. When a CRCO has occurred, the losses of the group can be carried over only against post-CRCO income of members of the original group. The Court in *Wolter Construction Co.* explained the CRCO limitation as follows:

"A 'consolidated return change of ownership' is defined generally in Section 1.1502–1(g) of the Treasury Regulations as a more than 50 percentage point change in ownership in the common parent corporation that occurs during a two-year period. If a consolidated return change of ownership occurs, then under section 1.1502–21(d) of the Regulations, the net operating losses attributable to the common parent before the change (together with the net operating losses attributable to the other corporations, if any, that were members of the group before the change) may be carried over to consolidated return years ending after the change only to the extent that the common parent (and the other corporations that were members of the group before the change) contribute to the consolidated taxable income of the group. This limitation hampers the tax avoidance motive of a party which infuses new capital into the common parent with the intention of having it acquire profitable subsidiaries." (1036)

In Rev. Rul. 84–33, 1984–1 Cum. Bull. 186, in a year in which a CRCO occurred, the common parent of an affiliated group filing a consolidated return formed two new subsidiaries by transferring a separate operating division of the parent corporation to each subsidiary. The Internal Revenue Service held that net operating losses of the parent corporation could be carried forward and used against income of the two subsidiaries even though the subsidiaries were technically not in existence as members of the consolidated group prior to the year in which the CRCO occurred. The Service concluded that the contributions of the new subsidiaries to consolidated taxable income should be treated as attributable to old members of the affiliated group because the assets and businesses of the new subsidiaries were derived solely from the parent corporation, an old member of the group.

4. *Reverse Acquisition*

Since the SRLY limitation does not apply in the case of a change of ownership of the common parent, and a CRCO occurs only if ten or fewer stockholders increase their percentage interests by more than 50 percent, there remains the possibility that the assets of a profitable corporation may be merged into the common parent in exchange for more than 50 percent of the stock of the common parent of the loss group. However, Regulations, section 1.1502–1(f)(3), treat this transaction as a "reverse acquisition" to deny the net operating loss carryover against the profits of the "acquired corporation." In *Wolter Construction Co.* the court rejected the taxpayer's argument that the common parent exception to the SRLY limitation and the reverse acquisition exception to the exception were intended to insure that loss carryovers were available only to the stockholders who owned the corporation when the losses were incurred, and that this policy should be applied to allow use of losses by the common parent affiliated with its former sister corporation. The court described the reverse acquisition rule as follows: "In a typical reverse acquisition in the loss carryover context, substantially all the assets or stock of a profit corporation are nominally acquired by a loss corporation in exchange for more than 50 percent of the latter's stock, so that control of the loss corporation has shifted to the stockholders of the profit corporation as they existed prior to the acquisition. The Regulations essentially treat the loss corporation as having been acquired, and under Section 1.1502–1(f)(3) of the Treasury Regulations, all taxable years of the loss corporation prior to the reverse acquisition are treated as separate return limitation years, notwithstanding its status as the common parent corporation of the new affiliated group consisting of it and the profit corporation. Conversely, the separate return years of the profit corporation prior to the acquisition are not treated, in general, as the separate return limitation years. Accordingly, the net operating losses sustained by the loss corporation, but not the profit corporation, in its separate return years are subject to the carryover limitation contained in Section 1.1502–21(c). The purpose and effect of the reverse acquisition rules is to prevent trafficking in loss corporations. This is accomplished by redirecting the SRLY limitation to the ostensibly acquiring corporation. This 'simple technical rule thwarts the attempts of those who would seek to present that the ailing David is trying to improve its financial strength by drawing on the earning power of Goliath.' Gans [A Practical Guide to Consolidated Returns (1976)], supra at 828.2." (1035–1036.)

5. *Section 382 Limitation*

Finally, Regulations, section 1.1502–21(e), incorporate section 382. The legislative history to the 1986 amendments to section 382 indicates that the SRLY and CRCO rules of the consolidated return regulations will continue to apply. H. Rep. No. 99–841, 99th Cong., 2d Sess. II–194 (1986). Presumably, Regulations, section 1.1502–21(e), apply the limitation of section 382 to losses before they are carried over under the SRLY or CRCO limitation. Thus, if there has been an ownership change under section 382(g)(1) with respect to a corporation acquired by a member of a consolidated group and subject to SRLY or CRCO, losses subject to those limitations will also be limited in amount based on the fair market value of the acquired corporation as provided in section 382(b)(1).

Because of the attribution rules of section 382(1)(3), changes of ownership within an affiliated group will not result in an ownership change for purposes of section 382. However, an ownership change of the common parent will result in an ownership change for each member of the consolidated group so that the section 382 will limit the net operating loss of all members of the group.

6. *Built–In Deductions*

Regulations, sections 1.1502–15 and 1.1502–75(d)(3), deal with the problem of "built in" deductions. If losses are economically incurred in a prior separate return year but realized for tax purposes in a consolidated year, such losses may not be applied against consolidated income but may only be used to offset the income of the corporation which realized the loss. In Rev. Rul. 79–279, 1979–2 Cum. Bull. 316, the Internal Revenue Service held that built-in deductions include normal operating expenses accrued by a cash basis corporation in a separate return year but not paid until a year in which the corporation is included in a consolidated return. Regulations, section 1.1502–15(a)(2), provide that the term "built-in deductions" does not include items incurred in rehabilitating a loss corporation. The Regulation is thus more liberal with respect to post-acquisition losses than section 382 which limits built-in losses following an ownership change, discussed supra, page 959, or section 269 which, in the view of the Service, would completely disallow deductions for such losses if the section were applicable. Note that the section 382 limitation on built-in loss differs in terms of both the threshold test for its application and the time element for recognition of built-in loss. Regulations, sections 1.1502–15 and 1.1502–75(d)(3), will have to be coordinated with the built-in gain and loss rules of sections 382 and 384.

B. ELIMINATION OF INTERCORPORATE PROFITS UNDER THE CONSOLIDATED RETURN REGULATIONS

The original technique for the elimination of intercorporate gain on sales between affiliated corporations covered by the pre–1966 consolidated return Regulations involved a carryover basis for the transferred asset in the hands of the corporation purchasing the asset. See Regulations, section 1.1502–38A(b). This technique in effect deferred the recognition of gain until the asset was disposed of outside of the consolidated group. At that point, the deferred gain would be taken into account by the corporation making the outside sale. This approach, however, proved inadequate as it was possible to avoid recognition of the deferred gain in certain circumstances by a disposition of the stock of the corporation which had purchased an appreciated asset in a prior intercompany transaction. See for example Henry C. Beck Builders, Inc. v. Commissioner, 41 T.C. 616 (1964), in which the Tax Court rejected the Commissioner's attempt under the pre–1966 Regulations to tax the intercorporate profit at the time of the disposition of the subsidiary's stock. The court rejected the position taken by the Commissioner, as an interpretation of the then existing Regulations in Rev. Rul. 60–245, 1960–2 Cum. Bull. 267, that the previously eliminated intercompany profit was required to be recognized in the year in which the stock was sold to a party outside of the affiliated group. AMBAC Industries v. Commissioner, 487 F.2d 463 (2d Cir.1973), refused to follow *Beck Building* in a similar situation involving an operating loss.

The 1966 revision of the consolidated returns Regulations met the *Beck Builders* problem by providing in general that deferred gain must be taken into account when the group member which owns the property with respect to which gain has been deferred ceases to be a member of the affiliated group. Regulations, section 1.1502–13(f)(1)(iii). Thus, the sale of the subsidiary stock would result in the inclusion in income of the deferred gain in the year of sale. In addition, the Regulations provide that the closing out of the deferred transaction will result in income to the member which originally earned the income, in this case the parent, rather than to the member holding the property, which was the case under the carryover basis approach of the previous Regulations.

C. INVESTMENT ADJUSTMENTS

1. *General*

Regulations, section 1.1502–32, and Temporary Regulations, section 1.2502–32T, require, in general, that each member of the group owning stock in another member of the group adjust its basis for that stock annually to reflect, among other things, a proportionate share of any undistributed current earnings and profits or any deficit in current earnings and profits of the subsidiary. The purpose of the investment adjustment rule is to prevent gain or loss which has been recognized by the subsidiary from being recognized a second time as investment gain or loss by the parent upon disposition of the subsidiary's stock.

These adjustments relate poorly to consolidated income in many instances because sections 312(k) and (n), supra, page 464, require adjustments to earnings and profits for a number of items, including depreciation, inventory amounts, and installment sales, which differ from the amounts taken into account in computing taxable income or loss. These differences are timing differences which create a disparity between the amount of taxable gain or loss of the subsidiary which is consolidated with the income of the parent and the adjustments to the basis of the subsidiary stock. Under a literal application of the Regulations, the parent may realize an inappropriate reduction in the amount of gain or loss on the sale of the subsidiary stock. In Woods Investment Co. v. Commissioner, 85 T.C. 274 (1985), the Tax Court held that Regulations, section 1.1502–32(a), were to be applied literally. The court suggested that the Treasury could cure the problem by amending the Regulations.

Congress did not wait for the Regulations to be amended and in the 1987 Act added section 1503(e). For dispositions after October 15, 1987, solely for the purpose of determining gain or loss on the disposition of stock of a subsidiary, adjustments to the basis of subsidiary stock are made by computing earnings and profits under section 312 without reference to sections 312(k) and (n). Thus, for this limited purpose, earnings and profits are computed, for example, using accelerated cost recovery under section 168 rather than the slower depreciation mandated by section 312(k). As a result, the adjustments to the parent's basis in the subsidiary stock will track more closely the amount of income of the subsidiary included on the consolidated return. Section 1503(e) applies to taxable sales of the subsidiary's stock, to computation of substituted basis if the subsidiary's stock is disposed of in a nonrecognition transaction, and to computation of the amount of the loss deduction under section 165 if the subsidiary stock becomes worthless. Because a benefit similar to that in *Woods Investment Co.* sometimes can be obtained even though a consolidated return is not filed, section 301(e), supra, page 512, was amended by the 1987 Act to require a similar adjustment to the basis of stock where the selling corporation owns twenty percent or more of the stock of the subsidiary.

Section 1503(e) also provides that section 312(*l*)(1), which excludes from earnings and profits any discharge of indebtedness income that is excludable because the basis of property is reduced under section 1017, does not apply for purposes of computing the parent's basis in subsidiary stock upon a disposition. Where other tax attributes, such as net operating loss carryovers, are reduced by virtue of the exclusion of discharge of indebtedness income, earnings and profits are reduced.

2. *Loss Disallowance Rules*

In some cases, application of the investment adjustment rules conflicts with the principles of sections 311 and 336, discussed supra, pages 609 and 616, because they permit assets which are sold out of the consolidated group to obtain a step up in basis without the payment of a current corporate level tax. Suppose, for example, that S Corporation holds a single asset with a basis of $100 and a fair market value of $300. P Corporation purchases all of the stock of S Corporation for $300, and P and S Corporation elect to file a consolidated return. S Corporation then sells the asset for $300. S Corporation recognizes a $200 gain, and P Corporation increases its basis in the S Corporation stock from $300 to $500. P Corporation then sells the stock of S Corporation for $300, recognizing a $200 loss, which offsets the $200 gain. The tax on the sale of the assets effectively was eliminated by P Corporation's loss of the sale of the stock of S. This tax loss is artificial; it does not reflect any economic loss. The same problem arises if the asset is a depreciable asset which is consumed in the course of S Corporation's business.

A similar problem may arise where P Corporation forms S Corporation as a subsidiary and S Corporation thereafter incurs net operating losses which cannot be used currently on the consolidated return or S Corporation's assets decline in value. In this case, the economic loss at the subsidiary level has not resulted in any current tax deduction and the parent's basis for the subsidiary stock is not reduced. (Regulations, section 1.1502–29(b)(1)(ii) prevent a basis reduction for the unused NOL.) Accordingly, P Corporation would recognize a loss upon the sale of the stock of S Corporation. This loss is duplicated when after leaving the group, S Corporation uses its NOL or recognizes its unrealized losses.

Temporary Regulations, section 1.1502–20T, respond to these problems by disallowing *any* loss realized by any member of a consolidated group upon the disposition of the stock of a subsidiary. This broad rule applies to real economic losses as well as the artificial losses arising in the transactions described above. The loss disallowance rule does not apply, however, to the extent that gain also is recognized on the sale (such as where one block of stock is sold at a gain and another block is sold at a loss) or to the extent that the sale results in the recognition of deferred intercompany gain. Even though the loss on the sale of the subsidiary stock is disallowed as a deduction, the selling corporation nevertheless reduces its earnings and profits by the amount of the loss.

If an event other than a disposition causes the member of a group owning stock of another member of the group and the subsidiary to cease to be members of the same group ("deconsolidation"), then as a result of the deconsolidation, if the basis of the stock of the subsidiary is greater than its fair market value, the basis must be reduced to its fair market value immediately before the deconsolidation. Regulations, section 1.1502–20T(b).

Finally, Temporary Regulations, section 1.1502–20T(f), permit the parent of the group to elect to retain as a consolidated loss carryover of the group any loss incurred by a subsidiary which was not usable in the year incurred. However, the loss is treated as absorbed and for purposes of the investment adjustment rules the parent's basis in the stock of the subsidiary must be reduced by the amount of the loss. A double deduction thus is prevented.

D. OTHER ASPECTS OF CONSOLIDATED RETURNS

The materials in Chapters 16 and 17 considering sales and purchases of corporate enterprises under Subchapter C were written on the assumption that the corporations involved in the various transactions were not filing consolidated returns. In a sense, these Chapters could be rewritten entirely from the standpoint of corporations filing consolidated returns. Thus when consolidated returns are involved, the transactions we have examined so far must be reviewed against a new question: what special adjustments, if any, are required because of the fact that one or more of the parties to the transaction files consolidated returns? These issues and their resolution in the consolidated return context are complex and the following materials are intended to give some indication of the special problems raised in the corporate transactions considered in the preceding pages when consolidated returns are involved.

1. *Excess Loss Account*

Under Regulations, section 1.1502–11, the utilization by the consolidated group of the operating losses of a subsidiary is not limited by the group's current investment in the subsidiary. When the losses are utilized, however, the parent must, under Regulations, section 1.1502–32, make investment adjustments to its basis in the stock of the subsidiary and, when the deductions for the losses reduce the basis in the subsidiary stock below zero, a so-called "excess loss account" is established with respect to the subsidiary's stock. The excess loss account functions somewhat as a "negative basis" reflecting the fact that the group has been able to utilize current deductions in excess of the investment in the subsidiary.

The existence of an excess loss account has an important impact on a number of corporate transactions involving the stock of the subsidiary. For example, if the stock of the subsidiary later were simply sold to a third party outside the group, under Regulations, section 1.1502–19, the amount of gain realized by the parent on the transaction would include not only the sales proceeds received but also the amount of the parent's excess loss account for the subsidiary. The amount of gain on the sale resulting from the excess loss account is generally treated as capital gain if the stock is a capital asset. Arguably the gain attributable to the excess loss account should be treated as ordinary income when it represents deductions previously taken against ordinary income. However, the Regulations allow capital gain treatment apparently on the theory that, had the subsidiary realized the appreciation in its assets prior to the disposition, the earnings and profits so generated would have eliminated the excess loss account and this is in effect what is happening when the parent sells the stock at a gain. If the subsidiary were insolvent at the time of the disposition, however, then ordinary income results from the transaction. See Regulations, section 1.1502–19(a)(2)(ii). Covil Insulation Co. v. Commissioner, 65 T.C. 364 (1975), upheld the validity of Regulations, section 1.1502–19, and required the parent corporation to include as ordinary income the excess loss account with respect to a subsidiary whose stock had become worthless. Both the treatment of the stock's worthlessness as an income generating event with respect to the excess loss account and characterization of the gain as ordinary were "permissible exercise[s] of the rule-making power granted by section 1502."

The existence of an excess loss account also can affect transactions which would otherwise be tax-free. For example, the disposition of stock in a reorganization involving an unrelated corporation could trigger a recognition of gain if the subsidiary involved had generated an excess loss account. On the other hand, tax-free reorganizations within the group generally do not require the inclusion of the excess loss account in income; instead the excess loss account is applied to the stock received in the section 354 exchange, either reducing basis or adding to the excess loss account of that stock. A liquidation to which section 334(b) applies eliminates the excess loss account; here apparently the theory is that since the "normal" basis is eliminated in such a transaction, similar treatment should apply to the "negative" basis represented by the excess loss account. The transaction is in effect treated as if the parent had owned the subsidiary's assets directly from the beginning.

Other events such as the discontinuation of filing consolidated returns or the worthlessness of the stock of the subsidiary can also require the inclusion in income of the amount of the excess loss account. For example, in Garvey v. United States, 726 F.2d 1569 (Fed. Cir.1984), the parent corporation acquired stock of a subsidiary in a tax-free type (B) reorganization which resulted in a low carryover basis to the common parent. Subsequent to acquisition the subsidiary distributed $4.9 million in dividends out of pre-affiliation earnings and profits. Under Regulations, section 1.1502–32(b)(2)(iii)(b), the dividend distribution created an excess loss account which required the recognition of income when the group disaffiliated. The court rejected the taxpayer's argument that application of the Regulations unfairly created phantom income which, would not have existed had the group filed separate tax returns. The court pointed out that in electing consolidated treatment the taxpayer "must take the bitter with the sweet."[1]

2. *Deferred Intercompany Gain*

As in the case of excess loss accounts, deferred gain on intercompany transactions also can affect the income tax consequences of various corporate transactions. Under Regulations, section 1.1502–13(f)(1), deferred gain must generally be accounted for when either the selling member or the member which owns the property ceases to be a member of the group. Thus, the sale by the parent of the stock of its subsidiary or an otherwise tax-free reorganization outside the group might require the current inclusion in income of the relevant deferred intercompany gains. However, sale of the stock of a subsidiary within the group does not require recognition of deferred intercompany gain. Regulations, section 1.1502–13(f)(1). In Rev. Rul. 81–84, 1981–1 Cum. Bull. 451, the Service held that income realized on a sale of the stock of one member of the affiliated group to another because of the presence of an excess loss account represented deferred intercompany gain under Regulations, section 1.1502–13(c)(1). Thus, the selling member was allowed to defer recognition of the excess loss account attributable to stock of the transferred subsidiary.

Regulations, section 1.1502–14T, were added in 1988 to treat as deferred intercompany gain the gain realized by the distributing corporation under sections 311(b) and 336 on a distribution of appreciated property to a member of the consolidated group.[2] Deferred gain under this provision will be taken into account by the distributing corporation under the Regulations, section 1.1502–13(d) and (e), as the distributed property is depreciated or disposed of by the distributee.

1. Proposed Regulations, pending at the time of the *Garvey* transaction would have provided a basis adjustment in the case of a (B) reorganization. The court rejected the taxpayer's argument that the Commissioner was estopped from applying the existing Regulations, section 1.1502–32(b)(2)(iii)(b), because of the Proposed Regulation. When the Proposed Regulations were finalized in 1972, the relief for (B) reorganizations was not included.

2. The Regulations also apply to gain recognized under sections 341(f)(2) (gain recognized by an electing corporation under the collapsible corporation provisions), 453B (disposition of an installment obligation), and 1245 and 1250 (depreciation recapture).

3. *Earnings and Profits*

Special adjustments are required in the earnings and profits accounts of the parent corporation in a consolidated group to reflect the consolidated situation. If the parent of the group were not required to include in its earnings and profits the earnings and profits of subsidiaries in the group, a parent corporation with profitable subsidiaries and no earnings and profits of its own could make distributions to its stockholders on a tax-free basis under section 301 despite the fact that the group as a whole had current earnings. Beginning in 1976, Regulations, section 1.1502–33(c)(4), require that earnings and profits be computed on a consolidated basis even though the earnings have not been distributed by the subsidiary members of the group to the parent. Thus, the group's earnings and profits are consolidated in the parent for purposes of determining the extent to which distributions by the parent to its stockholders are dividends.

4. *Section 338*

Following a qualified stock acquisition and deemed sale under section 338, the target corporation bears the liability for any taxes generated by the deemed sale. However, section 338(h)(9) provides as a general rule that the target corporation in a section 338 transaction is not treated as a member of the selling affiliated group. Thus, tax liability for the deemed sale will not be reflected in the consolidated return of the selling group. Section 338(h)(10) provides a special rule under which, if the target was a member of a consolidated group prior to the sale, the parties can elect to have the transaction treated as if the target had sold its assets while a member of the selling consolidated group and the selling stockholder will recognize no gain on the sale of the target's stock. As a result, the selling stockholder will bear the tax liability for any gain recognized with respect to the section 338 sale. The existence of section 338(h)(10) allows the parties to keep the form of the transaction as a sale of stock but have the tax results of an asset sale. See supra, page 713.

Rev. Rul. 89–98, 1989–2, Cum. Bull. 219, holds that when a parent corporation has an excess loss account in a subsidiary's stock and the stock is sold in a transaction for which a section 338(h)(10) election is made, the excess loss account is eliminated rather than included in the parent's income. The section 338 transaction is treated as a deemed sale and section 332 liquidation for purposes of the consolidated return Regulations. The stock sale is ignored with the result that recognition of the excess loss account is not triggered.

5. *Mirror Transactions*

A transaction that engendered considerable controversy after the repeal of the *General Utilities* doctrine is the so-called "mirror transaction." The following example provides a simplified form of the mirror technique and the hoped for tax consequences prior to the 1987 Act. Suppose P Corporation decides to acquire T Corporation. T is a holding company with two operating subsidiaries, T–1 and T–2. The basis of the T–1 stock is $10, and the basis of the T–2 stock is $50. The fair market value of T–1 stock is $100 and the fair market value of T–2 stock is $200. The basis of T–1's assets is $10 and the basis of T–2's assets is $50. P desires to retain T–2 but does not want T–1. P, however, would like to avoid gain recognition on the disposition of T–1.

Accordingly, P forms two new subsidiaries, P–1 and P–2, contributing $100 in cash to P–1 and $200 in cash to P–2. Using the recently contributed cash, P–1 acquires one-third of the stock of T Corporation and P–2 acquires two-thirds of the stock of T Corporation. T Corporation is then liquidated, with the stock of T–1 going to P–1 and the stock of T–2 going to P–2. P–1 and P–2 could have qualified as 80 percent distributees under section 332 if the P group had made a consolidated return election. See Regulations, section 1.332–2(a) and 1.1502–34, which counted the members of an affiliated group as a single entity for purposes of the 80 percent control test of section 332. If the P group filed a consolidated return and made no section 338 election, then it was arguable before the 1987 Act that the liquidation was tax-free under sections 337 and 332, with the basis of T–1 and T–2 assets carrying over under section 334. P would then sell the stock of T–1 for $100 and recognize no gain or loss since its basis in the T–1 stock was $100. The basis of T–1 assets would remain $10. The same result might have been achieved before the 1987 Act under either section 304 or 355 by slightly altering the form of the transaction.

The 1987 Act amended sections 304, 337 and 355 to eliminate the possibility of using mirror transactions to achieve the above-described result. Section 337(c) provides that gain will be recognized on a liquidation distribution unless the 80 percent distributee requirement is satisfied by a corporation which *directly* owns 80 percent of the stock of the distributing corporation without regard to the consolidated return Regulations. The legislative history calls for Regulations to treat liquidation distributions to less than 80 percent distributees as a deferred intercompany transaction. H. Rep. No. 100–495, 100th Cong., 1st Sess. 968–969 (1987). Section 355(b)(2)(D), discussed supra, page 923, was amended to require as a prerequisite to the active trade or business requirement that control of the distributing corporation was not acquired in a taxable transaction within five years preceding a section 355 transaction. Section 304, discussed supra, page 592, was amended to require proper adjustments to stock basis and earnings and profits accounts in the case of a stock transfer subject to section 304(a) between members of an affiliated group.

E. REFERENCES

Lerner, Antes, Rosen, and Finkelstein, Federal Income Taxation of Corporations Filing Consolidated Returns (1988); Peel, Consolidated Tax Returns (1988); Crestol, Hennessey and Rua, The Consolidated Tax Return (1988); Dahlberg, Aggregate vs. Entity: Adjusting the Basis of Stock in a Subsidiary Filing a Consolidated Return, 42 Tax L. Rev. 547 (1987); Eisenberg, Consolidated Returns: Family Ties for Financial Gain, 64 Taxes 907 (1986); Axelrod, The Basis for Using E & P in Consolidated Return Basis Adjustments, 12 J. Corp. Tax'n 227 (1985); Symposium, Multiple Corporations: The Consolidated Return, 31 N.Y.U. Tax Inst. 451 (1973); Peel, The Consolidated Return Election—The Sword of Damocles, 28 N.Y.U. Tax Inst. 619 (1970).

PART IX

SPECIAL RULES TO PREVENT AVOIDANCE OF SHAREHOLDER LEVEL TAX

CHAPTER 25

PENALTY TAXES

INTRODUCTION

The Code contains three sets of provisions to prevent the use of a corporation to accumulate income in avoidance of progressive individual tax rates and to convert ordinary income at the corporate level into stockholder capital gain. First, the accumulated earnings tax of sections 531–537 imposes a penalty tax on corporate earnings which are accumulated beyond the reasonable needs of the business. Second, the personal holding company tax of sections 541–547 imposes a penalty tax on undistributed passive investment income of closely held holding companies. Finally, the collapsible corporation rules of section 341 are designed to prevent the conversion of unrealized corporate income into stockholder capital gain.

The changes in corporate income taxation brought about by the 1986 Act have rendered most aspects of the accumulated earnings tax, the personal holding company tax, and the collapsible corporation provisions obsolete. The modified flat-rate individual income tax, which is lower than the corporate tax rate, now discourages income accumulation at the corporate level. The absence of a preference for capital gains, at least for the time-being, and the requirement that corporate level built-in gain be taxed on liquidation of the corporation, eliminate the benefit of the collapsible corporation. Nonetheless, all three provisions remain in the Code and under some factual circumstances provide traps for the unwary. Perhaps the penalty provisions, especially the accumulated earnings tax, now best can be viewed as appropriate to accelerate full imposition of the two-level tax, but many believe they are no longer necessary.

SECTION 1: THE ACCUMULATED EARNINGS TAX

INTERNAL REVENUE CODE: Sections 531–537.

REGULATIONS: Sections 1.532–1(a); 1.533–1(a); 1.537–1(a), (b), –2, –3.

Sections 531 and 532 impose a tax of 28 percent on the "accumulated taxable income" of a corporation which has been formed or availed of for the purpose of avoiding the imposition of income tax on its shareholders, or the shareholders of another corporation, by permitting earnings and profits to accumulate instead of being distributed.[1] In Ivan Allen Company v. United States, 422 U.S. 617 (1975), the Court described the purpose and function of the accumulated earnings as follows:

"Under our system of income taxation, corporate earnings are subject to tax at two levels. First, there is the tax imposed upon the income of the corporation. Second, when the corporation, by way of a dividend, distributes its earnings to its shareholders, the distribution is subject to the tax imposed upon the income of the shareholders. Because of the disparity between the corporate tax rates and the higher gradations of the rates on individuals, a corporation may be utilized to reduce significantly its shareholders' overall tax liability by accumulating earnings beyond the reasonable needs of the business. Without some method to force the distribution of unneeded corporate earnings, a controlling shareholder would be able to postpone the full impact of income taxes on his share of the corporation's earnings in excess of its needs. * * *

"In order to foreclose this possibility of using the corporation as a means of avoiding the income tax on dividends to the shareholders, every revenue act since the adoption of the Sixteenth Amendment in 1913 has imposed a tax upon unnecessary accumulations of corporate earnings effected for the purpose of insulating shareholders.[8]

1. The constitutionality of the predecessor of the accumulated earnings tax, was sustained by the Supreme Court in Helvering v. National Grocery Co., 304 U.S. 282 (1938). The Court said that tax was on net income and the fact that the incidence was determined by a state of mind was not unknown to the tax field.

8. The accumulated earnings tax originated in § II A, Subdivision 2, of the Tariff Act of October 3, 1913, 38 Stat. 166. This imposed a tax on the shareholders of a corporation "formed or fraudulently availed of for the purpose of preventing the imposition of such tax through the medium of permitting such gains and profits to accumulate instead of being divided or distributed." Accumulations "beyond the reasonable needs of the business shall be prima facie evidence of a fraudulent purpose to escape such tax." Id., at 167. The same provision appeared as § 3 of the Revenue Act of 1916, 39 Stat. 758, and again as § 220 of the Revenue Act of 1918, 40 Stat. 1072 (1919), except that in the 1918 Act the word "fraudulently" was deleted. This change was effected inasmuch as the Senate felt that the former phraseology "has proved to be of little value, because it was necessary to its application that intended fraud on the revenue be established in each case." S.Rep. No. 617, 65th Cong., 3d Sess., 5 (1918).

This pattern of tax on the shareholders was changed with the Revenue Act of 1921, § 220, 42 Stat. 247. The incidence of the tax was shifted from the shareholders to the corporation itself. Judge Learned Hand opined that the change was due to doubts "as to the validity of taxing income which the taxpayers had never received, and in 1921 it was thought safer to tax the company itself." United Business Corp. v. Commissioner, 62 F.2d 754, 756 (CA2), cert. denied, 290 U.S. 635, 54 S.Ct. 53, 78 L.Ed. 552 (1933).

"The Court has acknowledged the obvious purpose of the accumulation provisions of the successive acts:

> 'As the theory of the revenue acts has been to tax corporate profits to the corporation, and their receipt only when distributed to the stockholders, the purpose of the legislation is to compel the company to distribute any profits not needed for the conduct of its business so that, when so distributed, individual stockholders will become liable not only for normal but for surtax on the dividends received.' Helvering v. Chicago Stock Yards Co., 318 U.S. 693, 699, 63 S.Ct. 843, 846, 87 L.Ed. 1086 (1943).

This was reaffirmed in United States v. Donruss Co., 393 U.S. 297, 303, 89 S.Ct. 501, 504, 21 L.Ed.2d 495 (1969).

"It is to be noted that the focus and impositions of the accumulated earnings tax is upon 'accumulated taxable income,' § 531. This is defined in § 535(a) to mean the corporation's 'taxable income,' as adjusted. The adjustments consist of the various items described in § 535(b), including federal income tax, the deduction for dividends paid defined in § 561, and the accumulated earnings credit defined in § 535(c). The adjustments prescribed by §§ 535(a) and (b) are designed generally to assure that a corporation's 'accumulated taxable income' reflects more accurately than 'taxable income' the amount actually available to the corporation for business purposes. This explains the deductions for dividends paid and for federal income taxes; neither of these enters into the computation of taxable income. Obviously, dividends paid and federal income taxes deplete corporate resources and must be recognized if the corporation's economic condition is to be properly perceived. Conversely, § 535(b)(3) disallows, for example, the deduction, available to a corporation for income tax purposes under § 243, on account of dividends received; dividends received are freely available for use in the corporation's business.

"The purport of the accumulated earnings tax structure established by §§ 531–537, therefore, is to determine the corporation's true economic condition before its liability for tax upon 'accumulated taxable income' is determined. The tax, although a penalty and therefore to be strictly construed, Commissioner v. Acker, 361 U.S. 87, 91, 80 S.Ct. 144, 147, 4 L.Ed.2d 127 (1959), is directed at economic reality.

* * *

"Accumulation beyond the reasonable needs of the business, by the language of § 533(a), is 'determinative of the purpose' to avoid tax with respect to shareholders unless the corporation proves the contrary by a preponderance of the evidence. The burden of proof, thus, is on the taxpayer. A rebuttable presumption is statutorily imposed. To be sure, we deal here, in a sense, with a state of mind. But it has been said that the statute, without the support of the presumption, would 'be practically unenforceable without it.' United Business Corp. v. Commissioner, 62 F.2d 754, 755 (CA2), cert. denied, 290 U.S. 635, 54 S.Ct. 53, 78 L.Ed. 552 (1933). What is required, then, is a comparison of accumulated earnings and profits with 'the reasonable needs of the

Although the statutory language has varied somewhat from time to time, the income tax law, since the change effected by the Revenue Act of 1921, consistently has imposed the tax on the corporation, rather than upon the shareholders. * * *

business.' Business *needs* are critical. And need, plainly, to use mathematical terminology, is a function of a corporation's liquidity, that is, the amount of idle current assets at its disposal. The question, therefore, is not how much capital of all sorts, but how much in the way of quick or liquid assets, it is reasonable to keep on hand for the business." (624–629)

Generally, the Commissioner has attempted to apply the accumulated earnings tax only to closely held corporations. The requirement that the corporation be formed or availed of to avoid shareholder tax is less likely to exist in the case of publicly owned companies. In some instances, the tax has been applied to widely held companies which were controlled by a small group of stockholders; [2] and the 1984 Act added section 532(c) to provide that the accumulated earnings tax is to be applied without regard to the number of stockholders.

ILLUSTRATIVE MATERIAL

A. THE RELATION BETWEEN THE PROSCRIBED ACCUMULATION "PURPOSE" AND THE REASONABLE NEEDS OF THE BUSINESS

In United States v. Donruss Co., 393 U.S. 297 (1969), the Court resolved a conflict as to whether, as urged by the Government, a taxpayer to rebut the presumption contained in section 533(a) must establish that tax avoidance with respect to the shareholders was not "one" of the purposes for the accumulation or whether, as some Courts of Appeals had held, the presumption could be rebutted by demonstrating that tax avoidance was not the "dominant, controlling, or impelling" purpose for the accumulation. The Court sustained the Government's position.

To understand the impact of the holding in *Donruss,* consider the situation of the taxpayer in that case on remand. Since the jury that decided the case below had already found that the accumulation was beyond the reasonable needs of the business, the presumption in section 533(a) that the purpose was to avoid income taxes with respect to the shareholders had been brought into play. It would thus now be up to the taxpayer to prove by a preponderance of the evidence the negative proposition that not one of the purposes of the accumulation was tax avoidance, an almost impossible task. Though the statute makes a finding of the proscribed purpose the crucial event for the imposition of the tax, the *Donruss* holding made the finding as to the reasonableness of the accumulation the determinative factor in the vast majority of cases. See e.g., Bahan Textile Machinery Co., Inc. v. United States, 453 F.2d 1100 (4th Cir.1972) (after an accumulation beyond the reasonable needs of the business was established, the taxpayer unsuccessfully tried to overcome the presumption as to purpose by showing that the controlling shareholder was "an overly cautious man, fearful of long-term

2. See Trico Products Corp. v. Commissioner, 137 F.2d 424 (2d Cir.1943) and Trico Products v. McGowan, 169 F.2d 343 (2d Cir.1948) (corporation owned by 2,000 stockholders but 74% of the stock was held by six stockholders). But in Golconda Mining Corp. v. Commissioner, 507 F.2d 594 (9th Cir.1974), the appellate court reversed the Tax Court's holding that the accumulated earnings tax was applicable to a corporation whose management group owned from 12% to 17% of the stock. The court held that the accumulated earnings tax could only apply where a relatively small group of stockholders exercised control, a situation which could exist only if a small group of stockholders owned more than 50% of the stock of the corporation.

debt and conservative in financial outlook"). Compare Bremerton Sun Publishing Co. v. Commissioner, 44 T.C. 566 (1965) ("Although we feel that the total accumulation was somewhat beyond the reasonable foreseeable business needs of petitioner, we are convinced that the only reason for the excessive retention of earnings was the conservative policies of the directors and not their concern for the surtax liability of [the shareholders]." (590)); Starman Investment, Inc. v. United States, 534 F.2d 834 (9th Cir.1976) (even if accumulation beyond reasonable needs, lack of tax avoidance motive precludes imposition of tax).

In Magic Mart, Inc. v. Commissioner, 51 T.C. 775 (1969), the court concluded that since accumulations beyond the reasonable needs of the business were not present, a finding as to the purpose of the accumulations was unnecessary in light of the credit in section 535(c) for reasonable accumulation, and the *Donruss* issue was not reached. In contrast to *Magic Mart,* some courts have apparently been of the view that, to escape tax, the accumulations, in addition to being reasonable in an objective sense, must have been *motivated* by business needs and not tax avoidance purposes. See Apollo Industries, Inc. v. Commissioner, 358 F.2d 867 (1st Cir.1966), remanding the case to the Tax Court for an answer to the following question: "[E]ven if accumulated earnings did not exceed reasonably anticipated business needs in one or both years, was avoidance of taxes on shareholders nevertheless a dominant purpose?" The Court of Appeals in *Donruss* apparently was of the same view (384 F.2d 292, 294 (6th Cir.1967)), though the cases it cited for this proposition were decided prior to the enactment of section 535(c). The Tax Court uniformly has taken the view that where the accumulations do not exceed the reasonable needs of the business so that a sufficient credit would be present quite apart from any issue as to the purpose for the accumulation, the issue as to the purpose of the accumulations is irrelevant. John P. Scripps Newspapers v. Commissioner, 44 T.C. 453 (1965); Dielectric Materials Co. v. Commissioner, 57 T.C. 587 (1972).

B. FACTORS BEARING ON REASONABLE BUSINESS NEEDS

1. *General*

Determining the "reasonable business needs" involves a complex factual inquiry into all aspects of the corporation's business. Courts generally start with the statement that they are reluctant to substitute their judgment for the business judgment of the management as to the need for the accumulations (see e.g., Dielectric Materials Co. v. Commissioner, 57 T.C. 587 (1972)), and then proceed with an exhaustive analysis of the corporation's financial and business history. While the cases are not easily classified, each turning on its own facts, they typically involve the factors discussed below.

2. *Accumulations for Expansion or Diversification*

(a) *Expansion*

The expansion or replacement of existing business facilities often is given as a justification for accumulations. Regulations, section 1.537–1(b)(1), require that the corporation "must have specific, definite, and feasible plans for the use of such accumulations." The courts have applied this requirement with varying degrees of strictness. See, e.g., Faber Cement Block Co., Inc. v. Commissioner, 50 T.C. 317 (1968) (A) (taxpayer's operations on its property constituted a nonconforming use under the local zoning ordinances and any expansion would have required an additional variance; accumulations over a long period of time for a proposed expansion were justified).

(b) *Diversification*

In addition to expansion of facilities, accumulations often are justified on the ground that they are needed to diversify the existing business. Regulations, section 1.537–3(a), define the "business" of a corporation very broadly as "not merely that which it has previously carried on but includ[ing], in general, any line of business which it may undertake." On the other hand, investments which are "unrelated" to the activities of the business of the taxpayer are an indication of unreasonable accumulations, Regulations, section 1.537–2(c)(4), and the line between an "unrelated investment" and the beginning of a new "business" is not a clear one. See, e.g., Electric Regulator Corp. v. Commissioner, 336 F.2d 339 (2d Cir.1964) (taxpayer produced a small patented voltage regulator which was quite successful commercially, resulting in large accumulated profits; taxpayer's justification for the accumulation based on the desire to develop new products was sustained); Hughes Inc. v. Commissioner, 90 T.C. 1 (1988) (purchase of an orange grove and interests in partnerships holding real estate were justified as part of efforts to diversify the business of owning and leasing improved real and tangible personal properties); J. Gordon Turnbull, Inc. v. Commissioner, 41 T.C. 358 (1963) (fact that an architectural and engineering firm invested large sums in real estate was found indicative of an accumulation beyond the reasonable needs of its business); Cataphote Corp. of Miss. v. United States, 535 F.2d 1225 (Ct. Cl.1976) (acquisition of 26 fractional working interests in oil and gas ventures by a corporation in the truck leasing business did not mean that the corporation was also in the oil and gas business for accumulated earnings tax purposes; the corporation did not have the necessary business responsibilities and the interests constituted mere investments unrelated to the active business of the corporation).

(c) *Valuation Aspects*

In Ivan Allen v. United States, 422 U.S. 617 (1975), supra, page 1064, the issue was whether in determining the reasonable needs of the business marketable securities owned by the corporation should be counted at cost, as the taxpayer asserted, or their net liquidation value as claimed by the Commissioner. The Court pointed out that the accumulated earnings tax itself is imposed only on accumulated taxable income, which includes only realized gains. The Court held, however, that in determining whether accumulations exceed the reasonable needs of the business the full value of readily available liquid assets should be taken into account.

The decision of the Supreme Court in *Ivan Allen* was correct from the standpoint of the policy behind the accumulated earnings tax. The actual value which the corporation could realize from its investments and distribute to its shareholders is the best measure of the amount and reasonableness of its total accumulation; the cost basis of the investments is not relevant to that determination. Nevertheless, taxpayers, the Internal Revenue Service, and the lower courts may experience some problems in implementing the Court's decision. The majority in *Ivan Allen* assumed that the proper time for valuation of the securities was the end of the taxable year of the corporation. In some instances, other dates, e.g., the date on which the Board of Directors makes its dividend decision for the year, might be more appropriate. There are also some technical problems. In other areas of the tax law, valuation of securities is made by taking a "blockage" factor into account, i.e., the size of the block of stock held by a particular shareholder can reduce the total value below a fair market value based on the quoted per share value because a single sale of the entire stock would depress the market. Valuation of closely held stock will present similar difficulties.

In footnote 5 of the *Ivan Allen* opinion, the majority noted that fair market value was stipulated by the parties on the basis of the market price minus the costs of selling and minus the capital gains tax that would be incurred on the sale. While the reduction for the selling costs is appropriate, it is less clear that the capital gain tax should be subtracted. What if, for example, the taxpayer had capital losses for the year in question sufficient to offset the unrealized appreciation?

The majority in *Ivan Allen* went to some length to emphasize that its opinion was directed toward "readily marketable portfolio securities." But, as the dissenters pointed out, the majority's "rationale is not so easily contained." If a corporation holds securities which are not readily marketable but are still unrelated to its business, the majority's reasoning appears equally applicable; the lack of marketability or difficulties in disposition would be relevant to the valuation issue but do not lead to the conclusion that cost basis should be employed. Likewise, a finding that investments in real estate, timber land, and other such assets are unrelated to the business of the corporation should call into play the fair market value approach adopted by the majority.

In footnote 9 of the opinion, the majority stated that it was expressing no view with respect to the valuation of items such as inventory or accounts receivable. Motor Fuel Carriers, Inc. v. Commissioner, 559 F.2d 1348 (5th Cir.1977), held that accounts receivable should be treated as liquid assets for accumulated earnings tax purposes and valued at fair market value.

3. *Working Capital Needs*

Regulations, section 1.537–2(b)(4), recognize the need to accumulate earnings "to provide necessary working capital for the business." The courts have struggled to develop standards for the determination of a reasonable allowance for working capital. The older cases allowed an accumulation of working capital to cover some arbitrary period of time, such as one year, or stressed the relationship between current liabilities and current assets in assessing working capital needs. The more recent cases, following the approach taken initially in Bardahl Mfg. Corp. v. Commissioner, 24 T.C.M. 1030 (1965), attempt to relate the corporation's need for working capital to its "operating cycle." In J.H. Rutter Rex Mfg. Co. v. Commissioner, 853 F.2d 1275 (5th Cir.1988), the court described the operating cycle approach as follows:

"An operating cycle for a manufacturing business like Rutter Rex is the period of time needed to convert cash into raw materials, raw materials into inventory, inventory into accounts receivable, and accounts receivable into cash. In other words, an operating cycle is the time a corporation's working capital is tied up in producing and selling its product. * * *

"The 'operating cycle' as originally formulated in *Bardahl Manufacturing* is broken down into two sub-cycles: an inventory cycle and an accounts receivable cycle. These cycles are measured in terms of days. An inventory cycle is the time necessary to convert raw materials into finished goods and to sell those goods. An accounts receivable cycle is the time necessary to convert the accounts receivable created by the sale of finished goods into cash. These two cycles are added together to determine the total number of days in the operating cycle. The number of days in the operating cycle is then divided by 365; the resulting fraction is multiplied by the amount of the corporation's operating expenses for one year, including costs of goods sold, selling expenses, general and administrative expenses, and estimated federal and state income tax payments (but excluding depreciation). The resulting figure is the amount of liquid assets necessary to meet the ordinary operating expenses for the complete operating cycle." (1286–1288.)

The *Bardahl* formula is also applied by taking account of a credit cycle. The credit cycle is based on the amount of time between the corporation's receipt of raw materials, supplies, labor, and other inputs, and the corporation's payment for these things. The deferral of payment reduces the corporation's need for capital and thus the credit cycle is subtracted from the operating cycle determined from inventory and receivables cycles. See C.E. Hooper, Inc. v. United States, 539 F.2d 1276 (Ct.Cl.1976). In *J.H. Rutter Rex Mfg. Co.,* supra, the taxpayer convinced the appellate court that application of a credit cycle to reduce its working capital needs was inappropriate because of the lack of evidence that the corporation utilized an extension of credit from its major suppliers to any significant degree.

Despite the seeming exactness of the operating cycle formula, its limitations must be recognized. See Dielectric Materials Co. v. Commissioner, 57 T.C. 587 (1972) (*Bardahl* formula not sufficiently "flexible" to take into account the fact that taxpayer had additional working capital needs in the light of a threatened labor dispute); Ready Paving and Construction Co. v. Commissioner, 61 T.C. 826 (1974) ("special investment warrants" received as payment for contracting work done for municipal governments constituted assets available for use as working capital under the *Bardahl* formula; correspondingly, the warrants did not constitute accounts receivable for determining the amount of accumulated earnings needed for working capital; consistent treatment of the items was required in both aspects of the *Bardahl* formula).

4. *Provision for Contingencies*

Fears, both real and imagined, of contingent liabilities also have been used to justify accumulations of earnings. In Halby Chemical Co., Inc. v. United States, 180 Ct.Cl. 584 (1967), the court allowed accumulations for self-insurance against the "enduring possibility of a disastrous fire or explosion" which could not adequately be covered by insurance because of the riskiness of taxpayer's operations. In Hughes Inc. v. Commissioner, 90 T.C. 1 (1988), a closely held corporation which rented warehouses to a publicly held corporation used accumulated earnings to purchase stock of the public corporation in order to prevent a hostile takeover of its lessee. The court said that investments in marketable securities which bear some relationship to a corporation's business are considered a proper business application of funds and may be accumulated with impunity. On the other hand, in Oyster Shell Products Corp. v. Commissioner, 313 F.2d 449 (2d Cir.1963), the taxpayer unsuccessfully attempted to justify accumulations on the ground that possible flooding of the river on which its operations were located could result in large expenses; the court rejected the argument as "conjured up" after the accumulated earnings tax issue was first raised by the Government.

Section 537(b)(4) specifically provides for the accumulation of a reserve for reasonably anticipated product liability losses.

5. *Accumulations to Fund Stock Redemptions*

If a redemption is treated as a dividend under section 301, no accumulated earnings tax issue arises since the distribution is fully taxed at the shareholder level. But redemptions taxed under section 302(b) and section 303 are not treated as dividends and thus raise an accumulated earnings tax issue. Pelton Steel Casting Co. v. Commissioner, 251 F.2d 278 (7th Cir. 1958), held that the accumulated earnings tax applied where the corporation accumulated income to redeem the stock of two of its three shareholders rather than paying its earnings out as dividends to all of the shareholders and, presumably, then redeeming the stock at a lower price. The purpose of the redemption was to prevent the redeemed shareholders from selling their stock to outsiders, which was found not to be a corporate business purpose.

Mountain State Steel Foundries, Inc. v. Commissioner, 284 F.2d 737 (4th Cir.1960), held that the accumulated earnings tax did not apply to earnings in 1951 through 1954 used to pay a promissory note issued by the corporation in redemption of 50 percent of its shares in 1950. The Court emphasized that there was a business purpose for the redemption because the redeemed shareholders, who were inactive, had conflicting interests regarding corporate management with the continuing shareholders, who were active.

Is a business purpose such as was found in *Mountain State Steel Foundries* sufficient to justify a preredemption accumulation, as occurred in *Pelton Steel Casting Co.*? The lower courts have found a proper "corporate purpose" sufficient to avoid the accumulated earnings tax in a number of situations involving minority shareholders or retiring employee-shareholders. See Ted Bates & Co., Inc. v. Commissioner, 24 T.C.M. 1346 (1965) (redemption made in order to assure "continuity of [taxpayer's] management"); Farmers & Merchants Investment Co. v. Commissioner, 29 T.C.M. 705 (1970) ("promotion of harmony in the conduct of the business"). In contrast, accumulations to redeem uncontentious large shareholders have been held subject to the tax. See John B. Lambert & Associates v. United States, 76–2 U.S.T.C. ¶ 9776 (Ct.Cl.1976); Lamark Shipping Agency, Inc. v. Commissioner, 42 T.C.M. 38 (1981).

Section 537(a)(2) specifically provides that accumulations to fund redemptions which qualify under section 303 are to meet the reasonable need of the business. However, section 537(b)(1) limits qualification under this rule to accumulations in the year the shareholder dies and subsequent years. Accumulations in years prior to the year of death cannot be justified by subsequent use for a section 303 redemption. See S.Rep. No. 91–522, 91st Cong., 1st Sess. 291 (1969).

6. *Shareholder Loans, Dividend Record and Shareholder Tax Bracket*

While the fact that the corporation has paid no dividends is, of course, not conclusive on the issue of the proscribed purpose, it is a factor. Failure to pay dividends together with loans to shareholders by the corporation indicate an availability of funds to make dividend distributions. See, e.g.,

Bahan Textile Machinery, Co. v. United States, 453 F.2d 1100 (4th Cir. 1972) (loans to shareholders and relatives "show not only that the company was dissipating funds which it claimed were needed for the business, but also indicated a purpose to distribute corporate profits indirectly rather than as dividends that would be taxable to the recipients").

In GPD, Inc. v. Commissioner, 60 T.C. 480 (1973), rev'd, 508 F.2d 1076 (6th Cir.1974), the Tax Court held that the corporation was subject to the accumulated earnings tax for a year in which there had been a decrease in the corporation's earnings and profits. The Tax Court took the position that since there was no accumulation of earnings and profits, the accumulated earnings tax could not apply, even though in that year, the corporation did have accumulated taxable income under section 535.[3] The Court of Appeals reversed the Tax Court and held that the legislative history of the accumulated earnings tax did not show any intent to require the accumulations of earnings and profits in the current year as a condition precedent to the imposition of the tax. The Court of Appeals observed that if the Tax Court position were adopted, and a corporation distributed the exact amount of its earnings and profits for a year, no accumulated earnings tax could be imposed on accumulated taxable income of the corporation in that year; on the other hand, one cent of undistributed earnings and profits for the year would subject the entire accumulated taxable income to the tax. Moreover, the Court of Appeals observed that the Tax Court rule in effect gave a corporation a double accumulated earnings tax credit, since a corporation would be protected both in the year of accumulation and also in the year in which the actual redemption reduced earnings and profits.

Atlantic Properties, Inc. v. Commissioner, 519 F.2d 1233 (1st Cir. 1975), involved a corporation owned by four equal shareholders but whose corporate charter required an 80 percent vote of the shareholders for any corporate action. Three of the shareholders desired to have the corporation adopt a policy of dividend distributions; one shareholder did not, in part because of the adverse tax consequences of the dividend distribution to him. The court held that the accumulated earnings tax applied since the corporation was availed of for a proscribed purpose, even though a majority of the shareholders did not agree with that purpose.

7. *Accumulations by and for Subsidiaries*

Regulations, section 1.537–3(b), provide that under certain circumstances the accumulated earnings of a parent corporation may be justified by the reasonably anticipated business needs of its subsidiary. In the converse situation, the Court of Appeals in Inland Terminals, Inc. v. United States, 477 F.2d 836 (4th Cir.1973), held that it was also possible to justify a controlled subsidiary's accumulated earnings with reference to the parent corporation's reasonably anticipated business needs which the parent corporation itself could not satisfy. On remand, the District Court held that the parent corporation's alternative diversification or relocation plans were such as would take all or substantially all of its own earnings and those of the subsidiary; thus the combined earnings of the two corporations did not exceed the reasonable needs of the parent's business. 73–2 U.S.T.C. ¶ 9724 (D.Md.1973).

3. Accumulated taxable income was present despite a reduction in earnings and profits because of stock redemptions, not being dividends, had no effect on the determination of accumulated taxable income.

In Chaney & Hope, Inc. v. Commissioner, 80 T.C. 263 (1983), the court held that accumulations for the business needs of a brother or sister corporation cannot generally be considered as accumulations to meet reasonable business needs because the business of the sister corporation is not the business of the corporation. The court also held, however, that the taxpayer could accumulate its earnings to meet the reasonably anticipated future needs of an expanded business to be conducted by its successor corporation, a sister corporation into which the taxpayer would be merged. Permissible accumulations were limited to earnings accumulated after the time plans for the merger became definite.

Suppose a parent corporation has no current or accumulated earnings and profits of its own but has a subsidiary with profitable operations. If the subsidiary distributed dividends to the parent which in turn paid dividends to its individual shareholders, the earnings and profits created for the parent by the receipt of the dividends would make the distributions paid to its individual shareholders taxable as dividends. If, rather than having the subsidiary pay dividends, the parent corporation borrows funds secured by the stock of the subsidiary and distributes the loan proceeds to its shareholders, the distributions would be tax-free to the individual shareholders under section 301(c)(2). Regulations proposed in 1968, but later withdrawn, attempted to meet this problem by providing that the subsidiary in this situation would be deemed to have been availed of for the purpose of avoiding tax with respect to the shareholders of the parent corporation.

C. PROCEDURAL ASPECTS

In addition to the presumptions in section 533, discussed above, section 534 sets forth a complicated allocation of the burden of proof on certain issues in proceedings in the Tax Court. The provision is intended to lighten the burden on the taxpayer faced with an accumulated earnings tax case. See, Senate Finance Committee Report, S.Rep. No. 83–1622, 83rd Cong., 2d Sess. 70–71 (1954).

The provision, however, has not been of much help to taxpayers because the Tax Court has been quite strict regarding the required content of the taxpayer's statement under section 534(c). It must contain adequate factual material and not simply "conclusory" statements. See, J.H. Rutter Rex Mfg. Co. v. Commissioner, 853 F.2d 1275, 1283 (5th Cir.1988), where the taxpayer's statement was found wanting because of its failure to quantify working capital needs and provide financial information supporting its claim. "Obviously the statute does not contemplate shifting the burden of proof when a taxpayer merely tells the Commissioner it is going to challenge the imposition of the accumulated earnings tax. There must be notice of the specific grounds and contentions." See also, Hughes Inc. v. Commissioner, supra, 90 T.C. 1 (1988) (taxpayer provided sufficient detail which, if proven, would support the alleged business needs for the accumulation with respect to some but not all of the grounds asserted).

Sections 561–563 provide a deduction for dividends paid within two and one-half months of the close of the taxable year, which dividends reduce the taxpayer's accumulated earnings and profits for the prior year for purposes of the accumulated earnings tax.

D. REFERENCES

Herwitz, Stock Redemptions and the Accumulated Earnings Tax, 74 Harv.L.Rev. 866 (1961); Doernberg, the Accumulated Earnings Tax: The Relationship Between Earnings and Profits and Accumulated Taxable Income in a Redemption Transaction, 34 U.Fla.L.Rev. 715 (1982); Horvitz and Hebble, The Effect of the Section 531 Penalty Tax on Accumulations of Earnings and Profits after TRA 86, 14 J.Corp. Tax'n 236 (1987); Kwall, Subchapter G of the Internal Revenue Code: Crusade Without a Cause? 5 Va.Tax Rev. 223 (1985).

SECTION 2. THE PERSONAL HOLDING COMPANY TAX

INTERNAL REVENUE CODE: Sections 541–547; 6501(f).

ILLUSTRATIVE MATERIAL

A. PERSONAL HOLDING COMPANY TAX GENERALLY

Section 541 imposes a special tax on the undistributed personal holding company income of a corporation which qualifies as a personal holding company. A corporation is classified as a personal holding company under section 542(a) if at least 60 percent of its adjusted ordinary gross income is personal holding company income and more than 50 percent in value of its stock is directly or indirectly owned by five or fewer individuals.

Historically, the personal holding company tax has been imposed on corporate income at the highest individual tax rate. The 1981 Act reduced the rate from 70 percent to 50 percent as a corollary to the reduction of the top individual marginal rate from 70 to 50 percent. Likewise, the 1986 Act reduced the personal holding company tax to 28 percent for taxable years beginning on or after January 1, 1988.

The tax operates as an automatic obstacle to corporate accumulations intended to avoid the individual tax on the shareholders, since it does not turn on the need, reasonableness, or purpose of an accumulation but instead is applied if its objective conditions are met. After 1986, the corporate tax structure no longer provides an inducement to accumulate earnings at corporate rates which, at 34 percent, are higher than the top individual marginal rate. Nonetheless, a closely held corporation with personal holding company income still may be subject to the penalty tax. Even an apparent operating company may unexpectedly find itself with a sufficiently high proportion of personal holding company income to trigger the tax. See Eller v. Commissioner, 77 T.C. 934 (1981). Similarly, an active corporation which is in the process of liquidating and selling its assets can become a personal holding company by virtue of the passive investment income that is generated by investments of the sales proceeds prior to distribution in liquidation. See Lachinski v. Commissioner, 51 T.C.M. 1665 (1986) (interest on installment sale of active business received pending liquidation triggered personal holding company tax; the court rejected the taxpayer's argument that personal holding company income is limited to passive rather than active income).

profits. Also the concept of "accumulation" is essentially absent from the personal holding company tax. On the other hand, if the corporation is a personal holding company, the accumulated earnings tax does not apply. Section 532(b)(1). But, as noted above, a corporation that avoids personal holding company status must still face the possibility that its accumulations will be reached under the accumulated earnings tax.

An active manufacturing company with some investment income may fall accidentally into personal holding company status. For manufacturing companies, "gross income" is not "gross receipts," but instead constitutes gross receipts less cost of goods sold. Thus, in a bad year in which the cost of goods sold exceeded gross receipts, the corporation might find itself with less than 40 percent of its adjusted ordinary gross income from non-personal holding income sources.

The at-risk provisions of section 465, limiting the taxpayer's ability to take deductions in connection with nonrecourse financing, apply to "closely held" corporations which meet the stock ownership requirements of section 542(a)(2). This in turn can have an impact on the calculation of adjusted ordinary gross income and thus on the status of the corporation as a personal holding company.

F. REFERENCES

Cook and Allen, *Eller* Considered: Are Substantial Services Irrelevant in Determining Personal Holding Company Rents, 10 J. Corp. Tax'n 139 (1983); Baumann, Jr., Deficiency Dividends and Other Solutions for Avoiding Personal Holding Company Tax, 59 J. Tax'n 202 (1983); Pratt and Wittenburg, Understanding and Avoiding the Personal Holding Company Tax: A Tax Planning Model, 53 Taxes 359 (1975); Harris, Recognizing Personal Holding Company Income: Section 543(a), 54 Taxes 646 (1976); Loening, Personal Holding Companies: Re–Viewing an Old Problem; New Implications, 29 N.Y.U. Tax Inst. 815 (1971); Liles, A New Look at Personal Holding Company Problems: The New Rules of the 1964 Act, 24 N.Y.U. Tax Inst. 863 (1966); Libin, Personal Holding Companies and the Revenue Act of 1964, 63 Mich. L. Rev. 421 (1965).

SECTION 3. COLLAPSIBLE CORPORATIONS

INTERNAL REVENUE CODE: Section 341.

ILLUSTRATIVE MATERIAL

A. SECTION 341 IN GENERAL

1. *General*

The collapsible corporation provisions of section 341 are intended to prevent a sale of corporate stock at capital gains rates before the corporation has realized the income from its activities. Section 341 provides in general that any gain recognized on the sale, exchange, or liquidation of the stock of a collapsible corporation (or on a distribution with respect to stock subject to section 301(c)(3)), which otherwise would be treated as capital gain, shall be treated as ordinary income. A collapsible corporation is defined in section 341(b) as a corporation formed or availed of principally for the manufacture, construction, production, or purchase of certain types of property (mostly ordinary income property), with a view to the sale or exchange by the shareholders of their stock, or to the liquidation of the corporation (its collapse), before the realization by the corporation of two-thirds of the income to be derived from the property. Clearly the threat of ordinary income treatment for capital gains is of little concern in the absence of a capital gains preference.

2. *Historical Background*

O'Brien v. Commissioner, 25 T.C. 376 (1955), illustrates the problem which originally led to enactment of section 341. The taxpayers, Pat O'Brien and Phil L. Ryan, were a movie actor and director interested in acquiring rights to the story "Pile Buck" for purposes of making a motion picture. O'Brien and Ryan, along with a third person, formed a corporation with cash contributions totalling $12,500. The corporation employed O'Brien to star in the picture, employed Ryan as the producer, hired actors and a director, entered into a distribution agreement with Columbia Pictures, and obtained bank financing for production costs. After completion of the film, the corporation was liquidated. The corporation's film rights, including the right to payments from Columbia under the distribution contract, were distributed to the taxpayers as a liquidation distribution. The taxpayers reported the difference between the value of the film rights and their basis in corporate stock as a capital gain.[11] The Commissioner asserted that the corporation was taxable on income earned from the motion picture under assignment of income principles and, as an alternative, that the corporation should recognize gain on distribution of the film rights under Commissioner v. Court Holding Company, 324 U.S. 331 (1945), supra, page 690, as if it had sold the movie rights before liquidation. The Tax Court refused to ignore the fact that the corporation had been liquidated before earning the income which the Commissioner sought to tax to it and rejected the Commissioner's position.[12] As a result, by collapsing the corporation before it earned income from production of the film, the taxpayers converted the corporation's earnings into capital gain of the stockholders.

Section 341 is a statutory attempt to cope with the tax avoidance potentials of the collapsible corporation device. The section first appeared in 1950 limited in its scope to what is now the "manufacture, construction or production" aspect of section 341(b). As such, the section was aimed at the single motion picture or real estate venture. In 1951 the section was amended to include the "purchase" aspect of section 341(b) so as to cover situations in which appreciated inventory, such as whiskey, was transferred to a corporation and the stock of the corporation then sold. In 1954 the presumptions of section 341(c) were added, making the section applicable where the corporation held inventory, unrealized receivables, or section 1231 assets which had appreciated 20 percent in value and which assets represented 50 percent of the total assets, unless the taxpayer could prove under section 341(b) that the corporation was not formed or availed of for the proscribed

11. This transaction was viable because when it occurred, the *General Utilities* doctrine, discussed supra, page 472, provided nonrecognition to the corporation with respect to any gain realized on the liquidating distribution.

12. The taxpayers also asserted that payments from Columbia Pictures in excess of the fair market value of the distributed film rights were capital gains. The Tax Court treated the payments as ordinary income by pointing out that the value of the contract rights distributed in liquidation was fixed. Since the liquidation was a closed transaction, payments in excess of the fixed value of the liquidation distribution were not received as liquidation distributions.

purpose. This addition attempts to replace the subjective test of section 341(b) with the objective criteria of section 341(c). In the case of a corporation with LIFO inventory, these rules can make the corporation collapsible though it has been in existence for many years. Regulations, sections 1.341–5(c)(1), and Rev.Rul. 56–244, 1956–1 Cum.Bull. 176, temper this result by finding a non-collapsible status if the volume of inventory is at an average level at the time of liquidation. The 1954 changes also extended the "purchase" aspect of section 341(b) to section 1231(b) assets, i.e., land and depreciable assets used in trade or business but not held for sale to customers. The provision apparently was aimed at improved real estate held for rental income but it also extends to television and motion picture films, patents, copyrights, and natural resources land, all of which would not necesarily require manufacturing, construction or production activity and which could appreciate in value over a short period. Also in 1954, the escape clause of section 341(d) for minority stockholders was lowered from 10 percent of stock ownership to 5 percent. The section 341(e) exception discussed below was added in 1958. In 1964, a further exception was added in section 341(f), discussed below. In 1984 section 341(b)(1)(A) was amended to replace the requirement that the corporation realize a "substantial part" of the income attributable to collapsible property, with an objective requirement that the corporation realize ⅔ of the income to be derived from collapsible property.

After 1986, the abuse targeted by section 341 is no longer possible. The requirement of section 336 that built-in gain be recognized by the distributing corporation on a liquidation and the elimination of preferential treatment for capital gains destroy the incentive to form or use a collapsible corporation. Nonetheless, the 1986 Act retains the collapsible corporation provisions, perhaps in anticipation of the return of the capital gains preference.

3. *General Scope*

The remedy of section 341 for the tax avoidance potential of the collapsible corporation is to treat the entire gain realized by the shareholder on the sale of the stock or liquidation of the corporation as ordinary income. This overshoots the mark to the extent that a portion of the gain, if realized at the corporate level, would have been capital gain or would not have been gain from collapsible activity. Section 341(d)(2) compensates for this defect to a limited extent by providing that section 341 is inapplicable unless more than 70 percent of the stockholder gain is attributable to the collapsible property. In addition, ordinary income will not result to the stockholder if two-thirds of the collapsible gain has been realized at the corporate level. Section 341(b)(1)(A). Hence, the price of avoidance of ordinary gain to the stockholder is ordinary gain to the corporation followed by capital gain to the stockholders.

Section 341 bristles with words and phrases whose applicability depends largely on the facts of the particular case: "formed or availed of principally for the purpose of;" "with a view to;" "gain attributable to the property so produced." As a consequence it has an *in terrorem* effect which restrains some adventures in tax avoidance, but it also may inhibit some transactions motivated by genuine business considerations.

Section 341 is not by its terms exclusive. Hence the Commissioner could resort to other arguments if a case does not fall within section 341.

But as the *O'Brien* decision indicates, the Commissioner's chances of success are not high in view of both the adoption of section 341 itself and the considerable detail with which the rules of that section are formulated. Many courts, disliking the escape from tax presented by the collapsible device, however, have seized on section 341 to find ordinary gain and appeared quite willing to give a favorable interpretation, from the Government's viewpoint, to the details of the section, although there were limits to this general statement. See e.g. Commissioner v. Kelley, 293 F.2d 904 (5th Cir.1961), interpreting the "substantial part" language of section 341(b)(1)(A) before amendment in 1984 to require realization of only one-third of the taxable income to be derived from collapsible property.

4. *Absence of Tax Avoidance Motive*

Taxpayers initially asserted that section 341 did not apply where the stockholders would have been entitled to capital gain treatment had they realized the gain in their individual capacities without employing the corporate form. This argument was accepted in United States v. Ivey, 294 F.2d 799 (5th Cir.1961), but rejected in Braunstein v. Commissioner, 305 F.2d 949 (2d Cir.1962). The Supreme Court resolved the issue in favor of the Commissioner in Braunstein v. Commissioner, 374 U.S. 65 (1963), a case involving the construction of a single apartment building for sale, with the stockholder not in the business of selling apartment buildings:

"There is nothing in the language or structure of the section to demand or even justify reading into these provisions the *additional* requirement that the taxpayer must in fact have been using the corporate form as a device to convert ordinary income into capital gain. If a corporation owns but one asset, and the shareholders sell their stock at a profit resulting from an increase in the value of the asset, they have 'gain attributable to' that asset in the natural meaning of the phrase regardless of their desire, or lack of desire, to avoid the bite of federal income taxes." (70)

B. TECHNICAL ASPECTS OF SECTION 341

1. *The "View" Requirement*

(a) *Must the Intent Be Principally to Collapse the Corporation or Principally to Manufacture, Construct, etc.*

The courts have held that while there must be a "view" to "collapse" the corporation, the requisite *principal* intent need only be to manufacture, construct, etc., the collapsible asset rather than to possess a view to engage in tax avoidance through the collapse of the corporation. In Weil v. Commissioner, 252 F.2d 805, 806 (2d Cir.1958) the court said, "We read the word 'principally' as modifying the phrase 'manufacture, construction, or production of property * * *.' Under this reading, the corporation may be treated as collapsible if 'manufacture, construction, or production' was a principal corporate activity even if the 'view to' collapse was not the principal corporate objective when the corporation was 'formed or availed of * * *.'" Burge v. Commissioner, 253 F.2d 765 (4th Cir.1958), and Mintz v. Commissioner, 284 F.2d 554 (2d Cir.1960), are in accord; see also Regulations, section 1.341–5(b)(3).

The Internal Revenue Service ordinarily will not issue an advance ruling on the issue whether a corporation is a collapsible corporation, that is whether it was formed or availed of with the requisite view, but will rule if the corporation has been in existence for at least twenty years or can demonstrate that it has realized two-thirds of the taxable income to be derived from collapsible property, and, during the twenty year period, has had substantially the same owners and has conducted substantially the same trade or business. Rev. Proc. 90–3, I.R.B. 1990–1, 54, section 4.01, par. 23.

(b) *Time at Which Collapsible View Must Be Held*

Regulations, section 1.341–2(a)(3), state that if the requisite "view" exists at any time during the manufacture, construction, etc., the section is satisfied. Thus the view need not exist before the collapsible activity is started but it must exist before it is completed. Some courts have thought the Treasury's interpretation too restrictive from the Government's standpoint, as the following excerpt from Glickman v. Commissioner, 256 F.2d 108 (2d Cir.1958), indicates:

"[The taxpayers] contend that * * * the requisite 'view' must exist when the corporation is formed or at least when construction is begun. We agree with Judge Parker's statement in [Burge v. Commissioner, 253 F.2d 765 (4th Cir., 1958)]: 'It is not necessary that the "view" exist when the corporation is formed. It is sufficient that it exist when the corporation is "availed of" * * *.' Since the corporation may at any time during its corporate life be 'availed of' for the proscribed purpose, subject, of course, to the limitations imposed by [section 341(b)(1)], it seems surprising that the Regulations have adopted a narrower interpretation of the statute, and require the requisite view to exist 'during the construction * * *' or to be 'attributable' to 'circumstances which reasonably could be anticipated at the time of such * * * construction.' We are disposed to disagree with so narrow an interpretation, but whether the Regulation is valid need not be determined now." (111) See also Sidney v. Commissioner, 273 F.2d 928 (2d Cir.1960). The Second Circuit, however, in Braunstein v. Commissioner, 305 F.2d 949 (2d Cir.1962), referred to the *Glickman* statement quoted above as "dictum." Most courts have adopted the position of the Regulations that the requisite view must arise prior to the completion of manufacture, construction, or production, see, e.g. Payne v. Commissioner, 268 F.2d 617 (5th Cir.1959); Tibbals v. United States, 362 F.2d 266 (Ct.Cl.1966); F.T.S. Associates, Inc. v. Commissioner, 58 T.C. 207 (1972); Jacobson v. Commissioner, 281 F.2d 703 (3d Cir.1960). As to the facts evidencing the time at which the "view" arises, see e.g. Manassas Airport Industrial Park, Inc. v. Commissioner, 66 T.C. 566 (1976) (view present when corporation's "policymakers considered dissolution a recognized possibility").

If the view to collapse arises only after the construction or production of the property has been completed, the corporation will not be treated as collapsible, thus making the factual determination of when construction or production is completed a crucial question. See e.g., Computer Services Corp. v. Commissioner, 63 T.C. 327 (1974) (production of computer program was completed before the time the taxpayers considered disposing of the stock, despite the fact that subsequent improvements and changes were still being made in the program at that time).

(c) *Change of Circumstances*

Regulations, section 1.341–2(a)(3), indicate that the requisite view will not exist where the sale, exchange, or distribution is attributable to circumstances arising after manufacture, construction, production, or purchase, "other than circumstances which reasonably could be anticipated at the time of such manufacture, construction, production, or purchase." In Commissioner v. Lowery, 335 F.2d 680 (3d Cir.1964), the taxpayer was a minority stockholder in two corporations which began the construction of apartment houses in 1950. Before construction was completed, the taxpayer was informed that more funds would be required to complete the projects. He did not have the additional funds and did not want to put more money in the projects. Therefore he sold his stock in the corporations in 1951 and 1952 to investors who were willing to put up the required funds. The corporations were never in fact liquidated. The court held for the taxpayer: "We are of the opinion that [section 341] contemplates a freedom of choice in reaching a decision to sell stock in determining whether a shareholder had the 'view' proscribed by the section, and that where a sale is compelled by circumstances beyond control the 'view' does not exist." (684) By basing its conclusion on the lack of the requisite view, the Court of Appeals did not have to deal with the Tax Court conclusion that section 341 does not apply to minority stockholders because a minority stockholder has no control over corporate policies and the "view" to be ascertained is that of the controlling stockholders, see (d) below.

In Commissioner v. Solow, 333 F.2d 76 (2d Cir.1964), a minority stockholder in 16 real estate corporations was forced to sell his stock because of a disagreement that arose between him and the majority stockholder, the majority stockholder insisting that the taxpayer sell his stock or he would cause the latter's financial ruin. The taxpayer "reluctantly agreed to the sale" and the court held that the requisite view was not present because of the coercive circumstances. But see Braunstein v. Commissioner, 305 F.2d 949 (2d Cir.1962) (unexpected decline in profitability did not constitute a change in circumstances).

(d) *Minority Stockholders*

Regulations, section 1.341–2(a)(2) (second sentence), provide that the intent to form or avail of a corporation for the proscribed purpose exists when such action is contemplated by persons in a position to determine the policies of the corporation by virtue of majority control or otherwise. In Goodwin v. United States, 320 F.2d 356 (Ct.Cl.1963), a minority stockholder's stock was redeemed in circumstances which would have made section 341 applicable. Following the Tax Court position in *Solow,* the court held that the predecessor of section 341 did not apply to the minority stockholder.

2. *Realization of Two–Thirds of the Taxable Income*

The opinion in Payne v. Commissioner, 268 F.2d 617 (5th Cir.1959), implies that under the pre–1985 "substantial part" standard if the "view" exists to distribute before a realization of a substantial part of the income the Commissioner need not show that the distribution was made before the actual realization of a substantial part. Under this analysis, if an initial distribution is made prior to the realization of two-thirds of the taxable income to be derived from the property and the requisite view existed, then the corporation remains a collapsible corporation even though at the time of later distributions, the corporation has earned more than two-thirds of its income. See Heft v. Commissioner, 294 F.2d 795 (5th Cir.1961):

"It may well be that shareholders who liquidate their corporation by a series of distributions may be caught under Section [341] even though most or even all of the corporation's income is eventually realized by the corporation and taxed to it, whereas by waiting until a substantial part of the income has been realized they could have avoided Section [341] and yet have acquired a major part of the corporation's property without the income attributable to it being taxed to the corporation. However, the statute is not directed at the avoidance of *corporate* income taxes. Section [341] is aimed at preventing taxpayers using a corporation to avoid individual stockholder gains from stock sales or corporate distributions from being accorded capital gain treatment. These are separate problems. Even if Section [341] applied except when one hundred per cent of the income was realized by the corporation, this would not entirely close the personal tax loophole; the corporate tax added to a capital gains tax could still be less than the regular income tax at a high bracket. To screen out the most flagrant cases abusing the favored capital gains treatment accorded to sales or exchanges of stock, Congress selected a test based on the sequence of transactions rather than a test geared to the amount of tax paid by the corporation. Under the chosen test, the statute unmistakably applies to the taxpayers in this case." (798).

Difficulties may be encountered in determining the amount of the total gain that is to be realized from the property for purposes of deciding whether a two-thirds of that gain has been realized at the time of the transaction in question. Thus, in the case of rental properties, is the gain to be realized confined to proceeds from sale of the property, or does it also include future rents? The courts in Commissioner v. Kelley, 293 F.2d 904 (5th Cir.1961), and in Payne v. Commissioner, 268 F.2d 617 (5th Cir.1959), seemed to indicate that the pre–1985 "substantial part" test required some estimate of the future operation of the property beyond an ascertainment of its value at the time of the transaction resulting in stockholder gain. See also Manassas Airport Industrial Park v. Commissioner, 66 T.C. 566 (1976), indicating the calculations appropriate to estimate the anticipated future expenses which would reduce the total gain to be realized and thus affect the amount of gain necessary to be realized to avoid collapsible status.

3. *What Constitutes the "Property"*

When more than one asset is held by the corporation, identification of the "property" with respect to which the two-thirds of income test of section 341(b)(1)(A) applies is an important aspect of the test. See Regulations, section 1.341–2(a)(4). A similar problem of identification of the collapsible property is presented by the "70–30" exception of section 341(d)(2) discussed, infra. In Rev. Rul. 68–476, 1968–2 Cum.Bull. 139, at the time of the sale of stock in a collapsible corporation, 60 percent of the gain was attributable to a building and the balance to a general increase in the value of land which had been purchased more than three years prior to the sale of the stock. The Ruling held that "property" under section 341(d)(2) encompassed both the land and the building, which comprised a "single unit of constructed real property." Hence, since all of the gain was attributable to such constructed property, the exception of section 341(d)(2) did not apply. See also Glickman v. Commissioner, 256 F.2d 108 (2d Cir.1958) (held in effect that as respects the 70% test both land and the building constructed on it were the collapsible property and not just the building so that appreciation attributable to the value of the land was collapsible gain).

Computer Services Corp. v. Commissioner, 63 T.C. 327 (1974), held that constructed property includes intangible assets produced by the taxpayer, in that case a computer program for the computerized preparation of income tax returns. It rejected the taxpayer's argument that the program was simply know-how and good will arising from its operation of a service business. *Manassas Airport Industrial Park, Inc.,* supra, page 1083, held that vacant land could be the object of "construction" and section 341 was not limited in its application to depreciable property.

4. *What Constitutes "Construction"*

Section 341(b)(2) requires a determination of what constitutes "construction." Abbott v. Commissioner, 258 F.2d 537 (3d Cir.1958), held that where land had been subdivided with installation of streets and utilities, etc., such acts constituted "construction." Rev.Rul. 56–137, 1956–1 Cum.Bull. 178, stated that the obtaining of a rezoning permit was a part of "construction" activity. See also Farber v. Commissioner, 312 F.2d 729 (2d Cir. 1963) (retention of architect, application for building permit, making of utility deposits and application for loan commitment constituted "construction"); Sproul Realty Co. v. Commissioner, 38 T.C. 844 (1962) (rezoning of land for commercial use, obtaining of lease commitments, hiring of architect and general contractor, and attempting to get permanent financing constituted "construction").

In Rev.Rul. 69–378, 1969–2 Cum.Bull. 49, a corporation leased land to a second corporation on which the latter was to construct a shopping center. The lessor corporation had the right to approve plans and share rents, and it agreed to subordinate its mortgage to enable the lessee to obtain a construction loan. The Ruling held that lessor corporation's activities were "integral steps" in the construction of the shopping center; the fact that it did not engage in physical construction of the shopping center was irrelevant and its activities constituted "construction." However, where the lessor does not assist in the financing of the construction or participate in the profits of the lessee, no "construction" by the lessor will be deemed to take place. Rev. Rul. 77–306, 1977–2, Cum.Bull. 103.

It is also important under section 341(b)(3) and (d)(3) to determine when construction is completed. In Rev.Rul. 69–378, supra, construction was not completed from the standpoint of the lessor corporation until the date of actual completion of construction of the shopping center (even though its activities with respect to the property had ended with the subordination of its mortgage one year earlier). Rev.Rul. 63–114, 1963–1 Cum.Bull. 74, held that minor alterations in the three years following completion of construction of an office building, which alterations did not increase the rental space or the character of the building and did not increase the fair market value of or the net income from the property, did not constitute "construction;" section 341(d)(3) would be satisfied three years from the date of the completion of the office building. Rev.Rul. 72–422, 1972–2 Cum.Bull. 211, indicated that neither the amount expended for alterations nor the ratio of the cost of alterations to the original cost of the property are determinative factors under Rev.Rul. 63–114. See also Rev. Rul. 64–125, 1964–1 Cum.Bull. 131 (unsuccessful oil and gas exploration activities carried on after completion of successful wells did not constitute additional "construction"); Rev.Rul. 68–472, 1968–2 Cum.Bull. 138 (restoration of building destroyed by fire to extent that the criteria of Rev.Rul. 63–

114 were satisfied did not constitute "construction"). In Weil v. Commissioner, 28 T.C. 809 (1957), aff'd per curiam, 252 F.2d 805 (2d Cir.1958), a shopping center was held not completed since the construction of a retaining wall and the completion of a parking lot still remained to permit effective operation, the Tax Court saying that final completion would not be fixed earlier than the time when the project was ready to begin earning a substantial part of the net income. This last aspect hardly seems the decisive factor; thus, the construction of some houses available for rent in a housing project before the remaining houses are built does not mark the completion of the construction. In King v. United States, 641 F.2d 253 (5th Cir.1981), the period of construction of a utility system was expanded to include construction of water and sewer pipe lines by related corporations. On completion, the related corporations contributed the completed pipe lines to the collapsible corporation.

5. *Transactions to Which Section 341 Applies*

Section 341 applies to sales or exchanges of the stock of a collapsible corporation; to distributions in complete or partial liquidation; and to distributions not in redemption of stock which are treated as sales or exchanges under section 301(c)(3)(A). Moreover, once such a collapsible distribution is made, the corporation is a collapsible one and a later sale of its stock is automatically covered regardless of whether the sale would independently meet the tests of section 341(b). Glickman v. Commissioner, 256 F.2d 108 (2d Cir.1958). Section 341 does not, however, appear to cover a section 302(a) redemption; the Regulations, section 1.341–1, refer to an "actual" sale or exchange, which presumably excludes the "treated as" exchange of section 302(a).

For section 341 to apply, gain must be recognized on the exchange of the stock of the collapsible corporation and if the stock is disposed of in a nonrecognition transaction section 341 will not apply. Rev.Rul. 73–378, 1973–2 Cum.Bull. 113 (section 341(a) was not triggered by an exchange of collapsible corporation stock for stock of the acquiring corporation in a reorganization; since the acquiring corporation was not itself a collapsible corporation, the collapsible "taint" disappeared entirely and gain on the subsequent disposition of the stock in the acquiring corporation by the former stockholder of the collapsible corporation was entitled to capital gain treatment).

6. *Section 341(d) Exceptions*

Section 341(d) provides three exceptions whereby stockholders of collapsible corporations can qualify for capital gain treatment despite the fact that the corporation is a collapsible corporation as defined in section 341(b).

The *first exception,* section 341(d)(1), a de minimis rule, protects from ordinary income treatment a stockholder owning (or considered as owning under the attribution rules specified in section 341(d)) five percent or less in value of the outstanding stock of a corporation.

Under the *second exception,* section 341(d)(2), section 341(a) will not apply to the gain recognized by a stockholder in a collapsible corporation unless more than 70 percent of such gain recognized by the stockholder during the taxable year is attributable to the manufacture, construction or production of the property, or purchase of property described in section 341(b)(3). The meanings of the terms "property" and "construction," discussed supra, are thus also important with respect to this exception. Taxpayers frequently have argued that in the case of land and a building, gain should be attributable to the increase in the value of the land for purposes of bringing more of the gain into the 30 percent side of the equation. Thus, in Benedek v. Commissioner, 429 F.2d 41 (2d Cir.1970), the taxpayer, relying on the 70 percent rule, asserted that distributions were attributable to an increase in land value and did not result from the construction of apartment houses. The court held that the test was "what caused the distributions, or what property—land or buildings—generated them?" The court concluded that the distributions were caused by and generated by the construction of the buildings and not by an increase in the value of the land. Loan proceeds distributed resulted from the construction and the shareholder's gain was therefore attributable entirely to construction. Similar results were reached in Farber v. Commissioner, 312 F.2d 729 (2d Cir.1963); Short v. Commissioner, 302 F.2d 120 (4th Cir. 1962); Mintz v. Commissioner, 284 F.2d 554 (2d Cir. 1960). In King v. United States, 641 F.2d 253 (5th Cir. 1981), the court held that the construction of pipelines undertaken by related corporations and contributed to a collapsible corporation contributed to the gain attributable to construction realized on sale of the collapsible corporation stock. The court also concluded that the corporation's actual construction of utility facilities enhanced the value of its other assets, including franchises, customer lists and connection lines, so that gain on these assets was attributable to the construction. Finally, the 1984 Act added the last sentence to section 341(d) calling for Regulations treating inventory type property as a single item of property for purposes of the 70/30 test.

Under the *third exception,* section 341(d)(3), gain realized after the expiration of three years following the completion of manufacture, construction, production, or purchase of section 341(b)(3) property is protected from ordinary income treatment. The problems of time of completion of manufacture or construction discussed, supra, page 1086, thus also are involved in this exception. Rev. Rul. 60–68, 1960–1 Cum. Bull. 151, held that if the sale of stock for cash would result in ordinary income under section 341, then the same result follows if a section 453 election is made; the fact that receipt of an installment occurs more than three years after the time limit of section 341(d)(3) does not affect the ordinary income treatment. But where an executory contract of sale was entered into within the three-year period the taxpayer was able to utilize the exception of section 341(d)(3) where the closing date occurred after the expiration of the three-year period and the burdens and benefits of ownership remained with the seller until the closing date. Rev. Rul. 79–235, 1979–2 Cum. Bull. 135, provides that the three year period with respect to property received in a like-kind exchange under section 1031 in exchange for property constructed by the taxpayer begins to run on the date that construction of the original property was completed.

Suppose that a part of a stockholder's gain is protected under the exception of section 341(d)(3) and he attempts to use the "70–30" exception for the balance of the gain. Does the amount qualifying under the section 341(d)(3) exception fall on the 70 percent or the 30 percent side of the equation? Rev. Rul. 65–184, 1965–2 Cum. Bull. 91, held that the two exceptions operate independently; the exception in section 341(d)(2) does not become applicable simply because 30 percent or more of the gain of the stockholder is attributable to property to which the exception of section 341(d)(3) applies.

7. *Section 341(e) Exception*

Section 341(b)(3)(D) extends section 341 to the purchase of section 1231(b) assets, i.e., land and depreciable property used in business but not held for sale to customers. This means that although an individual who owns such assets outright would have had capital gain, the same individual as a stockholder of a corporation owning such assets could end up with ordinary income on sale of its stock or on liquidation. To prevent this result, section 341(e) provides a general exception to section 341. If the tests of section 341(e) are met, the corporation is not a collapsible corporation. If the tests are not met, then the other provisions of section 341 still must be applied to see if collapsible status exists.

Section 341(e) is extremely complicated. Speaking very generally, as long as the unrealized appreciation of those assets of the corporation which, if sold either by the corporation or any stockholder owning more than 20 percent of its stock would result in ordinary income (other than assets which result in ordinary income because of the application of the various recapture rules specified in section 341(e)(12)), does not exceed 15 percent of the corporation's net worth, then the rules of section 341(e) may apply and the corporation will not be a collapsible corporation as respects the sale or exchange of stock by any stockholder who also meets an additional test described below. This is the "general corporate test" of Regulations, section 1.341–6(a)(4). In determining the stockholder ownership percentages under section 341(e), the attribution rules specified in section 341(e)(8) are applicable.

Once the "general corporate test" is met, the "specific stockholder test" of Regulations, section 1.341–6(a)(5), also must be satisfied. This test recalculates the 15 percent ceiling on ordinary income assets (so-called subsection (e) assets) of the "general corporate test" by recharacterizing certain assets, not otherwise considered to be ordinary income assets, with reference to the shareholder in question. Thus, for example, a more than 5 percent but less than 20 percent stockholder would have the ordinary or capital status of a corporate asset tested, as respects the particular stockholder, but not other stockholders, by what its character would be in that stockholder's hands if the stockholder were a more than 20 percent stockholder. (This is to prevent a dealer from obtaining capital asset status by placing the assets in a corporation along with other non-dealer stockholders.) A more than 20 percent stockholder will have the status of a corporate asset tested, as respects that individual, but no other stockholders, by considering the stockholder as owning certain assets of other corporations in which the stockholder has a substantial interest. (This to prevent an individual from using a separate corporation for each venture to avoid dealer status.) Regulations, section 1.341–6(a)(5)(ii), (c)(3)(ii), and (d). Further, certain of the refinements in section 341(e)(4) are designed to prevent the stockholders of a corporation with depreciable, depletable or amortizable assets from liquidating the corporation, paying a capital gain tax, and thus securing a stepped-up basis for the assets. This latter policy extends also to a sale of the stock of such a corporation to related persons, so that such a sale is not a transaction protected by section 341(e). See section 341(e)(8).

Section 341(e) and the Regulations thereunder must be studied with great care by the tax advisor since this relief provision, where operable, completely removes the collapsible corporation "taint" for the stockholder. The Regulations under section 341(e) clarify many of the uncertainties in the statutory language. There remains, however, a certain aura of unreality to the section even under the Regulations. For example, in applying the specific stockholder test to determine whether a more than 20 percent stockholder is a dealer, a stockholder who is not a dealer may be deemed to be a dealer by hypothesizing what the stockholder would have done with respect to corporate property if he had owned it. See Regulations, section 1.341–6(b)(4).

8. *Section 341(f) Exception*

Section 341(f), provides relief from the collapsible corporation rules with respect to sales by a stockholder of a collapsible corporation if the corporation consents to recognize the gain upon a subsequent disposition of the "subsection (f) assets," as defined in section 341(f)(4). If the corporation files its consent, then shares sold by a stockholder within six months of the date of the corporation's consent will be protected from section 341(a)(2). Rev. Rul. 69–32, 1969–1 Cum. Bull. 100, specifies the rules for the filing of the requisite consent by the corporation. The general purpose of section 341(f) was to give relief to current stockholders if there is assurance that gain would ultimately be recognized by the corporation at the corporate level. Since, after 1986, a corporation is required to recognize gain on any distribution of corporate assets, there is no corporate level cost to making an election under section 341(f). But then again, since corporate level gain must be recognized on any distribution made after 1986, no corporation can be formed or availed of to collapse after that date without recognition of corporate level gain.

C. REFERENCES

Ginsburg, Collapsible Corporations—Revisiting an Old Misfortune, 33 Tax L. Rev. 307 (1978); Axelrad, Collapsible Corporations and Collapsible Partnerships, 1960 So. Calif. Tax Inst. 269; Chodorow and DeCastro, How to Use the "70–30" Exception to Avoid Collapsible Corporation Treatment, 21 J. Tax 258 (1964); Holden, The Collapsible Corporation: What, Why, How; Understanding the Creature as a Protection Against Unfortunate Tax Results, 34 N.Y.U. Tax Inst. 11 (1976).

INDEX

References are to pages

†